Y0-EIA-625

INTERACTIVE CASEBOOK SERIES[SM]

CRIMINAL PROCEDURE: ADJUDICATIVE

A Contemporary Approach

FOURTH EDITION

Russell L. Weaver
PROFESSOR OF LAW & DISTINGUISHED UNIVERSITY SCHOLAR
UNIVERSITY OF LOUISVILLE
LOUIS D. BRANDEIS SCHOOL OF LAW

John M. Burkoff
PROFESSOR OF LAW EMERITUS
UNIVERSITY OF PITTSBURGH SCHOOL OF LAW

Catherine Hancock
GEOFFREY C. BIBLE & MURRAY H. BRING PROFESSOR OF CONSTITUTIONAL LAW
TULANE UNIVERSITY SCHOOL OF LAW

WEST ACADEMIC

To Laurence, Ben and Kate, with love

RLW

Dedicated with love to Nancy, Amy & Sean,
David & Emmy, Emma, Molly,
Hannah, and Cyrus

JMB

For Peter, Elizabeth, Caitlin, Margaret, Josh & Forrest, with love

CH

Preface

This fourth edition of our interactive criminal procedure casebook continues the tradition of our prior criminal procedure casebook (which went through five editions in a non-interactive format), but continues to a fourth edition in the interactive format.

As with the prior books, our primary goal was to create a "teacher's book"—a book that contains thought provoking problems (referred to as "hypos" or "Food for Thought" in the Interactive Casebook Series) designed to stimulate thought and produce interesting classroom discussion. The hypos and Food for Thought are woven throughout the chapters and are designed to help students learn doctrine, illuminate trends in the law, and ultimately produce better learning. A secondary goal was to include a focus on teaching "skills." Many of the hypos place students in practical situations that they are likely to encounter in practice, and therefore encourage students to think about how they might handle those situations in real-life.

However, the interactive format allows us to offer a number of other features, including live hyperlinks and the ability to access the material interactively. Students will also find a variety of boxes in the text of the principal cases, Some of these boxes involve "food for thought" questions that will help them understand how to address the more complex questions that arise in the "points for discussion" material and in the hypotheticals. The boxes also provide information about topics such as the attorneys' strategies in the cases and links to online sources that illustrate various facets of the litigation. There are also "FYI," and "Take Note" boxes. Also included are multiple choice questions that allow students to test their understanding and comprehension of the issues presented.

As with any book, tradeoffs are necessary. In order to prevent the book from being unduly voluminous and unwieldy, we have chosen not to include encyclopedic notes and references like those found in other books. The inclusion of too many notes impedes learning. Moreover, in the criminal procedure area, students have numerous high-quality secondary sources available to them, and students can consult those sources for expanded scholarly discussions of the law. By limiting the scope of notes, we were able to include more hypotheticals and to provide greater opportunity for critical thinking.

We welcome input from faculty and students who use this book. You can contact us at the following e-mail addresses: Professor Russell Weaver (russ.weaver@louisville.edu); Professor John Burkoff (burkoff@pitt.edu); and Professor Catherine Hancock (chancock@law.tulane.edu).

We give thanks to the many people who assisted us in the creation and revision of this book, including our research assistants and secretaries. We are particularly grateful to students who helped us find and correct errors. Finally, we are thankful to our spouses, significant others, and children who supported us through the various stages of this project.

RLW, JMB, CH

Acknowledgments

Excerpts from the following articles have been reprinted by permission:

Jeffrey Bellin, "Theories of Prosecution," 108 CALIF. L. REV. 1203, 1204–09, 1211–15 (2020). © 2020 by the California Law Review, Inc. Reprinted from the California Law Review 108 CALIF. L. REV. 1203 (2020). By permission of the California Law Review.

Jenny E. Carroll, "If Only I Had Known: The Challenges of Representation," 89 FORDHAM L. REV. 2447, 2447–48, 2453–54, 2458–62, 2464–65 (2021).

Eric Fish, "Against Adversary Prosecution," 103 IOWA L. REV. 1419, 1420–23, 1424–26 (2018).

Bruce Green & Ellen Yaroshefsky, "Prosecutorial Accountability 2.0," 92 NOTRE DAME L. REV. 51, 114–16 (2016). Vol. 92 NOTRE DAME LAW REVIEW, Page 51 (2016). Reprinted with permission. © Notre Dame Law Review, University of Notre Dame.

Andrew Guthrie Ferguson "Courts Without Court," 75 VAND. L. REV. 1461, 1462–65, 1521–22 (2022).

W. William Hodes, "Seeking the Truth Versus Telling the Truth at the Boundaries of the Law: Misdirection, Lying, and 'Lying With an Explanation,' " 44 S. TEX. L. REV. 53, 57–62 (2002).

John D. King, "Gamesmanship and Criminal Process," 58 AM. CRIM. L. REV. 47, 48–51, 57–58, 59 (2021).

Richard Klein, "The Role of Defense Counsel in Ensuring a Fair Justice System," 36 THE CHAMPION 38, 38–39, 43–44 (June 2012).

Robert P. Mosteller, "Why Defense Attorneys Cannot, But Do, Care About Innocence," 50 SANTA CLARA L. REV. 1, 3–4, 40–41, 58–59, 60–62 (2010).

Deborah L. Rhode, "The Future of the Legal Profession: Institutionalizing Ethics," 44 CASE W. RES. L. REV. 665, 667–73 (1994).

Meghan J. Ryan, "Criminal Justice Secrets," 59 Am. Crim. L. Rev. 1541, 1542–46, 1596 (2022).

Abbe Smith, "Defending Those People," 10 OHIO ST. J. CRIM. L. 277, 283–285, 287–288, 290–291, 298, 300, 301 (2012).

Features of This Casebook

Throughout the book you will find various text boxes on either side of the page. These boxes provide information that will help you to understand a case or cause you to think more deeply about an issue.

 For More Information These boxes point you to resources to consult for more information on a subject.

 What's That? These boxes explain the meaning of special legal terms that appear in the main text. Black's Law Dictionary definitions may be accessed by clicking on the hyperlinked term in the text.

 Take Note Here you will be prompted to take special notice of something that deserves further thought or attention.

 See It These boxes point you to visual information that is relevant to the material in the text.

 It's Latin to Me The law is fond of Latin terms and phrases; when you encounter these for the first time, this box will explain their meaning.

 Food for Thought These boxes pose questions that prompt you to think about issues raised by the material.

 Practice Pointer Here you will find advice relevant to legal practice typically inspired by the actions (or inactions) of legal counsel in the cases or simply prompted by an important issue being discussed.

 FYI A self-explanatory category that shares useful or simply interesting information relevant to material in the text.

 Hear It These boxes point you to an audio file that is relevant to the material in the text.

 Ethical Issue These boxes present relevant real-world situations that potentially cause ethical conflicts and pose questions relating to those situations.

Go Online If there are relevant online resources that are worth consulting in relation to any matter being discussed, these boxes will direct you to them.

 Test Your Knowledge These boxes contain hyperlinks to online assessment questions that will help you test your understanding of the material in each chapter.

 Global View These boxes offer comparative and international law perspectives.

 Who's That? These boxes provide biographical information about a person mentioned in the text.

 Major Themes A discussion of some of the deeper themes and issues pertaining to the topic covered in that chapter.

 Make the Connection When concepts or discussions that pertain to information covered in other law school courses appear in a case or elsewhere in this text, often you will find this text box to indicate the course in which you can study those topics. Here you may also be prompted to connect information in the current case to material that you have covered elsewhere in this course.

Table of Contents

Table of Cases

The principal cases are in bold type.

Page numbers 1–38 and 163–840, set out below,
are found in Weaver, Burkoff, and Hancock's
Criminal Procedure, A Contemporary Approach (4th ed. 2024).

CRIMINAL PROCEDURE: ADJUDICATIVE

A Contemporary Approach

FOURTH EDITION

CHAPTER 9

Introduction to the Adversary System

Unlike criminal justice systems in many parts of the world, the American criminal justice system is an adversary system. A criminal defendant's guilt or innocence is determined as a result of the adversarial arguments and presentations of evidence by a prosecutor and defense counsel, overseen by a neutral and impartial judge.

While such a system has the immediate virtue of familiarity to most Americans, it is difficult if not impossible to argue that this method of adjudication is the *only* fair way to determine the guilt or innocence of criminal defendants. Indeed, some commentators argue that the American adversarial system, in practice if not in theory, is not truly fair at all. In the face of such criticisms, it is worthwhile to consider whether or not an adversary criminal adjudication model is and continues to be the most appropriate way to try criminal defendants in this country. And, even if we decide on balance that it is optimal, what does that mean in terms of the appropriate roles of defense counsel and prosecutors?

A. Costs & Benefits

Richard Klein—The Role of Defense Counsel In Ensuring a Fair Justice System

36 THE CHAMPION 38, 38–39, 43–44 (June 2012).

Warrior for justice. Maybe this is overly romanticized, but it is how I see the role of the criminal defense attorney. The defense attorney is on the front lines doing, if not God's work, surely something quite close to it. And, as is true with anything that important, the work is anything but easy. Obstacles, barriers, and road blocks are on the path.

Who's That?

Richard Klein is Bruce K. Gould Distinguished Professor of Law at Touro Law Center. He worked for ten years as a trial attorney with the Criminal Defense Division of the Legal Aid Society of New York, New York County.

Defense counsel may accurately be considered law enforcers. While representing a lone individual against all the power of the state, counsel must "police the police" to determine if there has been an unconstitutional search, a coerced confession, an unlawfully suggestive lineup, or the fabrication of testimony. Defense counsel must attempt to ensure that the prosecutor is adhering to the professional requirement not merely to convict, but to do justice and comply with his obligations to turn over exculpatory material to the defense. Perhaps most challenging of all is the need to remind the judge of the constitutional mandate as well as the professional obligation to protect the rights of the defendant rather than treat him as a docket number to be quickly processed and sent to jail.

Supreme Court decisions are replete with statements about how crucial it is to have a defense attorney represent the person who is accused of crime:

Even the intelligent and educated layman has small and sometimes no skill in the science of law. If charged with crime, he is incapable, generally, of determining for himself whether the indictment is good or bad. He is unfamiliar with the rules of evidence. Left without the aid of counsel he may be put on trial without a proper charge, and convicted upon incompetent evidence, or evidence irrelevant to the issue or otherwise inadmissible. He lacks both the skill and knowledge adequately to prepare his defense, even though he have a perfect one. He requires the guiding hand of counsel at every step in the proceedings against him. Without it, though he be not guilty, he faces the danger of conviction because he does not know how to establish his innocence. If that be true of men of intelligence, how much more true is it of the ignorant and illiterate, or those of feeble intellect.

Take Note

Don't miss the "religious" imagery here. Many lawyers, judges, and legal commentators believe that criminal defense counsel should be "zealots" for their clients. A "zealot" is, of course, a person who is fanatical and uncompromising in pursuit of his or her religious, political, or other ideals. Indeed, many argue that zealousness is an obligation that outweighs the importance of a criminal trial as a (supposed) search for truth. Are you troubled by a professional obligation of this sort?

It is somewhat odd to be doing (almost) God's work, yet to have so few people acknowledge the vital import of the work. When we challenge the validity of the search of a home by the police, we are not just representing a single individual. When vigorous advocacy informs the police that they will not be able to "get away with" an illegal, unconstitutional search of a particular person's home, the benefits accrue to and protect us all. If we did not keep them honest, or as honest as we can keep them, there would be nothing to deter the police from entering any of our homes at will.

One can succeed, probably, in not committing a crime, but may not be as successful in not being charged with a crime.

It is appropriate to view the role of the criminal defense attorney as, in some ways, that of a constitutional lawyer. We attempt to protect clients from violations of their Fourth Amendment rights by unlawful searches and seizures, their Fifth Amendment rights by coerced confessions, their Sixth Amendment rights by a lawyer who is not totally effective in all respects, and their Eight Amendment right to not be subjected to a sentence that is grossly disproportionate to the crime committed. We attempt to compensate for the severe racial disparities of those arrested and prosecuted by combating the prosecutorial and judicial abuse of discretion against minorities and to secure the equal protection of the laws. And underlying it all is our commitment to due process and our sometimes desperate struggles to have criminal proceedings that are fundamentally fair.

These battles are against odds that certainly appear to be overwhelming at times. The discrepancy between the resources available to the prosecutor and those for counsel for the indigent is legendary. The prosecutor has not only the tools of an office that is better funded, but typically has police department investigators and laboratory technicians available as well. Eighty percent of prosecutions nationwide are against indigents who are represented by a public defender's office, a private not-for-profit corporation such as a legal aid society, or court-appointed private attorneys.

Food for Thought

A successful suppression motion typically results in the suppression of "truth," e.g. the defendant really *did* "possess" the suppressed drugs and she really was "guilty" of possession of narcotics; *or* the defendant really *did* kill his victim as his now-suppressed, un-*Mirandized*, inculpatory statement baldly conceded. Are the values of our adversary system sufficiently important to us that they outweigh the value of ascertaining the truth in criminal proceedings? What do you think?

Things are certainly not getting easier. The recession has hit the criminal defense bar with full force. As states find themselves with fewer available funds, indigent defense monies are hard hit. Fire departments, police, schools, parks and libraries all have their constituents who fight aggressively against cutbacks. There is virtually no constituency for the indigent defendant charged with crime—none, except the Sixth Amendment.

Watching an arraignment in many of the large urban areas throughout the country can be an embarrassment for anyone concerned with a fair justice system. It can be assembly line justice at its worst. Human being after human being parades in front of the judge. Often, the only information brought before the court is what is in the police report. The prosecutor informs the judge of the accusation, and the judge assumes guilt. The defense counsel often has little or no information to add; there is no presumption of innocence. It is hard for anyone involved in this process to maintain their dignity. What is the proper response for the defender who is most concerned with a fair justice system? Defense counsel should strive to ensure that there is an awareness that these courts need to be concerned with preserving the due process protections of the Constitution.

The title of this article assumes that there is a fair justice system in America, but it is hard to claim that justice is fair for many of our clients. The lack of adequate funding for indigent defense services is sorely lacking and, therefore, many defenders have such extensive caseloads as to bring into doubt whether the mandate of *Gideon* has been met. No defender can provide effective assistance to his clients if he simply has too many of them.

Our work is so extraordinarily crucial. We struggle against all odds to bring truth to "Equal Justice Under the Law," when we see the reality of the treatment of the minorities and the poor by the criminal justice system. We fight for "Liberty and Justice for All," when we know that some of our clients have no liberty and are incarcerated in overcrowded jails simply because they have no funds for bail and, therefore, cannot afford liberty. The Sixth Amendment right to counsel does not serve merely to supplement other constitutional rights. It is the basic right that serves to enable an individual to exercise his other constitutional rights. Counsel is there to ensure that

Food for Thought

Do you agree? Does our criminal justice system operate in such a way that unfairness is intrinsic for many defendants? Can you imagine a criminal justice system (in the American context) that works differently . . . and works fairly, to boot?

the procedural protections, which exist on paper, are actually applied. This is no easy task. The best of us, the most passionate of us, the most committed of us, go beyond just perceiving the job as one that "the adversary system and our constitution requires to be done;" we add, "by me."

W. William Hodes—Seeking the Truth Versus Telling the Truth At the Boundaries of the Law: Misdirection, Lying, and "Lying With An Explanation"

44 S. TEX. L. REV. 53, 57–62 (2002).

One of the most brutal clashes between competing values is that between "truth" and "justice," with implications for the very nature of the legal system itself. Finding the truth and then resolving disputes on the basis of that truth ranks very highly in our value system. But so does achieving justice, even though justice as Peter defines it, it will often be purchased at Paul's expense, and even though some of the truth is frequently obscured or even sacrificed along the way. And, of course,

Who's That?

W. William Hodes is Professor of Law Emeritus at the Indiana University Robert H. McKinney School of Law.

the elusive and essentially fatuous concept of "the whole truth" is always lost in the fog of adversarial combat.

The tension between truth on the one hand, and justice on the other-the latter often equated in our culture simply with winning-has long engaged both the legal profession and the public. This clash of values arises most dramatically in the context of high profile criminal trials, which correspondingly receive the most media attention and public debate.

The public is offended enough when a criminal defense is based on suppression of evidence or some other legal or "technical" defense. But that pales in comparison to the outrage expressed when it appears that the defense lawyers knew the truth of a client's factual guilt, but nonetheless attempted to achieve an acquittal on the merits. This is often seen as a form of "lying," and it must be conceded that the lawyer's plan in such a case is to induce the jury to come to a conclusion that the lawyer knows is factually wrong, namely that someone other than the accused physically did the deeds in question.

Defense lawyers, on the other hand, and allies in the bar generally, are typically angered by such attacks, and point to a lawyer's obligation-rooted in both professional ethics and in the Sixth Amendment to the United States Constitution-to use all legal means to mount a defense, whether or not the client is known to be factually guilty. More important, for present purposes, they reject any claim that they have "lied," if no false evidence has been introduced, and if they have engaged only in argumentation, pointing out inconsistencies and trying to punch logical holes in the government's case, and suggesting alternative "narratives" that the jury is free to accept or reject.

Take Note

Hodes clearly strikes a more "moderate" tone than Professor Klein in the preceding article excerpt, but note that he still contends that the present balance between zealous representation and concern for the truth has been struck correctly.

This quarrel can be seen as no more than a variant on the distinction between active and passive behavior, but I prefer the shorthand implicit in the title of this essay-that while lawyers must tell the truth, they are not required to seek the truth or to aid in the search. Instead, they are often required by their roles to work to obscure inconvenient truths and to prevent the truth from coming out.

Moreover, although I have my moments of queasiness, like everyone else, and although I struggle along with everyone else to locate the exact boundary line between truth and justice, I am convinced that the law of lawyering has drawn this particular line roughly where it ought to be drawn.

Deborah L. Rhode—The Future of the Legal Profession: Institutionalizing Ethics

44 CASE W. RES. L.REV. 665, 667–73 (1994).

The central norm of contemporary American legal practice is one of neutral partisanship; the attorney's role is to advance client interests "zealously within the bounds of the law" regardless of the attorney's own assessment of their underlying merits. Although lawyers have certain obligations as officers of the court, these are quite limited and largely track the prohibitions on criminal and fraudulent conduct that govern all participants in the legal process.

Who's That?

The late Deborah L. Rhode was the Ernest W. McFarland Professor of Law and the Director of the Center on the Legal Profession at Stanford University.

This neutral partisanship model rests on two assumptions. The first is that an adversarial clash between two zealous advocates is the best way to discover truth and to promote accurate legal decision making. A second assumption is that partisan advocacy provides the most effective protection for individual rights. [The] first assumption, that an adversarial clash yields accurate outcomes, is not self-evident. As many commentators have observed, this is not how most countries adjudicate disputes, how most professionals investigate facts, or even how most lawyers conduct inquiries outside the courtroom.

In an adversarial model, the merits prevail only if the contest is a balanced one—that is, if each side has roughly equal access to relevant legal information, resources, and capabilities. Yet how often a fully balanced contest occurs in practice is open to doubt. American lawyers practice in a social order that tolerates vast disparities in wealth, makes most litigation enormously expensive, and allocates civil legal assistance almost entirely through market mechanisms. Under these circumstances, one would expect that the "haves" generally come out ahead.

Among defenders of current partisan norms, the conventional "solution" to the problem of unequal advocacy "is not to impose on counsel the burden of representing interests other than those of his client, but rather to take appropriate steps to ensure that all interests are effectively represented." Exactly what those steps might be have never been satisfactorily elaborated. Inequalities in access have been seriously confronted only at a rhetorical level.

The unqualified pursuit of client interests carries obvious costs: It obstructs the decision-making process, imposes unnecessary delays and expense, and deters meritorious claims. In response to such criticisms, proponents of neutral partisanship typically invoke a second line of defense. Whatever its effectiveness or efficiency in promoting truth, this partisan framework is an indispensable safeguard of individual rights. On this view, respect for clients' autonomy implies respect for their pursuit of legal claims and demands largely undivided loyalty from their legal advisors. By absolving attorneys from accountability for clients' acts, the traditional advocacy role encourages representation of those most vulnerable to public prejudice and state oppression. The promise of non-judgmental advocacy may also encourage legal consultation by those most in need of ethical counseling. Any alternative system, it is argued, would threaten "rule by an oligarchy of lawyers." To demand that attorneys judge, rather than simply defend, their clients would be "equivalent to saying that saints must have a monopoly of lawsuits" and that the lawyers should have a monopoly of deciding who qualifies for sainthood.

From an ethical standpoint, this justification for neutral partisanship presents two central difficulties. First, it conflates legal and moral entitlements; it assumes that society wishes to permit whatever lawmakers do not prohibit. Yet some conduct that is clearly antithetical to broader public interests may nonetheless remain legal-either because prohibitions appear too difficult or costly to enforce, or because decision makers are too uninformed, overworked, or pressured by special interests. Although lawyers may have no special moral expertise, they at least have a more disinterested perspective than clients on the ethical dimensions of certain practices. Attorneys can accept moral responsibility without necessarily imposing it. Unless the lawyer is the last in town, his or her refusal of the neutral partisan role may simply impose on clients the psychological and financial cost of finding alternative counsel.

A second problem with rights-based justifications for partisanship is that they fail to explain why the rights of clients should trump those of all other parties whose interests are inadequately represented.

Food for Thought

Professor Rhode took issue with other commentators' "neutral partisanship model" of criminal defense counsel's role, noting, *inter alia*, the costs of what she deemed to be *excessively* partisan practices. Perhaps her strongest criticism was that such a model "fail[s] to explain why the rights of clients should trump those of all other parties whose interests are inadequately represented." What is your position on this question? Should criminal defense counsel consider interests other than his or her client's? Whose? The victim's? The victim's family's? The community's? Which community? Would you prefer a justice system where defense counsel is obliged to determine the client's guilt and, in essence, disclose it to the court? Doesn't such a system at least have the virtue of better producing the truth? Or does it? Is there any actor in such a (hypothesized) system who will make the effort to insure that the defendant is being treated fairly? Is that important? More or as important as discovering the truth? At the very minimum, you should see how hard these policy choices are to make.

Much of the appeal of rights-based justifications for partisanship draws on the lawyer's role in criminal defense proceedings. Yet such proceedings are distinctive in their potential for governmental oppression and in their impact on individual life, liberty, and reputation. For the same reasons that our constitutional traditions impose special protections for criminal cases, most commentators suggest that the justifications for neutral partisanship are strongest in that context.

Hypo: *Role of Judge*

Should judges have a greater role in the trial process in order to insure fairness and increase the odds of discovering the truth? What do you think? Would our system benefit from more intervention and tighter control by the trial judge? Less strategic posturing by counsel? Such dramatic changes in our system—even if we agree that they are desirable—may not be possible in a practical sense given defendants' constitutional rights in our system, e.g. the Sixth Amendment right to effective assistance of counsel. Would you be willing to trade away (the current scope of) some of these rights for a more efficient and less adversarial criminal justice system?

John D. King—Gamesmanship and Criminal Process

58 AM. CRIM. L. REV. 47, 48–51, 57–58, 59 (2021).

We first learn formal structures of rules and norms of conduct through games and sports. Notions of fair play, sportsmanship, and cheating are developed from an early age on basketball courts, playgrounds, and soccer fields. Today, as many critique the legitimacy of the American criminal justice system in several different respects, those who care about the integrity of the criminal justice system can learn from ideas and philosophies of fairness and cheating in the sports context. Specifically, the idea of "gamesmanship" in criminal procedure has fruitful analogies in the world of sport. In the adversarial world of American criminal adjudication, prosecutors and defense

Who's That?

John King is James P. Morefield Professor of Law at Washington and Lee University School of Law and is Director of both Experiential Education and the Criminal Justice Clinic. Prior to law teaching, he was a supervising attorney at the D.C. Public Defender Service.

attorneys occasionally accuse each other of "playing games" instead of playing fair. But what one person would characterize as gamesmanship, another would characterize as zealously using the rules to the advantage of one's client or cause. And whereas "cheating" (in the sense of violating the constitutional or statutory rules that govern criminal practice) provides relatively clear lines of acceptability, the more interesting and difficult questions instead involve the aggressive use of rules that might violate some sense of decorum or culture, but stay within the formal rules of engagement.

The concept of gamesmanship is notoriously tricky to define, but one useful definition from the Journal of the Philosophy of Sport is "a strategy designed for winning regardless of athletic excellence." Translated to the criminal litigation context, this idea might imperfectly be expressed as "a strategy designed for winning regardless of the factual and legal merits of the case." Such a definition resonates with the negative connotations of the term in litigation: one side may use it to accuse the other side of engaging in tactics that have nothing to do with the true goal or ultimate systemic objective of the litigation. Others looking at the concept of gamesmanship from a philosophical angle have found a meaningful distinction between "the rules of the game" and "the code of fair play." The code of fair play, which is an unwritten set of shared expectations among the participants about the range of acceptable behavior, overlaps but is not co-extensive with the official rules of the game. Some actions do not violate the rules but would offend notions of fair play, while other actions that violate the rules would not be seen as outside of the code of fair play. One such example is the intentional foul in basketball, which is against the rules of the game but is in no way seen as violating notions of fair play. Conversely, some litigators take the position that objecting during an opponent's opening statement or closing argument to a jury violates some shared expectation or norm of conduct, although doing so is certainly within the official rules of engagement and in fact might be necessary to enforce those formal rules.

Although usually invoked in a pejorative sense in sport and in criminal practice, gamesmanship can serve an important and productive purpose. By clarifying the boundaries of acceptable practice and by bringing into stark relief the limitations of existing rules, gamesmanship forces us to establish and defend which objectives are essential and which values are central to a system. Only where a practice of gamesmanship subverts or undermines an overarching goal is it problematic. The overall professed goals of the criminal justice system are familiar: the ascertainment of truth and application of just verdicts within a system that protects individual rights and human dignity. If gamesmanship subverts these ends, it should be discouraged in criminal litigation. But the prescription depends entirely on how one defines the goals of the system within which gamesmanship is deployed. Often, what appears to be gamesmanship may be perfectly aligned with a broader goal and so should not only be tolerated but also encouraged.

An important caveat in comparing sports to criminal litigation is the asymmetry in role and resources between the contestants. Although a general requirement of sport is that each participant faces the same restrictions, is bound by the same rules, and pursues the same goals, our tradition of criminal justice assigns different objectives to prosecutors and defense lawyers. Because of these different roles, rules of gamesmanship should apply differently to the different players in the criminal justice system. Defense lawyers are bound, as a matter of ethics, to pursue the interests of their clients and to use whatever legal and ethical means are available to them to achieve their clients' goals. Prosecutors, on the other hand, are required not primarily to be advocates, but to be "ministers of justice." In a very real sense, then, prosecutors and defense lawyers are—or at least should be—playing different games. Some kinds of strategic behavior by defense lawyers can be acceptable and even socially productive while the same kinds of behavior by prosecutors would be inconsistent with their institutional role and therefore unacceptable.

In addition to the different roles assigned, an imbalance of resources that virtually always favors the prosecution provides another justification for limiting the use of gamesmanship by prosecutors. The real problem facing our criminal courts is not one of excessive zeal and gamesmanship by defense lawyers but rather a system of mass processing that undervalues zeal, due process, and adversarial testing of evidence. Aggressive application of procedural rules by defense lawyers can help to restore some of the balance to the adversarial process.

In our seemingly boundless appetite for watching sports, Americans generally accept without much debate the legitimacy—if not always the accuracy—of the process of rule enforcement in sports. On the other hand, many have called into question the fairness, neutrality, and legitimacy of the American criminal justice system.

Recognizing that gamesmanship is not only an inevitable but also a positive and productive force in both sports and criminal litigation, reformers should take action to curb a specific practice only when it conflicts with a broad and fundamental goal of the criminal justice system. But where a practice is at odds with some important value or objective, legislatures and courts should alter procedural rules and penalties to eliminate these specific forms of gamesmanship. In this process, however, we should remain cognizant of the different roles assigned to prosecutors and defense lawyers in criminal litigation and the particularly corrosive effect that prosecutorial gamesmanship can have on the legitimacy of the criminal justice system.

Food for Thought

Do you agree that "gamesmanship is not only an inevitable but also a positive and productive force in both sports and criminal litigation?" Is that so obvious?

The critical difference between sports and legal contests is the ultimate objective of each: while sporting contests are all about deciding which of the competitors best displayed mastery of a skill during the contest, trials are about (in addition to a normative moral determination) what happened outside of the courtroom, and should seek to minimize or eliminate the skill of the litigators as a factor in the outcome. The overall objectives of the system should dictate the specific procedural rules of engagement:

> The usual justification for the adversary system is that truth will emerge from a rule-bound contest between two opponents presided over by a passive umpireal judge. But if the central goal is truth-seeking, why should the prosecutor, with his greater resources and access to witnesses, not have the responsibility for putting all the evidence on the table, including that which is favorable to an accused? Because they are asked to be not only advocates but also "ministers of justice," instances of prosecutors involved in gamesmanship pose a special threat to the legitimacy of the criminal justice system. The practice of prosecutors making obviously pretextual arguments in order to prevent people of color from serving on criminal juries, for example, undermines confidence in the integrity of the system. Gamesmanship can be corrosive to the public's trust in a system, whether a system of sports rules or criminal justice. When official actors are seen as behaving arbitrarily or unjustly, the legitimacy of the system is questioned by those who use it. As that legitimacy is called into question, rates of compliance with the law fall.

Meghan J. Ryan—*Criminal Justice Secrets*

59 AM. CRIM. L. REV. 1541, 1542–46, 1596 (2022).

Our criminal justice system is cloaked in immense secrecy. From beginning to end, covert operators and legal rules hide the inner workings of the system. Undercover police officers and confidential informants work surreptitiously to arm the government with secret information. Covert technologies such as Stingray cell phone trackers further provide the government with information it can use to uncover criminal activity and convict criminal offenders. Prosecutors

> **Who's That?**
>
> Meghan Ryan is Altshuler Distinguished Teaching Professor and Professor of Law at SMU Dedman School of Law.

attack criminal suspects in secret grand jury proceedings without allowing these prospective defendants the opportunity to defend themselves. Prosecutors engage in plea-bargaining behind closed doors, preventing defendants the opportunity to fairly compare the prosecutors' plea offers with those offered to similarly situated defendants. Even "discovery" proceedings are full of secrecy. Under the Supreme Court's due process jurisprudence, prosecutors are required to disclose only minimal evidence to criminal defendants, and violations of even this basic demand are rampant. That means that evidence exculpating defendants is often hidden from defendants, judges, juries, and the public more broadly. Beyond hiding exculpatory evidence, prosecutors are also using secret evidence to convict criminal defendants. Breathalyzer and some DNA evidence, for example, are based upon source codes and algorithms to which defendants are generally denied access because they are categorized as trade secrets. This means that defendants lack the opportunity to truly challenge this evidence in court. Further, secrecy obscures jury deliberations on the evidence. These deliberations happen behind closed doors and, even if there is evidence of juror misconduct infecting the discussions, this information ordinarily cannot be used to legally undercut the verdict that was reached. Instead, jury deliberations ordinarily remain a black box. Extensive secrecy even shrouds criminal punishment. The government fails to disclose some aspects of incarceration, such as jail operating procedures and lethal injection protocols, claiming that those details constitute trade secrets. It even hides the particulars of the ultimate punishment, masking the identities of executioners and lethal injection drugs, as well as death row inmates' physical reactions to the drugs.

There are some justifications for this extensive secrecy. Most of them relate to the government's prosecutorial interests. For example, more surveillance evidence of criminal wrongdoing assists the government in uncovering and punishing this behavior. Secrecy also helps prosecutors by easing the burdens associated with disclosing information such as the details of plea bargains or immaterial exculpatory evidence. But secrecy also serves prosecutors' interests in securing convictions, regardless of whether those convictions further the broader goal of achieving justice. For example, a prosecutor's refusal to disclose certain exculpatory evidence places the defendant at an informational disadvantage about the strength of the prosecutor's case, making it easier for the prosecutor to secure a plea agreement. By withholding this evidence, prosecutors may also give a skewed picture to the judge and jury about the strength of the government's case and thus have a greater likelihood of prevailing at trial. Finally, commentators sometimes justify government secrecy in certain segments of the criminal justice system as a practice that protects witnesses and other third parties. One example of such third-party protection is masking the identities of confidential informants from criminal defendants to avoid witness intimidation. Another is invoking trade secret protection to guard the underlying source codes and algorithms of breathalyzer devices and probabilistic genotyping systems, which, in turn, protects the profit motives of these programs' developers.

Despite these asserted justifications for shrouding the workings of our criminal justice system, this extensive secrecy is contrary to the system's transparency roots. At the time of the Founding, transparency in criminal justice was extremely important. This is reflected in the various constitutional provisions guaranteeing transparency in criminal proceedings. For example, the Sixth Amendment provides criminal defendants with the rights to a public trial and to be judged by a jury of their peers. The Amendment also guarantees that defendants cannot be kept in the dark about the charges against them and that there cannot be secret witnesses against the accused—

defendants have the right to confront witnesses against them. Openness in criminal proceedings was embedded in English common law, and the Founders' focus on transparency intensified as a reaction to outrageous historical actions such as those of the English Court of Star Chamber, which involved covertly extracting witness testimony—sometimes through torturous means. Transparency in criminal proceedings has always been considered essential to ensuring fairness and, relatedly, to instilling confidence in the fairness of the system. Such transparency can also provide a necessary civic education and spark new innovations to improve the system. Blocking the citizenry from accessing the various facets of our criminal justice system contravenes these transparency roots of the system and also strips the system of the much needed benefits that transparency provides.

Not only is the overwhelming amount of secrecy in today's criminal justice system contrary to our transparency foundations, but it also poses some very real, concrete constitutional concerns. The government's extensive surveillance network, and the secrecy of that surveillance, raises constitutional concerns under the Fourth Amendment. Grand jury secrecy, while once a useful defendant protection practice may now actually hurt the defendant more than it helps. Secrecy in plea-bargaining raises equal protection concerns by creating an environment in which similarly situated defendants may very well be treated differently due to a variety of factors, such as race, sex, gender, economic status, or prosecutorial retaliation. The system's significant limitations on discovery and prosecutors' resulting tendency to hide exculpatory evidence lead to situations in which defendants' due process rights may be violated and defendants may be convicted on incomplete and misleading evidence. The secrecy surrounding some of the evidence prosecutors use to convict defendants at trial—such as breathalyzer results and certain DNA evidence—implicates both confrontation and due process concerns. Because defendants are denied access to the underlying source codes and algorithms for the computer programs producing these results, and because courts have found this information to be protected by trade secret law, defendants are unable to confront these witnesses against them—whether those be the program developers or the programs themselves. Further, denying defendants access to this information contravenes due process guarantees by stripping defendants of an opportunity to mount a sufficient defense and denying them access to potentially exculpatory *Brady* material. The secrecy surrounding jury deliberations means that bias or juror misconduct may infect jury verdicts, undercutting a defendant's right to an impartial jury. Finally, the constitutional concerns of criminal justice secrecy even reach into the realm of punishment, where denying access to information about the details of incarceration or inmates' impending executions creates questions about whether the sentence contravenes the Eighth Amendment ban on cruel and unusual punishments. Secrecy hides the true intensity of a punishment, raising concerns about whether sentencers not privy to this information can impose a constitutionally proportionate punishment. Secrecy about the details of punishment could also be masking the imposition of torturous punishment—something clearly prohibited by the Eighth Amendment. And masking the true nature of punishment exacerbates the possibility of imposing unconstitutional punishment: if the public is unaware of the true nature of punishment, citizens' moral views on the punishment cannot inform legislation, yet state legislation is a significant factor in courts' determinations of whether a punishment is unconstitutionally cruel and unusual.

Each of these constitutional concerns resulting from the secrecy cloaking the criminal justice system is important. Further, the accumulation of secrecy from each step of the criminal process creates a monstrous wall of secrecy that criminal defendants face. Not only are defendants confronting prosecutors hiding exculpatory evidence or being convicted based on secret evidence, but defendants are facing secrecy at every step of the criminal justice process. The system is so replete with constitutional problems that the particularly identified, often compound, constitutional questions at issue should be viewed more critically.

Food for Thought

Do you agree with Professor Ryan's contention that secrecy in the criminal justice system is endemic and problematic? Isn't it possible that complete transparency would be even more problematic? What do you think?

The many levels of secrecy—all the way from the moment an investigation begins to the final moments of punishment—create serious constitutional concerns. The Fourth, Fifth, Sixth, and Eighth Amendments were drafted and ratified to protect individuals' privacy rights, ensure transparency and fairness in criminal proceedings, and prohibit torturous punishment. But the secret practices pervasive within today's criminal justice system push against these constitutional guarantees. Not only do the individual acts of secrecy create constitutional concerns, but the accumulation of all these constitutionally questionable practices creates a real constitutional quagmire. This tangle of constitutional problems dictates that we must begin dismantling this system of secrecy. The dismantling is likely something that we must do slowly, brick by brick; but reevaluating the need for secrecy at each step of the criminal justice system is necessary. Certainly, secrecy may sometimes be justified, and, in beginning to tear down the immense wall of secrecy within the system, we must once again be careful not to create unintended consequences that may be damaging to effective law enforcement and defendants' constitutional rights. But, over time, secrecy has grown and there has not necessarily been a careful consideration of the advantages and disadvantages of that secrecy. It is now time to revisit the constitutional rules surrounding the secrecy that has become ubiquitous within our criminal justice system despite our Founding Fathers' sincere belief in the transparency of the American criminal justice system.

Andrew Guthrie Ferguson—Courts Without Court

75 VAND. L. REV. 1461, 1462–65, 1521–22 (2022).

The criminal legal system in America is largely broken. In big cities and rural counties, too many cases chase too few resources, resulting in a bureaucratic indifference to mass incarceration. The result is a system of plea bargains, mandatory minimums, fines, fees, and punitive social control arising from misdemeanors and low-level felonies. Defense lawyers have little time to investigate, write motions, and vet experts, let alone advise clients. Trials are rare. Defendants have little faith in the system. And almost everyone toiling in the trenches knows that criminal courts have failed to live up to the promise of equal justice for all.

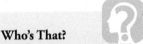

Who's That?

Andrew Guthrie Ferguson is Professor of Law, American University Washington College of Law. Prior to law teaching, Professor Ferguson worked as a supervising attorney at the D.C. Public Defender Service.

In the midst of this broken criminal legal system, what happens when the courts just shut down? The COVID-19 pandemic physically closed courts, locked down jails, incapacitated lawyers, killed judges, and scared jurors away from service. Most fundamentally, court systems turned into virtual courts, conducting proceedings on Zoom or other commercial online platforms. Lawyers adapted to an online practice, conducting motions hearings, bail hearings, pleas, and sentencings mediated by a screen in their homes, miles away from the physical courthouse.

A radical disruption occurred. Court-centered factfinding processes dating back centuries were threatened. In the place of the familiar criminal justice system taught in law school and portrayed in the media, a new video streaming system emerged

Food for Thought

How does the proliferation of virtual court proceedings fit with Professor Ryan's arguments about secrecy in the criminal justice system? Does is make the criminal proceedings even more secretive? Or more open and accessible? What do you think?

(and began expanding). Based largely on available consumer-oriented technology and born out of a public health emergency, this virtual system of online criminal courts sprung into being. With little planning, less academic debate, and almost no input from impacted communities, what the public used to think of as criminal court started becoming a virtual proxy of the real thing.

And, as with many innovations, many of these virtual measures will outlast the immediate crisis, reshaping traditional practices and creating a new normal. Arguments for efficiency and convenience will enshrine some online innovations as the preferred way of running criminal dockets. Online hearings—connecting judges, lawyers, and defendants in virtual courtrooms—will become part of ordinary criminal practice.

Physically moving away from the courthouse decreases the centrality of a judge-based carceral system. Reorganizing court scheduling reduces the centrality of the judge as organizer. Developing external monitoring technologies recenters accountably mechanisms away from internal court systems. A move to online courts thus presents an opportunity to decenter and disrupt judicial power. At the same time, the rules of trial should not be so easily shifted online. The constitutional principles supporting criminal trials—while not fixed—likely will be difficult to adapt to online equivalents.

Food for Thought

Are you as sanguine about this potential changes as Professor Ferguson is? What was your experience during the COVID-19 Pandemic? Are you as optimistic about the value of virtual court proceedings?

The end result is a criminal legal system that may step back from trying to solve social problems through a centralized court system and perhaps even ask hard questions about why we are asking courts to solve social problems in the first place. Court-centered solutionism makes less sense when the courthouse and the judge no longer play the same central role in the process. Community-based solutions appear more appealing when the work of criminal justice is happening outside of court. As communities look to reshape government and police power in other ways, the shift to online courts might offer a way to literally and metaphorically redirect power away from the courthouse and into the community. At a minimum, reexamining criminal courts through the prism of virtual experimentation allows society to ask deep questions about our reliance on criminal judges to solve issues arising from poverty, structural inequality, and social ills.

Exercise: *Observe Criminal Proceedings*

Spend at least half a day observing a criminal trial or hearings at your local courthouse. Write a paper briefly reporting the nature of your observations and addressing all of the following questions where they are applicable: Were defense counsel and the prosecutor contentious in their advocacy? Should they have been more zealous or adversarial in their advocacy? In what ways did the outcome of the proceedings you observed turn on the adversarial manner of presentation of arguments and/or evidence? What difference do you think it would have made if the proceedings had taken place in a less adversarial fashion?

B. Defense Counsel's Role

Accepting the present reality, i.e. that criminal trials take place in an adversary setting, what does adversariness mean *in practice* for defense counsel? Is it possible to be an able and effective defense attorney and to be a "good person" at the same time? Is it possible to stay emotionally healthy?

Robert P. Mosteller—Why Defense Attorneys Cannot, But Do, Care About Innocence

50 SANTA CLARA L. REV. 1, 3–4, 40–41, 58–59, 60–62 (2010).

Defense counsel focus on what is useful to the conduct of their representation that relates to innocence—its proof. When such proof is available, they develop it and present it. Assuredly, when innocence is not present, they defend anyway, but their reaction is connected to the irrelevance of guilt to the duty to represent the client and does not dictate the irrelevance of innocence.

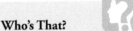

Who's That?

Robert Mosteller is the J. Dickson Phillips Distinguished Professor of Law Emeritus at the University of North Carolina. He worked for seven years with the Washington, D.C. Public Defender Service where he was Director of Training and Chief of the Trial Division.

Belief in innocence without proof is a different matter. Unlike prosecutors, defense attorneys lack the power to dismiss a case because they believe the defendant is, or may be, innocent. In the courtroom, their belief is treated as inadmissible, and therefore it is functionally irrelevant. In contrast to guilt, where defense attorneys may have unique personal knowledge because the client unequivocally admitted guilt to them, a client's impassioned protestation of innocence hardly constitutes knowledge of innocence. Usually, the evidence defense attorneys possess that is not also available to the prosecution merely supports the likelihood of innocence, but does not prove it.

My experience is that defense attorneys do care about innocence when they see it or they think they see it. However, defenders who search among their clients for those who are innocent are inviting personal and professional destruction. A defender's belief in her client's innocence must be backed by evidence; otherwise, it largely only torments the defender and interferes with the performance of the attorney's professional duty to all of her other clients. Furthermore, because this can become disabling, it can harm even a client the defender believes to be innocent.

In the end, I conclude that the concern for innocence will likely continue to be handled individually by attorneys responding to the torment by giving special attention to those clients, and attempting to limit the damage that special attention may cause to others who they represent.

In meeting hundreds of clients and examining their cases, attentive defense attorneys build a knowledge base, which enables most to analyze criminal cases with skill and judgment. One also develops a cynical side and sees the world as a hard place. Optimists—those who believe in the possibility of human perfection and consider most of their clients innocent or perfectible—do not survive long. Although I rationally understood that I could not actually know which clients were the innocent ones, I now recognize that I had a false sense of confidence that I would have a relatively accurate inclination of innocence, which I suspect many defenders share. My suspicion is that this false confidence arose from a self-protective instinct designed to lower the pressure of the work, which was much easier if the system's expectation that all clients were guilty was true.

I do not assume that many of my clients were innocent, but what I have come to appreciate more over time is that I could not tell the innocent from the large percentage that were guilty. This point may be criticized because I have no proof that I had any other innocent client beyond those who were discovered. I do not know.

In assessing the possible impact that a focus on guilt and innocence might have on defenders, some typology of the motivations of defenders is helpful. I suggest there are four major categories: (1) The Tester of Factual or Legal Guilt, (2) The Rights Protector, (3) The Protector of and Aid to the Downtrodden, and (4) The Competitor.

The first category—The Tester of Factual or Legal Guilt—is the one most directly involved in this article. The motivation of these lawyers roughly centers on the arguments that determining facts is often difficult, leading to inherent uncertainty as to factual guilt, and thus, despite the good faith efforts of prosecutors, conviction of the innocent remains a reality. As a result, defense lawyers are needed to protect the factually innocent. Even if we know what happened, many cases turn on issues of human motivation and responsibility, which may remain uncertain or which may properly be viewed from different perspectives. Thus, lawyers also play this role, even when the issue is legal guilt rather than factual innocence. Finally, in death penalty cases, defense attorneys are critical to reaching an appropriate judgment as to punishment.

Global View

A number of countries around the world have begun a transition to a more adversarial criminal justice system, including adopting the concept of appointed public defenders for indigent clients. But the U.S. public defender system hasn't always been a successful transplant in other countries. Consider the example of Chile. *See* John D. King, *The Public Defender as International Transplant*, 38 U. PA. J. INT'L L. 831 (2017).

The second category—The Rights Protector—houses arguments flowing from the command of the Sixth Amendment under our adversarial system for equal justice and the contention that in protecting those least loved, defenders support the foundation of the liberties of all. The third category—The Protector of the Downtrodden—contains elements of social work and political cause. Most of those charged with crimes come from impoverished backgrounds and present a host of social maladies. Somewhere in the mix of motivations to enter defender work is likely at least the potential for empathy for defendants who typically come from impoverished backgrounds and may be members of racial minority groups. Few defenders are likely drawn to the work to perform a social work function, but in reality, much of a defender's work has this function. For those who endure, success in the social work function often becomes a fulfilling element of the job. The fourth category—The Competitor—captures the personal ego satisfaction that sustains litigators. It is the selfish joy of winning. For defenders, this joy may be more infrequent because the prosecution typically has the stronger case, but the victories are more enjoyable when they come to an underdog.

At PDS [the Washington, D.C. Public Defender Service], as I assume with public defenders generally, we had no clearly articulated justifications for our work either at an office-wide level or individually. I saw and felt elements of all four of the motivational categories described above. The most common articulation was the systemic justification set out in the second category—"The Protector of Rights." We certainly believed that a major consequence and purpose of our work was to keep the criminal justice process honest, which should help those who are innocent, but our focus was on the immediate goal of maintaining a fair process. We were, in this way, lawyers working for a cause. Thus, working for a larger cause is somewhere in their motivation, but for most defenders, that is not what sustains them on a day-to-day basis.

In her insightful article, Repression and Denial in Criminal Lawyering, 9 Buff. Crim. L. Rev. 339, 359 (2006), Professor Susan Bandes examines the emotional and psychological impact upon defenders of representing largely, but not universally, guilty individuals, many of whom have caused pain to others and face the prospect of harsh punishment themselves. On the support side of the ledger, Bandes, drawing from numerous personal accounts of defenders, notes the central focus and sustaining motivation is the client: "One common thread among those who maintain a commitment to defense work is the importance of the connection to one's client, and the importance of keeping his needs concrete and immediate."

Food for Thought

What do you think about Professor Mosteller's description of the types of PD motivations? Overly simplistic? Or . . . right on? If you are considering criminal defense practice after law school, which of these might apply to you? And given the fact that many, many civil practice clients are every bit as unpleasant, culpable, and discomfiting, do you think that criminal defense practice is really a more emotionally demanding setting in which to practice law?

860 — CRIMINAL PROCEDURE: ADJUDICATIVE *A Contemporary Approach* —

As Professor Bandes describes, the lawyers at the Public Defender Service most centrally represented people in need—we had clients and saw ourselves as their vigorous and loyal lawyers. Representing clients is the obvious centerpiece of what public defenders do. Lawyers, no doubt, go into defender work because they are drawn to a general cause, but the sense of mission at PDS was not felt immediately as being to a cause—the cause of justice—but to individual clients. We defended the guilty and innocent alike, but we tried to win cases and more particularly to do our best for our clients, whom we saw principally as clients and individuals rather than consciously recognizing them as either guilty or innocent clients.

Hypo: *Defending Bad Guys*

How do you feel about representing criminal defendants who you believe (or know) have committed serious or, often, heinous offenses? Could you do it? Should you do it? How do you feel about others doing it? Do you respect the people who have the fortitude to engage in such a practice, or do you look down upon them? Are you comfortable with criminal defense counsel's coping mechanism of "not knowing" whether his or her client is guilty? Maybe this is the moment to reflect on these issues and decide whether you screwed up and should have gone into the family dry-cleaning business instead of coming to law school.

Abbe Smith—Defending Those People

10 OHIO ST. J. CRIM. L. 277, 283–285, 287–288, 290–291, 298, 300, 301 (2012).

I am drawn to people in trouble. Maybe this is because I had a little sister who was often in trouble. My sister had "problems" as a young child. Once, in kindergarten, she was finger-painting. When it was time to clean up and move to the next activity, the teacher said, "Okay, class. Time to put everything away." My sister ignored her. The teacher approached my sister and, calling her by name, directed her to put the paints away. My sister kept painting. When the teacher repeated her request, my sister picked up her paint-covered hands and wiped them on the teacher's dress.

Who's That?

Abbe Smith is Scott K. Ginsburg Professor of Law, Director of the Criminal Defense & Prisoner Advocacy Clinic, and Co-Director of the E. Barrett Prettyman Fellowship Program, at Georgetown University Law Center. Professor Smith began her legal career at the Defender Association of Philadelphia, where she was an Assistant Defender, a member of the Special Defense Unit, and a Senior Trial Attorney.

I grew up intervening on my sister's behalf, fighting her battles—at home, school, and in the neighborhood. Sometimes I literally fought for her. There was a red-haired boy named Alan who, in second grade, called my sister a name. I gave him a bloody lip, which got me sent to the principal's office. This was my first and only visit to the principal. It was worth it.

I don't think I've punched anyone since. I tend to fight my battles in court.

From that point on, it wasn't a great leap to others in trouble. I mean "trouble" broadly, not just the kind my sister got in, or the kind that lands people in the criminal justice system. I feel a natural sympathy for people in difficulty or distress. It doesn't matter who they are. The fact that they are in trouble is what makes me want to defend them.

This is ironic since patience is generally not my strong suit—I can be brusque and dismissive. I am not known for my attention span—I tend to lose interest quickly (except when it's me who's talking, then I'm riveted). I have many more flaws: I can be a smart aleck, sarcasm is second nature, I don't suffer fools gladly. If I am any guide, you don't need to be the nicest person on earth to want to help people in trouble.

I am probably nicer to people in trouble than I am to ordinary people—even more so if I don't know them. No one should take from this kindness to strangers any great meaning, biblical or otherwise. I might be nicer to strangers only in comparison to people I know. I laugh when a friend or family member takes a pratfall. I can barely stop laughing long enough to help them up.

I seem to broadcast a certain receptiveness to trouble. I am regularly accosted and confided in by people with problems: on the street, in the subway, and at the grocery store. This is multiplied many times in the courthouse. It never fails: the anxious person with a summons, subpoena, or son in jail manages to find me. I don't know why this is.

Ordinarily, I am not terribly interested in "needy" people. I don't have the stamina to weed through layers of need. But with people in criminal trouble there is a built-in narrative that draws me in—something happened and something else will happen to resolve it one way or another. It doesn't need to be a serious or high profile crime for there to be a good story: A gripping tale of comedy, tragedy, theater.

Most of those accused and convicted of crime are poor. Disproportionate numbers are nonwhite. There are now more black people currently under the control of the criminal justice system than were enslaved in 1850. I suppose this is why "nobody really cares" about the quality of criminal justice in the United States, or the fact that we currently lock up more people than any other nation on earth in the "history of the free world." Who gives a damn about a bunch of poor, black people in prison?

I do. And so does every public defender in America—or at least they should.

I often tell students I became a criminal lawyer because I read the book To Kill a Mockingbird (and saw the movie version) too many times as an impressionable child. For me, there is no more compelling figure than Atticus Finch, the archetypal criminal lawyer defending a wrongly accused poor black man. That Gregory Peck played Finch in the movie only contributes to his iconic stature.

Criminal defenders are, by and large, poverty lawyers. You can't spend any amount of time in criminal court and not see that it is a poor people's court. You can't step foot in a jail or prison and not notice they are full of poor people.

But I confess that I am also drawn to any underdog—the little guy, not the big one; David, not Goliath; the Cubs, not the Yankees. I often tell students that growing up a Chicago Cubs fan probably helped pave my life path. Moreover, some criminal justice underdogs were once top dogs. That's the terrifying thing about a criminal prosecution—the once mighty can suddenly be brought low. Although I have represented very few non-indigent clients, the fear, anxiety, and vulnerability that accompany a criminal accusation transcend class.

There's also something fun about fighting for the underdog in criminal court: the stakes are high, the battle hard-fought, the outcome uncertain. The lines are also refreshingly clear. Defenders fight for underdogs against the enormous power of the State. It's the Good Fight.

What's more, we have to be that much better—tougher, smarter, more creative, more resourceful—in order to level the playing field. As one writer puts it: "It's always a stacked deck for the state and often the defense attorney's very best work is simply not good enough to overcome the power and the might." This can be frightening, but it is also exciting. Sometimes you can literally beat the government. There's nothing more thrilling than this, nothing more intoxicating. The wins help keep you going.

But the thing about siding with the underdog is you don't always win—in fact mostly you don't—and it can be devastating when the government puts a human being under your care in a steel cage or kills them. Each defender has to figure out a reason to continue the fight. The opportunity to challenge authority on behalf of another—in fact, the duty to do so—is oddly satisfying and somehow freeing. It doesn't feel that way when I have to confront authority on my own behalf. Then I fold like a cheap tent. But for a client, I am easily indignant and outraged. I tone it down because those feelings are not necessarily the most effective advocacy. But I am happy to go toe-to-toe with prosecutors, police officers, probation officers, and parole officers for a client if I have to—likewise with judges: I am willing to court contempt if need be.

For all of these reasons—the fact that I'm drawn to people in trouble, underdogs, and the guilty, and I enjoy challenging authority—I am what might be called a natural defender. But that doesn't mean there's nothing hard about it. There is plenty that's hard about it. The hardest part is the randomness of justice and the pervasiveness of injustice. Too much depends on the luck of the draw: which lawyer, prosecutor, judge, or jury you happen to get. And too much depends on the resources of the accused.

In her classic article on criminal defense, Barbara Babcock concludes that the real question is not "How can you defend the guilty?" but "Why don't you defend the guilty?" She means two things by this. First, that lawyers who are supposed to be defending the accused often fail to do so because of crushing caseloads and lack of resources. Second, that there should be more lawyers doing criminal defense. Babcock believes that the criminal justice system and the legal profession would be better off if more lawyers did criminal work.

Food for Thought

Does this article excerpt make you think that criminal defense attorneys—and maybe prosecutors, too—are drawn to the different sides of criminal justice practice in some part for psychological, characterological, and/or emotional reasons? Is that a surprise to you? And if there is some truth to this notion, what accounts for lawyers who move from defense to prosecutorial practice, and vice versa? Schizophrenic?

All of this is true. But I would add one more thing: There is nothing more stimulating, fun, challenging, and rewarding than representing people accused or convicted of crime.

FYI

You might be interested in looking at what Professor Smith has to say about whether it is possible to be a feminist and a criminal defense lawyer. Note her own answer: "The answer to the question I pose in this Essay is literally self-evident, for I am both a feminist and a criminal defense lawyer. I have been both of these things for more than thirty years. So yes, of course, one can be a feminist and a criminal defense lawyer: here I am." Abbe Smith, *Can You Be a Feminist and a Criminal Defense Lawyer?*, 57 AM. CRIM. L. REV. 1569 (2020).

Hypo: *Withholding Evidence*

Two part-time public defenders, brothers George and Walter Stenhach, were appointed to represent Richard Buchanan who was charged in Potter County, Pennsylvania, with murder. In discussing the events surrounding the alleged homicide with George Stenhach, Buchanan revealed the locations of some pieces of physical evidence. An investigator for the brothers went to one of the locations and discovered a broken rifle stock which had apparently been used in the homicide. The investigator retrieved and turned the stock over to the Stenhach brothers who withheld it from the prosecution on the theory that "they were obligated to retain the rifle stock to protect their client." During Buchanan's murder trial, the prosecution learned of the existence of the rifle stock and the trial judge subsequently ordered the Stenhach brothers to produce it, which they did. After Buchanan was convicted of murder, the Stenhach brothers were themselves charged with various criminal offenses relating to obstruction of justice.

Do you think that the Stenhach brothers were guilty of criminal activity on these facts or were they, instead, simply acting zealously and professionally in the best interests of their client? Does it make any difference in your analysis that the prosecutor never asked the Stenhach brothers, formally or informally, to produce any relevant evidence that they may have had in their possession? Would it make any difference in your analysis if the evidence that the Stenhach brothers withheld was testimonial rather than physical, e.g. Buchanan's confidential statements to them confessing to the crime? *See Commonwealth v. Stenhach*, 356 Pa.Super. 5, 514 A.2d 114 (1986).

Jenny E. Carroll—If Only I Had Known: The Challenges of Representation

89 FORDHAM L. REV. 2447, 2447–48, 2453–54, 2458–62, 2464–65 (2021).

I began my career as a public defender in the fall of 1998. I was twenty-seven years old and one year out of law school. I had spent the intervening year as a law clerk to a federal district court judge in my home state of Texas. To become a public defender, I did not stay home, however. I moved to what I perceived at the time to be the center of public defense work—Washington, D.C.—to become an E. Barrett Prettyman Fellow at Georgetown University Law Center. In Washington, D.C., far from my rural home in the Rio Grande Valley of Texas, I brought my ideals of criminal systems. As I began my career, I imagined that my commitment and the commitment of those like me to adversarial representation could render these systems just. Instead, in the courtrooms of the Superior Court of the District of Columbia and later in King County, Washington, I bore witness to the complexities of representative systems.

Who's That?

Jenny Carroll is Wiggins, Childs, Quinn & Pantazis Professor of Law at the University of Alabama School of Law. As she discusses in this article excerpt, she is a former public defender.

A system grounded in advocacy by necessity places burdens on the representative. Justice Fortas's description of the criminal defense lawyer as standing between the client and a cruel system is simultaneously awe-inspiring and dauntingly problematic. It is not surprising that such a description would inspire a legion of defense attorneys to seize the mantle of a representative. It is also not surprising that this description would lead to critiques of systems that ultimately failed both those it sought to represent and the attorneys doing the representing; not all of them and not always but painfully often.

One such critique is that the procedural safeguard of representation quiets community discomfort with criminal systems. In this critique, a lawyer does not stand between the client and the overwhelming power of the criminal process. Instead, the lawyer stands between the public and that process to obscure the realities of a system that fall disproportionally on marginalized populations. The lawyer is a salve for a collective conscience that may (or may not) wonder if the system is fair after all. To paraphrase the U.S. Supreme Court in *Strickland v. Washington*, effective counsel is not just the accused's representative, she is the body in the room that makes the rest of us feel as if the outcome was just and correct.

This myth of the defense attorney as a shield in unjust systems creates impossible expectations of the lawyer. The attorney must use skill and advocacy to ensure that innocent clients are acquitted and the same skill and advocacy (though likely exercised in a different fashion) to ensure that the rights of the guilty are protected. This is a near impossible balance to strike. In my time as defense counsel, I witnessed colleagues, good lawyers and people, struggle under the weight of these expectations. But I saw just as often the same good lawyers and people struggle as they tried to provide rigorous representation to clients who fit neither the category of guilt or of innocence. Guilty and innocent clients are alike in that they are rarely only guilty or innocent.

In each of these cases, the burden of representation is not just the lawyer's shortcomings but the peril of representation itself. Not only is representation premised on false dichotomies of guilt and innocence and not only does it serve as both a means of assuaging collective guilt over an unjust system and as a means of actually arriving at some truth, but the ultimate balance representation asks an attorney to engage in is to tell a story not her own in the hopes of urging legal systems to recognize the human dignity of the represented, even as those systems seek to dehumanize that person with their punitive aims.

Others have explored the phenomenon of secondary or vicarious trauma on those engaged in criminal defense work. Such trauma refers to the effect of vicarious and repeated exposure to highly emotional experiences. Perhaps unsurprisingly, studies focused on criminal defense attorneys reveal a high rate of secondary trauma. One such study notes that in the course of their practices, defense attorneys are constantly exposed to traumatic events, including descriptions, visual depictions, and reenactments of such events. Coupled with high caseloads; often unsympathetic police, prosecutors, and courts; and a lack of funding for defense work, it comes as no surprise that defense attorneys show higher rates of secondary traumatic stress symptoms than other trauma workers. The good work of representing the criminally accused is not just hard work, it is traumatic work.

Those who study secondary trauma chronicle its effects on lawyers. Defense attorneys may experience post-traumatic stress disorder symptoms, such as emotional numbing and physiological hyperarousal. Attorneys may attempt to distance themselves from traumatic events. Such distancing may affect both attorneys' ability to connect with their clients and the legal advice attorneys give and litigation strategies they adopt. Attorneys may also suffer from function impairment or engage in self-destructive behavior in response to their secondary trauma. Some will experience burnout, which is "the psychological syndrome of emotional exhaustion, depersonalization, and reduced personal accomplishment." These studies and the work that interprets them is important not only because they identify the occurrence and result of secondary trauma related to defense work but also because they offer concrete suggestions to heal such trauma.

These studies, however, fail to contemplate the full traumatic exposure of defense attorneys on two levels. First, they fail to touch the full extent of the trauma that defense attorneys witness. For many clients, criminal systems are one more stop in a long line of systems that marginalize and complicate their daily existence. From housing and food insecurity, to mental health issues, to intergenerational poverty, to immigration concern, and on and on, I never represented a client who did not bring with them a lifetime of trauma that would continue long after my representation ceased. Second, and not unrelated, these studies contemplate trauma drawn from attorney-client interaction and the case itself. Defense attorneys' traumatic exposure is not limited, however, to the stories clients or witnesses might tell them or the horrors that evidence might reveal. A defense attorney's traumatic exposure includes bearing witness to criminal systems' cruelty to clients and acknowledging the attorney's own complicity in such systems. In this, defense attorneys are in unique positions, as they have both a short view and a long view of the power of criminal law and the systems upon which it relies. They have a literal and figurative seat at the table as both advocates and witnesses to the impact of criminal systems and their disparities.

As a new lawyer, I did not need to read studies on racial bias in policing, prosecution, or sentencing to understand that these systems disproportionately impacted Black and Brown communities. I saw it every day in the courtrooms in which I worked and in my own caseload as a public defender. I did not need a study to tell me that criminal systems had intergenerational impacts or that they maintained economic inequities—I saw it every day. I did not need a study to tell me that the bail system was broken, plea systems were coercive, or that every rule I diligently learned in law school and beyond offered precious little of the promised protections for my clients. I did not need an abolition movement to tell me that criminal systems were overused to horrific effect or that no one ever got better in jail, prison, or juvenile lockup. I was there in courtrooms, in clients' neighborhoods and living rooms, and in jailhouse visits. I saw it. I saw it on my clients' faces and I saw it on their families' and communities' collective face. I saw it all. And I was part of it.

This is the duplicity of defense work that secondary trauma studies miss. To speak of the hazards and the toll of representation, before or in the time of a public health crisis, is to offer a description of systems that imagines the defense lawyer as simultaneously protecting the accused against the power of those systems, while also working within the system itself to ensure that business always proceeds as usual. This balance was never right for me. Between clients and court, I found myself torn between competing needs and obligations.

The court demanded my efficient participation. Judges demanded allegiance to the rules and rulings that defined when, how, and which stories were told in the court-room. In the process, a forced but efficient narrative emerged. The theory of the case was built around defined elements and told between the borders of evidentiary rules defining what was relevant and by extension admissible. I was amazed to learn the first time I picked a jury on behalf of a client that the judge could not only limit the types of questions I could ask the people who would eventually sit in judgment of my client but could also limit the amount of time I had to ask those questions. How, in the thirty allotted minutes, could I know with any certainty if the jurors I chose could be impartial? How, with limited and obscure questions, could I know if the jurors I chose could put aside implicit biases they might not even know they possessed and explicit biases they embraced in their lives when they heard the disjointed narrative of the trial through witnesses and arguments? Judge and supervisor alike told me I had to learn to trust the system. The court's docket was long, and a trial was a vortex in which time disappeared. So, I learned to hurry through jury selections, opening statements, closing arguments, and even objections, hoping in the process that I told enough of my client's story to produce the desired result. More common hearings—the endless arraignments, status conferences, plea entries, and sentencing hearings—revealed both a similar curtailment of the client's narrative and an allegiance to efficiency.

Even as judges and rules curtailed my clients' narratives, for my clients, criminal courts were different than other political moments. Ironically, for many of my clients, the systems which I viewed as indifferent or consciously exclusive of their narrative, offered a mechanism of empowerment that had previously been elusive. The entry into criminal court systems was an entry into a formal world that carried with it formal "protections" of counsel. Once arraigned, defendants were appointed counsel.

In jail visitor rooms through glass, over the phone, or in face-to-face meetings, I met the men, women, and children I would represent and they met me.

In that initial meeting, I explained the parameters of my representation—my appointment as the public defender on this case and this case alone (i.e., I could not and would not handle divorce, child custody, or eviction disputes; I could not make social security finally pay out a claim or find out who kept stealing things off the front porch), attorney-client privilege, and the process to expect going forward (plea, trial, or dismissal).

These initial meetings often went poorly. Why should they not? Except for my repeat clients, these clients I met didn't know me, but they often knew or knew of the system they had entered. Their neighborhoods were full of stories of "public pretend-ers"—sorry lawyers who were public defenders because they could not get another job or they worked to convict or shuffle cases through quickly without protecting the client. And who was I? I did not sound or look like them. The disadvantage of my Texas upbringing was a reliance on words like "y'all" and descriptions of what I was "fixin' to do" that rang discordant out of my mouth to my Pacific Northwest and Washington, D.C., clients. (Although, my contrarian skepticism of police born of years lived on the Texas-Mexico border rang true). In response to their doubts, I worked to win their trust. I began to print my résumé and take it to meetings. I began explaining that I chose to be a public defender. For many clients, we made progress together, mainly because I spent time listening to them and they took time to trust me and tell me their stories, even when we both knew there might be little I could do.

In those meetings, we talked about more than their cases. We talked about lives broken by poverty, substance dependency, over-policing, racism, sexism, and LGBTQ-IA+ bias (even though I didn't know the acronym at the time). They told me stories that had nothing to do with the world in which I had grown up that nonetheless resonated with themes of a government simultaneously overwhelmingly grand in its promise and cruelty. Those meetings, even when they went badly, offered many of my clients something they lacked in the outside, non-criminal-procedure-bound world— an advocate. I was their advocate. They did not have to come up with a theory of their defense, contest the constitutionality of a search, or find a treatment facility on their own, though sometimes they did all three. That was my job. When the judge yelled at someone in the courtroom, it was usually at me, not my client. When the prosecu-tor behaved badly, I objected, argued, and fought. When the police or a lay witness slid sideways on the witness stand to evade a question or duck a contradiction, I straightened them up with all the skills I had been taught in cross-examination and nimble advocacy. Many clients loved the performance that was every court hearing, not because we won (to the contrary, we lost again and again) but because they had a performer in the arena. And every public defender I know tells the story of the client who invited them to Sunday dinner after the win and consoled them—the lawyer—at the bars of the lockup when they lost, for exactly the same reason. It was the standing up that mattered in the end. In our common ground and our uncommon ground, I increasingly saw myself as failing not because I could not do my job but because my job was not the job that was needed or one at which anyone could succeed. The time I spent with my clients taught me to look beyond the narrow role of representation criminal legal systems allotted me and them. The time I spent representing them taught me that the duplicity of my role created an internal conflict that was both unique to the job and often created distress.

In the end, what I loved about being a lawyer were the same things that ultimately made me want to stop—the lives of the people I knew. The weight of those lives came to feel like something I could no longer bear as other life obligations pulled me in different directions. My clients' stories, my role as the person who bridged the chasm between their lives and the formal systems in which they found themselves ensnared, my own complicity in helping criminal legal systems shuffle one more client through, all have stuck with me. They taught me that I was not the representative my clients needed even as I did my best for them. Or more accurately, I was not the only representative they needed.

Food for Thought

Do the points made in this article make you question the way in which lawyers are trained in law school? Or the way in which you are being trained right now? Would a (or your) legal education be more valuable or useful to one's future clients if there was a focus on helping clients in a more holistic fashion? Or is that a task for professionals other than and in addition to lawyers? What do you think?

I have carried the people I represented with me long after I have forgotten their names and they have likely forgotten mine. And in this portage, I have come to accept that I was a conduit to systems that sought to crush them in the first place. True representation for my clients lay in their own communities, where their acts and harms and aching absences were not measured in criminal histories or offense classifications but in lived remembrances and in the cruel, compromising work of figuring out how to exist after the one awful moment that brought the criminal referral in the first place. In thinking of a new model of criminal systems, a new model of representation seems necessary.

This is not the Essay I intended to write when first approached to write for a symposium about attorneys' mental health. I meant to write a "typical" law review article full of citations and distant observations about law and lives. Instead, I found myself returning again and again to what I could not find in the literature I read: an account of what it was to be a lawyer and the burdens that carried. I found myself returning again and again to not only the stories of my clients but to my story as their representative. So, this is the Essay I wrote. Even as I wrote it, it felt, and still feels, risky. It is personal, not objective. I hear in the back of my head the editorial push to banish the first person from law reviews. I hear the critique that it is emotional, not analytical; anecdotal and therefore not accurate or universal. Even in the face of that self-critique, this Essay is, for all its emotion and anecdotal memory, my experience and perhaps that is what I find missing even as I feel I have laid parts of myself bare to write it. Such a personal account can never be universal, nor is it meant to be. It is meant to say: if you read something here that resonates, that feels like what you feel, I give it word and form not to claim it but to convey that I, too, am here. I, too, felt it in all its introspective contradiction and fraught telling.

In reading over it, it strikes me as depressing. Friends and colleagues who have read it call to say they are sorry or worried. They did not realize how hard things were, or they did and they are lost or overwhelmed. They call to share their own stories or to wring their hands and search for therapy helplines over telephone lines and across years of their own guilt or despair. They remind me that in this work, either as an essayist or a defender, I was and am never alone. A former client who I let read it commented that it was "not nearly as funny as I remember you being." This is a client to whom I wrote for the last sixteen years as she waited out her twenty-two-year sentence. I assured her I was never truly that funny over a prison phone call that warned it was recorded so she and I could not forget where she was and that I was no longer her attorney. She suggested I needed a vacation. The irony of her statement was not lost on me.

Whatever the impression this Essay may leave, let me assuage the impression that I am or was sad for the work I did as a public defender. I was not and I am not. It was hard work. And I am frustrated that it was work in systems that I now realize, with the benefit of age and hindsight, I could never "win" in (at least not in ordinary ways—I negotiated far more guilty pleas than I won "not guilty" verdicts). At the same time, however, it is work I am glad I did and continue to toil over because it was and is the work of imagining the world as something different than what I, or my clients, know. It is the work of claiming space and words. It is the work of resistance and community building. It is the exhausting, terrifying, honest, exhilarating work of representing.

C. The Prosecutor's Role

Prosecutors, like defense counsel, often struggle with the appropriate contours of their role in the American adversarial criminal justice system. If "justice" requires that criminal defense counsel defend their clients' zealously, does the same hold true for prosecutors? Do—should—prosecutors have professional duties that differ from those assigned to defense counsel? And how do we—should we—regulate prosecutors' exercise of those duties?

Eric Fish—Against Adversary Prosecution

103 IOWA L. REV. 1419, 1420–23, 1424–26 (2018).

In the book *Just Mercy*, attorney Bryan Stevenson recounts the true story of his long struggle to exonerate Walter McMillian, a man sentenced to death for a murder he did not commit.[1] In one scene of the book, Stevenson meets with the newly elected district attorney for Monroe County, Alabama, where

Who's That?

Eric Fish is Acting Professor of Law at UC Davis School of Law. Previously, he was a federal public defender in San Diego and San Francisco.

McMillian had been convicted. Hoping to convince the prosecutor to agree to reopen the case, Stevenson describes the (rather overwhelming) evidence he has gathered to show his client's innocence. After some discussion, the prosecutor angrily replies: "[M]y job is to defend this conviction."

Implicit in this prosecutor's statement is a particular view of his role: that he is a partisan lawyer tasked with obtaining and preserving convictions. The literature on American prosecutors suggests that this view is commonly held. Prosecutors, as well as the general public, see the criminal justice system as an adversarial contest between two sides. The government wins this contest if the defendant is convicted and punished. The government loses if the defendant is acquitted or the conviction is later vacated. Consequently, the prosecutor is expected to advocate zealously for conviction and punishment. This means they must make strategic decisions that will maximize the likelihood of victory, just as a private lawyer would act strategically on behalf of their client.

Of course, prosecutors are not supposed to be mere adversaries in our system—they also have a special duty to "seek justice." The American Bar Association's ("ABA") Model Rules of Professional Conduct instruct that "[a] prosecutor has the responsibility of a minister of justice and not simply that of an advocate," and that this responsibility entails ensuring "that the defendant is accorded procedural justice." Prosecutors are thus described as having a "dual role." They must seek convictions and punishments in an adversary contest, while also working to ensure the fairness of that contest.

But these two roles are in conflict with one another. Adversarial lawyering is essentially amoral—it requires acting strategically to win litigation, however the client defines victory, regardless of the lawyer's own ethical commitments. Seeking justice, however, requires choosing what substantive values to pursue. And so these two roles push prosecutors in different directions. For any particular choice a prosecutor makes in a case—e.g., adding a count, offering plea-bargain terms, revealing evidence to the

---

[1]   *See generally* Bryan Stevenson, *Just Mercy: A Story of Justice and Redemption* (2014).

defendant, fighting a post-conviction innocence claim—they must decide whether they will strategically maximize their likelihood of victory (which might be defined as securing or preserving a conviction, obtaining a significant punishment, or some other outcome), or instead make room for values like mercy, due process, and proportionality.

This tension, combined with the powerful cultural and professional forces that push prosecutors to seek convictions and harsh punishments, causes adversarialism to dominate American prosecution. This adversary zeal is not just an academic concern—it has significant consequences for the administration of criminal justice. Prosecutors who see their professional goal as strategically maximizing convictions, or punishments, are more likely to use their charging and plea-bargaining discretion to secure guilty pleas and excessive sentences. Indeed, recent empirical scholarship suggests that prosecutorial charging decisions have been a driving force behind the growth of the American prison population over the last 20 years. Adversarial prosecutors are also more likely to ignore evidence of innocence and to fight meritorious post-conviction innocence claims. Studies of exonerations suggest that prosecutorial overzealousness plays a major role in wrongful convictions. How we define the prosecutor's role is thus one of the most important design questions in our criminal justice system.

I argue that the role ethics of American prosecutors should be reconceived as non-adversarial. Analogous to prosecutors in countries with inquisitorial criminal justice systems, like France and Germany, American prosecutors should not think that their goal is to win a case by securing conviction and punishment. Indeed, the argument for non-adversarial prosecution is stronger in the American system than it is in inquisitorial systems. This is because, in America, the prosecutor effectively wields more power than a judge—he or she dictates case outcomes by making charging decisions, controlling pre-trial investigation, and extending plea-bargain offers. By contrast, in inquisitorial systems the judge has power to investigate cases and control the presentation of facts, and prosecutors' charging discretion and plea-bargaining power are sharply constrained. This makes it ironic that American prosecutors are adversarial, while inquisitorial prosecutors are not. Adversary prosecution is uniquely dangerous in a system where the prosecutor is the most important decision-maker.

However, rejecting adversary prosecution, and thereby embracing the pursuit of justice as American prosecutors' sole mandate, is only the first step. This proposed non-adversarial role must itself be unpacked, because there are many values that prosecution could serve in the name of justice. In particular, one crucial question is whether prosecutors themselves will dictate the system's value choices, or whether they will implement policies set by other actors. For example, again by analogy to inquisitorial systems, American prosecutors might think of themselves as neutral conduits for the law. This would require outside institutions like courts, legislatures, and sentencing commissions to impose rules that govern prosecutors' decision-making, and for prosecutors to fit the facts of each case into these externally established rules. Such an ethic might be described as "positivist"—it divests prosecutors of moral agency and turns them into neutral law enforcers. However, as a practical matter, the American system gives prosecutors too much discretion for them to act as morally neutral bureaucrats at every stage of the criminal justice process. American prosecutors have nearly unconstrained discretion to decide on charges and set plea terms. In making such decisions prosecutors must determine, either through established office policies or individual choices, how they are going to weigh the different values that these decisions implicate. This Article thus proposes that "seeking justice" can itself be viewed as containing a dual role for American prosecutors. Where established rules and standards constrain prosecutors' discretion, they should neutrally apply those rules and standards. Where they exercise discretion, they should make value choices for which they are held morally accountable.

American prosecutors should not be viewed as adversary attorneys. [First,] prosecutors in the American system wield an immense amount of power. They have nearly unilateral control over charging decisions, they determine the evidence that will be used against the defendant, and they set the terms of plea-bargain negotiations. Given this power, it is dangerous for prosecutors to think of their job as "winning" cases.

Food for Thought

What do you think about this argument that American prosecutors should not be viewed as adversarial? Does it make sense when and if criminal defense attorneys are adversarial? Maybe criminal defense attorneys should be more concerned about "justice," too. What do you think?

Second, American prosecutors do not have "clients" in any normal sense. While victims are sometimes given a voice in the criminal justice process, the prosecutor is not their lawyer. And while it is conventionally said that the prosecutor represents the state (or "the people"), that does not logically entail an ethic of adversarial conviction-seeking, and if anything lends support to a non-adversarial role. Thus, to the extent that adversary lawyering can be justified by reference to the lawyer's relationship with their client, such a justification is unavailable to prosecutors. Third, American prosecutors have nearly unlimited discretion to bring charges or not bring charges according to their moral views about what conduct is worthy of punishment. Thus, to the extent that adversarialism is justified by rule-of-law values because it removes moral discretion from law enforcement, this justification is also unavailable to American prosecutors. Finally, the strongest argument in favor of adversarial prosecution is that the litigation contest helps to generate facts and legal arguments. Unlike in inquisitorial systems, American courts rely primarily on the parties to present evidence and brief legal issues. However, this argument contains two important caveats. The first is that non-adversarial prosecutors can still generate and present the relevant evidence and arguments, though perhaps not with the same competitive zeal. The second is that only a relatively small number of criminal cases are resolved after an adversary trial (much less one with an effective defense), and so it would be perverse to let prosecutors' role in trial practice justify a general ethic of adversary combat.

My thesis is in one sense a significant departure from the current system. It calls for us to reorient prosecutors' role morality such that they do not think of convictions and punishments as victories, and acquittals as defeats. In another sense, this reorientation is already implicit in the way the legal profession describes prosecutors' professional ideal: as "seeking justice," at least in part. But the continued legitimacy of adversarial prosecution interferes with the search for justice. When a prosecutor goes too far in their partisan zeal—trying to preserve an incorrect conviction or adding charges against a defendant to secure a harsher plea—this is thought of as simply an extension of the prosecutor's legitimate desire to win. It should instead be considered a betrayal of their role. Describing prosecutors as having a dual role, however, legitimizes the partisan half of that duality, and restricts criticism of prosecutors to cases where they break the rules. The duty to seek justice should mean more than avoiding misconduct. Bringing theoretical clarity to prosecutors' professional role can help us to build a system of ethics that contains a more robust conception of the duty to seek justice.

Hypo: *Voir Dire*

When a prosecutor is engaging in the *voir dire* process, should he or she seek to seat jurors who appear to favor the government's case (as the defense will be doing in reverse), or does the duty to "do justice" mean, at least as a matter of theory, that prosecutors should seek to seat only neutral and seemingly unbiased jurors?

Bruce Green & Ellen Yaroshefsky—Prosecutorial Accountability 2.0

92 NOTRE DAME L. REV. 51, 114–16 (2016).

Attention to prosecutorial misconduct has grown in the Internet era. Traditionally, prosecutorial misconduct was viewed as episodic, where the perception was that only a few "rogue prosecutors" engaged in such conduct. Historically, there was limited examination of the issue beyond some defense organizations and a few judges, and regulation of prosecutorial conduct, either by courts or disciplinary authorities, was scant. Discipline within prosecutors' offices was considered ineffective. It was difficult to obtain information about prosecutorial misconduct in cases and, to the extent the issues were exposed, discussions reached a limited audience.

This has changed significantly in the Internet era. The rhetorical shift has moved toward the perception that prosecutorial misconduct is recurring and systemic. Moreover, there has been a regulatory shift toward examining prosecutorial conduct more broadly. Judges more readily express skepticism about prosecutorial compliance with law and ethics rules, and legislative reform has targeted prosecutorial conduct, most notably in areas regarding compliance with discovery in criminal cases. Even disciplinary authorities have stepped up action against errant prosecutors.

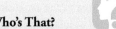

Who's That?

Bruce Green is the Louis Stein Chair at Fordham Law School, where he directs the Louis Stein Center for Law and Ethics. Ellen Yaroshefsky is Howard Lichtenstein Distinguished Professor in Legal Ethics, and Executive Director of the Monroe H. Freedman Institute for the Study of Legal Ethics at Hofstra Law School.

The reasons for the shift in attention to prosecutorial misconduct are multiple and interrelated. We have highlighted five necessary social conditions, beginning with the obvious one—the recurrence of prosecutorial misconduct.

Second, failings of the criminal justice system are front and center in the American discourse. Over-criminalization, mass incarceration, racial disparity in policing, and a myriad of other criminal justice concerns are the fodder of daily news stories. Many of these implicate prosecutors' work, especially their exercise of discretion in investigation, charging, plea bargaining, and sentencing. Concern about prosecutorial conduct is no longer limited to intentional lawbreaking.

Third, hundreds of DNA exonerations and the work of innocence projects exposing the causes of wrongful convictions have prompted public and professional discourse about the prosecutorial responsibility to avert wrongful convictions. Years of litigation, scientific research, and policy work exposed cases where prosecutors relied upon faulty eyewitness identification, false confessions, bad science, and police misconduct in obtaining criminal convictions of innocent people. Many of those cases also involved intentional and negligent failure to disclose evidence favorable to the defense.

FYI

Barry Scheck and Peter Neufeld, who met as public defenders at the Bronx Legal Aid Society, started the Innocence Project in 1992 as a legal clinic at Benjamin N. Cardozo School of Law. The idea was simple: If DNA technology could prove people guilty of crimes, it could also prove that people who had been wrongfully convicted were innocent. Since 1992, Innocence Project efforts have resulted in 375 DNA exonerations of convicted prisoners, including 21 who served time on Death Row. *See* https://innocenceproject.org/exonerated.

Fourth, academic scholarship, particularly in the social sciences, has demonstrated deficiencies in the criminal justice process that prosecutors can ameliorate, and deficiencies in prosecutors' decisionmaking. The scholarship has contributed to the expansion of concern from deliberate prosecutorial wrongdoing to a concept of misconduct that encompasses both negligent wrongdoing and failures to take reasonable measures to ensure the fairness and reliability of the criminal process.

Fifth, as a consequence of and contributor to increased public attention to prosecutorial misconduct, reform organizations slowly built momentum toward discovery reform and other reform directed at prosecutors' conduct.

However, it is unlikely that any of these conditions, individually or collectively, would have resulted in the rhetorical and regulatory shift we describe but for a change in the medium by which prosecutors' conduct is catalogued and debated and made a subject of reform. Information technology has served as a catalyst for change. The Internet has expanded public exposure to wrongful conviction cases, the fault lines in the criminal justice system, the misconduct of prosecutors, and work of reform organizations. Blogs, listservs, Twitter, evolving sites, and new applications contribute to a flurry and exchange of information that was impossible in the pre-Internet days.

There has been a shifting discourse about prosecutorial misconduct, its causes, and potential remedies. Attention to the issue has not waned in the past decade. If anything, public attention is relatively constant and sustained by Internet exposure of new cases, issues, proposed reforms, and new programs. Slowly, but in significant measure, courts, legislatures, and disciplinary authorities have responded to the call for enhanced accountability measures. One cannot predict the future, but the inevitable increase in the sources, availability, and dissemination of information suggests that at the very least, information technology will continue to fuel a movement toward expanded judicial, legislative, and disciplinary regulation of prosecutors and attention to systemic changes in the role of prosecutors in our criminal justice system.

Hypo: *Prosecutors' Duty to Rape Victims & Their Families*

American Bar Association (ABA) Standards for Criminal Justice, Prosecution Function Standard 3–3.4(i) (4th ed. 2017) provides, *inter alia*, that "consistent with any specific laws or rules governing victims, the prosecutor should provide victims of serious crimes, or their representatives, an opportunity to consult with and to provide information to the prosecutor, prior to making significant decisions such as whether or not to prosecute, to pursue a disposition by plea, or to dismiss charges."

Go Online

You can take a look at all of the current ABA Standards for Criminal Justice, including the Prosecution and Defense Function Standards at https://www.americanbar.org/groups/criminal_justice/standards/.

Since the victim of an alleged criminal offense is not the prosecutor's "client," do you think it appropriate in the following situations for a prosecutor to either consider the victim's (or the victim's representatives') input or to require the victim's (or representatives') approval before taking the action proposed:

A) A rape victim does not want her attacker to be prosecuted because she fears the humiliation and embarrassment of having to recount the circumstances of the rape on the witness stand;

B) A rape victim does not want her attacker to be prosecuted because she fears that he or friends of his will harm her or her family;

C) The family of a murdered victim wants the prosecutor to seek the death penalty in a homicide prosecution;

D) The family of a murdered victim wants the prosecutor not to seek the death penalty in a homicide prosecution;

E) An armed robbery victim does not want the prosecution to offer the defendant a proposed plea bargain which would not include incarceration. (Should it make a difference in this situation how strong the prosecution thinks its case is?)

In addition to ethical constraints and quandaries, prosecutors must operate in a setting where they often do not control their own investigative resources. In considering the following excerpt discussing this issue in the federal setting, consider the ways in which this dynamic might influence prosecutorial decision-making.

Jeffrey Bellin—Theories of Prosecution

108 CALIF. L. REV. 1203, 1204–09, 1211–15 (2020).

Scholars view prosecutors as "the most powerful officials in the criminal justice system," and blame them for "[m]uch of what is wrong with American criminal justice." But there is typically something missing from the accounts. An abundant literature highlights the failings of the nation's prosecutors. Yet when it comes to setting out principles

Who's That?

Jeffrey Bellin is Professor of Law at William & Mary Law School. Professor Bellin previously served as a prosecutor in the United States Attorney's Office in D.C.

to govern how prosecutors should act, the commentary offers only platitudes. A 1935 Supreme Court opinion famously reminds prosecutors that it is their special duty to ensure "that justice shall be done." After that, the consensus crumbles. Despite all the attention paid to prosecutors in recent years, the primary guidance on the prosecutorial function remains a timeworn Rorschach test.

Commentators traditionally viewed the absence of concrete rules governing prosecutorial discretion as a blight on the criminal justice landscape, contributing to overly punitive and often racist criminal justice outcomes. Yet in recent years, with the ascension of unapologetically "progressive prosecutors," commentary on prosecutorial power developed a new dimension. In 2017, for example, newly elected Orlando District Attorney Aramis Ayala announced that her office would no longer seek the death penalty. Over one hundred prominent law professors and public officials signed an open letter of support. Efforts to override Ayala's decision, they wrote, threatened prosecutors' "extremely broad discretion to decide when, and how, to prosecute" and "compromise[d] the prosecutorial independence upon which the criminal justice system depends." Around the same time, Baltimore's chief prosecutor, Marilyn Mosby, became a "proxy for a nation reeling with outrage and disbelief" when she swiftly initiated ultimately unsuccessful criminal charges against six police officers involved in the death of Freddie Gray. In a "clip that would echo across the country," Mosby explained to supporters, "I have heard your calls for 'no justice, no peace!' " Most recently, Mosby, along with other big-city prosecutors like District Attorneys Larry Krasner (Philadelphia) and Cyrus Vance (Manhattan) announced that their offices would no longer enforce marijuana possession laws. Krasner explained the decision as "the right thing to do"; Vance's stated goal was "to reduce inequality and unnecessary interactions with the criminal justice system." Mosby highlighted the laws' ineffectiveness: "When I ask myself: Is the enforcement and prosecution of marijuana possession making us safer as a city? [T]he answer is emphatically 'no.' "

These prosecutors are not aberrations. They are prominent representatives of a national movement to leverage prosecutorial power to achieve criminal justice reform. A recent New York Times editorial captures the excitement, embracing the new wave of "state and local prosecutors who are open to rethinking how they do their enormously influential jobs." In light of legislative obstacles, the Times editorialized, this "wiser generation" of prosecutors is "the best chance for continued reform." These developments bring renewed urgency to a long-unanswered question: What is the role of the American prosecutor? Given the centrality of prosecutors to academic writing of the past decade, the lack of an answer is striking.

The curious absence of a normative theory of prosecutorial behavior is best explained by the runaway success of the vacuous ideal that reigns in its place. The conventional view of the prosecutorial role derives from an iconic passage in *Berger v. United States*. There, a unanimous Supreme Court rebuked a prosecutor who made "improper insinuations and assertions calculated to mislead the jury." A prosecutor, the Court explained, represents "a sovereignty whose obligation to govern impartially is as compelling as its obligation to govern at all; and whose interest, therefore, in a criminal prosecution is not that it shall win a case, but that justice shall be done."

Although earlier statements to similar effect can be found, jurists, attorneys, and commentators seize upon the *Berger* passage as "the most authoritative and eloquent description in U.S. law of the role of the prosecutor in administering criminal justice." The American Bar Association (ABA) adopts this formulation (and little else) in its Model Rules of Professional Conduct, instructing prosecutors to act as "minister[s] of justice." The largest association of state prosecutors, the National District Attorneys Association (NDAA), similarly describes the prosecutor as "an independent administrator of justice." Following these organizations' lead, the "legal profession has left much of a prosecutor's day-to-day decisionmaking unregulated, in favor of this catch-all 'seek justice' admonition."

It is hard to object to *Berger's* iconic description of prosecutors. No one can deny the appeal of justice, Merriam-Webster's 2018 "word of the year." Federal prosecutors work in the "Department of Justice." Superheroes operate out of the "Hall of Justice." School children pledge allegiance to a nation dedicated to "justice for all." It's a great slogan. The problem is that philosophers have been trying to define "justice" for thousands of years and report little progress. John Stuart Mill considered justice to be a placeholder for other considerations, which explained why "so many things appear either just or unjust, according to the light in which they are regarded." This observation becomes particularly salient in the grey landscapes of the criminal law, where justice has little uncontested content. Reformers urge prosecutors to seek justice by dispensing mercy, while their opponents wield the same slogan to endorse severity. As Abbe Smith points out: "The concept could not be more ambiguous and subject to multiple interpretations." Other commentators pile on: "When the ABA advises prosecutors to act as 'ministers of justice' or 'administrators of justice,' it is using juris-babble that is practically meaningless to prosecutors and to the ABA itself."

There is, then, a strong case for developing a normative theory of the prosecutorial role. But what? There are numerous justice themes that prosecutors invoke in the course of their duties: public safety ("tough justice"), serving constituents ("popular justice"), and, most recently, ending mass incarceration ("social justice").But these rhetorical appeals are typically too indeterminate to generate concrete guidance for prosecutors deciding whether to initiate and how to pursue specific cases. The law is the most likely place to look for this kind of guidance—and prosecutors sometimes invoke their adherence to the law to explain unpopular decisions. Yet scholars vigorously resist such an approach, urging prosecutors to exercise their discretion when necessary to sidestep the law's commands. Closely tying prosecutorial discretion to substantive law, they contend, will result in wooden formalism and needless severity. These are all good points. But they undergird a hard bargain. Our long experiment with justice as the prosecutorial touchstone has not produced an abundance of leniency or, in the eyes of many commentators, justice. And given the widely recognized dangers of unbridled prosecutorial discretion, it seems worthwhile to explore alternatives.

This Article explores the possibility of using existing legal rules to construct a coherent normative theory of prosecution—and primarily state and local prosecution, the locus of American criminal law. It crafts a "servant-of-the-law" model of prosecution that takes its name from an undeveloped intuition expressed in the same Supreme Court opinion that tasks prosecutors with ensuring "that justice shall be done." There, the Court also emphasized that the prosecutor is "in a peculiar and very definite sense the servant of the law." Parallels can be drawn to the perception of prosecutors in continental Europe, although those legal systems are so distinct that isolated comparisons of the prosecutorial function tend to obscure rather than clarify. The Article retains a domestic focus, explaining how a servant-of-the-law orientation would change American prosecutorial behavior. In so doing, it highlights potential benefits for our criminal justice system of shifting the dominant conception of the prosecutorial role from an "advocate for justice" to a "servant of the law." Perhaps the greatest benefit is determinacy. By stripping away any pretense that prosecutors possess sweeping responsibility for justice, a servant-of-the-law model lays the groundwork for both overarching principles and concrete guidance for how prosecutors best serve the law in specific situations.

Food for Thought

Do you find this "servant-of-the-law approach useful? Is it clear to you *which* laws should serve as the groundwork for this approach? And which laws should or need not?

Serving the law is a clearer assignment than seeking justice. But it is by no means easy. Prosecutors will always be torn by competing tensions, as is the law. This tension could lead to an equanimity of purpose rather than the adversarial mindset at the root of modern prosecutorial excess. The law criminalizes certain conduct and sets penalty ranges upon conviction. But the law also dictates a process by which convictions must be obtained, including a heavy burden of proof. The law guarantees criminal defendants a right to counsel and asks neutral factfinders to resolve disputes. A prosecutor viewing this whole fabric as "the law" that must be served would be indifferent to wins and losses. Such a prosecutor succeeds when a jury convicts; succeeds when the jury acquits; and succeeds when dismissing a case due to insufficient evidence or an unlawful search or interrogation. As the Supreme Court explained in another context: "The criminal goes free, if he must, but it is the law that sets him free." A prosecutor with a professional identity as a servant of the law would find satisfaction in that result.

This understanding of the prosecutor as a servant of the law, rather than an advocate for justice, would clarify and, in some areas, transform the traditional conception of the prosecutor's role. Importantly, this reconceptualization might be accepted (or spurned) across the political spectrum because it does not fit neatly into either "side" of the criminal justice debate. It will nudge prosecutors toward severity when the background law is severe and towards leniency when the background law is lenient. It could make prosecutors less adversarial and more cooperative with defense counsel and judges. At its core, this reconceptualization narrows the rhetorical scope of the prosecutorial function, placing the focus on other actors, and ultimately the system itself, to ensure that justice is done.

Importantly, a prosecutor who embraces the servant-of-the-law model would not robotically enforce every criminal statute in every case. Most obviously, the prosecutor would decline to prosecute cases with insufficient evidence to prove the defendant's guilt. This would include cases that depend on police officers with credibility problems, jailhouse informants, coerced confessions, flawed identification procedures, or questionable forensic science. The servant-of-the-law prosecutor would also preference defendant-protective state and federal constitutional provisions over the mechanical enforcement of criminal statutes. Thus, the prosecutor would decline to trigger bail conditions, charges, or sentencing enhancements that would violate constitutional provisions such as the Eighth Amendment's proportionality principle, or its prohibition of excessive bail or fines. The prosecutor would also rework plea practices to ensure that defendants are not coerced to waive their Sixth Amendment right to a jury trial.

Perhaps most significantly, in light of the weighty due process and discovery requirements that attach to even the most petty criminal case, servant-of-the-law prosecutors would freely dismiss minor cases in response to resource constraints. For example, in an age of police body cameras, even the smallest case requires a prosecutor to gather and review the body camera footage from officers who responded to the incident and interacted with the defendant or victim. Prosecutors who cannot satisfy the legal obligations attendant to every case on their docket must dismiss cases until they can. Given the breadth of American criminal laws, all prosecutors decline to pursue some offenses to preserve resources for more consequential prosecutions. Servant-of-the-law prosecutors, keenly aware of the legal obligations that inhere in every prosecution, would be no exception.

A servant-of-the-law model will not resolve all prosecutorial choices, but it would provide a default position for the American prosecutor, a much-needed starting point for crafting nuanced rules and guidance. In light of the complexity of American criminal justice, deviations from the default would be expected. However, these deviations would be recognizable and thus more likely to be accompanied by transparent and consistent explanations.

With the beginnings of a concrete normative theory of prosecutorial behavior in hand, the question becomes whether such a theory is preferable to the malleability of the "do justice" status quo. A shift in orientation may prove unpalatable to both prosecutors who prefer the freedom to do "what is right" and reformers inspired by prosecutors' potential power to unilaterally disarm the criminal justice system. But over the long term, more narrowly channeling the power of prosecutors could be preferable to continued expansion. And many (if not most) of the goals of the prosecutor-driven criminal justice reform movement could be advanced by reorienting prosecutors as less adversarial servants of the law.

Executive Summary

Adversary System. The American criminal justice system is an adversary system where a criminal defendant's guilt or innocence is determined as a result of the adversarial arguments and presentations of evidence by a prosecutor and defense counsel, overseen by a neutral and impartial judge.

Defense Counsels' Dilemma. Criminal defense counsel need to represent their clients effectively, whether or not they know that they are or may be guilty. Nonetheless, representing guilty clients as if they are innocent often can be troubling for defense counsel (and their families) personally, emotionally, and sometimes professionally.

Prosecutors' Dilemma. Prosecutors are supposed to fight crime and convict the guilty. However, they are also supposed to "seek justice, not victory" or be a "servant of the law," and this obligation counsels prosecutors not to try to win at all costs, a stricture that can be difficult for prosecutors to follow personally, emotionally, and professionally.

Major Themes

a. Defense Counsel as Zealots—Many criminal defense counsel believe that they must or should represent their clients "zealously." But sometimes zealous representation of criminal defendants raises concerns about real or apparent conflicts with defense counsel's simultaneous role as an officer of the court.

b. Prosecutor's Clients—Prosecutors are said to be "ministers of justice," "servants of the law," whose clients are *all* of the people in their jurisdiction, not the victims of a crime. But sometimes it can be difficult for prosecutors to resist the urge to act in just as adversarial a fashion as criminal defense counsel, considering primarily the victims' interests, whether or not securing a conviction actually reflects the overall community's interests.

c. **Due Process vs. Truth**—The American criminal justice system sometimes values adherence to proper procedures, e.g. avoiding police misconduct, over finding the truth, e.g. determining whether the defendant is actually innocent or guilty. This important and overriding systemic respect for fair and lawful methods of proceeding creates a persistent tension in the criminal justice system, however, and it sometimes results in public misunderstanding of—and displeasure with—events that may take place in a criminal prosecution, e.g. the suppression of otherwise inculpatory evidence.

Test Your Knowledge

To assess your understanding of the material in this chapter, click here to take a quiz.

CHAPTER 10

Initial Appearance &
Pretrial Release

A. Initial Appearance

Following an arrest and administrative "booking," the accused must be brought before a judge or other judicial officer (e.g., a magistrate) for a proceeding usually called a "first appearance" "initial appearance," "presentment," or "preliminary arraignment." There are three main determinations that take place at the initial appearance: a determination of probable cause, a determination regarding bond, and appointment of counsel if necessary.

Federal Rule of Criminal Procedure 5(d) is typical of most rules setting the procedures for the initial appearance in court. Under Rule 5(d), the judge must inform the accused of the following: the charges; the right to remain silent; the right to request or retain an attorney; the fact that any statements that he/she makes may be used against him/her; the circumstances under which the accused

Take Note

In many jurisdictions, no charging document may be issued by the prosecuting authority at the time of the initial appearance. Instead, the court makes determinations regarding probable cause and bond based on sworn information from the police.

may secure pretrial release; the right to a preliminary hearing; a reasonable time to consult with an attorney; & the setting or denying bail.

FYI

When there is a charging document from the prosecutor, and the charging document is an indictment, or when an indictment is unnecessary, the defendant normally enters a plea to the charges, usually "Not Guilty" at this early stage of the case. If a defendant chooses to stand mute, the court, by rule or its inherent authority, enters a not guilty plea on the defendant's behalf.

In some jurisdictions, including in the federal courts, at the initial appearance an accused is charged by the prosecuting authority by way of a complaint or similar document. Whether there is a charging document from the prosecution or simply an accusation from the police (commonly referred to as a "police charge"), the court must make the defendant aware of the accusation(s) against him.

Most jurisdictions require that the accused be brought before the nearest available judicial officer without unnecessary delay. Many jurisdictions have a provision like Fed. R. Crim. P. 5, which permits the judicial officer to conduct the initial appearance by video teleconference with the defendant's consent. Under Fed. R. Crim. P. 5, the judge also has flexibility as to the district in which the initial appearance may be held. In *United States v. Alvarez-Sanchez*, 511 U.S. 350 (1994), the Court held that the period of delay in federal courts usually is measured from the time the accused is arrested on federal charges. An unreasonable delay between arrest and the initial appearance may violate due process. In evaluating an allegation of unreasonable delay, courts analyze the amount of time that has passed as well as how and why the delay occurred.

Take Note

Confessions that are obtained during periods of unnecessary delay prior to the initial appearance may be inadmissible. For example, under 18 U.S.C. § 3501, delay is one of several statutory factors considered in deciding whether a confession was given voluntarily during the period of unreasonable delay. *See McNabb v. United States*, 318 U.S. 332 (1943); *Mallory v. United States*, 354 U.S. 449 (1957).

Point for Discussion

Assignment of Counsel

In *Rothgery v. Gillespie County, Texas,* 554 U.S. 191 (2008), the Court made clear that a defendant's Sixth Amendment right to counsel attaches at the initial appearance, regardless of whether there is a formal charging document. *See also* Fed. R. Crim. P. 44. In many jurisdictions, while specific counsel may be "appointed," that may not actually happen at the initial appearance, thereby creating the possibility that defendant will not have an assigned attorney for an extended period of time. In such situations, there is usually one attorney from the local public defenders' office who will stand in and represent all indigent defendants at first appearances. In more urban or larger jurisdictions, this may mean twenty or more defendants at once. However, sometimes there is no counsel present at the first appearance.

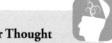

Food for Thought

What problems do you see if counsel is not present at the initial appearance? What role should a lawyer play at that stage? What problems might be created by the fact that a single lawyer stands in for all defendants? What should the remedy be for the lack of counsel at the first appearance?

Gerstein v. Pugh

420 U.S. 103 (1975).

MR. JUSTICE POWELL delivered the opinion of the Court.

In March 1971 respondents Pugh and Henderson were arrested in Dade County, Fla. Each was charged with several offenses under a prosecutor's information. Pugh was denied bail because one of the charges against him carried a potential life sentence, and Henderson remained in custody because he was unable to post a $4,500 bond.

Hear It

You can hear the oral argument in *Gerstein* at: http://www.oyez.org/cases/1970-1979/1973/1973_73_477.

In Florida, indictments are required only for prosecution of capital offenses. Prosecutors may charge all other crimes by information, without a prior preliminary hearing and without obtaining leave of court. Florida courts have held that the filing of an information foreclosed the suspect's right to a preliminary hearing. They have also held that *habeas corpus* could not be used, except perhaps in exceptional circumstances, to test the probable cause for detention under an information. The only possible methods for obtaining a judicial determination of probable cause were a special statute allowing a preliminary hearing after 30 days and arraignment, which the District Court found was often delayed a month or more after arrest. As a result, a person charged by information could be detained for a substantial period solely on the decision of a prosecutor. This case presents two issues: whether a person arrested and held for trial on an information is entitled to a judicial determination of probable cause for detention, and if so, whether the adversary hearing ordered by the District Court and approved by the Court of Appeals is required by the Constitution.

Take Note

Defendants were arrested without a warrant. Had they been arrested on a warrant, *Gerstein* held that an arrest warrant previously issued by a magistrate would satisfy the probable cause determination for the imposition of bail, temporarily detaining a defendant.

To implement the Fourth Amendment's protection against unfounded invasions of liberty and privacy, the Court has required that the existence of probable cause be decided by a neutral and detached magistrate whenever possible. The classic statement of this principle appears in *Johnson v. United States*, 333 U.S. 10, 13 (1948): "The point of the Fourth Amendment, which often is not grasped by zealous officers, is not that it denies law enforcement the support of the usual inferences which reasonable men draw from evidence. Its protection consists in requiring that those inferences be drawn by a neutral and detached magistrate instead of being judged by the officer engaged in the often competitive enterprise of ferreting out crime." Maximum protection of individual rights could be assured by requiring a magistrate's review of the factual justification prior to any arrest, but such a requirement would constitute an intolerable handicap for legitimate law enforcement. While the Court has expressed a preference for arrest warrants when feasible it has never invalidated an arrest supported by probable cause solely because the officers failed to secure a warrant.

A policeman's on-the-scene assessment of probable cause provides legal justification for arresting a person suspected of crime, and for a brief period of detention to take the administrative steps incident to arrest. Once the suspect is in custody, the reasons that justify dispensing with the magistrate's neutral judgment evaporate. There no longer is any danger that the suspect will escape or commit further crimes while the police submit their evidence to a magistrate. While the State's reasons for taking summary action subside, the suspect's need for a neutral determination of probable cause increases significantly. The consequences of prolonged detention may be more serious than the interference occasioned by arrest. Pretrial confinement may imperil the suspect's job, interrupt his source of income, and impair his family relationships. Even pretrial release may be accompanied by burdensome conditions that effect a significant restraint of liberty. When the stakes are this high, the detached judgment of a neutral magistrate is essential if the Fourth Amendment is to furnish meaningful protection from unfounded interference with liberty. Accordingly, we hold that the Fourth Amendment requires a judicial determination of probable cause as a prerequisite to extended restraint of liberty following arrest.

Both the District Court and the Court of Appeals held that the determination of probable cause must be accompanied by the full panoply of adversary safeguards—counsel, confrontation, cross-examination, and compulsory process for witnesses. A full preliminary hearing of this sort is modeled after the procedure used in many States to determine whether the evidence justifies going to trial under an information or presenting the case to a grand jury. These adversary safeguards are not essential for the probable cause determination required by the Fourth Amendment. The sole issue is whether there is probable cause for detaining the arrested person pending further proceedings. This issue can be determined reliably without an adversary hearing. The standard is the same as that for arrest. That standard—probable cause to believe the suspect has committed a crime—traditionally has been decided by a magistrate in a nonadversary proceeding on hearsay and written testimony, and the Court has approved these informal modes of proof.

The use of an informal procedure is justified not only by the lesser consequences of a probable cause determination but also by the nature of the determination itself. It does not require the fine resolution of conflicting evidence that a reasonable-doubt or even a preponderance standard demands, and credibility determinations are seldom crucial in deciding whether the evidence supports a reasonable belief in guilt. This is not to say that confrontation and cross-examination might not enhance the reliability of probable cause determinations in some cases. In most cases, their value would be too slight to justify holding, as a matter of constitutional principle, that these formalities and safeguards designed for trial must also be employed in making the Fourth Amendment determination of probable cause. Because of its limited function and its nonadversary character, the probable cause determination is not a "critical stage" in the prosecution that would require appointed counsel. The Court has identified as "critical stages" those pretrial procedures that would impair defense on the merits if the accused is required to proceed without counsel. *Coleman v. Alabama*, 399 U.S. 1 (1970); *United States v. Wade*, 388 U.S. 218 (1967). The Fourth Amendment probable cause determination is addressed only to pretrial custody. To be sure, pretrial custody may affect the defendant's ability to assist in preparation of his defense, but this does not present the high probability of substantial harm identified as controlling in *Wade* and *Coleman*.

Although the Constitution does not require an adversary determination of probable cause, we recognize that state systems of criminal procedure vary widely. There is no single preferred pretrial procedure, and the nature of the probable cause determination usually will be shaped to accord with a State's pretrial procedure viewed as a whole. Whatever procedure a State may adopt, it must provide a fair and reliable determination of probable cause as a condition for any significant pretrial restraint of liberty,[26]

Food for Thought

Is the Court right? Why is this not a "critical stage"? Why aren't some adversarial safeguards necessary at this point since defendant is in court? Is there something between what the District Court required and what the Court here suggests, which is reliance on an *ex parte* determination of probable cause by a judicial officer without the opportunity for a lawyer representing the defense to point out any problems or defects?

and this determination must be made by a judicial officer either before or promptly after arrest.

We agree with the Court of Appeals that the Fourth Amendment requires a timely judicial determination of probable cause as a prerequisite to detention. As we do not agree that the Fourth Amendment requires the adversary hearing outlined in the District Court's decree, we reverse in part and remand to the Court of Appeals for further proceedings consistent with this opinion.

It is so ordered.

---

[26] Because the probable cause determination is not a constitutional prerequisite to the charging decision, it is required only for those suspects who suffer restraints on liberty other than the condition that they appear for trial. There are many kinds of pretrial release and many degrees of conditional liberty. We cannot define specifically those that would require a prior probable cause determination, but the key factor is significant restraint on liberty.

Make the Connection

This case was brought as a civil rights action under U.S.C. § 1983, as was *Rothgery*. However, the Court suggests in *Gerstein* that the case could have been brought as a pretrial petition for a writ of *habeas corpus* challenging the pretrial detention as unlawful under the Fourth Amendment. Lawyers and judges usually think of *habeas corpus* petitions as solely designed to address post-conviction constitutional issues, but that is not the case.

Points for Discussion

a. The *Gerstein* Proceeding

At a *Gerstein* hearing, hearsay and written testimony are permitted if those statements have been sworn to under oath. While the *Gerstein* determination is not an adversarial proceeding and the accused has no right to be present, to have counsel, or to question witnesses, the initial appearance often includes the

Because of the similarity between the timing of the initial appearance and the *Gerstein* determination following a warrantless arrest, a judge may conduct both proceedings at the time of the initial appearance.

accused and counsel, and counsel may be allowed to point out defects in the government's presentation.

b. A Finding of No Probable Cause

When a court determines that there is no probable cause, the defendant must be released from custody on that charge. A finding of no probable cause does not foreclose a later prosecution.

c. The Forty-Eight Hour Rule

In *County of Riverside v. McLaughlin*, 500 U.S. 44 (1991), the Court held that absent "emergency or other extraordinary circumstances" the judicial determination of probable cause must occur as "soon as is reasonably feasible, but in no event later than 48 hours after arrest."

Make the Connection

What happens if defendant is arrested under a warrant and the affidavit does not establish probable cause, or the judicial officer finds probable cause at the first appearance, but the officer is wrong? Does defendant have a constitutional remedy? *Gerstein* does not answer these questions but does the Fourth Amendment require a remedy?

Hypo: *Did the Police Comply with* Riverside?

The police arrest Johnson for murder on a Saturday at 11:00 a.m. as he is fleeing the scene of a homicide. The police hold Johnson for interrogation until Monday morning while they complete their investigation. In this jurisdiction, the court holds first appearances at 10:00 a.m. and at 3:00 p.m. every day Monday through Friday, but only at 5:00 p.m. on Saturdays, Sundays and holidays. Monday morning, the police take Frank to court for the 10:00 a.m. initial appearance session. Did the police comply with *Riverside*? See *Lopez v. City of Chicago*, 464 F. 3d 711 (7th Cir. 2006).

B. Pretrial Release

A defendant's pretrial release from custody typically is in exchange for a pledge of something of value designed to insure he will appear in court and will comply with the court's orders in a pending criminal case. Bail is the Anglo-American criminal justice system's solution to the problem of how to handle

> **FYI**
>
> In *Walker v. City of Calhoun,* 901 F.3d 1245 (11th Cir. 2018), the court held that indigents could be held for forty-eight hours before receiving a bail hearing.

an accused, who is presumed innocent, during the period between arrest and trial. Conceptually, bail accommodates the defendant's interest in pretrial liberty (consistent with the presumption of innocence) and society's interest in assuring that the accused is present for trial so that the case can be properly adjudicated. In each case, a judge must decide whether to grant pretrial release, and if so, what monetary amount and/or conditions of release are needed to assure the defendant's presence. There are a variety of release conditions that a court may impose.

Points for Discussion

a. Recognizance Bond

Release on recognizance (ROR) is a long-standing practice, and for good reason. If the defendant is likely return to court, even without the imposition of conditions, the bond requirement may not be needed, and may impose a substantial and unnecessary hardship upon a defendant of limited resources. Perhaps for this reason, the law acknowledges the power of the courts to release a defendant on recognizance, and indeed entitles a defendant to ROR unless the court finds that something more is required to insure the defendant's appearance in court. In other words, under the law, although not necessarily in practice, release on recognizance should be the norm or "default" position.

b.   Unsecured Bond

An unsecured bond is a pledge by defendant to be liable for a specified sum if he breaches a material release condition. The unsecured bond is advantageous over release on PR when defendant is a person of means. The bond gives the defendant a financial stake in obeying court orders and thus helps insure the defendant's appearance.

c.   Release on Nonfinancial Conditions

The court has the power and flexibility to place nonfinancial conditions on the defendant if they are limited to conditions designed to insure the presence of the accused at future court proceedings. Courts must impose the least onerous conditions that will insure defendant's presence in court. Such conditions may include, but are not limited to, placing defendant in the custody of a person or agency, placing restrictions upon travel, association or place of abode, drug testing or treatment, enrollment in school or pursuit of employment, electronic monitoring,

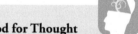

Food for Thought

A bail reform law prioritizes non-monetary methods of bail. The law requires a court to measure a defendant's flight risk and imposes conditions such as house arrest, wearing a monitor, and other restrictions on movement. Defendant agreed to home detention and electronic monitoring. However, after a few months, he believes that his movements are overly restricted, and demands that he be given the option of posting cash bail. The judge denies the motion. Is defendant entitled to cash bail? *See Holland v. Rosen*, 895 F.3d 272 (3d Cir. 2018).

or requiring confinement at home, a jail, a halfway house or other facility during specified hours.

d.   Cash Bond

A defendant may be released from custody by depositing cash (or its equivalent) in the amount of the bail with the court. The money is deposited by the clerk in an escrow account and is returned, usually minus an administrative fee, at the conclusion of the proceedings if the accused has appeared as directed. A major advantage of a cash

In *Daves v. Dallas County*, 984 F.3d 381 (5th Cir. 2020), the court upheld a lower court order blocking Dallas County from detaining indigent arrestees who cannot afford to pay cash bail. The trial court judge noted "a clear showing of routine wealth-based detention." However, the decision was vacated. *Daves v. Dallas County*, 988 F.3d 834 (5th Cir., en banc, 2021).

bond is that it gives defendant an immediate stake in appearing for court proceedings. In the event of non-appearance, defendant faces an immediate financial loss, rather than some sort of distant civil liability, as would be true under an unsecured bond. Moreover, if defendant does appear in court as ordered, the money may be recovered rather than retained by the bondsman who may have done little to advance the justice system's interests. A cash bond may also be available for forfeiture or for application to indebtedness upon judgment in the case.

e. Personal Surety Bond

The defendant may also be able to obtain release by pledging his real property (or arranging for his/her friends to pledge theirs). If defendant fails to appear in court, the property is forfeited. If defendant appears as directed, the property or any lien on the real estate is released at the conclusion of the proceedings.

f. Surety Bond

The court may require defendant to post a bond underwritten by one or more sureties. This is the classic bail bond situation. The defendant or his or her family or friends pay a fee, typically 10%, to a bondsman, and the bondsman posts

Take Note

While bail bondsmen may have made sense in earlier times, the need for bondsmen is obsolete with the advent of modern policing and computer systems: 1) once the bondsman is paid his fee, the bond no longer provides the defendant with an incentive to appear; 2) in actual practice, bondsmen do very little because a defendant who fails to appear is usually returned to court by law enforcement; 3) even if a bondsman does attempt to return defendant to court, it is questionable whether public safety is advanced by "Dog the Bounty Hunter" going out into the community armed with a gun to protect his own money. Isn't this better handled by trained law enforcement?

Food for Thought

Compare the differences between cash and surety bonds. Is there any advantage of one over the other for criminal justice purposes? Why might judges prefer surety bonds? Is there a rational basis for that preference?

the entire amount of the bond with the court. The bondsman keeps the 10% as a fee at the conclusion of the case. If defendant fails to appear in court, the bondsman is on the hook for the bond amount and therefore has an incentive to find the defendant and get him to court, much in the vein of Old West bounty hunters.

1. Release Determinations

Stack v. Boyle

342 U.S. 1 (1951).

MR. CHIEF JUSTICE VINSON delivered the opinion of the Court.

Indictments have been returned in the Southern District of California charging the twelve petitioners with conspiring to violate the Smith Act, 18 U.S.C. (Supp. IV) §§ 371, 2385. Upon their arrest, bail was fixed for each petitioner in the widely varying amounts of $2,500, $7,500, $75,000 and $100,000. On motion of petitioner Schneiderman following arrest in New York, his bail was reduced to $50,000 before his removal to California. On motion of the Government to increase bail in the case of other petitioners, bail was fixed in the District Court for the Southern District of California in the uniform amount of $50,000 for each petitioner.

Petitioners moved to reduce bail on the ground that bail as fixed was excessive under the Eighth Amendment.[1] In support of their motion, petitioners submitted statements as to their financial resources, family relationships, health, prior criminal records, and other information. The only evidence offered by the Government was a certified record showing that four persons previously convicted under the Smith Act in the Southern District of New York had forfeited bail. No evidence was produced relating those four persons to the petitioners in this case. At a hearing on the motion, petitioners were examined by the District Judge and cross-examined by an attorney for the Government. Petitioners' factual statements stand uncontroverted. After their motion to reduce bail was denied, petitioners filed applications for *habeas corpus* in the District Court. The writs were denied. The Court of Appeals for the Ninth Circuit affirmed.

From the passage of the Judiciary Act of 1789 to the present Federal Rules of Criminal Procedure, Rule 46 (a)(1), federal law has unequivocally provided that a person arrested for a non-capital offense *shall* be admitted to bail. This traditional right to freedom before conviction permits the unhampered preparation of a defense, and serves to prevent the infliction of punishment prior to conviction. *See Hudson v. Parker*, 156 U.S. 277 (1895). Unless this right to bail before trial is preserved, the presumption of innocence, secured only after centuries of struggle, would lose its meaning.

The right to release before trial is conditioned upon the accused's giving adequate assurance that he will stand trial and submit to sentence if found guilty. *Ex parte*

---

[1]   Excessive bail shall not be required, nor excessive fines imposed, nor cruel and unusual punishments inflicted." U.S. CONST., AMEND. VIII.

Milburn, 9 Pet. 704 (1835). Like the ancient practice of securing the oaths of responsible persons to stand as sureties for the accused, the modern practice of requiring a bail bond or the deposit of a sum of money subject to forfeiture serves as additional assurance of the presence of an accused. Bail set at a figure higher than an amount reasonably calculated to fulfill this purpose is "excessive" under the Eighth Amendment. Since the function of bail is limited, the fixing of bail for any individual defendant must be based upon standards relevant to the purpose of assuring the presence of that defendant. The traditional standards as expressed in the Federal Rules of Criminal Procedure are to be applied in each case to each defendant. In this case petitioners are charged with offenses under the Smith Act. Upon conviction, petitioners face imprisonment of not more than five years and a fine of not more than $10,000. Bail for each petitioner has been fixed in a sum much higher than that usually imposed for offenses with like penalties and yet there has been no factual showing to justify such action. The Government asks the courts to depart from the norm by assuming, without evidence, that each petitioner is a pawn in a conspiracy and will, in obedience to a superior, flee the jurisdiction. To infer from the fact of indictment alone a need for bail in an unusually high amount is an arbitrary act. Such conduct would inject into our system of government the very principles of totalitarianism which Congress was seeking to guard against in passing the statute under which petitioners have been indicted. If bail in an amount greater than that usually fixed for serious charges of crimes is required in the case of any of the petitioners, that is a matter to which evidence should be directed in a hearing so that the constitutional rights of each petitioner may be preserved. In the absence of such a showing, the fixing of bail before trial in these cases cannot be squared with the statutory and constitutional standards for admission to bail.

The Court concludes that bail has not been fixed by proper methods in this case and that petitioners' remedy is by motion to reduce bail, with right of appeal. Accordingly, the judgment of the Court of Appeals is vacated and the case is remanded to the District Court with directions to vacate its order denying petitioners' applications for writs of *habeas corpus* and to dismiss the applications without prejudice. Petitioners may move for reduction of bail in the criminal proceeding so that a hearing may be held for the purpose of fixing reasonable bail for each petitioner.

By MR. JUSTICE JACKSON, whom MR. JUSTICE FRANKFURTER joins dissenting.

The principles governing bail have been misunderstood or too casually applied in these cases and they should be returned to the Circuit Justice or the District Courts for reconsideration in the light of standards which it is our function to determine.

Admission to bail, as it has evolved in Anglo-American law, is not a device for keeping persons in jail upon mere accusation until it is found convenient to give them a trial. The spirit of the procedure is to enable them to stay out of jail until a

Food for Thought

The view of bail articulated in this opinion is not reflective of what the vast majority of judges actually do in setting bond. For example, when a judge sets a million dollar bond for an indigent defendant in a murder or rape case, does the judge expect defendant to post the bond, giving him an adequate incentive to return to court, or does he expect that the accused will stay in jail?

trial has found them guilty. Without this conditional privilege, even those wrongly accused are punished by a period of imprisonment while awaiting trial and are handicapped in consulting counsel, searching for evidence and witnesses, and preparing a defense. To open a way of escape from this handicap and possible injustice, Congress commands allowance of bail for one under charge of any offense not punishable by death, Fed. Rules Crim. Proc., 46 (a)(1) providing: "A person arrested for an offense not punishable by death shall be admitted to bail" before conviction.

Admission to bail always involves a risk that the accused will take flight. That is a calculated risk which the law takes as the price of our system of justice. We know that Congress anticipated that bail would enable some escapes, because it provided a procedure for dealing with them. Fed. Rules Crim. Proc., 46 (f). In allowance of bail, the duty of the judge is to reduce the risk by fixing an amount reasonably calculated to hold the accused available for trial and its consequence. Fed. Rules Crim. Proc., 46 (c). But the judge is not free to make the sky the limit, because the Eighth Amendment to the Constitution says: "Excessive bail shall not be required." Congress has reduced this generality in providing more precise standards, stating that "the amount shall be such as in the judgment of the commissioner or court or judge or justice will insure the presence of the defendant, having regard to the nature and circumstances of the offense charged, the weight of the evidence against him, the financial ability of the defendant to give bail and the character of the defendant." Fed. Rules Crim. Proc., 46(c).

It is complained that the District Court fixed a uniform blanket bail chiefly by consideration of the nature of the accusation and did not take into account the difference in circumstances between different defendants. If this occurred, it is a clear violation of Rule 46 (c). Each defendant stands before the bar of justice as an individual. Even on a conspiracy charge defendants do not lose their separateness or identity. While it might be possible that these defendants are identical in financial ability, character and relation to the charge—elements Congress has directed to be regarded in fixing bail—it violates the law of probabilities. Each accused is entitled to any benefits due to his good record, and misdeeds or a bad record should prejudice only those who are guilty of them. The question when application for bail is made relates to each one's trustworthiness to appear for trial and what security will supply reasonable assurance of his appearance.

But the protest charges, and the defect in the proceedings below appears to be, that, provoked by the flight of certain Communists after conviction, the Government demands and public opinion supports a use of the bail power to keep Communist defendants in jail before conviction. Thus, the amount is said to have been fixed not as a reasonable assurance of their presence at the trial, but as an assurance they would remain in jail. There seems reason to believe that this may have been the spirit to which the courts below have yielded, and it is contrary to the policy and philosophy of bail. This is not to say that every defendant is entitled to such bail as he can provide, but he is entitled to an opportunity to make it in a reasonable amount. I think the matter should be reconsidered by the appropriate judges in the traditional spirit of bail procedure.

Go Online

To learn more about the relationship between high money bonds and poverty, race and pretrial detention, *see*: http://www.bjs.gov/content/pub/pdf/prfdsc.pdf; http://www.pretrial.org; http://www.npr.org/2010/01/21/122725771/Bail-Burden-Keeps-U-S-Jails-Stuffed-With-Inmates.

Food for Thought

Does the bail system threaten justice by encouraging innocent defendants to plead guilty? In *Curry v. Yachera*, 835 F.3d 373 (3d Cir. 2016), defendant, who was convicted of using an old receipt to falsely return items to Walmart, remained in jail for two months because he could not post bail. During that time, his child was born, he lost his job, and was at risk of losing his home and car. In desperation, he decided to plead no contest to the charge in order to get out of jail. He then sought to sue the arresting officer for malicious prosecution. Should the action be precluded since he pleaded no contest to the charge?

FYI

Nielsen v. Preap, 139 S.Ct. 954 (2019), dealt with a federal law which provided that aliens who have committed certain dangerous crimes, as well as those who have connections to terrorism, must be arrested and held without a bond hearing except in one limited situation. The Court rejected the Ninth Circuit's holding that a bond hearing is required if an alien is not immediately arrested after being released from custody on other charges. In *Jennings v. Rodriguez*, 138 S.Ct. 830 (2018), the Court held that federal law does not place a six month limit on the detention of immigrants, or give detained immigrants the right to periodic bond hearings during the course of their detention.

Hypo 1: *Proper Bond?*

Joe is charged with theft in a jurisdiction where he has lived all his life. He lives with his wife and children, and has a steady job at a local manufacturing plant but no savings. The court sets a bond of $10,000 cash or surety. Is the bond amount proper? What if instead, Joe was arrested and charged with armed robbery after being identified by two witnesses and bond is set at $50,000? In each case, what are the best defense and prosecution arguments?

Take Note

In *ODonnell v. Harris County*, 892 F.3d 147 (5th Cir. 2018), the court held that Harris County, Texas' bail system is likely oppressive and unconstitutional as applied to indigent arrestees. The evidence showed that the county does not hold bail hearings within 24 hours. When they occur, the hearings last for only a few seconds, and arrestees are not allowed to present any evidence regarding their ability to pay bond. Following the denial of bail, prosecutors offer a plea bargain, involving a sentence of time served. 90% of the time, indigent defendants are expected to pay the maximum bail on the non-mandatory schedule of bail amounts, and the bail amounts imposed are secured rather than unsecured. The court held that courts must do a case-by-case evaluation of each arrestee's circumstances, provide them a bond hearing within 48 hours, and provide a reasoned decision by an impartial decisionmaker.

Hypo 2: *Escalating Priors*

Steve is charged with possession of cocaine. Steve recently moved to this jurisdiction from out of state to live with his girlfriend. Steve has no prior convictions and no assets. The court sets a bond of $5,000 cash or surety. What are the arguments for and against this bond? Does it change the analysis if Steve has two prior misdemeanor convictions, one for criminal trespass and one for simple assault? What if, instead of those two convictions, Steve has two prior felony convictions that significantly enhance the potential sentence he could receive upon conviction for possession of cocaine? In the last two situations what additional information might you want regarding the cases?

Hypo 3: *A Question of Assets*

Barbara is an executive at a large national bank who is charged with defrauding the bank and its customers out of millions of dollars. She is single and has no family, but owns a multi-million-dollar downtown condo, a brand new Lexus, and has stocks, bonds, and cash totaling $2.5 million. What arguments for bail will the defense and prosecution make?

Food for Thought

Should there be a right to bail post-conviction, but prior to sentencing? *See State v. Patel*, 171 A.3d 1037 (Conn. 2017). Prior to his conviction, Patel was free on $1 million bail. Following his conviction, bail was revoked. Should defendant have a right to bail following conviction? Is there any longer a presumption of innocence?

Hypo 4: *The Addict Mother*

Thirty-six-year-old Susan is charged with burglary. She is a heroin addict, and has a record of seven prior convictions, five for theft and two for possession of narcotics. She works part-time and lives with her three children and her husband who is a high school math teacher. The court is contemplating setting a $15,000 cash or surety bond, which she does not have the financial ability to pay. What position(s) will the defense advance on Susan's behalf? How should the prosecution respond?

Hypo 5: *Same Crime, Same Bond*

Two men rob a convenience store and are quickly arrested. David is single, unemployed, and mostly lives with his parents but stays "off and on" with his girlfriend. John is married with one infant child and has a steady job at McDonalds. The detective has brought both men in for questioning. David immediately asserts his right to remain silent and is booked for robbery and taken to court that day for his initial appearance. Bond is set at $25,000 which must be provided by a commercial surety. John waives his rights and eventually confesses that he and David robbed the store together. As a result of the interrogation, John isn't brought to court for his initial appearance until the next day. The prosecutor informs the magistrate about David's bond, and the magistrate immediately sets John's bond at the same amount. What statutory and/or constitutional arguments can John's attorney make to challenge the bail? How might the prosecution respond?

Food for Thought

Michael is twenty-three years old and shares an apartment with three other men in their 20s and one of their girlfriends. None of them have steady employment, but rather do odd jobs. Based on tips, the police set up an observation post at a street corner near the apartment that is known for narcotics activity. The police see Michael walk up to a man later identified as Patrick standing near the corner, and hand Patrick money. Patrick then signals to another man who retrieves a small, ziplock plastic bag containing an off-white rock-like substance from a bush. The man hands the bag to Michael and leaves. The police radio a description of Michael to other officers who stop and arrest Michael on his way back to the apartment. A search of Michael yields the plastic bag along with a small pipe. The substance tests positive for cocaine. The police also arrest Patrick at the corner but the other man gets away. A search of Patrick yields about $700 in cash. In the bush, police locate a large plastic bag containing twenty-five small ziplock bags each containing crack cocaine. The magistrate sets Michael's bond at $2500 cash or surety. Patrick's bond is set at $50,000 cash or surety. Do these bonds make sense? What arguments can be made for and against these bonds?

Hypo 6: *Funds Used to Hire Lawyer*

Susan is a twenty-two-year-old single mother of three children who is charged with theft. She has one prior conviction for possession of marijuana. Susan has a full-time waitressing job and has managed to put about $1000 of her tips into a savings account. Susan's best friend looks for an attorney to take Susan's case and finally one agrees to take it for $750. The attorney shows up for the initial appearance, but when the judge learns about Susan's employment and savings account the judge sets bond at $2500 cash or surety. What arguments might her attorney make on a motion to reconsider the bond? What if no attorney will agree to take the case for less than $2500 so Susan is instead represented by a public defender?

> ## Hypo 7: *Wealthy Parents*
>
> Frank is a twenty-one-year-old full-time college student. Pursuant to a valid search warrant, the police search his dorm room and find fifty individually packaged ziplock bags each containing twenty-five dollars' worth of marijuana. Frank is arrested and charged with possession with intent to distribute marijuana. Frank has no car or other large assets (just a two-year-old computer, clothes and other small personal belongings). His mother is a cardiologist and his father is a successful business executive and they are quite wealthy with combined yearly earnings around $1 million. They own a large suburban home (paid off) and a Lexus and an Audi. They are paying Frank's way through college, including his $40,000 per year tuition and expenses through their savings and income. As soon as Frank is arrested, he contacts his parents and they retain the best lawyer in town for $25,000. The judge sets Frank's bond at $100,000. What are the arguments in favor and against this amount?

2. The Bail Reform Act

Most states rely upon statutes to define the circumstances under which an accused may obtain pretrial release. The Bail Reform Act of 1984 (18 U.S.C. §§ 3141–3150) governs release determinations in federal courts, and may serve as a reference. For minor misdemeanors, many jurisdictions provide a uniform schedule of bail, though even then defendants may alternatively avail themselves of the regular bail provisions.

An initial determination is made by the court about whether the accused is a flight or safety risk. If not, § 3142(b) mandates a recognizance bond or an unsecured appearance bond. If the court believes that the accused presents either risk, the court must inquire whether the risk can be minimized by measures short of pretrial detention, *i.e.*, by imposing conditions under § 3142(c), after considering the § 3142(g) factors. If the risk can be minimized, the court tailors conditions to address the risk. Under particular circumstances, including a serious risk that the defendant will not appear, the defendant may be subject to pretrial detention without the possibility of release, § 3142(e)–(g). Section 3142(c)(2) prohibits the imposition of financial conditions that are so burdensome that the defendant is effectively subject to preventive detention. Does that mean that a court cannot set a bail that the defendant cannot meet immediately? Although the Court has never firmly resolved the issue, one Circuit held in *United States v. Mantecon-Zayas*, 949 F.2d 548 (1st Cir. 1991) that a court can impose a financial condition exceeding a defendant's means as long as the amount of bail is reasonably necessary to assure defendant's presence at trial.

3. Pretrial Detention

The Bail Reform Act of 1984 not only governs pretrial release decisions but, for the first time in our nation's history, explicitly authorized the government to hold a defendant charged with an ordinary criminal offense in jail pending trial without any means for release—so called "preventive detention." Title 18 U.S.C. § 3142 authorizes a judicial officer to order the detention of a defendant pending trial if the prosecution demonstrates by clear and convincing evidence that no release conditions will reasonably assure the safety of the community or assure the defendant's appearance at future court proceedings. It was only a matter of time before the United States Supreme Court reviewed the constitutionality of this novel and controversial statute.

FYI

Regardless of the type of release, it is always subject to the condition that the person not commit another crime. § 3142(b). When a defendant commits a crime while released, an independent, mandatory, consecutive, additional sentence (up to ten years for felonies and one year for misdemeanors) is imposed after conviction. § 3147. In addition, the sentencing judge may increase the sentence for crimes committed while on pretrial release. *United States Sentencing Commission, Federal Sentencing Guidelines Manual,* §§ 2J1.7, 4A1.3. However, a separate prosecution for contempt for violation of the release order raises complicated double jeopardy issues.

United States v. Salerno

481 U.S. 739 (1987).

CHIEF JUSTICE REHNQUIST delivered the opinion of the Court.

The Bail Reform Act of 1984 (Act) allows a federal court to detain an arrestee pending trial if the Government demonstrates by clear and convincing evidence after an adversary hearing that no release conditions "will reasonably assure the safety of any other person and the community." The United States Court of Appeals for the Second Circuit struck down this provision of the Act as facially unconstitutional, because, in that court's words, this type of pretrial detention violates "substantive due process."

Hear It

You can hear the oral argument in Salerno at: http://www.oyez.org/cases/1980-1989/1986/1986_86_87.

Responding to "the alarming problem of crimes committed by persons on release," Congress formulated the Bail Reform Act of 1984, 18 U.S.C. § 3141 et seq. (1982 ed., Supp. III), as the solution to a bail crisis in the federal courts. The Act represents the National Legislature's considered response to numerous perceived deficiencies in the federal bail process. By providing for sweeping changes in both the way federal courts consider bail applications and the circumstances under which bail is granted, Congress hoped to "give the courts adequate authority to make release decisions that give appropriate recognition to the danger a person may pose to others if released." To this end, § 3141(a) of the Act requires a judicial officer to determine whether an arrestee shall be detained. Section 3142(e) provides that "if, after a hearing pursuant to the provisions of subsection (f), the judicial officer finds that no condition or combination of conditions will reasonably assure the appearance of the person as required and the safety of any other person and the community, he shall order the detention of the person prior to trial." Section 3142(f) provides the arrestee with a number of procedural safeguards. He may request the presence of counsel at the detention hearing, he may testify and present witnesses in his behalf, as well as proffer evidence, and he may cross-examine other witnesses appearing at the hearing. If the judicial officer finds that no conditions of pretrial release can reasonably assure the safety of other persons and the community, he must state his findings of fact in writing, § 3142(i), and support his conclusion with "clear and convincing evidence," § 3142(f).

The judicial officer is not given unbridled discretion in making the detention determination. Congress has specified the considerations relevant to that decision. These factors include the nature and seriousness of the charges, the substantiality of the Government's evidence against the arrestee, the arrestee's background and characteristics, and the nature and seriousness of the danger posed by the suspect's release. § 3142(g). Should a judicial officer order detention, the detainee is entitled to expedited appellate review of the detention order. §§ 3145(b), (c).

Respondents Anthony Salerno and Vincent Cafaro were arrested on March 21, 1986, after being charged in a 29-count indictment alleging various Racketeer Influenced and Corrupt Organizations Act (RICO) violations, mail and wire fraud offenses, extortion, and various criminal gambling violations. The RICO counts alleged 35 acts of racketeering activity, including fraud, extortion, gambling, and conspiracy to commit murder. At respondents' arraignment, the Government moved to have Salerno and Cafaro detained pursuant to § 3142(e), on the ground that no condition of release would assure the safety of the community or any person. The District Court held a hearing at which the Government made a detailed proffer of evidence. The Government's case showed that Salerno was the "boss" of the Genovese crime family of La Cosa Nostra and that Cafaro was a "captain" in the Genovese family. According to the Government's proffer, based in large part on conversations intercepted by a court-ordered wiretap, respondents had participated in wide-ranging conspiracies to aid their illegitimate enterprises through violent means. The Government also offered the testimony of two of its trial witnesses, who would assert that Salerno personally participated in two murder conspiracies. Salerno opposed the motion for detention, challenging the credibility of the Government's witnesses. He offered the testimony of several character witnesses as well as a letter from his doctor stating that he was

Take Note

These particular defendants—dangerous and notorious mafia crime bosses—presented the Court with the best scenario for preventive detention. Indeed, by the time the case reached the Supreme Court, the Court did not have to decide the case: Salerno had been convicted and sentenced and Cafaro had been released at the government's request because he had agreed to be a government informant (apparently making him no longer dangerous in the government's eyes). The issue of preventive detention was therefore moot for both defendants. Yet the Court decided the issue anyway because it presented such a compelling case for preventive detention.

suffering from a serious medical condition. Cafaro presented no evidence at the hearing, but instead characterized the wiretap conversations as merely "tough talk."

A facial challenge to a legislative Act is the most difficult challenge to mount successfully, since the challenger must establish that no set of circumstances exists under which the Act would be valid. The fact that the Bail Reform Act might operate unconstitutionally under some conceivable set of circumstances is insufficient to render it wholly invalid, since we have not recognized an "overbreadth" doctrine outside the limited context of the First Amendment. *Schall v. Martin*, 467 U.S. 253 (1984). Respondents have failed to shoulder their heavy burden to demonstrate that the Act is "facially" unconstitutional.

Respondents present two grounds for invalidating the Bail Reform Act's provisions permitting pretrial detention on the basis of future dangerousness. First, they rely upon the Court of Appeals' conclusion that the Act exceeds the limitations placed upon the Federal Government by the Due Process Clause of the Fifth Amendment. Second, they contend that the Act contravenes the Eighth Amendment's proscription against excessive bail. We treat these contentions in turn.

The Due Process Clause of the Fifth Amendment provides that "No person shall . . . be deprived of life, liberty, or property, without due process of law." This Court has held that the Due Process Clause protects individuals against two types of government action. So-called "substantive due process" prevents the government from engaging in conduct that "shocks the conscience," *Rochin v. California*, 342 U.S. 165 (1952), or interferes with rights "implicit in the concept of ordered liberty," *Palko v. Connecticut*, 302 U.S. 319 (1937). When government action depriving a person of life, liberty, or property survives substantive due process scrutiny, it must still be implemented in a fair manner. *Mathews v. Eldridge*, 424 U.S. 319 (1976). This requirement has traditionally been referred to as "procedural" due process. Respondents argue that the Act violates substantive due process because the pretrial detention it authorizes constitutes impermissible punishment before trial. *See Bell v. Wolfish*, 441 U.S. 520 (1979). The Court of Appeals assumed that pretrial detention under the Bail Reform Act is regulatory, not penal, and we agree. The mere fact that a person is detained does not inexorably lead to the conclusion that the government has imposed punishment. To determine whether a restriction on liberty constitutes impermissible punishment or permissible regulation, we look to legislative intent. Unless Congress expressly intended to impose punitive restrictions, the punitive/regulatory distinction turns on "whether an alternative purpose to which the restriction may rationally be connected is assignable for it, and whether it appears excessive in relation to the alternative purpose assigned to it." *Schall v. Martin*, 467 U.S. at 269. We conclude that the detention imposed by the Act falls on the regulatory side of the dichotomy. The legislative history of the Bail Reform Act clearly indicates that Congress did not formulate the pretrial detention provisions as punishment for dangerous individuals. Congress instead perceived pretrial detention as a potential solution to a pressing societal problem. There is no doubt that preventing danger to the community is a legitimate regulatory goal.

Nor are the incidents of pretrial detention excessive in relation to the regulatory goal Congress sought to achieve. The Bail Reform Act carefully limits the circumstances under which detention may be sought to the most serious of crimes. *See* 18 U.S.C. § 3142(f). The arrestee is entitled to a prompt detention hearing, and the maximum length of pretrial detention is limited by the stringent time limitations of the Speedy Trial Act. *See* 18 U.S.C. § 3161 *et seq.* Moreover, as in *Schall v. Martin*, the conditions of confinement envisioned by the Act "appear to reflect the regulatory purposes relied upon by the" Government. The statute requires that detainees be housed in a "facility separate, to the extent practicable, from persons awaiting or serving sentences or being held in custody pending appeal." 18 U.S.C. § 3142(i)(2). We conclude, therefore, that the pretrial detention contemplated by the Bail Reform Act is regulatory in nature, and does not constitute punishment before trial in violation of the Due Process Clause.

The Court of Appeals nevertheless concluded that "the Due Process Clause prohibits pretrial detention on the ground of danger to the community as a regulatory measure, without regard to the duration of the detention." Respondents characterize the Due Process Clause as erecting an impenetrable "wall" in this area that "no governmental interest—rational, important, compelling or otherwise—may surmount." We do not think the Clause lays down any such categorical imperative. The Government's regulatory interest in community safety can, in appropriate circumstances, outweigh an individual's liberty interest. For example, in times of war or insurrection, when society's interest is at its peak, the Government may detain individuals whom the Government believes to be dangerous. *See Ludecke v. Watkins*, 335 U.S. 160 (1948). Even outside the exigencies of war, we have found that sufficiently compelling governmental interests can justify detention of dangerous persons. Thus, we have found no absolute constitutional barrier to detention of potentially dangerous resident aliens pending deportation proceedings. *Carlson v. Landon*, 342 U.S. 524 (1952). We have also held that the government may detain mentally unstable individuals who present a danger to the public, *Addington v. Texas*, 441 U.S. 418 (1979), and dangerous defendants who become incompetent to stand trial, *Jackson v. Indiana*, 406 U.S. 715 (1972); *Greenwood v. United States*, 350 U.S. 366 (1956). We have approved of post arrest regulatory detention of juveniles when they present a continuing danger to the community. *Schall v. Martin, supra.* Even competent adults may face substantial liberty restrictions as a result of the operation of our criminal justice system. If the police suspect an individual of a crime, they may arrest and hold him until a neutral magistrate determines whether probable cause exists. *Gerstein v. Pugh*, 420 U.S. 103 (1975). Finally, an arrestee may be incarcerated until trial if he presents a risk of flight, *see Bell v. Wolfish*, 441 U.S., at 534, or a danger to witnesses.

Respondents characterize these cases as exceptions to the "general rule" of substantive due process that the government may not detain a person prior to a judgment of guilt in a criminal trial. Such a "general rule" may freely be conceded, but these cases show a sufficient number of exceptions to the rule that the congressional action challenged here can hardly be characterized as totally novel. Given the well-established authority of the government, in special circumstances, to restrain individuals' liberty prior to or even without criminal trial and conviction, the present statute providing for pretrial detention on the basis of dangerousness must be evaluated in precisely the same manner that we evaluated the laws in the cases discussed above.

The government's interest in preventing crime by arrestees is both legitimate and compelling. In *Schall* we recognized the strength of the State's interest in preventing juvenile crime. This general concern with crime prevention is no less compelling when the suspects are adults. Indeed, "the harm suffered by the victim of a crime is not dependent upon the age of the perpetrator." *Schall v. Martin.* The Bail Reform Act of 1984 responds to an even more particularized governmental interest than the interest we sustained in *Schall.* The statute we upheld in Schall permitted pretrial detention of any juvenile arrested on any charge after a showing that the individual might commit some undefined further crimes. The Bail Reform Act, in contrast, narrowly focuses on a particularly acute problem in which the Government interests are overwhelming. The Act operates only on individuals who have been arrested for a specific category of extremely serious offenses. 18 U.S.C. § 3142(f). Congress specifically found that these individuals are far more likely to be responsible for dangerous acts in the community after arrest. Nor is the Act by any means a scattershot attempt to incapacitate those who are merely suspected of these serious crimes. The Government must first of all demonstrate probable cause to believe that the charged crime has been committed by the arrestee, but that is not enough. In a full-blown adversary hearing, the Government must convince a neutral decisionmaker by clear and convincing evidence that no conditions of release can reasonably assure the safety of the community or any person. 18 U.S.C. § 3142(f). While the Government's general interest in preventing crime is compelling, even this interest is heightened when the Government musters convincing proof that the arrestee, already indicted or held to answer for a serious crime, presents a demonstrable danger to the community. Under these narrow circumstances, society's interest in crime prevention is at its greatest.

On the other side of the scale is the individual's strong interest in liberty. We do not minimize the importance and fundamental nature of this right. But this right may, in circumstances where the government's interest is sufficiently weighty, be subordinated to the greater needs of society. Congress' careful delineation of the circumstances under which detention will be permitted satisfies this standard. When the Government proves by clear and convincing evidence that an arrestee presents an identified and articulable threat to an individual or the community, consistent with the Due Process Clause, a court may disable the arrestee from executing that threat. Under these circumstances, we cannot categorically state that pretrial detention "offends some principle of justice so rooted in the traditions and conscience of our people as to be ranked as fundamental." *Snyder v. Massachusetts*, 291 U.S. 97 (1934).

Finally, we dispose of respondents' facial challenge to the Bail Reform Act. To sustain them against such a challenge, we need only find them "adequate to authorize the pretrial detention of at least some persons charged with crimes," *Schall, supra*, at 264, whether or not they might be insufficient in some circumstances. They pass that test. As we stated in *Schall*, "there is nothing inherently unattainable about a prediction of future criminal conduct." Under the Bail Reform Act, the procedures by which a judicial officer evaluates the likelihood of future dangerousness are designed to further the accuracy of that determination. Detainees have a right to counsel at the detention hearing. 18 U.S.C. § 3142(f). They may testify in their own behalf, present information by proffer or otherwise, and cross-examine witnesses who appear at the hearing. The judicial officer charged with the responsibility of determining the appropriateness of detention is guided by statutorily enumerated factors, which include the nature and the circumstances of the charges, the weight of the evidence, the history and characteristics of the putative offender, and the danger to the community. § 3142(g). The Government must prove its case by clear and convincing evidence. § 3142(f). Finally, the judicial officer must include written findings of fact and a written statement of reasons for a decision to detain. § 3142(i). The Act's review provisions provide for immediate appellate review of the detention decision. Given the legitimate and compelling regulatory purpose of the Act and the procedural protections it offers, the Act is not facially invalid under the Due Process Clause of the Fifth Amendment.

Respondents also contend that the Bail Reform Act violates the Excessive Bail Clause of the Eighth Amendment. We think that the Act survives a challenge founded upon the Eighth Amendment. The Eighth Amendment addresses pretrial release by providing merely that "excessive bail shall not be required." This Clause, of course, says nothing about whether bail shall be available at all. Respondents nevertheless contend that this Clause grants them a right to bail calculated solely upon considerations of flight. They rely on *Stack v. Boyle*, 342 U.S. 1 (1951), in which the Court stated that "bail set at a figure higher than an amount reasonably calculated [to ensure the defendant's presence at trial] is 'excessive' under the Eighth Amendment." In respondents' view, since the Bail Reform Act allows a court essentially to set bail at an infinite amount for reasons not related to the risk of flight, it violates the Excessive Bail Clause. Respondents concede that the right to bail they have discovered in the Eighth Amendment is not absolute. A court may, for example, refuse bail in capital cases. A court may refuse bail when the defendant presents a threat to the judicial process by intimidating witnesses. Respondents characterize these exceptions as consistent with what they claim to be the sole purpose of bail—to ensure the integrity of the judicial process. While a primary function of bail is to safeguard the courts' role in adjudicating the guilt or innocence of defendants, we reject the proposition that the Eighth Amendment categorically prohibits the government from pursuing other admittedly compelling interests through regulation of pretrial release. The Court in *Stack* had no occasion to consider whether the Excessive Bail Clause requires courts to admit all defendants to bail, because the statute before the Court in that case allowed defendants to be bailed. Thus, the Court had to determine only whether bail was excessive if set at a sum greater than that necessary to ensure the arrestees' presence at trial. *Stack* is illuminated by the holding just four months later in *Carlson v. Landon*, 342 U.S. 524, 545 (1952): "The bail clause was lifted with slight changes from the English Bill of Rights Act. In England that clause has never been thought to accord a right to bail in all cases, but merely to provide that bail shall not be excessive in those cases where it is proper to grant bail. When this clause was carried over into our Bill of Rights, nothing was said that indicated any different concept. The Eighth Amendment has not prevented Congress from defining the classes of cases in which bail shall be allowed in this country. Thus, in criminal cases bail is not compulsory where the punishment may be death. Indeed, the very language of the Amendment fails to say all arrests must be bailable."

Carlson v. Landon was a civil case, and we need not decide today whether the Excessive Bail Clause speaks at all to Congress' power to define the classes of criminal arrestees who shall be admitted to bail. Even if we were to conclude that the Eighth Amendment imposes some substantive limitations on the National Legislature's powers in this area, we would still hold that the Bail Reform Act is valid. Nothing in the text of the Bail Clause limits permissible Government considerations solely to questions of flight. The only arguable substantive limitation of the Bail Clause is that the Government's proposed conditions of release or detention not be "excessive" in light of the perceived evil. Of course, to determine whether the Government's response is excessive, we must compare that response against the interest the Government seeks to protect by means of that response. Thus, when the Government has admitted that its only interest is in preventing flight, bail must be set by a court at a sum designed to ensure that goal, and no more. *Stack v. Boyle, supra.* When Congress has mandated detention on the basis of a compelling interest other than prevention of flight, as it has here, the Eighth Amendment does not require release on bail.

In our society liberty is the norm, and detention prior to trial or without trial is the carefully limited exception. The provisions for pretrial detention in the Bail Reform Act of 1984 fall within that carefully limited exception. The Act authorizes detention prior to trial of arrestees charged with serious felonies who are found after an adversary hearing to pose a threat to the safety of individuals or to the community which no condition of release can dispel. The numerous procedural safeguards detailed above must attend this adversary hearing. We are unwilling to say that this congressional determination, based as it is upon that primary concern of every government—a concern for the safety and indeed the lives of its citizens—on its face violates either the Due Process Clause of the Fifth Amendment or the Excessive Bail Clause of the Eighth Amendment.

The judgment of the Court of Appeals is therefore *reversed*.

JUSTICE MARSHALL, with whom JUSTICE BRENNAN joins, dissenting.

This case [involves] a statute in which Congress declares that a person innocent of any crime may be jailed indefinitely, pending the trial of allegations which are legally presumed to be untrue, if the Government shows to the satisfaction of a judge that the accused is likely to commit crimes, unrelated to the pending charges, at any time in the future. Such statutes, consistent with the usages of tyranny and the excesses of what bitter experience teaches us to call the police state, have long been thought incompatible with the fundamental human rights protected by our Constitution. This decision disregards basic principles of justice established centuries ago and enshrined beyond the reach of governmental interference in the Bill of Rights.

The majority divides the discussion into two sections, one concerned with the substantive guarantees implicit in the Due Process Clause, and the other concerned with the protection afforded by the Excessive Bail Clause of the Eighth Amendment. On the due process side appears an argument concerning the distinction between regulatory and punitive legislation. The majority concludes that the Act is a regulatory rather than a punitive measure. The major premise is that "unless Congress expressly intended to impose punitive restrictions, the punitive/regulatory distinction turns on 'whether an alternative purpose to which the restriction may rationally be connected is assignable for it, and whether it appears excessive in relation to the alternative purpose assigned to it.' " The majority finds that "Congress did not formulate the pretrial detention provisions as punishment for dangerous individuals," but instead was pursuing the "legitimate regulatory goal" of "preventing danger to the community." Concluding that pretrial detention is not an excessive solution to the problem of preventing danger to the community, the majority thus finds that no substantive element of the guarantee of due process invalidates the statute. The majority proceeds as though the only substantive right protected by the Due Process Clause is a right to be free from punishment before conviction. The majority's technique for infringing this right is simple: merely redefine any measure which is claimed to be punishment as "regulation," and, magically, the Constitution no longer prohibits its imposition. Because the Due Process Clause protects other substantive rights which are infringed by this legislation, the majority's argument is an exercise in obfuscation.

The Eighth Amendment states that "excessive bail shall not be required." The majority declares that: "this Clause says nothing about whether bail shall be available at all." If excessive bail is imposed the defendant stays in jail. The same result is achieved if bail is denied altogether. Whether the magistrate sets bail at $1 billion or refuses to set bail at all, the consequences are indistinguishable. It would be mere sophistry to suggest that the Eighth Amendment protects against the former decision, and not the latter. But perhaps, the majority says the Bail Clause is addressed only to the Judiciary. The text of the Amendment, which provides simply that "excessive bail shall not be required, nor excessive fines imposed, nor cruel and unusual punishments inflicted," provides absolutely no support for the majority's speculation that both courts and Congress are forbidden to inflict cruel and unusual punishments, while only the courts are forbidden to require excessive bail.

The majority concedes that "when the Government has admitted that its only interest is in preventing flight, bail must be set by a court at a sum designed to ensure that goal, and no more." But, the majority says, "when Congress has mandated detention on the basis of a compelling interest other than prevention of flight, as here, the Eighth Amendment does not require release on bail." The majority does not ask, as a result of its disingenuous analysis, if there are any substantive limits contained in both the Eighth Amendment and the Due Process Clause which render this system of preventive detention unconstitutional. The answer is apparent and, to the majority, inconvenient.

Title 18 U.S.C. § 3142(j) provides that "nothing in this section shall be construed as modifying or limiting the presumption of innocence." But the very purpose of this statute is an abhorrent limitation of the presumption of innocence. The majority's untenable conclusion that the present Act is constitutional arises from a specious denial of the role of the Bail Clause and the Due Process Clause in protecting the invaluable guarantee afforded by the presumption of innocence. "The principle that there is a presumption of innocence in favor of the accused is the undoubted law, axiomatic and elementary, and its enforcement lies at the foundation of the administration of our criminal law." *Coffin v. United States*, 156 U.S. 432, 453 (1895). Our society's belief, reinforced over the centuries, that all are innocent until the state has proved them to be guilty, like the companion principle that guilt must be proved beyond a reasonable doubt, is "implicit in the concept of ordered liberty," *Palko v. Connecticut*, 302 U.S. 319 (1937), and is established beyond legislative contravention in the Due Process Clause. *See In re Winship*, 397 U.S. 358 (1970).

The statute before us declares that persons who have been indicted may be detained if a judicial officer finds clear and convincing evidence that they pose a danger to individuals or to the community. The statute does not authorize the Government to imprison anyone it has evidence is dangerous; indictment is necessary. Under this statute an untried indictment somehow acts to permit a detention, based on other charges, which after an acquittal would be unconstitutional. The conclusion is inescapable that the indictment has been turned into evidence, if not that the defendant is guilty of the crime charged, then that left to his own devices he will soon be guilty of something else. To be sure, an indictment is not without legal consequences. It establishes that there is probable cause to believe that an offense was committed, and that the defendant committed it. Upon probable cause a warrant for the defendant's arrest may issue; a period of administrative detention may occur before the evidence of probable cause is presented to a neutral magistrate. *See Gerstein v. Pugh*, 420 U.S. 103 (1975). Once a defendant has been committed for trial he may be detained in custody if the magistrate finds that no conditions of release will prevent him from becoming a fugitive. But in this connection the charging instrument is evidence of nothing more than the fact that there will be a trial, and "release before trial is conditioned upon the accused's giving adequate assurance that he will stand trial and submit to sentence if found guilty. The modern practice of requiring a bail bond or the deposit of a sum of money subject to forfeiture serves as additional assurance of the presence of an accused." *Stack v. Boyle*, 342 U.S. 1, 4 (1951).

The finding of probable cause conveys power to try, and the power to try imports of necessity the power to assure that the processes of justice will not be evaded or obstructed. "Pretrial detention to prevent future crimes against society at large is not justified by any concern for holding a trial on the charges for which a defendant has been arrested." *Salerno*, 794 F.2d 64, 73 (2d Cir. 1986). The detention purportedly authorized by this statute bears no relation to the Government's power to try charges supported by a finding of probable cause, and thus the interests it serves are outside the scope of interests which may be considered in weighing the excessiveness of bail under the Eighth Amendment. It is not a novel proposition that the Bail Clause plays a vital role in protecting the presumption of innocence. Reviewing the application for bail pending appeal by members of the American Communist Party convicted under the Smith Act, 18 U.S.C. § 2385, Justice Jackson wrote: "Grave public danger is said to result from what the defendants may be expected to do, in addition to what they have done since their conviction. If I assume that defendants are disposed to commit every opportune disloyal act helpful to Communist countries, it is still difficult to reconcile with traditional American law the jailing of persons by the courts because of anticipated but as yet uncommitted crimes. Imprisonment to protect society from predicted but unconsummated offenses is unprecedented in this country and fraught with danger of excesses and injustice." *Williamson v. United States*, 95 L. Ed. 1379, 1382 (1950). As Chief Justice Vinson wrote for the Court in *Stack v. Boyle*: "Unless the right to bail before trial is preserved, the presumption of innocence, secured only after centuries of struggle, would lose its meaning."

There is a connection between the peculiar facts of this case and the evident constitutional defects in the statute which the Court upholds. Respondent Cafaro was originally incarcerated for an indeterminate period at the request of the Government, which believed (or professed to believe) that his release imminently threatened the safety of the community. That threat apparently vanished, from the Government's point of view, when Cafaro agreed to act as a covert agent of the Government. There could be no more eloquent demonstration of the coercive power of authority to imprison upon prediction, or of the dangers which the almost inevitable abuses pose to the cherished liberties of a free society. "It is a fair summary of history to say that the safeguards of liberty have frequently been forged in controversies involving not very nice people." *United States v. Rabinowitz*, 339 U.S. 56, 69 (1950) (Frankfurter, J., dissenting). Honoring the presumption of innocence is difficult; sometimes we must pay substantial social costs as a result of our commitment to the values we espouse. But at the end of the day the presumption of innocence protects the innocent; the shortcuts we take with those whom we believe to be guilty injure only those wrongfully accused and, ultimately, ourselves.

Throughout the world today there are men, women, and children interned indefinitely, awaiting trials which may never come or which may be a mockery of the word, because their governments believe them to be "dangerous." Our Constitution, whose construction began two centuries ago, can shelter us forever from the evils of such unchecked power. Today the Court applies itself to an ominous exercise in demolition. Theirs is truly a decision which will go forth without authority, and come back without respect. I dissent.

JUSTICE STEVENS, dissenting.

There may be times when the Government's interest in protecting the safety of the community will justify the brief detention of a person who has not committed any crime. It is difficult to accept the proposition that the Government is without power to detain a person when it is a virtual certainty that he or she would otherwise kill a group of innocent people in the immediate future. Nonetheless, the provision of the Bail Reform Act allowing pretrial detention on the basis of future dangerousness is unconstitutional. A pending indictment may not be given any weight in evaluating an individual's risk to the community or the need for immediate detention. If the evidence of imminent danger is strong enough to warrant emergency detention, it should support that preventive measure regardless of

Food for Thought

Who has the better argument, the majority or the dissent? What reasoning is most persuasive and why? In terms of the kinds of cases to which they apply, are the preventive detention provisions of the Bail Reform Act of 1984 as limited as the majority asserts? What happens when these provisions are replicated on the State level?

whether the person has been charged, convicted, or acquitted of some other offense. Justice Marshall has demonstrated that the fact of indictment cannot, consistent with the presumption of innocence and the Eighth Amendment's Excessive Bail Clause, be used to create a special class, the members of which are, alone, eligible for detention because of future dangerousness.

Points for Discussion

a. High Money Bonds Versus Preventive Detention

After *Salerno*, many States adopted similar preventive detention statutes. Nevertheless, in most States, the use of these statutes is relatively limited, and there continue to be many defendants held in jail pretrial on money bonds that they are financially unable to satisfy. Why do you think this is? In this respect, are there actually any advantages to the defendant in using the preventive detention scheme in the Bail Reform Act of 1984? If so, what are they?

b. Crimes of Violence

Under § 3142(f)(1)(A), the United States Attorney can seek preventive detention in any case that "involves a crime of violence." Is the crime of being a felon in possession of a firearm "a crime of violence" eligible for preventive detention? What are the arguments in favor of and against this interpretation? Compare *United States v. Ingle,* 454 F.3d 1082 (10th Cir. 2006) with *United States v. Dillard,* 214 F. 3d 88 (2d Cir. 2000).

Hypo 1: *A Case for Preventive Detention?*

Defendant is charged with drug trafficking and illegal possession of firearms. A firearm was present in defendant's residence when police executed a search warrant and the firearm was in close proximity to drugs that defendant was alleged to have distributed. Some years ago, defendant was sentenced to ten years' probation for theft, burglary, and auto burglary; that probation was successfully completed. He also had convictions for obstructing an officer, trafficking in marijuana and marijuana paraphernalia, public intoxication, and failure to return rental property, for which prison sentences were imposed. All of the convictions occurred at least five years ago. Defendant has family ties in the area, including responsibility for his minor child. Under the preventive detention provision of the Bail Reform Act, what arguments will the prosecution make in favor of pretrial detention? What arguments will the defense make in opposition?

> ### Hypo 2: *Another Case for Preventive Detention?*
>
> Defendant has no prior criminal record, but was recently arrested for drug trafficking. He is 27 years old, has lived his entire life in Pennsylvania, and has a history of steady employment. He worked in his father's construction business after graduating from high school nine years ago, and has worked as a personal fitness trainer for the past 2 years. He has close ties to his family. Until last year, he lived with his parents. His younger sister stated that since his arrest, she has maintained his apartment and would offer to help her brother post a bond and supervise her brother if he is released. She indicated that her parents are also willing to provide support. She also found someone willing to employ defendant should he be released. Finally, the DEA agents who arrested defendant said that upon his arrest, he expressed concern about his parents' reaction to his arrest because his brother had been murdered in a drug-related incident last year. Defendant's only assets are $400 in a checking account and a Pontiac valued at approximately $200. Defendant was apprehended during a government sting operation. A confidential informant, who cooperated with the government in hope of obtaining more lenient treatment, called defendant and asked him to meet him at a hotel. The informant then produced a kilo of cocaine to sell to defendant. When he indicated that he had no money, the informant gave him the kilo on consignment. Under the Bail Reform Act, what are the prosecutor's best arguments in favor of preventive detention? What are the defense arguments in opposition?

Executive Summary

No Unnecessary Delay Between Arrest and Appearance. An accused must be taken before a judge without unnecessary delay following arrest.

Notice & Advice at First Appearance. The judge must advise the accused about the charges and several constitutional rights.

***Gerstein* Probable Cause Finding.** Under *Gerstein*, a judge must make a determination of probable cause prior to setting or denying bail pending trial.

No Probable Cause Finding Does Not Bar Further Proceedings. Whether a court finds probable cause at first appearance has no effect on whether the proceedings against the defendant go forward.

No Excessive Bail. The Eighth Amendment prohibits excessive bail. Bail becomes excessive when it is set higher than reasonably necessary to assure a defendant's appearance at trial.

Preventive Detention by Statute. By federal statute and some state statutes, a defendant can be preventatively detained prior to trial if the prosecution makes a showing that the defendant presents a danger to the community.

Preventive Detention Constitutional. Preventive detention was held constitutional by the Supreme Court in *United States v. Salerno,* 481 U.S. 739 (1987).

Major Themes

a. **Lack of Counsel**—The right to counsel attaches at an accused's initial appearance in court but an accused may nonetheless not actually have counsel in court representing his interests during proceedings where a judge or magistrate makes important decisions regarding probable cause to detain the accused pretrial and the amount of bond.

b. **Bail**—While *Stack v. Boyle* holds that bail is set in order to guarantee return to court, state judges and magistrates nonetheless set bail in amounts that accused persons cannot make.

c. **Preventive Detention**—*Salerno*'s facts and holding would have indicated a much more limited use of preventive detention, holding defendant in jail pretrial, in opposition to the current practice in many states of allowing preventive detention for many different felonies and for persons with no prior record of violence or dangerousness.

For More Information

- RUSSELL L. WEAVER, JOHN M. BURKOFF, CATHERINE HANCOCK & STEVEN I. FRIEDLAND, PRINCIPLES OF CRIMINAL PROCEDURE Ch. 9 (8th ed. 2024).

- WAYNE R. LAFAVE, JEROLD H. ISRAEL, NANCY J. KING & ORIN S. KERR, CRIMINAL PROCEDURE (6th ed. 2017).

Test Your Knowledge

To assess your understanding of the material in this chapter, click here to take a quiz.

CHAPTER 11

Prosecutorial Discretion

A. Introduction

A major feature of prosecutorial power is the exercise of discretion regarding whether to bring charges against a suspect, and, if charges are initiated, what to charge. This aspect of prosecutorial power is a very significant but often overlooked component of the prosecutor's broad powers. Prosecutors have considerable leeway in making strategic decisions, a power that can be controversial in high-profile cases, such as those involving the shooting deaths by Officer Darryl Wilson and neighborhood watchman George Zimmerman. In those cases, the prosecutorial decisions regarding Wilson, who shot teenager Michael Brown, and Zimmerman, who shot teenager Trayvon Martin, were controversial. Of course, the greater the prosecutorial discretion, the greater the potential for abuse. Recurring questions arise about how much power prosecutors ought to be able to wield and what limits or checks should be placed on that power. High profile cases often raise issues relating to decisions whether to prosecute, as well as regarding the nature and scope of charges.

Points for Discussion

a.   *Zimmerman & Martin*

A controversial case that raised prosecutorial discretion issues was *Florida v. Zimmerman*, a case involving the shooting of unarmed teenager Trayvon Martin on February 26, 2012, by neighborhood watchman volunteer, George Zimmerman, in Sanford, Florida. After a trial of a little more than a month, the jury acquitted Zimmerman, who claimed self-defense. A preliminary issue involved the process by which charges should have been initiated—through a grand jury derived from the public or an information filed by the prosecutor? The Governor of Florida appointed a special prosecutor who decided to charge Zimmerman with second-degree murder instead of seeking a Grand Jury indictment. The charging process, like many other aspects of the case, was controversial. There were those who thought the case should have gone to a grand jury. Others thought the defendant was over-charged based on the facts. The media provided numerous reports and experts, flooding the internet and airwaves with commentary. After the case was tried and Zimmerman was acquitted, the prosecutor's discretion in charging was obscured by the decision.

b. *United States v. John Edwards*

John Edwards, a former senator from North Carolina and presidential candidate, was indicted by a Grand Jury in 2011 for violating federal campaign finance laws.

The violations primarily stemmed from his cover-up of a sexual affair during his presidential campaign in 2006. After a lengthy pre-trial run-up involving motions and discovery, he was tried in federal court in Greensboro, NC. The jury acquitted him of one charge and hung on five other counts, leading to a mistrial. The government decided not to retry him on the remaining counts.

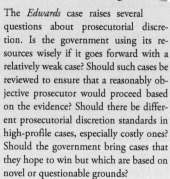

Food for Thought

The *Edwards* case raises several questions about prosecutorial discretion. Is the government using its resources wisely if it goes forward with a relatively weak case? Should such cases be reviewed to ensure that a reasonably objective prosecutor would proceed based on the evidence? Should there be different prosecutorial discretion standards in high-profile cases, especially costly ones? Should the government bring cases that they hope to win but which are based on novel or questionable grounds?

c. *Wilson & Brown*

In 2014, a confrontation between Officer Darryl Wilson and teenager Michael Brown left Brown dead. The prosecutor, Robert P. McCulloch, of St. Louis County, resisted the appointment of a special prosecutor and asked a Grand Jury to see if there was probable cause to believe Wilson had committed a crime. The officer essentially alleged self-defense, and witnesses before the Grand Jury gave conflicting stories. In the end, the Grand Jury refused to return a true bill. One of the controversial issues focused on prosecutorial discretion. Usually, a prosecutor seeks indictment for a specific crime, and offers a minimal number of witnesses in a largely one-sided affair, especially given that the defense does not have an attorney in the Grand Jury room and cannot cross-examine any witnesses. In this case, the prosecutor offered all of the evidence and witnesses it found to the Grand Jury so that the jury would be free to draw its own conclusions about what happened. By not returning a true bill, the Grand Jury (or at least four of the jurors (9 of 12 were needed to find probable cause)) found no probable cause to believe a crime had been committed by the officer. While the prosecutor could offer additional evidence or seek an alternative route, McCulloch declined to prosecute in light of the Grand Jury's decision.

d. *United States v. Blankenship*

Periodically, a coal mine disaster occurs with workers getting trapped and killed far below ground. It is unusual to see the management of the company held criminally responsible. In 2010, there was an explosion in the Upper Big Branch mine in West

Virginia which caused methane gas to surge through two miles of tunnels, killing 29 miners. The explosion was allegedly caused by unlawful conditions, including high levels of coal dust in the mine. In late 2014, the then CEO of Massey Energy, one of the largest coal companies in the United States and the company that owned the mine, Mr. Donald L. Blankenship, was indicted on criminal charges related to that event. The Grand Jury found probable cause to believe that Mr. Blankenship engaged in conspiracy, fraud, and numerous safety violations and returned a true bill in the form of the indictment. Federal prosecutors in Charleston, West Virginia, then moved forward on the charges. Trip Gabriel, *West Virginia Coal Country Sees New Era as Donald Blankenship Is Indicted*, N.Y. Times (Nov. 30, 2014). For a copy of the indictment, *see*: http://www.nytimes.com/2014/12/01/us/west-virginia-coal-country-sees-new-era-as-a-mine-boss-is-indicted.html.

Hypo: *Charging Choices*

Three men, Al (age 46) Peter (age 19), and James (age 16), decide to rob a local convenience store one November morning in southern Georgia. Al tells the others how easy it will be and how they will never put anyone in danger, especially because they will not have any weapons. After robbing the proprietor of the convenience store of $2,000, the men decide to rob a jewelry store down the street, where they net $5,000. They do not threaten the sole employee in the store. They all get into Al's car and he drives them to Atlanta, where, after getting gas, they rob another jewelry store at Al's urging. When the proprietor of this jewelry store starts to reach into a drawer, Al, takes out of his pocket a starter's pistol that looks like a real gun but fires blanks, points it at the proprietor, and says, "Do not move!" The proprietor quickly closes the drawer, which has a loaded gun in it. As the men are driving away, they are caught by the police. After a quick pat-down at the scene, Peter is found to have two marijuana joints in his pocket. A) With what crimes would you charge them if you are the prosecutor assigned to the case? B) Should a prosecutor's personal views about marijuana matter if given discretion on how to charge the possession of the substance? C) What should be the proper penalty for each participant? D) What, if any, plea bargains would you accept?

* * *

These questions pose dilemmas for prosecutors that are within the purview of prosecutorial discretion. From whether to charge, to how to charge and how to dispose of cases, prosecutors have considerable leeway in making strategic decisions. Of course, the greater this prosecutorial power is, the greater the possibility of abuse.

B. Overview of Prosecutorial Discretion

Prosecutors have broad discretion about when and whether to investigate and prosecute cases. Broad discretion is required as a matter of separation of powers because prosecutors are part of the Executive Branch. Courts have repeatedly held that the decision to prosecute is particularly ill-suited to judicial review. Among the discretionary factors that are not easily reviewable are decisions on whether and how to charge because they involve the strength of the case, the prosecution's general deterrence value, the State's enforcement priorities, and the case's relationship to the State's overall enforcement plans. As Congress and state legislatures have criminalized more and more behavior and provided duplicative ways in which to charge criminals, the prosecutor has arguably become the most powerful figure in the criminal justice system, inviting both vigorous critique and defense of the prosecutor's role. While discretion can be dangerous, so is rigidity because it precludes individualized treatment of individuals based on common sense.

Food for Thought

You are the new state budget chief. You have a budget surplus of $1 million which you must allocate to the following three areas: hiring additional police officers; hiring more prosecutors; hiring additional prison guards. How would you allocate the funds? What are your rationales for doing so?

Why is prosecutorial discretion so important? While specific circumstances can dictate what is fair in criminal cases, so can a scarcity of resources. As one commentator recently stated, "Procedural justice is undermined because over-policing increases the number of cases in lower criminal courts, overwhelming prosecutors, defenders, and judges." K. Babe Howell, *Prosecutorial Discretion and the Duty to Seek Justice in an Overburdened System*, 27 GEO. J. L. ETHICS 285 (2014).

Some regard prosecutorial discretion as a necessity, both in terms of pragmatism and jurisprudence. Then-Professor, now U.S. Third Circuit Court of Appeals Judge Stephanos Bibas, in his article, *The Need for Prosecutorial Discretion*, 19 TEMP. POL. & CIV. RTS. L. REV. 369 (2009–2010), argues that U.S. criminal court dockets are so congested that prosecutors have no choice but to "plea bargain away most of their cases." He notes that legislatures often "pass overbroad and overlapping criminal statutes instead of drawing them so narrowly that some scoundrels might escape." The breadth of these laws necessarily leaves prosecutors with discretion which they exercise in different ways. For example, prosecutors might choose not to prosecute more minor offenses (e.g., jaywalking or speeders who are only slightly above the speed limit) in favor of prosecuting more serious offenses (e.g., murder). However, some prosecutors will charge defendants with more minor offenses in an effort to encourage potential witnesses to turn state's evidence. However, prosecutorial discretion is hardly limited to the question of whether or not to charge a defendant with a crime. If a defendant is convicted, the prosecutor has discretion regarding whether to recommend a high sentence, a low sentence, or even probation.

Bibas believes that prosecutorial discretion is not simply a function of scarce resources. He notes that, in some European countries (e.g., Germany) "prosecutors are supposed to charge and prosecute all defendants for whom they have enough evidence of guilt." *Id.* He notes that some U.S. jurisdictions take a similar approach. However, he also argues that "justice" requires the exercise of discretion so that prosecutors can make "fine-grained moral evaluations and distinctions." Judges and juries should make more of these judgment calls than they do now, but prosecutors also play an important role. He notes that, even though some jurisdictions ban "weapons" from school grounds, it would make no sense to prosecute a grandmother who sends a birthday cake, and a knife to cut it, to school with her granddaughter.

The fact that prosecutors have broad discretion creates the potential for abuse. Under constitutionally imposed rules, prosecutors are required to disclose exculpatory evidence to defendants. *See Editorial—Justice and Prosecutorial Misconduct?, N.Y. Times* (Dec. 28, 2011). However, there is evidence suggesting that prosecutors do not always turn over exculpatory evidence, and that they rarely suffer consequences for their failure to do so. As the Court recognized in *Berger v. United States*, 295 U.S. 78 (1935), a "prosecutor is the representative not of an ordinary party to a controversy but a sovereignty whose obligation to govern impartially is as compelling as its obligation to govern at all; and whose interest, therefore, in a criminal prosecution is not that it shall win a case, but that justice shall be done." The ultimate objective is that "guilt shall not escape or innocence suffer." However, while a prosecutor may "strike hard blows, he is not at liberty to strike foul ones. It is as much his duty to refrain from improper methods calculated to produce a wrongful conviction as it is to use every legitimate means to bring about a just one." Moreover, prosecutors have a "nullification power" that they can use to nullify a "law by not bringing charges when they should, or by bringing different charges than they should," as well as by deciding the venue where a case will be litigated.

Prosecutorial discretion is not always cabined by decisions on whether to charge at all or what charges to bring, but rather by how to conduct the prosecution. Sometimes, prosecutors do things that transgress acceptability. This was the case in the following case which involved prosecutorial ethics, discretion and the use of the internet. In *Bowen*, police officers were convicted of felonies relating to the killing of several unarmed men after Hurricane Katrina in New Orleans and then orchestrating a cover-up. The primary issue in the government's appeal, was whether anonymous on-line posting by government prosecutors would, when discovered, warrant a new trial.

United States v. Bowen

799 F.3d 336 (5th Cir. 2015).

EDITH H. JONES, CIRCUIT JUDGE:

In the anarchy following Hurricane Katrina, a group of heavily armed New Orleans police officers were dispatched to the Danziger Bridge in response to an emergency call reporting shots being fired at police. There, amid chaos, they shot and killed two unarmed men, one of them developmentally disabled, and wounded four unarmed civilians. The police then allegedly orchestrated a cover-up to deny what happened. Some of those involved were tried by the state, but a mistrial was ordered. The federal government took over the prosecution and bungled it. Five former officers have been convicted of serious crimes and received lengthy sentences. Yet the district court granted a new trial.

The reasons for granting a new trial are novel and extraordinary. No less than three high-ranking federal prosecutors are known to have been posting online, anonymous comments to newspaper articles about the case throughout its duration. The government makes no attempt to justify the prosecutors' ethical lapses, which the court described as having created an "online 21st century carnival atmosphere." Not only that, but the government inadequately investigated and substantially delayed the ferreting out of information about its in-house contributors to the anonymous postings. Cooperating defendants called to testify by the government lied, an FBI agent overstepped, defense witnesses were intimidated from testifying, and inexplicably gross sentencing disparities resulted from the government's plea bargains and charging practices.

We are well aware of our duty normally to affirm convictions that are tainted only by harmless error. In this extraordinary case, harmless error cannot even be evaluated because the full consequences of the federal prosecutors' misconduct remain uncertain after less-than-definitive DOJ internal investigations. The trial was permeated by the cumulative effect of the additional irregularities found by the district court. The grant of a new trial was not an abuse of the district court's discretion.

Emotions ran high as the prosecution progressed. Local news coverage of the impending federal indictments was punctuated by press leaks "from unnamed sources" that tended to favor the government. One cooperating defendant, Lehrmann, signed a confidential plea agreement, and a magistrate judge sealed the Information. One day before Lehrmann was scheduled to enter the plea in open court, the Associated Press and the *New Orleans Times-Picayune*, the local paper, published articles announcing that fact. The district court ordered the government to attempt to find the leak, but the order bore no fruit. Concomitantly, commenters on the website for the *New*

Orleans Times Picayune vigorously debated the significance of the case and the guilt of the individual perpetrators and the entire New Orleans Police Department.

During the interim between the verdict and sentencing, events reflecting shocking breaches of prosecutorial ethics were revealed and then compounded by further breaches. The district court was led on a "legal odyssey" when another target of federal investigation in New Orleans discovered that a high-ranking Assistant United States Attorney, Senior Trial Counsel Sal Perricone, had been posting comments to Nola.com under multiple assumed names. Perricone's comments were inflammatory, highly opinionated, and pro-prosecution. Perricone's comments were soon tied to the Danziger Bridge prosecutions and were shown to have begun well before the indictments and continued through trial. He castigated the defendants and their lawyers and repeatedly chastised the NOPD. Within ten days of the revelation of Perricone's comments, he resigned as an AUSA, and then-United States Attorney Jim Letten issued a press release attempting to confine any online misconduct to Perricone alone. [At] the district court's first hearing on these allegations occurred in June 2012. Letten was flanked by his First Assistant United States Attorney and Chief of the Office's Criminal Division Jan Mann as he promised "gospel truth" that no one else had commented on stories related to pending cases. [That statement turned out to be incorrect because Mann herself had done so.] After the hearing, Mann was tasked by Letten to conduct the investigations within the New Orleans office. She reported back to the district court with assurances that Perricone was the sole culprit in the USAO and that the defense was likely responsible for press leaks. These reports failed to overcome the district court's concerns. The district court's [noted that] Perricone, now a private citizen, had not been questioned under oath by Mann. The catalog of Perricone's comments reflected those he composed as "HenryL.Mencken_1951" but did not include comments he submitted under alternative monikers. In the first week of August, an extensive interview of Perricone was published in *New Orleans Magazine*. The interview [revealed] that Perricone had actually posted comments about pending USAO matters under not one but several assumed names. At [an] October 10, 2012 status conference, Perricone raised questions about the possible involvement of the local FBI in press leaks and about online monikers that he did not use, specifically those of "eweman" and certain variations on "campstblue." Postings under these additional names had come to the district court's attention because their content implied they might have been written by insiders to the prosecution.

Before [the court] could take testimony from another former AUSA, a lawsuit was filed alleging that Jan Mann had been commenting, as "eweman." About forty inappropriate comments under this moniker had appeared on the Nola.com website from 2011 until Perricone was exposed in March 2012. The suit alleged that "approximately 63 percent of the posts by [First AUSA Mann] appear with comments posted by Perricone, and they frequently reply to express consistency with the points of view expressed by the other." It took four days, plus a specific request by the district court, before Letten informed the district court that Jan Mann had "much to his surprise" admitted her activity on Nola.com. [A subsequent hearing] yielded insights into the possible knowledge of other AUSAs and office personnel about Perricone's comments. He specifically insinuated that Mann and her husband, AUSA Jim Mann, as friends of Perricone, knew about the commenting. Bernstein from DOJ assured the district court that, having interviewed current and former members of "the prosecution team," she was told that none of them had been posting comments. She contended that because the postings were anonymous, the district court had conducted a thorough jury *voir dire*, and Jan Mann's postings on the Danziger Bridge case apparently post-dated the trial, "the conduct at issue had no effect on the validity" of the verdict against the defendants.

Afterwards, the district court made significant preliminary findings: (1) Certain members of the USAO monitored and reviewed Nola.com articles, in particular the "comment" postings, and shared them with other members of the office; (2) Some members of the USAO determined that the posts suspiciously seemed to contain confidential, privileged, or sensitive information about a variety of cases in which the office was involved; (3) Certain members of the USAO commented to each other on their suspicions, particularly concerning commenters named "legacyusa" and "HenryL.Mencken_1951," and linked those posts possibly to Perricone; (4) Two individuals in the office emailed each other only a week before the Lohman plea and four months before the Danziger Bridge indictments, and indicated that comments concerning the Danziger Bridge incident were written by people "who know a little bit too much about our office . . ."; and (5) Jan Mann supervised the responses to the district court's attempts to ascertain the extent of online commenting within the office to that point. The district court worried, particularly in light of the belated identification of Jan Mann as "eweman," whether these were the only unauthorized comments from within the office. The district court reiterated its concern that at least one cooperating defendant felt coerced into pleading guilty, that the sentences meted out to defendants were shockingly disparate, that FBI Agent William Bezak had used coercive tactics against a defense witness, and that the defense was deprived of live testimony by at least three witnesses who refused to testify at trial when DOJ targeted them for possible perjury charges. Three years after trial, however, not one of those people had actually been charged with a crime.

Two weeks after this order, Letten resigned as United States Attorney, and both Jan Mann and her husband Jim retired. The DOJ appointed two attorneys—FAUSA John Horn and AUSA Charysse Alexander—to conduct an investigation ranging from the New Orleans office of the United States Attorney to the Criminal Division of DOJ. [Their] reports [revealed] startling information. Neither Jan Mann nor her husband had ever been placed under oath when being interviewed, and each had refused to execute affidavits. Jan Mann's interview [was] incomplete. [There was] a carefully worded reference to comments about the trial posted by a DOJ Civil

Rights Division employee (pseudonym "Dipsos") "who had first-hand knowledge of the Danziger Bridge case but was not a member of the prosecution team." That this employee was, *inter alia*, "walled off from the prosecution team and was prohibited from having any substantive discussion about the investigation with any member of the prosecution team or any supervisor over the prosecution team." "Dipsos" [was later] revealed to be Ms. Karla Dobinski, [who was part] of the "prosecution team." Dobinski is disturbingly vague in her OPR interview about how many other people in her department were aware of her commenting and whether "Dipsos" was her only moniker. DOJ refused to follow up with the newspaper reporters who had written articles referencing "two people familiar with the investigation" and "a source close to the probe" concerning the Lohman plea leak.

The disparity between the punishment meted out to cooperating defendants and those who went to trial is stark. The cooperating defendants' participation seems comparable, yet the government threw the book at those who went to trial by stacking firearms charges. As a result of the charging disparity, those who went to trial have been sentenced from thirty-eight to sixty-five years in prison, while the cooperating defendants garnered from five to eight years. In addition to Hunter, another cooperating defendant, Hills, had fired at people on the bridge. Hills pled guilty to misprision/obstruction charges and was sentenced to six and a half years in prison, but he had earlier denied his guilt to his supervisor. He explained that he had to take the plea deal as "the best [he] could get." A third cooperating defendant, Barrios, was the only defendant who pled out but was not presented as a witness by the government. Barrios had been present at the bridge and changed his statements about whether he fired on the civilians. Barrios received a five-year sentence. When he testified for the defense, he had to contradict his wife's statements that he had been forced to admit guilt despite his innocence.

Also troubling was the saga of cooperating defendant Jeffrey Lehrmann, who received only a three-year sentence for misprision of a felony. Yet Lehrmann worked hand in glove with Kaufman, who was charged with multiple felonies and received a six-year sentence. In crafting false evidence, Lehrmann went so far as to create a fictitious witness, "Lakeisha Smith," to fortify the defendant officers' stories about the shooting. Lehrmann also falsely charged crimes against Lance Madison, the brother of a murdered, disabled victim. Lehrmann received his favorable plea deal even after he had lied to the federal grand jury. Even more surprising, Lehrmann had been hired as a federal ICE agent during the pendency of the Danziger Bridge investigation and worked as a federal agent for nearly four years. His federal employment terminated several months after his formal guilty plea. Finally, the district court pointed to its understanding that at least three potential defense witnesses refused to testify following prosecution threats to bring perjury charges against them. As the district court explained, since these witnesses had earlier testified to the grand jury, their transcripts could be offered at trial, but transcripts are never as powerful as live witnesses. In any event, not one of those people was later charged.

In granting the defendants' Rule 33 motion, the district court principally relied on footnote nine of *Brecht v. Abrahamson*, which reserves the possibility that a new trial can in some egregious circumstances be mandated for certain "trial-type" errors even without a showing of prejudice to the defendants. 507 U.S. 619, 638 n. 9 (1993). The court also concluded that the defendants were in fact prejudiced. The motion for new trial here was granted because "the interest of justice so requires," Fed.R.Crim.P. 33(a), and the motion was specifically based on newly discovered evidence. Fed.R.Crim.P. 33(b)(1). Newly discovered evidence need not relate only to guilt or innocence, but may be relevant to any controlling issue of law. If a court finds "that a miscarriage of justice may have occurred at trial, . . . this is classified as such an 'exceptional case' as to warrant granting a new trial in the interest of justice." *United States v. Robertson*, 110 F.3d 1113, 1120 n. 11 (5th Cir.1997). A miscarriage of justice harms the substantial rights of a defendant, and it may consist of errors and omissions considered for their cumulative effect on the trial proceedings. *United States v. Barrett*, 496 F.3d 1079, 1121 (10th Cir.2007).

The government acknowledges significant, repeated misconduct by Perricone and Jan Mann and, to a lesser extent, Dobinski. The government concedes that Perricone "intentionally committed professional misconduct" violating (a) federal regulations restricting extrajudicial statements by DOJ personnel relating to civil and criminal proceedings, (b) DOJ policies, and (c) court and state bar rules of professional conduct. The government acknowledges that besides his postings in this case, Perricone posted "thousands" of anonymous comments on various topics over the course of several years. As to Jan Mann, the government admits that her postings on Nola.com of "anonymous comments about Department of Justice matters" violated the same rules, although the results of her postings relating to the Danziger Bridge prosecution are mitigated because they allegedly occurred after the trial had concluded. The government also admits that Mann acted dishonestly during the new trial proceedings when she misrepresented facts and allowed them to be misrepresented to the district court. The government rejects Perricone's and Mann's repeated assertions that their private, anonymous online commenting could be separated from their professional public duties. Dobinski was prohibited from participating anonymously in a public forum discussing the case, because "several sources of authority broadly prohibit Department attorneys from making any extrajudicial statements regarding a pending matter." Contending that her comments were innocuous and "not intentional" misconduct, the government acknowledges only that Dobinski exercised "poor judgment" in posting comments during the trial. What the government nowhere confronts is the incomplete, dilatory, and evasive nature of its efforts to respond to the district court's inquiries about the full extent of online activity by government employees and the source of the Lohman plea leak. The district court doggedly pursued the truth about these matters, but to this day the government has never fully answered the district court's legitimate questions.

The district court concluded that the government's protracted misconduct required a new trial. In *Brecht*, the Supreme Court held that to obtain relief on collateral review, a habeas petitioner must establish that the constitutional trial error had a "substantial and injurious effect or influence in determining the jury's verdict." *Id.* at 637 (quoting *Kotteakos v. United States*, 328 U.S. 750, 776 (1946)). In other words, the habeas petitioner must establish actual prejudice. The Court distinguished such "trial errors," which occur during the presentation of a case to the jury, from "structural defects" in the prosecution, like denial of counsel, that require automatic reversal of a conviction. The Court also stated that its holding: "does not foreclose the possibility that in an unusual case, a deliberate and especially egregious error of the trial type, *or one that is combined with a pattern of prosecutorial misconduct,* might so infect the integrity of the proceeding as to warrant the grant of habeas relief, even if it did not substantially influence the jury's verdict." The district court found that the government's pervasive misconduct so contaminated every phase of the prosecution that this case, unique "in nature [and] in scope," fit "squarely within" *Brecht's* prejudice exception.

Most decisions considering the possibility of *Brecht* footnote nine "hybrid" error have declined to grant relief to defendants, because most of the complaints have involved pure trial error. As the Court noted in *Brecht*, when the errors occur during the presentation of the case to the jury, they are amenable to harmless error review "because they may be quantitatively assessed in the context of the evidence as a whole, to determine the effect on the trial." But "not every error . . . is easily shoe-horned into one of those neat categories. The 'nature, context, and significance of the violation,' for instance, may determine whether automatic reversal or the harmless error analysis is appropriate." Courts must therefore decide where, along the spectrum of errors, those which are not clearly trial type or structural may fall.

Here, the breadth of the government's misconduct and continued obfuscation makes this the "unusual case" contemplated by *Brecht*. The online commenting alone, which breached all standards of prosecutorial ethics, gave the government a surreptitious advantage in influencing public opinion, the venire panel, and the trial itself. By degrees, the district court was led to conclude that what it had previously considered to be isolated missteps was actually evidence of a pattern of misconduct that permeated every stage of the prosecution. Because the government refused to adequately investigate its errors, covered up what it knew to be misleading omissions, and in some instances lied directly to the court, the district court could neither uncover the extent of the prosecution's transgressions nor determine the severity of the prejudice suffered by the defendants.

The government's unrelenting efforts thus prevented the district court from evaluating the fairness of defendants' trial and thrust the prosecution into the rare territory of *Brecht* hybrid error. Trial errors can be evaluated for harmlessness precisely because the nature and extent of the harm is ascertainable from a review of the record. Here, the ability of trial and appellate courts to evaluate the effect of the anonymous comments has been thwarted by the government's subsequent lack of cooperation. There is a fundamental imbalance between the knowledge of the prosecutors, and the defendants and courts, concerning the true extent and significance of the ongoing commenting. This case thus presents the unclassifiable and pervasive errors to which the Supreme Court referred in *Brecht* when it identified a category of errors capable of infecting the integrity of the prosecution to a degree warranting a new trial irrespective of prejudice. Our conclusion is reinforced by overarching standards of prosecutorial conduct and the nature of their breach. Prosecutors maintain the integrity, fairness and objectivity of the criminal justice system in part by refraining from speaking in public about pending and impending cases except in very limited circumstances. The government's own list of applicable regulations and ethical rules demonstrates that the prosecutors' obligation of silence extends beyond "confidential and grand jury matters" and beyond the "prosecution team" narrowly defined to include only those who participate in a particular case. Further, there is no dividing line between the prosecutors' professional and private lives with respect to these duties. Had Perricone, Mann, or Dobinski frequented a bar or habitually called in to a radio talk show and blown off steam about the Danziger Bridge prosecution in the terms they used online, their misconduct would have been the same as it is with their anonymous online commentary.

Although 'statements to the press may be an integral part of a prosecutor's job, and . . . may serve a vital public function,' that function is strictly limited by the prosecutor's overarching duty to do justice.' Insulating the prosecution and trial from bias, prejudice, misinformation, and evidence revealed outside the courtroom are crucial to the fairness of our processes. Equally important, the prosecutor must respect the presumption of innocence even as he seeks to bring a defendant to justice. In short, the prosecutors' misconduct was so incongruous with their duties buttresses our conclusion that this is the rare case involving *Brecht* error.

While a demonstration of prejudice is ordinarily a prerequisite for the grant of a new trial, the Supreme Court specifically identified the type of extraordinary errors that will dispense with this burden. Such errors occurred here. Prosecutorial misconduct commenced even before indictments were handed down and continued throughout trial and into the post-trial proceedings, and that misconduct affected the prosecution and trial in ways that cannot be fully evaluated due to the government's mishandling of the investigation into cyberbullying. The online anonymous postings, whether the product of lone wolf commenters or an informal propaganda campaign, gave the prosecution a tool for public castigation of the defendants that it could not have used against them otherwise, and in so doing deprived them of a fair trial. The district court's steady drip of discoveries of misconduct infecting every stage of this prosecution, combined with the government's continued obfuscation and deceit, renders this the rare case in which imposition of the *Brecht* remedy is necessary.

Even when a district court finds that misconduct occurred, it must normally find that the misconduct in question actually prejudiced the defense. Prejudice depends on the extent to which the particular misconduct contributed to a guilty verdict. The district court was unable to capture the extent of prejudice during jury selection or trial because the tainted source of the comments had not yet been revealed. However, the district court found that seven of twelve seated jurors had visited the Nola.com website in the months preceding trial. Jurors who visited the website appeared to have a lower opinion of NOPD officers' honesty. The district court believed that the government pressured cooperating defendants to seek plea deals and then to shade their testimony against the others. The district court reiterated that government threats of perjury charges against defense witnesses, which had never materialized, prompted several not to testify at the trial. The facts that the government engaged in misconduct, which took place off the record but in public, and that the misconduct was directed at the public but defies investigation because of the government's tactics, should tip toward a finding of prejudice. On-the-record misconduct can be easily evaluated; the misconduct here cannot. Furtive misconduct should not escape remedy simply because it was furtive.

A prosecutor's status enhances the credibility of public comments and magnifies the adverse consequences of the commenter's inappropriate remarks. The prosecutor's comments implicate his or her inside knowledge of prosecutorial activity as they explain the significance of particular events during a case. Bias or vindictiveness in the prosecutor's comments, reflected repeatedly in Perricone's postings, cast doubt on the integrity of the process, as did Jan's Mann's online questioning of the district court's motives in a related Danziger Bridge prosecution. Dobinski's contributions encouraged and approved one-sided reports about the trial. All of these experienced, high-level prosecutors were well aware that they were forbidden, legally and ethically, from making in public the statements they communicated online. They all knew that employment sanctions should be imposed for their activities if undertaken publicly.

Although the government does not deny the impropriety of online anonymous comments about pending cases, it downplays their prejudicial effects. The government overlooks that potential harm extends not just to jurors but others involved in the case. Inflammatory and biased online comments to news articles must have affected the participants' approaches to their defense, testimony, or decisions to testify. That there was some influence, although unquantifiable, seems inescapable. These prosecutors created an air of bullying against the defendants whose rights they, especially Dobinski, were sworn to respect. The impact is felt not only by the defendants but by codefendants pressed to plead guilty or defense witnesses dissuaded from testifying. Preventing mob justice is precisely the goal of prosecutorial ethical constraints. The government should not be able to shelter under a banner of "no prejudice proved." The district court did not err in finding that the defendants were prejudiced by the government's misconduct. Defendants are entitled to a new trial.

AFFIRMED; REMANDED FOR TRIAL.

The government also argues that official and professional discipline were adequate to rebuke Perricone, Jan Mann, and Dobinski and should have sufficed in lieu of a new trial. Like the district court, we disagree. Whether those who committed misconduct were disciplined simply does not bear on whether the defendants received a fair trial. It is clear from Perricone, Mann, and Dobinski's testimony that none of them is particularly remorseful about the misconduct, and they claimed to believe their individual First Amendment rights were separable from their positions of public trust. Perricone and Jan Mann both resigned from office with benefits as far as the record shows, although they were referred for professional discipline to the State Bar of Louisiana. Dobinski remains in federal employment with only a bare reproof for her online commenting. Their misdeeds are compounded by the government's insouciant investigation, which leaves open only three inferences concerning this prosecutorial breakdown: the government is not serious about controlling extracurricular, employment-related online commenting by its officials; the government feared what it might uncover by a thorough and timely investigation; or the government's investigation was incompetent. Exerting professional discipline on three individual government lawyers does nothing to solve the systemic problem, and it is not a sufficient answer to the miscarriage of justice in this case.

EDWARD C. PRADO, CIRCUIT JUDGE, dissenting:

I agree that the actions of the government attorneys demean the integrity of the judiciary and merit the most severe sanctions. But we "cannot permit" these considerations "to alter our analysis, for we are not at liberty to ignore the mandate" of the Federal Rules of Criminal Procedure "in order to obtain 'optimal' results," *Carlisle v. United States*, 517 U.S. 416, 430 (1996). In the present case, the district court had authority to consider—and we have authority to review—*only* a motion for a new trial based on newly discovered evidence. Neither the district court nor the majority opinion applied the appropriate standard: "In order to warrant a new trial on the basis of newly discovered evidence, defendant must demonstrate that (1) the evidence is newly discovered and was unknown to the defendant at the time of trial; (2) failure to detect the evidence was not due to a lack of diligence by the defendant; (3) the evidence is not merely cumulative or impeaching; (4) the evidence is material; and (5) *the evidence introduced at a new trial would probably produce an acquittal.* Unless all factors are met, the motion should be denied." In sum, I would conclude that the district court abused its discretion in granting a new trial. The district court erred in not applying our established Rule 33(b)(1) standard, and the defendants have not carried their heavy burden to prove that "the evidence introduced at a new trial would probably produce an acquittal," *Bowler*, 252 F.3d at 747. In holding otherwise, the majority opinion puts us at odds with binding Fifth Circuit precedent as well as authority from our sister circuits.

C. The Decision to Investigate or Charge

1. Discretionary Authority

Prosecutors have broad discretion—rather than an obligation or a duty—about when and whether to investigate and/or to prosecute. Arguably, broad discretion is required as a matter of separation of powers because prosecutors are part of the Executive Branch. With numerous criminal statutes providing different levels of punishment, should prosecutors have the power to select which statutes to enforce?

United States v. Batchelder

442 U.S. 114 (1979).

MR. JUSTICE MARSHALL delivered the opinion of the Court.

At issue are two overlapping provisions of the Omnibus Crime Control and Safe Streets Act of 1968. Both prohibit convicted felons from receiving firearms, but each authorizes different maximum penalties. We must determine whether a defendant convicted of the offense carrying the greater penalty may be sentenced only under the more lenient provision when his conduct violates both statutes.

Respondent, a previously convicted felon, was found guilty of receiving a firearm that had traveled in interstate commerce, in violation of 18 U.S.C. § 922(h). The District Court sentenced him under 18 U.S.C. § 924(a) to five years' imprisonment, the maximum term authorized for violation of § 922(h). The Court of Appeals affirmed the conviction but remanded for resentencing.

Who's That?

Thurgood Marshall was an associate justice on the United States Supreme Court for 24 years, from 1967–1991. The first African-American justice, he was well-known before his appointment to the high court, having won many arguments before the same court, including *Brown v. Board of Education* in his role as chief counsel and executive director for the NAACP Legal Defense Fund. He also was the Solicitor General, appointed by President Lyndon Johnson.

The majority recognized that respondent had been indicted and convicted under § 922(h) and that § 924(a) permits five years' imprisonment. However, noting that the substantive elements of § 922(h) and 18 U.S.C.App. § 1202(a) are identical as applied to a convicted felon who unlawfully receives a firearm, the court interpreted the Act to allow no more than the 2-year maximum sentence provided by § 1202(a). This Court has previously noted the partial redundancy of §§ 922(h) and 1202(a), both as to the conduct they proscribe and the individuals they reach. However, we find nothing in the language, structure, or legislative history of the Act to suggest that because of this overlap, a defendant convicted under § 992(h) may be imprisoned for no more than the maximum term specified in § 1202(a). As we read the Act, each substantive statute, in conjunction with its own sentencing provision, operates independently of the other.

In construing § 1202(a) to override the penalties authorized by § 924(a), the Court of Appeals invoked the well-established doctrine that ambiguities in criminal statutes must be resolved in favor of lenity. Although this principle of construction applies to sentencing as well as substantive provisions, in the instant case there is no ambiguity to resolve. Respondent unquestionably violated § 922(h), and § 924(a) unquestionably permits five years' imprisonment for such a violation. Nor can § 1202(a) be interpreted as implicitly repealing § 924(a) whenever a defendant's conduct might violate both Titles. In this case, the penalty provisions are fully capable of coexisting because they apply to convictions under different statutes. Finally, the maxim that statutes should be construed to avoid constitutional questions offers no assistance here. We find no constitutional infirmities. It is a fundamental tenet of due process that "no one may be required at peril of life, liberty or property to speculate as to the meaning of penal statutes." A criminal statute is therefore invalid if it "fails to give a person of ordinary intelligence fair notice that his contemplated conduct is forbidden." So too, vague sentencing provisions may pose constitutional questions if they do not state with sufficient clarity the consequences of violating a given criminal statute. The provisions here unambiguously specify the activity proscribed and the penalties available upon conviction. That this particular conduct may violate both Titles does not detract from the notice afforded by each. This Court has long recognized that when an act violates more than one criminal statute, the Government may prosecute under either so long as it does not discriminate against any class of defendants. The provisions at issue plainly demarcate the range of penalties that prosecutors and judges may seek and

Food for Thought

A prosecutor in a large urban city wishes to provide diversion, meaning non-prosecution of charges, for all persons who have no prior serious criminal offenses on their criminal records. A) Would this be an appropriate policy? Is there an alternative policy that you might impose if you were the prosecutor? B) What articulable criteria would you use for your decision-making process? (Examples of such criteria are provided in Part E. infra.)

impose. In light of that specificity, the power that Congress has delegated to those officials is no broader than the authority they routinely exercise in enforcing the criminal laws. Having informed the courts, prosecutors, and defendants of the permissible punishment alternatives available under each Title, Congress has fulfilled its duty.

Accordingly, the judgment of the Court of Appeals is reversed.

* * *

Immigration. Prosecutorial discretion arises in many places and contexts. During the Trump administration, the immigration context assumed a higher profile, particularly given President Trump's posture concerning deportation. In immigration cases, prosecutorial discretion involves the power to choose whether to seek deportation of a person, to denaturalize persons who lied to immigration officials in the process of becoming a citizen, and to prosecute those that person violate federal law which subjects a person to prison if the person "knowingly procures or attempts to procure, contrary to any law, the naturalization of any person." In *Maslenjak v. United States,* the Court heard oral argument regarding whether a naturalized person can be stripped of citizenship based on an immaterial lie. The justices were not sure a clear line could be drawn between materiality and immateriality. As Justice Anthony Kennedy stated at the oral argument, "You can have a statement that everyone thinks is immaterial, it's subjectively immaterial, but it might have a causal connection at the end of the day."

2. Criteria for the Exercise of Discretion

While not binding on a prosecutor's decision regarding whether or who to investigate or charge, and at what level, the American Bar Association has adopted standards intended to assist prosecutors in the principled exercise of their investigatory and charging discretion. Consider two examples of policy questions that arise regarding discretion. First, should the age and medical status of suspects be regarded as relevant criteria in determining whether and how to prosecute? If so, how? Second, should the criteria for the prosecutor's exercise of discretion be disclosed to the defense or the public?

In *Inmates of Attica Correctional Facility v. Rockefeller,* 477 F.2d 375 (2d Cir. 1973), the court held that the federal judiciary, even at the behest of crime victims, lack the authority to compel federal and state officials to investigate and prosecute persons who have violated criminal statutes. Because prosecutors possess discretion (rather than an obligation or duty) to investigate and prosecute, they are not legally bound to do either. From the perspective of the separation of powers, the Judicial Branch should not be interfering with the executive prerogatives of prosecutors who are part of the Executive Branch. As the court points out, we do not want courts to become "superprosecutors", without anyone to check the exercise (and abuse) of such authority.

Hypo 1: *Homicide Charge*

Suppose that Terry, a Hispanic-American, is a neighborhood watch coordinator for his gated community. Terry sees Alan, a young African American, who he does not recognize. Terry calls the local police to report suspicious behavior, saying that the person is cutting between houses, but not engaging in any criminal behavior. After the phone call, there is a violent confrontation between the two individuals. During the incident, Terry shoots Alan in the chest, killing him. Terry claims self-defense. Assume that the law states in pertinent part: "A person is justified in using force, except deadly force, against another when and to the extent that the person reasonably believes that such conduct is necessary to defend himself or herself or another against the other's imminent use of unlawful force. However, a person is justified in the use of deadly force and does not have a duty to retreat if he or she reasonably believes that such force is necessary to prevent imminent death or great bodily harm to himself or herself or another or to prevent the imminent commission of a forcible felony. If you decide to charge Terry with homicide, would you seek a Grand Jury indictment or charge the case yourself by information (if you are not required by law to seek an indictment for the crimes charged)? If you don't feel that you can fairly make a decision based on these limited facts, what further facts would you ask the police to obtain? How would these additional facts influence your exercise of discretion?

Hypo 2: *More Decisions*

What decisions would you make as a prosecutor in each of the following scenarios—and why?

A) Dr. Jack Kevorkian, who believes strongly in euthanasia, flies to your jurisdiction and obtains drugs for a woman to help her 72-year-old husband take his own life. The husband has terminal cancer. Your jurisdiction's Crimes Code contains a section which provides that "a person who intentionally aids or solicits another to commit suicide is guilty of a felony punishable by up to 10 years in prison if the person's conduct causes such suicide or an attempted suicide." Should you charge Dr. Kevorkian and/or the deceased's spouse?

B) The day after a defendant is arrested for the sexual abuse of a 10-year-old boy, the boy's distraught mother shoots and kills defendant at his arraignment. She tells you that she bought the gun that morning in order to kill the deceased. The state's Crimes Code provides that: an intentional, premeditated killing is first-degree murder; an otherwise malicious killing is second-degree murder; and a provoked killing is voluntary manslaughter, although the provocation must be "sudden." With what, if anything, do you charge the mother?

C) A woman who was physically and emotionally abused by her husband for three years kills him by pouring gasoline on him and lighting a match while he is passed out in an alcoholic stupor. The last time he abused her was three days earlier. Your jurisdiction's Crimes Code does not expressly recognize a "battered spouse" defense, and its self-defense provisions require that a defendant establish, *inter alia,* that he or she used defensive deadly force in response to the "imminent" use of deadly force against her. Do you charge her with murder?

D) A college student, Anthony, spies on his new roommate, making a secret tape of the student while that student is on a date in their dormitory room. The student posts the tape to his Facebook page. When the roommate finds out, an altercation ensues. Assume that Anthony is charged with battery and invasion of privacy. Also assume that Anthony's immigration status would be adversely affected by a plea of guilty to a felony or misdemeanor charge. What criteria would you use for determining whether and with what to charge Anthony? Would you take his immigration status into account?

D. Prosecutorial Discretion in Plea Bargaining

Prosecutorial discretion frequently comes into play in plea bargaining—when prosecutors and attorneys for the accused—or the accused directly, if she is unrepresented—attempt to reach an alternate disposition to a trial. It is the functional equivalent of settlement negotiations in civil cases.

The bargaining generally involves discussions regarding the specific type of crime to be charged, as well as the degree and potential outcomes (jail? probation? diversion?), and it will come as no surprise that most criminal cases do not go to trial and are instead resolved through plea bargaining agreements between prosecutors and defendants. For example, in 2011, fewer than 1 in 40 criminal cases went to trial.

According to one commentator: "Beginning in the 1960s, and escalating thereafter, Congress and most state legislatures, largely in response to public pressure, decreed that those convicted of crimes would serve ever-longer prison sentences. In the federal system, this trend involved mandatory minimum sentences, sentencing guidelines, and the abolition of parole. Faced with the knowledge that their clients, if convicted after trial, would be sentenced to very long periods of incarceration, prudent defense counsel increasingly sought to negotiate plea bargains that would allow their clients to obtain lower sentences by pleading guilty to lesser counts or narrower charges, or in exchange for other sentencing concessions. The result was an increase in the percentage of criminal cases resolved by guilty pleas; such pleas now account for ninety-seven percent of all federal criminal convictions and ninety-four percent of all state criminal convictions." Jed. S. Rakoff, Frye *and* Lafler: *Bearers of Mixed Messages*, 122 YALE L.J. ONLINE 25 (2012).

The risk from plea bargaining is that an innocent defendant will plead guilty to a crime that he did not commit. *See* Gary Fields & John Emshwiller, *Federal Guilty Pleas Soar as Bargains Trump Trials*, Wall St. Journal, U.S. News Section. A.1 (Sept. 23, 2012). Defendants sometimes plead guilty (even when innocent) because they fear that, if they do not, they may be convicted and spend years or decades in prison. By pleading guilty, defendants sometimes receive lesser sentences. Prosecutors can exacerbate these fears by overcharging defendants. Indeed, in 2011, guilty pleas were entered in 97% of all federal cases, an increase of 84% from 1990. At the same time, because of a crackdown on various crimes, the number of prosecutions increased two-fold. Sometimes, defendants pleaded guilty without attempting to discover whether the prosecution has exculpatory evidence. As a result, some have begun to question whether plea bargains should be allowed or should be more carefully scrutinized. Some believe that defendants who plea bargain should receive the same types of protection that they would have received had they gone to trial.

Point for Discussion

Effective Assistance of Counsel

In 2012, the Court decided two cases that involved plea bargaining. These cases intersect with other areas of criminal procedure, but have some relevance in the plea bargaining context. In particular, the cases show that in the plea bargaining arena, defendants have constitutional rights. Moreover, even if prosecutors exercise their discretion properly, the Sixth Amendment right to counsel still limits what bargaining will suffice for a permissible outcome. In the first case, *Missouri v. Frye*, 566 U.S. 134 (2012), the Court considered whether the Sixth Amendment right to the effective assistance of counsel extends to the consideration and negotiation of plea agreements. The Court held that it did. Because 95% of cases result in plea bargains, the Court held that it was improper to think that only the trial process protects criminal defendants against errors in the pre-trial phase. As Justice Kennedy noted, plea bargaining, "is not some adjunct to the criminal justice system, it is the criminal justice system." In *Lafler v. Cooper*, 566 U.S. 156 (2012), the Court considered a *habeas corpus* claim, involving an alleged violation of the Six Amendment right to the effective assistance of counsel, specifically whether a state court's application of the right to effective assistance was contrary to the standard set forth in *Strickland v. Washington*, 466 U.S. 668 (1984). In the trial court, defendant Cooper rejected two plea offers and chose to go to trial. The Court concluded that when a defendant claims that ineffective assistance of counsel led to the improper rejection of a plea offer, defendant has the burden of showing by a reasonable probability that the prejudice resulting from a more severe conviction and sentence after trial would not have occurred but for the ineffective assistance.

Ineffective assistance is an extremely important aspect of the process. When he was Attorney General of the United States, John Ashcroft issued a memo limiting the authority of prosecutors to enter into plea bargains. *See* David Rosenzweig, *L.A. Attorneys Divided on Ashcroft Directive: Some Defense Lawyers Fear That Placing Restrictions on Prosecutors Who are Seeking Plea Bargains Will Strain the System*, L.A. TIMES p. B2 (October 17, 2003). Some commentators have suggested that the entire criminal justice system might collapse if the new memo limited and constrained plea bargaining. *Id.* In Los Angeles, at the time, some 97.2% of all cases were settled through plea bargaining (the rate is 96% nationally). *Id.* As a result, if only a fraction of defendants who currently plead guilty were to choose trials because prosecutors had become uncompromising, the courts would be inundated in no time, said defense lawyers." *Id.* The Ashcroft policy altered a policy previously issued by former Attorney General Janet Reno in 1993 which "allowed prosecutors engaged in plea negotiations to make individualized assessments of the circumstances and seriousness of a crime and whether the sentence would be appropriate." *Id.* However, the Reno memo left intact "a requirement that prosecutors proceed on the most serious 'readily provable' charges and not arrive at a plea agreement 'that fails to reflect the seriousness of the defendant's conduct.'" *Id.* So, the Ashcroft memo seemed designed to limit prosecutorial discretion.

Food for Thought

What would happen if a prosecutor's office prohibited plea bargaining and allowed only straight pleas of guilty, dismissal, or diversion? For example, consider the statement by the then District Attorney of the Bronx, New York, Robert T. Johnson, made on November 24, 1992: "Last week, I directed my staff not to plea bargain any case which had been indicted by a grand jury. Of course, defendants are free to plead to the crimes as charged in the indictment, or to attempt to negotiate a plea before an indictment results. This direction was met by protests from some that the system would collapse. In my view, this objection demonstrates the need for the system to take stock of itself and answer this question: is it actually accomplishing what it was designed to accomplish? For if the system really will collapse unless we plea bargain, then there must be something terribly wrong with the system. It means that those charged with crime have a stranglehold on the rest of us; it means that society has ceded control to those it has accused of violating its laws; and it means that our system is running us, instead of the other way around."

E. Pretrial Diversion for Defendants

In addition to exercising discretion with respect to who and when to investigate and who, what, and whether to charge, prosecutors in many jurisdictions also possess substantial authority to divert accused persons to pretrial intervention (PTI) programs. In effect, prosecutors have essentially the same unfettered discretion with respect to a diversion decision as they possess in deciding who to investigate or to charge. The prosecutor is presumed to have considered all relevant factors in making his or her decision. In *State v. Rosario*, 566 A.2d 1173 (App. Div. 1989) (distinguished by *State v. Green*, 997 A.2d 242 (2010)), the court upheld the discretion of a prosecutor to refuse to consent to the defendant's participation in a diversion program. Evidence that Rosario had used his residence as a source of narcotics trafficking, even though he was not charged with trafficking, justified the prosecutor's refusal to consent to diversion: "Abandonment of the prosecution would be more harmful to society than admission into the diversion program would be beneficial to defendant."

Typically, the successful completion by an accused of the conditions set for entry into a PTI program results in dismissal of the charges that led to the PTI diversion. Concomitantly, failure to meet those PTI requirements results in the prosecutorial office taking the charges to trial. The National District Attorneys Association has created a set of model standards for the prosecutorial exercise of discretion relating to PTI referrals, standards which have not been expressly adopted in any jurisdiction, but which will illustrate the sorts of concerns and criteria prosecutors should have and use in deciding how to exercise this discretion.

National District Attorneys Association—National Prosecution Standards

STANDARDS 4–3.1 through 4–3.8 (3d ed. 2009).

Diversion

4–3.1 Prosecutorial Responsibility: The decision to divert cases from the criminal justice system should be the responsibility of the prosecutor. The prosecutor should, within the exercise of his or her discretion, determine whether diversion of an offender to a treatment alternative best serves the interests of justice.

4–3.2 Diversion Alternatives: A prosecutor should be aware and informed of the scope and availability of all alternative diversion programs. The prosecutor's office should take steps to help ensure that all diversion programs are credible and effective. . . .

4–3.4 Information Gathering: The prosecutor should have all relevant investigative information, personal data, case records, and criminal history information necessary to render sound and reasonable decisions on diversion of individuals from the criminal justice system. The chief prosecutor should take steps to ensure the enactment of appropriate legislation and court rules to enable the prosecutor to obtain such information from appropriate agencies.

4–3.5 Factors to Consider: The prosecutor may divert individuals from the criminal justice system when he or she considers it to be in the interest of justice and beneficial to both the community and the individual. Factors which may be considered in this decision include: a. The nature and severity of the offense; b. Any special characteristics or difficulties of the offender; c. Whether the defendant is a first-time offender; d. The likelihood that the defendant will cooperate with and benefit from the diversion program; e. Whether an available program is appropriate to the needs of the offender; f. The impact of diversion upon the community; g. Recommendations of the relevant law enforcement agency; h. The likelihood that the defendant will recidivate; i. The extent to which diversion will enable the defendant to maintain employment or remain in school; j. The opinion of the victim; k. Provisions for restitution; l. The impact of the crime on the victim; and m. Diversion decisions with respect to similarly situated defendants.

4–3.6 Diversion Procedures: The process of diverting a defendant should include the following procedures: a. A signed agreement or court record specifying all requirements of the accused; b. A signed waiver of speedy trial requirements, where applicable; c. The right of the prosecutor, for a designated time period, to proceed with the criminal case when, in the prosecutor's judgment, such action would be in the interest of justice; d. Appropriate mechanisms to safeguard the prosecution of the case, such as admissions of guilt, stipulations of facts, and depositions of witnesses.

Commentary

An alternative available to prosecutors in the processing of a criminal complaint is that of diversion—the channeling of criminal defendants and even potential defendants, into programs that may not result in a criminal conviction. The purposes of diversion programs include: Unburdening court dockets and conserving judicial resources for more serious cases; & Reducing the incidence of offender recidivism by providing community-based rehabilitation that would be more effective and less costly than the alternatives available in continued criminal prosecution.

Food for Thought

What is your opinion of the appropriateness of the guidance factors set forth in NDAA Standard 4–3? Are all of these factors appropriate for a prosecutor's consideration given the fact that there is unlikely to be any judicial review? Is it appropriate for a prosecutor, for example, to take account of the political impact of a decision to divert an accused into an otherwise available PTI program: Is the "political reaction" of individuals in the community (including, perhaps, whether or not to vote for the prosecutor in the next election) different from the "community reaction" which Standard 4–3 provides should be appropriate for the prosecutor to consider? In your opinion, are there other factors not set forth in Standard 4–3 that should be considered by a prosecutor in making these decisions? What are they?

Determination of the appropriateness of diversion in a specified case will involve a subjective determination that, after consideration of all circumstances, the offender and the community will both benefit more by diversion than by prosecution. Equally important as protecting the rights of the individual is the necessity to protect the interests of society. It must be remembered that the individual involved in the diversion process is accused of having committed a criminal act and is avoiding prosecution only because an alternative procedure is thought to be more appropriate and more beneficial.

Hypo: *The Ray Rice Case*

Ray Rice, a running back with the National Football League (NFL) Baltimore Ravens, was videotaped on Valentine's Day weekend, 2014, punching and knocking out his then-fiancée, and now wife—in an elevator of an Atlantic City Hotel and Casino. Rice was indicted for aggravated assault on March 27, 2014, and then accepted into a diversion program on May 23, 2014. For the elevator video, *see* http://www.tmz.com/videos/0_ekaflcqq/. For Judge Jones' arbitration decision of Rice's appeal of his NFL suspension, go to: https://s3.amazonaws.com/s3.documentcloud.org/documents/1372767/judge-ruling-ray-rice-decision.pdf. Based on the NDAA standards above, was the granting of diversion appropriate? What would you have done?

F. Selective Prosecution

As a result of the broad discretion that prosecutors exercise in prosecuting criminal cases, there is the potential for abuse of discretion. Misuse of discretion especially presents itself when a prosecutor, with the requisite amount of probable cause, purposefully chooses to pursue a case because of the defendant's race, religion, or some other arbitrary criteria.

Wayte v. United States

470 U.S. 598 (1985).

JUSTICE POWELL delivered the opinion of the Court.

The question is whether a passive enforcement policy under which the Government prosecutes only those who report themselves as having violated the law, or who are reported by others, violates the First and Fifth Amendments.

On July 2, 1980, pursuant to his authority under § 3 of the Military Selective Service Act, the President issued Presidential Proclamation No. 4771. This Proclamation directed male citizens and certain male residents born during 1960 to register with the Selective Service System during the week of July 21, 1980. Petitioner fell within that class but did not register. Instead, he wrote several letters to Government officials, including the President, stating that he had not registered and did not intend to do so. Petitioner's letters were added to a Selective Service file of young men who advised that they had failed to register or who were reported by others as having failed to register. Selective Service adopted a policy of passive enforcement under which it would investigate and prosecute only the cases of nonregistration contained in this file. In furtherance of this policy, Selective Service sent a letter on June 17, 1981, to each reported violator who had not registered and for whom it had an address. The letter explained the duty to register, and warned that a violation could result in criminal prosecution and specified penalties. On July 20, 1981, Selective Service transmitted to the Department of Justice, for investigation and potential prosecution, the names of petitioner and 133 other young men identified under its passive enforcement system—all of whom had not registered. At two later dates, it referred the names of 152 more young men similarly identified. After screening out the names of those who appeared not to be in the class required to register, the Department of Justice referred the remaining names to the Federal Bureau of Investigation for additional inquiry and to the United States Attorneys for the districts in which the nonregistrants resided. Petitioner's name was one of those referred.

Pursuant to Department of Justice policy, those referred were not immediately prosecuted. Instead, the appropriate United States Attorney was required to notify identified nonregistrants by registered mail that, unless they registered within a specified time, prosecution would be considered. In addition, an FBI agent was sent to interview the nonregistrant. This effort to persuade nonregistrants to change their minds became known as the "beg" policy. Under it, young men who registered late were not prosecuted, while those who never registered were investigated further by the Government. Pursuant to the "beg" policy, the United States Attorney for the Central District of California sent petitioner a letter on October 15, 1981, urging him to register or face possible prosecution. Petitioner failed to respond. On December 9, 1981, the Department of Justice instructed all United States Attorneys not to begin seeking indictments against nonregistrants until further notice. On January 7, 1982, the President announced a grace period to afford nonregistrants a further opportunity to register without penalty. This grace period extended until February 28, 1982. Petitioner still did not register. Over the next few months, the Department decided to begin prosecuting those young men who, despite the grace period and "beg" policy, continued to refuse to register. It recognized that under the passive enforcement system those prosecuted were "liable to be vocal proponents of nonregistration" or persons "with religious or moral objections." It also recognized that prosecutions would "undoubtedly result in allegations that the case was brought in retribution for the nonregistrant's exercise of his first amendment rights." The Department was advised, however, that Selective Service could not develop a more "active" enforcement system for some time. Because of this, the Department decided to begin seeking indictments under the passive system without further delay. On May 21, 1982, United States Attorneys were notified to begin prosecution of nonregistrants. On June 28, 1982, FBI agents interviewed petitioner, and he continued to refuse to register. Accordingly, an indictment was returned against him for knowingly and willfully failing to register with the Selective Service. Petitioner moved to dismiss the indictment on the ground of selective prosecution. He contended that he and the other indicted nonregistrants were "vocal" opponents of the registration program who had been impermissibly targeted (out of an estimated 674,000 nonregistrants) for prosecution on the basis of their exercise of First Amendment rights. [The federal district court found that the government had engaged in impermissible selective prosecution; the Ninth Circuit Court of Appeals reversed.]

In our criminal justice system, the Government retains "broad discretion" as to whom to prosecute. "So long as the prosecutor has probable cause to believe that the accused committed an offense defined by statute, the decision whether to prosecute, and what charge to file or bring before a grand jury, generally rests entirely in his discretion." This broad discretion rests largely on the recognition that the decision to prosecute is particularly ill-suited to judicial review. Such factors as the strength of the case, the prosecution's general deterrence value, the Government's enforcement priorities, and the case's relationship to the Government's overall enforcement plan are not readily susceptible to the kind of analysis the courts are competent to undertake. Judicial supervision in this area, moreover, entails systemic costs of particular concern. Examining the basis of a prosecution delays the criminal proceeding, threatens to chill law enforcement by subjecting the prosecutor's motives and decision-making to outside inquiry, and may undermine prosecutorial effectiveness by revealing the Government's enforcement policy. All these are substantial concerns that make the courts properly hesitant to examine the decision whether to prosecute. As we noted in a slightly different context, although prosecutorial discretion is broad, it is not " 'unfettered.' Selectivity in the enforcement of criminal laws is subject to constitutional constraints." In particular, the decision to prosecute may not be "deliberately based upon an unjustifiable standard such as race, religion, or other arbitrary classification," including the exercise of protected statutory and constitutional rights.

It is appropriate to judge selective prosecution claims according to ordinary equal protection standards. These standards require petitioner to show both that the passive enforcement system had a discriminatory effect and that it was motivated by a discriminatory purpose. All petitioner has shown here is that those eventually prosecuted, along with many not prosecuted, reported themselves as having violated the law. He has not shown that the enforcement policy selected nonregistrants for prosecution on the basis of their speech. Indeed, he could not have done so given the way the "beg" policy was carried out. The Government did not prosecute those who reported themselves but later registered. Nor did it prosecute those who protested registration but did not report themselves or were not reported by others. In fact, the Government did not even investigate those who wrote letters to Selective Service criticizing registration unless their letters stated affirmatively that they had refused to comply with the law. The Government, on the other hand, did prosecute people who reported themselves or were reported by others but who did not publicly protest. These facts demonstrate that the Government treated all reported nonregistrants similarly. It did not subject vocal nonregistrants to any special burden. Indeed, those prosecuted in effect selected themselves for prosecution by refusing to register after being reported and warned by the Government.

Even if the passive policy had a discriminatory effect, petitioner has not shown that the Government intended such a result. The evidence he presented demonstrated only that the Government was aware that the passive enforcement policy would result in prosecution of vocal objectors and that they would probably make selective prosecution claims. As we have noted, however: " 'Discriminatory purpose' implies more than intent as awareness of consequences. It implies that the decisionmaker selected or reaffirmed a particular course of action at least in part 'because of,' not merely 'in spite of,' its adverse effects upon an identifiable group." In the present case, petitioner has not shown that the Government prosecuted him *because of* his protest activities. Absent such a showing, his claim of selective prosecution fails.

> **Take Note**
>
> Sometimes, politics is alleged to be the real reason for a prosecution. For example, Professor Alan Dershowitz of Harvard Law School claimed that the felony prosecution of conservative filmmaker and author Dinesh D'Souza involved an improper use of prosecutorial discretion. Jacob Gershman, *Dershowitz Says D'Souza Case "Smacks of Selective Prosecution,"* Wall St. Journal Law Blog (Jan. 31, 2014).

We conclude that the Government's passive enforcement system together with its "beg" policy violated neither the First nor Fifth Amendment. Accordingly, we affirm the judgment of the Court of Appeals.

It is so ordered.

JUSTICE MARSHALL, with whom JUSTICE BRENNAN joins, dissenting.

Wayte presents an equal protection challenge. Wayte argues that the scheme purposefully singled out these individuals as a result of their exercise of First Amendment rights. The claim is that the "passive" enforcement system was designed to discriminate against those who exercised their First Amendment rights. Such governmental action cannot stand if undertaken with discriminatory intent. "For an agent of the State to pursue a course of action whose objective is to penalize a person's reliance on his legal rights is 'patently unconstitutional.' " If the Government intentionally discriminated in defining the pool of potential prosecutees, it cannot immunize itself from liability merely by showing that it used permissible methods in choosing whom to prosecute from this previously tainted pool.

United States v. Armstrong

517 U.S. 456 (1996).

CHIEF JUSTICE REHNQUIST delivered the opinion of the Court.

In this case, we consider the showing necessary for a defendant to be entitled to discovery on a claim that the prosecuting attorney singled him out for prosecution on the basis of his race. We conclude that respondents failed to show that the Government declined to prosecute similarly situated suspects of other races.

Practice Pointer

When a trial court denies a defense motion to compel discovery, the standard applied by many appellate courts is abuse of discretion, *see, e.g., United States v. Hirsch*, 360 F.3d 860 (8th Cir. 2004), while a few courts apply a *de novo* standard of review, *see, e.g., United States v. James*, 257 F.3d 1173 (10th Cir. 2001).

Respondents were indicted in the United States District Court for the Central District of California on charges of conspiring to possess with intent to distribute more than 50 grams of cocaine base (crack) and conspiring to distribute the same, in violation of 21 U.S.C. §§ 841 and 846, and federal firearms offenses. For three months prior to the indictment, agents had infiltrated a suspected crack distribution ring by using confidential informants. On seven separate occasions during this period, the informants bought a total of 124.3 grams of crack from respondents and witnessed respondents carrying firearms during the sales. The agents searched the hotel room in which the sales were transacted, arrested respondents Armstrong and Hampton in the room, and found more crack and a loaded gun. The agents later arrested the other respondents. Respondents filed a motion for discovery to support their selective prosecution claim. The motion was opposed by the Government, but granted by the District Court. [This] Court considered whether this discovery request was warranted.

A selective-prosecution claim is not a defense on the merits to the criminal charge itself, but an independent assertion that the prosecutor has brought the charge for reasons forbidden by the Constitution. Our cases delineating the necessary elements to prove a claim of selective prosecution have taken great pains to explain that the standard is a demanding one. These cases afford a "background presumption" that the showing necessary to obtain discovery should itself be a significant barrier to the litigation of insubstantial claims.

A selective-prosecution claim asks a court to exercise judicial power over a "special province" of the Executive. The Attorney General and United States Attorneys retain " 'broad discretions' 'to enforce the Nation's criminal laws.' " They have this latitude because they are designated by statute as the President's delegates to help him discharge his constitutional responsibility to 'take Care that the Laws be faithfully executed.' " In the ordinary case, "so long as the prosecutor has probable cause to believe that the accused committed an offense defined by statute, the decision whether or not to prosecute, and what charge to file or bring before a grand jury, generally rests entirely in his discretion." Of course, a prosecutor's discretion is "subject to constitutional constraints." One of these constraints, imposed by the equal protection component of the Due Process Clause of the Fifth Amendment, is that the decision whether to prosecute may not be based on "an unjustifiable standard such as race, religion, or other arbitrary classification." A defendant may demonstrate that the administration of a criminal law is "directed so exclusively against a particular class of persons with a mind so unequal and oppressive" that the system of prosecution amounts to "a practical denial" of equal protection of the law.

In order to dispel the presumption that a prosecutor has not violated equal protection, a criminal defendant must present "clear evidence to the contrary." The high standard stems from a concern not to unnecessarily impair the performance of a core executive constitutional function. "Examining the basis of a prosecution delays the criminal proceeding, threatens to chill law enforcement by subjecting the prosecutor's motives and decisionmaking to outside inquiry, and may undermine prosecutorial effectiveness by revealing the Government's enforcement policy." The requirements for a selective-prosecution claim draw on "ordinary equal protection standards." The claimant must demonstrate that the federal prosecutorial policy "had a discriminatory effect and that it was motivated by a discriminatory purpose." To establish a discriminatory effect in a race case, the claimant must show that similarly situated individuals of a different race were not prosecuted. If discovery is ordered, the Government must assemble from its own files documents which might corroborate or refute the defendant's claim. Discovery thus imposes many of the costs present when the Government must respond to a *prima facie* case of selective prosecution. It will divert prosecutors' resources and may disclose the Government's prosecutorial strategy. The justifications for a rigorous standard for the elements of a selective-prosecution claim thus require a correspondingly rigorous standard for discovery in aid of such a claim. The Courts of Appeals "require some evidence tending to show the existence of the essential elements of the defense," discriminatory effect and discriminatory intent.

In this case we consider what evidence constitutes "some evidence tending to show the existence" of the discriminatory effect element. The Court of Appeals held that a defendant may establish a colorable basis for discriminatory effect without evidence that the Government has failed to prosecute others who are similarly situated to the defendant. It was mistaken. The vast majority of the Courts of Appeals require the defendant to produce some evidence that similarly situated defendants of other races could have been prosecuted, but were not, and this requirement is consistent with our equal protection case law. As the three-judge panel explained, " 'selective prosecution' implies that a selection has taken place." We think the required threshold—a credible showing of different treatment of similarly situated persons—adequately balances the Government's interest in vigorous prosecution and the defendant's interest in avoiding selective prosecution.

Respondents' "study" did not constitute "some evidence tending to show the existence of the essential elements of" a selective-prosecution claim. The study failed to identify individuals who were not black, could have been prosecuted for the offenses for which respondents were charged, but were not prosecuted. This omission was not remedied by respondents' evidence in opposition to the Government's motion for reconsideration. The newspaper article which discussed the discriminatory effect of federal drug sentencing laws, was not relevant to an allegation of discrimination in decision prosecuted. This omission was not evidence in opposition to the reconsideration. The newspaper article, discriminatory effect of federal drug sentencing laws, was not relevant to an allegation of discrimination in decisions to prosecute. Respondents' affidavits, which recounted one attorney's conversation with a drug treatment center employee and the experience of another attorney defending drug prosecutions in state court, recounted hearsay and reported personal conclusions based on anecdotal evidence. The judgment of the Court of Appeals is therefore reversed, and the case is remanded for proceedings consistent with this opinion.

It is so ordered.

JUSTICE STEVENS, dissenting.

The facts presented to the District Court in support of respondents' claim that they had been singled out for prosecution because of their race were not sufficient to prove that defense. I am persuaded that the District Judge did not abuse her discretion when she concluded that the factual showing was sufficiently disturbing to require some response from the United States Attorney's Office. Perhaps the discovery order was broader than necessary, but I cannot agree with the Court's conclusion that no inquiry was permissible. The District Judge's order should be evaluated in light of three circumstances that underscore the need for judicial vigilance over certain types of drug prosecutions. First, the Anti-Drug Abuse Act of 1986 and subsequent legislation established a regime of extremely high penalties for the possession and distribution of so-called "crack" cocaine. Second, the disparity between the treatment of crack cocaine and powder cocaine is matched by the disparity between the severity of the punishment imposed by federal law and that imposed by state law for the same conduct. Finally, the brunt of the elevated federal penalties falls heavily on blacks. While 65% of the persons who have used crack are white, in 1993 they represented only 4% of the federal offenders convicted of trafficking in crack. Eighty-eight percent of such defendants were black. The extraordinary severity of the penalties and the troubling racial patterns of enforcement give rise to a special concern about the fairness of charging practices for crack offenses. Evidence tending to prove that black defendants charged with distribution of crack are prosecuted in federal court, whereas members of other races charged with similar offenses are prosecuted in state court, warrants close scrutiny by the federal judges. In my view, the District Judge, who has sat on both the federal and the state benches in Los Angeles, acted well within her discretion to call for the development of facts that would demonstrate what standards, if any, governed the choice of forum where similarly situated offenders are prosecuted. In this case, the evidence was sufficiently disturbing to persuade the District Judge to order discovery that might help explain the conspicuous racial pattern of cases before her.

United States v. Bass

536 U.S. 862 (2002).

PER CURIAM.

A federal grand jury in the Eastern District of Michigan returned a superseding indictment charging respondent with, *inter alia*, the intentional firearm killings of two individuals. The United States filed a notice of intent to seek the death penalty. Respondent, who is black, alleged that the Government had determined to seek the death penalty against him because of his race. He moved to dismiss the death penalty notice and, in the alternative, for discovery of information relating to the Government's capital charging practices. The District Court granted the motion for discovery, and after the Government informed the court that it would not comply with the discovery order, the court dismissed the death penalty notice. A divided panel of the United States Court of Appeals for the Sixth Circuit affirmed. We grant the petition for a writ of certiorari and now summarily reverse.

In *United States v. Armstrong*, we held that a defendant who seeks discovery on a claim of selective prosecution must show some evidence of both discriminatory effect and discriminatory intent. We need go no further in the present case than consideration of the evidence supporting discriminatory effect. *Armstrong* says that the defendant must make a "credible showing" that "similarly situated individuals of a different race were not prosecuted." The Sixth Circuit concluded that respondent had made such a showing based on nationwide statistics demonstrating that "the United States charges blacks with a death-eligible offense more than twice as often as it charges whites" and that the United States enters into plea bargains more frequently with whites than it does with blacks. Even assuming that the *Armstrong* requirement can be satisfied by a nationwide showing (as opposed to a showing regarding the record of the decisionmakers in respondent's case), raw statistics regarding overall charges say nothing about charges brought against *similarly situated defendants*. And the statistics regarding plea bargains are even less relevant, since respondent *was* offered a plea bargain but declined it. Under *Armstrong*, because respondent failed to submit relevant evidence that similarly situated persons were treated differently, he was not entitled to discovery.

Food for Thought

Neither *Armstrong* nor *Bass* specified how the showing of "some evidence" of discriminatory effect could be satisfied, *e.g.*, by affidavit, by other admissible documentation, or by specific allegations. In *McNeil v. State*, 685 A.2d 839 (1996), the court suggested that presentation of verifiable facts in some form would be sufficient as long as it went beyond a mere general allegation of prosecutorial misconduct. Thus, even if a defense motion to dismiss for selective prosecution were not supported by an affidavit, it would nevertheless suffice if it was verifiable by review of the court file. In *United States v. Alameh*, 341 F.3d 167 (2d Cir. 2003), statistical evidence and affidavits showed increased prosecutions of people with Arab names after September 11, 2001, but the court held that was insufficient to support discovery because most of the investigation had occurred prior to that date.

The Sixth Circuit's decision is contrary to *Armstrong* and threatens the "performance of a core executive constitutional function." For that reason, we reverse.

Hypo 1: *Latin Kings*

"King Paradise," a/k/a George Boyd, retained you to represent him following his federal indictment for racketeering and murder. You have filed motions to dismiss the indictment due to selective prosecution and to gain access to information about governmental charging policies. The indictment charges George and all of the "Kings" who are officers and have prior criminal histories (*e.g.*, King Guy, King Bullet, King Humpty, King Biz); they are also the older male members of the local chapter of the Almighty Latin King Nation. Among the other members of the local chapter who were not indicted are its only three women members, who were officers and associates (commonly referred to as, you guessed it, "Queens") of the Latin Kings. In the Latin Kings organization, because women are prohibited from holding positions of authority, the highest office open to women is "Secretary," who is responsible for keeping records of the meetings. George indicates that some of the unindicted male members and all of the female members will testify for the Government. Evaluate whether the court will deny your motions.

Hypo 2: *Selective Prosecution*

Following discovery of a large and violent crack cocaine conspiracy, the United States Attorney indicted 25 persons, all African Americans. Of the 55 unindicted persons who were involved in the conspiracy, 50 are African American and five are white. Twenty-five African Americans were granted immunity from prosecution as were three whites. Defendant Sterling moved to dismiss the indictment, claiming that he had been selected for prosecution because of his race. He argued that the five unindicted white persons were similarly situated to him and that more than 90% of those indicted in the metro area since 1992 for crack cocaine trafficking are African Americans. An officer in the local police department testified that he did not choose individuals: "They choose to violate the law themselves. And when they violate the law, if we can prove it, we prosecute them, regardless of their race, sex, where they were born, or their family identity." He also testified about the reason that each white conspirator identified in Sterling's motion had not been indicted: one had agreed to work undercover, another was a target but the evidence against him was still insufficient, and the third had proven himself to be truthful and cooperative with the investigation. The trial court concluded that Sterling had made a nonfrivolous showing in raising a claim of selective prosecution and ordered the prosecution to respond to Sterling's formal requests for discovery into its criteria for selecting whom to prosecute. The court also found that Sterling and the unindicted white conspirators were "similarly situated" for a selective prosecution claim and that Sterling's statistical data made a nonfrivolous showing of discriminatory intent. Do you agree?

G. Vindictive Prosecution

The line between selective and vindictive prosecution is not always clear. The court in the following case takes pains to describe the criteria.

United States v. Brown

862 F.Supp.2d 1276 (N.D. Ala. 2012).

Memorandum Opinion and Order.

Vindictive prosecution is distinguishable from selective prosecution in that vindictive prosecution arises when the severity of the charges against a defendant is increased after the defendant exercises a constitutional right after criminal charges have begun, while selective prosecution occurs when a person is prosecuted based on an immutable personal characteristic, such as race or religion, or in response to some constitutionally-protected act that a person has done prior to the criminal charge being brought against him.

Claims of selective prosecution have been recognized by the Supreme Court for well over a century. In *Yick Wo v. Hopkins*, 118 U.S. 356 (1886), two Chinese subjects raised challenges under the Fourteenth Amendment's Equal Protection Clause to their incarceration for violating a San Francisco ordinance requiring operators of laundries in wooden buildings to obtain a permit from the city. About 200 Chinese owners of wooden laundries had been denied permits, whereas 80 non-Chinese owners had been granted permits to carry on their businesses under similar conditions. The Court reversed the convictions, declaring: "Though the law itself be fair on its face and impartial in appearance, if it is applied and administered by public authority with an evil eye and an unequal hand, so as practically to make unjust and illegal discriminations between persons in similar circumstances, material to their rights, the denial of equal justice is within the prohibition of the Constitution." In other words, a decision to prosecute that is "deliberately based upon an unjustifiable standard such as race, religion, or other arbitrary classification" is a denial of equal protection. *Oyler v. Boles*, 368 U.S. 448, 456 (1962). The ban on discriminatory prosecution is not limited to the states but also applies to the federal government under the Fifth Amendment's Due Process Clause. As noted by the Magistrate Judge, in *Wayte*, the Supreme Court set out the constitutional constraints on prosecutorial discretion as follows: "Although prosecutorial discretion is broad, it is not 'unfettered.' Selectivity in the enforcement of criminal laws is subject to constitutional constraints. The decision to prosecute may not be 'deliberately based upon an unjustifiable standard such as race, religion, or other arbitrary classification,' including the exercise of protected statutory and constitutional rights." *Wayte v. United States*, 470 U.S. 598, 608. *Wayte* instructs that selective prosecution cases are to be "judged according to ordinary equal protection standards." Unless the equal protection claim is based on an overtly discriminatory classification, "these standards require petitioner to show both that the passive enforcement system had a discriminatory effect and that it was motivated by a discriminatory purpose."

"As long as the prosecutor has probable cause to believe the accused has committed a crime, the courts have no authority to interfere with a prosecutor's decision to prosecute." *United States v. Barner*, 441 F. 3d 1310, 1315 (11th Cir. 2006). The prosecutor will violate due process, however, if he obtains new charges out of vindictiveness, *i.e.*, a "desire to punish a person for exercising his statutory or constitutional rights." *Id.* There are two ways to prove a prosecutorial vindictiveness claim: (1) by showing that a presumption of vindictiveness arises from the government's conduct; or (2) by showing actual vindictiveness. *See, e.g., United States v. Saltzman*, 537 F.3d 353 (5th Cir. 2008).

Brown's claim of vindictive prosecution is based on his allegation that he was prosecuted when others who are similarly situated were not because, before the charge he seeks to have dismissed was brought: (1) Brown was the victim of an assault by a BOP guard for which the guard had entered a guilty plea; (2) Brown had filed a civil suit in relation to that assault; (3) prison personnel were aware of those facts; and (4) Brown wrote an "inordinate number" of grievances against prison staff. However, even assuming that Brown has asserted a claim of presumptive or actual vindictiveness, he has failed to show the existence of either.

"A prosecutor's decision to seek heightened charges after a defendant successfully appeals his conviction for the same conduct is presumed to be vindictive." *Barner*, 441 F. 3d at 1315. There is, however, no automatic presumption of vindictiveness when a prosecutor decides to increase charges after a defendant exercises a legal right in the pretrial context. *Barner*, 441 F. 3d at 1316. Although the Eleventh Circuit has not definitively determined whether the presumption of vindictiveness can ever arise in the pretrial—much less precharge—context, a presumption could arise in the pretrial context only if the facts of the case "form a realistic likelihood of vindictiveness." *Barner*, 441 F.3d at 1318. For such a presumption to arise, defendant must first show that his exercise of pretrial rights was followed by charges of increased severity. If this threshold showing is made, defendant then must identify other factors to raise a realistic likelihood of vindictiveness.

To establish actual vindictiveness, a defendant must prove that: (1) the prosecutor wanted to punish the defendant for exercising his rights (animus); and (2) the prosecutor's animus caused the prosecutor to bring charges of increased severity (causation). *See Barner*, 441 F. 3d at 1322. A showing of actual vindictiveness is "exceedingly difficult to make." Moreover, it would be unduly burdensome on any person challenging a prosecution as vindictive to limit the motive which must be shown to the subjective motive of the actual prosecutor, or even to the United States Attorneys office. *Simms v. United States*, 41 A.3d 482 (D.C. Court of Appeals, 2012) (To impose a 'personal stake' requirement unduly constricts the inquiry of prosecutorial vindictiveness, which is not limited to the motives of an individual prosecutor and may focus on the motivations of the government as an institution.").

Not surprisingly, *Brown* has not established actual vindictiveness. Brown has not alleged a set of circumstances showing that "a reasonable likelihood of vindictiveness exists." *Goodwin*, 457 U.S. at 373. All *Brown* has done is shown that he was assaulted by a guard, the guard was prosecuted and plead guilty, Brown filed a civil suit related to the assault, and Brown was indicted for assaulting a guard by throwing feces and urine in the guard's face although other inmates who had engaged in similar assaults were not indicted. Thus, the Government was not required to come up with a reasonable explanation for the difference in Brown's treatment. *See Simms*, 41 A.3d 482. Government's obligation to answer or explain allegations of prosecutorial vindictiveness does not arise unless "the accumulation of circumstances of record, without more, give rise to a realistic likelihood of prosecutorial vindictiveness."

Points for Discussion

a. Causing a Retrial

Should there be a presumption of vindictiveness when a prosecutor increases criminal charges after a defendant exercises a constitutional right that causes a retrial after conviction? Suppose that Goodwin was charged with several misdemeanor and petty offenses, including assault on a United States Park Policeman. He initiated plea negotiations with the prosecutor, but later stated that he did not wish to plead guilty and desired a trial by jury. The case was transferred to the District Court and responsibility for the prosecution was assumed by an Assistant United States Attorney. About six weeks later, after reviewing the case, the prosecutor obtained a four-count indictment charging respondent with one felony count of forcibly assaulting a federal officer and three related counts. A jury convicted respondent on the felony count and on one misdemeanor count. Should a presumption of vindictiveness have attached to this case? *See United States v. Goodwin*, 457 U.S. 368 (1982).

b. Different Prosecutors

Should a presumption of vindictiveness arise if the defendant can prove that separate prosecutors filed related indictments? Can a persuasive argument be made that the vindictiveness is institutional rather than personal? *See Thigpen v. Roberts*, 468 U.S. 27, 31 (1984), where the Court noted that the addition of another prosecutor changed "little," but then stated: "It might be argued that if two different prosecutors are involved, a presumption of vindictiveness, which arises in part from assumptions about the individual's personal stake in the proceedings, is inappropriate. On the other hand, to the extent the presumption reflects 'institutional pressure that might subconsciously motivate a vindictive prosecutorial response to defendant's exercise of his right to obtain a retrial of a decided question,' it does not hinge on the continued involvement of a particular individual. A district attorney burdened with the retrial of an already-convicted defendant might be no less vindictive because he did not bring the initial prosecution. Indeed, *Blackledge* referred frequently to actions by 'the State,' rather than 'the prosecutor.' We need not determine the correct rule when two independent prosecutors are involved, however."

c. Mistrial

Should a presumption of vindictiveness exist when the prosecutor brings additional charges after a mistrial but before a retrial? *See, e.g., United States v. Poole*, 407 F.3d 767 (6th Cir. 2005) (no presumption of vindictiveness for adding charges following a mistrial due to a hung jury).

Hypo: *Vindictive Extra Count*

Three defendants were indicted for narcotics and firearms offenses. At their initial appearance, two of the defendants requested that they be released on bail pending trial, but the government was strongly opposed. The third defendant had turned state's evidence and had been threatened. The government responded by placing her in the federal witness protection program and urged that the other two defendants not be released on bail. Based on testimony regarding the threats, the magistrate denied bail and remanded the two defendants to federal custody. The jailed defendants appealed that decision to the district judge who released them on bond. Two days later, the Assistant United States Attorney sought and obtained a superseding indictment charging defendants with an additional conspiracy count. Should the conspiracy charge be dismissed as vindictive?

d. Malicious Prosecution

Usually, a prosecutor enjoys immunity when exercising prosecutorial discretion, but there might be an alternative path to a lawsuit. After Freddy Gray died while being transported by the police in Baltimore in 2015, District Attorney Marilyn Mosby filed charges against six police officers. Three of the cases resulted in acquittal and three were dismissed. Five of the officers filed suit in federal court for malicious prosecution, among other grounds. A federal judge refused to dismiss the case against Mosby at this juncture because her office asserted it did its own investigative work and therefore functioned as an investigator in part, and not as a prosecutor. *See, e.g.*, Justin Fenton,

"Judge Orders Discovery and Depositions to Move Forward in Mosby Malicious Prosecution Lawsuit," *Baltimore Sun*, Maryland News (Feb. 3, 2017). Available at: https://www.baltimoresun.com/news/crime/bs-md-ci-mosby-lawsuit-discovery-20170203-story.html.

Executive Summary

Prosecutorial Discretion Is Designed to Promote Fairness. Discretion is built into the system in the investigative and prosecution phases to allow the system to be flexible enough to mold itself around the facts of individual cases. This flexibility promotes fairness.

Prosecutors Have Broad Discretion. Prosecutors have discretion over when and how to investigate a potential case and how to charge it.

Use of Grand Juries. While some jurisdictions require grand juries in certain types of cases, such as a capital murder case, prosecutors have the option of using a grand jury to determine whether charges are appropriate.

Discretion Has Limits. Prosecutors cannot use their discretion in violation of the law, particularly the Constitution.

No Selective Prosecution. Prosecutors cannot prosecute defendants based on immutable characteristics, such as race or national origin, in violation of equal protection principles.

No Vindictive Prosecution. Prosecutors cannot penalize defendants for exercising their constitutional or statutory rights after proceedings have commenced by subsequently increasing charges.

Major Themes

a. Discretion Is Widespread—Prosecutorial discretion exists in many aspects of the criminal justice system, from investigating leads, to plea bargaining, to calling witnesses, to sentencing allocution.

b. Discretion Can Be Controversial—Prosecutorial discretion, particularly whether and how to charge cases, can be controversial, indicating a need to limit and guide discretion, when appropriate.

c. Selective and Vindictive Prosecution—Certain types of misuse of discretion are not permitted, such as selective and vindictive prosecution.

For More Information

- RUSSELL L. WEAVER, JOHN M. BURKOFF, CATHERINE HANCOCK & STEVEN I. FRIEDLAND, PRINCIPLES OF CRIMINAL PROCEDURE, Ch. 10 (8th ed. 2024).

- D. Lieb, Note, *Vindicating Vindictiveness: Prosecutorial Discretion and Plea Bargaining, Past and Future,* 123 YALE L. J. 1014 (2014), http://www.yalelawjournal.org/note/vindicating-vindictiveness-prosecutorial-discretion-and-plea-bargaining-past-and-future.

Test Your Knowledge

To assess your understanding of the material in this chapter, click here to take a quiz.

CHAPTER 12

Case Screening: Preliminary Hearings & Grand Juries

A. Introduction

There are three basic processes by which a case is screened for a determination whether to proceed to a formal prosecution. First, a prosecutor has discretion to decide whether to file formal charges. The two other processes are preliminary hearings and grand juries. Both the preliminary hearing and grand jury review examine whether the government has shown the quantum of proof required to proceed to trial. Both processes only require proof of probable cause (as opposed to proof beyond a reasonable doubt) that a crime has been committed and that a particular defendant committed the crime.

Take Note

Preliminary hearings and grand juries differ in important respects. Preliminary hearings are public, while grand jury proceedings are secret. Preliminary hearings are adversary proceedings in which the defense can challenge the prosecution's case while grand juries normally hear only the prosecution's case and prospective defendants and defense counsel are excluded from the proceedings. Judges preside over preliminary hearings while grand jury proceedings are run by the prosecution and involve little judicial participation. Finally, judges determine the sufficiency of the evidence in preliminary hearings, while grand jurors (citizens of the local community) make this determination in grand jury proceedings.

B. Preliminary Hearings

In most jurisdictions, the accused may request that the judge conduct an adversarial hearing to determine whether there is probable cause to believe that a crime has been committed and that the defendant committed it. Recall that the *Gerstein* determination of probable cause discussed in Chapter 10 may be *ex parte*, without any input from the defendant. Federal Rule of Criminal Procedure 5.1, which is typical, specifies that a defendant who requests one should have a preliminary hearing within 10 days, if he or she is incarcerated, and within 20 days if he or she is not. Without a finding of probable cause, the accused must be released from custody as well as from any bail obligation.

In *Coleman v. Alabama*, <u>399 U.S. 1 (1970)</u>, the Court held that when a state grants the accused a preliminary hearing, the Sixth Amendment right to counsel applies. The Court noted that counsel is necessary to try to rebut the showing of probable cause, discover the prosecution's case, build a record for later impeachment, preserve the testimony of witnesses who are unavailable for trial, and make effective arguments on matters like the necessity for bail.

Points for Discussion

a. Screening

Whether or not the preliminary hearing serves a screening function for the prosecution depends on the circumstances. Some prosecutors' offices spend substantial resources before the first appearance, or before a formal charge is filed, screening the case for merit and will not bring charges that are weak. As a result, the screening for meritorious prosecutions has already been done before the preliminary hearing. In federal court, and in state cases involving a grand jury indictment, the accused is usually not entitled to a preliminary hearing. The grand jury will have already determined that there is probable cause to go forward. For example, 18 U.S.C. § 3060(e) provides that no preliminary hearing is required for an arrested person if at any time subsequent to the initial appearance of that person and prior to the date fixed for the preliminary examination, an indictment is returned.

Practice Pointer

The importance to the defense of the limited discovery accessible through the preliminary hearing depends in large part on the availability of alternative discovery procedures. For example, if prior statements of prospective witnesses and the arresting officer's report are readily accessible, the hearing's discovery possibilities may be relatively unimportant. On the other hand, if state law and practice, like federal practice, provide for little pretrial discovery, the preliminary hearing may serve as an important discovery device. Similarly, if discovery does not occur until after the critical time for plea negotiations, the preliminary hearing may serve as the main discovery device for the large percentage of cases resolved by guilty pleas.

If a prosecutor's office does not engage in significant screening in advance of the preliminary hearing, and does not proceed through an indictment, then the preliminary hearing may indeed serve a screening function. With the opportunity to hear from witnesses in the case (typically a police officer), it may become apparent that the charge lacks probable cause or that the prosecution's case is weak and not worth pursuing. Normally, a finding of no probable cause at a preliminary hearing does not preclude future prosecution of the case, especially if further investigation unearths additional evidence.

b. Pretrial Discovery

In practice, the preliminary hearing may provide defense counsel with a valuable discovery technique as it listens to the prosecution present its case. Defense counsel may also have the opportunity to cross-examine the prosecution's witnesses at the hearing, and subpoena other potential witnesses to testify as defense witnesses.

c. Future Impeachment

Extensive cross-examination of prosecution witnesses at the preliminary hearing stage may be of value to the defense even though there is little likelihood of successfully challenging the prosecution's showing of probable cause and little to be gained by way of discovery. The skilled interrogation of witnesses can be a vital impeachment tool which lays the foundation for cross-examination at trial. Witnesses are more likely to make damaging admissions or contradictory statements at the preliminary hearing because they are less thoroughly briefed for that proceeding than they are for trial. In addition, the more witnesses say before trial, the more likely that they will makes statements that are inconsistent with their trial testimony and their previous statements.

Practice Pointer

Of course, if the defense engages in cross-examination to lay the foundation for future impeachment, it takes risks. By focusing on potential weaknesses in a witness's testimony, the prosecution can rehabilitate the witness for trial, and the witness may state at trial that she was confused at the preliminary hearing, but now is clear and certain. Cross-examination may also harden a witness's position, making the witness less able to retreat to a more friendly position. Finally, if the witness is unavailable at trial, the earlier testimony can be used, and the perpetuated testimony may be more damaging than that which would have existed without the cross-examination.

d. Perpetuation of Testimony

Although the preliminary hearing testimony of a prosecution witness who is unavailable for trial can be admitted at trial, that testimony must be reconciled with the defendant's constitutional right of confrontation. Preliminary hearing testimony may be admissible as substantive evidence at trial if: 1) it was given under oath; 2) the declarant is unavailable to testify at trial; and 3) a reasonable opportunity, whether exercised or not, for cross-examination on substantially

Take Note

Given all of the possible strategies for a defense attorney at a preliminary hearing, the motives and extent of cross-examination of a witness at a preliminary hearing may be different from the motives and extent of cross-examination of that same witness at a future trial. If so, then it may violate the Confrontation Clause to allow the preliminary hearing testimony of that witness to come in as evidence at trial in lieu of live testimony and cross-examination at trial.

the same issues was afforded the opposing party at the preliminary hearing. *See Crawford v. Washington*, 541 U.S. 36 (2004), and its progeny.

e.   Pretrial Release

Where bail is set at the initial appearance on the basis of sketchy facts, the preliminary hearing provides the judge with the first extensive adversary examination of the facts. The testimony may persuade the court to reduce or increase bail, or impose other terms or conditions of pretrial release. The hearing also insures that a person who has been unjustifiably accused will be promptly released from custody or from bail obligations.

f.   Plea Bargaining

A preliminary hearing may be an "educational experience" for the defendant who does not accept defense counsel's opinion that the prosecution has such a strong case that a negotiated plea is in the defendant's best interest. Conversely, the proof at the hearing may provide insufficient evidence of the charged offenses, and lead to a reduction of excessive charges. It thereby may serve as a check against the prosecutorial practice of "overcharging" (by the number of charges and/or the severity of charges) in anticipation of plea negotiations. However, this latter function is mitigated by the fact that a finding of no probable cause at the preliminary hearing does not necessarily preclude the later filing of the charge.

Practice Pointer

There is typically no reason a defendant would waive a preliminary hearing as it is an important avenue of discovery. However, on occasion, a prosecutor may offer more robust "open file" discovery in return for the defendant's waiver of the preliminary hearing. In those cases, a defendant receives the benefit of better discovery and may decide to waive the hearing.

g.   Motion to Dismiss

At the close of the prosecution's case at a preliminary hearing, defense counsel should move to dismiss the charges based upon the prosecution's failure to establish: 1) That an offense was committed; 2) That the accused is the one who committed it; 3) That proper venue is lacking (usually, the place where the offense took place); & 4) for jurisdictional purposes. If the judge denies defense counsel's motion for a dismissal, as will usually be the case, the defense may move the court to reduce the original charge to a lesser offense (e.g., from a felony to a misdemeanor), or have the accused plead guilty to the reduced charge, thereby disposing of the case. If the accused is permitted to enter a guilty plea to an amended charge that involves a lesser-included offense of the original charge, double jeopardy principles will prevent the prosecution from reinstituting the original charge against the accused.

Hypo 1: *Present the Alibi?*

The F.B.I. arrests Jack Penny for bank robbery on October 21 at approximately 11:00 a.m. Penny, who is detained pretrial, contacts you to represent him. From the documents you have been able to obtain, it appears that someone robbed the employees of a federally insured bank in a small town about seventy-five miles from the city where your client resides. From the photographs taken by the bank camera, the F.B.I. identified Penny and arrested him. Several employees of the bank identified him in a line-up held on October 23. Penny has told you that, during the late morning of October 21, he was visiting his hometown methadone center receiving his weekly dosage. You corroborate this information with the receptionist on duty at that time. At the preliminary hearing, the Assistant U.S. Attorney presents his evidence, and bank employees identify Penny as he sits next to you at counsel table in the small courtroom. You dutifully conduct your cross-examination of the prosecution witnesses, but are unable to make much progress in challenging their identifications. At the conclusion of the government's case, you move to dismiss the charges because there was inadequate proof of probable cause, but you are unsuccessful. Now should you present the testimony of the receptionist or your client?

Hypo 2: *Present the Driver?*

Four men are driving at 2:00 a.m. The police conduct a traffic stop and discover a gun under the driver's seat which is also accessible to the back seat passenger, Ronald Martin. Martin is charged with unlawful possession of a firearm. You are appointed to represent Martin who has been released on personal recognizance. He tells you that when the officer approached the car, he asked the driver if he had any guns or drugs, and the driver stated that he had a gun and turned over both the gun and the registration papers for the gun. The driver confirms this and agrees to testify if necessary. At the preliminary hearing, the prosecution offers the testimony of a police officer who testifies to the simple fact of the gun being found near Martin, and claims the existence of probable cause to believe that Martin possessed a gun. Should you call the driver to testify? Why or why not?

Hypo 3: *Call the Eyewitness?*

You are the prosecutor for the preliminary hearing on a robbery charge. You have a police officer available to testify to the facts of the robbery, as well as to the fact that there was an eyewitness identification of the defendant as the robber. Should you also call the eyewitness to the robbery? Why or why not?

Hypo 4: *A Domestic Violence Victim*

You are a prosecutor assigned to domestic violence cases. You conduct a preliminary hearing in a case where a man beat his girlfriend of five years, a woman who is also the mother of their children. This is not the first time this defendant has been arrested for beating this same victim. However, he has not been convicted for any of the assaults. You have the police officer who arrested the defendant and can testify to what the victim told him about the beating. Should you also call the victim to testify? Why or why not?

C. Grand Juries

The grand jury, which has existed since the ancient common law, originated as a body of local citizens who helped examine possible crimes in the community. This investigative function has been characterized as a sword to root out crime. However, by the time of the American Revolution, the colonists, and ultimately the founding fathers, rejected the grand jury as a sword because the British authorities had engaged in malicious prosecutions, particularly involving charges of sedition and libel against the King. Hence, the founding fathers viewed the grand jury as a shield to protect citizens against unfounded prosecutions. In this Chapter, you will see that the two functions of the grand jury ebb and flow with the times.

FYI

Many states have either eliminated grand juries, allowing prosecution by information, or permit the prosecutor to choose between grand jury indictment and information. Other states require indictment by a grand jury for only certain offenses (usually serious felonies) and permit prosecution by information for less serious charges. Those states that use grand juries may have rules comparable to the federal rules, permitting defendants to waive the right to indictment and proceed by information.

In the federal system, the view that the grand jury acts as a "shield" or "screen" against improper prosecutions is embodied in U.S. Constitution, Amendment V which provides: "No person shall be held to answer for a capital, or otherwise infamous crime, unless on a presentment or indictment of a Grand Jury." The grand jury requirement has not been "incorporated" and made applicable to the States through the Due Process Clause of the Fourteenth Amendment. *See Hurtado v. California*, 110 U.S. 516 (1884). As a result, the individual states have their own statutory or constitutional provisions regarding grand juries. In general, there are two methods by which the prosecution can formally charge a defendant with a crime: by grand jury indictment or by information. An information is a charge drawn up by the prosecutor which is not submitted to a grand jury, and which may or may not be screened by a judicial officer at a preliminary hearing.

Points for Discussion

a. Selection of the Grand Jury

Grand juries can differ greatly in their composition and selection processes in individual jurisdictions. At common law, the grand jury was comprised of twenty-three persons, at least twelve of whom had to agree in order to indict an individual for a criminal offense. Today, federal grand juries consist of between sixteen and twenty-three jurors, twelve of whom must agree to indict the defendant. Other jurisdictions utilize much smaller grand juries, although all jurisdictions require that an indictment be based on the concurrence of at least a majority of the grand jurors empaneled to review the charges.

The process of selecting grand jurors begins with the court's summoning of a number of persons qualified to serve as grand jurors. The qualifications for grand jury service are set out in the jurisdiction's statutes and are normally similar to or identical to the requirements for regular jury service, and require that the prospective grand juror be: 1) a citizen of the jurisdiction; 2) reside in the jurisdiction; 3) be over eighteen years of age; and 4) be a person of honesty, intelligence, and good demeanor. Purging the grand jury is the

Take Note

Defense counsel do not participate in the selection of grand juries. Thus, any deficiencies in the composition of a grand jury must be raised when the defendant is brought to trial (objections cannot be raised for the first time on appeal). A timely and well-founded pretrial objection allows the trial court to void the indictment and send the prosecutor back to a lawfully constituted grand jury. Challenges to the composition of the grand jury are made by a motion to dismiss or quash the indictment. Generally, courts have recognized only two proper grounds for objecting to the composition of a grand jury: 1) one or more of the grand jurors failed to meet the statutory qualifications for service; or 2) the process for selecting grand jurors violated constitutional standards, *i.e.*, usually discrimination based on suspect classifications such as race and gender.

process of narrowing the number of qualified grand jurors to the number of jurors who will actually serve. The process eliminates otherwise qualified grand jurors who have legitimate excuses for not serving, such as health problems, family obligations and the like.

Although the States are not required to utilize grand juries, if they choose to do so, the Equal Protection Clause of the U.S. Constitution requires that no State may deliberately and systematically exclude individuals because of race, class, gender, or national origin. *Taylor v. Louisiana*, 419 U.S. 522 (1975). The basic elements of an equal protection challenge to the grand jury are the same as required for challenges to the trial jury. Constitutional infirmities in the composition of a grand jury may invalidate a conviction even though the trial jury was legally constituted and guilt was established beyond a reasonable doubt. *Vasquez v. Hillery*, 474 U.S. 254 (1986).

FYI

In *State v. Vega-Larregui*, 248 A.3d 1124 (N.J. 2021), the court held that, during the pandemic, the state could hold virtual grand jury proceedings. The court rejected the argument that the grand jury did not contain a "fair cross-section" of the community because some potential jurors might have been excluded because of the lack of a computer or internet access. However, the court provided jurors with the equipment they needed, and even trained them. The court also rejected the argument that the proceedings were not secret, viewing that argument as "speculative." The court emphasized that the online proceedings were temporary until the pandemic subsided.

Hypo 1: *Project Exile*

The police observed defendant Jones, an African American, drive in the wrong direction on a one-way street. An officer stops defendant's vehicle and finds that his driver's license is suspended. During a search subsequent to the stop, the police officer discovers marijuana, a nine-millimeter pistol, and drug paraphernalia in the vehicle. However, a program designated "Project Exile" results in the transfer of Jones' case to a federal grand jury which issues a four-count indictment. The federal indictment covers precisely the same conduct originally prosecuted in the state proceedings. Project Exile is jointly undertaken by the prosecutor for the City of Richmond, Virginia and the United States Attorney for the Eastern District of Virginia. Although Richmond has only three percent of the State's population, it accounts for twenty-seven percent of the State's homicides. The stated goal of Project Exile is to reduce violent crime by federally prosecuting firearm-related crimes whenever possible. The parties are unable to obtain precise empirical data concerning the race of Project Exile defendants or the racial composition of the relevant grand jury pools. However, the parties agree that the vast majority, and perhaps as many as ninety percent, of the defendants prosecuted under Project Exile are African American. The jury pool for the Circuit Court for the City of Richmond is approximately seventy-five percent African American. The jury pool for the Richmond Division of the Eastern District of Virginia is drawn from a broader geographic area. In contrast to the state jury pool, it is only about ten percent African American. At a local Bench-Bar Conference discussing the issue, an Assistant United States Attorney stated that one goal of Project Exile is to avoid "Richmond juries." As defense counsel for Mr. Jones, what arguments would you make in a motion to quash the indictment issued by the federal grand jury? As the prosecutor, how would you respond to the motion to quash?

Hypo 2: *Foreperson Selection*

Assume a system where grand jurors are selected at random and the supervising judge chooses the foreperson for the grand jury. The judge chooses the foreperson from the venire (the entire pool) and not from those who were already selected to serve. Assume that for the past twenty years, no black person has ever been chosen to be foreperson even though the pool is 20% black. What arguments will you make to dismiss the indictment? What are the likely responses by the prosecution? *See Campbell v. Louisiana,* 523 U.S. 392 (1998).

b.   Scope of Grand Jury Investigation

Once a grand jury is selected and empanelled, the judge will charge the grand jury. This charge may include the judge's statements about the general state of the Union, as well as suggestions about particular matters that will come before the grand jury. All judges, however, will caution the grand jury to maintain the secrecy of its proceedings. Once the judge has charged the grand jury, the prosecutor will lead the jury in its investigation of alleged criminal offenses. Unlike preliminary hearings, the judge does not preside over grand jury proceedings.

The prosecutor chooses which cases to present to a grand jury and which witnesses to call. After the presentation of witnesses and evidence, the prosecutor instructs the grand jury on the elements of the offenses and the grand jury decides whether to return an indictment,

> **Take Note**
>
> The grand jury's refusal to return a true bill does not preclude the prosecutor from resubmitting the evidence to another grand jury. Double Jeopardy does not protect the accused from undergoing successive grand jury investigations.

a written accusation of crime prepared by the prosecutor. If the grand jury agrees that the evidence establishes probable cause for a charge, it will return a "true bill" of indictment upon which the accused will face trial. If the grand jury concludes that the evidence does not establish probable cause, it will return "no true bill." Very rarely, a grand jury may go beyond the prosecutor's direction and investigate additional crimes. More commonly, the grand jury follows the prosecutor's lead. Because the prosecution typically presents only its own witnesses and its own side of the case, the grand jury virtually always returns an indictment.

c. Rare Decision Not to Indict

On August 9, 2014, Michael Brown, an unarmed black teenager, was shot and killed by Darren Wilson, a white police officer, in Ferguson, Missouri. The incident set off waves of protests around the country. Some witnesses claimed Brown was shot while he was doing nothing and his arms were up in the air. Police witnesses said Brown was shot after struggling for Darren Wilson's gun. The St. Louis County Prosecutor convened a grand jury to decide whether to indict the officer for the killing. The typical grand jury hears all testimony in a single day, typically involving only a few prosecution witnesses, usually police officers, no defense witnesses or the defendant, and is instructed on potential charges by the prosecutor. In the *Brown* case, the grand jury listened to evidence for 25 days, with over 60 witnesses, mainly defense, including four hours of testimony by the defendant, and the Prosecutor did not suggest any charges. The grand jury decided not to indict. Given that the grand jury's purpose is to screen cases for probable cause and not to decide guilt, was the Prosecutor's use of the grand jury proper?

See It

Shortly after the grand jury in Ferguson, Missouri decided not to indict, on December 3, 2014, a grand jury in Staten Island decided not to indict a white police officer who killed Eric Garner, an unarmed black man, by using an unauthorized chokehold causing him to suffocate to death. There was debate about what had occurred in Ferguson, but the entire incident was captured on video: http://www.theguardian.com/us-news/video/2014/dec/04/i-cant-breathe-eric-garner-chokehold-death-video.

d. Grand Jury Secrecy

Unlike most stages of a criminal prosecution, grand jury proceedings are conducted in secret. The secrecy requirement is designed to serve five important objectives: 1) to prevent the escape of those whose indictment may be contemplated; 2) to insure the utmost freedom to the grand jury in its deliberations, and to prevent persons subject to indictment or their friends from importuning the grand jurors; 3) to prevent subornation of perjury or tampering with the witnesses who may testify before the grand jury and later appear at the trial of those indicted by it; 4) to encourage free and untrammeled disclosures by persons who have information with respect to the commission of crimes; 5) to protect the innocent accused who is exonerated from disclosure of the fact that he has been under investigation, and from the expense of standing trial where there was no probability of guilt. *United States v. Procter & Gamble Co.*, 356 U.S. 677, 681 (1958). Whether, and to what extent, these stated reasons are the current and actual motivations for maintaining grand jury secrecy is open to question. Federal Rule of Criminal Procedure 6(e)(3)(D) follows the Patriot Act, § 203, to allow disclosure of Grand Jury information that "involves foreign intelligence or counterintelligence" to intelligence, defense, national security, or immigration officials.

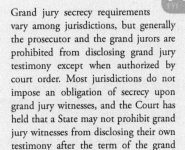

Grand jury secrecy requirements vary among jurisdictions, but generally the prosecutor and the grand jurors are prohibited from disclosing grand jury testimony except when authorized by court order. Most jurisdictions do not impose an obligation of secrecy upon grand jury witnesses, and the Court has held that a State may not prohibit grand jury witnesses from disclosing their own testimony after the term of the grand jury has ended. *Butterworth v. Smith*, 494 U.S. 624 (1990).

1. The Grand Jury as a Shield

In the federal system, the constitutional requirement for a grand jury indictment has continuing vitality. When a properly constituted grand jury returns an indictment, courts will not review the adequacy of the evidence presented to the grand jury. In *Wood v. Georgia*, 370 U.S. 375, 390 (1962), the Court described the grand jury as "a primary security to the innocent against hasty, malicious and oppressive persecution; it serves the invaluable function in our society of standing between the accuser and the accused, whether the latter be an individual, minority group, or other, to determine whether a charge is founded upon reason or was dictated by an intimidating power or by malice and personal ill will." However, the *Wood* perspective has given way over the years as issues of crime control and punishment have loomed large since the 1980s War on Crime. The shield function has eroded in rhetoric and the sword function has become primary again. The majority view is that the shielding function of the grand jury, while attractive rhetoric, is illusory in practice. Statistics show that grand juries rarely refuse to indict, an under-

See It

The prosecutor who conducted the grand jury proceedings in the high-profile shooting death of Michael Brown in Ferguson took the unusual step of releasing volumes of transcripts to the public after the grand jury controversially decided not to indict. You can see and read them at: http://www.nytimes.com/interactive/2014/11/25/us/evidence-released-in-michael-brown-case.html.

standable result in light of the fact that grand jury proceedings are not adversarial. Without the presence of defense counsel to challenge the government's evidence or to present exculpatory evidence, the proceeding is more like a football game where only one team is on the field.

United States v. Williams

504 U.S. 36 (1992).

JUSTICE SCALIA delivered the opinion of the Court.

The question in this case is whether a district court may dismiss an otherwise valid indictment because the Government failed to disclose to the grand jury "substantial exculpatory evidence", in its possession.

Hear It

You can hear the oral argument in *Williams* at: http://www.oyez.org/cases/1990-1999/1991/1991_90_1972.

Respondent John H. Williams, Jr., a Tulsa, Oklahoma, investor, was indicted by a federal grand jury on seven counts of "knowingly making a false statement or report for the purpose of influencing the action of a federally insured financial institution," in violation of 18 U.S.C. § 1014 (1988 ed., Supp. 11). According to the indictment, between September 1984 and November 1985 Williams supplied four Oklahoma banks with "materially false" statements that variously overstated the value of his current assets and interest income in order to influence the banks' actions on his loan requests. Shortly after arraignment, the District Court granted Williams' motion for disclosure of all exculpatory portions of the grand jury transcripts. Upon reviewing this material, Williams demanded that the District Court dismiss the indictment, alleging that the Government failed to fulfill its obligation to present "substantial exculpatory evidence" to the grand jury. His contention was that evidence which the Government had chosen not to present to the grand jury—in particular, Williams' general ledgers and tax returns, and Williams' testimony in his contemporaneous Chapter 11 bankruptcy proceeding—disclosed that, for tax purposes and otherwise, he had regularly accounted for the "notes receivable" (and the interest on them) in a manner consistent with the Balance Sheet and the Income Statement. This, he contended, belied an intent to mislead the banks, and thus directly negated an essential element of the charged offense. The District Court found, after a hearing, that the withheld evidence was "relevant to an essential element of the crime charged," created "a reasonable doubt about respondent's guilt," and thus "rendered the grand jury's decision to indict gravely suspect." The Court of Appeals affirmed the District Court's order. Under these circumstances, the Tenth Circuit concluded, it was not an abuse of discretion for the District Court to require the Government to begin anew before the grand jury. We granted certiorari.

Bank of Nova Scotia v. United States, 487 U.S. 250 (1988), makes clear that the supervisory power can be used to dismiss an indictment because of misconduct before the grand jury, at least where that misconduct amounts to a violation of one of those "few, clear rules which were carefully drafted and approved by this Court and by Congress to ensure the integrity of the grand jury's functions." We did not hold in *Bank of Nova Scotia*, however, that the courts' supervisory power could be used, not merely as a means of enforcing or vindicating legally compelled standards of prosecutorial conduct before the grand jury, but as a means of prescribing those standards of prosecutorial conduct in the first instance—just as it may be used as a means of establishing standards of prosecutorial conduct before the courts themselves. It is this latter exercise that respondent demands. Because the grand jury is an institution separate from the courts, over whose functioning the courts do not preside, we think it clear that, as a general matter at least, no such "supervisory" judicial authority exists, and that the disclosure rule applied here exceeded the Tenth Circuit's authority.

"Rooted in long centuries of Anglo-American history," the grand jury is mentioned in the Bill of Rights, but not in the body of the Constitution. It has not been textually assigned, therefore, to any of the branches described in the first three Articles. In fact, the whole theory of its function is that it belongs to no branch of the institutional government, serving as a kind of buffer or referee between the Government and the people. Although the grand jury normally operates in the courthouse and under judicial auspices, its institutional relationship with the judicial branch has traditionally been at arm's length. Judges' direct involvement in the functioning of the grand jury has generally been confined to the constitutive one of calling the grand jurors together and administering their oaths of office.

We have insisted that the grand jury remain "free to pursue its investigations unhindered by external influence or supervision so long as it does not trench upon the legitimate rights of any witness called before it." Recognizing this tradition of independence, the Fifth Amendment's "constitutional guarantee presupposes an investigative body 'acting independently of either prosecuting attorney or judge'." Given the grand jury's operational separateness from its constituting court, we have been reluctant to invoke the judicial supervisory power as a basis for prescribing modes of grand jury procedure. Over the years, we have received many requests to exercise supervision over the grand jury's evidence-taking process, but we have refused all, including some more appealing than the one presented today. Any power federal courts may have to fashion, on their own initiative, rules of grand jury procedure is a very limited one, not remotely comparable to the power they maintain over their own proceedings. It would not permit judicial reshaping of the grand jury institution, substantially altering the traditional relationships between the prosecutor, the constituting court, and the grand jury itself.

Requiring the prosecutor to present exculpatory as well as inculpatory evidence would alter the grand jury's historical role, transforming it from an accusatory to an adjudicatory body. Imposing upon the prosecutor a legal obligation to present exculpatory evidence in his possession would be incompatible with this system. If a "balanced" assessment of the matter is the objective, surely the first thing to be done—rather than requiring the prosecutor to say what he knows in defense of the target of the investigation—is to entitle the target to tender his own defense. To require the former while denying (as we do) the latter would be quite absurd. It would also be pointless, since it would merely invite the target to circumnavigate the system by delivering his exculpatory evidence to the prosecutor, whereupon it would have to be passed on to the grand jury—unless the prosecutor is willing to take the chance that a court will not deem the evidence important enough to qualify for mandatory disclosure. Respondent insists that courts must require the modern prosecutor to alert the grand jury to the nature and extent of the available exculpatory evidence, because otherwise the grand jury "merely functions as an arm of the prosecution." We reject the attempt to convert a nonexistent duty of the grand jury itself into an obligation of the prosecutor. The authority of the prosecutor to seek an indictment has long been understood to be "coterminous with the authority of the grand jury to entertain the prosecutor's charges." If the grand jury has no obligation to consider all "substantial exculpatory" evidence, we do not understand how the prosecutor can be said to have a binding obligation to present it.

Respondent's proposal positively contradicts the "common law" of the Fifth Amendment grand jury. Motions to quash indictments based upon the sufficiency of the evidence relied upon by the grand jury were unheard of at common law in England. The traditional American practice was described by Justice Nelson as follows: "No case has been cited, nor have we been able to find any, furnishing an authority for looking into and revising the judgment of the grand jury upon the evidence, for the purpose of determining whether or not the finding was founded upon sufficient proof, or whether there was a deficiency in respect to any part of the complaint." It would make little sense, we think, to abstain from reviewing the evidentiary support for the grand jury's judgment while scrutinizing the sufficiency of the prosecutor's presentation. A complaint about the quality or adequacy of the evidence can always be recast as a complaint that the prosecutor's presentation was "incomplete" or "misleading." Our words in *Costello* bear repeating: Review of facially valid indictments on such grounds "would run counter to the whole history of the grand jury institution, and neither justice nor the concept of a fair trial requires it."

Respondent argues that a rule requiring the prosecutor to disclose exculpatory evidence to the grand jury would, by removing from the docket unjustified prosecutions, save valuable judicial time. That depends upon what the ratio would be between unjustified prosecutions eliminated and grand jury indictments challenged—for the latter as well as the former consume "valuable judicial time." If there is an advantage to the proposal, Congress is free to prescribe it. Courts have no authority to prescribe such a duty pursuant to their inherent supervisory authority over their own proceedings. The judgment of the Court of Appeals is accordingly reversed and the cause remanded for further proceedings consistent with this opinion.

JUSTICE STEVENS, with whom JUSTICE BLACKMUN and JUSTICE O'CONNOR join, and with whom JUSTICE THOMAS joins as to Parts II and III, dissenting.

The prosecutor is not required to place all exculpatory evidence before the grand jury. A grand jury proceeding is an *ex parte* investigatory proceeding to determine whether there is probable cause to believe a violation of the criminal laws has occurred, not a trial. Requiring the prosecutor to ferret out and present all evidence that could be used at trial to create a reasonable doubt as to the defendant's guilt would be inconsistent with the purpose of the grand jury proceeding and would place significant burdens on the investigation. But that does not mean that the prosecutor may mislead the grand jury into believing that there is probable cause to indict by withholding clear evidence to the contrary. "When a prosecutor conducting a grand jury inquiry is personally aware of substantial evidence which directly negates the guilt of a subject of the investigation, the prosecutor must present or otherwise disclose such evidence to the grand jury before seeking an indictment against such a person." U.S. Dept. of Justice, United States Attorneys' Manual, Title 9, ch. 11, & 9–11.233, 88 (1988). Whether the evidence withheld in this case directly negates respondent's guilt, I need not resolve my doubts because the Solicitor General did not ask the Court to review the nature of the evidence withheld. Instead, he asked us to decide the legal question whether an indictment may be dismissed because the prosecutor failed to present exculpatory evidence. I believe the answer to that question is yes, if the withheld evidence would plainly preclude a finding of probable cause.

Make the Connection

In Constitutional Law, you likely learned the importance of originalism to justices like Justice Scalia as a method for interpreting the Constitution. In history classes, you might have learned that the Founding Fathers were deeply skeptical of prosecutions by the Crown for crimes like seditious libel. There is little doubt that the founders believed the grand jury was a shield and not a sword, preventing abuses of wrongful and unjust charging. It is not at all clear that originalism dictates that the founders would have agreed that substantial exculpatory information in the hands of the prosecution should not have to be presented to a grand jury.

Points for Discussion

a. Admissibility of "Inadmissible Evidence"

The Court set the stage for *Williams* in two prior cases. In *Costello v. United States*, 350 U.S. 359 (1956), the Court held that hearsay is admissible in a grand jury proceeding. The holding rested on the assumption that the "accused will get his fair, judicial, hearing at his trial." But if the grand jury is to protect the innocent against oppression and unjust prosecution, should a defendant be compelled to go to trial to prove the insufficiency of the charge? The Second Circuit described the effect of an investigation as follows: "A wrongful indictment is no laughing matter; often it works a grievous irreparable injury to the person indicted. The stigma cannot be easily erased. In the public mind, the blot on a man's escutcheon, resulting from such a public accusation of wrongdoing, is seldom wiped out by a subsequent judgment of not guilty. Frequently, the public remembers the accusation, and still suspects guilt, even after an acquittal." *In re Fried*, 161 F.2d 453 (2d Cir.1947) (concurring opinion).

In the second case, *United States v. Calandra*, 414 U.S. 338, 349 (1974), the Court indicated that the *Costello* rationale barred a challenge to an indictment which was based on unconstitutionally obtained evidence. In *Calandra* the district court held that the defendant "need not answer any of the grand jury's questions based on" evidence obtained from an unconstitutional search. The Court reversed, stating: "This extension of the exclusionary rule would seriously impede the grand jury. Because the grand jury does not finally adjudicate guilt or innocence, it has traditionally been allowed to pursue its investigative and accusatorial functions unimpeded by the evidentiary and procedural restrictions applicable to a criminal trial. Permitting witnesses to invoke the exclusionary rule before a grand jury would precipitate adjudication of issues hitherto reserved for the trial on the merits and would delay and disrupt grand jury proceedings."

Food for Thought

Should the prosecutor have an obligation to disclose that: 1) The accused did not have a motive to commit the crime? 2) The State's witnesses have criminal records? 3) The testimony of an eyewitness is potentially biased? 4) The testimony of an eyewitness is contradicted by other witnesses? 5) The accused denied involvement in the crime? 6) A reliable alibi witness is available to testify? 7) Reliable exculpatory physical evidence is available? 8) The prosecution's main witness has recanted her testimony? 9) The target of the grand jury's investigation was insane at the time of the offense?

b. What Is Exculpatory?

Despite the *Williams* decision, most state courts have imposed a duty on prosecutors to disclose exculpatory evidence to the grand jury when the prosecutor has the evidence in her file. *See, e.g., State v. Hogan*, 144 N.J. 216, 676 A.2d 533 (1996).

Most state courts impose a limited duty on the prosecutor to inform the grand jury of evidence which directly negates the guilt of the accused and is clearly exculpatory.

c. Duty to Present Possible Defenses?

In a later opinion arising from the same facts, the appellate court in *State v. Hogan*, 336 N.J.Super. 319, 764 A.2d 1012, 1025 (2001) opined:

> In our view, a prosecutor's obligation to instruct the grand jury on possible defenses is a corollary to his responsibility to present exculpatory evidence. The extent of the prosecutor's duty must be defined with reference to the role of the grand jury—to protect the innocent, and bring to trial those who may be guilty. The question of whether a particular defense need be charged depends upon its potential for eliminating a needless or unfounded prosecution. The appropriate distinction is between exculpatory and mitigating defenses. An exculpatory defense is one that would, if believed, result in a finding of no criminal liability, *i.e.*, a complete exoneration. The rule accords with common sense and promotes the ability of a grand jury to filter out cases that should never be tried. We adopt that rule to the extent that it defines the existence of the prosecutor's duty. The first question is when such a duty arises. We do not believe that the prosecutor has the obligation on his own meticulously to sift through the entire record of investigative files to see if some combination of facts and inferences might rationally sustain a defense or justification. The rule should be that it is only when the facts known to the prosecutor clearly indicate or clearly establish the appropriateness of an instruction that the duty of the prosecution arises.

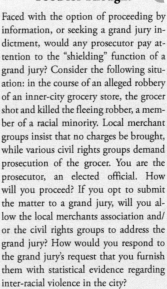

Food for Thought

Faced with the option of proceeding by information, or seeking a grand jury indictment, would any prosecutor pay attention to the "shielding" function of a grand jury? Consider the following situation: in the course of an alleged robbery of an inner-city grocery store, the grocer shot and killed the fleeing robber, a member of a racial minority. Local merchant groups insist that no charges be brought, while various civil rights groups demand prosecution of the grocer. You are the prosecutor, an elected official. How will you proceed? If you opt to submit the matter to a grand jury, will you allow the local merchants association and/or the civil rights groups to address the grand jury? How would you respond to the grand jury's request that you furnish them with statistical evidence regarding inter-racial violence in the city?

d. Non-Constitutional Errors Cured by Conviction at Trial

In *United States v. Mechanik*, 475 U.S. 66 (1986), the grand jury process violated Fed. R. Crim. P. 6(d) by allowing two witnesses to be present in the grand jury room at the same time. The issue was raised after defendant was convicted at a jury trial. The Court held that "the petit jury's subsequent guilty verdict means not only that there was probable cause to believe that the defendants were guilty as charged, but also that they were in fact guilty as charged beyond a reasonable doubt. Measured by the petit jury's verdict, then, any error in the grand jury proceeding connected with the charging decision was harmless beyond a reasonable doubt." Errors of constitutional dimension can be challenged, however. *See, e.g., Campbell v. Louisiana*, 523 U.S. 392 (1998) (equal protection claim).

e. Dismissal of Grand Jury

May the court dismiss a grand jury? Refuse to extend its term? Refuse to issue or enforce subpoenas requested by the grand jury? Some jurisdictions permit the judge to dismiss the grand jury at any time; other jurisdictions prohibit dismissal because of a fear that a judge will thwart a legitimate investigation, particularly an investigation into government corruption. Refusal to extend the grand jury term or to enforce its subpoenas are forms of controlling a runaway grand jury.

2. The Grand Jury as a Sword

In practice, the grand jury's potential to "shield" innocent citizens is often subordinate to its functioning as a "sword" to root out crime through use of its investigative authority. Rather than viewing grand jury indictment as an unnecessary burden, many prosecutors favor use of grand jury proceedings in hopes of uncovering additional evidence. They seek to use the grand jury's broad subpoena powers over witnesses and documents.

> **FYI**
>
> During the early stages of the Watergate investigation, Federal District Judge Sirica was hailed as a hero for extending the grand jury's term until it could pierce the suspected cover-up.

A witness who is not a target of a grand jury investigation and who is subpoenaed to appear before a grand jury has no general right to remain silent or to refuse to cooperate. Nor is a subpoena to appear before a grand jury a "seizure" of the person under the Fourth Amendment. *United States v. Dionisio*, 410 U.S. 1 (1973). In the absence of a constitutional provision such as the Fifth Amendment privilege against self-incrimination or a common law communication privilege, the witness "must tell what he knows" or risk being punished for contempt. *Branzburg v. Hayes*, 408 U.S. 665 (1972). The contempt sanction makes the grand jury subpoena particularly useful in obtaining statements from persons who will not voluntarily furnish information to the police. Failure to comply with a grand jury subpoena may constitute contempt, but in the federal system it may also subject the party to prosecution for violating 18 U.S.C. § 1503, which prohibits "corruptly influencing, obstructing, or impeding, or endeavoring to influence, obstruct, or impede, the due administration of justice." *See United States v. Erickson*, 561 F. 3d 1150 (10th Cir. 2009). Even when an individual invokes the privilege against self-incrimination, the prosecutor may, if authorized by law, grant the witness immunity and thus force an answer to its question.

a.   Fifth Amendment Rights Applicable to Testimony

Any witness who is called to testify before a grand jury may assert the Fifth Amendment privilege against self-incrimination. Whether and under what circumstances the courts will uphold a witness's assertion of the privilege, and decline to compel the witness to testify under the threat of contempt and possible incarceration has been the subject of considerable dispute and litigation.

Hoffman v. United States

341 U.S. 479 (1951).

MR. JUSTICE CLARK delivered the opinion of the Court.

Petitioner has been convicted of criminal contempt for refusing to obey a federal court order requiring him to answer certain questions asked in a grand jury investigation. He raises here important issues as to the application of the privilege against self-incrimination under the Fifth Amendment, claimed to justify his refusal.

A special federal grand jury was convened at Philadelphia on September 14, 1950. The pertinent interrogation, in which [Hoffman] refused to answer, follows:

"Q. What do you do now, Mr. Hoffman?

A.   I refuse to answer.

Q. Have you been in the same undertaking since the first of the year?

A.   I don't understand the question.

Q. Have you been doing the same thing you are doing now since the first of the year?

A.   I refuse to answer.

Q. Do you know Mr. William Weisberg?

A.   I do.

Q. How long have you known him?

A. Practically twenty years, I guess.

Q. When did you last see him?

A. I refuse to answer.

Q. Have you seen him this week?

A. I refuse to answer.

Q. Do you know that a subpoena has been issued for Mr. Weisberg?

A. I heard about it in Court.

Q. Have you talked with him on the telephone this week?

A. I refuse to answer.

Q. Do you know where Mr. William Weisberg is now?

A. I refuse to answer."

> **FYI**
>
> Hoffman was more than willing to stand by his refusal to answer and serve five months in jail while his lawyers litigated to protect his right to refuse to answer. For Hoffman, the consequences of answering and incriminating himself and others might have jeopardized his life.

It was stipulated that petitioner declined to answer on the ground that his answers might tend to incriminate him of a federal offense.

Petitioner's claim of privilege was challenged by the Government in the Federal District Court for the Eastern District of Pennsylvania, which found no real and substantial danger of incrimination to petitioner and ordered him to return to the grand jury and answer. Petitioner stated in open court that he would not obey the order, and on October 5 was adjudged in criminal contempt and sentenced to five months imprisonment.

This is another of five proceedings before this Court during the present Term in each of which the privilege against self-incrimination has been asserted in the course of federal grand-jury investigations. A number of similar cases have been considered recently by the lower courts. The increase in such litigation emphasizes the continuing necessity that prosecutors and courts alike be "alert to repress" any abuses of the investigatory power invoked, bearing in mind that while grand juries "may proceed, either upon their own knowledge or upon the examination of witnesses, to inquire whether a crime cognizable by the court has been committed," *Hale v. Henkel,* 201 U.S. 43, 65 (1906), yet "the most valuable function of the grand jury has been not only to examine into the commission of crimes, but to stand between the prosecutor and the accused," *id.* at 59. Enforcement officials taking the

> **FYI**
>
> The other four proceedings mentioned here were related to McCarthy Era investigations into purported communist activities. They involved prosecutions of persons who refused to answer the government's questions regarding Communist connections.

initiative in grand-jury proceedings and courts charged with their superintendence should be sensitive to the considerations making for wise exercise of such investigatory power, not only where constitutional issues may be involved but also where the noncoercive assistance of other federal agencies may render it unnecessary to invoke the compulsive process of the grand jury.

The Fifth Amendment declares in part that "No person shall be compelled in any criminal case to be a witness against himself." This guarantee against testimonial compulsion, like other provisions of the Bill of Rights, "was added to the original Constitution in the conviction that too high a price may be paid even for the unhampered enforcement of the criminal law and that, in its attainment, other social objects of a free society should not be sacrificed." *Feldman v. United States,* 322 U.S. 487, 489 (1944). This provision of the Amendment must be accorded liberal construction in favor of the right it was intended to secure.

The privilege extends to answers that would in themselves support a conviction under a federal criminal statute but likewise embraces those which would furnish a link in the chain of evidence needed to prosecute the claimant for a federal crime. But this protection must be confined to instances where the witness has reasonable cause to apprehend danger from a direct answer. The witness is not exonerated from answering merely because he declares that in so doing he would incriminate himself. It is for the court to say whether his silence is justified, and to require him to answer if "it clearly appears to the court that he is mistaken." *Temple v. Commonwealth,* 75 Va. 892, 899 (1881). However, if the witness, upon interposing his claim, were required to prove the hazard in the sense in which a claim is usually required to be established in court, he would be compelled to surrender the very protection which the privilege is designed to guarantee. To sustain the privilege, it need only be evident from the implications of the question, in the setting in which it is asked, that a responsive answer to the question or an explanation of why it cannot be answered might be dangerous because injurious disclosure could result. The trial judge in appraising the claim "must be governed as much by his personal perception of the peculiarities of the case as by the facts actually in evidence." *See* Taft, J., in *Ex parte Irvine,* 74 F. 954, 960 (C.C.S.D. Ohio 1896).

The judge who ruled on the privilege had himself impaneled the special grand jury to investigate "rackets" in the district. He explained to the jury that "the Attorney General's office has come into this district to conduct an investigation that will run the gamut of all crimes covered by federal statute." "If rackets infest or encrust our system of government," he instructed, "just as any blight attacks any other growth, it withers and dies." Subpoenas had issued for some twenty witnesses, but only eleven had been served; as the prosecutor put it, he was "having trouble finding some big shots." Several of those who did appear and were called into the grand-jury room before petitioner had refused to answer questions until ordered to do so by the court. The prosecutor had requested bench warrants for eight of the nine who had not appeared the first day of the session, one of whom was William Weisberg. Petitioner had admitted having known Weisberg for about twenty years. In addition, counsel for petitioner had advised the court that "It has been broadly published that petitioner has a police record." The court should have considered, in connection with the business questions, that the chief occupation of some persons involves evasion of federal criminal laws, and that truthful answers by petitioner to these questions might have disclosed that he was engaged in such proscribed activity.

The court should have recognized, in considering the Weisberg questions, that one person with a police record summoned to testify before a grand jury investigating the rackets might be hiding or helping to hide another person of questionable repute sought as a witness. The Government may inquire of witnesses before the grand jury as to the whereabouts of unlocated witnesses; ordinarily the answers to such questions are harmless if not fruitless. But of the seven questions relating to Weisberg (of which three were answered), three were designed to draw information as to petitioner's contacts and connection with the fugitive witness; and the final question, perhaps an afterthought of the prosecutor, inquired of Weisberg's whereabouts at the time. All of them could easily have required answers that would forge links in a chain of facts imperiling petitioner with conviction of a federal crime. The three questions, if answered affirmatively, would establish contacts between petitioner and Weisberg during the crucial period when the latter was eluding the grand jury; and in the context of these inquiries the last question might well have called for disclosure that Weisberg was hiding away on petitioner's premises or with his assistance. Petitioner could reasonably have sensed the peril of prosecution for federal offenses ranging from obstruction to conspiracy.

Take Note

If a witness has a valid Fifth Amendment privilege, the prosecutor can still obtain the witness's testimony by giving the witness immunity from prosecution.

It was not "perfectly clear, from a careful consideration of all the circumstances in the case, that the witness is mistaken, and that the answers cannot possibly have such tendency" to incriminate. *Temple v. Commonwealth*, 75 Va. 892, 898 (1881). "The immediate and potential evils of compulsory self-disclosure transcend any difficulties that the exercise of the privilege may impose on society in the detection and prosecution of crime." *United States v. White*, 322 U.S. 694, 698 (1944). Pertinent here is the observation of Mr. Justice Brandeis for this Court in *McCarthy v. Arndstein*, 266 U.S. 34, 42 (1924): "If Congress should hereafter conclude that a full disclosure by the witnesses is of greater importance than the possibility of punishing them for some crime in the past, it can, as in other cases, confer the power of unrestricted examination by providing complete immunity."

Reversed.

Points for Discussion

a.   A Fifth Amendment Privilege for Claimed Innocence?

In *Ohio v. Reiner*, 532 U.S. 17, 21 (2001), the Court stated that, "We have never held that the privilege is unavailable to those who claim innocence. To the contrary, we have emphasized that one of the Fifth Amendment's 'basic functions is to protect innocent men "who otherwise might be ensnared by ambiguous circumstances." ' "

b.   *Miranda* Warnings?

There is no requirement that a grand jury witness who might have a Fifth Amendment privilege be given *Miranda* warnings. *United States v. Mandujano*, 425 U.S. 564 (1976). As a matter of practice, good prosecutors typically warn a witness that the witness need not answer any questions that may incriminate the witness and that the witness is entitled to a lawyer.

c.   Warnings to Targets?

In *United States v. Washington*, 431 U.S. 181, 188 (1977), the Court held that a witness need not be warned that he is a target of the grand jury investigation: "After being sworn, respondent was explicitly advised that he had a right to remain silent and that any statements he did make could be used to convict him of crime. It is inconceivable that such a warning would fail to alert him to his right to refuse to answer any questions which might incriminate him. Even in the presumed psychologically coercive atmosphere of police custodial interrogation, *Miranda* does not require that any additional warnings be given simply because the suspect is a potential defendant; indeed, such suspects are potential defendants more often than not. Respondent points out that unlike one subject to custodial interrogation, whose arrest should inform him only too clearly that he is a potential criminal defendant, a grand jury witness may well be unaware that he is targeted for possible prosecution. While this may be so, it is an overdrawn generalization. In any case, events here prior to questioning by the prosecutor clearly put respondent on notice that he was a suspect in the motorcycle theft."

d. Sixth Amendment Right to Counsel

The Court has indicated, though never explicitly held, that a witness before a grand jury has no Sixth Amendment right to be represented by counsel. *See Anonymous v. Baker*, 360 U.S. 287 (1959). While that means that an indigent person has no right to counsel at the State's expense, citizens can choose to employ counsel at their own expense. Whatever the status of a Sixth Amendment or Due Process right to counsel at grand jury proceedings, consultation between a witness and counsel may be necessary so that the witness may determine whether to invoke the Fifth Amendment privilege against self-incrimination in response to a particular question. In such situations, the witness has a right to consult with an attorney outside the grand jury room.

Take Note

This right to consult with, but not have counsel present, often leads to almost farcical scenes in which the grand jurors pose a question to a witness who then asks to be excused so that he may consult with his attorney in the hallway. The witness will repeat the question to the attorney who will advise whether the question calls for self-incrimination. The witness will return to the grand jury room, inform the grand jury of whether he will answer the question; this scenario may be repeated after each question is posed. Some courts permit the witness to consult with counsel after each question, *see, e.g., United States v. George*, 444 F.2d 310 (6th Cir.1971), while other courts deem this to be obstructionist and limit the witness to consulting with counsel on only three or four questions, *see, e.g., In re Tierney*, 465 F.2d 806 (5th Cir.1972). Some states explicitly permit counsel to be in the grand jury room when the witness is a target or has a Fifth Amendment privilege. *See, e.g.,* La C.Cr.P. Art. 433A(2) (2013).

e. Witness Protection Against Perjury

In *United States v. Sarihifard*, 155 F. 3d 301 (4th Cir. 1998), the Court recognized the possibility of perjury entrapment when a witness is called more than once before the grand jury and held that a witness called multiple times is entitled to review their prior transcripts. The Court held in *Rehberg v. Paulk*, 566 U.S. 356 (2012), that, as a state actor, a grand jury witness is entitled to absolute immunity from a § 1983 civil suit brought by the grand jury target claiming that the witness conspired to present false testimony before the grand jury.

f. Fifth Amendment & Compliance with *Subpoena Duces Tecum*

A grand jury may issue a *subpoena duces tecum* which is a command to a person to produce writings or objects described in the subpoena. A subpoena issued by a grand jury is presumed reasonable and the burden is on the recipient to prove that requiring compliance would be unreasonable. *United States v. R. Enterprises, Inc.*, <u>498 U.S. 292 (1991)</u>. The only constitutional limitations on *subpoenas duces tecum* or other grand jury investigative powers are the constitutional rights of individual witnesses, particularly the Fifth Amendment right against self-incrimination. This area of the law is very complex.

With respect to *subpoenas duces tecum* for written materials, the Fifth Amendment applies to the person producing the materials subpoenaed when three conditions are met: 1) the government seeks to "compel" compliance with its demand that the person produce documents or tangible items; 2) the compelled material is "testimonial" in nature; and 3) the material "incriminates" the person required to produce it. The requirements that the material be both "compelled" and "testimonial" in nature has led the Court to distinguish between the *creation* of and *production* of the document. When the government seeks documents previously created by the defendant, the act of creation is deemed to have been voluntary, not compelled. The act of producing the voluntarily created documents, however, may be deemed "testimonial" *only* if the act establishes incriminating aspects *unrelated* to the contents of the document. For example, the act of production may establish the existence of the documents; defendant's control over the documents; or may constitute authentication of the documents, *i.e.*, that the documents are those described by the subpoena. In such cases, the Fifth Amendment privilege may apply to the production of the documents even if the documents were voluntarily created. *See Fisher v. United States*, <u>425 U.S. 391 (1976)</u>.

Doe v. United States

<u>487 U.S. 201 (1988)</u>.

JUSTICE BLACKMUN delivered the opinion of the Court.

This case presents the question whether a court order compelling a target of a grand jury investigation to authorize foreign banks to disclose records of his accounts, without identifying those documents or acknowledging their existence, violates the target's Fifth Amendment privilege against self-incrimination.

Hear It

You can hear the oral argument in *Doe* at: http://www.oyez.org/cases/1980-1989/1987/1987_86_1753.

Appearing before the grand jury pursuant to a subpoena directing him to produce records of transactions in accounts at three named banks in the Cayman Islands and Bermuda, petitioner produced some records and testified that no additional records were within his possession. When questioned about the existence of additional records, he invoked the Fifth Amendment privilege against self-incrimination. Grand jury subpoenas then were issued to United States branches of each of the banks, but the banks refused to comply because their governments' laws prohibited disclosure of account records without the customer's consent. The prosecution then filed a motion with the district court requesting that petitioner be ordered to sign forms stating that he was "directing any bank at which I may have a bank account of any kind or at which a corporation has a bank account of any kind upon which I am authorized to draw" to deliver records of those accounts to the grand jury. The form specifically noted that petitioner's directive was being made pursuant to court order, and that the directive was intended to provide compliance with the bank secrecy laws of the Cayman Islands and Bermuda. Petitioner refused to sign the consent directive on self-incrimination grounds, and after being held in contempt, sought appellate review. The Court of Appeals affirmed.

Petitioner's sole claim is that his execution of the consent forms directing the banks to release records as to which the banks believe he has the right of withdrawal has independent testimonial significance that will incriminate him, and that the Fifth Amendment prohibits governmental compulsion of that act. The question is whether the act of executing the form is a "testimonial communication." The parties disagree about the meaning of "testimonial" and whether the consent directive fits the proposed definitions. Petitioner contends that a compelled statement is testimonial if the Government could use the content of the speech or writing, as opposed to its physical characteristics, to further a criminal investigation of the witness. The second half of petitioner's "testimonial" test is that the statement must be incriminating, which is a separate requirement for invoking the privilege. Thus, Doe contends, in essence, that every written and oral statement significant for its content is necessarily testimonial for purposes of the Fifth Amendment. Under this view, the consent directive is testimonial because it is a declarative statement of consent made by Doe to the foreign banks, a statement that the Government will use to persuade the banks to produce potentially incriminating account records that would otherwise be unavailable to the grand jury.

While the Court in *Fisher v. United States*, 425 U.S. 391 (1976) and *United States v. Doe*, 465 U.S. 605 (1984) did not purport to announce a universal test for determining the scope of the privilege, it also did not purport to establish a more narrow boundary applicable to acts alone. The Court applied basic Fifth Amendment principles. An examination of the Court's application of these principles indicates the Court's recognition that, in order to be testimonial, an accused's communication must explicitly or implicitly relate a factual assertion or disclose information. Only then is a person compelled to be a "witness" against himself. This understanding is perhaps most clearly revealed in cases in which the Court has held that certain acts, though incriminating, are not within the privilege. Thus, a suspect may be compelled to furnish a blood sample, to provide a handwriting exemplar or a voice exemplar, to stand in a lineup, and to wear particular clothing. These decisions are grounded on the proposition that "the privilege protects an accused only from being compelled to testify against himself, or otherwise provide the State with evidence of a testimonial or communicative nature." *Schmerber v. California*, 384 U.S. 757, 761 (1966). It is the "extortion of information from the accused," the attempt to force him "to disclose the contents of his own mind," that implicates the Self-Incrimination Clause. "Unless some attempt is made to secure a communication—written, oral or otherwise—upon which reliance is to be placed as involving the accused's consciousness of the facts and the operations of his mind in expressing it, the demand made upon him is not a testimonial one."

It is consistent with the history of and the policies underlying the Self-Incrimination Clause to hold that the privilege may be asserted only to resist compelled explicit or implicit disclosures of incriminating information. Historically, the privilege was intended to prevent the use of legal compulsion to extract from the accused a sworn communication of facts which would incriminate him. Such was the process of the ecclesiastical courts and the Star Chamber—the inquisitorial method of putting the accused upon his oath and compelling him to answer questions designed to uncover uncharged offenses, without evidence from another source. The major thrust of the policies undergirding the privilege is to prevent such compulsion. The Court in *Murphy v. Waterfront Comm'n of New York Harbor*, 378 U.S. 52, 55 (1964) explained that the privilege is founded on: "[1] our unwillingness to subject those suspected of crime to the cruel trilemma of self-accusation, perjury or contempt; [2] our preference for an accusatorial rather than an inquisitorial system of criminal justice; [3] our fear that self-incriminating statements will be elicited by inhumane treatment and abuses; [4] our sense of fair play which dictates 'a fair state-individual balance by requiring the government to leave the individual alone until good cause is shown for disturbing him and by requiring the government in its contest with the individual to shoulder the entire load,'; [5] our respect for the inviolability of the human personality and of the right of each individual 'to a private enclave where he may lead a private life,'; [6] our distrust of self-deprecatory statements; and [7] our realization that the privilege, while sometimes 'a shelter to the guilty,' is often 'a protection to the innocent.' " These policies are served when the privilege is asserted to spare the accused from having to reveal, directly or indirectly, his knowledge of facts relating him to the offense or from having to share his thoughts and beliefs with the Government.

We are not persuaded that our articulation of the privilege fundamentally alters the power of the Government to compel an accused to assist in his prosecution. There are very few instances in which a verbal statement, either oral or written, will not convey information or assert facts. The vast majority of verbal statements thus will be testimonial and, to that extent, will fall within the privilege. Furthermore, there are many restrictions on the Government's prosecutorial practices in addition to the Self-Incrimination Clause. Indeed, there are other protections against governmental efforts to compel an unwilling suspect to cooperate in an investigation, including efforts to obtain information from him. We are confident that these provisions, together with the Self-Incrimination Clause, will continue to prevent abusive investigative techniques.

We turn to consider whether Doe's execution of the consent directive at issue here would have testimonial significance. It would not, because neither the form, nor its execution, communicates any factual assertions, implicit or explicit, or conveys any information to the Government. The consent directive is not "testimonial." It is carefully drafted not to make reference to a specific account, but only to speak in the hypothetical. Thus, the form does not acknowledge that an account in a foreign financial institution is in existence or that it is controlled by petitioner. Nor does the form indicate whether documents or any other information relating to petitioner are present at the foreign bank, assuming that such an account does exist. The form does not even identify the relevant bank. Although the executed form allows the Government access to a potential source of evidence, the directive does not point the Government toward hidden accounts or otherwise provide information that will assist the prosecution in uncovering evidence. The Government must locate that evidence "by the independent labor of its officers." The Government is not relying upon the "truthtelling" of Doe's directive to show the existence of, or his control over, foreign bank account records.

Given the consent directive's phraseology, petitioner's compelled act of executing the form has no testimonial significance either. By signing the form, Doe makes no statement, explicit or implicit, regarding the existence of a foreign bank account or his control over any such account. Nor would his execution of the form admit the authenticity of any records produced by the bank. Not only does the directive express no view on the issue, but because petitioner did not prepare the document, any statement by Doe to the effect that it is authentic would not establish that the records are genuine. Authentication evidence would have to be provided by bank officials. We read the directive as equivalent to a statement by Doe that, although he expresses no opinion about the existence of, or his control over, any such account, he is authorizing the bank to disclose information relating to accounts over which, in the bank's opinion, Doe can exercise the right of withdrawal. When forwarded to the bank along with a subpoena, the executed directive, if effective under local law, will simply make it possible for the recipient bank to comply with the Government's request to produce such records. If the Government obtains bank records after Doe signs the directive, the only factual statement made by anyone will be the bank's implicit declaration, by its act of production in response to the subpoena, that it believes the accounts to be petitioners'. *Cf. Fisher.* The fact that the bank's customer has directed the disclosure of his records "would say nothing about the correctness of the bank's representations." Indeed, the Second and Eleventh Circuits have concluded that consent directives virtually identical to the one here are inadmissible as an admission by the signator of either control or existence.

JUSTICE STEVENS, dissenting.

A defendant can be compelled to produce material evidence that is incriminating. Fingerprints, blood samples, voice exemplars, handwriting specimens or other items of physical evidence may be extracted from a defendant against his will. But can he be compelled to use his mind to assist the prosecution in convicting him of a crime? I think not. He may in some cases be forced to surrender a key to a strong box containing incriminating documents, but I do not believe he can be compelled to reveal the combination to his wall safe—by word or deed.

The document the Government seeks to extract from John Doe purports to order third parties to take action that will lead to the discovery of incriminating evidence. The directive itself may not betray any knowledge petitioner may have about the circumstances of the offenses being investigated by the Grand Jury, but it nevertheless purports to evidence a reasoned decision by Doe to authorize action by others. The forced execution of this document differs from the forced production of physical evidence just as human beings differ from other animals. If John Doe can be compelled to use his mind to assist the Government in developing its case, he will be forced "to be a witness against himself." The fundamental purpose of the Fifth Amendment was to mark the line between the kind of inquisition conducted by the Star Chamber and what we proudly describe as our accusatorial system of justice. It reflects "our respect for the inviolability of the human personality." In my opinion that protection gives John Doe the right to refuse to sign the directive authorizing access to the records of any bank account that he may control. Accordingly, I respectfully dissent.

Food for Thought

What is the basis for Justice Stevens' distinction between what he concedes is permissible—forcing the defendant "to surrender a key to a strong box containing incriminating documents"—and what he considers impermissible—compelling the defendant "to reveal the combination to his wall safe by word or deed?" Does it matter if the combination to the safe has been memorized (and must be disclosed by the defendant's verbal statement) or if the combination was written on a piece of paper that the defendant is ordered to physically surrender to the government? Is there a meaningful distinction between a physical act (deemed non-testimonial) and a mental process (deemed testimonial)?

Food for Thought

The Fifth Amendment privilege only protects testimonial evidence from a witness. A blood test is not testimonial because it is not a communication from the witness's mind but rather a naturally occurring element in the body. *Schmerber v. California*, 384 U.S. 757 (1966). What about the following: 1) A compelled voice exemplar from a witness, where the witness was told to read a portion of a transcript of an intercepted conversation into a recording device. The grand jury scrutinized the exemplars in an attempt to identify the voices in the intercepted conversation. *See United States v. Dionisio*, 410 U.S. 1 (1973); 2) A videotape of a compelled sobriety test where the witness exhibited slurred speech, the witness could not walk in a straight line, the witness was asked the date of his sixth birthday and could not remember, or the witness could not touch his nose with his index finger. *See Pennsylvania v. Muniz*, <u>496 U.S. 582 (1990)</u>.

Hypo: *Computers & Incrimination*

How would the Court deal with the following court orders to a defendant? 1) Tell us what is on the computer disk you prepared on September 1; 2) Surrender the disk to the U.S. Attorney; or 3) Surrender the password and code used to encrypt the disk.

Points for Discussion

a.   What Is the Corporate Custodian of Records to Do?

Collective entities such as corporations, partnerships, and labor unions have no Fifth Amendment privilege against self-incrimination. In *Braswell v. United States*, 487 U.S. 99 (1988), the Court held that the custodian of records of a collective entity cannot resist a subpoena for entity records by claiming the privilege against self-incrimination on behalf of the corporation. The corporate custodian has no privilege as to the corporate records, even though the act of production may be personally incriminating. Because the Court has used a fiction (*i.e.*, the corporate employee acts only as an agent when asked to produce corporate documents in response to a subpoena), the Court addressed the issue of personal incrimination for the custodian. To ensure that the compelled act does not violate the custodian's personal Fifth Amendment privilege, the government cannot disclose to the jury who produced the documents. If the jury is not told that the custodian produced the records, the act of production by the custodian merely implies possession and authentication by the corporation but not by the custodian. Therefore, production of the corporate documents is not incriminating to the custodian.

b. Use of "Compelled" Disclosures in Subsequent Proceedings

If the court upholds a witness's assertion of the Fifth Amendment privilege, or if the prosecutor (or other authority seeking evidence such as Congress) agrees that the witness has a valid Fifth Amendment privilege, it is not the end of the matter. The prosecutor (or Congress or other lawful authority) may still seek to compel disclosure by granting the witness immunity from prosecution. The theory here is that the Fifth Amendment only protects a person from being compelled to be a witness against himself at a criminal proceeding. If the "witness" cannot be prosecuted because she has been granted immunity, then anything that she is compelled to disclose cannot violate the Fifth Amendment privilege because it cannot be used in a subsequent prosecution. Therefore, while the witness has been "compelled" to disclose, she has not been compelled to be a "witness" at a criminal proceeding because there will not be a subsequent criminal prosecution due to the grant of immunity.

Historically, two types of immunity have developed. Originally, what has come to be known as transactional immunity was thought to be necessary in order to overcome a valid assertion of Fifth Amendment privilege. Under transactional immunity, the witness is given complete immunity from criminal prosecution for any offenses committed in connection with the criminal incident(s) for which the immunity has been granted. In other words, the witness simply cannot be prosecuted for anything in connection with the incident(s). For almost 200 years, transactional immunity was the sole type of immunity. It was during the Watergate era, however, that attorneys at the Department of Justice came up with the concept of use immunity.

> **FYI**
>
> Ironically, use immunity arose on the watch of President Richard Nixon's Attorney General John Mitchell, who was subsequently jailed for his role in the Watergate scandals.

Under use immunity, anything that witnesses are compelled to say or disclose cannot be "used" against them at a subsequent criminal proceeding. However, a subsequent criminal proceeding is not completely barred (as under transactional immunity). Instead, the witness may be prosecuted for offenses committed in connection with the criminal incident(s) about which they were compelled to testify, as long as the compelled disclosures are not used, and the prosecution is based entirely on other evidence completely separate and apart from any compelled disclosures. *See*

> **Practice Pointer**
>
> For a defense lawyer representing an individual with a potential privilege, it is important to raise the privilege regardless of whether the judge upholds the privilege. This is because if the judge denies the privilege and the defendant has to testify, that testimony is compelled and cannot be used against him in a future proceeding.

Kastigar v. United States, 406 U.S. 441 (1972). Since *Kastigar*, this form of immunity has come to be known as "use and derivative use immunity" because *Kastigar* requires not only that no compelled disclosures be directly used at a subsequent criminal prosecution, but also that no compelled disclosures be indirectly used as leads or otherwise to obtain other evidence. In other words, all of the evidence used at a subsequent criminal prosecution must be completely independent of any compelled disclosures. A pretrial hearing, sometimes referred to as a "*Kastigar*" hearing, may be necessary in order to determine compliance.

United States v. Hubbell

530 U.S. 27 (2000).

JUSTICE STEVENS delivered the opinion of the Court.

The questions presented concern the scope of a witness' protection against compelled self-incrimination: (1) whether the Fifth Amendment privilege protects a witness from being compelled to disclose the existence of incriminating documents that

Hear It

You can hear the oral argument in *Hubbell* at: http://www.oyez.org/cases/1990-1999/1999/1999_99_166.

the Government is unable to describe with reasonable particularity; and (2) if the witness produces such documents pursuant to a grant of immunity, whether 18 U.S.C. § 6002 prevents the Government from using them to prepare criminal charges against him.

This proceeding arises out of the second prosecution of respondent, Webster Hubbell, commenced by the Independent Counsel appointed in August 1994 to investigate possible violations of federal law relating to the Whitewater Development Corporation. The first prosecution was terminated pursuant to a plea bargain. In December 1994, respondent pleaded guilty to charges of mail fraud and tax evasion arising out of his billing practices as a member of an Arkansas law firm from 1989 to 1992, and was sentenced to 21 months in prison. In the plea agreement, respondent promised to provide the Independent Counsel with "full, complete, accurate, and truthful information" about matters relating to the Whitewater investigation.

The second prosecution resulted from the Independent Counsel's attempt to determine whether respondent had violated that promise. In October 1996, while respondent was incarcerated, the Independent Counsel served him with a subpoena duces tecum calling for the

FYI

The Whitewater investigation is famous for ultimately leading to the exposure of President Bill Clinton's affair with Monica Lewinsky, as well as to subsequent impeachment proceedings.

production of 11 categories of documents before a grand jury sitting in Little Rock, Arkansas. On November 19, he appeared before the grand jury and invoked his Fifth Amendment privilege against self-incrimination. In response to questioning by the prosecutor, respondent refused "to state whether there are documents within my possession, custody, or control responsive to the Subpoena." Thereafter, the prosecutor produced an order, previously obtained from the District Court pursuant to 18 U.S.C. § 6003(a), directing him to respond to the subpoena and granting him immunity "to the extent allowed by law." Respondent then produced 13,120 pages of documents and records and responded to a series of questions that established that those were all of the documents in his custody or control that were responsive to the commands in the subpoena, with the exception of a few documents he claimed were shielded by the attorney-client and attorney work-product privileges.

The contents of the documents produced by respondent provided the Independent Counsel with the information that led to this second prosecution. A grand jury returned a 10-count indictment charging respondent with various tax-related crimes and mail and wire fraud. The District Court dismissed the indictment relying, in part, on the ground that the Independent Counsel's use of the subpoenaed documents violated § 6002 because all of the evidence he would offer against respondent at trial derived either directly or indirectly from the testimonial aspects of respondent's immunized act of producing those documents. Noting that the Independent Counsel had admitted that he was not investigating tax-related issues when he issued the subpoena, and that he had "learned about the unreported income and other crimes from studying the records' contents, 'the District Court characterized the subpoena as the quintessential fishing expedition.' " The Court of Appeals vacated the judgment and remanded for further proceedings. The majority concluded that the District Court had incorrectly relied on the fact that the Independent Counsel did not have prior knowledge of the contents of the subpoenaed documents. The question the District Court should have addressed was the extent of the Government's independent knowledge of the documents' existence and authenticity, and of respondent's possession or control of them. It explained:

> On remand, the district court should hold a hearing in which it seeks to establish the extent and detail of the Government's knowledge of Hubbell's financial affairs (or of the paperwork documenting it) on the day the subpoena issued. It is only then that the court will be in a position to assess the testimonial value of Hubbell's response to the subpoena. Should the Independent Counsel prove capable of demonstrating with reasonable particularity a prior awareness that the exhaustive litany of documents sought in the subpoena existed and were in Hubbell's possession, then the wide distance evidently traveled from the subpoena to the substantive allegations contained in the indictment would be based upon legitimate intermediate steps. To the extent that the information conveyed through Hubbell's

compelled act of production provides the necessary linkage, however, the indictment deriving therefrom is tainted.

In the opinion of the dissenting judge, the majority failed to give full effect to the distinction between the contents of the documents and the limited testimonial significance of the act of producing them. In his view, as long as the prosecutor could make use of information contained in the documents or derived therefrom without any reference to the fact that respondent had produced them in response to a subpoena, there would be no improper use of the testimonial aspect of the immunized act of production. In other words, the constitutional privilege and the statute conferring use immunity would only shield the witness from the use of any information resulting from his subpoena response "beyond what the prosecutor would receive if the documents appeared in the grand jury room or in his office unsolicited and unmarked, like manna from heaven."

On remand, the Independent Counsel acknowledged that he could not satisfy the "reasonable particularity" standard prescribed by the Court of Appeals and entered into a conditional plea agreement with respondent. In essence, the agreement provides for the dismissal of the charges unless this Court's disposition of the case makes it reasonably likely that respondent's "act of production immunity" would not pose a significant bar to his prosecution. The case is not moot because the agreement also provides for the entry of a guilty plea and a sentence that will not include incarceration if we should reverse and issue an opinion that is sufficiently favorable to the Government to satisfy that condition. Despite that agreement, we granted the Independent Counsel's petition for a writ of certiorari in order to determine the precise scope of a grant of immunity with respect to the production of documents in response to a subpoena. We now affirm.

It is useful to preface our analysis of the constitutional issue with a restatement of certain propositions that are not in dispute. The term "privilege against self-incrimination" is not an entirely accurate description of a person's constitutional protection against being "compelled in any criminal case to be a witness against himself." The word "witness" in the constitutional text limits the relevant category of compelled incriminating communications to those that are "testimonial" in character. As Justice Holmes observed, there is a significant difference between the use of compulsion to extort communications from a defendant and compelling a person to engage in conduct that may be incriminating. Even though the act may provide incriminating evidence, a criminal suspect may be compelled to put on a shirt, to provide a blood sample or handwriting exemplar, or to make a recording of his voice. The act of exhibiting such physical characteristics is not the same as a sworn communication by a witness that relates either express or implied assertions of fact or belief.

More relevant is the settled proposition that a person may be required to produce specific documents even though they contain incriminating assertions of fact or belief because the creation of those documents was not "compelled" within the meaning of the privilege. It is clear that respondent Hubbell could not avoid compliance with the subpoena served on him merely because the demanded documents contained incriminating evidence, whether written by others or voluntarily prepared by himself. We have made it clear that the act of producing documents in response to a subpoena may have a compelled testimonial aspect. "The act of production" itself may implicitly communicate "statements of fact." By "producing documents in compliance with a subpoena, the witness would admit that the papers existed, were in his possession or control, and were authentic." Moreover, as in this case, when the custodian of documents responds to a subpoena, he may be compelled to take the witness stand and answer questions designed to determine whether he has produced everything demanded by the subpoena. The answers to those questions, as well as the act of production itself, may certainly communicate information about the existence, custody, and authenticity of the documents. Whether the constitutional privilege protects the answers to such questions, or protects the act of production itself, is a question that is distinct from the question whether the unprotected contents of the documents themselves are incriminating.

Finally, the phrase "in any criminal case" in the text of the Fifth Amendment might have been read to limit its coverage to compelled testimony that is used against the defendant in the trial itself. It has, however, long been settled that its protection encompasses compelled statements that lead to the discovery of incriminating evidence even though the statements themselves are not incriminating and are not introduced into evidence. Thus, a half-century ago we held that a trial judge had erroneously rejected a defendant's claim of privilege on the ground that his answer to the pending question would not itself constitute evidence of the charged offense. As we explained: "The privilege afforded not only extends to answers that would in themselves support a conviction under a federal criminal statute but likewise embraces those which would furnish a link in the chain of evidence needed to prosecute the claimant for a federal crime." *Hoffman v. United States*, 341 U.S. 479, 486 (1951). Compelled testimony that communicates information that may "lead to incriminating evidence" is privileged even if the information itself is not inculpatory. *Doe v. United States*, 487 U.S. 201, 208 (1988). It is the Fifth Amendment's protection against the prosecutor's use of incriminating information derived directly or indirectly from the compelled testimony of the respondent that is of primary relevance in this case.

Acting pursuant to 18 U.S.C. § 6002, the District Court entered an order compelling respondent to produce "any and all documents" described in the grand jury subpoena and granting him "immunity to the extent allowed by law." In *Kastigar v. United States*, 406 U.S. 441 (1972), we upheld the constitutionality of § 6002 because the scope of the "use and derivative-use" immunity that it provides is coextensive with the scope of the constitutional privilege against self-incrimination. The "compelled testimony" in this case is not to be found in the contents of the documents produced in response to the subpoena. It is, rather, the testimony inherent in the act of producing those documents. The disagreement between the parties focuses entirely on the significance of that testimonial aspect. The Government correctly emphasizes that the testimonial aspect of a response to a subpoena duces tecum does nothing more than establish the existence, authenticity, and custody of items that are produced. The Government is entirely correct that it would not have to advert to respondent's act of production in order to prove the existence, authenticity, or custody of any documents that it might offer in evidence at a criminal trial; indeed, the Government disclaims any need to introduce any of the documents produced by respondent into evidence in order to prove the charges against him. It follows, according to the Government, that it has no intention of making improper "use" of respondent's compelled testimony.

The question is not whether the response to the subpoena may be introduced into evidence at his criminal trial. That would surely be a prohibited "use" of the immunized act of production. But the fact that the Government intends no such use of the act of production leaves open the separate question whether it has already made "derivative use" of the testimonial aspect of that act in obtaining the indictment against respondent and in preparing its case for trial. It clearly has. It is apparent from the text of the subpoena that the prosecutor needed respondent's assistance both to identify potential sources of information and to produce those sources. Given the breadth of the description of the 11 categories of documents called for by the subpoena, the collection and production of the materials demanded was tantamount to answering a series of interrogatories asking a witness to disclose the existence and location of particular documents fitting certain broad descriptions. The assembly of literally hundreds of pages of material in response to a request for "any and all documents reflecting, referring, or relating to any direct or indirect sources of money or other things of value received by or provided to" an individual or members of his family during a 3-year period, is the functional equivalent of the preparation of an answer to either a detailed written interrogatory or a series of oral questions at a discovery deposition. Entirely apart from the contents of the 13,120 pages of materials that respondent produced in this case, it is undeniable that providing a catalog of existing documents fitting within any of the 11 broadly worded subpoena categories could provide a prosecutor with a "lead to incriminating evidence," or "a link in the chain of evidence needed to prosecute."

The record makes clear that that is what happened in this case. The documents were produced before a grand jury sitting in the Eastern District of Arkansas in aid of the Independent Counsel's attempt to determine whether respondent had violated a commitment in his first plea agreement. The use of those sources of information eventually led to the return of an indictment by a grand jury sitting in the District of Columbia for offenses that apparently are unrelated to that plea agreement. What the District Court characterized as a "fishing expedition" did produce a fish, but not the one that the Independent Counsel expected to hook. The testimonial aspect of respondent's act of producing subpoenaed documents was the first step in a chain of evidence that led to this prosecution. The documents did not magically appear in the prosecutor's office like "manna from heaven." They arrived there only after respondent asserted his constitutional privilege, received a grant of immunity, and— under compulsion of the District Court's order—took the mental and physical steps necessary to provide the prosecutor with an accurate inventory of the many sources of potentially incriminating evidence sought by the subpoena. It was only through respondent's truthful reply to the subpoena that the Government received the incriminating documents of which it made "substantial use in the investigation that led to the indictment." For these reasons, we cannot accept the Government's submission that respondent's immunity did not preclude its derivative use of the produced documents because its "possession of the documents was the fruit only of a simple physical act—the act of producing the documents." It was necessary for respondent to make extensive use of "the contents of his own mind" in identifying the hundreds of documents responsive to the requests in the subpoena. The assembly of those documents was like telling an inquisitor the combination to a wall safe, not like being forced to surrender the key to a strongbox. The Government's anemic view of respondent's act of production as a mere physical act that is principally non-testimonial in character and can be entirely divorced from its "implicit" testimonial aspect so as to constitute a "legitimate, wholly independent source" (as required by *Kastigar*) for the documents produced simply fails to account for these realities.

The constitutional privilege against self-incrimination protects the target of a grand jury investigation from being compelled to answer questions designed to elicit information about the existence of sources of potentially incriminating evidence. That constitutional privilege has the same application to the testimonial aspect of a response to a subpoena seeking discovery of those sources. The Government arguably conceded that respondent's act of production in this case had a testimonial aspect that entitled him to respond to the subpoena by asserting his privilege against self-incrimination. The Government has argued that the communicative aspect of respondent's act of producing ordinary business records is insufficiently "testimonial" to support a claim of privilege because the existence and possession of such records by any businessman is a "foregone conclusion" under our decision in *Fisher v. United States*, 425 U.S. 391 (1976). This argument misreads *Fisher* and ignores our subsequent decision in *United States v. Doe*, 465 U.S. 605 (1984).

Whatever the scope of this "foregone conclusion" rationale, the facts of this case plainly fall outside of it. While in *Fisher* the Government already knew that the documents were in the attorneys' possession and could independently confirm their existence and authenticity through the accountants who created them, here the Government has not shown that it had any prior knowledge of either the existence or the whereabouts of the 13,120 pages of documents produced by respondent. The Government cannot cure this deficiency through the overbroad argument that a businessman such as respondent will always possess general business and tax records that fall within the broad categories described in this subpoena. The Doe subpoenas also sought several broad categories of general business records, yet we upheld the finding that the act of producing those records would involve testimonial self-incrimination.

Given our conclusion that respondent's act of production had a testimonial aspect, at least with respect to the existence and location of the documents sought by the Government's subpoena, respondent could not be compelled to produce those documents without first receiving a grant of immunity under § 6003. As we construed § 6002 in *Kastigar*, such immunity is co-extensive with the constitutional privilege. *Kastigar* requires that respondent's motion to dismiss the indictment on immunity grounds be granted unless the Government proves that the evidence it used in obtaining the indictment and proposed to use at trial was derived from legitimate sources "wholly independent" of the testimonial aspect of respondent's immunized conduct in assembling and producing the documents described in the subpoena. The Government does not claim that it could make such a showing. Rather, it contends that its prosecution of respondent must be considered proper unless someone—presumably respondent—shows that "there is some substantial relation between the compelled testimonial communications implicit in the act of production (as opposed to the act of production standing alone) and some aspect of the information used in the investigation or the evidence presented at trial." We could not accept this submission without repudiating the basis for our conclusion in *Kastigar* that the statutory guarantee of use and derivative-use immunity is as broad as the constitutional privilege itself. This we are not prepared to do.

Accordingly, the indictment against respondent must be dismissed. The judgment of the Court of Appeals is affirmed. *It is so ordered.*

Points for Discussion

a.   Foregone Conclusion

What is the nature of the foregone conclusion discussion in *Hubbell*? In *Fisher v. United States*, 425 U.S. 391 (1976), and other cases, the Court has discussed this concept: "It is doubtful that implicitly admitting the existence and possession of the papers rises to the level of testimony within the protection of the Fifth Amendment. The papers belong to the accountant, were prepared by him, and are the kind usually prepared by an accountant working on the tax returns of his client. Surely the Government is in no way relying on the 'truthtelling' of the taxpayer to prove the existence of or his access to the documents. The existence and location of the papers are a foregone conclusion and the taxpayer adds little or nothing to the sum total of the

Government's information by conceding that he in fact has the papers. Under these circumstances by enforcement of the summons "no constitutional rights are touched. The question is not of testimony but of surrender." Besides noting that the papers were of the kind usually prepared by an accountant, the Court never explained why the existence and location of the accountant's work papers were a foregone conclusion. *Doe* also tied authenticity to the foregone conclusion. Authenticity concerns whether a document is genuine, rather than a forgery or fabrication. The act of production confirms that the person responding to the subpoena believes the documents are those described in the subpoena.

b. Prosecution's Burden

In *In re Grand Jury Subpoena, Dated April 18, 2003*, 383 F. 3d 905 (9th Cir. 2004), the court held that the trial court erred in concluding that the prosecution had proved that the existence, possession, and authenticity of the documents was a foregone conclusion, as well as in refusing to examine the documents *in camera* to determine whether the act of producing them would be incriminating:

> The government was not required to have actual knowledge of the existence and location of each and every responsive document; the government was required, however, to establish the existence of the documents sought and Doe's possession of them with "reasonable particularity" before the existence and possession of the documents could be considered a foregone conclusion and production therefore would not be testimonial. Although the government possessed extensive knowledge about Doe's price-fixing activities as a result of interviews with cooperating witnesses and Doe's own incriminating statements made to federal agents on April 26, 2003, it is the government's knowledge of the existence and possession of the actual documents, not the information contained therein, that is central to the foregone conclusion inquiry. The breadth of the subpoena far exceeded the government's knowledge about the actual documents that Doe created or possessed during his former employment and that he retained after he terminated his employment. The government probably could identify with sufficient particularity the existence of e-mails between Doe and some of his competitors, e-mails between Doe and his superiors regarding pricing, phone records corroborating that Doe spoke to his competitors, and records establishing meetings with certain competitors because Doe made substantial admissions to investigators during his living room interview regarding these documents. The government, however, failed to draft the subpoena narrowly to identify the documents that it could establish with reasonable particularity. Thus, the subpoena's breadth far exceeded the reasonably particular knowledge that the government actually possessed when it served the subpoena on Doe.

The authenticity prong of the foregone conclusion doctrine requires the government to establish that it can independently verify that the compelled documents "are in fact what they purport to be." Independent verification not only requires the government to show that the documents sought to be compelled would be admissible independent of the witness' production of them, but also inquires into whether the government is compelling the witness to use his discretion in selecting and assembling the responsive documents, and thereby tacitly providing identifying information that is necessary to the government's authentication of the subpoenaed documents. Although the government could probably authenticate the writing on Doe's handwritten documents through handwriting analysis, it made little effort to demonstrate how anyone beside Doe could sift through his handwritten notes, personal appointment books, and diaries to produce what Doe's attorney estimates may be 4,500 documents. Such a response by Doe would provide the government with the identifying information that it would need to authenticate these documents. Doe's notes to himself would be difficult, if not impossible, to authenticate by anyone besides Doe. In this case, the government has failed to demonstrate that it can authenticate the documents so broadly described in the subpoena without the identifying information that Doe would provide by using his knowledge and judgment to sift through, select, assemble, and produce the documents.

c.   Oliver North Prosecution

For another good illustration of the *Kastigar* problem, regarding whether, after disclosures made pursuant to a grant of immunity, a subsequent criminal prosecution may go forward, *see United States v. North*, 910 F.2d 843 (D.C. Cir. 1990). In that case, Oliver North was prosecuted for violating the Boland Amendments, which barred the United States government from providing resources to rebels (so called "Contras") battling the Nicaraguan government. Congress conducted hearings to investigate whether President Reagan's administration was violating these provisions. Retired Colonel Oliver North, then a member of the National Security Administration staff, was subpoenaed to testify and asserted his Fifth Amendment privilege. Congress decided that getting to the truth of whether the Reagan administration was violating the law was more important than criminal prosecution and decided to grant North immunity (use and derivative use) in order to compel his testimony. North provided extensive testimony on how the administration had violated the law by funneling money from secret sales of weapons to Iran to the Contras in Nicaragua. Special Prosecutor Lawrence Walsh subsequently prosecuted North for his lead role in violating the Boland Amendments. North was convicted but his conviction was subsequently overturned by the D.C. Circuit because in the appellate court's view, the prosecution had failed to satisfy the dictates of *Kastigar* by demonstrating that every piece of its evidence was obtained wholly independent of North's testimony. While the D.C. Circuit wrote about the prosecution's "heavy burden" under *Kastigar* to show an independent source for each piece of evidence, the decision came in a divided 2–1 opinion in which the two judges in the majority were Reagan appointees. North was a high official in the Reagan administration and, according to news accounts, other higher administration officials, such as Secretary of Defense Caspar Weinberger may have been implicated. Whether *Kastigar* provides much protection to run of the mill defendants is questionable.

Executive Summary

Screening a Case. There are three basic ways in which a case may be "screened" to determine whether it will proceed: 1) by the prosecution within the prosecutor's office; 2) through a preliminary hearing; or (3) through a grand jury.

Preliminary Hearing. A preliminary hearing is an adversary proceeding that occurs in open court, is presided over by a judge, and the accused has the right to counsel, to cross examine witnesses presented by the prosecution, and to present evidence.

A Lack of Probable Cause Is Not a Barrier to Prosecution. A finding of no probable cause by the judge at a preliminary hearing does not necessarily preclude the prosecution from prosecuting the charge.

Effect of Indictment. The return of an indictment establishes probable cause and may eliminate the accused's right to a preliminary hearing.

Unbiased Grand Juror Selection. Grand jurors must be selected without systematic exclusion of individuals based on race, gender, or national origin.

Rules on Disclosure of Grand Jury Testimony. The prosecutor and grand jurors are generally prohibited from disclosing grand jury testimony to others, but witnesses are not prohibited from disclosing their own testimony.

No Court Review of Grand Jury Findings. Courts will not review the adequacy of evidence presented to a grand jury.

Evidence Submitted to Grand Jury. Hearsay testimony and evidence obtained in violation of the Fourth Amendment are admissible in grand jury proceedings, and prosecutors have no constitutional duty to present exculpatory evidence to a grand jury.

Fifth Amendment Privilege. In response to a grand jury subpoena to testify or subpoena duces tecum, a person may claim that compliance with the subpoena would violate the Fifth Amendment right against self-incrimination.

Immunity. A prosecutor may grant a witness "use" immunity in order to overcome a witness's assertion of a Fifth Amendment privilege and compel the witness to testify or comply with a subpoena duces tecum.

Overcoming Fifth Amendment Privilege. In order to overcome an assertion of a Fifth Amendment privilege with respect to a subpoena duces tecum, a prosecutor must show that at the time the subpoena issued, the government knew that the material sought existed, knew who had the material, and knew that the material sought was that described by the subpoena.

Major Themes

a. Discretion—The main source for screening whether a case will go forward is the vast discretion of the prosecutor whether to charge. The preliminary hearing rarely leads to a dismissal of the charges, and the grand jury rarely refuses to return an indictment.

b. Sword—While the grand jury was born of the founders' interest in having it serve as a shield to governmental over-reaching in charging, it rarely if ever serves that purpose now. It is a sword in the prosecution's possession used to investigate and bring charges in serious or high profile cases.

c. Immunity—In high profile or complex investigations, in order to gain important information through testimony in the grand jury, the prosecution has complete discretion to offer a witness who may incriminate himself transactional or use immunity.

For More Information

- RUSSELL L. WEAVER, JOHN M. BURKOFF, CATHERINE HANCOCK & STEVEN I. FRIEDLAND, PRINCIPLES OF CRIMINAL PROCEDURE Ch. 11 (8th ed. 2024).

- WAYNE R. LAFAVE, JEROLD H. ISRAEL, NANCY J. KING & ORIN S. KERR, CRIMINAL PROCEDURE (6th ed. 2017).

Test Your Knowledge

To assess your understanding of the material in this chapter, click here to take a quiz.

CHAPTER 13

Discovery & Disclosure

Discovery in criminal cases is conceptually similar to discovery in civil cases: it is the process by which information is exchanged between the parties, which in a criminal case are the prosecution and the defense. This exchange of information is to be contrasted with other avenues for gathering information, such as factual investigation. In practice, however, criminal and civil discovery are very different. While discovery in civil cases is broad and evenly pursued, the prosecution holds the vast majority of the information in criminal cases. The reason for this is partly structural—the prosecution gathers information from the police, who report to the scene of the crime and investigate immediately; the defense is not able to begin investigating the crime until the defendant obtains counsel (who has access to an investigator), and that may not occur until weeks or months after the crime is committed. In addition, law enforcement possesses formal statutory authority to investigate criminal activity and the defense does not. The other reason for the uneven balance is the availability of resources. The prosecution has a plethora of government agents at its disposal for investigation, forensic examination and other expertise. The typical criminal defense attorney is a public defender, who is often underpaid, overworked and under-resourced. Therefore, discovery disputes most often involve a defendant trying to obtain information from the prosecution, and most litigation in the discovery area involves allegations that the prosecution failed to disclose information.

Practice Pointer

It is crucial that defense counsel be aware of how discovery obligations are triggered in a particular jurisdiction. In the federal court and in many state jurisdictions, the requirement to disclose information is triggered simply by a request for information by the opposing party, usually in writing and pursuant to a statute that sets forth what must be disclosed. Further, some jurisdictions require a party to assert that it has engaged in diligent efforts to obtain the discovery by request or other means before he party can file a motion for discovery from the opposing party. On the other hand, some state jurisdictions provide that a party's obligation to provide discovery pursuant to statute is only triggered by filing a formal discovery motion with the court.

There are two sources for the right to discovery: constitutional and statutory. The United States Constitution sets a floor, giving minimal rights of discovery to a criminal defendant through the Due Process Clause of the Fifth Amendment. *See Armstrong v. Manzo*, 380 U.S. 545 (1965). Every jurisdiction also has a statute governing criminal discovery that sets forth various types of information that must be given to the other party. Most meaningful discovery will come from statutory requirements as opposed to the Constitutional obligations.

The arraignment process is an important part of the discovery process. An arraignment is the court proceeding whereby the accused is given formal notice of the charges against him through the reading of the indictment or information, and the accused enters a plea. The arraignment is not to be confused with the first appearance, where formal charges are often not yet filed. The defendant's right to statutory discovery is usually not triggered until arraignment and entry of a plea of not guilty.

There are two basic discovery issues under the United States Constitution. One involves the defendant's due process right to notice of the charges, and the other involves the defendant's due process right to discover exculpatory evidence.

A. Notice & Motion for Bill of Particulars

After the defendant is arraigned on charges in open court, he or she may seek additional information about the charges by filing a motion for a bill of particulars. This motion is limited to clarifying the charging document, whether indictment or information, so that the defendant has adequate notice of the charges. *See Armstrong v. Manzo*, 380 U.S. 545 (1965) (defendant's right to notice of charges is basic to due process). For example, defendant may request information regarding the date, time and place of the alleged incident(s), the nature of the alleged acts which comprise the elements of the charged crime, or which subsection of a multi-sectioned criminal statute forms the basis of the charge. "The decisive consideration in each case is whether the matter claimed to be left out of the indictment has deprived the accused of a substantial right and subjects him to danger of being tried upon a charge for which he has not been indicted." *Ward v. Commonwealth*, 138 S.E.2d 293 (1964).

Practice Pointer

Given the limited information obtained by a bill of particulars, such motions are rarely filed in routine criminal cases because that information is usually clear in those cases. It is more likely that a defense attorney will seek a bill of particulars in a case in which the charges are either very serious, such as in a capital case, or very complex, such as in conspiracy or RICO prosecutions, and the attorney needs clarification of basic information about the charges.

B. Discovery of Exculpatory Evidence

By far, the largest area of contention and confusion between prosecutors and defense attorneys is the requirement set forth in *Brady v. Maryland*, 373 U.S. 83 (1963), and its progeny. Loosely stated, these cases hold that the prosecution has an obligation under the Due Process Clause to disclose exculpatory information. However, the parameters of this obligation are contested. The issue often arises when a defendant learns of withheld information after conviction.

Brady v. Maryland

373 U.S. 83 (1963).

Opinion of the Court by MR. JUSTICE DOUGLAS.

Petitioner and a companion, Boblit, were found guilty of murder in the first degree and sentenced to death. At his trial Brady took the stand and admitted his participation in the crime, but he claimed that Boblit did the actual killing. In his summation to the jury, Brady's counsel conceded that Brady was guilty of murder in the first degree, asking only that the jury return that verdict "without capital punishment." Prior to the trial petitioner's counsel had requested the prosecution to allow him to examine Boblit's extrajudicial statements. Several of those statements were shown to him; but one dated July 9, 1958, in which Boblit admitted the actual homicide, was withheld by the prosecution and did not come to petitioner's notice until after he had been tried, convicted, and sentenced, and after his conviction had been affirmed.

We agree with the Maryland Court of Appeals that suppression of this confession was a violation of the Due Process Clause of the Fourteenth Amendment. This ruling is an extension of *Mooney v. Holohan*, 294 U.S. 103, 112 (1935), where the Court ruled on what nondisclosure by a prosecutor violates due process: "if a State has contrived a conviction through the pretense of a trial which in truth is but used as a means of depriving a defendant of liberty through a deliberate deception of court and jury by the presentation of testimony known to be perjured. Such a contrivance by a State to procure the conviction and imprisonment of a defendant is as inconsistent with the rudimentary demands of justice as is the obtaining of a like result by intimidation." In *Pyle v. Kansas,* 317 U.S. 213, 215

Take Note

The undisclosed statement did not exculpate Brady of the crime of first-degree murder—he was an accomplice to the felony and so was liable for felony-murder even if Boblit did the killing. The statement was potentially relevant to whether he received a life sentence or capital punishment.

(1942), we phrased the rule in broader terms: "Petitioner's papers set forth allegations that his imprisonment resulted from perjured testimony, knowingly used by the State authorities to obtain his conviction, and from the deliberate suppression of evidence favorable to him. These allegations sufficiently charge a deprivation of rights guaranteed by the Federal Constitution, and, if proven, would entitle petitioner to release from his present custody." The Third Circuit has construed that statement in *Pyle v. Kansas* to mean that the "suppression of evidence favorable" to the accused was sufficient to amount to a denial of due process. In *Napue v. Illinois*, 360 U.S. 264, 269 (1959), we extended the test formulated in *Mooney* v. *Holohan* when we said: "The same result obtains when the State, although not soliciting false evidence, allows it to go uncorrected when it appears."

We hold that the suppression by the prosecution of evidence favorable to an accused upon request violates due process where the evidence is material to guilt or to punishment, irrespective of the good faith or bad faith of the prosecution. The principle of *Mooney* is not punishment of society for misdeeds of a prosecutor but avoidance of an unfair trial to the accused. Society wins not only when the guilty are convicted but when criminal trials are fair; our system of justice suffers when any accused is treated unfairly. An inscription on the walls of the Department of Justice states the proposition candidly: "The United States wins its point whenever justice is done its citizens in the courts." A prosecution that withholds evidence on demand of an accused which, if made available, would tend to exculpate him or reduce the penalty helps shape a trial that bears heavily on the defendant. That casts the prosecutor in the role of an architect of a proceeding that does not comport with standards of justice, even though his action is not "the result of guile."

Affirmed.

Take Note

In *Juniper v. Zook*, 876 F.3d 551 (4th Cir. 2017), defendant was convicted of murder based on the testimony of two witnesses who testified under a grant of immunity that they saw defendant in the home where the murders occurred with the murder weapon in his hands. Prosecutors failed to provide defendant with the report of a neighbor who was outside when she heard gun shots and saw a man run away from the scene of the crime. The neighbor, who could not identify defendant as the perpetrator based on a photo array, gave testimony that contradicted the other witnesses regarding the time of the gunshots, the getaway vehicle, and the perpetrator's description. The court concluded that the failure to disclose the statement "significantly undermined the reliability of the jury's conviction."

United States v. Bagley

473 U.S. 667 (1985).

JUSTICE BLACKMUN announced the judgment of the Court and delivered an opinion of the Court except as to Part III.

In *Brady v. Maryland*, 373 U.S. 83 (1963), this Court held that "the suppression by the prosecution of evidence favorable to an accused upon request violates due process where the evidence is material either to guilt or punishment." The issue in the present case

Hear It

You can hear the oral argument in *Bagley* at: http://www.oyez.org/cases/1980-1989/1984/1984_84_48.

concerns the standard of materiality to be applied in determining whether a conviction should be reversed because the prosecutor failed to disclose requested evidence that could have been used to impeach Government witnesses.

In October 1977, respondent Hughes Anderson Bagley was indicted in the Western District of Washington on 15 charges of violating federal narcotics and firearms statutes. On November 18, 24 days before trial, respondent filed a discovery motion. The sixth paragraph of that motion requested: "The names and addresses of witnesses that the government intends to call at trial. Also the prior criminal records of witnesses, and any deals, promises or inducements made to witnesses in exchange for their testimony." The Government's two principal witnesses at the trial were James F. O'Connor and Donald E. Mitchell. O'Connor and Mitchell were state law-enforcement officers employed by the Milwaukee Railroad as private security guards. Between April and June 1977, they assisted the federal Bureau of Alcohol, Tobacco and Firearms (ATF) in conducting an undercover investigation of respondent. The Government's response to the discovery motion did not disclose that any "deals, promises or inducements" had been made to O'Connor or Mitchell. In apparent reply to a request in the motion's ninth paragraph for "copies of all Jencks Act material," the Government produced a series of affidavits that O'Connor and Mitchell had signed between April 12 and May 4, 1977, while the undercover investigation was in progress. These affidavits recounted in detail the undercover dealings that O'Connor and Mitchell were having at the time with respondent. Each affidavit concluded with the statement, "I made this statement freely and voluntarily without any threats or rewards, or promises of reward having been made to me in return for it." Respondent waived his right to a jury trial and was tried before the court in December 1977. At the trial, O'Connor and Mitchell testified about both the firearms and the narcotics charges. On December 23, the court found respondent guilty on the narcotics charges, but not guilty on the firearms charges.

[In a subsequent *habeas corpus* action, the district court found that the prosecution had failed to disclose the existence of agreements with O'Connor and Mitchell to pay them for their testimony if it proved to be useful. These agreements would have provided impeachment material when O'Connor and Mitchell testified.] The District Court found beyond a reasonable doubt, however, that had the existence of the agreements been disclosed during trial, the disclosure would have had no effect upon its finding that the Government had proved beyond a reasonable doubt that respondent was guilty of the offenses for which he had been convicted. The District Court reasoned: Almost all of the testimony of both witnesses was devoted to the firearms charges in the indictment. Respondent was acquitted on those charges. The testimony of O'Connor and Mitchell concerning the narcotics charges was relatively very brief. On cross-examination, respondent's counsel did not seek to discredit their testimony as to the facts of distribution but rather sought to show that the controlled substances came from supplies that had been prescribed for respondent's personal use. The answers of O'Connor and Mitchell to this line of cross-examination tended to be favorable to respondent. Thus, the claimed impeachment evidence would not have been helpful to respondent and would not have affected the outcome of the trial. Accordingly, the District Court denied respondent's motion to vacate his sentence.

The holding in *Brady v. Maryland* requires disclosure only of evidence that is both favorable to the accused and "material either to guilt or to punishment." The *Brady* rule is based on the requirement of due process. Its purpose is not to displace the adversary system as the primary means by which truth is uncovered, but to ensure that a miscarriage of justice does not occur. Thus, the prosecutor is not required to deliver his entire file to defense counsel, but only to disclose evidence favorable to the accused that, if suppressed, would deprive the defendant of a fair trial. In *Brady* and *United States v. Agurs*, 427 U.S. 97 (1976), the prosecutor failed to disclose exculpatory evidence. In the present case, the prosecutor failed to disclose evidence that the defense might have used to impeach the Government's witnesses by showing bias or interest. Impeachment evidence, as well as exculpatory evidence, falls within the *Brady* rule. Such evidence is "evidence favorable to an accused," so that, if disclosed and used effectively, it may make the difference between conviction and acquittal. The constitutional error, if any, in this case was the Government's failure to assist the defense by disclosing information that might have been helpful in conducting the cross-examination. Such suppression of evidence amounts to a constitutional violation only if it deprives the defendant of a fair trial. Consistent with "our overriding concern with the justice of the finding of guilt," a constitutional error occurs, and the conviction must be reversed, only if the evidence is material in the sense that its suppression undermines confidence in the outcome of the trial.

It remains to determine the standard of materiality applicable to the nondisclosed evidence. *Agurs* distinguished three situations involving the discovery, after trial, of information favorable to the accused that had been known to the prosecution but unknown to the defense. The first situation was the prosecutor's knowing use of perjured testimony or, equivalently, the prosecutor's knowing failure to disclose that testimony used to convict the defendant was false. "A conviction obtained by the knowing use of perjured testimony is fundamentally unfair, and must be set aside if there is any reasonable likelihood that the false testimony could have affected the judgment of the jury." Although this rule is stated in terms that treat the knowing use of perjured testimony as error subject to harmless-error review, it may as easily be stated as a materiality standard under which the fact that testimony is perjured is considered material unless failure to disclose it would be harmless beyond a reasonable doubt. *Agurs* justified this standard of materiality on the ground that the knowing use of perjured testimony involves prosecutorial misconduct and, more importantly, involves "a corruption of the truth-seeking function of the trial process." At the other extreme is the situation in *Agurs*, where defendant does not make a *Brady* request and the prosecutor fails to disclose evidence favorable to the accused. The Court rejected a harmless-error rule, because under that rule every nondisclosure is treated as error, thus imposing on the prosecutor a constitutional duty to deliver his entire file to defense counsel. At the same time, the Court rejected a standard that would require the defendant to demonstrate that the evidence if disclosed probably would have resulted in acquittal: "If the standard applied to the usual motion for a new trial based on newly discovered evidence were the same when the evidence was in the State's possession as when it was found in a neutral source, there would be no special significance to the prosecutor's obligation to serve the cause of justice." The standard of materiality applicable in the absence of a specific *Brady* request is therefore stricter than the harmless-error standard but more lenient to the defense than the newly-discovered-evidence standard. The third situation identified by *Agurs* is where the defense makes a specific request and the prosecutor fails to disclose responsive evidence. The Court did not define the standard of materiality applicable in this situation, but suggested that the standard might be more lenient to the defense than in the situation in which the defense makes no request or only a general request: "When the prosecutor receives a specific and relevant request, the failure to make any response is seldom, if ever, excusable."

The Court has relied on and reformulated the *Agurs* standard for the materiality of undisclosed evidence in two subsequent cases arising outside the *Brady* context. In neither case did the Court's discussion of the *Agurs* standard distinguish among the three situations described in *Agurs*. In *Strickland v. Washington*, 466 U.S. 668 (1984), the Court held that a new trial must be granted when evidence is not introduced because of the incompetence of counsel only if "there is a reasonable probability that, but for counsel's unprofessional errors, the result of the proceeding would have been different." The *Strickland* Court defined a "reasonable probability" as "a probability sufficient to undermine confidence in the outcome." We find the *Strickland* formulation of the *Agurs* test for materiality sufficiently flexible to cover the "no request," "general request," and "specific request" cases of prosecutorial failure to disclose evidence favorable to the accused: The evidence is material only if there is a reasonable probability that, had the evidence been disclosed to the defense, the result of the proceeding would have been different. A "reasonable probability" is a probability sufficient to undermine confidence in the outcome.

The Government suggests that a materiality standard more favorable to the defendant reasonably might be adopted in specific request cases. The Government notes that an incomplete response to a specific request not only deprives the defense of certain evidence, but also has the effect of representing to the defense that the evidence does not exist. In reliance on this misleading representation, the defense might abandon lines of independent investigation, defenses, or trial strategies that it otherwise would have pursued. We agree that the prosecutor's failure to respond fully to a *Brady* request may impair the adversary process in this manner. The more specifically the defense requests certain evidence, thus putting the prosecutor on notice of its value, the more reasonable it is for the defense to assume from the nondisclosure that the evidence does not exist, and to make pretrial and trial decisions on the basis of this assumption. This possibility of impairment does not necessitate a different standard of materiality, however, for under the *Strickland* formulation the reviewing court may consider directly any adverse effect that the prosecutor's failure to respond might have had on the preparation or presentation of the defendant's case. The reviewing court should assess the possibility that such effect might have occurred in light of the totality of the circumstances and with an awareness of the difficulty of reconstructing in a post-trial proceeding the course that the defense and the trial would have taken had the defense not been misled by the prosecutor's incomplete response.

There is a significant likelihood that the prosecutor's response to respondent's discovery motion misleadingly induced defense counsel to believe that O'Connor and Mitchell could not be impeached on the basis of bias or interest arising from inducements offered by the Government. Defense counsel asked the prosecutor to disclose any inducements that had been made to witnesses, and the prosecutor failed to disclose that the possibility of a reward had been held out to O'Connor and Mitchell if the information they supplied led to "the accomplishment of the objective sought to be obtained to the satisfaction of the Government." This possibility of a reward gave O'Connor and Mitchell a direct, personal stake in respondent's conviction. The fact that the stake was not guaranteed through a promise or binding contract, but was expressly contingent on the Government's satisfaction with the end result, served only to strengthen any incentive to testify falsely in order to secure a conviction.

The District Court found beyond a reasonable doubt that, had the information that the Government held out the possibility of reward to its witnesses been disclosed, the result of the criminal prosecution would not have been different. If this finding were sustained, the information would be immaterial even under the standard of materiality applicable to the prosecutor's knowing use of perjured testimony. Although the holding of the Court of Appeals was that the nondisclosure in this case required automatic reversal, the Court of Appeals "disagreed" with the District Court's finding of harmless error. In particular, the Court of Appeals disagreed with the factual premise on which this finding expressly was based. The District Court reasoned that O'Connor's and Mitchell's testimony was exculpatory on the narcotics charges. The Court of Appeals concluded, after reviewing the record, that O'Connor's and Mitchell's testimony was in fact inculpatory on those charges. Accordingly, we reverse the judgment of the Court of Appeals and remand to that court for a determination whether there is a reasonable probability that, had the inducement offered by the Government to O'Connor and Mitchell been disclosed to the defense, the result of the trial would have been different.

JUSTICE WHITE, with whom THE CHIEF JUSTICE and JUSTICE REHNQUIST join, concurring in part and concurring in the judgment.

"Evidence is material only if there is a reasonable probability that, had the evidence been disclosed to the defense, the result of the proceeding would have been different." Given the flexibility of the standard and the inherently factbound nature of the cases to which it will be applied, I see no reason to attempt to elaborate on the relevance to the inquiry of the specificity of the defense's request for disclosure, either generally or with respect to this case. I would hold simply that the proper standard is one of reasonable probability and the Court of Appeals' failure to apply this standard necessitates reversal.

JUSTICE MARSHALL, with whom JUSTICE BRENNAN joins, dissenting.

When the Government withholds from a defendant evidence that might impeach the prosecution's only witnesses, that failure to disclose cannot be deemed harmless error. Once the prosecutor suspects that certain information might have favorable implications for the defense, either because it is potentially exculpatory or relevant to credibility, I see no reason why he should not be required to disclose it. Favorable evidence indisputably enhances the truth-seeking process at trial. And it is the job of the defense, not the prosecution, to decide whether and in what way to use arguably favorable evidence. In addition, to require disclosure of all evidence that might reasonably be considered favorable to the defendant would have the precautionary effect of assuring that no information of potential consequence is mistakenly overlooked. A clear rule of this kind, coupled with a presumption in favor of disclosure, also would facilitate the prosecutor's admittedly difficult task by removing a substantial amount of unguided discretion.

I cannot agree with the Court that the due process right to favorable evidence recognized in *Brady* was intended to become entangled in prosecutorial determinations of the likelihood that particular information would affect the outcome of trial. I recognize that a failure to divulge favorable information should not result in reversal in all cases. The benefits of disclosure may at times be tempered by the state's legitimate desire to avoid retrial when error has been harmless. However, in making the determination of harmlessness, I would apply our normal constitutional error test and reverse unless it is clear beyond a reasonable doubt that the withheld evidence would not have affected the outcome of the trial.

JUSTICE STEVENS, dissenting.

Food for Thought

For years, defense attorneys have maintained that *Bagley's* materiality standard is strictly for appellate courts to apply in determining whether a *Brady* violation warranting reversal has occurred, and that at the trial level the question is simply whether the information is favorable to the defense. In other words, materiality cannot be known before all of the evidence is in, but only on a review of the complete record on appeal. As one appellate court explained, at the trial level "no one has the gift of prophecy. To argue that the [trial] court [or prosecutor] can apply a material-to-outcome test before trial is to argue a contradiction." *Lewis v. United States*, 408 A.2d 303, 307 (D.C. 1979). *See* Discussion Point f below for some views of current Justices on the issue.

Two situations in which the rule applies are those demonstrating the prosecution's knowing use of perjured testimony, and the prosecution's suppression of favorable evidence specifically requested by the defendant. In both situations, the prosecution's deliberate nondisclosure constitutes constitutional error—the conviction must be set aside if the suppressed or perjured evidence was "material" and there was "any reasonable likelihood" that it "could have affected" the outcome of the trial. The combination of willful prosecutorial suppression of evidence and the potential "corruption of the truth-seeking function of the trial process" requires that result. Suppression in response to a request is far more serious than mere nondisclosure of evidence in which the defense has expressed no particular interest.

Food for Thought

Assume you are Bagley's defense attorney on remand. Assume that O'Connor and Mitchell were the only prosecution witnesses linking Bagley to the narcotics. Articulate your argument to the Court that there is a reasonable probability that the outcome of the trial would have been different if you had known of the impeaching evidence. What difficulties are there in making this argument? Now articulate your argument under the dissent's desired harmless error standard—that the prosecution cannot prove beyond a reasonable doubt that the outcome would not have been different with the impeaching evidence. Which standard makes more sense and why? What values does each standard serve?

Turner v. United States

582 U.S. 313 (2017).

JUSTICE BREYER delivered the opinion of the Court.

In *Brady v. Maryland*, 373 U.S. 83 (1963), this Court held that the government violates the Constitution's Due Process Clause "if it withholds evidence that is favorable to the defense and material to the defendant's guilt or punishment." *Smith v. Cain*, 565 U.S. 73, 75 (2012). In 1985 petitioners were tried together for the kidnaping, armed robbery, and murder of Catherine Fuller. Long after petitioners' convictions became final, it emerged that the Government possessed evidence that it failed to disclose to the defense. The question is whether that evidence was "material" under *Brady*. The D.C. Superior Court, after a 16-day hearing, determined that the withheld evidence was not material. The D.C. Court of Appeals reached the same conclusion, and affirmed. We reach the same conclusion.

A grand jury indicted the seven petitioners—Timothy Catlett, Russell Overton, Levy Rouse, Kelvin Smith, Charles Turner, Christopher Turner, and Clifton Yarborough—and several others for the kidnaping, robbery, and murder of Catherine Fuller. The evidence showed that on October 1, 1984, at around 4:30 p.m., Catherine Fuller left her home to go shopping. At around 6 p.m., William Freeman, a street vendor, found Fuller's body inside an alley garage between Eighth and Ninth Street N. E., just a few blocks from Fuller's home. Fuller had been robbed, severely beaten, and sodomized with an object that caused extensive internal injuries. The Government advanced the theory that Fuller had been attacked in the alley by a large group of individuals, including petitioners; codefendants Steve Webb, Alfonso Harris, and Felicia Ruffin; as well as by Calvin Alston and Harry Bennett. The Government's evidentiary centerpiece consisted of testimony by Alston and Bennett, who confessed to participating in the offense and who cooperated with the Government in return for leniency. Although the testimony of Alston and Bennett diverged on minor details, it was consistent in stating that, and describing how, Fuller was attacked by a sizable group of individuals, including petitioners and themselves.

> **FYI**
>
> Before *Bagley*, in *Giglio v. United States*, 405 U.S. 150 (1972), the Court made clear that *Brady* applies not only to evidence that affirmatively helps show that the defendant is innocent of the crime but also to evidence which merely weakens or undermines the strength of the prosecution's case, such as impeachment evidence. In *Giglio*, the impeachment evidence was a deal between the prosecution and its main witness—that the witness would receive favorable treatment on other charges in return for his testimony. *Bagley* then held that all impeachment evidence was subject to disclosure, not just deals with prosecution witnesses.

Alston testified that at about 4:10 p.m. on the day of the murder, he arrived in a park on H Street. He found a group of people there. It included petitioners Levy Rouse, Russell Overton, Christopher Turner, Charles Turner, Kelvin Smith, Clifton Yarborough, and Timothy Catlett, as well as several codefendants and others. Those in the group were talking and singing while Catlett was banging out a beat. Alston suggested "getting paid" by robbing someone. Catlett, Overton, Rouse, Smith, Charles Turner, Christopher Turner, Yarborough, and several others agreed. Alston pointed at Catherine Fuller, who was walking on the other side of H Street near the corner of H and Eighth Streets. Those in the group were "game for getting paid." Alston, Rouse, Yarborough, and Charles Turner crossed H Street moving toward Eighth Street and followed Fuller down Eighth Street. The rest of the group crossed H Street and moved toward Ninth Street. When Alston's group approached Fuller, Charles Turner shoved her into an alley that runs between Eighth and Ninth Streets. Charles Turner, Rouse, and Alston began punching Fuller. They were soon joined by Christopher Turner, Smith, and others. All of them continued to hit and kick Fuller until she fell to the ground. Rouse and Charles Turner then carried Fuller to the center of the alley and dropped her in front of a garage located at the point where the alley joins another, perpendicular alley that runs toward I Street. Someone dragged Fuller into the garage. Alston, Rouse, Charles Turner, Overton, Yarborough, and Catlett followed. Others stood outside. Members of the group tore Fuller's clothes off and struggled over her change purse. Overton and Charles Turner then held Fuller's legs, and Alston, Catlett, Harris, and Yarborough stood around her while Rouse sodomized her with a foot-long pipe. Shortly after, the group dispersed and left the alley.

Harry Bennett's testimony was similar. Bennett also described a group attack. He had gone to the H Street park, where he saw Rouse, Overton, Christopher Turner, Smith, Catlett, and others gathered. Alston was talking to the group about "getting paid" and said "let's go get that lady." At that point Alston, Rouse, Overton, and Webb crossed H Street and approached Fuller, while Catlett, Christopher Turner, Charles Turner, and Harris followed in a separate group. Bennett added that he went to the corner of Eighth and H Streets to watch for police. He then went into the alley and joined the group in kicking and beating Fuller. He testified that at least 12 people were there, with some beating Fuller and others watching or picking up her jewelry. Overton then dragged Fuller into the garage, and Bennett, Rouse, Christopher Turner, Charles Turner, Catlett, Smith, Harris, and Webb followed, as did some "girls." Alston and Steve Webb held Fuller's legs, and Rouse sodomized her with a pole. The group then dispersed.

The Government presented several other witnesses who corroborated aspects of Alston's and Bennett's testimony, including the fact that Fuller was attacked by a group. Melvin Montgomery testified that he was in the H Street park on the afternoon of the murder. He saw Overton, Catlett, Rouse, Charles Turner, and others gathered there. The group was being noisy and singing a song about needing money. Somebody then said they were "going to get that one," and Montgomery saw that Overton was pointing to a woman standing on the corner of Eighth Street. Overton, Catlett, Rouse, Charles Turner, and others crossed H Street. Some headed toward Eighth Street while others went toward Ninth Street. Montgomery did not follow them. Maurice Thomas, then 14 years old, testified that he witnessed the attack. Thomas lived in the neighborhood and knew many of the defendants. As he was walking home, he glanced down the Eighth Street alley and saw a group surrounding Fuller. Thomas saw Catlett pat Fuller down and then hit her. He then saw everyone in the group join in hitting her. Thomas said he knew Catlett, Yarborough, Rouse, Charles Turner, Christopher Turner, and Smith and recognized them in the group. Thomas heard Fuller calling for help. He ran home where he found his aunt, who told him not to tell anyone what he saw. Later that day, Thomas saw Catlett at a corner store, and heard Catlett say to someone that they "had to kill her" because "she spotted someone he was with." On the afternoon of the murder, Carrie Eleby and Linda Jacobs were looking for petitioner Smith, who was Eleby's boyfriend, near the corner of H and Eighth Streets. They heard screams coming from where a "gang of boys" was beating somebody near the garage in the alley. Eleby and Jacobs approached the group. Eleby recognized Christopher Turner, Smith, Catlett, Rouse, Overton, Alston, and Webb kicking Fuller while Yarborough stood nearby. Both Eleby and Jacobs testified that they saw Rouse sodomize Fuller with a pole. Eleby added that Overton held Fuller's legs. Finally, the Government played a videotape of a recorded statement that Yarborough, one of the petitioners, had given to detectives approximately two months after the murder. Names were redacted. The video shows Yarborough describing in detail how he was part of a large group that forced Fuller into the alley, jointly robbed and assaulted her, and dragged her into the garage.

None of the defendants testified, nor did any of them try to rebut the prosecution witnesses' claim that Fuller was killed in a group attack. Rather, each petitioner pursued what was essentially a "not me, maybe them" defense, namely, that he was not part of the group that attacked Fuller. Each tried to establish this defense by impeaching witnesses who had placed that particular petitioner at the scene. Some provided evidence that Eleby and Jacobs had used PCP the day of Fuller's murder. Some tried to establish alibis for the time of Fuller's death. The jury convicted all seven petitioners, along with codefendant Steve Webb (who subsequently died). The jury acquitted codefendants Alfonso Harris and Felicia Ruffin. On appeal, the D.C. Court of Appeals affirmed petitioners' convictions, though it remanded for resentencing. The trial court resentenced petitioners to the same amount of prison time.

The *Brady Claims*. In 2010, petitioners pursued postconviction proceedings to vacate their convictions or be granted a new trial. After petitioners' convictions became final, it emerged that the Government possessed certain evidence that it had withheld from the defense at the time of trial. Petitioners discovered other withheld evidence in their review of the trial prosecutor's case file, which the Government turned over to petitioners in the course of the postconviction proceedings. Petitioners contended that the withheld evidence was both favorable and material, entitling them to relief under *Brady*. The D.C. Superior Court rejected those claims, finding that "none of the undisclosed information was material." The D.C. Court of Appeals affirmed.

At issue were the following seven specific pieces of evidence: 1. *The identity of James McMillan.* Freeman, the vendor who discovered Fuller's body in the alley garage, testified at trial that, while he was waiting for police to arrive, he saw two men run into the alley and stop near the garage for about five minutes before running away when an officer approached. One of the men had a bulge under his coat. Early in the trial, codefendant Harris' counsel had requested the identity of the two men to confirm that her client was not one of them. But the Government refused to disclose the men's identity. In their postconviction review of the prosecutor's files, petitioners learned that Freeman had identified the two men he saw in the alley as James McMillan and Gerald Merkerson. McMillan lived in a house which opens in the back onto a connecting alley. In the weeks following Fuller's murder, but before petitioners' trial, McMillan was arrested for beating and robbing two women in the neighborhood. Neither attack included a sexual assault. Separately, petitioners learned that seven years after petitioners' trial, McMillan had robbed, sodomized, and murdered a young woman in an alley. 2. *The interview with Willie Luchie.* The prosecutor's notes also recorded an undisclosed interview with Willie Luchie, who told the prosecutor that he and three others walked through the alley on their way to an H Street liquor store between 5:30 and 5:45 p.m. on the evening of the murder. As the group walked by the garage, Luchie "heard several groans" and "remembers the doors to the garage being closed." Another person in the group recalled "hearing some moans," while the other two persons did not recall hearing anything unusual. The group continued walking without looking into the garage or otherwise investigating the source of the sounds. They did not see McMillan or any other person in the alley when they passed through. 3. *The interviews with Ammie Davis.* Undisclosed notes written by a police officer and the prosecutor refer to two interviews with Ammie Davis, who had been arrested for disorderly conduct a few weeks after Fuller's murder. Davis initially told a police investigator that she had seen another individual, James Blue, beat Fuller to death in the alley. Shortly thereafter, she said she only saw Blue grab Fuller and push her into the alley. Davis also said that a girlfriend, whom she did not name, accompanied her. She promised to call the investigator with more details, but she did not do. About 9 months later (after petitioners were indicted but 11 weeks before trial), a prosecutor learned of the investigator's notes and interviewed Davis. The prosecutor's notes state that Davis did not provide any more details, except to say that the girlfriend who accompanied her was nicknamed "Shorty." About two months later, shortly before petitioners' trial, Blue murdered Davis in an unrelated drug dispute. During the post-conviction evidentiary hearing, the prosecutor who interviewed Davis testified that he did not disclose Davis' statement because she acted "playful" and "not serious" during the interview and he found her to be "totally incredible." Additionally, the prosecutor stated that he knew Davis had previously falsely accused Blue of a different murder, and on another occasion had falsely accused a different individual of a different murder. 4. *Impeachment of Kaye Porter and Carrie Eleby.* Kaye Porter accompanied Eleby during an initial interview with homicide detectives. Porter agreed with Eleby that she had also heard Alston state that he was involved in robbing Fuller. An undisclosed prosecutorial note states that in a later interview with detectives, Porter stated that she did not actually recall hearing Alston's statement and just went along with what Eleby said. The note also states that Eleby likewise admitted that she had lied about Porter being present during Alston's statement and had asked Porter to support her. 5. *Impeachment of Carrie Eleby.* A prosecutor's undisclosed note revealed that Eleby said she had been high on PCP during a January 9, 1985, meeting with investigators. 6. *Impeachment of Linda Jacobs.* An undisclosed note of an interview with Linda Jacobs said that the detective had "questioned her hard," and that she had "vacillated" about what she saw. The prosecutor recalled that the detective "kept raising his voice" and was "smacking his hand on the desk" during the interview. 7. *Impeachment of Maurice Thomas.* An undisclosed note of an interview with Maurice Thomas' aunt stated that she "does not recall Maurice ever telling her anything such as this."

The Government does not contest petitioners' claim that the withheld evidence was "favorable to the accused, either because it is exculpatory, or because it is impeaching." *Strickler v. Greene*, 527 U.S. 263, 281 (1999). Neither does the Government contest petitioners' claim that it "suppressed" the evidence, "either willfully or inadvertently." It does concede that the *Brady* rule's "overriding concern is with the justice of the finding of guilt," *United States v. Bagley*, 473 U.S. 667, 678 (1985), and that the Government's "interest in a criminal prosecution is not that it shall win a case, but that justice shall be done," *Kyles v. Whitley*, 514 U.S. 419, 439 (1995). The Government assured the Court that subsequent to petitioners' trial, it has adopted a "generous policy of discovery" in criminal cases under which it discloses any "information that a defendant might wish to use." Petitioners and the Government do contest the materiality of the undisclosed *Brady* information. "Evidence is 'material' within the meaning of *Brady* when there is a reasonable probability that, had the evidence been disclosed, the result of the proceeding would have been different." *Cone v. Bell*, 556 U.S. 449, 469 (2009). "A 'reasonable probability' of a different result" is one in which the suppressed evidence "undermines confidence in the outcome of the trial." *Kyles, supra,* at 434. In other words, petitioners are entitled to a new trial only if they "establish the prejudice necessary to satisfy the 'materiality' inquiry." *Strickler, supra,* at 282.

The issue before us is legally simple but factually complex. We must examine the trial record, "evaluate" the withheld evidence "in the context of the entire record," and determine in light of that examination whether "there is a reasonable probability that, had the evidence been disclosed, the result of the proceeding would have been different." We agree with the lower courts that there was no such reasonable probability. Petitioners' main argument is that, had they known about McMillan's identity and

Luchie's statement, they could have challenged the Government's basic theory that Fuller was killed in a group attack. Petitioners contend that they could have raised an alternative theory, namely, that a single perpetrator (or two at most) had attacked Fuller. According to petitioners, the groans that Luchie and his companion heard when they walked through the alley between 5:30 and 5:45 p.m. suggest that the attack was taking place inside the garage at that moment. The fact that the garage was small and that Luchie's group saw no one in the alley could bolster a "single attacker" theory. Freeman's recollection that one garage door was open when he found Fuller's body at around 6 p.m., combined with Luchie's recollection that both doors were shut around 5:30 or 5:45 p.m., could suggest that one or two perpetrators were in the garage when Luchie walked by but left before Freeman arrived. McMillan's identity as one of the men Freeman saw enter the alley after Freeman discovered Fuller's body would have revealed McMillan's criminal convictions in the months before petitioners' trial. Petitioners argue that together, this evidence would have permitted the defense to knit together a theory that the group attack did not occur at all—and that it was actually McMillan, alone or with an accomplice, who murdered Fuller. They add that they could have used the investigators' failure to follow up on Ammie Davis' claim about James Blue, and the various pieces of withheld impeachment evidence, to suggest that an incomplete investigation had ended up accusing the wrong persons.

Considering the withheld evidence "in the context of the entire record," it is too little, too weak, or too distant from the main evidentiary points to meet *Brady's* standards. McMillan's guilt (or that of any other single, or near single, perpetrator) is inconsistent with petitioners' guilt only if there was no group attack. But a group attack was the very cornerstone of the Government's case. The witnesses may have differed on minor details, but virtually every witness agreed that Fuller was killed by a large group of perpetrators. The evidence was such that, even though petitioners knew that Freeman saw two men enter the alley after he discovered Fuller's body, that one appeared to have a bulky object hidden under his coat, and that both ran when the police arrived, none of the petitioners attempted to mount a defense that implicated those men as alternative perpetrators acting alone.

Is it reasonably probable that adding McMillan's identity, and Luchie's ambiguous statement that he heard groans but saw no one, could have led to a different result at trial? It is not. The problem for petitioners is that their current alternative theory would have had to persuade the jury that both Alston and Bennett falsely confessed to being active participants in a group attack that never occurred; that Yarborough falsely implicated himself in that group attack and, through coordinated effort or coincidence, gave a highly similar account of how it occurred; that Thomas, a disinterested witness who recognized petitioners when he happened upon the attack and heard Catlett refer to it later that night, wholly fabricated his story; that both Eleby and Jacobs likewise testified to witnessing a group attack that did not occur; and that

Montgomery in fact did not see petitioners and others, as a group, identify Fuller as a target and leave the park to rob her.

With respect to the undisclosed impeachment evidence, it was largely cumulative of impeachment evidence petitioners had used at trial. The jury heard multiple times about Eleby's frequent PCP use, including Eleby's own testimony that she and Jacobs had smoked PCP shortly before they witnessed Fuller's attack. It would not have surprised the jury to learn that Eleby used PCP on yet another occasion. Porter was a minor witness who was also impeached at trial with evidence about changes in her testimony over time, leaving little added significance to the note that she changed her mind about having agreed with Eleby's claims. The jury was also well aware of Jacobs' vacillation, as she was impeached on the stand with her shifting stories about what she witnessed. Knowledge that a detective raised his voice during an interview with her would have added little more. Nor do we see how the note about the statement by Thomas' aunt could have mattered much, given the facts that neither side chose to call the aunt as a witness and that the jury already knew, from Thomas' testimony, that his aunt had told him not to tell anyone what he saw. As for James Blue, petitioners argue that the investigators' delay in following up on Ammie Davis' statement could have led the jury to doubt the thoroughness of the investigation. But this likelihood is seriously undercut by notes about Davis' demeanor and lack of detail, and by her prior false accusations that Blue committed a different murder and that yet another person committed yet a different murder.

We do not suggest that impeachment evidence is immaterial with respect to a witness who has already been impeached with other evidence. We conclude only that in the context of this trial, with respect to these witnesses, the cumulative effect of the withheld evidence is insufficient to "undermine confidence" in the jury's verdict. On the basis of our review, we agree that there is not a "reasonable probability" that the withheld evidence would have changed the outcome of petitioners' trial. The judgment of the D.C. Court of Appeals, accordingly, is affirmed.

It is so ordered.

JUSTICE KAGAN, with whom JUSTICE GINSBURG joins, dissenting.

The Government knew about but withheld the evidence of an alternative perpetrator—and so prevented the defendants from coming together to press that theory of the case. If the Government's non-disclosure was material, this Court's decision in *Brady* demands a new trial. In light of the evidence, the majority argues, the transformed defense stood little chance of persuading a juror to vote to acquit. That conclusion is not indefensible: The Government put on quite a few witnesses who said that the defendants committed the crime. But the majority gets the answer wrong. With the undisclosed evidence, the whole tenor of the trial would have changed. Rather than relying on a "not me, maybe them" defense, defendants would have relentlessly impeached the Government's (thoroughly impeachable) witnesses and offered the jurors a way to view the crime in a different light. That could well have flipped one or more jurors—which is all *Brady* requires.

The majority and I agree on the exculpatory or impeaching evidence suppressed in this case. We also agree that such evidence ought to be disclosed to defendants as a matter of course. Turning over exculpatory materials is a core responsibility of all prosecutors—whose professional interest and obligation is not to win cases but to ensure justice is done. Finally, we agree on the legal standard by which to assess the materiality of undisclosed evidence for purposes of applying the constitutional rule: Courts are to ask whether there is a "reasonable probability" that disclosure of the evidence would have led to a different outcome—*i.e.*, an acquittal or hung jury rather than a conviction. I part ways with the majority in applying that standard to the evidence withheld in this case. That evidence falls into three basic categories. Taken together, the materials would have recast the trial significantly—so as to "undermine confidence" in the guilty verdicts reached in their absence. *Kyles*, 514 U.S., at 434.

First, the Government suppressed information identifying a possible alternative perpetrator. Defendants knew that, shortly before the police arrived, witnesses had observed two men acting suspiciously near the alleyway garage where Catherine Fuller's body was found. They did not know—because the Government never told them—that a witness had identified one of those men as James McMillan. With that information, defendants would have discovered that in the weeks following Fuller's murder, McMillan assaulted and robbed two other women of comparable age in the same neighborhood. Using *that* information, defendants would have united around a common defense. They would have pointed their fingers at McMillan (rather than at each other), arguing that he committed Fuller's murder as part of a string of similar crimes. Second, the Government suppressed witness statements suggesting that one or two perpetrators—not a large group—carried out the attack. Those statements were given by two individuals who walked past the garage around the time of Fuller's death. They told the police that they heard groans coming from inside the garage; and one remarked that the garage's doors were closed. Introducing that evidence would have sown doubt about the Government's group-attack narrative, because that many people couldn't have fit inside the small garage. The questions thus raised would have further supported the defendants' theory that McMillan (and perhaps an accomplice) had committed the murder. Third and finally, the Government suppressed a raft of evidence discrediting its investigation and impeaching its witnesses. Undisclosed files, for example, showed that the police took more than nine months to look into a witness's claim that a man named James Blue had murdered Fuller. Evidence of that kind of negligence could easily have led jurors to wonder about the competence of the police work done in the case. Other withheld documents revealed that one of the Government's main witnesses was high on PCP when she met with investigators to identify participants in the crime—and that she also encouraged a friend to lie to the police to support her story. Using that sort of information, defendants could have undercut the Government's witnesses—even while presenting their own account of the murder.

The majority argues that "none of the accused attempted to mount an alternative-perpetrator defense" and that such a defense would have challenged "the very cornerstone of the Government's case." The defendants didn't offer an alternative-perpetrator defense because the Government prevented them from learning what made it credible: that one of the men seen near the garage had a record of assaulting and robbing middle-aged women, and that witnesses would back up the theory that only one or two individuals had committed the murder. Moreover, that defense had game-changing potential exactly *because* it challenged the cornerstone of the Government's case. Without the withheld evidence, defendants had little choice but to accept the Government's framing of the crime as a group attack—and argue only that *he* wasn't there. That meant defendants often worked at cross-purposes. Each defendant not identified by a Government witness sought to bolster that witness's credibility, no matter the harm to his co-defendants. Credible alternative-perpetrator evidence would have allowed the defendants to escape this cycle of mutually assured destruction. By enabling defendants to jointly attack the Government's "cornerstone" theory, the withheld evidence would have reframed the case presented to the jury.

The majority claims, an alternative-perpetrator defense would have had no realistic chance of changing the outcome because the Government had ample evidence of a group attack, including five witnesses who testified that they had participated in it or seen it happen. But the Government's case wasn't the slam-dunk the majority suggests. No physical evidence tied any of the defendants to the crime—a highly surprising fact if, as the Government claimed, more than ten people carried out a spur-of-the-moment, rampage-like attack in a confined space. The Government's five eyewitnesses had some serious credibility deficits. Two had been charged as defendants, and agreed to testify only in exchange for favorable plea deals. Two admitted they were high on PCP at the time. (one was also high when she later met with police to identify the culprits.) One was an eighth-grader whose own aunt contradicted parts of his trial testimony. Even in the absence of an alternative account of the crime, the jury took more than a week—and many dozens of votes—to reach its final verdict. Had defendants offered a unified counter-narrative, based on the withheld evidence, one or more jurors could well have concluded that the Government had not proved its case beyond a reasonable doubt. The Government got the case it most wanted—the one in which the defendants, each in an effort to save himself, formed something of a circular firing squad. The Government avoided the case it most feared—the one in which the defendants acted jointly to show that a man known to assault women like Fuller committed her murder. The difference between the two cases lay in the Government's files—evidence of obvious relevance that prosecutors nonetheless chose to suppress. I think it could have mattered to the trial's outcome. For that reason, I respectfully dissent.

Points for Discussion

a. Prosecutorial Duty to Seek Evidence from Prosecution Team

In *Kyles v. Whitley*, <u>514 U.S. 419 (1995)</u>, the Court clarified that the duty to turn over exculpatory evidence to the defense encompasses a duty to actively seek out any such evidence from the extended members of the prosecution "team," *i.e.*, "others acting on the government's behalf in the case, including the police." In *Kyles*, the prosecution failed to learn of exculpatory evidence in the hands of the police who investigated the case. While the state argued that the prosecution should not be held responsible for exculpatory evidence the police did not disclose to it, the Court responded, "any argument for excusing a prosecutor from disclosing what he does not happen to know about boils down to a plea to substitute the police for the prosecutor, and even for the courts themselves, as the final arbiters of the government's obligation to ensure fair trials."

b. Disclosure of Confidential Information

Defendant's right to *Brady* evidence generally overcomes statutory rules of privilege or confidentiality. *See Davis v. Alaska*, 415 U.S. 308 (1974) (withholding of presumptively confidential juvenile criminal record violated defendant's Confrontation Clause right to impeach the witness with the record); *Pennsylvania v. Ritchie*, 480 U.S. 39 (1987) (holding that, while a criminal defendant charged with child abuse cannot conduct an unsupervised search of child welfare agency confidential files to find exculpatory evidence, defendant could request specific information, and the trial court could decide the exculpatory value of the evidence in chambers); *Roviaro v. United States*, 353 U.S. 53 (1957) (establishing an exception to the general rule against disclosure of an informant's identity, holding that "where the disclosure of an informer's identity is relevant and helpful to the defense of an accused, or is essential to a fair determination of a cause, the privilege of nondisclosure must give way.")

c. Disclosure of Inadmissible Evidence

In *Wood v. Bartholmew*, 526 U.S. 1 (1995), the Court held that the failure to disclose a polygraph test showing that a prosecution witness had lied did not have to be disclosed under *Brady* because the polygraph test results would have been inadmissible at trial. Since *Wood*, lower courts have divided over whether all inadmissible evidence must automatically be excluded from *Brady* analysis. In *Commonwealth v. Willis*, 46 A.3d 648 (Pa. 2012), the Pennsylvania Supreme Court summarized the division among the lower courts as involving three approaches: some hold that inadmissible evidence is immaterial as a matter of law. *See Hoke v. Netherland*, 92 F.3d 1350 (4th Cir. 1996); *State v. Pena*, 353 S.W.3d 797 (Tex. Crim. App. 2011); others hold that evidence that is inadmissible at trial may be material under *Brady* if it would lead to admissible evidence. *See, e.g., United States v. Gil*, 297 F.3d 93 (2d Cir. 2002); *United States v. Sudikoff*, 36 F. Supp. 2d 1196 (C.D. Cal. 1999); a third group would treat the admissibility of derivative evidence as simply one factor to consider in the totality of the circumstances regarding whether the disclosure would have "put the whole case in such a different light as to undermine confidence in the verdict." *See, e.g., United States v. Sipe*, 388 F.3d 471 (5th Cir. 2004). In *Willis*, a plurality of the Pennsylvania Supreme Court agreed on the third approach.

d. The *Bagley* Materiality Standard

In *Smith v. Cain*, 565 U.S. 73 (2012), a prosecutor withheld a police report that undermined its case. The police report had prior inconsistent statements of the sole eyewitness indicating he could not identify anyone from the killing. Although the *Smith* opinion is rather short and unexceptional, the oral argument was extremely illuminating on the issue of whether the materiality standard from *Bagley* should be applied in a trial or pretrial setting. In other words, if the prosecution has exculpatory evidence or information, can the prosecution nonetheless not disclose the evidence or information, taking the position that the evidence or information is not "material" under *Bagley*—that is, there is no reasonable probability that disclosure will alter the result of the proceeding? The Court has never decided this issue in a written opinion. In oral argument in *Smith*, however, members of the Court expressed their strong belief that the standard for disclosure at trial is not the standard for discerning error on appeal. The Justices were incredulous that the prosecutor's office argued that undisclosed exculpatory information, which was helpful to the defense, did not need to be disclosed because it was not "material" under *Bagley*. An excerpt from the oral argument demonstrates the Justices' view:

Hear It

To listen to the oral argument in *Smith*, go to: http://www.oyez.org/cases/2010-2019/2011/2011_10_8145.

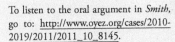

JUSTICE SOTOMAYOR: Tell me why [the witness's statements] didn't on their face constitute *Brady* materials that needed to be turned over. What's the legal principle that doesn't make them *Brady*?

[PROSECUTOR]: Because if they had been presented—if those statements had been presented to defense—or presented to a jury, the—the outcome would have remained the same. The jury—

JUSTICE GINSBURG: How do you know? How do you know? How can you possibly know? The jury is supposed to decide on the credibility of this witness.

JUSTICE KENNEDY: With all respect I think you misspoke when you—you were asked what is—the test for when material must be turned over. You said whether or not there's a reasonable probability—reasonable likelihood—pardon me—a reasonable probability that the result would have been different. That's the test for when there has been a *Brady* violation. You don't determine your *Brady* obligation by the test for the *Brady* violation. You're transposing two very different things. That's incorrect.

JUSTICE KAGAN: Did your office ever consider just confessing error in this case? You've had a bunch of time to think about it. You know?

[PROSECUTOR]: Your Honor, we believe that we have an argument that these statements are not material.

JUSTICE SCALIA:—you stop fighting as to whether it should be turned over? Of course, it should have been turned over. . . . Why don't you give that up?

e. Remedying *Brady* Violations

Just nine months before *Smith*, the Court considered another case of withheld exculpatory evidence from the same prosecutor's office—Orleans Parish District Attorney. In *Connick v. Thompson*, <u>563 U.S. 51 (2011)</u>, John Thompson sued Orleans Parish District Attorney Harry Connick, Sr. and his office alleging that their deliberate indifference to *Brady* violations and failure to train caused the *Brady* violation in his case which led to his spending 14 years on death row in solitary confinement. The jury awarded Thompson $14 million in damages. A deeply divided Court reversed. Justice Thomas wrote for the majority that, because Thompson did not allege a pattern of violations (although there had been four reversals of convictions from that office on *Brady* violations), and his theory of recovery was based on the egregiousness of one violation, the single incident by a rogue prosecutor was not the result of a failure to train. Justice Thomas indicated that prosecutors are given tools in law school and beyond to ensure they can follow *Brady*'s dictates. The four-member dissent disagreed that this was a one-violation case, cataloguing the many *Brady* violations, and arguing that Connick's office demonstrated a deliberate indifference to *Brady* violations and training. Harry Connick testified that he had "stopped reading law books and looking at opinions" after being elected District Attorney in 1974 and that there was a need for *Brady* training in the office. Not only did the dissent find training absent, and the understanding of *Brady* in the office deficient, it concluded that there is no requirement in law school or the Bar exam that future lawyers learn *Brady*.

f.   *Brady* & Guilty Pleas

In *United States v. Ruiz*, 536 U.S. 622 (2002), the Court held that prosecutors are not required to disclose impeachment information relating to informants or other witnesses before entering into a binding plea agreement with a criminal defendant. Although constitutional fair trial guarantees provide that defendants have the right to receive exculpatory impeachment material for trial, Justice Breyer stated that a defendant who pleads guilty foregoes a fair trial and various other constitutional guarantees. *See* Chapter 16, Guilty Pleas, *infra*.

g.   Post-Conviction Discovery of Exculpatory Evidence

There is a division of opinion regarding whether prosecutors must turn over exculpatory evidence that comes to light post-conviction. While the American Bar Association amended Model Rule 3.8 to require the disclosure of such evidence, some courts disagree. *See Commission for Lawyer Discipline v. Hanna*, 513 S.W.3d 175 (Tex. App. 2016).

Food for Thought

Which of the following pieces of information must be disclosed by the prosecution? A) The main homicide detective in a murder case was accused in another murder case of fabricating a police report. That accusation is being investigated by the police department's internal investigation unit; B) In a murder prosecution, a prosecution witness with an unrelated pending charge asks the prosecutor whether she can help him get out of that charge. The prosecutor responds that she can make no promises; C) A police report indicating that an eyewitness to the murder initially tells the police she cannot identify the killer. (Subsequently, she identifies the defendant and says she was just too scared the first time they asked.); D) Information that the police first pursued another suspect in the murder, but that investigation was dropped when the suspect's alibi was confirmed. Prosecutors are obligated to turn over favorable evidence in a timely manner. In deciding what is timely, consider the prosecutions' reasons for wanting to turn over the evidence later and the defense attorney's reasons for needing the evidence earlier to make effective use of it. Go back through the examples in this Hypo, assuming it is favorable, consider whether it would be "timely" to turn over that information just before trial.

Hypo 1: *Police Activity Sheet*

James Lambert was convicted and sentenced to death for the murder of two patrons during a robbery of Prince's Lounge. One of the main prosecution witnesses was Bernard Jackson who admitted being involved in the robbery and who named Lambert and Bruce Reese as his accomplices. The state failed to disclose a "police activity sheet" which noted that a photo display containing a photo of Lawrence Woodlock was shown to two witnesses to the robbery but no identification was made. The sheet noted that Woodlock was named as a co-defendant by Bernard Jackson. The defense argues that the sheet is exculpatory because it suggested that someone other than him or in addition to him committed the crime, and could have been used to further impeach Jackson who named Woodlock as an accomplice before he named Lambert. The state argues that the activity sheet contains nothing more than an "ambiguously worded notation" because Jackson was under investigation at the time for at least 13 armed robberies of bars and that he was more likely to name Woodlock as a codefendant in one of those other robberies, considering the police never pursued Woodlock for this charge. What do you think? See *Wetzel v. Lambert*, 565 U.S. 520 (2012).

Hypo 2: *Failure to Disclose*

A witness, who testified for the prosecution, lied when he testified that he had quit selling illegal drugs. However, the prosecution failed to reveal to the defense that the witness had lied. The witness' testimony was detailed, purported to convey first-hand information, and corroborated the testimony of other witnesses. However, the prosecution's witnesses were an assortment of "questionable characters," one of whom was named "Scotty Toohigh." Was there a *Brady* violation when the prosecution failed to reveal that defendants had lied? See *United States v. Walter*, 870 F.3d 622 (7th Cir. 2017).

C. Preservation of Evidence

Under normal circumstances, the duty to disclose evidence encompasses the duty to preserve evidence once it comes within the custody and control of the government. However, what should be the consequences of the government's failure to meet its preservation responsibility.

Arizona v. Youngblood

488 U.S. 51 (1988).

CHIEF JUSTICE REHNQUIST delivered the opinion of the Court.

Respondent Larry Youngblood was convicted by a Pima County, Arizona, jury of child molestation, sexual assault, and kidnaping. The Arizona Court of Appeals reversed his conviction on the ground that the State had failed to preserve semen samples from the victim's body and clothing. We granted certiorari

Hear It

You can hear the oral argument in *Youngblood* at: http://www.oyez.org/cases/1980-1989/1988/1988_86_1904.

to consider the extent to which the Due Process Clause of the Fourteenth Amendment requires the State to preserve evidentiary material that might be useful to a criminal defendant.

On October 29, 1983, David L., a 10-year-old boy, attended a church service with his mother. After he left the service at about 9:30 p.m., the boy went to a carnival behind the church, where he was abducted by a middle-aged man of medium height and weight. The assailant drove the boy to a secluded area near a ravine and molested him. He then took the boy to an unidentified, sparsely furnished house where he sodomized the boy four times. Afterwards, the assailant tied the boy up while he went outside to start his car. Once the assailant started the car, albeit with some difficulty, he returned to the house and again sodomized the boy. The assailant then sent the boy to the bathroom to wash up before he returned him to the carnival. He threatened to kill the boy if he told anyone about the attack. The entire ordeal lasted about 1½ hours. After the boy made his way home, his mother took him to Kino Hospital. At the hospital, a physician treated the boy for rectal injuries. The physician also used a "sexual assault kit" to collect evidence of the attack. The Tucson Police Department provided such kits to all hospitals in Pima County for use in sexual assault cases. Under standard procedure, the victim of a sexual assault was taken to a hospital, where a physician used the kit to collect evidence. The kit included paper to collect saliva samples, a tube for obtaining a blood sample, microscopic slides for making smears, a set of Q-Tip-like swabs, and a medical examination report. The physician used the swab to collect samples from the boy's rectum and mouth. He then made a microscopic slide of the samples. The doctor also obtained samples of the boy's saliva, blood, and hair. The physician did not examine the samples. The police placed the kit in a secure refrigerator at the police station. At the hospital, the police also collected the boy's underwear and T-shirt. This clothing was not refrigerated or frozen. Nine days after the attack, on November 7, 1983, the police asked the boy to pick out his assailant from a photographic lineup. The boy identified respondent as the assailant.

Respondent was not located by the police until four weeks later; he was arrested on December 9, 1983.

On November 8, 1983, Edward Heller, a police criminologist, examined the sexual assault kit. He testified that he followed standard department procedure, which was to examine the slides and determine whether sexual contact had occurred. After he determined that such contact had occurred, the criminologist did not perform any other tests, although he placed the assault kit back in the refrigerator. He testified that tests to identify blood group substances were not routinely conducted during the initial examination of an assault kit and in only about half of all cases in any event. He did not test the clothing at this time. Respondent was indicted on charges of child molestation, sexual assault, and kidnaping. The State moved to compel respondent to provide blood and saliva samples for comparison with the material gathered through the use of the sexual assault kit, but the trial court denied the motion on the ground that the State had not obtained a sufficiently large semen sample to make a valid comparison. The prosecutor then asked the State's criminologist to perform an ABO blood group test on the rectal swab sample in an attempt to ascertain the blood type of the boy's assailant. This test failed to detect any blood group substances. In January 1985, the police criminologist examined the boy's clothing for the first time. He found one semen stain on the boy's underwear and another on the rear of his T-shirt. The criminologist tried to obtain blood group substances from both stains using the ABO technique, but was unsuccessful. He also performed a P-30 protein molecule test on the stains, which indicated that only a small quantity of semen was present on the clothing; it was inconclusive as to the assailant's identity. The Tucson Police Department had just begun using this test, which was then used in slightly more than half of the crime laboratories in the country.

Respondent's principal defense was that the boy erred in identifying him as the perpetrator of the crime. In this connection, both a criminologist for the State and an expert witness for respondent testified as to what might have been shown by tests performed on the samples shortly after they were gathered, or by later tests performed on the samples from the boy's clothing had the clothing been properly refrigerated. The court instructed the jury that if they found the State had destroyed or lost evidence, they might "infer that the true fact is against the State's interest." The jury found respondent guilty as charged, but the Arizona Court of Appeals reversed the conviction. It stated that "when identity is an issue and the police permit the destruction of evidence that could eliminate the defendant as the perpetrator, such loss is material to the defense and is a denial of due process." The Court of Appeals concluded on the basis of the expert testimony at trial that timely performance of tests with properly preserved semen samples could have produced results that might have completely exonerated respondent. The Court of Appeals reached this conclusion even though it did "not imply any bad faith on the part of the State." The Supreme Court of Arizona denied the State's petition for review, and we granted certiorari. We now reverse.

Our most recent decision in this area of the law, *California v. Trombetta*, 467 U.S. 479 (1984), arose out of a drunk-driving prosecution in which the State had introduced test results indicating the concentration of alcohol in the blood of two motorists. Defendants sought to suppress the test results on the ground that the State had failed to preserve the breath samples used in the test. We rejected this argument for several reasons: first, "the officers were acting in 'good faith and in accord with their normal practice,' second, in light of the procedures actually used the chances that preserved samples would have exculpated the defendants were slim, and, third, even if the samples might have shown inaccuracy in the tests, defendants had 'alternative means of demonstrating their innocence.' " In the present case, the likelihood that the preserved materials would have enabled the defendant to exonerate himself appears to be greater than it was in *Trombetta*, but here, unlike *Trombetta*, the State did not attempt to make any use of the materials in its own case in chief.

Our decisions in related areas have stressed the importance for constitutional purposes of good or bad faith on the part of the Government when the claim is based on loss of evidence attributable to the Government. In *United States v. Marion*, 404 U.S. 307 (1971), we said that "no actual prejudice to the conduct of the defense is alleged or proved, and there is no showing that the Government intentionally delayed to gain some tactical advantage over appellees or to harass them." Similarly, in *United States v. Valenzuela-Bernal*, 458 U.S. 858 (1982), we considered whether the Government's deportation of two witnesses who were illegal aliens violated due process. We held that the prompt deportation of the witnesses was justified "upon the Executive's good-faith determination that they possess no evidence favorable to the defendant in a criminal prosecution."

The Due Process Clause of the Fourteenth Amendment, as interpreted in *Brady*, makes the good or bad faith of the State irrelevant when the State fails to disclose to the defendant material exculpatory evidence. But the Due Process Clause requires a different result when we deal with the failure of the State to preserve evidentiary material of which no more can be said than that it could have been subjected to tests, the results of which might have exonerated the defendant. Part of the reason for the difference in treatment is found in the observation made by the Court in *Trombetta*, that "whenever potentially exculpatory evidence is permanently lost, courts face the treacherous task of divining the import of materials whose contents are unknown and, very often, disputed." Part of it stems from our unwillingness to read the "fundamental fairness" requirement of the Due Process Clause as imposing on the police an undifferentiated and absolute duty to retain and to preserve all material that might be of conceivable evidentiary significance in a particular prosecution. We think that requiring a defendant to show bad faith on the part of the police both limits the extent of the police's obligation to preserve evidence to reasonable bounds and confines it to that class of cases where the interests of justice most clearly require it, *i.e.*, those cases in which the police themselves by their conduct indicate that the evidence could form a basis for exonerating the defendant. We therefore hold that unless a criminal defendant can show bad faith on the part of the police, failure to preserve potentially useful evidence does not constitute a denial of due process of law.

In this case, the police collected the rectal swab and clothing on the night of the crime; respondent was not taken into custody until six weeks later. The failure of the police to refrigerate the clothing and to perform tests on the semen samples can at worst be described as negligent. None of this was concealed from respondent at trial, and the evidence—such as it was—was made available to respondent's expert who declined to perform any tests on the samples. The Arizona Court of Appeals noted that there was no suggestion of bad faith on the part of the police. It follows, therefore, that there was no violation of the Due Process Clause. The Arizona Court of Appeals also referred somewhat obliquely to the State's "inability to quantitatively test" certain semen samples with the newer P-30 test. If the court meant the Due Process Clause is violated when the police fail to use a particular investigatory tool, we strongly disagree. The situation here is no different than a prosecution for drunken driving that rests on police observation alone; the defendant is free to argue to the finder of fact that a breathalyzer test might have been exculpatory, but the police do not have a constitutional duty to perform any particular tests.

The judgment of the Arizona Court of Appeals is reversed, and the case is remanded for further proceedings not inconsistent with this opinion.

Reversed.

JUSTICE STEVENS, concurring in the judgment.

Three factors are of critical importance. First, at the time the police failed to refrigerate the victim's clothing, and thus negligently lost potentially valuable evidence, they had at least as great an interest in preserving the evidence as did the person later accused of the crime. Second, although it is not possible to know whether the lost evidence would have revealed any relevant information, it is unlikely that defendant was prejudiced by the State's omission. In examining witnesses and in her summation, defense counsel impressed upon the jury the fact that the State failed to preserve the evidence and that the State could have conducted tests that might well have exonerated defendant. The trial judge instructed the jury: "If you find that the State has allowed to be destroyed or lost any evidence whose content or quality are in issue, you may infer that the true fact is against the State's interest." As a result, the uncertainty as to what the evidence might have proved was turned to the defendant's advantage. Third, the fact that no juror chose to draw the permissive inference that proper preservation of the evidence would have demonstrated that the defendant was not the assailant suggests that the lost evidence was "immaterial." In declining defense counsel's and the court's invitations to draw the permissive inference, the jurors in effect indicated that, in their view, the other evidence at trial was so overwhelming that it was highly improbable that the lost evidence was exculpatory. Presumably, in a case involving a closer question as to guilt or innocence, the jurors would have been more ready to infer that the lost evidence was exculpatory. With these factors in mind, I concur. I do not join the Court's opinion because it states that "unless a criminal defendant can show bad faith on the part of the police, failure to preserve potentially useful evidence does not constitute a denial of due process of law." There may be cases in which the defendant is unable to prove that the State acted in bad faith but in which the loss or destruction of evidence is so critical to the defense as to make a criminal trial fundamentally unfair. This, however, is not such a case.

JUSTICE BLACKMUN, with whom JUSTICE BRENNAN and JUSTICE MARSHALL join, dissenting.

The Constitution requires that criminal defendants be provided with a fair trial, not merely a "good faith" try at a fair trial. Respondent, by what may have been nothing more than police ineptitude, was denied the opportunity to present a full defense. That ineptitude deprived respondent of his guaranteed right to due process of law. The evidence which was allowed to deteriorate was "constitutionally material," and its absence significantly prejudiced respondent.

Police action affirmatively aimed at cheating the process undoubtedly violates the Constitution. But to suggest that this is the only way in which the Due Process Clause can be violated cannot be correct. Police action that results in a defendant's receiving an unfair trial constitutes a deprivation of due process. *Brady* ruled that "the suppression by the prosecution of evidence favorable to an accused upon request violates due process where the evidence is material either to guilt or to punishment, irrespective of the good faith or bad faith of the prosecution." *Brady* went on to explain that the principle underlying earlier cases is "not punishment of society for misdeeds of a prosecutor but avoidance of an unfair trial to the accused." The failure to turn over material evidence "casts the prosecutor in the role of an architect of a proceeding that does not comport with standards of justice, even though, as in the present case, his action is not 'the result of guile.' " In *Trombetta*, the Court also relied on *United States v. Agurs*, which required a prosecutor to turn over to the defense evidence that was "clearly supportive of a claim of innocence" even without a defense request. The Court noted that the prosecutor's duty was not

Food for Thought

Why should the good faith or the bad faith of the police matter when the issue is loss of evidence that could have proven innocence? In 2000, Youngblood's attorneys requested testing of the degraded semen sample through the technology of DNA testing. The testing excluded Youngblood and he was exonerated. Does that information influence your view of what the standard should be for loss of evidence today, at least in particular kinds of cases where DNA testing is possible?

one of constitutional dimension unless the evidence was such that its "omission deprived the defendant of a fair trial." *Agurs* thus made plain that the prosecutor's state of mind is *not* determinative. Rather, the proper standard must focus on the materiality of the evidence, and that standard "must reflect our overriding concern with the justice of the finding of guilt."

Brady and *Agurs* could not be more clear in their holdings that a prosecutor's bad faith in interfering with a defendant's access to material evidence is *not* an essential part of a due process violation. Nor did *Trombetta* create such a requirement. *Trombetta* demonstrates that the absence of bad faith does not end the analysis. The determination in *Trombetta* that the prosecution acted in good faith and according to normal practice merely prefaced the primary inquiry, which centers on the "constitutional materiality" of the evidence itself. There is nothing in *Trombetta* that intimates that good faith alone should be the measure. As *Agurs* points out, it makes no sense to overturn a conviction because a malicious prosecutor withholds information that he mistakenly believes to be material, but which actually would have been of no help to the defense. In the same way, it makes no sense to ignore the fact that a defendant has been denied a fair trial because the State allowed evidence that was material to the defense to deteriorate beyond the point of usefulness, simply because the police were inept rather than malicious.

I doubt that the "bad faith" standard creates the bright-line rule sought by the majority. Apart from the inherent difficulty a defendant would have in obtaining evidence to show a lack of good faith, the line between "good faith" and "bad faith" is anything but bright, and the majority's formulation may create more questions than it answers. What constitutes bad faith for these purposes? Does a defendant have to show actual malice, or would recklessness, or the deliberate failure to establish standards for maintaining and preserving evidence, be sufficient? Does "good faith police work" require a certain minimum of diligence, or will a lazy officer, who does not walk the few extra steps to the evidence refrigerator, be considered to be acting in good faith?

Point for Discussion

Distinguishing *Youngblood*

At least one state has distinguished the *Youngblood* situation, where the results of the testing are not known, from the situation where it is known it would have been favorable to the defense. In *Galbraith v. Commonwealth*, 446 S.E.2d 633 (1994), the court stated that, "If it is clear that, had the evidence been properly preserved, it would have formed a basis for exonerating the defendant, then absent a showing to the contrary we must assume that the police were not acting in good faith."

Hypo 1: *Discovery of File of Exoneree*

Kurt Cross is prosecuted for aggravated rape and convicted. Years later, Cross is exonerated through DNA testing. The result of the DNA test is run through the CODIS database (storing DNA profiles of convicted felons) and there is a "match" with the DNA profile of Gregory Forman. The prosecution now charges Forman with the aggravated rape. Under *Brady*, Forman's lawyer requests the prosecution's file from Cross's previous prosecution. After a diligent search and investigation, the prosecution cannot find the Cross file. What result under *Youngblood*?

Hypo 2: *Lost Gun & Bullet*

In a murder investigation, a bullet is recovered from the decedent's body. The police execute a search warrant on suspect Frank Girard's house. A gun is located in a dresser drawer and taken to the crime laboratory. The lab finds a "match" between the bullet and the gun. An officer transporting the gun and bullet back to the courthouse is in an accident while crossing a bridge. The accident is not the officer's fault, but nonetheless, it causes the evidence he is carrying to fall into the river below never to be seen or found again. At trial, the state introduces the ballistics report about the match over the defendant's objection. What are the defendant's options in terms of motions that might be made to the court? If the ballistics report comes in and the defendant is convicted, what result on appeal?

D. Discovery Under Rules & Statutes

Most jurisdictions provide statutory discovery that is more extensive than what the Constitution requires, but less than what is granted in civil cases. For example, very few jurisdictions provide for depositions of witnesses. While states vary, most state discovery rules are variations on <u>Federal Rule of Criminal Procedure 16</u>. The rules and statutes provide for discovery in a number of generalized areas as follows: defendant's own statements to law enforcement, whether written, oral or recorded; defendant's own criminal records; documents and tangible evidence, such as weapons, clothing, drugs, photographs and the like, intended for use at trial; scientific evidence and reports intended for use at trial. Some subsidiary rules also include: other crimes evidence (Fed. R. Evid. 404(b)); co-defendants' statements; co-conspirators' statements.

Food for Thought

Why are there such strict limits on disclosure by the prosecution? Why is the presumption exclusion from discovery and not open file discovery, where the prosecution must disclose information unless the prosecution can give valid reasons why that material should not be turned over? What are the benefits of open file discovery?

Federal and most State discovery rules do not require prosecutors to disclose witness statements or even the identity of witnesses, the general rationale being the importance of witness safety. The defense is often not entitled to police reports either, although redacted reports are typically turned over as the most efficient way for busy prosecutors to comply with their discovery obligations. Generally, the prosecution cannot seek reciprocal discovery from the defendant until the defendant has sought discovery first through a request or motion. Disclosure under discovery rules is considered an ongoing obligation as parties learn about and gather new evidence and information. Discretion is normally left to the court to on how and whether to sanction a party for noncompliance with discovery rules. Noncompliance does not always result in exclusion of the evidence.

Points for Discussion

a. The Jencks Act

In the federal system, the *Jencks* rule strikes an accommodation between protecting witnesses from possible pretrial harassment and providing the defense with an opportunity to impeach witnesses who have made statements inconsistent with their trial testimony. In *Jencks v. United States*, 353 U.S. 657 (1957), the Court exercised its supervisory power over federal courts to require disclosure of prior statements by witnesses *after* they testify. Congress then enacted the Jencks Act, 18 U.S.C. § 3500, and the essence of the Jencks Act is now contained in Rule 26.2 of the Federal Rules of Criminal Procedure. The Jencks Act and Rule 26.2 require both parties—the prosecution and the defense—to provide to the opposition prior statements by its own witnesses. In order to qualify as "Jencks" and trigger disclosure, the statement must: 1) be that of a witness called by the party possessing the statement; 2)

Food for Thought

Suppose that the government introduces the out-of-court statements of the defendant's unindicted co-conspirator, who has fled the country and cannot be called to the witness stand. Could you invoke the Jencks Act to obtain any prior statements by the co-conspirator? Federal Rule of Evidence 806 equates hearsay with live testimony to the extent that if an out-of-court statement is admitted, the opposing party may impeach the statement with "any evidence which would be admissible for those purposes if the declarant had testified as a witness." In light of Rule 806, can you invoke the Jencks Act to obtain other statements made by the co-conspirator after he "testifies" via hearsay?

have been contemporaneously recorded (whether by means of writing, audio, or video); and 3) relate to the subject matter of the witness' testimony.

b. *Jencks* & Non-Testifying Witnesses

The Second and Fourth Circuits have held that the underlying "witness safety" purposes of the Jencks Act require that non-testifying declarants be treated like testifying government witnesses, thus their statements are shielded from pretrial discovery. *In re United States*, 834 F.2d 283 (2d Cir.1987); *United States v. Roberts*, 811 F.2d 257 (4th Cir.1987) (en banc). Does this inconsistent judicial interpretation of the Jencks Act allow the government to employ a "Heads I win. Tails you lose" approach, *i.e.* when defendants seek pretrial discovery, courts shield hearsay from disclosure by ruling that hearsay declarants are "witnesses" under the Jencks Act, but when defendants seek discovery at trial, courts deny disclosure on grounds that declarants are not witnesses within the meaning of the Jencks Act?

Hypo: *Videotape Request*

Your client was caught in a major DEA "sting" operation focusing on the manufacture and sale of PCP. Your client allegedly delivered certain controlled chemicals often used in the manufacture of PCP, and was paid for these chemicals with a large quantity of PCP. The exchange was made with Melvin Jones, an undercover agent of the Drug Enforcement Agency. You interviewed Mr. Jones who related that your client was merely one of many persons who had purchased drugs and chemicals during the two-month sting. Your client denies dealing with Mr. Jones, and you question whether Mr. Jones can remember the details of this one alleged "drug-deal" during a lengthy sting operation involving many people. You are aware that the DEA often uses a hidden video camera to record its sting operations. You would like to discover if there is any record of the alleged exchange between your client and Mr. Jones. On what grounds can you request disclosure of any existing videotape? In addition to, or in place of the videotape, can you request disclosure of: the identity of any other DEA agents or law enforcement officials who were present and observed the alleged exchange? any summary or memorandum of the exchange prepared by law enforcement officials? The identity of other defendants who had dealings with the DEA sting operation within a one-week period of your client's alleged exchange? The status of charges against other defendants prosecuted because of the sting operation? any plea bargains struck between the prosecution and these other defendants?

E. Discovery by the Prosecution

Many jurisdictions give the prosecution an unconditional right to be notified prior to trial that the defendant intends to raise the defense of insanity and to present expert testimony to support this claim. Such provisions allow the prosecution the time to prepare its own expert witnesses to rebut the claim. Federal Rule 12.1 embodies the approach utilized by a majority of states. Federal Rules of Criminal Procedure 12.2, 12.3 and 12.4 also mandate, respectively, the disclosure of defendant's intent to raise the defense of alibi, an actual or believed exercise of public authority on behalf of a law enforcement or federal intelligence agency, or the names of corporate parties with an interest in the case.

Williams v. Florida

399 U.S. 78 (1970).

JUSTICE WHITE delivered the opinion of the Court.

Prior to his trial for robbery in the State of Florida, petitioner filed a "Motion for a Protective Order," seeking to be excused from the requirements of Rule 1.200 of the Florida Rules of Criminal Procedure, 33 F.S.A. That rule requires a defendant, on written demand of the prosecuting attorney, to give notice in advance of trial if the defendant intends to claim an alibi, and to furnish the prosecuting attorney with information as to the place where he claims to have been and with the names and addresses of the alibi witnesses he intends to use. In his motion petitioner openly declared his intent to claim an alibi, but objected to the further disclosure requirements on the ground that the rule "compels the Defendant in a criminal case to be a witness against himself" in violation of his Fifth and Fourteenth Amendment rights. The motion was denied.

Hear It

You can hear the oral argument in *Williams* at: http://www.oyez.org/cases/1960-1969/1969/1969_927.

(Note that a separate issue argued in this case, the constitutionality of a jury of less than twelve, is covered in Chapter 17.)

Florida's notice-of-alibi rule is in essence a requirement that a defendant submit to a limited form of pretrial discovery by the State whenever he intends to rely at trial on the defense of alibi. In exchange for the defendant's disclosure of the witnesses he proposes to use to establish that defense, the State in turn is required to notify the defendant of any witnesses it proposes to offer in rebuttal to that defense. Both sides are under a continuing duty promptly to disclose the names and addresses of additional witnesses bearing on the alibi as they become available. The threatened sanction for failure to comply is the exclusion at trial of the defendant's alibi evidence—except for his own testimony—or, in the case of the State, the exclusion of the State's evidence offered in rebuttal of the alibi.

In this case, following the denial of his Motion for a Protective Order, petitioner complied with the alibi rule and gave the State the name and address of one Mary Scotty. Mrs. Scotty was summoned to the office of the State Attorney on the morning of the trial, where she gave pretrial testimony. At the trial, Mrs. Scotty, petitioner, and petitioner's wife all testified that the three of them had been in Mrs. Scotty's apartment during the time of the robbery. On two occasions during cross-examination of Mrs. Scotty, the prosecuting attorney confronted her with her earlier deposition in which she had given dates and times that in some respects did not correspond with the dates and times given at trial. Mrs. Scotty adhered to her trial story, insisting that she had been mistaken in her earlier testimony. The State also offered in rebuttal the testimony of one of the officers investigating the robbery who claimed that Mrs. Scotty had asked him for directions on the afternoon in question during the time when she claimed to have been in her apartment with petitioner and his wife.

We need not linger over the suggestion that the discovery permitted the State against petitioner in this case deprived him of "due process" or a "fair trial." Florida law provides for liberal discovery by the defendant against the State, and the notice-of-alibi rule is itself carefully hedged with reciprocal duties requiring state disclosure to the defendant. Given the ease with which an alibi can be fabricated, the State's interest in protecting itself against an eleventh-hour defense is both obvious and legitimate. Reflecting this interest, notice-of-alibi provisions, dating at least from 1927, are now in existence in a substantial number of States. The adversary system of trial is hardly an end in itself; it is not yet a poker game in which players enjoy an absolute right always to conceal their cards until played. We find ample room in that system, at least as far as "due process" is concerned, for the instant Florida rule, which is designed to enhance the search for truth in the criminal trial by insuring both the defendant and the State ample opportunity to investigate certain facts crucial to the determination of guilt or innocence.

Petitioner's major contention is that he was "compelled to be a witness against himself" contrary to the commands of the Fifth and Fourteenth Amendments because the notice-of-alibi rule required him to give the State the name and address of Mrs. Scotty in advance of trial and thus to furnish the State with information useful in convicting him. No pretrial statement of petitioner was introduced at trial; but armed with Mrs. Scotty's name and address and the knowledge that she was to be petitioner's alibi witness, the State was able to take her deposition in advance of trial and to find rebuttal testimony. Also, requiring him to reveal the elements of his defense is claimed to have interfered with his right to wait until after the State had presented its case to decide how to defend against it. We conclude, as has apparently every other court that has considered the issue, that the privilege against self-incrimination is not violated by a requirement that the defendant give notice of an alibi defense and disclose his alibi witnesses.

The defendant in a criminal trial is frequently forced to testify himself and to call other witnesses in an effort to reduce the risk of conviction. When he presents his witnesses, he must reveal their identity and submit them to cross-examination which in itself may prove incriminating or which may furnish the State with leads to incriminating rebuttal evidence. That the defendant faces such a dilemma demanding a choice between complete silence and presenting a defense has never been thought an invasion of the privilege against compelled self-incrimination. The pressures generated by the State's evidence may be severe but they do not vitiate the defendant's choice to present an alibi defense and witnesses to prove it, even though the attempted defense ends in catastrophe for the defendant. However "testimonial" or "incriminating" the alibi defense proves to be, it cannot be considered "compelled" within the meaning of the Fifth and Fourteenth Amendments.

Very similar constraints operate on the defendant when the State requires pre-trial notice of alibi and the naming of alibi witnesses. Nothing in such a rule requires the defendant to rely on an alibi or prevents him from abandoning the defense; these matters are left to his unfettered choice. That choice must be made, but the pressures that bear on his pretrial decision are of the same nature as those that would induce him to call alibi witnesses at the trial: the force of historical fact beyond both his and the State's control and the strength of the State's case built on these facts. Response to that kind of pressure by offering evidence or testimony is not compelled self-incrimination transgressing the Fifth and Fourteenth Amendments.

The notice-of-alibi rule in no way affected petitioner's crucial decision to call alibi witnesses or added to the legitimate pressures leading to that course of action. At most, the rule only compelled petitioner to accelerate the timing of his disclosure, forcing him to divulge at an earlier date information that the petitioner from the beginning planned to divulge at trial. Nothing in the Fifth Amendment privilege entitles a defendant as a matter of constitutional right to await the end of the State's case before announcing the nature of his defense, any more than it entitles him to await the jury's verdict on the State's case-in-chief before deciding whether or not to take the stand himself.

Food for Thought

A defendant's filing of a Notice of Alibi does not bind him to that defense. If the defendant does not pursue the alibi at trial, the prosecution cannot use the Notice and subsequent withdrawal against him. Why do you think that is?

Petitioner concedes that absent the notice-of-alibi rule the Constitution would raise no bar to the court's granting the State a continuance at trial on the ground of surprise as soon as the alibi witness is called. Nor would there be self-incrimination problems if, during that continuance, the State was permitted to do precisely what it did here prior to trial: take the deposition of the witness and find rebuttal evidence. But if so utilizing a continuance is permissible under the Fifth and Fourteenth Amendments, then surely the same result may be accomplished through pretrial discovery, as it was here, avoiding the necessity of a disrupted trial. We decline to hold that the privilege against compulsory self-incrimination guarantees the defendant the right to surprise the State with an alibi defense.

JUSTICE BLACK, with whom JUSTICE DOUGLAS joins, concurring in part and dissenting in part.

The Court today holds that a State can require a defendant in a criminal case to disclose in advance of trial the nature of his alibi defense and give the names and addresses of witnesses he will call to support that defense. This requirement, the majority says, does not violate the Fifth Amendment prohibition against compelling a criminal defendant to be a witness against himself. Although this case involves only a notice-of-alibi provision, the decision means that a State can require a defendant to disclose in advance of trial any and all information he might possibly use to defend himself at trial. This decision, in my view, is a radical and dangerous departure from the historical and constitutionally guaranteed right of a defendant in a criminal case to remain completely silent, requiring the State to prove its case without any assistance of any kind from the defendant himself.

Food for Thought

Other than notices of an insanity or alibi defense, many states condition the prosecution's right to discovery upon whether the defense has been granted discovery. The defense may then be required to provide the prosecutor with an opportunity to inspect or copy any physical evidence or reports of any scientific expert or test that the defense intends to use at trial. Why is it that the prosecution's right to reciprocal discovery is dependent on its compliance with its own discovery obligation first? Why isn't it simply a two-way street?

F. Regulation of Discovery

The criminal defendant's right to pretrial discovery may be in conflict with the privacy rights of victims or other third parties. All jurisdictions empower the court to issue protective orders or limit the scope and terms of discovery, subject of course to constitutional limitations. If either party fails to comply with the court's discovery orders the court generally has a number of options for dealing with the violation.

Ethical Issue

Regardless of whether the identity of the opposing party's witness is learned through discovery or through investigation, a witness does not "belong" to either side and cannot be instructed not to speak with the opposing party. The American Bar Association, Model Rules of Professional Conduct, 3.4(a) provides: "A lawyer shall not unlawfully obstruct another party's access to evidence or unlawfully alter, destroy or conceal a document or other material having potential evidentiary value. A lawyer shall not counsel or assist another to do such act."

Possible sanctions authorized in various states include: instruct the jury to assume the accuracy of certain facts that might have been established through the non-disclosed material; hold the offending party in contempt of court; declare a mistrial; or, in the case of a violation by the government, dismiss the prosecution. The least drastic and preferred remedy for violations of discovery orders is to order immediate disclosure and offer a continuance for the party to examine the material.

Point for Discussion

Preclusion Sanction

In *Taylor v. Illinois*, <u>484 U.S. 400 (1988)</u>, a trial court became frustrated when it found repeated and blatant discovery violations by the defense. When the defense attorney called a witness to testify whose identity had not been disclosed to the prosecution despite repeated requests, the trial court refused to allow the witness to testify. The Court held that the extreme sanction of precluding the witness's testimony did not violate the defendant's Sixth Amendment right to present witnesses on his behalf under the Compulsory Process Clause. In dissent, Justices Brennan, Marshall and Blackmun argued that it would have been fairer and more effective to directly sanction the offending attorney: "Deities may be able to visit the sins of the father on the son, but I cannot agree that courts should be permitted to visit the sins of the lawyer on the innocent client."

Executive Summary

Bill of Particulars. The defendant may move for a bill of particulars if the charging instrument does not give sufficient notice of the charges.

Prosecutor's Duty to Disclose Exculpatory Information. A prosecutor must disclose to the defendant exculpatory and impeachment information before trial.

Statutory Discovery by Defendant. Statutory and procedural rules allow the defendant to request information from the prosecution about defendants' statements to law enforcement, and documents and tangible objects, reports of scientific tests.

Reciprocal Discovery by Prosecution. If a defendant requests and obtains information from the prosecution, the prosecution may obtain disclosure of documents and tangible objects as well as reports of scientific evidence in the possession of the defense and intended for use at trial.

Alibi Demand. Most jurisdictions permit the prosecution pretrial discovery about a defendant's alibi or a defendant's mental condition.

Sanctions for Discovery Violations. A court has discretion to refuse to allow a party to introduce evidence at trial that was not produced pursuant to pretrial discovery rules.

Major Themes

a. Duty to Disclose—If the prosecution withholds information that is favorable to the defense and material to the defendant's guilt or punishment, the conviction violates due process and must be reversed.

b. Materiality—Favorable information is "material" if it had a reasonable probability of changing the outcome of the trial or sentence.

c. Pre-Trial Disclosure—While the Court's case law indicates in dicta that the standard for whether the prosecutor must disclose favorable information before trial is the same as the standard for reversal on appeal (i.e., whether there was a reasonable probability the withheld evidence would have made a difference in the outcome), the ethical rules, common sense, and five Justices of the Court in a recent oral argument, all indicate that the prosecutor's duty at trial is simply to disclose favorable information without reference to outcome or prejudice.

d. Team—The prosecutor's duty to disclose favorable evidence at trial includes evidence in the hands of any member of the prosecution team, including the police.

e. Guilty Plea—The prosecution does not have to disclose impeachment information prior to a guilty plea, but the Court has not yet ruled on whether it has to disclose non-impeachment exculpatory information for a valid guilty plea.

For More Information

- Russell L. Weaver, John M. Burkoff, Catherine Hancock & Steven I. Friedland, Principles of Criminal Procedure Ch. 12 (8th ed. 2024).

- Wayne R. LaFave, Jerold H. Israel, Nancy J. King & Orin S. Kerr, Criminal Procedure (6th ed. 2017).

Test Your Knowledge

To assess your understanding of the material in this chapter, click here to take a quiz.

CHAPTER 14

Joinder & Severance

A. Introduction

Joinder and severance of defendants or offenses revolve around the prosecution's charging instruments, such as the indictment or information. The primary issue is whether principles of fairness require that offenses or defendants should be joined or severed from the same charging instruments and cases. Most state criminal procedure rules as well as the Federal Rules of Criminal Procedure allow a prosecutor to combine offenses or defendants simply by charging multiple offenses and defendants in the same indictment or information.[1] In addition,

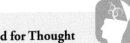

> **Food for Thought**
>
> Joinder is really a marriage of claims or defendants, combining for better or worse for a trip through the criminal system. Severance is really a divorce, separating cases and claims for good.

if offenses or parties are charged separately but initially *could* have been joined together in a single indictment or information, the criminal rules give a trial judge the discretion to do so, with or without a motion. This delayed joinder is called consolidation of the charges.

The importance of joinder and severance cannot be overstated. It is an important decision that often lies within the prosecutor's discretion. As one commentator has noted: "The way in which the prosecutor chooses to combine offenses or defendants in a single indictment is perhaps second in importance only to his decision to prosecute. Whether a defendant is tried *en masse* with many other participants in an alleged crime, or in a separate trial of his own, will often be decisive of the outcome. Equally decisive may be the number of offenses which are cumulated against a single defendant, particularly if they are unconnected." 8 MOORE'S FEDERAL PRACTICE 8-3 (Cipes ed. 1993).

Joint trials play an important role in the criminal justice system because they can promote efficiency and serve the interests of justice (*i.e.*, avoiding the shame and

---

[1] When charging multiple offenses in a single charging document, each crime must be alleged in a separate count. A prosecutor must be careful to avoid charging separate crimes in a single count because to do so will cause the count to be duplicitous.

unfairness of inconsistent verdicts). They also can save state funds, reduce inconvenience to witnesses and law enforcement authorities, and reduce delays in bringing defendants to trial.

Go Online

To better understand joinder and severance, it is useful to become acquainted with charging instruments. The main charging instruments are informations, pieces of paper filed by the prosecutor, and indictments, returned by grand juries. For the Federal Rule of Criminal Procedure on charging instruments, *see* Fed. R. Crim. P. 7: http://www.law.cornell.edu/rules/frcrmp/rule_7. For an actual indictment, go to: https://www.justice.gov/sites/default/files/usao-edpa/legacy/2014/10/22/liciardello_indictment.pdf.

Joint trials also offer strategic opportunities. Prosecutors might have the ability to paint a more complete picture of events, involving all or many of the defendants associated with a single case. Prosecutors also have greater opportunities to compare and contrast the stories and arguments of individual defendants, and even to pit them against each other. On the other hand, defendants can be obscured sometimes when multiple parties are in the same courtroom and juries can compare the relative blameworthiness of behavior.

Once multiple offenses or defendants are joined, either by charging document or by court order, the defense or prosecution may ask the court to sever one or more of them. A motion for severance may be based on misjoinder of either offenses or defendants, sometimes based on the idea that the joinder rules have not been followed. In federal courts, even if joinder is otherwise proper, a pretrial motion to sever under Fed. R. Crim. P. 14 may assert prejudicial joinder. Rule 14 leaves the determination of risk of prejudice, and any remedy that may be necessary, to the sound discretion of the trial, court. If prejudice develops at trial after a motion to sever has been overruled, the defendant should renew the motion and move for a mistrial.

Go Online

Some famous joint trials included Lewis Powell and David Herold (coconspirators in the killing of Abraham Lincoln); Sacco and Vanzetti; and Leopold and Loeb. http://law2.umkc.edu/faculty/projects/ftrials/SaccoV/SaccoV.htm; http://law2.umkc.edu/faculty/projects/ftrials/lincolnconspiracy/lincolnaccount.html.

B. Joinder & Severance of Offenses

The decision to join or sever offenses can have a significant impact on how cases are approached and tried. Public policy, especially fairness and efficiency concerns, underlies joinder and severance analysis. How people are tried matters, and fairness of process is of the utmost importance.

When a defendant is charged with multiple offenses, procedural rules usually govern the joinder and severance of offenses, as well as whether there will be a single trial or several trials. In general, the rules give the prosecution the discretion to charge in a single prosecution all of the offenses that a defendant allegedly committed in a closely connected series of events within the same time sequence. Conversely, the rules permit the defendant to seek a severance of offenses that have been joined. Rules like <u>Fed. R. Crim. P. 8(a)</u> are typical, allowing, but not requiring, joinder of offenses. It states that two or more offenses may be charged against a defendant if they are based upon: 1) the same act or transaction (*e.g.,* a rape and assault); or 2) a series of acts or transactions constituting a common scheme (*e.g.,* armed robbery, auto theft, possession of weapon); or 3) offenses that are of similar character (*e.g.,* bank robberies in same neighborhood two months apart).

Make the Connection

In addition to joinder and severance issues, the exercise of prosecutorial discretion to join or not join offenses or defendants may have constitutional consequences. These consequences relate primarily to Fifth Amendment Double Jeopardy and collateral estoppel issues, discussed in Chapter 21, as well as Sixth Amendment Confrontation Clause matters, discussed in Chapter 18.

Take Note

The "same or same series of acts or transactions" requirement comes up often in this and other procedural areas. This is the type of language referred to as "boiler plate," meaning often used language in a particular area. In this instance, though, it is a very significant part of the rules and concerns the nexus of the conduct in question.

Because the rule is permissive rather than mandatory, a defendant has no right to have all alleged offenses tried together. However, a defendant's motion to consolidate charges under <u>Fed. R. Crim. P. 13</u> may succeed *if* the charges could have been brought together under Rule 8(a). Rule 13 states in part: "The court may order two or more indictments or informations or both to be tried together if the offenses, and the defendants if there is more than one, could have been joined in a single indictment or information." Joinder is usually upheld when the crimes are closely related in character, circumstances, and time. One example of a common scheme or plan is when the offenses show a near identical *modus operandi* and the offenses occur within such a close proximity of time and location to each other that there can be little doubt that the offenses were committed by the same person. A second type of case arises when the crimes are somewhat similar in nature but are closely related to an overall scheme.

The efficiency realized from joining "same act" offenses or "same series" offenses may vanish when the only basis for the joinder is the similarity of charged offenses which were committed in different places, at different times, or in different ways.

When evidence of one offense is not admissible at the trial of another offense, joinder is inefficient, and separate trials are preferable. Case law suggests, however, that if evidence of each crime is simple and distinct, though not admissible in separate trials, joinder may be proper if the trial judge properly instructs the jury about the dangers of cumulating evidence. If evidence of one crime *is* admissible at the trial of the other, the court may not find the joinder of offenses prejudicial and determine that separate trials of the similar offenses are unnecessary.

Arguably, any joinder of offenses is prejudicial to some extent, but where joinder is otherwise proper under the rules of procedure, defendant must prove prejudice to justify and obtain a severance. There are several general discretionary considerations which may persuade a court to grant severance. First, when the case is such that there is a risk that the jury will consider the defendant a "bad person" or infer a criminal propensity by the defendant simply because he is charged with so many offenses. Second, when proof of one charge may "spill over" and assist in a conviction on another charge. Unless there is a high probability of an acquittal on one count, courts will usually deny a severance on this ground. *See, e.g., United States v. Moyer*, 313 F.3d 1082 (8th Cir. 2002) (joinder of crimes not prejudicial solely because evidence of some crimes is stronger than evidence of other crimes). Third, when the defendant wishes to testify about one offense, but not about another offense. *See, e.g., United States v. Saadey*, 393 F.3d 669 (6th Cir. 2005) (defendant failed to show trial court how testifying about one charge would violate his Fifth Amendment privilege against self-incrimination on another charge when he had asserted that the charges were unrelated). In this situation, defendant must convince the trial judge that he has important testimony to give concerning one count, but that there is a strong need to assert the Fifth Amendment Privilege Against Self-Incrimination and refrain from testifying on the other count. Finally, when the defendant may wish to assert antagonistic defenses to the joinable charges. For example, if he is charged with two assaults, he may want to claim an alibi as to one assault and insanity as to the other. Because one of the defenses is likely to diminish the credibility of the other, prejudice may be asserted in support of a motion for a severance. The following case illustrates the fact that the test for joinder of offenses is about a fair trial as much as it is about the same, similar or connected transaction test of Fed. R. Cr. P. 8(a).

Practice Pointer

It is up to the prosecutor or defendant to *move* for joinder or severance. It is not up to the judge to try the case for the parties. Generally, motions will be filed in writing and then sometimes argued, as compared to a simple objection, which is often only oral and usually about the admissibility of evidence. Sometimes motions and objections are inappropriately mixed, so that a party objects to the joinder of parties or offenses, instead of moving to have joinder or severance.

United States v. Angell

2017 WL 1364893 (D. Utah, Apr. 12, 2017).

DISTRICT JUDGE CLARK WADDOUPS.

Before the court is Defendant Misty Angell's Motion for Separate Trial, in which Defendant argues that the counts against her were improperly joined in the indictment or, alternatively, that the two counts should be severed to avoid prejudice to her defense. Defendant was charged by a two-count indictment. The indictment accuses her of mail theft and simple possession of methamphetamine. The government alleges [that] approximately five grams of methamphetamine were found in Defendant's possession during prebooking for her arrest for mail theft. That arrest occurred seven days after Defendant was observed stealing mail from mailboxes in Magna, Utah. Defendant was not employed at the time of the charged conduct. The government represented to the court during the status conference on the day Defendant filed the motion to sever that the arresting officer would testify regarding both counts. Defendant has not at this time presented a contrary factual account.

Federal Rule of Criminal Procedure 8(a) permits joinder of multiple charges against a defendant in the same indictment. Such joinder is proper "if the offenses charged are of the same or similar character, or are based on the same transaction, or are connected with or constitute parts of a common scheme or plan." Fed. R. Crim. P. 8(a). Joinder is proper here because the facts demonstrate that the charges are based on the same act or transaction and are connected as part of a common plan. Defendant argues for misjoinder, claiming that the charged conduct is not "connected in any way." Her argument focuses on the dissimilarity between drug possession and theft and the lack of overlapping evidence between the two counts. But the charged offenses were separated by a mere seven days—a substantially shorter period than in the case Defendant relies upon to argue that time between criminal acts can justify misjoinder, *see United States v. Chavis*, 296 F.3d 450 (6th Cir. 2002) (joinder improper when gun purchased two years prior to possession of cocaine and there was no evidence or allegation that the two offenses connected), and a shorter time than in many cases in which courts have held joinder was proper, *see, e.g., United States v. Bagby*, 696 F.3d 1074, 1086 (10th Cir. 2012) (plain error not to sever counts of drug possession and ammunition possession when the ammunition and drugs were found three months apart in different locations); *United States v. Holland*, 10 F.3d 696, 697, 699 (10th Cir. 1993) (affirming joinder when gun and drug possession were separated by three months). While theft and drug use are not the same conduct, there is a logical inference that Defendant committed the theft to facilitate drug use, because Defendant had no income.

Defendant will not be so prejudiced as to require severance. Severance is necessary when a defendant's "right to a fair trial is threatened or actually deprived." *United*

States v. Johnson, 130 F.3d 1420, 1427 (10th Cir. 1997). Severance is appropriate when there is a serious risk that joinder would "compromise a specific trial right" of the defendant or "prevent the jury from making a reliable judgment about guilt or innocence." *Zafiro v. United States*, 506 U.S. 534, 539 (1993); *Valentine*, 706 F.2d at 290. Defendants are not prejudiced simply because severance would have given them a better chance of acquittal. Where the jury can be instructed to consider the charges separately, courts have presumed their ability to do so and have thus denied severance. Defendant argues that failure to sever would require a later trial date in violation of her rights under the Speedy Trial Act. Her motion to sever, however, tolls the Speedy Trial Act, and the currently scheduled trial date is within the Speedy Trial period. She then claims that introduction of evidence of the drugs in support of Count Two of the indictment "would severely impact Ms. Angell's ability to receive a fair trial on Count One." While evidence of one count may in theory influence juror thinking on the other count, that does not rise to the level of prejudice where the court can, and will in this case, issue a limiting instruction to the jury. In sum, severance is not necessary to avoid prejudice to the defense in this case.

Defendant's Motion for Separate Trial is hereby DENIED. The two counts will be tried together according to the schedule set out in the final pretrial order.

Hypo 1: *Permissible Joinder?*

In the following situations, determine whether joinder is permissible under the applicable criminal procedure rule (meaning federal, the state where you attend law school or the state where you intend to practice). If joinder is permissible, determine whether the joinder under that rule is nonetheless prejudicial: A) Tom Slime is charged in a single indictment with the rape of one of his daughters in 2009 and a separate rape of his stepdaughter in 2006; B) Dick is charged with robbing Smith's Drug Store on July 1, 2014, with assaulting Jim Johnson on February 3, 2005, and with being a career criminal (two or more prior felony convictions); C) Harry is charged with sixteen robberies over a 28-month period. The robberies were committed in the same manner and at about the same time of day by a man wearing similar clothing.

Hypo 2: *Severance*

In the early hours of June 19, Tom allegedly entered a convenience store, brandished a 12-inch knife, and demanded that the clerk hand over all the money in the store's two cash registers. Two weeks later, in the early morning of July 3, Tom allegedly returned to the store, demanded that another clerk hand over money from the same registers, and threatened the clerk with the jagged edge of a broken bottle. After the robberies, each clerk gave slightly different descriptions of the robber. Later, both clerks picked Tom out of a photographic display. A) As defense counsel for Tom, describe the arguments you would make in a motion to the court for a severance of the two robbery counts based upon prejudicial joinder. B) If you are the prosecutor in the case, how would you respond to Tom's motion? C) As the trial judge, how would you rule on Tom's motion for a severance of the robbery charges?

C. Joinder & Severance of Defendants

1. Joinder of Defendants Under the Rules

Criminal procedure rules address joinder and severance procedures in situations when multiple defendants are jointly alleged to have committed one or more crimes. The policy behind this type of rule is to improve judicial economy, since one trial is faster and less expensive than two. The joinder of defendants is permissive, and severance is discretionary with the court. When multiple defendants are jointly charged, a severance may be available based upon specific allegations of prejudice. A more general request for severance may be grounded on the proposition that defendants should not have been joined in the first place. This is similar to the problem that arises when there is misjoinder of unrelated offenses.

Take Note

While the rules might overlap, it is important to distinguish the joinder of defendants from the joinder of claims, particularly regarding the policy concerns and practical impact underlying each type of rule.

In most jurisdictions, joinder of defendants is permitted when the defendants allegedly participated either in the same act or transaction or in the same series of acts or transactions. Unlike the rules on joinder of offenses, before defendants can be joined, they must have committed offenses which are part of the same series of acts rather than being of a similar character. Joinder of defendants looks to the factual connecting link. Where the link is part of some larger plan, or there is some commonality of proof, joinder is permitted. Even when the connecting link is absent, and joinder is not permitted under the rules, misjoinder is subject to harmless error analysis. *United States v. Lane*, 474 U.S. 438 (1986). Most procedural rules also provide that defendants may be charged in one or more counts together or separately, but each defendant does not have to be charged in each count. *See, e.g.,* Fed. R. Crim. P. 8(b).

Assuming that joinder is proper under the applicable rules, severance of defendants may be based upon specific allegations of prejudice that may result from a joint trial. The prejudicial aspects of a joint trial are commonly considered as 1) the "spill over" effect of one defendant's heinous conduct affecting the jury's view of the other co-defendants; and 2) the dangers of any one attorney not having total control over the defense. While the prosecution is unified, the defense is fragmented because each defendant has an attorney and each attorney's view of the case may differ. Specific grounds for severance of defendants for factual prejudice relate to: 1) the weight or type of proof as to one defendant; 2) antagonistic defenses or positions; 3) the desire to call the codefendant as a witness; and 4) the confession of a codefendant. When there is a great disparity in the weight or type of the evidence against the defendants, with the evidence against one or more defendants far more damaging than the evidence against the moving defendant, severance may be appropriate. Otherwise, the guilt of others may "rub off" on the moving defendant. For example, a defendant being tried for a single offense may seek a severance from being jointly tried with a defendant who is charged with both the same offense as the other defendant and with being a recidivist.

If antagonistic defenses are alleged as the basis for a motion for separate trials, the moving defendant must show that the antagonism with a codefendant will mislead or confuse the jury, thereby rendering his defense ineffective. In *Zafiro v. United States*, 506 U.S. 534 (1993), the Court rejected a bright line test that severance is required whenever defendants have mutually antagonistic defenses. The four *Zafiro* defendants did not articulate any specific instances of prejudice but merely argued that the "very nature of their defenses, without more, prejudiced them." Writing for the Court, Justice O'Connor responded that "it is well settled that defendants are not entitled to a severance merely because they may have a better chance of acquittal in separate trials." Instead, a court: "should grant a severance only if there is a serious risk that a joint trial would compromise a specific right of one of the defendants, or prevent the jury from making a reliable judgment about guilt or innocence. Such a risk might occur when evidence that the jury should not consider against a defendant and that would not be admissible if a defendant were tried alone is admitted against a codefendant. For example, evidence of a codefendant's wrongdoing in some circumstances erroneously could lead a jury to conclude that a defendant was guilty. When many defendants are tried together in a complex case and they have markedly different degrees of culpability, this risk of prejudice is heightened. Evidence that is probative of a defendant's guilt but technically admissible only against a codefendant also might present a risk of prejudice. Conversely, a defendant might suffer prejudice if essential exculpatory evidence that would be available to a defendant tried alone were unavailable in a joint trial."

Even if there is some risk of prejudice, it may be curable with proper instructions. Justice O'Connor noted that the trial court in *Zafiro* instructed the jury to give separate consideration to each defendant, and that each defendant was entitled to have his or her case judged only on the basis of the evidence applicable to him/her. Thus, the instructions "sufficed to cure any possibility of prejudice."

The problem of calling a codefendant as a witness may conflict with the codefendant's privilege against self-incrimination. If the cases are severed, and the codefendant's trial is held first, the self-incrimination problem might be eliminated by virtue of a conviction or acquittal. Courts faced with severance motions based on the prospect of calling a codefendant often require specific statements of 1) a bona fide need for the codefendant's testimony, 2) the substance of the codefendant's testimony, 3) the exculpatory nature and effect of the codefendant's testimony, and 4) the likelihood that the codefendant will in fact testify at a separate trial. For example, in *United States v. Hall*, 473 F.3d 1295 (10th Cir. 2007), the court upheld a denial of severance because the exculpatory value of the codefendant's testimony was minimal.

Point for Discussion

Sufficient Prejudice

Consider whether sufficient prejudice is present in a trial of two defendants when: 1) One defendant testifies and the other does not; 2) Evidence is introduced that is competent as to one defendant but inadmissible as to another; 3) One defendant claims merely to have been present at the crime scene and the other claims entrapment; 4) The chances for acquittal for one defendant are better if there are separate trials; 5) The expense or strain of a joint trial is harmful to the defendant.

Food for Thought

What effect should a court give to each of the following when ruling on a motion to sever based upon the ground of calling a codefendant? 1) The sufficiency of a showing that the codefendant would testify at a severed trial. 2) The degree to which the exculpatory testimony would be cumulative. 3) Judicial economy. 4) The likelihood that the testimony would be substantially impeached.

Hypo 1: *Permissible but Prejudicial?*

In the following situations, determine whether the joinder of defendants is permissible under the applicable criminal procedure rules, and if so whether the joinder, though permissible, is nonetheless prejudicial. A) In two counts of a ten-count indictment, the prosecutor has charged Joan and Buffy with illegally trafficking in controlled substances. In the remaining counts, Joan alone is charged with trafficking in controlled substances on eight other occasions. B) The prosecution charges Jill, Sally, and others with trafficking illegally in controlled substances. Jill's defense is that she merely aided and abetted the other defendants; Sally's defense is entrapment. C) Alice and Deborah face multiple criminal tax charges arising from their business ventures. Alice is willing to give exculpatory evidence for Deborah, but without a severance of her case from Deborah's, she will invoke her privilege against self-incrimination.

Hypo 2: *Arguing a Motion*

Charles asks his friend Phil if he knows where he can purchase cocaine. Phil asks his friend Harry, who in turn finds Dave, who offers to sell a kilogram of cocaine to Charles for $25,000. Late one night, the four men meet in a parking lot to consummate the transaction. Charles gives Dave the cash for the drugs, thinking that Dave has already given the drugs to Phil. When Dave and Harry quickly drive off in Dave's car, Charles asks Phil for the drugs. Phil replies that he does not have them and that he thought that Dave had given them to Charles when Charles paid. Phil and Charles jump into Phil's pickup truck and start chasing Dave and Harry. During the chase, both cars collide with another vehicle, killing the two occupants. No cocaine is found in Dave's car. Immediately after he is arrested, Charles gives the police a statement in which he describes the drug sale gone bad, and implicates Dave as the culprit. The prosecutor charges Charles and Dave each with two counts of wanton murder, and also charges Dave with trafficking in a controlled substance and theft by deception. The prosecutor allows Phil and Harry to plead guilty to minor offenses in return for their testimony at Charles' and Dave's trial. The law provides that wanton murder occurs when a defendant operates a motor vehicle under circumstances manifesting extreme indifference to human life and kills another person. Trafficking in cocaine occurs when a defendant sells, transfers or possesses cocaine with intent to sell. One way in which theft by deception may occur is when a defendant creates a false impression as to his intention and obtains the property of another with intent to deceive that person of the property. Nothing in the statutes or their legislative histories indicates that cumulative punishments for trafficking and theft by deception are permitted.

A) As defense counsel for Charles, describe the nature of the arguments you would make in a motion to the court for a severance of his wanton murder charge from Dave's charges. If you are the prosecutor in the case, how would you respond to Charles' motion? As the trial judge, how would you rule?

B) As the trial judge, how would you rule on Dave's motion: 1) To compel the prosecution to elect between prosecuting him for trafficking or for theft by deception because they are the same offense; and 2) To exclude his name or any reference to his participation from Charles' statement when it is introduced during the prosecution's case-in-chief?

2. Impact of Severance

Severance of defendants involves calculating the relative interests of the government and the defense. The authors of an empirical study involving the impact of severance in a case reached these conclusions:

> In addition to offering empirical findings, we have argued that courts currently miscalculate the defense and governmental interests when deciding whether to sever. In particular, we claim that judges undervalue the defendants' interests, in part because they may assume that defendants are trying to gain some tactical or unfair advantage from separate trials. This fear seems exaggerated; we could not identify any illegitimate reason why a defendant would seek severance. At the same time, the fear of increased trials in a world of more generous severance also seems overdone. More severance would undoubtedly lead to some increase in the number of proceedings, but given the predictive effect of the first trial outcome on the rest of the cases, it is questionable whether all, or even most, subsequent trials would find their way to the courtroom.

Andrew D. Leipold and Hossein A. Abbasi, *The Impact of Joinder and Severance on Federal Cases: An Empirical Study*, 59 Vand. L. Rev. 349 (2006).

Executive Summary

Rationale. Joinder and severance issues involve issues of fairness and efficiency.

Basic Definitions. Joinder involves combining offenses or defendants in the same proceeding; severance involves separating them into separate proceedings. Joinder and severance can apply to both offenses and defendants.

Strategies & Tactics. As a general rule, prosecutors prefer to join defendants for the resulting efficacy, completeness of the narrative, and potential impact on the jury. Defendants generally prefer to be tried separately to avoid guilt by association.

Joinder or Severance of Offense. The same positioning of defendants is not so clear for offenses, where joinder of offenses might depend on the circumstances. Often, defendants prefer to have charges consolidated in order to give the prosecution only "one bite at the apple." There is a lower standard for motions made pretrial as compared to motions made during trial.

Major Themes

a. **Start with the Pleadings**—Joinder of offenses and defendants commences with the pleadings but often continues as an issue up to and through the trial. Joinder of offenses and defendants depends on the circumstances of the case and will be impermissible if prejudice will result.

b. **"Same Transaction or Series of Transactions"**—Joinder of offenses often is based on the same transactions or series of transactions (or the offenses are of a similar character).

c. **Delays**—Delayed joinder is also permitted, and is called consolidation.

d. **Severance Considerations and Context**—Severance of defendants or offenses often depends on the evidence, whether disparity or quantity differentials will cause prejudice for one or more defendants. It also depends on process, whether the defenses offered by a defendant are sufficiently antagonistic to warrant separation of defendants or offenses.

For More Information

- For a recent opinion on joinder and severance, *see Microsoft Corp. v. Surfcast, Inc.,* Case IPR 2014-00271 (Patent Trial and Appeal Board).

- RUSSELL L. WEAVER, JOHN M. BURKOFF, CATHERINE HANCOCK & STEVEN I. FRIEDLAND, PRINCIPLES OF CRIMINAL PROCEDURE Ch. 13 (8th ed. 2024).

- Article: http://www.natlawreview.com/article/microsoft-corporation-v-surfcast-inc-decision-denying-institution-and-motion-joinder.

- Opinion: http://ptabtrialblog.com/wp-content/uploads/2014/06/IPR2014-00271-Decision-Denying-Institution-and-Motion-for-Joinder-20140613.pdf.

Test Your Knowledge

To assess your understanding of the material in this chapter, click here to take a quiz.

CHAPTER 15

Pre-Charge Delay &
Speedy Trial

A. Delay in Bringing the Charge

To establish a federal due process violation based on pre-charge delay, a defendant must show that: 1) the delay resulted in actual prejudice to the ability of the defense to present its case; and 2) the prosecution's conduct was intentional and motivated by an intent to harass the defendant or to gain a tactical advantage over the defendant. In each case, the reasons for the delay and the prospective impact on a trial are relevant. The burden of proving prosecutorial intent and of establishing actual prejudice is a heavy one.

Take Note

Defendants have two constitutional rights related to issues of delay. First, the Due Process Clauses of the Fifth and Fourteenth Amendments offer some protection to an accused for delay between commission of the crime and arrest, indictment, or information, whichever comes first. Second, the Sixth Amendment protects a defendant from undue delay in bringing the case to trial after charging. The Sixth Amendment states, in relevant part, "In all criminal prosecutions, the accused shall enjoy the right to a speedy . . . trial." This Chapter covers pre-charge delay, delay implicating the Sixth Amendment speedy trial right, and delay implicating the statutory rights created by the federal Speedy Trial Act.

United States v. Lovasco

431 U.S. 783 (1977).

MR. JUSTICE MARSHALL delivered the opinion of the Court.

On March 6, 1975, respondent was indicted for possessing eight firearms stolen from the United States mails, and for dealing in firearms without a license. The offenses were alleged to have occurred between July 25 and August 31, 1973, more than 18 months before the indictment was filed. Respondent moved to dismiss the indictment due to the delay. The District Court conducted a hearing at which respondent sought to prove that the delay was unnecessary and that it had prejudiced his defense. Respondent presented a Postal Inspector's report on his investigation that was prepared one month after the crimes were committed, and a stipulation concerning the post-report progress of the probe. The report stated, in brief, that within the first month of the investigation respondent had admitted to Government agents that he had possessed and then sold five of the stolen guns, and that the agents had developed strong evidence linking respondent to the remaining three weapons. The report also stated that the agents had been unable to confirm or refute respondent's claim that he

Hear It

You can hear the oral argument in *Lovasco* at: http://www.oyez.org/cases/1970-1979/1976/1976_75_1844.

had found the guns in his car after visiting his son, a mail handler, at work. The stipulation the Assistant United States Attorney entered indicated that little additional information concerning the crimes was uncovered in the 17 months following the preparation of the Inspector's report.

To establish prejudice, respondent testified that he had lost the testimony of two material witnesses due to the delay. The first witness, Tom Stewart, died more than a year after the alleged crimes occurred. Respondent claimed that Stewart had been his source for two or three of the guns. The second witness, respondent's brother, died in April 1974, eight months after the crimes were completed. Respondent testified that his brother was present when respondent called Stewart to secure the guns, and witnessed all of respondent's sales. Respondent did not state how the witnesses would have aided the defense had they been willing to testify.

The Government made no systematic effort to explain its long delay. The Assistant United States Attorney did expressly disagree with defense counsel's suggestion that the investigation had ended after the Postal Inspector's report was prepared. The prosecutor stated that it was the Government's theory that respondent's son, who had access to the mail at the railroad terminal from which the guns were "possibly stolen," was responsible for the thefts. Finally, the prosecutor elicited somewhat cryptic testimony from the Postal Inspector indicating that the case "as to these particular weapons involves other individuals"; that information had been presented to a grand jury "in regard to this case other than on the day of the indictment itself"; and that he had spoken to the prosecutors about the case on four or five occasions.

Following the hearing, the District Court found that by October 2, 1973, the date of the Postal Inspector's report, "the Government had all the information relating to defendant's alleged commission of the offenses charged against him," and that the 17-month delay before the case was presented to the grand jury "had not been explained or justified" and was "unnecessary and unreasonable." The court also found that "as a result of the delay defendant has been prejudiced by reason of the death of Tom Stewart, a material witness on his behalf." Accordingly, the court dismissed the indictment. The Eighth Circuit Court of Appeals affirmed. We granted certiorari and reverse.

In *United States v. Marion*, 404 U.S. 307 (1971), this Court considered the significance, for constitutional purposes, of a lengthy preindictment delay. We held that as far as the Speedy Trial Clause of the Sixth Amendment is concerned, such delay is wholly irrelevant, since our analysis of the language, history, and purposes of the Clause persuaded us that only "a formal indictment or information or else the actual restraints imposed by arrest and holding to answer a criminal charge engage the particular protections" of that provision. We went on to note that statutes of limitations, which provide predictable, legislatively enacted limits on prosecutorial delay, provide "the primary guarantee, against bringing overly stale criminal charges." But we did acknowledge that the "statute of limitations does not fully define defendants' rights with respect to the events occurring prior to indictment," and that the Due Process Clause has a limited role to play in protecting against oppressive delay.

Marion makes clear that proof of prejudice is generally a necessary but not sufficient element of a due process claim, and that the due process inquiry must consider the reasons for the delay as well as the prejudice to the accused. It requires no extended argument to establish that prosecutors do not deviate from "fundamental conceptions of justice" when they defer seeking indictments until they have probable cause to believe an accused is guilty; indeed it is unprofessional conduct for a prosecutor to recommend an indictment on less than probable cause. It should be equally obvious that prosecutors are under no duty to file charges as soon as probable cause exists but before they are satisfied they will be able to establish the suspect's guilt beyond a reasonable doubt. To impose such a duty "would have a deleterious effect both upon the rights of the accused and upon the ability of society to protect itself." From the perspective of potential defendants, requiring prosecutions to commence when probable cause is established is undesirable because it would increase the likelihood of unwarranted charges being filed, and would add to the time during which defendants stand accused but untried. From the perspective of law enforcement officials, a requirement of immediate prosecution upon probable cause is equally unacceptable because it could make obtaining proof of guilt beyond a reasonable doubt impossible by causing potentially fruitful sources of information to evaporate before they are fully exploited. From the standpoint of the courts, such a requirement is unwise because it would cause scarce resources to be consumed on cases that prove to be insubstantial, or that involve only some of the responsible parties or some of the criminal acts. Thus, no one's interests would be well served by compelling prosecutors to initiate prosecutions as soon as they are legally entitled to do so.

It might be argued that once the Government has assembled sufficient evidence to prove guilt beyond a reasonable doubt, it should be constitutionally required to file charges promptly, even if its investigation of the entire criminal transaction is not complete. Adopting such a rule would have many of the same consequences as adopting a rule requiring immediate prosecution upon probable cause. First, compelling a prosecutor to file public charges as soon as the requisite proof has been developed against one participant on one charge would cause numerous problems in those cases in which a criminal transaction involves more than one person or more than one illegal act. In some instances, an immediate arrest or indictment would impair the prosecutor's ability to continue his investigation, thereby preventing society from bringing lawbreakers to justice. In other cases, the prosecutor would be able to obtain additional indictments despite an early prosecution, but the necessary result would be multiple trials involving a single set of facts. Such trials place needless burdens on defendants, law enforcement officials, and courts. Second, insisting on immediate prosecution once sufficient evidence is developed to obtain a conviction would pressure prosecutors into resolving doubtful cases in favor of early and possibly unwarranted prosecutions. The determination of when the evidence available to the prosecution is sufficient to obtain a conviction is seldom clear-cut, and reasonable persons often will reach conflicting conclusions. In the instant case, since respondent admitted possessing at least five of the firearms, the primary factual dispute was whether respondent knew the guns were stolen as required by 18 U.S.C. § 1708. Not surprisingly, the Postal Inspector's report contained no direct evidence on this issue. The decision whether to prosecute, therefore, required a necessarily subjective evaluation of the strength of the circumstantial evidence available and the credibility of respondent's denial. Even if a prosecutor concluded that the case was weak and further investigation appropriate, he would have no assurance that a reviewing court would agree. To avoid the risk that a subsequent indictment would be dismissed for preindictment delay, the prosecutor might feel constrained to file premature charges, with all the disadvantages that would entail. Finally, requiring the Government to make charging decisions immediately upon assembling evidence sufficient to establish guilt would preclude the Government from giving full consideration to the desirability of not prosecuting in particular cases. The decision to file criminal charges, with the awesome consequences it entails, requires consideration of a wide range of factors in addition to the strength of the Government's case, in order to determine whether prosecution would be in the public interest. Prosecutors often need more information than proof of a suspect's guilt before deciding whether to seek an indictment. Again the instant case provides a useful illustration. Although proof of the identity of the mail thieves was not necessary to convict respondent of the possessory crimes with which he was charged, it might have been crucial in assessing respondent's culpability, as distinguished from his legal guilt. If further investigation were to show that respondent had no role in or advance knowledge of the theft and simply agreed, out of paternal loyalty, to help his son dispose of the guns once respondent discovered his son had stolen them, the United States Attorney might have decided not to prosecute, especially since respondent was over 60 years old and had no prior criminal record. Requiring prosecution once the evidence of guilt is clear could prevent a prosecutor from awaiting the information necessary for such a decision.

We would be reluctant to adopt a rule which would have these consequences absent a clear constitutional command to do so. We can find no such command in the Due Process Clause of the Fifth Amendment. Investigative delay is fundamentally unlike delay undertaken by the Government solely "to gain tactical advantage over the accused," *United States v. Marion*, 404 U.S., at 324, precisely because investigative delay is not so one-sided.[17] Rather than deviating from elementary standards of "fair play and decency," a prosecutor abides by them if he refuses to seek indictments until he is completely satisfied that he should prosecute and will be able promptly to establish guilt beyond a reasonable doubt. Penalizing prosecutors who defer action for these reasons would subordinate the goal of "orderly expedition" to that of "mere speed." This the Due Process Clause does not require. We therefore hold that to prosecute a defendant following investigative delay does not deprive him of due process, even if his defense might have been somewhat prejudiced by the lapse of time.

Food for Thought

When and how did Justice Marshall decide that due process gives him leeway rather than a restriction in his analysis of pre-charge delay cases?

In *Marion* we could not determine in the abstract the circumstances in which preaccusation delay would require dismissing prosecutions. In the intervening years so few defendants have established that they were prejudiced by delay that neither this Court nor any lower court has had a sustained opportunity to consider the constitutional significance of various reasons for delay. We therefore leave to the lower courts the task of applying the settled principles of due process that we have discussed to the particular circumstances of individual cases. We simply hold that in this case the lower courts erred in dismissing the indictment.

Reversed.

Food for Thought

The Court observed the impossibility of deciding in the abstract when due process relief is required, and it left to the lower courts the task of applying "settled principles of due process" to the particular circumstances of individual cases. How settled could those principles have been if the courts were lacking in the experience of deciding the significance of various reasons for delay?

---

[17]   In *Marion* the Government conceded that a "tactical" delay would violate the Due Process Clause. The Government renews that concession here: "A due process violation might also be made out upon a showing of prosecutorial delay incurred in reckless disregard of circumstances, known to the prosecution, suggesting that there existed an appreciable risk that delay would impair the ability to mount an effective defense." However, there is no evidence of recklessness here.

Points for Discussion

a. Prosecutorial Intent

Suppose a defendant is able to show prejudice from the delay between the crime and the arrest, how can the defendant prove an improper prosecutorial motive? Occasionally, courts decide that proof of prejudice to the defense is sufficient to afford the defendant a dismissal of the charge, without a showing of improper prosecutorial motive. *See, e.g., Howell v. Barker,* 904 F.2d 889 (4th Cir. 1990); *State v. Cyr,* 588 A.2d 753 (Me. 1991).

Take Note

In *Jauch v. Choctaw County,* 874 F.3d 425 (5th Cir. 2017), although defendant was arrested based on a warrant, based on probable cause, the prosecution waited 96 days before bringing her before a judge. The delay was caused by the sheriff who decided that she must wait until the court convened for its next term. On due process grounds, the court concluded that the delay was unconstitutional, noting that an "indefinite pre-trial detention without an arraignment or other court appearance offends fundamental principles of justice deeply rooted in the conscience of our people."

b. Statutes of Limitations

Besides constitutional restrictions on charging defendants, there may be statutes of limitations for felonies or misdemeanors. In *United States v. Marion,* 404 U.S. 307 (1971), the Court stated: "The purpose of a statute of limitations is to limit exposure to prosecution to a fixed period of time and to protect individuals from having to defend themselves against charges when the basic facts may have become obscured by the passage of time. Such a time limit may also have the salutary effect of encouraging law enforcement officials promptly to investigate suspected criminal activity." Many states have no time limit within which felony charges must be brought. The limitations period for many federal felonies is five years. *See* 18 U.S.C. § 3282. By contrast, misdemeanor charges typically must be commenced within a time certain, *e.g.,* one year, from the last act constituting the offense.

Take Note

When a defendant alleges, without substantiation, prejudice from witnesses' faded memories, the defendant's inability to locate witnesses, the loss of evidence, or the refusal of witnesses to testify, courts generally refuse to find substantial prejudice to the defendant's ability to present a defense at trial. *See, e.g., United States v. Gilbert,* 266 F. 3d 1180 (9th Cir.2001) (no showing of how testimony of "lost" witnesses would have assisted defendant).

Hypo: *A Case for Unconstitutional Pre-Indictment Delay?*

In 1990, Sue acquired a building in Metro that she converted into a country-western nightclub known as Sue's. The nightclub opened in early 1991, but was damaged severely by fire two months later. The fire was arson. Sue was alone at the time and claims that the fire was started by a masked man who accosted her at the nightclub, stole all the money, tied her to a chair, and started the fire. Sue escaped after she began to smell smoke, and went to a nearby convenience store for help. Store clerks later stated that Sue appeared to have been beaten and her hands were tied with wire. The police took a number of pictures of Sue's face showing cuts and bruises. Local police and fire departments and Sue's insurance carrier conducted extensive investigations to determine the origin and cause of the fire. Even though the insurance investigators were suspicious of Sue's story, they paid her insurance claim during the summer of 1991. In May 1996, a grand jury indicted Sue and an associate on charges of arson. Between April 1991 and May 1996 there were no new developments in the case—no new evidence was found, no new studies were conducted, and no new witnesses or statements about the fire were made available to authorities. During this time, the police lost the photos of Sue's injuries and one of the two store clerks moved and could not be found. Prior to trial, Sue moved to dismiss the indictment on the ground that the pre-charge delay and the State's loss of potentially exculpatory evidence had prejudiced her case. The court reserved judgment on the motion until after trial. During the trial, the State entered evidence showing that Sue was heavily in debt, that she set the fire to her business intentionally in order to collect insurance proceeds, and that she inflicted her own injuries to support her story that a robber set the fire. Sue testified and also put on a store clerk who testified about her injuries and her tied hands. The jury found Sue guilty of arson. The trial judge then granted Sue's pretrial motion to dismiss the indictment on the ground of prejudicial pre-indictment delay. Do you agree with the decision? If the standard for appellate review is whether the trial judge's factual and legal findings were clearly erroneous, will the prosecutor be successful on appeal of the trial judge's grant of the dismissal?

B. Delay in Bringing Defendant to Trial

An accused's right to a speedy trial is guaranteed by the Sixth Amendment. Because a defendant has no duty to bring himself to trial, the prosecution has the duty of executing the right. The right is designed to spare the accused those penalties and disabilities that spring from delays in the criminal process, as well as to provide protection for society's interest in effective prosecution. *Dickey v. Florida*, 398 U.S. 30 (1970). The constitutional right to a speedy trial protects the accused from arrest through trial, but does not apply to sentencing (i.e., once a defendant has been found guilty at trial or has pleaded guilty to criminal charges). *Betterman v. Montana*, 578 U.S. 437 (2016). The speedy trial right helps to implement the presumption of innocence and hence loses force upon conviction. The following case illustrates the Court's balancing inquiry for deciding whether the right has been violated.

Barker v. Wingo

407 U.S. 514 (1972).

MR. JUSTICE POWELL delivered the opinion of the Court.

The right to a speedy trial is generically different from any of the other rights enshrined in the Constitution for the protection of the accused. In addition to the general concern that all accused persons be treated according to decent and fair procedures, there is a societal interest in providing a speedy trial which exists separate from, and at times in opposition to, the interests of the accused. The inability of courts to provide a prompt trial has contributed to a large backlog of cases in urban courts which, among other things, enables defendants to negotiate more effectively for pleas of guilty to lesser offenses and otherwise manipulate the system. In addition, persons released on bond for lengthy periods awaiting trial have an opportunity to commit other crimes. It must be of little comfort to the residents of Christian County, Kentucky, to know that Barker was at large on bail for over four years while accused of a vicious and brutal murder of which he was ultimately convicted. Moreover, the longer an accused is free awaiting trial, the more tempting becomes his opportunity to jump bail and escape. Finally, delay between arrest and punishment may have a detrimental effect on rehabilitation.

Hear It

You can hear the oral argument in *Barker v. Wingo* at: http://www.oyez.org/cases/1970-1979/1971/1971_71_5255.

If an accused cannot make bail, he is generally confined, as was Barker for 10 months, in a local jail. This contributes to the overcrowding and generally deplorable state of those institutions. Lengthy exposure to these conditions "has a destructive effect on human character and makes rehabilitation of the individual offender much more difficult." At times the result may even be violent rioting. Finally, lengthy pretrial detention is costly. The cost of maintaining a prisoner in jail varies from $3 to $9 per day, and this amounts to millions across the Nation. In addition, society loses wages which might have been earned, and it must often support families of incarcerated breadwinners.

A second difference between the right to speedy trial and the accused's other constitutional rights is that deprivation of the right may work to the accused's advantage. Delay is not an uncommon defense tactic. As the time between the commission of the crime and trial lengthens, witnesses may become unavailable or their memories may fade. If the witnesses support the prosecution, its case will be weakened, sometimes seriously so. And it is the prosecution which carries the burden of proof. Thus, unlike the right to counsel or the right to be free from compelled self-incrimination, deprivation of the right to speedy trial does not *per se* prejudice the accused's ability to defend himself.

Take Note

While the right to a speedy trial applies equally to both defendants who are detained and those who are out on bond, most appellate courts do not take seriously a speedy trial claim unless the defendant is or was incarcerated. Courts assume (usually correctly) that if the defendant is at liberty, the defense is either primarily or equally responsible for the delay or at least has acquiesced in the delay.

Finally, and perhaps most importantly, the right to speedy trial is a more vague concept than other procedural rights. It is impossible to determine with precision when the right has been denied. We cannot definitely say how long is too long in a system where justice is supposed to be swift but deliberate. As a consequence, there is no fixed point in the criminal process when the State can put the defendant to the choice of either exercising or waiving the right to a speedy trial. If, for example, the State moves for a 60-day continuance, granting that continuance is not a violation of the right to speedy trial unless the circumstances of the case are such that further delay would endanger the values the right protects. It is impossible to do more than generalize about when those circumstances exist. There is nothing comparable to the point in the process when a defendant exercises or waives his right to counsel or his right to a jury trial. The amorphous quality of the right also leads to the unsatisfactorily severe remedy of dismissal of the indictment when the right has been deprived. This is indeed a serious consequence because it means that a defendant who may be guilty of a serious crime will go free, without having been tried. Such a remedy is more serious than an exclusionary rule or a reversal for a new trial, but it is the only possible remedy.

Perhaps because the speedy trial right is so slippery, two rigid approaches are urged upon us as ways of eliminating some of the uncertainty which courts experience in protecting the right. The first suggestion is that we hold that the Constitution requires a criminal defendant to be offered a trial within a specified time period. The result of such a ruling would have the virtue of clarifying when the right is infringed and of simplifying courts' application of it. Recognizing this, some legislatures have enacted laws, and some courts have adopted procedural rules which more narrowly define the right. The United States Court of Appeals for the Second Circuit has promulgated rules for the district courts in that Circuit establishing that the government must be ready for trial within six months of the date of arrest, except in unusual circumstances, or the charge will be dismissed. This type of rule is also recommended by the American Bar Association. But such a result would require this Court to engage in legislative or rulemaking activity, rather than in the adjudicative process to which we should confine our efforts. We do not establish procedural rules for the States, except when mandated by the Constitution. We find no constitutional basis for holding that the speedy trial right can be quantified into a specified number of days or months. The States, of course, are free to prescribe a reasonable period consistent with constitutional standards, but our approach must be less precise.

The second suggested alternative would restrict consideration of the right to those cases in which the accused has demanded a speedy trial. Most States have recognized what is loosely referred to as the "demand rule," although eight States reject it. It is not clear precisely what is meant by that term. Some [courts] have regarded the rule within the concept of waiver, whereas others have viewed it as a factor to be weighed in assessing whether there has been a deprivation of the speedy trial right. We refer to the former approach as the demand-waiver doctrine. The demand-waiver doctrine provides that a defendant waives any consideration of his right to speedy trial for any period prior to which he has not demanded a trial. Under this rigid approach, a prior demand is a necessary condition to the consideration of the speedy trial right. Such an approach, by presuming waiver of a fundamental right from inaction, is inconsistent with this Court's pronouncements on waiver of constitutional rights. The Court has defined waiver as "an intentional relinquishment or abandonment of a known right or privilege." *Johnson* v. *Zerbst,* 304 U.S. 458, 464 (1938). Courts should "indulge every reasonable presumption against waiver," *Aetna Ins. Co.* v. *Kennedy,* 301 U.S. 389, 393 (1937), and they should "not presume acquiescence in the loss of fundamental rights," *Ohio Bell Tel. Co.* v. *Public Utilities Comm'n,* 301 U.S. 292, 307 (1937). In *Carnley* v. *Cochran,* 369 U.S. 506 (1962), we held: "Presuming waiver from a silent record is impermissible. The record must show, or there must be an allegation and evidence which show, that an accused was offered counsel but intelligently and understandably rejected the offer. Anything less is not waiver." In excepting the right to speedy trial from the rule of waiver we have applied to other fundamental rights, courts that have applied the demand-waiver rule have relied on the assumption that delay usually works for the benefit of the accused and on the absence of any readily ascertainable time in the criminal process for a defendant to be given the choice of exercising or waiving his right. But it is not necessarily true that delay benefits the defendant. There are cases in which delay harms the defendant's ability to defend himself. Moreover, a defendant confined to jail prior to trial is obviously disadvantaged by delay as is a defendant released on bail but unable to lead a normal life because of community suspicion and his own anxiety.

The nature of the speedy trial right does make it impossible to pinpoint a precise time in the process when the right must be asserted or waived, but that fact does not argue for placing the burden of protecting the right solely on defendants. A defendant has no duty to bring himself to trial; the State has that duty as well as the duty of insuring that the trial is consistent with due process. Moreover, for the reasons earlier expressed, society has a particular interest in bringing swift prosecutions, and society's representatives are the ones who should protect that interest.

It is noteworthy that such a rigid view of the demand-waiver rule places defense counsel in an awkward position. Unless he demands a trial early and often, he is in danger of frustrating his client's right. If counsel is willing to tolerate some delay because he finds it reasonable and helpful in preparing his own case, he may be unable to obtain a speedy trial for his client at the end of that time. Since under the demand-waiver rule no time runs until the demand is made, the government will have whatever time is otherwise reasonable to bring the defendant to trial after a demand has been made. Thus, if the first demand is made three months after arrest in a jurisdiction which prescribes a six-month rule, the prosecution will have a total of nine months—which may be wholly unreasonable under the circumstances. The result is likely to be either an automatic, *pro forma* demand made immediately after appointment of counsel or delays which, but for the demand-waiver rule, would not be tolerated. Such a result is not consistent with the interests of defendants, society, or the Constitution.

We reject, therefore, the rule that a defendant who fails to demand a speedy trial forever waives his right. This does not mean that defendant has no responsibility to assert his right. The better rule is that the defendant's assertion of or failure to assert his right to a speedy trial is one of the factors to be considered in an inquiry into the deprivation of the right. Such a formulation avoids the rigidities of the demand-waiver rule and the resulting possible unfairness in its application. It allows the trial court to exercise a judicial discretion based on the circumstances, including due consideration of any applicable formal procedural rule. It would permit, for example, a court to attach a different weight to a situation in which the defendant knowingly fails to object from a situation in which his attorney acquiesces in long delay without adequately informing his client, or from a situation in which no counsel is appointed. It would also allow a court to weigh the frequency and force of the objections as opposed to attaching significant weight to a purely *pro forma* objection.

The rule we announce today, which comports with constitutional principles, places the primary burden on the courts and the prosecutors to assure that cases are brought to trial. If delay is attributable to the defendant, then his waiver may be given effect under standard waiver doctrine, the demand rule aside. We, therefore, reject both of the inflexible approaches—the fixed-time period because it goes further than the Constitution requires; the demand-waiver rule because it is insensitive to a right which we have deemed fundamental. The approach we accept is a balancing test, in which the conduct of both the prosecution and the defendant are weighed.[29] A balancing test necessarily compels courts to approach speedy trial cases on an *ad hoc*

---

[29]   Nothing we have said should be interpreted as disapproving a presumptive rule adopted by a court in the exercise of its supervisory powers which establishes a fixed time period within which cases must normally be brought.

basis. We can do little more than identify some of the factors which courts should assess in determining whether a particular defendant has been deprived of his right. We identify four such factors: Length of delay, the reason for the delay, the defendant's assertion of his right, and prejudice to the defendant.

The length of the delay is to some extent a triggering mechanism. Until there is some delay which is presumptively prejudicial, there is no necessity for inquiry into the other factors that go into the balance. Nevertheless, because of the imprecision of the right to speedy trial, the length of delay that will provoke such an inquiry is necessarily dependent upon the peculiar circumstances of the case.[31] The delay that can be tolerated for an ordinary street crime is considerably less than for a serious, complex conspiracy charge.

Closely related to length of delay is the reason the government assigns to justify the delay. Different weights should be assigned to different reasons. A deliberate attempt to delay the trial in order to hamper the defense should be weighted heavily against the government. A more neutral reason such as negligence or overcrowded courts should be weighted less heavily but nevertheless should be considered since the ultimate responsibility for such circumstances must rest with the government rather than with the defendant. Finally, a valid reason, such as a missing witness, should serve to justify appropriate delay.

We have already discussed the third factor, the defendant's responsibility to assert his right. Whether and how a defendant asserts his right is closely related to the other factors. The strength of his efforts will be affected by the length of the delay, to some extent by the reason for the delay, and most particularly by the personal prejudice, which is not always readily identifiable, that he experiences. The more serious the deprivation, the more likely a defendant is to complain. The defendant's assertion of his speedy trial right is entitled to strong evidentiary weight in determining whether the defendant is being deprived of the right. We emphasize that failure to assert the right will make it difficult for a defendant to prove that he was denied a speedy trial.

A fourth factor is prejudice to the defendant. Prejudice, of course, should be assessed in the light of the interests of defendants which the speedy trial right was designed to protect. This Court has identified three such interests: (i) to prevent oppressive pretrial incarceration; (ii) to minimize anxiety and concern of the accused; and (iii) to limit the possibility that the defense will be impaired. Of these, the most serious is the last, because the inability of a defendant adequately to prepare his case skews the fairness of the entire system. If witnesses die or disappear during a delay, the prejudice is obvious. There is also prejudice if defense witnesses are unable to recall

---

[31] For example, the First Circuit thought a delay of nine months overly long, absent a good reason, in a case that depended on eyewitness testimony. *United States v. Butler*, 426 F.2d 1275 (1970).

accurately events of the distant past. Loss of memory, however, is not always reflected in the record because what has been forgotten can rarely be shown.

We have discussed previously the societal disadvantages of lengthy pretrial incarceration, but obviously the disadvantages for the accused who cannot obtain his release are even more serious. The time spent in jail awaiting trial has a detrimental impact on the individual. It often means loss of a job; it disrupts family life; and it enforces idleness. Most jails offer little or no recreational or rehabilitative programs. The time spent in jail is simply dead time. Moreover, if a defendant is locked up, he is hindered in his ability to gather evidence, contact witnesses, or otherwise prepare his defense.[35] Imposing those consequences on one who has not yet been convicted is serious. It is especially unfortunate for those who are ultimately found to be innocent. Even if an accused is not incarcerated prior to trial, he is still disadvantaged by restraints on his liberty and by living under a cloud of anxiety, suspicion, and often hostility.

Food for Thought

Why must prejudice be a factor? Do you agree that the anxiety and "lack of repose" from pending charges for the non-incarcerated defendant is not that serious compared to other constitutional violations? Should the fact that a defendant is incarcerated pretrial for months without good reason for the delay become a constitutional violation without regard to prejudice? As a practical matter, courts only become interested in the delay if there is prejudice to the defense. Of course, that is the hardest showing for a defendant—how does he prove he would have found a helpful witness or evidence when there now appears to be no helpful witness or evidence?

We regard none of the four factors identified above as either a necessary or sufficient condition to the finding of a deprivation of the right of speedy trial. Rather, they are related factors and must be considered together with such other circumstances as may be relevant. In sum, these factors have no talismanic qualities; courts must still engage in a difficult and sensitive balancing process. But, because we are dealing with a fundamental right of the accused, this process must be carried out with full recognition that the accused's interest in a speedy trial is specifically affirmed in the Constitution.

---

[35] There is statistical evidence that persons who are detained between arrest and trial are more likely to receive prison sentences than those who obtain pretrial release, although other factors bear upon this correlation. *See* Wald, *Pretrial Detention and Ultimate Freedom: A Statistical Study,* 39 N.Y.U.L. Rev. 631 (1964).

FYI

In *United States v. Tigano*, 880 F.3d 602 (2d Cir. 2018), defendant was locked up for almost seven years before he was brought to trial. The delay was caused by a request for unnecessary competency examinations, governmental delays in producing plea offers, and the trial court's failure to prioritize the case. In addition, defendant's lawyer failed to push for a speedy trial after rejecting a plea offer. The court deemed the delay to be excessive. Likewise, in *United States v. Oliva*, 909 F.3d 1292 (11th Cir. 2018), a two-year delay between indictment and trial was deemed to be permissible. The delay was caused by the negligence of the prosecution. In particular, a state law enforcement official incorrectly was unfamiliar with the federal indictment and arrest procedure.

Points for Discussion

a.   CIA Interrogation

In *United States v. Ghailani*, 733 F.3d 29 (2d Cir. 2013), the Second Circuit held that a five-year delay due to the detention and interrogation of the defendant by the CIA did not count against the government under the Sixth Amendment's Speedy Trial Clause. The Court reasoned that the government does not have to choose between national security and criminal prosecution.

b.   Reasons for the Delay

Courts weigh delays intended to gain a trial advantage more heavily against the prosecution than unintentional delays resulting from institutional dysfunction. Neutral reasons such as negligence and overcrowded calendars weigh less heavily, but are still considered because responsibility for such conditions rests with the prosecution. Delays attributable to court appointed defense counsel are not to be counted against the State. *Vermont v. Brillon*, 556 U.S. 81 (2009).

FYI

The right to a speedy trial attaches at the earlier of the date of the indictment or information, or the date of the arrest, *i.e.*, when the person becomes "accused." Similarly, the right to a speedy trial attaches when a detainer is lodged against an accused in custody on other charges. Once the right to a speedy trial attaches, it continues until the charges are dismissed.

c.   Delay Caused by Lack of Defense Funding

In *Boyer v. Louisiana*, 569 U.S. 238 (2013), the Court split 5–4 in favor of dismissing the case. The issue the Court was asked to take up was "whether a state's failure to fund counsel for an indigent defendant for five years, particularly where failure was the direct result of the prosecution's choice to seek the death penalty, should be weighed against the state for speedy trial purposes." The Louisiana courts had answered no, that funding was a circumstance out of the prosecution's control. For the four dissenters, Justice Sotomayor wrote that *Barker's* reasoning "requires that a delay caused by a State's failure to provide funding for an indigent's defense must count against the State, and not the accused. We held there that even a more 'neutral reason' for a delay such as 'overcrowded courts' should be weighed against the State, because 'the ultimate responsibility for such circumstances' lies squarely with the state system as a whole."

d. Role of Speedy Trial Demand

Take Note

In *United States v. MacDonald*, 456 U.S. 1 (1982), the Court held that the time period between dismissal of charges and reinstatement of those charges is a part of the pre-charge period to which the Sixth Amendment right to a speedy trial is inapplicable. *MacDonald* was deemed controlling in *United States v. Loud Hawk*, 474 U.S. 302 (1986), where the Court held that the time during which the prosecution appealed a dismissal, while the defendants were not incarcerated and not subject to bail, did not count in the Sixth Amendment speedy trial analysis. The Court stated that an interlocutory appeal is "ordinarily a valid reason that justifies the delay."

A defendant's failure to demand a speedy trial undercuts the defendant's constitutional argument. By contrast, a vigorous and timely assertion of the right provides strong evidence that the defendant is interested in a speedy disposition. A court will not treat a claim seriously that a trial started too late unless the defendant continuously has sought a speedy trial. *See, e.g., United States v. Vachon*, 869 F.2d 653 (1st Cir.1989) (defendant did not assert right until two days before trial after thirteen-month delay).

Food for Thought

If a defendant is denied a speedy trial but is found not guilty, does the defendant have any remedy? If so, what? If not, should there be one?

e. Harsh Remedy

Barker expressly stated that dismissal with prejudice is the only possible remedy for a violation of the Sixth Amendment speedy trial right. Trial courts therefore cannot devise less extreme remedies such as a sentence reduction. *Strunk v. United States*, 412 U.S. 434 (1973). The re-prosecution prohibition undoubtedly results in courts finding fewer constitutional violations because of the extreme nature of the remedy. An alternative disposition is to find a violation of the relevant speedy trial statute (*e.g.*, 18 U.S.C. § 3161 *et seq.*) or the relevant docket control rule (*e.g.*, Fed.R.Crim.P. 48(b)), both of

Take Note

In the following Sixth Amendment speedy trial case, notice the extent to which the Court has altered *Barker's* balancing test. The Court stated that an interlocutory appeal is "ordinarily a valid reason that justifies the delay."

which may prescribe dismissal without prejudice as an available method of enforcement. Still another remedy is to provide a writ of mandamus to compel a trial court to set a trial date for the defendant's case.

Food for Thought

While defendant remains in jail, it takes fifteen months for the prosecution to bring defendant to trial on a firearms charge. However, during that time, defendant was being prosecuted on state charges, and federal prosecutors were waiting for the state proceedings to conclude. In addition, defendant failed to assert his right to a speedy trial. Has defendant's right to a speedy trial been impaired? Would it matter whether any evidence was lost during the delay? *See United States v. Nixon*, 919 F.3d 1265 (10th Cir.), *cert. denied*, *Nixon v. United States*, 140 S.Ct. 242 (2019).

Hypo: *Discovery and Translation Issues*

An Uzbek immigrant was charged with providing material support to the Islamic Jihad Union, but was held in detention and not brought to trial for 6.5 years. The government sought to justify the delay on the basis that defendant sought broad discovery from the prosecution. In addition, the case involved 39,000 audio recordings in Russian, Ubek and Tajik which had to be translated and any release of the audio had to comply with the Classified Information Procedures Act. Is a 6.5 year delay excessive under the circumstances? *See United States v. Muhtorov*, 20 F.4th 558 (10th Cir. 2021).

Doggett v. United States

505 U.S. 647 (1992).

JUSTICE SOUTER delivered the opinion of the Court.

In this case we consider whether the delay of 8½ years between petitioner's indictment and arrest violated his Sixth Amendment right to a speedy trial. We hold that it did.

On February 22, 1980, petitioner Marc Doggett was indicted for conspiring with several others to import and distribute cocaine. Douglas Driver, the

Hear It

You can hear the oral argument in *Doggett* at: http://www.oyez.org/cases/1990-1999/1991/1991_90_857.

Drug Enforcement Administration's principal agent investigating the conspiracy, told the United States Marshal's Service that the DEA would oversee the apprehension of Doggett and his confederates. On March 18, 1980, two police officers set out under Driver's orders to arrest Doggett at his parents' house in Raleigh, North Carolina, only to find that he was not there. His mother told the officers that he had left for Colombia four days earlier. To catch Doggett on his return to the United States, Driver sent word of his outstanding arrest warrant to all United States Customs stations and to a number of law enforcement organizations. He also placed Doggett's name in the Treasury Enforcement Communication System (TECS), a computer network that helps Customs agents screen people entering the country, and in the National Crime Information Center computer system, which serves similar ends. The TECS entry expired that September, however, and Doggett's name vanished from the system. In September 1981, Driver found out that Doggett was under arrest on drug charges in Panama and, thinking that a formal extradition request would be futile, simply asked Panama to "expel" Doggett to the United States. Although the Panamanian authorities promised to comply when their own proceedings had run their course, they freed Doggett the following July and let him go to Colombia, where he stayed with an aunt for several months. On September 25, 1982, he passed unhindered through Customs in New York City and settled down in Virginia. Since his return to the United States, he has married, earned a college degree, found a steady job as a computer operations manager, lived openly under his own name, and stayed within the law.

Doggett's travels abroad had not wholly escaped the Government's notice, however. In 1982, the American Embassy in Panama told the State Department of his departure to Colombia, but that information, for whatever reason, eluded the DEA, and Agent Driver assumed for several years that his quarry was still serving time in a Panamanian prison. Driver never asked DEA officials in Panama to check into Doggett's status, and only after his own fortuitous assignment to that country in 1985 did he discover Doggett's departure for Colombia. Driver then simply assumed Doggett had settled there, and he made no effort to track Doggett down, either abroad or in the United States. Thus Doggett remained lost to the American criminal justice system until September 1988, when the Marshal's Service ran a simple credit check on several thousand people subject to outstanding arrest warrants and, within minutes, found out where Doggett lived and worked. On September 5, 1988, nearly 6 years after his return to the United States and 8½ years after his indictment, Doggett was arrested.

He naturally moved to dismiss the indictment, arguing that the Government's failure to prosecute him earlier violated his Sixth Amendment right to a speedy trial. The Federal Magistrate hearing his motion applied the criteria for assessing speedy trial claims set out in *Barker v. Wingo*, 407 U.S. 514 (1972): "length of delay, the reason for the delay, the defendant's assertion of his right, and prejudice to the defendant." The Magistrate found that the delay between Doggett's indictment and arrest was long enough to be "presumptively prejudicial," that the delay "clearly was attributable to the negligence of the government," and that Doggett could not be faulted for any delay in asserting his right to a speedy trial, there being no evidence that he had known of the charges against him until his arrest. The Magistrate also found, however, that Doggett had made no affirmative showing that the delay had impaired his ability to mount a successful defense or had otherwise prejudiced him. In his recommendation to the District Court, the Magistrate contended that this failure to demonstrate particular prejudice sufficed to defeat Doggett's speedy trial claim. The District Court took the recommendation and denied Doggett's motion.

The Sixth Amendment guarantees that, "in all criminal prosecutions, the accused shall enjoy the right to a speedy trial." On its face, the Speedy Trial Clause is written with such breadth that, taken literally, it would forbid the government to delay the trial of an "accused" for any reason at all. Our cases have qualified the literal sweep of the provision by specifically recognizing the relevance of four separate enquiries: whether delay before trial was uncommonly long, whether the government or the criminal defendant is more to blame for that delay, whether, in due course, the defendant asserted his right to a speedy trial, and whether he suffered prejudice as the delay's result.

The first of these is actually a double enquiry. Simply to trigger a speedy trial analysis, an accused must allege that the interval between accusation and trial has crossed the threshold dividing ordinary from "presumptively prejudicial" delay, since, by definition, he cannot complain that the government has denied him a "speedy" trial if it has, in fact, prosecuted his case with customary promptness. If the accused makes this showing, the court must then consider, as one factor among several, the extent to which the delay stretches beyond the bare minimum needed to trigger judicial examination of the claim. This latter enquiry is significant to the speedy trial analysis because the presumption that pretrial delay has prejudiced the accused intensifies over time. In this case, the extraordinary 8½ year lag between Doggett's indictment and arrest clearly suffices to trigger the speedy trial enquiry;[1] its further significance within that enquiry will be dealt with later.

As for *Barker*'s second criterion, the Government claims to have sought Doggett with diligence. The findings of the courts below are to the contrary, and we review trial court determinations of negligence with considerable deference. The Government gives us nothing to gainsay the findings that have come to us, and we see nothing fatal to them in the record. For six years, the Government's investigators made no serious effort to test their progressively more questionable assumption that Doggett was living abroad, and they could have found him within minutes. While the Government's

---

[1] Depending on the nature of the charges, the lower courts have found postaccusation delay "presumptively prejudicial" as it approaches one year. "Presumptive prejudice" does not necessarily indicate a statistical probability of prejudice; it simply marks the point at which courts deem the delay unreasonable enough to trigger the *Barker* enquiry.

lethargy may have reflected no more than Doggett's relative unimportance in the world of drug trafficking, it was still findable negligence, and the finding stands.

The Government goes against the record in suggesting that Doggett knew of his indictment years before he was arrested. Were this true, *Barker*'s third factor, concerning invocation of the right to a speedy trial, would be weighed heavily against him. But the Government is trying to revisit the facts. At the hearing on Doggett's speedy trial motion, it introduced no evidence challenging the testimony of Doggett's wife, who said that she did not know of the charges until his arrest, and of his mother, who claimed not to have told him or anyone else that the police had come looking for him. The Government is left, then, with its principal contention: that Doggett fails to make out a successful speedy trial claim because he has not shown precisely how he was prejudiced by the delay between his indictment and trial.

Unreasonable delay between formal accusation and trial threatens to produce more than one sort of harm, including "oppressive pretrial incarceration," "anxiety and concern of the accused," and "the possibility that the accused's defense will be impaired" by dimming memories and loss of exculpatory evidence. Of these forms of prejudice, "the most serious is the last, because the inability of a defendant adequately to prepare his case skews the fairness of the entire system." Doggett claims this kind of prejudice, and there is probably no other kind that he can claim, since he was subjected neither to pretrial detention nor, he has successfully contended, to awareness of unresolved charges against him.

The Government answers Doggett's claim by citing the proposition that the Speedy Trial Clause does not significantly protect a criminal defendant's interest in fair adjudication. Once triggered by arrest, indictment, or other official accusation, the speedy trial enquiry must weigh the effect of delay on the accused's defense just as it has to weigh any other form of prejudice that *Barker* recognized.

As an alternative to limiting *Barker*, the Government claims Doggett has failed to make any affirmative showing that the delay weakened his ability to raise specific defenses, elicit specific testimony, or produce specific items of evidence. Though Doggett did indeed come up short in this respect, consideration of prejudice is not limited to the specifically demonstrable, and, as it concedes, affirmative proof of particularized prejudice is not essential to every speedy trial claim. *Barker* explicitly recognized that impairment of one's defense is the most difficult form of speedy trial prejudice to prove because time's erosion of exculpatory evidence and testimony "can rarely be shown." Though time can tilt the case against either side, one cannot generally be sure which of them it has prejudiced more severely. Thus, we generally have to recognize that excessive delay presumptively compromises the reliability of a trial in ways that neither party can prove or, for that matter, identify. While such presumptive prejudice cannot alone carry a Sixth Amendment claim without regard to the other

Barker criteria, it is part of the mix of relevant facts, and its importance increases with the length of delay.

This brings us to an enquiry into the role that presumptive prejudice should play in the disposition of Doggett's speedy trial claim. We begin with hypothetical and somewhat easier cases and work our way to this one. Our speedy trial standards recognize that pretrial delay is often both inevitable and wholly justifiable. The government may need time to collect witnesses against the accused, oppose his pretrial motions, or, if he goes into hiding, track him down. We attach great weight to such considerations when balancing them against the costs of going forward with a trial whose probative accuracy the passage of time has begun by degrees to throw into question. In this case, if the Government had pursued Doggett with reasonable diligence from his indictment to his arrest, his speedy trial claim would fail. Indeed, that conclusion would generally follow as a matter of course however great the delay, so long as Doggett could not show specific prejudice to his defense.

The Government concedes that Doggett would prevail if he could show that the Government had intentionally held back in its prosecution of him to gain some impermissible advantage at trial. *Barker* stressed that official bad faith in causing delay will be weighed heavily against the government, and a bad-faith delay the length of this negligent one would present an overwhelming case for dismissal. Between diligent prosecution and bad-faith delay, official negligence in bringing an accused to trial occupies the middle ground. While not compelling relief in every case where bad-faith delay would make relief virtually automatic, neither is negligence tolerable simply because the accused cannot demonstrate exactly how it has prejudiced him. It was on this point that the Court of Appeals erred.

Barker made it clear that "different weights are to be assigned to different reasons" for delay. Although negligence is to be weighed more lightly than a deliberate intent to harm the accused's defense, it still falls on the wrong side of the divide between acceptable and unacceptable reasons for delaying a criminal prosecution once it has begun. Such is the nature of the prejudice presumed that the weight we assign to official negligence compounds over time as the presumption of evidentiary prejudice grows. Thus, our toleration of negligence varies inversely with its protractedness, and its consequent threat to the fairness of the accused's trial. Condoning prolonged and unjustifiable delays in prosecution would penalize many defendants for the state's fault and encourage the government to gamble with the interests of criminal suspects assigned a low prosecutorial priority. The Government can hardly complain too loudly, for persistent neglect in concluding a criminal prosecution indicates an uncommonly feeble interest in bringing an accused to justice; the more weight the Government attaches to securing a conviction, the harder it will try to get it.

To warrant granting relief, negligence unaccompanied by particularized trial prejudice must have lasted longer than negligence demonstrably causing such prejudice. But the Government's egregious persistence in failing to prosecute Doggett is clearly sufficient. The lag between Doggett's indictment and arrest was 8½ years, and he would have faced trial 6 years earlier than he did but for the Government's inexcusable oversights. The portion of the delay attributable to the Government's negligence far exceeds the threshold needed to state a speedy trial claim; indeed, we have called shorter delays "extraordinary." When the Government's negligence thus causes delay six times as long as that generally sufficient to trigger judicial review, and when the presumption of prejudice, albeit unspecified, is neither extenuated, as by the defendant's acquiescence, nor persuasively rebutted, the defendant is entitled to relief.

We reverse the judgment of the Court of Appeals and remand the case for proceedings consistent with this opinion.

Justice O'Connor, dissenting.

The Court of Appeals properly balanced the considerations set forth in *Barker v. Wingo*. Although the delay between indictment and trial was lengthy, petitioner did not suffer any anxiety or restriction on his liberty. The only harm to petitioner from the lapse of time was potential prejudice to his

Take Note

Footnote 1 offered a crucial new marker of a one-year delay for a presumption of prejudice for the lower courts.

ability to defend his case. We have not allowed such speculative harm to tip the scales. Instead, we have required a showing of actual prejudice to the defense before weighing it in the balance. As we stated in *United States v. Loud Hawk*, 474 U.S. 302, 315 (1986), the "possibility of prejudice is not sufficient to support respondents' position that their speedy trial rights were violated. In this case, delay is a two-edged sword. It is the Government that bears the burden of proving its case beyond a reasonable doubt. The passage of time may make it difficult or impossible for the Government to carry this burden." The Court of Appeals followed this holding, and I believe we should as well. For this reason, I respectfully dissent.

Justice Thomas, with whom The Chief Justice and Justice Scalia join, dissenting.

Odd facts make odd law. Doggett's 8½-year odyssey from youthful drug dealing in the tobacco country of North Carolina, through stints in a Panamanian jail and in Colombia, to life as a computer operations manager, homeowner, and registered voter in suburban Virginia, is extraordinary. Even more extraordinary is the Court's conclusion that the Government denied Doggett his Sixth Amendment right to a speedy trial despite the fact that he has suffered none of the harms that the right was designed to prevent. In my view, the choice presented is not a hard one. *Barker*'s suggestion that preventing prejudice to the defense is a fundamental and independent objective of the Clause is plainly dictum. Never, until today, have we confronted a case where a defendant subjected to a lengthy delay after indictment nonetheless failed to suffer any substantial impairment of his liberty. *Barker* simply did not contemplate such an unusual situation. Moreover, to the extent that the *Barker* dictum purports to elevate considerations of prejudice to the defense to fundamental and independent status under the Clause, it cannot be deemed to have survived our subsequent decisions. Therefore, I see no basis for the Court's conclusion that Doggett is entitled to relief under the Speedy Trial Clause simply because the Government was negligent in prosecuting him and because the resulting delay may have prejudiced his defense.

Does the Clause protect a right to repose, free from secret or unknown indictments? In my view, it does not. There is no basis for concluding that the disruption of an accused's life years after the commission of his alleged crime is an evil independently protected by the Speedy Trial Clause. Such disruption occurs regardless of whether the individual is under indictment during the period of delay. Thus, had Doggett been indicted shortly before his 1988 arrest rather than shortly after his 1980 crime, his repose would have been equally shattered—but he would not have even a colorable speedy-trial claim. To recognize a constitutional right to repose is to recognize a right to be tried speedily after the offense. That would, of course, convert the Speedy Trial Clause into a constitutional statute of limitations—a result with no basis in the text or history of the Clause or in our precedents.

Food for Thought

Both *Barker* and *Doggett*, like most (if not all) speedy trial cases, come to the Court on appeal after conviction. Is there anything a defendant who is being denied a speedy trial can do pretrial? What?

Today's opinion, I fear, will transform the courts into boards of law-enforcement supervision. For the Court compels dismissal of the charges against Doggett not because he was harmed in any way by the delay between his indictment and arrest, but simply because the Government's efforts to catch him are found wanting. Our Constitution neither contemplates nor tolerates such a role. I respectfully dissent.

Food for Thought

Does *Doggett* offer insight into the interrelationships among the *Barker* factors? For example, if the reason for the delay is the reasonable diligence of the government, a defendant's speedy trial claim probably will fail unless there is a showing of specific prejudice. Conversely, if the reason for the delay is the prosecution's attempt to gain some impermissible tactical advantage, a rebuttal presumption of prejudice exists. As a prosecutor, how would you rebut the presumption of prejudice? If the reason for the delay is the prosecution's negligence, is some showing of prejudice by the defendant necessary or is a presumption of prejudice created? What is the distinction between governmental negligence and bad faith?

Points for Discussion

a. Shorter Delays in "Uncomplicated Cases"

In weighing the four *Barker* factors, a court may well find a shorter delay less tolerable in a minor, less complicated, case. In *State v. Cahill*, 61 A.3d 1278 (N.J. 2013), for example, the New Jersey Supreme Court held that a 16-month delay in a DWI case violated the defendant's right to a speedy trial. The defendant's failure to assert the right was outweighed by the state's complete failure to justify the long delay in a straightforward, uncomplicated quasi-criminal matter.

b. Lack of Speedy Trial Demand by Counsel

In the absence of a demand by defense counsel, does the demand "requirement" result in the defendant paying for the omission of counsel? Is a successful claim of ineffective assistance of counsel necessary to relieve the defendant of the failure to make a demand for a speedy trial? Should the defendant's failure to request a speedy trial be treated differently when the defendant is representing herself?

c. Mistrials

States are divided over whether the speedy trial clock continues to tick or whether it restarts after the declaration of a mistrial. What are the arguments in favor of restarting the clock? Against? If the clock keeps running, how should the mistrial factor into the speedy trial analysis? *See, e.g., Goncalves v. State*, 404 S.W.3d 180 (Ky. 2013).

Food for Thought

In *Reed v. Farley*, 512 U.S. 339 (1994), the Court, citing *Barker*, asserted: "A showing of prejudice is required to establish a violation of the Sixth Amendment Speedy Trial Clause, and that necessary ingredient is entirely missing here." Does *Reed* further modify or rebalance the statements in *Doggett* about the interrelationship of the *Barker* factors?

Hypo 1: *Speedy Trial & Retrials*

A man is convicted of sexually assaulting his young daughter, but the conviction is overturned because of a confrontation clause violation. Regarding his retrial, the man contends that he had an independent and absolute right to a speedy trial which he contended precluded continuances or exceptions. The prosecution claims that a delay was justified by the primary witness's refusal to cooperate, as well as by the fact that she had married, changed her name, and had moved, making it difficult to locate her. The prosecution located her in California, and moved for a continuance, claiming that they had exercised due diligence in trying to locate her. Would it violate the right to a speedy trial to grant the continuance under these circumstances? *See Mosley v. People*, 392 P.3d 1198 (Colo. 2017).

Hypo 2: *Locating the Defendant*

In early 2006, Bob and John arranged to purchase cocaine from Sam. Sam, acting as a "middleman," set up a meeting with Bob, John and a cocaine supplier, who in fact was an undercover federal agent working with the police. The meeting took place on March 30, 2006, at which time Bob and John were arrested by the federal agent on suspicion of state law drug violations. Because of the amount of drugs involved, the police requested federal prosecution. John was soon released from custody. A federal indictment was returned on May 8, 2006. John, however, was not arrested until October 16, 2007. Metro Police Officer Bill Green testified that during the time between John's indictment and arrest, he spent several nights looking for John, including watching John's house, which Green said looked vacant. At one point, Green knocked on John's door, but John's wife said he was at work. Green left a message with John's wife, but did not mention that John was under federal indictment. In June, 2006, Green suspended efforts to locate John, under the impression that United States Marshals would take over the case. In October, 2007, Green happened to drive by John's house, saw that the lights were on, and knocked on the door. John answered, and was arrested. John moves to dismiss the indictment because of unconstitutional delay. The United States, of course, opposes the motion. What are the merits of the motion to dismiss? Would you grant it?

Food for Thought

Defendant is indicted for murder, but it takes 21 months for the prosecution to bring him to trial. Defendant claims that his right to a speedy trial was infringed by the delay. Defendant's attorney did not initially object to the delay, and even agrees that the reason for the delay (to obtain a DNA analysis regarding a hat) involves a "crucial piece of evidence." Defendant eventually filed a *pro se* motion objecting to the delay, but he still was not brought to trial until a year later. During this time, the prosecutor repeatedly contacted the DNA lab for details. In addition, defendant was already in jail on state charges. When the DNA analysis came back, there was no link between defendant and the crime. Under the *Barker* factors, is dismissal for undue delay appropriate? *See Miles v. Jordan*, 988 F.3d 916 (6th Cir. 2021).

Hypo 3: *Clerical Error*

Willie was indicted on April 23, 2006, for polluting streams near his home. After indictment, the state moves for three continuances of six months each to allow the prosecutor additional time to prepare her case. In addition, the trial judge's clerk forgets to redocket the case for trial for one year. During this two and a half year time frame, public opinion has become less tolerant of water pollution. In October 2008, Willie is found guilty by a jury and sentenced to ten years. Willie's counsel objects to the proceedings before and during trial, but the trial judge denies his motions to dismiss. Willie wants you to help him file an appeal. What speedy trial arguments will you make on Willie's behalf? Are they likely to be successful?

Food for Thought

Cooley was indicted by a grand jury in August, 2019, and an arrest warrant was entered into the National Crime Information Center (NCIC) system. Fourteen months later (October, 2020), the FBI realized that the warrant had been inadvertently removed from the system and reentered it. In March, 2021, officers arrested Cooley and scheduled his trial for July, 2021. After two continuances, which were sought by Cooley's co-defendants and to which Cooley did not object, the case was tried in December, 2021. Under the circumstances, did the prosecution violate Cooley's right to a speedy trial? *See United States v. Cooley*, 63 F.4th 1173 (8th Cir. 2023).

C. Statutory Prompt Disposition Provisions

In addition to the constitutional speedy trial standard, many state legislatures and the Congress have enacted speedy trial legislation that establishes specific time limits for completing stages of a criminal prosecution. For example, the federal Speedy Trial Act (18 U.S.C. § 3161 *et seq.*) requires that an arrested defendant be formally charged within thirty days after arrest and that the defendant's trial begin within seventy days after the formal charge is filed. In addition, the trial cannot begin earlier than thirty days from the date the defendant first appears before the court unless the defendant consents in writing to an earlier trial. Unlike the constitutional standard that makes the passage of time a "triggering mechanism," the statute makes the passage of time dispositive of whether there is a violation. Many speedy trial statutes, like the federal Act, do not require a defendant to show either a demand for a speedy trial or that the effect of the delay was prejudicial.

Certain types of pretrial delays are automatically excluded from the computation of legislative time limits, including periods of delay like the absence or unavailability of the defendant or an essential witness (as long as it is not the result of a lack of due diligence), delays resulting from the joinder of a codefendant, and delays resulting from "other proceedings" involving the defendant. In *Henderson v. United States*, 476 U.S. 321 (1986), the Court held that Congress intended the "other proceedings" provision to require exclusion of all delays attributable to pendency of pretrial motions regardless of whether the delays are reasonably necessary. 18 U.S.C. § 3161(h)(1)(D) covers the delay from the filing of any pretrial motion through the hearing or other disposition of the motion. The running of the 70-day period from indictment to trial stops upon the filing of the pretrial motion, regardless of whether it actually causes a delay in starting the trial. *See United States v. Tinklenberg*, 563 U.S. 647 (2011). However, time granted by the trial court to *prepare* pretrial motions is not necessarily automatically excludable. *See Bloate v. United States*, 559 U.S. 196 (2010). To give trial judges some flexibility, continuances may be granted when the "ends of justice" outweigh the interest of the public and the defendant in a speedy trial. By contrast, a court cannot grant a continuance for delays caused by general congestion of the court calendar, or by the prosecution's failure to prepare diligently or obtain available witnesses.

To compute whether there has been a statutory violation, the court calculates the gross elapsed days and subtracts the number of days attributable to excludable time, leaving the net elapsed days. If the Act's time limits are not met, the charges against a defendant must be dismissed. The key determination for the trial judge is whether the dismissal must be with or without prejudice ("with prejudice" means the prosecution cannot re-bring the charges later). As stated in 18 U.S.C. §§ 3162(a)(1)–(2), the judge should consider three factors in exercising discretion to dismiss charges with or without prejudice: 1) the seriousness of the offense; 2) the circumstances leading to dismissal; and 3) the effect of reprosecution on the administration of justice and the speedy trial legislation. In *United States v. Taylor*, 487 U.S. 326 (1988), the Court held that it is an abuse of discretion for the trial judge to fail to consider each statutory factor and explain other factors relied upon in deciding whether to dismiss charges.

Points for Discussion

a. Waiver of Speedy Trial

Is a defendant permitted to waive the requirements of the Speedy Trial Act? For example, can a defendant execute a written waiver of speedy trial rights based on an "ends of justice" continuance under § 3161(h)(8)? In *Zedner v. United States*, 547 U.S. 489 (2006), the Court stated that, under § 3162(a)(2), a waiver of the right to dismissal for a past statutory violation occurs when a defendant fails to file a motion for dismissal before trial or before entering a guilty plea. However, that provision does not indicate that Congress intended to permit prospective

> **FYI**
>
> The STA requires that the trial begin within seventy days of the filing of an information or indictment, or of the date the defendant appears before an officer of the court in which the charge is pending, whichever is later.

waivers, *i.e.,* a defendant cannot opt out of the Act's requirements prior to a violation. The Act was intended to serve public interests that would be subverted by an interpretation that allowed prospective waivers.

> ### Food for Thought
>
> The Speedy Trial Act (STA) requires that an information or indictment be filed within thirty days after arrest or service of a summons on the defendant. Does the thirty-day period begin to run when a defendant is arrested and released without being charged and then is indicted after the thirty-day period has run? *See United States v. Gaskin,* 364 F. 3d 438 (2d Cir. 2004).

b. Superseding Indictment

Does the filing of a superseding indictment for offenses charged affect the seventy-day period? *See United States v. Apperson,* 441 F. 3d 1162 (10th Cir. 2006).

c. Pretrial Period

What trial event constitutes the end of the pretrial period? *See United States v. Rodriguez,* 63 F. 3d 1159 (1st Cir. 1995).

Food for Thought

After the Speedy Trial Act's time limit has passed, the trial court grants a detained defendant's motion to dismiss. As the defendant is about to be released, the government refiles a new indictment. Can the government keep the defendant in custody? Compare *United States v. Tirasso*, 532 F.2d 1298 (9th Cir. 1976), with *United States v. Worthy*, 699 F.3d 661 (1st Cir. 2012).

Hypo: A State Statutory Problem

The state of Pennsylvania failed to prosecute the defendant for kidnapping and rape within the one-year statutory period. The preliminary hearing judge failed to forward the case to the court's central docketing system; the state failed to follow up and track the case itself; and the defendant did not mention the issue until he moved for a speedy trial dismissal just after the one-year period. Should the case be dismissed on speedy trial grounds? *See Commonwealth v. Bradford*, 46 A.3d 693 (Pa. 2012).

Executive Summary

Pre-Charge Delay. Due process may protect an accused from delay between the crime and the earlier of an arrest, indictment or information.

Speedy Trial Right. The Sixth Amendment speedy trial right protects a defendant from delay from the earlier of arrest or formal charge to trial.

When Violated. A balancing of the length of the delay, reasons for the delay, assertion of the speedy trial right, and any prejudice from the delay determines whether there is a violation of the constitutional right to a speedy trial under the Sixth Amendment.

Speedy Trial Statutes. Most jurisdictions, including the federal law, have speedy trial statutes that measure a violation exclusively by the lapse of a specific length of time, after subtracting time attributable to specific types of excludable delay.

Major Themes

a. Defense Burden—While there is a due process right against undue pretrial delay, it is almost impossible for a defendant to meet the burden of proving that the prosecutor's delay in charging was in bad faith and resulted in actual prejudice to the defendant's ability to present a case.

b. Prejudice—While there are four *Barker v. Wingo* factors for courts to consider, by far the most important to most courts is the ability of the defendant to show prejudice from the delay. Without prejudice, courts are reluctant to grant the extreme remedy for a speedy trial delay, which is dismissal. *Doggett* gave defendants the benefit of a presumption of prejudice if the delay has reached one year.

For More Information

- Russell L. Weaver, John M. Burkoff, Catherine Hancock & Steven I. Friedland, Principles of Criminal Procedure Ch. 14 (8th ed. 2024).

- Wayne R. LaFave, Jerold H. Israel, Nancy J. King & Orin S. Kerr, Criminal Procedure (6th ed. 2017).

Test Your Knowledge

To assess your understanding of the material in this chapter, click here to take a quiz.

CHAPTER 3

The Right to Counsel

A. Generally

In 1938, the United States Supreme Court held that federal defendants who could not afford an attorney had a constitutional right to appointed counsel under the Sixth Amendment. *Johnson v. Zerbst*, 304 U.S. 458 (1938). Justice Black, writing for the majority, emphasized that "the Sixth Amendment stands as a constant admonition that if the constitutional safeguards it provides be lost, justice will not 'still be done.' It embodies a realistic recognition of the obvious truth that the average defendant does not have the professional legal skills to protect himself when brought before a tribunal with power to take his life or liberty, wherein the prosecution is presented by experienced and learned counsel. The Sixth Amendment withholds from federal courts, in all criminal proceedings, the power and authority to deprive an accused of his life or liberty unless he has or waives the assistance of counsel."

Betts v. Brady

316 U.S. 455 (1942).

MR. JUSTICE ROBERTS delivered the opinion of the Court.

Smith Betts was indicted for robbery in the Circuit Court of Carroll County, Maryland. Due to lack of funds he was unable to employ counsel, and so informed the judge at his arraignment. He requested that counsel be appointed for him. The judge advised him that this could not be done as it was not the practice in Carroll County to appoint counsel for indigent defendants save in prosecutions for murder and rape.

Without waiving his asserted right to counsel the petitioner pleaded not guilty and elected to be tried without a jury. At his request witnesses were summoned in his behalf. He cross-examined the State's witnesses and examined his own. The latter gave testimony tending to establish an alibi. Although afforded the opportunity, he did not take the witness stand. The judge found him guilty and imposed a sentence of eight years.

Was the petitioner's conviction and sentence a deprivation of his liberty without due process of law, in violation of the Fourteenth Amendment, because of the court's refusal to appoint counsel at his request?

The Sixth Amendment of the national Constitution applies only to trials in federal courts. The due process clause of the Fourteenth Amendment does not incorporate, as such, the specific guarantees found in the Sixth Amendment although a denial by a State of rights or privileges specifically embodied in that and others of the first eight amendments may, in certain circumstances, or in connection with other elements, operate, in a given case, to deprive a litigant of due process of law in violation of the Fourteenth. The phrase due process of law formulates a concept less rigid and more fluid than those envisaged in other specific and particular provisions of the Bill of Rights. Its application is less a matter of rule. Asserted denial is to be tested by an appraisal of the totality of facts in a given case. That which may, in one setting, constitute a denial of fundamental fairness, shocking to the universal sense of justice, may, in other circumstances, and in the light of other considerations, fall short of such denial. In the application of such a concept there is always the danger of falling into the habit of formulating the guarantee into a set of hard and fast rules the application of which in a given case may be to ignore the qualifying factors therein disclosed.

The question we are now to decide is whether due process of law demands that in every criminal case, whatever the circumstances, a State must furnish counsel to an indigent defendant. Is the furnishing of counsel in all cases whatever dictated by natural, inherent, and fundamental principles of fairness? The answer to the question may be found in the common understanding of those who have lived under the Anglo-American system of law. By the Sixth Amendment the people ordained that, in all criminal prosecutions, the accused should "enjoy the right to have the Assistance of Counsel for his defense." We have construed the provision to require appointment of counsel in all cases where a defendant is unable to procure the services of an attorney, and where the right has not been intentionally and competently waived. Though, as we have noted, the Amendment lays down no rule for the conduct of the States, the question recurs whether the constraint laid by the Amendment upon the national courts expresses a rule so fundamental and essential to a fair trial, and so, to due process of law, that it is made obligatory upon the states by the Fourteenth Amendment. Relevant data on the subject are afforded by constitutional and statutory provisions subsisting in the colonies and the states prior to the inclusion of the Bill of Rights in the national Constitution, and in the constitutional, legislative, and judicial history of the States to the present date.

The Constitutions of the thirteen original States, as they were at the time of federal union, exhibit great diversity in respect of the right to have counsel in criminal cases. It is evident that the constitutional provisions to the effect that a defendant should be "allowed" counsel or should have a right "to be heard by himself and his counsel," or that he might be heard by "either or both," at his election, were intended to do away with the rules which denied representation, in whole or in part, by counsel in criminal prosecutions, but were not aimed to compel the State to provide counsel for a defendant.

The constitutions of all the States, presently in force, save that of Virginia, contain provisions with respect to the assistance of counsel in criminal trials. Those of nine States may be said to embody a guarantee textually the same as that of the Sixth Amendment, or of like import. In the fundamental law of most States, however, the language used indicates only that a defendant is not to be denied the privilege of representation by counsel of his choice.

This demonstrates that, in the great majority of the States, it has been the considered judgment of the people, their representatives and their courts that appointment of counsel is not a fundamental right, essential to a fair trial.

On the contrary, the matter has generally been deemed one of legislative policy. In the light of this evidence, we are unable to say that the concept of due process incorporated in the Fourteenth Amendment obligates the States, whatever may be their own views, to furnish counsel in every such case. Every court has power, if it deems proper, to appoint counsel where that course seems to be required in the interest of fairness.

In this case there was no question of the commission of a robbery. The State's case consisted of evidence identifying the petitioner as the perpetrator. The defense was an alibi. Petitioner called and examined witnesses to prove that he was at another place at the time of the commission of the offense. The simple issue was the veracity of the testimony for the State and that for the defendant. As Judge Bond says, the accused was not helpless, but was a man forty-three years old, of ordinary intelligence, and ability to take care of his own interests on the trial of that narrow issue. He had once before been in a criminal court, pleaded guilty to larceny and served a sentence and was not wholly unfamiliar with criminal procedure.

Make the Connection

Recall the discussion in Chapter 2(A) of the pre-incorporation "fundamental rights" approach to determining individual rights in the states. This is a perfect example. The Court here won't require states to respect Bill of Rights provisions unless they are "fundamental and necessary" to due process or "shocking to the universal sense of justice." What does this actually mean in this setting? What significance do you think we should give today to the fact that, when the Constitution was adopted, indigent defendants did not have the right to counsel?

It is quite clear that in Maryland, if the situation had been otherwise and it had appeared that the petitioner was, for any reason, at a serious disadvantage by reason of the lack of counsel, a refusal to appoint would have resulted in the reversal of a judgment of conviction.

Food for Thought

Is this accurate? Do you believe that a person who previously pleaded guilty in a criminal matter would now be somewhat familiar with criminal procedure? Really?

To deduce from the due process clause a rule binding upon the states in this matter would be to impose upon them a requirement without distinction between criminal charges of different magnitude or in respect of courts of varying jurisdiction. "Presumably it would be argued that trials in the Traffic Court would require it." And indeed it was said by petitioner's counsel both below and in this court, that as the Fourteenth Amendment extends the protection of due process to property as well as to life and liberty, if we hold with the petitioner, logic would require the furnishing of counsel in civil cases involving property.

As we have said, the Fourteenth Amendment prohibits the conviction and incarceration of one whose trial is offensive to the common and fundamental ideas of fairness and right, and while want of counsel in a particular case may result in a conviction lacking in such fundamental fairness, we cannot say that the Amendment embodies an inexorable command that no trial for any offense, or in any court, can be fairly conducted and justice accorded a defendant who is not represented by counsel.

The judgment is *Affirmed*.

MR. JUSTICE BLACK, dissenting, with whom MR. JUSTICE DOUGLAS and MR. JUSTICE MURPHY concur.

The petitioner, a farm hand, out of a job and on relief, was indicted in a Maryland state court on a charge of robbery. He was too poor to hire a lawyer. He so informed the court and requested that counsel be appointed to defend him. His request was denied. Put to trial without a lawyer, he conducted his own defense, was found guilty, and was sentenced to eight years' imprisonment. The court below found that the petitioner had "at least an ordinary amount of intelligence." It is clear from his examination of witnesses that he was a man of little education.

If this case had come to us from a federal court, it is clear we should have to reverse it, because the Sixth Amendment makes the right to counsel in criminal cases inviolable by the Federal Government. I believe that the Fourteenth Amendment made the Sixth applicable to the states. But this view, although often urged in dissents, has never been accepted by a majority of this Court and is not accepted today.

This Court has declared that due process of law is denied if a trial is conducted in such manner that it is "shocking to the universal sense of justice" or "offensive to the common and fundamental ideas of fairness and right." On another occasion, this Court has recognized that whatever is "implicit in the concept of ordered liberty" and "essential to the substance of a hearing" is within the procedural protection afforded by the constitutional guaranty of due process. The right to counsel in a criminal proceeding is "fundamental."

An historical evaluation of the right to a full hearing in criminal cases, and the dangers of denying it, were set out in the *Powell v. Alabama*, 287 U.S. 45 (1932), case, where this Court said: "What does a hearing include? Historically and in practice, in our own country at least, it has always included the right to the aid of counsel when desired and provided by the party asserting the right. Even the intelligent and educated layman lacks both the skill and knowledge adequately to prepare his defense, even though he have a perfect one. He requires the guiding hand of counsel in every step in the proceedings against him. Without it, though he be not guilty, he faces the danger of conviction because he does not know how to establish his innocence."

A practice cannot be reconciled with "common and fundamental ideas of fairness and right," which subjects innocent men to increased dangers of conviction merely because of their poverty. Whether a man is innocent cannot be determined from a trial in which, as here, denial of counsel has made it impossible to conclude, with any satisfactory degree of certainty, that the defendant's case was adequately presented.

Gideon v. Wainwright

372 U.S. 335 (1963).

MR. JUSTICE BLACK delivered the opinion of the Court.

Petitioner was charged in a Florida state court with having broken and entered a poolroom with intent to commit a misdemeanor. This offense is a felony under Florida law. Appearing in court without funds and without a lawyer, petitioner asked the court to appoint counsel for him, whereupon the following colloquy took place:

"The COURT: Mr. Gideon, I am sorry, but I cannot appoint Counsel to represent you in this case. Under the laws of the State of Florida, the only time the Court can appoint Counsel to represent a Defendant is when that person is charged with a capital offense. I am sorry, but I will have to deny your request to appoint Counsel to defend you in this case.

"The DEFENDANT: The United States Supreme Court says I am entitled to be represented by Counsel."

Put to trial before a jury, Gideon conducted his defense about as well as could be expected from a layman. He made an opening statement to the jury, cross-examined the State's witnesses, presented witnesses in his own defense, declined to testify himself, and made a short argument "emphasizing his innocence to the charge contained in the Information filed in this case." The jury returned a verdict of guilty, and petitioner was sentenced to serve five years in the state prison. Gideon subsequently filed a *habeas corpus* petition attacking his conviction on the ground that the trial court's refusal to appoint counsel for him was unconstitutional. The Florida Supreme Court denied him any relief without opinion. Since 1942, when *Betts v. Brady* was decided by a divided Court, the problem of a defendant's federal constitutional right to counsel in a state court has been a continuing source of controversy and litigation in both state and federal courts.

The Sixth Amendment provides: "In all criminal prosecutions, the accused shall enjoy the right to have the Assistance of Counsel for his defense." We have construed this to mean that in federal courts counsel must be provided for defendants unable to employ counsel unless the right is competently and intelligently waived. *Betts* argued that this right is extended to indigent defendants in state courts by the Fourteenth Amendment. In response the Court stated that, while the Sixth Amendment laid down "no rule for the conduct of the States, the question recurs whether the constraint laid by the Amendment upon the national courts expresses a rule so fundamental and essential to a fair trial, and so, to due process of law, that it is made obligatory upon the States by the Fourteenth Amendment." In order to decide whether the Sixth Amendment's guarantee of counsel is of this fundamental nature, the Court in *Betts* set out and considered "relevant data on the subject afforded by constitutional and statutory provisions subsisting in the colonies and the states prior to the inclusion of the Bill of Rights in the national Constitution, and in the constitutional, legislative, and judicial history of the States to the present date." On the basis of this historical data the Court concluded that "appointment of counsel is not a fundamental right, essential to a fair trial." It was for this reason the *Betts* Court refused to accept the contention that the Sixth Amendment's guarantee of counsel for indigent federal defendants was extended to or, in the words of that Court, "made obligatory upon the states by the Fourteenth Amendment." Plainly, had the Court concluded that appointment of counsel for an indigent criminal defendant was "a fundamental right, essential to a fair trial," it would have held that the Fourteenth Amendment requires appointment of counsel in a state court, just as the Sixth Amendment requires in a federal court.

See It

You can watch the legendary actor, Henry Fonda, do a terrific job of playing the role of Clarence Gideon in the 1980 made-for-TV film, *Gideon's Trumpet*, based on the book by Anthony Lewis. *See* http://www.imdb.com/title/tt0080789/.

We accept *Betts v. Brady*'s assumption, based as it was on our prior cases, that a provision of the Bill of Rights which is "fundamental and essential to a fair trial" is made obligatory upon the States by the Fourteenth Amendment. We think the Court in *Betts* was wrong, however, in concluding that the Sixth Amendment's guarantee of counsel is not one of these fundamental rights.

The fact is that in deciding as it did—that "appointment of counsel is not a fundamental right, essential to a fair trial"—the Court in *Betts v. Brady* made an abrupt break with its own well-considered precedents. In returning to these old precedents, sounder we believe than the new, we but restore constitutional principles established to achieve a fair system of justice. Not only these precedents but also reason and reflection require us to recognize that in our adversary system of criminal justice, any person haled into court, who is too poor to hire a lawyer, cannot be assured a fair trial unless counsel is provided for him. This seems to us to be an obvious truth. Governments, both state and federal, quite properly spend vast sums of money to establish machinery to try defendants accused of crime. Lawyers to prosecute are everywhere deemed essential to protect the public's interest in an orderly society. Similarly, there are few defendants charged with crime, few indeed, who fail to hire the best lawyers they can get to prepare and present their defenses. That government hires lawyers to prosecute and defendants who have the money hire lawyers to defend are the strongest indications of the wide-spread belief that lawyers in criminal courts are necessities, not luxuries. The right of one charged with crime to counsel may not be deemed fundamental and essential to fair trials in some countries, but it is in ours. From the very beginning, our state and national constitutions and laws have laid great emphasis on procedural and substantive safeguards designed to assure fair trials before impartial tribunals in which every defendant stands equal before the law. This noble ideal cannot be realized if the poor man charged with crime has to face his accusers without a lawyer to assist him. A defendant's need for a lawyer is nowhere better stated than in the moving words of Mr. Justice Sutherland in *Powell v. Alabama*, 287 U.S. 45 (1932):

> "The right to be heard would be, in many cases, of little avail if it did not comprehend the right to be heard by counsel. Even the intelligent and educated layman has small and sometimes no skill in the science of law. If charged with crime, he is incapable, generally, of determining for himself whether the indictment is good or bad. He is unfamiliar with the rules of evidence. Left without the aid of counsel he may be put on trial without a proper charge, and convicted upon incompetent evidence, or evidence irrelevant to the issue or otherwise inadmissible. He lacks both the skill and knowledge adequately to prepare his defense, even though he have a perfect one. He requires the guiding hand of counsel at every step in the proceedings against him. Without it, though he be not guilty, he faces the danger of conviction because he does not know how to establish his innocence."

The Court in *Betts v. Brady* departed from the sound wisdom upon which the Court's holding in *Powell v. Alabama* rested. Florida, supported by two other States, has asked that *Betts v. Brady* be left intact. Twenty-two States, as friends of the Court, argue that *Betts* was "an anachronism when handed down" and that it should now be overruled.

We agree. *Reversed.*

MR. JUSTICE HARLAN, concurring.

Food for Thought

Why do you think that the Attorneys General from twenty-two states filed an *Amicus* Brief *in Gideon's behalf* rather than supporting the state of Florida? Do you think they were simply convinced at this point in time that *Betts* was wrongly decided? Or could they have had some tactical motivation for taking this position?

When we hold a right or immunity to be "implicit in the concept of ordered liberty" and thus valid against the States, we do not automatically carry over an entire body of federal law and apply it in full sweep to the States. Any such concept would disregard the frequently wide disparity between the legitimate interests of the States and of the Federal Government, the divergent problems that they face, and the significantly different consequences of their actions.

Points for Discussion

a. **Providing Indigent Services**

Indigent defense systems provide representation using:

- governmental public defender office, which provides representation through publicly operated governmental offices where staff are government employees funded by the state or county governments

- governmental conflict public defender office, which provides representation in cases where legal conflicts exist through a publicly operated governmental office and where staff are government employees

- nongovernmental public defender office, which provides representation through written contracts between some governmental entity and a nonprofit entity. Staff are not government employees

- contract system, which provides representation through contracts or other agreements between a governmental entity and one or more private attorneys or law firms that operate for-profit

- assigned or appointed counsel system, which provides representation through individual attorneys or law firms. These attorneys are assigned or appointed on a case-by-case basis.

Two-thirds of all reported criminal cases were closed by public defender offices. In 2013, state-administered indigent defense systems served an estimated 103,778,710 residents. The median number of cases closed per state was 75,560. In 2013, public defenders closed 67% of cases, followed by assigned counsel (20%), contract counsel (13%), and conflict counsel (<1%). Suzanne M. Strong, "State-Administered Indigent Defense Systems, 2013," U.S. Department of Justice Special Report (November 2016), https://bjs.ojp.gov/content/pub/pdf/saids13.pdf.

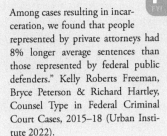

Among cases resulting in incarceration, we found that people represented by private attorneys had 8% longer average sentences than those represented by federal public defenders." Kelly Roberts Freeman, Bryce Peterson & Richard Hartley, Counsel Type in Federal Criminal Court Cases, 2015–18 (Urban Institute 2022).

County-based public defender offices received more than 4 million cases in 2007. About three-quarters (73%) of county-based public defender offices exceeded the maximum recommended limit of cases received per attorney in 2007. County-based offices employed a median of 7 litigating public defenders. Donald J. Farole, Jr. & Lynn Langton, County-based and Local Public Defender Offices, 2007 (U.S. Dept. Of Justice, Bur. Of Justice Statistics, Sept. 2010), https://www.bjs.gov/content/pub/pdf/clpdo07.pdf. State governments spent $2.3 billion on indigent defense in 2012. Erinn Herberman and Tracey Kyckelhahn, State Government Indigent Defense Expenditures, FY 2008–2012—Updated (U.S. Dept. Of Justice, Bur. Of Justice Statistics, October 24, 2014), http://www.bjs.gov/content/pub/pdf/sgide0812.pdf.

Court-appointed counsel represented 66% of federal felony defendants in 1998. U.S. Dept. of Justice, Bur. of Justice Statistics, Defense Counsel in Criminal Cases (November 2000). However,

> federal appellate and district judges express high regard for public defenders but low regard for court-appointed counsel and retained counsel. Retained counsel represent 25% and court-appointed counsel 33% of federal criminal defendants. If the quality of legal representation matters to criminal case outcomes, as recent studies suggest, a majority of indigent federal criminal defendants may be serving longer sentences by virtue of not having been represented by a federal public defender. The Constitution has been interpreted to place a floor under the quality of assistance of counsel tolerated in criminal cases, but one federal district judge described the work of defense attorneys other than public defenders as "exceedingly poor."

Richard A. Posner & Albert H. Yoon, *What Judges Think of the Quality of Legal Representation*, 63 STANFORD LAW REVIEW 317, 341–42 (2011).

Unfortunately, skyrocketing caseloads and inadequate funding for such programs has led to what some commentators deem "a crisis of extraordinary proportions in many states throughout the country." Richard Klein & Robert Spangenberg, *The Indigent Defense Crisis* 25 (ABA Section of Criminal Justice 1993). *See also id.* ("Justice often does not reach impoverished urban centers or poor rural counties where limited funding for indigent defense cannot provide effective representation to those accused of crime."); Stephen B. Bright, *Turning Celebrated Principles Into Reality*, CHAMPION 6 (January/February 2003):

> No constitutional right is celebrated so much in the abstract and observed so little in reality as the right to counsel. While leaders of the judiciary, legal profession and government give speeches every Law Day about the essential role of lawyers in protecting the individual rights of people accused of crimes, many states have yet to create and fund adequately independent programs for providing legal representation. As a result, some people—even people accused of felonies—enter guilty pleas and are sentenced to imprisonment without any representation. Others languish in jail for weeks or months—often for longer than any sentence they would receive—before being assigned a lawyer. Many receive only perfunctory representation—sometimes nothing more than hurried conversations with a court-appointed lawyer outside the courtroom or even in open court—before entering a guilty plea or going to trial. The poor person who is wrongfully convicted may face years in prison, or even execution, without any legal assistance to pursue avenues of post-conviction review.

See also Ethan Bronner, *Right to Lawyer Can Be Empty Promise for Poor*, New York Times p. A1 (March 16, 2013) ("The Legal Services Corporation says there are more than 60 million Americans—35 percent more than in 2005—who qualify for its services. But it calculates that 80 percent of the legal needs of the poor go unmet.");

Food for Thought

Do these comments and statistics make you wonder whether the *Gideon* decision has actually worked to accomplish what the Court thought or hoped that it would accomplish? Should more public monies be spent on indigent defense services? Is this realistic as a political matter?

Attorney General Eric Holder, Jr., *Defendants' legal rights undermined by budget cuts*, Washington Post (August 22, 2013) ("Despite the promise of the court's ruling in *Gideon*, the U.S. indigent defense systems—which provide representation to those who cannot afford it—are in financial crisis, plagued by crushing caseloads and insufficient resources."); Tony Schick, *Oregon lawmakers consider bill to overhaul public defense system*, Oregon Public Broadcasting

(May 1, 2023), https://www.opb.org/article/2023/04/03/oregon-legislature-bill-to-overhaul-public-defense-system/ ("Oregon lawmakers are considering a bill to overhaul the state's long-troubled public defense system. The state has too few attorneys to represent everyone charged with a crime, leaving many people without the adequate legal counsel they are guaranteed by the U.S. Constitution. That includes thousands of people charged with crimes who have no defense attorney.").

See further Matt Apuzzo, *Holder Backs Suit in New York Faulting Legal Service for Poor*, New York Times p. A1 (Sept. 25, 2014):

Attorney General Eric H. Holder Jr., who last year declared a crisis in America's legal-defense system for the poor, is supporting a class-action lawsuit that accuses Gov. Andrew M. Cuomo and the State of New York of perpetuating a system that violates the rights of people who cannot afford to hire lawyers. The lawsuit claims that public defenders in New York are so overworked and overmatched that poor people essentially receive no legal defense at all. It describes a system in which indigent defendants navigate courts nearly alone, relying on spotty advice from lawyers who do not have the time or money to investigate their cases or advise them properly. Because of substandard legal aid, children are taken from their parents, defendants in minor cases are jailed for long periods and people are imprisoned for crimes for which they might have been acquitted, the civil rights lawyers who filed the suit said.

Although the United States is not a party to the case, Mr. Holder is using the same core legal arguments as the plaintiffs and the weight of the federal government to resolve what he sees as deep-seated unfairness in local criminal courts. His views will bring national attention to a case that has mainly been of interest in New York. After Mr. Holder weighed in last year in a similar case in Washington State, the judge strongly rebuked the public-defense systems in two cities there and ordered improvements.

FYI

Difficulties in providing indigent services does not necessarily equate with lesser quality services. *See, e.g.,* Brian J. Ostrom & Jordan Bowman, "Examining the Effectiveness of Indigent Defense Team Services: A Multisite Evaluation of Holistic Defense in Practice, Project Summary," p. 49, U.S. Dept. of Justice, Office of Justice Programs (February 2020), https://www.ncjrs.gov/pdffiles1/nij/grants/254549.pdf: "The enhanced efficiency gained by holistic and traditional public defenders in Minnesota does not come at the expense of their clients. Public defenders, both holistic and traditional, are as successful as privately retained attorneys in achieving favorable outcomes for their clients. The conviction rates, dismissal rates, acquittal rates at trial, charge reduction rates, incarceration rates, and length of prison sentences for their clients are similar to the outcomes associated with privately retained counsel, with few substantive differences."

If the New York lawsuit succeeds, the state could be forced to take over the public-defense system, which is now run by county governments. Such an outcome would also quite likely encourage similar lawsuits, and, in turn, additional intervention by the Justice Department.

Mr. Holder has made the right to legal representation part of a broad effort to address inequities in the criminal justice system. He has pushed to reduce harsh sentences that were adopted during the country's crack epidemic, for example, and to eliminate mandatory-minimum sentences for nonviolent drug crimes.

"To truly guarantee adequate representation for low-income defendants, we must ensure that public defenders' caseloads allow them to do an effective job," Mr. Holder said in a statement. "The Department of Justice is committed to addressing the inequalities that unfold every day in America's courtrooms."

And, finally, see Sara Mayeux, "Our Rickety Public Defense System Has Finally Collapsed. Here's How to Fix It," The Nation (May 9, 2016), https://www.thenation.com/article/archive/our-rickety-public-defense-system-has-finally-collapsed-heres-how-to-fix-it/:

The persistence of crisis conditions in indigent defense suggests that the causes are deeply entrenched, and not a temporary reflection of shifting political views or economic vicissitudes. One long-term historical factor helping to explain America's weak commitment to indigent defense is the legal profession's own prestige hierarchy, which has long valorized advising corporations more than helping ordinary people. A second factor undermining indigent defense is simply the structure of American federalism. The New Orleans judge who recently ordered the release of defendants awaiting counsel wrote, by way of explanation, that "constitutional rights are not contingent on budget demands." But in practice, constitutional rights are often hamstrung by state-level budgets.

b.   Excessive Caseloads & Appointments

In *State ex rel. Missouri Public Defender Com'n v. Waters*, 370 S.W.3d 592 (Mo. 2012), the Missouri Supreme Court ruled that a trial court exceeded its lawful authority by appointing the state public defender's office to represent a defendant in contravention of an administrative rule permitting a district defender office to decline additional appointments when it has been certified as being on limited availability after exceeding its caseload capacity for at least three consecutive calendar months. The court reasoned that overburdened defense counsel is ineffective counsel and simply put, a judge may not appoint counsel when the judge is aware that, for whatever reason, counsel is unable to provide effective representation to a defendant. Effective, not just pro forma, representation is required by the Missouri and federal constitutions.

Does this make sense to you? Should (can?) courts force state or local governments to spend more on indigent defense, essentially making a "political" choice as between public spending priorities?

c.   **Who Is an "Indigent"?**

The Supreme Court has never defined "indigency" for purposes of an indigent criminal defendant's right to the appointment of counsel. States use varying formulae and income levels to define indigency for these purposes. The American Bar Association, in ABA Standards for Criminal Justice, Providing Defense Services Standard 5–7.1 (3d ed. 1992), has recommended the following standard be applied: "Counsel should be provided to persons who are financially unable to obtain adequate representation without substantial hardship. Counsel should not be denied because of a person's ability to pay part of the cost of representation, because friends or relatives have resources to obtain counsel, or because bond has been or can be posted."

d.   **Making the Indigent's Family Pay**

The Massachusetts Supreme Judicial Court has held that rules of court requiring the income of an otherwise indigent's defendant's girlfriend and mother to be attributed to him did not violate his right to counsel, and that it was not unconstitutional to place the burden of proving indigency on the defendant himself. *Com. v. Fico*, 462 Mass. 737, 971 N.E.2d 275 (2012). *See also Com. v. Porter*, 462 Mass. 724, 971 N.E.2d 291 (2012) (rule allowing defendant's spouse's income to be attributed to him for purposes of determining indigency held constitutional); *Com. v. Mortimer*, 462 Mass. 749, 971 N.E.2d 283 (2012) (rule allowing defendant's spouse's income to be attributed to him for purposes of determining indigency held constitutional). Is this fair? What do you think?

See further People v. Greer, 2022 CO 5, 502 P.3d 1012, 1019 (Colo. 2022) ("income from members of a defendant's household who contribute monetarily to the household should be excluded from an indigency determination when such income is unavailable to the defendant").

Food for Thought

Can public defenders refuse to take additional cases until they are "caught up" with existing cases, and simply ask judges to appoint private attorneys at state expense? What else can they do? Should they (can they) sue the state (their employers) for relief? *See, e.g.,* Dave Collins, *Public defenders feel squeeze: Conn. cuts create caseload worries,* BOSTON GLOBE (July 21, 2011), ("The public defenders' office cut all 30 of its per diem independent contractor positions last week, including 16 lawyers, and laid off 12 temporary employees, including seven lawyers. All 42 of those workers helped keep caseload levels down, but needed to be cut regardless of any union savings deal. To meet the savings mandated by the Legislature, the public defenders' office is proposing laying off 24 full-time employees and eliminating another nine jobs through attrition or retirements. The agency has not decided yet how many of those positions will be lawyers or when the job cuts will be made."); Deborah Yetter, *State's Public Defender Can't Refuse Cases, Court Rules,* LOUISVILLE COURIER-JOURNAL, A-1, c. 1–6 (Sept. 20, 2008).

Argersinger v. Hamlin

407 U.S. 25 (1972).

MR. JUSTICE DOUGLAS delivered the opinion of the Court.

Petitioner, an indigent, was charged in Florida with carrying a concealed weapon, an offense punishable by imprisonment up to six months, a $1,000 fine, or both. The Florida Supreme Court followed the line we marked out in *Duncan v. Louisiana*, 391 U.S. 145, 159, as respects the right to trial by jury and held that the right to court-appointed counsel extends only to trials "for non-petty offenses punishable by more than six months imprisonment." We reverse.

The right to trial by jury, also guaranteed by the Sixth Amendment by reason of the Fourteenth, was limited by Duncan to trials where the potential punishment was imprisonment for six months or more. But the right to trial by jury has a different genealogy and is brigaded with a system of trial to a judge alone. While there is historical support for limiting the "deep commitment" to trial by jury to "serious criminal cases," there is no such support for a similar limitation on the right to assistance of counsel.

The Sixth Amendment extended the right to counsel beyond its common-law dimensions. But there is nothing in the language of the Amendment, its history, or in the decisions of this Court, to indicate that it was intended to embody a retraction of the right in petty offenses wherein the common law previously did require that counsel be provided.

The assistance of counsel is often a requisite to the very existence of a fair trial. The requirement of counsel may well be necessary for a fair trial even in a petty-offense prosecution. We are by no means convinced that legal and constitutional questions involved in a case that actually leads to imprisonment even for a brief period are any less complex than when a person can be sent off for six months or more.

Beyond the problem of trials and appeals is that of the guilty plea, a problem which looms large in misdemeanor as well as in felony cases. Counsel is needed so that the accused may know precisely what he is doing, so that he is fully aware of the prospect of going to jail or prison, and so that he is treated fairly by the prosecution.

In addition, the volume of misdemeanor cases, far greater in number than felony prosecutions, may create an obsession for speedy dispositions, regardless of the fairness of the result. We must conclude, therefore, that the problems associated with misdemeanor and petty offenses often require the presence of counsel to insure the accused a fair trial. Mr. Justice Powell suggests that these problems are raised even in situations where there is no prospect of imprisonment. We need not consider the requirements of the Sixth Amendment as regards the right to counsel where loss of liberty is not involved, however, for here petitioner was in fact sentenced to jail. And, as we said in *Baldwin*, "the prospect of imprisonment for however short a time will seldom be viewed by the accused as a trivial or 'petty' matter and may well result in quite serious repercussions affecting his career and his reputation."

We hold, therefore, that absent a knowing and intelligent waiver, no person may be imprisoned for any offense, whether classified as petty, misdemeanor, or felony, unless he was represented by counsel at his trial.

We do not sit as an ombudsman to direct state courts how to manage their affairs but only to make clear the federal constitutional requirement. How crimes should be classified is largely a state matter. The fact that traffic charges technically fall within the category of "criminal prosecutions" does not necessarily mean that many of them will be brought into the class where imprisonment actually occurs.

Food for Thought

Does this holding make sense? How can a judge sensibly and fairly make the decision whether or not he or she is going to sentence the defendant (if convicted) to at least a day in jail *in advance of hearing the facts?*

Under the rule we announce today, every judge will know when the trial of a misdemeanor starts that no imprisonment may be imposed, even though local law permits it, unless the accused is represented by counsel. He will have a measure of the seriousness and gravity of the offense and therefore know when to name a lawyer to represent the accused before the trial starts.

Food for Thought

Is representation by a law student in criminal proceedings sufficient to meet the Sixth Amendment guarantee of the right to counsel? Would you want to have your spleen removed by a medical student? Is there a difference? What do you think? When he was alive, should we have arranged for a medical student to perform an endoscopy on Chief Justice Burger and *then* ask him if he thought this was adequate medical care? Too late now.

The run of misdemeanors will not be affected by today's ruling. But in those that end up in the actual deprivation of a person's liberty, the accused will receive the benefit of "the guiding hand of counsel" so necessary when one's liberty is in jeopardy.

Reversed.

MR. CHIEF JUSTICE BURGER, concurred in the result. MR. JUSTICE BRENNAN, with whom MR. JUSTICE DOUGLAS and MR. JUSTICE STEWART joined, concurred, adding:

Law students may provide an important source of legal representation for the indigent. More than 125 of the country's 147 accredited law schools have established clinical programs in which faculty supervised students aid clients in a variety of civil and criminal matters. These programs supplement practice rules enacted in 38 States authorizing students to practice law under prescribed conditions. Most of these regulations permit students to make supervised court appearances as defense counsel in criminal cases.

Given the huge increase in law school enrollments over the past few years, law students can be expected to make a significant contribution, quantitatively and qualitatively, to the representation of the poor in many areas.

MR. JUSTICE POWELL, with whom MR. JUSTICE REHNQUIST joins, concurring in the result.

The flat six-month rule of the Florida court and the equally inflexible rule of the majority opinion apply to all cases within their defined areas regardless of circumstances. It is precisely because of this mechanistic application that I find these alternatives unsatisfactory. Due process embodies principles of fairness rather than immutable line drawing as to every aspect of a criminal trial.

While counsel is often essential to a fair trial, this is by no means a universal

Food for Thought

Do you agree with Justice Powell? Was a "bright-line rule" really necessary here? Bright line rules are often appealing because they are seemingly easy to apply. However, sometimes these rules create anomalous results. It's hard to create a "one size fits all rule" and have it make sense in every situation. Case-by-case approaches, on the other hand, can produce unpredictable results and can be hard to apply. Which is better in this specific situation?

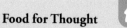

fact. Some petty offense cases are complex; others are exceedingly simple. Where the possibility of a jail sentence is remote and the probable fine seems small, or where the evidence of guilt is overwhelming, the costs of assistance of counsel may exceed the benefits. It is anomalous that the Court's opinion today will extend the right of appointed counsel to indigent defendants in cases where the right to counsel would rarely be exercised by nonindigent defendants. I would hold that the right to counsel in petty-offense cases is not absolute but is one to be determined by the trial courts exercising a judicial discretion on a case-by-case basis.

Points for Discussion

a. Right to Counsel for Fines?

In *Scott v. Illinois*, 440 U.S. 367 (1979), Scott was convicted of theft and fined $50 after a bench trial in which he was unrepresented. The Illinois statute set the maximum penalty for theft at a $500 fine and/or one year in jail. Scott challenged his conviction on the basis that *Argersinger* required the state to provide counsel whenever imprisonment was an *authorized* penalty. The Court rejected this challenge: "The central premise of *Argersinger*—that actual imprisonment is a penalty different in kind from fines or the mere threat of imprisonment—is eminently sound and warrants adoption of actual imprisonment as the line defining the constitutional right to appointment of counsel."

b. Suspended Sentences

In *Alabama v. Shelton*, 535 U.S. 654 (2002), the Supreme Court ruled 5-to-4 that the *Argersinger* and *Scott* day-in-jail rule applies to defendants who receive suspended sentences rather than actual incarceration. Shelton was convicted of assault and sentenced to 30 days in jail, but the trial court immediately suspended the sentence, placing him on probation for two years. The majority held that "the Sixth Amendment right to appointed counsel, as delineated in *Argersinger* and *Scott*, applies to a defendant in Shelton's situation. We hold that a suspended sentence that may 'end up in the actual deprivation of a person's liberty' may not be imposed unless the defendant was accorded 'the guiding hand of counsel' in the prosecution for the crime charged." The Court added that "a suspended sentence is a prison term imposed for the offense of conviction. Once the prison term is triggered, the defendant is incarcerated not for the probation violation, but for the underlying offense. The uncounseled conviction at that point 'results in imprisonment'; it 'ends up in the actual deprivation of a person's liberty.' This is precisely what the Sixth Amendment, as interpreted in *Argersinger* and *Scott*, does not allow."

c. **Sentence Enhancement with Uncounseled Conviction**

In *Baldasar v. Illinois*, 446 U.S. 222 (1980), the Supreme Court held that an uncounseled misdemeanor conviction, although lawful under *Scott*, could not be used to enhance a defendant's sentence for a subsequent misdemeanor conviction into a felony conviction under a sentencing enhancement statute. Subsequently, however, the Court reversed itself, overruling *Baldasar* and holding that "an uncounseled misdemeanor conviction, valid under *Scott* because no prison term was imposed, is also valid when used to enhance punishment at a subsequent conviction." *Nichols v. United States*, 511 U.S. 738, 749 (1994).

d. **When Right to Counsel Attaches**

Gideon and *Scott* focus upon the right to counsel at trial. The text of the Sixth Amendment embraces, however, "all criminal prosecutions," not just criminal trials. The Supreme Court has ruled, accordingly, that the right to counsel attaches prior to trial at any "critical stage of the criminal prosecution" after the "initiation of adversary judicial criminal proceedings—whether by way of formal charge, preliminary hearing, indictment, information, or arraignment." *Kirby v. Illinois*, 406 U.S. 682, 683, 689 (1972). A proceeding is a critical stage of the prosecution when "potential substantial prejudice to the defendant's rights inheres in the particular confrontation," and "the ability of counsel can help avoid that prejudice." *United States v. Wade*, 388 U.S. 218, 227 (1967). The right to counsel applies, for example, when a defendant appears at a sentencing proceeding, *Mempa v. Rhay*, 389 U.S. 128 (1967), when a defendant appears at a preliminary hearing, *Coleman v. Alabama*, 399 U.S. 1 (1970), and when a defendant first appears before a judge to be "told of the formal accusation against him and restrictions are imposed on his liberty," *Rothgery v. Gillespie County, Texas*, 554 U.S. 191, 194 (2008).

> **FYI**
>
> Based on California's Constitution, California's Supreme Court has decided indigent defendants are entitled to counsel during provisional appeals of in even minor criminal cases. *See Gardner v. Superior Court*, 6 Cal.5th 998, 245 Cal. Rptr.3d 58, 436 P.3d 946 (Cal. 2019).

e. Choosing Retained Defense Counsel

A criminal defendant with adequate resources has the right to retain counsel of his or her choice. *United States v., Gonzalez-Lopez*, 548 U.S. 140 (2006); *Chandler v. Fretag*, 348 U.S. 3 (1954). However, such retained counsel must be admitted to practice in the jurisdiction in which the trial is being held, unless the trial court exercises its discretion to grant counsel special admission to the Bar for purposes of that trial only ("*pro hac vice* admission"). *Leis v. Flynt*, 439 U.S. 438 (1979).

It's Latin to Me

Pro hac vice. A lawyer who has not been admitted to practice in a particular jurisdiction but who is admitted there temporarily for the purpose of conducting a particular case.

FYI

A trial court's order denying defendant the use of his retained counsel because counsel could not be available for three hours as he was attending a disciplinary proceeding was held to be a Sixth Amendment violation, and grounds for reversal of defendant's convictions and death sentence, entitling him to a new trial. *Randolph v. Secretary Pennsylvania Department of Corrections*, 5 F.4th 362, 379 (3d Cir. 2021), *cert. denied*, 142 S. Ct. 1461 (2022) ("One's right to choice of counsel is not without limits. Trial courts retain certain discretion to balance that right with the exigencies of administering criminal justice. But however broad a court's discretion may be, it is not broad enough to excuse the Sixth Amendment violation that occurred here.").

f. Indigents Have No Right to Choose Counsel

Unlike criminal defendants who have adequate resources to employ their own counsel, indigent defendants do not have a right to "choose" their counsel. As the Court explained in *Wheat v. United States*, 486 U.S. 153, 159 (1988), "the essential aim of the Sixth Amendment is to guarantee an effective advocate for each criminal defendant rather than to insure that a defendant will inexorably be represented by the lawyer whom he prefers. A defendant may not insist on representation by an attorney he cannot afford or who for other reasons declines to represent the defendant." A judge may, however, as a discretionary matter, appoint an attorney that an indigent defendant desires, assuming that such attorney is available and agrees to accept the (typically minimal) compensation that is provided for such appointed services.

Moreover, 18 U.S.C. § 3599 entitles indigent federal criminal defendants to the appointment of counsel in capital cases, including *habeas corpus* proceedings. In *Christeson v. Roper*, 574 U.S. 373 (2015), a majority of the Supreme Court held that a federal district court abused its discretion in denying a *habeas* petitioner's request for substitution of his federally-appointed counsel due to counsel's conflict of interest. Such motions for appointment of new counsel should be evaluated in the "interests of justice," the majority ruled, and substitution of counsel was necessary under that standard in *Christeson* where appointed counsel labored under what the Court deemed an "obvious conflict of interest."

Hypo 1: *License Revocation*

Does a respondent in a driver's license revocation proceeding have a right to appointed counsel? Would your answer be any different if the judge made it clear in advance that no jail time would be imposed?

Hypo 2: *Post-Verdict Motions*

After the criminal trial has concluded and the defendant has been convicted, does the defendant have a continuing right to be represented by appointed counsel for purposes of filing post-trial motions, like a motion for new trial, for example? What if the defendant represented himself at trial, waiving his right to appointed trial counsel? In that case, should his waiver mean that he has also lost the right to have counsel appointed to make post-trial motions for him? *See State v. Pitts*, 131 Hawai'i 537, 319 P.3d 456 (2014).

Hypo 3: *Special Relationship with Counsel*

Defendants Emily and William Harris, members of the "Symbionese Liberation Army," were charged with kidnaping, robbery, assault with a deadly weapon and false imprisonment. Defendants asked the trial judge to appoint attorneys Susan Johnson and Leonard Weinberg to represent them. Both attorneys were willing to undertake the representation, had represented defendants in a prior related proceeding, and purported to have a special relationship with defendants. Many of the witnesses in the prior proceeding were likely to be witnesses in this proceeding. The defendants also asserted that these attorneys shared their political and social beliefs so that there was a sense of mutual trust and confidence between them. In their view, to appoint "strangers" in whom they had no such confidence and trust would be to deprive them of a true representation of their interests. Should the judge grant defendants' motion to appoint these attorneys? How would you argue this case for the State? How might defendants respond? How would you rule? Suppose that the judge felt that it would be better to appoint other attorneys based on their reputation among the local bench and bar, their experience in the trial of capital cases, and the fact that the other attorneys were certified as criminal law specialists by the State Bar? *See Harris v. Superior Court*, 19 Cal.3d 786, 140 Cal. Rptr. 318, 567 P.2d 750 (In Banc, 1977).

Hypo 4: *Physical Assault on Counsel*

When should a trial judge deny an indigent defendant the right to counsel and force him or her to proceed pro se? Suppose that a defendant told his appointed counsel "I know how to get rid of you," and later physically assaulted him. If you were the judge, how should you proceed? If counsel wants to withdraw, should you release him, and, if so, are you obligated to appoint alternate counsel for the defendant, or can you force him to proceed *pro se*? *See State v. Holmes*, 302 S.W.3d 831 (Tenn. 2010).

B. Waiver of the Right to Counsel

Faretta v. California

422 U.S. 806 (1975).

MR. JUSTICE STEWART delivered the opinion of the Court.

The Sixth and Fourteenth Amendments of our Constitution guarantee that a person brought to trial in any state or federal court must be afforded the right to the assistance of counsel before he can be validly convicted and punished by imprisonment. This clear constitutional rule has emerged from a series of cases decided here over the last 50 years. The question before us now is whether a defendant in a state criminal trial has a constitutional right to proceed *without* counsel when he voluntarily and intelligently elects to do so. Stated another way, the question is whether a State may constitutionally hale a person into its criminal courts and there force a lawyer upon him, even when he insists that he wants to conduct his own defense. It is not an easy question, but we have concluded that a State may not constitutionally do so.

Anthony Faretta was charged with grand theft in an information filed in the Superior Court of Los Angeles County, Cal. At the arraignment, the Superior Court Judge assigned to preside at the trial appointed the public defender to represent Faretta. Well before the date of trial, however, Faretta requested that he be permitted to represent himself. Questioning by the judge revealed that Faretta had once represented himself in a criminal prosecution, that he had a high school education, and that he did not want to be represented by the public defender because he believed that office was "very loaded down with a heavy case load." The judge responded that he believed Faretta was "making a mistake" and emphasized that in further proceedings Faretta would receive no special favors. Nevertheless, after establishing that Faretta wanted to represent himself and did not want a lawyer, the judge, in a "preliminary ruling," accepted Faretta's waiver of the assistance of counsel. The judge indicated, however, that he might reverse this ruling if it later appeared that Faretta was unable adequately to represent himself.

It's Latin to Me

Sua sponte. Without prompting or suggestion; on its own motion.

Several weeks thereafter, but still prior to trial, the judge *sua sponte* held a hearing to inquire into Faretta's ability to conduct his own defense, and questioned him specifically about both the hearsay rule and the state law governing the challenge of potential jurors. After consideration of Faretta's answers, and observation of his demeanor, the judge ruled that Faretta had not made an intelligent and knowing waiver of his right to the assistance of counsel, and also ruled that Faretta had no constitutional right to conduct his own defense. The judge, accordingly, reversed his earlier ruling permitting self-representation and again appointed the public defender to represent Faretta. Faretta's subsequent request for leave to act as co-counsel was rejected, as were his efforts to make certain motions on his own behalf. Throughout the subsequent trial, the judge required that Faretta's defense be conducted only through the appointed lawyer from the public defender's office. At the conclusion of the trial, the jury found Faretta guilty as charged, and the judge sentenced him to prison. The California Court of Appeal affirmed the trial judge's ruling that Faretta had no federal or state constitutional right to represent himself.

In the federal courts, the right of self-representation has been protected by statute since the beginnings of our Nation. In *Adams v. U. S. ex rel. McCann*, 317 U.S. 269, 279 (1942), the Court recognized that the Sixth Amendment right to the assistance of counsel implicitly embodies a "correlative right to dispense with a lawyer's help." The defendant in that case, indicted for federal mail fraud violations, insisted on conducting his own defense without benefit of counsel. He also requested a bench trial and signed a waiver of his right to trial by jury. The prosecution consented to

Food for Thought

Why would a defendant want to proceed *pro se*? How can such a decision make sense? After all, few defendants are well versed in the criminal law, the rules of evidence, or in criminal procedure. So, how can they effectively represent themselves (or think that they can)?

the waiver of a jury, and the waiver was accepted by the court. The defendant was convicted, but the Court of Appeals reversed the conviction on the ground that a person accused of a felony could not competently waive his right to trial by jury except upon the advice of a lawyer. This Court reversed and reinstated the conviction, holding that "an accused, in the exercise of a free and intelligent choice, and with the considered approval of the court, may waive trial by jury, and so likewise may he competently and intelligently waive his Constitutional right to assistance of counsel."

The *Adams* case does not, of course, necessarily resolve the issue before us. It held only that "the Constitution does not force a lawyer upon a defendant." Whether the Constitution forbids a State from forcing a lawyer upon a defendant is a different question. But the Court in *Adams* did recognize, albeit in dictum, an affirmative right of self-representation:

"The right to assistance of counsel and the correlative right to dispense with a lawyer's help are not legal formalisms. They rest on considerations that go to the substance of an accused's position before the law.

"What were contrived as protections for the accused should not be turned into fetters. To deny an accused a choice of procedure in circumstances in which he, though a layman, is as capable as any lawyer of making an intelligent choice, is to impair the worth of great Constitutional safeguards by treating them as empty verbalisms.

"When the administration of the criminal law is hedged about as it is by the Constitutional safeguards for the protection of an accused, to deny him in the exercise of his free choice the right to dispense with some of these safeguards is to imprison a man in his privileges and call it the Constitution."

This Court's past recognition of the right of self-representation, the federal-court authority holding the right to be of constitutional dimension, and the state constitutions pointing to the right's fundamental nature form a consensus not easily ignored. We confront here a nearly universal conviction, on the part of our people as well as our courts, that forcing a lawyer upon an unwilling defendant is contrary to his basic right to defend himself if he truly wants to do so. This consensus is soundly premised. The right of self-representation finds support in the structure of the Sixth Amendment, as well as in the English and colonial jurisprudence from which the Amendment emerged. Because Sixth Amendment rights are basic to our adversary system of criminal justice, they are part of the "due process of law" that is guaranteed by the Fourteenth Amendment to defendants in the criminal courts of the States. The Sixth Amendment does not provide merely that a defense shall be made for the accused; it grants to the accused personally the right to make his defense. It is the accused, not counsel, who must be "informed of the nature and cause of the accusation," who must be "confronted with the witnesses against him," and who must be accorded "compulsory process for obtaining witnesses in his favor." Although not stated in the Amendment in so many words, the right to self-representation—to make one's own defense personally—is thus necessarily implied by the structure of the Amendment. The right to defend is given directly to the accused; for it is he who suffers the consequences if the defense fails.

The counsel provision supplements this design. It speaks of the "assistance" of counsel, and an assistant, however expert, is still an assistant. The language and spirit of the Sixth Amendment contemplate that counsel, like the other defense tools guaranteed by the Amendment, shall be an aid to a willing defendant—not an organ of the State interposed between an unwilling defendant and his right to defend himself personally. To thrust counsel upon the accused, against his considered wish, thus violates the logic of the Amendment. In such a case, counsel is not an assistant, but a master; and the right to make a defense is stripped of the personal character upon which the Amendment insists. It is true that when a defendant chooses to have a lawyer manage and present his case, law and tradition may allocate to the counsel the power to make binding decisions of trial strategy in many areas. This allocation can only be justified, however, by the defendant's consent, at the outset, to accept counsel as his representative. An unwanted counsel "represents" the defendant only through a tenuous and unacceptable legal fiction. Unless the accused has acquiesced in such representation, the defense presented is not the defense guaranteed him by the Constitution, for, in a very real sense, it is not *his* defense.

There can be no blinking the fact that the right of an accused to conduct his own defense seems to cut against the grain of this Court's decisions holding that the Constitution requires that no accused can be convicted and imprisoned unless he has been accorded the right to the assistance of counsel. For it is surely true that the basic thesis of those decisions is that the help of a lawyer is essential to assure the defendant a fair trial. And a strong argument can surely be made that the whole thrust of those decisions most inevitably lead to the conclusion that a State may constitutionally impose a lawyer upon even an unwilling defendant.

But it is one thing to hold that every defendant, rich or poor, has the right to the assistance of counsel, and quite another to say that a State may compel a defendant to accept a lawyer he does not want. The value of state-appointed counsel was not unappreciated by the Founders, yet the notion of compulsory counsel was utterly foreign to them. And whatever else may be said of those who wrote the Bill of Rights, surely there can be no doubt that they understood the inestimable worth of free choice.

It is undeniable that in most criminal prosecutions defendants could better defend with counsel's guidance than by their own unskilled efforts. But where the defendant will not voluntarily accept representation by counsel, the potential advantage of a lawyer's training and experience can be realized, if at all, only imperfectly. To force a lawyer on a defendant can only lead him to believe that the law contrives against him. Moreover, it is not inconceivable that in some rare instances, the defendant might in fact present his case more effectively by conducting his own defense. Personal liberties are not rooted in the law of averages. The right to defend is personal. The defendant,

Take Note

Footnote 46 is important. After the Court legitimized the concept of "standby counsel" here, the use of this technique became commonplace where defendants decided to "go *pro se*" in serious cases.

and not his lawyer or the State, will bear the personal consequences of a conviction. It is the defendant, therefore, who must be free personally to decide whether in his particular case counsel is to his advantage. And although he may conduct his own defense ultimately to his own detriment, his choice must be honored out of "that respect for the individual which is the lifeblood of the law."[46]

FYI

Is it *really* so foolish to want to represent oneself? *See, e.g.,* Erica J. Hashimoto, *Defending the Right to Self Representation: An Empirical Look at the* Pro Se *Felony Defendant*, 85 N.C. L. Rev. 423, 423–24 (2007):

> The data undermine both the assumption that most felony pro se defendants are ill-served by the decision to self-represent and the theory that most pro se defendants suffer from mental illness. Somewhat surprisingly, the data indicate that pro se felony defendants in state courts are convicted at rates equivalent to or lower than the conviction rates of represented felony defendants, and the vast majority of pro se felony defendants—nearly 80%—did not display outward signs of mental illness.

> The data also suggest an alternative explanation for the pro se phenomenon. The small, self-selected group of felony defendants who choose to represent themselves may make that choice because of legitimate concerns about court-appointed counsel. Without the right to represent themselves, those defendants would be in the untenable position of being represented by inadequate counsel with no alternative. When an accused manages his own defense, he relinquishes, as a purely factual matter, many of the traditional benefits associated with the right to counsel. For this reason, in order to represent himself, the accused must "knowingly

---

[46]   We are told that many criminal defendants representing themselves may use the courtroom for deliberate disruption of their trials. But the right of self-representation has been recognized from our beginnings by federal law and by most of the States, and no such result has thereby occurred. Moreover, the trial judge may terminate self-representation by a defendant who deliberately engages in serious and obstructionist misconduct. Of course, a State may—even over objection by the accused—appoint a 'standby counsel' to aid the accused if and when the accused requests help, and to be available to represent the accused in the event that termination of the defendant's self-representation is necessary.

The right of self-representation is not a license to abuse the dignity of the courtroom. Neither is it a license not to comply with relevant rules of procedural and substantive law. Thus, whatever else may or may not be open to him on appeal, a defendant who elects to represent himself cannot thereafter complain that the quality of his own defense amounted to a denial of "effective assistance of counsel."

> and intelligently" forgo those relinquished benefits. Although a defendant need not himself have the skill and experience of a lawyer in order competently and intelligently to choose self-representation, he should be made aware of the dangers and disadvantages of self-representation, so that the record will establish that "he knows what he is doing and his choice is made with eyes open."

Here, weeks before trial, Faretta clearly and unequivocally declared to the trial judge that he wanted to represent himself and did not want counsel. The record affirmatively shows that Faretta was literate, competent, and understanding, and that he was voluntarily exercising his informed free will. The trial judge had warned Faretta that he thought it was a mistake not to accept the assistance of counsel, and that Faretta would be required to follow all the "ground rules" of trial procedure. We need make no assessment of how well or poorly Faretta had mastered the intricacies of the hearsay rule and the California code provisions that govern challenges of potential jurors on *voir dire*. For his technical legal knowledge, as such, was not relevant to an assessment of his knowing exercise of the right to defend himself.

In forcing Faretta, under these circumstances, to accept against his will a state-appointed public defender, the California courts deprived him of his constitutional right to conduct his own defense. Accordingly, the judgment before us is vacated.

MR. JUSTICE BLACKMUN, with whom THE CHIEF JUSTICE and MR. JUSTICE REHNQUIST join, dissenting.

If there is any truth to the old proverb that "one who is his own lawyer has a fool for a client," the Court by its opinion today now bestows a *constitutional* right on one to make a fool of himself.

Point for Discussion

On Appeal

In *State v. Rafey*, 167 Wash.2d 644, 652, 222 P.3d 86, 89 (2009), the Washington Supreme Court recognized a convicted defendant's right to proceed *pro se* under the State of Washington's Constitution: "In both trial and appellate proceedings, courts must carefully balance the dissonant rights to counsel and to self-representation when a defendant seeks to proceed *pro se*." However, the court also warned that the right must be asserted in a timely manner. Are appellate proceedings so different from trial court proceedings that courts should *not* recognize a right to *pro se* representation in that setting? What do you think?

Hypo 1: *The Unabomber Case*

You are the federal judge assigned to hear the "Unabomber case." The defendant, Theodore Kaczynski, is the individual who was charged with having murdered a number of people with mail bombs. Defendant wants to conduct his own defense, but his own attorneys question his competency. The reality is that Kaczynski is very bright, but his sanity is questionable (to put it mildly). How do you decide whether Kaczynski is competent to represent himself? How much weight should you give to the fact that Kaczynski may not be insane, but is, any event, clearly not in sound mental health?

See It

Here's how the FBI described this case: "How do you catch a twisted genius who aspires to be the perfect, anonymous killer—who builds untraceable bombs and delivers them to random targets, who leaves false clues to throw off authorities, who lives like a recluse in the mountains of Montana and tells no one of his secret crimes? That was the challenge facing the FBI and its investigative partners, who spent nearly two decades hunting down this ultimate lone wolf bomber." *See* https://www.fbi.gov/history/famous-cases/unabomber.

Hypo 2: *Non-Investigating Great Advocate*

Defendant was represented at trial by a public defender. On several occasions during the trial, defendant expressed dissatisfaction with counsel's performance. Prior to jury selection, defendant filed a motion to dismiss his attorney. He claimed that his attorney was not investigating the case adequately. Defense counsel acknowledged the existence of some problems in investigating matters related to the case, but the judge nonetheless denied defendant's motion, noting that the defendant's attorney had been a "great advocate" for his client. Did the judge act properly? *State v. Flanagan*, 293 Conn. 406, 978 A.2d 64 (2009).

Iowa v. Tovar

541 U.S. 77 (2004).

JUSTICE GINSBURG delivered the opinion of the Court.

The Sixth Amendment safeguards to an accused who faces incarceration the right to counsel at all critical stages of the criminal process. The entry of a guilty plea, whether to a misdemeanor or a felony charge, ranks as a "critical stage" at which the right to counsel adheres. Waiver of the right to counsel, as of constitutional rights in the criminal process generally, must be a "knowing, intelligent act done with sufficient awareness of the relevant circumstances." This case concerns the extent to which a trial judge, before accepting a guilty plea from an uncounseled defendant, must elaborate on the right to representation.

Hear It

You can hear the oral argument in *Tovar* at http://www.oyez.org/cases/2000-2009/2003/2003_02_1541.

Beyond affording the defendant the opportunity to consult with counsel prior to entry of a plea and to be assisted by counsel at the plea hearing, must the court, specifically: (1) advise the defendant that "waiving the assistance of counsel in deciding whether to plead guilty entails the risk that a viable defense will be overlooked"; and (2) "admonish" the defendant "that by waiving his right to an attorney he will lose the opportunity to obtain an independent opinion on whether, under the facts and applicable law, it is wise to plead guilty"? The Iowa Supreme Court held both warnings essential to the "knowing and intelligent" waiver of the Sixth Amendment right to the assistance of counsel.

We hold that neither warning is mandated by the Sixth Amendment. The constitutional requirement is satisfied when the trial court informs the accused of the nature of the charges against him, of his right to be counseled regarding his plea, and of the range of allowable punishments attendant upon the entry of a guilty plea.

On November 2, 1996, respondent Felipe Edgardo Tovar, then a 21-year-old college student, was arrested in Ames, Iowa, for operating a motor vehicle while under the influence of alcohol (OWI). At arraignment, the court's inquiries of Tovar began: "Mr. Tovar appears without counsel and I see, Mr. Tovar, that you waived application for a court appointed attorney. Did you want to represent yourself at today's hearing?" Tovar replied: "Yes, sir." The court soon after asked: "How did you wish to plead?" Tovar answered: "Guilty." Tovar affirmed that he had not been promised anything or threatened in any way to induce him to plead guilty.

Conducting the guilty plea colloquy required by the Iowa Rules of Criminal Procedure, the court explained that, if Tovar pleaded not guilty, he would be entitled to a speedy and public trial by jury, and would have the right to be represented at that trial by an attorney, who "could help Tovar select a jury, question and cross-examine the State's witnesses, present evidence, if any, in his behalf, and make arguments to the judge and jury on his behalf." By pleading guilty, the court cautioned, "not only would Tovar give up his right to a trial of any kind on the charge against him, he would give up his right to be represented by an attorney at that trial." The court further advised Tovar that, if he entered a guilty plea, he would relinquish the right to remain silent at trial, the right to the presumption of innocence, and the right to subpoena witnesses and compel their testimony.

Turning to the particular offense with which Tovar had been charged, the court informed him that an OWI conviction carried a maximum penalty of a year in jail and a $1,000 fine, and a minimum penalty of two days in jail and a $500 fine. Tovar affirmed that he understood his exposure to those penalties. The court next explained that, before accepting a guilty plea, the court had to assure itself that Tovar was in fact guilty of the charged offense. To that end, the court informed Tovar that the OWI charge had only two elements: first, on the date in question, Tovar was operating a motor vehicle in the State of Iowa; second, when he did so, he was intoxicated. Tovar confirmed that he had been driving on the night he was apprehended and that he did not dispute the results of the intoxilyzer test administered by the police that night, which showed that his blood alcohol level exceeded the legal limit nearly twice over.

After the plea colloquy, the court asked Tovar if he still wished to plead guilty, and Tovar affirmed that he did. The court then accepted Tovar's plea, observing that there was "a factual basis" for it, and that Tovar had made the plea "voluntarily, with a full understanding of his rights, and of the consequences of pleading guilty."

On December 30, 1996, Tovar appeared for sentencing on the OWI charge. Noting that Tovar was again in attendance without counsel, the court inquired: "Mr. Tovar, did you want to represent yourself at today's hearing or did you want to take some time to hire an attorney to represent you?" Tovar replied that he would represent himself. The court then engaged in essentially the same plea colloquy on the suspension charge as it had on the OWI charge the previous month. After accepting Tovar's guilty plea, the court imposed the minimum sentence of two days in jail and a $500 fine, plus a surcharge and costs.

On March 16, 1998, Tovar was convicted of OWI for a second time. He was represented by counsel in that proceeding, in which he pleaded guilty. On December 14, 2000, Tovar was again charged with OWI, this time as a third offense. Represented by an attorney, Tovar pleaded not guilty.

In March 2001, through counsel, Tovar filed a motion arguing that Tovar's first OWI conviction, in 1996, could not be used to enhance the December 2000 OWI charge from a second-offense aggravated misdemeanor to a third-offense felony. Tovar did not allege that he was unaware at the November 1996 arraignment of his right to counsel prior to pleading guilty and at the plea hearing. Instead, he maintained that his 1996 waiver of counsel was invalid—not "full knowing, intelligent, and voluntary"—because he "was never made aware by the court of the dangers and disadvantages of self-representation."

The court denied Tovar's motion. Tovar then waived his right to a jury trial and was found guilty. On the OWI third-offense charge, he received a 180-day jail term, with all but 30 days suspended, three years of probation, and a $2,500 fine plus surcharges and costs. The Iowa Court of Appeals affirmed, but the Supreme Court of Iowa reversed, holding that the colloquy preceding acceptance of Tovar's 1996 guilty plea had been constitutionally inadequate. We granted certiorari and we now reverse.

The Sixth Amendment secures to a defendant who faces incarceration the right to counsel at all "critical stages" of the criminal process. A plea hearing qualifies as a "critical stage."

Because Tovar received a two-day prison term for his 1996 OWI conviction, he had a right to counsel both at the plea stage and at trial had he elected to contest the charge.

A person accused of crime, however, may choose to forgo representation. While the Constitution does not force a lawyer upon a defendant, it does require that any waiver of the right to counsel be knowing, voluntary, and intelligent. Tovar contends that his waiver of counsel at his first OWI plea hearing, was insufficiently informed, and therefore constitutionally invalid. In particular, he asserts that the trial judge did not elaborate on the value, at that stage of the case, of an attorney's advice and the dangers of self-representation in entering a plea.

Take Note

Note that, without much fanfare, the Court confirmed here that indigents have the right to counsel at guilty plea hearings.

We have described a waiver of counsel as intelligent when the defendant "knows what he is doing and his choice is made with eyes open." We have not, however, prescribed any formula or script to be read to a defendant who states that he elects to proceed without counsel. The information a defendant must possess in order to make an intelligent election will depend on a range of case-specific factors, including the defendant's education or sophistication, the complex or easily grasped nature of the charge, and the stage of the proceeding.

In Tovar's case, he first indicated that he waived counsel at his Initial Appearance, affirmed that he wanted to represent himself at the plea hearing, and declined the court's offer of "time to hire an attorney" at sentencing, when it was still open to him to request withdrawal of his plea. Does the Sixth Amendment require a court to give a rigid and detailed admonishment to a *pro se* defendant pleading guilty of the usefulness of an attorney, that an attorney may provide an independent opinion whether it is wise to plead guilty and that without an attorney the defendant risks overlooking a defense? This Court recently explained, in reversing a lower court determination that a guilty plea was not voluntary: "The law ordinarily considers a waiver knowing, intelligent, and sufficiently aware if the defendant fully understands the nature of the right and how it would likely apply in general in the circumstances—even though the defendant may not know the specific detailed consequences of invoking it." We have similarly observed: "If the defendant lacked a full and complete appreciation of all of the consequences flowing from his waiver, it does not defeat the State's showing that the information it provided to him satisfied the constitutional minimum."

In a collateral attack on an uncounseled conviction, it is the defendant's burden to prove that he did not competently and intelligently waive his right to the assistance of counsel. Tovar has never claimed that he did not fully understand the charge or the range of punishment for the crime prior to pleading guilty. Further, he has never "articulated with precision" the additional information counsel could have provided, given the simplicity of the charge. Nor does he assert that he was unaware of his right to be counseled prior to and at his arraignment. He suggests only that he "may have been under the mistaken belief that he had a right to counsel at trial, but not if he was merely going to plead guilty."

Food for Thought

As extensive as waiver-of-the-right-to-counsel colloquies may appear in theory, the reality is that many trial judges "fly through" them, and many other judges openly encourage such waivers. What effect to you think that the *Tovar* decision will have on that practical reality?

We note, finally, that States are free to adopt by statute, rule, or decision any guides to the acceptance of an uncounseled plea they deem useful. We hold only that the two admonitions the Iowa Supreme Court ordered are not required by the Federal Constitution.

For the reasons stated, the judgment of the Supreme Court of Iowa is reversed.

Indiana v. Edwards

554 U.S. 164 (2008).

JUSTICE BREYER delivered the opinion of the Court.

This case focuses upon a criminal defendant whom a state court found mentally competent to stand trial if represented by counsel but not mentally competent to conduct that trial himself. We must decide whether in these circumstances the Constitution forbids a State from insisting that the defendant proceed to trial with counsel, the State thereby denying the defendant the right to represent himself. We conclude that the Constitution does not forbid a State so to insist.

Hear It

You can hear the oral argument in *Edwards* at http://www.oyez.org/cases/2000-2009/2007/2007_07_208.

In July 1999 Ahmad Edwards tried to steal a pair of shoes from an Indiana department store. After he was discovered, he drew a gun, fired at a store security officer, and wounded a bystander. He was caught and then charged with attempted murder, battery with a deadly weapon, criminal recklessness, and theft. His mental condition subsequently became the subject of three competency proceedings and two self-representation requests, mostly before the same trial judge:

1. First Competency Hearing: August 2000. Five months after Edwards' arrest, his court-appointed counsel asked for a psychiatric evaluation. After hearing psychiatrist and neuropsychologist witnesses (in February 2000 and again in August 2000), the court found Edwards incompetent to stand trial and committed him to Logansport State Hospital for evaluation and treatment.

2. Second Competency Hearing: March 2002. Seven months after his commitment, doctors found that Edwards' condition had improved to the point where he could stand trial. Several months later, however, but still before trial, Edwards' counsel asked for another psychiatric evaluation. In March 2002, the judge held a competency hearing, considered additional psychiatric evidence, and (in April) found that Edwards, while "suffering from mental illness," was "competent to assist his attorneys in his defense and stand trial for the charged crimes."

3. Third Competency Hearing: April 2003. Seven months later but still before trial, Edwards' counsel sought yet another psychiatric evaluation of his client. And, in April 2003, the court held yet another competency hearing. Edwards' counsel presented further psychiatric and neuropsychological

evidence showing that Edwards was suffering from serious thinking difficulties and delusions. A testifying psychiatrist reported that Edwards could
understand the charges against him, but he was "unable to cooperate with
his attorney in his defense because of his schizophrenic illness"; "his delusions and his marked difficulties in thinking make it impossible for him to
cooperate with his attorney." In November 2003, the court concluded that
Edwards was not then competent to stand trial and ordered his recommit-
ment to the state hospital.

4.   First Self-Representation Request and First Trial: June 2005. About
eight months after his commitment, the hospital reported that Edwards'
condition had again improved to the point that he had again become competent to stand trial. And almost one year after that Edwards' trial began.
Just before trial, Edwards asked to represent himself. He also asked for a
continuance, which, he said, he needed in order to proceed pro se. The
court refused the continuance. Edwards then proceeded to trial represented
by counsel. The jury convicted him of criminal recklessness and theft but
failed to reach a verdict on the charges of attempted murder and battery.

5.   Second Self-Representation Request and Second Trial: December
2005. The State decided to retry Edwards on the attempted murder and
battery charges. Just before the retrial, Edwards again asked the court to
permit him to represent himself. Referring to the lengthy record of psychiatric reports, the trial court noted that Edwards still suffered from schizophrenia and concluded that "with these findings, he's competent to stand
trial but I'm not going to find he's competent to defend himself." The court
denied Edwards' self-representation request. Edwards was represented by
appointed counsel at his retrial. The jury convicted Edwards on both of the
remaining counts.

Subsequently, the Indiana Supreme Court concluded that this Court's precedents,
namely, *Faretta*, and *Godinez v. Moran*, 509 U.S. 389 (1993), required the State to
allow *Edwards* to represent himself. Our examination of this Court's precedents convinces us that those precedents frame the question presented, but they do not answer
it. The two cases that set forth the Constitution's "mental competence" standard,
Dusky v. United States, 362 U.S. 402 (1960), and *Drope v. Missouri*, 420 U.S. 162
(1975), specify that the Constitution does not permit trial of an individual who lacks
"mental competency." *Dusky* defines the competency standard as including both (1)
"whether" the defendant has "a rational as well as factual understanding of the proceedings against him" and (2) whether the defendant "has sufficient present ability
to consult with his lawyer with a reasonable degree of rational understanding." *Drope*
repeats that standard, stating that it "has long been accepted that a person whose
mental condition is such that he lacks the capacity to understand the nature and object

of the proceedings against him, to consult with counsel, and to assist in preparing his defense may not be subjected to a trial." Neither case considered the mental competency issue presented here, namely, the relation of the mental competence standard to the right of self-representation.

The Court's foundational "self-representation" case, *Faretta*, held that the Sixth and Fourteenth Amendments include a "constitutional right to proceed without counsel when" a criminal defendant "voluntarily and intelligently elects to do so." The sole case in which this Court considered mental competence and self-representation together is *Godinez*. That case focused upon a borderline-competent criminal defendant who had asked a state trial court to permit him to represent himself and to change his pleas from not guilty to guilty. The state trial court had found that the defendant met *Dusky*'s mental competence standard, that he "knowingly and intelligently" waived his right to assistance of counsel, and that he "freely and voluntarily" chose to plead guilty. And the state trial court had consequently granted the defendant's self-representation and change-of-plea requests. This Court "rejected the notion that competence to plead guilty or to waive the right to counsel must be measured by a standard that is higher than (or even different from) the *Dusky* standard." The decision to plead guilty, we said, "is no more complicated than the sum total of decisions that a represented defendant may be called upon to make during the course of a trial." Hence "there is no reason to believe that the decision to waive counsel requires an appreciably higher level of mental functioning than the decision to waive other constitutional rights." And even assuming that self-representation might pose special trial-related difficulties, "the competence that is required of a defendant seeking to waive his right to counsel is the competence to waive the right, not the competence to represent himself."

Godinez does not answer the question before us now. In *Godinez*, the higher standard sought to measure the defendant's ability to proceed on his own to enter a guilty plea; here the higher standard seeks to measure the defendant's ability to conduct trial proceedings. To put the matter more specifically, the *Godinez* defendant sought only to change his pleas to guilty, he did not seek to conduct trial proceedings, and his ability to conduct a defense at trial was expressly not at issue.

We assume that a criminal defendant has sufficient mental competence to stand trial (i.e., the defendant meets *Dusky*'s standard) and that the defendant insists on representing himself during that trial. We ask whether the Constitution permits a State to limit that defendant's self-representation right by insisting upon representation by counsel at trial on the ground that the defendant lacks the mental capacity to conduct his trial defense unless represented.

Several considerations taken together lead us to conclude that the answer to this question is yes. First, the Court's precedent points slightly in the direction of our affirmative answer. The Court's "mental competency" cases set forth a standard that focuses directly upon a defendant's "present ability to consult with his lawyer," a "capacity to consult with counsel," and an ability "to assist counsel in preparing his defense." These standards assume representation by counsel and emphasize the importance of counsel. They thus suggest (though do not hold) that an instance in which a defendant who would choose to forgo counsel at trial presents a very different set of circumstances, which in our view, calls for a different standard.

Second, the nature of the problem before us cautions against the use of a single mental competency standard for deciding both (1) whether a defendant who is represented by counsel can proceed to trial and (2) whether a defendant who goes to trial must be permitted to represent himself. Mental illness itself is not a unitary concept. It varies in degree. It can vary over time. It interferes with an individual's functioning at different times in different ways. The history of this case illustrates the complexity of the problem. In certain instances an individual may well be able to satisfy *Dusky*'s mental competence standard, for he will be able to work with counsel at trial, yet at the same time he may be unable to carry out the basic tasks needed to present his own defense without the help of counsel.

Third, in our view, a right of self-representation at trial will not "affirm the dignity" of a defendant who lacks the mental capacity to conduct his defense without the assistance of counsel. To the contrary, given that defendant's uncertain mental state, the spectacle that could well result from his self-representation at trial is at least as likely to prove humiliating as ennobling. Moreover, insofar as a defendant's lack of capacity threatens an improper conviction or sentence, self-representation in that exceptional context undercuts the most basic of the Constitution's criminal law objectives, providing a fair trial.

Further, proceedings must not only be fair, they must appear fair to all who observe them. An amicus brief reports one psychiatrist's reaction to having observed a patient (a patient who had satisfied *Dusky*) try to conduct his own defense: "How in the world can our legal system allow an insane man to defend himself?" The application of *Dusky*'s

> **FYI**
>
> Only a *minority* of states have followed Indiana's lead and determined that the competency standard to be met in order for a defendant to proceed *pro se* should be set higher than the competency standard to be met for merely standing trial represented by counsel.

basic mental competence standard can help in part to avoid this result. But given the different capacities needed to proceed to trial without counsel, there is little reason to believe that *Dusky* alone is sufficient. At the same time, the trial judge, particularly one such as the trial judge in this case, who presided over one of *Edwards*' competency hearings and his two trials, will often prove best able to make more fine-tuned mental capacity decisions, tailored to the individualized circumstances of a particular defendant.

We consequently conclude that the Constitution permits judges to take realistic account of the particular defendant's mental capacities by asking whether a defendant who seeks to conduct his own defense at trial is mentally competent to do so. That is to say, the Constitution permits States to insist upon representation by counsel for those competent enough to stand trial under Dusky but who still suffer from severe mental illness to the point where they are not competent to conduct trial proceedings by themselves.

Indiana has also asked us to adopt, as a measure of a defendant's ability to conduct a trial, a more specific standard that would "deny a criminal defendant the right to represent himself at trial where the defendant cannot communicate coherently with the court or a jury." We are sufficiently uncertain, however, as to how that particular standard would work in practice to refrain from endorsing it as a federal constitutional standard here. We need not now, and we do not, adopt it.

Indiana has also asked us to overrule *Faretta*. We decline to do so. We recognize that judges have sometimes expressed concern that *Faretta*, contrary to its intent, has led to trials that are unfair. But recent empirical research suggests that such instances are not common. *See, e.g.,* Hashimoto, Defending the Right of Self-Representation: An Empirical Look at the *Pro Se* Felony Defendant, 85 N.C.L.Rev. 423, 427, 428 (2007) (noting that of the small number of defendants who chose to proceed pro se, roughly 0.3% to 0.5%" of the total, state felony defendants in particular "appear to have achieved higher felony acquittal rates than their represented counterparts in that they were less likely to have been convicted of felonies"). At the same time, instances in which the trial's fairness is in doubt may well be concentrated in the 20 percent or so of self-representation cases where the mental competence of the defendant is also at issue. If so, today's opinion, assuring trial judges the authority to deal appropriately with cases in the latter category, may well alleviate those fair trial concerns.

Food for Thought

Is it *fair* to convict a *pro se* defendant of a crime when any reasonable person could see that he or she did not have the slightest idea what he or she was doing? What do you think?

For these reasons, the judgment of the Supreme Court of Indiana is vacated, and JUSTICE SCALIA, with whom JUSTICE THOMAS joins, dissenting.

The Constitution guarantees a defendant who knowingly and voluntarily waives the right to counsel the right to proceed pro se at his trial. A mentally ill defendant who knowingly and voluntarily elects to proceed pro se instead of through counsel receives a fair trial that comports with the Fourteenth Amendment. The Court today concludes that a State may nonetheless strip a mentally ill defendant of the right to represent himself when that would be fairer. In my view the Constitution does not permit a State to substitute its own perception of fairness for the defendant's right to make his own case before the jury—a specific right long understood as essential to a fair trial.

Because I think a defendant who is competent to stand trial, and who is capable of knowing and voluntary waiver of assistance of counsel, has a constitutional right to conduct his own defense, I respectfully dissent.

Points for Discussion

a. Pro Se Defendants, Mental Illness, & the Challenge for Trial Judges

Pro se defendants with mental problems are a real challenge for trial judges. Not only might such defendants do crazy and/or disruptive things in court, but the judge may have a reasonable fear that their lack of legal skills might lead to an unfair result. It is not surprising then to find trial judges, after *Edwards*, turning down an increasing number of putative *pro se* defendants' requests to represent themselves on competency grounds. Not only because it's "easier" on the judge, but also because of the judge's (perfectly legitimate) fears and doubts about the fairness of the proceedings. That said, as the *Edwards* Court made clear, *Faretta* is still good law. Criminal defendants do still have a constitutional right to represent themselves.

b. Waiver by Silence

What constitutes a good waiver? Suppose that the defendant fails to assert the right to counsel, and proceeds to represent himself or herself at trial. Has there been a waiver by virtue of the mere failure to make such an assertion? No. The Court has made it clear that such a waiver will not be presumed from mere silence. Trial judges, accordingly, need to take pains to make sure that waivers are clear on the record.

> **FYI**
>
> In *United States v. Balsiger*, 910 F.3d 942 (7th Cir. 2018), after defendant's lawyer died, he insisted on hiring a lawyer who would not be available for 18 months. Even though the trial judge made it clear that he would not delay the trial for 18 months, defendant repeatedly refused to choose another attorney. The judge did indicate that, if defendant chose another attorney, he would grant a continuance for a reasonable period of time so that counsel could prepare for trial. Finally, when defendant continued to fail to choose an alternate attorney, the judge concluded that he had waived his right to counsel and forced him to proceed *pro se*. The Seventh Circuit found that this was not a violation of his Sixth Amendment right to counsel: "The district court's decision to deny the continuance was neither unreasonable nor arbitrary."

c. **Good Waivers**

The *Faretta* Court talked about a "knowing and intelligent" waiver of counsel and the *Tovar* Court similarly spoke of a waiver made by a defendant who "knows what he is doing." But *Tovar* and *Faretta* don't *really* require that a defendant make an "intelligent" choice in the dictionary meaning of that word. As Justice Blackmun pointed out in his dissent in *Faretta*, few decisions to waive counsel can be regarded as truly intelligent in that sense. In most instances, criminal defendants do not know the rules of evidence, and have studied neither criminal law nor criminal procedure. Under these circumstances, can even a fully competent defendant make a truly "knowing" and "intelligent" waiver of the right to counsel? In any event, the Supreme Court requires only that the defendant be competent to make the waiver, and that he or she has been given sufficient information on which to base the waiver decision.

> **FYI**
>
> In *United States v. Watts*, 896 F.3d 1245 (11th Cir. 2018), defendant elected to proceed *pro se*, and decided that he would not testify in his own defense. Defendant changed his mind after both sides had rested in terms of their production of evidence. After the court refused to reopen the case so that he could testify, defendant objected that the trial judge did not adequately explain his right to testify. The 11th Circuit disagreed, noting that defendant was able to consult with his former attorney (who remained present in an advisory role) before deciding not to testify.

Hypo 1: *Judge's Dilemma #1*

Assuming that defendants are entitled to make a less than (truly) intelligent choice, how should they do so? A robbery defendant has stated that he is aware of his right to counsel, but that he prefers to proceed *pro se*. In light of *Faretta*'s requirement that a waiver be "knowing and intelligent," how should the trial judge proceed? Should the judge accept his request at face value? Should the judge interrogate him about his knowledge of the rules of evidence and the criminal law? Should it matter that the accused did not know, or was not able to recall, most (or any) of the exceptions to the hearsay rule? For that matter, can you recall them?

Hypo 2: *Judge's Dilemma #2*

If a *pro se* defendant has a valid objection to inadmissible evidence introduced by the prosecutor but fails to make the objection (because he or she doesn't know the applicable law), should the trial judge act *sua sponte* to keep the evidence out? Should the judge inform the *pro se* defendant of the law? Or should the judge say nothing and simply permit the prosecution to introduce otherwise inadmissible evidence

Hypo 3: *Defendant Changes His Mind*

Where an indigent defendant has waived his right to counsel multiple times, but then changes his mind after trial, and decides that he does want counsel after all for purposes of filing a motion for new trial, should the trial judge have the discretion to deny that request? Or must the trial judge grant that request automatically? What do you think is the appropriate rule given the existing precedent? *See Marshall v. Rodgers*, <u>569 U.S. 58 (2013)</u>.

Hypo 4: *New Judge Changes Waiver Ruling*

A new judge overturned another judge's denial of a murder defendant's pretrial *Faretta* motion for self-representation, intentionally ignoring the first judge's findings, including testimony she heard from three mental health experts, that defendant was not competent to validly waive counsel or represent himself. In the absence of new evidence of competence, do you think such a ruling was appropriate? *See People v. Waldon*, 14 Cal.5th 288, 522 P.3d 1059, 303 Cal. Rptr.3d 652 (2023).

Exercise: *Pro Se Request*

You are the law clerk to a trial judge. Defendant Jane Jones has been charged with arson in your court and has demanded to proceed *pro se* at trial. She was examined by a clinical psychologist one year ago who found that Jones suffered from "an active psychotic disorder of a paranoid type" and has "auditory hallucinations, delusions of a bizarre and persecutory nature, and is intent on using the legal process as a vehicle for acting out many of her paranoid psychotic preoccupations." After interrogating Jones at length, your judge has told you that she believes that Jones understands the seriousness of the charge filed against her and comprehends the disadvantages of proceeding *pro se*, and that Jones told her that although she heard voices in the past, she no longer does. The file also discloses that Jones has extensive familiarity with the courts in that she has previously filed seventeen motions in state court, eleven in federal court, and has instituted two Court of Claims actions, one for damages for false arrest and the other for an assault allegedly committed on her at a state mental institution. Your judge has asked you to provide her with a bench memo (of no longer than 5 double-spaced pages) that summarizes the applicable federal law on this subject and recommends to her whether or not she should permit Jones to proceed *pro se*.

* * *

The *Faretta* Court indicated in a footnote that trial judges could appoint "standby counsel" to assist *pro se* defendants in presenting their cases, or simply to be available when and if the *pro se* defendant decides that he or she would rather be represented by counsel. As the following decision illustrates, however, standby counsel's appropriate role remains controversial.

McKaskle v. Wiggins

465 U.S. 168 (1984).

JUSTICE O'CONNOR delivered the opinion of the Court.

In *Faretta v. California*, this Court recognized a defendant's Sixth Amendment right to conduct his own defense. The Court also held that a trial court may appoint "standby counsel" to assist the *pro se* defendant in his defense. Today we must decide what role standby counsel who is present at trial over the defendant's objection may play consistent with the protection of the defendant's *Faretta* rights.

Hear It

You can hear the oral argument in *McKaskle* at http://www.oyez.org/cases/1980-1989/1983/1983_82_1135.

Carl Edwin Wiggins was convicted of robbery and sentenced to life imprisonment as a recidivist. In his petition for federal *habeas corpus* relief, Wiggins argued that standby counsel's conduct deprived him of his right to present his own defense, as guaranteed by *Faretta*. The Court of Appeals held that Wiggins' Sixth Amendment right of self-representation was violated by the unsolicited participation of overzealous standby counsel: "The rule that we establish today is that court-appointed standby counsel is 'to be seen, but not heard.' By this we mean that he is not to compete with the defendant or supersede his defense. Rather, his presence is there for advisory purposes only, to be used or not used as the defendant sees fit." We do not accept the Court of Appeals' rule, and reverse its judgment.

A defendant's right to self-representation plainly encompasses certain specific rights to have his voice heard. The *pro se* defendant must be allowed to control the organization and content of his own defense, to make motions, to argue points of law, to participate in *voir dire*, to question witnesses, and to address the court and the jury at appropriate points in the trial. The record reveals that Wiggins was in fact accorded all of these rights.

Before trial Wiggins moved the trial court to order preparation of a transcript of the first trial. He, not standby counsel, then waived receipt of the transcript and announced ready for trial. He filed and argued at least 12 *pro se* motions in pretrial proceedings. Wiggins alone conducted the defense's *voir dire* of prospective jurors and made the opening statement for the defense to the jury.

Wiggins filed numerous *pro se* motions in the course of the trial. He cross-examined the prosecution's witnesses freely, and registered his own objections. Throughout the trial Wiggins selected the witnesses for the defense, examined them, decided that certain questions would not be asked by the defense, and decided which witnesses would not be called. Against counsel's advice, Wiggins announced that the defense rested. Wiggins filed his own requested charges to the jury, and made his own objections to the court's suggested charge. He obtained the removal of one of the court's proposed charges over counsel's express objection, approved the verdict form supplied to the jury, and gave a closing argument to the and he argued his case to the jury at that stage as well.

Wiggins' complaint is directed not at limits placed on *his* participation in the trial, for there clearly were none. Wiggins contends that his right to present his defense *pro se* was impaired by the distracting, intrusive, and unsolicited participation of counsel throughout the trial.

Faretta's logic indicates that no absolute bar on standby counsel's unsolicited participation is appropriate or was intended. The right to appear *pro se* exists to affirm the dignity and autonomy of the accused and to allow the presentation of what may, at least occasionally, be the accused's best possible defense. Both of these objectives can be achieved without categorically silencing standby counsel.

In determining whether a defendant's *Faretta* rights have been respected, the primary focus must be on whether the defendant had a fair chance to present his case in his own way. *Faretta* itself dealt with the defendant's affirmative right to participate, not with the limits on standby counsel's additional involvement. The specific rights to make his voice heard that Wiggins was plainly accorded form the core of a defendant's right of self-representation.

We recognize, nonetheless, that the right to speak for oneself entails more than the opportunity to add one's voice to a cacophony of others. As Wiggins contends, the objectives underlying the right to proceed *pro se* may be undermined by unsolicited and excessively intrusive participation by standby counsel. In proceedings before a jury the defendant may legitimately be concerned that multiple voices "for the defense" will confuse the message the defendant wishes to convey, thus defeating *Faretta's* objectives. Accordingly, the *Faretta* right must impose some limits on the extent of standby counsel's unsolicited participation.

First, the *pro se* defendant is entitled to preserve actual control over the case he chooses to present to the jury. This is the core of the *Faretta* right. If standby counsel's participation over the defendant's objection effectively allows counsel to make or substantially interfere with any significant tactical decisions, or to control the questioning of witnesses, or to speak instead of the defendant on any matter of importance, the *Faretta* right is eroded.

Take Note

The ABA in its Criminal Justice Standards, The Defense Function, Standard 4–5.3(b) (4th ed. 2017), has recommended that "defense counsel whose duty is to assist a *pro se* accused only when the accused requests assistance may bring to the attention of the accused steps that could be potentially beneficial or dangerous to the accused, but should not actively participate in the conduct of the defense unless requested by the accused or as directed to do so by the court."

Second, participation by standby counsel without the defendant's consent should not be allowed to destroy the jury's perception that the defendant is representing himself. The defendant's appearance in the status of one conducting his own defense is important in a criminal trial, since the right to appear *pro se* exists to affirm the accused's individual dignity and autonomy. In related contexts the courts have recognized that a defendant has a right to be present at all important stages of trial, that he may not normally be forced to appear in court in shackles or prison garb, and that he has a right to present testimony in his own behalf. Appearing before the jury in the status of one who is defending himself may be equally important to the *pro se* defendant. From the jury's perspective, the message conveyed by the defense may depend as much on the messenger as on the message itself. From the defendant's own point of view, the right to appear *pro se* can lose much of its importance if only the lawyers in the courtroom know that the right is being exercised.

Participation by standby counsel outside the presence of the jury engages only the first of these two limitations. A trial judge, who in any event receives a defendant's original *Faretta* request and supervises the protection of the right throughout the trial, must be considered capable of differentiating the claims presented by a *pro se* defendant from those presented by standby counsel. Accordingly, the appearance of a *pro se* defendant's self-representation will not be unacceptably undermined by counsel's participation outside the presence of the jury.

Thus, *Faretta* rights are adequately vindicated in proceedings outside the presence of the jury if the *pro se* defendant is allowed to address the court freely on his own behalf and if disagreements between counsel and the *pro se* defendant are resolved in the defendant's favor whenever the matter is one that would normally be left to the discretion of counsel.

Most of the incidents of which Wiggins complains occurred when the jury was not in the courtroom. In the jury's absence Wiggins' two standby counsel frequently explained to the trial judge their views and points of disagreement with Wiggins. Counsel made motions, dictated proposed strategies into the record, registered objections to the prosecution's testimony, urged the summoning of additional witnesses, and suggested questions that the defendant should have asked of witnesses. On several occasions Wiggins expressly adopted standby counsel's initiatives.

On several other occasions Wiggins strongly opposed the initiatives of counsel. He resisted counsel's suggestion that the trial be postponed so that the transcript of his prior trial could be prepared, and he waived counsel's right to a 10-day preparation period, which counsel wished to invoke. In the course of a pretrial discussion concerning a discovery request Wiggins indignantly demanded that counsel not participate further without invitation. Later, Wiggins successfully opposed the inclusion in the jury instructions of a charge that counsel felt should be included.

The most acrimonious exchange between standby counsel Graham and Wiggins occurred in the course of questioning a witness on *voir dire*. Wiggins suggests this exchange was typical of counsel's overbearing conduct, but he fails to place the incident in context. Wiggins had expressly agreed to have Graham conduct the *voir dire*, but Wiggins attempted to take over the questioning in midstream. Plainly exasperated, Graham used profanity and curtly directed Wiggins to "sit down."

Though several of these incidents are regrettable, we are satisfied that counsel's participation outside the presence of the jury fully satisfied the first standard we have outlined. Wiggins was given ample opportunity to present his own position to the court on every matter discussed. He was given time to think matters over, to explain his problems and concerns informally, and to speak to the judge off the record. Standby counsel participated actively, but for the most part in an orderly manner. Equally important, all conflicts between Wiggins and counsel were resolved in Wiggins' favor. The trial judge repeatedly explained to all concerned that Wiggins' strategic choices, not counsel's, would prevail. Not every motion made by Wiggins was granted, but in no instance was counsel's position adopted over Wiggins' on a matter that would normally be left to the defense's discretion.

Participation by standby counsel in the presence of the jury is more problematic. It is here that the defendant may legitimately claim that excessive involvement by counsel will destroy the appearance that the defendant is acting *pro se*. This, in turn, may erode the dignitary values that the right to self-representation is intended to promote and may undercut the defendant's presentation to the jury of his own most effective defense. Nonetheless, we believe that a categorical bar on participation by standby counsel in the presence of the jury is unnecessary.

In measuring standby counsel's involvement against the standards we have described, it is important not to lose sight of the defendant's own conduct. A defendant can waive his *Faretta* rights. Participation by counsel with a *pro se* defendant's express approval is, of course, constitutionally unobjectionable. A defendant's invitation to counsel to participate in the trial obliterates any claim that the participation in question deprived the defendant of control over his own defense. Such participation also diminishes any general claim that counsel unreasonably interfered with the defendant's right to appear in the status of one defending himself.

Although this is self-evident, it is also easily overlooked. A defendant like Wiggins, who vehemently objects at the beginning of trial to standby counsel's very presence in the courtroom, may express quite different views as the trial progresses. Even when he insists that he is not waiving his *Faretta* rights, a *pro se* defendant's solicitation of or acquiescence in certain types of participation by counsel substantially undermines later protestations that counsel interfered unacceptably.

The record in this case reveals that Wiggins' *pro se* efforts were undermined primarily by his own, frequent changes of mind regarding counsel's role. *Faretta* does not require a trial judge to permit "hybrid" representation of the type Wiggins was actually allowed. But if a defendant is given the opportunity and elects to have counsel appear before the court or jury, his complaints concerning counsel's subsequent unsolicited participation lose much of their force. A defendant does not have a constitutional right to choreograph special appearances by counsel. Once a *pro se* defendant invites or agrees to any substantial participation by counsel, subsequent appearances by counsel must be presumed to be with the defendant's acquiescence, at least until the defendant expressly and unambiguously renews his request that standby counsel be silenced.

Faretta rights are also not infringed when standby counsel assists the *pro se* defendant in overcoming routine procedural or evidentiary obstacles to the completion of some specific task, such as introducing evidence or objecting to testimony, that the defendant has clearly shown he wishes to complete. Nor are they infringed when counsel merely helps to ensure the defendant's compliance with basic rules of courtroom protocol and procedure. In neither case is there any significant interference with the defendant's actual control over the presentation of his defense. The likelihood that the defendant's appearance in the status of one defending himself will be eroded is also slight, and in any event it is tolerable. A defendant does not have a constitutional right to receive personal instruction from the trial judge on courtroom procedure. Nor does the Constitution require judges to take over chores for a *pro se* defendant that would normally be attended to by trained counsel as a matter of course.

Accordingly, we make explicit today what is already implicit in *Faretta*: A defendant's Sixth Amendment rights are not violated when a trial judge appoints standby counsel—even over the defendant's objection—to relieve the judge of the need to explain and enforce basic rules of courtroom protocol or to assist the defendant in overcoming routine obstacles that stand in the way of the defendant's achievement of his own clearly indicated goals. Participation by counsel to steer a defendant through the basic procedures of trial is permissible even in the unlikely event that it somewhat undermines the *pro se* defendant's appearance of control over his own defense.

At Wiggins' trial a significant part of standby counsel's participation both in and out of the jury's presence involved basic mechanics of the type we have described—informing the court of the whereabouts of witnesses, supplying Wiggins with a form needed to elect to go to the jury at the punishment phase of trial, explaining to Wiggins that he should not argue his case while questioning a witness, and so on. When Wiggins attempted to introduce a document into evidence, but failed to mark it for identification or to lay a predicate for its introduction, counsel, at the trial court's suggestion, questioned the witness to lay an appropriate predicate, and Wiggins then resumed his examination. Similarly, the trial judge repeatedly instructed Wiggins to consult with counsel, not with the court, regarding the appropriate procedure for summoning witnesses.

Notwithstanding Wiggins' several general objections to the presence and participation of counsel, we find these aspects of counsel's involvement irreproachable. None interfered with Wiggins' actual control over his defense; none can reasonably be thought to have undermined Wiggins' appearance before the jury in the status of a *pro se* defendant.

Putting aside participation that was either approved by Wiggins or attendant to routine clerical or procedural matters, counsel's unsolicited comments in front of the jury were infrequent and for the most part innocuous. On two occasions Graham interrupted a witness' answer to a question put by Wiggins. The first interruption was trivial. When the second was made the jury was briefly excused and subsequently given a cautionary instruction as requested by Graham. Wiggins made no objection. Standby counsel also moved for a mistrial three times in the presence of the jury. Each motion was in response to allegedly prejudicial questions or comments by the prosecutor. Wiggins did not comment on the first motion, but he opposed the following two. All three motions were immediately denied by the trial court. Regrettably, counsel used profanity to express his exasperation on the second occasion. Finally, counsel played an active role at the punishment phase of the trial. The record supplies no explanation for the sudden change in this regard. Wiggins made no objection to counsel's participation in this phase of the trial. We can only surmise that by then Wiggins had concluded that appearing *pro se* was not in his best interests.

The statements made by counsel during the guilt phase of the trial, in the presence of the jury and without Wiggins' express consent, occupy only a small portion of the transcript. Most were of an unobjectionable, mechanical sort. While standby counsel's participation at Wiggins' trial should not serve as a model for future trials, we believe that counsel's involvement fell short of infringing on Wiggins' *Faretta* rights. Wiggins unquestionably maintained actual control over the presentation of his own defense at all times.

We are also persuaded that Wiggins was allowed to appear before the jury in the status of one defending himself. At the outset the trial judge carefully explained to the jury that Wiggins would be appearing *pro se*. Wiggins, not counsel, examined prospective jurors on *voir dire*, cross-examined the prosecution's witnesses, examined his own witnesses, and made an opening statement for the defense. Wiggins objected to the prosecutor's case at least as often as did counsel. If Wiggins closing statement to the jury had to compete with one made by counsel, it was only because Wiggins agreed in advance to that arrangement.

By contrast, counsel's interruptions of Wiggins or witnesses being questioned by Wiggins in the presence of the jury were few and perfunctory. Most of counsel's uninvited comments were directed at the prosecutor. Such interruptions present little threat to a defendant's *Faretta* rights, at least when the defendant's view regarding those objections has not been clearly articulated. On the rare occasions that disagreements between counsel and Wiggins were aired in the presence of the jury the trial judge consistently ruled in Wiggins' favor. This was a pattern more likely to reinforce than to detract from the appearance that Wiggins was controlling his own defense. The intrusions by counsel at Wiggins' trial were simply not substantial or frequent enough to have seriously undermined Wiggins' appearance before the jury in the status of one representing himself.

Food for Thought

The majority concludes that its new test for the limits on standby counsel's participation was not violated in this case. Do you think this conclusion was correct, i.e. even if the test is just fine, was it really satisfied on these facts?

Faretta affirmed the defendant's constitutional right to appear on stage at his trial. We recognize that a *pro se* defendant may wish to dance a solo, not a *pas de deux*. Standby counsel must generally respect that preference. But counsel need not be excluded altogether, especially when the participation is outside the presence of the jury or is with the defendant's express or tacit consent. The defendant in this case was allowed to make his own appearances as he saw fit. In our judgment counsel's unsolicited involvement was held within reasonable limits.

The judgment of the Court of Appeals is therefore *Reversed*.

JUSTICE WHITE, with whom JUSTICE BRENNAN and JUSTICE MARSHALL join, dissenting.

The continuous and substantial intervention of standby counsel, despite Wiggins' repeated demands that he play a passive role, could not have had "anything but a negative impact on the jury. It also destroyed Wiggins' own perception that he was conducting *his* defense."

Under the Court's new test, it is necessary to determine whether the *pro se* defendant retained "actual control over the case he chose to present to the jury," and whether standby counsel's participation "destroyed the jury's perception that the defendant was representing himself." Although this test purports to protect all of the values underlying our holding in *Faretta*, it is unclear whether it can achieve this result.

As long as the *pro se* defendant is allowed his say, the first prong of the Court's test accords standby counsel at a bench trial or any proceeding outside the presence of a jury virtually untrammeled discretion to present any factual or legal argument to which the defendant does not object.

Although the Court is more solicitous of a *pro se* defendant's interests when standby counsel intervenes before a jury, the test's second prong suffers from similar shortcomings. To the extent that trial and appellate courts can discern the point at which counsel's unsolicited participation substantially undermines a *pro se* defendant's appearance before the jury, a matter about which I harbor substantial doubts, their decisions will, to a certain extent, "affirm the accused's individual dignity and autonomy." But they will do so incompletely, for in focusing on how the jury views the defendant, the majority opinion ignores *Faretta*'s emphasis on the defendant's own perception of the criminal justice system, and implies that the Court actually adheres to the result-oriented harmless error standard it purports to reject.

As a guide for standby counsel and lower courts, moreover, the Court's two-part test is clearly deficient. Instead of encouraging counsel to accept a limited role, the Court plainly invites them to participate despite their clients' contrary instructions until the clients renew their objections and trial courts draw the line. Trial courts required to rule on *pro se* defendants' objections to counsel's intervention also are left at sea. They clearly must prevent standby counsel from overtly muzzling their pro se clients and resolve certain conflicts in defendants'

Food for Thought

What more could the trial court have done in this case to protect Wiggin's pro se rights? One thing it could have done was to order standby counsel to remain silent, at least in front of the jury, unless spoken to or requested to speak by the defendant. Obviously, the majority was unwilling to impose that requirement. Would that have been a better result?

favor. But the Court's opinion places few, if any, other clear limits on counsel's uninvited participation; instead it requires trial courts to make numerous subjective judgments concerning the effect of counsel's actions on defendants' *Faretta* rights.

In short, I believe that the Court's test is unworkable and insufficiently protective of the fundamental interests we recognized in *Faretta*.

Hypo 1: *Meddling Law Professor*

Suppose that you graduated from law school, passed the bar (*congratulations!*), and were appointed to represent an indigent defendant in a criminal case. Your criminal procedure professor, interested to see how much you learned in law school, comes to observe. Unhappy with your performance, the professor offers interjections and suggestions while you are trying the case. Is a court likely to tolerate the professor's conduct? If not, should the court be any more willing to tolerate such conduct when a *pro se* defendant is involved as counsel? Is there a dispositive difference in these two situations?

Hypo 2: *Judicial Instructions*

Suppose that you are the judge in a criminal case involving a *pro se* defendant and standby counsel. Prior to trial, would you give standby counsel any special instructions regarding his or her role? What instructions? Suppose that counsel subsequently intrudes in the case inappropriately. How should you (still the trial judge) respond?

Hypo 3: *Standby Counsel's Role in Penalty Phase*

Defendant, who proceeded *pro se* at trial, was convicted of murder and faced the possibility of a death sentence. During the penalty phase of the proceeding, he elected not to present any evidence and instead relied in mitigation on the fact that he had confessed to some unsolved crimes and took responsibility for the murder for which he had been convicted. Standby counsel conducted his own mitigation investigation, and introduced mitigation evidence over defendant's objections, *inter alia*, establishing that defendant "was under the emotional or mental disturbance of cocaine dependency, and an antisocial personality disorder." Defendant was sentenced to death. Were the actions of standby counsel in presenting mitigation evidence over defendant's objections justified? Or did they unduly infringe upon defendant's Sixth Amendment right to proceed *pro se*? *Barnes v. State*, 29 So.3d 1010 (Fla. 2010).

Hypo 4: *Pro Se Defendant at Sidebar?*

Attorneys often "approach the Bench" and have conversations with the trial judge about various issues. This is called meeting "at sidebar." If a *pro se* defendant has standby counsel, should that *pro se* defendant have a right to participate in these sidebar conferences discussing legal issues instead of or in addition to standby counsel? Would it or should it make any difference if the defendant had previously been disruptive in court? *See Allen v. Com.*, 410 S.W.3d 125 (Ky. 2013).

C. Ineffective Assistance of Counsel

In *Powell v. Alabama*, 287 U.S. 45 (1932), the United States Supreme Court made it clear that a criminal defendant's constitutional right to counsel includes the right to the "effective" assistance of counsel.

However, the Court did not establish a test to determine when defense counsel violates the Sixth Amendment due to ineffective assistance of counsel until 1984.

FYI

Powell v. Alabama was the Supreme Court's decision in the widely-publicized "Scottsboro Boys" case, in which nine African-American teenagers were prosecuted for the rape of two white women. The trial court purported to appoint "all the members of the bar" to represent the defendants. But, despite the theoretical abundance of defense counsel, the reality was that no local lawyer would represent them. As a result, they were unrepresented at arraignment, and they were still unrepresented as late as the morning of trial. At that point, the judge hastily forced two lawyers to serve as counsel, but neither attorney was given time to prepare for trial, which began immediately. Unsurprisingly, the Scottsboro Boys were quickly convicted in a one-day trial and some were sentenced to death, and others received life sentences. But,

See It

Watch and listen to Emory's Charles Howard Candler Professor and Chair of African American Studies, Carol Anderson, movingly discuss the extraordinary circumstances of this case. *See* https://www.youtube.com/watch?v=TmsYL-mqx3wg.

in what can be seen as one of the earliest civil-rights decisions in this country, the Supreme Court reversed, holding that not only did the defendants have the right to counsel, but they were also entitled to the *effective* assistance of counsel, a right which they clearly had not received. (*Postscript:* Justice was only temporary. The defendants were re-convicted on remand, even though, in hindsight, the charges against them were clearly ludicrous and fabricated.)

Strickland v. Washington

466 U.S. 668 (1984).

JUSTICE O'CONNOR delivered the opinion of the Court.

This case requires us to consider the proper standards for judging a criminal defendant's contention that the Constitution requires a conviction or death sentence to be set aside because counsel's assistance at the trial or sentencing was ineffective.

During a 10-day period in September 1976, respondent planned and committed three groups of crimes, which included three brutal stabbing murders, torture, kidnaping, severe assaults, attempted murders, attempted extortion, and theft. After his two accomplices were arrested, respondent surrendered to police and voluntarily gave a lengthy statement confessing to the third of the criminal episodes. The State of Florida indicted respondent for kidnaping and murder and appointed an experienced criminal lawyer to represent him.

Hear It

You can hear the oral argument in *Strickland* at http://www.oyez.org/cases/1980-1989/1983/1983_82_1554.

Counsel actively pursued pretrial motions and discovery. He cut his efforts short, however, and he experienced a sense of hopelessness about the case, when he learned that, against his specific advice, respondent had also confessed to the first two murders. By the date set for trial, respondent was subject to indictment for three counts of first-degree murder and multiple counts of robbery, kidnaping for ransom, breaking and entering and assault, attempted murder, and conspiracy to commit robbery. Respondent waived his right to a jury trial, again acting against counsel's advice, and pleaded guilty to all charges, including the three capital murder charges.

In the plea colloquy, respondent told the trial judge that, although he had committed a string of burglaries, he had no significant prior criminal record and that at the time of his criminal spree he was under extreme stress caused by his inability to support his family. He also stated, however, that he accepted responsibility for the crimes. The trial judge told respondent that he had "a great deal of respect for people who are willing to step forward and admit their responsibility" but that he was making no statement at all about his likely sentencing decision.

Counsel advised respondent to invoke his right under Florida law to an advisory jury at his capital sentencing hearing. Respondent rejected the advice and waived the right. He chose instead to be sentenced by the trial judge without a jury recommendation.

In preparing for the sentencing hearing, counsel spoke with respondent about his background. He also spoke on the telephone with respondent's wife and mother, though he did not follow up on the one unsuccessful effort to meet with them. He did not otherwise seek out character witnesses for respondent. Nor did he request a psychiatric examination, since his conversations with his client gave no indication that respondent had psychological problems.

Counsel decided not to present and hence not to look further for evidence concerning respondent's character and emotional state. That decision reflected trial counsel's sense of hopelessness about overcoming the evidentiary effect of respondent's confessions to the gruesome crimes. It also reflected the judgment that it was advisable to rely on the plea colloquy for evidence about respondent's background and about his claim of emotional stress: the plea colloquy communicated sufficient information about these subjects, and by forgoing the opportunity to present new evidence on these subjects, counsel prevented the State from cross-examining respondent on his claim and from putting on psychiatric evidence of its own.

Counsel also excluded from the sentencing hearing other evidence he thought was potentially damaging. He successfully moved to exclude respondent's "rap sheet." Because he judged that a presentence report might prove more detrimental than helpful, as it would have included respondent's criminal history and thereby would have undermined the claim of no significant history of criminal activity, he did not request that one be prepared.

At the sentencing hearing, counsel's strategy was based primarily on the trial judge's remarks at the plea colloquy as well as on his reputation as a sentencing judge who thought it important for a convicted defendant to own up to his crime. Counsel argued that respondent's remorse and acceptance of responsibility justified sparing him from the death penalty. Counsel also argued that respondent had no history of criminal activity and that respondent committed the crimes under extreme mental or emotional disturbance, thus coming within the statutory list of mitigating circumstances. He further argued that respondent should be spared death because he had surrendered, confessed, and offered to testify against a codefendant and because respondent was fundamentally a good person who had briefly gone badly wrong in extremely stressful circumstances. The State put on evidence and witnesses largely for the purpose of describing the details of the crimes. Counsel did not cross-examine the medical experts who testified about the manner of death of respondent's victims.

The trial judge found several aggravating circumstances with respect to each of the three murders. He found that all three murders were especially heinous, atrocious, and cruel, all involving repeated stabbings. All three murders were committed in the course of at least one other dangerous and violent felony, and since all involved robbery, the murders were for pecuniary gain. All three murders were committed to avoid arrest for the accompanying crimes and to hinder law enforcement. In the course of one of the murders, respondent knowingly subjected numerous persons to a grave risk of death by deliberately stabbing and shooting the murder victim's sisters-in-law, who sustained severe—in one case, ultimately fatal—injuries.

With respect to mitigating circumstances, the trial judge made the same findings for all three capital murders. First, although there was no admitted evidence of prior convictions, respondent had stated that he had engaged in a course of stealing. In any case, even if respondent had no significant history of criminal activity, the aggravating circumstances "would still clearly far outweigh" that mitigating factor. Second, the judge found that, during all three crimes, respondent was not suffering from extreme mental or emotional disturbance and could appreciate the criminality of his acts. Third, none of the victims was a participant in, or consented to, respondent's conduct. Fourth, respondent's participation in the crimes was neither minor nor the result of duress or domination by an accomplice. Finally, respondent's age (26) could not be considered a factor in mitigation, especially when viewed in light of respondent's planning of the crimes and disposition of the proceeds of the various accompanying thefts.

In short, the trial judge found numerous aggravating circumstances and no (or a single comparatively insignificant) mitigating circumstance. He therefore sentenced respondent to death on each of the three counts of murder and to prison terms for the other crimes. The Florida Supreme Court upheld the convictions and sentences. In subsequent postconviction proceedings, a federal district court denied Strickland's petition for *habeas corpus*, but the court of appeals reversed.

In a long line of cases that includes *Powell v. Alabama*, 287 U.S. 45 (1932), *Johnson v. Zerbst*, 304 U.S. 458 (1938), and *Gideon v. Wainwright*, 372 U.S. 335 (1963), this Court has recognized that the Sixth Amendment right to counsel exists, and is needed, in order to protect the fundamental right to a fair trial. A fair trial is one in which evidence subject to adversarial testing is presented to an impartial tribunal for resolution of issues defined in advance of the proceeding. The right to counsel plays a crucial role in the adversarial system embodied in the Sixth Amendment, since access to counsel's skill and knowledge is necessary to accord defendants the ample opportunity to meet the case of the prosecution to which they are entitled.

The Court has recognized that "the right to counsel is the right to the effective assistance of counsel." Government violates the right to effective assistance when it interferes in certain ways with the ability of counsel to make independent decisions about how to conduct the defense. Counsel, however, can also deprive a defendant of the right to effective assistance, simply by failing to render "adequate legal assistance."

The Court has not elaborated on the meaning of the constitutional requirement of effective assistance in cases presenting claims of "actual ineffectiveness." In giving meaning to the requirement, however, we must take its purpose—to ensure a fair trial—as the guide. The benchmark for judging any claim of ineffectiveness must be whether counsel's conduct so undermined the proper functioning of the adversarial process that the trial cannot be relied on as having produced a just result.

The same principle applies to a capital sentencing proceeding such as that provided by Florida law. A capital sentencing proceeding like the one involved in this case is sufficiently like a trial in its adversarial format and in the existence of standards for decision, that counsel's role in the proceeding is comparable to counsel's role at trial—to ensure that the adversarial testing process works to produce a just result under the standards governing decision. For purposes of describing counsel's duties, therefore, Florida's capital sentencing proceeding need not be distinguished from an ordinary trial.

A convicted defendant's claim that counsel's assistance was so defective as to require reversal of a conviction or death sentence has two components. First, the defendant must show that counsel's

Food for Thought

Given the potential consequences of a capital sentencing hearing—*a sentence of death*—wouldn't it have been reasonable to have required defense counsel to do more than to provide merely *adequate* representation?

performance was deficient. This requires showing that counsel made errors so serious that counsel was not functioning as the "counsel" guaranteed the defendant by the Sixth Amendment. Second, the defendant must show that the deficient performance prejudiced the defense. This requires showing that counsel's errors were so serious as to deprive the defendant of a fair trial, a trial whose result is reliable. Unless a defendant makes both showings, it cannot be said that the conviction or death sentence resulted from a breakdown in the adversary process that renders the result unreliable.

The proper standard for attorney performance is that of reasonably effective assistance. When a convicted defendant complains of the ineffectiveness of counsel's assistance, the defendant must show that counsel's representation fell below an objective standard of reasonableness. More specific guidelines are not appropriate. The Sixth Amendment refers simply to "counsel," not specifying particular requirements of effective assistance. It relies instead on the legal profession's maintenance of standards sufficient to justify the law's presumption that counsel will fulfill the role in the adversary process that the Amendment envisions. The proper measure of attorney performance remains simply reasonableness under prevailing professional norms.

Representation of a criminal defendant entails certain basic duties. Counsel's function is to assist the defendant, and hence counsel owes the client a duty of loyalty, a duty to avoid conflicts of interest. From counsel's function as assistant to the defendant derive the overarching duty to advocate the defendant's cause and the more particular duties to consult with the defendant on important decisions and to keep the defendant informed of important developments in the course of the prosecution. Counsel also has a duty to bring to bear such skill and knowledge as will render the trial a reliable adversarial testing process.

These basic duties neither exhaustively define the obligations of counsel nor form a checklist for judicial evaluation of attorney performance. In any case presenting an ineffectiveness claim, the performance inquiry must be whether counsel's assistance was reasonable considering all the circumstances. Prevailing norms of practice as reflected in American Bar Association standards and the like, *e.g.*, ABA Standards for Criminal Justice 4–1.1 to 4–8.6 (2d ed. 1980) ("The Defense Function"), are guides to determining what is reasonable, but they are only guides. No particular set of detailed rules for counsel's conduct can satisfactorily take account of the variety of circumstances faced by defense counsel or the range of legitimate decisions regarding how best to represent a criminal defendant. Moreover, the purpose of the effective assistance guarantee of the Sixth Amendment is not to improve the quality of legal representation, although that is a goal of considerable importance to the legal system. The purpose is simply to ensure that criminal defendants receive a fair trial.

Judicial scrutiny of counsel's performance must be highly deferential. It is all too tempting for a defendant to second-guess counsel's assistance after conviction or adverse sentence, and it is all too easy for a court, examining counsel's defense after it has proved unsuccessful, to conclude that a particular act or omission of counsel was unreasonable. A fair assessment of attorney performance requires that every effort be made to eliminate the distorting effects of hindsight, to reconstruct the circumstances of counsel's challenged conduct, and to evaluate the conduct from counsel's perspective at the time. Because of the difficulties inherent in making the evaluation, a court must indulge a strong presumption that counsel's conduct falls within the wide range of reasonable professional assistance; that is, the defendant must overcome the presumption that, under the circumstances, the challenged action "might be considered sound trial strategy." There are countless ways to provide effective assistance in any given case. Even the best criminal defense attorneys would not defend a particular client in the same way.

The availability of intrusive post-trial inquiry into attorney performance or of detailed guidelines for its evaluation would encourage the proliferation of ineffectiveness challenges. Criminal trials resolved unfavorably to the defendant would increasingly come to be followed by a second trial, this one of counsel's unsuccessful defense. Counsel's performance and even willingness to serve could be adversely affected. Intensive scrutiny of counsel and rigid requirements for acceptable assistance could dampen the ardor and impair the independence of defense counsel, discourage the acceptance of assigned cases, and undermine the trust between attorney and client.

Thus, a court deciding an actual ineffectiveness claim must judge the reasonableness of counsel's challenged conduct on the facts of the particular case, viewed as of the time of counsel's conduct. A convicted defendant making a claim of ineffective assistance must identify the acts or omissions of counsel that are alleged not to have been the result of reasonable professional judgment. The court must then determine whether, in light of all the circumstances, the identified acts or omissions were outside the wide range of professionally competent assistance. In making that determination, the court should keep in mind that counsel's function, as elaborated in prevailing professional norms, is to make the adversarial testing process work in the particular case. At the same time, the court should recognize that counsel is strongly presumed to have rendered adequate assistance and made all significant decisions in the exercise of reasonable professional judgment.

These standards require no special amplification in order to define counsel's duty to investigate, the duty at issue in this case. As the Court of Appeals concluded, strategic choices made after thorough investigation of law and facts relevant to plausible options are virtually unchallengeable; and strategic choices made after less than complete investigation are reasonable precisely to the extent that reasonable professional judgments support the limitations on investigation. In other words, counsel has a duty to make reasonable investigations or to make a reasonable decision that makes particular investigations unnecessary. In any ineffectiveness case, a particular decision not to investigate must be directly assessed for reasonableness in all the circumstances, applying a heavy measure of deference to counsel's judgments.

The reasonableness of counsel's actions may be determined or substantially influenced by the defendant's own statements or actions. Counsel's actions are usually based, quite properly, on informed strategic choices made by the defendant and on information supplied by the defendant. In particular, what investigation decisions are reasonable depends critically on such information. For example, when the facts that support a certain potential line of defense are generally known to counsel because of what the defendant has said, the need for further investigation may be considerably diminished or eliminated altogether. And when a defendant has given counsel reason to believe that pursuing certain investigations would be fruitless or even harmful, counsel's failure to pursue those investigations may not later be challenged as unreasonable. In short, inquiry into counsel's conversations with the defendant may be critical to a proper assessment of counsel's investigation decisions, just as it may be critical to a proper assessment of counsel's other litigation decisions.

An error by counsel, even if professionally unreasonable, does not warrant setting aside the judgment of a criminal proceeding if the error had no effect on the judgment. The purpose of the Sixth Amendment guarantee of counsel is to ensure that a defendant has the assistance necessary to justify reliance on the outcome of the proceeding. Accordingly, any deficiencies in counsel's performance must be prejudicial to the defense in order to constitute ineffective assistance under the Constitution.

Conflict of interest claims aside, actual ineffectiveness claims alleging a deficiency in attorney performance are subject to a general requirement that the defendant affirmatively prove prejudice. The government is not responsible for, and hence not able to prevent, attorney errors that will result in reversal of a conviction or sentence. Attorney errors come in an infinite variety and are as likely to be utterly harmless in a particular case as they are to be prejudicial. They cannot be classified according to likelihood of causing prejudice. Nor can they be defined with sufficient precision to inform defense attorneys correctly just what conduct to avoid. Representation is an art, and an act or omission that is unprofessional in one case may be sound or even brilliant in another. Even if a defendant shows that particular errors of counsel were unreasonable, therefore, the defendant must show that they actually had an adverse effect on the defense.

It is not enough for the defendant to show that the errors had some conceivable effect on the outcome of the proceeding. Virtually every act or omission of counsel would meet that test, and not every error that conceivably could have influenced the outcome undermines the reliability of the result of the proceeding.

The appropriate test for prejudice finds its roots in the test for materiality of exculpatory information not disclosed to the defense by the prosecution, and in the test for materiality of testimony made unavailable to the defense by Government deportation of a witness. The defendant must show that there is a reasonable probability that, but for counsel's unprofessional errors, the result of the proceeding would have been different. A reasonable probability is a probability sufficient to undermine confidence in the outcome.

In making the determination whether the specified errors resulted in the required prejudice, a court should presume, absent challenge to the judgment on grounds of evidentiary insufficiency, that the judge or jury acted according to law. An assessment of the likelihood of a result more favorable to the defendant must exclude the possibility of arbitrariness, whimsy, caprice, "nullification," and the like. A defendant has no entitlement to the luck of a lawless decisionmaker, even if a lawless decision cannot be reviewed. The assessment of prejudice should proceed on the assumption that the decisionmaker is reasonably, conscientiously, and impartially applying the standards that govern the decision. It should not depend on the idiosyncrasies of the particular decisionmaker, such as unusual propensities toward harshness or leniency. Although these factors may actually have entered into counsel's selection of strategies and, to that limited extent, may thus affect the performance inquiry, they are irrelevant to the prejudice inquiry. Thus, evidence about the actual process of decision, if not part of the record of the proceeding under review, and evidence about, for example, a particular judge's sentencing practices, should not be considered in the prejudice determination.

The governing legal standard plays a critical role in defining the question to be asked in assessing the prejudice from counsel's errors. When a defendant challenges a conviction, the question is whether there is a reasonable probability that, absent the errors, the fact-finder would have had a reasonable doubt respecting guilt. When a defendant challenges a death sentence such as the one at issue in this case, the question is whether there is a reasonable probability that, absent the errors, the sentencer—including an appellate court, to the extent it independently reweighs the evidence—would have concluded that the balance of aggravating and mitigating circumstances did not warrant death.

In making this determination, a court hearing an ineffectiveness claim must consider the totality of the evidence before the judge or jury. A verdict or conclusion only weakly supported by the record is more likely to have been affected by errors than one with overwhelming record support. Taking the unaffected findings as a given, and taking due account of the effect of the errors on the remaining findings, a court making the prejudice inquiry must ask if the defendant has met the burden of showing that the decision reached would reasonably likely have been different absent the errors.

A number of practical considerations are important for the application of the standards we have outlined. Most important, in adjudicating a claim of actual ineffectiveness of counsel, a court should keep in mind that the principles we have stated do not establish mechanical rules. Although those principles should guide the process of decision, the ultimate focus of inquiry must be on the fundamental fairness of the proceeding whose result is being challenged. In every case the court should be concerned with whether, despite the strong presumption of reliability, the result of the particular proceeding is unreliable because of a breakdown in the adversarial process that our system counts on to produce just results.

To the extent that this has already been the guiding inquiry in the lower

> ### Take Note
>
> Note that to defeat a claim of ineffectiveness, all the government must do is to establish that the defendant has failed to satisfy *either* one of these tests, not both.

courts, the standards articulated today do not require reconsideration of ineffectiveness claims rejected under different standards. With regard to the prejudice inquiry, only the strict outcome-determinative test, among the standards articulated in the lower courts, imposes a heavier burden on defendants than the tests laid down today. The difference, however, should alter the merit of an ineffectiveness claim only in the rarest case.

Although we have discussed the performance component of an ineffectiveness claim prior to the prejudice component, there is no reason for a court deciding an ineffective assistance claim to approach the inquiry in the same order or even to address both components of the inquiry if the defendant makes an insufficient showing on one. If it is easier to dispose of an ineffectiveness claim on the ground of lack of sufficient prejudice, which we expect will often be so, that course should be followed. Courts should strive to ensure that ineffectiveness claims not become so burdensome to defense counsel that the entire criminal justice system suffers as a result.

Application of the governing principles is not difficult in this case. The facts as described above make clear that the conduct of respondent's counsel at and before respondent's sentencing proceeding cannot be found unreasonable. They also make clear that, even assuming the challenged conduct of counsel was unreasonable, respondent suffered insufficient prejudice to warrant setting aside his death sentence.

With respect to the performance component, the record shows that respondent's counsel made a strategic choice to argue for the extreme emotional distress mitigating circumstance and to rely as fully as possible on respondent's acceptance of responsibility for his crimes. Although counsel understandably felt hopeless about respondent's prospects, nothing in the record indicates that counsel's sense of hopelessness distorted his professional judgment. Counsel's strategy choice was well within the range of professionally reasonable judgments, and the decision not to seek more character or psychological evidence than was already in hand was likewise reasonable.

The trial judge's views on the importance of owning up to one's crimes were well known to counsel. The aggravating circumstances were utterly overwhelming. Trial counsel could reasonably surmise from his conversations with respondent that character and psychological evidence would be of little help. Respondent had already been able to mention at the plea colloquy the substance of what there was to know about his financial and emotional troubles. Restricting testimony on respondent's character to what had come in at the plea colloquy ensured that contrary character and psychological evidence and respondent's criminal history, which counsel had successfully moved to exclude, would not come in. On these facts, there can be little question, even without application of the presumption of adequate performance, that trial counsel's defense, though unsuccessful, was the result of reasonable professional judgment.

With respect to the prejudice component, the lack of merit of respondent's claim is even more stark. The evidence that respondent says his trial counsel should have offered at the sentencing hearing would barely have altered the sentencing profile presented to the sentencing judge. At most this evidence shows that numerous people who knew respondent thought he was generally a good person and that a psychiatrist and a psychologist believed he was under considerable emotional stress that did not rise to the level of extreme disturbance. Given the overwhelming aggravating factors, there is no reasonable probability that the omitted evidence would have changed the conclusion that the aggravating circumstances outweighed the mitigating circumstances and, hence, the sentence imposed. Indeed, admission of the evidence respondent now offers might even have been harmful to his case: his "rap sheet" would probably have been admitted into evidence, and the psychological reports would have directly contradicted respondent's claim that the mitigating circumstance of extreme emotional disturbance applied to his case.

Failure to make the required showing of either deficient performance or sufficient prejudice defeats the ineffectiveness claim. Here there is a double failure. More generally, respondent has made no showing that the justice of his sentence was rendered unreliable by a breakdown in the adversary process caused by deficiencies in counsel's assistance. Respondent's sentencing proceeding was not fundamentally unfair.

We conclude, therefore, that the District Court properly declined to issue a writ of *habeas corpus*. The judgment of the Court of Appeals is accordingly *Reversed*.

JUSTICE MARSHALL, dissenting.

My objection to the performance standard adopted by the Court is that it is so malleable that, in practice, it will either have no grip at all or will yield excessive variation in the manner in which the Sixth Amendment is interpreted and applied by different courts.

Food for Thought

Is the *Strickland* ineffectiveness test a sensible and fair one? Is it unreasonably difficult for a defendant to satisfy? Does or should the Sixth Amendment right to counsel require *more* from a defense representative?

I object to the prejudice standard adopted by the Court for two independent reasons. First, it is often very difficult to tell whether a defendant convicted after a trial in which he was ineffectively represented would have fared better if his lawyer had been competent. Seemingly impregnable cases can sometimes be dismantled by good defense counsel. On the basis of a cold record, it may be impossible for a reviewing court confidently to ascertain how the government's evidence and arguments would have stood up against rebuttal and cross-examination by a shrewd, well-prepared lawyer. The difficulties of estimating prejudice after the fact are exacerbated by the possibility that evidence of injury to the defendant may be missing from the record precisely because of the incompetence of defense counsel. In view of all these impediments to a fair evaluation of the probability that the outcome of a trial was affected by ineffectiveness of counsel, it seems to me senseless to impose on a defendant whose lawyer has been shown to have been incompetent the burden of demonstrating prejudice.

Second and more fundamentally, the assumption on which the Court's holding rests is that the only purpose of the constitutional guarantee of effective assistance of counsel is to reduce the chance that innocent persons will be convicted. In my view, the guarantee also functions to ensure that convictions are obtained only through fundamentally fair procedures. The majority contends that the Sixth Amendment is not violated when a manifestly guilty defendant is convicted after a trial in which he was represented by a manifestly ineffective attorney. I cannot agree. Every defendant is entitled to a trial in which his interests are vigorously and conscientiously advocated by an able lawyer.

Points for Discussion

a. Extrinsic Ineffectiveness

In a companion case to *Strickland, United States v. Cronic*, 466 U.S. 648 (1984), the Supreme Court rejected defendant's "extrinsic" claims of defense counsel's ineffectiveness in all but the rarest of cases. "Extrinsic" claims are those that focus upon alleged general problems with counsel or the case (e.g. counsel was too young and/or inexperienced, the case was too complex for this attorney and/or there was too little time to prepare) without accompanying claims of "actual" incidents of ineffectiveness. Cronic was indicted on mail fraud charges involving the transfer of over $9,400,000 in checks between banks in Florida and Oklahoma during a 4-month period. Shortly before the scheduled trial date, retained counsel withdrew. The court then appointed a young lawyer with a real estate practice to represent Cronic, but allowed counsel only 25 days for pretrial preparation even though it had taken the Government over four and one-half years to investigate the case and it had reviewed thousands of documents during that time. Cronic was subsequently convicted on 11 of the 13 counts in the indictment and received a 25-year sentence. The court of appeals overturned Cronic's conviction based on five extrinsic factors: "(1) The time afforded for investigation and preparation; (2) the experience of counsel; (3) the gravity of the charge; (4) the complexity of possible defenses; and (5) the accessibility of witnesses to counsel." The Supreme Court reversed, however, holding that a criminal defendant can "make out a claim of ineffective assistance only by pointing to specific errors made by trial counsel."

b. Ineffectiveness Claims in *Habeas Corpus* Proceedings

In *Kimmelman v. Morrison*, 477 U.S. 365 (1986), the Court refused to extend *Stone v. Powell*, 428 U.S. 465 (1976) to Sixth Amendment claims of ineffectiveness. In *Stone*, the Court held that exclusionary rule arguments relating to Fourth Amendment violations could not be asserted on collateral review in federal *habeas corpus* proceedings if the defendant had a full and fair opportunity to raise the issues in state court. In *Kimmelman*, the Court held that this rule did not apply to claims of ineffective assistance where the principal allegation and manifestation of inadequate representation was counsel's failure to file a timely motion to suppress evidence allegedly obtained in violation of the Fourth Amendment.

c. Ethics & Ineffectiveness

In *Nix v. Whiteside*, 475 U.S. 157 (1986), Whiteside was convicted of second degree murder. At trial, Whiteside claimed self-defense and wanted to testify that he had seen something metallic (presumably a gun) in the victim's hand. However, Whiteside's attorney concluded that the testimony would be perjury and "advised him that if he did do that it would be my duty to advise the Court of what he was doing and that I felt he was committing perjury." Counsel also stated that he would attempt to withdraw from representing Whiteside if he insisted on committing perjury. Following his conviction, Whiteside sought a writ of *habeas corpus*, claiming that the attorney's conduct deprived him of effective assistance of counsel. The Court rejected this argument:

> An attorney's ethical duty to advance the interests of his client is limited by an equally solemn duty to comply with the law and standards of professional conduct; it specifically ensures that the client may not use false evidence. Whether counsel's conduct is seen as a successful attempt to dissuade his client from committing the crime of perjury, or whether seen as a 'threat' to withdraw from representation and disclose the illegal scheme, his representation of Whiteside falls well within accepted standards of professional conduct and the range of reasonable professional conduct acceptable under *Strickland*.

Hypo 1: Cronic *Problems*

Does the *Cronic* presumption of effective assistance in the absence of a showing of actual, prejudicial errors make sense? When defense counsel is inexperienced and is given insufficient time and resources to prepare his case, is it really fair to simply presume that counsel functioned effectively? Shouldn't ineffective assistance be presumed sometimes? What if defendant's counsel showed up for trial drunk and occasionally went to sleep during the trial. In such a situation, should defendant really have to show that counsel committed specific errors in order to gain reversal?

Hypo 2: *Defense Counsel Ten Minutes Late*

Defendant Donald was charged, *inter alia*, with felony murder. At trial, his defense counsel returned late from a break in the proceedings, totally missing ten minutes of the trial. Donald was convicted and subsequently sentenced to life imprisonment. Do you think that defense counsel's absence during ten minutes of the trial was (or should be deemed to be) ineffective assistance under *Cronic*, entitling Donald to a new trial? *See Woods v. Donald*, 575 U.S. 312 (2015).

Hypo 3: *Missing Counsel*

Suppose that a defendant's attorney recommends that he talk to the police to explain his alibi to robbery/murder charges. However, counsel mistakenly believes that he cannot remain in the room during the questioning and therefore leaves. Notwithstanding counsel's absence, defendant explains his alibi and it leads the police to two witnesses who testify against him. Defendant is convicted. Should his conviction be reversed for ineffective assistance of counsel? *See People v. Frazier*, 2008 WL 782593 (Mich. Ct. App. 2008).

Hypo 4: *Failure to Object to Leg Restraints*

Was defense counsel ineffective under *Cronic* for failing to object to the fact that defendant was standing trial for first-degree murder while being forced by the sheriff to wear a leg restraint under his pants leg which prevented him from fully straightening his leg? Does it—should it—matter that the shackle was not visible to the jury? *See Zink v. State*, 278 S.W.3d 170 (Mo. 2009).

Hypo 5: *Limiting Communication with a Client*

Suppose that a criminal defendant is "physically intimidating" and "verbally abusive" towards his court-appointed attorney. May the lawyer place limitations on the client's ability to communicate with the lawyer, including only scheduled appointments and written communications. In imposing such limitations, can the lawyer meet his obligation to have "meaningful communication with the client?" *See* N.Y. State Bar Ass'n Commission on Professional Ethics, Op. 1144 (Jan. 29, 2018).

Missouri v. Frye

566 U.S. 134 (2012).

JUSTICE KENNEDY delivered the opinion of the Court.

The Sixth Amendment, applicable to the States by the terms of the Fourteenth Amendment, provides that the accused shall have the assistance of counsel in all criminal prosecutions. The right to counsel is the right to effective assistance of counsel. This case arises in the context of claimed ineffective assistance that led to the lapse of a prosecution offer of a plea bargain, a proposal that offered terms more lenient than the terms of the guilty plea entered later. The initial question is whether the constitutional right to counsel extends to the negotiation and con-

Hear It

You can hear the oral argument in *Frye* at http://www.oyez.org/cases/2010-2019/2011/2011_10_444.

sideration of plea offers that lapse or are rejected. If there is a right to effective assistance with respect to those offers, a further question is what a defendant must demonstrate in order to show that prejudice resulted from counsel's deficient performance.

In August 2007, respondent Galin Frye was charged with driving with a revoked license. Frye had been convicted for that offense on three other occasions, so the State of Missouri charged him with a class D felony, which carries a maximum term of imprisonment of four years. On November 15, the prosecutor sent a letter to Frye's counsel offering a choice of two plea bargains. The prosecutor first offered to recommend a 3-year sentence if there was a guilty plea to the felony charge, without a recommendation regarding probation but with a recommendation that Frye serve 10 days in jail as so-called "shock" time. The second offer was to reduce the charge to a misdemeanor and, if Frye pleaded guilty to it, to recommend a 90-day sentence. The misdemeanor charge of driving with a revoked license carries a maximum term of imprisonment of one year. The letter stated both offers would expire on December 28. Frye's attorney did not advise Frye that the offers had been made. The offers expired.

Frye's preliminary hearing was scheduled for January 4, 2008. On December 30, 2007, less than a week before the hearing, Frye was again arrested for driving with a revoked license. At the January 4 hearing, Frye waived his right to a preliminary hearing on the charge arising from the August 2007 arrest. He pleaded not guilty at a subsequent arraignment but then changed his plea to guilty. There was no underlying plea agreement. The state trial court accepted Frye's guilty plea. The prosecutor recommended a 3-year sentence, made no recommendation regarding probation, and requested 10 days shock time in jail. The trial judge sentenced Frye to three years in prison.

Frye filed for postconviction relief in state court. He alleged his counsel's failure to inform him of the prosecution's plea offer denied him the effective assistance of counsel. At an evidentiary hearing, Frye testified he would have entered a guilty plea to the misdemeanor had he known about the offer. A state court denied the postconviction motion, but the Missouri Court of Appeals reversed.

It is well settled that the right to the effective assistance of counsel applies to certain steps before trial. The "Sixth Amendment guarantees a defendant the right to have counsel present at all 'critical' stages of the criminal proceedings." Critical stages include arraignments, postindictment interrogations, postindictment lineups, and the entry of a guilty plea. With respect to the right to effective counsel in plea negotiations, a proper beginning point is to discuss two cases from this Court considering the role of counsel in advising a client about a plea offer and an ensuing guilty plea: *Hill v. Lockhart*, 474 U.S. 52 (1985); and *Padilla v. Kentucky*, 559 U.S. 356 (2010).

Hill established that claims of ineffective assistance of counsel in the plea bargain context are governed by the two-part test set forth in *Strickland*. In *Hill*, the decision turned on the second part of the *Strickland* test. There, a defendant who had entered a guilty plea claimed his counsel had misinformed him of the amount of time he would have to serve before he became eligible for parole. But the defendant had not alleged that, even if adequate advice and assistance had been given, he would have elected to plead not guilty and proceed to trial. Thus, the Court found that no prejudice from the inadequate advice had been shown or alleged.

In *Padilla*, the Court again discussed the duties of counsel in advising a client with respect to a plea offer that leads to a guilty plea. *Padilla* held that a guilty plea, based on a plea offer, should be set aside because counsel misinformed the defendant of the immigration consequences of the conviction. The Court made clear that "the negotiation of a plea bargain is a critical phase of litigation for purposes of the Sixth Amendment right to effective assistance of counsel." It also rejected the argument made by petitioner in this case that a knowing and voluntary plea supersedes errors by defense counsel.

When a plea offer has lapsed or been rejected, no formal court proceedings are involved. This underscores that the plea-bargaining process is often in flux, with no clear standards or time lines and with no judicial supervision of the discussions between prosecution and defense. Indeed, discussions between client and defense counsel are privileged. So the prosecution has little or no notice if something may be amiss and perhaps no capacity to intervene in any event. And, as noted, the State insists there is no right to receive a plea offer. For all these reasons, the State contends, it is unfair to subject it to the consequences of defense counsel's inadequacies, especially when the opportunities for a full and fair trial, or, as here, for a later guilty plea albeit on less favorable terms, are preserved.

The State's contentions are neither illogical nor without some persuasive force, yet they do not suffice to overcome a simple reality. Ninety-seven percent of federal convictions and ninety-four percent of state convictions are the result of guilty pleas. The reality is that plea bargains have become so central to the administration of the criminal

Take Note

Don't miss this important point. The five-justice majority in Frye recognized explicitly that plea bargaining—not an actual criminal trial—is "the name of the game" in U.S. criminal justice. That is how most criminal prosecutions are resolved, namely through pleas not in trials. Once the majority reached this conclusion, the holding that ineffective-assistance-of-counsel rules apply was ineluctable.

justice system that defense counsel have responsibilities in the plea bargain process, responsibilities that must be met to render the adequate assistance of counsel that the Sixth Amendment requires in the criminal process at critical stages. Because ours is for the most part a system of pleas, not a system of trials, it is insufficient simply to point to the guarantee of a fair trial as a backstop that inoculates any errors in the pretrial process. "To a large extent, horse trading between prosecutor and defense counsel determines who goes to jail and for how long. That is what plea bargaining is. It is not some adjunct to the criminal justice system; it is the criminal justice system." Scott & Stuntz, Plea Bargaining as Contract, 101 Yale L. J. 1909, 1912 (1992). In today's criminal justice system, therefore, the negotiation of a plea bargain, rather than the unfolding of a trial, is almost always the critical point for a defendant.

To note the prevalence of plea bargaining is not to criticize it. The potential to conserve valuable prosecutorial resources and for defendants to admit their crimes and receive more favorable terms at sentencing means that a plea agreement can benefit both parties. In order that these benefits can be realized, however, criminal defendants require effective counsel during plea negotiations. Anything less might deny a defendant effective representation by counsel at the only stage when legal aid and advice would help him.

The inquiry then becomes how to define the duty and responsibilities of defense counsel in the plea bargain process. This is a difficult question. Bargaining is, by its nature, defined to a substantial degree by personal style. The alternative courses and tactics in negotiation are so individual that it may be neither prudent nor practicable to try to elaborate or define detailed standards for the proper discharge of defense counsel's participation in the process. This case presents neither the necessity nor the occasion to define the duties of defense counsel in those respects, however. Here the question is whether defense counsel has the duty to communicate the terms of a formal offer to accept a plea on terms and conditions that may result in a lesser sentence, a conviction on lesser charges, or both.

This Court now holds that, as a general rule, defense counsel has the duty to communicate formal offers from the prosecution to accept a plea on terms and conditions that may be favorable to the accused. Any exceptions to that rule need not be explored here, for the offer was a formal one with a fixed expiration date. When defense counsel allowed the offer to expire without advising the defendant or allowing him to consider it, defense counsel did not render the effective assistance the Constitution requires. Under *Strickland*, the question then becomes what, if any, prejudice resulted from the breach of duty.

To show prejudice from ineffective assistance of counsel where a plea offer has lapsed or been rejected because of counsel's deficient performance, defendants must demonstrate a reasonable probability they would have accepted the earlier plea offer had they been afforded effective assistance of counsel. Defendants must also demonstrate a reasonable probability the plea would have been entered without the prosecution canceling it or the trial court refusing to accept it, if they had the authority to exercise that discretion under state law. To establish prejudice in this instance, it is necessary to show a reasonable probability that the end result of the criminal process would have been more favorable by reason of a plea to a lesser charge or a sentence of less prison time. In a case, such as this, where a defendant pleads guilty to less favorable terms and claims that ineffective assistance of counsel caused him to miss out on a more favorable earlier plea offer, *Strickland*'s inquiry into whether "the result of the proceeding would have been different," requires looking not at whether the defendant would have proceeded to trial absent ineffective assistance but whether he would have accepted the offer to plead pursuant to the terms earlier proposed.

In order to complete a showing of *Strickland* prejudice, defendants who have shown a reasonable probability they would have accepted the earlier plea offer must also show that, if the prosecution had the discretion to cancel it or if the trial court had the discretion to refuse to accept it, there is a reasonable probability neither the prosecution nor the trial court would have prevented the offer from being accepted or implemented. This further showing is of particular importance because a defendant has no right to be offered a plea, nor a federal right that the judge accept it. It can be assumed that in most jurisdictions prosecutors and judges are familiar with the boundaries of acceptable plea bargains and sentences. So in most instances it should not be difficult to make an objective assessment as to whether or not a particular fact or intervening circumstance would suffice, in the normal course, to cause prosecutorial withdrawal or judicial nonapproval of a plea bargain. The determination that there is or is not a reasonable probability that the outcome of the proceeding would have been different absent counsel's errors can be conducted within that framework.

These standards must be applied to the instant case. As regards the deficient performance prong of *Strickland*, the Court of Appeals found the "record is void of any evidence of any effort by trial counsel to communicate the formal Offer to Frye during the Offer window, let alone any evidence that Frye's conduct interfered with trial counsel's ability to do so." On this record, it is evident that Frye's attorney did not make a meaningful attempt to inform the defendant of a written plea offer before the offer expired. The Missouri Court of Appeals was correct that "counsel's representation fell below an objective standard of reasonableness." The Court of Appeals erred, however, in articulating the precise standard for prejudice in this context. As noted, a defendant in Frye's position must show not only a reasonable probability that he would have accepted the lapsed plea but also a reasonable probability that the prosecution would have adhered to the agreement and that it would have been accepted by the trial court. Frye can show he would have accepted the offer, but there is strong reason to doubt the prosecution and the trial court would have permitted the plea bargain to become final.

There appears to be a reasonable probability Frye would have accepted the prosecutor's original offer of a plea bargain if the offer had been communicated to him, because he pleaded guilty to a more serious charge, with no promise of a sentencing recommendation from the prosecutor.

The Court of Appeals failed, however, to require Frye to show that the first plea offer, if accepted by Frye, would have been adhered to by the prosecution and accepted by the trial court. Whether the prosecution and trial court are required to do so is a matter of state law, and it is not the place of this Court to settle those matters. The Court has established the minimum requirements of the Sixth Amendment as interpreted in *Strickland*, and States have the discretion to add procedural protections under state law if they choose. A State may choose to preclude the prosecution from withdrawing a plea offer once it has been accepted or perhaps to preclude a trial court from rejecting a plea bargain. In Missouri, it appears a plea offer once accepted by the defendant can be withdrawn without recourse by the prosecution. The extent of the trial court's discretion in Missouri to reject a plea agreement appears to be in some doubt.

Food for Thought

How in the world can the defendant prove whether the prosecution would have honored its bargain? Or whether the Court would accept it? Are proofs like this too high a burden for a defendant who has not been advised of a favorable plea bargain to meet?

We remand for the Missouri Court of Appeals to consider these state-law questions, because they bear on the federal question of *Strickland* prejudice. If, as the Missouri court stated here, the prosecutor could have canceled the plea agreement, and if Frye fails to show a reasonable probability the prosecutor would have adhered to the agreement, there is no *Strickland* prejudice. Likewise, if the trial court could have refused to accept the plea agreement, and if Frye fails to show a reasonable probability the trial court would have accepted the plea, there is no *Strickland* prejudice. In this case, given Frye's new offense for driving without a license on December 30, 2007, there is reason to doubt that the prosecution would have adhered to the agreement or that the trial court would have accepted it at the January 4, 2008, hearing, unless they were required by state law to do so.

The judgment of the Missouri Court of Appeals is vacated, and the case is remanded for further proceedings not inconsistent with this opinion.

JUSTICE SCALIA, with whom THE CHIEF JUSTICE, JUSTICE THOMAS, and JUSTICE ALITO join, dissenting.

The Court acknowledges that Frye's conviction was untainted by attorney error. Given the ultimate focus of our ineffective-assistance cases on the fundamental fairness of the proceeding whose result is being challenged, that should be the end of the matter.

The plea-bargaining process is a subject worthy of regulation, since it is the means by which most criminal convictions are obtained. It happens not to be, however, a subject covered by the Sixth Amendment, which is concerned not with the fairness of bargaining but with the fairness of conviction. The Constitution is not an all-purpose tool for judicial construction of a perfect world; and when we ignore its text in order to make it that, we often find ourselves swinging a sledge where a tack hammer is needed.

Food for Thought

Was Justice Scalia correct? Is "fairness" the "ultimate focus" of the Court's ineffective assistance cases?

In this case, the Court's sledge may require the reversal of perfectly valid, eminently just, convictions. I respectfully dissent.

Point for Discussion

Poor Advice

In the companion case of *Lafler v. Cooper*, 566 U.S. 156 (2012), the same 5-to-4 majority of the Supreme Court as in *Frye*, applied *Strickland* to a situation where a favorable plea offer was reported to the client (unlike *Frye*), but, on poor advice of counsel, was rejected. "In these circumstances," the majority ruled, "a defendant must show that but for the ineffective advice of counsel there is a reasonable probability that the plea offer would have been presented to the court (i.e., that the defendant would have accepted the plea and the prosecution would not have withdrawn it in light of intervening circumstances), that the court would have accepted its terms, and that the conviction or sentence, or both, under the offer's terms would have been less severe than under the judgment and sentence that in fact were imposed." Deficient performance was conceded, and the Court found prejudice because "respondent received a minimum sentence 3 1/2 times greater than he would have received under the plea." That said, the majority added:

> Even if a defendant shows ineffective assistance of counsel has caused the rejection of a plea leading to a trial and a more severe sentence, there is the question of what constitutes an appropriate remedy.

> The specific injury suffered by defendants who decline a plea offer as a result of ineffective assistance of counsel and then receive a greater sentence as a result of trial can come in at least one of two forms. In some cases, the sole advantage a defendant would have received under the plea is a lesser sentence. This is typically the case when the charges that would have been admitted as part of the plea bargain are the same as the charges the defendant was convicted of after trial. In this situation the court may conduct an evidentiary hearing to determine whether the defendant has shown a reasonable probability that but for counsel's errors he would have accepted the plea. If the showing is made, the court may exercise discretion in determining whether the defendant should receive the term of imprisonment the government offered in the plea, the sentence he received at trial, or something in between.

> In some situations it may be that resentencing alone will not be full redress for the constitutional injury. If, for example, an offer was for a guilty plea to a count or counts less serious than the ones for which a defendant was convicted after trial, or if a mandatory sentence confines a judge's sen-

tencing discretion after trial, a resentencing based on the conviction at trial may not suffice. In these circumstances, the proper exercise of discretion to remedy the constitutional injury may be to require the prosecution to reoffer the plea proposal. Once this has occurred, the judge can then exercise discretion in deciding whether to vacate the conviction from trial and accept the plea or leave the conviction undisturbed.

* * *

Since the reasonableness of defense counsel's conduct is a very fact-specific inquiry under *Strickland*, sometimes it may be perfectly reasonable for counsel to engage in counter-intuitive conduct for good reasons, e.g. actually conceding the defendant's guilt or abandoning an insanity defense. Then again, defense counsel's strategic decisions are not entirely immune from second guessing. In this regard, consider the following Supreme Court decisions:

Florida v. Nixon

543 U.S. 175 (2004).

JUSTICE GINSBURG delivered the opinion of the Court.

This capital case concerns defense counsel's strategic decision to concede, at the guilt phase of the trial, the defendant's commission of murder, and to concentrate the defense on establishing, at the penalty phase, cause for sparing the defendant's life. Any concession of that order, the Florida Supreme Court held, made without the defendant's express consent—however gruesome the crime and despite the strength of the evidence of guilt—automatically ranks as prejudicial ineffective assistance of counsel necessitating a new trial. We reverse the Florida Supreme Court's judgment.

Defense counsel undoubtedly has a duty to discuss potential strategies with the defendant. *See Strickland v. Washington*, 466 U.S. 668 (1984). But when a defendant, informed by counsel, neither consents nor objects to the course counsel describes as the most promising means to avert a sentence of death, counsel is not automatically barred from pursuing that course. The reasonableness of counsel's performance, after consultation with the defendant yields no response, must be judged in accord with the inquiry generally applicable to ineffective-assistance-of-counsel claims: Did counsel's representation "fall below an objective standard of reasonableness"? The Florida Supreme Court erred in applying, instead, a presumption of deficient performance, as well as a presumption of prejudice; that latter presumption, we have instructed, is reserved for cases in which counsel fails meaningfully to oppose the prosecution's case. A presumption of prejudice is not in order based solely on a defendant's failure to provide express consent to a tenable strategy counsel has adequately disclosed to and discussed with the defendant.

On Monday, August 13, 1984, near a dirt road in the environs of Tallahassee, Florida, a passing motorist discovered Jeanne Bickner's charred body. Bickner had been tied to a tree and set on fire while still alive. Her left leg and arm, and most of her hair and skin, had been burned away. The next day, police found Bickner's car, abandoned on a Tallahassee street corner, on fire. Police arrested 23-year-old Joe Elton Nixon later that morning, after Nixon's brother informed the sheriff's office that Nixon had confessed to the murder.

Questioned by the police, Nixon described in graphic detail how he had kidnaped Bickner, then killed her. He recounted that he had approached Bickner, a stranger, in a mall, and asked her to help him jumpstart his car. Bickner offered Nixon a ride home in her 1973 MG sports car. Once on the road, Nixon directed Bickner to drive to a remote place; en route, he overpowered her and stopped the car. Nixon next put Bickner in the MG's trunk, drove into a wooded area, removed Bickner from the car, and tied her to a tree with jumper cables. Bickner pleaded with Nixon to release her, offering him money in exchange. Concerned that Bickner might identify him, Nixon decided to kill her. He set fire to Bickner's personal belongings and ignited her with burning objects. Nixon drove away in the MG, and later told his brother and girlfriend what he had done. He burned the MG on Tuesday, August 14, after reading in the newspaper that Bickner's body had been discovered.

The State gathered overwhelming evidence establishing that Nixon had committed the murder in the manner he described. In late August 1984, Nixon was indicted in Leon County, Florida, for first-degree murder, kidnaping, robbery, and arson. Assistant public defender Michael Corin, assigned to represent Nixon, filed a plea of not guilty and deposed all of the State's potential witnesses. Corin concluded, given the strength of the evidence, that Nixon's guilt was not "subject to any reasonable dispute." Corin thereupon commenced plea negotiations, hoping to persuade the prosecution to drop the death penalty in exchange for Nixon's guilty pleas to all charges. Negotiations broke down when the prosecutors indicated their unwillingness to recommend a sentence other than death.

Faced with the inevitability of going to trial on a capital charge, Corin turned his attention to the penalty phase, believing that the only way to save Nixon's life would be to present extensive mitigation evidence centering on Nixon's mental instability. Experienced in capital defense, Corin feared that denying Nixon's commission of the kidnaping and murder during the guilt phase would compromise Corin's ability to persuade the jury, during the penalty phase, that Nixon's conduct was the product of his mental illness. Corin concluded that the best strategy would be to concede guilt, thereby preserving his credibility in urging leniency during the penalty phase.

Corin attempted to explain this strategy to Nixon at least three times. Although Corin had represented Nixon previously on unrelated charges and the two had a good relationship in Corin's estimation, Nixon was generally unresponsive during their discussions. He never verbally approved or protested Corin's proposed strategy. Corin eventually exercised his professional judgment to pursue the concession strategy. As he explained: "There are many times lawyers make decisions because they have to make them because the client does nothing."

When Nixon's trial began on July 15, 1985, his unresponsiveness deepened into disruptive and violent behavior. On the second day of jury selection, Nixon pulled off his clothing, demanded a black judge and lawyer, refused to be escorted into the courtroom, and threatened to force the guards to shoot him. An extended on-the-record colloquy followed Nixon's bizarre behavior, during which Corin urged the trial judge to explain Nixon's rights to him and ascertain whether Nixon understood the significance of absenting himself from the trial. Corin also argued that restraining Nixon and compelling him to be present would prejudice him in the eyes of the jury. When the judge examined Nixon on the record in a holding cell, Nixon stated he had no interest in the trial and threatened to misbehave if forced to attend. The judge ruled that Nixon had intelligently and voluntarily waived his right to be present at trial.

The guilt phase of the trial thus began in Nixon's absence. In his opening statement, Corin acknowledged Nixon's guilt and urged the jury to focus on the penalty phase:

"In this case, there won't be any question, none whatsoever, that my client, Joe Elton Nixon, caused Jeannie Bickner's death. That fact will be proved to your satisfaction beyond any doubt.

"This case is about the death of Joe Elton Nixon and whether it should occur within the next few years by electrocution or maybe its natural expiration after a lifetime of confinement.

"Now, in arriving at your verdict, in your penalty recommendation, for we will get that far, you are going to learn many facts about Joe Elton Nixon. Some of those facts are going to be good. That may not seem clear to you at this time. But, and sadly, most of the things you learn of Joe Elton Nixon are not going to be good. But, I'm suggesting to you that when you have seen all the testimony, heard all the testimony and the evidence that has been shown, there are going to be reasons why you should recommend that his life be spared."

During its case in chief, the State introduced the tape of Nixon's confession, expert testimony on the manner in which Bickner died, and witness testimony regarding Nixon's confessions to his relatives and his possession of Bickner's car and personal effects. Corin cross-examined these witnesses only when he felt their statements needed clarification and he did not present a defense case. Corin did object to the introduction of crime scene photographs as unduly prejudicial and actively contested several aspects of the jury instructions during the charge conference. In his closing argument, Corin again conceded Nixon's guilt and reminded the jury of the importance of the penalty phase: "I will hope to argue to you and give you reasons not that Mr. Nixon's life be spared one final and terminal confinement forever, but that he not be sentenced to die." The jury found Nixon guilty on all counts.

At the start of the penalty phase, Corin argued to the jury that "Joe Elton Nixon is not normal organically, intellectually, emotionally or educationally or in any other way." Corin presented the testimony of eight witnesses. Relatives and friends described Nixon's childhood emotional troubles and his erratic behavior in the days preceding the murder. A psychiatrist and a psychologist addressed Nixon's antisocial personality, his history of emotional instability and psychiatric care, his low IQ, and the possibility that at some point he suffered brain damage. The State presented little evidence during the penalty phase, simply incorporating its guilt-phase evidence by reference, and introducing testimony, over Corin's objection, that Nixon had removed Bickner's underwear in order to terrorize her.

In his closing argument, Corin emphasized Nixon's youth, the psychiatric evidence, and the jury's discretion to consider any mitigating circumstances; Corin urged that, if not sentenced to death, "Joe Elton Nixon would never be released from confinement." The death penalty, Corin maintained, was appropriate only for "intact human beings," and "Joe Elton Nixon is not one of those. He's never been one of those. He never will be one of those." Corin concluded: "You know, we're not around here all that long. And it's rare when we have the opportunity to give or take life. And you have that opportunity to give life. And I'm going to ask you to do that. Thank you." After deliberating for approximately three hours, the jury recommended that Nixon be sentenced to death.

In accord with the jury's recommendation, the trial court imposed the death penalty. Notably, at the close of the penalty phase, the court commended Corin's performance during the trial, stating that "the tactic employed by trial counsel was an excellent analysis of the reality of his case." The evidence of guilt "would have persuaded any jury beyond all doubt," and "for trial counsel to have inferred that Mr. Nixon was not guilty would have deprived counsel of any credibility during the penalty phase." The Florida Supreme Court subsequently reversed, finding ineffective assistance of counsel.

We granted certiorari to resolve an important question of constitutional law, i.e., whether counsel's failure to obtain the defendant's express consent to a strategy of conceding guilt in a capital trial automatically renders counsel's performance deficient, and whether counsel's effectiveness should be evaluated under *Cronic* or *Strickland*. We now reverse the judgment of the Florida Supreme Court.

An attorney undoubtedly has a duty to consult with the client regarding important decisions, including questions of overarching defense strategy. That obligation, however, does not require counsel to obtain the defendant's consent to every tactical decision. But certain decisions regarding the exercise or waiver of basic trial rights are of such moment that they cannot be made for the defendant by a surrogate. A defendant, this Court affirmed, has "the ultimate authority" to determine "whether to plead guilty, waive a jury, testify in his or her own behalf, or take an appeal." Concerning those decisions, an attorney must both consult with the defendant and obtain consent to the recommended course of action.

FYI

The Florida Supreme Court's decision in *Nixon* led to calls for the impeachment of three of the justices who decided that case. Given the outcome of the Supreme Court's unanimous ruling in *Nixon*, reversing the Florida Supreme Court, do you think that those calls were justified?

Corin was obliged to, and in fact several times did, explain his proposed trial strategy to Nixon. Given Nixon's constant resistance to answering inquiries put to him by counsel and court, Corin was not additionally required to gain express consent before conceding Nixon's guilt. The two evidentiary hearings conducted by the Florida trial court demonstrate beyond doubt that Corin fulfilled his duty of consultation by informing Nixon of counsel's proposed strategy and its potential benefits. Nixon's characteristic silence each time information was conveyed to him, in sum, did not suffice to render unreasonable Corin's decision to concede guilt and to home in, instead, on the life or death penalty issue.

Food for Thought

Suppose that, instead of remaining unresponsive, Nixon insisted that he was actually innocent (in the face of the same, overwhelming contrary evidence)? Would or should defense counsel in that instance have gone "all out" to try (futilely) to establish his innocence, thus creating a much higher risk of a death sentence?

Corin's concession of Nixon's guilt does not rank as a failure to function in any meaningful sense as the Government's adversary. Although such a concession in a run-of-the-mine trial might present a closer question, the gravity of the potential sentence in a capital trial and the proceeding's two-phase structure vitally affect counsel's strategic calculus. Attorneys representing capital defendants face daunting challenges in developing trial strategies, not least because the defendant's guilt is often clear. Prosecutors are more likely to seek the death penalty, and to refuse to accept a plea to a life sentence, when the evidence is overwhelming and the crime heinous. In such cases, "avoiding execution may be the best and only realistic result possible."

Counsel therefore may reasonably decide to focus on the trial's penalty phase, at which time counsel's mission is to persuade the trier that his client's life should be spared. Unable to negotiate a guilty plea in exchange for a life sentence, defense counsel must strive at the guilt phase to avoid a counterproductive course. In this light, counsel cannot be deemed ineffective for attempting to impress the jury with his candor and his unwillingness to engage in a useless charade.

Food for Thought

What if this had not been a capital case. Should the Court's ultimate holding have been the same? If Nixon had faced a potential sentence of 5 to 10 years in jail, for example, would defense counsel have been justified in sacrificing any chance at an acquittal, however remote, for a chance at arguing for a reduced sentence subsequently? What do you think?

To summarize, in a capital case, counsel must consider in conjunction both the guilt and penalty phases in determining how best to proceed. When counsel informs the defendant of the strategy counsel believes to be in the defendant's best interest and the defendant is unresponsive, counsel's strategic choice is not impeded by any blanket rule demanding the defendant's explicit consent. Instead, if counsel's strategy, given the evidence bearing on the defendant's guilt, satisfies the *Strickland* standard, that is the end of the matter; no tenable claim of ineffective assistance would remain.

Reversed.

Points for Discussion

a. Concession of Guilt over Defendant's Objections

In a more recent decision where "in contrast to *Nixon*, the defendant vociferously insisted that he did not engage in the charged acts and adamantly objected to any admission of guilt," the Supreme Court reached a different conclusion:

> We hold that a defendant has the right to insist that counsel refrain from admitting guilt, even when counsel's experienced-based view is that confessing guilt offers the defendant the best chance to avoid the death penalty. Guaranteeing a defendant the right "to have the Assistance of Counsel for his defence," the Sixth Amendment so demands. With individual liberty—and, in capital cases, life—at stake, it is the defendant's prerogative, not counsel's, to decide on the objective of his defense: to admit guilt in the

hope of gaining mercy at the sentencing stage, or to maintain his innocence, leaving it to the State to prove his guilt beyond a reasonable doubt.

McCoy v. Louisiana, 138 S.Ct. 1500 (2018).

The Court in *McCoy* explained its reasoning for this different result than in *Nixon* as follows:

> Just as a defendant may steadfastly refuse to plead guilty in the face of overwhelming evidence against her, or reject the assistance of legal counsel despite the defendant's own inexperience and lack of professional qualifications, so may she insist on maintaining her innocence at the guilt phase of a capital trial. These are not strategic choices about how best to achieve a client's objectives; they are choices about what the client's objectives in fact are.

In contrast, "Nixon's attorney did not negate Nixon's autonomy by overriding Nixon's desired defense objective, for Nixon never asserted any such objective. Nixon 'was generally unresponsive' during discussions of trial strategy, and 'never verbally approved or protested' counsel's proposed approach. Nixon complained about the admission of his guilt only after trial. McCoy, in contrast, opposed [his defense counsel's] assertion of his guilt at every opportunity, before and during trial, both in conference with his lawyer and in open court."

Does this distinction make sense to you? Recall that Nixon never actually agreed to his counsel's concession of his guilt. Does or should that make a difference?

b.   Advice About Defense

In *Knowles v. Mirzayance,* 556 U.S. 111 (2009), the Supreme Court concluded that defense counsel's advice to his client that he withdraw his insanity defense because it was "doomed to fail"—advice that was accepted by his client—was also not ineffective assistance of counsel. As the Court made clear, "we are aware of no 'prevailing professional norms' that prevent counsel from recommending that a plea be withdrawn when it is almost certain to lose. The law does not require counsel to raise every available nonfrivolous defense. Counsel also is not required to have a tactical reason—above and beyond a reasonable appraisal of a claim's dismal prospects for success—for recommending that a weak claim be dropped altogether." What do you think? Was this really the *effective* assistance of counsel?

Rompilla v. Beard

545 U.S. 374 (2005).

JUSTICE SOUTER delivered the opinion of the Court.

This case calls for specific application of the standard of reasonable competence required on the part of defense counsel by the Sixth Amendment. We hold that even when a capital defendant's family members and the defendant himself have suggested that no mitigating evidence is available, his lawyer is bound to make reasonable efforts to obtain and review material that counsel knows the prosecution will probably rely on as evidence of aggravation at the sentencing phase of trial.

On the morning of January 14, 1988, James Scanlon was discovered dead in a bar he ran in Allentown, Pennsylvania, his body having been stabbed repeatedly and set on fire. Rompilla was indicted for the murder and related offenses, and the Commonwealth gave notice of intent to ask for the death penalty. Two public defenders were assigned to the case.

The jury at the guilt phase of trial found Rompilla guilty on all counts, and during the ensuing penalty phase, the prosecutor sought to prove three aggravating factors to justify a death sentence: that the murder was committed in the course of another felony; that the murder was committed by torture; and that Rompilla had a significant history of felony convictions indicating the use or threat of violence. The Commonwealth presented evidence on all three aggravators, and the jury found all proven. Rompilla's evidence in mitigation consisted of relatively brief testimony: five of his family members argued in effect for residual doubt, and beseeched the jury for mercy, saying that they believed Rompilla was innocent and a good man. Rompilla's 14-year-old son testified that he loved his father and would visit him in prison. The jury acknowledged this evidence to the point of finding, as two factors in mitigation, that Rompilla's son had testified on his behalf and that rehabilitation was possible. But the jurors assigned the greater weight to the aggravating factors, and sentenced Rompilla to death. The Supreme Court of Pennsylvania affirmed both conviction and sentence. Subsequently, a District Court granted Rompilla's *habeas corpus* petition on ineffectiveness grounds, and the Third Circuit Court of Appeals reversed. We granted certiorari, and now reverse.

Ineffective assistance under *Strickland* is deficient performance by counsel resulting in prejudice, with performance being measured against an "objective standard of reasonableness," "under prevailing professional norms." This case, like some others recently, looks to norms of adequate investigation in preparing for the sentencing phase of a capital trial, when defense counsel's job is to counter the State's evidence of aggravated culpability with evidence in mitigation. In judging the defense's investigation, as in applying *Strickland* generally, hindsight is discounted by pegging adequacy to counsel's perspective at the time investigative decisions are made, and by giving a heavy measure of deference to counsel's judgments.

A standard of reasonableness applied as if one stood in counsel's shoes spawns few hard-edged rules, and the merits of a number of counsel's choices in this case are subject to fair debate. This is not a case in which defense counsel simply ignored their obligation to find mitigating evidence, and their workload as busy public defenders did not keep them from making a number of efforts, including interviews with Rompilla and some members of his family, and examinations of reports by three mental health experts who gave opinions at the guilt phase. None of the sources proved particularly helpful.

Rompilla's own contributions to any mitigation case were minimal. Counsel found him uninterested in helping, as on their visit to his prison to go over a proposed mitigation strategy, when Rompilla told them he was "bored being here listening" and returned to his cell. To questions about childhood and schooling, his answers indicated they had been normal, save for quitting school in the ninth grade. There were times when Rompilla was even actively obstructive by sending counsel off on false leads.

The lawyers also spoke with five members of Rompilla's family (his former wife, two brothers, a sister-in-law, and his son), and counsel testified that they developed a good relationship with the family in the course of their representation. The third and final source tapped for mitigating material was the cadre of three mental health witnesses who were asked to look into Rompilla's mental state as of the time of the offense and his competency to stand trial, but their reports revealed "nothing useful" to Rompilla's case, and the lawyers consequently did not go to any other historical source that might have cast light on Rompilla's mental condition.

When new counsel entered the case to raise Rompilla's postconviction claims, however, they identified a number of likely avenues the trial lawyers could fruitfully have followed in building a mitigation case. School records are one example, which trial counsel never examined in spite of the professed unfamiliarity of the several family members with Rompilla's childhood, and despite counsel's knowledge that Rompilla left school after the ninth grade. Others examples are records of Rompilla's juvenile and adult incarcerations, which counsel did not consult, although they were aware of their client's criminal record. And while counsel knew from police reports provided in pretrial discovery that Rompilla had been drinking heavily at the time of his offense, and although one of the mental health experts reported that Rompilla's troubles with alcohol merited further investigation, counsel did not look for evidence of a history of dependence on alcohol that might have extenuating significance.

Before us, trial counsel and the Commonwealth respond to these unexplored possibilities by emphasizing this Court's recognition that the duty to investigate does not force defense lawyers to scour the globe on the off-chance something will turn up; reasonably diligent counsel may draw a line when they have good reason to think further investigation would be a waste. The Commonwealth argues that the information trial counsel gathered from Rompilla and the other sources gave them sound reason to think it would have been pointless to spend time and money on the additional investigation espoused by postconviction counsel, and we can say that there is room for debate about trial counsel's obligation to follow at least some of those potential lines of enquiry. There is no need to say more, however, for a further point is clear and dispositive: the lawyers were deficient in failing to examine the court file on Rompilla's prior conviction.

There is an obvious reason that the failure to examine Rompilla's prior conviction file fell below the level of reasonable performance. Counsel knew that the Commonwealth intended to seek the death penalty by proving Rompilla had a significant history of felony convictions indicating the use or threat of violence, an aggravator under state law. Counsel further knew that the Commonwealth would attempt to establish this history by proving Rompilla's prior conviction for rape and assault, and would emphasize his violent character by introducing a transcript of the rape victim's testimony given in that earlier trial. There is no question that defense counsel were on notice, since they acknowledge that a "plea letter," written by one of them four days prior to trial, mentioned the prosecutor's plans. It is also undisputed that the prior conviction file was a public document, readily available for the asking at the very courthouse where Rompilla was to be tried.

It is clear, however, that defense counsel did not look at any part of that file, including the transcript, until warned by the prosecution a second time. In a colloquy the day before the evidentiary sentencing phase began, the prosecutor again said he would present the transcript of the victim's testimony to establish the prior conviction.

With every effort to view the facts as a defense lawyer would have done at the time, it is difficult to see how counsel could have failed to realize that without examining the readily available file they were seriously compromising their opportunity to respond to a case for aggravation. The prosecution was going to use the dramatic facts of a similar prior offense, and Rompilla's counsel had a duty to make all reasonable efforts to learn what they could about the offense. Reasonable efforts certainly included obtaining the Commonwealth's own readily available file on the prior conviction to learn what the Commonwealth knew about the crime, to discover any mitigating evidence the Commonwealth would downplay and to anticipate the details of the aggravating evidence the Commonwealth would emphasize. Without making reasonable efforts to review the file, defense counsel could have had no hope of knowing whether the prosecution was quoting selectively from the transcript, or whether there were circumstances extenuating the behavior described by the victim. The obligation to get the file was particularly pressing here owing to the similarity of the violent prior offense to the crime charged and Rompilla's sentencing strategy stressing residual doubt. Without making efforts to learn the details and rebut the relevance of the earlier crime, a convincing argument for residual doubt was certainly beyond any hope.

At argument the most that Pennsylvania (and the United States as amicus) could say was that defense counsel's efforts to find mitigating evidence by other means excused them from looking at the prior conviction file. And that, of course, is the position taken by the state postconviction courts. Without specifically discussing the prior case file, they too found that defense counsel's efforts were enough to free them from any obligation to enquire further.

We think this conclusion of the state court fails to answer the considerations we have set out, to the point of being an objectively unreasonable conclusion. It flouts prudence to deny that a defense lawyer should try to look at a file he knows the prosecution will cull for aggravating evidence, let alone when the file is sitting in the trial courthouse, open for the asking. No reasonable lawyer would forgo examination of the file thinking he could do as well by asking the defendant or family relations whether they recalled anything helpful or damaging in the prior victim's testimony. Nor would a reasonable lawyer compare possible searches for school reports, juvenile records, and evidence of drinking habits to the opportunity to take a look at a file disclosing what the prosecutor knows and even plans to read from in his case. Questioning a few more family members and searching for old records can promise less than looking for a needle in a haystack, when a lawyer truly has reason to doubt there is any needle there. But looking at a file the prosecution says it will use is a sure bet: whatever may be in that file is going to tell defense counsel something about what the prosecution can produce.

The dissent thinks this analysis creates a "rigid, per se" rule that requires defense counsel to do a complete review of the file on any prior conviction introduced, but that is a mistake. Counsel fell short here because they failed to make reasonable efforts to review the prior conviction file, despite knowing that the prosecution intended to introduce Rompilla's prior conviction not merely by entering a notice of conviction into evidence but by quoting damaging testimony of the rape victim in that case. The unreasonableness of attempting no more than they did was heightened by the easy availability of the file at the trial courthouse, and the great risk that testimony about a similar violent crime would hamstring counsel's chosen defense of residual doubt.

Since counsel's failure to look at the file fell below the line of reasonable practice, there is a further question about prejudice, that is, whether "there is a reasonable probability that, but for counsel's unprofessional errors, the result of the proceeding would have been different." We think Rompilla has shown beyond any doubt that counsel's lapse was prejudicial; Pennsylvania, indeed, does not even contest the claim of prejudice.

If the defense lawyers had looked in the file on Rompilla's prior conviction, it is uncontested they would have found a range of mitigation leads that no other source had opened up. In the same file with the transcript of the prior trial were the records of Rompilla's imprisonment on the earlier conviction, which defense counsel testified she had never seen. The prison files pictured Rompilla's childhood and mental health very differently from anything defense counsel had seen or heard. An evaluation by a corrections counselor states that Rompilla was "reared in the slum environment of Allentown, Pa. vicinity. He early came to the attention of juvenile authorities, quit school at 16, and started a series of incarcerations in and out Penna. often of assaultive nature and commonly related to over-indulgence in alcoholic beverages." The same file discloses test results that the defense's mental health experts would have viewed as pointing to schizophrenia and other disorders, and test scores showing a third grade level of cognition after nine years of schooling.

The accumulated entries would have destroyed the benign conception of Rompilla's upbringing and mental capacity defense counsel had formed from talking with Rompilla himself and some of his family members, and from the reports of the mental health experts. With this information, counsel would have become skeptical of the impression given by the five family members and would unquestionably have gone further to build a mitigation case. Further effort would presumably have unearthed much of the material postconviction counsel found, including testimony from several members of Rompilla's family, whom trial counsel did not interview. Judge Sloviter dissenting in the Third Circuit, summarized this evidence:

> "Rompilla's parents were both severe alcoholics who drank constantly. His mother drank during her pregnancy with Rompilla, and he and his brothers eventually developed serious drinking problems. His father, who had a vicious temper, frequently beat Rompilla's mother, leaving her bruised and black-eyed, and bragged about his cheating on her. His parents fought violently, and on at least one occasion his mother stabbed his father. He was abused by his father who beat him when he was young with his hands, fists, leather straps, belts and sticks. All of the children lived in terror. There were no expressions of parental love, affection or approval. Instead, he was subjected to yelling and verbal abuse. His father locked Rompilla and his brother Richard in a small wire mesh dog pen that was filthy and excrement filled. He had an isolated background, and was not allowed to visit other children or to speak to anyone on the phone. They had no indoor plumbing in the house, he slept in the attic with no heat, and the children were not given clothes and attended school in rags."

The jury never heard any of this and neither did the mental health experts who examined Rompilla before trial. While they found "nothing helpful to Rompilla's case," their postconviction counterparts, alerted by information from school, medical, and prison records that trial counsel never saw, found plenty of " 'red flags' " pointing up a need to test further. When they tested, they found that Rompilla "suffers from organic brain damage, an extreme mental disturbance significantly impairing several of his cognitive functions." They also said that "Rompilla's problems relate back to his childhood, and were likely caused by fetal alcohol syndrome and that Rompilla's capacity to appreciate the criminality of his conduct or to conform his conduct to the law was substantially impaired at the time of the offense."

These findings in turn would probably have prompted a look at school and juvenile records, all of them easy to get, showing, for example, that when Rompilla was 16 his mother "was missing from home frequently for a period of one or several weeks at a time." The same report noted that his mother "has been reported . . . frequently under the influence of alcoholic beverages, with the result that the children have always been poorly kept and on the filthy side which was also the condition of the home at all times." School records showed Rompilla's IQ was in the mentally retarded range.

Food for Thought

It may well be the case that the key fact to know in this case, like *Nixon*, is that this is a capital case. Is it possible that the Court is *sub silentio* requiring more of counsel in such cases than in non-capital cases given the gravity and finality of the potential penalty? If that is indeed the case, do you think that is an inappropriate approach? And if that is what a majority of the Court is really doing, should it just say so directly?

This evidence adds up to a mitigation case that bears no relation to the few naked pleas for mercy actually put before the jury, and although we suppose it is possible that a jury could have heard it all and still have decided on the death penalty, that is not the test. It goes without saying that the undiscovered mitigating evidence, taken as a whole, might well have influenced the jury's appraisal of Rompilla's culpability, and the likelihood of a different result if the evidence had gone in is sufficient to undermine confidence in the outcome actually reached at sentencing, *Strickland.*

The judgment of the Third Circuit is reversed, and Pennsylvania must either retry the case on penalty or stipulate to a life sentence.

JUSTICE O'CONNOR, concurring.

I write separately to put to rest one concern. The dissent worries that the Court's opinion "imposes on defense counsel a rigid requirement to review all documents in what it calls the 'case file' of any prior conviction that the prosecution might rely on at trial." But the Court's opinion imposes no such rule. Rather, today's decision simply applies our longstanding case-by-case approach to determining whether an attorney's performance was unconstitutionally deficient under *Strickland*. Trial counsel's performance in Rompilla's case falls short under that standard, because the attorneys' behavior was not "reasonable considering all the circumstances."

JUSTICE KENNEDY, with whom THE CHIEF JUSTICE, JUSTICE SCALIA, and JUSTICE THOMAS join, dissenting.

Today the Court brands two committed criminal defense attorneys as ineffective—"outside the wide range of professionally competent counsel"—because they did not look in an old case file and stumble upon something they had not set out to find. To reach this result, the majority imposes on defense counsel a rigid requirement to review all documents in what it calls the "case file" of any prior conviction that the prosecution might rely on at trial.

The majority's analysis contains barely a mention of *Strickland* and makes little effort to square today's holding with our traditional reluctance to impose rigid requirements on defense counsel. While the Court disclaims any intention to create a bright-line rule, this affords little comfort. The Court's opinion makes clear it has imposed on counsel a broad obligation to review prior conviction case files where those priors are used in aggravation—and to review every document in those files if not every single page of every document, regardless of the prosecution's proposed use for the prior conviction.

One of the primary reasons this Court has rejected a checklist approach to effective assistance of counsel is that each new requirement risks distracting attorneys from the real objective of providing vigorous advocacy as dictated by the facts and circumstances in the particular case. The Court's rigid requirement that counsel always review the case files of convictions the prosecution seeks to use at trial will be just such a distraction.

> **Food for Thought**
>
> The dissenters say this case creates a "rigid requirement." The majority say it does not. Which side is correct? Isn't it true after decision in *Rompilla* that defense counsel in a capital case must always look at the file documents relating to a prior offense if the prosecution indicates that it intends to rely on that conviction for purposes of sentence enhancement? If it is true, is that an inappropriate result?

Hypo: *Counsel Introduces Inadmissible Evidence*

Defense counsel introduced evidence of defendant's post-traumatic stress disorder (PTSD) even though evidence of PTSD was not admissible to negate intent for malice murder and voluntary manslaughter or to assist in proving self-defense, the offenses and the defense at issue in defendant's criminal trial.

> Counsel argued that evidence of PTSD was useful to explain defendant's conduct. But counsel admitted that the defense introduced "as much [mental health evidence] as we could get in not calling it PTSD . . . hoping to seek from the jury some—some—not nullification, but reduction of punishment." Defendant was nonetheless convicted. Was defense counsel constitutionally ineffective for doing this? What do you think? *See Bates v. State*, 313 Ga. 57, 867 S.E.2d 140 (2022).

Points for Discussion

a.   AEDPA

A 5-to-4 majority of the Supreme Court ruled in *Williams v. Taylor*, 529 U.S. 362, 412 (2000), that the Antiterrorism & Effective Death Penalty Act of 1996 ("AEDPA"), 28 U.S.C. § 2254, "places a new constraint on the power of a federal *habeas* court to grant a state prisoner's application for a writ of *habeas corpus* with respect to claims adjudicated on the merits in state court." More particularly, the Court held, under this new provision,

> the writ may issue only if one of the following two conditions is satisfied— the state-court adjudication resulted in a decision that (1) "was contrary to clearly established Federal law, as determined by the Supreme Court of the United States," or (2) "involved an unreasonable application of clearly established Federal law, as determined by the Supreme Court of the United States." Under the "contrary to" clause, a federal *habeas* court may grant the writ if the state court arrives at a conclusion opposite to that reached by this Court on a question of law or if the state court decides a case differently than this Court has on a set of materially indistinguishable facts. Under the "unreasonable application" clause, a federal *habeas* court may grant the writ if the state court identifies the correct governing legal principle from this Court's decisions but unreasonably applies that principle to the facts of the prisoner's case.

Subsequently, the Supreme Court added that "'clearly established Federal law' for purposes of the AEDPA includes only the holdings, as opposed to the *dicta*, of this Court's decisions." *See White v. Woodall*, 572 U.S. 415, 419 (2014). And the Supreme Court has also advised that the AEDPA also "prohibits the federal courts of appeals from relying on their own precedent to conclude that a particular constitutional principle is 'clearly established.'" *See Lopez v. Smith*, 574 U.S. 1, 2 (2014). More recently, the Supreme Court has opined that where a state court decision being reviewed in *habeas* proceedings includes little or no reasoning, "the federal court should 'look through' the unexplained decision to the last related state-court decision that does provide a relevant rationale. It should then presume that the unexplained decision adopted the same reasoning. But the State may rebut the presumption by showing that the unexplained affirmance relied or most likely did rely on different grounds than the lower state court's decision, such as alternative grounds for affirmance that were briefed or argued to the state supreme court or obvious in the record it reviewed." *Wilson v. Sellers*, 138 S. Ct. 1188, 1192 (2018).

Food for Thought

In *Brown v. Davenport*, 142 S. Ct. 1510 (2022), a 6-to-3 majority of the Supreme Court ruled that under the AEDPA, a state court's determination that a due process violation from defendant's shackling during trial was not prejudicial as it was neither contrary to nor an unreasonable application of clearly established federal law and, hence, not actionable as ineffective assistance of counsel, reversing the lower court's independent assessment of the error's prejudicial effect. What do you think?

Most significantly, the fact that a state court may have made an *incorrect* constitutional ruling on an ineffectiveness inquiry no longer suffices—under this AEDPA provision—to entitle a defendant to *habeas corpus* relief. *See, e.g. Woodford v. Visciotti*, 537 U.S. 19 (2002) ("Under the 'unreasonable application' clause, a federal *habeas* court may not issue the writ simply because that court concludes in its independent judgment that the state-court decision applied *Strickland* incorrectly. Rather, it is the *habeas* applicant's burden to show that the state court applied *Strickland* to the facts of his case in an objectively unreasonable manner.").

FYI

The Seventh Circuit has held that the Wisconsin Court of Appeals' conclusion that defense counsel's failure to produce for trial an individual who defendant claimed was the perpetrator of the home invasion and robbery for which he was convicted did not constitute deficient performance was an unreasonable application of clearly established federal law since there would have been strong corroboration of some "damning evidence" supporting this allegation had that individual testified. *Cook v. Foster*, 948 F.3d 896 (7th Cir. 2020).

In *Rompilla*, the dissenters argued that "the Pennsylvania Supreme Court gave careful consideration to Rompilla's Sixth Amendment claim and concluded that 'counsel reasonably relied upon their discussions with Rompilla and upon their experts to determine the records needed to evaluate his mental health and other potential mitigating circumstances.' This decision was far from unreasonable under the AEDPA." The majority concluded, however, not only that defense counsel were ineffective, but that the state court decision finding them *not* to have been ineffective "was contrary to, or involved an unreasonable application of, clearly established Federal law, as determined by the Supreme Court of the United States," pursuant to the AEDPA. What do you think? Do you agree?

See also *Shinn v. Kayer*, 141 S. Ct. 517, 520 (2020) ("When a state court has applied clearly established federal law to reasonably determined facts in the process of adjudicating a claim on the merits, a federal habeas court may not disturb the state court's decision unless its error lies 'beyond any possibility for fairminded disagreement.' "); *Sexton v. Beaudreaux*, 138 S. Ct. 2555, 2558 (2018), quoting *Harrington v. Richter*, 562 U.S. 86, 102 (2011) ("When, as here, there is no reasoned state-court decision on the merits, the federal court 'must determine what arguments or theories . . . could have supported the state court's decision; and then it must ask whether it is possible fairminded jurists could disagree that those arguments or theories are inconsistent with the holding in a prior decision of this Court.' ").

b. Decisional Consistency

Why was defense counsels' decision to focus on mitigation in the penalty phase of a capital case held in *Nixon* to be reasonable and the same decision held to be unreasonable in *Rompilla*? Does this difference in result make sense to you?

c. Limited Records for Review

In *Cullen v. Pinholster*, 563 U.S. 170 (2011), the Supreme Court ruled that an ineffectiveness inquiry in a federal *habeas corpus* proceeding under the AEDPA (*see* Point a, above) is limited to the record that was before the state court that adjudicated the claim on the merits; evidence that was presented only to the federal *habeas* court may not be considered. The *Cullen* majority conceded that "this test is 'difficult to meet,' and it is a 'highly deferential standard for evaluating state-court rulings, which demands that state-court decisions be given the benefit of the doubt.' "

The Supreme Court has also made clear that "whether a state court's decision resulted from an unreasonable legal or factual conclusion under the AEDPA does not require that there be an opinion from the state court explaining the state court's reasoning. Where a state court's decision is unaccompanied by an explanation, the *habeas* petitioner's burden still must be met by showing there was no reasonable basis for the state court to deny relief." *Harrington v. Richter*, 562 U.S. 86 (2011).

And in *Shinn v. Ramirez*, 142 S. Ct. 1718 (2022), a 6-to-3 majority of the Supreme Court added that a federal habeas court may not conduct an evidentiary hearing or otherwise consider evidence beyond the state-court record based on a claim of ineffective assistance of state postconviction counsel.

d. Mentally Ill Clients

In its 2007 decision in *Schriro v. Landrigan*, 550 U.S. 465 (2007), a 5-to-4 majority of the Supreme Court held that a federal district court did not abuse its discretion in declining to order a *habeas corpus* evidentiary hearing in a case where counsel failed to present significant mitigating evidence at a capital sentencing hearing where that failure was due to defendant's express request. As the majority pointed out, "it was not objectively unreasonable for the district court to conclude that a defendant who refused to allow the presentation of any mitigating evidence could not establish *Strickland* prejudice based on his counsel's failure to investigate further possible mitigating evidence." In dissent, Justice Stevens argued, however, that

> significant mitigating evidence—evidence that may well have explained respondent's criminal conduct and unruly behavior at his capital sentencing hearing—was unknown at the time of sentencing. Only years later did respondent learn that he suffers from a serious psychological condition that sheds important light on his earlier actions. The reason why this and other mitigating evidence was unavailable is that respondent's counsel failed to conduct a constitutionally adequate investigation.

What do you think? Should a mentally ill defendant's decisions against interest divest him of any opportunity to establish ineffective assistance after the fact?

e. Adequate Investigations

In *Bobby v. Van Hook*, 558 U.S. 4 (2009), the Supreme Court found that counsel was *not* ineffective for failing to adequately investigate and to present additional mitigating evidence at a capital sentencing hearing when defense counsel did present a great deal of evidence, but there could have been more:

> "Despite all the mitigating evidence the defense did present, Van Hook and the Court of Appeals fault his counsel for failing to find more. What his counsel did discover, the argument goes, gave them 'reason to suspect that much worse details existed,' and that suspicion should have prompted them to interview other family members-his stepsister, two uncles, and two aunts-as well as a psychiatrist who once treated his mother, all of whom 'could have helped his counsel narrate the true story of Van Hook's childhood experiences.' But there comes a point at which evidence from more distant relatives can reasonably be expected to be only cumulative, and the search for it distractive from more important duties. Given all the evidence they unearthed from those closest to Van Hook's upbringing and the experts who reviewed his history, it was not unreasonable for his counsel not to identify and interview every other living family member or every therapist who once treated his parents. This is not a case in which the defendant's attorneys failed to act while potentially powerful mitigating evidence stared them in the face or would have been apparent from documents any reasonable attorney would have obtained. It is instead a case, like *Strickland* itself, in which defense counsel's 'decision not to seek more' mitigating evidence

from the defendant's background 'than was already in hand' fell 'well within the range of professionally reasonable judgments.' "

Do you think this decision is consistent with the decision in *Rompilla*?

f.   Advice on Deportation Risk

In *Padilla v. Kentucky*, 559 U.S. 356 (2010), the Supreme Court ruled that in order to satisfy the performance prong of *Strickland*, "counsel must inform her client whether his guilty plea carries a risk of deportation." Padilla claimed that his counsel not only failed to advise him about the deportation consequences of his guilty plea to charged marijuana offenses, but told him that he did not have to worry about immigration status since he had been in the country so long. This advice was incorrect and, after his conviction, Padilla did indeed face deportation.

The Court held that "advice regarding deportation is not categorically removed from the ambit of the Sixth Amendment right to counsel. *Strickland* applies to Padilla's claim." That does not mean, the Court added, that criminal defense counsel must become experts on immigration law. Rather, "a criminal defense attorney need do no more than advise a noncitizen client that pending criminal charges may carry a risk of adverse immigration consequences."

The Supreme Court subsequently ruled that *Padilla* does not apply retroactively. *Chaidez v. United States*, 568 U.S. 342 (2013). Hence, a person whose conviction became final before *Padilla* was decided could not benefit from that decision.

g.   Don't Skimp on Experts

In *Hinton v. Alabama*, 571 U.S. 263 (2014), the Supreme Court unanimously found the conduct of defense counsel deficient where he failed to request additional funds to replace an inadequate "firearms and toolmark" expert. In *Hinton*, forensic comparisons of bullets recovered from the homicide defendant's revolver was critical evidence tying him to the crime scene. Operating under the mistaken belief that he could pay no more than $1,000, counsel went looking for a well-regarded expert, but found only one person who was willing to take the case for that amount of money. Counsel hired that expert even though he did not have the expertise he thought he needed, concluding that—for that amount of money—he was "stuck" with him. As expected, the expert's testimony was weak and largely discredited, defendant was convicted, and subsequently sentenced to death.

The Court concluded that defense counsel "knew that he needed more funding to present an effective defense, yet he failed to make even the cursory investigation of the state statute providing for defense funding for indigent defendants that would have revealed to him that he could receive reimbursement not just for $1,000 but for 'any expenses reasonably incurred.' An attorney's ignorance of a point of law that is fundamental to his case combined with his failure to perform basic research on that point is a quintessential example of unreasonable performance under *Strickland*."

That finding of inadequate performance did not, in and of itself, establish ineffective assistance. The case was remanded for a determination whether this deficient performance actually prejudiced the defendant. What would the defendant have to prove on remand to show that this deficient performance prejudiced him?

Note that the Supreme Court subsequently held, applying the AEDPA deferential standard (*see Point a, supra*), that state postconviction counsel was not ineffective in concluding that trial counsel was not deficient in failing to hire an expert to develop penalty-phrase mitigation evidence even though there was funding to retain such an expert. *Dunn v. Reeves*, 141 S. Ct. 2405, 2410 (2021) ("we have often explained that strategic decisions—including whether to hire an expert—are entitled to a "strong presumption" of reasonableness"). *And see Ferguson v. City of Charleston*, 141 S. Ct. 2405 (2021) (failure to hire expert held not ineffective; "counsel's choice regarding experts involved a strategic decision entitled to a presumption of reasonableness").

* * *

What exactly constitutes "prejudice" under *Strickland*? Consider the following decisions:

Glover v. United States

531 U.S. 198 (2001).

JUSTICE KENNEDY delivered the opinion of the Court.

Petitioner, Paul Glover, contends that the trial court erred in a Sentencing Guidelines determination. The legal error, petitioner alleges, increased his prison sentence by at least 6 months and perhaps by 21 months. We must decide whether this would be "prejudice" under *Strickland v. Washington*, 466 U.S. 668 (1984). We reverse and remand for further proceedings.

Glover was the Vice President and General Counsel of the Chicago Truck Drivers, Helpers, and Warehouse Workers Union (Independent). Glover used his control over the union's investments to enrich himself and his co-conspirators through kickbacks. The presentence investigation report recommended that the convictions for labor racketeering, money laundering, and tax evasion be grouped together under United States Sentencing Commission, Guidelines Manual § 3D1.2 (Nov.1994), which allows the grouping of "counts involving substantially the same harm." The

District Court ruled that the money laundering counts should not be grouped with Glover's other offenses. Glover's attorneys did not submit papers or offer extensive oral arguments contesting the no-grouping argument and, accordingly, Glover's offense level was increased by two levels, yielding a concomitant increase in the sentencing range. Glover was sentenced to 84 months in prison, which was in the middle of the Guidelines range of 78 to 97 months. On appeal, Glover's counsel (the same attorneys who represented him in District Court) did not raise the grouping issue. A short time after argument on Glover's appeal, a different panel of the Seventh Circuit held that, under some circumstances, grouping of money laundering offenses with other counts was proper under § 3D1.2. *United States v. Wilson*, 98 F.3d 281 (1996). A month later, the Seventh Circuit affirmed his conviction and sentence.

Glover filed a *pro se* motion to correct his sentence. The failure of his counsel to press the grouping issue, he argued, was ineffective assistance. The performance of counsel, he contended, fell below a reasonable standard both at sentencing, when his attorneys did not with any clarity or force contest the Government's argument, and on appeal, when they did not present the issue in their briefs or call the *Wilson* decision to the panel's attention following the oral argument. He further argued that absent the ineffective assistance, his offense level would have been two levels lower, yielding a Guidelines sentencing range of 63 to 78 months. Under this theory, the 84-month sentence he received was an unlawful increase of anywhere between 6 and 21 months.

The District Court denied Glover's motion and the Court of Appeals affirmed. It appears the Seventh Circuit relied on *Lockhart v. Fretwell*, 506 U.S. 364 (1993). *Lockhart* holds that in some circumstances a mere difference in outcome will not suffice to establish prejudice. But this Court explained last Term that our holding in Lockhart does not supplant the *Strickland* analysis. Our jurisprudence suggests that any amount of actual jail time has Sixth Amendment significance. *Argersinger v. Hamlin*, 407 U.S. 25 (1972).

Take Note

As difficult as it may sometimes be to establish the prejudice prong of the *Strickland* test, it is not impossible as the decision in *Glover* illustrates.

The Seventh Circuit's rule is not well considered in any event, because there is no obvious dividing line by which to measure how much longer a sentence must be for the increase to constitute substantial prejudice. Although the amount by which a defendant's sentence is increased by a particular decision may be a factor to consider in determining whether counsel's performance in failing to argue the point constitutes ineffective assistance, under a determinate system of constrained discretion such as the Sentencing Guidelines it cannot serve as a bar to a showing of prejudice. We hold that the Seventh Circuit erred in engrafting this additional requirement onto the prejudice branch of the *Strickland* test. This is not a case where trial strategies, in retrospect, might be criticized for leading to a harsher sentence. Here we consider the sentencing calculation itself, a calculation resulting from a ruling which, if it had been error, would have been correctable on appeal. We express no opinion on the ultimate merits of Glover's claim because the question of deficient performance is not before us, but it is clear that prejudice flowed from the asserted error in sentencing.

The judgment of the Seventh Circuit is reversed.

Buck v. Davis

580 U.S. 100 (2017).

CHIEF JUSTICE ROBERTS delivered the opinion of the Court.

A Texas jury convicted petitioner Duane Buck of capital murder. Under state law, the jury could impose a death sentence only if it found that Buck was likely to commit acts of violence in the future. Buck's attorney called a psychologist to offer his opinion on that issue. The psychologist testified that Buck probably would not engage in violent conduct. But he also stated that one of the factors pertinent in assessing a person's propensity for violence was his race, and that Buck was statistically more likely to act violently because he is black. The jury sentenced Buck to death.

Buck contends that his attorney's introduction of this evidence violated his Sixth Amendment right to the effective assistance of counsel. The Sixth Amendment right to counsel is the right to the effective assistance of counsel. A defendant who claims to have been denied effective assistance must show both that counsel performed deficiently and that counsel's deficient performance caused him prejudice.

Strickland's first prong sets a high bar. A defense lawyer navigating a criminal proceeding faces any number of choices about how best to make a client's case. The lawyer has discharged his constitutional responsibility so long as his decisions fall within the "wide range of professionally competent assistance." It is only when the lawyer's errors were "so serious that counsel was not functioning as the 'counsel' guaranteed by the Sixth Amendment" that *Strickland*'s first prong is satisfied.

The District Court determined that, in this case, counsel's performance fell outside the bounds of competent representation. We agree. Counsel knew that Dr. Quijano's report reflected the view that Buck's race disproportionately predisposed him to violent conduct; he also knew that the principal point of dispute during the trial's penalty phase was whether Buck was likely to act violently in the future. Counsel nevertheless (1) called Dr. Quijano to the stand; (2) specifically elicited testimony about the connection between Buck's race and the likelihood of future violence; and

(3) put into evidence Dr. Quijano's expert report that stated, in reference to factors bearing on future dangerousness, "Race. Black: Increased probability."

Given that the jury had to make a finding of future dangerousness before it could impose a death sentence, Dr. Quijano's report said, in effect, that the color of Buck's skin made him more deserving of execution. It would be patently unconstitutional for a state to argue that a defendant is liable to be a future danger because of his race. No competent defense attorney would introduce such evidence about his own client.

To satisfy *Strickland*, a litigant must also demonstrate prejudice—"a reasonable probability that, but for counsel's unprofessional errors, the result of the proceeding would have been different." Accordingly, the question before the District Court was whether Buck had demonstrated a reasonable probability that, without Dr. Quijano's testimony on race, at least one juror would have harbored a reasonable doubt about whether Buck was likely to be violent in the future. The District Court concluded that Buck had not made such a showing. We disagree.

In arguing that the jury would have imposed a death sentence even if Dr. Quijano had not offered race-based testimony, the State primarily emphasizes the brutality of Buck's crime and his lack of remorse. A jury may conclude that a crime's vicious nature calls for a sentence of death. In this case, however, several considerations convince us that it is reasonably probable—notwithstanding the nature of Buck's crime and his behavior in its aftermath—that the proceeding would have ended differently had counsel rendered competent representation.

Dr. Quijano testified on the key point at issue in Buck's sentencing. True, the jury was asked to decide two issues—whether Buck was likely to be a future danger, and, if so, whether mitigating circumstances nevertheless justified a sentence of life imprisonment. But the focus of the proceeding was on the first question. Much of the penalty phase testimony was directed to future dangerousness, as were the summations for both sides. The jury, consistent with the focus of the parties, asked during deliberations to see the expert reports on dangerousness.

Deciding the key issue of Buck's dangerousness involved an unusual inquiry. The jurors were not asked to determine a historical fact concerning Buck's conduct, but to render a predictive judgment inevitably entailing a degree of speculation. Buck, all agreed, had committed acts of terrible violence. Would he do so again?

Buck's prior violent acts had occurred outside of prison, and within the context of romantic relationships with women. If the jury did not impose a death sentence, Buck would be sentenced to life in prison, and no such romantic relationship would be likely to arise. A jury could conclude that those changes would minimize the prospect of future dangerousness.

But one thing would never change: the color of Buck's skin. Buck would always be black. And according to Dr. Quijano, that immutable characteristic carried with it an "increased probability" of future violence. Here was hard statistical evidence—from an expert—to guide an otherwise speculative inquiry.

And it was potent evidence. Dr. Quijano's testimony appealed to a powerful racial stereotype—that of black men as "violence prone." In combination with the substance of the jury's inquiry, this created something of a perfect storm. Dr. Quijano's opinion coincided precisely with a particularly noxious strain of racial prejudice, which itself coincided precisely with the central question at sentencing. The effect of this unusual confluence of factors was to provide support for making a decision on life or death on the basis of race.

This effect was heightened due to the source of the testimony. Dr. Quijano took the stand as a medical expert bearing the court's imprimatur. The jury learned at the outset of his testimony that he held a doctorate in clinical psychology, had conducted evaluations in some 70 capital murder cases, and had been appointed by the trial judge (at public expense) to evaluate Reasonable jurors might well have valued his opinion concerning the central question before them.

For these reasons, we cannot accept the District Court's conclusion that the introduction of any mention of race during the penalty phase was "de minimis." There were only two references to race in Dr. Quijano's testimony—one during direct examination, the other on cross. But when a jury hears expert testimony that expressly makes a defendant's race directly pertinent on the question of life or death, the impact of that evidence cannot be measured simply by how much air time it received at trial or how many pages it occupies in the record. Some toxins can be deadly in small doses.

The effect of Dr. Quijano's testimony on Buck's sentencing cannot be dismissed as "de minimis." Buck has demonstrated prejudice.

The judgment of the United States Court of Appeals for the Fifth Circuit is reversed, and the case is remanded for further proceedings consistent with this opinion.

> **FYI**
>
> *Consider* Lisa M. Saccomano, *Defining the Proper Role of "Offender Characteristics" in Sentencing Decisions: A Critical Race Theory Perspective*, 56 Am. Crim. L. Rev. 1693 (2019) ("I argue that white cultural values are deeply embedded in the practice of weighing offender characteristic factors at sentencing, such that judges often cite the incidents of privilege in mitigation, e.g., educational attainment and employment status. Similarly, judges often cite the incidents of disadvantage in aggravation.").

Points for Discussion

a. Quick Plea Advice Not Ineffective

In *Premo v. Moore*, 562 U.S. 115 (2011), the Supreme Court concluded that a state postconviction court's conclusion that defense counsel did not perform deficiently in advising his client, Moore, to enter a quick no-contest plea to felony murder, without having brought a motion to suppress one of his confessions, was neither an unreasonable application of clearly established federal law, nor was the conclusion that he was not prejudiced unreasonable:

> The state court here reasonably could have determined that Moore would have accepted the plea agreement even if his confession had been ruled inadmissible. By the time the plea agreement cut short investigation of Moore's crimes, the State's case was already formidable and included two witnesses to an admissible confession. Had the prosecution continued to investigate, its case might well have become stronger. At the same time, Moore faced grave punishments. His decision to plead no contest allowed him to avoid a possible sentence of life without parole or death. The bargain counsel struck was thus a favorable one—the statutory minimum for the charged offense—and the decision to forgo a challenge to the confession may have been essential to securing that agreement.

b. Insufficient Investigation Not Necessarily Prejudicial

In *Wong v. Belmontes*, 558 U.S. 15 (2009), the Court held that Belmontes was not prejudiced by the fact that defense counsel may have been ineffective for failing to investigate and present sufficient mitigating evidence during the penalty phase of his capital trial:

> It is hard to imagine expert testimony and additional facts about Belmontes' difficult childhood outweighing the facts of the victim's murder. It becomes even harder to envision such a result when the evidence that Belmontes had committed another murder—'the most powerful imaginable aggravating evidence,' is added to the mix. The notion that the result could have been different if only counsel had put on more than the nine witnesses he did, or called expert witnesses to bolster his case, is fanciful.

However, the Supreme Court subsequently emphasized that "we have never limited the prejudice inquiry under *Strickland* to penalty phase cases in which there was only 'little or no mitigation evidence' presented." *Sears v. Upton*, 561 U.S. 945 (2010). As the *Sears* Court explained:

To assess the probability of a different outcome under *Strickland*, we consider the totality of the available mitigation evidence—both that adduced at trial, and the evidence adduced in the *habeas* proceeding—and reweigh it against the evidence in aggravation. That standard will necessarily require a court to "speculate" as to the effect of the new evidence—regardless of how much or how little mitigation evidence was presented during the initial penalty phase. This is the proper prejudice standard for evaluating a claim of ineffective representation in the context of a penalty phase mitigation investigation.

Subsequently, in *Andrus v. Texas*, 140 S. Ct. 1875, 1881–82 (2020), another capital case, the Court held:

> It is unquestioned that under prevailing professional norms at the time of trial, counsel had an obligation to conduct a thorough investigation of the defendant's background. Counsel in a death-penalty case has a duty to make reasonable investigations or to make a reasonable decision that makes particular investigations unnecessary. In any ineffectiveness case, a particular decision not to investigate must be directly assessed for reasonableness in all the circumstances, applying a heavy measure of deference to counsel's judgments.

> Here, the habeas record reveals that Andrus' counsel fell short of his obligation in multiple ways: First, counsel performed almost no mitigation investigation, overlooking vast tranches of mitigating evidence. Second, due to counsel's failure to investigate compelling mitigating evidence, what little evidence counsel did present backfired by bolstering the State's aggravation case. Third, counsel failed adequately to investigate the State's aggravating evidence, thereby forgoing critical opportunities to rebut the case in aggravation. Taken together, those deficiencies effected an unconstitutional abnegation of prevailing professional norms.

Why do you think that so many Supreme Court ineffective-assistance-of-counsel decisions arise out of capital sentencing hearings? Is it because counsel in that setting is often so bad or because judges are less concerned about achieving finality in those cases? Or is neither of those reasons persuasive?

c.   **Changing Technology & Ineffectiveness**

In *Wright v. Van Patten*, 552 U.S. 120 (2008), the Supreme Court concluded that defense counsel's participation in a plea hearing (no contest) by speaker phone—rather than in person—was not presumptively prejudicial to his client: "Our precedents do not clearly hold that counsel's participation by speaker phone should be treated as a complete denial of counsel, on par with total absence. Even if we agree with Van

Patten that a lawyer physically present will tend to perform better than one on the phone, it does not necessarily follow that mere telephone contact amounted to total absence or prevented counsel from assisting the accused, so as to entail application of *Cronic*. The question is not whether counsel in those circumstances will perform less well than he otherwise would, but whether the circumstances are likely to result in such poor performance that an inquiry into its effects would not be worth the time." Do you agree? Should the same result apply when defense counsel appears at trial by way of video conferencing? Or, sometime in the future, during another Pandemic perhaps, when defense counsel "appears" virtually, but not corporally?

d.   Convicting the Innocent

A 2014 study estimates that if all death-sentenced defendants remained under sentence of death indefinitely, at least 4.1% of them would ultimately be exonerated. *See* Samuel R. Gross, Barbara O'Brien, Chen Huc, and Edward H. Kennedy, Proceedings of the National Academy of Science of the United States of America, *Rate of false conviction of criminal defendants who are sentenced to death*, http://www.pnas.org/content/111/20/7230.full (2014). As of May 1, 2023, 3,307 individuals have been found to have been wrongly convicted of a crime since 1989, and later cleared of all the charges against them based on new evidence of innocence. *See* National Registry of Exonerations, https://www.law.umich.edu/special/exoneration/Pages/about.aspx. *See also, e.g.*, Illinois abolishes death penalty; cites wrongful convictions, The Washington Times (March 9, 2011) ("Illinois abolished the death penalty Wednesday, more than a decade after the state imposed a moratorium on executions out of concern that innocent people could be put to death by a justice system that had wrongly condemned 13 men."). Does this suggest that the Court's approach to ineffective assistance is too strict, too difficult to establish? But, on the other hand, aren't *some* erroneous convictions inevitable? Or not?

e.   Structural Error & Ineffectiveness

Some trial errors are known as "structural errors," errors that cannot be deemed to be harmless. The purpose of the structural error doctrine is to ensure that certain basic, constitutional guarantees define the framework of any criminal trial. One such basic constitutional guarantee is the right to a public trial.

In *Weaver v. Massachusetts*, 582 U.S. 286 (2017), the issue arose of the relationship between this kind of structural error and an ineffectiveness claim. During Weaver's trial on state criminal charges, the courtroom was completely occupied by potential jurors and closed to the public for two days of the jury selection process. Defense counsel neither objected to the closure at trial nor raised the issue on direct review. As a result, the Court was faced with "the question whether invalidation of the conviction is required, or if the prejudice inquiry is altered when the structural error is raised in the context of an ineffective-assistance-of-counsel claim."

The Court reasoned that

although the public-trial right is structural, it is subject to exceptions. Though these cases should be rare, a judge may deprive a defendant of his right to an open courtroom by making proper factual findings in support of the decision to do so. The fact that the public-trial right is subject to these exceptions suggests that not every public-trial violation results in fundamental unfairness. Thus, when a defendant raises a public-trial violation via an ineffective-assistance-of-counsel claim, *Strickland* prejudice is not shown automatically. Instead, the burden is on the defendant to show either a reasonable probability of a different outcome in his or her case or to show that the particular public-trial violation was so serious as to render his or her trial fundamentally unfair.

Hence, the Supreme Court ruled, "in the context of a public-trial violation during jury selection, where the error is neither preserved nor raised on direct review but is raised later via an ineffective-assistance-of-counsel claim, the defendant must demonstrate prejudice to secure a new trial." In *Weaver*, the Court held that Weaver failed to do this, i.e. he did not establish a reasonable probability that the jury would not have convicted him if his attorney had objected to the closure of the courtroom.

Do you think this is a sensible test? Why should a defendant whose trial was subject to a structural error, the failure to receive a basic constitutional guarantee, have to prove that he or she was prejudiced thereby? More importantly, just how would a defendant go about proving such prejudice? As Justice Breyer, joined by Justice Kagan, argued in dissent:

In my view, we should not require defendants to take on a task that is normally impossible to perform. Nor would I give lower courts the unenviably complex job of deciphering which structural errors really undermine fundamental fairness and which do not—that game is not worth the candle. I would simply say that just as structural errors are categorically insusceptible to harmless-error analysis on direct review, so too are they categorically insusceptible to actual-prejudice analysis in Strickland claims. A showing that an attorney's constitutionally deficient performance produced a structural error should consequently be enough to entitle a defendant to relief.

What do you think?

f. Failure to File Appeal

In *Garza v. Idaho*, <u>139 S.Ct. 738 (2019)</u>, the Supreme Court held that "prejudice is presumed when counsel's constitutionally deficient performance deprives a defendant of an appeal that he otherwise would have taken." Indeed, the *Garza* Court found ineffective assistance to have existed in the absence of a prejudice inquiry simply because "Garza's attorney rendered deficient performance by not filing the notice of appeal in light of Garza's clear requests." Or as the Court restated the underlying point, "the rule is the one compelled by our precedent: When counsel's deficient performance forfeits an appeal that a defendant otherwise would have taken, the defendant gets a new opportunity to appeal." The *Garza* Court added, "we hold today that this presumption applies even when the defendant has signed an appeal waiver."

Hypo 1: *Failure to Challenge Government's Use of Flawed Scientific Evidence*

Defense counsel failed to challenge the government's use of Comparative Bullet Lead Analysis (CBLA) at defendant's first-degree murder trial in 1995. Although no longer generally accepted after 2003, CBLA evidence was commonly used at that time. Was defense counsel ineffective for failing to challenge the prosecution's use of that questionable evidence? Does it make sense to judge the reasonableness of defense counsel's conduct many years later, in hindsight? *See Maryland v. Kulbicki*, <u>577 U.S. 1 (2015)</u>.

Hypo 2: *Failure to Suppress*

Defendant is on trial for possession of narcotics. The prosecution has overwhelming evidence of guilt in the form of cocaine found in defendant's home. However, the evidence was obtained as a result of an illegal search. As in *Premo*, set out above, defense counsel fails to file a suppression motion and defendant is convicted. Was counsel ineffective under either *Strickland* or *Cronic*? *See, e.g., State v. Silvers*, <u>587 N.W.2d 325 (Neb. 1998)</u>.

Hypo 3: *Demeaning Client*

Should ineffectiveness have been presumed where defense counsel referred to his client during trial as a "big, menacing Black guy?" *See Mallard v. Warden, New Hampshire State Prison*, 175 N.H. 565, 294 A.3d 229 (2023).

Hypo 4: *Failure to Reveal Plea Offer*

The prosecution offered defendant's counsel a ten year plea deal on charges of felony murder, robbery and conspiracy. However, counsel failed to convey the offer to defendant in a timely manner. After defendant took the stand and testified in her own behalf, the prosecutor withdrew the offer. Was counsel ineffective for failing to convey the plea offer in a timely manner? *See Helmedach v. Commissioner*, 329 Conn. 726, 189 A.3d 1173 (2018).

Hypo 5: *Failure to Appear*

Do you think that criminal defense counsel should be deemed to be automatically ineffective when he failed to show up for most of the direct and cross-examination of an important prosecution witness—a victim—without any excuse for his absence? What if counsel failed to show up for any of the cross-examination? Would it make any difference in your analysis if counsel was prepared to finish the cross-examination, but asked for a recess to review what he had missed before proceeding? *See McKnight v. State*, 320 S.C. 356, 465 S.E.2d 352 (1995).

Hypo 6: *Prior Convictions*

Defendant is convicted of armed robbery. He had been convicted of this crime twice before. During *voir dire*, defense counsel asked the members of the venire whether they could judge defendant fairly and with an open mind if they learned he had been convicted of armed robbery twice previously. At no other point in the trial was the subject of defendant's prior convictions mentioned. Was counsel ineffective because he mentioned them during *voir dire*?

Hypo 7: *Failure to Advise*

Defense counsel failed to inform his client, who was considering pleading guilty to a drug offense, that the client's prior conviction for a narcotics paraphernalia offence would qualify as a sentencing enhancement mandating imprisonment for not less than five years. On advice of counsel, defendant pled guilty to manufacturing methamphetamine, second offense, and was sentenced to seven years' imprisonment. After *Padilla*, discussed above, was this ineffective assistance of counsel? *See Berry v. State*, 381 S.C. 630, 675 S.E.2d 425 (2009).

Hypo 8: *Failure to Call Eyewitness*

Do you think that trial counsel was ineffective where he failed to call an eyewitness to the shooting at issue even though he knew that her statements would contradict the eyewitness upon whom the prosecution's entire case relied, he knew that she had not identified the defendant on the night of the shooting, and he also knew that the witness had not identified the defendant later when she examined a photo array? Can you think of any tactical reason at all why counsel might have failed to put a witness like this on the stand? *See State v. Jenkins*, 355 Wis.2d 180, 848 N.W.2d 786 (2014).

Hypo 9: *You Get What You Pay for*

Massachusetts suffered from a shortage of lawyers willing to accept indigent appointments. The trial court concluded that the unavailability of lawyers was directly related to inadequate levels of compensation. Suppose that you are a trial court judge and you have a number of indigent defendants who are entitled to counsel but who remain unrepresented. What remedies are available to you? Should you: 1) order attorneys to accept indigent cases at prevailing compensation rates; 2) order the state to pay attorneys more for indigent representation; or 3) order that defendants be released and their cases be dismissed without prejudice? *See Lavallee v. Justices in the Hampden Superior Court*, 442 Mass. 228, 812 N.E.2d 895 (2004).

Hypo 10: *Investigating Ineffective Assistance*

You were recently admitted to the Bar of your state and are engaged in an active criminal law practice. As *pro bono* work, you take an occasional "innocence case," one in which you have serious doubts about whether someone was fairly convicted of a crime. One day, J.T. Booker comes to see you about his brother, John, who is on death row having been convicted of a brutal rape and murder. J.T. tells you that John could not have committed the rape or the murder because he was in another city at the time of the crime. J.T. is so sincere, and so convinced of his brother's innocence, that you decide to take the case. Suppose that you may want to pursue an ineffective assistance of claim with respect to trial counsel's performance. What steps would you take in order to decide whether ineffective assistance actually existed, and whether you should assert this claim? What types of evidence would be useful to you? How would you go about obtaining such evidence? How would you begin?

Hypo 11: *Failure to Advise Defendant to Be Contrite*

Defendant pled guilty to Assault Second Degree and Endangering the Welfare of a Child. Counsel, who met with his client only briefly and for the very first time on the day of sentencing, had not discussed with him the desirability of his expressing his contrition for the crimes he committed. The sentencing judge sentenced defendant to 18 years in prison, emphasizing as a basis for the heavy sentence defendant's lack of contrition in his allocution. Was defense counsel ineffective for not advising his client to express his contrition or, if he wasn't actually contrite, not to engage in allocution? *See Harden v. State*, <u>180 A.3d 1037 (Del. 2018)</u>.

Exercise: *IAC Claim*

Defendant Larry Hall was convicted at trial along with a codefendant, G., of the rape and murder of a young woman. The crime was one of a series of similar, seemingly-random abductions, rapes, and grisly murders of young women which took place during 1981 and 1982. Hall's defense at trial—which was apparently not credited by the jury—was strictly one of factual innocence. Hall was sentenced to death. His conviction and death sentence were affirmed on direct appeal.

Hall has now sought postconviction relief in state court, arguing that he is entitled to a new trial because of the ineffective assistance of his trial counsel, Kyle LaBomba (which he did not raise in his direct appeal since LaBomba was also his appellate counsel and failed to question his own ineffectiveness). The postconviction court denied Hall the opportunity for an evidentiary hearing on his claim of LaBomba's ineffectiveness, concluding that he did not make a sufficient showing of arguable ineffectiveness to justify such a hearing. Hall has appealed this decision to a state appellate court, arguing that he is entitled to a hearing. Attached to his appeal papers are affidavits from a number of psychiatrists which claim that he was psychotic and "psychologically adrift" at the time of the rape and murder for which he was sentenced to death and, further, that he was under the influence of the co-defendant, Linda Sanders, who initiated all of the crimes and "possessed a Charles Manson-like persona, subjugating Hall to her will."

Hall argues that LaBomba was ineffective in that he failed to raise any psychiatric defenses at trial. More important, Hall argues in his appeal papers that LaBomba failed even to obtain any psychiatric evaluation of Hall to assess whether or not such a defense might be tenable. It is Hall's argument that he is at least entitled to an evidentiary hearing at which he should be given an opportunity to show that LaBomba was constitutionally ineffective in failing to investigate and raise psychiatric defenses to these charges.

Half of you will be assigned to the defense, half to the prosecution. Prepare a brief (1 to 2 pages) outline of the arguments which support your side of the issue on appeal whether Hall should be entitled to such an evidentiary hearing on LaBomba's ineffectiveness.

D. Conflicts of Interest

In *Strickland*, the Court stated that when an attorney represents clients with conflicting interests, a limited presumption of incompetence can arise. *Cuyler* squarely presents that issue.

Cuyler v. Sullivan

446 U.S. 335 (1980).

MR. JUSTICE POWELL delivered the opinion of the Court.

The question presented is whether a state prisoner may obtain a federal writ of *habeas corpus* by showing that his retained defense counsel represented potentially conflicting interests.

Hear It

You can hear the oral argument in *Cuyler* at http://www.oyez.org/cases/ 1970-1979/1979/1979_78_1832.

Respondent John Sullivan was indicted with Gregory Carchidi and Anthony DiPasquale for the first-degree murders of John Gorey and Rita Janda. The victims, a labor official and his companion, were shot to death in Gorey's second-story office at the Philadelphia headquarters of Teamsters' Local 107. Francis McGrath, a janitor, saw the three defendants in the building just before the shooting. They appeared to be awaiting someone, and they encouraged McGrath to do his work on another day. McGrath ignored their suggestions. Shortly afterward, Gorey arrived and went to his office. McGrath then heard what sounded like firecrackers exploding in rapid succession. Carchidi, who was in the room where McGrath was working, abruptly directed McGrath to leave the building and to say nothing. McGrath hastily complied. When he returned to the building about 15 minutes later, the defendants were gone. The victims' bodies were discovered the next morning.

Two privately retained lawyers, G. Fred DiBona and A. Charles Peruto, represented all three defendants throughout the state proceedings that followed the indictment. Sullivan accepted representation from the two lawyers retained by his codefendants because he could not afford to pay his own lawyer. At no time did Sullivan or his lawyers object to the multiple representation. Sullivan was the first defendant to come to trial. The evidence against him was entirely circumstantial, consisting primarily of McGrath's testimony. At the close of the Commonwealth's case, the defense rested without presenting any evidence. The jury found Sullivan guilty and fixed his penalty at life imprisonment. The Pennsylvania Supreme Court affirmed his conviction by an equally divided vote. Sullivan's codefendants, Carchidi and DiPasquale, were acquitted at separate trials. In subsequent postconviction proceedings, a federal district court denied Sullivan's request for *habeas corpus* relief, but the Third Circuit Court of Appeals reversed, finding a conflict of interest sufficient to raise Sixth Amendment concerns.

We come to Sullivan's claim that he was denied the effective assistance of counsel guaranteed by the Sixth Amendment because his lawyers had a conflict of interest. In *Holloway v. Arkansas*, 435 U.S. 475 (1978), a single public defender represented three defendants at the same trial. The trial court refused to consider the appointment of separate counsel despite the defense lawyer's timely and repeated assertions that the interests of his clients conflicted. This Court recognized that a lawyer forced to represent codefendants whose interests conflict cannot provide the adequate legal assistance required by the Sixth Amendment. Given the trial court's

> **FYI**
>
> The *Holloway* Court established that where counsel has brought the issue of potential conflict to a trial court's attention and the trial court failed properly to respond to the motion, e.g. by failing to either grant it or to ascertain the potentiality of a conflict at an appropriate hearing, in contrast to ordinary ineffectiveness inquiries, reversal of a defendant's conviction is "automatic," even in the absence of a demonstration of prejudice. As the Supreme Court subsequently reiterated this rule: "*Holloway* creates an automatic reversal rule where defense counsel is forced to represent codefendants over his timely objection, unless the trial court has determined that there is no conflict." *Mickens v. Taylor*, 535 U.S. 162, 168 (2002).

failure to respond to timely objections, however, the Court did not consider whether the alleged conflict actually existed. It simply held that the trial court's error unconstitutionally endangered the right to counsel.

Holloway requires state trial courts to investigate timely objections to multiple representation. But nothing in our precedents suggests that the Sixth Amendment requires state courts themselves to initiate inquiries into the propriety of multiple representation in every case. Defense counsel have an ethical obligation to avoid conflicting representations and to advise the court promptly when a conflict of interest arises during the course of trial. Absent special circumstances, therefore, trial courts may assume either that multiple representation entails no conflict or that the lawyer and his clients knowingly accept such risk of conflict as may exist. Unless the trial court knows or reasonably should know that a particular conflict exists, the court need not initiate an inquiry.

Holloway reaffirmed that multiple representation does not violate the Sixth Amendment unless it gives rise to a conflict of interest. Since a possible conflict inheres in almost every instance of multiple representation, a defendant who objects to multiple representation must have the opportunity to show that potential conflicts impermissibly imperil his right to a fair trial. But unless the trial court fails to afford such an opportunity, a reviewing court cannot presume that the possibility for conflict has resulted in ineffective assistance of counsel. Such a presumption would preclude multiple representation even in cases where "a common defense gives strength against a common attack."

In order to establish a violation of the Sixth Amendment, a defendant who raised no objection at trial must demonstrate that an actual conflict of interest adversely affected his lawyer's performance. In *Glasser v. United States*, 315 U.S. 60 (1942), for example, the record showed that defense counsel failed to cross-examine a prosecution witness whose testimony linked Glasser with the crime and failed to resist the presentation of arguably inadmissible evidence. The Court found that both omissions resulted from counsel's desire to diminish the jury's perception of a codefendant's guilt. Indeed, the evidence of counsel's "struggle to serve two masters could not seriously

FYI

American Bar Association Standards for Criminal Justice Defense Function Standard 4–1.7(d) (4th ed. 2015) provides as follows:

Except where necessary to secure counsel for preliminary matters such as initial hearings or applications for bail, a defense counsel (or multiple counsel associated in practice) should not undertake to represent more than one client in the same criminal case. When there is not yet a criminal case, such multiple representation should be engaged in only when, after careful investigation and consideration, it is clear either that no conflict is likely to develop at any stage of the matter, or that multiple representation will be advantageous to each of the clients represented and that foreseeable conflicts can be waived.

evidence, was overwhelming and uncontradicted; the prosecutor had no need for petitioner's eyewitness testimony to persuade the jury to convict Stevens and to sentence him to death. Mr. Burger tried to negotiate a plea with the district attorney for a life sentence. He flatly refused to even discuss it in any terms.

The argument that his partner's representation of Stevens inhibited Leaphart from arguing petitioner's lesser culpability because such reliance would be prejudicial to Stevens is also unsupported. Because the trials were separate, Leaphart would have had no particular reason for concern about the possible impact of the tactics in petitioner's trial on the outcome of Stevens' trial.

c. *Mickens v. Taylor*

In *Mickens v. Taylor*, <u>535 U.S. 162 (2002)</u>, involving defense counsel who had been representing his client's victim at the time of the victim's death, Justice Scalia ruled for the 5-to-4 majority that reversal need not be automatic every time a trial court fails to inquire into a potential conflict:

> The rule applied when the trial judge is not aware of the conflict (and thus not obligated to inquire) is that prejudice will be presumed only if the conflict has significantly affected counsel's performance—thereby rendering the verdict unreliable, even though *Strickland* prejudice cannot be shown. The trial court's awareness of a potential conflict neither renders it more likely that counsel's performance was significantly affected nor in any other way renders the verdict unreliable. Since this was not a case in which (as in *Holloway*) counsel protested his inability simultaneously to represent multiple defendants; and since the trial court's failure to make the *Sullivan*-mandated inquiry does not reduce the petitioner's burden of proof; it was at least necessary, to void the conviction, for petitioner to establish that the conflict of interest adversely affected his counsel's performance.

Suppose that, in *Mickens*, the attorney had informed the trial judge of his prior representation of Hall, stated that he was conflicted, asked to be replaced, and the trial judge dismissed the request without further inquiry. Would automatic reversal be required in that case?

d. **Waiver of Conflicts**

In *Wheat v. United States*, <u>486 U.S. 153 (1988)</u>, defendant Wheat was charged with participating in a drug distribution conspiracy. Also charged were Gomez-Barajas and Bravo, who were represented by attorney Iredale. Gomez-Barajas was tried and acquitted on drug charges overlapping with those against Wheat. To avoid a trial on other charges, Gomez-Barajas offered to plead guilty to tax evasion and illegal importation of merchandise. At the commencement of Wheat's trial, the plea had not been accepted and could have been withdrawn. Bravo decided to plead guilty to one count of transporting marijuana. After the plea was accepted, Iredale notified the court that he had been asked to defend Wheat. When the Government objected because of a possible conflict of interest, the trial court refused to allow the representation. Wheat's conviction was upheld on appeal:

> A defendant may not insist on retaining an attorney who has a previous or ongoing relationship with an opposing party, even when the opposing party is the Government. Where a court justifiably finds an actual conflict of interest, it may decline a proffer of waiver, and insist that defendants be separately represented. The court must be allowed substantial latitude in refusing waivers of conflicts of interest not only in those rare cases where an actual conflict may be demonstrated before trial, but in the more common cases where a potential for conflict exists which may or may not burgeon into an actual conflict as the trial progresses.

e.   **Sex with Clients**

In *Commonwealth v. Stote*, 456 Mass. 213, 922 N.E.2d 768 (2010), the Supreme Judicial Court of Massachusetts concluded that no unconstitutional conflict of interest existed where defense counsel at trial was discovered to have had an intimate relationship with an assistant district attorney (ADA) in the appellate division of the prosecutor's office, and a previous intimate relationship with the actual trial prosecutor. The court found that no *actual* conflict of interest existed with respect to the ongoing relationship as both defense counsel and the ADA swore that no confidential information about defendant was disclosed, and there was nothing in the record to suggest otherwise. The ADA added, moreover, that she had no involvement in the Commonwealth's appeal and knew nothing about the case, and this averment was corroborated by the trial prosecutor. Moreover, the court found that no conflict of interest existed with respect to defense counsel's prior relationship, which had ended seventeen years before trial, noting that "the trial judge pointed out that defense counsel 'had no hesitation whatsoever in lambasting the trial prosecutor for her alleged transgressions at trial' and concluded that 'he vigorously represented the defendant both at trial and on appeal.' "

Do these conclusions make sense to you? Does the fact that defense counsel "lambasted" the prosecutor at trial, for example, really indicate the absence of a conflict? What if defense counsel and the trial prosecutor were married or simply living together? Would that or should that make a difference? Should the defendant at least have been informed of that fact? What do you think?

Hypo 1: *Counsel Facing Disciplinary Complaints*

Defendants filed state bar disciplinary complaints against their respective defense counsel the week before trial. They claimed that their counsel had refused their requests to file motions to dismiss based upon speedy trial objections. Counsel moved to withdraw the day before trial based upon the conflict presented by the disciplinary complaints, but the trial court denied their requests finding no merit to their speedy trial claims. Defendants were convicted of mail fraud, conspiracy to commit mail fraud, aggravated identity theft, conspiracy to commit identity theft, and illegal monetary transactions. They now claim they were denied the effective assistance of counsel based on the conflict of interest posed by the pending disciplinary complaints against their lawyers. Were they? *United States v. Gandy*, 926 F.3d 248 (6th Cir. 2019).

Hypo 2: *Defense Counsel Also Police Officer*

While representing defendant, defense counsel was concurrently employed as a police officer outside the city in which the defendant's alleged crimes were committed, a fact not disclosed to his client. Is this *per se* ineffective assistance due to a conflict? What do you think? *See Diaz v. Commissioner of Correction*, 344 Conn. 365, 279 A.3d 147 (2022).

Hypo 3: *Retained Counsel & Ineffectiveness*

Should a non-indigent defendant be able to complain that his or her retained counsel was "ineffective?" As a general rule, non-indigent defendants have the right to choose the counsel they prefer (subject, of course, to their ability to pay the attorney's fees and the attorney's willingness to take the case). If the non-indigent chooses poorly and counsel commits prejudicial error, should that conviction be reversed for ineffectiveness?

Hypo 4: *Lump Sum Fees & Conflicts*

Has defense counsel rendered ineffective assistance of counsel as a result of a conflict of interest when he was paid a lump sum amount for his representation of a client rather than on an hourly basis? Defendant argued that this compensation agreement created an inherent and irreconcilable conflict of interest because both counsel's compensation and the costs for investigative and expert services were covered by a lump sum fee. Defendant asserted that this circumstance created a financial disincentive for counsel to adequately investigate and prepare his case. What do you think? *See People v. Doolin*, 45 Cal.4th 390, 87 Cal. Rptr.3d 209, 198 P.3d 11 (2009).

E. The *Griffin-Douglas* Doctrine

In *Griffin v. Illinois*, 351 U.S. 12 (1956), the Supreme Court concluded that an indigent prisoner appealing from conviction in state court had a Fourteenth Amendment right (under both the due process and equal protection clauses) to a free transcript of the trial proceedings where such transcripts were often a practical necessity for securing an appeal. In a plurality opinion, writing for four justices, Justice Black concluded that "there can be no equal justice where the kind of trial a man [*sic*] gets depends on the amount of money he has. Destitute defendants must be afforded as adequate appellate review as defendants who have money enough to buy transcripts."

Thereafter, the Court held in *Douglas v. California*, 372 U.S. 353 (1963), a companion case to *Gideon*, that indigent convicted defendants have a Fourteenth Amendment right (under both the due process and equal protection clauses) to the assistance of counsel on a first appeal where the state has granted them the right to appeal (as opposed to those instances where entitlement to appeal is only discretionary). Justice Douglas opined that "where the merits of the one and only appeal an indigent has as of right are decided without benefit of counsel, we think an unconstitutional line has been drawn between rich and poor."

Food for Thought

As then-Justice Rehnquist acknowledged in *Ross v. Moffitt*, indigent defendants are "somewhat handicapped" as compared to more affluent defendants by that decision, requiring only an "adequate"—but not an *equal*—opportunity to present one's claims. Does the Constitution require that the government address and relieve such handicaps?

Subsequently, the Court declined to extend this so-called "*Griffin-Douglas* Doctrine" so as to require a Fourteenth Amendment entitlement to counsel by indigents in discretionary state appeals and applications for review to the Supreme Court, holding that "the duty of the State under our cases is not to duplicate the legal arsenal that may be privately retained by a criminal defendant in a continuing effort to reverse his conviction, but only to assure the indigent defendant an adequate opportunity to present his claims fairly in the context of the State's appellate process." *Ross v. Moffitt*, 417 U.S. 600, 616 (1974).

The Supreme Court's 2005 decision in *Halbert v. Michigan* made it clear, however, that *Ross* did not supplant the Court's *Griffin-Douglas* commitment to equal justice for rich and poor:

Halbert v. Michigan

545 U.S. 605 (2005).

JUSTICE GINSBURG delivered the opinion of the Court.

In 1994, Michigan voters approved a proposal amending the State Constitution to provide that "an appeal by an accused who pleads guilty or nolo contendere shall be by leave of the court." Thereafter, several Michigan state judges began to deny appointed appellate counsel to indigents convicted by plea. Rejecting challenges based on the Equal Protection and Due Process Clauses of the Fourteenth Amendment to the Federal Constitution, the Michigan Supreme Court upheld this practice.

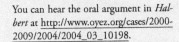

Hear It

You can hear the oral argument in *Halbert* at http://www.oyez.org/cases/2000-2009/2004/2004_03_10198.

Petitioner Antonio Dwayne Halbert, convicted on his plea of nolo contendere, sought the appointment of counsel to assist him in applying for leave to appeal to the Michigan Court of Appeals. The state trial court and the Court of Appeals denied Halbert's requests for appointed counsel, and the Michigan Supreme Court declined review.

Michigan Court of Appeals review of an application for leave to appeal, Halbert contends, ranks as a first-tier appellate proceeding requiring appointment of counsel under *Douglas v. California*, 372 U.S. 353 (1963). Michigan urges that appeal to the State Court of Appeals is discretionary and, for an appeal of that order, *Ross v. Moffitt*, 417 U.S. 600 (1974), holds counsel need not be appointed. Today, we conclude that Halbert's case is properly ranked with *Douglas* rather than *Ross*. Accordingly, we hold that the Due Process and Equal Protection Clauses require the appointment of counsel for defendants, convicted on their pleas, who seek access to first-tier review in the Michigan Court of Appeals.

The Federal Constitution imposes on the States no obligation to provide appellate review of criminal convictions. Having provided such an avenue, however, a State may not "bolt the door to equal justice" to indigent defendants. *Griffin* held that, when a State conditions an appeal from a conviction on the provision of a trial transcript, the State must furnish free transcripts to indigent defendants who seek to appeal. *Douglas* relied on *Griffin*'s reasoning to hold that, in first appeals as of right, States must appoint counsel to represent indigent defendants. *Ross* held, however, that a State need not appoint counsel to aid a poor person in discretionary appeals to the State's highest court, or in petitioning for review in this Court.

Cases on appeal barriers encountered by persons unable to pay their own way, we have observed, "cannot be resolved by resort to easy slogans or pigeonhole analysis." Our decisions in point reflect both equal protection and due process concerns. The equal protection concern relates to the legitimacy of fencing out would-be appellants based solely on their inability to pay core costs, while the due process concern homes in on the essential fairness of the state-ordered proceedings.

Two considerations were key to our decision in *Douglas* that a State is required to appoint counsel for an indigent defendant's first-tier appeal as of right. First, such an appeal entails an adjudication on the "merits." Second, first-tier review differs from subsequent appellate stages at which the claims have once been presented by appellate counsel and passed upon by an appellate court.

In *Ross*, we explained why the rationale of *Douglas* did not extend to the appointment of counsel for an indigent seeking to pursue a second-tier discretionary appeal to the North Carolina Supreme Court or, thereafter, certiorari review in this Court. The North Carolina Supreme Court, in common with this Court we perceived, does not sit as an error-correction instance. Principal criteria for state high court review, we noted, included "whether the subject matter of the appeal has significant public interest, whether the cause involves legal principles of major significance to the jurisprudence of the State, and whether the decision below is in probable conflict" with the court's precedent. Further, we pointed out, a defendant who had already benefitted from counsel's aid in a first-tier appeal as of right would have, "at the very least, a transcript or other record of trial proceedings, a brief on his behalf in the Court of Appeals setting forth his claims of error, and in many cases an opinion by the Court of Appeals disposing of his case."

Halbert's case is framed by these two prior decisions of this Court concerning state-funded appellate counsel, *Douglas* and *Ross*. The question before us is essentially one of classification: With which of those decisions should the instant case be aligned? We hold that *Douglas* provides the controlling instruction. Two aspects of the Michigan Court of Appeals' process following plea-based convictions lead us to that conclusion. First, in determining how to dispose of an application for leave to appeal, Michigan's intermediate appellate court looks to the merits of the claims made in the application. Second, indigent defendants pursuing first-tier review in the Court of Appeals are generally ill equipped to represent themselves.

A defendant who pleads guilty or nolo contendere in a Michigan court does not thereby forfeit all opportunity for appellate review. Although he relinquishes access to an appeal as of right, he is entitled to apply for leave to appeal, and that entitlement is officially conveyed to him. Of critical importance, the tribunal to which he addresses his application, the Michigan Court of Appeals, unlike the Michigan Supreme Court, sits as an error-correction instance.

Whether formally categorized as the decision of an appeal or the disposal of a leave application, the Court of Appeals' ruling on a plea-convicted defendant's claims provides the first, and likely the only, direct review the defendant's conviction and sentence will receive. Parties like Halbert, however, are disarmed in their endeavor to gain first-tier review. As the Court in *Ross* emphasized, a defendant seeking State Supreme Court review following a first-tier appeal as of right earlier had the assistance of appellate counsel. The attorney appointed to serve at the intermediate appellate court level will have reviewed the trial court record, researched the legal issues, and prepared a brief reflecting that review and research. The defendant seeking second-tier review may also be armed with an opinion of the intermediate appellate court addressing the issues counsel raised. A first-tier review applicant, forced to act *pro se*, will face a record unreviewed by appellate counsel, and will be equipped with no attorney's brief prepared for, or reasoned opinion by, a court of review.

Persons in Halbert's situation are particularly handicapped as self-representatives. Approximately 70% of indigent defendants represented by appointed counsel plead guilty, and 70% of those convicted are incarcerated. Sixty-eight percent of the state prison population did not complete high school, and many lack the most basic literacy skills. Seven out of ten inmates fall in the lowest two out of five levels of literacy—marked by an inability to do such basic tasks as write a brief letter to explain an error on a credit card bill, use a bus schedule, or state in writing an argument made in a lengthy newspaper article. Many, Halbert among them, have learning disabilities and mental impairments.

Navigating the appellate process without a lawyer's assistance is a perilous endeavor for a layperson, and well beyond the competence of individuals, like Halbert, who have little education, learning disabilities, and mental impairments. Appeals by defendants convicted on their pleas may involve myriad and often complicated substantive issues, and may be no less complex than other appeals. One who pleads guilty or nolo contendere may still raise on appeal constitutional defects that are irrelevant to his factual guilt, double jeopardy claims requiring no further factual record, jurisdictional defects, challenges to the sufficiency of the evidence at the preliminary examination, preserved entrapment claims, mental competency claims, factual basis claims, claims that the state had no right to proceed in the first place, including claims that a defendant was charged under an inapplicable statute, and claims of ineffective assistance of counsel.

While the State has a legitimate interest in reducing the workload of its judiciary, providing indigents with appellate counsel will yield applications easier to comprehend. Michigan's Court of Appeals would still have recourse to summary denials of leave applications in cases not warranting further review. And when a defendant's case presents no genuinely arguable issue, appointed counsel may so inform the court.

For the reasons stated, we vacate the judgment of the Michigan Court of Appeals and remand the case for further proceedings not inconsistent with this opinion.

JUSTICE THOMAS, with whom JUSTICE SCALIA joins, and with whom the CHIEF JUSTICE joins in part, dissenting.

The majority holds that Michigan's system is constitutionally inadequate. It finds that all plea-convicted indigent defendants have the right to appellate counsel when seeking leave to appeal. *Douglas*, however, does not support extending the right to counsel to any form of discretionary review, as *Ross v. Moffitt*, and later cases make clear. Moreover, Michigan has not engaged in the sort of invidious discrimination against indigent defendants that *Douglas* condemns. Michigan has done no more than recognize the undeniable difference between defendants who plead guilty and those who maintain their innocence, in an attempt to divert resources from largely frivolous appeals to more meritorious ones. The majority substitutes its own policy preference for that of Michigan voters, and it does so based on an untenable reading of *Douglas*.

Today the Court confers on defendants convicted by plea a right nowhere to be found in the Constitution or this Court's cases. It does so at the expense of defendants whose claims are, on average, likely more meritorious. I respectfully dissent.

* * *

One of the most significant applications of the *Griffin-Douglas* Doctrine in the criminal justice system involves the question of what assistance—other than defense counsel—the government must provide to indigent defendants.

Ake v. Oklahoma

470 U.S. 68 (1985).

JUSTICE MARSHALL delivered the opinion of the Court.

The issue in this case is whether the Constitution requires that an indigent defendant have access to the psychiatric examination and assistance necessary to prepare an effective defense based on his mental condition, when his sanity at the time of the offense is seriously in question.

Late in 1979, Glen Burton Ake was arrested and charged with murdering a couple and wounding their two children. His behavior at arraignment, and in other prearraignment incidents at the jail, was so bizarre that the trial judge, *sua sponte*, ordered him to be examined by a psychiatrist "for the purpose of advising with the Court as to his impressions of whether the Defendant may need an extended period of mental observation." The examining psychiatrist reported: "At times Ake appears to be frankly delusional. He claims to be the 'sword of vengeance' of the Lord and that he will sit at the left hand of God in heaven." He diagnosed Ake as a probable paranoid schizophrenic and recommended a prolonged psychiatric evaluation to determine whether Ake was competent to stand trial.

In March, Ake was committed to a state hospital to be examined with respect to his "present sanity," i.e., his competency to stand trial. On April 10, less than six months after the incidents for which Ake was indicted, the chief forensic psychiatrist at the state hospital informed the court that Ake was not competent to stand trial. The court then held a competency hearing, at which a psychiatrist testified:

> "Ake is a psychotic. His psychiatric diagnosis was that of paranoid schizophrenia—chronic, with exacerbation, that is with current upset, and that in addition he is dangerous. Because of the severity of his mental illness and because of the intensities of his rage, his poor control, his delusions, he requires a maximum security facility within—I believe—the State Psychiatric Hospital system."

The court found Ake to be a "mentally ill person in need of care and treatment" and incompetent to stand trial, and ordered him committed to the state mental hospital.

Six weeks later, the chief forensic psychiatrist informed the court that Ake had become competent to stand trial. At the time, Ake was receiving 200 milligrams of Thorazine, an antipsychotic drug, three times daily, and the psychiatrist indicated that, if Ake continued to receive that dosage, his condition would remain stable. The State then resumed proceedings against Ake.

At a pretrial conference in June, Ake's attorney informed the court that his client would raise an insanity defense. To enable him to prepare and present such a defense adequately, the attorney stated, a psychiatrist would have to examine Ake with respect to his mental condition at the time of the offense. During Ake's 3-month stay at the state hospital, no inquiry had been made into his sanity at the time of the offense, and, as an indigent, Ake could not afford to pay for a psychiatrist. Counsel asked the court either to arrange to have a psychiatrist perform the examination, or to provide funds to allow the defense to arrange one. The trial judge rejected counsel's argument that the Federal Constitution requires that an indigent defendant receive the assistance of a psychiatrist when that assistance is necessary to the defense, and he denied the motion for a psychiatric evaluation at state expense.

Ake was tried for two counts of murder in the first degree, a crime punishable by death in Oklahoma, and for two counts of shooting with intent to kill. At the guilt phase of trial, his sole defense was insanity. Although defense counsel called to the stand and questioned each of the psychiatrists who had examined Ake at the state hospital, none testified about his mental state at the time of the offense because none had examined him on that point. The prosecution, in turn, asked each of these psychiatrists whether he had performed or seen the results of any examination diagnosing Ake's mental state at the time of the offense, and each doctor replied that he had not. As a result, there was no expert testimony for either side on Ake's sanity at the time of the offense. The jurors were then instructed that Ake could be found not guilty by reason of insanity if he did not have the ability to distinguish right from wrong at the time of the alleged offense. They were further told that Ake was to be presumed sane at the time of the crime unless he presented evidence sufficient to raise a reasonable doubt about his sanity at that time. If he raised such a doubt in their minds, the jurors were informed, the burden of proof shifted to the State to prove sanity beyond a reasonable doubt. The jury rejected Ake's insanity defense and returned a verdict of guilty on all counts.

At the sentencing proceeding, the State asked for the death penalty. No new evidence was presented. The prosecutor relied significantly on the testimony of the state psychiatrists who had examined Ake, and who had testified at the guilt phase that Ake was dangerous to society, to establish the likelihood of his future dangerous behavior. Ake had no expert witness to rebut this testimony or to introduce on his behalf evidence in mitigation of his punishment. The jury sentenced Ake to death on each of the two murder counts, and to 500 years' imprisonment on each of the two counts of shooting with intent to kill.

The Oklahoma Court of Criminal Appeals upheld Ake's conviction on appeal. We hold that when a defendant has made a preliminary showing that his sanity at the time of the offense is likely to be a significant factor at trial, the Constitution requires that a State provide access to a psychiatrist's assistance on this issue if the defendant cannot otherwise afford one.

This Court has long recognized that when a State brings its judicial power to bear on an indigent defendant in a criminal proceeding, it must take steps to assure that the defendant has a fair opportunity to present his defense. This elementary principle, grounded in significant part on the Fourteenth Amendment's due process guarantee of fundamental fairness, derives from the belief that justice cannot be equal where, simply as a result of his poverty, a defendant is denied the opportunity to participate meaningfully in a judicial proceeding in which his liberty is at stake. In recognition of this right, this Court held almost 30 years ago that once a State offers to criminal defendants the opportunity to appeal their cases, it must provide a trial transcript to an indigent defendant if the transcript is necessary to a decision on the merits of the appeal. *Griffin v. Illinois*, 351 U.S. 12 (1956). Since then, this Court has held that an indigent defendant may not be required to pay a fee before filing a notice of appeal of his conviction, that an indigent defendant is entitled to the assistance of counsel at trial, and on his first direct appeal as of right, and that such assistance must be effective.

Meaningful access to justice has been the consistent theme of these cases. We recognized long ago that mere access to the courthouse doors does not by itself assure a proper functioning of the adversary process, and that a criminal trial is fundamentally unfair if the State proceeds against an indigent defendant without making certain that he has access to the raw materials integral to the building of an effective defense. Thus, while the Court has not held that a State must purchase for the indigent defendant all the assistance that his wealthier counterpart might buy, it has often reaffirmed that fundamental fairness entitles indigent defendants to "an adequate opportunity to present their claims fairly within the adversary system." To implement this principle, we have focused on identifying the basic tools of an adequate defense or appeal, and we have required that such tools be provided to those defendants who cannot afford to pay for them.

To say that these basic tools must be provided is, of course, merely to begin our inquiry. In this case we must decide whether, and under what conditions, the participation of a psychiatrist is important enough to preparation of a defense to require the State to provide an indigent defendant with access to competent psychiatric assistance in preparing the defense. Three factors are relevant to this determination. The first is the private interest that will be affected by the action of the State. The second is the governmental interest that will be affected if the safeguard is to be provided. The third is the probable value of the additional or substitute procedural safeguards that are sought, and the risk of an erroneous deprivation of the affected interest if those safeguards are not provided.

The private interest in the accuracy of a criminal proceeding that places an individual's life or liberty at risk is almost uniquely compelling. Indeed, the host of safeguards fashioned by this Court over the years to diminish the risk of erroneous conviction stands as a testament to that concern. The interest of the individual in the outcome of the State's effort to overcome the presumption of innocence is obvious and weighs heavily in our analysis.

We consider, next, the interest of the State. Oklahoma asserts that to provide Ake with psychiatric assistance on the record before us would result in a staggering burden to the State. We are unpersuaded by this assertion. Many States, as well as the Federal

Government, currently make psychiatric assistance available to indigent defendants, and they have not found the financial burden so great as to preclude this assistance. This is especially so when the obligation of the State is limited to provision of one competent psychiatrist, as it is in many States, and as we limit the right we recognize today. At the same time, it is difficult to identify any interest of the State, other than that in its economy, that weighs against recognition of this right. The State's interest in prevailing at trial—unlike that of a private litigant—is necessarily tempered by its interest in the fair and accurate adjudication of criminal cases. Thus, also unlike a private litigant, a State may not legitimately assert an interest in maintenance of a strategic advantage over the defense, if the result of that advantage is to cast a pall on the accuracy of the verdict obtained. We therefore conclude that the governmental interest in denying Ake the assistance of a psychiatrist is not substantial, in light of the compelling interest of both the State and the individual in accurate dispositions.

Last, we inquire into the probable value of the psychiatric assistance sought, and the risk of error in the proceeding if such assistance is not offered. We begin by considering the pivotal role that psychiatry has come to play in criminal proceedings. More than 40 States, as well as the Federal Government, have decided either through legislation or judicial decision that indigent defendants are entitled, under certain circumstances, to the assistance of a psychiatrist's expertise. These statutes and court decisions reflect a reality that we recognize today, namely, that when the State has made the defendant's mental condition relevant to his criminal culpability and to the punishment he might suffer, the assistance of a psychiatrist may well be crucial to the defendant's ability to marshal his defense. In this role, psychiatrists gather facts, through professional examination, interviews, and elsewhere, that they will share with the judge or jury; they analyze the information gathered and from it draw plausible conclusions about the defendant's mental condition, and about the effects of any disorder on behavior; and they offer opinions about how the defendant's mental condition might have affected his behavior at the time in question.

Psychiatry is not an exact science, and psychiatrists disagree widely and frequently on what constitutes mental illness, on the appropriate diagnosis to be attached to given behavior and symptoms, on cure and treatment, and on likelihood of future dangerousness.

Food for Thought

In this day and age when it may appear that no two psychological experts ever hold the same viewpoint, what accounts for the lower courts' reluctance to provide such services? The obvious answer is the slippery slope. If you provide a psychiatrist, then won't you need to provide investigators, and medical examiners, and accident reconstruction professionals, and ballistics experts, and DNA specialists, and jury consultants, etc., etc. When have you left the realm of "basic tools' and simply provided a "defense consultant" (as Justice Rehnquist worries in his omitted dissent). At a time when it stretches governmental units' budgets simply to provide indigents with appointed counsel, where would the money come from for such "extravagances"?

Perhaps because there often is no single, accurate psychiatric conclusion on legal insanity in a given case, juries remain the primary fact-finders on this issue, and they must resolve differences in opinion within the psychiatric profession on the basis of the evidence offered by each party. When jurors make this determination about issues that inevitably are complex and foreign, the testimony of psychiatrists can be crucial and a virtual necessity if an insanity plea is to have any chance of success. In so saying, we neither approve nor disapprove the widespread reliance on psychiatrists but instead recognize the unfairness of a contrary holding in light of the evolving practice.

The foregoing leads inexorably to the conclusion that, without the assistance of a psychiatrist to conduct a professional examination on issues relevant to the defense, to help determine whether the insanity defense is viable, to present testimony, and to assist in preparing the cross-examination of a State's psychiatric witnesses, the risk of an inaccurate resolution of sanity issues is extremely high. With such assistance, the defendant is fairly able to present at least enough information to the jury, in a meaningful manner, as to permit it to make a sensible determination.

We therefore hold that when a defendant demonstrates to the trial judge that his sanity at the time of the offense is to be a significant factor at trial, the State must, at a minimum, assure the defendant access to a competent psychiatrist who will conduct an appropriate examination and assist in evaluation, preparation, and presentation of the defense. This is not to say, of course, that the indigent defendant has a constitutional right to choose a psychiatrist of his personal liking or to receive funds to hire his own. Our concern is that the indigent defendant have access to a competent psychiatrist for the purpose we have discussed, and as in the case of the provision of counsel we leave to the States the decision on how to implement this right.

Ake also was denied the means of presenting evidence to rebut the State's evidence of his future dangerousness. The foregoing discussion compels a similar conclusion in the context of a capital sentencing proceeding, when the State presents psychiatric evidence of the defendant's future dangerousness. We have repeatedly recognized the defendant's compelling interest in fair adjudication at the sentencing phase of a capital case. The State, too, has a profound interest in assuring that its ultimate sanction is not erroneously imposed, and we do not see why monetary considerations should be more persuasive in this context than at trial.

We turn now to apply these standards to the facts of this case. On the record before us, it is clear that Ake's mental state at the time of the offense was a substantial factor in his defense, and that the trial court was on notice of that fact when the request for a court-appointed psychiatrist was made. In addition, Ake's future dangerousness was a significant factor at the sentencing phase. The state psychiatrist who treated Ake at the state mental hospital testified at the guilt phase that, because of his mental illness, Ake posed a threat of continuing criminal violence. This testimony raised the issue of Ake's future dangerousness, which is an aggravating factor under Oklahoma's capital sentencing scheme, and on which the prosecutor relied at sentencing. We therefore conclude that Ake also was entitled to the assistance of a psychiatrist on this issue and that the denial of that assistance deprived him of due process.

Accordingly, we reverse and remand for a new trial.

Point for Discussion

Volunteer Psychologist Insufficient

In *McWilliams v. Dunn*, 582 U.S. 183 (2017), a 5-to-4 majority of the Supreme Court held that Alabama failed to meet its obligations under *Ake v. Oklahoma* to provide a capital murder defendant, McWilliams, with access to a mental health expert to assist in the evaluation, preparation, and presentation of his defense at sentencing. Alabama argued that the State was exempted from its obligations under *Ake* because McWilliams already had the assistance of a psychologist from the University of Alabama who had volunteered to help defense counsel "in her spare time." Justice Breyer ruled for the majority that "even if the episodic assistance of an outside volunteer could relieve the State of its constitutional duty to ensure an indigent defendant access to meaningful expert assistance, no lower court has held or suggested that that psychologist was available to help, or might have helped, McWilliams at the judicial sentencing proceeding, the proceeding here at issue. Alabama does not refer to any specific record facts that indicate that she was available to the defense at this time."

"No one denies that the conditions that trigger application of *Ake* are present," the majority added, as "McWilliams is and was an 'indigent defendant,' his 'mental condition' was 'relevant to the punishment he might suffer, and that 'mental condition,' i.e., his 'sanity at the time of the offense,' was 'seriously in question.' " Consequently, the Constitution, as interpreted in *Ake*, required the State to provide McWilliams with "access to a competent psychiatrist who will conduct an appropriate examination and assist in evaluation, preparation, and presentation of the defense."

Hypo 1: *Additional Assistance*

Defendant James Kelly was convicted of the robbery, rape and murder of a college student who was working as a pizza delivery person and who had delivered a pizza to Kelly's girlfriend's apartment. He was sentenced to death. On appeal, Kelly contended that the trial judge erred by denying his pretrial request for provision of a private investigator and other experts. The trial judge had concluded that *Ake* does not give a defendant a constitutional right to any expert other than a psychiatrist. Kelly argued that, although he had consensual sex with the victim, he did not kill her, and that a private investigator would have enabled him to find key (unnamed) witnesses who would have helped to confirm his story. Moreover, he argued that he should have been provided with: 1) a forensic expert to assess the truthfulness of the prosecution's forensic experts (who "matched" his DNA with DNA found in the victim's vagina and on the victim's underwear and jeans); and 2) a medical expert to "go over" the medical examiner's report. Do you think that the trial court's ruling was correct? *See Rogers v. Oklahoma*, 890 P.2d 959 (Okla. Cr. App. 1995).

Hypo 2: *Transcript of Co-Defendant's Trial*

Should a defendant have the right under the *Griffin-Douglas* Doctrine to be provided with a free copy of his *co-defendant's* trial transcript when the two of them have had separate trials but the facts all arose out of the same incident? *See State v. Scott*, 131 Hawai'i 333, 319 P.3d 252 (2013).

Hypo 3: *Right to Delayed Appeal of Conviction?*

Defendant, convicted of aggravated murder, filed a notice of appeal eighteen years after the time to take a direct appeal had expired. He argues that the denial of a delayed appeal denied him due process of law and equal protection of the laws under *Griffin-Douglas* as an appeal is a "necessary tool." Do you think that this is a tenable argument under this line of cases? Why or why not? *See Sexton v. Wainright*, 2021 WL 779115 (S.D. Ohio 2021).

Executive Summary

Right to Counsel. People have a right to the assistance of counsel for their defense at all critical stages of the proceedings when they are charged with a criminal offense, and if they are indigent and cannot afford counsel, one will be appointed for them.

Indigent Appointments. Indigent criminal defendants are only entitled to appointment of counsel when they will receive a punishment of at least one day in jail, whether or not that sentence is suspended.

Waiver of Right to Counsel. A waiver of the right to counsel must be knowing and intelligent.

Right to Proceed *Pro Se*. Competent criminal defendants have the right to waive the assistance of counsel and to represent themselves at trial (deemed "proceeding *pro se*").

Standby Counsel. Standby counsel may be appointed to assist a *pro se* criminal defendant in his or her defense, but counsel must endeavor to preserve the *pro se* defendant's actual control over the case, and is not allowed to destroy the jury's perception that the defendant is representing himself or herself.

Ineffective Assistance of Counsel. To obtain a reversal of a conviction on grounds of ineffective assistance under the seminal *Strickland* decision, a convicted defendant must show *both* that defense counsel's performance was deficient in that it fell below an objective standard of reasonableness *and* that counsel's deficient performance was prejudicial in that there was a reasonable probability that, absent counsel's errors, the fact-finder would have had a reasonable doubt respecting his or her guilt.

Conflicts of Interest. In order to establish ineffectiveness based upon defense counsel's conflict of interest, a defendant who raised no objection at trial must demonstrate that an actual conflict of interest adversely affected his or her lawyer's performance.

Other Assistance Beyond Counsel. An indigent criminal defendant has a right under the Fourteenth Amendment to assistance other than representation by a lawyer when that assistance constitutes a basic tool of an adequate defense or appeal, such as access to a psychological expert where defendant's sanity will be a significant issue at trial.

Major Themes

a. Indigent Representation Unequal—Although indigent criminal defendants are entitled to appointed counsel, they do not have the right to counsel of their choice, nor representation at every point in the proceedings, nor the full array of resources available to someone who can afford to retain his or her own attorney.

b. Ineffectiveness Difficult to Establish—Although criminal defendants are entitled to receive the effective assistance of counsel, ineffectiveness under the *Strickland* two-part test is extremely difficult to establish, and very few convictions are reversed on this basis.

For More Information

- Zohra Ahmed, *The Right to Counsel in a Neoliberal Age*, 69 U.C.L.A. L. Rev. 442 (2022).

- American Bar Association, GIDEON's Broken Promise: America's Continuing Quest for Equal Justice (2004).

- Mary Sue Backus & Paul Marcus, The Right to Counsel in Criminal Cases: A National Crisis (2006).

- John M. Burkoff & Nancy M. Burkoff, Ineffective Assistance of Counsel (Thomson Reuters/West, annual editions).

- David Cole, No Equal Justice (1999).

- David Harris, *The Constitution and Truth Seeking: A New Theory on Expert Services for Indigent Defendants*, 83 J. Crim. L. & C. 469 (1992).

- Bruce R. Jacob, *Memories of and Reflections About Gideon v. Wainwright*, 33 Stetson L. Rev. 181 (2003).

- Janet Moore, *The Antidemocratic Sixth Amendment*, 91 Wash. L. Rev. 1705 (2016).

- Shaun Ossei-Owusu, *The Sixth Amendment Facade: The Racial Evolution of the Right to Counsel*, 167 U. Pa. L. Rev. 1161 (2019).

- Anne Bowen Poulin, *The Role of Standby Counsel in Criminal Cases: In the Twilight Zone of the Criminal Justice System*, 75 N.Y.U. L. Rev. 676 (2000).

- John Rappaport, *The Structural Function of the Sixth Amendment Right to Counsel of Choice*, 2016 Sup. Ct. Rev. 117 (2016).

- Kathryn A. Sabbeth & Jessica K. Steinberg, *The Gender of Gideon*, 69 U.C.L.A. L. Rev. 1130 (2023).

- Abbe Smith, *Defending* Gideon, 26 U.C. Davis Soc. Just. L. Rev. 235 (2022).

- Abbe Smith, *The Difference in Criminal Defense and the Difference It Makes*, 11 Wash.U. J.L.& Pol'y 83 (2003).

- Ken Strutin, *From Poverty to Personhood:* Gideon *Unchained*, 45 Mitchell Hamline L. Rev. 266 (2019).

- James Tomkovicz, The Right to the Assistance of Counsel (Greenwood Press 2002).

- Russell L. Weaver, John M. Burkoff, Catherine Hancock & Steven I. Friedland, Principles of Criminal Procedure Ch. 3 (8th ed. 2024).

Test Your Knowledge

To assess your understanding of the material in this chapter, <u>click here</u> to take a quiz.

CHAPTER 16

Guilty Pleas

A. Introduction

After an indictment or criminal information has been filed, the defendant is typically arraigned on the charging document and is asked to enter a plea in open court. At that time, the defendant may plead guilty, not guilty, or, in many jurisdictions—if permitted by the court in the interests of justice—enter a plea of *nolo contendere*, indicating that he or she is simply not contesting the charges. *See, e.g.,* Fed.R.Crim.P. 11(b). Generally a "nolo plea" (as they are commonly called) is identical to a guilty plea except that a nolo plea cannot be used as an admission of guilt against the defendant in a subsequent civil proceeding. In most jurisdictions, instead of pleading guilty or not guilty (or entering a nolo plea), the defendant can invoke a psychological condition by pleading "not guilty by reason of insanity" or, in some jurisdictions, "guilty but mentally ill."

FYI

According to the Bureau of Justice Statistics of the U.S. Department of Justice (BJS), of the estimated 1,132,290 felons convicted in state courts in 2006, the vast majority (94%) of those sentenced for a felony pleaded guilty. The remaining 6% were found guilty either by a jury (4%) or by a judge in a bench trial (2%). BJS, Felony Sentences in State Court, 2006, https://www.bjs.gov/content/pub/pdf/fssc06st.pdf (last visited 12/14/14). Moreover, "the predominance of guilty pleas is not new in the criminal justice system. A study in Connecticut covering 75 years (1880 to 1954) concludes that between 1880 and 1910 10% of all convictions were obtained by trial." U.S. Department of Justice, Report to the Nation on Crime and Justice 83 (2d ed. 1988).

In many states, a defendant may enter a conditional guilty plea, reserving the right to appeal specified pretrial motions without having to proceed to a complete trial in order to preserve the issues for appeal. *See, e.g.,* Fed.R.Crim.P. 11(a)(2). Conditional pleas generally require that the court and the prosecutor approve the conditional guilty plea, and any defendant who prevails on appeal may later withdraw the conditional plea.

B. Policy Concerns

Most cases in which criminal charges are filed are resolved by a guilty plea and never go to trial. In deciding to plead guilty, defendant gives up his right to a trial, and (of course) the possibility of an acquittal. In response, the prosecution usually agrees to a lower sentence for defendant, and sometimes agrees to convict defendant of only less serious charges. On balance, those who agree to plead guilty serve shorter sentences than those who do not. *See* Robert E. Scott & William J. Stuntz, *Plea Bargaining as Contract*, 101 YALE L.J. 1909 (1992).

Who's That?

Robert Scott is a Professor of Law at Columbia Law School. You can read about him at https://www.law.columbia.edu/faculty/robert-scott. William Stuntz was a Professor of Law at Harvard Law School until he passed away in 2011. You can read about him at http://www.nytimes.com/2011/03/21/us/21stuntz.html.

Of course, the plea bargaining process produces unique results. While many perceive the criminal justice process as involving elaborate trials—in which there is a clash of lawyers through argument, the production of witnesses, and the production of physical evidence—plea bargains essentially involve little more than agreements between the prosecution and the defense. The vast majority of cases are resolved through this bargaining/contract process which have enormous real world consequences that place individuals in prison, sometimes for long prison terms. They are entered into because the prosecution seeks to avoid the risk and expense of a trial, with the possibility of an acquittal, and the defendant receives a guarantee of a lower sentence. Moreover, since plea bargains are so much more efficient than trials, prosecutors can handle far more cases through plea bargaining than they could handle if all cases had to be tried.

The plea bargaining process has been subject to numerous criticisms. Unlike defendants who go to trial, and whose cases are subject to elaborate investigation and fact-finding processes, defendants who enter into plea bargains are subjected to only limited investigation and fact-finding. Fearing more severe punishments, poor defendants often agree to plead guilty and forego the right to a trial. As a result, they may never find out about exculpatory evidence that may exist in the prosecutor's file. Because of the limited nature of the process, judges often do not have sufficient information to decide whether to accept or reject a plea deal. Although most "legal scholars oppose plea bargaining," most "participants generally approve of it." *Id*.

The absence of complete information complicates the plea bargaining process. Since most criminal defendants assert their innocence, prosecutors may have difficulty distinguishing between guilty defendants and innocent defendants. Moreover, truly innocent defendants may find it difficult to signal their innocence to prosecutors. As a result, prosecutors may not be able to accurately calculate the possibility that a given defendant will be convicted at trial. By contrast, defendants have reasons to be risk adverse and plead guilty despite their innocence. Thus, there is no assurance that the plea bargaining process will produce satisfactory or desirable results. These factors can distort the process:

Food for Thought

What do you think? Is plea bargaining good for the criminal justice system, a necessary evil, or a feature that needs to be eliminated, whether due to the unequal bargaining power between the parties or the risk of innocent persons pleading guilty?

> By failing to enforce prosecutors' sentencing promises, the law encourages courts to raise sentences in precisely those cases where the defendant is most likely to be innocent. By under protecting against defense attorney error, the law increases the chances of risk averse innocent defendants accepting deals that treat them as certain convictions. And by permitting prosecutorial manipulation of broad mandatory sentencing statutes, the doctrine reduces prosecutors' incentives to separate innocent from guilty defendants at the charging stage. All these effects are unnecessary. By following appropriate contract models, one can devise different rules that reduce the harm to innocent defendants and meanwhile reduce transaction costs and inefficiency for everyone else.

Id.

Points for Discussion

a. Bargain as Contract

Courts have generally applied the law of contracts to plea agreements. *See, e.g., United States v. Vaval*, 404 F. 3d 144 (2d Cir.2005). As such, one or both parties may breach the agreement, although determining the existence of a breach tends to be very fact-specific. Some courts have held that due process requires that any ambiguity in the terms of an agreement should be construed against the prosecution, consistent with the defendant's reasonable understanding of the agreement. *See, e.g., United States v. Guzman*, 318 F. 3d 1191 (10th Cir. 2003); *United States v. Bownes*, 405 F. 3d 634 (7th Cir. 2005) (although plea agreements are generally analyzed under contract law, analogy to contract law is not complete because guilty plea involves waiver of fundamental constitutional rights).

Several of the Court's decisions have analyzed plea bargains as contracts. In *Ricketts v. Adamson*, 483 U.S. 1 (1987), Ricketts was charged with first-degree murder. Ricketts and the prosecutor reached an agreement whereby Ricketts agreed that, in

1084 — CRIMINAL PROCEDURE: ADJUDICATIVE *A Contemporary Approach* —

return for a guilty plea to the lesser charge of second-degree murder, he would testify against two other individuals allegedly involved in the murder. He agreed to do so "in any Court, State or Federal, when requested by proper authorities against any and all parties involved in the murder." Further, "should defendant refuse to testify or should he at any time testify untruthfully then this entire agreement is null and void and the original charge will be automatically reinstated." The state trial court accepted the plea agreement and found Ricketts guilty of second-degree murder. Ricketts then testified as obligated under the agreement, and both other individuals were convicted of first-degree murder. Ricketts was sentenced, but then the convictions of the two other individuals were reversed by an appellate court and a new trial was ordered. The State again sought Ricketts' testimony but he refused, claiming he had fulfilled his side of the bargain and his obligation was met. The State disagreed and called him to testify but he refused, claiming a Fifth Amendment privilege. The State then reinstituted the first-degree murder charge against Ricketts and he claimed that a retrial violated double jeopardy. A majority of the Court rejected this claim and held that the defendant had violated the agreement, which thereby removed the double jeopardy bar to prosecution of Ricketts on the first-degree murder charge.

Whereas *Ricketts* is a case where the defendant breached the contract, *Santobello v. New York*, 404 U.S. 257 (1971), is one where the prosecution failed to uphold its end of the bargain. The State charged Santobello with two felony counts. After negotiations, the prosecution agreed to permit petitioner to plead guilty to a lesser-included offense that would carry a maximum prison sentence of one year. The prosecutor agreed to make no recommendation as to the actual sentence within the one-year maximum. At sentencing, another prosecutor had replaced the prosecutor who negotiated the plea. The new prosecutor recommended the maximum one-year sentence, denied knowledge of any agreement, and the court sentenced Santobello to one year. The Court held that "the interests of justice and appropriate recognition of the duties of the prosecution in relation to promises made in the negotiation of pleas of guilty will be best served" by recognizing the breach of agreement and remanding the case for an appropriate solution. In so holding the Court underscored the legitimate value of plea bargains:

> This record represents another example of an unfortunate lapse in orderly prosecutorial procedures, in part, no doubt, because of the enormous increase in the workload of the often understaffed prosecutor's offices. The heavy workload may well explain these episodes, but it does not excuse them. The disposition of criminal charges by agreement between the prosecutor and the accused, sometimes loosely called "plea bargaining," is an essential component of the administration of justice. Properly administered, it is to be encouraged. If every criminal charge were subjected to a full-scale trial, the States and the Federal Government would need to multiply by many times the number of judges and court facilities. Disposition of

charges after plea discussions is not only an essential part of the process but a highly desirable part for many reasons. It leads to prompt and largely final disposition of most criminal cases; it avoids much of the corrosive impact of enforced idleness during pre-trial confinement for those who are denied release pending trial; it protects the public from those accused persons who are prone to continue criminal conduct even while on pretrial release; and, by shortening the time between charge and disposition, it enhances whatever may be the rehabilitative prospects of the guilty when they are ultimately imprisoned.

> In *Commonwealth v. Francis*, 79 N.E.3d 1045 (Mass. 2017), Francis was convicted in 1967 of first degree murder. When the conviction was reversed, he entered into an agreement to plead guilty to second degree murder in exchange for the opportunity to immediately seek parole. When the plea agreement fell apart, because the judge refused to consider parole for someone not yet in prison, Francis withdrew his guilty plea and was retried for first degree murder. When he was convicted a second time, and sentenced to life in prison without the possibility for parole, he argued that he should be allowed to take advantage of the original plea deal. The Massachusetts courts disagreed.

b. Remedies for Breach?

If a defendant is able to prove that the prosecution has breached a plea agreement, what is the appropriate remedy? Withdrawal of the plea? Specific performance of the agreement? Alteration of the sentence? In *Santobello*, the issue of the appropriate remedy was left to the discretion of the trial court. Should the defendant who seeks specific performance be required to prove prejudice? *See, e.g., United States v. Manzo*, 675 F. 3d 1204 (9th Cir. 2012) (court orders specific performance of plea agreement where government promised a certain base offense level under the Sentencing Guidelines and reneged by going along with the presentence report which grouped the offenses together and came up with a higher base level).

Take Note

Ordinarily, statements made in plea bargaining negotiations are treated as confidential, and admissions cannot be used against the accused. However, in *United States v. Bauzo-Santiago*, 876 F.3d 13 (1st Cir. 2017), in which defendant made an unsolicited admission of guilt to the judge, as part of a request for new counsel, the court held that the admission could be used against the defendant.

Food for Thought

Defendant Carlton Legall executed a plea agreement with the government in which both sides agreed not to appeal if Legall's sentence for the offense of conspiracy to import a controlled substance fell within a range of 120 to 135 months imprisonment. The district court sentenced Legall to 135 months and he appealed, claiming that the federal sentencing guidelines permit an appeal when the sentence is in violation of a statutory provision as this one was since the trial judge imposed this sentence without a proper specification of reasons. The government agrees that an appeal would normally be appropriate in these circumstances except that Legall waived his right to appeal from a sentence in this range in his plea agreement. Who is right? Why? Should it matter that the 135-month sentence may be illegal under the applicable sentencing guidelines? *United States v. Yemitan*, 70 F. 3d 746 (2d Cir.1995).

Hypo: *Reneging on the Plea Deal*

Defendant agreed to plead guilty in exchange for the government's promise to authorize a sentence below the statutory minimum. However, by the time of sentencing, it was clear that defendant was continuing to engage in criminal conduct. As a result, although the government recommended a reduced sentence, it refused to recommend one below the statutory minimum. The judge, who concluded that the plea agreement required "full cooperation," including disclosure of defendant's ongoing criminal activity, refused to give a sentence below the statutory minimum. What remedy should be available to defendant? *See United States v. E.F.*, 920 F.3d 682 (10th Cir. 2019).

c.   Sentencing Recommendations

In a federal plea agreement between a defendant and the government under Fed.R.Crim.P. 11(c)(1)(B), the prosecutor may be responsible for making a nonbinding sentencing recommendation to the court. In *United States v. Benchimol*, 471 U.S. 453 (1985), the Court held that the prosecutor does not have to "enthusiastically" defend its sentencing recommendation. Is a promise by the government to recommend a sentence at the low end of the sentencing guideline range breached when the government recommendation is in the presentence report but it does not affirmatively advocate that sentence to the trial court? Yes, said the appellate court in *United States v. Barnes*, 278 F. 3d 644 (6th Cir. 2002). On the other hand, when the government keeps its promise about not making a sentencing recommendation, courts usually do not preclude additional comments as long as a specific sentence is not recommended. *See, e.g., Colvin v. Taylor*, 324 F. 3d 583 (8th Cir.2003) (no breach when prosecutor rebutted factual assertions that supported defendant's request); *United States v. Gerace*,

997 F.2d 1293 (9th Cir.1993) (no breach when prosecutor was silent at sentencing but opposed leniency at later probation revocation hearing).

d.   Binding on Non-Party Authorities?

Assuming that a plea agreement exists between a defendant and the prosecution, who is bound by that agreement? In *Santobello*, the successor of the prosecutor who made a promise to the defendant was bound by that promise. Generally, a plea agreement in a state prosecution is not binding on prosecutors in other jurisdictions or on officials in other parts of the same jurisdiction if they are not parties to the agreement. *See, e.g., Montoya v. Johnson*, 226 F. 3d 399 (5th Cir. 2000) (binding on federal officials).

e.   Fleeing Defendant

After entry of a negotiated guilty plea but prior to sentencing, a defendant flees by failing to appear for sentencing. He is later caught and brought back to court. Under the circumstances, may the government renege on its obligations under the agreement if there is no express provision regarding flight? If the government does renege, can defendant back out of the agreement and insist on a trial? *See United States v. Hallahan*, 744 F.3d 497 (7th Cir. 2014).

* * *

Some argue that the plea bargaining process is unfair to minority groups, especially when they are confronted by police who sometimes arrest and charge minorities based on "suspicious" activity rather than based on probable cause. *See* Chester Mirsky, *Plea Reform is No Bargain*, *Newsday* p.70 (City edition, March 4, 1994). The vast majority of these cases are resolved through plea bargains. When these defendants do plead guilty, judges are inclined to accept the pleas for a variety of reasons. Sadly, some courts may not rigorously examine the evidence to make sure that defendants are actually guilty. Rather, they may assume guilt based on a defendant's race or socio-economic status.

Food for Thought

In one jurisdiction, local rules require that a plea bargain involve conviction for the most serious charge in an indictment, thereby eliminating the possibility of defendants receiving a lesser sentence based on a reduced charge. Is such an approach desirable? Might such an approach help ensure that drug dealers and violent individuals receive more severe sentences? Might such a rule discourage defendants from engaging in plea bargaining because they will receive less benefit? If so, what is the potential impact on the criminal justice system? Might cases languish longer? Might defendants remain in jail longer? Might the prosecution's evidence disappear or go stale as time passes? Can such a policy be manipulated to continue "business as usual?"

C. The Legal Requirements of a Valid Guilty Plea

In order for a guilty plea to be constitutionally valid, three requirements must be satisfied. The plea must have been made "knowingly" and "voluntarily," and there must be a "factual basis" for the plea. *See Boykin v. Alabama*, 395 U.S. 238 (1969). To ensure that a valid guilty plea satisfies these basic constitutional requirements, most states follow procedures similar to those set out in Federal Rule of Criminal Procedure 11. These procedures are usually satisfied by a "colloquy" (a conversation) in open court between the trial judge, the defendant and the prosecution.

Boykin v. Alabama

395 U.S. 238 (1969).

MR. JUSTICE DOUGLAS delivered the opinion of the Court.

In the spring of 1966, within the period of a fortnight, a series of armed robberies occurred in Mobile, Alabama. The victims, in each case, were local shopkeepers open at night who were forced by a gunman to hand over money. While robbing one grocery store, the assailant fired his gun once, sending a bullet through a door into the ceiling. A few days earlier in a drugstore, the robber had allowed his gun to discharge in such a way that the bullet, on ricochet from the floor, struck a customer in the leg. Shortly thereafter, a local grand jury returned five indictments against petitioner, a 27-year-old Negro, for common law robbery—an offense punishable in Alabama by death. Before the matter came to trial, the court determined that petitioner was indigent and appointed counsel to represent him. Three days later, at his arraignment, petitioner pleaded guilty to all five indictments. The judge asked no questions of petitioner concerning his plea, and petitioner did not address the court. Trial strategy may of course make a plea of guilty seem the desirable course. But the record is wholly silent on that point and throws no light on it.

Hear It

You can hear the oral argument in *Boykin* at: http://www.oyez.org/cases/1960-1969/1968/1968_642.

Alabama provides that when a defendant pleads guilty, "the court must cause the punishment to be determined by a jury" (except where it is required to be fixed by the court) and may "cause witnesses to be examined, to ascertain the character of the offense." In the present case a trial of that dimension was held, the prosecution presenting its case largely through eyewitness testimony. Although counsel for petitioner engaged in cursory cross-examination, petitioner neither testified himself nor presented testimony concerning his character and background. There was nothing to indicate that he had a prior criminal record. In instructing the jury, the judge stressed that petitioner had pleaded guilty in five cases of robbery, defined as "the felonious taking of money from another against his will by violence or by putting him in fear carrying from ten years minimum in the penitentiary to the supreme penalty of death by electrocution." The jury, upon deliberation, found petitioner guilty and sentenced him to die on each of the five indictments. The Alabama Supreme Court affirmed.

It was error, plain on the record, for the trial judge to accept petitioner's guilty plea without an affirmative showing that it was intelligent and voluntary. A plea of guilty is more than a confession which admits that the accused did various acts; it is itself a conviction; nothing remains but to give judgment and determine punishment. Admissibility of a confession must be based on a "reliable determination on the voluntariness issue which satisfies the constitutional rights of the defendant." The requirement that the prosecution spread on the record the prerequisites of a valid waiver is no constitutional innovation. In *Carnley v. Cochran*, 369 U.S. 506, we dealt with a problem of waiver of the right to counsel, a Sixth Amendment right. We held: "Presuming waiver from a silent record is impermissible. The record must show, or there must be an allegation and evidence which show, that an accused was offered counsel but intelligently and understandingly rejected the offer. Anything less is not waiver."

We think that the same standard must be applied to determining whether a guilty plea is voluntarily made. A plea of guilty is more than an admission of conduct; it is a conviction. Ignorance, incomprehension, coercion, terror, inducements, subtle or blatant threats might be a perfect cover-up of unconstitutionality. The question of an effective waiver of a federal constitutional right in a proceeding is of course governed by federal standards. Several federal constitutional rights are involved in a waiver that takes place when a plea of guilty is entered in a state criminal trial. First, is the privilege against compulsory self-incrimination guaranteed by the Fifth Amendment and applicable to the States by reason of the Fourteenth. Second, is the right to trial by jury. Third, is the right to confront one's accusers. We cannot presume a waiver of these three important federal rights from a silent record.

What is at stake for an accused facing death or imprisonment demands the utmost solicitude of which courts are capable in canvassing the matter with the accused to make sure he has a full understanding of what the plea connotes and of its consequence. When the judge discharges that function, he leaves a record adequate for any review that may be later sought and forestalls the spin-off of collateral proceedings that seek to probe murky memories.

Reversed.

FYI

In *United States v. King-Gore*, 875 F.3d 1141 (D.C. Cir. 2017), defendant met with the prosecution for an "off the record" meeting and was promised that any statements that he made would not be used against him. During that meeting, defendant made incriminating statements, suggesting that he was a drug wholesaler. After defendant pled guilty, the prosecutor used those statements against him. On appeal, defendant's sentence was overturned and the case was remanded for a new sentencing hearing.

Points for Discussion

a. Rule 11 & *Boykin*

The Court regards the Fed.R.Crim.P. 11(b)(1)(C)–(E) list of rights as merely a codification of *Boykin*'s requirements regarding the waiver of constitutional rights. *Libretti v. United States*, <u>516 U.S. 29 (1995)</u>. The reading of these rights and their knowing and voluntary waiver is often called the *Boykin* inquiry. The trial judge will confirm that the defendant is knowingly and voluntarily waiving various rights, including the right to a judge or jury trial where the prosecution would be required to prove every element of every offense beyond a reasonable doubt, the right to have counsel cross-examine the prosecution's witnesses, the right to call witnesses in his defense, and the right to appeal errors in the trial if there is a conviction.

Food for Thought

Defendant pleaded guilty to distributing sexually explicit photos of his minor daughter. Although the court initially accepted his plea, despite defendant's apparent confusion regarding the court's questions regarding his guilt, defendant thereafter chose to withdraw the plea. Defendant then changed his mind, and said that he wanted to plead guilty to one of the charges against him, but did not specify which one. The court accepted the plea without informing defendant about his rights and the consequences of a guilty plea. Did the court handle the guilty plea properly? *See United States v. Olson*, 880 F.3d 873 (7th Cir. 2018).

b. No Constitutional Right to a Deal

A defendant has no constitutional right to plea bargain with the prosecutor. *Weatherford v. Bursey*, <u>429 U.S. 545 (1977)</u>. Indeed, prosecutors have discretion to plea bargain with some defendants but not with others. Similarly, prosecutors have discretion to offer "package deals" (often referred to as "wired" deals) to all defendants or no deal at all. *See United States v. Crain*, <u>33 F. 3d 480 (5th Cir. 1994)</u>. Prosecutors nevertheless cannot base the decision to plea bargain on unjustifiable standards such as race, religion or other arbitrary classification. *Bordenkircher v. Hayes*, <u>434 U.S. 357 (1978)</u>. *See* Chapter 11 on Prosecutorial Discretion.

c. **What Is "Knowing"?**

The trial judge has an obligation to determine whether defendant understands what he is doing when he decides to plead guilty. In *Godinez v. Moran*, 509 U.S. 389, 396–402 (1993), the Court held that the competency standard for pleading guilty is no higher than the competency standard for standing trial:

> A criminal defendant may not be tried unless he is competent and he may not plead guilty unless he does so "competently and intelligently." In *Dusky v. United States*, 362 U.S. 402 (1960), we held that the standard for competence to stand trial is whether the defendant has "sufficient present ability to consult with his lawyer with a reasonable degree of rational understanding" and has "a rational as well as factual understanding of the proceedings against him." While we have described the standard for competence to stand trial, we have never expressly articulated a standard for competence to plead guilty. Even assuming that there is some meaningful distinction between the capacity for "reasoned choice" and a "rational understanding" of the proceedings, we reject the notion that competence to plead guilty must be measured by a standard that is higher than (or even different from) the *Dusky* standard.

> We begin with the guilty plea. A defendant who stands trial is likely to be presented with choices that entail relinquishment of the same rights that are relinquished by a defendant who pleads guilty: He will ordinarily have to decide whether to waive his "privilege against compulsory self-incrimination" by taking the witness stand; if the option is available, he may have to decide whether to waive his "right to trial by jury"; and, in consultation with counsel, he may have to decide whether to waive his "right to confront his accusers" by declining to cross-examine witnesses for the prosecution. A defendant who pleads not guilty faces still other strategic choices: In consultation with his attorney, he may be called upon to decide, among other things, whether (and how) to put on a defense and whether to raise one or more affirmative defenses. In sum, all criminal defendants—not merely those who plead guilty—may be required to make important decisions once criminal proceedings have been initiated. While the decision to plead guilty is undeniably a profound one, it is no more complicated than the sum total of decisions that a defendant may be called upon to make during the course of a trial. (The decision to plead guilty is also made over a shorter period of time, without the distraction and burden of a trial.) We can conceive of no basis for demanding a higher level of competence for those defendants who choose to plead guilty. If the *Dusky* standard is adequate for defendants who plead not guilty, it is necessarily adequate for those who plead guilty. Requiring that a criminal defendant be competent has a modest aim:

It seeks to ensure that he has the capacity to understand the proceedings and to assist counsel. While psychiatrists and scholars may find it useful to classify the various kinds and degrees of competence, and while States are free to adopt competency standards that are more elaborate than the *Dusky* formulation, the Due Process Clause does not impose these additional requirements.

d. Voluntariness & Knowledge of Elements

Can a guilty plea be voluntary if the defendant is unaware of the essential elements of the offense to which he is pleading? In *Henderson v. Morgan*, 426 U.S. 637, 644 (1976), the Court held that a plea was involuntary when neither defense counsel nor the trial court explained to defendant that intent was an element of second-degree murder:

> We assume that the prosecutor had overwhelming evidence of guilt. We also accept petitioner's characterization of the competence of respondent's counsel and of the wisdom of their advice to plead guilty to a charge of second-degree murder. Nevertheless, such a plea cannot support a judgment of guilt unless it was voluntary in a constitutional sense. Clearly the plea could not be voluntary in the sense that it constituted an intelligent admission that he committed the offense unless the defendant received "real notice of the true nature of the charge against him, the first and most universally recognized requirement of due process." *Smith v. O'Grady*, 312 U.S. 329, 334. There is nothing in this record that can serve as a substitute for either a finding after trial, or a voluntary admission, that respondent had the requisite intent. Defense counsel did not purport to stipulate to that fact; they did not explain to him that his plea would be an admission of that fact; and he made no factual statement or admission necessarily implying that he had such intent. In these circumstances it is impossible to conclude that his plea to the unexplained charge of second-degree murder was voluntary.

Should the trial judge be able to rely on defense counsel disclosing the important elements of the offense to the defendant? In *Bradshaw v. Stumpf*, 545 U.S. 175 (2005), the Court held that "where a defendant is represented by competent counsel, the court usually may rely on that counsel's assurance that the defendant has been properly informed of the nature and elements of the charge to which he is pleading guilty."

e. Factual Basis for the Plea

In *McCarthy v. United States*, 394 U.S. 459 (1969), the Court noted that the requirement of agreeing to a factual basis protects a defendant from pleading voluntarily without realizing that her conduct is not actually within the charge. In court, after the judge makes the proper *Boykin* inquiries to ensure that the defendant is entering the plea knowingly and voluntarily, the judge turns to the prosecutor to provide the factual basis for the plea. The prosecutor reads a short statement of facts, which may be a police report, of what would have been proven had the case gone to trial, and then the judge asks the defendant if the facts are true. The defendant may disagree with some of the stated facts, but the plea will be valid as long as the facts necessary to constitute the elements of the charge are agreed upon.

f.   *Alford* Plea

A court may, in its discretion, accept a plea when there is a factual basis for the charges even though the defendant asserts his innocence. In *North Carolina v. Alford*, 400 U.S. 25 (1970), Alford was indicted for first-degree murder, a capital offense. His appointed counsel questioned witnesses who Alford said would substantiate his claim of innocence. The witnesses did not support Alford's story but instead gave statements that strongly indicated his guilt. Faced with strong evidence of guilt and no substantial evidentiary support for the claim of innocence, Alford's attorney recommended that he plead guilty, but left the ultimate decision to Alford himself. The prosecutor agreed to accept a plea of guilty to a charge of second-degree murder, and Alford pleaded guilty to the reduced charge. The Court approved this plea:

> State and lower federal courts are divided upon whether a guilty plea can be accepted when it is accompanied by protestations of innocence and hence contains only a waiver of trial but no admission of guilt. Some courts, giving expression to the principle that "our law only authorizes a conviction where guilt is shown," require that trial judges reject such pleas. But others have concluded that they should not "force any defense on a defendant in a criminal case," particularly when advancement of the defense might "end in disaster." Since "guilt, or the degree of guilt, is at times uncertain and elusive," "an accused, though believing in or entertaining doubts respecting his innocence, might reasonably conclude a jury would be convinced of his guilt and that he would fare better in the sentence by pleading guilty." As one state court observed nearly a century ago, "reasons other than the fact that he is guilty may induce a defendant to so plead, and he must be permitted to judge for himself in this respect."

> We cannot perceive any material difference between a plea that refuses to admit commission of the criminal act and a plea containing a protestation of innocence when, as in the instant case, a defendant intelligently concludes that his interests require entry of a guilty plea and the record before the judge contains strong evidence of actual guilt. Here the State had a strong case of first-degree murder against Alford. Whether he realized or disbelieved his guilt, he insisted on his plea because in his view he had absolutely nothing to gain by a trial and much to gain by pleading. Because of

the overwhelming evidence against him, a trial was precisely what neither Alford nor his attorney desired. Confronted with the choice between a trial for first-degree murder, on the one hand, and a plea of guilty to second-degree murder, on the other, Alford quite reasonably chose the latter and thereby limited the maximum penalty to a 30-year term. When his plea is viewed in light of the evidence against him, which substantially negated his claim of innocence and which further provided a means by which the judge could test whether the plea was being intelligently entered, its validity cannot be seriously questioned. In view of the strong factual basis for the plea demonstrated by the State and Alford's clearly expressed desire to enter it despite his professed belief in his innocence, we hold that the trial judge did not commit constitutional error in accepting it.

Food for Thought

Alford pleas are atypical. Why do you think that is? How do you think the judge, who will sentence the defendant, views an *Alford* plea? Is it appropriate for the judge to take into account a defendant's lack of admission of guilt as a reason to increase the sentence? *See* Chapter 20, Sentencing, *infra*.

Whether a prosecutor agrees to an *Alford* plea and whether the trial court accepts one is discretionary.

g. The Judge's Role

Fed.R.Crim.P. 11(c)(1) prohibits the judge from participating in plea negotiations. In federal court, the plea negotiation takes place solely between the prosecution and the defendant. While the judge may decide whether to accept a plea negotiated between the prosecution and the defense, the judge cannot participate in the process. *See, e.g., United States v. Hemphill,* 748 F.3d 666 (5th Cir. 2014) (holding trial court's comments about strength of prosecution's evidence and reference to fate befallen similarly situated defendants constituted improper participation in plea negotiations).

Professor Albert Alschuler made the following argument on the trial judge's role:

Apologists for plea bargaining often contend that, when a plea agreement satisfies the parties, no one else can have legitimate reason for complaint. A bargain that a defendant, advised by able counsel, finds advantageous cannot properly be criticized on the ground that it is unfair to him, and if occasional cases of incompetence or corruption are set aside, the prosecutor's acquiescence in the bargain insures that it is fair to the state as well. A jurisprudential assessment of this argument would require consideration of the concept of voluntariness, of the goals of criminal proceedings, of the mechanisms by which those goals can best be achieved, and, perhaps, of the reasons for prohibiting a variety of consensual arrangements in other contexts. It is sufficient for present purposes to note that one who accepts this central argument for plea bargaining cannot consistently oppose judicial participation in the process, for judicial bargaining apparently meets with the approval of most defense attorneys and a great many prosecutors. At the very least, if the consent of the parties is regarded as determinative, a trial judge should be permitted to negotiate with a defense attorney when both the prosecutor and the defendant acquiesce in this procedure. If the opponents of judicial

Food for Thought

Federal courts have interpreted Rule 11's prohibition on judicial involvement in plea negotiations to include a prohibition on letting the parties know what sentence the court would impose under a particular plea. This would seem to deprive meaning from the constitutional requirement that a plea reflect the accused's "knowing and intelligent waiver of constitutional rights." What could be more important to the accused than knowing what sentence would be imposed upon pleading guilty? And as far as contract law goes, isn't this a bit like negotiating over a purchase without knowing either the price or the value of the thing being purchased?

bargaining are unwilling to create this exception to the prohibition that they propose, some of them must apparently reconsider the significance that the consent of the parties should have in criminal proceedings.

Albert Alschuler, *The Trial Judge's Role in Plea Bargaining, Part I*, 76 COLUM. L. REV. 1059, 1152 (1976). Do you agree or disagree with this excerpt? Why? Do you think that there is something "unseemly" or otherwise inappropriate about judges being involved in plea bargaining? If so, is that a commentary on the judicial role or on plea bargaining itself?

h. Collateral Consequences

Fed.R.Crim.P. 11(b)(1) lists some consequences of a guilty plea (*e.g.,* mandatory minimum penalty & maximum possible penalty). A defendant need not be advised of every collateral consequence of a guilty plea (*e.g.,* loss of government benefits, voting rights, housing, professional licensing), but the Court held in *Padilla v. Kentucky*, 559 U.S. 356 (2010), that ineffective assistance of counsel occurs when a

In State courts, the source of most of the nation's criminal justice action, where dockets have large backlogs and resources are vastly less than in the federal system, there are generally no impediments to active judicial participation in plea negotiations, and most plea bargains involve a guaranteed sentence agreed upon by all participants, including the judge.

defendant's lawyer does not advise a client of deportation risks, including advising in general terms if the exact immigration consequences are unclear.

What about mandatory sex offender registration obligations? Must a guilty plea advisory warn defendants of this consequence? Courts have split on the issue. *See, e.g., People v. Fonville*, 804 N.W.2d 878 (Mich. App. 2011) (warning required because sex offender registration is like deportation in that it is a serious and intimately-connected consequence of conviction); *People v. Gravino*, 928 N.E.2d 1048 (N.Y. 2010) (pre-*Padilla* case holding that because registration is a "collateral" and not "direct" consequence, warning not required).

i. Presumption of Validity

When a prior conviction based upon a guilty plea is used to enhance the defendant's sentence for the current offense, in the absence of a transcript of the prior guilty plea proceeding, the burden is on the defendant to show a *Boykin* violation. The *Boykin* "presumption of invalidity" is trumped by the presumption of regularity attaching to final judgments. *Parke v. Raley*, 506 U.S. 20 (1992).

j. Contract Null if Court Rejects Plea

In *United States v. Hyde*, 520 U.S. 670 (1997), the Court observed that the Federal Rules: "explicitly envision a situation in which the defendant performs his side of the bargain (the guilty plea) before the Government is required to perform its side (here, the motion to dismiss four counts). If the court accepts the agreement and thus the Government's promised performance, then the contemplated agreement is complete and the defendant gets the benefit of his bargain. But if the court rejects the Government's promised performance, then the agreement is terminated and the defendant has the right to back out of his promised performance (the guilty plea), just as a binding contractual duty may be extinguished by the nonoccurrence of a condition subsequent.

k. Use of Statements Made in Plea Negotiations

Notwithstanding Fed.R.Crim.P. 11(f)'s general prohibition on the admissibility of plea-statements, the Court in *United States v. Mezzanatto*, 513 U.S. 196 (1995), held that a defendant could agree prior to plea discussions that any statement he made during those discussions could be used to impeach any contradictory statement he might make if the case is tried. The Court found that waiver is not inconsistent with the rule's goal of encouraging voluntary settlement, because it "makes no sense to conclude that mutual settlement will be encouraged by precluding negotiation over an issue that may be particularly important to one of the parties to the transaction."

l. Involuntariness as Basis for Negating Plea

One of the few grounds upon which a guilty plea may be set aside is if a court determines that it was involuntary. In *Brady v. United States*, 397 U.S. 742 (1970), the Court held that, in order to establish involuntariness, defendant must prove that the fear of the possible consequences of not pleading guilty destroyed the ability to balance the risks and benefits of going to trial. The Court found that Brady's plea was voluntary even though it was motivated by his desire to avoid the death penalty.

Food for Thought

Under Rule 11, defendants can withdraw a guilty plea prior to sentencing if they "can show a fair and just reason for requesting a withdrawal." In one case, the judge mistakenly stated that the mandatory minimum term of supervised release for the crime with which defendant was charged was five years when it was actually ten. Defendant was ultimately sentenced to fifteen years in prison and ten years of supervised release. Defendant seeks to withdraw his plea, claiming that he was misled by the judge's misstatement and therefore that his plea was not "knowing" and "intelligent." Under these circumstances, should defendant be allowed to withdraw his plea? What if the evidence suggests that the misstatement was not "material" in the sense that defendant would have entered into the plea agreement anyway? *See United States v. Freeman*, 17 F.4th 255 (2nd Cir. 2021).

Hypo: *Withdrawal of Plea?*

Jonathan Pollard, an Intelligence Research Specialist with the United States Navy, admitted to spying for the Israeli government. Ultimately, he pleaded guilty to one count of conspiracy to deliver national defense information to a foreign government. Anne Pollard, Jonathan Pollard's wife, was also implicated in the affair. Despite the fact that Anne Pollard had a debilitating gastrointestinal disorder prior to her arrest, and was seriously ill, losing forty pounds over a period of three months while confined in jail after her arrest, the government refused to offer her a plea agreement unless Jonathan Pollard also pleaded guilty. Such plea arrangements are commonly called "wired pleas," *i.e.,* each plea is inextricably linked to the other; if one defendant fails to abide by his or her plea agreement terms, both plea deals fail. After Anne Pollard served three years in prison and was paroled and moved to Israel, Jonathan Pollard sought to withdraw his plea arguing that the government overreached by using unconstitutional pressure (his concern about his wife's health) to force him to plead guilty, in effect, coercing an involuntary plea. Do you think this is a good argument? Why? Should it make any difference that Pollard did not contest his actual guilt?

United States v. Ruiz

536 U.S. 622 (2002).

JUSTICE BREYER delivered the opinion of the Court.

In this case we primarily consider whether the Fifth and Sixth Amendments require federal prosecutors, before entering into a binding plea agreement with a criminal defendant, to disclose "impeachment information relating to any informants or other witnesses." We hold that the Constitution does not require that disclosure.

After immigration agents found 30 kilograms of marijuana in Angela Ruiz's luggage, federal prosecutors offered her what is known in the Southern District of California as a "fast track" plea bargain. That bargain asks a defendant to waive indictment, trial, and an appeal. In return, the Government agrees to recommend to the sentencing judge a two-level departure downward from the otherwise applicable United States Sentencing Guidelines sentence. In Ruiz's case, a two-level departure downward would have shortened the ordinary Guidelines-specified 18-to-24-month sentencing range by 6 months, to 12-to-18 months. The prosecutors' proposed plea agreement contains a set of detailed terms. Among other things, it specifies that "any known information establishing the factual innocence of the defendant" "has been turned over to the defendant," and it acknowledges the Government's "continuing duty to provide such information." At the same time it requires that the defendant "waive the right" to receive "impeachment information relating to any informants or other witnesses" as well as the right to receive information supporting any affirmative defense the defendant raises if the case goes to trial. Because Ruiz would not agree to this last-mentioned waiver, the prosecutors withdrew their bargaining offer. The Government then indicted Ruiz for unlawful drug possession. Despite the absence of any agreement, Ruiz ultimately pleaded guilty. At sentencing, Ruiz asked the judge to grant her the same two-level downward departure that the Government would have recommended had she accepted the "fast track" agreement. The Government opposed her request, and the District Court denied it, imposing a standard Guideline sentence instead. The Ninth Circuit vacated the District Court's sentencing determination. The Ninth Circuit pointed out that the Constitution requires prosecutors to make certain impeachment information available to a defendant before trial. It decided that this obligation entitles defendants to receive that same information before they enter into a plea agreement. The Ninth Circuit also decided that the Constitution prohibits defendants from waiving their right to that information. And it held that the prosecutors' standard "fast track" plea agreement was unlaw-

Hear It

You can hear the oral argument in *Ruiz* at: http://www.oyez.org/cases/2000-2009/2001/2001_01_595.

ful because it insisted upon that waiver. We granted the Government's petition for certiorari.

The constitutional question concerns a federal criminal defendant's waiver of the right to receive exculpatory impeachment material from prosecutors—a right that the Constitution provides as part of its basic "fair trial" guarantee. *See* U.S. Const., Amdts. 5, 6. *See also Brady v. Maryland*, 373 U.S. 83 (1963) (Due process requires prosecutors to "avoid an unfair trial" by making available "upon request" evidence "favorable to an accused where the evidence is material either to guilt or to punishment"); *Giglio v. United States*, 405 U.S. 150, 154 (1972) (exculpatory evidence includes "evidence affecting" witness "credibility," where the witness' "reliability" is likely "determinative of guilt or innocence"). When a defendant pleads guilty he or she, of course, forgoes not only a fair trial, but also other accompanying constitutional guarantees. *Boykin v. Alabama*, 395 U.S. 238 (1969) (pleading guilty implicates the Fifth Amendment privilege against self-incrimination, the Sixth Amendment right to confront one's accusers, and the Sixth Amendment right to trial by jury). Given the seriousness of the matter, the Constitution insists, among other things, that the defendant enter a guilty plea that is "voluntary" and that the defendant must make related waivers "knowingly, intelligently, and with sufficient awareness of the relevant circumstances and likely consequences." We must decide whether the Constitution requires that preguilty plea disclosure of impeachment information. We conclude that it does not.

Food for Thought

The Court here seems unable to see why an innocent person would plead guilty. Can you? Is the Court's discounting of this possibility warranted?

Due process considerations, the very considerations that led this Court to find trial-related rights to exculpatory and impeachment information in *Brady* and *Giglio*, argue against the existence of the "right" that the Ninth Circuit found here. This Court has said that due process considerations include not only (1) the nature of the private interest at stake, but also (2) the value of the additional safeguard, and (3) the adverse impact of the requirement upon the Government's interests. *Ake v. Oklahoma*, 470 U.S. 68 (1985). Here, the added value of the Ninth Circuit's "right" to a defendant is often limited, for it depends upon the defendant's independent awareness of the details of the Government's case. And in any case, as the proposed plea agreement at issue here specifies, the Government will provide "any information establishing the factual innocence of the defendant" regardless. That fact, along with other guilty-plea safeguards, diminishes the force of Ruiz's concern that, in the absence of impeachment information, innocent individuals, accused of crimes, will plead guilty.

At the same time, a constitutional obligation to provide impeachment information during plea bargaining, prior to entry of a guilty plea, could seriously interfere

FYI

Ruiz is a federal case. To the extent there is any legitimacy to the Court's assumptions in *Ruiz* about the lack of costs to innocent defendants and the high costs to the government, those assumptions are not as warranted in state criminal cases. While in the vast majority of federal cases, involving drug, gun and white-collar offenses, the witnesses are government agents or are known to the defendant, state criminal prosecutions rely far more heavily on civilian witnesses.

with the Government's interest in securing those guilty pleas that are factually justified, desired by defendants, and help to secure the efficient administration of justice. The Ninth Circuit's rule risks premature disclosure of Government witness information, which, the Government tells us, could "disrupt ongoing investigations" and expose prospective witnesses to serious harm. And the careful tailoring that characterizes most legal Government witness disclosure requirements suggests recognition by both Congress and the Federal Rules Committees that such concerns are valid. *See, e.g.*, 18 U.S.C. § 3432 (witness list disclosure required in capital cases three days before trial with exceptions); § 3500 (Government witness statements ordinarily subject to discovery only after testimony given); Fed. Rule Crim. Proc. 16(a)(2) (embodies limitations of 18 U.S.C. § 3500).

Consequently, the Ninth Circuit's requirement could force the Government to abandon its "general practice" of not "disclosing to a defendant pleading guilty information that would reveal the identities of cooperating informants, undercover investigators, or other prospective witnesses." It could require the Government to devote substantially more resources to trial preparation prior to plea bargaining, thereby depriving the plea-bargaining process of its main resource-saving advantages. Or it could lead the Government instead to abandon its heavy reliance upon plea bargaining in a vast number—90% or more—of federal criminal cases. We cannot say that the Constitution's due process requirement demands so radical a change in the criminal justice process in order to achieve so comparatively small a constitutional benefit.

These considerations, taken together, lead us to conclude that the Constitution does not require the Government to disclose material impeachment evidence prior to entering a plea agreement with a criminal defendant. In addition, we note that the "fast track" plea agreement requires a defendant to waive her right to receive information the Government has regarding any "affirmative defense" she raises at trial. We do not believe the Constitution requires provision of this information to the defendant prior to plea bargaining. In the context of this agreement, the need for this information is more closely related to the *fairness* of a trial than to the *voluntariness* of the plea; the value in terms of the defendant's added awareness of relevant circumstances is ordinarily limited; yet the added burden imposed upon the Government by requiring its provision well in advance of trial (often before trial preparation begins) can be serious, thereby significantly interfering with the administration of the plea bargaining process.

For these reasons the decision of the Court of Appeals for the Ninth Circuit is reversed.

Points for Discussion

a. Non-Impeachment Evidence

The facts of *Ruiz* do not reach the issue of a guilty plea where a defendant agrees to forego discovery of withholding non-impeachment exculpatory evidence, such as evidence indicating someone else may have committed the crime. Should such an agreement be treated differently? What about evidence that would undermine the identification of an eyewitness? Is that covered by *Ruiz*? Is that impeachment evidence? *Compare Matthew v. Johnson,* 201 F.3d 353 (5th Cir. 2000) (holding defendants cannot challenge guilty pleas on basis on undisclosed *Brady* information) *with State v. Heubler,* 275 P.3d 91 (Nev. 2012) (holding defendants can challenge guilty pleas on basis of withheld non-impeachment or affirmatively exculpatory evidence).

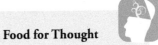

Food for Thought

Are there valid interests to be protected by requiring prosecutors to disclose all exculpatory evidence before a guilty plea, or, similarly, behind not allowing defendants to waive the right to this disclosure?

b. Pre-Plea Request

Does *Ruiz* apply when a defendant already had made a pre-plea discovery request for any potentially *exculpatory* evidence in the state's control? Should the court require the prosecutor to provide the defendant with the evidence before accepting the plea? *See, e.g., State v. Harris,* 266 Wis.2d 200, 667 N.W.2d 813 (App. 2003) (defendant allowed to withdraw guilty plea when prosecutor failed to disclose exculpatory information prior to entry of plea).

Hypo: *Exculpatory Evidence*

Even though *Ruiz* holds that the prosecution does not have to disclose impeachment evidence prior to entering into a plea deal, should it have to disclose evidence that proves defendant's innocence? *See Alvarez v. City of Brownsville,* 904 F.3d 382 (5th Cir. 2018).

D. Plea Negotiation Roles

Some have argued that, during the plea bargaining process, prosecutors must play multiple roles: 1) "administrator" in the sense of disposing of cases in the "fastest, most efficient manner"; 2) "advocate" in the sense of trying "to maximize both the number of convictions and the severity of the sentences that are imposed after conviction"; "judge" in the sense that the prosecutor may be trying to do the 'right thing' for the defendant in view of the defendant's social circumstances or in view of the peculiar circumstances of his crime—with the qualification, of course, that the 'right thing' will not be done unless the defendant pleads guilty; "legislator" because he "may grant concessions because the law is "too harsh," not only for this defendant but for all defendants." *See* Albert W. Alschuler, *The Prosecutor's Role in Plea Bargaining*, 36 U. CHI. L.REV. 50, 52–53 (1968).

Point for Discussion

ABA Standards

The relevant portions of the ABA Prosecution Function Standards warn prosecutors against misleading criminal defendants in plea discussions. However, law enforcement personnel are entitled under existing Fifth, Sixth and Fourteenth Amendment law to "mislead" accused defendants who have properly received *Miranda* warnings, *e.g.*, about inculpatory statements supposedly made by co-defendants or the existence of fingerprints supposedly left at the scene of the crime. Do the ethics rules conflict with prevailing constitutional law? If so, which body of law or rules should a prosecutor follow?

Some argue that there is a widespread perception that criminal attorneys are romantic figures who serve as "an antidote to the fear, ignorance, and bewilderment of the impoverished and uneducated defendant, not only in the courtroom but throughout the criminal process." *See* Albert W. Alschuler, *The Defense Attorney's Role in Plea Bargaining*, 84 YALE L.J. 1179, 1181 (1975). The hope is that "a guilty plea is truthful, based on consent, and entered with an awareness of the consequences and of the defendant's rights." Alschuler argues that the economics of criminal defense work tend to undercut this romantic image. Some lawyers are able to develop "a reputation as an outstanding trial lawyer" that allows them to attract wealthy clients who can pay higher fees. Many other criminal defense attorneys handle "a large volume of cases for less-than-spectacular fees," and that is usually accomplished by having lots of clients agree to plea bargains. Indeed, lawyers never make much money on cases that they try. As one prominent attorney said, "A guilty plea is a quick buck." *Id.* As another attorney noted "Half of the regular defense bar are guys who plead out constantly." As another lawyer said "Of the lawyers who sometimes appear in criminal cases, there are no more than five whom I would hire. There may be 30 others who do a more-or-less conscientious job. And there are probably 50 or 55 cop-out lawyers." Another believed that there are a number of lawyers "who hustle business, never see their clients, and plead all of them guilty." Nevertheless, "at least half of all defense attorneys never take a case intending to prepare for trial." *Id.* As a result, although plea bargaining seems to occur in "an atmosphere of informed choice," the participating parties (private defense attorneys, public defenders, and appointed attorneys) "are all subject to bureaucratic pressures and conflicts of interest that seem unavoidable in any regime grounded on the guilty plea." *Id.*

Alschuler goes on to argue that, unless it is possible to remedy these defects in the plea bargaining process, "we must either endure these abuses or else restructure our criminal justice system to eliminate the overwhelming importance of the defendant's choice of plea, a choice that is usually bent to the purposes of defense attorneys and other participants in the criminal justice system rather than to the interests of the defendant or society." *Id.* He concludes: "The problem of providing adequate resources for criminal courts, for prosecutor and defender offices, and for other criminal justice agencies is undeniably difficult. Nevertheless, even the poorest and most primitive societies manage to guarantee a right to trial, and it is hard to believe that our nation cannot find the resources to guarantee this right as well. Rather than rationalize the familiar, the cheap, and the easy, it may be time to reassert the judgment of the framers of the Sixth Amendment: the cost of jury trials is worth paying." *Id.*

Food for Thought

Professor Alschuler describes the problems defense attorneys encounter in the plea bargaining system. What are the pressures and problems prosecutors (the executive branch), judges, and legislators confront? Consider the pressures on judges to move overcrowded dockets and obtain resources to run their courts. Judges know well that setting high bail amounts that result in incarceration of defendants pretrial force quicker guilty pleas, and that guilty pleas allow for the imposition of fines and fees that are relied upon to finance the court system. Legislators pass draconian sentencing schemes, and prosecutors can leverage those schemes to force defendants to plead guilty regardless of a meritorious defense or actual innocence.

Exercise: *Plea Bargaining*

Your class should be split evenly between those assigned the role of prosecutors and those assigned to be defense counsel, and negotiate regarding the fate of Peter Lane who is observed by police in an area known for drug dealing. The police see him talking to known addicts, and at one point they see him reach into his front right pocket and pull something out and give it to someone. The officers cannot see what Peter pulled out and there is no exchange of items. An officer approaches Peter and puts him against the wall for a frisk. Upon feeling a plastic baggie in Peter's front right pocket, which in the officer's experience feels like it contains rocks consistent with cocaine, the officer pulls the baggie out of Peter's pocket. The officer finds that it contains six rocks of cocaine. The officer arrests Peter.

The prosecutor assigned to the charging division charged Peter with possession with intent to distribute cocaine which carries a maximum term of imprisonment of 10 years and a mandatory minimum of one year. Simple possession of cocaine carries a maximum term of imprisonment of five years and no mandatory minimum. Peter has one prior arrest for possession of cocaine where the case was dismissed and one prior conviction for simple assault.

At a time to be set by your professor, prosecutors and defense counsel should simulate a meeting between the two sides (a meeting requested by defense counsel) to discuss whether there might be a plea deal. Both sides should come to class having prepared a "pre-negotiation memorandum," referring to, *inter alia*: A) the considerations (policy, political, ethical, moral, penological, community, etc.) relevant to this charging decision (from the defendant's side and from the State's side respectively); B) what additional information, if any, about Peter Lane should be acquired by defense counsel or the District Attorney's Office to better determine an appropriate plea; C) strengths and weaknesses in the State's case; D) specific recommendations for the deal, and arguments in support thereof.

Two student observers should monitor each of the plea negotiation sessions. The observers should draft a memorandum analyzing what they observed, *e.g.*, how did the negotiation proceed?; was a fair resolution reached?; how could each of the sides have better maximized their respective positions?

E. Withdrawing a Guilty Plea

It is not uncommon for a defendant who has previously tendered a guilty plea to subsequently seek to withdraw that plea, whether it is days, months, or even years later. There are innumerable reasons why a defendant might later seek to withdraw his or her guilty plea beyond just the prosecutor's failure to abide by the agreement. Such reasons range from mere second thoughts about the strategic thinking (defendant's and/or defense counsel's) that resulted in a guilty plea, to dissatisfaction with or surprise at the severity of the sentence received, to the emergence of new evidence or new witnesses (or the disappearance of evidence or witnesses). However, once properly tendered, a defendant does not generally have the right to withdraw a guilty plea. Nonetheless, prior to the imposition of sentence, most courts can and do permit withdrawal if the defendant presents "any fair and just" reason to do so. After the imposition of sentence, withdrawal is rarely permitted absent a finding of manifest injustice or a miscarriage of justice. *See* Fed.R.Crim.P. 11(d)(2).

In *United States v. Hyde*, 520 U.S. 670 (1997), the Court reversed a case in which the trial court permitted defendant to withdraw a guilty plea after acceptance of a plea but before sentencing, without offering any justification. The Court observed:

> After the defendant has sworn in open court that he actually committed the crimes, after he has stated that he is pleading guilty because he is guilty, after the court has found a factual basis for the plea, and after the court has explicitly announced that it accepts the plea, the Court of Appeals would allow the defendant to withdraw his guilty plea simply on a lark. The Advisory Committee, in adding the "fair and just reason" standard to Rule 32(e) in 1983, explained why this cannot be so: "Given the great care with which pleas are taken under revised Rule 11, there is no reason to view pleas so taken as merely 'tentative,' subject to withdrawal before sentence whenever the government cannot establish prejudice. Were withdrawal automatic in every case where the defendant decided to alter his tactics and present his theory of the case to the jury, the guilty plea would become a mere gesture, a temporary and meaningless formality reversible at the defendant's whim. In fact, however, a guilty plea is no such trifle, but a "grave and solemn act," which is "accepted only with care and discernment." We think the Court of Appeals' holding would degrade the otherwise serious act of pleading guilty into something akin to a move in a game of chess.

If the reason a defendant pleaded guilty was that he or she relied on the incompetent legal or tactical advice of defense counsel, where he or she can demonstrate that "there is a reasonable probability that, but for counsel's errors, defendant would not have pleaded guilty and would have insisted on going to trial," the guilty plea may be withdrawn based upon ineffective assistance of counsel. *Hill v. Lockhart*, 474 U.S. 52, 59 (1985).

FYI

In *United States v. Ladue*, 866 F.3d 978 (8th Cir. 2017), the court refused to allow defendant to withdraw a guilty plea. Defendant plead guilty to two counts of aggravated sexual abuse in exchange for the government's agreement to drop charges of aggravated sexual abuse of a child under the age of 12, thereby avoiding a mandatory minimum sentence of 30 years in prison. At his plea hearing, defendant stated that he was aware that he faced a possible sentence of 360 months to life in prison. Defendant sought to withdraw because the trial court judge was not explicit about the fact that, in pleading guilty to two counts of aggravated sexual abuse, he would be ineligible for parole. The court viewed his claim—that the decisive factor in his decision to plead guilty was his eligibility for parole—as uncredible. Also, defendant's counsel informed him, in advance of the plea, that he could not expect probation.

F. The Consequences of a Guilty Plea

When a defendant decides to plead guilty, defendant relinquishes many rights, including various appeal rights. But does defendant preserve the right to raise certain issues on appeal?

Class v. United States

138 S.Ct. 798 (2018).

JUSTICE BREYER delivered the opinion of the Court.

A federal grand jury indicted petitioner, Rodney Class, for possessing firearms in his locked jeep, which was parked in a lot on the grounds of the United States Capitol in Washington, D.C. *See* 40 U.S.C. § 5104(e)(1). Class, appearing *pro se*, asked the Federal District Court for the District of Columbia to dismiss the indictment. Class alleged that the statute violates the Second Amendment. He also raised a due process claim, arguing that he was denied fair notice that weapons were banned in the parking lot. The District Court denied both claims. Class pleaded guilty. A written plea agreement set forth the terms of Class' guilty plea, including several rights that he expressly agreed to waive. Those express waivers included: (1) defenses based upon the statute of limitations; (2) several specified trial rights; (3) the right to appeal a sentence at or below the judicially determined, maximum sentencing guideline range; (4) most collateral attacks on the conviction and sentence; and (5) various rights to request or receive information concerning the investigation and prosecution of his criminal case. At the same time, the plea agreement expressly enumerated categories of claims that Class could raise on appeal, including claims based upon (1) newly discovered evidence; (2) ineffective assistance of counsel; and (3) statutes providing for sentence reductions. Finally, the plea agreement stated under the heading "Complete Agreement": "No agreements, promises, understandings, or representations have been made by the parties or their counsel other than those contained in writing herein, nor will any such agreements be made unless committed to writing and signed." The agreement said nothing about the right to raise on direct appeal a claim that the statute of conviction was unconstitutional. The District Court held a plea hearing during which it reviewed the terms of the plea agreement (with Class present and under oath) to ensure the validity of the plea. *See* Fed. Rule Crim. Proc. 11(b); *United States v. Ruiz*, 536 U.S. 622 (2002). After providing Class with the required information and warnings, the District Court accepted his guilty plea. Class was sentenced to 24 days imprisonment followed by 12 months of supervised release. Class appealed. He repeated his constitutional claims that the statute violates the Second Amendment and the Due Process Clause because it fails to give fair notice of which areas fall within the Capitol Grounds where firearms are banned. The Court of Appeals held that Class could not raise his constitutional claims because, by pleading guilty, he had waived them. The question is whether a guilty plea by itself bars a federal criminal defendant from challenging the constitutionality of the statute of conviction on direct appeal. It does not.

Fifty years ago this Court stated that a defendant's "plea of guilty did not waive his previous constitutional claim." *Haynes v. United States*, 390 U.S. 85, 87 (1968). In *Blackledge v. Perry*, 417 U.S. 21 (1974), North Carolina indicted and convicted Jimmy Perry on a misdemeanor assault charge. When Perry exercised his right under a North Carolina statute to a *de novo* trial in a higher court, the State reindicted him, but this time the State charged a felony, which carried a heavier penalty, for the same conduct. Perry pleaded guilty. He then sought *habeas* relief on the grounds that the reindictment amounted to an unconstitutional vindictive prosecution. The State argued that Perry's guilty plea barred him from raising his constitutional challenge. This Court held that it did not. The Court noted that a guilty plea bars appeal of many claims, including some "antecedent constitutional violations" related to events (say, grand jury proceedings) that "occurred prior to entry of the guilty plea." "The nature of the underlying constitutional infirmity is markedly different" from a claim of vindictive prosecution, which implicates "the very power of the State" to prosecute the defendant. Accordingly, "the right" Perry "asserts and we accept the right not to be haled into court upon the felony charge" since "the very initiation of the proceedings" against Perry "operated to deprive him due process of law." In *Menna v. New York*, 423 U.S. 61 (1975) (*per curiam*), after Menna served a 30-day jail term for refusing to testify before a grand jury, the State of New York charged him once again for (what Menna argued was) the same crime. Menna pleaded guilty, but subsequently appealed arguing that the new charge violated the Double Jeopardy Clause. U.S. Const., Amdt. 5. The lower courts held that Menna's constitutional claim had been "waived." Citing *Blackledge*, the Court held that Menna's claim amounted to a claim that "the State may not convict" him "no matter how validly his factual guilt is established." Menna's "guilty plea, therefore, did not bar the claim."

These holdings reflect an understanding of the nature of guilty pleas which stretches back nearly 150 years. In 1869 Justice Ames wrote for the Supreme Judicial Court of Massachusetts: "The plea of guilty is a confession of the facts charged in the indictment, and of the evil intent imputed to the defendant. It is a waiver also of all merely technical and formal objections of which the defendant could have availed himself by any other plea or motion. But if the facts alleged and admitted do not constitute a crime against the laws of the Commonwealth, the defendant is entitled to be discharged." Decisions of federal and state courts throughout the 19th and 20th centuries reflect a similar view of the nature of a guilty plea. We have reaffirmed the *Menna-Blackledge* doctrine and refined its scope. In *United States v. Broce*, 488 U.S. 563 (1989), defendants pleaded guilty to two separate indictments in a single proceeding which "on their face" described two separate bid-rigging conspiracies. They later sought to challenge their convictions on double jeopardy grounds, arguing that they had only admitted to one conspiracy. Citing *Blackledge* and *Menna*, this Court repeated that a guilty plea does not bar a claim on appeal "where on the face of the record the court had no power to enter the conviction or impose the sentence." However, because the defendants could not "prove their claim by relying on those indictments and the existing record" and "without contradicting those indictments," this Court held that their claims were "foreclosed by the admissions inherent in their guilty pleas."

Unlike the claims in *Broce*, Class' constitutional claims here do not contradict the terms of the indictment or the written plea agreement. They are consistent with Class' knowing, voluntary, and intelligent admission that he did what the indictment alleged. Those claims can be "resolved without any need to venture beyond that record." Nor do Class' claims focus upon case-related constitutional defects that "occurred prior to the entry of the guilty plea." *Blackledge*, 417 U.S., at 30. They could not "have been 'cured' through a new indictment by a properly selected grand jury." Because the defendant has admitted the charges against him, a guilty plea makes the latter kind of constitutional claim "irrelevant to the constitutional validity of the conviction." *Haring v. Prosise*, 462 U.S. 306, 321 (1983). But the cases make clear that a defendant's guilty plea does not make irrelevant the kind of constitutional claim Class seeks to make. The claims at issue here do not fall within any of the categories of claims that Class' plea agreement forbids him to raise on direct appeal. They challenge the Government's power to criminalize Class' (admitted) conduct. They thereby call into question the Government's power to "constitutionally prosecute" him. A guilty plea does not bar a direct appeal in these circumstances.

The Government contends that by entering a guilty plea, Class inherently relinquished his constitutional claims. A guilty plea does implicitly waive some claims, including some constitutional claims. However, Class' valid guilty plea does not bar direct appeal of his constitutional claims in these circumstances. A valid guilty plea "forgoes not only a fair trial, but also other accompanying constitutional guarantees." While those "simultaneously" relinquished rights include the privilege against compulsory self-incrimination, the jury trial right, and the right to confront accusers, *McCarthy v. United States*, 394 U.S. 459 (1969), they do not include "a waiver of privileges which exist beyond the confines of the trial." *Mitchell v. United States*, 526 U.S. 314, 324 (1999). Here, Class' statutory right to appeal his conviction "cannot be characterized as part of the trial." A valid guilty plea renders irrelevant—and thereby prevents the defendant from appealing—the constitutionality of case-related government conduct that takes place before the plea is entered. *See, e.g., Haring, supra*, at 320 (a valid guilty plea "results in the defendant's loss of any meaningful opportunity to challenge the admissibility of evidence obtained in violation of the Fourth Amendment"). Neither can the defendant later complain that the indicting grand jury was unconstitutionally selected. But those kinds of claims are not at issue here. Finally, a valid guilty plea relinquishes any claim that would contradict the "admissions necessarily made upon entry of a voluntary plea of guilty." *Broce, supra*, at 573. But the constitutional claim here is consistent with Class' admission that he engaged in the conduct alleged in the indictment. Class' challenge does not deny that he engaged in the conduct to which he admitted. Instead, like the defendants in *Blackledge* and *Menna*, he seeks to raise a claim which, "judged on its face," would extinguish the government's power to "constitutionally prosecute" defendant if the claim were successful.

The Government and the dissent point to Rule 11(a)(2) of the Federal Rules of Criminal Procedure, which governs "conditional" guilty pleas. The Rule states: "Conditional Plea. With the consent of the court and the government, a defendant may enter a conditional plea of guilty or *nolo contendere*, reserving in writing the right to have an appellate court review an adverse determination of a specified pre-trial motion. A defendant who prevails on appeal may then withdraw the plea." The Government and the dissent argue that Rule 11(a)(2) means that "a defendant who pleads guilty cannot challenge his conviction on appeal on a forfeitable or waivable ground that he failed to present to the district court or failed to reserve in writing." They point to the notes of the Advisory Committee that drafted the text of Rule 11(a)(2). In particular, the dissent points to the suggestion that an unconditional guilty plea constitutes a waiver of "nonjurisdictional defects," while the Government points to the drafters' statement that they intended the Rule's "conditional plea procedure to conserve prosecutorial and judicial resources and advance speedy trial objectives," while ensuring "much needed uniformity in the federal system on this matter." The Government adds that its interpretation of the Rule furthers these basic purposes. Just as defendants must use Rule 11(a)(2)'s procedures to preserve, for instance, Fourth Amendment unlawful search-and-seizure claims, so must they use it to preserve the constitutional claims here. The problem is that, by its own terms, the Rule itself does not say whether it sets forth the exclusive procedure for a defendant to preserve a constitutional claim following a guilty plea. The drafters' notes acknowledge that the "Supreme Court has held that certain kinds of constitutional objections may be raised after a plea of guilty." Advisory Committee's Notes, at 912. The notes specifically refer to the "*Menna-Blackledge* doctrine." They add that the Rule "should not be interpreted as either broadening or narrowing that doctrine or as establishing procedures for its application."

The Government argues that Class "expressly waived" his right to appeal his constitutional claim. The Government concedes that the written plea agreement, which sets forth the "Complete Agreement" between Class and the Government does not contain this waiver. Rather, the Government relies on the fact that during the Rule 11 plea colloquy, the District Court Judge stated that, under the written plea agreement, Class was "giving up [his] right to appeal [his] conviction." Class agreed. We do not see why the District Court Judge's statement should bar Class' constitutional claims. Under these circumstances, Class' acquiescence neither expressly nor implicitly waived his right to appeal his constitutional claims.

For these reasons, we hold that Class may pursue his constitutional claims on direct appeal. The contrary judgment of the Court of Appeals for the District of Columbia Circuit is reversed, and the case is remanded for further proceedings consistent with this opinion.

It is so ordered.

JUSTICE ALITO, with whom JUSTICE KENNEDY and JUSTICE THOMAS join, dissenting.

The Federal Constitution does not prohibit the waiver of the rights Class asserts. Most personal constitutional rights may be waived. No federal statute or rule bars waiver. Rule 11 of the Federal Rules of Criminal Procedure makes it clear that, with one exception, a defendant who enters an unconditional plea waives all nonjurisdictional claims. Subdivision (a)(2) allows a defendant, "with the consent of the court and the government," to "enter a conditional plea of guilty or *nolo contendere*, reserving in writing the right to have an appellate court review an adverse determination of a specified pretrial motion." Subdivision (a)(2) was adopted against the backdrop of decisions of this Court holding that a guilty plea generally relinquishes all defenses to conviction. Rule 11 actually bars the raising of such claims.

The Advisory Committee's Notes on Rule 11 specify that Rule 11(a)(2) "has no application" to the "*Menna-Blackledge* doctrine." In *Blackledge*, the Court held that a defendant who pleaded guilty could challenge his conviction on the ground that his right to due process was violated by a vindictive prosecution. The most natural way to understand *Blackledge* would be to say that an argument survives a guilty plea if it attacks the court's jurisdiction. But that cannot be what *Blackledge* meant. Blackledge had been tried in state court for a state-law offense, and the jurisdiction of state courts to entertain such prosecutions is purely a matter of state law. Second, a rule that jurisdictional defects alone survive a guilty plea would not explain *Blackledge*. Arguments attacking a court's subject-matter jurisdiction can neither be waived nor forfeited. But the due process right at issue in Blackledge was perfectly capable of being waived or forfeited. Most constitutional defenses, if successfully asserted in a pretrial motion, deprive the prosecution of the "power" to proceed to trial or secure a conviction. If that remedial consequence converted them all into rights not to be prosecuted, *Blackledge* would have no discernible limit. *Menna* may be worse. *United States v. Broce*,

488 U.S. 563 (1989). *Broce* involved two defendants who pleaded guilty but sought to attack their convictions on double jeopardy grounds. The Court held that their guilty pleas prevented them from litigating their claims. "By entering a plea of guilty, the accused is not simply stating that he did the acts described in the indictment; he is admitting guilt of a substantive crime." It makes no difference whether defendant "may not have correctly appraised the constitutional significance of certain historical facts." A defendant's decision to plead guilty necessarily extinguishes whatever "potential defenses" he might have asserted to show that it would be unlawful to hold him liable for his conduct. So much for *Menna*. As for *Blackledge*, by holding that the defendants' double jeopardy rights were extinguished by their pleas, *Broce* necessarily rejected the idea that a right not to be tried survives an unconditional guilty plea. *Broce* was content to distinguish those cases on the ground that they involved defendants who could succeed on appeal without going beyond "the existing record," whereas the defendants in Broce would have to present new evidence.

The Court repeats that an argument survives if it "implicates 'the very power of the State' to prosecute the defendant," but this shibboleth is no more intelligible now than it was in *Blackledge*. Would this rule permit a defendant to argue that his prosecution is barred by a statute of limitations or the Speedy Trial Act? Presumably yes. By admitting commission of the acts alleged in an indictment or complaint, defendant would not concede that the charge was timely. What about the argument that a defendant's conduct does not violate the statute of conviction? The rule barring only those claims inconsistent with the facts alleged in the indictment or complaint would appear to permit the issue to be raised on appeal, but the Court says that a defendant who pleads guilty "has admitted the charges against him." The Court says that a guilty plea precludes a defendant from litigating "the constitutionality of case-related government conduct that takes place before the plea is entered." This category is most mysterious. Class was arguing that the Government violated the Constitution at the moment when it initiated his prosecution. That sounds like he is trying to attack "the constitutionality of case-related government conduct that took place before the plea was entered." Yet the Court holds that he may proceed.

The governing law in the present case is Rule 11 of the Federal Rules of Criminal Procedure. Under that Rule, an unconditional guilty plea waives all nonjurisdictional claims with the possible exception of the "*Menna-Blackledge* doctrine." That doctrine is vacuous, has no sound foundation, and produces nothing but confusion. I fear that today's decision will bedevil the lower courts.

Executive Summary

Types of Pleas. In many jurisdictions, a defendant may enter either a plea of not guilty, *nolo contendere*, guilty, guilty but mentally ill, not guilty by reason of insanity, an *Alford* plea, or a conditional guilty plea.

Knowing & Voluntary Plea. A judge must address a defendant personally in open court to determine if a plea is voluntary and if the defendant understands the rights being waived by entering the plea.

Factual Basis Required. There must be a factual basis for the plea stated on the record.

Competency to Plead Guilty. To enter a guilty plea a defendant must be competent which is determined by the same standards as competency to stand trial.

Withdrawing a Guilty Plea. Procedural rules may allow to defendant to withdraw a guilty plea under specified circumstances, though it is much easier to withdraw a guilty plea prior to sentencing than after a sentence has been imposed.

Non-Disclosure of Impeachment Evidence. Prosecutors may withhold impeachment evidence regarding prosecution witnesses prior to entry of a guilty plea.

Major Themes

a. Vast Majority—The role of prosecutors and defense attorneys in criminal cases is largely one of negotiating pleas; the vast majority of charged defendants plead guilty on lesser charges as opposed to risk more severe sentences by proceeding to trial.

b. Contracts—Promises or agreements that form the basis of a plea generally must be fulfilled as under the law of contracts. Both sides of the agreement must fulfill their promises.

For More Information

- RUSSELL L. WEAVER, JOHN M. BURKOFF, CATHERINE HANCOCK & STEVEN I. FRIEDLAND, PRINCIPLES OF CRIMINAL PROCEDURE Ch. 15 (8th ed. 2024).

- WAYNE R. LAFAVE, JEROLD H. ISRAEL, NANCY J. KING & ORIN S. KERR, CRIMINAL PROCEDURE (6th ed. 2017).

Test Your Knowledge

To assess your understanding of the material in this chapter, <u>click here</u> to take a quiz.

CHAPTER **17**

Jury Trials

A. Right to Jury Trial

The Sixth Amendment provides in pertinent part that "in all criminal prosecutions an accused shall enjoy the right to a speedy and public trial, by an impartial jury of the State and district wherein the crime shall have been committed." Further, Article III of the Constitution states that "the trial of all crimes . . . shall be by jury; and such trial shall be held in the state where the said crimes shall have been committed." In *Duncan v. Louisiana*, 391 U.S. 145 (1968), the Court held that the right to trial by jury is a fundamental right that is applicable to the states through the Due Process Clause of the Fourteenth Amendment.

In *Duncan,* defendant was convicted of simple battery, a misdemeanor under Louisiana law, a crime punishable by a maximum of two years' imprisonment and a $300 fine. Appellant sought trial by jury, but the trial judge denied the request because the state constitution granted jury trials only when capital punishment or imprisonment at hard labor may be imposed. Appellant was convicted and sentenced to serve 60 days in the parish prison and was required to pay a fine of $150. Justice White upheld the defendant's right to a jury trial, with the following broad reasoning:

> The guarantees of jury trial in the Federal and State Constitutions reflect a profound judgment about the way in which law should be enforced and justice administered. A right to jury trial is granted to criminal defendants in order to prevent oppression by the Government. Those who wrote our constitutions knew from history and experience that it was necessary to protect against unfounded criminal charges brought to eliminate enemies and against judges too responsive to the voice of higher authority. The framers of the constitutions strove to create an independent judiciary but insisted upon further protection against arbitrary action. Providing an accused with the right to be tried by a jury of his peers gave him an inestimable safeguard against the corrupt or overzealous prosecutor and against the compliant, biased, or eccentric judge. If the defendant preferred the common-sense judgment of a jury to the more tutored but perhaps less sympathetic reaction of the single judge, he was to have it. Beyond this, the jury trial provisions

in the Federal and State Constitutions reflect a fundamental decision about the exercise of official power—a reluctance to entrust plenary powers over the life and liberty of the citizen to one judge or to a group of judges. Fear of unchecked power, so typical of State and Federal Governments in other respects, found expression in the criminal law in this insistence upon community participation in the determination of guilt or innocence. The deep commitment of the Nation to the right of jury trial in serious criminal cases as a defense against arbitrary law enforcement qualifies for protection under the Due Process Clause of the Fourteenth Amendment, and must therefore be respected by the States.

In determining whether the length of the authorized prison term or the seriousness of other punishment is enough in itself to require a jury trial, we refer to objective criteria, chiefly the existing laws and practices in the Nation. In the federal system, petty offenses are defined as those punishable by no more than six months in prison and a $500 fine. In 49 of the 50 States, crimes subject to trial without a jury (which occasionally include simple battery) are punishable by no more than one year in jail. We need not, however, settle the exact location of the line between petty offenses and serious crimes. It is sufficient to hold that a crime punishable by two years in prison is, based on past and contemporary standards in this country, a serious crime and not a petty offense. Consequently, appellant was entitled to a jury trial and it was error to deny it.

Food for Thought

You learned in Chapter 16 that approximately 95% of defendants charged with crimes plead guilty rather than risk trial. Does this mean that the judgment of guilt or innocence is largely entrusted to the unchecked decisions of a prosecutor? Does the right to a jury trial have meaning in this context?

Blanton v. City of North Las Vegas

489 U.S. 538 (1989).

JUSTICE MARSHALL delivered the opinion of the Court.

The issue in this case is whether there is a constitutional right to a trial by jury for persons charged under Nevada law with driving under the influence of alcohol (DUI). Nev.Rev.Stat. § 484.379(1) (1987). We hold that there is not.

DUI is punishable by a minimum term of two days' imprisonment and a maximum term of six months' imprisonment. Alternatively, a trial court may order defendant "to perform 48 hours of work for the community while dressed in distinctive garb which identifies him" as a DUI offender. Defendant also must pay a fine ranging from $200 to $1,000. In addition, defendant automatically loses his driver's license for 90 days, and he must attend, at his own expense, an alcohol abuse education course. Repeat DUI offenders are subject to increased penalties.

Petitioners Melvin R. Blanton and Mark D. Fraley were charged with DUI in separate incidents. Neither petitioner had a prior DUI conviction. The North Las Vegas, Nevada, Municipal Court denied their respective pretrial demands for a jury trial. On appeal, the Eighth Judicial District Court denied Blanton's request for a jury trial but, a month later, granted Fraley's. Blanton then appealed to the Supreme Court of Nevada, as did respondent city of North Las Vegas with respect to Fraley. After consolidating the two cases along with several others raising the same issue, the Supreme Court concluded, *inter alia*, that the Federal Constitution does not guarantee a right to a jury trial for a DUI offense because the maximum term of incarceration is only six months and the maximum possible fine is $1,000. We granted *certiorari* to consider whether petitioners were entitled to a jury trial, and now affirm.

Hear It

You can listen to the oral argument in *Blanton* at: http://www.oyez.org/cases/1980-1989/1988/1988_87_1437.

It has long been settled that "there is a category of petty crimes or offenses which is not subject to the Sixth Amendment jury trial provision." *Duncan v. Louisiana*, 391 U.S. 145, 159 (1968). In determining whether a particular offense should be categorized as "petty," our early decisions focused on the nature of the offense and on whether it was triable by a jury at common law. In recent years, we have sought more "objective indications of the seriousness with which society regards the offense." *Frank v. United States*, 395 U.S. 147, 148 (1969). "We have found the most relevant such criteria in the severity of the maximum authorized penalty." *Baldwin v. New York*, 399 U.S. 66, 68 (1970) (plurality opinion). In fixing the maximum penalty for a crime, a legislature "includes within the definition of the crime itself a judgment about the seriousness of the offense."

In using the word "penalty," we do not refer solely to the maximum prison term authorized for a particular offense. A legislature's view of the seriousness of an offense also is reflected in the other penalties that it attaches to the offense. We thus examine "whether the length of the authorized prison term or the seriousness of other punishment is enough in itself to require a jury trial." *Duncan*, 391 U.S., at 161. Primary emphasis must be placed on the maximum authorized period of incarceration. Penalties such as probation or a fine may engender "a significant infringement of personal freedom," but they cannot approximate in severity the loss of liberty that a prison term entails. Because incarceration is an "intrinsically different" form of punishment, it is the most powerful indication whether an offense is "serious."

Following this approach, our decision in *Baldwin* established that a defendant is entitled to a jury trial whenever the offense for which he is charged carries a maximum authorized prison term of greater than six months. The possibility of a sentence exceeding six months is "sufficiently severe by itself" to require the opportunity for a jury trial. A prison term of six months or less will seldom be viewed by the defendant as "trivial or 'petty.' " But we found that the disadvantages of such a sentence, "onerous though they may be, may be outweighed by the benefits that result from speedy and inexpensive nonjury adjudications." Although we did not hold in *Baldwin* that an offense carrying a maximum prison term of six months or less automatically qualifies as a "petty" offense, we do find it appropriate to presume for purposes of the Sixth Amendment that society views such an offense as "petty." A defendant is entitled to a jury trial in such circumstances only if he can demonstrate that any additional statutory penalties, viewed in conjunction with the maximum authorized period of incarceration, are so severe that they clearly reflect a legislative determination that the offense in question is a "serious" one.

Applying these principles, it is apparent that petitioners are not entitled to a jury trial. The maximum authorized prison sentence for first-time DUI offenders does not exceed six months. A presumption therefore exists that the Nevada Legislature views DUI as a "petty" offense for purposes of the Sixth Amendment. Considering the additional statutory penalties, we do not believe that the Nevada Legislature has clearly indicated that DUI is a "serious" offense. It is immaterial that a first-time DUI offender may face a minimum term of imprisonment. In settling on six months' imprisonment as the constitutional demarcation point, we have assumed that a defendant convicted of the offense in question would receive the maximum authorized prison sentence. It is not constitutionally determinative, therefore, that a particular defendant may be required to serve some amount of jail time less than six months. Likewise, it is of little moment that a defendant may receive the maximum prison term because of the prohibitions on plea bargaining and probation. As for the 90-day license suspension, it will be irrelevant if it runs concurrently with the prison sentence, which we assume for present purposes to be the maximum of six months.[9] We are also unpersuaded by the fact that, instead of a prison sentence, a DUI offender may be ordered to perform 48 hours of community service dressed in clothing identifying him as a DUI offender. Even assuming the outfit is the source of some embarrassment, such a penalty will be less embarrassing and less onerous than six months in jail. As

Food for Thought

Do you agree with the Court that the combination of sanctions described in the first paragraph of the decision is not sufficiently "serious"? Does the Court give guidelines for what is "serious" enough to require a jury trial besides the maximum jail time?

---

[9]   It is unclear whether the license suspension and prison sentence run concurrently. The requirement that an offender attend an alcohol abuse education course can only be described as *de minimis*.

for the possible $1,000 fine, it is well below the $5,000 level set by Congress in its most recent definition of a "petty" offense, and petitioners do not suggest that this congressional figure is out of step with state practice for offenses carrying prison sentences of six months or less. Finally, we ascribe little significance to the fact that a DUI offender faces increased penalties for repeat offenses. Recidivist penalties of the magnitude imposed for DUI are commonplace and, in any event, petitioners do not face such penalties here.

Viewed together, the statutory penalties are not so severe that DUI must be deemed a "serious" offense for purposes of the Sixth Amendment. It was not error, therefore, to deny petitioners jury trials. Accordingly, the judgment of the Supreme Court of Nevada is

Affirmed.

Points for Discussion

a. Six Months or Less

In *United States v. Nachtigal*, 507 U.S. 1 (1993), the Court relied on *Blanton* in holding that a DUI charge with a maximum penalty of six months' imprisonment, a $5,000 fine, a five-year term of probation, and other penalties was not constitutionally serious. The Court reiterated *Blanton*'s presumption that offenses for which the maximum authorized period of incarceration is six months or less are presumptively "petty." That legislative judgment, plus the possibility of a probationary sentence or a $5,000 fine, was not sufficiently severe to overcome the presumption. *See Richter v. Fairbanks*, 903 F.2d 1202 (8th Cir. 1990), the court found that a possible 15-year driver's license revocation for a third DUI offense justified a jury trial even though the maximum authorized sentence was six months.

b. Aggregate Terms

In *Lewis v. United States*, 518 U.S. 322 (1996), the Court held that the scope of the federal jury trial right does not change when a defendant faces a potential aggregate prison term in excess of six months because multiple petty offenses are charged: "By setting the maximum authorized prison term at six months, the legislature categorized the offense as petty. The fact that Lewis was charged with two counts of a petty offense does not revise the legislative judgment as to the gravity of the particular offense, nor does it transform the petty offense into a serious one."

c. Contempt Proceedings

Contempt proceedings are at least quasi-criminal in nature, and a jury must be afforded before a sentence of confinement for more than six months may be imposed for a post-verdict finding of contempt. In *Codispoti v. Pennsylvania*, <u>418 U.S. 506 (1974)</u>, the Court held that a contemnor has a right to a jury trial if the aggregate sentences imposed on multiple contempt convictions is more than six months even though each count is only punishable up to six months. *Lewis* distinguished *Codispoti* because the legislature usually has not set a specific penalty for criminal contempt. Instead, "courts use the severity of the penalty actually imposed as the measure of the character of the offense."

d. Jury Trials & Fines

Is a jury trial constitutionally required when the authorized statutory punishment is six months or less, but the penalty includes a fine? Does *Blanton* suggest that the magnitude of a fine may take the case out of the "petty offense" category? Many courts apply the federal statutory standard of a fine of $5,000 or less as the petty offense upper limit. A jury trial is required when a court imposes serious fines for criminal contempt. In *International Union, United Mine Workers of Am. v. Bagwell*, <u>512 U.S. 821 (1994)</u>, the Court held that contempt fines of $52 million for violation of a labor injunction were criminal and were subject to the jury trial right. However, the Court reiterated the long-accepted idea that direct contempt in the presence of the court is subject to immediate summary adjudication without jury trial.

e. Juvenile Court

Juvenile court proceedings against a youthful offender are not considered to be criminal in nature, and there is no right to a jury trial in such proceedings. *McKeiver v. Pennsylvania*, <u>403 U.S. 528 (1971)</u>.

f. Bench Trials

Virtually all jurisdictions allow the constitutional right to a jury trial to be waived by the defendant in favor of a bench trial in most circumstances, although a defendant does not have a constitutional right to a bench trial. *Patton v. United States*, <u>281 U.S. 276 (1930)</u>. Consequently, statutory rules like Fed. R. Crim. Pro. 23, which require a prosecutor's consent to a bench trial, are constitutional. In *Singer v. United States*, <u>380 U.S. 24 (1965)</u>, the Court left open the possibility that the right to waive could belong to the defendant alone: "We need not determine whether there might be some circumstances where a defendant's reasons for wanting to be tried by a judge alone are

Food for Thought

A determination that a waiver is made voluntarily with a full understanding of its consequences must precede the acceptance of a waiver by the court. *See Singer v. United States, supra*. Assuming that the prosecutor and the court are willing to concur in defendant's decision to waive a jury trial, what strategic considerations may affect a defendant's decision to do so?

so compelling that the Government's insistence on trial by jury would result in the denial to a defendant of an impartial trial."

g. Sentencing Enhancements & Jury Trials

In *Apprendi v. New Jersey*, 530 U.S. 466 (2000), the Court struck down a sentencing law enabling a judge to lengthen a jury-imposed sentence by two years if the judge determined it to be a hate crime. The Court held that, other than the fact of a prior conviction, any fact increasing the penalty beyond the prescribed statutory maximum, whether the statute calls it an element or a sentencing factor, must be submitted to a jury, and proved beyond a reasonable doubt. *See* Chapter 20, Sentencing, *infra*.

Hypo: *Waiver of the Right to Trial by Jury*

Although the right to trial by jury can be waived, courts generally require that the waiver be voluntary, knowing and intelligent. Suppose that discussions regarding defendant's waiver of the right to jury trial occurred only when the judge and the attorneys were present, but never when defendant was present. Although the defense lawyer stipulated that defendant would waive his right to trial by jury, the trial judge made clear that the waiver must be signed by defendant. It was not. If the case proceeds to trial without a jury, can defendant later object that he never validly waived his right to a jury trial? *See United States v. Laney*, 881 F.3d 1100 (9th Cir. 2018).

B. Jury Size & Unanimity

Williams v. Florida

399 U.S. 78 (1970).

MR. JUSTICE WHITE delivered the opinion of the Court.

[Williams's motion to impanel a 12-person jury, rather than the six-person jury provided by Florida law in noncapital cases, was denied. Thereafter he was convicted of robbery and sentenced to life imprisonment.]

In *Duncan v. Louisiana*, 391 U.S. 145 (1968), we held that the Fourteenth Amendment guarantees a right to trial by jury in all criminal cases that—were they in a federal court—would come within the Sixth Amendment's guarantee. Petitioner's trial for robbery on July 3, 1968, clearly falls within the scope of that holding. The question is whether the constitutional guarantee of a trial by "jury" necessarily requires trial by exactly 12 persons, rather than some lesser number—in this case six. We hold that the 12-man panel is not a necessary ingredient of "trial by jury," and that respondent's refusal to impanel more than the six members provided for by Florida law did not violate petitioner's Sixth Amendment rights as applied to the States through the Fourteenth.

We had occasion in *Duncan v. Louisiana* to review the history of the development of trial by jury in criminal cases. That history revealed a long tradition attaching great importance to the concept of relying on a body of one's peers to determine guilt or innocence as a safeguard against arbitrary law enforcement. That same history affords little insight into the considerations that gradually led the size of that body to be

Hear It

You can listen to the oral argument in *Williams* at: http://www.oyez.org/cases/1960-1969/1969/1969_927.

generally fixed at 12. Some have suggested that the number 12 was fixed upon simply because that was the number of the presentment jury from the hundred, from which the petit jury developed. Other, less circular for the number 12 have been given, "but they were all brought forward after the number was fixed," and rest on little more than mystical or superstitious insights into the significance of "12." Lord Coke's explanation that the "number of twelve is much respected in holy writ, as 12 apostles, 12 stones, 12 tribes, etc.," is typical. In short, while sometime in the 14th century the size of the jury at common law came to be fixed generally at 12, that particular feature of the jury system appears to have been a historical accident, unrelated to the great purposes which gave rise to the jury in the first place. The question is whether this accidental feature of the jury has been immutably codified into our Constitution.

The relevant inquiry must be the function that the particular feature performs and its relation to the purposes of the jury trial. Measured by this standard, the 12-man requirement cannot be regarded as an indispensable component of the Sixth Amendment. The purpose of the jury trial, as we noted in *Duncan*, is to prevent oppression by the Government.

Food for Thought

Is the mode of analysis used by Justice White consistent with the Court's current emphasis on applying text and history? Does this affect the outcome in these cases?

Given this purpose, the essential feature of a jury obviously lies in the interposition between the accused and his accuser of the commonsense judgment of a group of laymen, and in the community participation and shared responsibility that results from that group's determination of guilt or innocence. The performance of this role is not a function of the particular number of the body that makes up the jury. To be sure, the number should probably be large enough to promote group deliberation, free from outside attempts at intimidation, and to provide a fair possibility for obtaining a representative cross-section of the community. But we find little reason to think that these goals are in any meaningful sense less likely to be achieved when the jury numbers six, than when it numbers 12—particularly if the requirement of unanimity is retained. Certainly the reliability of the jury as a factfinder hardly seems likely to be a function of its size. It might be suggested that the 12-man jury gives a defendant a greater advantage since he has more "chances" of finding a juror who will insist on acquittal and thus prevent conviction. But the advantage might just as easily belong to the State, which also needs only one juror out of twelve insisting on guilt to prevent acquittal. What few experiments have occurred—usually in the civil area—indicate that there is no discernible difference between the results reached by the two different-sized juries. In short, neither currently available evidence nor theory suggests that the 12-man jury is necessarily more advantageous to the defendant than a jury composed of fewer members.

FYI

Despite the *Williams* holding— that the federal constitution does not require that a jury be composed of twelve members—many state constitutions require a twelve-person jury for all felony prosecutions and a six-person jury for misdemeanor prosecutions.

Similarly, while in theory the number of viewpoints represented on a randomly selected jury ought to increase as the size of the jury increases, in practice the difference between the 12-man and the six-man jury in terms of the cross-section of the community represented seems likely to be negligible. Even the 12-man jury cannot insure representation of every distinct voice in the community, particularly given the use of the peremptory challenge.

Point for Discussion

Six-Person Jury

In *Ballew v. Georgia*, 435 U.S. 223 (1978), the Court used empirical data to establish a constitutional minimum of six-person juries and to reject a jury of only five persons as violative of the Sixth and Fourteenth Amendments:

> Recent empirical data suggest that progressively smaller juries are less likely to foster effective group deliberation. At some point, this decline leads to inaccurate fact-finding and incorrect application of the common sense of the community to the facts. Generally, a positive correlation exists between group size and the quality of both group performance and group

productivity. A variety of explanations have been offered for this conclusion. Several are particularly applicable in the jury setting. The smaller the group, the less likely are members to make critical contributions necessary for the solution of a given problem. Because most juries are not permitted to take notes, memory is important for accurate jury deliberations. As juries decrease in size, they are less likely to have members who remember each of the important pieces of evidence or argument. Furthermore, the smaller the group, the less likely it is to overcome the biases of its members to obtain an accurate result. The data now raise doubts about the accuracy of the results achieved by smaller and smaller panels. The data suggest that the verdicts of jury deliberation in criminal cases will vary as juries become smaller, and that the variance amounts to an imbalance to the detriment of one side, the defense. What has just been said about the presence of minority viewpoint as juries decrease in size foretells problems not only for jury decisionmaking, but also for the representation of minority groups in the community. We do not pretend to discern a clear line between six members and five. But the assembled data raise substantial doubt about the reliability and appropriate representation of panels smaller than six. Because of the fundamental importance of the jury trial to the American system of criminal justice, any further reduction that promotes inaccurate and possibly biased decisionmaking, that causes untoward differences in verdicts, and that prevents juries from truly representing their communities, attains constitutional significance.

FYI

Under the Federal Rules of Criminal Procedure, may a case proceed to judgment without 12 jurors when an alternate juror is available? In *United States v. Brown*, 784 F.3d 1301 (9th Cir. 2015), the court concluded that the F.R.Cr.P. gives judges discretion about how to proceed. In *Brown*, the trial judge opted not to seat an alternate juror because, following a five-day trial involving a 14 count indictment, jurors had already deliberated for more than a day and asked five substantive questions. Seating an alternate would have required the jury to start its deliberations anew. The Ninth Circuit upheld the trial court judge's decision.

Ramos v. Louisiana

140 S.Ct. 1390 (2020).

JUSTICE GORSUCH announced the judgment of the Court and delivered the opinion of the Court with respect to Parts I, II-A, III, and IV-B-1, an opinion with respect to Parts II-B, IV-B-2, and V, in which JUSTICE GINSBURG, JUSTICE BREYER, and JUSTICE SOTOMAYOR join, and an opinion with respect to Part IV-A, in which JUSTICE GINSBURG and JUSTICE BREYER join.

Accused of a serious crime, Evangelisto Ramos insisted on his innocence and invoked his right to a jury trial. Eventually, 10 jurors found the evidence against him persuasive. But a pair of jurors believed that the State of Louisiana had failed to prove Mr. Ramos's guilt beyond reasonable doubt; they voted to acquit. In 48 States and federal court, a single juror's vote to acquit is enough to prevent a conviction. But not in Louisiana. Along with Oregon, Louisiana has long punished people based on 10-to-2 verdicts. So instead of the mistrial he would have received almost anywhere else, Mr. Ramos was sentenced to life in prison without the possibility of parole.

Louisiana first endorsed nonunanimous verdicts for serious crimes at a constitutional convention in 1898. According to one committee chairman, the avowed purpose of that convention was to "establish the supremacy of the white race," and the resulting document included many of the trappings of the Jim Crow era: a poll tax, a combined literacy and property ownership test, and a grandfather clause that in practice exempted white residents from the most onerous of these requirements. Nor was it only the prospect of African-Americans voting that concerned the delegates. Just a week before the convention, the U.S. Senate passed a resolution calling for an investigation into whether Louisiana was systemically excluding African-Americans from juries. Seeking to avoid unwanted national attention, and aware that this Court would strike down any policy of overt discrimination against African-American jurors as a violation of the Fourteenth Amendment, the delegates sought to undermine African-American participation on juries in another way. With a careful eye on racial demographics, the convention delegates sculpted a "facially race-neutral" rule permitting 10-to-2 verdicts in order "to ensure that African-American juror service would be meaningless." Adopted in the 1930s, Oregon's rule permitting nonunanimous verdicts can be similarly traced to the rise of the Ku Klux Klan and efforts to dilute "the influence of racial, ethnic, and religious minorities on Oregon juries." In fact, no one before us contests any of this; courts in both Louisiana and Oregon have frankly acknowledged that race was a motivating factor in the adoption of their States' respective nonunanimity rules.

We took this case to decide whether the Sixth Amendment right to a jury trial—as incorporated against the States by way of the Fourteenth Amendment—requires a unanimous verdict to convict a defendant of a serious offense.

I

The Sixth Amendment promises that "in all criminal prosecutions, the accused shall enjoy the right to a speedy and public trial, by an impartial jury of the State and district wherein the crime shall have been committed, which district shall have been previously ascertained by law." The Amendment goes on to preserve other rights for criminal defendants but says nothing else about what a "trial by an impartial jury" entails. Still, the promise of a jury trial surely meant *something*—otherwise, there would have been no reason to write it down. Nor would it have made any sense to spell out the places from which jurors should be drawn if their powers as jurors could be freely abridged by statute. Imagine a constitution that allowed a "jury trial" to mean nothing but a single person rubberstamping convictions without hearing any evidence—but simultaneously insisting that the lone juror come from a specific judicial district "previously ascertained by law." And if that's not enough, imagine a constitution that included the same hollow guarantee *twice*—not only in the Sixth Amendment, but also in Article III. The text and structure of the Constitution clearly suggest that the term "trial by an impartial jury" carried with it *some* meaning about the content and requirements of a jury trial.

One of these requirements was unanimity. The requirement of juror unanimity emerged in 14th century England and was accepted as a vital right protected by the common law. As Blackstone explained, no person could be found guilty of a serious crime unless "the truth of every accusation should be confirmed by the unanimous suffrage of twelve of his equals and neighbors, indifferently chosen, and superior to all suspicion."[10] A "verdict, taken from eleven, was no verdict" at all. This same rule applied in the young American States. Six State Constitutions explicitly required unanimity. Another four preserved the right to a jury trial in more general terms. But state courts appeared to regard unanimity as an essential feature of the jury trial.

It was against this backdrop that James Madison drafted and the States ratified the Sixth Amendment in 1791. By that time, unanimous verdicts had been required for about 400 years. Influential, postadoption treatises confirm this understanding. Nor is this a case where the original public meaning was lost to time and only recently recovered. This Court has, repeatedly and over many years, recognized that the Sixth Amendment requires unanimity. This Court has long explained that the Sixth Amendment right to a jury trial is "fundamental to the American scheme of justice" and incorporated against the States under the Fourteenth Amendment.[23] This Court has long explained, too, that incorporated provisions of the Bill of Rights bear the same content when asserted against States as they do when asserted against the federal government. So if the Sixth Amendment's right to a jury trial requires a unanimous verdict to support a conviction in federal court, it requires no less in state court.

---

[10]   4 W. BLACKSTONE, COMMENTARIES ON THE LAWS OF ENGLAND 343 (1769).
[23]   *Duncan v. Louisiana*, 391 U. S. 145, 148 (1968).

II

A

In 1972, the Court confronted these States' unconventional schemes for the first time—in *Apodaca* v. *Oregon*[25] and a companion case, *Johnson* v. *Louisiana*.[26] Ultimately, the Court could do no more than issue a badly fractured set of opinions.

B

In the years following *Apodaca*, both Louisiana and Oregon chose to continue allowing nonunanimous verdicts. But their practices have always stood on shaky ground. Really, no one has found a way to make sense of it. In later cases, this Court has labeled *Apodaca* an "exception," "unusual," and in any event "not an endorsement" of Justice Powell's view of incorporation. At the same time, we have continued to recognize the historical need for unanimity.

III

Sensibly, Louisiana doesn't dispute that the common law required unanimity. Instead, it argues that the drafting history of the Sixth Amendment reveals an intent by the framers to leave this particular feature behind. But this snippet of drafting history could just as easily support the opposite inference.

IV

A

[The Court rejected the notion that stare decisis required affirmance of the conviction.]

V

The judgment of the Court of Appeals is *Reversed.*

Justice Sotomayor, concurring as to all but Part IV-A.

The majority vividly describes the legacy of racism that generated Louisiana's and Oregon's laws. Today, Louisiana's and Oregon's laws are fully—and rightly—relegated to the dustbin of history.

Justice Kavanaugh, concurring in part.

---

[25]   406 U. S. 404 (plurality opinion).
[26]   406 U.S. 356.

I agree with the Court that the time has come to overrule *Apodaca*.

JUSTICE THOMAS, concurring in the judgment.

I agree [that] Ramos' felony conviction by a nonunanimous jury was unconstitutional. I write separately because I would resolve this case based on the Court's longstanding view that the Sixth Amendment includes a protection against nonunanimous felony guilty verdicts, without undertaking a fresh analysis of the meaning of "trial . . . by an impartial jury."

Points for Discussion

a.   Federal Rule on Unanimity

In federal cases, unanimous jury verdicts are required by the Federal Rules unless the parties stipulate otherwise. *See* Fed. R. Crim. P. 31.

> **FYI**
>
> In the State of Washington, although a jury must be unanimous in finding that defendant committed the crime with which he was charged, it need not be unanimous on the question of how he committed the crime. In *State v. Woodlyn*, 188 Wash.2d 157, 392 P.3d 1062 (Wash. 2017), defendant was convicted of second-degree theft, but that crime could have been committed in one of two ways: wrongfully obtaining the property or obtaining control of the property by deception. Defendants are entitled to unanimous verdicts only on the question of guilt.

b.   Uncertain Verdicts

In *Schad v. Arizona*, 501 U.S. 624 (1991), defendant was convicted of first-degree murder and sentenced to death. First-degree murder included both premeditated and felony-murder theories, and the prosecution offered proof on both. With a general verdict, it was uncertain whether the jury had been unanimous about premeditated murder. A plurality of the Court said that the issue "is one of the permissible limits in defining criminal conduct, not one of jury unanimity," and held that Schad's due process rights had not been violated when the trial court grouped felony murder and premeditated murder as alternative ways of committing the single crime of first-degree murder.

In *Richardson v. United States*, 526 U.S. 813 (1999), a federal statute prohibits engaging in a continuing criminal enterprise, which is defined as a violation of the drug statutes where the "violation is part of a continuing series of violations." 21 U.S.C § 848. The Court had to decide whether the phrase "series of violations" refers to one element—a "series"—or whether it creates several elements, or violations, each of which requires unanimity. If the Court concluded that the former approach applied, the jury would simply have to find that the defendant engaged in a series of violations, without regard to whether there was jury unanimity about which violations constituted the series. The Court opted for the latter formulation, and held that a jury must agree unanimously not only that a defendant committed a "continuing series of violations" but also which specific violations made up that "continuing series of violations."

c. Deadlocked Jury

In some instances the jury will report that it is "hung" and is unable to reach a unanimous verdict. If this situation continues the judge may declare a mistrial. A mistrial because of a hung jury usually does not bar a retrial of the defendant. *See* Chapter 21, Double Jeopardy, *infra*. When a jury reports that it is unable to reach a verdict, but the trial court believes that further deliberations may be useful, the court may give the jury what is commonly called an anti-deadlock instruction. Such an instruction is normally given only once, as more than one such instruction can be considered coercive. Judges often give what is known as an "Allen charge," named after the decision in *Allen v. United States*, 164 U.S. 492 (1896). In *Allen*, the Court repeated the approved instruction as follows:

> Although the verdict must be the verdict of each individual juror, and not a mere acquiescence in the conclusion of his fellows, yet they should examine the question submitted with candor, and with a proper regard and deference to the opinions of each other; that it was their duty to decide the case if they could conscientiously do so; that they should listen, with a disposition to be convinced, to each other's arguments; that, if much the larger number were for conviction, a dissenting juror should consider whether his doubt was a reasonable one which made no impression upon the minds of so many men, equally honest, equally intelligent with himself. If, on the other hand, the majority were for acquittal, the minority ought to ask themselves whether they might not reasonably doubt the correctness of a judgment which was not concurred in by the majority.

Some judges opt for a less "coercive" charge. *See also Lowenfield v. Phelps*, 484 U.S. 231 (1988) (a supplemental instruction, which does not speak specifically to minority jurors but does serve the purpose of avoiding a retrial, is permissible after consideration of the context and circumstances in which it is given). While an anti-deadlock instruction may usually be read only once, a judge may send a jury back to continue deliberations without instruction multiple times. There is considerable debate about how often a judge can do this without being coercive. When a jury has been kept together until it appears that there is no probability of agreement upon a verdict, the court may discharge the jury without a verdict.

d. Inconsistent Verdicts

In a trial involving multiple charges, the jury may convict on one or more counts and acquit on others. Inconsistency in the verdict is typically not grounds for a retrial. For example, a jury might decide to convict a defendant of a homicide charge, when the homicide was accomplished with a firearm, and acquit of the charge of illegal possession of a firearm, even if obviously proven. Some states place limits on inconsistent verdicts, but they are rare and specialized.

Food for Thought

In *Ramos v. Louisiana*, 140 S.Ct. 1390 (2020), the Court held that jury verdicts must be unanimous, concluding that the non-unanimous rule was based on racial animus. In *Edwards v. Vannoy*, 141 S.Ct. 1547 (2021), the Court held that *Ramos* should not be retroactively applied to those seeking collateral review of prior convictions based on non-unanimous verdicts. Did *Edwards* reach the correct decision? After all, if non-unanimous requirements were based on racial animus, shouldn't *Ramos'* unanimity requirement be applied retroactively?

C. Selecting Prospective Jurors

In most states, the master list for prospective jurors is drawn from voter registration lists for the county or a list of persons over the age of eighteen holding valid drivers' licenses issued in the county or a compilation from both sources. A computer periodically may generate a randomized jury list of prospective jurors. A court that conducts felony trials will summon as many potential jurors for jury service as deemed necessary for the number of trials requiring juries. The total number of people drawn for jury service on any given day may be called the "jury pool" or the "jury venire." Of that group, the group called to a courtroom for jury selection is called either the "jury panel" or the "jury venire," depending on the usage of the terms in that courthouse. The people actually selected to serve on a jury comprise the "petit jury."

Each person drawn for jury service may be served with a summons directing him or her to report at a specified time and place and to be available for jury service for a period of time. Often, the summons is accompanied by a jury qualification form that must be completed and returned. The form may seek information about the person's address, date of birth, level of education, employer, and members of the immediate family. The form also may seek information about whether the person has ever sued or been sued, as well as information which could statutorily disqualify the person from serving as a juror, *e.g.,* citizenship, inability to speak and understand English, physical or mental disabilities which may prevent effective jury service, a current indictment or a past felony conviction against the prospective juror, or recent jury service. Unless the court determines that the information contained on the form must be kept confidential, or its use restricted in the interest of justice, the information is generally made available to the parties or their attorneys.

1. The Fair Cross-Section Requirement

The Sixth Amendment grants to criminal defendants the right to a "jury of the State and district wherein the crime shall have been committed." From this language has evolved the concept that the petit jury in a criminal case must be selected from a fair cross-section of the community where the crime occurred. Note that this requirement applies only to the jury panel from which the petit jury is selected. The jury that actually decides the case does not have to reflect a cross-section of the community. *Holland v. Illinois*, 493 U.S. 474 (1990). As discussed, *infra*, the Equal Protection Clause of the Fourteenth Amendment dictates restrictions on the composition of the petit jury.

The purposes of the cross-section requirement are: 1) avoiding "the possibility that the composition of juries would be arbitrarily skewed in such a way as to deny criminal defendants the benefit of the common-sense judgment of the community;" 2) avoiding an "appearance of unfairness;" and 3) ensuring against deprivation of "often historically disadvantaged groups of their right as citizens to serve on juries in criminal cases." *Lockhart v. McCree*, 476 U.S. 162 (1986). Most of the early fair cross-section cases concerned the systematic exclusion of racial or ethnic groups from the jury panel. Later cases recognized violations of the fair cross-section requirement on the basis of gender. The Court also found that a petit jury must be selected from a representative cross-section of the community because it is a fundamental aspect of the jury trial guarantee in the Sixth Amendment. A cross-section of the community is composed of "large, distinctive groups" which play "major roles in the community."

Duren v. Missouri

439 U.S. 357 (1979).

MR. JUSTICE WHITE delivered the opinion of the Court.

In *Taylor v. Louisiana*, 419 U.S. 522 (1975), this Court held that systematic exclusion of women during the jury-selection process, resulting in jury pools not "reasonably representative" of the community, denies a criminal defendant his right, under the Sixth and Fourteenth Amendments, to a petit jury selected from a fair cross section of the community. Under the system invalidated in *Taylor*, a woman could not serve on a jury unless she filed a written declaration of her willingness to do so. As a result, although 53% of the persons eligible for jury service were women, less than 1%

of the 1,800 persons whose names were drawn from the jury wheel during the year in which appellant Taylor's jury was chosen were female. At the time of our decision in *Taylor* no other State provided that women could not serve on a jury unless they volunteered to serve. However, five States, including Missouri, provided an automatic exemption from jury service for any women requesting not to serve. Subsequent to *Taylor*, three of these States eliminated this exemption. Only Missouri and Tennessee continue to exempt women from jury service upon request. Today we hold that such systematic exclusion of women that results in jury venires averaging less than 15% female violates the Constitution's fair-cross-section requirement.

Petitioner Duren was indicted in 1975 in the Circuit Court of Jackson County, Mo., for first-degree murder and first-degree robbery. In a pretrial motion to quash his petit jury panel and again in a post-conviction motion for a new trial, he contended that his right to trial by a jury chosen from a fair cross section of his community was denied by provisions of Missouri law granting women who so request an automatic exemption from jury service. Both motions were denied.

The jury-selection process in Jackson County begins with the annual mailing of a questionnaire to persons randomly selected from the Jackson County voter registration list. Approximately 70,000 questionnaires were mailed in 1975. The questionnaire contains a list of occupations and other categories which are the basis under Missouri law for either disqualification[9] or exemption[10] from jury service. Included on the questionnaire is a paragraph prominently addressed "TO WOMEN" that states in part: "Any woman who elects not to serve will fill out this paragraph and mail this questionnaire to the jury commissioner at once." The names of those sent questionnaires are placed in the master jury wheel for Jackson County, except for those returning the questionnaire who indicate disqualification or claim an applicable exemption. Summonses are mailed on a weekly basis to prospective jurors randomly drawn from the jury wheel. The summons, like the questionnaire, contains special directions to men over 65 and to women, this time advising them to return the summons by mail if they desire not to serve. The practice is that even those women who do not return the summons are treated as having claimed exemption if they fail to appear for jury service on the appointed day. Other persons seeking to claim an exemption at this stage must make written or personal application to the court.

According to the 1970 census, 54% of the adult inhabitants of Jackson County were women. For the periods June–October 1975 and January–March 1976, 11,197

---

[9] Felons, illiterates, attorneys, judges, members of the Armed Forces, and certain others are ineligible for jury service.

[10] In addition to women, the following are exempted from jury service upon request: persons over age 65, medical doctors, clergy, teachers, persons who performed jury service within the preceding year, "any person whose absence from his regular place of employment would, in the judgment of the court, tend materially and adversely to affect the public safety, health, welfare or interest," and "any person upon whom service as a juror would in the judgment of the court impose an undue hardship."

persons were summoned and that 2,992 of these or 26.7%, were women. Of those summoned, 741 women and 4,378 men appeared for service. Thus, 14.5% (741 of 5,119) of the persons on the post summons weekly venires during the period in which petitioner's jury was chosen were female. In March 1976, when petitioner's trial began, 15.5% of those on the weekly venires were women (110 of 707). Petitioner's jury was selected from a 53-person panel on which there were 5 women; all 12 jurors chosen were men. The Missouri Supreme Court affirmed.

In certain crucial respects the Missouri Supreme Court misconceived the nature of the fair-cross-section inquiry set forth in *Taylor*. In holding that "petit juries must be drawn from a source fairly representative of the community," we explained that: "jury wheels, pools of names, panels, or venires from which juries are drawn must not systematically exclude distinctive groups in the community and thereby fail to be reasonably representative thereof." In order to establish a *prima facie* violation of the fair-cross-section requirement, defendant must show (1) that the group alleged to be excluded is a "distinctive" group in the community; (2) that the representation of this group in venires from which juries are selected is not fair and reasonable in relation to the number of such persons in the community; and (3) that this underrepresentation is due to systematic exclusion of the group in the jury-selection process.

With respect to the first part of the *prima facie* test, Taylor without doubt established that women "are sufficiently numerous and distinct from men" so that "if they are systematically eliminated from jury panels, the Sixth Amendment's fair-cross-section requirement cannot be satisfied."

The second prong of the *prima facie* case was established by petitioner's statistical presentation. Initially, defendant must demonstrate the percentage of the community made up of the group alleged to be underrepresented, for this is the conceptual benchmark for the Sixth Amendment fair-cross-section requirement. In *Taylor*, the State stipulated that 53% of the population eligible for jury service was female, while petitioner Duren has relied upon a census measurement of the actual percentage of women in the community (54%). Although the Missouri Supreme Court speculated that changing population patterns between 1970 and 1976 and unequal voter registration by men and women rendered the census figures a questionable frame of reference, there is no evidence to suggest that the 1970 census data significantly distorted the percentage of women in Jackson County at the time of trial. Petitioner's presentation was clearly adequate *prima facie* evidence of population characteristics for the purpose of making a fair-cross-section violation. Given petitioner's proof that in the relevant community slightly over half of the adults are women, we disagree with the conclusion of the court below that jury venires containing approximately 15% women are "reasonably representative" of this community. If the percentage of women appearing on jury pools in Jackson County had precisely mirrored the percentage of women in the population, more than one of every two prospective jurors would have been female. In fact, less than one of every six prospective jurors was female; 85% of the average jury was male. Such a gross discrepancy between the percentage of women in jury venires and the percentage of women in the community requires the conclusion that women were not fairly represented in the source from which petit juries were drawn in Jackson County.

In order to establish a *prima facie* case, it was necessary for petitioner to show that the underrepresentation of women, generally and on his venire, was due to their systematic exclusion in the jury-selection process. Petitioner's proof met this requirement. His undisputed demonstration that a large discrepancy occurred not just occasionally but in every weekly venire for a period of nearly a year manifestly indicates that the cause of the underrepresentation was systematic—that is, inherent in the particular jury-selection process utilized. Duren's statistics and other evidence also established when in the selection process the systematic exclusion took place. There was no indication that underrepresentation of women occurred at the first stage of the selection process—the questionnaire canvass of persons randomly selected from the relevant voter registration list. The first sign of a systematic discrepancy is at the next stage—the construction of the jury wheel from which persons are randomly summoned for service. Less than 30% of those summoned were female, demonstrating that a substantially larger number of women answering the questionnaire claimed either ineligibility or exemption from jury service. Moreover, at the summons stage women were not only given another opportunity to claim exemption, but also were presumed to have claimed exemption when they did not respond to the summons. Thus, the percentage of women at the final, venire, stage (14.5%) was much lower than the percentage of women who were summoned for service (26.7%). The resulting disproportionate and consistent exclusion of women from the jury wheel and at the venire stage was quite obviously due to the system by which juries were selected. Petitioner demonstrated that the underrepresentation of women in the final pool of prospective jurors was due to the operation of Missouri's exemption criteria—whether the automatic exemption for women or other statutory exemptions—as implemented in Jackson County. Women were therefore systematically underrepresented within the meaning of *Taylor*.

Once defendant has made a *prima facie* showing of an infringement of his constitutional right to a jury drawn from a fair cross section of the community, the State bears the burden of justifying this infringement by showing attainment of a fair cross section to be incompatible with a significant state interest. Assuming, arguendo, that the exemptions mentioned would justify failure to achieve a fair community cross section on jury venires, the State must demonstrate that these exemptions caused the underrepresentation. The record contains no such proof, and mere suggestions or assertions to that effect are insufficient.

Chapter 17 Jury Trials

The other possible cause of the disproportionate exclusion of women on Jackson County jury venires is, of course, the automatic exemption for women. Neither the Missouri Supreme Court nor respondent has offered any substantial justification for this exemption. Counsel for respondent ventured that the only state interest advanced by the exemption is safeguarding the important role played by women in home and family life. But exempting all women because of the preclusive domestic responsibilities of some women is insufficient justification for their disproportionate exclusion on jury venires. What we stated in *Taylor* with respect to the system there challenged is equally applicable to Missouri's "opt out" exemption: "It is untenable to suggest these days that it would be a special hardship for each and every woman to perform jury service or that society cannot spare any women from their present duties. This may be the case with many, and it may be burdensome to sort out those who should be exempted from those who should serve. But that task is performed in the case of men and the administrative convenience in dealing with women as a class is insufficient justification for diluting the quality of community judgment represented by the jury in criminal trials. If it was ever the case that women were unqualified to sit on juries or were so situated that none of them should be required to perform jury service, that time has long since passed."

We recognize that a State may have an important interest in assuring that those members of the family responsible for the care of children are available to do so. An exemption appropriately tailored to this interest would survive a fair-cross-section challenge. However, the constitutional guarantee to a jury drawn from a fair cross section of the community requires that States exercise proper caution in exempting broad categories of persons from jury service. Although most occupational and other reasonable exemptions may inevitably involve some degree of overinclusiveness or underinclusiveness, any category expressly limited to a group in the community of sufficient magnitude and distinctiveness so as to be within the fair-cross-section requirement—such as women—runs the danger of resulting in underrepresentation sufficient to constitute a *prima facie* violation of that constitutional requirement. We repeat the observation made in *Taylor* that it is unlikely that reasonable exemptions, such as those based on special hardship, incapacity, or community needs, "would pose substantial threats that the remaining pool of jurors would not be representative of the community."

> **FYI**
>
> Justice Rehnquist alone dissented in both *Taylor* and *Duren*, lamenting in *Duren*, "Eventually, the Court will insist that women be treated identically to men for purposes of jury selection.

Points for Discussion

a. Who Is "Distinctive"?

A jury panel from which a cognizable class of citizens has been systematically excluded is not a representative jury. Thus far, the Court has not extended the category of those classes of citizens who are "distinctive" beyond the constitutionally "suspect classes" (*e.g.,* racial minorities and women). *See Castaneda v. Partida*, 430 U.S. 482 (1977) (racial minorities constitute such a class). Young adults and college students are not a distinctive group. Likewise, the exclusion of young people that results from the intermittent recompiling of the jury lists has been justified in the interest of judicial economy. *See Hamling v. United States*, 418 U.S. 87 (1974).

Food for Thought

If convicted felons are excluded from jury service, how might you argue that they represent a "distinctive" class under *Taylor*?

b. Unvaccinated Jurors

In *United States v. Colon*, 64 F.4th 589 (4th Cir. 2023), the court held that a trial court judge could exclude jurors who were not vaccinated against Covid-19 without violating the fair cross-section guarantee. The trial took place during the height of the Delta variant of Covid-19 in 2021. The court concluded that the unvaccinated individuals posed a risk to other jurors and anyone else in the courtroom.

2. Jury Selection Process

In the typical large urban courthouse, a large pool of 300 to 500 people is called on any given day for potential jury service. When a judge informs the clerk that a jury is needed, the clerk randomly calls out the numbers of forty to seventy jurors to participate in the *voir dire*, or jury selection, process. As their names are called, the jurors are tentatively seated in the jury box to be examined under oath concerning their qualifications. If jurors are excused from service following their examination, the judge's clerk draws additional names until they are replaced.

Because of its central role in the selection of a fair and impartial jury, the *voir dire* examination is one of the most important parts of the trial. Its importance is augmented by the fact that it is the first opportunity afforded to counsel to address the jury in connection with the case. Impressions that the jurors have about the case and about counsel at the conclusion of the examination may last throughout the entire trial.

There are two kinds of challenges to jurors. The first is known as a "challenge for cause." A challenge for cause can be made, and will be sustained by the judge, whenever it appears that a juror will not be able to be fair and impartial in a case. That may happen by the juror's own admission or through questioning that makes the bias known. Examples of categories of inquiries plumbed for challenges for cause are: prior knowledge about the parties, judge, witnesses, or the crime; attitudes or prejudices that will likely have a bearing on the case; prior experience as a crime victim, a law enforcement officer, or as a juror; inability to follow the presumption of innocence or other rules of law. The number of jurors who may be struck by challenges for cause is unlimited.

Practice Pointer

The purposes of *voir dire* examination are to determine any possible basis for challenging jurors for cause, to develop background information that can be considered so that peremptory challenges can be exercised intelligently, to learn about jurors' backgrounds and receptiveness to particular arguments, and to educate jurors about the law and factors at issue in the case.

If there are reasonable grounds to believe that a juror cannot render a fair and impartial verdict, the juror shall be excused for cause. However, disqualification is not required merely because a juror does not understand or immediately accept every legal concept presented during *voir dire*. The test is not whether a juror agrees with the law when it is presented; it is whether, after having heard all of the evidence, the prospective juror can adjust his views to the requirements of the law and render a fair and impartial verdict. Even if the parties fail to make a challenge for cause, the court has an affirmative duty to explore undisclosed information of which it is aware affecting the qualification of an individual juror. The court may exercise considerable discretion in deciding whether to excuse an individual juror for cause. Usually, to show prejudice from any abuse of discretion in denying a for cause challenge, the party challenging the juror must first use all peremptory challenges. *Ross v. Oklahoma*, 487 U.S. 81 (1988).

The other kind of challenge to jurors is the peremptory challenge. While peremptory challenges are not constitutionally required, the peremptory challenge is so historically ingrained that every jurisdiction provides parties with a set number of peremptory challenges. The parties can exercise their peremptory challenges without giving any reason whatsoever (with the limited exception described in Part 3, *infra*). If multiple defendants are being tried, each defendant gets his own set of peremptories, and the prosecution, in turn, gets its allotted number for each defendant added together.

FYI

In 2021, Arizona became the first state to prohibit peremptory challenges. The Chief Justice of Arizona's Supreme Court described the action as follows: "Eliminating peremptory strikes of jurors will reduce the opportunity for misuse of the jury selection process and will improve jury participation and fairness."

In federal court, the judge typically asks the questions and conducts the *voir dire*, and the lawyers have a very limited role. In most state courts, the judges permit far more involvement by the lawyers. Even if the court conducts the examination, the parties are often entitled to submit supplemental inquiries. Moreover, the initial responses of individual jurors to questions may require further inquiry. There are also some questions, such as those covering sensitive matters, which are best conducted through a private examination of individual jurors, either at the bench or in the judge's chambers. As another example, the ABA Standards Relating to Fair Trial and Free Press, §§ 3, 4, recommends the separate examination of jurors concerning pretrial publicity in order to avoid the incidental exposure of other members of the panel to affirmative responses.

Hypo: *The Equivocal Juror*

On *voir dire*, a prospective juror states that she will "try to be fair." Before making that statement, she discloses the fact that she has been the victim of a similar crime. When the judge asks follow-up questions regarding her ability to be fair, she responds that she "might" be able to put aside her prior experience, and that she would "want to put her personal stuff aside." Should the juror be excused if she cannot unequivocally state that she can and will be fair? *See United States v. Kechedzian*, 902 F.3d 1023 (9th Cir. 2018).

3. Constitutional Limits on Peremptory Challenges

Traditionally, a party could exercise peremptory challenges without offering any justification or explanation. The issue eventually arose, however, regarding the constitutionality of striking potential jurors based on race. In *Swain v. Alabama*, 380 U.S. 202 (1965), the Court held that the defendant's showing that no African American had served on a petit jury for a number of years did not give rise to an inference of systematic discrimination on the part of the State through its use of peremptory challenges. However, in the

Food for Thought

Why do you think parties get peremptory challenges?

watershed case of *Batson v. Kentucky*, <u>476 U.S. 79 (1986)</u>, the Court rejected that conclusion. In *Batson*, the Court described the basic principles that apply to challenges against the exercise of peremptory challenges based on race:

A defendant may establish a *prima facie* case of purposeful discrimination in selection of the petit jury solely on evidence concerning the prosecutor's exercise of peremptory challenges at the defendant's trial. To establish such a case, the defendant first must show that he is a member of a cognizable racial group, and that the prosecutor has exercised peremptory challenges to remove from the venire members of the defendant's race. Second, the defendant is entitled to rely on the fact, as to which there can be no dispute, that peremptory challenges constitute a jury selection practice that permits "those to discriminate who are of a mind to discriminate." Finally, defendant must show that these facts and any other relevant circumstances raise an inference that the prosecutor used that practice to exclude veniremen from the petit jury on account of their race. This combination of factors in the empanelling of the petit jury, as in the selection of the venire, raises the necessary inference of purposeful discrimination.

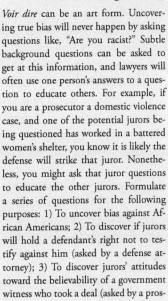

Food for Thought

Voir dire can be an art form. Uncovering true bias will never happen by asking questions like, "Are you racist?" Subtle background questions can be asked to get at this information, and lawyers will often use one person's answers to a question to educate others. For example, if you are a prosecutor a domestic violence case, and one of the potential jurors being questioned has worked in a battered women's shelter, you know it is likely the defense will strike that juror. Nonetheless, you might ask that juror questions to educate the other jurors. Formulate a series of questions for the following purposes: 1) To uncover bias against African Americans; 2) To discover if jurors will hold a defendant's right not to testify against him (asked by a defense attorney); 3) To discover jurors' attitudes toward the believability of a government witness who took a deal (asked by a prosecutor).

In deciding whether defendant has made the requisite showing, the trial court should consider all relevant circumstances. For example, a "pattern" of strikes against black jurors included in the particular venire might give rise to an inference of discrimination. Similarly, the prosecutor's questions and statements during *voir dire* examination and in exercising his challenges may support or refute an inference of discriminatory purpose. These examples are merely illustrative. We have confidence that trial judges, experienced in supervising *voir dire*, will be able to decide if the circumstances concerning the prosecutor's use of peremptory challenges creates a *prima facie* case of discrimination against black jurors.

Once defendant makes a *prima facie* showing, the burden shifts to the State to come forward with a neutral explanation for challenging black jurors. Though this requirement imposes a limitation in some cases on the full peremptory character of the historic challenge, we emphasize that the prosecutor's explanation need not rise to the level justifying exercise of a challenge for cause. But the prosecutor may not rebut the defendant's *prima facie* case of discrimination by stating merely that he challenged jurors of the defendant's race on the assumption—or his intuitive judgment—that they would be partial to the defendant because of their shared race. The core guarantee of equal protection, ensuring citizens that their State will not discriminate on account of race, would be meaningless were we to approve the exclusion of jurors on the basis of such assumptions, which arise solely from the jurors' race. Nor may the prosecutor rebut the defendant's case merely by denying that he had a discriminatory motive or "affirming his good faith in making individual selections." If these general assertions were accepted as rebutting a defendant's *prima facie* case, the Equal Protection Clause "would be but a vain and illusory requirement." The prosecutor therefore must articulate a neutral explanation related to the particular case to be tried. The trial court then will have the duty to determine if the defendant has established purposeful discrimination.

After *Batson*, several cases significantly broadened its scope. First, in *Powers v. Ohio*, <u>499 U.S. 400 (1991)</u>, a white defendant alleged that the prosecutor used peremptory challenges to exclude African American jurors based on their race. Using third-party standing principles, the Court held that the white defendant had standing to assert an equal protection claim on behalf of the excluded African American jurors. Second, the Court held that a criminal defendant cannot engage in purposeful discrimination in the exercise of peremptory challenges. *Georgia v. McCollum*, <u>505 U.S. 42 (1992)</u>. The Court relied on *Powers* to find that the prosecution had third-party standing to assert the equal protection rights of excluded jurors. "As the representative of all its citizens, the State is the logical and proper party to assert the invasion of the constitutional rights of the excluded jurors in a criminal trial." Third, the Court emphasized that *Batson* applied to both race and gender. In *Hernandez v. New York*, <u>500 U.S. 352 (1991)</u>, the Court found that Hispanics have a right to be free from discrimination in jury selection. Then, in

Food for Thought

While clearly illegal under *Batson*, is there any legitimacy to a decision to strike a juror based on his or her race? Assume the parties receive very little printed information about the jurors and the judge conducts a fairly limited *voir dire* to determine only strikes for cause. If you represent an African American man accused of a crime against a white person, would you consider striking white jurors? Is there a legitimate purpose?

J.E.B. v. Alabama ex rel. T.B., 511 U.S. 127 (1994), the Court held that the Equal Protection Clause forbids the exercise of a peremptory challenge based upon the gender of a prospective juror.

A generation after *Batson*, the Court continued to offer guidance to lower courts for applying the steps of the constitutional analysis.

Take Note

Under *Batson*, is a judge required to undertake a comparative examination of struck jurors against jurors who were not struck? In *Chamberlin v. Fisher*, 885 F.3d 832 (5th Cir. 2018), the court held that a comparative examination was not required. A trial judge need only ensure that a juror was dismissed for a permissible reason.

Miller-El v. Dretke

545 U.S. 231 (2005).

JUSTICE SOUTER delivered the opinion of the Court.

The numbers describing the prosecution's use of peremptories [in defendant's capital murder trial] are remarkable. Out of 20 black members of the 108-person venire panel for Miller-El's trial, only 1 served. Although 9 were excused for cause or by agreement, 10 were peremptorily struck by the prosecution. More powerful than these bare statistics are side-by-side comparisons of some black venire panelists who were struck and white panelists allowed to serve. If a prosecutor's proffered reason for striking a black panelist applies just as well to an otherwise-similar nonblack who is permitted to serve, that is evidence tending to prove purposeful discrimination to be considered at *Batson*'s third step. The prosecution used its second peremptory strike to exclude Billy Jean Fields, a black man who expressed unwavering support for the death penalty. On the questionnaire filled out by all panel members before individual examination on the stand, Fields said that he believed in capital punishment, and during questioning he disclosed his belief that the State acts on God's behalf when it imposes the death penalty. "Therefore, if the State exacts death, then that's what it should be." He testified that he had no religious or philosophical reservations about the death penalty and that the death penalty deterred crime. He twice averred, without apparent hesitation, that he could sit on Miller-El's jury and make a decision to impose this penalty. Although at one point, Fields indicated that the possibility of rehabilitation might be relevant to the likelihood that a defendant would commit future acts of violence, he responded to ensuing questions by saying that although he believed anyone could be rehabilitated, this belief would not stand in the way of a decision to impose the death penalty.

Hear It

You can listen to the oral argument in *Miller-El* at: http://www.oyez.org/cases/2000-2009/2004/2004_03_9659.

Fields was struck peremptorily by the prosecution, with prosecutor James Nelson offering a race-neutral reason: "We have concern with reference to some of his statements as to the death penalty in that he said that he could only give death if he thought a person could not be rehabilitated and he later made the comment that any person could be rehabilitated if they find God or are introduced to God and the fact that we have a concern that his religious feelings may affect his jury service in this case." Thus, Nelson simply mischaracterized Fields's testimony. He represented that Fields said he would not vote for death if rehabilitation was possible, whereas Fields unequivocally stated that he could impose the death penalty regardless of the possibility of rehabilitation. Perhaps Nelson misunderstood, but unless he had an ulterior reason for keeping Fields off the jury we think he would have proceeded differently. In light of Fields's outspoken support for the death penalty, we expect the prosecutor would have cleared up any misunderstanding by asking further questions before getting to the point of exercising a strike.

If, indeed, Fields's thoughts on rehabilitation did make the prosecutor uneasy, he should have worried about a number of white panel members he accepted with no evident reservations. Sandra Hearn said that she believed in the death penalty "if a criminal cannot be rehabilitated and continues to commit the same type of crime." Hearn went so far as to express doubt that at the penalty phase of a capital case she could conclude that a convicted murderer "would probably commit some criminal acts of violence in the future." "People change," she said, making it hard to assess the risk of someone's future dangerousness. "The evidence would have to be awful strong." But the prosecution did not respond to Hearn the way it did to Fields, and without delving into her views about rehabilitation with any further question, it raised no objection to her serving on the jury. White panelist Mary Witt said she would take the possibility of rehabilitation into account in deciding at the penalty phase of the trial about a defendant's probability of future dangerousness, but the prosecutors asked her no further question about her views on reformation, and they accepted her as a juror. Latino venireman Fernando Gutierrez, who served on the jury, said that he would consider the death penalty for someone who could not be rehabilitated, but the prosecutors did not question him further about this view. In sum, nonblack jurors whose remarks on rehabilitation could well have signaled a limit on their willingness to impose a death sentence were not questioned further and drew no objection, but the prosecution expressed apprehension about a black juror's belief in the possibility of reformation even though he repeatedly stated his approval of the death penalty and testified that he could impose it according to state legal standards even when the alternative sentence of life imprisonment would give a defendant (like everyone else in the world) the opportunity to reform. In sum, when we look for nonblack jurors similarly situated to Fields, we find strong similarities as well as some differences. But the differences seem far from significant, particularly when we read Fields's *voir dire* testimony in its entirety. Upon that reading, Fields should have been an ideal juror in the eyes of a prosecutor seeking a death sentence, and the prosecutors' explanations for the strike cannot reasonably be accepted.

The prosecution's proffered reasons for striking Joe Warren, another black venireman, are comparably unlikely. Warren gave this answer when he was asked what the death penalty accomplished: "I don't know. It's really hard to say because I know sometimes you feel that it might help to deter crime and then you feel that the person is not really suffering. You're taking the suffering away from him. So it's like I said, sometimes you have mixed feelings about whether or not this is punishment or, you know, you're relieving personal punishment." The prosecution said nothing about these remarks when it struck Warren from the panel, but prosecutor Paul Macaluso referred to this answer as the first of his reasons when he testified at the later *Batson* hearing: "I thought [Warren's statements on *voir dire*] were inconsistent responses. At one point he says, you know, on a case-by-case basis and at another point he said, well, I think—I got the impression, at least, that he suggested that the death penalty was an easy way out, that they should be made to suffer more." On the face of it, the explanation is reasonable from the State's point of view, but its plausibility is severely undercut by the prosecution's failure to object to other panel members who expressed views much like Warren's. Sandra Jenkins, whom the State accepted (but who was struck by the defense) testified that she thought "a harsher treatment is life imprisonment with no parole." Leta Girard, accepted by the State (but also struck by the defense) gave her opinion that "living sometimes is a worse—is worse to me than dying would be." The fact that Macaluso's reason also applied to these other panel members, most of them white, none of them struck, is evidence of pretext.

The suggestion of pretext is not mitigated much by Macaluso's explanation that Warren was struck when the State had 10 peremptory challenges left and could afford to be liberal in using them. If that were the explanation for striking Warren and later accepting panel members who thought death would be too easy, the prosecutors should have struck Sandra Jenkins, whom they examined and accepted before Warren. Indeed, the disparate treatment is the more remarkable for the fact that the prosecutors repeatedly questioned Warren on his capacity and willingness to impose a sentence of death and elicited statements of his ability to do so if the evidence supported that result and the answer to each special question was yes, whereas the record before us discloses no attempt to determine whether Jenkins would be able to vote for death in spite of her view that it was easy on the convict. Yet the prosecutors accepted the white panel member Jenkins and struck the black venireman Warren.

When illegitimate grounds like race are in issue, a prosecutor simply has got to state his reasons as best he can and stand or fall on the plausibility of the reasons he gives. A *Batson* challenge does not call for a mere exercise in thinking up any rational basis. If the stated reason does not hold up, its pretextual significance does not fade because a trial judge, or an appeals court, can imagine a reason that might not have been shown up as false.

The whole of the *voir dire* testimony subject to consideration casts the prosecution's reasons for striking Warren in an implausible light. Comparing his strike with the treatment of panel members who expressed similar views supports a conclusion that race was significant in determining who was challenged and who was not. We do not decide whether there were white jurors who expressed ambivalence just as much as these black members of the venire panel. There is no need to go into these instances, for the prosecutors' treatment of Fields and Warren supports stronger arguments that *Batson* was violated.

The case for discrimination goes beyond these comparisons to include broader patterns of practice during the jury selection. The prosecution's shuffling of the venire panel, its enquiry into views on the death penalty, its questioning about minimum acceptable sentences: all indicate decisions probably based on race. Finally, the appearance of discrimination is confirmed by widely known evidence of the general policy of the Dallas County District Attorney's Office to exclude black venire members from juries at the time Miller-El's jury was selected. The first clue to the prosecutors' intentions, distinct from the peremptory challenges themselves, is their resort during *voir dire* to a procedure known in Texas as the jury shuffle. In the State's criminal practice, either side may literally reshuffle the cards bearing panel members' names, thus rearranging the order in which members of a venire panel are seated and reached for questioning. Once the order is established, the panel members seated at the back are likely to escape *voir dire* altogether, for those not questioned by the end of the week are dismissed. In this case, the prosecution and then the defense shuffled the cards at the beginning of the first week of *voir dire*; the record does not reflect the changes in order. At the beginning of the second week, when a number of black members were seated at the front of the panel, the prosecution shuffled. At the beginning of the third week, the first four panel members were black. The prosecution shuffled, and these black panel members ended up at the back. Then the defense shuffled, and the black panel members again appeared at the front. The prosecution requested another shuffle, but the trial court refused. Finally, the defense shuffled at the beginning of the fourth and fifth weeks of *voir dire*; the record does not reflect the panel's racial composition before or after those shuffles. The State notes that there might be racially neutral reasons for shuffling the jury, but no racially neutral reason has ever been offered, and nothing stops the suspicion of discriminatory intent from rising to an inference.

The next body of evidence that the State was trying to avoid black jurors is the contrasting *voir dire* questions posed respectively to black and nonblack panel members, on two different subjects. First, there were the prosecutors' statements preceding questions about a potential juror's thoughts on capital punishment. Some of these prefatory statements were cast in general terms, but some followed the so-called graphic script, describing the method of execution in rhetorical and clinical detail. It is intended, Miller-El contends, to prompt some expression of hesitation to consider the death penalty and thus to elicit plausibly neutral grounds for a peremptory strike of a potential juror subjected to it, if not a strike for cause. If the graphic script is given to a higher proportion of blacks than whites, this is evidence that prosecutors more often wanted blacks off the jury, absent some neutral and extenuating explanation. Of the 10 nonblacks whose questionnaires expressed ambivalence or opposition, only 30% received the graphic treatment. But of the seven blacks who expressed ambivalence or opposition, 86% heard the graphic script. The reasonable inference is that race was the major consideration when the prosecution chose to follow the graphic script.

The same is true for another kind of disparate questioning, which might fairly be called trickery. The prosecutors asked members of the panel how low a sentence they would consider imposing for murder. Most potential jurors were told that Texas law provided for a minimum term of five years, but some were not, and if a panel member then insisted on a minimum above five years, the prosecutor would suppress his normal preference for tough jurors and claim cause to strike.

It is entirely true that prosecutors struck a number of nonblack members of the panel (as well as black members) for cause or by agreement before they reached the point in the standard *voir dire* sequence to question about minimum punishment. But this is no answer; 8 of the 11 nonblack individuals who voiced opposition or ambivalence were asked about the acceptable minimum only after being told what state law required. Hence, only 27% of nonblacks questioned on the subject who expressed these views were subjected to the trick question, as against 100% of black members. The implication of race in the prosecutors' choice of questioning cannot be explained away.

In the course of drawing a jury to try a black defendant, 10 of the 11 qualified black venire panel members were peremptorily struck. At least two of them, Fields and Warren, were ostensibly acceptable to prosecutors seeking a death verdict, and Fields was ideal. The prosecutors' chosen race-neutral reasons for the strikes do not hold up and are so far at odds with the evidence that pretext is the fair conclusion, indicating the very discrimination the explanations were meant to deny. The strikes that drew these incredible explanations occurred in a selection process replete with evidence that the prosecutors were selecting and rejecting potential jurors because of race. At least two of the jury shuffles conducted by the State make no sense except as efforts to delay consideration of black jury panelists to the end of the week, when they might not even be reached. The State has never offered any other explanation. Nor has the State denied that disparate lines of questioning were pursued: 53% of black panelists but only 3% of nonblacks were questioned with a graphic script meant to induce qualms about applying the death penalty (and thus explain a strike), and 100% of blacks but only 27% of nonblacks were subjected to a trick question about the minimum acceptable penalty for murder, meant to induce a disqualifying answer. The State's attempts to explain the prosecutors' questioning of particular witnesses on nonracial grounds fit the evidence less well than the racially discriminatory hypothesis.

If anything more is needed for an undeniable explanation of what was going on, history supplies it. The prosecutors took their cues from a 20-year old manual of tips on jury selection, as shown by their notes of the race of each potential juror. By the time a jury was chosen, the State had peremptorily challenged 12% of qualified nonblack panel members, but eliminated 91% of the black ones. It blinks reality to deny that the State struck Fields and Warren, included in that 91%, because they were black. The strikes correlate with no fact as well as they correlate with race, and they occurred during a selection infected by shuffling and disparate questioning that race explains better than any race-neutral reason advanced by the State. The State's pretextual positions confirm Miller-El's claim, and the prosecutors' own notes proclaim that the Sparling Manual's emphasis on race was on their minds when they considered every potential juror.

The state court's conclusion that the prosecutors' strikes of Fields and Warren were not racially determined is wrong to a clear and convincing degree; the state court's conclusion was unreasonable as well as erroneous. The judgment of the Court of Appeals is reversed, and the case is remanded for entry of judgment for petitioner together with orders of appropriate relief.

It is so ordered.

JUSTICE BREYER, concurring.

In *Batson v. Kentucky*, 476 U.S. 79 (1986), the Court adopted a burden-shifting rule designed to ferret out the unconstitutional use of race in jury selection. In his separate opinion, Justice Thurgood Marshall predicted that the Court's rule would not achieve its goal. The only way to "end the racial discrimination that peremptories inject into the jury-selection process," he concluded, was to "eliminate peremptory challenges entirely." Today's case reinforces Justice Marshall's concerns. This case illustrates the practical problems of proof that Justice Marshall described. Miller-El marshaled extensive evidence of racial bias. Despite the strength of his claim, Miller-El's challenge has resulted in 17 years of largely unsuccessful and protracted litigation—including 8 different judicial proceedings and 8 different judicial opinions, and involving 23 judges, of whom 6 found the *Batson* standard violated and 16 the contrary.

The complexity of this process reflects the difficulty of finding a legal test that will objectively measure the inherently subjective reasons that underlie use of a peremptory challenge. *Batson* seeks to square this circle by (1) requiring defendants to establish a prima facie case of discrimination, (2) asking prosecutors then to offer a race-neutral explanation for their use of the peremptory, and then (3) requiring defendants to prove that the neutral reason offered is pretextual. But *Batson* embodies defects intrinsic to the task. At *Batson*'s first step, litigants remain free to misuse peremptory challenges as long as the strikes fall below the *prima facie* threshold level. At *Batson*'s second step, prosecutors need only tender a neutral reason, not a "persuasive, or even plausible" one. *Purkett v. Elem*, 514 U.S. 765 (1995) (per curiam). Most importantly, at step three, *Batson* asks judges to engage in the awkward, sometime hopeless, task of second-guessing a prosecutor's instinctive judgment—the underlying basis for which may be invisible even to the prosecutor exercising the challenge. Given the inevitably clumsy fit between any objectively measurable standard and the subjective decisionmaking at issue, I am not surprised to find studies and anecdotal reports suggesting that, despite *Batson*, the discriminatory use of peremptory challenges remains a problem.

Practical problems of proof to the side, peremptory challenges seem increasingly anomalous in our judicial system. The use of race-and gender-based stereotypes in the jury-selection process seems better organized and more systematized than ever before. *See, e.g.,* Post, *A Loaded Box of Stereotypes: Despite "Batson," Race, Gender Play Big Roles in Jury Selection*, NAT. L. J., Apr. 25, 2005, pp. 1, 18 (discussing common reliance on race and gender in jury selection). For example, one jury-selection guide counsels attorneys to perform a "demographic analysis" that assigns numerical points to characteristics such as age, occupation, and marital status—in addition to race as well as gender. *See* V. STARR & A. MCCORMICK, JURY SELECTION 193 (3d ed. 2001). Thus, in a hypothetical dispute between a white landlord and an African American tenant, the authors suggest awarding two points to an African-American venire member while subtracting one point from her white counterpart. *Id.,* at 197. These examples reflect a professional effort to fulfill the lawyer's obligation to help his or her client. Nevertheless, the outcome in terms of jury selection is the same as it would be were the motive less benign. As long as that is so, the law's anti-discrimination command and a peremptory jury-selection system that permits or encourages the use of stereotypes work at cross-purposes.

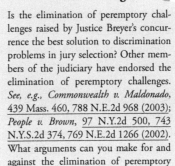

Food for Thought

Is the elimination of peremptory challenges raised by Justice Breyer's concurrence the best solution to discrimination problems in jury selection? Other members of the judiciary have endorsed the elimination of peremptory challenges. *See, e.g., Commonwealth v. Maldonado*, 439 Mass. 460, 788 N.E.2d 968 (2003); *People v. Brown*, 97 N.Y.2d 500, 743 N.Y.S.2d 374, 769 N.E.2d 1266 (2002). What arguments can you make for and against the elimination of peremptory strikes?

I recognize that peremptory challenges have a long historical pedigree. They may help to reassure a party of the fairness of the jury. But long ago, Blackstone recognized the peremptory challenge as an "arbitrary and capricious species of a challenge." 4

W. BLACKSTONE, COMMENTARIES ON THE LAWS OF ENGLAND 346 (1769). If used to express stereotypical judgments about race, gender, religion, or national origin, peremptory challenges betray the jury's democratic origins and undermine its representative function. *See* 1 A. DE TOCQUEVILLE, DEMOCRACY IN AMERICA 287 (H. Reeve transl. 1900). In light of the considerations I have mentioned, I believe it necessary to reconsider *Batson*'s test and the peremptory challenge system as a whole. With that qualification.

Flowers v. Mississippi

139 S.Ct. 2228 (2019).

JUSTICE KAVANAUGH delivered the opinion of the Court.

In *Batson v. Kentucky*, 476 U.S. 79 (1986), this Court ruled that a State may not discriminate on the basis of race when exercising peremptory challenges against prospective jurors in a criminal trial. The events that gave rise to this case took place in Winona, Mississippi, a small town in Mississippi. The town is about 53 percent black and 46 percent white. In 1996, Bertha Tardy, Robert Golden, Derrick Stewart, and Carmen Rigby were murdered at the Tardy Furniture store. All four worked at the store. Three of the victims were white; one was black. In 1997, the State charged Curtis Flowers with murder. Flowers is black. Since then, Flowers has been tried six separate times for the murders.

Other than voting, serving on a jury is the most substantial opportunity that most citizens have to participate in the democratic process. This case arises at the intersection of the peremptory challenge and the Equal Protection Clause. Ratified in 1868 in the wake of the Civil War, the Equal Protection Clause of the Fourteenth Amendment provides that no State shall "deny to any person within its jurisdiction the equal protection of the laws." A primary objective of the Equal Protection Clause was "the freedom of the slave race, the security and firm establishment of that freedom, and the protection of the newly-made freeman and citizen from the oppressions of those who had formerly exercised unlimited dominion over him." *Slaughter-House Cases*, 21 L.Ed. 394 (1873). In 1880, the Court decided *Strauder v. West Virginia*, 100 U.S. 303. That case concerned a West Virginia statute that allowed whites only to serve as jurors. The Court held the law unconstitutional. The Fourteenth Amendment required "that the law in the States shall be the same for the black as for the white; that all persons, whether colored or white, shall stand equal before the laws of the States, and, in regard to the colored race, for whose protection the amendment was primarily designed, that no discrimination shall be made against them by law because of their color." "The very fact that colored people are singled out and expressly denied by a statute all right to participate in the administration of the law, as jurors, because of their color, though they are citizens, and may be in other respects fully qualified, is practically a brand upon them, affixed by the law, an assertion of their inferiority, and a stimulant to that race prejudice which is an impediment to securing to individuals of the race that equal justice which the law aims to secure to all others."

After *Strauder*, even though laws barring blacks from serving on juries were unconstitutional, many jurisdictions employed discriminatory tools to prevent black persons from being called for jury service. When those tactics failed, or were invalidated, prosecutors could still exercise peremptory strikes in individual cases to remove most or all black prospective jurors. The freedom to exercise peremptory strikes for any reason meant that "the problem of racial exclusion from jury service" remained "widespread" and "deeply entrenched." 5 U. S. Commission on Civil Rights Report 90 (1961). Defense counsel could use—and routinely did—peremptory challenges to strike all black prospective jurors in cases involving white defendants and black victims. In the aftermath of *Strauder*, the exclusion of black jurors became more covert and less overt—often accomplished through peremptory challenges. In *Batson*, the Court emphasized that "the central concern" of the Fourteenth Amendment "was to put an end to governmental discrimination on account of race." *Batson* noted that Swain had left prosecutors' peremptory challenges "largely immune from constitutional scrutiny." Under *Batson*, once a *prima facie* case of discrimination has been shown, the State must provide race-neutral reasons for its peremptory strikes. The trial judge must determine whether the prosecutor's stated reasons were the actual reasons or instead were a pretext for discrimination.

Four parts of *Batson* warrant particular emphasis here. First, *Batson* rejected *Swain*'s insistence that a defendant demonstrate a history of racially discriminatory strikes in order to make out a claim of race discrimination. A criminal defendant could show "purposeful discrimination in selection of the petit jury solely on evidence concerning the prosecutor's exercise of peremptory challenges at the defendant's trial." Second, *Batson* rejected *Swain*'s statement that a prosecutor could strike a black juror based on an assumption or belief that the black juror would favor a black defendant. Third, *Batson* did not accept the argument that race-based peremptories should be permissible because black, white, Asian, and Hispanic defendants and jurors were "equally" subject to race-based discrimination. Each removal of an individual juror because of his or her race is a constitutional violation. Fourth, *Batson* did not accept the argument that race-based peremptories are permissible because both the prosecution and defense could employ them in any individual case and in essence balance things out. Even a single instance of race discrimination against a prospective juror is impermissible. Because blacks are a minority in most jurisdictions, prosecutors often have more peremptory strikes than there are black prospective jurors on a particular panel. Equal justice under law requires a criminal trial free of racial discrimination in the jury selection process. *Batson* ended the widespread practice in which prosecutors could (and often would) routinely strike all black prospective jurors in cases involving black defendants. *Batson* sought to protect the rights of defendants and jurors, and to enhance public confidence in the fairness of the criminal justice system.

In the decades since *Batson*, this Court's cases have vigorously enforced and reinforced the decision, and guarded against any backsliding. A defendant of any race may raise a *Batson* claim, and a defendant may raise a *Batson* claim even if the defendant and the excluded juror are of different races. Moreover, *Batson* now applies to gender discrimination, to a criminal defendant's peremptory strikes, and to civil cases.

Batson's holding raised several important evidentiary and procedural issues, three of which we underscore. First, our precedents allow criminal defendants raising *Batson* challenges to present a variety of evidence to support a claim that a prosecutor's peremptory strikes were made on the basis of race. Defendants may present: statistical evidence about the prosecutor's use of peremptory strikes against black prospective jurors as compared to white prospective jurors in the case; evidence of a prosecutor's disparate questioning and investigation of black and white prospective jurors in the case; side-by-side comparisons of black prospective jurors who were struck and white prospective jurors who were not struck in the case; a prosecutor's misrepresentations of the record when defending the strikes during the *Batson* hearing; relevant history of the State's peremptory strikes in past cases; or other relevant circumstances that bear upon the issue of racial discrimination. Second, the job of enforcing *Batson* rests first and foremost with trial judges. Once a *prima facie* case of racial discrimination has been established, the prosecutor must provide race-neutral reasons for the strikes. The trial court must consider the prosecutor's explanations in light of all of the relevant facts and circumstances, and in light of the arguments of the parties. The trial judge must determine whether the prosecutor's proffered reasons are the actual reasons, or whether the proffered reasons are pretextual and the prosecutor instead exercised peremptory strikes on the basis of race. The ultimate inquiry is whether the State was "motivated in substantial part by discriminatory intent." *Foster*, 136 S.Ct., at 1754. Third, "since the trial judge's findings largely will turn on evaluation of credibility, a reviewing court ordinarily should give those findings great deference." *Batson*, 476 U.S. at 98.

The Constitution forbids striking even a single prospective juror for a discriminatory purpose. *See Foster*, 136 S.Ct., at 1747. The question is whether the trial court erred in concluding that the State was not "motivated in substantial part by discriminatory intent" when exercising peremptory strikes at Flowers' sixth trial. Because this case arises on direct review, we owe no deference to the Mississippi Supreme Court, as distinct from the trial court. Four categories of evidence loom large in assessing the *Batson* issue in Flowers' case: (1) the history from Flowers' six trials, (2) the prosecutor's striking of five of six black prospective jurors at the sixth trial, (3) the prosecutor's dramatically disparate questioning of black and white prospective jurors at the sixth trial, and (4) the prosecutor's proffered reasons for striking one black juror (Carolyn

Wright) while allowing other similarly situated white jurors to serve on the jury at the sixth trial.

In Flowers' first trial, the prosecutor successfully used peremptory strikes against all of the black prospective jurors. Flowers faced an all-white jury. In Flowers' second trial, the prosecutor tried again to strike all of the black prospective jurors, but the trial court decided that the State could not strike one of those jurors. The jury consisted of 11 white jurors and 1 black juror. In Flowers' third trial, there were 17 black prospective jurors. The prosecutor used 15 out of 15 peremptory strikes against black prospective jurors. After one black juror was struck for cause and the prosecutor ran out of strikes, one black juror remained. The jury again consisted of 11 white jurors and 1 black juror. In Flowers' fourth trial, the prosecutor used 11 out of 11 peremptory strikes against black prospective jurors. Because of the large number of black prospective jurors at the trial, the prosecutor ran out of peremptory strikes before it could strike all black prospective jurors. The jury for that trial consisted of seven white jurors and five black jurors, and the jury was unable to reach a verdict. There is no available information about the race of prospective jurors in the fifth trial. The jury consisted of nine white jurors and three black jurors, and the jury was unable to reach a verdict. Stretching across Flowers' first four trials, the State employed its peremptory strikes to remove as many black prospective jurors as possible. The State appeared to proceed as if *Batson* had never been decided. The State's relentless, determined effort to rid the jury of black individuals strongly suggests that the State wanted to try Flowers before a jury with as few black jurors as possible, and ideally before an all-white jury. The trial judge did not sufficiently account for the history when considering Flowers' *Batson* claim. The State's actions in the first four trials necessarily inform our assessment of the State's intent going into Flowers' sixth trial. We cannot ignore that history.

We turn now to Flowers' sixth trial. As *Batson* noted, a " 'pattern' of strikes against black jurors included in the particular venire might give rise to an inference of discrimination." At trial, 26 prospective jurors were presented to potentially serve on the jury. Six prospective jurors were black. The State accepted one black prospective juror—Alexander Robinson. The State struck the other five black prospective jurors. The resulting jury consisted of 11 white jurors and 1 black juror. The State's use of peremptory strikes in Flowers' sixth trial followed the same pattern as the first four trials, with one modest exception: the State accepted one black juror. Given the history, that alone cannot insulate the State from a *Batson* challenge. In *Miller-El II*, this Court skeptically viewed the State's decision to accept one black juror, explaining that a prosecutor might do so in an attempt "to obscure the otherwise consistent pattern of opposition to" seating black jurors. The State's decision to strike five of the six black prospective jurors is further evidence suggesting that the State was motivated in substantial part by discriminatory intent.

As *Batson* explained, "the prosecutor's questions and statements during *voir dire* examination and in exercising his challenges may support or refute an inference of discriminatory purpose." The questioning occurred through an initial group *voir dire* and then more in-depth follow-up questioning by the prosecutor and defense counsel of individual prospective jurors. The State asked the five black prospective jurors who were struck a total of 145 questions. By contrast, the State asked the 11 seated white jurors a total of 12 questions. On average, the State asked 29 questions to each struck black prospective juror. The State asked an average of one question to each seated white juror. Disparate questioning can be probative of discriminatory intent. *See Miller-El v. Cockrell*, 537 U.S. 322 (2003) (*Miller-El I*). As *Miller-El I* stated, "if disparate questioning is determined by race, it is likely that a justification for a strike based on the resulting divergent views would be pretextual. The State argues that it questioned black and white prospective jurors differently only because of differences in the jurors' characteristics. The record refutes that explanation. Dianne Copper was a black prospective juror who was struck. The State asked her 18 follow-up questions about her relationships with Flowers' family and witnesses in the case. Pamela Chesteen was a white juror whom the State accepted for the jury. Although the State asked questions of Chesteen during group *voir dire*, the State asked her no individual follow-up questions about her relationships with Flowers' family, even though the State was aware that Chesteen knew several members of Flowers' family. Similarly, the State asked no individual follow-up questions to four other white prospective jurors who, like Copper, had relationships with defense witnesses, even though the State was aware of those relationships. Likewise, the State conducted disparate investigations of certain prospective jurors. Tashia Cunningham, who is black, stated that she worked with Flowers' sister, but that the two did not work closely together. To try to disprove that statement, the State summoned a witness to challenge Cunningham's testimony. The State did not conduct similar investigations of white prospective jurors.

It is reasonable for the State to ask follow-up questions or to investigate the relationships of jurors to the victims, potential witnesses, and the like. But white prospective jurors who were acquainted with the Flowers' family or defense witnesses were not questioned extensively by the State or investigated. White prospective jurors who admitted that they or a relative had been convicted of a crime were accepted without apparent further inquiry by the State. The difference in the State's approaches to black and white prospective jurors was stark. Disparate questioning and investigation of prospective jurors on the basis of race can arm a prosecutor with seemingly race-neutral reasons to strike the prospective jurors of a particular race. The prosecutor's dramatically disparate questioning of black and white prospective jurors—if it rises to a certain level of disparity—can supply a clue that the prosecutor may have been seeking to paper the record and disguise a discriminatory intent. To be clear, disparate questioning or investigation alone does not constitute a *Batson* violation. Disparate questioning or investigation of black and white prospective jurors may reflect ordinary race-neutral considerations. But disparate questioning or investigation can, along with other evidence, inform the trial court's evaluation of whether discrimination occurred. Here, along with the historical evidence from the earlier trials, as well as the State's striking of five of six black prospective jurors at the sixth trial, the dramatically disparate questioning and investigation of black prospective jurors and white prospective jurors strongly suggests that the State was motivated in substantial part by a discriminatory intent.

In combination with the other facts and circumstances, the record of jury selection at the sixth trial shows that the peremptory strike of at least one of the black prospective jurors (Carolyn Wright) was motivated in substantial part by discriminatory intent. The Constitution forbids striking even a single prospective juror for a discriminatory purpose. Comparing prospective jurors who were struck and not struck can be an important step in determining whether a *Batson* violation occurred. *See Snyder*, 552 U.S. at 483. The comparison can suggest that the prosecutor's proffered explanations for striking black prospective jurors were a pretext for discrimination. When a prosecutor's "proffered reason for striking a black panelist applies as well to an otherwise-similar nonblack panelist who is permitted to serve, that is evidence tending to prove purposeful discrimination." *Foster*, 136 S.Ct., at 1754. Although a defendant ordinarily will try to identify a similar white prospective juror whom the State did not strike, a defendant is not required to identify an identical white juror for the comparison to be suggestive of discriminatory intent. *Miller-El II*, 545 U.S. at 247.

Carolyn Wright was a black prospective juror who was strongly in favor of the death penalty as a general matter. And she had a family member who was a prison security guard. Yet the State exercised a peremptory strike against Wright. The State said it struck Wright in part because she knew several defense witnesses and had worked at Wal-Mart where Flowers' father also worked. Winona is a small town. Wright had some sort of connection to 34 people involved in Flowers' case, both on the prosecution witness side and the defense witness side. But three white prospective jurors—Pamela Chesteen, Harold Waller, and Bobby Lester—also knew many individuals involved in the case. Chesteen knew 31 people, Waller knew 18 people, and Lester knew 27 people. Yet the State did not ask Chesteen, Waller, and Lester individual follow-up questions about their connections to witnesses. If the State were concerned about prospective jurors' connections to witnesses, the State presumably would have used individual questioning to ask those potential white jurors whether they could remain impartial despite their relationships. A "State's failure to engage in any meaningful *voir dire* examination on a subject the State alleges it is concerned about is evidence suggesting that the explanation is a sham and a pretext for discrimination." *Miller-El II*, 545 U.S. at 246.

Both Carolyn Wright and Archie Flowers, defendant's father, had worked at the local Wal-Mart. But there was no evidence that they worked together or were close. Importantly, the State did not ask individual follow-up questions to determine the nature of their relationship. Wright said she did not know whether Flowers' father still worked at Wal-Mart, which "supports an inference that Wright and Flowers did not have a close working relationship." White prospective jurors also had relationships with members of Flowers' family. Indeed, white prospective juror Pamela Chesteen stated that she had provided service to Flowers' family members at the bank and that she knew several members of the Flowers family. White prospective juror Bobby Lester worked at the same bank and also encountered Flowers' family members. Although Chesteen and Lester were questioned during group *voir dire*, the State did not ask Chesteen or Lester individual follow-up questions in order to explore the depth of their relationships with Flowers' family. Instead of striking those jurors, the State accepted them for the jury. Both Chesteen and Lester were later struck by the defense. But the State's acceptance of Chesteen and Lester necessarily informs our assessment of the State's intent in striking similarly situated black prospective jurors.

The State noted that Wright had once been sued by Tardy Furniture for collection of a debt 13 years earlier. Wright said that the debt was paid off and that it would not affect her evaluation of the case. The victims worked at Tardy Furniture. But the State did not explain how Wright's 13-year-old, paid-off debt to Tardy Furniture could affect her ability to serve impartially as a juror in this quadruple murder case. The "State's unsupported characterization of the lawsuit is problematic." In any event, the State did not purport to rely on that reason alone as the basis for the Wright strike. The State explained that it exercised a peremptory strike against Wright because she had worked with one of Flowers' sisters. That was incorrect. When a prosecutor mis-states the record in explaining a strike, that misstatement can be another clue showing discriminatory intent. The State made apparently incorrect statements to justify the strikes of black prospective jurors Tashia Cunningham, Edith Burnside, and Flancie Jones. The State contradicted Cunningham's earlier statement that she had only a working relationship with Flowers' sister by inaccurately asserting that Cunningham and Flowers' sister were close friends. The State asserted that Burnside had tried to cover up a Tardy Furniture suit. She had not. And the State explained that it struck Jones in part because Jones was Flowers' aunt. That, too, was not true. The State's pattern of factually inaccurate statements about black prospective jurors suggests that the State intended to keep black prospective jurors off the jury. *See Foster*, 136 S.Ct., at 1754. To be sure, the back and forth of a *Batson* hearing can be hurried, and prosecu-tors can make mistakes when providing explanations. That is entirely understandable, and mistaken explanations should not be confused with racial discrimination. But when considered with other evidence of discrimination, a series of factually inaccurate explanations for striking black prospective jurors can be telling.

In a different context, the Wright strike might be deemed permissible. But we must examine the whole picture. The overall context here requires skepticism. We must examine the Wright strike in light of the history of the State's use of peremptory strikes in the prior trials, the State's decision to strike five out of six black prospective jurors at Flowers' sixth trial, and the State's vastly disparate questioning of black and white prospective jurors during jury selection. In light of all the facts and circumstances, the trial court clearly erred in ruling that the State's peremptory strike of Wright was not motivated in substantial part by discriminatory intent. All that we decide is that all of the relevant facts and circumstances taken together establish that the trial court at Flowers' sixth trial committed clear error in concluding that the State's peremptory strike of black prospective juror Carolyn Wright was not motivated in substantial part by discriminatory intent. In reaching that conclusion, we break no new legal ground. We simply enforce and reinforce *Batson* by applying it to the extraordinary facts of this case.

We reverse the judgment of the Supreme Court of Mississippi, and we remand the case for further proceedings not inconsistent with this opinion.

It is so ordered.

JUSTICE ALITO, concurring.

Viewing the totality of the circumstances, petitioner's capital conviction cannot stand.

JUSTICE THOMAS, with whom JUSTICE GORSUCH joins as to Parts I, II, and III, dissenting.

The majority focuses its discussion on potential juror Carolyn Wright, but the State offered multiple race-neutral reasons for striking her. Wright lost a lawsuit to Tardy Furniture soon after the murders, and a garnishment order was issued against her. Wright claimed the lawsuit "would not affect her evaluation of the case." But the potential bias is obvious. The "victims" did not merely "work at Tardy Furniture." Bertha Tardy owned Tardy Furniture. Following her murder, her daughter and son-in-law succeeded her as owners; they sued Wright, and the daughter testified at this trial. Neither the trial court nor Flowers suffered from any confusion as to how losing a lawsuit to a trial witness and daughter of a victim might affect a juror. The majority suggests that the State did not adequately explain how the lawsuit could affect Wright. But it is obvious, and the State did spell it out.

The majority completely ignores the State's race-neutral explanations for striking the other four black jurors. Tashia Cunningham stated repeatedly that she "didn't believe in the death penalty" and would "not even consider" it. When pressed, she vacillated, saying that she "didn't think" she could consider the death penalty but then, "I might. I don't know. I might." Opposition to the death penalty is plainly a valid, race-neutral reason for a strike. Moreover, Cunningham knew Flowers' sister, having worked with her on an assembly line for several years. She testified that they did not work in close proximity, but a supervisor testified that they actually worked "side by side." This misstatement and the fact that Cunningham worked with Flowers' sister are valid, race-neutral reasons. Edith Burnside knew Flowers personally. Flowers had visited in her home, lived one street over, and played basketball with her sons. Burnside also testified repeatedly that she "could not judge anyone," no "matter what the case was," and that her "problem with judging" could "affect her judgment" here. Finally, she too was sued by Tardy Furniture soon after the murders, and a garnishment order was entered against her. Dianne Copper had worked with both Flowers' father and his sister for "a year or two" each. She agreed that because of these relationships and others with various defense witnesses, she might "lean toward" Flowers and would be unable to "come with an open mind." She also said that deciding the case on "the evidence only" would make her "uncomfortable." Finally, as to Flancie Jones, Flowers conceded that he "did not challenge her strike" and that "the State's bases for striking Jones appear to be race neutral." Because any argument as to Jones "was not raised below, it is waived." Even if Flowers had not waived this argument, this strike was obviously supported by race-neutral reasons. Jones was related to Flowers in several ways. She was late to court on multiple occasions. On her juror questionnaire, she said she was "strongly against the death penalty," but when asked about her opposition, said, "I guess I'd say anything to get off" jury duty. She admitted that she was not necessarily "being truthful" on her questionnaire but refused to provide her actual view on the death penalty, saying, "I—really and truly don't want to be here." In terms of race-neutral validity, these five strikes are not remotely close calls. Each strike was supported by multiple race-neutral reasons articulated by the State at the *Batson* hearing and supported by the record. Only by ignoring these facts can the Court assert that "the State's decision to strike five of the six black prospective jurors is further evidence suggesting that the State was motivated in substantial part by discriminatory intent." The majority has no response whatsoever to the State's race-neutral explanations and, for four of the five strikes, does not dispute the state courts' conclusion that race played no role at all. For *Batson* purposes, these strikes might as well have been exercised against white jurors. Yet the majority illegitimately counts them all against the State.

Here, neither the majority nor Flowers has identified any nonstruck white jurors remotely similar to any of the struck black jurors. The majority points to white jurors Pamela Chesteen and Bobby Lester, who worked at the Bank of Winona and therefore had interacted with several members of Flowers' family as bank customers. That comparison is untenable. Lester testified that working at the bank meant he and Chesteen "saw everyone in town." "A bank teller, who waits on customers at a bank," has a "substantially different" relationship from someone who "works at the same business establishment with members of the defendant's family." "A coworker relationship" and "employee/ customer relationship are distinguishable." The majority mentions none of this. Next, the majority contends that white jurors Chesteen, Lester, and Harold Waller, like Wright, "knew many individuals involved in the case." Yet the majority concedes that Wright knew more individuals than any of them. And the more relevant statistic from the State's perspective is how many defense witnesses a juror knows, since that knowledge suggests a greater connection to the defendant. By Flowers' own count, Wright knew substantially more defense witnesses than the three white jurors. Wright knew 19 defense witnesses, while Chesteen knew 14 and Lester and Waller knew around 6 each.

Additional relevant differences existed between Wright and the three white jurors. Wright had been sued by a witness and member of the victim's family, and worked at the same store as the defendant's father. Chesteen was friends with the same member of the victim's family and also knew another victim's wife. The trial court found that Chesteen "had a much closer relationship with members of the victims' families than she had with anyone in Flowers' family." Likewise, Waller knew victim Carmen Rigby and her husband; their children attended school with his daughter, and "they were involved in school activities together." He served on the school board with Rigby. And victim Bobo Stewart "went to school with Waller's daughter," and Waller knew his family. Similarly, Lester had been friends with Rigby's husband "for years," and he "knew her family." Lester's wife taught Stewart first grade. Lester was related by marriage to Bertha Tardy and had known the Tardy family his entire life, growing up with Bertha's daughter. His daughter had just graduated with Bertha's grandson, and they were friends. As Lester put it, "I have a lot of connections to the victims' families." Given that these prospective jurors were favorable for the State, it is hardly surprising that the State would not affirmatively "use individual questioning to ask these potential white jurors whether they could remain impartial despite their relationships" with victims' families or prosecution witnesses for to do so could invite defense strikes. Revealingly, Flowers' counsel exhaustively questioned these three white jurors—treating them much differently than Wright. Flowers' counsel asked Wright only a handful of questions, all of which sought to confirm that she could judge impartially.

The majority next discovers "clues" of racial discrimination in minor factual mistakes supposedly made by the State during the *Batson* hearing. Flowers forfeited this argument by failing to present it to the trial court. Even if Flowers had not forfeited his argument, it is devoid of merit. The *Batson* hearing was conducted immediately after *voir dire*, before a transcript was available. Counsel relied on handwritten notes taken during a fast-paced, multiday *voir dire* involving 156 potential jurors. Still, the majority comes up with only a few mistakes, and they are either imagined or utterly trivial. Tellingly, Flowers' counsel, although aided by "many interns," made many more mistakes.

The majority asserts that the State engaged in "dramatically disparate" questioning based on race. By the majority's count, "the State asked the five black prospective jurors who were struck a total of 145 questions" and "the 11 seated white jurors a total of 12 questions." The majority's statistical "evidence" is irrelevant and misleading. First, the majority finds that only one juror—Carolyn Wright—was struck on the basis of race, but it neglects to mention that the State asked her only five questions. Second, both sides asked a similar number of questions to the jurors they peremptorily struck. This is to be expected—a party will often ask more questions of jurors whose answers raise potential problems. Flowers asked the jurors he struck—all white—an average of about 40 questions, and the State asked the black jurors it struck an average of about 28 questions. The number of questions asked by the State to these jurors is not evidence of race discrimination.

The majority appears to assume that the only relevant difference between the black jurors and seated white jurors is their race. But reality is not so simple. Deciding whether a statistical disparity is caused by a particular factor requires controlling for other potentially relevant variables; otherwise, the difference could be explained by other influences. Yet the majority's raw comparison of questions does not control for any of the important differences between struck and seated jurors. Most fundamentally, the majority's statistics are divorced from the realities of this case. Winona is a very small town, and "this was the biggest crime that had ever occurred" there. Moreover, Flowers' family was "very, very prominent" in Winona's black community. "Flowers has a number of brothers and sisters. His parents are well-known. His father is apparently one of the most well-thought of people in this community. Countless numbers of African-Americans have come in and said they could not sit in judgment because of their knowledge of Mr. Flowers, and they could not be fair and impartial." Flowers' counsel stated that when Flowers' father "was working as a greeter at Wal-Mart," there was "probably not a person in Winona who wouldn't have said, 'Mr. Archie's my friend.'" "The overwhelming majority" of potential black jurors "stated that they could not sit in judgment of him because of kinships, friendships, and family ties." According to Flowers, "seventy-five percent of the total qualified venire, sixty-three percent of the venire members actually tendered for acceptance or rejection as jurors, and forty percent of the persons empanelled as jurors or alternates (six of 15) were personally acquainted with either the defendant or one or more of the decedents or their families and/or had actual opinions as to guilt or innocence formed prior to the trial." Before peremptory strikes even started, the venire had gone from 42% to 28% black. Any "statistical abnormality" "is strictly because of the prominence of Flowers' family." Flowers' counsel admitted that she was not "surprised" by the reduction given the circumstances and the experiences in the previous trials.

The state courts appropriately viewed the parties' questioning in light of these circumstances. The majority wonders why "the State spent far more time questioning the black prospective jurors" and concludes that "no one can know." But even Flowers admits that "more African-American jurors knew the parties, most of the State's follow-up questions pertained to relevant matters, and more questions were asked of jurors who had personal relationships about the case, or qualms about the death penalty." The State's questions refute the majority's suggestion that the State did not "not ask white prospective jurors the same questions." The State asked all potential jurors whether Tardy Furniture sued them, and only Wright and Burnside answered in the affirmative. Two of five questions to Wright and around eight questions to Burnside followed up on this lawsuit. All potential jurors were asked whether they knew Flowers' father, and no white jurors had worked with him at Wal-Mart. Two of Wright's remaining three questions followed up on this relationship. The State asked all potential jurors whether anyone lived in the areas around Flowers' house, and no white jurors answered in the affirmative. Seven questions to Copper—another black prospective juror—and three to Burnside followed up on this geographic proximity. Copper's remaining questions were mostly about her working with Flowers' father and sister and her statement that she would lean in Flowers' favor. Burnside's remaining questions were mostly about Flowers' visits to her house and her statement that she could not judge others. The State asked all potential jurors whether anyone was related to Flowers' family, and only Jones, a black prospective juror, answered affirmatively, leading to about 18 follow-up questions. Jones' remaining questions were mostly about her being late to court and her untruthful answer regarding the death penalty on the jury questionnaire. Finally, nearly all of Cunningham's questions were about her work with Flowers' sister. Any reasonable prosecutor would have followed up on these issues, and the majority does not cite even a single question that it thinks suggests racial discrimination.

The majority's comparison of the State's questions to Copper with its questions to several white jurors is baseless. As an initial matter, Flowers forfeited this argument by not making it at the trial court. And "a retrospective comparison of jurors based on a cold appellate record may be very misleading when alleged similarities were not raised at trial" because "an exploration of the alleged similarities at the time of trial might have shown that the jurors in question were not really comparable." *Snyder*, 552 U.S. at 483. Even if Flowers had not forfeited this argument, it is meritless. Copper worked with two of Flowers' family members and testified that she could "lean toward" Flowers and would not decide the case "with an open mind." These answers justified heavier questioning than was needed for Chesteen, the white bank teller who occasionally served Flowers' family members. Moreover, the State did ask Chesteen and Lester, a white juror who also worked at the bank, "follow-up questions about their relationships with Flowers' family." I have already addressed Lester and Waller, and why the State did not need to ask them more questions. The majority also references Larry Blaylock and Marcus Fielder, two white prospective jurors who "had relationships with defense witnesses." As for Blaylock, the majority makes no attempt to say what those "relationships" were, presumably because the only relationship discussed at the *Batson* hearing was Blaylock's 30-year friendship with the prosecutor's primary investigator—whom the defense planned to call as a hostile witness. The investigator was also his uncle by marriage, and the defense asked Blaylock some 46 questions. Likewise, Fielder's only relationship discussed at the *Batson* hearing was his work for a prosecution witness who had investigated the murders. The defense felt it necessary to ask Fielder about 30 follow-up questions. Despite the majority's focus on Copper, no one could compare the State's need to question her with its need to question these jurors.

The majority complains that the State had a witness testify that Cunningham worked closely with Flowers' sister. According to the majority, "the State apparently did not conduct similar investigations of white prospective jurors." Putting aside that the majority offers no record support for this claim, the majority does not tell us what investigation was performed, much less which white jurors could or should have been similarly investigated. The State made one call to Cunningham's employer on the morning of the hearing to ask a single question: Where did Cunningham work in relation to Flowers' sister? I see no reason to assume that the State failed to conduct any other single-phone-call "investigations" in this high-profile trial. Nor am I aware of white jurors who worked in any proximity to Flowers' family members. If the majority is going to infer racial bias from the State's attempt to present the truth in court—particularly in a case where juror perjury had been a problem, it ought to provide a sound basis for its criticism.

Finally, the majority asserts that "white prospective jurors who admitted that they or a relative had been convicted of a crime were accepted without apparent further inquiry by the State." The majority cites nothing to support this assertion, and the record does not support it. Three of the struck black jurors had relatives with a criminal conviction. The State asked no questions to either Copper or Cunningham on this point, and it asked three questions to Burnside about her son's robbery conviction. The State treated white jurors similarly. For example, the State asked three questions to Suzanne Winstead about a nephew's drug charges, four questions to Sandra Hamilton about crimes of her first cousins, and two questions to Larry Blaylock about a cousin who committed murder. Because any "disparate questioning or investigation of black and white prospective jurors" "reflects ordinary race-neutral considerations," this factor provides no evidence of racial discrimination in jury selection.

The evidence overwhelmingly supports the conclusion that the State did not engage in purposeful race discrimination. Any competent prosecutor would have struck the jurors struck below. Indeed, some of the jurors' conflicts might even have justified for-cause strikes. But the question us is not whether we "would have decided the case differently," but instead whether the state courts were clearly wrong. The answer to that question is obviously no. The ultimate question in *Batson* cases— whether the prosecutor engaged in purposeful discrimination—"involves an evaluation of the prosecutor's credibility," and "the best evidence of discriminatory intent often will be the demeanor of the attorney who exercises the challenge." *Snyder*, 552 U.S. at 477. The question also turns on "a juror's demeanor," "making the trial court's firsthand observations of even greater importance." *Ibid.* "Only the trial judge can be aware of the variations in demeanor and tone of voice that bear so heavily on the listener's understanding of and belief in what is said." *Anderson v. Bessemer City*, 470

U.S. 564, 575 (1985). Because the trial court is best situated to resolve the sensitive questions in a *Batson* challenge, "a trial court's ruling on the issue of discriminatory intent must be sustained unless it is clearly erroneous." *Snyder, supra*, at 477. Our review is particularly deferential where, as here, "an intermediate court reviews, and affirms, a trial court's factual findings." *Easley, supra*, at 242. "Where there are two permissible views of the evidence, the factfinder's choice between them cannot be clearly erroneous." *Anderson, supra*, at 574. The notion that it is "impermissible" to adopt the view of the evidence that I have outlined above is incredible. Besides being supported by carefully reasoned opinions from both the trial court and the Mississippi Supreme Court—opinions that consider all relevant facts and circumstances—that view is at a minimum consistent with the factual record. At the *Batson* hearing, the State offered "a coherent and facially plausible story that is not contradicted" by the record, and the trial court's "decision to credit" such a story "can virtually never be clear error." *Anderson, supra*, at 575. The trial court reasonably understood the supposedly "dramatically disparate" questioning to be explained by the circumstances of this case—circumstances that the majority does not dispute. The majority apparently thinks that it is in a better position than the trial court to judge the tone of the questions and answers, the demeanor of the attorneys and jurors, the courtroom dynamic, and the culture of Winona, Mississippi.

The State exercised 50 peremptory strikes in Flowers' previous trials. 49 of those strikes were race neutral. [In] Flowers' first trial, the State exercised peremptory strikes on five black jurors and seven white jurors. The trial court found that Flowers had not made out even a *prima facie Batson* case, much less showed purposeful race discrimination in any of the State's strikes. Thus, all of the State's strikes in this trial were race neutral. [At] the second trial, the State exercised peremptory strikes on five black jurors and two white jurors; the trial court disallowed one of the State's strikes under *Batson*. Flowers was convicted and apparently did not appeal on *Batson* grounds. [In the] "third" trial, the State struck 15 black jurors. The trial court found no *Batson* violations. On appeal, Flowers did not challenge four of the strikes, and the Mississippi Supreme Court unanimously upheld the trial court's ruling as to nine of the other strikes. Thus, the Court is wrong multiple times over to say that the Mississippi Supreme Court "concluded that the State had again violated *Batson* by discriminating on the basis of race in exercising all 15 of its peremptory strikes against 15 black prospective jurors." That court unanimously concluded that 13 strikes were race neutral, and a majority concluded that the remaining two strikes did not violate *Batson*. Therefore, all 15 strikes were race neutral. In the next two trials, Flowers apparently did not even allege a *Batson* violation. In the "fourth" trial, the State struck 11 black jurors but did not exercise its three remaining strikes; five black jurors were seated. In the "fifth" trial, the State struck five jurors, but Flowers is unable to identify the race of these jurors, and three black jurors were seated. Thus, up to the present trial, the State had sought to exercise 50 peremptory strikes, 36 on potential black jurors. In this trial, the State struck five black jurors and one white juror; one black juror sat on the jury, and one black juror was an alternate.

Points for Discussion

a. Explaining *Miller-El*

After *Miller-El*, it seems clear that not all members of a racial group must be excluded from a jury in order for *Batson* to apply. How would you describe to a colleague the basis of the Court's holding? Which step(s) in the three-step *Batson* analysis are addressed by Justice Souter?

b. The "Neutral" Explanation

Batson does not require that the neutral explanation for peremptorily striking a potential juror be derived from *voir dire*, nor does the neutral explanation have to rise to a level sufficient to satisfy a strike for cause. Instead, a prosecutor may use her own personal knowledge concerning a juror and information supplied from outside sources. The test is not whether the information is true or false; it is whether she has a good-faith belief in the information and whether she can articulate the reason to the trial court in a race-neutral or gender-neutral way that does not violate the defendant's constitutional rights. The trial court then decides whether the prosecutor has acted with a prohibited intent.

Hypo: *A McCullom* Challenge

In *Gilchrist v. Maryland*, 667 A.2d 876 (Md.1995), before the jury box was full, each side exercised one peremptory challenge. After twelve jurors were seated, defense counsel then continues to exercise peremptory challenges as each new prospective juror is seated. All of the peremptory challenges were used by the defense against white prospective jurors. After the seventh prospective juror was peremptorily challenged by defense counsel, the prosecutor objected, arguing that the defense was attempting to remove all white prospective jurors from the jury in violation of *Batson*. The following colloquy occurred out of the hearing of the jury. As you read the transcript, consider whether there was a *McCollum* violation? Did the prosecutor establish a *prima facie* case? Did the trial judge find a *prima facie* case? Were the explanations given by defense counsel racially neutral?

THE COURT: Which juror are you questioning or do you want to go through a reason for each one of them?

ASSISTANT STATE'S ATTORNEY: For each one.

THE COURT: All right. That's seven jurors you've struck. They were all white. Let's go through them one by one and give me the reasons you struck them. [Two of the jurors were challenged by the defendant because they were crime victims, and the one juror was challenged because the defendant was uncomfortable with the way the juror stared at him. The court found that these were acceptable explanations. The conversation moved on to the other strikes.]

DEFENSE COUNSEL: Judge, I personally, by looking at her—I see jurors in the box and I look at the way they relate to each other.

THE COURT: Well, how did she look?

DEFENSE COUNSEL: She reminded me of my Catholic School teacher that I didn't particularly like. Her look at the other people who were in the jury box.

DEFENSE COUNSEL: Judge, the next juror was young. I didn't think particularly he would be a strong juror for my case by looking at him.

THE COURT: And why was that?

DEFENSE COUNSEL: Because I look at the way he fits into the persons that are on the panel. And what I'm trying to accomplish from the look of him, from the way he sat—

THE COURT: Well, how did he look from the way he was sitting that made you feel he was not good, other than the fact he was white and young?

DEFENSE COUNSEL: Well, he—number one, most of the jurors would look at my client and look over at the table. He was just like sitting there not relating to anything in the room.

THE COURT: Because he wasn't relating to your client?

DEFENSE COUNSEL: Not relating to anything or anyone in the room. Frankly, I don't think he even wanted to be here.

THE COURT: For the next juror?

DEFENSE COUNSEL: Why? He was—I don't have anything written on here.

THE COURT: Let the record reflect he was a young white male in a navy blazer and khaki slacks.

DEFENSE COUNSEL: I believe he was—I remember him, Judge, and . . . we say he was unacceptable.

THE COURT: And why was that?

DEFENSE COUNSEL: His clothing, his manner.

THE COURT: What was wrong with his clothing and his manner?

DEFENSE COUNSEL: Well, his manner and his clothing suggest to me that he wouldn't be able to relate to my client because in this particular case there are—there is the police officer's word against my client's word. My client may very well testify. And because of those things—

THE COURT: Well, how does his clothing have anything to do with it? I don't make the connection.

DEFENSE COUNSEL: The clothing, Judge, means when you go to Brooks Brothers and buy a suit, and maybe not the suit—

THE COURT: The people who go to Brooks Brothers are more likely to believe police than defendants; is that what you're saying?

DEFENSE COUNSEL: Not necessarily so. But given the little information I have about them, I must make judgments about these individuals.

THE COURT: Well, what—well, all right. That's right. So what information did you have that required you to strike him?

DEFENSE COUNSEL: He's a student. We don't know what he's studying—

THE COURT: Well, we could have asked him.

DEFENSE COUNSEL: Well, some courts don't let you bring them up and ask them.

THE COURT: But you didn't ask.

DEFENSE COUNSEL: He seems rather studious.

THE COURT: Well, so what if he's studious? He's 21 years old.

DEFENSE COUNSEL: Right. He has 16 years of education.

THE COURT: Right.

DEFENSE COUNSEL: That means he's done his college.

THE COURT: Right.

DEFENSE COUNSEL: Those are my reasons.

THE COURT: When you say that someone comes in a navy blazer and khaki slacks, and because he's a student and because of his address that's a reason for striking him—

DEFENSE COUNSEL: I said I don't know anything about his address because I don't know the address. But, Judge, that could have been a black man. Are we saying that black men don't wear blazers and khaki pants?

Food for Thought

In *Gibson v. State*, 117 S.W.3d 567 (Tex.Ct.App.2003), the defense made a *Batson* challenge. As you read the following colloquy, ask yourself: is it different in any respect from the previous colloquy? Did the judge make the right decision on the challenge? Are you satisfied with the "race neutral" reasons given in both this and the previous case?

THE COURT: Now, you have a *Batson* challenge, [Defense Counsel]. Would you tell me the jurors that you challenge or believe the State struck for racial reasons? I'd like the number only, please, and I will take judicial notice that the Defendant is—the Defendant's race.

DEFENSE COUNSEL: Your Honor, that would go to Juror Number 6 and 11.

THE COURT: Thank you, sir. Will the State give me a race neutral reason why you struck Juror Number 6?

PROSECUTOR: Judge, I struck [Juror 6] among other reason because he's a substance abuse counselor.

THE COURT: Okay.

PROSECUTOR: And he told us as much during *voir dire*.

PROSECUTOR: Judge, I struck Juror 11 because she had spoken up and said that she would require more than one witness to testify.

THE COURT: All right.

DEFENSE COUNSEL: Your Honor, in response to that, [Juror 7] stated the same thing, that he would need more evidence than one witness though he was not struck by the State.

THE COURT: All right. Can you answer that, please?

PROSECUTOR: I can, Judge. He qualified his answer—And we can go back to the record. But he qualified his record at one point and said, but if there is more evidence I would be okay. And, in fact, there is more evidence in this case. I can't state strongly enough, Judge—I don't want to—We want to give Mr. Gibson a fair trial and if there's anything here that's not fair—

THE COURT: Well, that's what I'm trying to find out. You struck Number 11 for the reason you stated and did not strike Number 7 for the reason you stated; is that correct?

PROSECUTOR: That is correct with the caveat I just added.

THE COURT: Okay, I'm going to deny the *Batson* challenge. He's given race neutral reasons. Yes, sir.

DEFENSE COUNSEL: Just as a request to clarify your ruling. Their reason for striking [Juror 11], that he needed more evidence and the similar and same reason [Juror 7] was not struck, is that—has he given a sufficient race neutral reason to strike [Juror 11]?

THE COURT: In my judgment he has. They're pre-emptory [sic] challenges and he's given a race neutral reason.

c. *Batson's* Logic

Batson demands that litigants be color-blind. However, they do not always act in a color-blind manner, and will often use race as a proxy for beliefs and biases, the same as they use a person's occupation or how they dress. When a defense attorney assumes that white jurors will be less sympathetic to his African American client than African American jurors, is that racism or common sense? Given the ease with which litigants can give "race neutral" reasons for strikes, what value does *Batson* serve? Would you keep it?

> Sometimes a Batson violation is easy to spot. In Foster v. Chatman, 578 U.S. 468 (2016), the Court found a clear violation in a 30-year-old death penalty case. Not only did the state exercise its peremptory strikes against all four prospective black jurors that were qualified to serve, but the Court found the prosecutor's strikes of two black jurors were motivated by discriminatory intent, given shifting explanations, misrepresentations of the record and a prosecutor file focused on the race of the potential jurors, including placement of the letter "B" next to black jurors' names and a statement next to one that "if it comes down to having to pick one of the black jurors this one might be okay."

---

d. Deficient Performance

A state petitioner on *habeas* makes a claim of ineffective assistance of counsel because his trial counsel chose to strike all women jurors on the belief women would be biased against the defendant in a sexual assault case. The federal court held that violating *Batson* is always deficient performance by counsel (even when allegedly violated for the benefit of the defendant) and normally would be prejudicial *per se*, as *Batson* violations are always structural error. *See Winston v. Boatwright*, 649 F. 3d 618 (7th Cir. 2011) (upholding conviction, however, as it was not clearly established at the time that the state court should not have used harmless error analysis.)

Hypo 1: *Gender Plus*

Defense counsel raised a *Batson* objection after the prosecutor used all peremptory strikes to remove men from the jury pool. The judge then asked the prosecutor to explain the challenges. The prosecutor candidly admitted that he considered gender, but claimed that other factors such as age, education and employment motivated the strikes as well. The trial court concluded that the fact that the four strikes were all males did not establish a *prima facie* case of discrimination, and the court accepted the prosecutor's explanation that he had relied on "other rationales" in making his strikes. On appeal, as an appellate judge, how would you rule? Did defense counsel establish a *prima facie* case? If so, did the explanations offered by the prosecutor explain his decision related to each juror and explain why each of the jurors should not be on the jury? *See State v. Jagodinsky*, 209 Wis.2d 577, 563 N.W.2d 188 (App.1997).

Hypo 2: *Racial Strikes & the KKK*

On April 13, the Ku Klux Klan held a rally on the steps of the local courthouse. Although the rally itself occurred without incident, a member of the Klan, Karl Kody, a 25-year-old unemployed Caucasian, was arrested for wanton endangerment as he left the gathering when he swung his uniform at a crowd of people who were protesting the Klan's presence. At his jury trial, Karl's attorney, Kalvin Cline, used all three of the defense's available peremptory challenges to remove African Americans from the jury. After the defense used its peremptory challenges, no African American jurors remained on the jury. Articulate the real reason Cline struck those jurors. How might Cline distinguish his strikes of African Americans from the *Batson* rationale? Would he succeed?

Hypo 3: Batson *Violation?*

In a capital murder case involving a black defendant, the prosecution used the vast majority of its early peremptory challenges against black jurors. It accepted two black jurors, but only after defense counsel's repeated objections and after it was running out of peremptory strikes. In addition, in its earlier strikes, the prosecution did not strike a white juror who was essentially similar to two of the black jurors who were struck. Did the prosecutor act unconstitutionally based on race? *See Chamberlin v. Fisher*, 855 F.3d 657 (5th Cir. 2017).

Hypo 4: *Striking Females in Stalker Cases*

A woman is charged with "stalking" a man that she met online. During jury selection, the prosecution struck only females from the jury. When the defense challenged the strikes, the prosecution offered gender-neutral reasons for the strikes, including age, health and apparent disinterest in the legal process. Did the strikes involve improper gender discrimination? *See People v. Beauvais*, 393 P.3d 509 (Colo. 2017).

D. The No Impeachment Rule

Peña-Rodriguez v. Colorado

<u>580 U.S. 206 (2017)</u>.

JUSTICE KENNEDY delivered the opinion of the Court.

The jury is a central foundation of our justice system and our democracy as a necessary check on governmental power. The jury, over the centuries, has been an inspired, trusted, and effective instrument for resolving factual disputes and determining ultimate questions of guilt or innocence in criminal cases. Its judgments find acceptance in the community, an acceptance essential to respect for the rule of law. The jury is a tangible implementation of the principle that the law comes from the people.

In the era of our Nation's founding, the right to a jury trial already had existed and evolved for centuries, through and alongside the common law. The jury was considered a fundamental safeguard of individual liberty. *See* THE FEDERALIST No. 83, p. 451 (B. Warner ed. 1818) (A. Hamilton). The right to a jury trial in criminal cases was part of the Constitution as first drawn, and it was restated in the Sixth Amendment. Art. III, § 2, cl. 3; Amdt. 6. By operation of the Fourteenth Amendment, it is applicable to the States. *Duncan v. Louisiana*, 391 U.S. 145 (1968).

Like all human institutions, the jury system has its flaws, yet experience shows that fair and impartial verdicts can be reached if the jury follows the court's instructions and undertakes deliberations that are honest, candid, robust, and based on common sense. A general rule has evolved to give substantial protection to verdict finality and to assure jurors that, once their verdict has been entered, it will not later be called into question based on the comments or conclusions they expressed during deliberations. This principle, centuries old, is referred to as the no-impeachment rule. The instant case presents the question whether there is an exception to the no-impeachment rule when, after the jury is discharged, a juror comes forward with compelling evidence that another juror made clear and explicit statements indicating that racial animus was a significant motivating factor in his or her vote to convict.

In 2007, in the bathroom of a Colorado horse-racing facility, a man sexually assaulted two teenage sisters. The girls told their father and identified the man as an employee of the racetrack. The police located and arrested petitioner. Each girl separately identified petitioner as the man who had assaulted her. The State charged petitioner with harassment, unlawful sexual contact, and attempted sexual assault on a child. Before the jury was empanelled, members of the venire were repeatedly asked whether they believed that they could be fair and impartial. None of the empanelled jurors expressed any reservations based on racial or any other bias. And none asked to speak with the trial judge. After a 3-day trial, the jury found petitioner guilty of unlawful sexual contact and harassment, but it failed to reach a verdict on the attempted sexual assault charge. When the jury was discharged, the court gave them this instruction, as mandated by Colorado law: "The question may arise whether you may now discuss this case with the lawyers, defendant, or other persons. For your guidance the court instructs you that whether you talk to anyone is entirely your own decision. If any person persists in discussing the case over your objection, or becomes critical of your service either before or after any discussion has begun, please report it to me."

Following the discharge of the jury, petitioner's counsel entered the jury room to discuss the trial with the jurors. Two jurors remained to speak with counsel in private. They stated that, during deliberations, another juror had expressed anti-Hispanic bias toward petitioner and petitioner's alibi witness. Petitioner's counsel reported this to the court and, with the court's supervision, obtained sworn affidavits from the two jurors. The affidavits described a number of biased statements made by another juror, identified as Juror H.C. According to the two jurors, H.C. told the other jurors that he "believed the defendant was guilty because, in H.C.'s experience as an ex-law enforcement officer, Mexican men had a bravado that caused them to believe they could do whatever they wanted with women." The jurors reported that H.C. stated his belief that Mexican men are physically controlling of women because of their sense of entitlement, and further stated, "I think he did it because he's Mexican and Mexican men take whatever they want." According to the jurors, H.C. further explained that, in his experience, "nine times out of ten Mexican men were guilty of being aggressive toward women and young girls." Finally, the jurors recounted that Juror H.C. said that he did not find petitioner's alibi witness credible because, among other things, the witness was "an illegal." (In fact, the witness was a legal resident of the United States.)

After reviewing the affidavits, the trial court acknowledged H.C.'s apparent bias. But the court denied petitioner's motion for a new trial, noting that "the actual deliberations that occur among the jurors are protected from inquiry under Colorado Rule of Evidence 606(b)." Like its federal counterpart, Colorado's Rule 606(b) generally prohibits a juror from testifying as to any statement made during deliberations in a proceeding inquiring into the validity of the verdict. *See* Fed. Rule Evid. 606(b). The Colorado Rule reads as follows:"(b) Inquiry into validity of verdict or indictment. Upon an inquiry into the validity of a verdict or indictment, a juror may not testify as to any matter or statement occurring during the course of the jury's deliberations or to the effect of anything upon his or any other juror's mind or emotions as influencing him to assent to or dissent from the verdict or indictment or concerning his mental processes in connection therewith. But a juror may testify about (1) whether extraneous prejudicial information was improperly brought to the jurors' attention, (2) whether any outside influence was improperly brought to bear upon any juror, or

(3) whether there was a mistake in entering the verdict onto the verdict form. A juror's affidavit or evidence of any statement by the juror may not be received on a matter about which the juror would be precluded from testifying." Colo. Rule Evid. 606(b) (2016)." The verdict deemed final, petitioner was sentenced to two years' probation and was required to register as a sex offender. A divided panel of the Colorado Court of Appeals affirmed petitioner's conviction. The Colorado Supreme Court affirmed. The prevailing opinion relied on two decisions of this Court rejecting constitutional challenges to the federal no-impeachment rule as applied to evidence of juror misconduct or bias. *See Tanner v. United States*, 483 U.S. 107 (1987). This Court granted certiorari to decide whether there is a constitutional exception to the no-impeachment rule for instances of racial bias.

At common law jurors were forbidden to impeach their verdict, either by affidavit or live testimony. This rule originated in *Vaise v. Delaval*, 1 T.R. 11, 99 Eng. Rep. 944 (K.B. 1785). There, Lord Mansfield excluded juror testimony that the jury had decided the case through a game of chance. The Mansfield rule, as it came to be known, prohibited jurors, after the verdict was entered, from testifying either about their subjective mental processes or about objective events that occurred during deliberations. American courts adopted the Mansfield rule as a matter of common law, though not in every detail. Some jurisdictions adopted a different, more flexible version of the no-impeachment bar known as the "Iowa rule." Under that rule, jurors were prevented only from testifying about their own subjective beliefs, thoughts, or motives during deliberations. Jurors, however, could testify about objective facts and events occurring during deliberations, in part because other jurors could corroborate that testimony. An alternative approach, referred to as the federal approach, stayed closer to the original Mansfield rule. Under this version, the no-impeachment bar permitted an exception only for testimony about events extraneous to the deliberative process, such as reliance on outside evidence—newspapers, dictionaries, and the like—or personal investigation of the facts.

This Court's early decisions did not establish a clear preference for a particular version of the no-impeachment rule. In *United States v. Reid*, 12 How. 361, 13 L.Ed. 1023 (1852), the Court appeared open to the admission of juror testimony that the jurors had consulted newspapers during deliberations, but in the end it barred the evidence because the newspapers "had not the slightest influence" on the verdict. Reid warned that juror testimony "ought always to be received with great caution." Yet it added an important admonition: "cases might arise in which it would be impossible to refuse" juror testimony "without violating the plainest principles of justice." In a following case the Court required the admission of juror affidavits stating that the jury consulted information that was not in evidence, including a prejudicial newspaper article. *Mattox v. United States*, 146 U.S. 140 (1892). The Court suggested that the admission of juror testimony might be governed by a more flexible rule, one permitting jury testimony even where it did not involve consultation of prejudicial extraneous information. Later, however, the Court rejected the more lenient Iowa rule. In *McDonald v. Pless*, 238 U.S. 264 (1915), the Court affirmed the exclusion of juror testimony about objective events in the jury room. There, the jury allegedly had calculated a damages award by averaging the numerical submissions of each member. As the Court explained, admitting that evidence would have "dangerous consequences": "no verdict would be safe" and the practice would "open the door to the most pernicious arts and tampering with jurors." Yet the Court reiterated its admonition from *Reid*, cautioning that the no-impeachment rule might recognize exceptions "in the gravest and most important cases" where exclusion of juror affidavits might well violate "the plainest principles of justice."

The common-law development of the no-impeachment rule reached a milestone in 1975, when Congress adopted the Federal Rules of Evidence, including Rule 606(b). Congress, like the *McDonald* Court, rejected the Iowa rule. Instead it endorsed a broad no-impeachment rule, with only limited exceptions. The Advisory Committee drafted a rule reflecting the Iowa approach, prohibiting admission of juror testimony only as it related to jurors' mental processes in reaching a verdict. The Department of Justice, however, expressed concern. The Advisory Committee then drafted the more stringent version now in effect, prohibiting all juror testimony, with exceptions only where the jury had considered prejudicial extraneous evidence or was subject to other outside influence. Rules of Evidence for United States Courts and Magistrates, 56 F.R.D. 183 (1972). The Court adopted this second version and transmitted it to Congress. The House favored the Iowa approach, but the Senate expressed concern that it did not sufficiently address the public policy interest in the finality of verdicts. Siding with the Senate, the Conference Committee adopted, Congress enacted, and the President signed the Court's proposed rule. The substance of the Rule has not changed since 1975, except for a 2006 modification.

The current version of Rule 606(b) states as follows: "(1) *Prohibited Testimony or Other Evidence*. During an inquiry into the validity of a verdict or indictment, a juror may not testify about any statement made or incident that occurred during the jury's deliberations; the effect of anything on that juror's or another juror's vote; or any juror's mental processes concerning the verdict or indictment. The court may not receive a juror's affidavit or evidence of a juror's statement on these matters. (2) *Exceptions*. A juror may testify about whether: (A) extraneous prejudicial information was improperly brought to the jury's attention; (B) an outside influence was improperly brought to bear on any juror; or (C) a mistake was made in entering the verdict on the verdict form." This version of the no-impeachment rule has substantial merit. It promotes full and vigorous discussion by providing jurors with considerable assurance that after being discharged they will not be summoned to recount their deliberations, and they will not otherwise be harassed or annoyed by litigants seeking to challenge the verdict. The rule gives stability and finality to verdicts.

Some version of the no-impeachment rule is followed in every State and the District of Columbia. Variations make classification imprecise, but, as a general matter, 42 jurisdictions follow the Federal Rule, while 9 follow the Iowa Rule. Within both classifications there is a diversity of approaches. Nine jurisdictions that follow the Federal Rule have codified exceptions other than those listed in Federal Rule 606(b). At least 16 jurisdictions, 11 of which follow the Federal Rule, have recognized an exception to the no-impeachment bar under the circumstances the Court faces here: juror testimony that racial bias played a part in deliberations. Only one State other than Colorado has addressed this issue and declined to recognize an exception for racial bias. *See Commonwealth v. Steele*, 961 A.2d 786 (2008).

The federal courts are governed by Federal Rule 606(b). Various Courts of Appeals have had occasion to consider a racial bias exception and have reached different conclusions. Three have held or suggested there is a constitutional exception for evidence of racial bias. One court of appeals has declined to find an exception, reasoning that other safeguards inherent in the trial process suffice to protect defendants' constitutional interests. Another has suggested in the *habeas* context that an exception for racial bias was not clearly established but indicating in dicta that no such exception exists. One Court of Appeals has held that evidence of racial bias is excluded by Rule 606(b), without addressing whether the Constitution may at times demand an exception. In addressing the scope of the common-law no-impeachment rule before Rule 606(b)'s adoption, the *Reid* and *McDonald* Courts noted the possibility of an exception to the rule in the "gravest and most important cases." *Reid*, 12 How., at 366; *McDonald*, 238 U.S., at 269. Yet since the enactment of Rule 606(b), the Court has addressed the precise question whether the Constitution mandates an exception to it in just two instances.

In its first case, *Tanner*, 483 U.S. 107, the Court rejected a Sixth Amendment exception for evidence that some jurors were under the influence of drugs and alcohol during the trial. Central to the Court's reasoning were the "long-recognized and very substantial concerns" supporting "the protection of jury deliberations from intrusive inquiry." *Tanner* echoed *McDonald*'s concern that, if attorneys could use juror testimony to attack verdicts, jurors would be "harassed and beset by the defeated party," thus destroying "all frankness and freedom of discussion and conference." The Court was concerned, moreover, that attempts to impeach a verdict would "disrupt the finality of the process" and undermine both "jurors' willingness to return an unpopular verdict" and "the community's trust in a system that relies on the decisions of laypeople." *Tanner* outlined existing, significant safeguards for the defendant's right to an impartial and competent jury beyond post-trial juror testimony. *Voir dire* provides an opportunity for the court and counsel to examine members of the venire for impartiality. As a trial proceeds, the court, counsel, and court personnel have some opportunity to learn of any juror misconduct. Before the verdict, jurors themselves can report misconduct to the court. These procedures do not undermine the stability of a verdict once rendered. Even after the trial, evidence of misconduct other than juror testimony can be used to attempt to impeach the verdict. Balancing these interests and safeguards against the defendant's Sixth Amendment interest in that case, the Court affirmed the exclusion of affidavits pertaining to the jury's inebriated state.

The second case was *Warger*. The Court again rejected the argument that the jury trial right required an exception to the no-impeachment rule. *Warger* involved a civil case where, after the verdict was entered, the losing party sought to proffer evidence that the jury forewoman had failed to disclose prodefendant bias during *voir dire*. As in *Tanner*, the Court put substantial reliance on existing safeguards for a fair trial. The Court stated: "Even if jurors lie in *voir dire* in a way that conceals bias, juror impartiality is adequately assured by the parties' ability to bring to the court's attention any evidence of bias before the verdict is rendered, and to employ nonjuror evidence even after the verdict is rendered." In *Warger*, the Court did reiterate that the no-impeachment rule may admit exceptions. As in *Reid* and *McDonald*, the Court warned of "juror bias so extreme that, almost by definition, the jury trial right has been abridged." "If and when such a case arises," the Court indicated it would "consider whether the usual safeguards are or are not sufficient to protect the integrity of the process." The recognition in *Warger* that there may be extreme cases where the jury trial right requires an exception to the no-impeachment rule must be interpreted in context as a guarded, cautious statement. This caution is warranted to avoid formulating an exception that might undermine the jury dynamics and finality interests the no-impeachment rule seeks to protect. Today, the Court must decide whether the Constitution requires an exception to the no-impeachment rule when a juror's statements indicate that racial animus was a significant motivating factor in his or her finding of guilt.

It must become the heritage of our Nation to rise above racial classifications that are so inconsistent with our commitment to the equal dignity of all persons. This imperative to purge racial prejudice from the administration of justice was given new force and direction by the ratification of the Civil War Amendments. "The central purpose of the Fourteenth Amendment was to eliminate racial discrimination emanating from official sources in the States." *McLaughlin v. Florida*, 379 U.S. 184, 192 (1964). In the years before and after the ratification of the Fourteenth Amendment, racial discrimination in the jury system posed a particular threat both to the promise of the Amendment and to the integrity of the jury trial. "Almost immediately after the Civil War, the South began a practice that would continue for many decades: All-white juries punished black defendants particularly harshly, while simultaneously refusing to punish violence by whites, including Ku Klux Klan members, against blacks and Republicans." In the years 1865 and 1866, all-white juries in Texas decided a total of 500 prosecutions of white defendants charged with killing African-Americans. All 500 were acquitted. The stark and unapologetic nature of race-motivated outcomes challenged the American belief that "the jury was a bulwark of liberty," and prompted

Congress to pass legislation to integrate the jury system and to bar persons from eligibility for jury service if they had conspired to deny the civil rights of African-Americans. Members of Congress stressed that the legislation was necessary to preserve the right to a fair trial and to guarantee the equal protection of the laws.

The duty to confront racial animus in the justice system is not the legislature's alone. Time and again, this Court has been called upon to enforce the Constitution's guarantee against state-sponsored racial discrimination in the jury system. Beginning in 1880, the Court interpreted the Fourteenth Amendment to prohibit the exclusion of jurors on the basis of race. *Strauder v. West Virginia*, 100 U.S. 303 (1880). The Court has repeatedly struck down laws and practices that systematically exclude racial minorities from juries. To guard against discrimination in jury selection, the Court has ruled that no litigant may exclude a prospective juror on the basis of race. *Batson v. Kentucky*, 476 U.S. 79 (1986). In an effort to ensure that individuals who sit on juries are free of racial bias, the Court has held that the Constitution at times demands that defendants be permitted to ask questions about racial bias during *voir dire*. The unmistakable principle underlying these precedents is that discrimination on the basis of race, "odious in all aspects, is especially pernicious in the administration of justice." *Rose v. Mitchell*, 443 U.S. 545, 555 (1979). The jury is to be "a criminal defendant's fundamental 'protection of life and liberty against race or color prejudice.' " *McCleskey v. Kemp*, 481 U.S. 279, 310 (1987). Permitting racial prejudice in the jury system damages "both the fact and the perception" of the jury's role as "a vital check against the wrongful exercise of power by the State." *Powers v. Ohio*, 499 U.S. 400, 411 (1991).

This case lies at the intersection of the Court's decisions endorsing the no-impeachment rule and its decisions seeking to eliminate racial bias in the jury system. The two lines of precedent need not conflict. Racial bias of the kind alleged in this case differs in critical ways from the compromise verdict in *McDonald,* the drug and alcohol abuse in *Tanner,* or the pro-defendant bias in *Warger*. The behavior in those cases is troubling and unacceptable, but each involved anomalous behavior from a single jury—or juror—gone off course. Jurors are presumed to follow their oath, and neither history nor common experience show that the jury system is rife with mischief of these or similar kinds. To attempt to rid the jury of every irregularity of this sort would be to expose it to unrelenting scrutiny. "It is not clear that the jury system could survive such efforts to perfect it."

The same cannot be said about racial bias, a familiar and recurring evil that, if left unaddressed, would risk systemic injury to the administration of justice. Racial bias implicates unique historical, constitutional, and institutional concerns. An effort to address the most grave and serious statements of racial bias is not an effort to perfect the jury but to ensure that our legal system remains capable of coming closer to the promise of equal treatment under the law that is so central to a functioning democracy. Racial bias is distinct in a pragmatic sense. In past cases this Court has relied on other safeguards to protect the right to an impartial jury. Some of those safeguards can disclose racial bias. *Voir dire*, observation of juror demeanor and conduct during trial, juror reports before the verdict, and nonjuror evidence after trial are important mechanisms. Yet their operation may be compromised, or they may prove insufficient. This Court has noted the dilemma faced by trial court judges and counsel in deciding whether to explore potential racial bias at *voir dire*. Generic questions about juror impartiality may not expose specific attitudes or biases that can poison jury deliberations. More pointed questions "could well exacerbate whatever prejudice might exist without substantially aiding in exposing it."

The stigma that attends racial bias may make it difficult for a juror to report inappropriate statements during the course of juror deliberations. It is one thing to accuse a fellow juror of having a personal experience that improperly influences her consideration of the case. It is quite another to call her a bigot. The recognition that certain of the *Tanner* safeguards may be less effective in rooting out racial bias than other kinds of bias is not dispositive. All forms of improper bias pose challenges to the trial process. But there is a sound basis to treat racial bias with added precaution. A constitutional rule that racial bias in the justice system must be addressed—including after the verdict has been entered—is necessary to prevent a systemic loss of confidence in jury verdicts, a confidence that is a central premise of the Sixth Amendment trial right.

The Court now holds that where a juror makes a clear statement that indicates he or she relied on racial stereotypes or animus to convict a criminal defendant, the Sixth Amendment requires that the no-impeachment rule give way in order to permit the trial court to consider the evidence of the juror's statement and any resulting denial of the jury trial guarantee. Not every offhand comment indicating racial bias or hostility will justify setting aside the no-impeachment bar to allow further judicial inquiry. For the inquiry to proceed, there must be a showing that one or more jurors made statements exhibiting overt racial bias that cast serious doubt on the fairness and impartiality of the jury's deliberations and resulting verdict. To qualify, the statement must tend to show that racial animus was a significant motivating factor in the juror's vote to convict. Whether that threshold showing has been satisfied is a matter committed to the substantial discretion of the trial court in light of all the circumstances, including the content and timing of the alleged statements and the reliability of the proffered evidence.

The practical mechanics of acquiring and presenting such evidence will no doubt be shaped and guided by state rules of professional ethics and local court rules, both of which often limit counsel's post-trial contact with jurors. These limits seek to provide jurors some protection when they return to their daily affairs after the verdict has been entered. But while a juror can always tell counsel they do not wish to discuss the case, jurors may come forward of their own accord. That is what happened here. In this case the alleged statements by a juror were egregious and unmistakable in their reliance on racial bias. Not only did juror H.C. deploy a dangerous racial stereotype to conclude petitioner was guilty and his alibi witness should not be believed, but he encouraged other jurors to join him in convicting on that basis.

Petitioner's counsel did not seek out the two jurors' allegations of racial bias. Pursuant to Colorado's mandatory jury instruction, the trial court set limits on juror contact and encouraged jurors to inform the court if anyone harassed them about their role in the case. With the understanding that they were under no obligation to speak, the jurors approached petitioner's counsel, within a short time after the verdict, to relay their concerns about H.C.'s statements. Pursuant to local court rules, petitioner's counsel then sought and received permission from the court to contact the two jurors and obtain affidavits limited to recounting the exact statements made by H.C. that exhibited racial bias. While the trial court concluded that Colorado's Rule 606(b) did not permit it even to consider the resulting affidavits, the Court's holding today removes that bar. When jurors disclose an instance of racial bias as serious as the one involved in this case, the law must not wholly disregard its occurrence.

The Court relies on the experiences of the 17 jurisdictions that have recognized a racial-bias exception to the no-impeachment rule—some for over half a century—with no signs of an increase in juror harassment or a loss of juror willingness to engage in searching and candid deliberations. The experience of these jurisdictions, and the experience of the courts going forward, will inform the proper exercise of trial judge discretion in these and related matters. This case does not ask, and the Court need not address, what procedures a trial court must follow when confronted with a motion for a new trial based on juror testimony of racial bias. The Court also does not decide the appropriate standard for determining when evidence of racial bias is sufficient to require that the verdict be set aside and a new trial be granted.

There are standard and existing processes designed to prevent racial bias in jury deliberations. The advantages of *voir dire* have already been noted. Other safeguards deserve mention. Trial courts, often at the outset of the case and again in their final jury instructions, explain the jurors' duty to review the evidence and reach a verdict in a fair and impartial way, free from bias of any kind. Some instructions are framed by trial judges based on their own learning and experience. Model jury instructions likely take into account these continuing developments and are common across jurisdictions. Instructions may emphasize the group dynamic of deliberations by urging jurors to share their questions and conclusions with their colleagues. Probing and thoughtful deliberation improves the likelihood that jurors can confront the flawed nature of reasoning that is prompted or influenced by improper biases, whether racial or otherwise. These dynamics help ensure that the exception is limited to rare cases.

The Nation must continue to make strides to overcome race-based discrimination. The progress that has already been made underlies the Court's insistence that blatant racial prejudice is antithetical to the functioning of the jury system and must be confronted in egregious cases like this one despite the general bar of the no-impeachment rule. It is the mark of a maturing legal system that it seeks to understand and to implement the lessons of history. The Court now seeks to strengthen the broader principle that society can and must move forward by achieving the thoughtful, rational dialogue at the foundation of both the jury system and the free society that sustains our Constitution.

The judgment of the Supreme Court of Colorado is reversed, and the case is remanded for further proceedings not inconsistent with this opinion.

It is so ordered.

JUSTICE THOMAS, dissenting.

The Court's holding cannot be squared with the original understanding of the Sixth or Fourteenth Amendments. The common-law right to a jury trial did not guarantee a defendant the right to impeach a jury verdict with juror testimony about juror misconduct, including "a principal species of juror misbehaviour"—"notorious partiality." 3 BLACKSTONE 388. Although partiality was a ground for setting aside a jury verdict, the English common-law rule did not allow jurors to supply evidence of that misconduct. *Rex v. Almon,* 5 Burr. 2687, 98 Eng. Rep. 411 (K.B.).[4]

At the time of the founding, the States took mixed approaches to this issue. Many States followed Lord Mansfield's no-impeachment rule and refused to receive juror affidavits. By the time the Fourteenth Amendment was ratified, Lord Mansfield's no-impeachment rule had become firmly entrenched in American law. The vast majority of States adopted the rule as a matter of common law. Our common-law history does not establish that—in either 1791 (when the Sixth Amendment was ratified) or 1868 (when the Fourteenth Amendment was ratified)—a defendant had the right to impeach a verdict with juror testimony of misconduct. In fact, such evidence was prohibited. Perhaps good reasons exist to curtail or abandon the no-impeachment rule. Some States have and others have not. Ultimately, that question should be left to the political process. The Court today ends the political process and imposes a uniform, national rule. The Constitution does not require such a rule. Neither should we. I dissent.

---

[4]   Prior to 1770, juror affidavits were sometimes received to impeach a verdict on the ground of juror misbehavior, although only "with great caution." *McDonald v. Pless,* 238 U.S. 264, 268 (1915). But "previous to our Revolution, and at least as early as 1770, the doctrine in England was distinctly the other way, and has so stood ever since." 3 T. WATERMAN, A TREATISE ON THE PRINCIPLES OF LAW AND EQUITY WHICH GOVERN COURTS IN THE GRANTING OF NEW TRIALS IN CASES CIVIL AND CRIMINAL 1429 (1855).

JUSTICE ALITO, with whom THE CHIEF JUSTICE and JUSTICE THOMAS join, dissenting.

For centuries, it has been the judgment of experienced judges, trial attorneys, scholars, and lawmakers that allowing jurors to testify after a trial about what took place in the jury room would undermine the system of trial by jury that is integral to our legal system. Juries occupy a unique place in our justice system. When jurors retire to deliberate, they enter a space that is not regulated. Jurors are ordinary people. They are expected to speak, debate, argue, and make decisions the way ordinary people do in their daily lives. Our Constitution places great value on this way of thinking, speaking, and deciding. The jury trial right protects parties in court cases from being judged by a special class of trained professionals who do not speak the language of ordinary people and may not understand or appreciate the way ordinary people live their lives. To protect that right, the door to the jury room has been locked, and the confidentiality of jury deliberations has been closely guarded. Today, with the admirable intention of providing justice for one criminal defendant, the Court not only pries open the door; it rules that respecting the privacy of the jury room, as our legal system has done for centuries, violates the Constitution. This is a startling development. The Court justifies its decision on the ground that the nature of the confidential communication at issue—a clear expression of what the Court terms racial bias—is uniquely harmful to our criminal justice system.

The firm no-impeachment approach taken in *McDonald* came to be known as "the federal rule." This approach categorically bars testimony about jury deliberations, except where it is offered to demonstrate that the jury was subjected to an extraneous influence (for example, an attempt to bribe a juror). Some jurisdictions, notably Iowa, adopted a more permissive rule. The Iowa rule allowed jurors to "testify as to events or conditions which might have improperly influenced the verdict, even if these took place during deliberations within the jury room." Debate between proponents of the federal rule and the Iowa rule emerged during the framing and adoption of Federal Rule of Evidence 606(b). In the end the strict federal approach was retained. The process that culminated in the adoption of Federal Rule of Evidence 606(b. Recognizing the importance of Rule 606(b), this Court has twice rebuffed efforts to create a Sixth Amendment exception. Today, the Court creates a constitutional exception to no-impeachment rules.

The Court contends that the effectiveness of *voir dire* is questionable in cases involving racial bias because pointed questioning about racial attitudes may highlight racial issues and thereby exacerbate prejudice. The suggestion that *voir dire* is ineffective in unearthing bias runs counter to decisions of this Court holding that *voir dire* on the subject of race is constitutionally required in some cases, mandated as a matter of federal supervisory authority in others, and typically advisable in any case if a defendant requests it. Even the majority recognizes the "advantages of careful *voir dire*" as a "process designed to prevent racial bias in jury deliberations." Reported decisions substantiate that *voir dire* can be effective. Thus, while *voir dire* is not a magic cure, there are good reasons to think that it is a valuable tool.

The majority argues that "racial bias may make it difficult for a juror to report inappropriate statements during the course of juror deliberations" because it is difficult to "call another juror a bigot." Jurors *do* report biased comments made by fellow jurors prior to the beginning of deliberations. Even if there is something to the distinction that the Court makes between pre- and post-verdict reporting, it is debatable whether the difference is significant enough to merit different treatment. Post-verdict reporting is both more disruptive and may be the result of extraneous influences. A juror who is initially in the minority but is ultimately persuaded by other jurors may have second thoughts after the verdict and may be angry with others on the panel who pressed for unanimity. If a verdict is unpopular with a particular juror's family, friends, employer, co-workers, or neighbors, the juror may regret his or her vote and may feel pressured to rectify what the jury has done.

The thrust of the opinion is that the Constitution is less tolerant of racial bias than other forms of juror misconduct, but it is hard to square this argument with the nature of the Sixth Amendment right. What the Sixth Amendment protects is the right to an "impartial jury." Nothing in the text or history of the Amendment or in the inherent nature of the jury trial right suggests that the extent of the protection provided by the Amendment depends on the nature of a jury's partiality or bias. "Racial bias implicates unique historical, constitutional, and institutional concerns." But it is hard to see what that has to do with the scope of an *individual criminal defendant's* Sixth Amendment right to be judged impartially. Recasting this as an equal protection case would not provide a ground for limiting the holding to cases involving racial bias. At a minimum, cases involving bias based on any suspect classification—such as national origin or religion—would merit equal treatment. So would bias based on sex, or the exercise of the First Amendment right to freedom of expression or association. Indeed, convicting a defendant on the basis of any irrational classification would violate the Equal Protection Clause. The Court says that only "clear" expressions of bias must be admitted, but judging whether a statement is sufficiently "clear" will often not be easy. Under today's decision it will be difficult for judges to discern the dividing line between those that are "clearly" based on racial or ethnic bias and those that are at least somewhat ambiguous.

Today's decision—especially if it is expanded in ways that seem likely—will invite the harms that no-impeachment rules were designed to prevent. As the Court explained in *Tanner,* "post verdict scrutiny of juror conduct" will inhibit "full and frank discussion in the jury room." Today's ruling will also prompt losing parties and their friends, supporters, and attorneys to contact and seek to question jurors, and this pestering may erode citizens' willingness to serve on juries. Where post-verdict approaches are permitted or occur, there is almost certain to be an increase in harassment, arm-twisting, and outright coercion. The majority's approach will undermine the finality of verdicts. Accusations of juror bias—which may be "raised for the first time days, weeks, or months after the verdict"—can "seriously disrupt the finality of the process." *Tanner, supra*, at 120. The Court's only response is that some jurisdictions already make an exception for racial bias, and the Court detects no signs of "a loss of juror willingness to engage in searching and candid deliberations." The Court's decision is well-intentioned. It seeks to remedy a flaw in the jury trial system, but it is questionable whether our system of trial by jury can endure this attempt to perfect it.

In addition to the question of whether a jury's verdict can be impeached, a verdict might be challenged under certain circumstances. For example, in *English v. Berghuis* 900 F.3d 804 (6th Cir. 2018), in a sexual assault case, a juror failed to disclose that she had been sexually assaulted when she was eight years old. The court concluded that the nondisclosure should be treated as deliberate, leading to an inference of bias, and required a reversal of defendant's conviction.

Hypo 1: *The Juror's Blog*

During a criminal trial of a man charged with fraud, a blog was found to contain numerous negative comments about the defendant. When it became clear that a juror had posted a comment on the blog, the court made inquiry and determined that the individual was a juror who had been removed from the jury. Later, a second juror posted anonymous comments that referred to the removed juror and comments that she had made during the trial: "Mama June, and those who were there know what I'm talking about, she was spouting about the 'shots in the dark' blog since day one. It's why she conveniently got 'sick' and didn't finish her service. Several other jurors told her to stfu and got annoyed. 'Idiot' doesn't describe the half of it." Does the fact that one juror appeared to be talking about the blog to other jurors during the trial justify holding a hearing regarding to determine what happened? *See United States v. Zimny*, 846 F.3d 458 (1st Cir. 2017).

A juror's independent research regarding a case can provide the basis for overturning a conviction and requiring a new trial. However, in *Jeffries v. State*, 397 P.3d 21 (Nev. 2017), when the judge found out about the independent research, and instructed jurors not to consider the outside information, defendant's conviction was not overturned.

1182 — CRIMINAL PROCEDURE: ADJUDICATIVE *A Contemporary Approach* —

Hypo 2: *Removing All Reading Material*

A jury deliberated for 11 hours, but was unable reach a verdict. When the judge learned that one juror was doing crossword puzzles, rather than deliberating, the judge ordered all reading material removed from the jury room. Within minutes, the jury returned with a verdict of "guilty." Did the judge act improperly in ordering the removal of the crossword puzzle and all reading material? *See Brewster v. Hetzel*, 913 F.3d 1042 (11th Cir. 2019).

Food for Thought

Defendant, who was in an interracial marriage, was being tried for the murder of his wife. During *voir dire*, the court learned that a prospective juror does not support interracial marriage. Suppose that the juror indicates that he is able to set aside his bias and to decide the case based on the evidence presented during the trial. Would the judge commit error by deciding to seat the juror? *See Thomas v. Lumpkin*, 995 F.3d 432 (5th Cir. 2021).

Hypo 3: *The Racist Juror*

Defendant was convicted of murder, tried, and sentenced to death. Following the verdict, one of the jurors said that his study of the Bible made him wonder whether "black people even have souls." That juror swore in an affidavit that "there are two types of black people: black folks and niggers." He also stated that defendant was in the latter group and that he should "get the electric chair for what he did," and that he should receive the death penalty as "an example to other blacks who kill blacks." Can the jury's verdict of "guilty" be impeached? *See Tharpe v. Ford*, 898 F.3d 1342, *cert. denied*, 139 S.Ct. 911 (2019).

Executive Summary

Right to a Jury Trial. A defendant has a Sixth Amendment right to a jury trial when the authorized maximum punishment for a charge exceeds six months.

Less than Six Months but "Serious." For offenses with shorter authorized sentences, no jury trial right exists unless the other statutory penalties, such as fines, are so severe as to render the offense "serious."

Jury of Twelve Not Required. A jury of twelve persons is not constitutionally mandated in State court proceedings and juries may be composed of as few as six persons, but a jury of six must be unanimous.

Unanimity Required. Unanimity is constitutionally required in both federal and State court proceedings.

Fair Cross-Section Requirement. Prospective jurors must be selected from a fair cross-section of the population of the place where the crime was committed. Exclusion of large distinctive groups from jury service, such as women or on the basis of race, violates the constitution.

Challenges for Cause. Prospective trial jurors may be questioned during *voir dire* to determine whether they can be excluded from the jury for cause because they cannot be fair and impartial.

Peremptory Challenges. Peremptory challenges to jurors may be based on any reason or no reason at all except that neither party can exercise peremptory challenges to exclude jurors based on race or gender.

The No Impeachment Rule. As a general rule, jury verdicts are not subject to challenge or impeachment. There are limited exceptions, including situations when a jury's verdict is influenced by racial bias.

Major Themes

a. Limited Right—While the Court has recognized the great importance of a trial by jury to the founders, it has nonetheless chipped away at the edges of the right using a historical analysis (not agreed upon by all members of the Court), resulting in conclusions that the right never applied to all offenses, and never required unanimity nor a jury of twelve persons.

b. Jury Selection—Jury selection procedures are governed by several constitutional rights, from a fairly limited right to a jury chosen from a fair-cross section of the community, to the right to an impartial jury, allowing the court to remove jurors for cause who could not be fair, and the right of jurors to equal protection of the laws, such that neither the prosecution nor the defense can strike jurors based on race or gender.

For More Information

- RUSSELL L. WEAVER, JOHN M. BURKOFF, CATHERINE HANCOCK & STEVEN I. FRIEDLAND, PRINCIPLES OF CRIMINAL PROCEDURE Ch. 16 (8th ed. 2024).

- WAYNE R. LAFAVE, JEROLD H. ISRAEL, NANCY J. KING & ORIN S. KERR, CRIMINAL PROCEDURE (6th ed. 2017).

Test Your Knowledge

To assess your understanding of the material in this chapter, click here to take a quiz.

CHAPTER 18

The Confrontation Clause

A. Introduction

The Sixth Amendment provides that: "In all criminal prosecutions, the accused shall enjoy the right . . . to be confronted with the witnesses against him." The Confrontation Clause protects criminal defendants by affording them the opportunity to confront the witnesses against them at trial as part of the truth seeking process. What "confronting witnesses" means, however, is far from clear. Instead, the phrase long has depended on judicial interpretation, especially by the Court. The Clause protects the accused in federal court cases directly through the Sixth Amendment, and in state court cases through the Fourteenth Amendment's Due Process Clause.

Over the past several decades, two distinct threads of Confrontation Clause analysis have developed. One thread involves the potential exclusion of hearsay statements offered by the prosecution against defendants in criminal cases. Another thread involves whether defendants in sexual assault cases have the right to be face-to-face with child witnesses.

> **What's That?**
>
> Hearsay is an out-of-court statement offered to prove the truth of the matter asserted. Fed. R. Evid. 801. Under the rules of evidence, hearsay is generally excluded. Fed. R. Evid. 802. Even so, there are a litany of exceptions to the hearsay rule. *See* Fed. R. Evid. 803 and 804. Hearsay statements raise both evidentiary issues and Confrontation Clause questions. This chapter is concerned only with the Confrontation Clause.

The hearsay statement thread of Confrontation Clause analysis was well-established until it was wrested from its moorings in *Crawford v. Washington*, 541 U.S. 36 (2004), and became the subject of renewed interest and volatility. In *Crawford*, Justice Scalia altered the foundation of when and how the Clause applied. *Crawford* divided the constitutional firmament for hearsay statements into two categories: testimonial hearsay and everything else. The Confrontation Clause now focused only on testimonial statements, not the remainder.

Crawford's new structure emphasized the defendant's ability to examine a declarant about his hearsay statements. If the statement is regarded as testimonial, then defendant must have an opportunity to examine the declarant about the statement; it is not necessary that the accused in fact examine the declarant. If the declarant is available at trial, the declarant generally must be called as a witness. If the declarant is not available, no matter how firmly rooted or reliable the testimonial statements are, the statements only will be admissible if the defendant had a prior opportunity to cross-examine the now unavailable declarant. Otherwise the statements are excluded from evidence under the Confrontation Clause.

Take Note

The pre-*Crawford* Confrontation Clause approach applied to all hearsay and was focused on the reliability of the statement. As the Court held in its seminal decision in *Ohio v. Roberts*, 448 U.S. 56 (1980), if the hearsay was located within a "firmly rooted" exception or had "particularized guarantees of trustworthiness," it was considered to have presumptive reliability. *Roberts'* reliability analysis no longer governs, replaced instead by the testimonial hearsay inquiry of *Crawford*. In effect, instead of changing the oil in a car, *Crawford* seemingly traded in the entire vehicle for replacement.

Crawford's meaning has developed as a result of a case-by-case analysis in hundreds of subsequent state and federal cases, including several Court cases. For example, after *Crawford*, Justice Scalia recognized a significant exclusion under the Confrontation Clause for statements made for the primary purpose of responding to an on-going emergency, as compared to statements relating the facts of a past crime. *Davis v. Washington*, 547 U.S. 813 (2006).

What's That?

Since the lynchpin of the *Crawford* analysis is whether a statement is considered to be testimonial, the definition of this term is critical. What is included in the testimonial statements category, though, has not been starkly illuminated by the Court, but rather revolves around context. Justice Scalia in Crawford indicated that affidavits, statements produced by custodial police interrogation, depositions, courtroom testimony, and "statements that were made under circumstances which would lead an objective witness reasonably to believe that the statement would be available for use at a later trial" are included. These statements thus could be formal, as evidenced by affidavits, or informal, such as those made during on-the-street police questioning.

Even if statements are deemed to be testimonial and the Confrontation Clause applies, the accused still can waive his or her rights either explicitly or implicitly. One type of implied waiver involves forfeiture by wrongdoing, when an accused intentionally prevents a declarant from testifying is precluded from using the Confrontation Clause as a shield.

The second thread of Confrontation Clause analysis applies to sexual assault cases involving children. This thread usually concerns the circumstances under which victimized children testify at a trial, if at all. Significant issues revolve around the meaning of "face-to-face" confrontation.

> **FYI**
>
> The fact that a hearsay statement survives Confrontation Clause analysis does not guarantee that it will be admissible at trial. Under the rules of evidence, the prohibition against hearsay, and other potential exclusions, could render the evidence inadmissible.

B. Modern Hearsay Thread Confrontation Clause Analysis

Modern "hearsay" Confrontation Clause analysis revolves around the following decision which raises constitutional issues based on the text and the framers' intent.

Crawford v. Washington

541 U.S. 36 (2004).

JUSTICE SCALIA delivered the opinion of the Court.

On August 5, 1999, Kenneth Lee was stabbed at his apartment. Police arrested petitioner later that night. After giving petitioner and his wife *Miranda* warnings, detectives interrogated each of them twice. Petitioner eventually confessed that he and Sylvia had gone in search of Lee because he was upset over an earlier incident in which Lee had tried to rape her. The two found Lee at his apartment, and a fight ensued in which Lee was stabbed in the torso and petitioner's hand was cut. Petitioner claimed that he saw something in Lee's hand, possibly a weapon, right before he stabbed him. Sylvia generally corroborated petitioner's story about the events

Who's That?

Justice Scalia was appointed to the Court as an Associate Justice by President Ronald Reagan in 1986 and served until his death in 2016. With nine children, he was a former professor at the University of Virginia Law School and judge on the D.C. Circuit Court of Appeals. His interest in the Confrontation Clause is apparent, if only from the number and importance of his Confrontation opinions. Often labeled a textualist, who tries to divine meaning from the text of statutes and the Constitution, he was known for asking many questions during oral arguments and sometimes wrote sharp-tongued dissents.

leading up to the fight, but her account of the fight was arguably different—particularly with respect to whether Lee had drawn a weapon before petitioner assaulted him. She denied seeing anything in Lee's hands.

The State charged petitioner with assault and attempted murder. At trial, he claimed self-defense. Sylvia did not testify because of the state marital privilege, which generally bars a spouse from testifying without the other spouse's consent. In Washington, this privilege does not extend to a spouse's out-of-court statements admissible under a hearsay exception, so the State sought to introduce Sylvia's tape-recorded statements to the police as evidence that the stabbing was not in self-defense. Noting that Sylvia had admitted she led petitioner to Lee's apartment and thus facilitated the assault, the State invoked the hearsay exception for statements against penal interest. Petitioner countered that, state law notwithstanding, admitting the evidence would violate his federal constitutional right to be "confronted with the witnesses against him." Amdt. 6. According to our description of that right in *Ohio v. Roberts*, 448 U.S. 56 (1980), it does not bar admission of an unavailable witness's statement against a criminal defendant if the statement bears "adequate 'indicia of reliability.' " To meet that test, evidence must either fall within a "firmly rooted hearsay exception" or bear "particularized guarantees of trustworthiness." The trial court admitted the statement, offering several reasons why it was trustworthy. The Washington Court of Appeals reversed concluding that, although Sylvia's statement did not fall under a firmly rooted hearsay exception, it bore guarantees of trustworthiness. We granted certiorari to determine whether the State's use of Sylvia's statement violated the Confrontation Clause.

Hear It

Listen to the oral argument of *Crawford* at: http://www.oyez.org/cases/2000-2009/2003/2003_02_9410.

The Sixth Amendment's Confrontation Clause provides that, "in all criminal prosecutions, the accused shall enjoy the right . . . to be confronted with the witnesses against him." We have held that this bedrock procedural guarantee applies to both federal and state prosecutions. *Roberts* says that an unavailable witness's out-of-court statement may be admitted so long as it has "adequate indicia of reliability"—*i.e.,* falls within a "firmly rooted hearsay exception" or bears "particularized guarantees of trustworthiness." Petitioner argues that this test strays from the original meaning of the Confrontation Clause.

The Constitution's text does not alone resolve this case. One could plausibly read "witnesses against" a defendant to mean those who actually testify at trial, those whose statements are offered at trial, or something in-between. We must turn to the historical background of the Clause to understand its meaning. English common law tradition is one of live testimony in court subject to adversarial testing. *See* 3 W. BLACKSTONE, COMMENTARIES ON THE LAWS OF ENGLAND 373–374 (1768). Many declarations of rights adopted around the time of the Revolution guaranteed a right of confrontation. *See* VIRGINIA DECLARATION OF RIGHTS § 8 (1776). The proposed Federal Constitution, however, did not. When there was an outcry against this omission, the First Congress responded by including the Confrontation Clause in the proposal that became the Sixth Amendment. Early state decisions shed light upon the original understanding of the common-law right. *State v. Webb*, 2 N.C. 103 (1794) (per curium), held: "It is a rule of the common law, founded on natural justice, that no man shall be prejudiced by evidence which he had not the liberty to cross examine."

This history supports two inferences about the meaning of the Sixth Amendment. First, the principal evil at which the Confrontation Clause was directed was the civil-law mode of criminal procedure, and particularly its use of *ex parte* examinations as evidence against the accused. It was these practices that the Crown deployed in notorious treason cases and that the founding-era rhetoric decried. The Sixth Amendment must be interpreted with this focus in mind. We reject the view that the Confrontation Clause applies of its own force only to in-court testimony, and that its application to out-of-court statements introduced at trial depends upon "the law of Evidence for the time being." Leaving the regulation of out-of-court statements to the law of evidence would render the Confrontation Clause powerless to prevent even the most flagrant inquisitorial practices. This focus suggests that not all hearsay implicates the Sixth Amendment's core concerns. An off-hand, overheard remark might be unreliable evidence and thus a good candidate for exclusion under hearsay rules, but it bears little resemblance to the civil-law abuses the Confrontation Clause targeted. On the other hand, *ex parte* examinations might sometimes be admissible under modern hearsay rules, but the Framers would not have condoned them. The text of the Confrontation Clause reflects this focus. It applies to "witnesses" against the accused—in other words, those who "bear testimony." "Testimony" is typically "a solemn declaration or affirmation made for the purpose of establishing or proving some fact." An accuser who makes a formal statement to government officers bears testimony in a sense that a person who makes a casual remark to an acquaintance does not.

Various formulations of this core class of "testimonial" statements exist: "*ex parte* in-court testimony or its functional equivalent—that is, affidavits, custodial examinations, prior testimony that the defendant was unable to cross-examine, or similar pretrial statements that declarants would reasonably expect to be used prosecutorially," "extrajudicial statements contained in formalized testimonial materials, such as affidavits, depositions, prior testimony, or confessions," *White v. Illinois*, 502 U.S. 346 (1992) (Thomas, J., concurring); "statements that were made under circumstances which would lead an objective witness reasonably to believe that the statement would be available for use at a later trial." Statements taken by police officers in the course of interrogations are also testimonial under even a narrow standard. That interrogators are police officers rather than magistrates does not change the picture. Even if the Sixth Amendment is not solely concerned with testimonial hearsay, that is its primary object, and interrogations by law enforcement officers fall squarely within that class.

The historical record supports a second proposition: that the Framers would not have allowed admission of testimonial statements of a witness who did not appear at trial unless he was unavailable to testify, and defendant had had a prior opportunity for cross-examination. The text of the Sixth Amendment does not suggest any open-ended exceptions from the confrontation requirement to be developed by the courts. Rather, the "right to be confronted with the witnesses against him" is most naturally read as a reference to the right of confrontation at common law, admitting only those exceptions established at the time of the founding. As the English authorities reveal, the common law in 1791 conditioned admissibility of an absent witness's examination on unavailability and a prior opportunity to cross-examine. The Sixth Amendment therefore incorporates those limitations.

We do not read the historical sources to say that a prior opportunity to cross-examine was merely a sufficient, rather than a necessary, condition for admissibility of testimonial statements. They suggest that this requirement was dispositive, and not merely one of several ways to establish reliability. Our case law has been largely consistent with these two principles. In *Mattox v. United States*, 156 U.S. 237 (1895), we relied on the fact that the defendant had had, at the first trial, an adequate opportunity to confront the witness. Even our recent cases hew closely to the traditional line. *Ohio v. Roberts*, 448 U.S., at 67, admitted testimony from a preliminary hearing at which the defendant had examined the witness. *Lilly v. Virginia*, excluded testimonial statements that the defendant had had no opportunity to test by cross-examination. *Bourjaily v. United States*, 483 U.S. 171 (1987), admitted statements made unwittingly to an FBI informant after applying a more general test that did not make prior cross-examination an indispensable requirement. Our cases have thus remained faithful to the Framers' understanding: Testimonial statements of witnesses absent from trial have been admitted only where the declarant is unavailable, and only where the defendant has had a prior opportunity to cross-examine. When the declarant appears for cross-examination at trial, the Confrontation Clause places no constraints at all on the use of his prior testimonial statements. *See Tennessee v. Street*, 471 U.S. 409 (1985).

Although our decisions have generally been faithful to the original meaning of the Confrontation Clause, the same cannot be said of our rationales. *Roberts* conditions the admissibility of all hearsay evidence on whether it falls under a "firmly rooted hearsay exception" or bears "particularized guarantees of trustworthiness." This test departs from the historical principles identified above in two respects.   It applies the same mode of analysis whether or not the hearsay consists of *ex parte* testimony. This often results in close constitutional scrutiny in cases that are far removed from the core concerns of the Clause. At the same time, the test is too narrow: It admits statements that *do* consist of *ex parte* testimony upon a mere finding of reliability. This malleable standard fails to protect against paradigmatic confrontation violations.

Where testimonial statements are involved, we do not think the Framers meant to leave the Sixth Amendment's protection to the vagaries of the rules of evidence, much less to amorphous notions of "reliability." Admitting statements deemed reliable by a judge is fundamentally at odds with the right of confrontation. Dispensing with confrontation because testimony is obviously reliable is akin to dispensing with jury trial because a defendant is obviously guilty. This is not what the Sixth Amendment prescribes. The legacy of *Roberts* vindicates the Framers' wisdom in rejecting a general reliability exception. The framework is so unpredictable that it fails to provide meaningful protection from even core confrontation violations. Reliability is an amorphous, if not entirely subjective, concept. Whether a statement is deemed reliable depends heavily on which factors the judge considers and how much weight he accords each of them. Some courts wind up attaching the same significance to opposite facts.

The unpardonable vice of the *Roberts* test is not its unpredictability, but its demonstrated capacity to admit core testimonial statements that the Confrontation Clause plainly meant to exclude. One recent study found that, after *Lilly,* appellate courts admitted accomplice statements to the authorities in 25 out of 70 cases—more than one-third of the time. Courts have invoked *Roberts* to admit other sorts of plainly testimonial statements despite the absence of any opportunity to cross-examine. To add insult to injury, some of the courts that admit untested testimonial statements find reliability in the very factors that *make* the statements testimonial. One court relied on the fact that the witness's statement was made to police while in custody on pending charges—the theory being that this made the statement more clearly against penal interest and thus more reliable. That inculpating statements are given in a testimonial setting is not an antidote to the confrontation problem, but rather the trigger that makes the Clause's demands most urgent.

Roberts' failings were on full display in the proceedings below. Sylvia Crawford made her statement while in police custody, herself a potential suspect in the case. Indeed, she had been told that whether she would be released "depended on how the investigation continues." In response to often leading questions from police detectives, she implicated her husband in Lee's stabbing and arguably undermined his self-defense claim. Despite this, the trial court admitted her statement, listing several reasons why it was reliable. In reversing, the Court of Appeals listed several *other* reasons why the statement was *not* reliable. The State Supreme Court relied on the interlocking character of the statement and disregarded every other factor the lower courts had considered. The case is thus a demonstration of *Roberts'* unpredictable and inconsistent application. Each of the courts also made assumptions that cross-examination might well have undermined.

To reverse the Washington Supreme Court's decision after conducting our own reliability analysis would perpetuate what the Sixth Amendment condemns. The Constitution prescribes a procedure for determining the reliability of testimony in criminal trials, and we lack authority to replace it with one of our own devising. The Framers knew that judges, like other government officers, could not always be trusted to safeguard the rights of the people. Where nontestimonial hearsay is at issue, it is wholly consistent with the Framers' design to afford the States flexibility in their development of hearsay law—as does *Roberts,* and as would an approach that exempted such statements from Confrontation Clause scrutiny altogether. Where testimonial evidence is at issue, the Sixth Amendment demands what the common law required: unavailability and a prior opportunity for cross-examination. We leave for another day any effort to spell out a comprehensive definition of "testimonial." Whatever else the term covers, it applies at a minimum to prior testimony at a preliminary hearing, before a grand jury, or at a former trial; and to police interrogations.

In this case, the State admitted Sylvia's testimonial statement against petitioner, despite the fact that he had no opportunity to cross-examine her. That alone is sufficient to make out a violation of the Sixth Amendment. *Roberts* notwithstanding, we decline to mine the record in search of indicia of reliability. Where testimonial statements are at issue, the only indicium of reliability sufficient to satisfy constitutional demands is the one the Constitution actually prescribes: confrontation.

The judgment of the Washington Supreme Court is reversed, and the case is remanded for further proceedings not inconsistent with this opinion.

It is so ordered.

CHIEF JUSTICE REHNQUIST, with whom JUSTICE O'CONNOR joins, concurring in the judgment.

I dissent. The Court's distinction between testimonial and nontestimonial statements is no better rooted in history than our current doctrine. Testimonial statements such as accusatory statements to police officers would have been disapproved of in the 18th century, not necessarily because they resembled *ex parte* affidavits or depositions as the Court reasons, but more likely because they were not made under oath. *See King v. Woodcock*, 1 Leach 500, 503, 168 Eng. Rep. 352, 353 (1789). Without an oath, one usually did not get to the second step of whether confrontation was required. While the Framers were mainly concerned about sworn affidavits and depositions, it does not follow that they

Who's That?

Chief Justice Rehnquist, considered a conservative justice, was originally appointed to the Supreme Court as an Associate Justice by President Richard Nixon in 1971. He was elevated to Chief Justice in 1986 by President Ronald Reagan, where he remained until his death in 2005. Justice Rehnquist presided over many important cases, including *Bush v. Gore,* and the impeachment trial of President Bill Clinton. He oversaw a very different Supreme Court than his predecessor, Chief Justice Burger, or successor, Chief Justice Roberts.

were similarly concerned about the Court's broader category of testimonial statements. Unsworn testimonial statements were treated no differently at common law than were nontestimonial statements, and it seems to me any classification of statements as testimonial beyond that of sworn affidavits and depositions will be somewhat arbitrary, merely a proxy for what the Framers might have intended had such evidence been liberally admitted as substantive evidence like it is today. I therefore see no reason why the distinction the Court draws is preferable to our precedent. Exceptions to confrontation have always been derived from the experience that some out-of-court statements are just as reliable as cross-examined in-court testimony due to the circumstances under which they were made.

"Cross-examination may be superfluous; it may be sufficiently clear that the statement is free enough from the risk of inaccuracy and untrustworthiness, so that the test of cross-examination would be a work of supererogation." 5 WIGMORE § 1420, at 251. In choosing the path it does, the Court of course overrules *Roberts,* a case decided nearly a quarter of a century ago. The Court grandly declares that "we leave for another day any effort to spell out a comprehensive definition of 'testimonial,' "But the thousands of federal prosecutors and the tens of thousands of state prosecutors need answers as to what beyond the specific kinds of "testimony" the Court lists is covered by the new rule. They need them now, not months or years from now. Rules of criminal evidence are applied every day in courts throughout the country, and parties should not be left in the dark. The result the Court reaches follows inexorably from *Roberts* and its progeny without any need for overruling that line of cases. In *Idaho v. Wright,* 497 U.S. 805 (1990), we held that an out-of-court statement was not admissible simply because the truthfulness of that statement was corroborated by other evidence at trial. A citation to *Wright,* would suffice. This would be a far preferable course.

> In *Commonwealth v. Adonsoto,* 475 Mass. 497, 58 N.E.3d 305 (Mass. 2016), the court held that all station house interviews with non-English speaking suspects that are conducted through an interpreter must be recorded. The court concluded that the recording would help courts gauge the reliability of the translation, but also provides a basis for evaluating the truth of the testimony for Confrontation Clause purposes. The court noted that Massachusetts police are already required to record interrogations.

Point for Discussion

Expecting to Bear Witness

Other federal courts subsequently articulated their understanding of testimonial statements. The Court observed in *United States v. Dargan,* 738 F.3d 643 (4th Cir. 2013): "As *Crawford* and later cases make clear, a statement must be 'testimonial' to be excludable under the Confrontation Clause. The primary determinant of a statement's testimonial quality is 'whether a reasonable person in the declarant's position would have expected his statements to be used at trial—that is, whether the declarant would have expected or intended to "bear witness" against another in a later proceeding.' *Crawford*, 541 U.S. at 52. This definition flows from the Court's recognition that 'the principal evil at which the Confrontation Clause was directed was the civil-law mode of criminal procedure, and particularly its use of *ex parte* examinations as evidence against the accused.' "

Hypo 1: *Does* Crawford *Apply to Pretrial Suppression Hearings?*

Jones was stopped by the police for erratic driving. In the audiotape of the initial conversation between Officer Pelts and Jones after the stop, Pelts could be heard stating, "I saw you cross over the center line twice, in violation of the law. That is why I stopped you." Jones was arrested for DUI and the possession of guns. In a subsequent suppression hearing, the audiotape is offered by the prosecution because Officer Pelts has since passed away. Jones claims that admission of the tape violates his Confrontation Clause rights. Should the court admit the tape? *State v. Zamzow*, 374 Wis.2d 220 (2017).

Food for Thought

At defendant's trial, the prosecution asked questions regarding a witness' history of domestic violence with the murdered victim. On cross-examination, defendant sought to question the witness in detail regarding the domestic violence. The trial court refused to allow extensive examination on the theory that it would "confuse the jury." Was it appropriate for the judge to limit the scope of the cross-examination? *See Rhodes v. Dittmann*, 903 F.3d 646 (7th Cir. 2018).

Hypo 2: *Testimonial Statements*

Please consider whether the following statements are "testimonial" and therefore within the scope of the Confrontation Clause:

A) An eighty-year-old woman is battered and injured in her apartment by a younger woman who asks for money and ransacks the apartment. The assailant leaves the scene, and the police are called. After the police arrive, the police officer talks with the bruised woman and calls emergency medical services to help treat her and prepare for transport to the hospital. During the conversation, the woman provides a description of her assailant. Missing additional forensic evidence, such as fingerprints, hairs, or fibers, the victim's statements are important to the prosecution's case. At the defendant's trial for battery with a deadly weapon and robbery, the victim is unavailable to testify. Are the victim's statements to the police testimonial?

B) Defendants Donnie and Charlie are selling drugs at a local schoolyard. When a police officer stops Charlie and questions him, Charlie responds with an alibi to the effect that he and Donnie are working for a charity, seeking donations. After more questioning, Charlie inadvertently admits to committing the crime and then confesses. Were Charlie's statements testimonial? Explain.

C) Jones is prosecuted for selling large quantities of counterfeit goods. At trial, the prosecution calls Detective Peabody who testifies that the accused was not at first a suspect but became one after interviewing Jones' former roommate, Manfred. Manfred had been hit by a car and was in a coma at the time of trial. Did Detective Peabody's testimony violate defendant's rights? Could the appellate court consider whether defendant's rights were violated if the defense attorney did not object or in any other way preserve the question for appeal?

D) In a sexual assault case, the prosecution offers the testimony of a psychiatric social worker regarding what various complainants told her concerning assaults against them. Most of the people who were the sources of the information testified at trial. Some of the sources did not testify. The evidence presented by the social worker about the assaults was not duplicated by other sources or physical evidence. Was the testimony permissible under the Confrontation Clause? What if some statements were made for the purposes of medical treatment? Would these statements still be regarded as testimonial?

E) A victim of an armed robbery spoke to the police shortly after the crime and identified defendant, who was in custody, as the perpetrator. The victim was bleeding profusely and did not have time to reflect on or think about the statement concerning the events surrounding the attack. At the time of the declarant's statement, defendant had been arrested. At trial, the declarant was unavailable to testify. If a judge decides that these statements meet the excited utterance requirements under Federal Rule of Evidence 803(2), should the statement be admitted on behalf of the prosecution?

F) On March 4th, a bank was robbed in downtown Greensboro. The suspect was George Peabody, a student, who claimed at trial that he was in class at the date and time of the robbery. The prosecutor offers the statement of defendant's teacher who told a detective before trial that she checked the class rolls and that defendant was not in class at that day and time. The defense attorney objects, claiming that the detective's testimony violated the Confrontation Clause. Was the testimony about the teacher's search of the class rolls testimonial? Why or why not?

Hypo 3: *Availability to Testify*

How should the following situations be handled under the Confrontation Clause: A) Suzie had been married to Decker for 10 years when she was asked by the police about the whereabouts and conduct of her husband on a certain date. After Suzie spoke voluntarily with the police, her husband was charged with two counts of burglary. At trial, the prosecution called Suzie to the witness stand, but she invoked the spousal testimony privilege and refused to testify. The prosecution wants to read her statement to the jury over the defense objection. Should the trial court admit the testimony? B) At trial, a witness was called to the stand in an armed robbery case to establish the existence of other prior robberies with the same modus operandi. The witness, a co-defendant, raised the Fifth Amendment and refused to answer any questions. The prosecutor was allowed to read the witness' prior statement which was made to the police during interrogation. Was the prosecutor's conduct permissible?

Hypo 4: *Opportunity to Examine*

Arthur Smitts is charged with grand theft auto. Before trial, the prosecution takes a discovery deposition of a witness who does not testify at trial. Defendant was permitted to attend the deposition by stipulation of both parties. Would Smitts have a viable Confrontation Clause claim if he did not attend the deposition and never cross-examined the witness? Explain.

Hemphill v. New York

595 U.S. 140 (2022).

JUSTICE SOTOMAYOR delivered the opinion of the Court.

In April 2006, Ronnell Gilliam and several other individuals got into a physical fight near Tremont Avenue in the Bronx. Shortly after the fight, someone fired a 9-millimeter handgun. The bullet killed a 2-year-old child sitting in a nearby minivan. Police officers determined that Gilliam was involved and that Nicholas Morris, Gilliam's best friend, had been at the scene. Officers searched Morris' apartment. On Morris' nightstand, the officers found a 9-millimeter cartridge and three .357-caliber bullets. Three witnesses identified Morris as the shooter [at] a police lineup. The police arrested Morris the next day and observed bruising on his knuckles consistent with fist fighting. Gilliam surrendered and identified Morris as the shooter. Gilliam later returned to the police station and recanted, stating that Hemphill, Gilliam's cousin, had in fact been the shooter. Investigators initially did not credit Gilliam's recantation; instead, the State charged Morris with the child's murder and for possession of a 9-millimeter handgun. After opening statements at Morris' trial, the State decided not to oppose Morris' application for a mistrial to allow the State to reconsider the charges against him. Six weeks later, the State agreed to dismiss the murder charges against Morris if he pleaded guilty to criminal possession of a weapon. But rather than having Morris plead to the charge in the existing indictment for possession of a 9-millimeter handgun, the State filed a new charge alleging that Morris had possessed a .357-magnum revolver, a different type of firearm than the one used to kill the victim. In exchange for this plea, the prosecution recommended a sentence of time served.

In 2011, the State learned that Hemphill's DNA matched a sample from a blue sweater that police had recovered in a search of Gilliam's apartment shortly after the crime. Eyewitnesses had described the shooter as wearing a blue shirt or sweater. In 2013, Hemphill was arrested and indicted for the murder. At trial, Hemphill pursued a third-party culpability defense by blaming Morris for the shooting. Hemphill's counsel noted that officers had recovered 9-millimeter ammunition from Morris' nightstand hours after a 9-millimeter bullet killed the victim. The State did not object, but later contended that Hemphill's argument had been misleading because officers also had found .357-caliber bullets on the nightstand and because Morris ultimately pleaded guilty to possessing a .357 revolver. Morris, however, was unavailable to testify at Hemphill's trial. As a result, the State sought to introduce the transcript of Morris' plea allocution to suggest that he had possessed only a .357 revolver. Hemphill's counsel objected, arguing that the plea allocution was "clearly hearsay" and that Hemphill was being "deprived of an opportunity for cross-examination." The [trial] court relied on *People v. Reid*, 19 N. Y. 3d 382, 971 N. E. 2d 353. In *Reid*, New York's highest court held that a criminal defendant could "open the door" to evidence that would otherwise be inadmissible under the Confrontation Clause if the evidence was "reasonably necessary to correct a misleading impression" made by the defense's "evidence or argument." The trial court applied *Reid* as follows: "A significant aspect of the defense in this case is that Morris, who was originally prosecuted for this homicide, was, in fact, the actual shooter and that the defendant, Hemphill, was excluded as the shooter. There is, however, evidence contrary to the argument presented by the defense in this case. In my judgment, the defense's argument, which in all respects is appropriate and under the circumstances of this case probably a necessary argument to make, nonetheless, opens the door to evidence offered by the State refuting the claim that Morris was, in fact, the shooter." Based on this ruling, the State published to the jury the portions of the transcript of Morris' plea hearing containing Morris' admission to possessing a .357 revolver and his counsel's statements that he was doing so against counsel's advice in order to get out of jail immediately. Hemphill premised his closing argument, like the rest of his defense, on the theory that Morris was the shooter. The State, in its closing, cited Morris' plea allocution and emphasized that possession of a .357 revolver, not murder, was "the crime Morris actually committed." The jury found Hemphill guilty. The Court of Appeals affirmed. This Court granted certiorari.

One of the bedrock constitutional protections afforded to criminal defendants is the Confrontation Clause of the Sixth Amendment, which states: "In all criminal prosecutions, the accused shall enjoy the right . . . to be confronted with the witnesses against him." The State does not dispute that Morris' plea allocution was testimonial, meaning that it implicated Hemphill's rights under the Confrontation Clause. The State attempts to characterize the *Reid* rule as a mere "procedural rule" that "treats the misleading door-opening actions of counsel as the equivalent of failing to object to the confrontation violation." So construed, the *Reid* rule limits only the manner of asserting the confrontation right, not its substantive scope. The door-opening principle incorporated in *Reid* is a substantive principle of evidence that dictates what material is relevant and admissible in a case. The principle requires a trial court to determine whether one party's evidence and arguments, in the context of the full record, have created a "misleading impression" that requires correction with additional material from the other side. If *Crawford* stands for anything, it is that the history, text, and purpose of the Confrontation Clause bar judges from substituting their own determinations of reliability for the method the Constitution guarantees. The Clause "commands, not that evidence be reliable, but that reliability be assessed by testing in the crucible of cross-examination." *Crawford*, 541 U. S., at 61. It "thus reflects a judgment, not only about the desirability of reliable evidence, but about how reliability can best be determined." *Ibid.* "A mere judicial determination" regarding the reliability of evidence is no substitute for the "constitutionally prescribed method of assessing reliability." The upshot is that the role of the trial judge is not, for Confrontation Clause purposes, to weigh the reliability or credibility of testimonial hearsay evidence; it is to ensure that the Constitution's procedures for testing the reliability of that evidence are followed. The trial court violated this principle by admitting unconfronted, testimonial hearsay against Hemphill simply because the judge deemed his presentation to have created a misleading impression that the testimonial hearsay was reasonably necessary to correct. For Confrontation Clause purposes, it was not for the judge to determine whether Hemphill's theory that Morris was the shooter was unreliable, incredible, or otherwise misleading in light of the State's proffered, unconfronted plea evidence. Nor, under the Clause, was it the judge's role to decide that this evidence was reasonably necessary to correct that misleading impression. Such inquiries are antithetical to the Confrontation Clause.

The State insists that the *Reid* rule is necessary to safeguard the truth-finding function of courts because it prevents the selective and misleading introduction of evidence. Even as it has recognized and reaffirmed the vital truth-seeking function of a trial, the Court has not allowed such considerations to override the rights the Constitution confers upon criminal defendants. The Court has not held that defendants can "open the door" to violations of constitutional requirements merely by making evidence relevant to contradict their defense. The Sixth Amendment speaks with clarity: "In all criminal prosecutions, the accused shall enjoy the right to be confronted with the witnesses against him." It admits no exception for cases in which the trial judge believes unconfronted testimonial hearsay might be reasonably necessary to correct a misleading impression. Courts may not overlook its command, no matter how noble the motive. The State warns that a reversal will leave prosecutors without recourse to protect against abuses of the confrontation right. State and federal hearsay rules generally preclude all parties from introducing unreliable, out-of-court statements for the truth of the matter asserted. Even for otherwise admissible evidence, "well-established rules," such as Federal Rule of Evidence 403, "permit trial judges to exclude evidence if its probative value is outweighed by certain other factors such as unfair prejudice, confusion of the issues, or potential to mislead the jury." *Holmes v. South Carolina*, 547 U. S. 319, 326 (2006). If a court admits evidence before its misleading or unfairly prejudicial nature becomes apparent, it generally retains the authority to withdraw it, strike it, or issue a limiting instruction as appropriate.

Finally, the Court does not decide the validity of the common-law rule of completeness as applied to testimonial hearsay. Under that rule, a party "against whom a part of an utterance has been put in, may in his turn complement it by putting in the remainder." *Beech Aircraft Corp. v. Rainey*, 488 U. S. 153 (1988) (quoting 7 J. WIGMORE, EVIDENCE § 2113, p. 653 (J. Chadbourn rev. 1978)). The parties agree that the rule of completeness does not apply to the facts of this case, as Morris' plea allocution was not part of any statement that Hemphill introduced. Whether and under what circumstances that rule might allow the admission of testimonial hearsay against a criminal defendant presents different issues that are not before this Court.

The Confrontation Clause requires that the reliability and veracity of the evidence against a criminal defendant be tested by cross-examination, not determined by a trial court. The trial court's admission of unconfronted testimonial hearsay over Hemphill's objection, on the view that it was reasonably necessary to correct Hemphill's misleading argument, violated that fundamental guarantee. The judgment of the New York Court of Appeals is reversed, and the case is remanded for further proceedings not inconsistent with this opinion.

It is so ordered.

JUSTICE ALITO, with whom JUSTICE KAVANAUGH joins, concurring.

When a defendant introduces the statement of an unavailable declarant, he commits himself to the trier of fact's examination of what the declarant has to say on that subject. The remainder of the declarant's statement or statements—and any other statements by the same declarant on the same subject—are fair game. Defendant cannot reasonably claim otherwise, given his tactical choice to put the declarant's statements on the relevant subject in contention despite his unavailability for cross-examination. Having made the choice to introduce the statements of an unavailable declarant, defendant cannot be heard to complain that he cannot cross-examine that declarant with respect to the remainder of that statement or the declarant's related statements on the same subject.

C. Distinguishing Testimonial Statements from Statements Made for the Primary Purpose of Resolving an On-Going Emergency

The Court was confronted by the difficulty of how to categorize statements made by persons for the purpose of resolving on-going emergency situations, such as statements made during 911 calls. Should these statements be considered "testimonial," and therefore subject to the Confrontation Clause?

Hammon v. Indiana; Davis v. Washington

547 U.S. 813 (2006).

JUSTICE SCALIA delivered the opinion of the Court.

These cases require us to determine when statements made to law enforcement personnel during a 911 call or at a crime scene are "testimonial" and thus subject to the requirements of the Sixth Amendment's Confrontation Clause.

Hear It

You can hear the oral argument in *Hammon* at: http://www.oyez.org/cases/2000-2009/2005/2005_05_570.

The relevant statements in *Davis v. Washington* were made to a 911 emergency operator on February 1, 2001. In the ensuing conversation, the operator ascertained that the 911 caller McCottry was involved in a domestic disturbance with her former boyfriend Adrian Davis, the petitioner in this case:

"911 Operator: Hello.

"Complainant: Hello.

"911 Operator: What's going on?

"Complainant: He's here jumpin' on me again.

"911 Operator: Listen to me carefully. Do you know his last name?

"Complainant: It's Davis.

"911 Operator: Davis? Okay, what's his first name?

"Complainant: Adrian

"Complainant: Martell. He's runnin' now."

McCottry described the context of the assault, after which the operator told her that the police were on their way. The police arrived within four minutes of the 911 call and observed McCottry's shaken state, the "fresh injuries on her forearm and her face," and her "frantic efforts to gather her belongings and her children so that they could leave the residence." The State charged Davis with felony violation of a domestic no-contact order. "The State's only witnesses were the two police officers who responded to the 911 call. Both officers testified that McCottry exhibited injuries that appeared to be recent, but neither officer could testify as to the cause of the injuries." McCottry presumably could have testified as to whether Davis was her assailant, but she did not appear. Over Davis's objection, based on the Confrontation Clause of the Sixth Amendment, the trial court admitted the recording of her exchange with the 911 operator, and the jury convicted him. The Washington Court of Appeals and Supreme Court of Washington affirmed. We granted certiorari.

In *Hammon v. Indiana,* police responded late on the night of February 26, 2003, to a "reported domestic disturbance" at the home of Hershel and Amy Hammon. They found Amy alone on the front porch, appearing "somewhat frightened," but she told them that "nothing was the matter." She gave them permission to enter the house, where an officer saw "a gas heating unit in the corner of the living room" that had "flames coming out of the partial glass front. Hershel, meanwhile, was in the kitchen. He told the police "that he and his wife had 'been in an argument' but 'everything was fine now' and the argument 'never became physical.' " By this point Amy had come back inside. After hearing Amy's account, the officer "had her fill out and sign a battery affidavit." Amy handwrote the following: "Broke our Furnace & shoved me down on the floor into the broken glass. Hit me in the chest and threw me down. Broke our lamps & phone. Tore up my van where I couldn't leave the house. Attacked my daughter." The State charged Hershel with domestic battery and with violating his probation. Amy was subpoenaed, but she did not appear at his subsequent bench trial. The State called the officer who had questioned Amy, and asked him to recount what Amy told him and to authenticate the affidavit. Hershel's counsel repeatedly objected to the admission of this evidence. Nonetheless, the trial court admitted the affidavit as a "present sense impression," and Amy's statements as "excited utterances" that "are expressly permitted in these kinds of cases even if the declarant is not available to testify," The officer thus testified that Amy: "informed me that she and Hershel had been in an argument. That he became irrate [sic] over the fact of their daughter going to a boyfriend's house. The argument became physical after being verbal. She informed me Mr. Hammon had pushed her onto the ground, had shoved her head into the broken glass of the heater and that he had punched her in the chest twice I believe." The trial judge found Hershel guilty on both charges, and the Indiana Court of Appeals affirmed in relevant part. The Indiana Supreme Court also affirmed, concluding that Amy's statement was admissible for state-law purposes as an excited utterance, that "a 'testimonial' statement is one given or taken in significant part for purposes of preserving it for potential future use in legal proceedings," where "the motivations of the questioner and declarant are the central concerns," and that Amy's oral statement was not "testimonial" under these standards. It also concluded that, although the affidavit was testimonial and thus wrongly admitted, it was harmless beyond a reasonable doubt, largely because the trial was to the bench. We granted certiorari.

The Confrontation Clause of the Sixth Amendment provides: "In all criminal prosecutions, the accused shall enjoy the right to be confronted with the witnesses against him." In 2004, we held that this provision bars "admission of testimonial statements of a witness who did not appear at trial unless he was unavailable to testify, and the defendant had had a prior opportunity for cross-examination." A critical portion of this holding is the phrase "testimonial statements." Only statements of this sort cause the declarant to be a "witness" within the meaning of the Confrontation Clause. It is the testimonial character of the statement that separates it from other hearsay that, while subject to traditional limitations upon hearsay evidence, is not subject to the Confrontation Clause.

Our opinion in *Crawford* set forth "various formulations" of the core class of "testimonial" statements, but found it unnecessary to endorse any of them, because "some statements qualify under any definition." Among those, we said, were "statements taken by police officers in the course of interrogations. Questioning that generated the deponent's statement in *Crawford*—which was made and recorded while she was in police custody, after having been given *Miranda* warnings as a possible suspect herself—"qualifies under any conceivable definition" of an "interrogation," We therefore did not define that term, except to say that "we use it in its colloquial, rather than any technical legal, sense," and that "one can imagine various definitions, and we need not select among them in this case." It suffices to decide the present cases to hold as follows: Statements are non-testimonial when made in the course of police interrogation under circumstances objectively indicating that the primary purpose of the interrogation is to enable police assistance to meet an ongoing emergency. They are testimonial when the circumstances objectively indicate that there is no such ongoing emergency, and that the primary purpose of the interrogation is to establish or prove past events potentially relevant to later criminal prosecution.

We must decide whether the Confrontation Clause applies only to testimonial hearsay; and, if so, whether the recording of a 911 call qualifies as an interrogation by law enforcement officers. The answer to the first question was suggested in *Crawford*: "The text of the Confrontation Clause reflects this focus on testimonial hearsay. It applies to 'witnesses' against the accused—in other words, those who 'bear testimony.' 1 N. WEBSTER, AN AMERICAN DICTIONARY OF THE ENGLISH LANGUAGE (1828). 'Testimony,' in turn, is typically 'a solemn declaration or affirmation made for the purpose of establishing or proving some fact.' An accuser who makes a formal statement to government officers bears testimony in a sense that a person who makes a casual remark to an acquaintance does not." A limitation so clearly reflected in the text of the constitutional provision must fairly be said to mark out not merely its "core," but its perimeter.

We are not aware of any early American case invoking the Confrontation Clause or the common-law right to confrontation that did not clearly involve testimony as thus defined. Even our later cases, conforming to the reasoning of *Roberts*, never in practice dispensed with the Confrontation Clause requirements of unavailability and prior cross-examination in cases that involved testimonial hearsay, *Crawford*, 541 U.S., at 57–59, with one arguable exception (discussing *White v. Illinois*, 502 U.S. 346). Where our cases did dispense with those requirements—even under the *Roberts* approach—the statements at issue were clearly nontestimonial. *See, e.g., Bourjaily v. United States*, 483 U.S. 171, 181 (1987) (statements made unwittingly to a Government informant).

Food for Thought

Does *White v. Illinois* undermine the Court's review of precedent?

The question before us in *Davis* is whether, objectively considered, the interrogation that took place in the course of the 911 call produced testimonial statements. When we said in *Crawford* that "interrogations by law enforcement officers fall squarely within the class" of testimonial hearsay, we had in mind interrogations solely directed at establishing the facts of a past crime, in order to identify (or provide evidence to convict) the perpetrator. The product of such interrogation, whether reduced to a writing signed by the declarant or embedded in the memory (and perhaps notes) of the interrogating officer, is testimonial. A 911 call, on the other hand, and at least the initial interrogation conducted in connection with a 911 call, is ordinarily not designed primarily to "establish or prove" some past fact, but to describe current circumstances requiring police assistance.

The difference between the interrogation in *Davis* and the one in *Crawford* is apparent on the face of things. In *Davis,* McCottry was speaking about events *as they were actually happening,* rather than "describing past events," *Lilly v. Virginia,* 527 U.S. 116 (1999) (plurality opinion). Sylvia Crawford's interrogation, on the other hand, took place hours after the events she described had occurred. Moreover, any reasonable listener would recognize that McCottry (unlike Sylvia Crawford) was facing an ongoing emergency. Although one *might* call 911 to provide a narrative report of a crime absent any imminent danger, McCottry's call was plainly a call for help against bona fide physical threat. Third, the nature of what was asked and answered in *Davis,* again viewed objectively, was such that the elicited statements were necessary to be able to *resolve* the present emergency, rather than simply to learn (as in *Crawford*) what had happened in the past. That is true even of the operator's effort to establish the identity of the assailant, so that the dispatched officers might know whether they would be encountering a violent felon. Finally, the difference in the level of formality between the two interviews is striking. Crawford was responding calmly, at the station house, to a series of questions, with the officer-interrogator taping and making notes of her answers; McCottry's frantic answers were provided over the phone, in an environment that was not tranquil, or even (as far as any reasonable 911 operator could make out) safe.

We conclude that the circumstances of McCottry's interrogation objectively indicate its primary purpose was to enable police assistance to meet an ongoing emergency. She simply was not acting as a *witness;* she was not *testifying.* What she said was not "a weaker substitute for live testimony" at trial, *United States v. Inadi,* 475 U.S. 387, 394 (1986), like Lord Cobham's statements in *Raleigh's Case,* 2 How. St. Tr. 1 (1603), or Jane Dingler's *ex parte* statements against her husband in *King v. Dingler,* 2 Leach 561, 168 Eng. Rep. 383 (1791), or Sylvia Crawford's statement in *Crawford.* In each of those cases, the *ex parte* actors and the evidentiary products of the *ex parte* communication aligned perfectly with their courtroom analogues. McCottry's emergency statement does not. No "witness" goes into court to proclaim an emergency and seek help.

Davis seeks to cast McCottry in the unlikely role of a witness by pointing to English cases. None of them involves statements made during an ongoing emergency.

In *King v. Brasier*, 1 Leach 199, 168 Eng. Rep. 202 (1779), a young rape victim, "immediately on her coming home, told all the circumstances of the injury" to her mother. The case would be helpful to Davis if the relevant statement had been the girl's screams for aid as she was being chased by her assailant. But by the time the victim got home, her story was an account of past events. This is not to say that a conversation which begins as an interrogation to determine the need for emergency assistance cannot "evolve into testimonial statements," once that purpose has been achieved. In this case, after the operator gained the information needed to address the exigency of the moment, the emergency appears to have ended (when Davis drove away from the premises). The operator then told McCottry to be quiet, and proceeded to pose a battery of questions. It could readily be maintained that, from that point on, McCottry's statements were testimonial, not unlike the "structured police questioning" that occurred in *Crawford*. This presents no great problem. Through *in limine* procedure, they should redact or exclude the portions of any statement that have become testimonial, as they do, for example, with unduly prejudicial portions of otherwise admissible evidence. Davis's jury did not hear the *complete* 911 call, although it may well have heard some testimonial portions. We were asked to classify only McCottry's early statements identifying Davis as her assailant, and we agree that they were not testimonial. That court also concluded that, even if later parts of the call were testimonial, their admission was harmless beyond a reasonable doubt. Davis does not challenge that holding, and we assume it to be correct.

Determining the testimonial or nontestimonial character of the statements that were the product of the interrogation in *Hammon* is a much easier task, since they were not much different from the statements we found to be testimonial in *Crawford*. It is entirely clear from the circumstances that the interrogation was part of an investigation into possibly criminal past conduct—as, indeed, the testifying officer expressly acknowledged. There was no emergency in progress; the interrogating officer testified that he heard no arguments or crashing and saw no one throw or break anything. When the officer questioned Amy for the second time, and elicited the challenged statements, he was not seeking to determine (as in Davis) "what is happening," but rather "what happened." Objectively viewed, the primary, if not sole, purpose of the interrogation was to investigate a possible crime—which is, of course, precisely what the officer should have done. It is true that the *Crawford* interrogation was more formal. But Amy's interrogation was formal enough that Amy's interrogation was conducted in a separate room, away from her husband (who tried to intervene), with the officer receiving her replies for use in his "investigation." What we called the "striking resemblance" of the *Crawford* statement to civil-law *ex parte* examinations is shared by Amy's statement here. Both declarants were actively separated from the defendant—officers forcibly prevented Hershel from participating in the interrogation. Both statements deliberately recounted, in response to police questioning, how potentially criminal past events began and progressed. Both took place sometime after the events described were over.

Respondents in both cases contend that the nature of the offenses charged in these two cases—domestic violence—requires greater flexibility in the use of testimonial evidence. This particular type of crime is notoriously susceptible to intimidation or coercion of the victim to ensure that she does not testify at trial. When this occurs, the Confrontation Clause gives the criminal a windfall. We may not, however, vitiate constitutional guarantees when they have the effect of allowing the guilty to go free. But when defendants seek to undermine the judicial process by procuring or coercing silence from witnesses and victims, the Sixth Amendment does not require courts to acquiesce. We reiterate what we said in *Crawford:* that "the rule of forfeiture by wrongdoing extinguishes confrontation claims on essentially equitable grounds." That is, one who obtains the absence of a witness by wrongdoing forfeits the constitutional right to confrontation.

Absent a finding of forfeiture by wrongdoing, the Sixth Amendment operates to exclude Amy Hammon's affidavit. The Indiana courts may determine on remand whether such a claim of forfeiture is properly raised and, if so, whether it is meritorious.

We affirm the judgment of the Supreme Court of Washington. We reverse the judgment of the Supreme Court of Indiana, and remand the case to that court for proceedings not inconsistent with this opinion.

It is so ordered.

JUSTICE THOMAS, concurring in the judgment in part and dissenting in part.

In *Crawford v. Washington*, 541 U.S. 36 (2004), we abandoned the general reliability inquiry we had long employed to judge the admissibility of hearsay evidence under the Confrontation Clause, describing that inquiry as "*inherently,* and therefore *permanently,* unpredictable." Today, a mere two years after the Court decided *Crawford,* it adopts an equally unpredictable test, under which district courts are charged with divining the "primary purpose" of police interrogations. Besides being difficult to apply, this test characterizes as "testimonial," and therefore inadmissible, evidence that bears little resemblance to what we have recognized as the evidence targeted by the Confrontation Clause. Because neither of the cases before the Court would implicate the Confrontation Clause under an appropriately targeted standard, I concur only in the judgment in *Davis* and dissent from the Court's resolution of *Hammon*.

Neither the 911 call at issue in *Davis* nor the police questioning at issue in *Hammon* is testimonial under the appropriate framework. Neither the call nor the questioning is itself a formalized dialogue. Nor do any circumstances surrounding the taking of the statements render those statements sufficiently formal to resemble the Marian examinations; the statements were neither *Mirandized* nor custodial, nor accompanied by any similar indicia of formality. Finally, there is no suggestion that the prosecution attempted to offer the women's hearsay evidence at trial in order to evade confrontation. Accordingly, the statements in both cases are nontestimonial and admissible under the Confrontation Clause. Because the standard adopted by the Court today is neither workable nor a targeted attempt to reach the abuses forbidden by the Clause, I concur in *Davis* and dissent from the Court's resolution of *Hammon.*

Hypo 1: *Primary Purpose of Interrogation*

How does the Confrontation Clause apply to the following two situations: A) A victim of domestic violence places a 911 call to the police for help. The first part of the call involves the imminent safety of the caller. When it is established that the perpetrator rode away on a bicycle, the rest of the call concerns the identity of the perpetrator and the relevant circumstances. A timely objection has been lodged. You are the judge. Would you admit testimony regarding the 911 call? B) The county coroner conducts an autopsy on a 72-year-old male. After the autopsy, the coroner concludes that the decedent died from strangulation. The prosecution offers a forensic pathologist to testify about the autopsy report in a subsequent murder case. Is the report testimonial? Is the primary purpose of the report to create evidence for trial? If not, what is the primary purpose?

Hypo 2: *Judicial Error*

How would the Confrontation Clause apply to the following two situations: A) Defendant is on trial for eluding a police officer after being pulled over for a traffic violation and then driving off, creating a wild and dangerous chase through a highly populated area. The declarant, while being questioned by the police after the defendant was arrested, informed the police that she loaned defendant her car. Declarant also provides considerable information about the defendant's state of mind. The Court admitted the declarant's statement over objection, saying it was part of "an on-going emergency" and that it met the excited utterance foundation and was important to the prosecution's case, establishing how defendant obtained the car and the motive for driving off. If you are an appellate court judge who must decide whether the admission of the declarant's statements was harmless error, how would you rule? B) A police officer at a valid traffic stop discovers a baggie containing a white substance in plain view. Based on what he sees, the officer arrests defendant for the possession of cocaine. At trial for possession with intent to distribute cocaine, a report by a non-testifying chemist is offered in evidence without objection during the testimony of the arresting officer. On appeal, petitioner claims that it was unconstitutional and plain error to admit the evidence. How should the appellate court rule on the claim of error?

Michigan v. Bryant

562 U.S. 344 (2011).

Justice Sotomayor delivered the opinion of the Court.

At respondent Richard Bryant's trial, the court admitted statements that the victim, Anthony Covington, made to police officers who discovered him mortally wounded in a gas station parking lot. A jury convicted Bryant of second-degree murder. On appeal, the Supreme Court of Michigan held that the Sixth Amendment's Confrontation Clause rendered Covington's statements inadmissible testimonial hearsay, and reversed Bryant's conviction. We granted certiorari. We hold that the circumstances of the interaction between Covington and the police objectively indicate that the "primary purpose of the interrogation" was "to enable police assistance to meet an ongoing emergency." *Davis*, 547 U.S., at 822. Therefore, Covington's identification and description of the shooter and the location of the shooting were not testimonial statements, and their admission at Bryant's trial did not violate the Confrontation Clause. We vacate and remand.

Who's That?

Sonia Sotomayor was appointed as an Associate Justice of the Supreme Court by President Obama in 2009, replacing David Souter. She first served as a federal district court judge, appointed by President George H.W. Bush. A graduate of Princeton University and Yale Law School, she was an assistant district attorney and international commercial litigator while in practice.

This case requires further explanation of the "ongoing emergency" circumstance. Because *Davis* and *Hammon* arose in the domestic violence context, that was the situation "we had immediately in mind." We now face a new context: a nondomestic dispute, involving a victim found in a public location, suffering from a fatal gunshot wound, and a perpetrator whose location was unknown at the time the police located the victim. To determine whether the "primary purpose" of an interrogation is "to enable police assistance to meet an ongoing emergency," which would render the resulting statements non-testimonial, we objectively evaluate the circumstances in which the encounter occurs and the statements and actions of the parties. An objective analysis of the circumstances of an encounter and the statements and actions of the parties to it provides the most accurate assessment of the "primary purpose of the interrogation." The circumstances in which an encounter occurs—*e.g.,* at or near the scene of the crime versus at a police station, during an ongoing emergency or afterwards—are clearly matters of objective fact. The statements and actions of the parties must also be objectively evaluated. That is, the relevant inquiry is not the subjective or actual purpose of the individuals involved in a particular encounter, but rather the purpose that reasonable participants would have had, as ascertained from the individuals' statements and actions and the circumstances in which the encounter occurred.

Whether an ongoing emergency exists is simply one factor—albeit an important factor—that informs the ultimate inquiry regarding the "primary purpose" of an interrogation. Another factor is the importance of *informality* in an encounter between a victim and police. Formality is not the sole touchstone of our primary purpose inquiry because, although formality suggests the absence of an emergency and therefore an increased likelihood that the purpose of the interrogation is to "establish or prove past events potentially relevant to later criminal prosecution," informality does not necessarily indicate the presence of an emergency or the lack of testimonial intent. As we explain the questioning in this case occurred in an exposed, public area, prior to the arrival of emergency medical services, and in a disorganized fashion. All of those facts make this case distinguishable from the formal station-house interrogation in *Crawford.*

In addition, the statements and actions of both the declarant and interrogators provide objective evidence of the primary purpose of the interrogation. *Davis* requires a combined inquiry that accounts for both the declarant and the interrogator. In many instances, the primary purpose of the interrogation will be most accurately ascertained by looking to the contents of both the questions and the answers. If the police say to a victim, "Tell us who did this to you so that we can arrest and prosecute them," the victim's response that "Rick did it," appears purely accusatory because by virtue of the phrasing of the question, the victim necessarily has prosecution in mind when she answers. The combined approach also ameliorates problems that could arise from looking solely to one participant. Predominant among these is the problem of mixed motives on the part of both interrogators and declarants. Police officers in our society function as both first responders and criminal investigators. Their dual responsibilities may mean that they act with different motives simultaneously or in quick succession. *See New York v. Quarles*, 467 U.S. 649 (1984).

As the context of this case brings into sharp relief, the existence and duration of an emergency depend on the type and scope of danger posed to the victim, the police, and the public. We first examine the circumstances in which the interrogation occurred. The parties disagree over whether there was an emergency when the police arrived at the gas station. The record reveals little about the motive for the shooting. What Covington did tell the officers was that he fled Bryant's back porch, indicating that he perceived an ongoing threat. The police did not know, and Covington did not tell them, whether the threat was limited to him. The potential scope of the dispute and therefore the emergency stretches more broadly than those at issue in *Davis* and *Hammon* and encompasses a threat potentially to the police and the public.

This is also the first of our post-*Crawford* Confrontation Clause cases to involve a gun. The physical separation that was sufficient to end the emergency in *Hammon* was not necessarily sufficient to end the threat in this case; Covington was shot through the back door of Bryant's house. Bryant's argument that there was no ongoing emergency because "no shots were being fired," surely construes ongoing emergency too narrowly. There was an ongoing emergency here where an armed shooter, whose motive for and location after the shooting were unknown, had mortally wounded Covington within a few blocks and a few minutes of the location where the police found Covington. For their part, the police responded to a call that a man had been shot. They did not know why, where, or when the shooting had occurred. Nor did they know the location of the shooter or anything else about the circumstances in which the crime occurred. The questions they asked—"what happened, who shot him, and where the shooting occurred,"—were the exact type of questions necessary to allow the police to "assess the situation, the threat to their own safety, and possible danger to the potential victim" and to the public, including to allow them to ascertain "whether they would be encountering a violent felon," *Davis* at 827. In other words, they solicited the information necessary to enable them "to meet an ongoing emergency exception." Nothing in Covington's responses indicated to the police that, contrary to their expectation upon responding to a call reporting a shooting, there was no emergency or that a prior emergency had ended. Covington did indicate that he had been shot at another location about 25 minutes earlier, but he did not know the location of the shooter at the time the police arrived and he gave no indication that the shooter, having shot at him twice, would be satisfied that Covington was only wounded. In fact, Covington did not indicate any possible motive for the shooting, and thereby gave no reason to think that the shooter would not shoot again if he arrived on the scene. As in *Davis,* "initial inquiries" may "*often* produce nontestimonial statements. The initial inquiries in this case resulted in the type of nontestimonial statements we contemplated in *Davis.*

Finally, we consider the informality of the situation and the interrogation. This situation is more similar, though not identical, to the informal, harried 911 call in *Davis* than to the structured, station-house interview in *Crawford.* The situation was fluid and somewhat confused: the officers arrived at different times; apparently each, upon arrival, asked Covington "what happened?"; and, contrary to the dissent's portrayal, they did not conduct a structured interrogation. The informality suggests that the interrogators' primary purpose was simply to address what they perceived to be an ongoing emergency, and the circumstances lacked any formality that would have alerted Covington to or focused him on the possible future prosecutorial use of his statements. Because the circumstances of the encounter as well as the statements and actions of Covington and the police objectively indicate that the "primary purpose of the interrogation" was "to enable police assistance to meet an ongoing emergency," Covington's identification and description of the shooter and the location of the shooting were not testimonial hearsay. The Confrontation Clause did not bar their admission at Bryant's trial.

For the foregoing reasons, we hold that Covington's statements were not testimonial and that their admission at Bryant's trial did not violate the Confrontation Clause. We leave for the Michigan courts to decide on remand whether the statements' admission was otherwise permitted by state hearsay rules. The judgment of the Supreme Court of Michigan is vacated, and the case is remanded for further proceedings not inconsistent with this opinion.

Food for Thought

Is *Michigan v. Bryant* consistent with *Hammon* and *Davis*? Apply *Bryant* to the hypos after *Hammon* and *Davis* to see if it invariably leads to the same results.

It is so ordered.

JUSTICE THOMAS, concurring in the judgment.

Covington's questioning by police lacked sufficient formality and solemnity for his statements to be considered "testimonial." *See Crawford v. Washington*, 541 U.S. 3 (2004). In determining whether Covington's statements to police implicate the Confrontation Clause, the Court evaluates the "primary purpose" of the interrogation. The majority's analysis which relies on what the police knew when they arrived at the scene, the specific questions they asked, the particular information Covington conveyed, the weapon involved, and Covington's medical condition illustrates the uncertainty that this test creates for law enforcement and the lower courts. I have criticized the primary-purpose test as "an exercise in fiction" that is "disconnected from history" and "yields no predictable results." Rather than attempting to reconstruct the "primary purpose" of the participants, I would consider the extent to which the interrogation resembles those historical practices that the Confrontation Clause addressed. This interrogation bears little if any resemblance to the historical practices that the Confrontation Clause aimed to eliminate. Covington thus did not "bear testimony" against Bryant, and the introduction of his statements at trial did not implicate the Confrontation Clause. I concur in the judgment.

JUSTICE SCALIA, dissenting.

Today's tale—a story of five officers conducting successive examinations of a dying man with the primary purpose, not of obtaining and preserving his testimony regarding his killer, but of protecting him, them, and others from a murderer somewhere on the loose—is so transparently false that professing to believe it demeans this institution. But reaching a patently incorrect conclusion on the facts is a relatively benign judicial mischief; it affects, after all, only the case at hand. In its vain attempt to make the incredible plausible, today's opinion distorts our Confrontation Clause jurisprudence and leaves it in a shambles. Instead of clarifying the law, the Court makes itself the obfuscator of last resort. Because I continue to adhere to the Confrontation Clause that the People adopted, as described in Crawford, I dissent.

A declarant-focused inquiry is the only inquiry that would work in every fact pattern implicating the Confrontation Clause. An inquiry into an officer's purposes would make no sense when a declarant blurts out "Rick shot me" as soon as the officer arrives on the scene. I see no reason to adopt a different test—one that accounts for an officer's intent—when the officer asks "what happened" before the declarant makes his accusation. (The identity of an interrogator, and the content and tenor of his questions, can bear upon whether a declarant intends to make a solemn statement, and envisions its use at a criminal trial. But none of this means that the interrogator's purpose matters.)

> **FYI**
>
> A commentator has suggested that Justice Sotomayor might have been reinstating the *Ohio v. Roberts* reliability analysis when she said, "Implicit in *Davis* is the idea that because the prospect of fabrication in statements given for the primary purpose of resolving that emergency is presumably significantly diminished, the Confrontation Clause does not require such examinations to be subject to the crucible of cross-examination." The commentator noted, "This logic of focusing on whether there is an ongoing emergency such as to render a statement non-testimonial is not unlike that justifying the excited utterance exception in hearsay law." I. Bennett Capers, "Reading *Michigan v. Bryant*, "Reading" Justice Sotomayor," 123 YALE L. FORUM 427 (2014).

Looking to the declarant's purpose, this is an absurdly easy case. Roughly 25 minutes after Anthony Covington had been shot, Detroit police responded to a 911 call reporting that a gunshot victim had appeared at a neighborhood gas station. They quickly arrived at the scene, and in less than 10 minutes five different Detroit police officers questioned Covington about the shooting. Each asked him a similar battery of questions: "what happened" and when, "who shot the victim," and "where" did the shooting take place. After Covington would answer, they would ask follow-up questions, such as "how tall is" the shooter. The battery relented when the paramedics arrived and began tending to Covington's wounds. From Covington's perspective, his statements had little value except to ensure the arrest and eventual prosecution of Richard Bryant. He knew the "threatening situation" had ended six blocks away and 25 minutes earlier when he fled from Bryant's back porch. Bryant had not confronted him face-to-face before he was mortally wounded, instead shooting him through a door. Even if Bryant had pursued him, and after seeing that Covington had ended up at the gas station was unable to confront him there before the police arrived, it was entirely beyond imagination that Bryant would again open fire while Covington was surrounded by five armed police officers.

And Covington knew the shooting was the work of a drug dealer, not a spree killer who might randomly threaten others.

The Court's distorted view creates an expansive exception to the Confrontation Clause for violent crimes. Because Bryant posed a continuing threat to public safety in the Court's imagination, the emergency persisted for confrontation purposes at least until the police learned his "motive for and location after the shooting." It may have persisted until the police "secured the scene of the shooting" two-and-a-half hours later. In *Crawford*, this Court noted that, in the law we inherited from England, there was a well-established exception to the confrontation requirement: The cloak protecting the accused against admission of out-of-court testimonial statements was removed for dying declarations. This historic exception, we recalled in *Giles v. California*, 554 U.S. 353 (2008), applied to statements made by a person about to die and aware that death was imminent. Were the issue properly tendered here, I would take up the question whether the exception for dying declarations survives our recent Confrontation Clause decisions.

> **FYI**
>
> Should "dying declarations" be admitted into evidence if the defendant has been given no right to confrontation? Although some states have held that dying declarations cannot be admitted after *Crawford*, in *Davis v. State*, 207 So.3d 142 (Fl. 2016), *cert. denied*, 137 S. Ct. 2218 (2017), the court held that such declarations are admissible.

Hypo: *Shotgun*

Defendant was tried for the unlawful possession of a shotgun. At trial, an investigating police officer testified that she was at the scene after a 911 call when the victim returned to the scene and told the officer that the accused had a gun which he pointed at her, and she identified the accused in the process. A timely objection was made to the investigator's testimony. The judge permitted a brief *voir dire* of the witness to determine whether the victim's statements were testimonial. You are asked to conduct the *voir dire*, meaning a brief cross-examination of the witness, in this case outside the hearing of the jury. What questions would you ask about the location of the defendant when the victim's statements were made? What other questions might you ask about the incident in question?

* * *

An important and evolving focus of courts in the aftermath of *Crawford* has been the development of the "primary purpose" test in determining whether evidence is testimonial. If the primary purpose of the evidence is to create an out-of-court substitute for trial testimony, it will fall within the ambit of the Confrontation Clause. On the other hand, if the evidence is intended to help resolve an on-going emergency or for some other purpose, it is not testimonial. *Ohio v. Clark* provides a good summary of the winding road leading to the current stasis of the rule.

Ohio v. Clark

576 U.S. 237 (2015).

JUSTICE ALITO delivered the opinion of the Court.

Darius Clark, who went by the nickname "Dee," lived in Cleveland, Ohio, with his girlfriend, T.T., and her two children: L.P., a 3-year-old boy, and A.T., an 18-month-old girl. Clark was T.T.'s pimp, and he would regularly send her on trips to Washington, D. C., to work as a prostitute. In March 2010, T.T. went on one such trip, and she left the children in Clark's care. The next day, Clark took L.P. to preschool. In the lunchroom, one of L.P.'s teachers, Ramona Whitley, observed that L.P.'s left eye appeared bloodshot. She asked him "what happened," and he initially said nothing. Eventually, however, he told the teacher that he "fell." When they moved into the brighter lights of a classroom, Whitley noticed "red marks, like whips of some sort," on L.P.'s face. She notified the lead teacher, Debra Jones, who asked L.P., "Who did this? What happened to you?" According to Jones, L.P. "seemed kind of bewildered" and "said something like, Dee, Dee." Jones asked L.P. whether Dee is "big or little," to which L.P. responded that "Dee is big." Jones then brought L.P. to her supervisor, who lifted the boy's shirt, revealing more injuries. Whitley called a child abuse hotline to alert authorities about the suspected abuse. When Clark arrived at the school, he denied responsibility for the injuries and quickly left with L.P. The next day, a social worker found the children at Clark's mother's house and took them to a hospital, where a physician discovered additional injuries suggesting child abuse. L.P. had a black eye, belt marks on his back and stomach, and bruises all over his body. A.T. had two black eyes, a swollen hand, and a large burn on her cheek, and two pigtails had been ripped out at the roots of her hair. Clark moved to exclude testimony about L.P.'s out-of-court statements under the Confrontation Clause. The trial court denied the motion, ruling that L.P.'s responses were not testimonial statements covered by the Sixth Amendment. The jury found Clark guilty on all counts except for one assault count related to A.T., and it sentenced him to 28 years' imprisonment. Clark appealed his conviction, and a state appellate court reversed on the ground that the introduction of L.P.'s out-of-court statements violated the Confrontation Clause. The Supreme Court of Ohio affirmed. We granted certiorari and reverse.

The Sixth Amendment's Confrontation Clause, which is binding on the States through the Fourteenth Amendment, provides: "In all criminal prosecutions, the accused shall enjoy the right . . . to be confronted with the witnesses against him." In *Ohio v. Roberts*, 448 U. S. 56, 66 (1980), we interpreted the Clause to permit the admission of out-of-court statements by an unavailable witness, so long as the statements bore "adequate 'indicia of reliability.'" Such indicia are present, we held, if "the evidence falls within a firmly rooted hearsay exception" or bears "particularized guarantees of trustworthiness." Our more recent cases have labored to flesh out what it means for a statement to be "testimonial." In *Davis v. Washington and Hammon v. Indiana*, 547 U. S. 813 (2006), which we decided together, we dealt with statements given to law enforcement officers by the victims of domestic abuse. The victim in *Davis* made statements to a 911 emergency operator during and shortly after her boyfriend's violent attack. In Hammon, the victim, after being isolated from her abusive husband, made statements to police that were memorialized in a "battery affidavit." We held that the statements in *Hammon* were testimonial, while the statements in *Davis* were not. Announcing what has come to be known as the "primary purpose" test, we explained: "Statements are nontestimonial when made in the course of police interrogation under circumstances objectively indicating that the primary purpose of the interrogation is to enable police assistance to meet an ongoing emergency. They are testimonial when the circumstances objectively indicate that there is no such ongoing emergency, and that the primary purpose of the interrogation is to establish or prove past events potentially relevant to later criminal prosecution."

In *Michigan v. Bryant*, 562 U. S. 344 (2011), we further expounded on the primary purpose test. The inquiry, we emphasized, must consider "all of the relevant circumstances." The existence vel non of an ongoing emergency is not the touchstone of the testimonial inquiry." Instead, "whether an ongoing emergency exists is simply one factor that informs the ultimate inquiry regarding the 'primary purpose' of an interrogation." One additional factor is "the informality of the situation and the interrogation." A "formal station-house interrogation," like the questioning in Crawford, is more likely to provoke testimonial statements, while less formal questioning is less likely to reflect a primary purpose aimed at obtaining testimonial evidence against the accused. In determining whether a statement is testimonial, "standard rules of hearsay, designed to identify some statements as reliable, will be relevant." In the end, the question is whether, in light of all the circumstances, viewed objectively, the "primary purpose" of the conversation was to "create an out-of-court substitute for trial testimony."

In this case, we consider statements made to preschool teachers, not the

Food for Thought

Defendant, who is charged with murder, takes the stand to testify that her dead boyfriend committed the murder. Before the boyfriend committed suicide, he had issued a statement, indicating that the murder was defendant's idea and that she forced him to go along. Can the boyfriend's statement be admitted, over defendant's objection, without running afoul of the Confrontation Clause? *See People v. Hopson*, 396 P.3d 1054 (Cal. 2017).

police. We are presented with the question we have repeatedly reserved: whether statements to persons other than law enforcement officers are subject to the Confrontation Clause. Because at least some statements to individuals who are not law enforcement officers could conceivably raise confrontation concerns, we decline to adopt a categorical rule excluding them from the Sixth Amendment's reach. Nevertheless, such statements are much less likely to be testimonial than statements to law enforcement officers. Considering all the relevant circumstances here, L.P.'s statements clearly were not made with the primary purpose of creating evidence for Clark's prosecution. Thus, their introduction at trial did not violate the Confrontation Clause.

We reverse the judgment of the Supreme Court of Ohio and remand the case for further proceedings not inconsistent with this opinion.

It is so ordered.

Point for Discussion

Ohio v. Clark's Progeny

After Ohio v. Clark, lower courts were left with the task of determining whether hearsay evidence was testimonial in the sense that the primary purpose of the evidence was to create an out-of-court substitute for trial testimony—or whether the primary purpose was for some other purpose such as addressing an on-going emergency. In *Oregon v. Rafeh*, 361 Ore. 423 (2017), the Oregon Supreme Court considered whether a document was testimonial and subject to Confrontation Clause scrutiny. The Court found that the document, a certification of notice given, was not testimonial:

The Driver and Motor Vehicle Services Division (DMV) of the Department of Transportation suspended defendant's driver's license for three years for refusing to submit voluntarily to a blood alcohol test. Approximately two and one-half years later, defendant was stopped while driving without a license, and the state charged her with driving while suspended (DWS). The question that this case presents is whether the federal Confrontation Clause prohibits the admission, in defendant's DWS trial, of an earlier certification that defendant had been given notice that the state intended to suspend her driver's license. The trial court admitted the certification over defendant's objection, and the jury found her guilty of DWS. The Court of Appeals summarily affirmed. We affirm the Court of Appeals decision and the trial court's judgment.

The question in Bryant and in Crawford was whether police officers were seeking to create "an out-of-court substitute" for testimony in a criminal trial. To accept defendant's expansive interpretation of the Confrontation

Clause, not only would we have to overlook the context in which the statements on which he relies were made, but we also would have to ignore the Court's holding in Clark that only out-of-court statements made or elicited primarily for use in a criminal proceeding are testimonial. Following Clark and Copeland, we conclude that the certification in the Implied Consent Combined Report was not made for "the primary purpose of assisting in defendant's prosecution." Rather, the primary purpose of the certification is administrative. It confirmed that defendant had received sufficient notice for DMV to proceed with an administrative license suspension hearing. The decision whether to suspend defendant's license was undertaken to ensure the safety of the other drivers on the state's roads, much in the same way that the child's statement in Clark identifying who had harmed him was elicited to protect the child from further harm. Indeed, the challenged certification—that defendant had been given a copy of the report as written notice—would have no relevance to a prosecution for DUII. The prospect that the certification might become relevant in some future prosecution for DWS turns on far too many contingencies to say that the certification's primary purpose was for use in a criminal proceeding.

A similar issue arose in *United States v. Fryberg*, 854 F. 3d 1126 (9th Cir. 2017), which involved a completed return of notice of a hearing on the restraining order. In that case before a tribal court, a key question was whether the defendant had received notice of a hearing on a restraining order. The government offered in evidence a document, the completed return of service showing notice, and not witness testimony. The question was whether that return was testimonial within the Confrontation Clause. The Court ruled that "the admission of the return of service did not violate either the rule against hearsay or the Confrontation Clause of the Sixth Amendment, and we affirm Defendant's conviction." A predicate question involved whether the return of service complied with the hearsay limits imposed by the Federal Rules of Evidence. The Court held that it did. The Court found that the officer was "under a legal duty to report when he completed the return of service," and that the service was a ministerial part of the officer's duties, making the service document a public record under Fed. R. Evid. 803(8)(A)(ii). The Court's reasoning on the Confrontation Clause issue was more nuanced:

"A business or public record is not 'testimonial' due to 'the mere possibility' that it could be used in a later criminal prosecution." *United States v. Morales*, 720 F.3d 1194, 1200 (9th Cir. 2013). The inquiry is whether the primary purpose of the record is "for use as evidence at a future criminal trial." Here, the primary purpose of the return of service was to inform the tribal court that Defendant had been served with notice of the hearing on the protection order, which enabled the hearing to proceed. Perhaps it was foreseeable to Officer Echevarria that the return of service might later be used in a criminal trial to establish the fact that Defendant had been served with notice, but that fact does not necessarily render the return of service It is generally true that one who violates a domestic violence protection order is subject to criminal penalties. Had the Government not produced a copy of the return of service but, instead, attempted to introduce a 2015 affidavit signed by Officer Echevarria stating that he had served Defendant with notice in 2002, this case would be closer to Bustamante. As it is, however, the Government introduced the return of service itself, a contemporaneous document owing its existence primarily to the tribal court's administrative needs. We hold that the admission of the return of service did not violate Defendant's rights under the Confrontation Clause.

Food for Thought

At defendant's trial for sex trafficking, the prosecution seeks to introduce police body camera footage which depicts a woman (defendant's co-conspirator, Moore) yelling that defendant was prostituting young girls. Moore entered into a plea deal with the government and was not called as a witness at defendant's trial. Were Moore's statements testimonial so that defendant has the right to confront her at trial? *See United States v. Graham*, 47 F.4th 561 (7th Cir. 2022).

D. Expert Reports & Confrontation

It is common for the prosecution to use experts and their reports in criminal cases. Experts testify about the *modus operandi* of criminal operations, and test for contraband substances in laboratories across the country. Prior to *Crawford*, experts could submit their test results as part of reliable reports under the hearsay exception recognized in state and federal courts alike, the public records exception. *See, e.g.*, Fed. R. Evid. 803(8).

Melendez-Diaz v. Massachusetts

557 U.S. 305 (2009).

JUSTICE SCALIA delivered the opinion of the Court, joined by JUSTICE STEVENS, JUSTICE SOUTER, JUSTICE THOMAS, and JUSTICE GINSBURG.

The Massachusetts courts admitted into evidence affidavits reporting the results of forensic analysis which showed that material seized by the police and connected to the defendant was cocaine. The question is whether those affidavits are "testimonial," rendering the affiants "witnesses" subject to the defendant's right of confrontation under the Sixth Amendment.

In 2001, Boston police officers arrested several men in a drug sting, one of whom was petitioner Luis Melendez-Diaz. The officers placed all three men in a police cruiser. During the short drive to the police station, the officers observed their passengers fidgeting and making furtive movements in the back of the car. After depositing the men at the station, they searched the police cruiser and found a plastic bag containing 19 smaller plastic bags hidden in the partition between the front and back seats. They submitted the seized evidence to a state laboratory required by law to conduct chemical analysis upon police request. Melendez-Diaz was charged with distributing cocaine and with trafficking in cocaine in an amount between 14 and 28 grams. At trial, the prosecution placed into evidence the bags seized from Wright and from the police cruiser. It also submitted three "certificates of analysis" showing the results of the forensic analysis performed on the seized substances. The certificates reported the weight of the seized bags and stated that the bags "have been examined with the following results: The substance was found to contain: Cocaine." The certificates were sworn to before a notary public by analysts at the State Laboratory Institute of the Massachusetts Department of Public Health, as required under Massachusetts law. Petitioner objected to the admission of the certificates, asserting that our Confrontation Clause decision required the analysts to testify in person. The objection was overruled, and the certificates were admitted pursuant to state law as "prima facie evidence of the composition, quality, and the net weight of the narcotic analyzed." The jury found Melendez-Diaz guilty. He appealed, contending, among other things, that admission of the certificates violated his Sixth Amendment right to be confronted with the witnesses against him. We granted certiorari.

The Sixth Amendment to the United States Constitution, made applicable to the States via the Fourteenth Amendment, provides that "in all criminal prosecutions, the accused shall enjoy the right . . . to be confronted with the witnesses against him." In *Crawford,* after reviewing the Clause's historical underpinnings, we held that it guarantees a defendant's right to confront those "who 'bear testimony' " against him. A witness's testimony against a defendant is thus inadmissible unless the witness appears at trial or, if the witness is unavailable, the defendant had a prior opportunity for cross-examination. Our opinion described the class of testimonial statements covered by the Confrontation Clause as follows: "Various formulations of this core class of testimonial statements exist: *ex parte* in-court testimony or its functional equivalent-that is, material such as affidavits, custodial examinations, prior testimony that the defendant was unable to cross-examine, or similar pretrial statements that declarants would reasonably expect to be used prosecutorially; extrajudicial statements . . . contained in formalized testimonial materials, such as affidavits, depositions, prior testimony, or confessions; statements that were made under circumstances which would lead an objective witness reasonably to believe that the statement would be available for use at a later trial."

There is little doubt that the documents at issue fall within the "core class of testimonial statements." The documents, while denominated by Massachusetts law "certificates," are quite plainly affidavits: "declarations of facts written down and sworn to by the declarant before an officer authorized to administer oaths." BLACK'S LAW DICTIONARY 62 (8th ed.2004). They are incontrovertibly a "solemn declaration or affirmation made for the purpose of establishing or proving some fact." *Crawford, supra,* at 51. The substance found in the possession of Melendez-Diaz and his code-fendants was cocaine-the precise testimony the analysts would be expected to provide if called at trial. The "certificates" are functionally identical to live, in-court testimony, doing "precisely what a witness does on direct examination." *Davis v. Washington,* 547 U.S. 813, 830 (2006).

Here, not only were the affidavits "made under circumstances which would lead an objective witness reasonably to believe that the statement would be available for use at a later trial," but under Massachusetts law the *sole purpose* of the affidavits was to provide "prima facie evidence of the composition, quality, and the net weight" of the analyzed substance, Mass. Gen. Laws, ch. 111, § 13. The analysts were aware of the affidavits' evidentiary purpose, since that purpose was reprinted on the affidavits themselves. In short, under *Crawford* the analysts' affidavits were testimonial statements, and the analysts were "witnesses" for purposes of the Sixth Amendment. Absent a showing that the analysts were unavailable to testify at trial *and* that petitioner had a prior opportunity to cross-examine them, petitioner was entitled to "be confronted with" the analysts at trial.

The vast majority of the state-court cases the dissent cites in support of its claim that established precedent is being swept away, and not surprisingly nearly all of them rely on our decision in *Ohio v. Roberts,* 448 U.S. 56 (1980), or its since-rejected theory that unconfronted testimony was admissible as long as it bore indicia of reliability. Five of them postdated and expressly relied on *Roberts.* In faithfully applying *Crawford,* we are not overruling settled jurisprudence. It is the dissent that seeks to overturn precedent by resurrecting *Roberts* a mere five years after it was rejected in *Crawford.*

The dissent contends that a "conventional witness recalls events observed in the past, while an analyst's report contains near-contemporaneous observations of the test." It is doubtful that the analyst's reports could be characterized as reporting "near-contemporaneous observations"; the affidavits were completed almost a week after the tests were performed. (the tests were performed on November 28, 2001, and the affidavits sworn on December 4, 2001). Regardless, the dissent misunderstands the role that "near-contemporaneity" has played in our case law. The dissent notes that that factor was given "substantial weight" in *Davis,* but in fact that decision *disproves* the dissent's position. There the Court considered the admissibility of statements made to police officers responding to a report of a domestic disturbance. By the time officers arrived the assault had ended, but the victim's statements-written and oral-were sufficiently close in time to the alleged assault that the trial court admitted her affidavit as a "present sense impression." *Davis*, 547 U.S., at 820. Though the witness's statements in *Davis* were "near-contemporaneous" to the events she reported, we nevertheless held that they could *not* be admitted absent an opportunity to confront the witness. A second reason the dissent contends that the analysts are not "conventional witnesses" (and thus not subject to confrontation) is that they "observed neither the crime nor any human action related to it." The dissent provides no authority for this particular limitation of the type of witnesses subject to confrontation. The dissent's novel exception would exempt all expert witnesses-a hardly "unconventional" class of witnesses. Respondent and the dissent may be right that there are other ways-and in some cases better ways-to challenge or verify the results of a forensic test. But the Constitution guarantees one way: confrontation. We do not have license to suspend the Confrontation Clause when a preferable trial strategy is available. Nor is it evident that what respondent calls "neutral scientific testing" is as neutral or as reliable as respondent suggests. Forensic evidence is not uniquely immune from the risk of manipulation. A forensic analyst responding to a request from a law enforcement official may feel pressure-or have an incentive-to alter the evidence in a manner favorable to the prosecution.

Confrontation is one means of assuring accurate forensic analysis. While an honest analyst will not alter his testimony when forced to confront the defendant, the same cannot be said of the fraudulent analyst. This case is illustrative. The affidavits submitted by the analysts contained only the bare-bones statement that "the substance was found to contain: Cocaine." At the time of trial, petitioner did not know what tests the analysts performed, whether those tests were routine, and whether interpreting their results required the exercise of judgment or the use of skills that the analysts may not have possessed. The same is true of many other types of forensic evidence commonly used in criminal prosecutions. "There is wide variability across forensic science disciplines with regard to techniques, methodologies, reliability, types and numbers of potential errors, research, general acceptability, and published material." National Academy Report S-5.

Respondent argues that the analysts' affidavits are admissible without confrontation because they are "akin to the types of official and business records admissible at common law." But the affidavits do not qualify as traditional official or business records, and even if they did, their authors would be subject to confrontation nonetheless. Documents kept in the regular course of business may ordinarily be admitted at trial despite their hearsay status. *See* Fed. Rule Evid. 803(6). But that is not the case if the regularly conducted business activity is the production of evidence for use at trial. Our decision in *Palmer v. Hoffman*, 318 U.S. 109 (1943), made that distinction clear. There we held that an accident report provided by an employee of a railroad company did not qualify as a business record because, although kept in the regular course of the railroad's operations, it was "calculated for use essentially in the court, not in the business." The analysts' certificates-like police reports generated by law enforcement officials-do not qualify as business or public records for precisely the same reason. *See* Rule 803(8) (defining public records as "excluding, however, in criminal cases matters observed by police officers and other law enforcement personnel").

Respondent asserts that we should find no Confrontation Clause violation because petitioner had the ability to subpoena the analysts. But that power-whether pursuant to state law or the Compulsory Process Clause-is no substitute for the right of confrontation. Unlike the Confrontation Clause, those provisions are of no use to the defendant when the witness is unavailable or simply refuses to appear. More fundamentally, the Confrontation Clause imposes a burden on the prosecution to present its witnesses, not on the defendant to bring those adverse witnesses into court. Finally, respondent asks us to relax the requirements of the Confrontation Clause to accommodate the "necessities of trial and the adversary process." It is not clear whence

Food for Thought

Suppose five analysts each do pieces of the DNA testing. Do all of the analysts have to testify? Does it matter if an analyst does only a small part of the testing in a laboratory, but it is an important link in the chain? What if the work the analyst does in the testing process involves the use of judgment or discretion? Must the analyst testify?

we would derive the authority to do so. Many States have already adopted the constitutional rule we announce today, and there is no evidence that the criminal justice system has ground to a halt in the States that, one way or another, empower a defendant to insist upon the analyst's appearance at trial. Indeed, in Massachusetts itself, a defendant may subpoena the analyst to appear at trial, and yet there is no indication that obstructionist defendants are abusing the privilege.

This case involves little more than the application of our holding in *Crawford*. The Sixth Amendment does not permit the prosecution to prove its case via *ex parte* out-of-court affidavits, and the admission of such evidence against Melendez-Diaz was error. We therefore reverse the judgment of the Appeals Court of Massachusetts and remand the case for further proceedings not inconsistent with this opinion.

It is so ordered.

JUSTICE THOMAS, concurring.

I write separately to note that I continue to adhere to my position that "the Confrontation Clause is implicated by extrajudicial statements only insofar as they are contained in formalized testimonial materials, such as affidavits, depositions, prior testimony, or confessions." *White v. Illinois*, 502 U.S. 346, 365, (1992). I join the Court's opinion because the documents at issue "are quite plainly affidavits." They "fall within the core class of testimonial statements" governed by the Confrontation Clause.

JUSTICE KENNEDY, with whom THE CHIEF JUSTICE, JUSTICE BREYER, and JUSTICE ALITO join, dissenting.

Until today, scientific analysis could be introduced into evidence without testimony from the "analyst" who produced it. This rule has been established for at least 90 years. It extends across at least 35 States and six Federal Courts of Appeals. Yet the Court undoes it based on two recent opinions that say nothing about forensic analysts: *Crawford* and *Davis*. The Court makes no attempt to acknowledge the real differences between laboratory analysts who perform scientific tests and other, more conventional witnesses—"witnesses" being the word the Framers used in the Confrontation Clause. Because *Crawford* and *Davis* concerned typical witnesses, the Court should have done the sensible thing and limited its holding to witnesses as so defined. Indeed, as Justice THOMAS warned in *Davis,* the Court's approach has become "disconnected from history and unnecessary to prevent abuse." The Court's reliance on the word "testimonial" is of little help for that word does not appear in the text of the Clause.

The Court dictates to the States, as a matter of constitutional law, an as-yet-undefined set of rules governing what kinds of evidence may be admitted without in-court testimony. Indeed, under today's opinion the States bear an even more onerous burden than they did before *Crawford*. The Court's opinion suggests this will be a body of formalistic and wooden rules, divorced from precedent, common sense, and the underlying purpose of the Clause. Before the results of a scientific test may be introduced into evidence, the defendant has the right to confront the "analyst." There is no accepted definition of analyst, and there is no established precedent to define that

Food for Thought

Suppose the Court agreed with Justice Ginsburg 9–0. Would that change the importance and impact of the case? Has the Confrontation Clause analysis been obscured by disagreements between the justices regarding the shape of the doctrine?

term. Outside this narrow category, the range of other scientific tests that may be affected by the Court's new confrontation right is staggering. For the sake of negligible benefits, the Court threatens to disrupt forensic investigations across the country and to put prosecutions nationwide at risk of dismissal based on erratic, all-too-frequent instances when a particular laboratory technician, now invested by the Court's new constitutional designation as the analyst, simply does not or cannot appear. The Court's holding is a windfall to defendants, one that is unjustified by any demonstrated deficiency in trials, any well-understood historical requirement, or any established constitutional precedent. I respectfully dissent.

Point for Discussion

Melendez-Diaz on Remand

On remand, the prosecutor argued that the defense failed to make the identity of the substance a live issue in the case and therefore the admission of the drug certificates were harmless beyond a reasonable doubt. The Court disagreed, finding there was harm and that "the defense was hardly in a position to argue that the substances were not cocaine. *See Commonwealth v. Melendez-Diaz,* 921 N.E.2d 108 (Mass. App. 2010) *on remand from sub nom. Massachusetts v. Melendez-Diaz,* 557 U.S. 305 (2009).

Bullcoming v. New Mexico

564 U.S. 647 (2011).

Petitioner Donald Bullcoming was arrested on charges of driving while intoxicated (DWI). Principal evidence against Bullcoming was a forensic laboratory report certifying that Bullcoming's blood-alcohol concentration was well above the threshold for aggravated DWI. At trial, the prosecution did not call as a witness the analyst who signed the certification. Instead, the State called another analyst who was familiar with the laboratory's testing procedures, but had neither participated in nor observed the test on Bullcoming's blood sample. The Court concluded that the Confrontation Clause was violated: "We hold that surrogate testimony of that order does not meet the constitutional requirement. The accused's right is to be confronted with the analyst who made the certification, unless that analyst is unavailable at trial, and the accused had an opportunity, pretrial, to cross-examine that particular scientist."

Hypo 1: *Who Must Testify*

A forensic chemist testified about mass spectrometer testing of controlled substances. The test examines the color produced by controlled substances and creates a graph that can be analyzed by an expert chemist. The chemist who testified was not the chemist who did the analysis of the drugs. While the testifying chemist did not give her own opinion about the analysis, she did summarize and explain the analysis performed by her colleague who wrote the report. The colleague was unavailable for trial. The testifying chemist described how peer reviews of expert opinions and test results yield inferences about the type as well as weight of the illegal drug. Is this testimony permitted? Why or why not? Suppose that Dr. Melinda Kite did the testing of narcotics in the testing laboratory, while Dr. Shamus Treadstone did the recording and analysis. Lab assistant Horris Houston was in charge of the entry of data, finalizing all reports. In the case of the lab report on Sample 26X4T, which was the main evidence in the case of the government prosecution of defendant, all of the above individuals participated in the drug sample concerning Austin's case. Who must the prosecution call to testify to satisfy *Melendez-Diaz*? Why?

Hypo 2: "*Who Done It*"?

The police find a body in a remote wilderness in Montana. They do all kinds of testing in a nearby laboratory, including regarding blood, hair, and bite marks. After five analysts participate in the testing, a report is written. All five analysts write their name on the report as "contributors." Twenty years later, after the DNA from the samples is entered into a nation-wide registry, a hit occurs, and defendant is accused of murder. At trial, can the government offer the twenty-year-old report without any of the five analysts who helped to prepare it? Explain.

Hypo 3: *Breathalyzer Calibration Records*

Should a court treat breathalyzer calibration records as testimonial? Assume that these records are created regularly as a part of police procedure and as required by applicable regulations and statutes. Are these records investigative, or do they simply reflect the operability of the breathalyzers? Are they reflective of objective facts or have sufficient human input to categorize them as investigatory? *See People v. Pealer*, 20 N.Y.App. 447 (2013).

Hypo 4: *Field Test Tales*

A police officer, Sgt. Smith, testified at defendant's criminal trial for possession of marijuana and other contraband. The officer stated that she field-tested the substance in accordance with her training, and the test was positive for the controlled substance in question. Defendant objected, claiming that *Melendez-Diaz* required the person who trained the Sgt. Smith to testify as well. Is defendant correct? *See Newman v. United States*, 49 A.3d 321 (D.C. 2012).

E. The Basis of Expert Testimony

Another corollary issue that arose regarding *Crawford*'s meaning related to the applicability of the Confrontation Clause to the bases of expert testimony. Experts regularly rely on inadmissible evidence, including hearsay. Is this practice consistent with *Crawford*? Would the bases of expert testimony depend on whether the reliance was brought to the jury's attention? Whether the hearsay was being offered for the truth of the matter asserted? Or simply whether the hearsay was considered testimonial? The next case attempted to answer these questions, but with a fractured court, perhaps illustrating that the Confrontation Clause analysis remains in a state of flux.

What's That?

As you might recall from your Evidence Law course, expert testimony is admissible if it meets certain prerequisites, showing that the expert is qualified and demonstrating that the theory upon which the expert is testifying is reliable. *See* Fed. R. Evid. 702. The basis for the expert's opinion might not necessarily be admissible in evidence. Instead, it simply must be "reasonably relied on" by an expert in the particular field. Sometimes the bases for the expert's opinions can be offered to show how the expert reached her conclusions even if the evidence is otherwise inadmissible. *See* Fed. R. Evid. 703.

Williams v. Illinois

567 U.S. 50 (2012).

JUSTICE ALITO announced the judgment of the Court and delivered an opinion, in which THE CHIEF JUSTICE, JUSTICE KENNEDY, and JUSTICE BREYER join.

In this case, we decide whether *Crawford v. Washington*, 541 U.S. 36 (2004), precludes an expert witness from testifying in a manner that has long been allowed under the law of evidence. Specifically, does *Crawford* bar an expert from expressing an opinion based on facts about a case that have been made known to the expert but about which the expert is not competent to testify? We also decide whether *Crawford* substantially impedes the ability of prosecutors to introduce DNA evidence and thus effectively relegate the prosecution in some cases to reliance on older, less reliable forms of proof.

In petitioner's bench trial for rape, the prosecution called an expert who testified that a DNA profile produced by an outside laboratory, Cellmark, matched a profile produced by the state police lab using a sample of petitioner's blood. On direct examination, the expert testified that Cellmark was an accredited laboratory and that Cellmark provided the police with a DNA profile. The expert also explained the notations on documents admitted as business records, stating that, according to the records, vaginal swabs taken from the victim were sent to and received back from Cellmark. The expert made no other statement that was offered for the purpose of identifying the sample of biological material used in deriving the profile or for the purpose of establishing how Cellmark handled or tested the sample. Nor did the expert vouch for the accuracy of the profile that Cellmark produced.

We conclude that this form of expert testimony does not violate the Confrontation Clause because that provision has no application to out-of-court statements that are not offered to prove the truth of the matter asserted. When an expert testifies for the prosecution in a criminal case, the defendant has the opportunity to cross-examine the expert about any statements that are offered for their truth. Out-of-court statements that are related by the expert solely for the purpose of explaining the assumptions on which that opinion rests are not offered for their truth and thus fall outside the scope of the Confrontation Clause. Applying this rule to the present case, we conclude that the expert's testimony did not violate the Sixth Amendment.

Even if the report produced by Cellmark had been admitted into evidence, there would have been no Confrontation Clause violation. The Cellmark report is very different from the sort of extrajudicial statements, such as affidavits, depositions, prior testimony, and confessions that the Confrontation Clause was originally understood to reach. The report was produced before any suspect was identified. The report was sought not for the purpose of obtaining evidence to be used against petitioner, who was not even under suspicion at the time, but for the purpose of finding a rapist who was on the loose. The profile that Cellmark provided was not inherently inculpatory. On the contrary, a DNA profile is evidence that tends to exculpate all but one of the more than 7 billion people in the world today.

In this case, a young woman, L.J., had been raped in Chicago, Illinois, in 2000. Various DNA testing occurred, and a perpetrator was identified and prosecuted. At a bench trial, various experts testified about their DNA analysis. A forensic specialist, Sandra Lambatos, also testified. Lambatos testified that she had compared samples tested by others, a practice she said was "commonly accepted" when it came to "one DNA expert relying on records from another DNA expert." One of the samples was prepared by Cellmark Diagnostics Laboratory, an "accredited crime lab." Lambatos then testified that as a result of the comparison, the defendant could not be excluded as a perpetrator. The trial court found petitioner guilty of the charges against him. The state appeals court and Illinois Supreme Court affirmed the decision.

The Confrontation Clause of the Sixth Amendment provides that, "in all criminal prosecutions, the accused shall enjoy the right . . . to be confronted with the witnesses against him." Our decision in *Crawford* has resulted in a steady stream of new cases. Two of these decisions involved scientific reports. In *Melendez-Diaz*, the defendant was arrested and charged with distributing and trafficking in cocaine. The trial court admitted into evidence three "certificates of analysis" from the state forensic laboratory stating that the bags contained cocaine. The Court held that the admission of these certificates, which were executed under oath before a notary, violated the Sixth Amendment. They were "quite plainly affidavits" used to prove the truth of the matter they asserted. In *Bullcoming*, we held that another scientific report could not be used as substantive evidence against the defendant unless the analyst who prepared and certified the report was subject to confrontation. The Court declined to accept a surrogate expert's testimony, despite the fact that the testifying analyst was a "knowledgeable representative of the laboratory" who could "explain the lab's processes and the details of the report." The Court stated simply: "The accused's right is to be confronted with the analyst who made the certification." In concurrence, Justice Sotomayor highlighted the importance of the fact that the forensic report had been admitted into evidence for the purpose of proving the truth of the matter it asserted. "We would face a different question," she observed, "if asked to determine the constitutionality of allowing an expert witness to discuss others' testimonial statements if the testimonial statements were not themselves admitted as evidence." We now confront that question.

It has long been accepted that an expert witness may voice an opinion based on facts concerning the events at issue in a particular case even if the expert lacks firsthand knowledge of those facts. At common law, courts developed two ways to deal with this situation. An expert could rely on facts that had already been established in the record. Because it was not always possible to proceed in this manner, and because record evidence was often disputed, courts developed the alternative practice of allowing an expert to testify in the form of a "hypothetical question." Under this approach, the expert would be asked to assume the truth of certain factual predicates, and was then asked to offer an opinion based on those assumptions. There is a long tradition of the use of hypothetical questions in American courts. Modern rules of evidence continue to permit experts to express opinions based on facts about which they lack personal knowledge, but these rules dispense with the need for hypothetical questions. Under both the Illinois and the Federal Rules of Evidence, an expert may base an opinion on facts that are "made known to the expert at or before the hearing," but such reliance does not constitute admissible evidence of this underlying information. Fed. R. Evid. 703. *Crawford*, while departing from prior Confrontation Clause precedent in other respects, took pains to reaffirm the proposition that the Confrontation Clause "does not bar the use of testimonial statements for purposes other than establishing the truth of the matter asserted." 541 U.S. at 59.

The principal argument advanced to show a Confrontation Clause violation concerns the phrase that Lambatos used when she referred to the DNA profile that the ISP lab received from Cellmark. In the view of the dissent, the following is the critical portion of Lambatos' testimony, with the particular words that the dissent finds objectionable italicized: "Q. Was there a computer match generated of the male

DNA profile *found in semen from the vaginal swabs of L.J.* to a male DNA profile that had been identified as having originated from Sandy Williams? A. Yes, there was." According to the dissent, the phrase violated petitioner's confrontation right because Lambatos lacked personal knowledge that the profile produced by Cellmark was based on the vaginal swabs taken from the victim, L.J. As the dissent acknowledges, there would have been "nothing wrong with Lambatos's testifying that two DNA profiles—the one shown in the Cellmark report and the one derived from Williams's blood—matched each other; that was a straightforward application of Lambatos's expertise." Thus, if Lambatos' testimony had been slightly modified as follows, the dissent would see no problem: "Q Was there a computer match generated of the male DNA profile produced by Cellmark found in semen from the vaginal swabs of L.J. to a male DNA profile that had been identified as having originated from Sandy Williams? A. Yes, there was."

The defect in this argument is that under Illinois law (like federal law) it is clear that the putatively offending phrase in Lambatos' testimony was not admissible for the purpose of proving the truth of the matter asserted—*i.e.*, that the matching DNA profile was "found in semen from the vaginal swabs." There is no reason to think that the trier of fact took Lambatos' answer as substantive evidence to establish where the DNA profiles came from.

The dissent's argument would have force if petitioner had elected to have a jury trial. In that event, there would have been a danger of the jury's taking Lambatos' testimony as proof that the Cellmark profile was derived from the sample obtained from the victim's vaginal swabs. Absent an evaluation of the risk of juror confusion and careful jury instructions, the testimony could not have gone to the jury. This case, however, involves *a bench trial* and we must assume that the trial judge understood that the portion of Lambatos' testimony to which the dissent objects was not admissible to prove the truth of the matter asserted. The dissent reaches the truly remarkable conclusion that the wording of Lambatos' testimony confused the trial judge. This argument reflects a profound lack of respect for the acumen of the trial judge. We conclude that petitioner's Sixth Amendment confrontation right was not violated.

Even if the Cellmark report had been introduced for its truth, we would nevertheless conclude that there was no Confrontation Clause violation. The abuses that the Court has identified as prompting the adoption of the Confrontation Clause shared the following two characteristics: (a) they involved out-of-court statements having the primary purpose of accusing a targeted individual of engaging in criminal conduct and (b) they involved formalized statements such as affidavits, depositions, prior testimony, or confessions. The Cellmark report is very different. It plainly was not prepared for the primary purpose of accusing a targeted individual. In identifying the primary purpose of an out-of-court statement, we apply an objective test. We look for the primary purpose that a reasonable person would have ascribed to the statement, taking into account all of the surrounding circumstances.

Here, the primary purpose of the Cellmark report, viewed objectively, was not to accuse petitioner or to create evidence for use at trial. When the ISP lab sent the sample to Cellmark, its primary purpose was to catch a dangerous rapist who was still at large, not to obtain evidence for use against petitioner, who was neither in custody nor under suspicion at that time. Similarly, no one at Cellmark could have possibly known that the profile that it produced would turn out to inculpate petitioner—or

Food for Thought

Why isn't face-to-face confrontation indispensable? Are the justices "watering down" the right by saying that it is just a "preference"?

for that matter, anyone else whose DNA profile was in a law enforcement database. Under these circumstances, there was no "prospect of fabrication" and no incentive to produce anything other than a scientifically sound and reliable profile. It is also significant that in many labs, numerous technicians work on each DNA profile. ("Approximately 10 Cellmark analysts were involved in the laboratory work in this case"). When the work of a lab is divided up in such a way, it is likely that the sole purpose of each technician is simply to perform his or her task in accordance with accepted procedures.

For the two independent reasons explained above, we conclude that there was no Confrontation Clause violation in this case. Accordingly, the judgment of the Supreme Court of Illinois is

Affirmed.

JUSTICE THOMAS, concurring in the judgment.

I agree with the plurality that the disclosure of Cellmark's out-of-court statements through the expert testimony of Sandra Lambatos did not violate the Confrontation Clause. I reach this conclusion solely because Cellmark's statements lacked the requisite "formality and solemnity" to be considered " 'testimonial' " for purposes of the Confrontation Clause. *See Michigan v. Bryant,* 131 S.Ct. 1143 (2011) (Thomas, J., concurring).

JUSTICE KAGAN, with whom JUSTICE SCALIA, JUSTICE GINSBURG, and JUSTICE SOTO-MAYOR join, dissenting.

Some years ago, the State of California prosecuted a man named John Kocak for rape. At a preliminary hearing, the State presented testimony from an analyst at the Cellmark Diagnostics Laboratory—the same facility used to generate DNA evidence in this case. The analyst had extracted DNA from a bloody sweatshirt found at the crime scene and then compared it to two control samples—one from Kocak and one from the victim. The analyst's report identified a single match: As she explained on direct examination, the DNA found on the sweatshirt belonged to Kocak. But after undergoing cross-examination, the analyst realized she had made a mortifying error. She took the stand again, but this time to admit that the report listed the victim's control sample as coming from Kocak, and Kocak's as coming from the victim. So the DNA on the sweatshirt matched not Kocak, but the victim herself. In trying Kocak, the State would have to look elsewhere for its evidence. Our Constitution contains a mechanism for catching such errors—the Sixth Amendment's Confrontation Clause. That Clause, and the Court's recent cases interpreting it, require that testimony against a criminal defendant be subject to cross-examination. That command applies with full force to forensic evidence of the kind involved in both the Kocak case and this one. In two decisions in the last three years, this Court held that if a prosecutor wants to introduce the results of forensic testing into evidence, he must afford the defendant an opportunity to cross-examine an analyst responsible for the test.

Under our Confrontation Clause precedents, this is an open-and-shut case. The State of Illinois prosecuted Sandy Williams for rape based in part on a DNA profile created in Cellmark's laboratory. Yet the State did not give Williams a chance to question the analyst who produced that evidence. Instead, the prosecution introduced the results of Cellmark's testing through an expert witness who had no idea how they were generated. That approach—no less (perhaps more) than the confrontation-free methods of presenting forensic evidence we have formerly banned—deprived Williams of his Sixth Amendment right to "confront . . . the witnesses against him." The Court today disagrees, though it cannot settle on a reason why. Justice Alito, joined by three other Justices, advances two theories—that the expert's summary of the Cellmark report was not offered for its truth, and that the report is not the kind of statement triggering the Confrontation Clause's protection. Five Justices specifically reject every aspect of its reasoning and every paragraph of its explication. Justice Thomas contends that the Cellmark report is non-testimonial on a different rationale. No other Justice joins his opinion or subscribes to the test he offers. That creates five votes to approve admission of the Cellmark report, but not a single good explanation. I would choose another path—to adhere to the simple rule established in our decisions, for the good reasons we have previously given. Because defendants like Williams have a constitutional right to confront the witnesses against them, I dissent from the Court's fractured decision.

The report at issue here shows a DNA profile produced by an analyst at Cellmark's laboratory, allegedly from a vaginal swab taken from a young woman, L.J., after she was raped. That report is identical to the one in *Bullcoming* (and *Melendez-Diaz*) in "all material respects." (Once again, the report was made to establish " 'some fact' in a criminal proceeding"—here, the identity of L.J.'s attacker). Once again, it details the results of forensic testing on evidence gathered by the police. Viewed side-by-side with the *Bullcoming* report, the Cellmark analysis has a comparable title; similarly describes the relevant samples, test methodology, and results; and likewise includes the signatures of laboratory officials. Under this Court's prior analysis, the substance of the report could come into evidence only if Williams had a chance to cross-examine the responsible analyst.

But that is not what happened. Instead, the prosecutor used Sandra Lambatos—a state-employed scientist who had not participated in the testing—as the conduit for this piece of evidence. Lambatos came to the stand after two other state analysts testified about forensic tests they had performed. One recounted how she had developed a DNA profile of Sandy Williams from a blood sample drawn after his arrest. Another told how he had confirmed the presence of (unidentified) semen on the vaginal swabs taken from L.J. All this was by the book: Williams had an opportunity to cross-examine both witnesses about the tests they had run. But of course, the State still needed to supply the missing link—it had to show that DNA found in the semen on L.J.'s vaginal swabs matched Williams's DNA. To fill that gap, the prosecutor could have called the analyst from Cellmark to testify about the DNA profile she had produced from the swabs. But instead, the State called Lambatos as an expert witness and had her testify that the semen on those swabs contained Sandy Williams's DNA:

"Q. Was there a computer match generated of the male DNA profile found in semen from the vaginal swabs of L.J. to a male DNA profile that had been identified as having originated from Sandy Williams?

"A. Yes, there was.

"Q. Did you compare the semen from the vaginal swabs of L.J. to the male DNA profile from the blood of Sandy Williams?

"A. Yes, I did. "Q. Is the semen identified in the vaginal swabs of L.J. consistent with having originated from Sandy Williams?

"A. Yes."

And so it was Lambatos, rather than any Cellmark employee, who informed the trier of fact that the testing of L.J.'s vaginal swabs had produced a male DNA profile implicating Williams.

Lambatos's testimony is functionally identical to the "surrogate testimony" that New Mexico proffered in Bullcoming, which did nothing to cure the problem identified in *Melendez-Diaz*. Like the surrogate witness in Bullcoming, Lambatos "could not convey what the actual analyst knew or observed about the events, i.e., the particular test and testing process he employed." *Bullcoming*, 131 S. Ct. at 2715. That is sufficient to resolve this case. "When the State elected to introduce" the substance of

Cellmark's report into evidence, the analyst who generated that report "became a witness" whom Williams "had the right to confront." *Bullcoming*, 131 S. Ct. at 2716.

Point for Discussion

Expert Testimony After *Williams*

What does *Williams* mean for expert testimony? There were at least a dozen cases pending before the Court seeking clarification of *Williams*, a case that exemplifies the difficulties of creating coherence from a multiplicity of doctrinal rationales. The splintered Court, with a 4–1–4 plurality, left many questions about the admissibility of experts testifying to statements by non-testifying persons and left lower courts grasping for a predictable pronouncement to follow. While there is a rule courts follow for plurality decisions—e.g., "when a fragmented Court decides a case and no single rationale explaining the result enjoys the assent of five Justices, the holding of the Court may be viewed as the position taken by those members who concurred in the judgments on the narrowest grounds." *Marks v. United States*, 430 U.S. 188, 193 (1977)—no such clear lowest common denominator is apparent in Williams. What statements are admissible, and under what rationale, is still open to debate.

Hypo: *Drugged Victim*

Two ladies in their mid-70s were convicted of murdering two elderly men six years apart to collect life insurance proceeds. The women lived in Los Angeles and were listed as beneficiaries on several life insurance policies taken out on the men. The women ran the men over with their cars and collected more than half a million dollars. At trial, the prosecution alleged that at least one of the men was drugged beforehand. A laboratory director testified that blood analysis reports showed that one of the men had a drug in his blood that caused drowsiness. The director did not perform the tests in the reports. Did the laboratory director's testimony violate the accused's Confrontation Clause rights? Explain.

F. Other Confrontation Issues

1. The *Bruton* Rule

Samia v. United States

599 U.S. 635 (2023).

JUSTICE THOMAS delivered the opinion of the Court.

Prosecutors have long tried criminal defendants jointly where the defendants are alleged to have engaged in a common criminal scheme. When prosecutors seek to introduce a nontestifying defendant's confession implicating his codefendants, a constitutional concern may arise. The Confrontation Clause of the Sixth Amendment states that, "in all criminal prosecutions, the accused shall enjoy the right to be confronted with the witnesses against him." In *Bruton v. United States*, 391 U.S. 123 (1968), this Court "held that a defendant is deprived of his rights under the Confrontation Clause when his nontestifying codefendant's confession naming him as a participant in the crime is introduced at their joint trial, even if the jury is instructed to consider that confession only against the codefendant." *Richardson v. Marsh*, 481 U.S. 200, 201 (1987). We must determine whether the Confrontation Clause bars the admission of a nontestifying codefendant's confession where (1) the confession has been modified to avoid directly identifying the nonconfessing codefendant and (2) the court offers a limiting instruction that jurors may consider the confession only with respect to the confessing codefendant. Considering longstanding historical practice, the general presumption that jurors follow their instructions, and the relevant precedents, we conclude that it does not.

Petitioner Adam Samia traveled to the Philippines to work for crime lord Paul LeRoux. While there, LeRoux tasked Samia, Joseph Hunter, and Carl Stillwell with killing Catherine Lee, a local real-estate broker who LeRoux believed had stolen money from him. Lee was found dead shortly thereafter, shot twice in the face. LeRoux was arrested by the U. S. Drug Enforcement Administration (DEA) and became a cooperating witness for the Government. Hunter, Samia, and Stillwell were arrested thereafter. During a search of Samia's home, law enforcement found a camera containing surveillance photographs of Lee's home as well as a key to the van in which Lee had been murdered. During Stillwell's arrest, law enforcement found a cell phone containing thumbnail images of Lee's dead body. During a postarrest interview with DEA agents, Stillwell waived his rights under *Miranda v. Arizona*, 384 U.S. 436 (1966), and gave a confession. Stillwell admitted that he had been in the van when Lee was killed, but he claimed that he was only the driver and that Samia had shot Lee. The Government charged all three men in a multicount indictment. Samia and Stillwell were charged with conspiracy to commit murder-for-hire, conspiracy to murder and kidnap in a foreign country, causing death with a firearm during and in relation to a crime of violence, and conspiracy to launder money. Hunter was charged with all but the money-laundering count. The Government tried all three men jointly. While Hunter and Stillwell admitted that they had participated in the murder, Samia maintained his innocence. Prior to trial, the Government moved *in limine* to admit Stillwell's confession. But, because Stillwell would not testify and the full confession inculpated Samia, the Government proposed that an agent testify as to the content of Stillwell's confession in a way that eliminated Samia's name while avoiding any obvious indications of redaction. The District Court granted the Government's motion but required further alterations.

At trial, the Government's theory was that Hunter had hired Samia and Stillwell to pose as real-estate buyers and visit properties with Lee. The Government also sought to prove that Samia, Stillwell, and Lee were in a van that Stillwell was driving when Samia shot Lee. In accordance with the court's ruling on its motion *in limine*, the Government presented testimony about Stillwell's confession through DEA Agent Eric Stouch. Stouch recounted the key portion of Stillwell's confession implicating Samia as follows: "Q. Did Stillwell say where [the victim] was when she was killed? A. Yes. He described when the *other person* he was with pulled the trigger on that woman in a van that he and Mr. Stillwell was driving." Other portions of Stouch's testimony also used the "other person" descriptor to refer to someone with whom Stillwell had traveled and lived and who carried a particular firearm. During Stouch's testimony, the [court] instructed the jury that his testimony was admissible only as to Stillwell and should not be considered as to Samia or Hunter. The [court] provided a similar limiting instruction before the jury began its deliberations. The jury convicted Samia and his codefendants on all counts. The District Court sentenced Samia to life plus 10 years' imprisonment.

Samia argued [on appeal] that the admission of Stillwell's confession—even as altered and with a limiting instruction—was constitutional error because other evidence and statements enabled the jury to immediately infer that the "other person" described in the confession was Samia himself. During opening statements, the Government asserted that Stillwell drove the van while Samia "was in the passenger seat," and that Samia pulled a gun, "turned around, aimed carefully and shot Lee." He also pointed out that "Stillwell admitted to driving the car while the man he was with turned around and shot Lee." So, even though Samia's position in the van and shooting of Lee were relevant to the Government's theory of the case with or without Stillwell's confession, Samia argued that those statements would allow the jury to infer that he was the "other person" in Stillwell's confession. The Government had elicited testimony that Samia and Stillwell coordinated their travel to the Philippines and lived together there. There was testimony that he had the type of gun that was used to shoot Lee. In its closing argument, the Government argued that video evidence showing

Hunter speaking about hiring two men to murder Lee was "admissible against all three defendants," allowing the jury to infer that Samia and Stillwell were co-conspirators. Finally, while discussing Stillwell's confession, the prosecution recounted how Stillwell "described a time when the other person he was with in the Philippines pulled the trigger on that woman in a van that Stillwell was driving." The Second Circuit rejected Samia's view. We granted certiorari to determine whether the admission of Stillwell's altered confession, subject to a limiting instruction, violated Samia's rights under the Confrontation Clause.

The Sixth Amendment's Confrontation Clause guarantees the right of a criminal defendant "to be confronted with the witnesses against him." This Clause forbids the introduction of out-of-court "testimonial" statements unless the witness is unavailable and the defendant has had the chance to cross-examine the witness previously. See *Crawford v. Washington*, 541 U.S. 36 (2004). Because Stillwell's formal, *Mirandized* confession which the Government sought to introduce, is testimonial, it falls within the Clause's ambit. Nonetheless, the Confrontation Clause applies only to witnesses "against the accused." *Crawford*, 541 U.S., at 50. "Ordinarily, a witness whose testimony is introduced at a joint trial is not considered to be a witness 'against' a defendant if the jury is instructed to consider that testimony only against a codefendant." *Richardson*, 481 U.S., at 206. This rule is consistent with the text of the Clause, historical practice, and the law's reliance on limiting instructions in other contexts.

For most of our Nation's history, longstanding practice allowed a nontestifying codefendant's confession to be admitted in a joint trial so long as the jury was properly instructed not to consider it against the nonconfessing defendant. While some courts would omit the defendant's name or substitute a reference to "another person," it is unclear whether any courts considered such alterations to be necessary. In any event, the combination of such alterations and an appropriate limiting instruction was generally sufficient to permit the introduction of such confessions. S. PHILLIPPS, LAW OF EVIDENCE 82 (1816). Our legal system presumes that jurors will "attend closely the particular language of such instructions in a criminal case and strive to understand, make sense of, and follow" them. *United States v. Olano*, 507 U.S. 725 (1993). In *Bruton*, this Court "recognized a narrow exception to" the presumption that juries follow their instructions, holding "that a defendant is deprived of his Sixth Amendment right of confrontation when the facially incriminating confession of a nontestifying codefendant is introduced at their joint trial," even with a proper instruction. *Richardson*, 481 U.S., at 207. In *Richardson v. Marsh*, the Court "declined to extend *Bruton*" to "confessions that do not name the defendant." *Id.*, at 211. *Gray v. Maryland*, 523 U.S. 185 (1998), later qualified *Richardson* by holding that certain obviously redacted confessions might be "directly accusatory," and thus fall within *Bruton*'s rule, even if they did not specifically use a defendant's name. Thus, the precedents distinguish between confessions that directly implicate a defendant and those that do so indirectly. Under these precedents, and consistent with the longstanding historical practice discussed above, the introduction of Stillwell's altered confession coupled with a limiting instruction did not violate the Confrontation Clause.

In *Bruton*, the Court considered the joint trial of George Bruton and William Evans for armed postal robbery. During two pretrial interrogations, Evans confessed to a postal inspector that he and Bruton—whom he implicated by name—had committed the robbery. The confession was introduced at trial, coupled with a limiting instruction that it not be used against Bruton. "Because of the substantial risk that the jury, despite instructions to the contrary, looked to the incriminating extrajudicial statements in determining Bruton's guilt, admission of Evans' confession in this joint trial violated Bruton's right of cross-examination secured by the Confrontation Clause of the Sixth Amendment." The Court acknowledged that a defendant is "entitled to a fair trial but not a perfect one" and conceded that "it is not unreasonable to conclude that in many cases the jury can and will follow the trial judge's instructions to disregard certain information." "If it were true that the jury disregarded the reference to Bruton, no question would arise under the Confrontation Clause." Yet, "there are some contexts in which the risk that the jury will not, or cannot, follow instructions is so great, and the consequences of failure so vital to the defendant, that the practical and human limitations of the jury system cannot be ignored." Accordingly, "the introduction of Evans' confession posed a substantial threat to Bruton's right to confront the witnesses against him."

In *Richardson*, the Court declined to expand *Bruton* to a redacted confession that inculpated defendant only when viewed in conjunction with other evidence. There, Clarissa Marsh, Benjamin Williams, and Kareem Martin were charged with assault and murder. Marsh and Williams were tried jointly. The State introduced Williams' confession, taken by police shortly after his arrest. "The confession was redacted to omit all reference to Marsh—indeed, to omit all indication that anyone other than Martin and Williams participated in the crime." The confession largely corroborated the victim's testimony and described a conversation between Williams and Martin as they drove to the scene of the crime: "According to Williams, Martin said that he would have to kill the victims after the robbery." The trial judge instructed the jury not to use [the confession] against Marsh in any way, an instruction reiterated in the jury charge at the conclusion of trial. In her testimony, however, Marsh volunteered that, during the drive to the crime scene, she "knew that Martin and Williams were talking' but could not hear the conversation because 'the radio was on and the speaker was in her ear." Both Marsh and Williams were convicted. This Court noted that, "ordinarily, a witness whose testimony is introduced at a joint trial is not considered to be a witness 'against' a defendant if the jury is instructed to consider that testimony only against a codefendant," emphasizing the "almost invariable assumption that jurors follow their instructions." It then explained that *Bruton* represented a "narrow exception." Whereas the confession in *Bruton* had " 'expressly implicated' the defendant and his accomplice," the confession in *Richardson* "was not incriminating on its face, and became so only when linked with evidence introduced later at trial." The former evidence, the Court explained, is "more vivid" and thus "more difficult to thrust out of mind." Additionally, in the case of inferential incrimination, the Court posited that "the judge's instruction may well be successful in dissuading the jury from entering onto the path of inference," leaving "no incrimination to forget."

Gray confronted a question *Richardson* expressly left open: whether a confession altered "by substituting for the defendant's name in the confession a blank space or the word 'deleted' " violated the Confrontation Clause. In *Gray*, the Court considered Anthony Bell's confession to Baltimore police, implicating himself, Kevin Gray, and co-conspirator Jacquin Vanlandingham in a murder. The prosecution sought to introduce the confession at trial, and the trial judge required that it be redacted to use the word "deleted" or "deletion" whenever Gray's or Vanlandingham's names appeared. At trial, the prosecution had a police detective read the confession aloud to the jury verbatim, substituting the words "deleted" or "deletion" for Gray's or Vanlandingham's names.[3] "Immediately after" the detective finished reading the confession, "the prosecutor asked, 'after he gave you that information, you subsequently were able to arrest Mr. Kevin Gray; is that correct?' The officer responded, 'That's correct.' " In instructing the jury at the close of trial, the judge specified that Bell's confession was evidence only against Bell, admonishing the jury not to use the confession as evidence against Gray. The jury convicted Bell and Gray. This Court held that the confession was inadmissible under *Bruton*. "Unlike *Richardson*'s redacted confession, Bell's confession referred directly to the 'existence' of the nonconfessing defendant." The Court concluded that, when a redacted confession "simply replaces a name with an obvious blank space or a word such as 'deleted' or a symbol or other similarly obvious indications of alteration," the evidence "so closely resembles *Bruton*'s unredacted statements that the law must require the same result." "Obvious blanks" would cause jurors to speculate as to whom the omitted individual may be, "lifting their eyes to the nonconfessing defendant, sitting at counsel table, to find what will seem the obvious answer," as the judge's "instruction will provide an obvious reason for the blank." It also reasoned that "statements redacted to leave a blank or some other similarly obvious alteration" were "directly accusatory," "pointing directly to the defendant in a manner similar to Evans' use of Bruton's name or to a testifying codefendant's accusatory finger." While the Court "conceded that *Richardson* placed outside the scope of *Bruton*'s rule those statements that incriminate inferentially," it explained that "inference pure and simple cannot make the critical difference, for if it did, then *Richardson* would also place outside *Bruton*'s scope confessions that use shortened first names, nicknames, and descriptions as unique as the 'red-haired, bearded, one-eyed man-with-a-limp.' " The Court elaborated: "That being so, *Richardson* must depend in significant part upon the kind of, not the simple fact of, inference. *Richardson*'s inferences involved statements that did not refer directly to the defendant himself and

---

[3] The prosecution also introduced a written copy of the confession with Gray's and Vanlandigham's names omitted, "leaving in their place blank white spaces separated by commas."

which became incriminating 'only when linked with evidence introduced later at trial.' The inferences at issue here involve statements that, despite redaction, obviously refer directly to someone, often obviously the defendant, and which involve inferences that a jury ordinarily could make immediately, even were the confession the very first item introduced at trial." Finally, the Court stressed that its holding, which addressed only obviously redacted confessions, was sufficiently narrow to avoid "unnecessarily leading prosecutors to abandon the relevant confession or joint trial."

Viewed together, the Court's precedents distinguish between confessions that directly implicate a defendant and those that do so indirectly. *Richardson* explicitly declined to extend *Bruton*'s "narrow exception" to the presumption that jurors follow their instructions beyond those confessions that occupy the former category. *Gray* qualified but confirmed this legal standard, reiterating that the *Bruton* rule applies only to "directly accusatory" incriminating statements, as distinct from those that do "not refer directly to the defendant" and "become incriminating only when linked with evidence introduced later at trial." Neither *Bruton*, *Richardson*, nor *Gray* provides license to flyspeck trial transcripts in search of evidence that could give rise to a collateral inference that the defendant had been named in an altered confession.

The District Court's admission of Stillwell's confession, accompanied by a limiting instruction, did not run afoul of this Court's precedents. Stillwell's confession was redacted to avoid naming Samia, satisfying *Bruton*'s rule. And, it was not redacted in a manner resembling the confession in *Gray*; the neutral references to some "other person" were not akin to an obvious blank or the word "deleted." In fact, the redacted confession is strikingly similar to a hypothetical modified confession we looked upon favorably in *Gray*, where we posited that, instead of saying "he, deleted, deleted, and a few other guys," the witness could easily have said "me and a few other guys." Accordingly, it "falls outside the narrow exception *Bruton* created." *Richardson*, 481 U.S., at 208. Moreover, it would not have been feasible to further modify Stillwell's confession to make it appear that he had acted alone. Stillwell was charged with conspiracy and did not confess to shooting Lee. Consequently, the evidence of coordination between Stillwell and Lee's killer (whether Samia or not) was necessary to prove an essential element of the Government's case. Editing the statement to exclude mention of the "other person" may have made it seem as though Stillwell and Lee were alone in the van at the time Lee was shot. Such a scenario may have led the jurors—who sat in judgment of both Samia and Stillwell—to conclude that Stillwell was the shooter, an obviously prejudicial result. Expanding the *Bruton* rule in the way Samia proposes would be inconsistent with longstanding practice and our precedents. It would also work an unnecessary and imprudent change in law, resulting in precisely the practical effects that the Court rejected in *Richardson*. The Confrontation Clause rule that Samia proposes would require federal and state trial courts to conduct extensive pretrial hearings to determine whether the jury could infer from the Government's case in its entirety that the defendant had been named in an altered confession. That approach would be burdensome and "far from foolproof," and we decline to endorse it.

In a criminal trial, all evidence that supports the prosecution's theory of the case is, to some extent, mutually reinforcing. Thus, the likely practical consequence of Samia's position would be to mandate severance whenever the prosecution wishes to introduce the confession of a nontestifying codefendant in a joint trial. But that is "too high" a price to pay. Joint trials have long "played a vital role in the criminal justice system," preserving government resources and allowing victims to avoid repeatedly reliving trauma. Further, joint trials encourage consistent verdicts and enable more accurate assessments of relative culpability. Also, separate trials "randomly favor the last-tried defendants who have the advantage of knowing the prosecution's case beforehand." *Richardson*, 481 U.S., at 210. Samia offers that the Government may choose to forgo use of the confession entirely, thereby avoiding the need for severance. But confessions are "essential to society's compelling interest in finding, convicting, and punishing those who violate the law." *Ibid.* The Confrontation Clause ensures that defendants have the opportunity to confront witnesses against them, but it does not provide a freestanding guarantee against the risk of potential prejudice that may arise inferentially in a joint trial. Here, the Clause was not violated by the admission of a nontestifying codefendant's confession that did not directly inculpate the defendant and was subject to a proper limiting instruction.

We therefore affirm the judgment of the Court of Appeals.

It is so ordered.

JUSTICE KAGAN, with whom JUSTICE SOTOMAYOR and JUSTICE JACKSON join, dissenting.

Bruton's application turned on the effect a confession is likely to have on the jury. In *Richardson*, we approved the admission of a confession "redacted to eliminate not only a co-defendant's name, but any reference to his or her existence." Despite that redaction, the confession served to incriminate the co-defendant later in the trial, when her own testimony placed her in a car ride that the confession described. But we thought that a confession that incriminated only "by connection" with subsequent evidence was neither so "vivid" nor so "powerful" as a confession that "incriminated on its face." For that reason, the jury was more "likely to obey the instruction" to disregard the confession as to the co-defendant. But we held in *Gray* that the calculus is different when a confession "refers directly to the 'existence' of the nonconfessing defendant," even though not by name. Such a confession points a finger at a co-defendant, so the jury can "immediately" and "vividly" grasp how it implicates her. The impact is similar to naming the defendant. The confession's "powerfully incriminating" effect "creates a special, and vital, need for cross-examination"—just as if "the codefendant pointed directly to the defendant in the courtroom."

According to the prosecution's theory, Paul LeRoux, the head of a transnational criminal organization, ordered the killing; and Hunter, one of LeRoux's managers, hired Samia and Stillwell as hitmen. Before trial, Stillwell confessed to federal agents that both he and Samia were present at the murder, but told them that Samia was the triggerman. On that version, Samia shot the victim in a van that Stillwell was driving. At trial, one of the agents testified about Stillwell's confession, replacing Samia's name with placeholders like "somebody else" and "the other person." When the prosecutor asked the agent what Stillwell said about his arrival in the Philippines, the agent answered: "He stated that he had met somebody else there." When asked whether Stillwell had recounted the crime, the agent testified: "Yes. He described a time when the other person pulled the trigger on that woman in a van that he and Mr. Stillwell was driving." From the jury's perspective, the identity of the triggerman would have been obvious. The jury knew from the start of trial that there were just three defendants. It knew based on the prosecutor's opening statement that those defendants were on trial for offenses related to a death in the Philippines. And it knew the role that each defendant allegedly played in the crime: Hunter had hired Stillwell and Samia as hitmen, and those two men carried out the murder. In fact, the prosecutor began his opening statement with the exact sequence of events Stillwell described in his interview. Any reasonable juror would have realized immediately—and without reference to other evidence—that "the other person" who "pulled the trigger" was Samia. That fact makes Stillwell's confession inadmissible under *Bruton*. The agent's testimony pointed a finger straight at Samia, no less than if the agent had used Samia's name or called him "deleted."

The majority distinguishes "between confessions that directly implicate a defendant and those that do so indirectly." But *Bruton*'s application has always turned on a confession's inculpatory impact. A confession that swaps a phrase like "the other person" for a defendant's name may incriminate just as powerfully as one that swaps a blank space. *Gray* repudiates rather than supports the distinction adopted today. *Gray* explained that what should matter is not a confession's form but its effects. A jury, *Gray* noted, "will often react similarly" to the two kinds of confessions; the blank space (rather than name) is "not likely to fool anyone." But *Gray* was a gang assault involving six perpetrators, while only one other person was on trial with the confessing defendant. The "[m]e and a few other guys" phrase thus did not point a finger directly at the co-defendant, as "the other person" phrase here did at Samia. When a modified confession has an "accusatory" effect "similar" to one with names, the law "requires the same result."

The majority reaches for two props inconsistent with *Bruton*. One is the "presumption that jurors follow limiting instructions." The presumption does not apply when the evidence is an accusatory co-defendant confession. The government can simply replace [the codefendant's] name with "woman" or "man" and the *Bruton* issue will go away. But the serious Sixth Amendment problem remains. Defendants in joint trials will not have the chance to confront some of the most damaging witnesses against them. And a constitutional right once guaranteeing that opportunity will no longer.

Justice Jackson, dissenting.

I join Justice KAGAN's dissent. The introduction of a "testimonial" statement from an unavailable declarant violates the Confrontation Clause unless the defendant had a prior opportunity for cross-examination. Stillwell's statement to law enforcement was testimonial, Stillwell was unavailable, and Samia had no opportunity to cross-examine Stillwell. The default presumption should have been that Stillwell's confession was *not* admissible because the statement implicated Samia on its face, and Samia could not cross-examine the declarant.* Before today, this Court had never held that a limiting instruction, combined with a redaction that merely replaces the defendant's name, sufficiently "cures" the constitutional problem.

2. Forfeiture of Confrontation Clause Rights by Wrongdoing

In *Giles v. California*, 554 U.S. 353 (2008), the Court held that the right to Confrontation could be forfeited by wrongdoing. Giles was convicted of murder after the trial court permitted prosecutors to introduce hearsay statements made by the victim to a police officer who was responding to a domestic violence alert. At issue before the Court was whether the un-confronted testimony of the victim was properly admitted, or whether the forfeiture exception applied only when there was an intentional act to prevent the witness from testifying or simply an intentional criminal act that does not permit the witness to testify. The Court, led again by Justice Scalia, adopted the former approach because it was established at the founding of the Amendment that there must be conduct designed to prevent subsequent testimony. As applied to Giles, the intentionality of the criminal act does not suffice to show there was a design to prevent testimony at a subsequent time. Because defendant's intent was not considered in determining whether there was such a design, that issue was remanded to the lower court. As noted, the seminal Confrontation Clause case of Crawford v. Washington continues to produce a plethora of cases attempting to cabin and explain the scope of the Clause.

The Louisiana Supreme Court has held that witness intimidation creates "unavailability" under the "forfeiture by wrongdoing" doctrine of the Confrontation Clause, even if it is not violent. In *State v. Aguilar*, 2015 BL 303182 (La. 2015), the Court

---

* A codefendant's confession implicates a defendant's Sixth Amendment rights even if it does "not directly accuse [the defendant] of wrongdoing," but "rather is inculpatory only when taken together with other evidence," *Melendez-Diaz v. Massachusetts*, 557 U.S. 305, 313 (2009). That conclusion follows from the text of the Sixth Amendment, which guarantees the right of the accused to "confron[t]" "witnesses *against* him" (emphasis added), not just those witnesses who "facially incriminate" him.

concluded that domestic violence victims were unavailable after the defendant violated a protective order barring contact with the victims and the victims subsequently recanted their original testimony. The Court stated:

> The district court erred in denying the State's motion to introduce the victims' statements at trial pursuant to La. Code Evid. art. 804B(7), forfeiture by wrongdoing. The State established by a preponderance of the evidence that the victims (the defendant's girlfriend and their daughter) recanted their testimony and ultimately became uncooperative with the prosecution of the case after the defendant repeatedly violated the protective order forbidding the defendant from contact with the victims. The lower courts both found the victims were unavailable as witnesses within the meaning of La. Code Evid. art. 804A. Thus, to introduce the victims' out of court statements, the State was required to show that the defendant engaged or acquiesced in wrongdoing that was intended to, and did, procure the unavailability of the declarants as witnesses. La. Code Evid. art. 804B(7); Giles v. California, 554 U.S. 353 (2008).

> Contrary to the court of appeal's reasoning, there is no requirement in the code article that the defendant must engage in violence or employ threats of physical violence to cause fear in the victim in order to procure the witness's unavailability. The link between the defendant's actions and the victim's unavailability may be established when "a defendant puts forward to a witness the idea to avoid testifying, either by threats, coercion, persuasion, or pressure " Commonwealth v. Edwards, 830 N.E.2d 158 (2005). Here, the defendant, in violation of the protective order, repeatedly suggested and encouraged the victims to recant their statements to the police and to avoid testifying against him at trial, thereby applying pressure on the witnesses through persistent contact. Because the witnesses' unavailability is a logical outgrowth of the defendant's actions in this domestic violence case, the forfeiture by wrongdoing doctrine is properly applied. For these reasons, the trial court's ruling is reversed, and the matter is remanded to that court for further proceedings.

FYI

In *Colorado v. Janis*, 429 P.3d 1138 (Colo. 2018), defendant, who suffered from PTSD, chose to leave the courtroom right before the victim testified. Afterwards, she claimed a Confrontation Clause violation on the basis that the judge should have explained that she had the right to confront her accuser. The court rejected the challenged, concluding that defendant was aware of her right to be present. Defendant could have requested a recess, but did not.

Hypos: *The Intimidator & the Killer*

A) A man, known in the neighborhood as "the intimidator," was charged with brutally beating up another man who lived in the same neighborhood. Frank was an eyewitness who was interviewed by the prosecution in a discovery deposition, which the defendant was not permitted to attend, and was subpoenaed to testify at trial. Frank was visited by several friends of the accused who, in a not-so-subtle fashion, indicated he should be careful about what he said. When Frank showed up at trial, claiming that he could no longer speak, the prosecution offered the discovery deposition instead. How should the judge rule if the defense objects to the deposition?

B) Jones is prosecuted for murder of his ex-girlfriend. His ex texted others on several occasions about how scared she was of Jones, and she reported his threats to the police. On one occasion, the police visited her home and took down a statement. The prosecution wants to offer the various statements of the victim at Jones' trial. The defense objects. What ruling and why?

3. Impeachment Evidence

To what extent is impeachment evidence protected by the Confrontation Clause? In *Davis v. Alaska*, 415 U.S. 308 (1974), the Court held that a criminal defendant has the right to cross-examine prosecution witnesses about their convictions, including sometimes their juvenile adjudications, particularly to show bias if on probation. Chief Justice Burger observed that subject to "the broad discretion of a trial judge to preclude repetitive and unduly harassing interrogation, the cross-examiner has traditionally been allowed to impeach, *i. e.,* discredit, the witness." He added:

> Cross-examination is the principal means by which the believability of a witness and the truth of his testimony are tested. A more particular attack on the witness' credibility is effected by means of cross-examination directed toward revealing possible biases, prejudices, or ulterior motives of the witness as they may relate directly to issues or personalities in the case at hand. We cannot speculate as to whether the jury, as sole judge of the credibility of a witness, would have accepted this line of reasoning had counsel been permitted to fully present it. But we conclude that the jurors were entitled to have the benefit of the defense theory before them so that they

could make an informed judgment as to the weight to place on Green's testimony which provided "a crucial link in the proof of petitioner's act." *Douglas v. Alabama*, 380 U. S., at 419. The accuracy and truthfulness of Green's testimony were key elements in the State's case against petitioner. The claim of bias which the defense sought to develop was admissible to afford a basis for an inference of undue pressure because of Green's vulnerable status as a probationer, as well as of Green's possible concern that he might be a suspect in the investigation.

Subsequently, the Court reaffirmed the protection for cross-examination to uncover bias in *Olden v. Kentucky*, 488 U.S. 227 (1988). In *Olden*, a defendant accused of sexual assault attempted to cross-examine the complaining witness by impeaching the witness' credibility by revealing that the witness might have had a motive to lie about the assault to protect an on-going extra-marital affair. The defense was not permitted to do so and the state court appeal was denied based on harmless error. The Court, in a *per curiam* opinion, concluded that the denial violated defendant's Confrontation Clause rights and was not harmless error under *Chapman v. California*, 386 U.S. 18 (1967). The Court noted that "the correct inquiry is whether, assuming that the damaging potential of the cross-examination were fully realized, a reviewing court might nonetheless say that the error was harmless beyond a reasonable doubt." *Delaware v. Van Arsdall*, 475 U.S. 673, 679 (1986). The Court explained that exclusion of the impeachment evidence was not harmless:

> Petitioner has consistently asserted that he and Matthews engaged in consensual sexual acts and that complaining witness Matthews—out of fear of jeopardizing her relationship with Russell—lied when she told Russell she had been raped and has continued to lie since. It is plain to us that "a reasonable jury might have received a significantly different impression of the witness' credibility had defense counsel been permitted to pursue his proposed line of cross-examination." *Delaware v. Van Arsdall, supra*, at 680. Here, Matthews' testimony was central, indeed crucial, to the prosecution's case. Her story, which was directly contradicted by that of petitioner and Harris, was corroborated only by the largely derivative testimony of Russell, whose impartiality would also have been somewhat impugned by revelation of his relationship with Matthews. Finally, the State's case against petitioner was far from overwhelming. In sum, considering the relevant *Van Arsdall* factors within the context of this case, we find it impossible to conclude "beyond a reasonable doubt" that the restriction on petitioner's right to confrontation was harmless.

Hypo 1: *Corruption Evidence*

Defendant Jones was charged in a drive-by shooting murder case. Jones offered extrinsic bias and corruption evidence about a testifying police detective. In particular, the defense wanted to show that the officer was the subject of an on-going investigation about coaching witnesses in another case. If you are the judge, would you allow this evidence? *Compare Longus v. United States*, 52 A.3d 836 (D.C. 2012), where the Court found that a trial court's "refusal to allow questioning about facts indicative of a witness's bias from which the jury could reasonably draw adverse inferences of reliability is an error of constitutional dimension." Moreover, evidence from which the jury can infer bias may be presented not only through cross-examination, but also by the introduction of extrinsic evidence. *See In re C.B.N.*, 499 A.2d 1215, 1218 (D.C. 1985).

4. Interpreter Statements

The circuits are split over whether statements by non-testifying interpreters violate the Confrontation Clause. In the Fourth and Ninth Circuits, courts view interpreters as language conduits, meaning agents of the speaker, and their statements are not considered testimonial. *See United States v. Shibin*, 722 F.3d 233 (4th Cir. 2013); and *United States v. Romo-Chavez*, 681 F.3d 955, 961 (9th Cir. 2013)(stating that a translator was serving as a "mere conduit" for the statements of the defendant.). In *Shibin*, the defendant, a Somali, was tried for his involvement in the piracy of a ship off of the Somali coast. The defendant negotiated a ransom from the owners of the ship. After his involvement in another ship hijacking, Shibin was captured and brought to Virginia to stand trial. Shibin was convicted and appealed. He raised the Confrontation Clause as it related to the interpreter used for one of his witnesses as the basis for one of the grounds of alleged error. The Court rejected Shibin's claims: "Here, the statements were introduced as prior inconsistent statements. The interpreter was nothing more than a language conduit. He interpreted the statements of Salad Ali [the defendant's witness] and FBI Agent Coughlin, both of whom were subject to cross-examination." The Eleventh Circuit disagreed with the *Shibin* approach. In *United States v. Charles*, 722 F.3d 1319 (11th Cir. 2013), in an opinion issued shortly after the Fourth Circuit's opinion, the Court found that statements by interpreters were indeed testimonial and subject to the Confrontation Clause. The Court also found, though, that the trial court's failure to allow confrontation based on the facts of the case was not plain error.

5. Harmless Error

When does a violation of the Confrontation Clause constitute harmless error? In *Johnson v. Lamas*, 850 F.3d 119 (3d Cir. 2017), the Court observed, "to be entitled to *habeas* relief, a *habeas* petitioner must establish that the trial error "had a substantial and injurious effect or influence in determining the jury's verdict." *Brecht v. Abrahamson*, 507 U.S. 619, 637 (1993). Under this test, we may grant relief only if we have a "grave doubt" as to whether the error at trial had a substantial and injurious effect or influence. *Davis v. Ayala*, 576 U.S. 257, 267 (2015). In other words, "there must be more than a 'reasonable probability' that the error was harmful." *Id.* The Court provided a list of factors that assisted in its analysis: "Several factors guide our review of Confrontation Clause errors, including "the importance of the witness' testimony in the prosecution's case, whether the testimony was cumulative, the presence or absence of evidence corroborating or contradicting the testimony of the witness on material points, the extent of cross-examination otherwise permitted, and, of course, the overall strength of the prosecution's case. U.S. Const. Amend. 6."

Hypo: *Confrontation & Harmless Error*

Preston's alleged accomplice gave a statement to police that was admitted at trial against both Preston and the accomplice. However, at trial, the accomplice refused to testify. Preston's attorney failed to object to the admission of the statement. Might the failure be regarded as harmless error if there was lots of other evidence of Preston's guilt, and if the accomplice did not actually that Preston was the shooter? *See Preston v. Superintendent Graterford SCI*, 902 F.3d 365 (3d Cir. 2018).

G. Confrontation in Sexual Assault Cases

A special Confrontation Clause issue arises in sexual assault cases—what are the requirements for confrontation in testimony by a complaining witness? Is the Clause only satisfied by face-to-face confrontation or are alternatives permitted? In *Maryland v. Craig*, 497 U.S. 839 (1990), the Court held that a child witness in a child abuse case can testify outside the defendant's physical presence, through a closed circuit television. Justice O'Connor, for the Court, stated:

> We have never held that the Confrontation Clause guarantees criminal defendants the *absolute* right to a face-to-face meeting with witnesses against them at trial. Our precedents establish that "the Confrontation Clause reflects a *preference* for face-to-face confrontation at trial," a prefer-

ence that "must occasionally give way to considerations of public policy and the necessities of the case." Thus, though we reaffirm the importance of face-to-face confrontation with witnesses appearing at trial, we cannot say that such confrontation is an indispensable element of the Sixth Amendment's guarantee of the right to confront one's accusers. If the State makes an adequate showing of necessity, the state interest in protecting child witnesses from the trauma of testifying in a child abuse case is sufficiently important to justify the use of a special procedure that permits a child witness in such cases to testify at trial against a defendant in the absence of face-to-face confrontation with the defendant.

Hypo: *Remote Testimony*

Suppose a sexual abuse trial is scheduled and the complaining witness is: A) eight years old and her mother does not want her to testify in front of the defendant; B) 10 years old and nervous about testifying; C) 12 years old and on a long-planned vacation with her family. Would a remote studio location without face-to-face confrontation for the testimony suffice in any of these three situations? Why or why not?

Executive Summary

The Confrontation Clause's Application. The Confrontation Clause applies to both state and federal governments and has two strands—putative hearsay and face-to-face positioning.

Hearsay and Confrontation. The more volatile and dynamic analysis concerns hearsay. After *Crawford v. Washington*, the Clause only applies to testimonial statements, for which the Court has not provided a comprehensive definition. These statements include affidavits, *ex parte* statements, and any statements that are made to prove a fact that previously happened likely will fall within the embrace of the Clause, regardless of their reliability. Reliability was the lynchpin under the prior seminal case, *Ohio v. Roberts*, but was abandoned in *Crawford*.

The Initial Issue Is Whether the Statement Is Testimonial. The hearsay strand applies only to testimonial statements. If a statement is offered by the prosecution, the accused must first have had the opportunity to examine the subsequently unavailable declarant before the statement is potentially admitted.

Testimonial Statements Can Still Satisfy Confrontation Requirements. If a statement is testimonial, the accused must have been afforded the opportunity to examine the declarant. If the declarant testifies, that satisfies the Sixth Amendment. If the declarant is unavailable, the accused must have been afforded the opportunity to examine the witness.

Opportunity Does Not Require Examination. The accused can waive the opportunity to examine the witness—all that is required is an opportunity. Of course, it is generally beneficial to cross-examine the opponent's witnesses.

The Clause Does Not Apply to All Statements. The Clause does not apply to statements offered by the defense, including statements not offered for their truth, or statements made for the primary purpose of resolving an on-going emergency.

Admissibility Ultimately Depends on Evidentiary Rules. Even if a statement survives the Confrontation Clause analysis, evidentiary and other rules apply and could preclude admissibility.

Exceptions. The Confrontation Clause has several exceptions and the rights it affords can be waived by the accused, either expressly or implicitly. These exceptions include forfeiture by wrongdoing, which occurs when an accused intentionally renders a witness unavailable for testifying.

Major Themes

a. **Testimonial**—Hearsay must be testimonial for the Confrontation right to apply.

b. **Opportunity**—An accused must have the opportunity to cross-examine a declarant whose statement is testimonial, or a witness when the declarant is unavailable.

For More Information

- RUSSELL L. WEAVER, JOHN M. BURKOFF, CATHERINE HANCOCK & STEVEN I. FRIEDLAND, PRINCIPLES OF CRIMINAL PROCEDURE Ch. 17 (8th ed. 2024).

- *Confrontation Clause: Continuing Uncertainty For Expert Testimony Following Williams v. Illinois*, FEDERAL EVIDENCE REVIEW (6/17/2013).

- J. Smith, *Understanding the New Confrontation Clause Analysis:* Crawford, Davis, Melendez-Diaz, ADMINISTRATION OF JUSTICE BULLETIN, UNC SCHOOL OF GOVERNMENT (2010).

Test Your Knowledge

To assess your understanding of the material in this chapter, click here to take a quiz.

CHAPTER 19

Freedom of the Press & Fair Trials

Guarantees of expressive freedom and a fair trial are fundamental values in American society, but these guarantees do not always coexist harmoniously. Indeed, freedom of the press may both promote and undermine the criminal justice process. An unfettered right to free expression promotes self-government by exposing judicial or prosecutorial corruption or incompetence, and it can be a catalyst for reform by heightening the public's political awareness and understanding of the criminal process. Thus, the media's presence and influence avoid proceedings akin to the star chamber and practices inimical to fundamental fairness. But, while the press can serve many useful functions, its presence has the potential to disrupt and undermine the fairness of the trial process. Consider the following case.

A. Failing to Control the Press

Sheppard v. Maxwell

384 U.S. 333 (1966).

Mr. Justice Clark delivered the opinion of the Court.

Marilyn Sheppard, petitioner's pregnant wife, was bludgeoned to death in the upstairs bedroom of their lakeshore home in Bay Village, Ohio, a suburb of Cleveland. On the day of the tragedy, July 4, 1954, Sheppard pieced together the following story: after dinner Sheppard became drowsy and dozed off on a couch. The next thing he remembered was hearing his wife cry out in the early morning. He hurried upstairs and in the dim light saw a "form" standing next to his wife's bed. As he struggled with the "form" he was struck on the back of the neck and rendered unconscious. From the outset officials focused suspicion on Sheppard. After a search of the house and premises on the morning of the tragedy, Dr. Gerber, the Coroner, is reported to have told his men, "It is evident the doctor did this, so let's go get the confession out of him." On July 20th, the press opened fire with a front-page charge that somebody is "getting away with murder." The newspapers emphasized evidence that tended to incriminate Sheppard and pointed out discrepancies in his statements to authorities. At the same time, Sheppard made many public statements to the press and wrote feature articles asserting his innocence.

The case came to trial two weeks before the November general election at which the chief prosecutor was a candidate for common pleas judge and the trial judge, Judge Blythin, was a candidate to succeed himself. Twenty-five days before the case was set, 75 veniremen were called as prospective jurors. All three Cleveland newspapers published the names and addresses of the veniremen. As a consequence, anonymous letters and telephone calls, as well as calls from friends, regarding the impending prosecution were received by all of the prospective jurors. The courtroom in which the trial was held measured 26 by 48 feet. A long temporary table was set up inside the bar, in back of the single counsel table. It ran the width of the courtroom, parallel to the bar railing, with one end less than three feet from the jury box. Approximately 20 representatives of newspapers and wire services were assigned seats at this table by the court. Behind the bar railing there were four rows of benches. These seats were likewise assigned by the court for the entire trial. The first row was occupied by representatives of television and radio stations, and the second and third rows by reporters from out-of-town newspapers and magazines. One side of the last row, which accommodated 14 people, was assigned to Sheppard's family and the other to Marilyn's. The public was permitted to fill vacancies in this row on special passes only. Representatives of the news media used all the rooms on the courtroom floor, including the room where cases were ordinarily called and assigned for trial. Private telephone lines and telegraphic equipment were installed in these rooms so that reports from the trial could be speeded to the papers. Station WSRS was permitted to set up broadcasting facilities on the third floor of the courthouse next to the jury room, where the jury rested during recesses in the trial and deliberated. Newscasts were made from this room throughout the trial, and while the jury reached its verdict.

On the sidewalk and steps in front of the courthouse, television and newsreel cameras were occasionally used to take motion pictures of the participants in the trial, including the jury and the judge. Indeed, one television broadcast carried a staged interview of the judge as he entered the courthouse. In the corridors outside the courtroom there was a host of photographers and television personnel with flash cameras, portable lights and motion picture cameras. This group photographed the prospective jurors during selection of the jury. After the trial opened, the witnesses, counsel, and jurors were photographed and televised whenever they entered or left the courtroom. Sheppard was brought to the courtroom about 10 minutes before each session began; he was surrounded by reporters and extensively photographed for the newspapers and television. A rule of court prohibited picture-taking in the courtroom during the actual sessions of the court, but no restraints were put on photographers during recesses, which were taken once each morning and afternoon, with a longer period for lunch.

All of these arrangements with the news media and their massive coverage of the trial continued during the nine weeks of the trial. The courtroom remained crowded to capacity with representatives of news media. Their movement in and out of the courtroom often caused so much confusion that, despite the loud-speaker system installed in the courtroom, it was difficult for the witnesses and counsel to be heard. Furthermore, the reporters clustered within the bar of the small courtroom made confidential talk among Sheppard and his counsel almost impossible during the proceedings. They frequently had to leave the courtroom to obtain privacy. Many times when counsel wished to raise a point with the judge out of the hearing of the jury it was necessary to move to the judge's chambers. Even then, news media representatives so packed the judge's anteroom that counsel could hardly return from the chambers to the courtroom. The reporters vied with each other to find out what counsel and the judge had discussed, and often these matters later appeared in newspapers accessible to the jury.

The jurors were constantly exposed to the news media. Every juror, except one, testified at *voir dire* to reading about the case in the Cleveland papers or to having heard broadcasts about it. Seven of the 12 jurors had one or more Cleveland papers delivered in their home. Nor were there questions as to radios or television sets in the jurors' homes, but we must assume that most of them owned such conveniences. As the selection of the jury progressed, individual pictures of prospective members appeared daily. During the trial, pictures of the jury appeared over 40 times in the Cleveland papers alone. The court permitted photographers to take pictures of the jury in the box, and individual pictures of the members in the jury room. One newspaper ran pictures of the jurors at the Sheppard home when they went there to view the scene of the murder. Another paper featured the home life of an alternate juror. The day before the verdict was rendered—while the jurors were at lunch and sequestered by two bailiffs—the jury was separated into two groups to pose for photographs which appeared in the newspapers.

While we cannot say that Sheppard was denied due process by the judge's refusal to take precautions against the influence of pretrial publicity alone, the court's rulings must be considered against the setting in which the trial was held. We believe that the arrangements made by the judge with the news media caused Sheppard to be deprived of that "judicial serenity and calm to which he was entitled." Bedlam reigned at the courthouse during the trial and newsmen took over practically the entire courtroom, hounding most of the participants in the trial, especially Sheppard. At a temporary table within a few feet of the jury box and counsel table sat some 20 reporters staring at Sheppard and taking notes. The erection of a press table for reporters inside the bar is unprecedented. The bar of the court is reserved for counsel, providing them a safe place in which to keep papers and exhibits, and to confer privately with client and co-counsel. It is designed to protect the witness and the jury from any distractions, intrusions or influences, and to permit bench discussions of the judge's rulings away from the hearing of the public and the jury. Having assigned almost all of the available seats in the courtroom to the news media the judge lost his ability to supervise that environment.

The carnival atmosphere at trial could easily have been avoided since the courtroom and courthouse premises are subject to the control of the court. The presence of the press at judicial proceedings must be limited when it is apparent that the accused might otherwise be prejudiced or disadvantaged. Bearing in mind the massive pretrial publicity, the judge should have adopted stricter rules governing the use of the courtroom by newsmen, as Sheppard's counsel requested. The number of reporters in the courtroom itself could have been limited at the first sign that their presence would disrupt the trial. They certainly should not have been placed inside the bar. Furthermore, the judge should have more closely regulated the conduct of newsmen in the courtroom. For instance, the judge belatedly asked them not to handle and photograph trial exhibits lying on the counsel table during recesses.

Secondly, the court should have insulated the witnesses. All of the newspapers and radio stations interviewed prospective witnesses at will, and in many instances disclosed their testimony. A typical example was the publication of numerous statements by Susan Hayes, before her appearance in court, regarding her love affair with Sheppard. Although the witnesses were barred from the courtroom during the trial the full verbatim testimony was available to them in the press. This completely nullified the judge's imposition of the rule.

Thirdly, the court should have made some effort to control the release of leads, information, and gossip to the press by police officers, witnesses, and the counsel for both sides. The trial court might well have proscribed extrajudicial statements by any lawyer, party, witness, or court official which divulged prejudicial matters, such as the refusal of Sheppard to submit to interrogation or take any lie detector tests; any statement made by Sheppard to officials; the identity of prospective witnesses or their probable testimony; any belief in guilt or innocence; or like statements concerning the merits of the case. Being advised of the great public interest in the case, the mass coverage of the press, and the potential prejudicial impact of publicity, the court could also have requested the appropriate city and county officials to promulgate a regulation with respect to dissemination of information about the case by their employees. In addition, reporters who wrote or broadcast prejudicial stories, could have been warned as to the impropriety of publishing material not introduced in the proceedings.

Unfair and prejudicial news comment on pending trials has become increasingly prevalent. Due process requires that the accused receive a trial by an impartial jury free from outside influences. Given the pervasiveness of modern communications and the difficulty of effacing prejudicial publicity from the minds of the jurors, trial courts must take strong measures to ensure that the balance is never weighed against the accused. And appellate tribunals have the duty to make an independent evaluation of the circumstances. Of course, there is nothing that proscribes the press from reporting events that transpire in the courtroom. But where there is a reasonable likelihood that prejudicial news prior to trial will prevent a fair trial, the judge should continue the case until the threat abates, or transfer it to another county not so permeated with publicity. In addition, sequestration of the jury was something the judge should have raised *sua sponte* with counsel. If publicity during the proceedings threatens the fairness of the trial, a new trial should be ordered. But we must remember that reversals are but palliatives; the cure lies in those remedial measures that prevent the prejudice at its inception. The courts must take such steps by rule and regulation that will protect their processes from prejudicial outside interferences. Neither prosecutors, counsel for defense, the accused, witnesses, court staff nor enforcement officers coming under the jurisdiction of the court should be permitted to frustrate its function. Collaboration between counsel and the press as to information affecting the fairness of a criminal trial is not only subject to regulation, but is highly censurable and worthy of disciplinary measures.

Since the state trial judge did not fulfill his duty to protect Sheppard from the inherently prejudicial publicity which saturated the community and to control disruptive influences in the courtroom, we must reverse the denial of the *habeas* petition. The case is remanded to the District Court with instructions to issue the writ and order that Sheppard be released from custody unless the State puts him to its charges again within a reasonable time.

It is so ordered.

B. Pretrial Publicity & Defendant's Right to a Fair Trial

In order to preserve a defendant's right to a fair trial, there are several steps that a judge might take to limit the impact of media publicity.

1. Change of Venue

While a defendant has a right to a state criminal trial in the county of the crime, the defendant may desire a trial in another county and may file a motion for a change of venue. The right to request a change of venue belongs to either the defendant or the prosecution. Since venue is largely a creature of statute, statutory procedures should be followed before relief may be granted. On the other hand, a change of venue is a federally protected right which may require the court to overlook statutory procedures. *Groppi v. Wisconsin*, 400 U.S. 505 (1971). Statutes may permit each party only one application for a change of venue which must be timely made or it may be waived.

FYI

When potential jurors have read or heard prejudicial publicity, a trial judge should inquire into the nature and extent of the exposure. To prove juror partiality, a defendant must show that the publicity either actually prejudiced a juror or so pervaded the proceedings that it raised a presumption of inherent prejudice. In *Sheppard v. Maxwell*, the Court noted that "where there is a reasonable likelihood that prejudicial news prior to trial will prevent a fair trial, the judge should continue the case until the threat abates, or transfer it to another county not so permeated with publicity." During trial, a judge also has broad discretion to sequester the jury and caution the jurors to avoid media accounts of the proceedings.

After an application for a change of venue has been made, the court must determine whether the application establishes a *prima facie* case for granting a change of venue. If it does not, the application may be denied. If a *prima facie* showing has been made, the opposing party must then controvert the allegations or the change of venue must be granted. In making its determination the trial court has wide discretion which will not be disturbed if it is supported by sufficient evidence. In many instances the trial judge will defer a decision about the motion until *voir dire* has indicated whether there is a valid prospect of a fair trial for the defendant. Once in a while, however, circumstances suggest the need to grant the change of venue without the necessity of weighing the nature and extent of awareness about the defendant and the charge.

United States v. Lindh

212 F. Supp. 2d 541 (E.D. Va. 2002).

ELLIS, DISTRICT JUDGE.

John Phillip Walker Lindh is an American citizen who, according to the Indictment filed against him, joined certain foreign terrorist organizations in Afghanistan and served these organizations in combat against Northern Alliance and American forces until his capture in November 2001. Lindh sought dismissal of certain counts of the Indictment on a variety of grounds, including lawful combatant immunity and selective prosecution. Lindh also sought dismissal, or alternatively, transfer of venue, arguing that he could not receive a fair trial in this district owing to pre-trial publicity. All motions were denied. Lindh requests dismissal on the ground that the media attention surrounding this case has been so prejudicial as to deprive him of his Sixth Amendment right to a fair trial. He alternatively requests a transfer of venue to the Northern District of California, the district in which he spent his childhood and where he claims the pre-trial publicity has not been as prejudicial. Lindh also claims that the Northern District of California is more convenient for the parties and witnesses, pursuant to Rule 21(b), Fed.R.Crim.P.

The principles that govern resolution of this motion are clear and well settled. The Sixth Amendment guarantees that in all criminal prosecutions, the defendant shall enjoy the right to trial "by an impartial jury." In certain extraordinary, circumstances, this fundamental right to trial "by an impartial jury" may be compromised by the presence of pervasive and inflammatory pre-trial publicity. To warrant a dismissal of an indictment on this ground, a defendant must establish that he cannot obtain a fair trial anywhere in the country owing to prejudicial pre-trial publicity. *See United States v. Abbott Laboratories*, 505 F.2d 565 (4th Cir.1974). In other words, dismissal is appropriate only where a defendant establishes that prejudicial pre-trial publicity is "so widespread and pervasive that a change of venue would be ineffective to assure a defendant a fair trial." *Id.* In this regard, it is important to note that "sheer volume of publicity alone does not deny a defendant a fair trial." *United States v. Bakker*, 925 F.2d 728, 732 (4th Cir.1991).

Dismissal of an indictment as a remedy for prejudicial pre-trial publicity is severe and rarely warranted, as it is unlikely that fair and impartial jurors cannot be found in any district. The less severe remedy of transfer is also unwarranted unless a defendant can show that the pre-trial publicity in the district "is so inherently prejudicial that trial proceedings must be presumed to be tainted." *Bakker*, 925 F.2d at 732. Moreover, transfers of venue based on pre-trial publicity are not often granted, as "the effects of pre-trial publicity on the pool from which jurors are drawn is generally determined by a careful and searching *voir dire* examination." *United States v. McVeigh*, 918 F.Supp. 1467 (W.D.Okla.1996). "Only where *voir dire* reveals that an impartial jury cannot be impaneled would a change of venue be justified." *Bakker*, 925 F.2d at 732. "It is not required that jurors be totally ignorant of the facts and issues involved." *Id.* at 734. Rather, "it is sufficient if the juror can lay aside his impression or opinion and render a verdict based on the evidence presented in court." *Id.*

All prospective jurors in this case will be questioned carefully as to what they have seen or read or heard about the case and whether they have formed any opinions or impressions. No juror will be qualified to serve unless the Court is satisfied that the juror (i) is able to put aside any previously formed opinions or impressions, (ii) is prepared to pay careful and close attention to the evidence as it is presented in the case and finally (iii) is able to render a fair and impartial verdict based solely on the evidence adduced at trial and the Court's instructions of law.

Just as the sheer volume of pre-trial publicity in this case does not compel dismissal or transfer, neither does the nature of that publicity. The bulk of the pre-trial publicity relating to this case is factual, rather than inflammatory, and hence less likely to poison the venire pool. No doubt the publicity also includes some expressions of opinions on newspaper editorial pages or the Internet that were specifically designed to inflame or persuade readers. Yet, on the whole, the record does not warrant a conclusion that prejudicial pre-trial publicity has been so "inherently prejudicial that trial proceedings must be presumed to be tainted" or that Lindh cannot receive a fair trial. The proof will be the *voir dire* results; only those prospective jurors found to be capable of fair and impartial jury service after careful *voir dire* will be declared eligible to serve as jurors. Past experience provides reasonable assurance that more than a sufficient number of qualified, impartial jurors will be identified as a result of the *voir dire* in this case.

Nor are Lindh's expert reports—one prepared by Neil Vidmar and the other by Steven Penrod—to the contrary; neither persuasively supports dismissal of the Indictment or transfer to another district. Vidmar developed a survey interview questionnaire to assess the impact of pre-trial publicity in this case. He later supervised the Evans McDonough Company in conducting random telephone interviews of 400 individuals in this district and, for comparison purposes, 200 individuals in Chicago, Minneapolis, San Francisco and Seattle.[8] Penrod, on the other hand, conducted a content analysis of the pre-trial newspaper coverage concerning Lindh and other issues, as reported in the two major newspapers circulated in Alexandria (the Washington Post and the Washington Times) and, for comparison purposes, the two major newspapers circulated in Minneapolis (the Minneapolis Star Tribune and the St. Paul Pioneer Press).[9]

Despite Lindh's arguments, the Vidmar report actually supports the conclusion that Lindh is just as likely to receive a fair trial in this district as elsewhere in the country. Indeed, Vidmar concludes that "the stated attitudes of jury eligible respondents in Virginia toward Mr. Lindh between April 29 and May 2 did not differ from stated attitudes in the rest of the country." Moreover, approximately three quarters (74%) of the Northern Virginia residents who were polled indicated that they could be fair and impartial if seated as a juror at Lindh's trial. Significantly, this percentage exceeds the percentage reported by Vidmar for California (68.6%), the jurisdiction to which Lindh seeks a transfer. The fact that a number of the individuals polled in both Virginia and elsewhere knew someone injured or killed in the September 11, 2001

---

[8] Among the questions asked of the respondents were (i) what information they know about Lindh; (ii) whether they have a strongly favorable, somewhat favorable, somewhat unfavorable or strongly unfavorable opinion of Lindh; (iii) whether they view Lindh as a terrorist, a traitor, a confused young man or a person on a religious journey; (iv) whether they believe Lindh was involved in the death of CIA agent Spann; (v) whether they believe there is a connection between Lindh and the September 11, 2001 terrorist attacks; (vi) whether they knew someone who was killed or injured in the September 11, 2001 terrorist attacks; (vii) whether they believe Lindh is guilty, probably guilty, probably not guilty or definitely not guilty of the charges against him; (viii) whether they would consider a not guilty verdict very acceptable, acceptable, not acceptable or very unacceptable; (ix) what punishment they believe Lindh should receive if found guilty of the charges against him; and (x) whether they could be fair and impartial if seated as a juror at Lindh's trial.

[9] Specifically, the newspaper articles were coded as either favorable or unfavorable toward Lindh on a number of issues, including (i) the personal characteristics of Lindh; (ii) Lindh's connections to the Taliban, al Qaeda and bin Laden; (iii) Lindh's connection to the QIJ prison uprising resulting in the death of CIA agent Spann; (iv) the regional economic and emotional impact of the September 11, 2001 attack on the Pentagon; and (v) the instant charges against Lindh.

terrorist attacks does not warrant dismissal of the Indictment or a change of venue. Rather, such personal connections to the terrorist attacks are matters adequately addressed and dealt with during *voir dire*.

The Penrod report also does not support dismissal or transfer of the case. On more than half the subjects covered by the survey, the Minneapolis newspapers were either harsher in their assessment of Lindh or expressed "unfavorable" opinions to the same extent as did the Alexandria newspapers. On those subjects where the Alexandria newspapers were found to be less favorable toward Lindh than the Minneapolis newspapers, the percentages were often so close as to be statistically insignificant. It is worth noting that Lindh is not entitled to a "favorable" jury, as Penrod appears to suggest; nor is he entitled to a jury that has not been privy to any media reports regarding the instant prosecution, favorable or unfavorable. Rather, the Sixth Amendment guarantees Lindh, and all criminal defendants, a fair and impartial jury. Nothing in the studies and data Lindh submitted supports a conclusion that Lindh cannot receive a fair and impartial jury trial in this district.

Lindh's motion to transfer the case to the Northern District of California for purposes of convenience, pursuant to Rule 21(b) is equally unpersuasive. Contrary to Lindh's contentions, there are multiple reasons for concluding that transfer from this district is inappropriate, including the following: (i) the trial will proceed more expeditiously in this district; (ii) this district is equipped and prepared to cope with the significant security concerns; (iii) the prosecution team is comprised largely of attorneys from this district; (iv) the relevant documents are located in this district; (v) the defendant is present in this district, subject to security measures already in place; and (vi) a number of potential witnesses are located in or near this district. Moreover, the fact that four of Lindh's attorneys reside in California rather than in this district is an inconvenience of his own choosing. No claim can be made that competent and experienced counsel cannot be found in this district. Of course, Lindh has a Sixth Amendment right to select competent and experienced counsel from another district, which he has done, but he is not entitled to rely on the exercise of that right to effect a change of venue.

Neither a dismissal of the Indictment nor a transfer of venue is warranted in this case. Lindh has failed to meet his burden of establishing that the pre-trial publicity generated in this case, by both the government and the defense, "has been so inflammatory and prejudicial that a fair trial is absolutely precluded and the indictment should be dismissed without an initial attempt to see if an impartial jury can be impaneled." *Abbott*, 505 F.2d at 571. He has also failed to establish that a transfer of venue based on pre-trial publicity is appropriate, as the publicity is not "so inherently prejudicial that trial proceedings in this district must be presumed to be tainted."

Bakker, 925 F.2d at 732.[15] Nor is a transfer of venue for purposes of convenience warranted under Rule 21(b), Fed.R.Crim.P. Rather, the appropriate course of action is to continue the proceedings in this district and to conduct a thorough *voir dire* of all potential jurors to ensure the selection of a fair and impartial jury that is able to set aside any pre-conceived notions regarding this case and render an impartial verdict based solely on the evidence presented and the Court's instructions.

Points for Discussion

a. Factors Supporting a Change of Venue

Other factors may support a motion for a change of venue: 1) The peculiar influence which a trial participant may have in the community may also preclude a fair trial, even if a jury with no actual knowledge of the case could be empanelled; 2) A state of lawlessness which threatens to erupt into mob violence or which might influence the conduct of the trial may also form the basis for a change of venue; 3) The need to transfer defendant to another place for safekeeping pending trial may require a change of venue. Ultimately, the question remains whether an impartial jury might be had in the community, and neither pretrial publicity nor hostility on the part of some members of the community requires a change of venue if a fair and impartial jury may be empanelled and a fair trial held.

FYI

While a change of venue is frequently thought of as related to a fair trial, a somewhat different procedure may allow the transfer of venue to another county for purposes of a plea. The purpose of this transfer provision is to permit a defendant to plead guilty in one place based on charges pending in another place. Fed.R.Crim.P. 20 and many corresponding state rules allow a defendant physically located in one place to plead guilty to charges pending in another place. While the federal rule deals with avoiding transportation problems, there is an added benefit in that a defendant can dispose of multiple cases in a single court. For example, defendants are sometimes charged with multiple crimes, such as bad checks, that occur in several adjacent counties. By appropriate plea negotiations with the various prosecutors involved, the defendant may get a "package deal" on all of his pending charges. In this fashion a single judge may take the plea and impose sentence in consideration of all the charges. Attorneys who have clients with multi-county charges should consider suggesting to the District Attorney that the transfer provision be utilized to consolidate and dispose of the charges. The transfer provisions only apply when there is going to be a guilty plea. If the defendant changes his mind and pleads not guilty, the proceedings are transferred back to the county where the prosecution was initially commenced. Where transfer has to be terminated, any statement that the defendant may have made expressing his desire to plead guilty cannot be used against him.

---

[15] This case is easily distinguishable from *United States v. McVeigh*, 918 F. Supp. 1467 (W.D. Okla. 1996), where a transfer of venue was granted based on the impact of defendant's conduct—the bombing of the Murrah Federal Office Building in Oklahoma City. This unique and extraordinary local impact led the district judge to conclude that "there is so great a prejudice against these defendants in the State of Oklahoma that they cannot obtain a fair and impartial trial at any place [in] that state." The very courthouse where the case would have been tried suffered collateral damage from the bombing. None of the features that motivated transfer in McVeigh is present to the same degree in the instant case.

b. Choosing an Alternate Venue

Statutes differ regarding where a case should be sent if the court grants a motion for a change of venue. For example, if a state court determines that a case should be removed due to emergency conditions, it may transfer the case to any other county within the state in which a fair trial may be held. Or, a statute may provide that, if a court decides to grant a change of venue, it must transfer the case to an adjoining county if a fair trial can be held there. If the court finds that a fair trial cannot be had in any adjoining county, the case may then be transferred to the most convenient county in which a fair trial may be had. In your state, where is a judge allowed to transfer a case after granting a change of venue? With cable television and the internet, is there a strong likelihood that no place exists within a state where a defendant can receive a fair trial? The court to which a case is removed has the same jurisdiction to dispose of the case as the original court that ordered the transfer. If the indictment is dismissed, the grand jury in the county to which the case has been transferred may thereafter be able to prosecute the action as if the offense had been committed in that county originally. The original court making the transfer has no further jurisdiction to prosecute the action as long as the transfer is in effect.

Hypo 1: *The Drug Conspiracy*

Three defendants, all from New York City, are charged with conducting a drug conspiracy in a rural area. One defendant previously was convicted of killing an informer's girlfriend in Vermont state court. Pretrial publicity included local newspaper and television coverage of 1) the defendants' drug arrests, 2) the defendant's prior murder conviction, and 3) the effects of the victim's death on the community. Defendants contend that common knowledge of these events within the venue prevents a fair trial. During *voir dire*, the court excuses any jurors who either 1) knew of defendant's guilty verdict in the earlier trial for murder, or 2) had formed an opinion about the case that prevented their impartial deliberation. The court does not excuse jurors reporting exposure to pre-trial publicity who stated that they could try the case fairly. Defendants further argue that as three black men from New York City, they cannot obtain an impartial jury from a largely white population in a rural area. The court inquires whether any of the remaining panel members have beliefs about drugs, firearms, defendants' race, or the fact that defendants hailed from New York City, that would prevent their impartial deliberation; no juror so indicated. As a judge, how would you exercise your discretion in this case if the defendants seek a change of venue?

Hypo 2: *Extensive Pre-Trial Publicity*

Defendants, claiming extensive pretrial publicity, submit scores of national and local newspaper and magazine reports about drug-related issues. They also present radio and television news transcripts, describing the growing problem of drug availability for young children. Only about one-third of the articles mentioned the defendants, and those articles were primarily factual in nature, only once referring to confessions given by the defendants. As a judge, how would you exercise your discretion in this case if defendants seek a change of venue?

Hypo 3: *Pre-Trial Polling*

At the time of his arraignment, defendant moved for a change of venue. A public opinion survey filed with the motion indicated that in 100 calls, 98 persons had read or heard about the crime. Eighty-nine of the 100 polled were aware of defendant's name; 73 knew that he had been in prison previously; and 60 were aware of the charge. Ninety-three persons had heard both radio and television stories, some up to at least 100 such reports. Eighty-five considered defendant guilty, while 15 did not respond or stated they did not know. Sixty-five thought he would receive a fair trial in the county. Defendant renewed his motion during the course of *voir dire* as prospective jurors gave repeated voice to the community's widespread sentiment against him. All potential jurors, save one, knew about the case. Of the 153 or more jurors that were *voir dired* individually, 112 were excused because they had preconceived opinions about defendant's guilt, could not presume him innocent, or admitted to knowledge of his prior manslaughter conviction. Of 38 jurors who were accepted by the court to comprise the pool from which the trial jury would be selected, 19 had an initial opinion that he was guilty. As a judge, how would you exercise your discretion in this case if defendants seek a change of venue?

2. Due Process & Pretrial Publicity

Despite concerns about pretrial publicity and juror impartiality, jurors need not be completely ignorant of the facts and issues. A trial judge must assess the jurors' opinions to determine whether the jurors can impartially decide the case. In *Irvin v. Dowd*, 366 U.S. 717 (1961), petitioner was convicted of murder following a trial that was "extensively covered" by the news media and aroused "great excitement and indignation." The press reported defendant's prior convictions, his confession to 24 burglaries and six murders including the one for which he was tried, and his unaccepted offer to plead guilty in order to avoid the death sentence. The trial court granted a change of venue to an adjoining county. The court refused an additional request for change of venue on the basis that Indiana law provided for only a single change of venue. The Court reversed:

> The "pattern of deep and bitter prejudice" shown to be present throughout the community was clearly reflected in the sum total of the *voir dire* examination of a majority of the jurors finally placed in the jury box. Eight out of the 12 thought petitioner was guilty. With such an opinion permeating their minds, it would be difficult to say that each could exclude this preconception of guilt from his deliberations. The influence that lurks in an opinion once formed is so persistent that it unconsciously fights detachment from the mental processes of the average man. Where one's life is at stake—and accounting for the frailties of human nature—we can say that in light of the circumstances the finding of impartiality does not meet constitutional standards. Two-thirds of the jurors had an opinion that petitioner was guilty and were familiar with the material facts and circumstances involved, including the fact that other murders were attributed to him, some going so far as to say that it would take evidence to overcome their belief. One said that he "could not give the defendant the benefit of the doubt that he is innocent." Another stated that he had a "somewhat" certain fixed opinion as to petitioner's guilt. No doubt each juror was sincere when he said that he would be fair and impartial to petitioner, but psychological impact requiring such a declaration before one's fellows is often its father. Where so many, so many times, admitted prejudice, such a statement of impartiality can be given little weight. As one of the jurors put it, "You can't forget what you hear and see." With his life at stake, it is not requiring too much that petitioner be tried in an atmosphere undisturbed by so huge a wave of public passion and by a jury other than one in which two-thirds of the members admit, before hearing any testimony, to possessing a belief in his guilt.

Irvin was followed by a couple of other major decisions. In *Murphy v. Florida*, 421 U.S. 794 (1975), the Court upheld petitioner's conviction for breaking and entering a home, while armed, with intent to commit robbery and of assault with intent to commit robbery. There was extensive press coverage because petitioner had been involved in the theft of the Star of India sapphire from a museum in New York. His flamboyant lifestyle made him a continuing subject of press interest, and the press referred to him as "Murph the Surf." Relying on *Irvin*, *Rideau v. Louisiana*, 373 U.S. 723 (1963), and *Estes v. Texas*, 381 U.S. 532 (1965), as well as on *Sheppard*, the Court concluded that the *voir dire* showed that the jurors did not have undue hostility towards petitioner, the situation in the community was not regarded as "inflammatory," and the Court was unable to conclude that Murphy did not receive a fair trial.

Patton v. Yount, 467 U.S. 1025 (1984), was a murder case in which there had been publicity regarding Yount's prior conviction for murder, his confession, and his prior plea of temporary insanity, information not admitted into evidence at trial. The Court refused to overturn the conviction even though *voir dire* showed that all but 2 of 163 veniremen questioned about the case had heard of it, and 126 (77%) admitted they would carry an opinion into the jury box. 8 of the 14 jurors and alternates actually seated admitted that at some time they had formed an opinion as to Yount's guilt. The Court focused on the fact that a year and a half had elapsed between the reversal and the start of the second trial. During this period, the two local newspapers published an average of less than one article per month about the case. Many of these articles were extremely brief announcements of the trial dates and scheduling such as are common in rural newspapers. During the *voir dire* the newspapers published articles on an almost daily basis, but these were purely factual articles generally discussing not the crime or prior prosecution, but the prolonged process of jury selection. In short, the record of publicity in the months preceding, and at the time of, the second trial does not reveal the "barrage of inflammatory publicity immediately prior to trial," amounting to a "huge wave of public passion," that the Court found in *Irvin*.

Skilling v. United States

561 U.S. 358 (2010).

JUSTICE GINSBURG delivered the opinion of the Court.

In 2001, Enron Corporation, then the seventh highest-revenue-grossing company in America, crashed into bankruptcy. We consider whether pretrial publicity and community prejudice presented Skilling from obtaining a fair trial. Skilling, we hold, did not establish that a presumption of juror prejudice arose or that actual bias infected the jury that tried him.

Founded in 1985, Enron Corporation grew from its headquarters in Houston, Texas, into one of the world's leading energy companies. Skilling launched his career there in 1990 when Kenneth Lay, the company's founder, hired him to head an Enron subsidiary. Skilling steadily rose through the corporation's ranks, serving as president and chief operating officer, and then, beginning in February 2001, as chief executive officer. Six months later, on August 14, 2001, Skilling resigned from Enron. Less than four months after Skilling's departure, Enron spiraled into bankruptcy. The company's stock, which had traded at $90 per share in August 2000, plummeted to pennies per share in late 2001. Attempting to comprehend what caused the corporation's collapse, the U.S. Department of Justice formed an Enron Task Force, comprising prosecutors and FBI agents from around the Nation. The Government's investigation uncovered an elaborate conspiracy to prop up Enron's short run stock prices by overstating the company's financial well-being. In the years following Enron's bankruptcy, the Government prosecuted dozens of Enron employees who participated in the scheme. In time, the Government worked its way up the corporation's chain of command: On July 7, 2004, a grand jury indicted Skilling, Lay, and Richard Cause, Enron's former chief accounting officer for securities and wire fraud, and insider trading.

In November 2004, Skilling moved to transfer the trial to another venue; he contended that hostility toward him in Houston, coupled with extensive pretrial publicity, had poisoned potential jurors. Skilling, aided by media experts, submitted hundreds of news reports detailing Enron's downfall; he also presented affidavits from the experts he engaged portraying community attitudes in Houston in comparison to other potential venues. The U.S. District Court for the Southern District of Texas denied the motion. Despite "isolated incidents of intemperate commentary," the court observed, media coverage "had mostly been objective and unemotional," and the facts of the case were "neither heinous nor sensational." Moreover, "courts had commonly" favored "effective *voir dire* to ferret out any juror bias." Pretrial publicity about the case, the court concluded, did not warrant a presumption that Skilling would be unable to obtain a fair trial in Houston.

In the months leading up to the trial, the District Court solicited from the parties questions the court might use to screen prospective jurors. Unable to agree on a questionnaire's format and content, Skilling and the Government submitted dueling documents. On venire members' sources of Enron-related news, the Government proposed that they tick boxes from a checklist of generic labels such as "television," "newspaper," and "radio"; Skilling proposed more probing questions asking venire members to list the specific names of their media sources and to report on "what stood out in their minds" of "all the things they had seen, heard or read about Enron." The District Court rejected the Government's sparer inquiries in favor of Skilling's submission. Skilling's questions "were more helpful" "because they were generally open-ended and would allow the potential jurors to give us more meaningful information." The court converted Skilling's submission, with slight modifications, into a 77-question, 14-page document that asked prospective jurors about, *inter alia*, their sources of news and exposure to Enron-related publicity, beliefs concerning Enron and what caused its collapse, opinions regarding the defendants and their possible guilt or innocence, and relationships to the company and to anyone affected by its demise.[4]

In November 2005, the District Court mailed the questionnaire to 400 prospective jurors and received responses from nearly all the addressees. The court granted hardship exemptions to approximately 90 individuals, and the parties, with the court's approval, further winnowed the pool by excusing another 119 for cause, hardship, or physical disability. The parties agreed to exclude "each and every" prospective juror who said that a preexisting opinion about Enron or the defendants would prevent her from impartially considering the evidence at trial. Denying Skilling's request for attorney-led *voir dire,* the court promised to give counsel an opportunity to ask follow-up questions, and it agreed that venire members should be examined individually about pretrial publicity.

After questioning the venire as a group, the District Court brought prospective jurors one by one to the bench for individual examination. Although the questions varied, the process generally tracked the following format: The court asked about exposure to Enron-related news and the content of any stories that stood out in the prospective juror's mind. Next, the court homed in on questionnaire answers that raised a red flag signaling possible bias. The court then permitted each side to pose follow-up questions. Finally, after the venire member stepped away, the court entertained and ruled on challenges for cause. The court granted one of the Government's for-cause challenges and denied four; it granted three of the defendants' challenges and denied six. The parties agreed to excuse three additional jurors for cause and one for hardship.

Following a 4-month trial and nearly five days of deliberation, the jury found Skilling guilty of 19 counts, including the honest-services-fraud conspiracy charge, and not guilty of 9 insider-trading counts. The District Court sentenced Skilling to 292 months' imprisonment, 3 years' supervised release, and $45 million in restitution. On appeal, Skilling raised a host of challenges to his convictions, including the

---

[4]   Questions included the following: "What are your opinions about the compensation that executives of large corporations receive?"; "Have you, any family members, or friends ever worked for or applied for work with," "done business with," or "owned stock in Enron Corporation or any Enron subsidiaries and partnership?"; "Do you know anyone who has been negatively affected or hurt in any way by what happened at Enron?"; "Do you have an opinion about the cause of the collapse of Enron? If YES, what is your opinion? On what do you base your opinion?"; "Have you heard or read about any of the Enron cases? If YES, please tell us the name of all sources from which you have heard or read about the Enron cases."; "Have you read any books or seen any movies about Enron? If YES, please describe."; "Are you angry about what happened with Enron? If YES, please explain."; "Do you have an opinion about Jeffrey Skilling? If YES, what is your opinion? On what do you base your opinion?"; "Based on anything you have heard, read, or been told, do you have any opinion about the guilt or innocence of Jeffrey Skilling? If YES, please explain."; "Would any opinion you may have formed regarding Enron or any of the defendants prevent you from impartially considering the evidence presented during the trial of Jeffrey Skilling? If YES or UNSURE, please explain."; "Is there anything else you feel is important for the court to know about you?"

fair-trial arguments he presses here. The Fifth Circuit initially determined that the volume and negative tone of media coverage generated by Enron's collapse created a presumption of juror prejudice.

Pointing to "the community passion aroused by Enron's collapse and the vitriolic media treatment" aimed at him, Skilling argues that his trial "never should have proceeded in Houston." Even if it had been possible to select impartial jurors in Houston, "the truncated *voir dire* did almost nothing to weed out prejudices," he contends, so "far from rebutting the presumption of prejudice, the record below affirmatively confirmed it." Skilling's fair-trial claim thus raises two distinct questions. First, did the District Court err by failing to move the trial to a different venue based on a presumption of prejudice? Second, did actual prejudice contaminate Skilling's jury?

The Sixth Amendment secures to criminal defendants the right to trial by an impartial jury. By constitutional design, that trial occurs "in the State where the Crimes have been committed." Art. III, § 2, cl. 3. "The theory of our trial system is that the conclusions to be reached in a case will be induced only by evidence and argument in open court, and not by any outside influence, whether of private talk or public print." *Patterson v. Colorado ex rel. Attorney General of Colo.*, 205 U.S. 454, 462 (1907). When does the publicity attending conduct charged as criminal dim prospects that the trier can judge a case, as due process requires, impartially, unswayed by outside influence? Because most cases of consequence garner at least some pretrial publicity, courts have considered this question in diverse settings. We begin our discussion by addressing the presumption of prejudice from which the Fifth Circuit's analysis in Skilling's case proceeded.

The foundation precedent is *Rideau v. Louisiana*, 373 U.S. 723 (1963). Wilbert Rideau robbed a bank in a small Louisiana town, kidnapped three bank employees, and killed one of them. Police interrogated Rideau in jail without counsel present and obtained his confession. Without informing Rideau, no less seeking his consent, the police filmed the interrogation. On three separate occasions shortly before the trial, a local television station broadcast the film to audiences ranging from 24,000 to 53,000 individuals. Rideau moved for a change of venue, arguing that he could not receive a fair trial in the parish where the crime occurred, which had a population of approximately 150,000 people. The trial court denied the motion, and a jury eventually convicted Rideau. The Supreme Court of Louisiana upheld the conviction. We reversed. "What the people in the community saw on their television sets," we observed, "was Rideau, in jail, flanked by the sheriff and two state troopers, admitting in detail the commission of the robbery, kidnapping, and murder." "To the tens of thousands of people who saw and heard it," the interrogation "in a very real sense *was* Rideau's trial-at which he pleaded guilty." We therefore "did not hesitate to hold, without pausing to examine a particularized transcript of the *voir dire*," that "the kangaroo court proceedings" trailing the televised confession violated due process.

We followed *Rideau's* lead in two later cases in which media coverage manifestly tainted a criminal prosecution. In *Estes v. Texas*, 381 U.S. 532, 538 (1965), extensive publicity before trial swelled into excessive exposure during preliminary court proceedings as reporters and television crews overran the courtroom and "bombarded the community with the sights and sounds of" the pretrial hearing. The media's over-zealous reporting efforts, we observed, "led to considerable disruption" and denied the "judicial serenity and calm to which Billie Sol Estes was entitled." Similarly, in *Sheppard v. Maxwell*, 384 U.S. 333 (1966), news reporters extensively covered the story of Sam Sheppard, who was accused of bludgeoning his pregnant wife to death. "Bedlam reigned at the courthouse during the trial and newsmen took over practically the entire courtroom," thrusting jurors "into the role of celebrities." Pretrial media coverage, which we characterized as "months of virulent publicity about Sheppard and the murder," did not alone deny due process, we noted. But Sheppard's case involved more than heated reporting pretrial: We upset the murder conviction because a "carnival atmosphere" pervaded the trial. In each of these cases, we overturned a "conviction obtained in a trial atmosphere that was utterly corrupted by press coverage"; our decisions, however, "cannot be made to stand for the proposition that juror exposure to news accounts of the crime alone presumptively deprives the defendant of due process." *Murphy v. Florida*, 421 U.S. 794, 798 (1975). Prominence does not necessarily produce prejudice, and juror *impartiality* does not require *ignorance*.

Relying on *Rideau, Estes,* and *Sheppard,* Skilling asserts that we need not pause to examine the screening questionnaires or the *voir dire* before declaring his jury's verdict void. Important differences separate Skilling's prosecution from those in which we have presumed juror prejudice. First, we have emphasized the size and characteristics of the community in which the crime occurred. In *Rideau,* the murder was committed in a parish of only 150,000 residents. Houston, in contrast, is the fourth most populous city in the Nation: At the time of Skilling's trial, more than 4.5 million individuals eligible for jury duty resided in the Houston area. Given this large, diverse pool of potential jurors, the suggestion that 12 impartial individuals could not be empanelled is hard to sustain.[15] *See Mu'Min v. Virginia*, 500 U.S. 415 (1991); *Gentile v. State Bar of Nev.*, 501 U.S. 1030 (1991) (plurality opinion). Second, although news stories about Skilling were not kind, they contained no confession or other blatantly prejudicial information of the type readers or viewers could not reasonably be expected to shut from sight. Rideau's dramatically staged admission of guilt was likely imprinted indelibly in the mind of anyone who watched it. Pretrial publicity about Skilling was less memorable and prejudicial. No evidence of the smoking-gun variety invited prejudgment of his culpability. Third, unlike cases in which trial swiftly

---

[15] According to a survey commissioned by Skilling in conjunction with his first motion for a venue change, only 12.3% of Houstonians named him when asked to list Enron executives they believed guilty of crimes. In response to the follow-up question "what words come to mind when you hear the name Jeff Skilling?", two-thirds of respondents failed to say a single negative word: 43% either had never heard of Skilling or stated that nothing came to mind when they heard his name, and another 23% knew Skilling's name was associated with Enron but reported no opinion about him.

followed a widely reported crime, over four years elapsed between Enron's bankruptcy and Skilling's trial. Although reporters covered Enron-related news throughout this period, the decibel level of media attention diminished somewhat in the years following Enron's collapse. Finally, and of prime significance, Skilling's jury acquitted him of nine insider-trading counts. Similarly, earlier instituted Enron-related prosecutions yielded no overwhelming victory for the Government. In *Rideau, Estes,* and *Sheppard,* the jury's verdict did not undermine in any way the supposition of juror bias. It would be odd for an appellate court to presume prejudice in a case in which jurors' actions run counter to that presumption.

Skilling's trial shares little in common with those in which we approved a presumption of juror prejudice. The Fifth Circuit reached the opposite conclusion based on the magnitude and negative tone of media attention directed at Enron. But "pretrial publicity—even pervasive, adverse publicity—does not inevitably lead to an unfair trial." *Nebraska Press Assn. v. Stuart*, 427 U.S. 539, 554 (1976). In this case, news stories about Enron did not present the kind of vivid, unforgettable information we have recognized as particularly likely to produce prejudice, and Houston's size and diversity diluted the media's impact.[17] Nor did Enron's "sheer number of victims," trigger a presumption of prejudice. Although the widespread community impact necessitated careful identification and inspection of prospective jurors' connections to Enron, the extensive screening questionnaire and follow-up *voir dire* were well suited to that task. Hindsight shows the efficacy of these devices; jurors' links to Enron were either nonexistent or attenuated.

Finally, although a codefendant's "well-publicized decision to plead guilty" shortly before trial created a danger of juror prejudice, the District Court took appropriate steps to reduce that risk. The court delayed the proceedings by two weeks, lessening the immediacy of that development. During *voir dire,* the court asked about prospective jurors' exposure to recent publicity, including news regarding the codefendant. Only two venire members recalled the plea; neither mentioned the codefendant by name, and neither ultimately served on Skilling's jury. Although publicity about a codefendant's guilty plea calls for inquiry to guard against actual prejudice, it does not ordinarily—and did not here—warrant an automatic presumption of prejudice. Persuaded that no presumption arose, the District Court, in declining to order a venue change, did not exceed constitutional limitations.

We next consider whether actual prejudice infected Skilling's jury. *Voir dire,* Skilling asserts, did not adequately detect and defuse juror bias. "The record affirmatively confirms" prejudice, he maintains, because several seated jurors "prejudged his guilt." We disagree with Skilling's characterization of the *voir dire* and the jurors selected through it. No hard-and-fast formula dictates the necessary depth or breadth

---

[17]   Data submitted by Skilling in support of his first motion for a venue transfer suggested that a slim percentage of Enron-related stories specifically named him.

of *voir dire*. Jury selection, we have repeatedly emphasized, is "particularly within the province of the trial judge." *Ristaino v. Ross*, 424 U.S. 589, 594 (1976). Appellate courts making after-the-fact assessments of the media's impact on jurors should be mindful that their judgments lack the on-the-spot comprehension of the situation possessed by trial judges. Reviewing courts are properly resistant to second-guessing the trial judge's estimation of a juror's impartiality, for that judge's appraisal is ordinarily influenced by a host of factors impossible to capture fully in the record—among them, the prospective juror's inflection, sincerity, demeanor, candor, body language, and apprehension of duty. In contrast to the cold transcript received by the appellate court, the in-the-moment *voir dire* affords the trial court a more intimate and immediate basis for assessing a venire member's fitness for jury service. We consider the adequacy of jury selection in Skilling's case, therefore, attentive to the respect due to district-court determinations of juror impartiality and of the measures necessary to ensure that impartiality.

Skilling deems the *voir dire* insufficient because, he argues, jury selection lasted "just five hours," "most of the court's questions were conclusory, high-level, and failed adequately to probe jurors' true feelings," and the court "consistently took prospective jurors at their word once they claimed they could be fair, no matter what other indications of bias were present." Our review of the record yields a different appraisal. The District Court initially screened venire members by eliciting their responses to a comprehensive questionnaire drafted in large part by Skilling. That survey helped to identify prospective jurors excusable for cause and served as a springboard for further questions put to remaining members of the array. *Voir dire* thus was the "culmination of a lengthy process." In other Enron-related prosecutions, District Courts, after inspecting venire members' responses to questionnaires, completed the jury-selection process within one day. The District Court conducted *voir dire* aware of the greater-than-normal need, due to pretrial publicity, to ensure against jury bias. At Skilling's urging, the court examined each prospective juror individually, thus preventing the spread of any prejudicial information to other venire members. To encourage candor, the court repeatedly admonished that there were "no right and wrong answers to the questions." The court denied Skilling's request for attorney-led *voir dire* because, in its experience, potential jurors were "more forthcoming" when the court, rather than counsel, asked the question. The parties were accorded an opportunity to ask follow-up questions of every prospective juror brought to the bench for colloquy. Skilling's counsel declined to ask anything of more than half of the venire members questioned individually, including eight eventually selected for the jury, because, he explained, "the Court and other counsel have covered" everything he wanted to know.

Inspection of the questionnaires and *voir dire* of the individuals who actually served as jurors satisfies us that, notwithstanding the flaws Skilling lists, the selection process successfully secured jurors who were largely untouched by Enron's collapse. Eleven of the seated jurors and alternates reported no connection at all to Enron, while other jurors reported at most an insubstantial link. As for pretrial publicity, jurors and alternates specifically stated that they had paid scant attention to Enron-related news. The remaining two jurors indicated that nothing in the news influenced their opinions about Skilling. The questionnaires confirmed that, whatever community prejudice existed in Houston generally, Skilling's jurors were not under its sway. Although many expressed sympathy for victims of Enron's bankruptcy and speculated that greed contributed to the corporation's collapse, these sentiments did not translate into animus toward Skilling. When asked whether they "had an opinion about Jeffrey Skilling," none of the seated jurors and alternates checked the "yes" box. And in response to the question whether "any opinion they may have formed regarding Enron or Skilling would prevent" their impartial consideration of the evidence at trial, every juror—despite options to mark "yes" or "unsure"—instead checked "no."

The District Court, Skilling asserts, should not have "accepted at face value jurors' promises of fairness." In *Irvin v. Dowd*, 366 U.S. at 727, Skilling points out, we found actual prejudice despite jurors' assurances that they could be impartial. We disagree. The facts of *Irvin* are worlds apart from those presented here. Leslie Irvin stood accused of a brutal murder and robbery spree in a small rural community. In the months before Irvin's trial, "a barrage" of publicity was "unleashed against him," including reports of his confessions to the slayings and robberies. "Newspapers in which these stories appeared were delivered regularly to 95% of the dwellings in" the county where the trial occurred, which had a population of only 30,000; "radio and TV stations, which likewise blanketed that county, also carried extensive newscasts covering the same incidents." In this case, news stories about Enron contained nothing resembling the horrifying information rife in reports about Irvin's rampage of robberies and murders. Of key importance, Houston shares little in common with the rural community in which Irvin's trial proceeded, and circulation figures for Houston media sources were far lower than the 95% saturation level recorded in *Irvin*. Skilling's seated jurors, moreover, exhibited nothing like the display of bias shown in *Irvin*. In light of these large differences, the District Court had far less reason than did the trial court in *Irvin* to discredit jurors' promises of fairness.

The District Court, moreover, did not simply take venire members who proclaimed their impartiality at their word. All of Skilling's jurors had already affirmed on their questionnaires that they would have no trouble basing a verdict only on the evidence at trial. Nevertheless, the court followed up with each individually to uncover concealed bias. This face-to-face opportunity to gauge demeanor and credibility, coupled with information from the questionnaires regarding jurors' backgrounds, opinions, and sources of news, gave the court a sturdy foundation to assess fitness for jury service. The jury's not-guilty verdict on nine insider-trading counts after nearly five days of deliberation suggests the court's assessments were accurate. Skilling failed to show that his *voir dire* fell short of constitutional requirements.

In sum, Skilling failed to establish that a presumption of prejudice arose or that actual bias infected the jury that tried him. Jurors need not enter the box with empty heads in order to determine the facts impartially. "It is sufficient if the jurors can lay aside their impressions or opinions and render a verdict based on the evidence presented in court." Taking account of the full record, rather than incomplete exchanges selectively culled from it, we find no cause to upset the lower courts' judgment that Skilling's jury met that measure. We therefore affirm the Fifth Circuit's ruling that Skilling received a fair trial.

For the foregoing reasons, we affirm the Fifth Circuit's ruling on Skilling's fair-trial argument.

It is so ordered.

JUSTICE SOTOMAYOR, with whom JUSTICE STEVENS and JUSTICE BREYER join, concurring in part and dissenting in part.

The more intense the public's antipathy toward a defendant, the more careful a court must be to prevent that sentiment from tainting the jury. In this case, passions ran extremely high. The sudden collapse of Enron directly affected thousands of people in the Houston area and shocked the entire community. As Enron's one-time CEO, Skilling was at the center of the storm. Even if these extraordinary circumstances did not constitutionally compel a change of venue, they required the District Court to conduct a thorough *voir dire* in which prospective jurors' attitudes about the case were closely scrutinized. The District Court's inquiry lacked the necessary thoroughness and left serious doubts about whether the jury empanelled to decide Skilling's case was capable of rendering an impartial decision based solely on the evidence presented in the courtroom.

Local media coverage of the story saturated the community. The *Houston Chronicle*—the area's leading newspaper—assigned as many as 12 reporters to work on the story full time. The paper mentioned Enron in more than 4,000 articles during the 3-year period following the company's bankruptcy filing. Hundreds of articles discussed Skilling by name. Many stories conveyed and amplified the community's outrage at the top executives perceived to be responsible for the company's bankruptcy. There were also articles expressing sympathy toward and solidarity with the company's many victims. Skilling's media expert counted nearly a hundred victim-related stories in the Chronicle which poignantly described the gut-wrenching experiences of former employees who lost vast sums of money, faced eviction from their homes, could not afford Christmas gifts for their children, and felt "scared," "hurt," "humiliated," "help-less," and "betrayed." More than one-third of the prospective jurors (approximately 99 of 283 indicated that they or persons they knew had lost money or jobs as a result of the Enron bankruptcy. Two-thirds of the jurors (188 of 283) expressed views about

Enron or the defendants that suggested a potential predisposition to convict. As the tide of public enmity rises, so too does the danger that the prejudices of the community will infiltrate the jury. In selecting a jury, a trial court must take measures adapted to the intensity, pervasiveness, and character of the pretrial publicity and community animus. Reviewing courts must assess whether the trial court's procedures sufficed under the circumstances to keep the jury free from disqualifying bias.

The prospect of seating an unbiased jury in Houston was not so remote as to compel the conclusion that the District Court acted unconstitutionally in denying Skilling's motion to change venue. However, the devastating impact of Enron's collapse and the relentless media coverage demanded exceptional care on the part of the District Court to ensure the seating of an impartial jury. While the procedures employed by the District Court might have been adequate in the typical high-profile case, they did not suffice in the extraordinary circumstances of this case to safeguard Skilling's constitutional right to a fair trial before an impartial jury. Any doubt that the prevailing mindset in the Houston community remained overwhelmingly negative was dispelled by prospective jurors' responses to the written questionnaires. More than one-third of the prospective jurors either knew victims of Enron's collapse or were victims themselves, and two-thirds gave responses suggesting an ant defendant bias. In many instances their contempt for Skilling was palpable. Only a small fraction of the prospective jurors raised no red flags in their responses. And this was *before* Causey's guilty plea and the flurry of news reports that accompanied the approach of trial. Given the extent of the antipathy evident both in the community at large and in the responses to the written questionnaire, it was critical for the District Court to take "strong measures" to ensure the selection of "an impartial jury free from outside influences." *Sheppard*, 384 U.S. at 362. The District Court's 5-hour *voir dire* was manifestly insufficient to identify and remove biased jurors. The court asked very few prospective jurors any questions directed to their knowledge of or feelings about that event.

The court rarely asked prospective jurors to describe personal interactions they may have had about the case, or to consider whether they might have difficulty avoiding discussion of the case with family, friends, or colleagues during the course of the lengthy trial. The tidbits of information that trickled out on these subjects provided cause for concern. In response to general media-related questions, several prospective jurors volunteered that they had spoken with others about the case. The court did not seek elaboration about the substance of these interactions. Surely many prospective jurors had similar conversations, particularly once they learned upon receiving the written questionnaire that they might end up on Skilling's jury. Prospective jurors' personal interactions may well have left them with the sense that the community was counting on a conviction. On the few occasions when prospective jurors were asked whether they would feel pressure from the public to convict, they acknowledged that it might be difficult to return home after delivering a not-guilty verdict. Most prospective jurors were asked just a few yes/no questions about their general exposure to media coverage and a handful of additional questions concerning any responses to the written questionnaire that suggested bias. The court rarely sought to draw them out with open-ended questions about their impressions of Enron or Skilling and showed limited patience for counsel's follow-up efforts.

The District Court failed to make a sufficiently critical assessment of prospective jurors' assurances of impartiality. The District Court essentially took jurors at their word when they promised to be fair. Worse still, the District Court accepted declarations of impartiality that were equivocal on their face. The majority takes solace in the fact that most of the persons actually seated as jurors and alternates "specifically stated that they had paid scant attention to Enron-related news." These general declarations reveal little about the seated jurors' actual knowledge or views. Jurors who did not "get into details" of Enron's complicated accounting schemes, nevertheless knew the outline of the oft-repeated story, including that Skilling and Lay had been cast as the leading villains. When the District Court asked the prospective jurors as a group whether they had any reservations about their ability to presume innocence and put the Government to its proof, only two answered in the affirmative, and both were excused for cause. The District Court's individual questioning exposed disqualifying prejudices among numerous additional prospective jurors who had earlier expressed no concerns about their impartiality. It thus strikes me as highly likely that at least some of the seated jurors, despite stating that they could be fair, harbored similar biases that a more probing inquiry would likely have exposed. Jurors who act in good faith and sincerely believe in their own fairness may nevertheless harbor disqualifying prejudices.

Points for Discussion

a.   More on *Irvin v. Dowd*

Consider the following language from *Irvin v. Dowd*, 366 U.S. 717 (1961):

Although this Court has said that the Fourteenth Amendment does not demand the use of jury trials in a State's criminal procedure, every State has constitutionally provided trial by jury. In essence, the right to jury trial guarantees to the criminally accused a fair trial by a panel of impartial, "indifferent" jurors. The failure to accord an accused a fair hearing violates even the minimal standards of due process. In the ultimate analysis, only the jury can strip a man of his liberty or his life. In the language of Lord Coke, a juror must be as "indifferent as he stands unsworn." His verdict must be based upon the evidence developed at the trial. This is true, regardless of the heinousness of the crime charged, the apparent guilt of the offender or the station in life which he occupies. "The theory of the law is that a juror who has formed an opinion cannot be impartial." *Reynolds v. United States,*

98 U.S. 145, 155. It is not required, however, that the jurors be totally ignorant of the facts and issues involved. In these days of swift, widespread and diverse methods of communication, an important case can be expected to arouse the interest of the public in the vicinity, and scarcely any of those best qualified to serve as jurors will not have formed some impression or opinion as to the merits of the case. This is particularly true in criminal cases. To hold that the mere existence of any preconceived notion as to the guilt or innocence of an accused, without more, is sufficient to rebut the presumption of a prospective juror's impartiality would be to establish an impossible standard. It is sufficient if the juror can lay aside his impression or opinion and render a verdict based on the evidence presented in court.

b.   The Judicial Duty

When pretrial publicity threatens to prejudice a trial, the trial judge has a duty to ensure that prospective jurors have not formed preconceptions of the defendant's guilt. In *Mu'Min v. Virginia*, 500 U.S. 415 (1991), 8 of the 12 persons sworn as jurors answered on *voir dire* that they had read or heard something about the case. The defendant argued that his Sixth Amendment right to an impartial jury and his right to due process under the Fourteenth Amendment were violated because the trial judge refused to question further prospective jurors about the specific content of the news reports to which they had been exposed. Citing *Patton v. Yount* and *Irvin v. Dowd*, the Court found that it was sufficient for a trial judge to ask a panel of prospective jurors collectively and in groups of four whether they had formed opinions based on publicity.

United States v. Tsarnaev

595 U.S. 302 (2022).

JUSTICE THOMAS delivered the opinion of the Court.

On April 15, 2013, Dzhokhar and Tamerlan Tsarnaev planted and detonated two homemade pressure-cooker bombs near the finish line of the Boston Marathon. The blasts hurled nails and metal debris into the assembled crowd, killing three while maiming and wounding hundreds. Three days later, the brothers murdered a campus police officer, carjacked a graduate student, and fired on police who had located them in the stolen vehicle. Dzhokhar attempted to flee in the vehicle but inadvertently killed Tamerlan by running him over. Dzhokhar was soon arrested and indicted. A jury found Dzhokhar guilty of 30 federal crimes and recommended the death penalty for 6 of them. The District Court accordingly sentenced Dzhokhar to death. The Court of Appeals vacated the death sentence. We now reverse.

The Tsarnaev brothers immigrated to the United States in the early 2000s and lived in Massachusetts. Little more than a decade later, they were actively contemplating how to wage radical jihad. They downloaded and read al Qaeda propaganda, and, by December of 2012, began studying an al Qaeda guide to bomb making. On April 15, 2013, the brothers went to the Boston Marathon finish line on Boylston Street. They each brought a backpack containing a homemade pressure-cooker bomb packed with explosives inside a layer of nails, BBs, and other metal scraps. Tamerlan left his backpack in a crowd of spectators and walked away. Dzhokhar stood with his backpack outside the Forum, a nearby restaurant where spectators watched the runners from the sidewalk and dining patio. For four minutes, Dzhokhar surveyed the crowd. After speaking with Tamerlan by phone, Dzhokhar left his backpack among the spectators. Tamerlan then detonated his bomb. While the crowd looked toward the explosion, Dzhokhar walked the other way. After a few seconds, he detonated his bomb. Each detonation sent fire and shrapnel in all directions. The blast from Tamerlan's bomb shattered Krystle Campbell's left femur and mutilated her legs. She bled to death. Dzhokhar's bomb ripped open the legs of Boston University student Lingzi Lu. She too bled to death. Dzhokhar's and Tamerlan's bombs maimed and wounded hundreds of other victims. Many people lost limbs.

After fleeing the scene, the brothers returned to their normal lives. Dzhokhar attended his college classes the next day. He went to the gym with friends. He posted online that he was "a stress free kind of guy." Several days later, after the Federal Bureau of Investigation (FBI) released images of the suspected bombers, a friend saw the images and texted Dzhokhar. Dzhokhar responded: "Better not text me my friend. Lol." Recognizing that investigators were closing in on them, Dzhokhar met up with Tamerlan that evening. The brothers collected more homemade bombs and a handgun and loaded them into Tamerlan's car. While driving past the Massachusetts Institute of Technology, they saw 27-year-old campus police officer Sean Collier sitting in his patrol car. They approached his car and shot him five times at close range, including once between the eyes. With Collier dead, the brothers tried to steal his service pistol but were unable to remove it from the holster. They then carjacked and robbed another man, Dun Meng, who was driving his SUV home from work. When the brothers forced Meng to stop at a gas station for fuel and snacks, he fled on foot. The brothers made off with Meng's SUV.

Meng contacted the police, who used the SUV's GPS device to track the Tsarnaevs. When officers found the brothers in Watertown a few hours later, a street battle ensued. Tamerlan fired on the officers with a handgun, while Dzhokhar threw homemade bombs. When Tamerlan's handgun ran out of ammunition, officers subdued him. As they tried to handcuff Tamerlan, Dzhokhar returned to the SUV and sped towards the officers. They evaded the SUV. Tamerlan did not. Dzhokhar ran over Tamerlan and dragged him roughly 30 feet down the road. Tamerlan disentangled from the undercarriage when Dzhokhar rammed a police cruiser before escaping.

Tamerlan died soon after from his injuries. Dzhokhar abandoned the SUV a few blocks away. He found a covered boat in a nearby backyard. Taking shelter inside, he carved the words "stop killing our innocent people, and we will stop" into the planking. He also wrote a manifesto in pencil on the bulkhead of the boat's cockpit justifying his actions and welcoming his expected martyrdom. The next day, the boat's owner found him. Police eventually forced Dzhokhar out of the boat and arrested him.

A federal grand jury indicted Dzhokhar for 30 crimes, 17 of which were capital offenses. In preparation for jury selection, the parties jointly proposed a 100-question form to screen the prospective jurors. The District Court adopted almost all of them, including many that probed for bias. For example, some questions asked whether a prospective juror had a close association with law enforcement. Others asked whether a prospective juror had strong feelings about Islam, Chechens, or the several Central Asian regions with which the Tsarnaevs were connected. Still others asked whether the prospective juror had a personal connection to the bombing. Several questions probed whether media coverage might have biased a prospective juror. One question asked if the prospective juror had "formed an opinion" about the case because of what he had "seen or read in the news media." Others asked about the source, amount, and timing of the person's media consumption. Still another asked whether the prospective juror had commented or posted online about the bombings. The District Court did reject one media-related question. The proposed questionnaire had asked each prospective juror to list the facts he had learned about the case from the media and other sources. Concerned that such a broad, "unfocused" question would "cause trouble" by producing "unmanageable data" of minimal value that would come to dominate the entire *voir dire*, the District Court declined to include it in the questionnaire. After Dzhokhar objected, the District Court explained that the question was "too unguided."

Recognizing the intense public interest, the District Court summoned an expanded jury pool. In early January 2015, the court called 1,373 prospective jurors for the first round of jury selection. After reviewing their answers to the questionnaire, the court reduced the pool to 256. As jury selection began in earnest, Dzhokhar renewed his request that the court ask each juror about the content of the media he had consumed. The District Court again refused Dzhokhar's blanket request and instead permitted counsel to ask appropriate followup questions about a prospective juror's media consumption based on the answers to questions in the questionnaire or at *voir dire*. Several times, the court permitted Dzhokhar's attorneys to follow up on a prospective juror's earlier answers with specific questions about what the juror had seen or heard in the news. Over the course of three weeks of in-person questioning, the District Court and the parties reduced the 256 prospective jurors down to 12 seated jurors.

After the District Court seated the jury, the case went to trial. Dzhokhar did not contest his guilt and the jury thus returned a guilty verdict on all counts. When the sentencing proceedings finished, the jury concluded that Dzhokhar warranted the death penalty for 6 of the 17 death-penalty-eligible crimes, despite Dzhokhar's argument that Tamerlan was more culpable. The District Court sentenced Dzhokhar to death. The Court of Appeals vacated Dzhokhar's capital sentence. The Court of Appeals held that the District Court abused its discretion during jury selection by declining to ask every prospective juror what he learned from the media about the case. According to the panel, such questions were required by that court's 1968 decision in *Patriarca v. United States*, 402 F.2d 314 (CA1 1968), which had mandated this *voir dire* rule "in the exercise of [the court of appeals'] discretionary supervisory powers, not as a matter of constitutional law." We granted certiorari.

The Government argues that the Court of Appeals improperly vacated Dzhokhar's capital sentences based on the juror questionnaire. We agree. The Sixth Amendment guarantees "the accused" the right to a trial "by an impartial jury." The right to an "impartial" jury "does not require *ignorance*." *Skilling v. United States*, 561 U.S. 358, 381 (2010). Notorious crimes are "almost, as a matter of necessity, brought to the attention" of those informed citizens who are "best fitted" for jury duty. *Reynolds v. United States*, 98 U.S. 145 (1879). A trial court protects the defendant's Sixth Amendment right by ensuring that jurors have "no bias or prejudice that would prevent them from returning a verdict according to the law and evidence." *Connors v. United States*, 158 U.S. 408 (1895).

Jury selection falls "particularly within the province of the trial judge." *Skilling*, 561 U.S., at 386. A trial "judge's appraisal is ordinarily influenced by a host of factors impossible to capture fully in the record," such as a "prospective juror's inflection, sincerity, demeanor, candor, body language, and apprehension of duty." *Skilling*, 561 U.S., at 386. A trial court's broad discretion includes deciding what questions to ask prospective jurors. See *Mu'Min*, 500 U.S., at 427. A court of appeals reviews the district court's questioning of prospective jurors only for abuse of discretion. That discretion does not vanish when a case garners public attention. Indeed, "when pretrial publicity is at issue, 'primary reliance on the judgment of the trial court makes especially good sense.' " *Skilling*, 561 U.S., at 386 (quoting *Mu'Min*, 500 U.S., at 427). After all, "the judge 'sits in the locale where the publicity is said to have had its effect' and may base her evaluation on her 'own perception of the depth and extent of news stories that might influence a juror.' " *Ibid.* Because conducting *voir dire* is committed to the district court's sound discretion, there is no blanket constitutional requirement that it must ask each prospective juror what he heard, read, or saw about a case in the media. *Mu'Min*, 500 U.S., at 417. Instead, the district court's duty is to conduct a thorough jury-selection process that allows the judge to evaluate whether each prospective juror is "to be believed when he says he has not formed an opinion about the case." *Id.*, at 425.

The District Court did not abuse its broad discretion by declining to ask about the content and extent of each juror's media consumption regarding the bombings. The court recognized the significant pretrial publicity concerning the bombings, and reasonably concluded that the proposed media-content question was "unfocused," risked producing "unmanageable data," and would at best shed light on "preconceptions" that other questions already probed. At *voir dire*, the court explained that it did not want to be "too tied to a script" because "every juror is different" and had to be "questioned in a way that was appropriate" to the juror's earlier answers. The court was concerned that a media-content question had "the wrong emphasis," focusing on what a juror knew before coming to court, rather than on potential bias. Based on "years" of trial experience, the court concluded that jurors who came in with some prior knowledge would still be able to act impartially and "hold the government to its proof." The District Court's decision was reasonable and well within its discretion. If any doubt remained, the rest of the jury-selection process dispels it. The District Court summoned an expanded jury pool of 1,373 prospective jurors and used the 100-question juror form to cull that down to 256. The questionnaire asked prospective jurors what media sources they followed, how much they consumed, whether they had ever commented on the bombings in letters, calls, or online posts, and, most pointedly, whether any of that information had caused the prospective juror to form an opinion about Dzhokhar's guilt or punishment. The court then subjected those 256 prospective jurors to three weeks of individualized *voir dire* in which the court and both parties had the opportunity to ask additional questions and probe for bias. Dzhokhar's attorneys asked several prospective jurors what they had heard, read, or seen about the case in the media. The District Court also provided "emphatic and clear instructions on the sworn duty of each juror to decide the issues only on evidence presented in open court." *Skilling*, 561 U.S., at 388. The court reminded the prospective jurors that they "must be able to decide the issues in the case based on the information or evidence presented in the course of the trial, not on information from any other sources," an instruction the court gave during *voir dire* and repeated during the trial. The court's jury selection process was both eminently reasonable and wholly consistent with this Court's precedents.

The Court of Appeals erred in holding otherwise. As it saw things, its decision nearly 50 years prior in *Patriarca* had, pursuant to its "supervisory authority," required district courts presiding over high-profile cases to ask about the " 'kind and degree of the prospective juror's exposure to the case or the parties." This Court has held many times that a district court enjoys broad discretion to manage jury selection, including what questions to ask prospective jurors. See, *e.g.*, *Skilling*, 561 U.S., at 387, n. 20; *Mu'Min*, 500 U.S., at 427; *Ristaino*, 424 U.S., at 594; *Ham*, 409 U.S., at 527. Our cases establish that a reviewing court may set aside a district court's questioning only for an abuse of discretion. Rather than ask whether media-content questions were necessary in light of the District Court's exhaustive *voir dire*, the Court of Appeals handed down a purported legal rule that media-content questions are required in all high-profile cases, and then concluded that the District Court committed legal error when it failed to comply with that rule. But a court of appeals cannot supplant the district court's broad discretion to manage *voir dire* by prescribing specific lines of questioning, and thereby circumvent a well-established standard of review.

Dzhokhar Tsarnaev committed heinous crimes. The Sixth Amendment nonetheless guaranteed him a fair trial before an impartial jury. He received one. The judgment of the United States Court of Appeals for the First Circuit is reversed.

It is so ordered.

JUSTICE BARRETT, with whom JUSTICE GORSUCH joins, concurring.

The First Circuit asserted "supervisory power" to impose a procedural rule on the District Court. Because that rule (which required a district court to ask media-content questions on request in high-profile prosecutions) conflicts with our cases (which hold that a district court has broad discretion to manage jury selection), the First Circuit erred.

Hypo 1: *Seating an Unbiased Jury*

How is it possible to get an unbiased jury in a case that generates extensive national publicity? Numerous examples abound of cases in which there has been excessive press coverage. Examples include the Rodney King case in which news organizations played videos of the beating over and over to a national and international audience, and the O.J. Simpson case which received obsessive national attention. Does the fact that both trials resulted in not guilty verdicts (at least, the first Rodney King verdict was "not guilty") suggest that jurors can retain their independence despite extensive press coverage? Do those verdicts suggest that the press may have less impact than we suspect?

Food for Thought

In 2021, former Minneapolis police officer Derek Chauvin was tried for the murder of George Floyd. Floyd's death in 2020 set off nationwide protests regarding allegations of systemic racism. When Floyd came to trial, Minneapolis had lots of Black Lives Matter (BLM) protestors on Minneapolis streets. In addition, the week before the trial started, the City of Minneapolis entered into a $26 million settlement with Floyd's family, and President Biden stated that he hopes that the jury comes in with the "right verdict." Was it appropriate to try the case in Minneapolis, or should the judge have granted Chauvin's request for a change of venue? Under the circumstances, should the jury have been sequestered during the trial? What else might the judge have done to guarantee Chauvin a fair trial?

Hypo 2: *The Congresswoman's Exhortations*

The Chauvin case was complicated by the fact that the night before the case was submitted to the jury, California Congresswoman Maxine Waters flew to Minneapolis and exhorted those who were protesting on the streets. She told them that, if Chauvin is acquitted: "We got to stay on the street, we've got to get more active, we've got to get more confrontational." At the end of the trial, the judge stated: "Waters may have given you something on appeal that may result in this whole trial being overturned." If you were the judge in the case, how would you have handled Waters' remarks? Should you have *voir dired* the jury regarding its ability to keep an open mind regarding Chauvin's guilt or innocence? What else would you have done to ensure that Chauvin received a fair trial?

Food for Thought

Members of the Black Guerilla Family, a violent street gang, were on trial for racketeering, conspiracy to distribute illegal drugs, and murder. Several jurors were excused after they stated that the gang's propensity for retribution caused them to fear for their safety. The judge then talked to each of the other jurors individually and inquired whether they were able to remain impartial. Two jurors expressed fear and were excused. After they were convicted, defendants' appealed claiming that the judge should have asked each juror individually about one juror's fears. Did the judge act properly in his handling of *voir dire*? *See United States v. Smith*, 919 F.3d 825 (4th Cir. 2019).

Hypo 3: *Docudrama & Change of Venue*

In one month, the National Broadcasting Company plans to air a "docudrama" entitled "The Billionaire Boys Club." The docudrama portrays Joe Bobson planning and committing a murder, and suggests a possible motive for the murder. In addition, the docudrama show Bobson's involvement with a social group referred to as the "Billionaire Boys Club," and portrays "Bobson's personality, activities, and business affairs in ways that further connect him to this murder." Bobson has already been convicted of murdering one person, and is about to stand trial for the murder depicted in the docudrama. Bobson believes that the film will severely prejudice his right to a fair trial in the second case. In addition, since Bobson's conviction in the first case is on appeal, Bobson worries that the airing of the docudrama will prejudice his right to a fair trial in that case should it be retried. Suppose that you are Bobson's attorney in the criminal trial. What steps might you to take to ensure Bobson's right to a fair trial?

Hypo 4: *The Obligation to Voir Dire*

Defendants were charged with engaging in a pattern of racketeering activity involving participation in the "Chicago Outfit"—the long-running lineal descendant of Al Capone's gang—and engaging in extortion, obstruction of justice, and other crimes. In order to protect the jury, the judge granted jury members anonymity. The notoriety of the Outfit guaranteed extensive press coverage, resulting in an interview with the government's mob expert, name-calling by a victim's brother, a story that Marcello had been "humiliated" by his mistress's testimony, and an opinion piece saying that jurors would be "basically stupid" if they didn't convict defendants. The judge told the jurors not to pay attention to the media and not to do research on their own. As a result, the judge refused to *voir dire* the jury each time a new article was published. In the absence of evidence that jurors have disobeyed his orders, is a judge required to *voir dire* the jury after every inflammatory article is published? *See United States v. Schiro*, 679 F. 3d 521 (7th Cir. 2012).

C. Gagging the Press

Nebraska Press Association v. Stuart

427 U.S. 539 (1976).

MR. CHIEF JUSTICE BURGER delivered the opinion of the Court.

The respondent judge entered an order restraining the petitioners from publishing or broadcasting accounts of confessions or admission made by the accused or facts "strongly implicative" of the accused in a widely reported murder of six persons. We granted certiorari to decide whether the entry of such an order on the showing made before the state court violated the constitutional guarantee of freedom of the press.

On October 18, 1975, local police found the six members of the Henry Kellie family murdered in their home in Sutherland, Neb., a town of about 850 people. Police released the description of a suspect, Erwin Charles Simants, to the reporters who had hastened to the scene of the crime. Simants was arrested and arraigned the following morning, ending a tense night for this small rural community. The crime immediately attracted widespread news coverage, by local, regional, and national newspapers, radio and television stations. Three days after the crime, the County Attorney and Simants' attorney joined in asking the County Court to enter a restrictive order relating to "matters that may or may not be publicly reported or disclosed to the public," because of the "mass coverage by news media" and the "reasonable likelihood of prejudicial news which would make difficult, if not impossible, the impaneling of an impartial jury and tend to prevent a fair trial." The County Court heard oral argument but took no evidence; no attorney for members of the press appeared at this stage. The County Court granted the prosecutor's motion for a restrictive order the next day. The order prohibited everyone in attendance from "releasing or authorizing the release for public dissemination in any form or manner whatsoever any testimony given or evidence adduced"; the order also required members of the press to observe the Nebraska Bar-Press Guidelines. Simants' preliminary hearing was held the same day, open to the public but subject to the order. The County Court bound over the defendant for trial to the State District Court. The charges, as amended to reflect the autopsy findings, were that Simants had committed the murders in the course of a sexual assault.

Petitioners—several press and broadcast associations, publishers, and individual reporters—moved for leave to intervene in the District Court, asking that the restrictive order imposed by the County Court be vacated. The District Court conducted a hearing, at which the County Judge testified and newspaper articles about the *Simants* case were admitted in evidence. The District Judge granted petitioners' motion to intervene and entered his own restrictive order. The judge found "because of the nature of the crimes charged in the complaint that there is a clear and present danger that pre-trial publicity could impinge upon the defendant's right to a fair trial." The order applied only until the jury was impaneled, and specifically prohibited petitioners from reporting five subjects: (1) the existence or contents of a confession Simants had made to law enforcement officers, which had been introduced in open court at arraignment; (2) the fact or nature of statements Simants had made to other persons; (3) the contents of a note he had written the night of the crime; (4) certain aspects of the medical testimony at the preliminary hearing; and (5) the identity of the victims of the alleged sexual assault and the nature of the assault. It also prohibited reporting the exact nature of the restrictive order itself. Like the County Court's order, this order incorporated the Nebraska Bar-Press Guidelines. Finally, the order set out a plan for attendance, seating, and courthouse traffic control during the trial.

Prior restraints on speech and publication are the most serious and the least tolerable infringement on First Amendment rights. A criminal penalty or a judgment in a defamation case is subject to the whole panoply of protections afforded by deferring the impact of the judgment until all avenues of appellate review have been exhausted. Only after judgment has become final, correct or otherwise, does the law's sanction become fully operative. A prior restraint, by contrast and by definition, has an immediate and irreversible sanction. If it can be said that a threat of criminal or civil sanctions after publication "chills" speech, prior restraint "freezes" it at least for the time. The damage can be particularly great when the prior restraint falls upon the communication of news and commentary on current events. Truthful reports of public judicial proceedings have been afforded special protection against subsequent punishment.

We turn now to whether, as Learned Hand put it, "the gravity of the 'evil,' discounted by its improbability, justifies such invasion of free speech as is necessary to avoid the danger." We must examine the evidence before the trial judge when the order was entered to determine (a) the nature and extent of pretrial news coverage; (b) whether other measures would be likely to mitigate the effects of unrestrained pretrial publicity; and (c) how effectively a restraining order would operate to prevent the threatened danger. The precise terms of the restraining order are also important. We must then consider whether the record supports the entry of a prior restraint on publication, one of the most extraordinary remedies known to our jurisprudence. Our review of the pretrial record persuades us that the trial judge was justified in concluding that there would be intense and pervasive pretrial publicity concerning this case. He could also reasonably conclude, based on common man experience, that publicity might impair the defendant's right to a fair trial. He did not purport to say more, for he found only "a clear and present danger that pre-trial publicity *could* impinge upon the defendant's right to a fair trial." His conclusion as to the impact of such publicity on prospective jurors was of necessity speculative, dealing as he was with factors unknown and unknowable.

We find little in the record that goes to another aspect of our task, determining whether measures short of an order retraining all publication would have insured the defendant a fair trial. Although the entry of the order might be read as a judicial determination that other measures would not suffice, the trial court made no express findings to that effect; the Nebraska Supreme Court referred to the issue only by implication. Most of the alternatives to prior restraint of publication were discussed with obvious approval in *Sheppard v. Maxwell*: (a) change of trial venue to a place less exposed to the intense publicity that seemed imminent in Lincoln County; (b) postponement of the trial to allow public attention to subside; (c) searching questioning of prospective jurors, as Mr. Chief Justice Marshall used in the Aaron Burr Case, to screen out those with fixed opinions as to guilt or innocence; (d) the use of emphatic and clear instructions on the sworn duty of each juror to decide the issues only on evidence presented in open court. Sequestration of jurors is, of course, always available. Although that measure insulates jurors only after they are sworn, it also enhances the likelihood of dissipating the impact of pretrial publicity and emphasizes the elements of the jurors' oaths.

We must also assess the probable efficacy of prior restraint on publication as a workable method of protecting Simants' right to a fair trial, and we cannot ignore the reality of the problems of managing and enforcing pretrial restraining orders. The territorial jurisdiction of the issuing court is limited by concepts of sovereignty. The need for *in personam* jurisdiction also presents an obstacle to a restraining order that applies to publication at large as distinguished from restraining publication within a given jurisdiction. The events disclosed by the record took place in a community of 850 people. Without any news accounts being printed or broadcast, rumors would travel swiftly by word of mouth. One can only speculate on the accuracy of such reports, given the generative propensities of rumors; they could well be more damaging than reasonably accurate news accounts. But plainly a whole community cannot be restrained from discussing a subject intimately affecting life within it. Given these practical problems, it is far from clear that prior restraint on publication would have protected Simants' rights.

MR. JUSTICE BRENNAN, with whom MR. JUSTICE STEWART and MR. JUSTICE MARSHALL join, concurring in the judgment.

The right to a fair trial by a jury of one's peers is unquestionably one of the most precious and sacred safeguards enshrined in the Bill of Rights. Resort to prior restraints on the freedom of the press is a constitutionally impermissible method for enforcing that right; judges have at their disposal a broad spectrum of devices for ensuring that fundamental fairness is accorded the accused without necessitating so drastic an incursion on the equally fundamental and salutary constitutional mandate that discussion of public affairs in a free society cannot depend on the preliminary grace of judicial censors.

Points for Discussion

a.   The Heavy Presumption Against Gag Orders

Restraining the press from reporting on judicial proceedings is a method for protecting a defendant's right to a fair trial. However, gag orders implicate First Amendment interests. As a preemptive restriction upon expression, such methods trigger the "heavy presumption" that exists against the constitutionality of "any system of prior restraint." *New York Times Co. v. United States*, 403 U.S. 713, 714 (1971) (per curiam). They also impose upon government "a heavy burden of justification." Given the constitutional interest, when the goal is ensuring a fair trial, compelling regulatory interests are identifiable in the abstract. The Court has established standards allowing gag orders, but not when the risks to a fair trial are merely speculative but only when those risks are demonstrable. Even then, prior restraint is permissible, they can be imposed only after methods less burdensome to First Amendment interests have been found inapt.

b.   Juror Sequestration

Critics of prior restraint analysis fault the Court for exalting form over substantive values and risks. *See, e.g.,* James Calvin Jeffries, Jr., *Rethinking Prior Restraint*, 92 YALE L.J. 409 (1983). Insofar as the doctrinal deck is stacked in favor of First Amendment interests, concern with the deficiencies of less restrictive alternatives predictably magnifies. Questions have been raised with respect to whether sequestration, especially in lengthy trials, breeds a state of mind that is inimical to fairness. *See, e.g.,* Bernard P. Bell, *Closure of Pretrial Suppression Hearings: Resolving the Free Trial/ Free Press Conflict*, 51 FORDHAM L. REV. 1297, 1315 (1983) (noting costs and burdens of sequestration and potential for causing "juror resentment"). Even if the formalities of prior restraint were subtracted from the analysis, it is reasonable to assume that review still would be probing. Because profound interests of self-governance vie against fair trial concerns, as they do when access is at issue, logic ordains that review be no less searching than when closure is at stake.

Food for Thought

In a number of other countries (England and Canada), the courts restrict press coverage of pending criminal matters through the contempt power. *See* GEOFFREY ROBERTSON & ANDREW G.L. NICOL, MEDIA LAW: THE RIGHTS OF JOURNALISTS AND BROADCASTERS 161–85 (3d ed. 1992); *see also* David A. Anderson, *Democracy and the Demystification of Courts: An Essay*, REV. LITIG. 627, 639 (1995). Should U.S. courts be equally free to restrict such coverage?

Hypo: *More on Gag Orders*

Defendants are being prosecuted for corruption in a case involving allegations that some defendants bribed elected legislative representatives. The case generated very substantial media coverage, including a live blog and Twitter feed. Prosecutors had significant interactions with the press during the pretrial phase of the proceeding: a prosecutor held a press conference to announce the indictment; a prosecutor tipped the press off to the fact that defendant was going to be arrested at his home; and a prosecutor issued press releases when two of the defendants pled guilty. Attorneys for some defendants were particularly vocal during the first trial, and would talk to the press as they left the courthouse on a daily basis. During these news conferences, the attorneys would comment on the credibility of the witnesses, discuss trial strategy, and speculate as to the cooperating witnesses' motives in testifying. Updates concerning the trial were posted by the media on an almost minute-by-minute basis. One particular revelation at the first trial garnered national media attention (allegedly racist comments made by some elected officials about African American voters). At the first trial, the trial court tried to minimize jurors' exposure to the media by designating an area outside the courthouse for the media, and by instructing jurors to enter and exit the courthouse from the other side of the building. The court also set up an overflow room where journalists could watch the court proceedings via closed-circuit video; no televised images of the trial aired publicly. Once the jury was selected, the court issued preliminary jury instructions ordering jurors scrupulously to avoid media coverage of the trial. In the six months between the first trial and the retrial, the case remained a prominent feature of Alabama politics. A state senator cited his participation in the case in his primary campaign to unseat an incumbent member of the U.S. House of Representatives, and sent out anti-gambling campaign literature. For the retrial, *voir dire* focused extensively on potential jurors' knowledge of the first trial, but the jury was sequestered and jurors were instructed not to view media coverage about the trial. Shortly before the retrial, the government moved for a gag order which would provide that "apart from court hearings or filings, no participating attorney or any member of their trial team shall make any extrajudicial comments about questions, or commentary." Thus, the attorneys cannot inform the press that a specific witness would be testifying the next day or direct the press to examine a recent filing. If you are the judge, should you grant the gag order? *See United States v. McGregor*, 838 F.Supp.2d 1256 (M.D. Ala. March 14, 2012).

D. Press Access to Judicial Proceedings

Even though the courts cannot prohibit the press from reporting on a trial, must the courts give the press access to the proceeding? Trials themselves historically have been open to the press and public, and the Court has established a presumption in favor of access. *Globe Newspaper Co. v. Superior Court*, 457 U.S. 596, 607 (1982). Tradition, however, has not always cut in favor of open preliminary proceedings. In *Gannett, Inc. v. DePasquale*, 443 U.S. 368, 394 (1979), the Court upheld a trial judge's order closing a suppression hearing at the defendant's request. The outcome in *Gannett* reflected an understanding that the Sixth Amendment guarantee of a public trial accrued not to the press or public but to the defendants. The decision's bottom line was that the Sixth Amendment established no constitutional right for the press or public to attend a criminal trial. The determination rested on the premise "that the public interest is fully protected by the participants in the litigation."

One year after *Gannett*, a defendant's motion to close a trial was defeated by First Amendment concerns. In *Richmond Newspapers, Inc. v. Virginia*, 448 U.S. 555 (1980), eight justices endorsed the notion of an access right for the press and public even over the defendant's objections. Chief Justice Burger, stressing the presumptive openness of criminal trials, observed that the right to attend such proceedings "is implicit in guarantees of the First Amendment; without the freedom to attend such trials, which people have exercised for centuries, important aspects of freedom of speech and of the press could be eviscerated." Consistent with established First Amendment doctrine, access to trials was configured coextensively for the press and public.

Globe Newspaper Co. v. Superior Court

457 U.S. 596 (1982).

JUSTICE BRENNAN delivered the opinion of the Court.

Section 16A of Chapter 278 of the Massachusetts General Laws, as construed by the Massachusetts Supreme Judicial Court, requires trial judges, at trials for specific sexual offenses involving a victim under the age of 18, to exclude the press and general public from the courtroom during the testimony of that victim. The question presented is whether the statute thus construed violates the First Amendment as applied to the States through the Fourteenth Amendment.

The Court's recent decision in *Richmond Newspapers* firmly established for the first time that the press and general public have a constitutional right of access to criminal trials. Of course, this right of access to criminal trials is not explicitly mentioned in the First Amendment. But we have long eschewed any "narrow, literal conception" of the Amendment's terms, for the Framers were concerned with broad principles, and wrote against a background of shared values and practices. The First Amendment is thus broad enough to encompass those rights that, while not unambiguously enumerated in the very terms of the Amendment, are nonetheless necessary to the enjoyment of other First Amendment rights. To the extent that the First Amendment embraces a right of access to criminal trials, it is to ensure that this constitutionally protected "discussion of governmental affairs" is an informed one.

Two features of the criminal justice system, emphasized in the various opinions in *Richmond Newspapers*, serve to explain why a right of access to criminal trials is properly afforded protection by the First Amendment. First, the criminal trial historically has been open to the press and general public. "At the time when our organic laws were adopted, criminal trials both here and in England had long been presumptively open." Since that time, the presumption of openness has remained secure. Indeed, at the time of this Court's decision in *In re Oliver*, the presumption was so solidly grounded that the Court was "unable to find a single instance of a criminal trial conducted in

Food for Thought

Can the denial of a public trial be regarded as "harmless error?" In general, courts automatically reverse convictions when defendant has been denied the right to a public trial. However, suppose that a defendant, who has been charged with a quadruple murder, is given a public trial. However, at one point, the judge holds a discussion in chambers regarding possible justifications for excluding particular jurors. The discussion lasts only 10 minutes. During the discussion, the court reporter was present, the discussion was immediately announced afterwards, and there were no objections. Should there be an automatic reversal of defendant's conviction? *See State v. Schierman*, 415 P.3d 106 (Wash. 2018).

Hypo: *After-Hours Trial*

Suppose that a trial runs later than normal. Because the trial is being held "after hours," courthouse officials locked the doors to the courthouse before the court adjourned for the day. Spectators who had already been admitted to the courthouse, could observe the trial. However, others were not able to enter the courthouse or the courtroom. Does it matter how long the evening session went? Suppose, for example, that it went until midnight. Should a trial judge that holds an evening session be required to make sure that potential observers have a way to gain access to the courthouse? *See United States v. Anderson*, 881 F.3d 568 (7th Cir. 2018).

Press-Enterprise Co. v. Superior Court

478 U.S. 1 (1986).

CHIEF JUSTICE BURGER delivered the opinion of the Court.

The right to an open public trial is a shared right of the accused and the public, the common concern being the assurance of fairness. Only recently, in *Waller v. Georgia*, for example, we considered whether the defendant's Sixth Amendment right to an open trial prevented the closure of a suppression hearing over the defendant's objection. We noted that the First Amendment right of access would in most instances attach to such proceedings and that "the explicit Sixth Amendment right of the accused is no less protective of a public trial than the implicit First Amendment right of the press and public." When the defendant objects to the closure of a suppression hearing, therefore, the hearing must be open unless the party seeking to close the hearing advances an overriding interest that is likely to be prejudiced. Here, unlike *Waller*, the right asserted is not the defendant's Sixth Amendment right to a public trial since the defendant requested a *closed* preliminary hearing. Instead, the right asserted here is that of the public under the First Amendment. The California Supreme Court concluded that the First Amendment was not implicated because the proceeding was not a criminal trial, but a preliminary hearing. However, the First Amendment question cannot be resolved solely on the label we give the event, *i.e.*, "trial" or otherwise, particularly where the preliminary hearing functions much like a full-scale trial.

In California, to bring a felon to trial, the prosecutor has a choice of securing a grand jury indictment or a finding of probable cause following a preliminary hearing. Even when the accused has been indicted by a grand jury, however, he has an absolute right to an elaborate preliminary hearing before a neutral magistrate. The accused has the right to personally appear at the hearing, to be represented by counsel, to cross-examine hostile witnesses, to present exculpatory evidence, and to exclude illegally obtained evidence. If the magistrate determines that probable cause exists, the accused is bound over for trial; such a finding leads to a guilty plea in the majority of cases.

Unlike a criminal trial, the California preliminary hearing cannot result in the conviction of the accused and the adjudication is before a magistrate or other judicial officer without a jury. But these features, standing alone, do not make public access any less essential to the proper functioning of the proceedings in the overall criminal justice process. Because of its extensive scope, the preliminary hearing is often the final and most important step in the criminal proceeding. As the California Supreme Court has stated the preliminary hearing in many cases provides "the sole occasion for public observation of the criminal justice system." Similarly, the absence of a jury, long recognized as "an inestimable safeguard against the corrupt or overzealous prosecutor and against the complaint, biased, or eccentric judge," makes the importance of public access to a preliminary hearing even more significant. "People in an open society do not demand infallibility from their institutions, but it is difficult for them to accept what they are prohibited from observing."

Denying the transcript of a 41-day preliminary hearing would frustrate what we have characterized as the "community therapeutic value" of openness. Criminal acts, especially certain violent crimes, provoke public concern, outrage, and hostility. "When the public is aware that the law is being enforced and the criminal justice system is functioning, an outlet is provided for these understandable reactions and emotions." In sum:

> The value of openness lies in the fact that people not actually attending trials can have confidence that standards of fairness are being observed; the sure knowledge that anyone is free to attend gives assurance that established procedures are being followed and that deviations will become known. Openness thus enhances both the basic fairness of the criminal trial and the

appearance of fairness so essential to public confidence in the system. *Press-Enterprise I, supra,* at 508 (emphasis in original).

We therefore conclude that the qualified First Amendment right of access to criminal proceedings applies to preliminary hearings as they are conducted in California.

Points for Discussion

a.　Press Privilege?

Modern First Amendment doctrine has trumpeted the theme that the press and media have no special status or priority in accessing proceedings or information. This premise is consistent with determinations that the press has no special privilege, rooted in the First Amendment, against having to disclose sources when asked to identify them in grand jury proceedings. The Court, in *Branzburg v. Hayes,* 408 U.S. 665, 688 (1972) (plurality opinion), not only stressed that the grand jury has the "right to everyman's evidence" but repudiated the notion that the media's role as the public's proxy would be undermined if confidentiality of sources was not protected. Although the newsgathering function may be perceived as essential to effective functioning of the press, insofar as it facilitates enhanced public knowledge and understanding, the Court has been loath to develop penumbras of press freedom that might be the equivalent of what freedom of association is to freedom of speech.

FYI

Consistent with its refusal to protect functions that arguably advance the aims of press freedom in the grand jury context, the Court has resisted arguments for recognizing media access rights in various criminal justice venues and processes. Although acknowledging that freedom of the press is crucial to informed self-government, it has brooked no distinction between press and public when access to facilities or proceedings is at stake. Questions of access have arisen most notably in the context of prisons, pretrial proceedings and trials. The common constitutional denominator in each of those settings is a refusal to set separate standards for the press and public.

b.　More on Public Access to Preliminary Hearings

Nevertheless, *Press-Enterprise* emphasized the tradition of open preliminary hearings and their similarity to trials in the states. The relevance of First Amendment priorities thus was referenced not to national norms, as was the case with trials, but to state customs. At least when the nature and traditions of a preliminary hearing are congruent with a trial, it is predictable that First Amendment values will be a dominant factor. Justice Stevens criticized the ruling as inconsistent with *Gannett*'s determination that the press and public have no First Amendment right to attend

Take Note

In *Presley v. Georgia*, 558 U.S. 209 (2010), the Court held that trial courts must consider alternatives to closing courtrooms during *voir dire*, even if no one has identified such alternatives, because the "public has a right to be present whether or not any party has asserted the right" and "trial courts are obligated to take every reasonable measure to accommodate public attendance at criminal trials."

pretrial proceedings. Closure of pretrial hearings under *Press-Enterprise* is justifiable only if "specific findings are made that there is a substantial probability that the defendant's right to a fair trial will be prejudiced by publicity that closure would prevent, and reasonable alternatives to closure cannot adequately protect the defendant's free trial rights." Even if those standards were satisfied and proceedings were closed, First Amendment interests would not vanish. As the *Gannett* Court itself indicated, the judge must provide a transcript of the proceeding when the risk of prejudice abates. *Gannett Co., Inc. v. DePasquale*, 443 U.S. 368, 393 (1979).

c. **Public Access to *Voir Dire***

Once trumpeted, the values supporting open trials invariably exerted pressure against the logic of *Gannett* in the pretrial context. Several decisions over the course of the 1980s significantly broadened the scope of access in pretrial proceedings. In *Press-Enterprise Co. v. Superior Court (I)*, the Court extended the First Amendment zone of interest to include *voir dire*. *Press-Enterprise Co. v. Superior Court*, 464 U.S. 501, 505 (1984). Finding that jury selection in criminal trials was presumptively open, the Court stressed the public interest in openness referenced in *Globe Newspaper* and *Richmond Newspapers*. Consistent with those decisions, it noted that the presumption against closure could be overcome only by a higher interest and narrowly tailored method.

Hypo 1: *Closing Voir Dire*

21 defendants are charged with drug trafficking and racketeering although some defendants plead guilty prior to trial. Because there are so many defendants, and lawyers, the judge decides to close *voir dire* to the public because of "capacity limitations." The judge allows only the defendants, their attorneys, and court personnel to be present. None of the defendants object at the time. Neither do any members of the press or the public. Once the two days of jury selection are over, all remaining proceedings are open to the public. In addition, the judge made a transcript of the *voir dire* proceedings available to the public shortly after it ended. Was it permissible for the judge to close *voir dire* under

these circumstances? *See United States v. Williams*, 974 F.3d 320 (3d Cir. 2020); *Barrows v. United States*, 15 A.3d 673 (D.C. App. 2011).

Hypo 2: *Frisk & State Employee Identification*

Prison inmate Conrad Lilly was charged with two counts of assault on a public servant. He moved to transfer the trial proceedings from the courthouse at the prison to the public county courthouse. The trial judge denied the motion and Lilly pled guilty in a proceeding at the prison. For an outsider to observe the proceedings at the prison, he or she must pass through a front gate, where one is frisked, then through two razor wire fences and three locked metal doors. A person can only gain entry with a valid state employee ID or with approval from the warden on duty. No unaccompanied minors or persons who have been released from confinement within the past two years may enter. In Lilly's case, no one was actually excluded from the proceedings. Was Lilly denied his Sixth Amendment right to a public trial? *See Lilly v. State*, 365 S.W.3d 321 (Tex. Crim. App. 2012).

Hypo 3: *Closing the Trial*

In a drug trial, suppose that a police officer who served in an undercover capacity will give testimony against the defendant. The prosecution, concerned about the safety of the witness given threats against his life, wants to close the trial. Is closure permissible during the witness' testimony? Is the trial court required to consider alternatives to closure? If so, what might they be? *See Moss v. Colvin*, 845 F.3d 516 (2d Cir. 2017).

E. Broadcasting Legal Proceedings

Cameras in the courtroom have become a staple in state courts, but except for some experimentation in the civil context, have been disallowed at the federal level. The Judicial Conference, after overseeing an experiment with cameras in six federal districts and two courts of appeals, voted to maintain a policy against their presence. The Conference's report is set forth in M. Johnson, Federal Judicial Center, *Electronic Media Coverage of Federal Civil Proceedings, An Evaluation of the Pilot Program in*

FYI

The right of access to trials and pretrial hearings does not incorporate any freedom for the media to use a particular technology to cover such proceedings. To the contrary, even as cameras and other electronic instrumentalities have become increasingly common in state courts, the judiciary still exercises considerable control over the extent (if any) to which they may be used.

Six District Courts and Two Courts of Appeals (1994). There, a plurality of the Court concluded that televised proceedings entail "such a probability that prejudice will result that it is deemed inherently lacking in due process." *Estes v. Texas*, 381 U.S. 532, 542 (1965). In a concurring opinion of significant durability, Justice Harlan stressed the need for adaptability in the event future circumstances warranted it. As he put it:

Permitting television in the courtroom undeniably has mischievous potentialities for intruding upon the detached atmosphere which should surround the judicial process. Forbidding this innovation would doubtless impinge upon one of the valued attributes of our federalism by preventing the States from pursuing a novel course of procedural experimentation. My conclusion is that there is no constitutional requirement that television be allowed in the courtroom, and, at least as to a notorious criminal trial such as this one, the considerations against allowing television in the courtroom so far outweigh the countervailing factors advanced in support as to require a holding that what was done in this case infringed the fundamental right to a fair trial assured by the Due Process Clause of the Fourteenth Amendment. Some preliminary observations are in order: All would agree that at its worst, television is capable of distorting the trial process so as to deprive it of fundamental fairness. Cables, kleig lights, interviews with the principal participants, commentary on their performances, "commercials" at frequent intervals, special wearing apparel and makeup for the trial participants—certainly such things would not conduce to the sound administration of justice by any acceptable standard.

Take Note

As technology reinvented the electronic instrumentalities of trial coverage, so that intrusiveness and distraction were diminished, case law veered in the direction of Justice Harlan's concurring opinion. Responding to liberalized provisions for electronic coverage of judicial proceedings, the Court in *Chandler v. Florida* repudiated the notion that cameras in the courtroom *per se* offended due process.

Chandler v. Florida

449 U.S. 560 (1981).

CHIEF JUSTICE BURGER delivered the opinion of the Court.

The question is whether, consistent with constitutional guarantees, a state may provide for radio, television, and still photographic coverage of a criminal trial for public broadcast, notwithstanding the objection of the accused. The Florida Supreme Court concluded "that on balance there was more to be gained than lost by permitting electronic media coverage of judicial proceedings subject to standards for such coverage." The Florida court was of the view that because of the significant effect of the courts on the day-to-day lives of the citizenry, it was essential that the people have confidence in the process. It felt that broadcast coverage of trials would contribute to wider public acceptance and understanding of decisions. Consequently, after revising the 1977 guidelines to reflect its evaluation of the pilot program, the Florida Supreme Court promulgated a revised Canon 3A(7). The Canon provides: "Subject at all times to the authority of the presiding judge to (I) control the conduct of proceedings before the court, (ii) ensure decorum and prevent distractions, and (iii) ensure the fair administration of justice in the pending cause, electronic media and still photography coverage of public judicial proceedings in the appellate and trial courts of this state shall be allowed in accordance with standards of conduct and technology promulgated by the Supreme Court of Florida."

The implementing guidelines specify in detail the kind of electronic equipment to be used and the manner of its use. For example, no more than one television camera and only one camera technician are allowed. Existing recording systems used by court reporters are used by broadcasters for audio pickup. Where more than one broadcast news organization seeks to cover a trial, the media must pool coverage. No artificial lighting is allowed. The equipment is positioned in a fixed location, and it may not be moved during trial. Videotaping equipment must be remote from the courtroom. Film, videotape, and lenses may not be changed while the court is in session. No audio recording of conferences between lawyers, between parties and counsel, or at the bench is permitted. The judge has sole and plenary discretion to exclude coverage of certain witnesses, and the jury may not be filmed. The judge has discretionary power to forbid coverage whenever satisfied that coverage may have a deleterious effect on the paramount right of the defendant to a fair trial. The Florida Supreme Court has the right to revise these rules as experience dictates, or indeed to bar all broadcast coverage or photography in courtrooms.

Appellants rely on *Estes v. Texas*, and Chief Justice Warren's separate concurring opinion in that case. They argue that the televising of criminal trials is inherently a denial of due process, and they read *Estes* as announcing a *per se* constitutional rule to that effect. Chief Justice Warren's concurring opinion, joined by Justices Douglas and

Goldberg, indeed provides some support for appellants' position: "While I join the Court's opinion and agree that the televising of criminal trials is inherently a denial of due process, I desire to express additional views on why this is so. Our condemnation of televised criminal trials is not based on generalities or abstract fears. The record in this case presents a vivid illustration of the inherent prejudice of televised criminal trials and supports our conclusion that this is the appropriate time to make a definitive appraisal of television in the courtroom." If appellants' reading of *Estes* were correct, we would be obliged to apply that holding and reverse the judgment under review.

Justice Harlan's concurring opinion, upon which analysis of the constitutional holding of *Estes* turns, must be read as defining the scope of that holding; *Estes* is not to be read as announcing a constitutional rule barring still photographic, radio, and television coverage in all cases and under all circumstances. It does not stand as an absolute ban on state experimentation with an evolving technology, which, in terms of modes of mass communication, was in its relative infancy in 1964, and is, even now, in a state of continuing change.

Since we are satisfied that *Estes* did not announce a constitutional rule that all photographic or broadcast coverage of criminal trials is inherently a denial of due process, we turn to consideration, as a matter of first impression, of appellants' suggestion that we now promulgate such a *per se* rule. Not unimportant is the change in television technology since 1962, when Estes was tried. It is urged, and some empirical data are presented, that many of the negative factors found in *Estes*—cumbersome equipment, cables, distracting lighting, numerous camera technicians—are less substantial factors today than they were at that time. It is also significant that safeguards have been built into the experimental programs in state courts, and into the Florida program, to avoid some of the most egregious problems envisioned by the opinions in the *Estes* case. Florida admonishes its courts to take special pains to protect certain witnesses—for example, children, victims of sex crimes, some informants, and even the very timid witness or party—from the glare of publicity and the tensions of being "on camera."

Inherent in electronic coverage of a trial is a risk that the very awareness by the accused of the coverage and the contemplated broadcast may adversely affect the conduct of the participants and the fairness of the trial, yet leave no evidence of how the conduct or the trial's fairness was affected. Given this danger, it is significant that Florida requires that objections of the accused to coverage be heard and considered on the record by the trial court. In addition to providing a record for appellate review, a pretrial hearing enables a defendant to advance the basis of his objection to broadcast coverage and allows the trial court to define the steps necessary to minimize or eliminate the risks of prejudice to the accused. Experiments such as the one presented here may well increase the number of appeals by adding a new basis for claims to reverse, but this is a risk Florida has chosen to take after preliminary experimentation. The record does not indicate that appellants requested an evidentiary hearing to show adverse impact or injury. Nor does the record reveal anything more than generalized allegations of prejudice.

To say that appellants have not demonstrated that broadcast coverage is inherently a denial of due process is not to say that appellants were in fact accorded all of the protections of due process in their trial. As noted, a defendant has the right to show that the media's coverage of his case—printed or broadcast—compromised the ability of the jury to judge him fairly. Alternatively, a defendant might show that broadcast coverage of his particular case had an adverse impact on the trial participants sufficient to constitute a denial of due process. Neither showing was made in this case.

To demonstrate prejudice in a specific case a defendant must show something more than juror awareness that the trial is such as to attract the attention of broadcasters. No doubt the very presence of a camera in the courtroom made the jurors aware that the trial was thought to be of sufficient interest to the public to warrant coverage. Jurors, forbidden to watch all broadcasts, would have had no way of knowing that only fleeting seconds of the proceeding would be reproduced. But the appellants have not attempted to show with any specificity that the presence of cameras impaired the ability of the jurors to decide the case on only the evidence before them or that their trial was affected adversely by the impact on any of the participants of the presence of cameras and the prospect of broadcast.

Although not essential to our holding, we note that at *voir dire*, the jurors were asked if the presence of the camera would in any way compromise their ability to consider the case. Each answered that the camera would not prevent him or her from considering the case solely on the merits. The trial court instructed the jurors not to watch television accounts of the trial, and the appellants do not contend that any juror violated this instruction. The appellants have offered no evidence that any participant in this case was affected by the presence of cameras. In short, there is no showing that the trial was compromised by television coverage, as was the case in *Estes*.

Since *Chandler*, and notwithstanding federal repudiation of cameras following an experimentation period from 1991–94, electronic coverage has become common in state proceedings. At least 47 states allow cameras in their courtrooms.

Point for Discussion

Cameras in Federal Court Proceedings

Despite upholding broadcast and photographic coverage of criminal proceedings in state courts, Federal Rule of Criminal Procedure 53 states that such activity "shall not be permitted" in federal courtrooms. In *United States v. Moussaoui*, <u>205 F.R.D. 183 (E.D.Va. 2002)</u>, Court TV unsuccessfully sought to intervene in order to record and telecast the pretrial and trial proceedings:

> The words "shall not be permitted" make clear that this rule is mandatory, leaving the Court with no discretion to ignore the categorical ban. Nor can Rule 53 be rewritten or finessed through technical hairsplitting. Advances in broadcast technology have created new threats to the integrity of the fact finding process. The traditional public spectator or media representative who attends a federal criminal trial leaves the courtroom with his or her memory of the proceedings and any notes he or she may have taken. These spectators do not leave with a permanent photograph. However, once a witness' testimony has been televised, the witness' face has not just been publicly observed, it has also become eligible for preservation by VCR or DVD recording, digitizing by the new generation of cameras or permanent placement on Internet web sites and chat rooms. Today, it is not so much the small, discrete cameras or microphones in the courtroom that are likely to intimidate witnesses, rather, it is the witness' knowledge that his or her face or voice may be forever publicly known and available to anyone in the world.

> As the United States argues, this intimidation could lead foreign prosecution witnesses, outside the jurisdiction of the Court, to refuse to testify or withhold their full testimony out of reasonable fears for their personal safety. It could similarly lead witnesses favorable to the defense to refrain from coming forward for fear of being ostracized. The permanent preservation of images of law enforcement witnesses could also jeopardize their future careers or personal safety. How could an agent whose face was known throughout the world ever be able to work undercover or interview witnesses on the street effectively? Knowledge that the proceedings were being broadcast may also intimidate jurors. Excluding cameras and other recording devices from the courtroom will help preserve the anonymity of the jurors who are selected to serve and minimize the potential for a "popular verdict."

Executive Summary

Conflicting Values. Guarantees of expressive freedom and a fair trial are fundamental values in American society, but these guarantees do not always coexist harmoniously. Indeed, freedom of the press may both promote and undermine the criminal justice process. An unfettered right to free expression promotes self-government by exposing judicial or prosecutorial corruption or incompetence, and can be a catalyst for reform by heightening the public's political awareness and understanding of the criminal process. But, while the press can serve many useful functions, its presence has the potential to disrupt and undermine the fairness of the trial process.

Remedies for Prejudicial Publicity. "Where there is a reasonable likelihood that prejudicial news prior to trial will prevent a fair trial, the judge should continue the case until the threat abates, or transfer it to another county not so permeated with publicity." During trial, a judge also has broad discretion to sequester the jury, to caution jurors to avoid media accounts of the proceedings, and to provide clear instructions to jurors to decide the issues only on evidence presented in open court. Publicity alone does not deny a defendant a fair trial. The less severe remedy of transfer is also unwarranted unless a defendant can show that the pre-trial publicity in the district is so inherently prejudicial that trial proceedings must be presumed to be tainted. Gag orders are also disfavored.

Voir Dire. No juror will be disqualified from service unless the Court is satisfied that the juror (i) is unable to put aside any previously formed opinions or impressions, (ii) is not prepared to pay careful and close attention to the evidence as it is presented in the case and finally (iii) is unable to render a fair and impartial verdict based solely on the evidence adduced at trial and the Court's instructions of law.

Press Access to Judicial Proceedings. Trials historically have been open to the press and public, and the Court has established presumptions in favor of openness and access. Although the right of access to criminal trials is of constitutional stature, it is not absolute, but can only be impinged when there is a compelling governmental interest that is narrowly tailored to serve that interest. The right of access to trials and pretrial hearings does not incorporate any freedom for the media to use a particular technology to cover such proceedings. To the contrary, even as cameras and other electronic instrumentalities have become increasingly common in state courts, the judiciary still exercises considerable control over the extent (if any) to which they may be used.

Major Themes

a. Conflicting Values—Guarantees of expressive freedom and a fair trial are fundamental values in American society, but these guarantees do not always coexist harmoniously. Freedom of the press may both promote and undermine the criminal justice process. Substantial and prejudicial publicity can undermine a defendant's right to a fair trial.

b. Remedies for Prejudicial Publicity—Trial courts have a variety of remedies available to them to preserve the right to a fair trial against prejudicial publicity. The judge can continue the case until the threat abates, grant a change of venue to a different location, *voir dire* the jury, sequester the jury, and caution jurors to avoid media accounts of the proceedings. As a general rule, courts may not impose gag orders on the media. However, the right to access is not absolute and can be overridden by a compelling governmental interest, but the restriction must be narrowly tailored to serve that interest.

c. Press Coverage of Criminal Proceedings—However, the right of access to trials and pretrial hearings does not include the right to use any particular technology to cover such proceedings. To the contrary, even as cameras and other electronic instrumentalities have become increasingly common in state courts, the judiciary still exercises considerable control over the extent (if any) to which they may be used.

For More Information

- RUSSELL L. WEAVER, JOHN M. BURKOFF, CATHERINE HANCOCK & STEVEN I. FRIEDLAND, PRINCIPLES OF CRIMINAL PROCEDURE Ch. 18 (8th ed. 2024).

- WAYNE R. LAFAVE, JEROLD H. ISRAEL, NANCY J. KING & ORIN S. KERR, CRIMINAL PROCEDURE (6th ed. 2017).

Test Your Knowledge

To assess your understanding of the material in this chapter, click here to take a quiz.

CHAPTER 20

Sentencing

A. Sentencing Procedures

Formal sentencing consists of pronouncing sentence in accordance with the previous plea or adjudication of guilt.[1] If the defendant has been convicted, the case should proceed to sentencing without unreasonable delay. However, it is customary to postpone sentencing for a short period of time to enable the court to obtain a presentence report prepared by the probation office or other court officer. The report usually includes an analysis of the defendant's background, such as prior arrests and convictions, mental health issues, school and employment history, family history, and also may include a victim impact statement under appropriate circumstances. If defendant wishes to dispute any portion of the contents of the report, the court must afford a fair opportunity and a reasonable period of time to challenge it. However, the court normally need not disclose the sources of confidential information contained in the report.

Normally, the judge who presided at the trial conducts the sentencing. Unlike the evidentiary restrictions at trial, the judge can take into account a vast array of information in making the sentencing decision, including proffers by counsel, hearsay, prior bad acts of the defendant not admissible at trial, expressions of remorse and the like. The judge should consider the presentence report, sentencing alternatives if any, evidence concerning the nature and characteristics of the criminal conduct, and whether to run any multiple sentences on different counts concurrently (at the same time) or consecutively (when the second or subsequent sentence does not start until the first sentence is completed). In addition, the judge may weigh untruthfulness by the defendant or weigh a defendant's cooperation with law enforcement in favor of the defendant. The judge "must be permitted to consider

> **Food for Thought**
>
> Why at sentencing can the judge consider inadmissible evidence such as hearsay and arrests or other bad acts that did not result in a conviction? What are the arguments in favor of allowing this and what are the arguments against?

---

[1] This chapter addresses only non-capital sentencing and sentencing procedures. Capital sentencing procedures are highly specialized and have special constitutional requirements and limitations.

any and all information that reasonably might bear on the proper sentence for the particular defendant, given the crime committed." *Wasman v. United States*, <u>468 U.S. 559 (1984)</u>.

At the sentencing hearing, defendant must be given the right of allocution, which is the right to speak to the judge to identify any reason why the sentence should not be pronounced or why a particular sentence is appropriate. *See* <u>Fed. R. Crim. P. 32(i)(4) (A)(ii)</u>. This right affords regularity to the proceedings and reduces the likelihood of a subsequent attack on the judgment. Additionally, the judge must advise the defendant of his right to appeal his conviction.

In making a sentencing decision, a judge may impose, the maximum punishment (term of imprisonment and/or fine), or the mandatory minimum punishment, as dictated by the governing statute. Most statutes articulate a sentencing range that gives judges discretion to impose a penalty within that range. When there is no mandatory minimum term of imprisonment, the judge can consider alternatives to imprisonment. There are a variety of such alternatives.

Hypo: *Always the Same Sentence*

A New Jersey judge remarks in a status conference involving a first-degree murder charge that he routinely rejects pleas of 45 years imprisonment and instead "always" dishes out 60-year terms in first-degree murder cases. The judge also tells the defendant that he can "check his record" on that. A defendant previously convicted of first-degree murder by a jury and sentenced by this judge to 60 years learns about these statements and decides to appeal his sentence. Note that the judge did weigh aggravating and mitigating circumstances as required by the statute before declaring the sentence to be 60 years. Are the judge's statements a problem? *State v. McFarlane*, 134 A.3d 956 (N.J. 2016).

Points for Discussion

a. **Fines**

The punishment for a violation of the law may include a fine in addition to, or in some cases instead of, imprisonment. A court's authority to impose fines for violations of criminal statutes is set forth in the statutes themselves. The procedure for the collection of fines is governed largely by statute. Due to constitutional limitations, an indigent person may not usually be imprisoned for failure to pay the fine or costs. *See Bearden v. Georgia*, 461 U.S. 660 (1983). When the defendant seeks to appeal a fine, the trial judge may grant a stay of the payment and require bail.

b. Restitution

By statute, a person can be ordered to make restitution of property or its value to the victim in cases involving the taking of, injury to, or destruction of property. An order of restitution may defer payment until the person is released from custody. However, the decision by a trial judge not to use this remedy does not deprive the victim of a civil action for the damage sustained.

c. Forfeiture or Confiscation of Property

A person convicted of certain types of crimes, such as the possession of controlled substances, intoxicating liquors, eavesdropping devices, deadly weapons, gambling devices, and obscene matter, can be ordered to forfeit that property if it was used in the commission of an offense. Forfeitures, as payments in kind, are "fines" if they constitute punishment for an offense. *Austin v. United States*, 509 U.S. 602 (1993). Thus, the forfeiture of vehicles and property used to facilitate commission of drug trafficking is allowed because it serves as a punishment under the Eighth Amendment's Excessive Fines Clause.

> **FYI**
>
> Generally, under the Due Process Clause, the Government must provide notice and a meaningful opportunity to be heard before seizing real property that is subject to civil forfeiture. *United States v. James Daniel Good Real Property*, 510 U.S. 43 (1993). The Due Process Clause does not preclude forfeiture of property used for unlawful purposes by a defendant but which belongs to another person. *Bennis v. Michigan*, 516 U.S. 442 (1996).

d. Probation & Conditional Discharge

Probation is granted when the sentencing court suspends the execution or imposition of a sentence of imprisonment conditionally and releases the defendant under the supervision of a probation officer. Statutes may provide that probation is prohibited after convictions for certain offenses such as crimes of violence, sex offenses, and the like, or for offenders who have one or more prior felony convictions. Otherwise, many states require that a defendant be considered for probation and conditional discharge unless the court finds that imprisonment is necessary to protect the public. When a defendant is sentenced to a period of incarceration followed by probation (as opposed to parole), the sentence is referred to as a "split sentence" because part of the sentence is suspended and the sentence is "split" between time in prison and a period of probation.

Conditions of probation are usually stated in writing and furnished to the defendant. All defendants are required to refrain from committing another offense. They may also be subject to other conditions such as drug testing and treatment, restitution, counseling or any other condition that the court deems reasonably necessary to enable defendant to lead a law-abiding life. In addition to reasonable conditions, a court may require a defendant to submit to a period of imprisonment, such as weekends in the local jail. The court, the probation officer, or the prosecution may initiate proceedings to determine whether to revoke the probation because of a violation of its conditions.

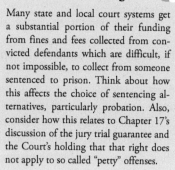

Food for Thought

Many state and local court systems get a substantial portion of their funding from fines and fees collected from convicted defendants which are difficult, if not impossible, to collect from someone sentenced to prison. Think about how this affects the choice of sentencing alternatives, particularly probation. Also, consider how this relates to Chapter 17's discussion of the jury trial guarantee and the Court's holding that that right does not apply to so called "petty" offenses.

e. Home Incarceration

Many states permit defendants convicted of minor offenses to serve all or part of a definite term of imprisonment through "home incarceration." The sentencing judge may have discretion to order home incarceration as a form of "split sentence" under which defendant serves part of the sentence at home and part of it in the local jail. As with probation and conditional discharge, a defendant under home incarceration must sign an agreement that lists all of the conditions of confinement.

f. Continuous Confinement for a Definite Term or Indeterminate Term

An indeterminate sentence is set within statutory limits, with the parole board having responsibility for deciding precisely when the defendant is eligible for early release. Many states use indeterminate sentences. A determinate sentence (also known as "flat time") is for a fixed period without the possibility of early release, but supervision often accompanies that release.

g. Capital Punishment

In *Panetti v. Quarterman*, 551 U.S. 930 (2007), the Court held that the Eighth Amendment to the U.S. Constitution prohibits the government from executing a prisoner whose mental illness prevents him from "rationally understanding" why the States seeks to impose that punishment. In *Madison v. Alabama*, 139 S.Ct. 718 (2019), the Court held that the Eighth Amendment did not necessarily preclude the execution of an individual who has no memory of committing his crime, or a prisoner suffering from dementia who is experiencing psychotic delusions. However, the Court remanded for consideration of whether defendant's mental illness prevents him from rationally understanding why the state is imposing the death penalty.

B. Proportionality of Punishment

The Eighth Amendment prohibits cruel and unusual punishments, which includes punishments that are deemed to be "excessive." In a series of cases, the Court has greatly restricted the judiciary's ability to find punishments excessive once set by legislatures.

Ewing v. California

538 U.S. 11 (2003).

JUSTICE O'CONNOR announced the judgment of the Court and delivered an opinion in which THE CHIEF JUSTICE and JUSTICE KENNEDY join.

In this case, we decide whether the Eighth Amendment prohibits the State of California from sentencing a repeat felon to a prison term of 25 years to life under the State's "Three Strikes and You're Out" law. According to the law, if the defendant has one prior "serious" or "violent" felony conviction, he must be sentenced to "twice the term otherwise provided as punishment for the current felony conviction." If the defendant has two or more prior "serious" or "violent" felony

Hear It

You can listen to the oral argument in *Ewing* at: http://www.oyez.org/cases/2000-2009/2002/2002_01_6978.

convictions, he must receive "an indeterminate term of life imprisonment." Defendants sentenced to life under the three strikes law become eligible for parole on a date calculated by reference to a "minimum term," which is the greater of (a) three times the term otherwise provided for the current conviction, (b) 25 years, or (c) the term determined by the court pursuant to § 1170 for the underlying conviction, including any enhancements.

On parole from a 9-year prison term, petitioner Gary Ewing walked into the pro shop of the El Segundo Golf Course in Los Angeles County on March 12, 2000. He walked out with three golf clubs, priced at $399 apiece, concealed in his pants leg. A shop employee, whose suspicions were aroused when he observed Ewing limp out of the pro shop, telephoned the police. The police apprehended Ewing in the parking lot. Ewing is no stranger to the criminal justice system. In 1984, at the age of 22, he pleaded guilty to theft. Only 10 months later, Ewing stole the golf clubs at issue. He was charged with, and ultimately convicted of, one count of felony grand theft of personal property in excess of $400. As required by the three strikes law, the prosecutor formally alleged, and the trial court found, that Ewing had been convicted previously of four serious or violent felonies for the three burglaries and the robbery in the Long Beach apartment complex. The trial judge determined that the grand theft should remain a felony. The court also ruled that the four prior strikes for the three burglaries and the robbery in Long Beach should stand. As a newly convicted felon with two or more "serious" or "violent" felony convictions in his past, Ewing was sentenced under the three strikes law to 25 years to life. The California Court of Appeal affirmed. Relying on our decision in *Rummel v. Estelle*, 445 U.S. 263 (1980), the court rejected Ewing's claim that his sentence was grossly disproportionate under the Eighth Amendment. Enhanced sentences under recidivist statutes like the three strikes law, the court reasoned, serve the "legitimate goal" of deterring and incapacitating repeat offenders. The Supreme Court of California denied Ewing's petition for review, and we granted certiorari. We affirm.

The Eighth Amendment, which forbids cruel and unusual punishments, contains a "narrow proportionality principle" that "applies to noncapital sentences." We have most recently addressed the proportionality principle as applied to terms of years in a series of cases beginning with *Rummel v. Estelle*. In *Rummel*, we held that it did not violate the Eighth Amendment for a State to sentence a three-time offender to life in prison with the possibility of parole. Like Ewing, Rummel was sentenced to a lengthy prison term under a recidivism statute. Rummel's two prior offenses were a 1964 felony for "fraudulent use of a credit card to obtain $80 worth of goods or services," and a 1969 felony conviction for "passing a forged check in the amount of $28.36." His triggering offense was a conviction for felony theft—"obtaining $120.75 by false pretenses."

Three years after *Rummel*, in *Solem v. Helm*, 463 U.S. 277, 279 (1983), we held that the Eighth Amendment prohibited "a life sentence without possibility of parole for a seventh nonviolent felony." The triggering offense in *Solem* was "uttering a 'no account' check for $100." We specifically stated that the Eighth Amendment's ban on cruel and unusual punishments "prohibits sentences that are disproportionate to the crime committed," and that the "constitutional principle of proportionality has been recognized explicitly in this Court for almost a century." The *Solem* Court explained that three factors may be relevant to a determination of whether a sentence is so disproportionate that it violates the Eighth Amendment: "(i) the gravity of the offense and the harshness of the penalty; (ii) the sentences imposed on other criminals in the same jurisdiction; and (iii) the sentences imposed for commission of the same crime in other jurisdictions." Applying these factors in *Solem*, we struck down defendant's sentence of life without parole. We noted the contrast between that sentence and the sentence in *Rummel*, pursuant to which the defendant was eligible for parole. We explicitly declined to overrule *Rummel*.

Eight years after *Solem*, we grappled with the proportionality issue again in *Harmelin v. Michigan*, 501 U.S. 957 (1991). Harmelin was not a recidivism case, but rather involved a first-time offender convicted of possessing 672 grams of cocaine. He was sentenced to life in prison without possibility of parole. A majority of the

Court rejected Harmelin's claim that his sentence was so grossly disproportionate that it violated the Eighth Amendment. The Court, however, could not agree on why his proportionality argument failed. Justice Scalia, joined by The Chief Justice, wrote that the proportionality principle was "an aspect of our death penalty jurisprudence, rather than a generalizable aspect of Eighth Amendment law." He would thus have declined to apply gross disproportionality principles except in reviewing capital sentences. Justice Kennedy, joined by two other [justices], concurred. Justice Kennedy recognized that "the Eighth Amendment proportionality principle also applies to noncapital sentences." He identified four principles of proportionality review—"the primacy of the legislature, the variety of legitimate penological schemes, the nature of our federal system, and the requirement that proportionality review be guided by objective factors"—that "inform the final one: The Eighth Amendment does not require strict proportionality between crime and sentence. Rather, it forbids only extreme sentences that are 'grossly disproportionate' to the crime." Justice Kennedy's concurrence also stated that *Solem* "did not mandate" comparative analysis "within and between jurisdictions."

The proportionality principles distilled in Justice Kennedy's concurrence guide our application of the Eighth Amendment in [this] context. Throughout the States, legislatures enacting three strikes laws made a deliberate policy choice that individuals who have repeatedly engaged in serious or violent criminal behavior, and whose conduct has not been deterred by more conventional approaches to punishment, must be isolated from society in order to protect the public safety. Though three strikes laws may be relatively new, our tradition of deferring to state legislatures in making and implementing such important policy decisions is longstanding. Our traditional deference to legislative policy choices finds a corollary in the principle that the Constitution "does not mandate adoption of any one penological theory." A sentence can have a variety of justifications, such as incapacitation, deterrence, retribution, or rehabilitation. Some or all of these justifications may play a role in a State's sentencing scheme. Selecting the sentencing rationales is generally a policy choice to be made by state legislatures, not federal courts.

When the California Legislature enacted the three strikes law, it made a judgment that protecting the public safety requires incapacitating criminals who have already been convicted of at least one serious or violent crime. California's justification is no pretext. Recidivism is a serious public safety concern in California and throughout the Nation. According to a recent report, approximately 67 percent of former inmates released from state prisons were charged with at least one "serious" new crime within three years of their release. The State's interest in deterring crime also lends some support to the three strikes law. We have long viewed both incapacitation and deterrence as rationales for recidivism statutes: "A recidivist statute's primary goals are to deter repeat offenders and, at some point in the life of one who repeatedly commits criminal offenses serious enough to be punished as felonies, to segregate that person from the rest of society for an extended period of time." *Rummel.* Four years after the passage of California's three strikes law, the recidivism rate of parolees returned to prison for the commission of a new crime dropped by nearly 25 percent.

Against this backdrop, we consider Ewing's claim that his three strikes sentence of 25 years to life is unconstitutionally disproportionate to his offense of "shoplifting three golf clubs." We first address the gravity of the offense compared to the harshness of the penalty. Ewing incorrectly frames the issue. The gravity of his offense was not merely "shoplifting three golf clubs." Rather, Ewing was convicted of felony grand theft for stealing nearly $1,200 worth of merchandise after previously having been convicted of at least two "violent" or "serious" felonies. Even standing alone, Ewing's theft should not be taken lightly. His crime was certainly not "one of the most passive felonies a person could commit." The Supreme Court of California has noted the "seriousness" of grand theft in the context of proportionality review. In weighing the gravity of Ewing's offense, we place on the scales not only his current felony, but also his long history of felony recidivism. Any other approach would fail to accord proper deference to the policy judgments that find expression in the legislature's choice of sanctions. In imposing a three strikes sentence, the State's interest is not merely punishing the offense of conviction, or the "triggering" offense: "It is in dealing in a harsher manner with those who by repeated criminal acts have shown that they are simply incapable of conforming to the norms of society as established by its criminal law." To give full effect to the State's choice of this legitimate penological goal, our proportionality review of Ewing's sentence must take that goal into account.

Ewing's sentence is justified by the State's public-safety interest in incapacitating and deterring recidivist felons, and amply supported by his own long, serious criminal record. Ewing has been convicted of numerous misdemeanor and felony offenses, served nine separate terms of incarceration, and committed most of his crimes while on probation or parole. His prior "strikes" were serious felonies including robbery and three residential burglaries. To be sure, Ewing's sentence is a long one. But it reflects a rational legislative judgment, entitled to deference, that offenders who have committed serious or violent felonies and who continue to commit felonies must be incapacitated. The State of California "was entitled to place upon Ewing the onus of one who is simply unable to bring his conduct within the social norms prescribed by the criminal law of the State." Ewing's is not "the rare case in which a threshold comparison of the crime committed and the sentence imposed leads to an inference of gross disproportionality."

Food for Thought

What values are espoused by Justice O'Connor in her opinion?

We hold that Ewing's sentence of 25 years to life in prison, imposed for the offense of felony grand theft under the three strikes law, is not grossly disproportionate and therefore does not violate the Eighth Amendment's prohibition on cruel and unusual punishments. The judgment of the California Court of Appeal is affirmed.

JUSTICE BREYER, with whom JUSTICE STEVENS, JUSTICE SOUTER, and JUSTICE GINSBURG join, dissenting.

In *Solem v. Helm*, the Court found grossly disproportionate a somewhat longer sentence imposed on a recidivist offender for triggering criminal conduct that was somewhat less severe. In my view, the differences are not determinative, and the Court should reach the same ultimate conclusion here.

The plurality applies Justice Kennedy's analytical framework in *Harmelin*. Courts faced with a "gross disproportionality" claim must first make "a threshold comparison of the crime committed and the sentence imposed." If a claim crosses that threshold—itself a rare occurrence—then the court should compare the sentence at issue to other sentences "imposed on other criminals" in the same, or in other, jurisdictions. The comparative analysis will "validate" or invalidate "an initial judgment that a sentence is grossly disproportionate to a crime." I believe that the case before us is a "rare" case—one in which a court can say with reasonable confidence that the punishment is "grossly disproportionate" to the crime.

Ewing's claim crosses the gross disproportionality "threshold." First, precedent makes clear that Ewing's sentence raises a serious disproportionality question. Ewing is a recidivist. Hence the two cases most directly in point are those in which the Court considered the constitutionality of recidivist sentencing: *Rummel* and *Solem*. Ewing's claim falls between these two cases. It is stronger than the claim presented in *Rummel*, where the Court upheld a recidivist's sentence as constitutional. It is weaker than the claim presented in *Solem*, where the Court struck down a recidivist sentence as unconstitutional.

Three kinds of sentence-related characteristics define the relevant comparative spectrum: (a) the length of the prison term in real time, i.e., the time that the offender is likely actually to spend in prison; (b) the sentence-triggering criminal conduct, i.e., the offender's actual behavior or other offense-related circumstances; and (c) the offender's criminal history. The length of the real prison term—the factor that explains the *Solem/Rummel* difference in outcome—places Ewing closer to *Solem* than to *Rummel*, though the greater value of the golf clubs that Ewing stole moves Ewing's case back slightly in *Rummel*'s direction. Overall, the comparison places Ewing's sentence well within the twilight zone between *Solem* and *Rummel*—a zone where the argument for unconstitutionality is substantial, where the cases themselves cannot determine the constitutional outcome. Second, Ewing's sentence on its face imposes one of the most severe punishments available upon a recidivist who subsequently engaged in one of the less serious forms of criminal conduct. I do not deny the seriousness of shoplifting, which costs retailers in the range of $30 billion annually. This case, of course, involves shoplifting by a recidivist. One might argue that any crime committed by a recidivist is a serious crime potentially warranting a 25-year sentence. But this Court rejected that view in *Solem*, and in *Harmelin*, with the recognition that "no penalty is *per se* constitutional." Third, some objective evidence suggests that many experienced judges would consider Ewing's sentence disproportionately harsh. The United States Sentencing Commission (having based the federal Sentencing Guidelines primarily upon its review of how judges had actually sentenced offenders) does not include shoplifting (or similar theft-related offenses) among the crimes that might trigger especially long sentences for recidivists.

A comparison of Ewing's sentence with other sentences requires answers to two questions. First, how would other jurisdictions (or California at other times, i.e.,

Food for Thought

As compared to Justice O'Connor, what values are espoused in the dissent?

without the three strikes penalty) punish the same offense conduct? Second, upon what other conduct would other jurisdictions (or California) impose the same prison term? Since hypothetical punishment is beside the point, the relevant prison time, for comparative purposes, is

real prison time, i.e., the time that an offender must actually serve. As to California, we know the following: First, between the end of World War II and 1994 (when California enacted the three strikes law), no one like Ewing could have served more than 10 years in prison. We know that for certain because the maximum sentence for Ewing's crime of conviction, grand theft, was for most of that period 10 years. The time that any offender actually served was likely far less than 10 years. Statistical data shows that the median time actually served for grand theft (other than auto theft) was about two years, and 90 percent of those convicted of that crime served less than three or four years.

Statistics suggest that recidivists of all sorts convicted during that same time period in California served a small fraction of Ewing's real-time sentence. On average, recidivists served three to four additional (recidivist-related) years in prison, with 90 percent serving less than an additional real seven to eight years. We know that California has reserved, and still reserves, Ewing-type prison time, i.e., at least 25 real years in prison, for criminals convicted of crimes far worse than was Ewing's. Statistics for the years 1945 to 1981, for example, indicate that typical (nonrecidivist) male first-degree murderers served between 10 and 15 real years in prison, with 90 percent of all such murderers serving less than 20 real years. Moreover, California, which has moved toward a real-time sentencing system (where the statutory punishment approximates the time served), still punishes far less harshly those who have engaged in far more serious conduct.

As to other jurisdictions, the United States, bound by the federal Sentencing Guidelines, would impose upon a recidivist, such as Ewing, a sentence that, in any ordinary case, would not exceed 18 months in prison. With three exceptions, we do not have actual time served by Ewing-type offenders in other States. We do know, that the law would make it legally impossible for a Ewing-type offender to serve more than 10 years in prison in 33 jurisdictions, as well as the federal courts, more than 15 years in 4 other States, and more than 20 years in 4 additional States. In nine other States, the law might make it legally possible to impose a sentence of 25 years or more—though that fact by itself, of course, does not mean that judges have actually done so.

Food for Thought

Does the O'Connor threesome or the dissent have the better argument under precedent? As a matter of policy? If you feel Ewing's punishment was wrong, what exactly was wrong with it?

Points for Discussion

a. Proportionality & Forfeiture

Proportionality limitations may apply to forfeitures as well. In *United States v. Bajakajian*, 524 U.S. 321 (1998), defendant was arrested while trying to take $357,144 on a flight to Cyprus, because he had failed to report that he possessed or had control of more than $10,000. After a bench trial on a criminal forfeiture charge, the trial court found the entire amount subject to forfeiture. The court, however, ordered only $15,000 forfeited, reasoning that forfeiture of more than that amount would be "grossly disproportional" to Bajakajian's culpability and thus unconstitutional under the Excessive Fines Clause. The court found that all of the money came from a lawful source and was to be used for a lawful purpose. The Court agreed that the forfeiture of currency permissible under the statute constituted punishment because the forfeiture only became possible upon conviction of willfully violating the reporting statute. After concluding that the forfeiture qualified as a "fine," and therefore "punishment," the Court turned to the question of excessiveness. Bajakajian's crime was "solely a reporting offense," and the harm Bajakajian's caused was "minimal" in the sense that the government would be deprived only of information that the $357,144 left the country. Thus, the gravity

Food for Thought

In *Timbs v. Indiana*, 139 S.Ct. 682 (2019), the Court held that the Eighth Amendment ban on "cruel and unusual punishments" applies to the civil forfeiture of a $42,000 Land Rover automobile. In that case, the maximum fine for defendant's drug offense was $10,000. Is it sufficiently proportionate to require forfeiture of a $42,000 automobile when the maximum fine for the underlying crime is $10,000?

of the crime compared to the amount in forfeiture sought would be "grossly dispro-portional" if the entire amount were forfeited.

b. Enhanced Sentences for Recidivists

Recidivist offender statutes like the one applied in *Ewing* are used by many states. A defendant is entitled to notice of being charged as a recidivist before the trial of the underlying substantive offense. A separate indictment meets this requirement just as does a separate count in the indictment charging the substantive offense to which it refers. It is common practice for the indictment to specify the nature, time and place of the prior conviction.

> **FYI**
>
> Assume a defendant is properly charged as a recidivist, and trial initially takes place on the underlying felony. During the trial, no mention is made of the prior convictions, except for impeachment. The determination of whether the defendant is a recidivist must occur in a separate proceeding from the trial on the underlying felony. This penalty phase usually is conducted with the same jury. The evidence at the hearing is very narrow. The only function of the jury is to hear proof of prior convictions and to determine if a defendant's record of recidivism warrants punishment. Accordingly, courts have denied defendants an opportunity to introduce evidence of mitigation. During the hearing, the prosecution must prove every element of the recidivist charge beyond a reasonable doubt. A defendant charged with being a recidivist may plead guilty to the charge.

c. Maximum Sentences for Juveniles

Under the Eighth Amendment's Cruel and Unusual Punishment Clause, a juve-nile cannot be sentenced to life without parole for non-homicide crimes. *Graham v. Florida*, 560 U.S. 48 (2010). The Eighth Amendment also forbids a sentencing scheme that *mandates* life without parole for any juvenile offender, regardless of the crime. *Miller v. Alabama*, 567 U.S. 460 (2012). In *Montgomery v. Louisiana*, 577 U.S. 190 (2016), the Court held that *Miller* was to be retroactively applied, potentially sending hundreds of inmates in several states back to court for resentencing.

d. Incorporation of the Prohibition Against Cruel & Unusual Punishment

In *Timbs v. Indiana*, 139 S.Ct. 682 (2019), the Court held that the Eighth Amendment's ban on "cruel and unusual punishment" applies to the states and also applies to *in rem* forfeitures. "This safeguard, we hold, is 'fundamental to our scheme of ordered liberty,' with 'deep roots in our history and tradition.' *McDonald v. Chicago*, 561 U.S. 742, 767 (2010)."

C. The Right to a Jury Trial Meets Sentencing

1. *Apprendi's* Sea Change

Throughout most of the U.S., legislatures gave trial judges considerable and broad discretion to sentence an individual convicted of a crime within a wide range of punishment. In addition, judges have broad authority to impose probation and suspend imprisonment when they thought it was warranted.

In the late 1970s and 1980s, during the War on Crime and the War on Drugs, legislatures began to adopt a new tough-on-crime attitude, and began to establish mandatory minimum terms of incarceration for certain kinds of crimes, eliminating judicial discretion to impose probation in those cases. Close on the heels of mandatory minimums, legislatures began to pass sentencing "enhancements", which allowed a judge to increase a penalty by a certain amount upon a finding, for example, that defendant used a firearm during the crime, that the crime was perpetrated on an elderly or very young victim, or the crime was perpetrated on a victim because of his or her race or ethnicity. As judicial discretion was narrowed and the plethora of sentencing enhancements grew, litigants seized upon the right to a trial by jury to attack the constitutionality of the enhancements.

In *Apprendi v. New Jersey,* 530 U.S. 466 (2000), the Court was confronted by a New Jersey hate crime statute which provided for an "extended term" of imprisonment if the trial judge found, by a preponderance of the evidence, that "the defendant in committing the crime acted with a purpose to intimidate an individual or group of individuals because of race, color, gender, handicap, religion, sexual orientation or ethnicity." With such a finding, the defendant's sentence could be extended by "between 10 and 20 years." After the trial court concluded that the crime was motivated by racial bias, Apprendi challenged his conviction on the basis that he had been denied his right to trial by jury on the sentence enhancement. The Court agreed:

> Just as the circumstances of the crime and the intent of the defendant at the time of commission were often essential elements to be alleged in the indictment, so too were the circumstances mandating a particular punishment. "Where a statute annexes a higher degree of punishment to a common-law felony, if committed under particular circumstances, an indictment for the offence, in order to bring the defendant within that higher degree of punishment, must expressly charge it to have been committed under those circumstances, and must state the circumstances with certainty and precision. 2 M. HALE, PLEAS OF THE CROWN." ARCHBOLD, PLEADING AND EVIDENCE IN CRIMINAL CASES, at 51. Nothing in this history suggests that it is impermissible for judges to exercise discretion—taking into consideration various factors relating both to offense and offender—in impos-

ing a judgment within the range prescribed by statute. Judges in this country have long exercised discretion of this nature in imposing sentence within statutory limits in the individual case. We do not suggest that trial practices cannot change in the course of centuries and still remain true to the principles that emerged from the Framers' fears "that the jury right could be lost not only by gross denial, but by erosion." But practice must at least adhere to the basic principles undergirding the requirements of trying to a jury all facts necessary to constitute a statutory offense, and proving those facts beyond reasonable doubt.

Our reexamination of our cases in this area, and of the history upon which they rely, confirms the opinion that we expressed in *Jones v. United States*, 526 U.S. 227 (1999). Other than the fact of a prior conviction, any fact that increases the penalty for a crime beyond the prescribed statutory maximum must be submitted to a jury, and proved beyond a reasonable doubt. With that exception, we endorse the statement of the rule set forth in the concurring opinions in that case: "It is unconstitutional for a legislature to remove from the jury the assessment of facts that increase the prescribed range of penalties to which a criminal defendant is exposed. It is equally clear that such facts must be established by proof beyond a reasonable doubt."

Points for Discussion

a. Aggravators & the Death Penalty

In *Ring v. Arizona*, 536 U.S. 584 (2002), the Court held that it was a violation of *Apprendi* for a sentencing judge sitting without a jury to find an aggravating circumstance necessary for imposition of the death penalty. When the judge made that finding, the defendant was exposed to a penalty greater than that authorized by the jury's verdict alone in violation of *Apprendi*.

b. Mandatory Minimums

Soon after *Apprendi* was decided, scores of challengers attempted to take advantage of what Justice O'Connor termed a "watershed change in constitutional law." While *Apprendi* made clear that a jury was required for a finding of facts which increased the statutory *maximum* sentence, it did not resolve whether a jury finding was also required for facts which increased the statutory *minimum* for a sentence. In 2002, the Court decided that *Apprendi* did not apply to mandatory minimum sentences. *Harris v. United States*, 536 U.S. 545 (2002). However, in 2013, the Court changed course. In *Alleyne v. United States*, 570 U.S. 99 (2013), the Court held that any fact that increases the mandatory minimum sentence for a crime is an "element" of the crime that must be submitted to a jury, and not a so-called "sentencing factor" that a judge alone can decide. Therefore, when a finding that a defendant had brandished, as opposed to merely carried, a firearm in connection with crime of violence would elevate a mandatory minimum term for the offense from five to seven years, it was therefore an "element" of a separate, aggravated offense that had to found by jury. According to the majority: "The essential Sixth Amendment inquiry is whether a fact is an element of the crime. When a finding of fact alters the legally prescribed punishment so as to aggravate it, the fact necessarily forms a constituent part of a new offense and must be submitted to the jury. It is no answer to say that the defendant could have received the same sentence with or without that fact. It is obvious that a defendant could not be convicted and sentenced for assault, if the jury only finds the facts for larceny, even if the punishments prescribed for each crime are identical. One reason is that each crime has different elements and a defendant can be convicted only if the jury has found each element of the crime of conviction." Justice Thomas was careful to add that nothing in the opinion was meant to circumscribe a judge's traditional discretion to take into account any facts and circumstances she found relevant to the offender or offense that affected her decision as to the appropriate sentence within the statutory range.

c.   Harmless Error

Apprendi violations are subject to constitutional harmless error analysis. *See Chapman v. California*, 386 U.S. 18 (1967). As with the failure to submit elements of a crime to the jury, the failure to submit a sentencing factor to the jury is not a "structural" error. *Washington v. Recuenco*, 548 U.S. 212 (2006).

d.   Findings for Consecutive Sentencing

In *Oregon v. Ice*, 555 U.S. 160 (2009), the Court held that it did not violate the Sixth Amendment (or *Apprendi*) for a judge to make factual findings for his decision to impose consecutive sentences as opposed to concurrent sentences.

e.   Imposition of Fine

In *Southern Union Co. v. United States*, 567 U.S. 343 (2012), the Court held that *Apprendi* extends to the imposition of criminal fines which are also a form of punishment. When the jury made a finding of guilt only on the charged offense—that Southern Union violated the Resource Conservation and Recovery Act of 1976 "on or about September 19, 2002 to October 19, 2004"—the trial court could not impose a fine for every day in that period because the jury never specifically found more than one day's violation.

2. *Blakely & Booker*

The next step in *Apprendi* litigation was an attack on sentencing guidelines. Sentencing guidelines came about because members of the criminal justice community and the public became dissatisfied with the wide disparity in sentencing practices among judges, amounting to different sentences for similarly situated individuals. In response to this disparity, and in league with the tough-on-crime attitude, the Federal Sentencing Guidelines were developed. The Guidelines were widely regarded as resulting in harsher penalties than were meted out under the previous sentencing scheme that gave judges wide latitude. The mandatory nature of the Guidelines also had the effect of cramping judges' ability to deal with inequities that were built into the system. Perhaps the most notorious of these inequities was the imposition of far more severe penalties on those who possessed or distributed crack cocaine, which was a largely African American population, than those who possessed or distributed powder cocaine, which was a whiter and wealthier population. Judges could consider fewer individualities of the defendant and virtually the only way for a defendant to get out from under severe Guidelines sentences was to cooperate with the prosecution, pursuant to Section 5K of the Sentencing Guidelines (lending the name "5K letters" to the prosecutor's letter to a judge detailing the cooperation). In *Blakely v. Washington*, 542 U.S. 296 (2004), the Court struck down Washington State's determinate sentencing scheme as a violation of the right to a trial by jury. That decision set the stage for the upset of the Federal Sentencing Guidelines in *Booker*.

United States v. Booker

543 U.S. 220 (2005).

JUSTICE STEVENS delivered the opinion of the Court in part [in which JUSTICE SCALIA, JUSTICE SOUTER, JUSTICE THOMAS, and JUSTICE GINSBURG join].

The question is whether an application of the Federal Sentencing Guidelines violated the Sixth Amendment. In each case, the courts below held that binding rules set forth in the Guidelines limited the severity of the sentence that the judge could lawfully impose on the defendant based on the facts found by the jury at his trial. In both cases the courts rejected, on the basis of our decision in *Blakely v. Washington*, 542 U.S. 296 (2004), the Government's recommended application of the Sentencing Guidelines because the proposed sentences were based on additional facts that the sentencing judge found by a preponderance of the evidence. We hold that both courts correctly concluded that the Sixth Amendment as construed in *Blakely* does apply to the Sentencing

Hear It

You can listen to the oral argument in *Booker* at: http://www.oyez.org/cases/2000-2009/2004/2004_04_104/.

Guidelines. In a separate opinion authored by Justice Breyer, the Court concludes that in light of this holding, two provisions of the Sentencing Reform Act of 1984 (SRA) that have the effect of making the Guidelines mandatory must be invalidated in order to allow the statute to operate in a manner consistent with congressional intent.

Respondent Booker was charged with possession with intent to distribute at least 50 grams of cocaine base (crack). Having heard evidence that he had 92.5 grams in his duffel bag, the jury found him guilty of violating 21 U.S.C. § 841(a)(1). That statute prescribes a minimum sentence of 10 years in prison and a maximum sentence of life for that offense. § 841(b)(1)(A)(iii). Based upon Booker's criminal history and the quantity of drugs found by the jury, the Sentencing Guidelines required the District Court Judge to select a "base" sentence of not less than 210 nor more than 262 months in prison. *See* United States Sentencing Commission, Guidelines Manual §§ 2D1.1(c)(4), 4A1.1 (Nov. 2003) (USSG). The judge held a post-trial sentencing proceeding and concluded by a preponderance of the evidence that Booker had possessed an additional 566 grams of crack and that he was guilty of obstructing justice. Those findings mandated that the judge select a sentence between 360 months and life imprisonment; the judge imposed a sentence at the low end of the range. Thus, instead of the sentence of 21 years and 10 months that the judge could have imposed on the basis of the facts proved to the jury beyond a reasonable doubt, Booker received a 30-year sentence.

The Seventh Circuit held that this application of the Sentencing Guidelines conflicted with our holding in *Apprendi v. New Jersey*, 530 U.S. 466 (2000), that "other than the fact of a prior conviction, any fact that increases the penalty for a crime beyond the prescribed statutory maximum must be submitted to a jury, and proved beyond a reasonable doubt." The majority relied on our holding in *Blakely v. Washington* that "the 'statutory maximum' for *Apprendi* purposes is the maximum sentence a judge may impose solely on the basis of the facts reflected in the jury verdict or admitted by the defendant." The court held that the sentence violated the Sixth Amendment, and remanded with instructions to sentence respondent within the sentencing range supported by the jury's findings or to hold a separate sentencing hearing before a jury. It has been settled throughout our history that the Constitution protects every criminal defendant "against conviction except upon proof beyond a reasonable doubt of every fact necessary to constitute the crime with which he is charged." *In re Winship*, 397 U.S. 358, 364 (1970). It is equally clear that the "Constitution gives a criminal defendant the right to demand that a jury find him guilty of all the elements of the crime with which he is charged." *United States v. Gaudin*, 515 U.S. 506, 511 (1995). These basic precepts, firmly rooted in the common law, have provided the basis for recent decisions interpreting modern criminal statutes and sentencing procedures.

In *Blakely v. Washington*, 542 U.S. 296 (2004), we dealt with a determinate sentencing scheme similar to the Federal Sentencing Guidelines. There the defendant pleaded guilty to kidnaping, a class B felony punishable by a term of not more than 10 years. Other provisions of Washington law, comparable to the Federal Sentencing Guidelines, mandated a "standard" sentence of 49-to-53 months, unless the judge found aggravating facts justifying an exceptional sentence. Although the prosecutor recommended a sentence in the standard range, the judge found that the defendant had acted with "deliberate cruelty" and sentenced him to 90 months. The application of Washington's sentencing scheme violated the defendant's right to have the jury find the existence of "any particular fact" that the law makes essential to his punishment. That right is implicated whenever a judge seeks to impose a sentence that is not solely based on "facts reflected in the jury verdict or admitted by the defendant." We rejected the State's argument that the jury verdict was sufficient to authorize a sentence within the general 10-year sentence for Class B felonies, noting that under Washington law, the judge was required to find additional facts in order to impose the greater 90-month sentence. Our precedents, we explained, make clear "that the 'statutory maximum' for *Apprendi* purposes is the maximum sentence a judge may impose solely on the basis of the facts reflected in the jury verdict or admitted by the defendant." The determination that the defendant acted with deliberate cruelty, like the determination in *Apprendi* that the defendant acted with racial malice, increased the sentence that the defendant could have otherwise received. Since this fact was found by a judge using a preponderance of the evidence standard, the sentence violated Blakely's Sixth Amendment rights.

As the dissenting opinions in *Blakely* recognized, there is no distinction of constitutional significance between the Federal Sentencing Guidelines and the Washington procedures at issue in that case. This conclusion rests on the premise, common to both systems, that the relevant sentencing rules are mandatory and impose binding requirements on all sentencing judges. If the Guidelines as currently written could be read as merely advisory provisions that recommended, rather than required, the selection of particular sentences in response to differing sets of facts, their use would not implicate the Sixth Amendment. We have never doubted the authority of a judge to exercise broad discretion in imposing a sentence within a statutory range. Indeed, everyone agrees that the constitutional issues presented by these cases would have been avoided entirely if Congress had omitted from the SRA the provisions that make the Guidelines binding on district judges; it is that circumstance that makes the Court's answer to the second question presented possible. For when a trial judge exercises his discretion to select a specific sentence within a defined range, the defendant has no right to a jury determination of the facts that the judge deems relevant.

The Guidelines as written are not advisory; they are mandatory and binding on all judges. While subsection (a) of § 3553 of the sentencing statute lists the Sentencing Guidelines as one factor to be considered in imposing a sentence, subsection (b) directs that the court "shall impose a sentence of the kind, and within the range" established by the Guidelines, subject to departures in specific, limited cases. Because they are binding on judges, we have consistently held that the Guidelines have the force and effect of laws.

The Guidelines permit departures from the prescribed sentencing range in cases in which the judge "finds that there exists an aggravating or mitigating circumstance of a kind, or to a degree, not adequately taken into consideration by the Sentencing Commission in formulating the guidelines that should result in a sentence different from that described." 18 U.S.C.A. § 3553(b)(1) (Supp.2004). At first glance, one might believe that the ability of a district judge to depart from the Guidelines means that she is bound only by the statutory maximum. Were this the case, there would be no *Apprendi* problem. Importantly, departures are not available in every case, and are unavailable in most. In most cases, as a matter of law, the Commission will have adequately taken all relevant factors into account, and no departure will be legally permissible.

Booker's case illustrates the mandatory nature of the Guidelines. The jury convicted him of possessing at least 50 grams of crack in violation of 21 U.S.C. § 841(b)(1)(A)(iii) based on evidence that he had 92.5 grams of crack in his duffel bag. The Guidelines specified an offense level of 32, which, given the defendant's criminal history category, authorized a sentence of 210-to-262 months. *See* USSG § 2D1.1(c)(4). Booker's is a run-of-the-mill drug case, and does not present any factors that were inadequately considered by the Commission. The sentencing judge would therefore have been reversed had he not imposed a sentence within the level 32 Guidelines range. Booker's actual sentence was 360 months, almost 10 years longer than the Guidelines range supported by the jury verdict alone. To reach this sentence, the judge found facts beyond those found by the jury: namely, that Booker possessed 566 grams of crack in addition to the 92.5 grams in his duffel bag. The jury never heard any evidence of the additional drug quantity, and the judge found it true by a preponderance of the evidence. As in *Blakely*, "the jury's verdict alone does not authorize the sentence. The judge acquires that authority only upon finding some additional fact." There is no relevant distinction between the sentence imposed pursuant to the Washington statutes in *Blakely* and the sentences imposed pursuant to the Federal Sentencing Guidelines in these cases.

The Government contends that *Blakely* is distinguishable because the Guidelines were promulgated by a commission rather than the Legislature; that principles of *stare decisis* require us to follow earlier decisions that are arguably inconsistent with *Blakely*; and that the application of *Blakely* to the Guidelines would conflict with separation of powers principles reflected in *Mistretta v. United States*, 488 U.S. 361 (1989). These arguments are unpersuasive. All of the foregoing support our conclusion that *Blakely* applies to the Sentencing Guidelines. In some cases jury fact-finding may impair the most expedient and efficient sentencing of defendants. But the interest in fairness and reliability protected by the right to a jury trial—a common-law right that defendants enjoyed for centuries and that is enshrined in the Sixth Amendment—has always outweighed the interest in concluding trials swiftly. Accordingly, we reaffirm our holding in *Apprendi*: Any fact (other than a prior conviction) which is necessary to support a sentence exceeding the maximum authorized by the facts established by a plea of guilty or a jury verdict must be admitted by the defendant or proved to a jury beyond a reasonable doubt.

JUSTICE BREYER delivered the opinion of the Court in part [in which THE CHIEF JUSTICE, JUSTICE O'CONNOR, JUSTICE KENNEDY, and JUSTICE GINSBURG join].

We answer the question of remedy by finding the provision of the federal sentencing statute that makes the Guidelines mandatory incompatible with today's constitutional holding. This provision must be severed and excised, as must one other statutory section which depends upon the Guidelines' mandatory nature. So modified, the federal sentencing statute makes the Guidelines effectively advisory. It requires a sentencing court to consider Guidelines ranges, but it permits the court to tailor the sentence in light of other statutory concerns as well.

We answer the remedial question by looking to legislative intent. We seek to determine what "Congress would have intended" in light of the Court's constitutional holding. In this instance, we must determine which of the two following remedial approaches is the more compatible with the legislature's intent as embodied in the 1984 Sentencing Act. One approach, that of Justice Stevens' dissent, would retain the Sentencing Act (and the Guidelines) as written, but would engraft onto the existing system today's Sixth Amendment "jury trial" requirement. The addition would change the Guidelines by preventing the sentencing court from increasing a sentence on the basis of a fact that the jury did not find (or that the offender did not admit). The other approach, which we adopt, would (through severance and excision of two provisions) make the Guidelines system advisory while maintaining a strong connection between the sentence imposed and the offender's real conduct—a connection important to the increased uniformity of sentencing that Congress intended its Guidelines system to achieve. Both approaches would significantly alter the system that Congress designed. But today's constitutional holding means that it is no longer possible to maintain the judicial fact-finding that Congress thought would underpin the mandatory Guidelines system that it sought to create and that Congress wrote into the Act in 18 U.S.C.A. §§ 3553(a) and 3661 (main ed. and Supp.2004).

Several considerations convince us that, were the Court's constitutional requirement added onto the Sentencing Act as currently written, the requirement would so transform the scheme that Congress created that Congress likely would not have intended the Act as so modified to stand. First, the statute's text states that "the court" when sentencing will consider "the nature and circumstances of the offense and the history and characteristics of the defendant." 18 U.S.C.A. § 3553(a)(1). The words "the court" mean "the judge without the jury," not "the judge working together with the jury." Second, Congress' basic statutory goal—a system that diminishes sentencing disparity—depends for its success upon judicial efforts to determine, and to base punishment upon, the real conduct that underlies the crime of conviction. That determination is particularly important where an act that meets the statutory definition can be committed in a host of different ways. Judges have long looked to real conduct when sentencing. Federal judges have long relied upon a presentence report, prepared by a probation officer, for information (often unavailable until after the trial) relevant to the manner in which the convicted offender committed the crime of conviction.

To engraft the Court's constitutional requirement onto the sentencing statutes would destroy the system. It would prevent a judge from relying upon a presentence report for factual information, relevant to sentencing, uncovered after the trial. In doing so, it would, even compared to pre-Guidelines sentencing, weaken the tie between a sentence and an offender's real conduct. It would thereby undermine the sentencing statute's basic aim of ensuring similar sentences for those who have committed similar crimes in similar ways. Several examples help illustrate the point. Imagine Smith and Jones, each of whom violates the Hobbs Act in very different ways. *See* 18 U.S.C. § 1951(a) (forbidding "obstructing, delaying, or affecting commerce or the movement of any article or commodity in commerce, extortion"). Smith threatens to injure a co-worker unless the co-worker advances him a few dollars from the interstate company's till; Jones, after similarly threatening the co-worker, causes far more harm by seeking far more money, by making certain that the co-worker's family is aware of the threat, by arranging for deliveries of dead animals to the co-worker's home to show he is serious, and so forth. The offenders' behavior is very different; the known harmful consequences of their actions are different; their punishments both before, and after, the Guidelines would have been different. But, under the dissenters' approach, unless prosecutors decide to charge more than the elements of the crime, the judge would have to impose similar punishments. Now imagine two former felons, Johnson and Jackson, each of whom engages in identical criminal behavior: threatening a bank teller with a gun, securing $50,000, and injuring an innocent bystander while fleeing the bank. Suppose prosecutors charge Johnson with one crime (say, illegal gun possession), and Jackson with another (say, bank robbery.) Before the Guidelines, a single judge faced with such similar real conduct would have been able (within statutory limits) to impose similar sentences upon the two similar offenders despite the different charges brought against them. The Guidelines themselves would ordinarily have required judges to sentence the two offenders similarly. But under the dissenters' system, in these circumstances the offenders likely would receive different punishments.

Third, the sentencing statutes, read to include the Court's Sixth Amendment requirement, would create a system far more complex than Congress could have intended. How would courts and counsel work with an indictment and a jury trial that involved not just whether a defendant robbed a bank but also how? Would the indictment have to allege, in addition to the elements of robbery, whether the defendant possessed a firearm, whether he brandished or discharged it, whether he threatened death, whether he caused bodily injury, whether any such injury was ordinary, serious, permanent or life threatening, whether he abducted or physically restrained anyone, whether any victim was unusually vulnerable, how much money was taken, and whether he was an organizer, leader, manager, or supervisor in a robbery gang? *See* USSG §§ 2B3.1, 3B1.1. If so, how could a defendant mount a defense against some or all such specific claims should he also try simultaneously to maintain that the Government's evidence failed to place him at the scene of the crime?

Plea bargaining would not significantly diminish the consequences of the Court's constitutional holding for the operation of the Guidelines. Rather, plea bargaining would make matters worse. Congress enacted the sentencing statutes in major part to achieve greater uniformity in sentencing, *i.e.,* to increase the likelihood that offenders who engage in similar conduct would receive similar sentences. The statutes reasonably assume that their efforts to move the trial-based sentencing process in the direction of greater sentencing uniformity would have a similar positive impact upon plea-bargained sentences, for plea bargaining takes place in the shadow of (*i.e.,* with an eye towards the hypothetical result of) a potential trial. That, too, is why Congress, understanding the realities of plea bargaining, authorized the Commission to promulgate policy statements that would assist sentencing judges in determining whether to reject a plea agreement after reading about the defendant's real conduct in a presentence report (and giving the offender an opportunity to challenge the report). This system has not worked perfectly; judges have often simply accepted an agreed-upon account of the conduct at issue. But compared to pre-existing law, the statutes try to move the system in the right direction, *i.e.,* toward greater sentencing uniformity. The Court's constitutional jury trial requirement, if patched onto the present Sentencing Act, would move the system backwards in respect both to tried and to plea-bargained cases. In tried cases, it would deprive the judge of the ability to use post-verdict-acquired real-conduct information; it would prohibit the judge from basing a sentence upon any conduct other than the conduct the prosecutor chose to charge; and it would put a defendant to a set of difficult strategic choices as to which prosecutorial claims he would contest. The sentence that would emerge in a case tried under such a system would likely reflect real conduct less completely, less accurately, and less often than did a pre-Guidelines, as well as a Guidelines, trial.

Because plea bargaining inevitably reflects estimates of what would happen at trial, plea bargaining under such a system would move in the wrong direction. In a sentencing system modified by the Court's constitutional requirement, plea bargaining would likely lead to sentences that gave greater weight, not to real conduct, but rather to the skill of counsel, the policies of the prosecutor, the caseload, and other factors that vary from place to place, defendant to defendant, and crime to crime. Compared to pre-Guidelines plea bargaining, plea bargaining of this kind would necessarily move federal sentencing in the direction of diminished, not increased, uniformity in sentencing. It would tend to defeat, not further, Congress' basic statutory goal.

Such a system would have particularly troubling consequences with respect to prosecutorial power. Until now, sentencing factors have come before the judge in the presentence report. But in a sentencing system with the Court's constitutional requirement engrafted onto it, any factor that a prosecutor chose not to charge at the plea negotiation would be placed beyond the reach of the judge. Prosecutors would thus exercise a power the Sentencing Act vested in judges: the power to decide, based on relevant information about the offense and the offender, which defendants merit heavier punishment. For these reasons, Congress, had it been faced with the constitutional jury trial requirement, likely would not have passed the same Sentencing Act. Hence the Act cannot remain valid in its entirety. Severance and excision are necessary.

We now turn to the question of which portions of the sentencing statute we must sever and excise as inconsistent with the Court's constitutional requirement. Although we believe that Congress would have preferred the total invalidation of the statute to the dissenters' remedial approach, we do not believe that the entire statute must be invalidated. Most of the statute is perfectly valid. We must sever and excise two specific statutory provisions: the provision that requires sentencing courts to impose a sentence within the applicable Guidelines range (in the absence of circumstances that justify a departure), *see* 18 U.S.C. § 3553(b)(1), and the provision that sets forth standards of review on appeal, including *de novo* review of departures from the applicable Guidelines range, *see* § 3742(e). With these two sections excised (and statutory cross-references to the two sections consequently invalidated), the remainder of the Act satisfies the Court's constitutional requirements. As the Court recognizes, the existence of § 3553(b)(1) is a necessary condition of the constitutional violation.

Without the "mandatory" provision, the Act nonetheless requires judges to take account of the Guidelines together with other sentencing goals. The Act still requires judges to consider the Guidelines "sentencing range established for an offense committed by the applicable category of defendant," the pertinent Sentencing Commission policy statements, the need to avoid unwarranted sentencing disparities, and the need to provide restitution to victims. And the Act nonetheless requires judges to impose sentences that reflect the seriousness of the offense, promote respect for the law, provide just punishment, afford adequate deterrence, protect the public, and effectively provide the defendant with needed educational or vocational training and medical care.

Despite the absence of § 3553(b)(1), the Act continues to provide for appeals from sentencing decisions (irrespective of whether the trial judge sentences within or outside the Guidelines range in the exercise of his discretionary power under § 3553(a)). We concede that the excision of § 3553(b)(1) requires the excision of a different, appeals-related section, namely § 3742(e), which sets forth standards of review on appeal. That section contains critical cross-references to the (now-excised) § 3553(b)(1) and consequently must be severed and excised for similar reasons.

Excision of § 3742(e), however, does not pose a critical problem for the handling of appeals. That is because a statute that does not explicitly set forth a standard of review may nonetheless do so implicitly. We infer appropriate review standards from related statutory language, the structure of the statute, and the "sound administration of justice." And in this instance those factors, in addition to the past two decades of appellate practice in cases involving departures, imply a practical standard of review already familiar to appellate courts: review for "unreasonableness." 18 U.S.C. § 3742(e)(3). The ball now lies in Congress' court. The National Legislature is equipped to devise and install, long-term, the sentencing system, compatible with the Constitution, that Congress judges best for the federal system of justice.

In respondent Booker's case, the District Court applied the Guidelines as written and imposed a sentence higher than the maximum authorized solely by the jury's verdict. The Court of Appeals held *Blakely* applicable to the Guidelines, concluded that Booker's sentence violated the Sixth Amendment, vacated the judgment of the District Court, and remanded for resentencing. We affirm the judgment of the Court of Appeals and remand the case. On remand, the District Court should impose a sentence in accordance with today's opinions.

[JUSTICE STEVENS dissented in part, arguing that the prosecution should be permitted to empanel juries to find "sentencing facts" that would increase a sentence above the maximum term of a presumptive range. JUSTICE SCALIA's dissenting opinion criticized the severance remedy, preferring a reasonableness standard.]

Points for Discussion

a. Appellate Advice for Prospective Trial Court Sentencing

For future cases, the circuits attempted to prescribe a sentencing method, after the mandatory nature of the Guidelines was determined unconstitutional:

> At this point, we can identify several essential aspects of *Booker* that concern the selection of sentences. First, the Guidelines are no longer mandatory. Second, the sentencing judge must consider the Guidelines and all of the other factors listed in section 3553(a). Third, consideration of the

Guidelines will normally require determination of the applicable Guidelines range, or at least identification of the arguably applicable ranges, and consideration of applicable policy statements. Fourth, the sentencing judge should decide, after considering the Guidelines and all the other factors set forth in section 3553(a), whether (i) to impose the sentence that would have been imposed under the Guidelines, i.e., a sentence within the applicable Guidelines range or within permissible departure authority, or (ii) to impose a non-Guidelines sentence. Fifth, the sentencing judge is entitled to find all the facts appropriate for determining either a Guidelines sentence or a non-Guidelines sentence.

United States v. Crosby, 397 F. 3d 103 (2d Cir. 2005).

b. What Is a "Reasonable" Sentence?

Justice Breyer's opinion (in part) in *Apprendi* held that the remedy for the constitutional violation was to make the Guidelines advisory and to replace *de novo* appellate review of sentences with a reasonableness standard of review. In *United States v. Fleming*, 397 F. 3d 95, 100 (2d Cir. 2005), the Second Circuit described how an appellate court would assess the reasonableness of a federal sentence:

The appellate function in this context should exhibit restraint, not micromanagement. In addition to their familiarity with the record, including the presentence report, district judges have discussed sentencing with a probation officer and gained an impression of a defendant from the entirety of the proceedings, including the defendant's opportunity for sentencing allocution. The appellate court proceeds only with the record. Although the brevity or length of a sentence can exceed the bounds of "reasonableness," we anticipate encountering such circumstances infrequently.

> **FYI**
>
> Given the predilection of many federal judges to adhere to the Guidelines, as well as the reluctance of other circuits to adhere to the principle of restraint espoused in the Second Circuit's decision in *Fleming* in reviewing sentences that depart from the Guidelines, Justice Breyer's fears that *Apprendi* meant the demise of the Sentencing Guidelines are not fully warranted.

In the pending case, the District Court sentenced a defendant who had served three sentences of imprisonment and was appearing for his third violation of a term of supervised release. Judge Gershon considered the current violations "massive." She noted that the Defendant had been given the benefit of a substantial departure for his cooperation in connection with his sentence on the prisoner assault charge. *See* U.S.S.G. § 7B1.4, comment. (n.4) ("Where the original sentence was the result of a downward departure (*e.g.,* as a reward for substantial assistance), an upward departure may be warranted."). She identified as the "primary purpose" of her sentence "the necessity for both punishment for Fleming's behavior and deterrence." The District Court's explanation was sufficient to facilitate appellate review. Under all the circumstances, we cannot say that the two-year sentence was unreasonable.

United States v. Haymond

139 S.Ct. 2369 (2019).

JUSTICE GORSUCH announced the judgment of the Court and delivered an opinion, in which JUSTICE GINSBURG, JUSTICE SOTOMAYOR, and JUSTICE KAGAN joined.

A jury found Andre Haymond guilty of possessing child pornography in violation of federal law. The law authorized a prison term of between zero and 10 years, and a period of supervised release of between 5 years and life. Because Haymond had no criminal history and was working to help support his mother who had suffered a stroke, the judge sentenced him to a prison term of 38 months, followed by 10 years of supervised release. After completing his prison sentence, an unannounced search of his computers and cellphone turned up 59 images that appeared to be child pornography. Based on that discovery, the government sought to revoke Mr. Haymond's supervised release and secure a new and additional prison sentence. A hearing followed before a district judge acting without a jury, and under a preponderance of the evidence rather than a reasonable doubt standard. The judge found it more likely than not that Mr. Haymond knowingly downloaded and possessed the remaining 13 images.

Under 18 U.S.C. § 3583(e)(3), enacted as part of the Sentencing Reform Act of 1984, a district judge who finds that a defendant has violated the conditions of his supervised release normally may (but is not required to) impose a new prison term up to the maximum period of supervised release authorized by statute for the defendant's original conviction, subject to certain limits. Under that provision, the judge would have been free to sentence Haymond to between zero and two additional years in prison. But, under § 3583(k), added to the Act in 2003 and amended in 2006, if a judge finds by a preponderance of the evidence that a defendant on supervised release committed one of several enumerated offenses, including the possession of child pornography, the judge must impose an additional prison term of at least five years and up to life without regard to the length of the prison term authorized for the defendant's initial crime of conviction. Because Haymond had committed an offense covered by § 3583(k), the judge felt bound to impose an additional prison term of at least five years. Were it not for § 3583(k)'s mandatory minimum, the judge added, he "probably would have sentenced in the range of two years or less." The Tenth Circuit concluded that § 3583(k) violated the Fifth and Sixth Amendments. We granted review.

Those who wrote our Constitution considered the right to trial by jury "the heart and lungs, the mainspring and the center wheel" of our liberties, without which "the body must die; the watch must run down; the government must become arbitrary." Letter from Clarendon to W. Pym (Jan. 27, 1766), in 1 PAPERS OF JOHN ADAMS 169 *. Taylor ed. 1977). Just as the right to vote sought to preserve the people's authority over their government's executive and legislative functions, the right to a jury trial sought to preserve the people's authority over its judicial functions. J. Adams, Diary Entry (Feb. 12, 1771), in 2 DIARY AND AUTOBIOGRAPHY OF JOHN ADAMS 3 (L. Butterfield ed. 1961). Toward that end, the Framers adopted the Sixth Amendment's promise that "in all criminal prosecutions the accused shall enjoy the right to a speedy and public trial, by an impartial jury." In the Fifth Amendment, they added that no one may be deprived of liberty without "due process of law." Together, these pillars of the Bill of Rights ensure that the government must prove to a jury every criminal charge beyond a reasonable doubt, an ancient rule that has "extended down centuries." *Apprendi v. New Jersey*, 530 U.S. 466, 477 (2000).

But when does a "criminal prosecution" arise implicating the right to trial by jury beyond a reasonable doubt? At the founding, a "prosecution" of an individual simply referred to "the manner of his formal accusation." 4 W. BLACKSTONE, COMMENTARIES ON THE LAWS OF ENGLAND 298 (1769). And the concept of a "crime" was a broad one linked to punishment, amounting to those "acts to which the law affixes punishment," or, stated differently, those "elements in the wrong upon which the punishment is based." 1 J. BISHOP, CRIMINAL PROCEDURE §§ 80, 84, pp. 51 (2d ed. 1872). Consistent with these understandings, juries in our constitutional order exercise supervisory authority over the judicial function by limiting the judge's power to punish. A judge's authority to issue a sentence derives from, and is limited by, the jury's factual findings of criminal conduct. In the early Republic, if an indictment or "accusation lacked any particular fact which the laws made essential to the punishment," it was treated as "no accusation" at all. 1 BISHOP § 87, at 55. And the "truth of every accusation" that was brought against a person had to "be confirmed by the unanimous suffrage of twelve of his equals and neighbours." 4 BLACKSTONE 343. It remains the case today that a jury must find beyond a reasonable doubt every fact "which the law makes essential to a punishment" that a judge might later seek to impose. *Blakely*, 542 U.S. at 304 (quoting 1 BISHOP § 87, at 55).

At common law, crimes tended to carry with them specific sanctions, and "once the facts of the offense were determined by the jury, the judge was meant simply to impose the prescribed sentence." *Alleyne v. United States*, 570 U.S. 99, 108 (2013) (plurality opinion). Even when judges did enjoy discretion to adjust a sentence based on judge-found aggravating or mitigating facts, they could not "swell the penalty above what the law had provided for the acts charged" and found by the jury. *Apprendi*, 530 U.S. at 519 (THOMAS, J., concurring). In time, legislatures adopted new laws allowing judges or parole boards to suspend part (parole) or all (probation) of a defendant's prescribed prison term and afford him a period of conditional liberty as an "act of grace," subject to revocation. But here the prison sentence a judge or parole board could impose for a parole or probation violation normally could not exceed the remaining balance of the term of imprisonment already authorized by the jury's verdict. So even these developments did not usually implicate the historic concerns of the Fifth and Sixth Amendments.

More recent legislative innovations have raised harder questions. In *Apprendi*, a jury convicted defendant of a gun crime that carried a maximum prison sentence of 10 years. But a judge sought to impose a longer sentence pursuant to a statute that authorized him to do so if he found, by a preponderance of the evidence, that the defendant had committed the crime with racial bias. *Apprendi* held this scheme unconstitutional: "Any fact that increases the penalty for a crime beyond the prescribed statutory maximum," this Court explained, "must be submitted to a jury, and proved beyond a reasonable doubt" or admitted by the defendant. Nor may a State evade this traditional restraint on the judicial power by simply calling the process of finding new facts and imposing a new punishment a judicial "sentencing enhancement." "The relevant inquiry is one not of form, but of effect—does the required judicial finding expose the defendant to a greater punishment than that authorized by the jury's guilty verdict?"

While "trial practices can change in the course of centuries and still remain true to the principles that emerged from the Framers' " design, *id.*, at 483, in the years since *Apprendi* this Court has not hesitated to strike down other innovations that fail to respect the jury's supervisory function. Still, these decisions left an important gap. In *Apprendi*, this Court recognized that "it is unconstitutional for a legislature to remove from the jury the assessment of facts that increase the prescribed range of penalties." By definition, a range of punishments includes not only a maximum but a minimum. Logically it would seem to follow that any facts necessary to increase a person's minimum punishment (the "floor") should be found by the jury no less than facts necessary to increase his maximum punishment (the "ceiling"). Before *Apprendi*, this Court had held that facts elevating the minimum punishment need not be proven to a jury beyond a reasonable doubt. Eventually, the Court confronted this anomaly in *Alleyne*. There, a jury convicted the defendant of a crime that ordinarily carried a sentence of five years to life in prison. But a separate statutory "sentencing enhancement" increased the mandatory minimum to seven years if the defendant "brandished" the gun. At sentencing, a judge found by a preponderance of the evidence that the defendant had indeed brandished a gun and imposed the mandatory minimum 7-year prison term. This Court reversed. Finding no basis in the original understanding of the Fifth and Sixth Amendments for *McMillan* and *Harris*, the Court expressly overruled those decisions and held that "the principle applied in *Apprendi* applies with equal force to facts increasing the mandatory minimum" as it does to facts increasing the statutory maximum penalty. Nor did it matter to *Alleyne*'s analysis that, even without the mandatory minimum, the trial judge would have been free to impose a 7-year sentence because it fell within the statutory sentencing range authorized by the jury's findings. Both the "floor" and "ceiling" of a sentencing range "define the legally prescribed penalty." Under our Constitution, when "a finding of fact alters the legally prescribed punishment so as to aggravate it" that finding must be made by a jury of the defendant's peers beyond a reasonable doubt. The Court observed that there can be little doubt that "elevating the low end of a sentencing range heightens the loss of liberty associated with the crime: The defendant's expected punishment has increased as a result of the narrowed range and the prosecution is empowered, by invoking the mandatory minimum, to require the judge to impose a higher punishment than he might wish."

Based on the facts reflected in the jury's verdict, Haymond faced a lawful prison term of between zero and 10 years under § 2252(b)(2). But a judge—acting without a jury and based only on a preponderance of the evidence—found that Mr. Haymond had engaged in additional conduct in violation of the terms of his supervised release. Under § 3583(k), that judicial factfinding triggered a new punishment in the form of a prison term of at least five years and up to life. So just like the facts the judge found at the defendant's sentencing hearing in *Alleyne*, the facts the judge found here increased "the legally prescribed range of allowable sentences" in violation of the Fifth and Sixth Amendments. In this case, that meant Haymond faced a minimum of five years in prison instead of as little as none. Nor did the absence of a jury's finding beyond a reasonable doubt only infringe the rights of the accused; it also divested the "people at large"—the men and women who make up a jury of a defendant's peers—of their constitutional authority to set the metes and bounds of judicially administered criminal punishments. *Blakely*, 542 U.S. at 306 (*quoting* Letter XV by the Federal Farmer (Jan. 18, 1788), in 2 THE COMPLETE ANTI-FEDERALIST 315, 320 (H. Storing ed. 1981)).

The government [points] out that *Alleyne* arose in a different procedural posture. The trial judge applied a "sentencing enhancement" based on his own factual findings at the defendant's initial sentencing hearing; meanwhile, Mr. Haymond received his new punishment from a judge at a hearing to consider the revocation of his term of supervised release. Our precedents, *Apprendi*, *Blakely*, and *Alleyne*, have repeatedly rejected efforts to dodge the demands of the Fifth and Sixth Amendments by the simple expedient of relabeling a criminal prosecution a "sentencing enhancement." Any "increase in a defendant's authorized punishment contingent on the finding of a fact" requires a jury and proof beyond a reasonable doubt "no matter" what the government chooses to call the exercise. *Ring*, 536 U.S. at 602. To be sure, founding-era prosecutions traditionally ended at final judgment. But at that time, generally, "questions of guilt and punishment both were resolved in a single proceeding" subject to the Fifth and Sixth Amendment's demands. Over time, procedures changed as legislatures sometimes bifurcated criminal prosecutions into separate trial and penalty phases. But none of these developments licensed judges to sentence individuals to punishments beyond the legal limits fixed by the facts found in the jury's verdict. To the contrary, we recognized in *Apprendi* and *Alleyne*, a "criminal prosecution" continues and the defendant remains an "accused" with all the rights provided by the Sixth Amendment, until a final sentence is imposed. This Court has recognized that supervised release punishments arise from and are "treated as part of the penalty for the initial offense." *Johnson v. United States*, 529 U.S. 694, 700 (2000). The defendant receives a term of supervised release thanks to his initial offense, and whether that release is later revoked or sustained, it constitutes a part of the final sentence. As at the initial sentencing hearing, that does not mean a jury must find every fact in a revocation hearing that may affect the judge's exercise of discretion within the range of punishments authorized by the jury's verdict. But it does mean that a jury must find any facts that trigger a new mandatory minimum prison term. This logic respects not only our precedents, but the original meaning of the jury trial right they seek to protect. The Constitution seeks to safeguard the people's control over the business of judicial punishments by ensuring that any accusation triggering a new and additional punishment is proven to the satisfaction of a jury beyond a reasonable doubt. By contrast, the view the government and dissent espouse would demote the jury from its historic role as "circuitbreaker in the State's machinery of justice," to "low-level gatekeeping," *Booker*, 543 U.S. at 230.

The government next suggests that Mr. Haymond's sentence for violating the terms of his supervised release was fully authorized by the jury's verdict. After all, the government observes, on the strength of the jury's findings the judge was entitled to impose as punishment a term of supervised release; and that term of supervised release was from the outset always subject to the possibility of judicial revocation and § 3583(k)'s mandatory prison sentence. Presto: Sixth Amendment problem solved. But in *Apprendi* and *Alleyne*, the jury's verdict triggered a statute that authorized a judge at sentencing to increase the defendant's term of imprisonment based on judge-found facts. This Court had no difficulty rejecting that scheme as an impermissible evasion of the historic rule that a jury must find all of the facts necessary to authorize a judicial punishment. And what was true there can be no less true here: A mandatory minimum 5-year sentence that comes into play only as a result of additional judicial factual findings by a preponderance of the evidence cannot stand. Treating Haymond's 5-year mandatory minimum prison term as part of his sentence for his original offense makes clear that it mirrors the unconstitutional sentencing enhancement in Alleyne. If the government were right, a jury's conviction on one crime would permit perpetual supervised release and allow the government to evade the need for another jury trial on any other offense the defendant might commit, no matter how grave the punishment. Instead of seeking a revocation of supervised release, the government could have chosen to prosecute Haymond under a statute mandating a term of imprisonment of 10 to 20 years for repeat child-pornography offenders. 18 U.S.C. § 2252(b)(2). But why bother with an old-fashioned jury trial for a new crime when a quick-and-easy "supervised release revocation hearing" before a judge carries a penalty of five years to life? This displacement of the jury's traditional supervisory role exemplifies the "Framers' fears that the jury right could be lost not only by gross denial, but by erosion." *Apprendi*, 530 U.S. at 483.

The government and the dissent accept that "postjudgment sentence-administration proceedings" can implicate the Fifth and Sixth Amendments. But, they contend, § 3583(k)'s supervised release revocation procedures are practically identical to historic parole and probation revocation procedures. Because those other procedures have usually been understood to comport with the Fifth and Sixth Amendments, they submit, § 3583(k)'s procedures must do so as well. But this argument rests on a faulty premise, overlooking a critical difference between § 3583(k) and traditional parole and probation practices. Before the Sentencing Reform Act of 1984, a federal criminal defendant could serve as little as a third of his assigned prison term before becoming eligible for release on parole. Or he might avoid prison altogether in favor of probation. If the defendant violated the terms of his parole or probation, a judge could send him to prison. But either way, a judge generally could sentence the defendant to serve only the remaining prison term authorized by statute for his original crime of conviction. A judge could not imprison a defendant for any longer than the jury's factual findings allowed—a result entirely harmonious with the Fifth and Sixth Amendments. All that changed beginning in 1984. That year, Congress overhauled federal sentencing procedures to make prison terms more determinate and abolish the practice of parole. Now, when a defendant is sentenced to prison he generally must serve the great bulk of his assigned term. In parole's place, Congress established the system of supervised release. But "unlike parole," supervised release wasn't introduced to replace a portion of the defendant's prison term, only to encourage rehabilitation after the completion of his prison term.

Where parole and probation violations generally exposed a defendant only to the remaining prison term authorized for his crime of conviction, as found by a unanimous jury under the reasonable doubt standard, supervised release violations subject to § 3583(k) can expose a defendant to an additional mandatory minimum prison term well beyond that authorized by the jury's verdict—all based on facts found by a judge by a mere preponderance of the evidence. § 3583(k) differs in this critical respect not only from parole and probation; it also represents a break from the supervised release practices that Congress authorized in § 3583(e)(3) and that govern most federal criminal proceedings today. Unlike those procedures, § 3583(k) alone requires a substantial increase in the minimum sentence to which a defendant may be exposed based only on judge-found facts under a preponderance standard. As we explained in *Alleyne* and reaffirm today, that offends the Fifth and Sixth Amendments' ancient protections.

The dissent suggests an analogy between revocation under § 3583(k) and prison disciplinary procedures that do not normally require the involvement of a jury. But while the Sixth Amendment surely does not require a jury to find every fact that the government relies on to adjust the terms of a prisoner's confinement (say, by reducing his privileges as a sanction for violating the prison rules), that does not mean the government can send a free man back to prison for years based on judge-found facts. A tradition of summary process in prison, where administrators face the "formidable task" of controlling a large group of potentially unruly prisoners, does not necessarily support the use of such summary process outside the prison walls. We have long held that prison regulations that impinge on the constitutional rights inmates would enjoy outside of prison must be "reasonably related to legitimate penological interests" in managing the prison. *Turner v. Safley,* 482 U.S. 78 (1987).

Our decision is limited to § 3583(k) and the *Alleyne* problem raised by its 5-year mandatory minimum term of imprisonment. Section § 3583(e), which governs supervised release revocation proceedings generally, does not contain any similar mandatory minimum triggered by judge-found facts. In most cases (including this one), combining a defendant's initial and post-revocation sentences under § 3583(e) will not yield a term of imprisonment that exceeds the statutory maximum term of imprisonment the jury has authorized for the original crime of conviction. That's because "courts rarely sentence defendants to the statutory maxima." *United States v. Caso,* 723 F.3d 215, 225 (C.A.D.C. 2013). So even if § 3583(e)(3) turns out to raise Sixth Amendment issues in a small set of cases, it hardly follows that "as a practical matter supervised-release revocation proceedings cannot be held" or that "the whole idea of supervised release must fall." Indeed, the vast majority of supervised release revocation proceedings under subsection (e)(3) would likely be unaffected.

Having concluded that the application of § 3583(k)'s mandatory minimum in this case violated Haymond's right to trial by jury, we face the question of remedy. The Tenth Circuit declared the last two sentences of § 3583(k) "unconstitutional and unenforceable." We believe the wiser course lies in returning the case to the court of appeals for the opportunity to address the government's remedial argument.

The judgment of the court of appeals is vacated, and the case is remanded for further proceedings.

It is so ordered.

JUSTICE BREYER, concurring in the judgment.

This specific provision of the supervised-release statute is unconstitutional. The consequences for violation of conditions of supervised release under § 3583(e), which governs most revocations, are limited by the severity of the original crime of conviction, not the conduct that results in revocation. § 3583(k)'s effects more closely resemble the punishment of new criminal offenses, but without granting a defendant the rights, including the jury right, that attend a new criminal prosecution.

In an ordinary criminal prosecution, a jury must find facts that trigger a mandatory minimum prison term.

JUSTICE ALITO, with whom THE CHIEF JUSTICE, JUSTICE THOMAS, and JUSTICE KAVANAUGH join, dissenting.

The replacement of parole with supervised release changed the form of federal sentences but not their substance. A pre-SRA sentence of nine years' imprisonment meant three years of certain confinement and six years of possible confinement depending on the defendant's conduct in the outside world after release from prison. Such a sentence is the substantive equivalent of a post-SRA sentence of three years' imprisonment followed by six years of supervised release. In both situations, the period of certain confinement (three years) and the maximum term of possible confinement (nine years) are the same. If anything, the defendant in the post-SRA case is treated more favorably because he is guaranteed release from prison after three years; his release is not dependent on a decision by a parole board. None of this matters in respondent's case because the sum of his original sentence (38 months) and the additional time imposed for violating supervised release (60 months) is less than 120 months. Under that rule, a term of supervised release could never be ordered for a defendant who is sentenced to the statutory maximum term of imprisonment, and only a short period of supervised release could be ordered for a defendant sentenced to a term of imprisonment that is close to the statutory maximum.

A parole revocation proceeding was not a "criminal prosecution" within the meaning of the Sixth Amendment, and revocation did not result in a new sentence. When a prisoner was paroled, the Executive was simply exercising the authority conferred by law to grant the defendant a conditional release from serving part of the sentence imposed after a guilty verdict. *Mistretta v. United States*, 488 U.S. 361 (1989). Supervised release is not fundamentally different and therefore should not be treated any differently for Sixth Amendment purposes. When a jury finds a federal defendant guilty of violating a particular criminal statute, the maximum period of confinement authorized is the maximum term of imprisonment plus the maximum term of supervised release. If a prisoner does not end up spending this full period in confinement, that is because service of part of the period is excused due to satisfactory conduct during the period of supervised release. At a parole revocation hearing, a parolee did not have a right to a jury trial. Neither the Confrontation Clause nor the formal rules of evidence had to be followed. Due process did not require proof beyond a reasonable doubt as is necessary at trial, and the Double Jeopardy Clause did not apply.

Respondent was no longer the "accused" while he served his term of supervised release. He was formerly the accused when he was duly indicted and tried for possession of child pornography. But after a jury convicted him and authorized the judge to sentence him to terms of imprisonment and supervised release, respondent was transformed into the convicted. And his status remained the same while he served his sentences, including during the proceeding to determine whether he had adhered to the conditions attached to the term of supervised release that was permitted by law and thus implicitly authorized by the jury's verdict. The principal reason for assigning a penalty to a supervised-release violation is not that the violative act is a crime (indeed, under other provisions in § 3583, the act need not even be criminal); rather, the violative act is a breach of trust. It makes little sense to treat respondent as the accused—i.e., one charged with a crime—when he has been charged not with a crime, but with violating the terms of a jury-authorized sentence that flowed from his original conviction. Prior to and at the time of the adoption of the Sixth Amendment, convicted criminals were often released on bonds and recognizances that made their continued liberty contingent on good behavior. If a prisoner released on such a bond did not exhibit good behavior, the courts had discretion to forfeit the bond (a loss of property) or to turn the individual over to the sheriff (a loss of liberty) until new conditions could be arranged. There is no evidence that there was a right to a jury trial at such proceedings, and the plurality does not even attempt to prove otherwise.

Point for Discussion

Plea Bargaining & Sentencing Guidelines

In *Hughes v. United States*, 138 S.Ct. 1765 (2018), Hughes was indicted on drug and gun charges for his participation in a conspiracy to distribute methamphetamine. The Government and Hughes negotiated a Type-C plea agreement whereby he agreed to plead guilty to two of the four charges (conspiracy to distribute methamphetamine and being a felon in possession of a gun); and in exchange the Government agreed to dismiss the other two charges and refrain from filing an information giving formal notification to the District Court of his prior drug felonies. The agreement stipulated that Hughes would receive a sentence of 180 months, but did not refer to any particular Guidelines range. Hughes entered his guilty plea in 2013. At the sentencing hearing, the court stated that it had "considered the plea agreement and the sentencing guidelines, particularly the provisions of § 3553(a)," and that it would "accept and approve the binding plea agreement." The court calculated Hughes' Guidelines range as 188 to 235 months in prison. When it imposed the agreed 180-month sentence the court reiterated that it was "a reasonable sentence in this case compatible with the advisory United States Sentencing Guidelines but in accordance with the mandatory matters the Court is required to consider in ultimately determining a sentence." Less than two months after the District Court sentenced Hughes, the Sentencing Commission adopted amendment 782 to the Guidelines. The amendment reduced the base offense level by two levels for most drug offenses. The Commission later made amendment 782 retroactive for defendants who already had been sentenced under the higher offense levels. Under the revised Guidelines, Hughes' sentencing range is

151 to 188 months—about three to four years lower than the range in effect when he was sentenced. Hughes filed a motion for a reduced sentence under § 3582(c)(2). The Court held that Hughes was entitled to a reduced sentence.

Executive Summary

Sentencing Alternatives. A variety of sentencing alternatives to incarceration are available for courts.

Proportionality Challenge. A criminal sentence may be challenged as grossly disproportionate under the Eighth Amendment.

Sentence Enhancements. Enhanced sentences for defendants with prior felony convictions may lead to a life sentence.

Due Process. Sentencing procedures must satisfy due process regarding judicial consideration of all information relating to the defendant.

Jury Requirements. Any factual information, other than a prior conviction where there was a right to a jury trial, that increases the maximum penalty for a crime must be charged in the charging instrument, submitted to a jury, and proved beyond a reasonable doubt.

Major Themes

a. **Judicial Discretion**—Unlike pretrial and trial procedures, sentencing procedures are bound by few rules as long as the sentencing judge stays within the sentencing range set by the legislature. A judge can take into account and consider almost any information, whether admissible or proven, which is relevant to punishment.

b. **Constitutional Limits**—The constitutional limits on a judge's sentencing discretion are the Eighth Amendment's prohibition on excessive punishment, which is practically no limit at all as it sets an extremely high bar for a showing of disproportionate punishment, and the right to a jury trial for the finding of facts that would increase a defendant's maximum sentencing exposure, which, unlike the Eighth Amendment, has led to substantial changes in sentencing procedures.

For More Information

- RUSSELL L. WEAVER, JOHN M. BURKOFF, CATHERINE HANCOCK & STEVEN I. FRIEDLAND, PRINCIPLES OF CRIMINAL PROCEDURE Ch. 19 (8th ed. 2024).

- DEBORAH YOUNG, PETER HOFFMAN, SIGMUND POPKO & THOMAS HUTCHINSON, FEDERAL SENTENCING LAW & PRACTICE (2014 ed.).

- Douglas A. Berman, Sentencing Law and Policy, sentencing.typepad.com.

- WAYNE R. LaFAVE, JEROLD H. ISRAEL, NANCY J. KING & ORIN S. KERR, CRIMINAL PROCEDURE (5th ed. 2009).

Test Your Knowledge

To assess your understanding of the material in this chapter, click here to take a quiz.

CHAPTER 21

Double Jeopardy

No person shall "be subject for the same offense to be twice put in jeopardy of life or limb."

—U.S. Const., Amdt. V

"At its core, the Double Jeopardy Clause reflects the wisdom of the founding generation that one's acquittal or conviction should satisfy the law."

—Justice Sonia Sotomayor, *Blueford v. Arkansas*, 566 U.S. 599, 609 (2012) (dissenting opinion)

A. Introduction

Double jeopardy doctrine is layered, complex, and nuanced, contrary to its compact reference in the Constitution. The initial determination that must be made is whether double jeopardy analysis is triggered by a particular charge or proceeding, especially a second or succeeding one. The clause applies only in criminal cases. It does not prevent criminal and civil punishment for the same offense—just no multiple criminal punishments. What constitutes a civil or criminal penalty is sometimes fuzzy, and the interpretation of legislative intent generally controls.

Make the Connection

Kansas v. Hendricks, 521 U.S. 346 (1997) involved the involuntary civil commitment of sex offenders following the completion of a criminal sentence. Justice Thomas distinguished what constituted civil from criminal actions, mostly deferring to the treatment accorded the action by the legislature that created it. Find it at the Oyez Project: http://www.oyez.org/cases/1990-1999/1996/1996_95_1649.

The Clause offers three primary protections: 1) against a second prosecution for the same offense following an acquittal; 2) against a second prosecution for the same offense after a conviction; and 3) against multiple punishments for the same offense.

Defendants usually have both federal and state constitutional protections against being placed in jeopardy twice for the same offense. While the Fifth Amendment double jeopardy protection directly applies only to the federal government, it also applies to the states through the Fourteenth Amendment. *Benton v. Maryland*, 395 U.S. 784 (1969).

Because the debates of the constitutional framers offer little guidance regarding the intended scope of double jeopardy protection, the courts have interpreted the clause in light of their understanding of its underlying purposes. The essence of the prohibition against double jeopardy is not that a defendant may incur a greater risk of being found guilty in a second trial than in a first trial, or that a second trial may be conducted prejudicially, but rather that the defendant cannot be forced to face the risk of conviction for an offense regarding which defendant previously has been placed on trial and in jeopardy.

Double jeopardy notions also are predicated on the principle that the United States has two sovereigns or governments. Thus, the state government can prosecute the same conduct that has been prosecuted in federal court, *Bartkus v. Illinois*, 359 U.S. 121 (1959), and, vice versa, the federal government can prosecute the same conduct that has been prosecuted in state court, *Abbate v. United States*, 359 U.S. 187 (1959), pursuant to federalism principles. These types of successive prosecutions generally do not violate double jeopardy principles.

A successful double jeopardy claim will bar a succeeding trial on an indictment or information or any punitive government act considered criminal in nature based on the first trial. The objection to the succeeding government action may be raised by a motion to dismiss at any time before trial. Although a failure to raise the objection before the second adjudication may operate as a waiver, it can be raised for the first time in a reviewing court if the double jeopardy issue can be decided as a matter of law on the facts established by the record. *Menna v. New York*, 423 U.S. 61 (1975).

One of the requirements for the attachment of jeopardy is that the court hearing the case must have jurisdiction. When the court exceeds its jurisdiction, a conviction is void, and there is no bar to a new trial.

"Wild Bill" Hickok and Double Jeopardy?

What does James Butler "Wild Bill" Hickok have to do with double jeopardy analysis? On August 2, 1876, Jack McCall murdered the 39-year-old Hickok by shooting him from behind because of a perceived slight. The shooting occurred in the town of Deadwood, South Dakota, where McCall was subsequently held for trial by local townspeople in an impromptu setting and acquitted. Shortly thereafter, McCall left for the Wyoming territory, where he was captured and returned to Yankton, in the South Dakota Territory where he was again tried for the murder. The South Dakota court found that there was no violation of double jeopardy as a result of the second trial because Deadwood, where the first trial occurred, was technically in what was then known as Indian territory, while the South Dakota trial was in U.S. territory. At the second trial, McCall was convicted and later executed. Go online: "This Day In History," The History Channel, http://www.history. com/this-day-in-history/wild-bill-hickok-is-murdered. Absent a facial jurisdictional defect, the original adjudication is presumed to have been within the court's jurisdiction. Likewise, a prior conviction or acquittal procured by the defendant to defraud the government of an opportunity to attain the proper sentence does not bar a new prosecution.

Take Note

The doctrine of dual sovereignty does not prohibit multiple prosecutions for the same offense by courts of different sovereigns. *See, e.g., Heath v. Alabama*, 474 U.S. 82 (1985) (successive prosecutions by different states permissible); *Bartkus v. People of State of Illinois*, 359 U.S. 121 (1959) (successive state and federal trials for same offense permissible). On the other hand, the dual sovereignty theory does not apply to state and municipal prosecutions for the same act because the state and the municipality are regarded as the same sovereign, regardless of how the state chooses to classify its governmental subunits: the subunits derive their power to exist from the sovereign. *See, e.g., Waller v. Florida*, 397 U.S. 387 (1970) (successive prosecutions for same offense based upon violations of state statute and local ordinance prohibited by double jeopardy).

B. Does Jeopardy Attach?

Double jeopardy bars a second prosecution only if jeopardy attached in the original proceeding. In a jury trial, jeopardy generally attaches when the jury is sworn. *Crist v. Bretz*, 437 U.S. 28 (1978). But what if there is no jury? If a case is tried before a judge, jeopardy attaches when the first witness is sworn. Jeopardy also attaches when the trial court accepts a guilty plea. Conversely, withdrawal of a guilty plea involves a waiver of double jeopardy protections against trial on the charge in the indictment or information. If a case is dismissed or terminated prior to the attachment of jeopardy, jeopardy has not attached, and the defendant may have to respond to the same criminal charges in subsequent proceedings.

FYI

The initial question in analyzing double jeopardy questions is whether jeopardy has attached. If jeopardy attached in the original proceeding, it leads to the question of whether the government is precluded from retrying or recharging the defendant. There are judicially-created standards for when jeopardy attaches and when a retrial is permitted. The standard for jeopardy attaching is singular and falls along a bright line. Courts generally find that if the jury has been empanelled and sworn, jeopardy has attached. The standard for the second question, whether a retrial is permitted, is a more nuanced matter.

Martinez v. Illinois

572 U.S. 833 (2014).

PER CURIAM.

The State of Illinois indicted Martinez in August 2006 on charges of aggravated battery and mob action against Avery Binion and Demarco Scott. But Martinez's trial date did not arrive for nearly four years. On July 20, 2009, the State moved to continue an August 3 trial date because it had not located the complaining witnesses, Binion and Scott. The State subpoenaed both men four days later, and the court rescheduled Martinez's trial to September 28. But the State sought another continuance, shortly before that date, because it still had not found Binion and Scott. The court rescheduled the trial to November 9, and the State reissued subpoenas. Still, the witnesses could not be located. On the morning of May 17, [the reset trial date], Binion and Scott were again nowhere to be found. At 8:30, when the trial was set to begin, the State asked for a brief continuance. The court offered to delay swearing the jurors until a complete jury had been empanelled and told the State that it could at that point either have the jury sworn or move to dismiss its case. When Binion and Scott still had not shown up after the jury was chosen, the court offered to call the other cases on its docket so as to delay swearing the jury a bit longer. But when all these delays had run out, Binion and Scott were still nowhere in sight. The State filed a written motion for a continuance, arguing that it was "unable to proceed" without Binion and Scott. The court denied that motion:

It's Latin to Me

What is "*per curiam*"? This means, in Latin, "by the court." A *per curiam* decision is issued by the court instead of specific judges. *Per curiam* decisions have been criticized as forsaking the tradition of individual accountability of judges, who usually sign the written opinions.

> "The case began on July 7, 2006. In two months we will be embarking upon half a decade of pending a Class 3 felony. Avery Binion, Jr., and Demarco Scott are well known in Elgin, both are convicted felons. One would believe that the Elgin Police Department would know their whereabouts. They were ordered to be in court today. The Court will issue body writs for both of these gentlemen.

> "In addition, the State's list of witnesses indicates twelve witnesses. Excluding Mr. Scott and Mr. Binion, that's ten witnesses. The Court would anticipate it would take every bit of today and most of tomorrow to get through ten witnesses. By then the People may have had a chance to execute the arrest warrant body writs for these two gentlemen. The Court will deny the

motion for continuance. I will swear the jury in 15, 20 minutes. Perhaps you might want to send the police out to find these two gentlemen."

After a brief recess, the court offered to delay the start of the trial for several more hours if the continuance would "be of any help" to the State. But when the State made clear that Binion and Scott's "whereabouts" remained "unknown," the court concluded that the delay "would be a further waste of time." The following colloquy ensued:

"THE COURT: It's a quarter to eleven and Binion and Scott have not appeared on their own will, so I'm going to bring the jury in now then to swear them.

"The Prosecutor: Okay. Your Honor, may I approach briefly?

"THE COURT: Yes.

"The Prosecutor: Your Honor, just so your Honor is aware, I know that it's the process to bring them in and swear them in; however, the State will not be participating in the trial. I wanted to let you know that.

"THE COURT: Very well. We'll see how that works."

The jury was then sworn. After instructing the jury, the court directed the State to proceed with its opening statement. The prosecutor demurred: "Your Honor, respectfully, the State is not participating in this case." After the defense waived its opening statement, the court directed the State to call its first witness. Again, the prosecutor demurred: "Respectfully, your Honor, the State is not participating in this matter." The defense then moved for a judgment of acquittal. The Court replied, "The Court will grant the motion for a directed finding and dismiss the charges."

The State appealed, arguing that the trial court should have granted a continuance. Martinez responded that the State's appeal was improper because he had been acquitted. The Illinois Appellate Court sided with the State, holding that jeopardy had never attached and that the trial court had erred in failing to grant a continuance. The Illinois Supreme Court granted review on the jeopardy issue and affirmed. It began by recognizing that "generally, in cases of a jury trial, jeopardy attaches when a jury is empanelled and sworn, as that is the point when the defendant is 'put to trial before the trier of the facts.' " But it reasoned that " 'rigid, mechanical' rules" should not govern the inquiry into whether jeopardy has attached. Rather, it opined, the relevant question is whether a defendant was "subjected to the hazards of trial and possible conviction." Here, the court concluded, Martinez "was never at risk of conviction"—and jeopardy therefore did not attach—because "the State indicated it would not participate prior to the jury being sworn Because Martinez was not placed in jeopardy," the court held, the trial court's entry of directed verdicts of not guilty did not constitute true acquittals. Indeed, the court remarked, the trial court repeatedly referred to its action as a "dismissal" rather than an acquittal.

This case presents two issues. First, did jeopardy attach to Martinez? Second, if so, did the proceeding end in such a manner that the Double Jeopardy Clause bars his retrial? Our precedents clearly dictate an affirmative answer to each question. There are few if any rules of criminal procedure clearer than the rule that "jeopardy attaches when the jury is empanelled and sworn." *Crist*, 437 U.S., at 35; *see also United States v. Martin Linen Supply Co.*, 430 U.S. 564 (1977). As *Crist* explains, "the precise point at which jeopardy attaches in a jury trial might have been open to argument before this Court's decision in *Downum v. United States*, 372 U.S. 734 (1963)," but *Downum* put any such argument to rest: Its holding "necessarily pinpointed the stage in a jury trial when jeopardy attaches, and it has since been understood as explicit authority for the proposition that jeopardy attaches when the jury is empanelled and sworn." The Illinois Supreme Court misread our precedents in suggesting that the swearing of the jury is anything other than a bright line at which jeopardy attaches. The Illinois Supreme Court's error was consequential, for it introduced confusion into what we have consistently treated as a bright-line rule. We have never suggested the exception perceived by the Illinois Supreme Court—that jeopardy may not have attached where, under the circumstances of a particular case, the defendant was not genuinely at risk of conviction. Martinez was subjected to jeopardy because the jury in his case was sworn.

The remaining question is whether the jeopardy ended in such a manner that the defendant may not be retried. There is no doubt that Martinez's jeopardy ended in a manner that bars his retrial: The trial court acquitted him of the charged offenses. "Perhaps the most fundamental rule in the history of double jeopardy jurisprudence has been that 'a verdict of acquittal could not be reviewed without putting a defendant twice in jeopardy, and thereby violating the Constitution.' " *Martin Linen*, 97 S.Ct. 1349. "Our cases have defined an acquittal to encompass any ruling that the prosecution's proof is insufficient to establish criminal liability for an offense." *Evans v. Michigan*, 133 S.Ct. 1069, 1074. After the State declined to present evidence against Martinez, his counsel moved for "directed findings of not guilty to both counts," and the court "granted the motion for a directed finding." That is a textbook acquittal: a finding that the State's evidence cannot support a conviction.

The Illinois Supreme Court thought otherwise. The court went on to "note that, in directing findings of not guilty," the trial court "referred to its action as a 'dismissal' rather than an acquittal." Under our precedents, that is immaterial. As in *Evans* and *Martin Linen*, the trial court's action was an acquittal because the court "acted on its view that the prosecution had failed to prove its case." *Evans*, 133 S.Ct., at 1078; Because Martinez was acquitted, the State cannot retry him. The functional rule adopted by the Illinois Supreme Court is not necessary to avoid unfairness to prosecutors or to the public. The Court repeatedly delayed that act to give the State additional time to find its witnesses. It had previously granted the State a number of continuances for the same purpose. Critically, the court told the State on the day of trial that it could "move to dismiss its case" before the jury was sworn. Had the State accepted that invitation, the Double Jeopardy Clause would not have barred it from recharging Martinez. Instead, the State participated in the selection of jurors and did not ask for dismissal before the jury was sworn. The State knew, or should have known, that an acquittal forever bars the retrial of the defendant when it occurs after jeopardy has attached. The Illinois Supreme Court's holding is understandable, given the significant consequence of the State's mistake, but it runs directly counter to our precedents and to the protection conferred by the Double Jeopardy Clause.

The judgment of the Supreme Court of Illinois is reversed, and the case is remanded for further proceedings not inconsistent with this opinion.

It is so ordered.

Hypo: *Does Jeopardy Attach?*

In the following situations, does double jeopardy apply? 1) Jonas is prosecuted for drug possession in his car. After obtaining a conviction, the prosecution sought forfeiture of the car under a civil forfeiture statute. *See Porter v. Coughlin*, 421 F.3d 141, 146 (2d Cir. 2005); 2) Felix is charged with failing to report transporting over $10,000 into the United States and making false statements to U.S. officials about the same. Felix is prosecuted for these acts under separate statutory provisions and given cumulative punishments. *See United States v. Woodward*, 469 U.S. 105 (1985) (*per curiam*); 3) Alberto is given consecutive sentences for possession with intent to distribute heroin and contempt of court, after committing a drug offense while on pre-trial release and after the court commanded the defendant to not commit any unlawful act. *See United States v. Henry*, 519 F.3d 68 (1st Cir. 2008).

While jurisdictions have allowed separate prosecutions for the same conduct in federal and state courts under the rationale that the federal and state governments are dual sovereigns, the doctrine is not beyond reproach. In the following case, the court found that a double jeopardy violation occurred when the state initiated prosecution for conduct the defendant had been prosecuted for and convicted of by the federal government.

State v. Robertson

2017 UT 27 (2017).

CHIEF JUSTICE DURRANT, opinion of the Court:

Defendant D. Chris Robertson was prosecuted and convicted by the federal government for possession of child pornography. The State of Utah subsequently charged him with twenty counts of sexual exploitation of a minor based on the same conduct. Robertson argues that Utah Code section 76–1–404 prohibits this subsequent state prosecution. That statute provides that—if a defendant's conduct establishes the commission of one or more offenses within the concurrent jurisdiction of this state and of another jurisdiction, federal or state, the prosecution in the other jurisdiction is a bar to a subsequent prosecution in this state if the former prosecution resulted in an acquittal, conviction, or termination of prosecution, and the subsequent prosecution is for the same offense or offenses. Under our previous interpretation of section 404, this statute would present no barrier to the current prosecution. In *State v. Franklin*, we concluded that section 404 incorporated the—dual sovereignty doctrine, a principle of double jeopardy law that permits subsequent prosecutions by different sovereigns, even for the—same offense. The court of appeals affirmed Robertson's convictions in accordance with this precedent.

Today, we reassess that earlier interpretation and conclude that it was wrongly decided. We overrule *Franklin* and hold that the legislature's use of the phrase—same offense in section 404 is an express rejection of the dual sovereignty doctrine. Properly interpreted, section 404 requires courts to employ only the *Blockburger-Sosa* test for determining whether two offenses are the—same offense. Under this test, two offenses are not the same if each requires proof of an element that the other does not. Because the charged offenses in his federal and state prosecutions are the—same offense under the *Blockburger-Sosa* test, and because the record shows that the state prosecution is based on the same conduct that was at issue in the initial federal prosecution, section 404, properly interpreted, prohibits the State from prosecuting Robertson. We therefore reverse the decision of the court of appeals.

[Defendant was found to have possessed child pornography and subsequently prosecuted and convicted in federal court. He was then charged in state court based on the same conduct.] We hold that—Same Offense in Section 76–1–404 Incorporates the *Blockburger-Sosa* Test but Rejects the Dual Sovereignty Doctrine, Overruling in Part *State v. Franklin* Having clarified the precedential value of *State v. Franklin*, we discuss whether our decision therein that Utah Code section 76–1–404 incorporated the dual sovereignty doctrine should be overruled. We do not overrule a prior interpretation of a statute lightly, out of respect for the *stare decisis* principles of—predictability and fairness. But even though overruling a prior interpretation of a statute is an—unusual step,—the doctrine of *stare decisis* is neither mechanical nor rigid as it relates to courts of last resort. We believe that the portion of *Franklin* interpreting the—same offense language of section 404 to incorporate the dual sovereignty doctrine should be overruled. Same offense, as used in section 404, should be interpreted as incorporating only the *Blockburger-Sosa* test and section 404 is an express rejection of the dual sovereignty doctrine.

We consider at least three factors when deciding whether to overrule a prior interpretation of a statute:—the plausibility of the existing interpretation given the statute, the degree to which that interpretation has worked itself into the state of the law, and the strength of the arguments for changing that interpretation. We discuss each factor and conclude that they weigh in favor of overruling *State v. Franklin*. Prior to deciding whether section 76–1–404 prohibits the State's prosecution of Robertson, we first address the State's argument that our decision to overrule *Franklin* should be applied prospectively. We conclude that section 404 is a substantive statute that creates an affirmative defense to avoid the dual sovereignty exception to double jeopardy and that the new interpretation announced in this case applies retroactively to cases on direct and collateral review. We apply our interpretation of section 404 to the facts of this case. We hold that the federal and state offenses are the same under *Blockburger-Sosa* and that the record shows that federal prosecution encompassed all of the conduct for which Robertson was subsequently prosecuted by the State.

The State Premised Its Prosecution of Robertson on Conduct that Constitutes the "Same Offense" for Which He Was Prosecuted Federally As discussed, Utah Code section 76–1–404 prohibits the State from prosecuting a defendant if the defendant has already been prosecuted in another jurisdiction provided two conditions are satisfied. First, the former prosecution must result in an acquittal, conviction, or termination of prosecution. The parties agree that Robertson's federal prosecution satisfies this requirement. The second condition requires that—the subsequent prosecution be for the same offense or offenses. It is on this condition that the parties disagree—whether the Utah prosecution can be said to be for the—same offense as the federal prosecution. Determining whether a prior foreign prosecution qualifies as the—same offense under section 404 requires a two-part analysis: whether the offenses for which an individual was prosecuted are the same under *Blockburger-Sosa* and, if they are, whether the conduct establishing the offenses is also the same. In this case, there is no dispute that the two relevant statutes are the—same offense under a *Blockburger-Sosa* analysis.

We do not reach the question whether there may be some exception to the general rule we adopt today. Robertson was charged in both federal and state court with possession of child pornography. The federal child pornography statute, 18 U.S.C. section 2252A(a)(5)(B) (2008), criminalizes the—knowing possession of—any material that contains an image of child pornography that has been transported using any means or facility of interstate or foreign commerce. The equivalent Utah statute, section 76–5a–3 (2004), makes it a crime to—knowingly possess. child pornography.

The definition of—child pornography is the same under both statutes. And though the federal offense requires proof of an element that the Utah statute does not—interstate commerce—the Utah statute does not require proof of an element that the federal statute does not. Thus, the Utah crime is a lesser-included offense of the federal offense, rendering it the—same offense under a *Blockburger-Sosa* analysis.

The language of the statute unmistakably operates as a legislative rejection of the dual sovereignty doctrine. We accordingly clarify today that section 404's use of—same offense encompasses only the *Blockburger-Sosa* test. Thus, section 404 prohibits Utah prosecutions following prosecutions in other jurisdictions so long as the offenses are the same under *Blockburger-Sosa* and the conduct at issue in the previous prosecution encompasses the same conduct at issue in the Utah prosecution, as informed by the relevant units of prosecution and evidence. The interpretation of section 404 that we announce today applies retroactively and, applying this interpretation to Robertson's case, we hold that section 404 prohibited the State from prosecuting him after the federal prosecution. We therefore reverse the court of appeals' decision.

C. Dual Sovereign Principle Applied

In *Denezpi v. United States*, 142 S.Ct. 1838 (2022), the U.S. prosecuted defendant under federal law (the Major Crimes Act) after having separately enforced the law of the Ute Mountain Ute Bribe. Defendant challenged the Major Crimes Act prosecution as a violation of Double Jeopardy. The government claimed that the dual sovereign principle applied. The twist is that the Ute court was a CFR ("Court of Indian Offenses") court, meaning that it was established by the Commissioner of Indian Affairs under the Code of Federal Regulation to adjudicate rules violations for the tribe. CFR judges (referred to as "magistrates") are appointed by the Department of Indian Affairs Assistant Secretary for Indian Affairs subject to a confirmation vote by the governing body of the tribe. The Assistant Secretary may remove magistrates for cause of his own accord or upon the recommendation of the tribal governing body. Federal regulations set forth a list of offenses that may be enforced in C.F.R. court, and a tribe's governing body may enact ordinances that, when approved by the Assistant Secretary, are enforceable in C.F.R. court and supersede conflicting federal regulations. Two members of the Navajo tribe were prosecuted for assault and battery, in violation of 6 Ute Mountain Ute Code § 2 (1988), terroristic threats, in violation of 25 C.F.R. § 11.402, and false imprisonment, in violation of 25 C.F.R. § 11.404. Defendant pleaded guilty to the assault and battery charge, and the prosecutor dismissed the other charges. Six months later, a federal grand jury in the District of Colorado indicted Denezpi on one count of aggravated sexual abuse in Indian country under the federal Major Crimes Act. The Court rejected Denezpi's motion to dismiss the indictment which was based on the Double Jeopardy Clause. The Court held that "a law is defined by the sovereign that makes it, expressing the interests that the sovereign wishes to vindicate. Because the sovereign source of a law is an inherent and distinctive feature of the law itself, an offense defined by one sovereign is necessarily a different offense from that of another sovereign." Thus, "the two offenses can be separately prosecuted without offending the Double Jeopardy Clause—even if they have identical elements and could not be separately prosecuted if enacted by a single sovereign. Before Europeans arrived on this continent, tribes 'were self-governing sovereign political communities' with 'the inherent power to prescribe laws for their members and to punish infractions of those laws. When a tribe enacts criminal laws, "it does so as part of its retained sovereignty and not as an arm of the Federal Government.' Thus, Wheeler's prosecution for a tribal offense did not bar his later prosecution for a federal offense. An offense defined by one sovereign is different from an offense defined by another. Thus, even if Denezpi is right that the Federal Government prosecuted his tribal offense, the Clause did not bar the Federal Government from prosecuting him under the Major Crimes Act too." Justice Gorsuch, joined by two other justices, dissented: "Unlike a tribal court operated by a Native American Tribe pursuant to its inherent sovereign authority, the Court of Indian Offenses is 'part of the Federal Government.' It is a creature of the Department of the Interior."

Gamble v. United States

<u>139 S.Ct. 1960 (2019)</u>.

JUSTICE ALITO delivered the opinion of the Court.

Our double jeopardy case law is complex, but the Clause means that those acquitted or convicted of a particular "offence" cannot be tried a second time for the same "offence." But what does the Clause mean by an "offence"? We have long held that a crime under one sovereign's laws is not "the same offence" as a crime under the laws of another sovereign. Under this "dual-sovereignty" doctrine, a State may prosecute a defendant under state law even if the Federal Government has prosecuted him for the same conduct under a federal statute. Or the reverse may happen. Terance Gamble, convicted by Alabama for possessing a firearm as a felon, now faces prosecution by the United States under its felon-in-possession law. Gamble asks us to overrule the dual-sovereignty doctrine. He contends that it departs from the founding-era understanding of the right enshrined by the Double Jeopardy Clause. We affirm that precedent.

A local police officer in Mobile, Alabama, pulled Gamble over for a damaged headlight. Smelling marijuana, the officer searched Gamble's car, where he found a loaded 9-mm handgun. Since Gamble had been convicted of second-degree robbery, his possession of the handgun violated an Alabama law providing that no one convicted of "a crime of violence" "shall own a firearm or have one in his or her possession." Ala. Code § 13A–11–72(a) (2015). After Gamble pleaded guilty to this state offense, federal prosecutors indicted him for the same instance of possession under a federal law—one forbidding those convicted of "a crime punishable by imprisonment for a term exceeding one year to ship or transport in interstate or foreign commerce, or possess in or affecting commerce, any firearm or ammunition." 18 U.S.C. § 922(g)(1).

Gamble moved to dismiss on one ground: The federal indictment was for "the same offence" as the one in his state conviction and thus exposed him to double jeopardy. Because this Court has long held that two offenses "are *not* the 'same offence'" for double jeopardy purposes if "prosecuted by different sovereigns," *Heath v. Alabama*, 474 U.S. 82, 92 (1985), the District Court denied Gamble's motion to dismiss. Gamble then pleaded guilty to the federal offense while preserving his right to challenge the denial of his motion to dismiss on double jeopardy grounds. The Eleventh Circuit affirmed. We granted certiorari.

Gamble contends that the Double Jeopardy Clause must forbid successive prosecutions by different sovereigns because that is what the founding-era common law did. Although the dual-sovereignty rule is often dubbed an "exception" to the double jeopardy right, it is not an exception at all. "The language of the Clause protects individuals from being twice put in jeopardy 'for the same *offence*,' not for the same *conduct* or *actions*," *Grady v. Corbin*, 495 U.S. 508, 529 (1990). As originally understood, an "offence" is defined by a law, and each law is defined by a sovereign. So where there are two sovereigns, there are two laws, and two "offences."

The first Congress, working on an earlier draft that would have banned "more than one trial or one punishment for the same offence," voted down a proposal to add "by any law of the United States." 1 Annals of Cong. 753 (1789). In rejecting this addition, Gamble surmises, Congress must have intended to bar successive prosecutions regardless of the sovereign bringing the charge. The private intent behind a drafter's rejection of one version of a text is shoddy evidence of the public meaning of an altogether different text. We see no reason to abandon the sovereign-specific reading of the phrase "same offence," from which the dual-sovereignty rule immediately follows.

Fidelity to the Double Jeopardy Clause's text does more than honor the formal difference between two distinct criminal codes. It honors the substantive differences between the interests that two sovereigns can have in punishing the same act. This principle comes into still sharper relief when we consider a prosecution for crimes committed abroad. A crime against two sovereigns constitutes two offenses because each sovereign has an interest to vindicate. We cemented that foundation 70 years after the last of those antebellum cases, in a decision upholding a federal prosecution that followed one by a State. *See United States v. Lanza*, 260 U.S. 377 (1922). For decades more, we applied our precedent without qualm or quibble.

The dissents contend that our dual-sovereignty rule errs in treating the Federal and State *Governments* as two separate sovereigns when in fact sovereignty belongs to the people. Yes, our Constitution rests on the principle that the people are sovereign, but that does not mean that they have conferred all the attributes of sovereignty on a single government. Instead, the people, by adopting the Constitution, "split the atom of sovereignty." *Alden v. Maine*, 527 U.S. 706, 751 (1999). "When the original States declared their independence, they claimed the powers inherent in sovereignty. The Constitution limited but did not abolish the sovereign powers of the States, which retained 'a residuary and inviolable sovereignty.' The Federalist No. 39, p. 245 ©. Rossiter ed. 1961). Thus, both the Federal Government and the States wield sovereign powers, and that is why our system of government is said to be one of 'dual sovereignty.' *Gregory v. Ashcroft*, 501 U.S. 452 (1991)." *Murphy v. National Collegiate Athletic Assn.*, 138 S.Ct. 1461 (2018).

It is true that the Republic is "ONE WHOLE." But there is a difference between the whole and a single part, and that difference underlies decisions as foundational to our legal system as *McCulloch v. Maryland*, 4 Wheat. 316, 4 L.Ed. 579 (1819). There, in terms so directly relevant as to seem presciently tailored to answer this very objection, Chief Justice Marshall distinguished precisely between "the people of a State" and "the people of all the States," between the "sovereignty which the people of a single state possess" and the sovereign powers "conferred by the people of the United States on the government of the Union," and thus between "the action of a part" and "the action of the whole." In short, *McCulloch*'s famous holding that a State may not tax the national bank rested on a recognition that the States and the Nation have different "interests" and "rights." The United States is a *federal* republic; it is not, contrary to Justice GORSUCH's suggestion, a unitary state like the United Kingdom.

Gamble and the dissents suggest that because the division of federal and state power was meant to promote liberty, it cannot support a rule that exposes Gamble to a second sentence. This argument fundamentally misunderstands the governmental structure established by our Constitution. Our federal system advances individual liberty in many ways. Among other things, it limits the powers of the Federal Government and protects certain basic liberties from infringement. But because the powers of the Federal Government and the States often overlap, allowing both to regulate often results in two layers of regulation. Taxation is an example that comes immediately to mind. It is not at all uncommon for the Federal Government to permit activities that a State chooses to forbid or heavily restrict—for example, gambling and the sale of alcohol. And a State may choose to legalize an activity that federal law prohibits, such as the sale of marijuana. So while our system of federalism is fundamental to the protection of liberty, it does not always maximize individual liberty at the expense of other interests. It is thus quite extraordinary to say that the venerable dual-sovereignty doctrine represents a "desecration" of federalism.

Gamble claims that our precedent contradicts the common-law rights that the Double Jeopardy Clause was originally understood to engraft onto the Constitution—rights stemming from the "common-law pleas of *auterfoits acquit* [former acquittal] and *auterfoits convict* [former conviction]." *Grady*, 495 U.S. at 530 (Scalia, J., dissenting). These pleas were treated as "reasons why the prisoner ought not to answer an indictment at all, nor put himself upon his trial for the crime alleged." 4 W. BLACKSTONE, COMMENTARIES ON THE LAWS OF ENGLAND 335 (1773) (Blackstone). Gamble argues that those who ratified the Fifth Amendment understood these common-law principles (which the Amendment constitutionalized) to bar a domestic prosecution following one by a foreign nation. For support, he appeals to early English and American cases and treatises. We have highlighted one hurdle to Gamble's reading: the sovereign-specific original meaning of "offence." But the doctrine of *stare decisis* is another obstacle. Here, Gamble's historical arguments must overcome *numerous* "major decisions of this Court" spanning *170 years*. Gamble's historical evidence must, at a minimum, be better than middling. It is not. The English cases are a muddle. Early state and federal cases are equivocal and downright harmful to Gamble's position. All told, this evidence does not establish that those who ratified the Fifth Amendment took it to bar successive prosecutions under different sovereigns' laws—much less do so with enough force to break a chain of precedent linking dozens of cases over 170 years.

Gamble's core claim is that early English cases reflect an established common-law rule barring domestic prosecution following a prosecution for the same act under a different sovereign's laws. But from the very dawn of the common law in medieval England until the adoption of the Fifth Amendment in 1791, there is not one reported decision barring a prosecution based on a prior trial under foreign law.

Gamble contends that the incorporation of the Double Jeopardy Clause should end the dual-sovereignty rule, but his analogy fails. The premises of the dual-sovereignty doctrine have survived incorporation intact. Incorporation meant that the States were now required to abide by this Court's interpretation of the Double Jeopardy Clause. But that interpretation has long included the dual-sovereignty doctrine, and there is no logical reason why incorporation should change it. The doctrine rests on the fact that only same-sovereign successive prosecutions are prosecutions for the "same offense," and that is just as true after incorporation as before.

Insofar as the expansion of the reach of federal criminal law has been questioned on constitutional rather than policy grounds, the argument has focused on whether Congress has overstepped its legislative powers under the Constitution. Eliminating the dual-sovereignty rule would do little to trim the reach of federal criminal law, and it would not even prevent many successive state and federal prosecutions for the same criminal conduct unless we also overruled the long-settled rule that an "offence" for double jeopardy purposes is defined by statutory elements, not by what might be described in a looser sense as a unit of criminal conduct. *See Blockburger v. United States*, 284 U.S. 299 (1932). Perhaps believing that two revolutionary assaults in the same case would be too much, Gamble has not asked us to overrule Blockburger along with the dual-sovereignty rule.

The judgment of the Court of Appeals for the Eleventh Circuit is affirmed.

It is so ordered.

JUSTICE THOMAS, concurring.

The founding generation foresaw very limited potential for overlapping criminal prosecutions by the States and the Federal Government. The Founders therefore had no reason to address the double jeopardy question that the Court resolves today. Given their understanding of Congress' limited criminal jurisdiction and the absence of an analogous dual-sovereign system in England, it is difficult to conclude that the People who ratified the Fifth Amendment understood it to prohibit prosecution by a State and the Federal Government for the same offense. We are not entitled to interpret the Constitution to align it with our personal sensibilities about "unjust" prosecutions.

JUSTICE GINSBURG, dissenting.

The Federal Government was able to multiply Gamble's time in prison because of the doctrine that, for double jeopardy purposes, identical criminal laws enacted by "separate sovereigns" are different "offences." An "offence," the argument runs, is the violation of a sovereign's law, the United States and each State are separate sovereigns, ergo successive state and federal prosecutions do not place a defendant in "jeopardy for the same offence." This "syllogism" is fatally flawed. The United States and its constituent States, unlike foreign nations, are "kindred systems," "parts of ONE WHOLE." The Federalist No. 82, p. 493 © Rossiter ed. 1961) (A. Hamilton). They compose one people, bound by an overriding Federal Constitution. The notion that the Federal Government and the States are separate sovereigns overlooks a basic tenet of our federal system. The doctrine treats *governments* as sovereign, with state power to prosecute carried over from years predating the Constitution. In the system established by the Federal Constitution, "ultimate sovereignty" resides in the *governed. Arizona State Legislature v. Arizona Independent Redistricting Comm'n*, 135 S.Ct. 2652 (2015). Insofar as a crime offends the "peace and dignity" of a sovereign, that "sovereign" is the people, the "original fountain of all legitimate authority," The Federalist No. 22, at 152 (A. Hamilton). States may be separate, but their populations are part of the people composing the United States.

The division of authority between the United States and the States was meant to operate as "a double security for the rights of the people." The Federalist No. 51, at 323 (J. Madison). The separate-sovereigns doctrine invokes federalism to withhold liberty. The Double Jeopardy Clause embodies a principle, "deeply ingrained" in our system of justice, "that the State with all its resources and power should not be allowed to make repeated attempts to convict an individual for an alleged offense, thereby subjecting him to embarrassment, expense and ordeal and compelling him to live in a continuing state of anxiety and insecurity, as well as enhancing the possibility that even though innocent he may be found guilty." *Green v. United States*, 355 U.S. 184, 187 (1957). From the standpoint of the individual who is being prosecuted," the liberty-denying potential of successive prosecutions, when Federal and State Governments prosecute in tandem, is the same as it is when either prosecutes twice.

Before incorporation, the separate-sovereigns doctrine had a certain logic: Without a carve-out for successive prosecutions by separate sovereigns, the Double Jeopardy Clause would have barred the Federal Government from prosecuting a defendant previously tried by a State, but would not have prevented a State from prosecuting a defendant previously tried by the Federal Government. Incorporation changed this. Operative against the States since 1969, when the Court decided *Benton v. Maryland*, 395 U.S. 784, the double jeopardy proscription now applies to the Federal Government and the States alike. The remaining office of the separate-sovereigns doctrine, then, is to enable federal and state prosecutors, proceeding one after the other, to expose defendants to double jeopardy. The Court regards incorporation as immaterial because application of the Double Jeopardy Clause to the States did not affect comprehension of the word "offence" to mean the violation of one sovereign's law. But the Court attributed a separate-sovereigns meaning to "offence" at least in part because the Double Jeopardy Clause did not apply to the States. Incorporation of the Clause should prompt the Court to consider the protection against double jeopardy from the defendant's perspective and to ask why each of two governments within the United States should be permitted to try a defendant once for the same offense when neither could try him or her twice.

The expansion of federal criminal law has exacerbated the problems created by the separate-sovereigns doctrine. In the last half century, federal criminal law has been extended pervasively into areas once left to the States. This new "age of 'cooperative federalism,' in which the Federal and State Governments are waging a united front against many types of criminal activity," provides new opportunities for federal and state prosecutors to "join together to take a second bite at the apple," *All Assets of G.P.S. Automotive*, 66 F. 3d at 498 (Calabresi, J., concurring). This situation might be less troublesome if successive prosecutions occurred only in "instances of peculiar enormity, or where the public safety demanded extraordinary rigor." *Fox*, 5 How. at 435. The run-of-the-mill felon-in-possession charges Gamble encountered indicate that, in practice, successive prosecutions are not limited to exceptional circumstances.

JUSTICE GORSUCH, dissenting.

This "separate sovereigns exception" to the bar against double jeopardy finds no meaningful support in the text of the Constitution, its original public meaning, structure, or history. Instead, the Constitution promises all Americans that they will never suffer double jeopardy. Mr. Gamble should win this case handily. Alabama prosecuted him for violating a state law that "prohibits a convicted felon from possessing a pistol" and sentenced him to a year in prison. But then the federal government, apparently displeased with the sentence, charged Mr. Gamble under 18 U.S.C. § 922(g)(1) with being a felon in possession of a firearm based on the same facts that gave rise to the state prosecution. Ultimately, a federal court sentenced him to 46 months in prison and three years of supervised release. Most any ordinary speaker of English would say that Mr. Gamble was tried twice for "the same offence," precisely what the Fifth Amendment prohibits.

As this Court explained long ago in *Blockburger v. United States*, "where the same act or transaction constitutes a violation of two distinct statutory provisions, the test to be applied to determine whether there are two offenses or only one, is whether each provision requires proof of a fact which the other does not." So if two laws demand proof of the same facts to secure a conviction, they constitute a single offense under our Constitution and a second trial is forbidden. That is exactly what we have here. That leaves the government and the Court to rest on the fact that distinct governmental entities, federal and state, enacted these identical laws. But the framers didn't conceive of the term "same offence" in some technical way as referring only to the same statute. The government insists that the separate sovereigns exception is compelled by the structure of our Constitution. But as Chief Justice Marshall explained, "the government of the Union is emphatically, and truly, a government of the people," and all sovereignty "emanates from them." *McCulloch v. Maryland*, 4 Wheat. 316, 404, 4 L.Ed. 579 (1819). Alexander Hamilton put the point this way: "The national and State systems are to be regarded" not as different sovereigns foreign to one another but "as ONE WHOLE." The Federalist No. 82, p. 494 ©. Rossiter ed. 1961). Under our Constitution, the federal and state governments are but two expressions of a single and sovereign people. When the "ONE WHOLE" people of the United States assigned different aspects of their sovereign power to the federal and state governments, they sought not to *multiply* governmental power but to *limit* it. "By denying any one government complete jurisdiction over all the concerns of public life, federalism protects the liberty of the individual from arbitrary power." *Bond v. United States*, 564 U.S. 211, 222 (2011). Today's Court invokes federalism not to protect individual liberty but to threaten it, allowing two governments to achieve together an objective denied to each. The separate sovereigns exception was wrong when it was invented, and it remains wrong today.

D. Double Jeopardy & Multiple Offenses

1. Generally

When the prosecution charges a defendant with multiple offenses, a double jeopardy issue might arise in determining whether the two charges are considered to be the "same offense." Thus, double jeopardy might arise not only in the traditional scenario involving successive prosecutions for related acts, but also in a single prosecution involving multiple offenses and punishments. A constitutional violation does not occur if the legislature intended to impose cumulative punishments for a single act that constitutes more than one crime. In *Missouri v. Hunter*, 459 U.S. 359 (1983), the Court held that "where a legislature specifically authorizes cumulative punishment under two statutes, the prosecutor may seek and the trial court or jury may impose cumulative punishment under such statutes in a single trial." *Hunter* held that to show legislative intent, the statutes defining the two offenses must require: 1) a "clearly expressed legislative intent" that supports the imposition of cumulative punishments; or 2) proof of different elements. Either the legislative history of the statute or the language or organization of a statute may reveal the legislative intent. "If the offenses are set forth in different statutes or in distinct sections of a statute, and each provision or section unambiguously sets forth punishment for its violation, then courts generally infer that Congress intended to authorize multiple punishments." *United States v. Gugino*, 860 F.2d 546, 549 (2d Cir.1988). In *Brown v. Ohio*, 432 U.S. 161 (1977), the Court suggested that the legislature may divide a continuous course of conduct into separate offenses, even for conduct which occurs within a very short period of time. *See, e.g.*, *Hennemeyer v. Commonwealth*, 580 S.W.2d 211 (Ky.1979), when the court held that six gunshots fired at police during a chase resulted in six different counts of wanton endangerment.

When the legislative intent to impose multiple charges or punishments is ambiguous, the test from *Blockburger v. United States*, 284 U.S. 299 (1932), governs whether multiple offenses and punishments in a single or successive prosecutions are constitutionally permissible. *Blockburger* held that two offenses do not constitute the same offense when *each* offense requires proof of elements that the other offense does not. The test may be satisfied despite substantial overlap in the evidence used to prove the offenses. In *United States v. Felix*, 503 U.S. 378 (1992), the Court held that an attempt to commit a substantive offense and a conspiracy to commit that offense are not the same offense for double jeopardy purposes even if they are based upon the same underlying facts. A conspiracy is distinct from the substantive offense that is the object of the conspiracy because the former requires proof of an agreement while the latter requires proof of an overt act.[1] On the other hand, two offenses *do* constitute the

---

[1]   When a single act affects multiple victims, different offenses are committed. If one person is killed and another is wounded by the same bullet, multiple criminal offenses have been committed. *See, e.g., Smith v. Commonwealth*, 734 S.W.2d 437 (Ky.1987).

same offense when only *one* of the offenses requires proof that the other offense does not. A lesser included offense is the same as the greater offense because by definition the greater offense includes all the elements of the lesser. Thus, multiple punishments following a single prosecution for both offenses are barred, in the absence of a clearly expressed legislative intent to the contrary.

Points for Discussion

a. Applying *Blockburger*

Applying the *Blockburger* test, the Court unanimously held that a charge of conspiracy to distribute controlled substances in violation of 21 U.S.C. § 846 is a lesser included offense of conducting a continuing criminal enterprise "in concert" with others in violation of 21 U.S.C. § 848 when the "in concert" element of the latter offense is based upon the same agreement as the conspiracy offense. *Rutledge v. United States*, 517 U.S. 292 (1996). Therefore, convictions of both charges in one trial violate double jeopardy, even when the trial court imposes concurrent life sentences. The Court remanded the case to the trial court to determine which conviction must be vacated.

b. The *Jeffers* Case

In *Jeffers v. United States*, 432 U.S. 137 (1977), a plurality of the Court found: "If the defendant expressly asks for separate trials on the greater and the lesser offenses, or, in connection with his opposition to trial together, fails to raise the issue that one offense might be a lesser included offense of the other, an exception to the same offense rule emerges. Although a defendant is normally entitled to have charges on a greater and a lesser offense resolved in one proceeding, there is no violation of the Double Jeopardy Clause when he elects to have the two offenses tried separately and persuades the trial court to honor his election."

Hypo 1: *Multiple & Same Offenses*

In each of the following examples, identify whether the multiple offenses charged in one indictment, and arising from the same transaction, constitute the "same offense" under *Hunter* or *Blockburger/Dixon*. In essence, could each listed offense have been committed, regardless of whether the other listed offense was committed? Use the applicable criminal law of your jurisdiction. The prosecutor charged: 1) Basil with rape and kidnapping arising from the same event; 2) Betty with wanton murder and driving while under the influence of controlled substances, based on the same course of conduct; 3) Larry with theft by deception and forgery. He entered into a CD burner rental agreement. The CD burner was valued at approximately $150. Larry forged the name of "Earl Wheeler," his cousin, on the rental agreement. After the CD burner was not returned pursuant to the rental agreement, theft by deception and forgery charges were brought against Larry; 4) Otis with DUI and attempted murder. Barney was on bike patrol in front of the Mayberry Hotel at 3 a.m., when he heard tires squealing. He rode to the back of the parking lot where he saw Otis driving a white F-10 truck with its headlights off. Otis was speeding to the back of a van several times as the van was leaving the parking lot. Otis then turned the F-10 truck in the direction of Barney, who told him twice to stop. As Barney pedaled his bike away from the truck, the truck hit the bike's back tire, spinning the bike around as Barney jumped off and hit the ground.

Food for Thought

Defendant was charged with manslaughter, the jury was empanelled, and heard the evidence. However, before they retired to consider its verdict, the jury saw a "menacing-looking man" in the courtroom. The jury reached a verdict which was not announced because jurors stated that they were frightened by the man. Nevertheless, the jury stated that its verdict was unaffected by the man's presence. Because of the situation, the judge declared a mistrial and sealed the verdict (which was "not guilty"). Does double jeopardy preclude the prosecution from trying defendant a second time? Did the jury have other options other than declaring a mistrial and sealing the verdict? If so, what were they? *See Gouveia v. Espinda*, 926 F.3d 1102 (9th Cir. 2019).

Hypo 2: *DUI-Related Offenses*

Defendant is charged with vehicular homicide for driving under the influence. Defendant is acquitted. Subsequently, defendant is charged with DUI based on the same facts. Would it violate the double jeopardy clause to try defendant for DUI after his acquittal for vehicular homicide? *See Reyna-Abarca v. People*, 2017 Co. 15, 390 P.3d 816 (Colo. 2017).

FYI

In another part of the Double Jeopardy universe lies *United States v. Faulkner*, 793 F.3d 752 (7th Cir. 2015), in which defendant pled guilty to charges under a 2011 indictment and received an enhanced sentence based on conduct used to bring another indictment in 2013. The Court found that the new indictment did not constitute multiple punishments, either on the facts or as a matter of law, and thus did not violate Double Jeopardy precepts. The court relied on *Witte v. United States*, 515 U.S. 389 (1995): "The Supreme Court has held that the "use of evidence of related criminal conduct to enhance a defendant's sentence for a separate crime within the authorized statutory limits does not constitute punishment for that conduct within the meaning of the Double Jeopardy Clause." *Witte*, 515 U.S. at 399. Thus, for purposes of the Double Jeopardy Clause, any use the judge made of evidence of Faulkner's involvement with controlled substances, gangs, and violence did not constitute "punishment" for that conduct, and thus a later conviction on the basis of that conduct does not violate the Clause."

Hypo 3: *Child Pornography Offenses*

Defendant is charged with and convicted of running a child-exploitation enterprise. He is also charged, based on the same facts, with conspiracy to distribute child pornography and conspiracy to sexually exploit a child. Are these three offenses considered to be a single offense, or can they be separately prosecuted and punished? *See United States v. Gries*, 877 F.3d 255 (7th Cir. 2017).

2. Collateral Estoppel & the Relitigation of Facts

As previously discussed, when there is a single criminal transaction or activity, it may be divided into multiple statutory crimes. If the prosecution chooses to divide the offenses into separate prosecutions or to bring the charges successively rather than simultaneously, an acquittal on one offense may preclude a trial on the other offense under the doctrine of collateral estoppel, also known as issue preclusion. This doctrine provides that determination of a factual issue in a defendant's favor at one proceeding may estop the prosecution from disputing the fact in another proceeding against the same defendant. Thus, when different offenses are charged and double jeopardy would normally not bar a second prosecution, collateral estoppel may, in effect, bar the second trial when a fact previously found in the defendant's favor is necessary to the second conviction.

For collateral estoppel to apply, the defendant must be contesting relitigation of an issue of ultimate fact previously determined in that defendant's favor by a valid and final judgment. The second prosecution must involve the same parties as the first trial. A defendant cannot estop the prosecution from relitigating a fact found against the prosecution in a proceeding against a different defendant. In *Standefer v. United States*, 447 U.S. 10 (1980), a unanimous Court held that one defendant's acquittal on a bribery charge did not preclude a later prosecution of another defendant for aiding and abetting the same bribery. Second, the fact finder must have "actually and certainly" determined the issue of fact in the earlier proceeding. For example, in *Schiro v. Farley*, 510 U.S. 222 (1994), a homicide case, the jury was given ten possible verdicts

Take Note

Collateral estoppel and *res judicata* are cousins—doctrines that prevent retrials. They have different focuses, however, on what is precluded from retrial, and differ in their elements. Collateral estoppel is about retrying facts while *res judicata* is about retrying legal claims. Collateral estoppel prevents the relitigation of an ultimate fact that has been necessarily and actually litigated, with a resolution, generally against the same party. *Res judicata* prevents a party from splitting and retrying claims subject to a final judgment on the merits in successive actions. Both doctrines also apply in the civil domain and are often taught in a Civil Procedure course.

and returned a verdict on only one of the verdict sheets, convicting the defendant for rape felony murder. Defendant claimed that the state was collaterally estopped from showing intentional killing (one of the other verdict sheet possibilities) as an aggravated factor supporting a death sentence. The Court held that "failure to return a verdict does not have collateral estoppel effect unless the record establishes that the issue was actually and necessarily decided in the defendant's favor."

The most difficult problem in applying collateral estoppel is ascertaining what facts were established in the earlier case. Because juries render general rather than special verdicts in most criminal cases, a determination of which facts support the verdict requires careful analysis of the trial record. Only those fact determinations essential to the first decision are conclusive in later proceedings. Not only must a court be able to determine that the fact issue was litigated in defendant's first trial, but also the nature of the reason for acquitting defendant in the earlier trial determines whether collateral estoppel applies in the current case. For example, assume that Donna Defendant is charged with assaults against two victims at the same time and place, but the offenses are not joined. If Donna is acquitted at the first trial for assaulting Victim #1 because there is doubt as to whether she was present at the time of the assaults, her acquittal acts as a collateral estoppel defense to the second assault charge. On the other hand, if the acquittal at the first trial resulted from doubt about whether Donna actually assaulted Victim #1, the prosecutor can still try to prove that Donna assaulted Victim #2.

Bravo-Fernandez v. United States

580 U.S. 5 (2016).

JUSTICE GINSBURG delivered the opinion of the Court.

This case concerns the issue-preclusion component of the Double Jeopardy Clause. In criminal prosecutions, as in civil litigation, the issue-preclusion principle means that "when an issue of ultimate fact has once been determined by a valid and final judgment, that issue cannot again be litigated between the same parties in any future lawsuit." *Ashe v. Swenson*, 397 U.S. 436, 443 (1970). Does issue preclusion apply when a jury returns inconsistent verdicts, convicting on one count and acquitting on another count, where both counts turn on the very same issue of ultimate fact? In such a case, this Court has held, both verdicts stand. The Government is barred by the Double Jeopardy Clause from challenging the acquittal, *see Green v. United States*, 355 U.S. 184 (1957), but because the verdicts are rationally irreconcilable, the acquittal gains no preclusive effect, *United States v. Powell*, 469 U.S. 57 (1984). Does issue preclusion attend a jury's acquittal verdict if the same jury in the same proceeding fails to reach a verdict on a different count turning on the same critical issue? This Court has answered yes, in those circumstances, the acquittal has preclusive force. *Yeager v. United States*, 557 U.S. 110 (2009). As "there is no way to decipher what a hung count represents," we reasoned, a jury's failure to decide "has no place in the issue-preclusion analysis." *Ibid.*

In the case before us, the jury returned irreconcilably inconsistent verdicts of conviction and acquittal. Without more, *Powell* would control. There could be no retrial of charges that yielded acquittals but, in view of the inconsistent verdicts, the acquittals would have no issue-preclusive effect on charges that yielded convictions. In this case, unlike *Powell*, the guilty verdicts were vacated on appeal because of error in the judge's instructions unrelated to the verdicts' inconsistency. Petitioners urge that, just as a jury's failure to decide has no place in issue-preclusion analysis, so vacated guilty verdicts should not figure in that analysis.

We hold otherwise. One cannot know from the jury's report why it returned no verdict. "A host of reasons" could account for a jury's failure to decide—"sharp disagreement, confusion about the issues, exhaustion after a long trial, to name but a few." *Yeager*, 557 U.S., at 121. But actual inconsistency in a jury's verdicts is a reality; vacatur of a conviction for unrelated legal error does not reconcile the jury's inconsistent returns. We therefore bracket this case with *Powell*, not *Yeager*, and affirm the judgment of the Court of Appeals, which held that issue preclusion does not apply when verdict inconsistency renders unanswerable "what the jury necessarily decided."

The doctrine of claim preclusion instructs that a final judgment on the merits "forecloses successive litigation of the very same claim." *New Hampshire v. Maine*, 532 U.S. 742, 748 (2001) The doctrine serves to "avoid multiple suits on identical entitlements or obligations between the same parties." 18 C. WRIGHT, A. MILLER, & E. COOPER, FEDERAL PRACTICE AND PROCEDURE § 4402, p. 9 (2d ed. 2002). Long operative in civil litigation, claim preclusion is also essential to the Constitution's prohibition against successive criminal prosecutions. No person, the Double Jeopardy Clause states, shall be "subject for the same offense to be twice put in jeopardy of life or limb." Amdt. 5. The Clause "protects against a second prosecution for the same offense after conviction"; as well, "it protects against a second prosecution for the same offense after acquittal." *North Carolina v. Pearce*, 395 U.S. 711, 717 (1969). "A verdict of acquittal in our justice system is final," the last word on a criminal charge, and therefore operates as "a bar to a subsequent prosecution for the same offense." *Green v. United States*, 355 U.S. 184, 188 (1957).

The allied doctrine of issue preclusion ordinarily bars relitigation of an issue of fact or law raised and necessarily resolved by a prior judgment. It applies in both civil and criminal proceedings, with an important distinction. In civil litigation, where issue preclusion and its ramifications first developed, the availability of appellate review is a key factor. In significant part, preclusion doctrine is premised on "an underlying confidence that the result achieved in the initial litigation was substantially correct." *Standefer v. United States*, 447 U.S. 10, 23 (1980). "In the absence of appellate review," we have observed, "such confidence is often unwarranted." *Standefer*, 447 U.S., at 23.

In civil suits, inability to obtain review is exceptional; it occurs typically when the controversy has become moot. In criminal cases, only one side (the defendant) has recourse to an appeal from an adverse judgment on the merits. The Government "cannot secure appellate review" of an acquittal, even one "based upon an egregiously erroneous foundation," *Arizona v. Washington*, 434 U.S. 497, 503 (1978). Juries enjoy an "unreviewable power to return a verdict of not guilty for impermissible reasons," for "the Government is precluded from appealing or otherwise upsetting such an acquittal by the Constitution's Double Jeopardy Clause." *United States v. Powell*, 469 U.S. 57, 63 (1984). The absence of appellate review of acquittals, we have cautioned, calls for guarded application of preclusion doctrine in criminal cases. *See Standefer*, 447 U.S., at 22. Particularly where it appears that a jury's verdict is the result of compromise, compassion, lenity, or misunderstanding of the governing law, the Government's inability to gain review "strongly militates against giving an acquittal issue preclusive effect." *Id.*, at 23.

This case requires us to determine whether an appellate court's *vacatur* of a conviction alters issue-preclusion analysis under the Double Jeopardy Clause. Three prior decisions guide our disposition. This Court first interpreted the Double Jeopardy Clause to incorporate the principle of issue preclusion in *Ashe v. Swenson*, 397 U.S. 436 (1970). *Ashe* involved a robbery of six poker players by a group of masked men. Ashe was charged with robbing one of the players, but a jury acquitted him "due to insufficient evidence." The State then tried Ashe again, this time for robbing another of the poker players. Aided by "substantially stronger" testimony from "witnesses who were for the most part the same," the State secured a conviction. We held that the second prosecution violated the Double Jeopardy Clause. Because the sole issue in dispute in the first trial was whether Ashe had been one of the robbers, the jury's acquittal verdict precluded the State from trying to convince a different jury of that very same fact in a second trial. *Ashe* explained that issue preclusion in criminal cases must be applied with "realism and rationality." To identify what a jury in a previous trial necessarily decided, a court must "examine the record of a prior proceeding, taking into account the pleadings, evidence, charge, and other relevant matter." This inquiry "must be set in a practical frame and viewed with an eye to all the circumstances of the proceedings." "The burden is on the defendant to demonstrate that the issue whose relitigation he seeks to foreclose was actually decided" by a prior jury's verdict of acquittal. *Schiro v. Farley*, 510 U.S. 222, 233 (1994).

In *United States v. Powell*, 469 U.S. 57, we held that a defendant cannot meet this burden when the same jury returns irreconcilably inconsistent verdicts on the question she seeks to shield from reconsideration. *Powell*'s starting point was our holding in *Dunn v. United States*, 284 U.S. 390 (1932), that a criminal defendant may not attack a jury's finding of guilt on one count as inconsistent with the jury's verdict of acquittal on another count. *Dunn* stated no exceptions to this rule, and after *Dunn* the Court had several times "alluded to the rule as an established principle," Nevertheless, several Courts of Appeals had "recognized exceptions," and Powell sought an exception for the verdicts of guilt she faced. At trial, a jury had acquitted Powell of various substantive drug charges but convicted her of using a telephone in "causing and facilitating" those same offenses. She appealed, arguing that "the verdicts were inconsistent, and that she therefore was entitled to reversal of the telephone facilitation convictions." Issue preclusion, she maintained, barred "acceptance of the guilty verdicts" on the auxiliary offenses because the same jury had acquitted her of the predicate felonies. Rejecting Powell's argument, we noted that issue preclusion is "predicated on the assumption that the jury acted rationally." When a jury returns irreconcilably inconsistent verdicts, we said, one can glean no more than that "either in the acquittal or the conviction the jury did not speak their real conclusions." Although it is impossible to discern which verdict the jurors arrived at rationally, "that does not show that they were not convinced of the defendant's guilt." In the event of inconsistent verdicts, it is just as likely that "the jury, convinced of guilt, properly reached its conclusion on one count, and then through mistake, compromise, or lenity, arrived at an inconsistent conclusion on the related offense." Because a court would be at a loss to know which verdict the jury "really meant," principles of issue preclusion are not useful, for they are "predicated on the assumption that the jury acted rationally and found certain facts in reaching its verdict." Holding that the acquittals had no preclusive effect on the counts of conviction, we reaffirmed *Dunn*'s rule, under which both Powell's convictions and her acquittals, albeit inconsistent, remained undisturbed.

Finally, in *Yeager v. United States*, 557 U.S. 110 (2009), we clarified that *Powell*'s holding on inconsistent verdicts does not extend to an apparent inconsistency between a jury's verdict of acquittal on one count and its inability to reach a verdict on another count. Yeager was tried on charges of fraud and insider trading. The jury acquitted him of the fraud offenses, which the Court of Appeals concluded must have reflected a finding that he "did not have any insider information that contradicted what was presented to the public." Yet the jury failed to reach a verdict on the insider-trading charges, as to which "the possession of insider information was likewise a critical issue of ultimate fact." Arguing that the jury had therefore acted inconsistently, the

Government sought to retry Yeager on the hung counts. We ruled that retrial was barred by the Double Jeopardy Clause. A jury "speaks only through its verdict." Any number of reasons—including confusion about the issues and sheer exhaustion, could cause a jury to hang. Accordingly, only "a jury's decisions, not its failures to decide," identify "what a jury necessarily determined at trial." Because a hung count reveals nothing more than a jury's failure to reach a decision, it supplies no evidence of the jury's irrationality. Hung counts, therefore, "have no place in the issue-preclusion analysis": When a jury acquits on one count while failing to reach a verdict on another count concerning the same issue of ultimate fact, the acquittal, and only the acquittal, counts for preclusion purposes. Given the preclusive effect of the acquittal, the Court concluded, Yeager could not be retried on the hung count.

We turn to the inconsistent verdicts rendered in this case. The prosecution stemmed from an alleged bribe paid by petitioner Juan Bravo-Fernandez (Bravo), an entrepreneur, to petitioner Hector Martínez-Maldonado (Martínez), then a senator serving the Commonwealth of Puerto Rico. The alleged bribe took the form of an all-expenses-paid trip to Las Vegas, including a $1,000 seat at a professional boxing match featuring a popular Puerto Rican contender. According to the Government, Bravo intended the bribe to secure Martínez' help in shepherding legislation through the Puerto Rico Senate that, if enacted, would "provide substantial financial benefits" to Bravo's enterprise. In the leadup to the Las Vegas trip, Martínez submitted the legislation for the Senate's consideration and issued a committee report supporting it; within a week of returning from Las Vegas, Martínez issued another favorable report and voted to enact the legislation.

Based on these events, a federal grand jury in Puerto Rico indicted petitioners for, *inter alia,* federal-program bribery, in violation of 18 U.S.C. § 666; conspiracy to violate § 666, in violation of § 371; and traveling in interstate commerce to further violations of § 666, in violation of the Travel Act, § 1952(a)(3)(A). Following a three-week trial, a jury convicted Bravo and Martínez of the standalone § 666 bribery offense, but acquitted them of the related conspiracy and Travel Act charges. Each received a sentence of 48 months in prison. The Court of Appeals for the First Circuit vacated the § 666 convictions for instructional error. In the First Circuit's view, the jury had been erroneously charged on what constitutes criminal conduct under that statute. The charge permitted the jury to find Bravo and Martínez "guilty of offering and receiving a gratuity," but, the appeals court held, § 666 proscribes only *quid pro quo* bribes, and not gratuities. True, the court acknowledged, the jury was instructed on both theories of bribery, and the evidence at trial sufficed to support a guilty verdict on either theory. But the Court of Appeals could not say with confidence that the erroneous charge was harmless, so it vacated the § 666 convictions and remanded for further proceedings.

On remand, relying on the issue-preclusion component of the Double Jeopardy Clause, Bravo and Martínez moved for judgments of acquittal on the standalone § 666 charges. They could not be retried on the bribery offense, they insisted, because the jury necessarily determined that they were not guilty of violating § 666 when it acquitted them of conspiring to violate § 666 and traveling in interstate commerce to further violations of § 666. That was so, petitioners maintained, because the only contested issue at trial was whether Bravo had offered, and Martínez had accepted, a bribe within the meaning of § 666. The District Court denied the motions. The First Circuit affirmed. We granted certiorari to resolve a conflict among courts on [whether] the issue-preclusion component of the Double Jeopardy Clause bars the Government from retrying defendants, like Bravo and Martínez, after a jury has returned irreconcilably inconsistent verdicts of conviction and acquittal, and the convictions are later vacated for legal error unrelated to the inconsistency? We affirm.

When a conviction is overturned on appeal, "the general rule is that the Double Jeopardy Clause does not bar reprosecution." *Justices of Boston Municipal Court v. Lydon*, 466 U.S. 294, 308 (1984). The ordinary consequence of vacatur, if the Government so elects, is a new trial shorn of the error that infected the first trial. This "continuing jeopardy" rule neither gives effect to the vacated judgment nor offends double jeopardy principles. Rather, it reflects the reality that the "criminal proceedings against an accused have not run their full course." *Ibid.* And by permitting a new trial post vacatur, the continuing-jeopardy rule serves both society's and criminal defendants' interests in the fair administration of justice. "It would be a high price indeed for society to pay were every accused granted immunity from punishment because of any defect sufficient to constitute reversible error in the proceedings leading to conviction." *United States v. Tateo*, 377 U.S. 463, 466 (1964). The rights of criminal defendants would suffer too, for "it is at least doubtful that appellate courts would be as zealous as they now are in protecting against the effects of improprieties at the trial or pretrial stage if they knew that reversal of a conviction would put the accused irrevocably beyond the reach of further prosecution." *Ibid.*

Bravo and Martínez ask us to deviate from the general rule that, post vacatur of a conviction, a new trial is in order. When a conviction is vacated on appeal, they maintain, an acquittal verdict simultaneously returned should preclude the Government from retrying the defendant on the vacated count. Our precedent, harmonious with issue-preclusion doctrine, opposes the foreclosure petitioners seek. Bravo and Martínez bear the burden of demonstrating that the jury necessarily resolved in their favor the question whether they violated § 666. But a defendant cannot meet that burden where the trial yielded incompatible jury verdicts on the issue the defendant seeks to insulate from relitigation. Here, the jury convicted Bravo and Martínez of violating § 666 but acquitted them of conspiring, and traveling with the intent, to violate § 666. The convictions and acquittals are irreconcilable because other elements of the Travel Act and conspiracy counts were not disputed. It is unknowable "which of the inconsistent verdicts—the acquittals or the convictions—'the jury really meant.' " In view of the Government's inability to obtain review of the acquittals, *Powell*, 469 U.S., at 68 the inconsistent jury findings weigh heavily against according those acquittals issue-preclusive effect.

That petitioners' bribery convictions were later vacated for trial error does not alter our analysis. The critical inquiry is whether the jury actually decided that Bravo and Martínez did not violate § 666. *Ashe* counsels us to approach that task with "realism and rationality," in particular, to examine the trial record "with an eye to all the circumstances of the proceedings." As the Court of Appeals explained, "the fact that the jury convicted Bravo and Martínez of violating § 666 would seem to be of quite obvious relevance" to this practical inquiry, "even though the convictions were later vacated." Because issue preclusion "depends on the jury's assessment of the facts in light of the charges presented at trial," a conviction overturned on appeal is "appropriately considered in our assessment of an acquittal verdict's preclusive effect." *United States v. Citron*, 853 F.2d 1055, 1061 (C.A.2 1988). Indeed, the jurors in this case might not have acquitted on the Travel Act and conspiracy counts absent their belief that the § 666 bribery convictions would stand.

Bravo and Martínez could not be retried on the bribery counts if the Court of Appeals had vacated their § 666 convictions because there was insufficient evidence to support those convictions. For double jeopardy purposes, a court's evaluation of the evidence as insufficient to convict is equivalent to an acquittal and therefore bars a second prosecution for the same offense. *See Burks v. United States*, 437 U.S. 1 (1978). But this is scarcely a case in which the prosecution "failed to muster" sufficient evidence in the first proceeding. *Burks*, 437 U.S., at 11. Quite the opposite. The evidence supported a guilty verdict on the gratuity theory *as well as* the *quid pro quo* theory. Vacatur was compelled for the sole reason that the First Circuit found the jury charge erroneous to the extent that it encompassed gratuities. Therefore, the general rule of "allowing a new trial to rectify trial error" applied. *Burks*, 437 U.S., at 14. Nor would retrial be tolerable if the trial error could resolve the apparent inconsistency in the jury's verdicts. But the instructional error here cannot account for the jury's contradictory determinations because the error applied equally to every § 666-related count.

As in *Powell*, "the problem is that the same jury reached inconsistent results." The convictions' later invalidation on an unrelated ground does not erase or reconcile that inconsistency: It does not bear on "the factual determinations actually and necessarily made by the jury," nor does it "serve to turn the jury's otherwise inconsistent and irrational verdict into a consistent and rational verdict." *People v. Wilson*, 852 N.W.2d 134, 151 (2014) (Markman, J., dissenting). Bravo and Martínez, therefore, cannot establish the factual predicate necessary to preclude the Government from retrying them on the standalone § 666 charges—that the jury in the first proceeding actually decided that they did not violate the federal bribery statute.

To support their argument for issue preclusion, Bravo and Martínez highlight our decision in *Yeager*. In *Yeager*, we recognized that hung counts "have never been accorded respect as a matter of law or history." That is also true of vacated convictions, they urge, so vacated convictions, like hung counts, should be excluded from the *Ashe* inquiry into what the jury necessarily determined. Asserting that we have "never held an invalid conviction relevant to or evidence of anything," Bravo and Martínez argue that taking account of a vacated conviction in our issue-preclusion analysis would impermissibly give effect to "a legal nullity." This argument misapprehends the *Ashe* inquiry. It is undisputed that petitioners' convictions are invalid judgments that may not be used to establish their guilt. The question is whether issue preclusion stops the Government from prosecuting them anew. On that question, Bravo and Martínez bear the burden of showing that the issue whether they violated § 666 has been "determined by a valid and final judgment of acquittal." *Yeager*, 557 U.S., at 119. To judge whether they carried that burden, a court must realistically examine the record to identify the ground for the § 666-based *acquittals*. *Ashe*, 397 U.S., at 444. A conviction that contradicts those acquittals is plainly relevant to that determination, no less so simply because it is later overturned on appeal for unrelated legal error: The split verdict—finding § 666 violated on the standalone counts, but not violated on the related Travel Act and conspiracy counts—tells us that, on one count or the other, "the jury did not follow the court's instructions," whether because of "mistake, compromise, or lenity." *Powell*, 469 U.S., at 65. Petitioners' acquittals therefore do not support the application of issue preclusion here.

Relying on *Yeager*, Bravo and Martínez contend that their vacated convictions should be ignored because, as with hung counts, "there is no way to decipher" what they represent. The § 666 convictions are meaningless, they maintain, because the jury was allowed to convict on the basis of conduct not criminal in the First Circuit—payment of a gratuity. This argument trips on *Yeager*'s reasoning. *Yeager* did not rest on a court's inability to detect the basis for a jury's decision. Rather, this Court reasoned that, when a jury hangs, there is *no decision,* hence no evidence of irrationality. A verdict of guilt, by contrast, *is* a jury decision, even if subsequently vacated on appeal. It therefore can evince irrationality. That is the case here. Petitioners do not dispute that the Government's evidence supported a guilty verdict on the *quid pro quo* theory, or that the gratuity instruction held erroneous by the Court of Appeals applied to every § 666-based offense. Because no rational jury could have reached conflicting verdicts on those counts, petitioners' § 666 convictions "reveal the jury's inconsistency—which is the relevant issue here—even if they do not reveal which theory of liability jurors relied upon in reaching those inconsistent verdicts." Because we do not know what the jury would have concluded had there been no instructional error, a new trial on the counts of conviction is in order. Bravo and Martínez have succeeded on appeal to that extent, but they are entitled to no more. The split verdict does not impede the Government from renewing the prosecution.

The Double Jeopardy Clause bars the Government from again prosecuting Bravo and Martínez on the § 666-based conspiracy and Travel Act offenses; "the acquittals themselves remain inviolate." Bravo and Martínez have also gained "the benefit of their appellate victory," a second trial on the standalone bribery charges, in which the Government may not invoke a gratuity theory. But issue preclusion is not a doctrine they can commandeer when inconsistent verdicts shroud in mystery what the jury necessarily decided.

For the reasons stated, the judgment of the Court of Appeals for the First Circuit is

Affirmed.

JUSTICE THOMAS, concurring.

As originally understood, the Double Jeopardy Clause does not have an issue-preclusion prong. "The English common-law pleas of *auterfoits acquit* and *auterfoits convict,* on which the Clause was based, barred only repeated 'prosecution for the same identical act *and* crime.' " "In *Ashe* the Court departed from the original meaning of the Double Jeopardy Clause, holding that it precludes successive prosecutions on distinct crimes when facts essential to conviction of the second crime have necessarily been resolved in the defendant's favor by a verdict of acquittal of the first crime." *Yeager*, supra, at 128 (Scalia, J., dissenting). "*Ashe* held only that the Clause sometimes bars successive prosecution of facts found during 'a prior proceeding.' " *Yeager*, however, "barred retrial on hung counts after what was not a prior proceeding but simply an earlier stage of the same proceeding." In an appropriate case, we should reconsider the holdings of *Ashe* and *Yeager.* Because the Court today declines to extend those cases, and reaches the correct result under the Clause's original meaning, I join its opinion.

Currier v. Virginia

138 S.Ct. 2144 (2018).

JUSTICE GORSUCH announced the judgment of the Court and delivered the opinion of the Court with respect to Parts I and II, and an opinion with respect to Part III, in which THE CHIEF JUSTICE, JUSTICE THOMAS, and JUSTICE ALITO join.

Michael Currier worried the prosecution would introduce prejudicial but probative evidence against him on one count that could infect the jury's deliberations on others. To address the problem, he agreed to sever the charges and hold two trials instead of one. After the first trial, Currier argued that the second would violate his right against double jeopardy. Can a defendant who agrees to have the charges against him considered in two trials successfully argue that the second trial offends the Fifth Amendment's Double Jeopardy Clause?

I

Police dredged up a safe full of guns from a Virginia river. Paul Garrison, the safe's owner, had reported it stolen from his home. Before the theft, Garrison said, it contained not just guns but also $71,000 in cash. The money was missing. [Garrison's] nephew quickly confessed. He pointed to Currier as his accomplice. A neighbor also reported that she saw Currier leave the Garrison home around the time of the crime. On the strength of this evidence, a grand jury indicted Currier for burglary, grand larceny, and unlawful possession of a firearm by a felon. The last charge followed Currier's previous convictions for burglary and larceny. Because the prosecution could introduce evidence of his prior convictions to prove the felon-in-possession charge, and worried that the evidence might prejudice the jury's consideration of the other charges, Currier and the government agreed to try the burglary and larceny charges first. The felon-in-possession charge could follow in a second trial. Some jurisdictions routinely refuse requests like this. They address the risk of prejudice with an instruction directing the jury to consider defendant's prior convictions only when assessing the felon-in-possession charge. Other jurisdictions allow parties to stipulate to the defendant's past convictions so the particulars of those crimes don't reach the jury's ears. Others take a more protective approach and view severance requests with favor. Because Virginia falls into this last group, the trial court granted the parties' joint request.

The trials followed. At the first, the prosecution produced the nephew and the neighbor who testified to Currier's involvement in the burglary and larceny. Currier argued that the nephew lied and the neighbor was unreliable and the jury acquitted. Before the second trial on the firearm charge, Currier argued [that] holding a second trial would amount to double jeopardy. Alternatively, he asked the court to forbid the government from relitigating any issue resolved in his favor at the first. He said the court should exclude from the new proceeding any evidence about the burglary and larceny. The court allowed the second trial to proceed unfettered. The jury convicted Currier on the felon-in-possession charge. Before the Virginia Court of Appeals, Currier repeated his double jeopardy arguments without success. The Virginia Supreme Court affirmed. We granted certiorari.

II

The Double Jeopardy Clause, applied to the States through the Fourteenth Amendment, provides that no person may be tried more than once "for the same offence." This guarantee recognizes the vast power of the sovereign, the ordeal of a criminal trial, and the injustice our criminal justice system would invite if prosecutors could treat trials as dress rehearsals until they secure the convictions they seek. *See Green v. United States*, 355 U.S. 871 (1957). The Clause was not written or originally understood to pose "an insuperable obstacle to the administration of justice" in cases where "there is no semblance of these types of oppressive practices." *Wade v. Hunter*, 336 U.S. 684, 688 (1949).

Currier suggests this Court's decision in *Ashe v. Swenson*, 397 U.S. 436 (1970), requires a ruling for him. There, the government accused a defendant of robbing six poker players in a game at a private home. At the first trial, the jury acquitted the defendant of robbing one victim. Then the State sought to try the defendant for robbing a second victim. This Court held the second prosecution violated the Double Jeopardy Clause. The Clause speaks of barring successive trials for the same offense. And the State sought to try defendant for a *different* robbery. But, the Court reasoned, because the first jury necessarily found that the defendant "was not one of the robbers," a second jury could not "rationally" convict the defendant of robbing the second victim without calling into question the earlier acquittal. In these circumstances, any relitigation of whether defendant participated as "one of the robbers" would be tantamount to the forbidden relitigation of the same offense resolved at the first trial. *Ashe* 's suggestion that the relitigation of an issue can sometimes amount to the impermissible relitigation of an offense represented a significant innovation in our jurisprudence. Some have argued that it sits uneasily with this Court's double jeopardy precedent and the Constitution's original meaning. *Ashe['s]* test is a demanding one. *Ashe* forbids a second trial only if to secure a conviction the prosecution must prevail on an issue the jury necessarily resolved in the defendant's favor in the first trial. A second trial "is not precluded simply because it is unlikely—or very unlikely—that the original jury acquitted without finding the fact in question." To say that the second trial is tantamount to a trial of the same offense as the first and thus forbidden by the Double Jeopardy Clause, we must be able to say that "it would have been *irrational* for the jury" in the first trial to acquit without finding in the defendant's favor on a fact essential to a conviction in the second. A critical difference immediately emerges between our case and *Ashe*. Even assuming that Currier's second trial qualified as the retrial of the same offense, he consented to it. Trying all three charges in one trial would have prevented any possible *Ashe* complaint Currier might have had.

In *Jeffers v. United States*, 432 U.S. 137 (1977), defendant sought separate trials on each of the counts against him to reduce the possibility of prejudice. The court granted his request. After the jury convicted defendant in the first trial of a lesser-included offense, he argued that the prosecution could not later try him for a greater offense. Historically, courts have treated greater and lesser-included offenses as the same offense for double jeopardy purposes, so a conviction on one normally precludes a later trial on the other. But it's different when the defendant consents to two trials. If a single trial on multiple charges would suffice to avoid a double jeopardy complaint, "there is no violation of the Double Jeopardy Clause when defendant elects to have the offenses tried separately and persuades the trial court to honor his election." If a defendant's consent to two trials can overcome concerns lying at the historic core of the Double Jeopardy Clause, it must overcome a double jeopardy complaint under *Ashe*. Nor does *Jeffers* suggest that the outcome should be different if the first trial yielded an acquittal rather than a conviction when a defendant consents to severance. While *Ashe*'s protections apply only to trials following acquittals, as a general rule, the Double Jeopardy Clause "protects against a second prosecution for the same offense after conviction" as well as "against a second prosecution for the same offense after acquittal." Because the Clause applies in both situations, consent to a second trial should have equal effect in both situations.

Holding otherwise would introduce an unwarranted inconsistency not just with *Jeffers* but with other precedents. In *United States v. Dinitz*, 424 U.S. 600 (1976), this Court held that a defendant's mistrial motion implicitly invited a second trial and was enough to foreclose any double jeopardy complaint. The Court rejected "the contention that the permissibility of a retrial depends on a knowing, voluntary, and intelligent waiver." None of the "prosecutorial or judicial overreaching" forbidden by the Constitution can be found when a second trial follows thanks to the defendant's motion. In *United States v. Scott*, 437 U.S. 82 (1978), this Court held that a defendant's motion effectively invited a retrial of the same offense, and "the Double Jeopardy Clause, which guards against Government oppression, does not relieve a defendant from the consequences of a voluntary choice." While relinquishing objections sometimes turns on state or federal procedural rules, consenting to two trials when one would have avoided a double jeopardy problem precludes any constitutional violation associated with holding a second trial. Defendant wins a potential benefit and experiences none of the prosecutorial "oppression" the Double Jeopardy Clause exists to prevent. Currier asks us to consider *Harris v. Washington*, 404 U.S. 55 (1971) (*per curiam*) and *Turner v. Arkansas*, 407 U.S. 366 (1972) (*per curiam*). But these cases merely applied *Ashe*'s test and concluded that a second trial was impermissible. They did not address the question whether double jeopardy protections apply if the defendant *consents* to a second trial.

Currier replies that he had no real choice but to seek two trials. Without a second trial, evidence of his prior convictions would have tainted the jury's consideration of the burglary and larceny charges. And Virginia law guarantees a severance in cases like his unless the defendant and prosecution agree to a single trial. But no one disputes that the Constitution permitted Virginia to try all three charges at once with appropriate cautionary instructions. So this isn't a case where defendant had to give up one constitutional right to secure another. Instead, Currier faced a lawful choice between two courses of action that each bore potential costs and rationally attractive benefits. It might have been a hard choice. But litigants every day face difficult decisions. Whether it's defendant who finds himself forced to choose between allowing an imperfect trial to proceed or seeking a second that promises its own risks. This Court has held that difficult strategic choices like these are "not the same as no choice," *United States v. Martinez-Salazar*, 528 U.S. 304 (2000), and the Constitution "does not forbid requiring" a litigant to make them, *McGautha v. California*, 402 U.S. 183 (1971).

III

Even if he voluntarily consented to the second trial, Currier argues that consent did not extend to the relitigation of any issues the first jury resolved in his favor. Currier says the court should have excluded evidence suggesting he possessed the guns in Garrison's home, leaving the prosecution to prove that he possessed them only later. Currier points to issue preclusion principles in civil cases and invites us to import into the criminal law through the Double Jeopardy Clause. In his view, the Clause should do more than bar the retrial of the same offense (or crimes tantamount to the same offense under *Ashe*); it should prevent the parties from retrying any issue or introducing any evidence about a previously tried issue. Even assuming that Currier's consent to *holding* a second trial didn't more broadly imply consent to the *manner* it was conducted, we reject his argument. Just last Term this Court warned that issue preclusion principles should have only "guarded application in criminal cases." *Bravo-Fernandez v. United States*, 137 S.Ct. 352, 358 (2016). That caution remains sound.

The Double Jeopardy Clause speaks not about prohibiting the relitigation of issues or evidence but offenses. Only in the Seventh Amendment—and only for civil suits—can we find anything resembling contemporary issue preclusion doctrine. The Double Jeopardy Clause took its cue from English common law pleas that prevented courts from retrying a criminal defendant previously acquitted or convicted of the crime in question. Those pleas barred only repeated "prosecution for the same identical act *and* crime," not the retrial of particular issues or evidence. In *Turner's Case,* 30 Kel. J. 30, 84 Eng. Rep. 1068 (K.B. 1663), a jury acquitted defendant of breaking into a home and stealing money from the owner. The court held that defendant could be tried later for the theft of money "stolen at the same time" from the owner's servant. In *Commonwealth v. Roby*, 12 Pickering 496 (Mass.1832), the court, invoking Blackstone, held that "in considering the identity of the offence, it must appear by the plea, that the offence charged in both cases was the same *in law* and *in fact*." A second prosecution isn't precluded "if the offences charged in the two indictments be perfectly distinct in point of law, *however nearly they may be connected in fact*." Another court ruled "that a man acquitted for stealing the horse hath yet been arraigned and convict for stealing the saddle, tho both were done at the same time." 2 Hale, *supra,* at 246. Early courts regularly confronted cases just like ours and expressly rejected the notion that the Double Jeopardy Clause barred the relitigation of issues or facts.

Under *Blockburger v. United States*, 284 U.S. 299 (1932), the courts apply much the same double jeopardy test they did at the founding. To prevent a second trial on a new charge, the defendant must show an identity of *statutory elements* between the two charges against him; it's not enough that "a substantial overlap exists in the *proof* offered to establish the crimes." *Iannelli v. United States*, 420 U.S. 770, 785 (1975). Of course, *Ashe* later pressed *Blockburger's* boundaries by suggesting that, in narrow circumstances, the retrial of an issue can be considered tantamount to the retrial of an offense. *See Yeager*, 557 U.S., at 119. But even there a court's ultimate focus remains on the practical identity of offenses, and the only available remedy is the traditional double jeopardy bar against the retrial of the same offense—not a bar against the relitigation of issues or evidence. Even at the outer reaches of our double jeopardy jurisprudence, this Court has never sought to regulate the retrial of issues or evidence in the name of the Double Jeopardy Clause. In *Dowling v. United States*, 493 U.S. 342 (1990), defendant faced charges of bank robbery. At trial, the prosecution introduced evidence of defendant's involvement in an earlier crime, even though the jury in that case had acquitted. Like Currier, defendant argued that the trial court should have barred relitigation of an issue resolved in his favor in an earlier case and therefore excluded evidence of the acquitted offense. But the Court refused the request and expressly "declined to extend *Ashe* to exclude in all circumstances, as defendant would have it, relevant and probative evidence that is otherwise admissible under the Rules of Evidence simply because it relates to alleged criminal conduct for which a defendant has been acquitted." If a second trial is permissible, the admission of evidence at that trial is governed by normal evidentiary rules—not by the terms of the Double Jeopardy Clause. "So far as merely evidentiary facts are concerned," the Double Jeopardy Clause "is inoperative." *Yates v. United States*, 354 U.S. 298, 338 (1957).

Any effort to transplant civil preclusion principles into the Double Jeopardy Clause would meet trouble. The Clause embodies a kind of "claim preclusion" rule. In civil cases, a claim generally may not be tried if it arises out of the same transaction or common nucleus of operative facts as another already tried. RESTATEMENT (SECOND) OF JUDGMENTS § 19 (1982). But in a criminal case, *Blockburger* precludes a trial on an offense only if a court has previously heard the same offense as measured by its statutory elements. This Court has emphatically refused to import into criminal double jeopardy law the civil law's more generous "same transaction" or same criminal "episode" test. It isn't even clear that civil preclusion principles would help Currier. Issue preclusion addresses the effect in a current case of a prior adjudication in *another case*. So it doesn't often have much to say about the preclusive effects of rulings "within the framework of a continuing action." Usually, the more flexible law of the case doctrine governs the preclusive effect of an earlier decision "within a single action." And that doctrine might counsel against affording conclusive effect to a prior jury verdict on a particular issue when the parties *agreed* to hold a second trial covering much the same terrain at a later stage of the proceedings. Even if issue preclusion is the right doctrine, its application usually depends "on 'an underlying confidence that the result achieved in the initial litigation was substantially correct.' " *Bravo-Fernandez*, 137 S.Ct., at 358 (quoting *Standefer v. United States*, 447 U.S. 10, 23 (1980)). The doctrine does not bar the relitigation of issues when "the party against whom preclusion is sought could not, as a matter of law, have obtained review of the judgment in the initial action." Restatement (Second) of Judgments § 28. In criminal cases, the government cannot obtain appellate review of acquittals.

Without text, history, or logic to stand on, the dissent leans heavily on a comparison to *Dowling*. In *Dowling*, the dissent emphasizes, the two trials involved different criminal episodes while the two trials here addressed the same set of facts. But *Dowling* did not rest its holding on this feature. If issue preclusion really did exist in criminal law, why wouldn't it preclude the retrial of *any* previously tried issue, regardless whether that issue stems from the same or a different "criminal episode"? Today, some state courts grant severance motions liberally to benefit defendants. But what would happen if this Court unilaterally increased the costs associated with severance in the form of allowing issue preclusion for defendants only? Granting a severance means a court must expend resources for two trials where the Constitution would have permitted one. Witnesses and victims must endure a more protracted ordeal. States sometimes accept these costs to protect a defendant from potential prejudice. But some jurisdictions might respond to any decision increasing the costs of severed trials by making them less freely available. By making severances more costly we might wind up making them rarer too.

Civil preclusion principles and double jeopardy are different doctrines, with different histories, serving different purposes. Historically, both claim and issue preclusion have sought to "promote judicial economy by preventing needless litigation." *Parklane Hosiery*, supra, at 326. That interest may make sense in civil cases where often only money is at stake. But the Double Jeopardy Clause and the common law principles it built upon govern *criminal* cases and concern more than efficiency. They aim, as we've seen, to balance vital interests against abusive prosecutorial practices with consideration to the public's safety. The Clause's terms and history simply do not contain the rights Currier seeks. Nor are we at liberty to rewrite those terms or that history. While the growing number of criminal offenses in our statute books may be cause for concern, no one should expect (or want) judges to revise the Constitution to address every social problem they perceive. The proper authorities, the States and Congress, are empowered to adopt new laws or rules experimenting with issue or claim preclusion in criminal cases if they wish. Some States have already done so. On these matters, the Constitution dictates no answers but entrusts them to a self-governing people to resolve.

The judgment of the Virginia Supreme Court is

Affirmed.

JUSTICE KENNEDY, concurring in part.

I join Parts I and II of the Court's opinion. When a defendant's voluntary choices lead to a second prosecution he cannot use the Double Jeopardy Clause, whether thought of as protecting against multiple trials or the relitigation of issues, to forestall that second prosecution.

JUSTICE GINSBURG, with whom JUSTICE BREYER, JUSTICE SOTOMAYOR, and JUSTICE KAGAN join, dissenting.

Currier's acquiescence in severance of the felon-in-possession charge does not prevent him from raising a plea of issue preclusion based on the jury acquittals of breaking and entering and grand larceny. Historically, the Court has safeguarded the right not to be subject to multiple trials for the "same offense." That claim-preclusive rule stops the government from litigating the "same offense" or criminal charge in successive prosecutions, regardless of whether the first trial ends in a conviction or an acquittal. *See Bravo-Fernandez v. United States*, 137 S.Ct. 352 (2016). To determine whether two offenses are the "same," this Court look to the offenses' elements. *Blockburger v. United States*, 284 U.S. 299 (1932). If each offense "requires proof of a fact which the other does not," *Blockburger* established, the offenses are discrete and the prosecution of one does not bar later prosecution of the other. If, however, two offenses are greater and lesser included offenses, the government cannot prosecute them successively. *See Brown*, 432 U.S., at 169. Also shielded by the Double Jeopardy Clause is the issue-preclusive effect of an acquittal. First articulated in *Ashe v. Swenson*, 397 U.S. 436 (1970), the issue-preclusive aspect of the Double Jeopardy Clause prohibits the government from relitigating issues necessarily resolved in a defendant's favor at an earlier trial presenting factually related offenses. Consequently, "after a jury determined by its verdict that he was not one of the robbers," the State could not "constitutionally hale him before a new jury to litigate that issue again." Issue preclusion ranks with claim preclusion as a Double Jeopardy Clause component. *Harris v. Washington*, 404 U.S. 55 (1971) (*per curiam*). Issue preclusion arms defendants against prosecutorial excesses, and preserves the integrity of acquittals, *see Yeager*, 557 U.S., at 118.

There is in Currier's case no suggestion that he expressly waived a plea of issue preclusion at a second trial, or that he failed to timely assert the plea. This Court "indulges every reasonable presumption against waiver of fundamental constitutional rights." *Johnson v. Zerbst*, 304 U.S. 458, 464 (1938). It has found "waiver by conduct" only where a defendant has engaged in "conduct inconsistent with the assertion of the right." *Pierce Oil Corp. v. Phoenix Refining Co.*, 259 U.S. 125, 129 (1922). For example, a defendant who "obtains the absence of a witness by wrongdoing" may "forfeit" or "waive" his Sixth Amendment right to confront the absent witness. *Davis v. Washington*, 547 U.S. 813 (2006). Currier took no action inconsistent with assertion of an issue-preclusion plea. Consenting to a second trial is not inconsistent with—and does not foreclose—defendant's gaining the issue-preclusive effect of an acquittal. The first trial established that Currier did not participate in breaking and entering the Garrisons' residence or in stealing their safe. The government can attempt to prove Currier possessed firearms through a means other than breaking and entering the Garrisons' residence and stealing their safe. But the government should not be permitted to show in the felon-in-possession trial what it failed to show in the first trial, *i.e.,* Currier's participation in the charged breaking and entering and grand larceny.

Food for Thought

Defendant is tried for first-degree murder, convicted, and sentenced to death. That conviction was reversed. Defendant was retried, convicted of second-degree murder, and sentenced to life in prison. That conviction was reversed as well. At his third trial, defendant was again convicted of second-degree murder with the jury finding that he had the specific intent to kill. Relying on *Ashe v. Swenson*, and the doctrine of collateral estoppel, defendant argued that the general verdict in the second trial precluded the finding of specific intent in the third trial. Is defendant correct? *See Langley v. Prince*, 926 F.3d 145 (5th Cir., en banc, 2019).

FYI

Evidence of a crime for which the defendant was acquitted sometimes may be introduced at a later trial involving the same circumstances. In *Dowling v. United States*, 493 U.S. 342 (1990), while prosecuting a defendant for bank robbery, the Court held that the prosecution may introduce relevant other acts of evidence of a burglary for which the defendant had been acquitted. The Court reasoned that the evidence was admissible at the robbery trial because the acquittal did not prove that defendant was innocent but only that there was a reasonable doubt about the defendant's guilt. The difference in burdens of proof was the key distinction for the Court: in the first trial, the government failed to show beyond a reasonable doubt that Dowling had committed the act; to introduce evidence of the same act in another trial, the government need show only that a jury could reasonably conclude that the defendant committed the first act.

3. Mistrial of Offenses & the "Continuation" of Jeopardy

What does it mean when a jury does not reach a verdict on a particular charge? Does that count as an acquittal or instead something else that would permit a retrial? Consider the following case.

Lemke v. Ryan

<u>719 F.3d 1093 (9th Cir. 2013).</u>

MR. JUSTICE BURNS delivered the opinion of the Court.

Petitioner Robert Lemke appeals the district court's denial of his petition for a writ of *habeas corpus* under 28 U.S.C.§ 2254. Lemke contends that subjecting him to retrial for felony murder violated the Double Jeopardy Clause because a jury earlier had impliedly acquitted him of the robbery underlying the felony murder charge. We conclude that the Arizona Court of Appeals' holding that double jeopardy did not bar Lemke's retrial was not "contrary to, or an unreasonable application of, clearly established Federal law, as determined by the Supreme Court of the United States." 28 U.S.C. § 2254(d)(1). Accordingly, we affirm.

Charles Chance was robbed and shot once in the chest. He died at the scene. Petitioner was indicted in Arizona state court on three counts stemming from that incident: (1) felony murder predicated on armed robbery; (2) armed robbery; and (3) conspiracy to commit armed robbery. At trial, the court instructed the jury that the armed robbery charge in Count II included the lesser offense of theft and, similarly, that the charge of conspiracy to commit armed robbery in Count III included the lesser charge of conspiracy to commit theft. In accordance with Arizona law, the trial court also provided a *LeBlanc* instruction, which allowed the jurors to consider a lesser included offense if, after reasonable effort, they could not agree on the greater charged offense. The jury was not instructed on any lesser included offense for Count I, felony murder. After seven days of deliberation, the jury returned guilty verdicts on the lesser included offenses of theft and conspiracy to commit theft. The jury left blank the verdict forms for armed robbery and conspiracy to commit armed robbery. As to felony murder predicated on armed robbery, the jury reported that it could not reach a verdict. The court declared a mistrial on the felony murder count and sentenced Lemke to a total of twenty-seven years' imprisonment for the theft and conspiracy convictions. The State then sought retrial on the felony murder count. Lemke moved for dismissal, arguing that double jeopardy barred his retrial for felony murder predicated on armed robbery. The trial court denied Lemke's motion, the Arizona Court of Appeals rejected Lemke's double jeopardy claim in a reasoned decision, and the Arizona Supreme Court denied review. Thereafter, Lemke pleaded guilty to felony murder in exchange for a concurrent life sentence with the possibility of parole after 25 years.

The Double Jeopardy Clause provides that no person shall "be subject for the same offence to be twice put in jeopardy of life or limb." U.S. Const. Amend. V. The claim preclusion aspect of the Double Jeopardy Clause bars successive prosecutions for charges that are, for double jeopardy purposes, the same offense. *United States v. Dixon*, 509 U.S. 688 (1993). The issue preclusion, or collateral estoppel, aspect of double jeopardy "precludes the Government from relitigating any issue that was necessarily decided by a jury's acquittal in a prior trial." *Yeager v. United States*, 557 U.S. 110 (2009). The Arizona Court of Appeals held that neither aspect of double jeopardy barred Lemke's retrial for felony murder. We now consider whether that conclusion constituted an unreasonable application of clearly established Supreme Court precedent, and we hold that it did not.

The Supreme Court has held that the Double Jeopardy Clause "protects against successive prosecutions for the same offense after acquittal or conviction." *Monge v. California*, 524 U.S. 721 (1998). Under this formulation and others put forth by the Court, the prosecution of Lemke for armed robbery felony murder after his implied acquittal of armed robbery was indeed prosecution for the "same offense." Precedent, however, does not clearly establish that, under the circumstances of his case, the continued prosecution was "successive" and therefore prohibited.

Two charges constitute the "same offense" for double jeopardy purposes unless "each provision requires proof of a fact which the other does not." *Blockburger v. United States*, 284 U.S. 299 (1932). The State admits that armed robbery and felony murder predicated on armed robbery are the "same offense" under the *Blockburger* test because the felony murder includes all of the elements of armed robbery. *See, e.g., Harris v. Oklahoma*, 433 U.S. 682 (1977) (holding that, for double jeopardy purposes, robbery with a firearm is the same offense as felony murder predicated on armed robbery). The Arizona Court of Appeals also assumed that, by convicting Lemke of theft and remaining silent as to the charge of armed robbery, the jury impliedly acquitted Lemke of armed robbery. The Arizona Court of Appeals was thus confronted with a situation in which the jury had convicted the defendant of theft, impliedly acquitted him of armed robbery, and deadlocked on felony murder, and all three of those charges constituted the "same offense" for double jeopardy purposes. Lemke argues that, once the Arizona Court of Appeals reached this point in its analysis, *Blockburger* compelled the court to hold that double jeopardy barred his retrial for felony murder. Under *Blockburger,* the offenses for which he was convicted (theft) and impliedly acquitted (armed robbery) are the "same offense" as felony murder. Accordingly, the State could not place him twice in jeopardy for the "same offense" by retrying him on the felony murder charge.

The Arizona Court of Appeals did not follow the straightforward approach that Lemke advocates. Citing *Richardson v. United States*, 468 U.S. 317, the court noted that the protections afforded by the Double Jeopardy Clause apply only after original jeopardy has terminated, and jeopardy "continues" on counts for which the jury has failed to reach a verdict. The Arizona Court of Appeals therefore held that, although jeopardy had terminated as to the armed robbery count of the indictment, it had never terminated as to the felony murder count. Thus, retrial for felony murder would not expose Lemke to a *successive* prosecution or place him "*twice* in jeopardy."

Case law from our sister circuits that conflicts with *Wilson* buttresses our conclusion that Lemke's double jeopardy claim is not founded on clearly established Supreme Court law. *See Carey v. Musladin*, 549 U.S. 70 (2006). Decisions from other circuits suggest that double jeopardy does not necessarily bar retrial on a hung count after jeopardy has terminated on a lesser included or greater inclusive offense charged in the same indictment. *See, e.g., United States v. Jackson*, 658 F.3d 145 (2d Cir. 2011); *Delgado v. Fla. Dep't of Corrections*, 659 F.3d 1311 (11th Cir. 2011); *United States v. Howe*, 538 F.3d 820 (8th Cir. 2008), *abrogated on other grounds by Yeager v. United States*, 557 U.S. 110 (2009). These cases cast doubt on the proposition that precedent clearly establishes that double jeopardy bars retrial on a deadlocked count once jeopardy has terminated on another count in the indictment that constitutes the "same offense." We conclude, therefore, that Lemke has failed to meet the requirement of 28 U.S.C. § 2254(d)(1) that the decision of the Arizona Court of Appeals rejecting double jeopardy claim preclusion "was contrary to, or involved an unreasonable application of, clearly established Federal law, as determined by the Court."

We also conclude that the Arizona Court of Appeals did not unreasonably apply clearly established federal law in holding that collateral estoppel did not bar Lemke's retrial for felony murder. Collateral estoppel would apply if Lemke's retrial for felony murder would involve "relitigating any issue that was necessarily decided by a jury's acquittal in a prior trial." *Yeager*, 557 U.S. at 119. In deciding whether an issue was "necessarily decided" by the jury, the court must "examine the record of a prior proceeding, taking into account the pleadings, evidence, charge, and other relevant matter, and conclude whether a rational jury could have grounded its verdict upon an issue other than that which the defendant seeks to foreclose from consideration." *Ashe v. Swenson*, 397 U.S. 436 (1970).

The Arizona Court of Appeals reasonably concluded that Petitioner could not carry his burden of demonstrating that the jury "necessarily decided" that he had not committed armed robbery. The court noted that "the *LeBlanc* instruction prevents us from knowing whether the jury unanimously acquitted defendant of armed robbery or simply could not agree." Although the jury's silence on armed robbery constituted an implied acquittal of that charge for the purposes of the claim preclusion aspect of double jeopardy, it does not have an issue preclusive effect unless the record indicates that the jury necessarily decided the issue in Lemke's favor. Here, the record did not establish that the jury had necessarily decided that Lemke did not commit armed robbery.

The judgment of the district court is *AFFIRMED*.

MR. JUSTICE BURNS concurring in part and dissenting in part.

I agree that the decision of the Arizona Court of Appeals rejecting Lemke's double jeopardy claim was not contrary to, or an unreasonable application of, clearly established Federal law. I don't agree that Lemke still had a double jeopardy claim left after he pled guilty to felony murder. Lemke signed a plea agreement in which he bargained away his right to pursue "any and all motions, defenses, objections or requests which he had made or raised, or could assert hereafter, to the court's entry of judgment against him." But after he got what he bargained for—namely, a favorable sentence—he reneged on his promise to drop his defenses and appeals. We shouldn't let him get away with such perfidy.

E. Termination of the Case by Dismissal, Mistrial or Acquittal

All jurisdictions provide statutory authority for the government to appeal from an adverse termination. *See, e.g.*, 18 U.S.C. § 3731. In the absence of a double jeopardy prohibition, the government can appeal under statutory authority and, if successful, can reprosecute the defendant.

Take Note

Once jeopardy has attached, the way in which a trial ends is critical to double jeopardy application. Whether the cessation of a trial is a dismissal or acquittal is important to resolving whether the government can appeal the adverse termination of the case, and whether the defendant can be reprosecuted. For example, if a case is terminated by mistrial, manifest necessity for the mistrial declaration is crucial for the prosecution to retry a defendant who objected to a mistrial. The assumption underlying the mistrial was that the reason for terminating the first trial was not a fatal defect to a second trial.

1. Termination of a Trial Because of Judicial Error

Can a premature ending to a trial due to a judicial error, namely an erroneous directed verdict of acquittal by a trial judge, be appealed and retried? Consider the following case.

Evans v. Michigan

568 U.S. 313 (2013).

JUSTICE SOTOMAYOR delivered the opinion of the Court.

When the State of Michigan rested its case at petitioner Lamar Evans' arson trial, the court entered a directed verdict of acquittal, based upon its view that the State had not provided sufficient evidence of a particular element of the offense. It turns out that the unproven "element" was not actually a required element at all. We must decide whether an erroneous acquittal such as this nevertheless constitutes an acquittal for double jeopardy purposes, which would mean that Evans could not be retried. This Court has previously held that a judicial acquittal premised upon a "misconstruction" of a criminal statute is an "acquittal on the merits that bars retrial." *Arizona v. Rumsey*, 467 U.S. 203 (1984). Seeing no meaningful constitutional distinction between a trial court's "misconstruction" of a statute and its erroneous addition of a statutory element, we hold that a midtrial acquittal in these circumstances is an acquittal for double jeopardy purposes as well.

The State charged Evans with burning "other real property," a violation of Mich. Comp. Laws § 750.73 (1981). The State's evidence suggested that Evans had burned down an unoccupied house. At the close of the State's case, Evans moved for a directed verdict of acquittal. He pointed the court to the applicable Michigan Criminal Jury Instructions, which listed as the "Fourth" element of the offense "that the building was not a dwelling house." The commentary to the Instructions emphasized, "an essential element is that the structure burned is not a dwelling house." Evans argued that Mich. Comp. Laws § 750.72 criminalizes common-law arson, which requires that the structure burned be a dwelling, while the provision under which he was charged, § 750.73, covers all other real property. Persuaded, the trial court granted the motion. The court explained that the "testimony of the homeowner was this was a dwelling house," so the non-dwelling requirement of Section 750.73 was not met.

On the State's appeal, the Michigan Court of Appeals reversed and remanded. Evans had conceded, and the court held, that under controlling precedent, burning "other real property" is a lesser included offense under Michigan law, and disproving the greater offense is not required. The court thus explained it was "undisputed that the trial court misperceived the elements of the offense with which Evans was charged and erred by directing a verdict." But the court rejected Evans' argument that the Double Jeopardy Clause barred retrial.

It has been half a century since we first recognized that the Double Jeopardy Clause bars retrial following a court-decreed acquittal, even if the acquittal is "based upon an egregiously erroneous foundation." *Fong Foo v. United States*, 369 U.S. 141 (*per curiam*). A mistaken acquittal is an acquittal nonetheless, and "a verdict of acquittal could not be reviewed, on error or otherwise, without putting a defendant twice in jeopardy, and thereby violating the Constitution." *United States v. Ball*, 163 U.S. 662, 671 (1896). Our cases have defined an acquittal to encompass any ruling that the prosecution's proof is insufficient to establish criminal liability for an offense. *See Burks v. United States*, 437 U.S. 1 (1978); *United States v. Martin Linen Supply Co.*, 430 U.S. 564 (1977). An "acquittal" includes "a ruling by the court that the evidence is insufficient to convict," a "factual finding that necessarily establishes the criminal defendant's lack of criminal culpability," and any other "ruling which relates to the ultimate question of guilt or innocence." *Scott*, 437 U.S. at 91. These sorts of substantive rulings stand apart from procedural rulings that may also terminate a case midtrial, which we generally refer to as dismissals or mistrials. Procedural dismissals include rulings on questions that "are unrelated to factual guilt or innocence," but "which serve other purposes," including "a legal judgment that a defendant, although criminally culpable, may not be punished" because of some problem like an error with the indictment.

The court below identified a "constitutionally meaningful difference" between this case and our previous decisions. Those cases, the court found, "involved evidentiary errors regarding the proof needed to establish a factual element of the crimes at issue," but still ultimately involved "a resolution regarding the sufficiency of the factual elements of the charged offense." When a court mistakenly "identifies an extraneous element and dismisses the case solely on that basis," however, it has "not resolved or even addressed any factual element necessary to establish" the offense. As a result, the court below reasoned, the case terminates "based on an error of law unrelated to the defendant's guilt or innocence on the elements of the charged offense," and thus falls outside the definition of an acquittal.

We fail to perceive the difference. This case, like our previous ones, involves an antecedent legal error that led to an acquittal because the State failed to prove some fact it was not actually required to prove. We hold that Evans' trial ended in an acquittal when the trial court ruled the State had failed to produce sufficient evidence of his guilt. The Double Jeopardy Clause thus bars retrial for his offense and should have barred the State's appeal. The judgment of the Supreme Court of Michigan is

Reversed.

JUSTICE ALITO, dissenting.

The Court holds that the Double Jeopardy Clause bars petitioner's retrial for arson because his attorney managed to convince a judge to terminate petitioner's first trial prior to verdict on the specious ground that the offense with which he was charged contains an imaginary "element" that the prosecution could not prove. The Court's decision makes no sense. It is not consistent with the original meaning of the

Double Jeopardy Clause; it does not serve the purposes of the prohibition against double jeopardy; and contrary to the Court's reasoning, the trial judge's ruling was not an "acquittal," which our cases have "consistently" defined as a decision that "actually represents a resolution, correct or not, of some or all of the factual *elements of the offense charged*." E.g., *Smith v. Massachusetts*, 543 U.S. 462 *(quoting United States v. Martin Linen Supply Co.*, 430 U.S. 564 (1977)). For no good reason, the Court deprives the State of Michigan of its right to have one fair opportunity to convict petitioner.

> **Food for Thought**
>
> Wrong! What if the attorney was correct in *Evans* about the extra element, but the Court mistakenly thought the element had been met by the state and proceeded to convict. Would a retrial be a violation of double jeopardy?

2. Reversal Based on Venue & Vicinage

In *Smith v. United States,* 599 U.S. 236 (2023), Smith's conviction was reversed because the prosecution occurred in the wrong venue and before a jury drawn from the wrong location. Defendant successfully challenged his conviction based on the Constitution's Venue Clause, Art. III, § 2, cl. 3 (the "Trial of all Crimes shall be held in the State where the . . . Crimes shall have been committed"), and its Vicinage Clause, Amdt. 6 ("the right to an impartial jury of the State and district wherein the crime shall have been committed."), and claimed that the fact that a jury had been empanelled precluded his retrial. The Court recited the longstanding rule that "when a defendant obtains a reversal of a prior, unsatisfied conviction, he may be retried in the normal course of events. Indeed, the "appropriate remedy for prejudicial trial error, in almost all circumstances, is simply the award of a retrial, not a judgment barring reprosecution" (except for violations of the Speedy Trial Clause). The Court noted that a "judicial decision on venue is fundamentally different from a jury's general verdict of acquittal. When a jury returns a general verdict of not guilty, its decision cannot be upset by speculation or inquiry into such matters by courts. To conclude otherwise would impermissibly authorize judges to usurp the jury right." However, "retrial is permissible when a trial terminates "on a basis unrelated to factual guilt or innocence of the offence. The reversal of a conviction based on a violation of the Venue or Vicinage Clauses, even when styled as a 'judgment of acquittal' under Rule 29, plainly does not resolve "the bottom-line question of 'criminal culpability.' " Instead, such a reversal is quintessentially a decision that 'the Government's case against the defendant must fail even though it might satisfy the trier of fact that he was guilty beyond a reasonable doubt.' "

3. Midtrial Dismissal of Charges

If a case or charge is dismissed before the conclusion of proceedings, even during a trial, whether a retrial of a case can occur is dependent on differing considerations. Who sought the dismissal, the prosecution or defense? Was the dismissal based on guilt or innocence or some other ground? Can the government appeal at all? Does it matter how the trial judge characterized her dismissal of the case or charge? These and other questions are considered in the following case.

United States v. Scott

437 U.S. 82 (1978).

MR. JUSTICE REHNQUIST delivered the opinion of the Court.

Respondent, a member of the police force in Muskegon, Mich., was charged in a three-count indictment with distribution of narcotics. Both before his trial, and twice during the trial, respondent moved to dismiss the two counts of the indictment which concerned transactions that took place during the preceding September, on the ground that his defense had been prejudiced by pre-indictment delay. At the close of the evidence, the court granted respondent's motion. Although the court did not explain its reasons for dismissing the second count, it explicitly concluded that respondent had "presented sufficient proof of prejudice with respect to Count I." The Government sought to appeal the dismissals of the first two counts to the United States Court of Appeals for the Sixth Circuit. That court, relying on *United States v. Jenkins*, 420 U.S. 358 (1975), concluded that any further prosecution of respondent was barred by the Double Jeopardy Clause of the Fifth Amendment, and therefore dismissed the appeal. The Government sought review only with regard to the dismissal of the first count. We granted certiorari to give further consideration to the applicability of the Double Jeopardy Clause to Government appeals from orders granting defense motions to terminate a trial before verdict. We reverse.

The problem presented by this case could not have arisen during the first century of this Court's existence. The Court has long taken the view that the United States has no right of appeal in a criminal case, absent explicit statutory authority. Such authority was not provided until the enactment of the Criminal Appeals Act, Act of Mar. 2, 1907, which permitted the United States to seek a writ of error in this Court from any decision dismissing an indictment on the basis of "the invalidity, or construction of the statute upon which the indictment is founded." In 1971, Congress adopted the current language of the Act, permitting Government appeals from any decision dismissing an indictment, "except that no appeal shall lie where the Double Jeopardy Clause of the United States Constitution prohibits further prosecution." 18 U.S.C. § 3731.

These, at least, are two venerable principles of double jeopardy jurisprudence. The successful appeal of a judgment of conviction, on any ground other than the insufficiency of the evidence to support the verdict, *Burks v. United States*, 437 U.S. 1, poses no bar to further prosecution on the same charge. A judgment of acquittal, whether based on a jury verdict of not guilty or on a ruling by the court that the evidence is insufficient to convict, may not be appealed and terminates the prosecution when a second trial would be necessitated by a reversal.

Although the primary purpose of the Double Jeopardy Clause was to protect the integrity of a final judgment, this Court has also developed a body of law guarding the separate but related interest of a defendant in avoiding multiple prosecutions even where no final determination of guilt or innocence has been made. Such interests may be involved in two different situations: the first, in which the trial judge declares a mistrial; the second, in which the trial judge terminates the proceedings favorably to the defendant on a basis not related to factual guilt or innocence.

Our opinion in *Burks* necessarily holds that there has been a "failure of proof," requiring an acquittal when the Government does not submit sufficient evidence to rebut a defendant's essentially factual defense of insanity, though it may otherwise be entitled to have its case submitted to the jury. The defense of insanity, like the defense of entrapment, arises from "the notion that Congress could not have intended criminal punishment for a defendant who has committed all the elements of a proscribed offense," *United States v. Russell*, 411 U.S. 423 (1973), where other facts established to the satisfaction of the trier of fact provide a legally adequate justification for otherwise criminal acts. Such a factual finding does "necessarily establish the criminal defendant's lack of criminal culpability," (Brennan, J., dissenting), under the existing law; the fact that "the acquittal may result from erroneous evidentiary rulings or erroneous interpretations of governing legal principles," affects the accuracy of that determination, but it does not alter its essential character. By contrast, the dismissal of an indictment for pre-indictment delay represents a legal judgment that a defendant, although criminally culpable, may not be punished because of a supposed constitutional violation.

In the present case, defendant successfully avoided such a submission of the first count of the indictment by persuading the trial court to dismiss it on a basis which did not depend on guilt or innocence. He was thus neither acquitted nor convicted, because he successfully undertook to persuade the trial court not to submit the issue of guilt or innocence to the jury which had been empanelled to try him. Defendant has not been "deprived" of his valued right to go to the first jury; only the public has been deprived of its valued right to "one complete opportunity to convict those who have violated its laws." *Arizona v. Washington.* No interest protected by the Double Jeopardy Clause is invaded when the Government is allowed to appeal and seek reversal of such a midtrial termination of the proceedings in a manner favorable to the defendant.[13] We, of course, do not suggest that a midtrial dismissal of a prosecution, in response to a defense motion on grounds unrelated to guilt or innocence, is necessarily improper. Such rulings may be necessary to terminate proceedings marred by fundamental error. But where a defendant prevails on such a motion, he takes the risk that an appellate court will reverse the trial court.

We pressed too far in *Jenkins*, the concept of the "defendant's valued right to have his trial completed by a particular tribunal." We now conclude that where the defendant himself seeks to have the trial terminated without any submission to either judge or jury as to his guilt or innocence, an appeal by the Government from his successful effort to do so is not barred by 18 U.S.C. § 3731.

FYI

In the three years between *Jenkins* and *Scott*, the Court's philosophy about Double Jeopardy changed—from shielding a defendant from the burden of multiple prosecutions (i.e., running the gauntlet twice), to preserving determinations only of innocence via an acquittal, but allowing retrials following dismissals or mistrials.

MR. JUSTICE BRENNAN, with whom MR. JUSTICE WHITE, MR. JUSTICE MARSHALL, and MR. JUSTICE STEVENS join, dissenting.

While the Double Jeopardy Clause often has the effect of protecting the accused's interest in the finality of particular favorable determinations, this is not its objective. For the Clause often permits Government appeals from final judgments favorable to the accused. The purpose of the Clause, which the Court today fails sufficiently to appreciate, is to protect the accused against the agony and risks attendant upon undergoing more than one criminal trial for any single offense. Society's "willingness to limit the Government to a single criminal proceeding to vindicate its very vital interest in enforcement of criminal laws" bespeaks society's recognition of the gross unfairness of requiring the accused to undergo the strain and agony of more than one trial for any single offense. The policies of the Double Jeopardy Clause mandate that the Government be afforded but one complete opportunity to convict an accused and that when the first proceeding terminates in a final judgment favorable to the defendant any retrial be barred. The rule as to acquittals can only be understood as simply an application of this larger principle.

---

[13]   It is entirely possible for a trial court to reconcile the public interest in the Government's right to appeal from an erroneous conclusion of law, with the defendant's interest in avoiding a second prosecution. In *Wilson*, the court permitted the case to go to the jury, which returned a verdict of guilty, but it dismissed the indictment for preindictment delay on the basis of evidence adduced at trial.

Food for Thought

As *Scott* states, an acquittal occurs when the judge's ruling represents a "resolution in the defendant's favor, correct or not, of some or all of the factual elements of the offense charged." In *Sanabria v. United States*, 437 U.S. 54 (1978), decided the same day as *Scott*, the Court held that when a defendant is acquitted at trial, he cannot be retried for the same charge, even if the legal rulings underlying the acquittal were erroneous. By contrast, the Court has held that the government may appeal the grant of *pretrial* motions to dismiss. *Serfass v. United States*, 420 U.S. 377 (1975). Even though a successful government appeal can lead to a new prosecution, the Double Jeopardy doctrine does not bar the appeal because jeopardy had not attached at the time the trial court dismissed the charges. The policy supporting this disposition is that the defendant is not running the gauntlet more than once, *i.e.*, a reprosecution does not provide a second chance for the prosecution because it has not yet had a first chance.

Hypo: *Appealing the Acquittal*

Defendants are charged with conspiracy and concealing material facts in a federal court case. Suppose, after trial has commenced, and during the prosecution's case, the district court judge concludes that the prosecutor's conduct is improper and that the prosecution's witnesses lack credibility. The judge then orders the jury to acquit the defendant, which it does, and a judgment of acquittal is promptly entered. The district court judge, however, does not have the power to direct the jury to render an acquittal. If the prosecutor appeals the acquittal, and wins, can the accused be retried? *See Fong Foo v. United States*, 369 U.S. 141 (1962).

4. Mistrials & Hung Juries

What if a jury deadlocks and a mistrial is declared? Can the defendant be retried? Does it matter whether the jury had indicated that it has reached certain conclusions regarding the charges? Are those indications conclusive for double jeopardy purposes?

Blueford v. Arkansas

566 U.S. 599 (2012).

CHIEF JUSTICE ROBERTS delivered the opinion of the Court.

The Double Jeopardy Clause protects against being tried twice for the same offense. The Clause does not, however, bar a second trial if the first ended in a mistrial. Before the jury concluded deliberations in this case, it reported that it was unanimous against guilt on charges of capital murder and first-degree murder, was deadlocked on manslaughter, and had not voted on negligent homicide. The court told the jury to continue to deliberate. The jury did so but still could not reach a verdict, and the court declared a mistrial. All agree that the defendant may be retried on charges of manslaughter and negligent homicide. The question is whether he may also be retried on charges of capital and first-degree murder.

Hear It

You can hear the oral argument in *Blueford* at: https://www.oyez.org/cases/2011/10-1320.

One-year-old Matthew McFadden, Jr., suffered a severe head injury while home with his mother's boyfriend, Alex Blueford. Despite treatment at a hospital, McFadden died a few days later. The State of Arkansas charged Blueford with capital murder, but waived the death penalty. The State's theory was that Blueford had injured McFadden intentionally, causing the boy's death "under circumstances manifesting extreme indifference to the value of human life." Ark. Code Ann. § 5–10–101(a)(9)(A) (Supp. 2011). The defense portrayed the death as the result of Blueford accidentally knocking McFadden onto the ground. The trial court instructed the jury that the charge of capital murder included three lesser offenses: first-degree murder, manslaughter, and negligent homicide.

Blueford's primary submission is that he cannot be retried for capital and first-degree murder because the jury actually acquitted him of those offenses, claiming it was an acquittal in substance, if not form. According to Blueford, the foreperson's announcement of the jury's unanimous votes on capital and first-degree murder represented just that: a resolution of some or all of the elements of those offenses in Blueford's favor. We disagree. The foreperson's report was not a final resolution of anything. The jurors went back to the jury room to deliberate further, even after the foreperson had delivered her report. When they emerged a half hour later, the foreperson stated only that they were unable to reach a verdict.

Blueford contends that there was no necessity for a mistrial on capital and first-degree murder, given the foreperson's report that the jury had voted unanimously against guilt on those charges. According to Blueford, the court should have taken "some action," whether through partial verdict forms or other means, to allow the jury to give effect to those votes, and then considered a mistrial only as to the remaining charges. We have never required a trial court, before declaring a mistrial because of a hung jury, to consider any particular means of breaking the impasse—let alone to consider giving the jury new options for a verdict. *See Renico v. Lett*, 559 U.S. 766 (2010). As permitted under Arkansas law, the jury's options in this case were limited to two: either convict on one of the offenses, or acquit on all. The instructions explained those options in plain terms, and the verdict forms likewise contemplated no other outcome. There were separate forms to convict on each of the possible offenses, but there was only one form to acquit, and it was to acquit on all of them. When the foreperson disclosed the jury's votes on capital and first-degree murder, the trial court did not abuse its discretion by refusing to add another option—that of acquitting on some offenses but not others. That, however, is precisely the relief Blueford seeks—relief the Double Jeopardy Clause does not afford him.

The jury did not convict Blueford of any offense, but it did not acquit him of any either. When the jury was unable to return a verdict, the trial court properly declared a mistrial and discharged the jury. As a consequence, the Double Jeopardy Clause does not stand in the way of a second trial on the same offenses.

The judgment of the Supreme Court of Arkansas is *Affirmed.*

Take Note

In *Oregon v. Kennedy*, 456 U.S. 667 (1982), the Court held that double jeopardy bars a second trial only if the conduct giving rise to the mistrial was prosecutorial or judicial conduct intended to provoke defendant into moving for a mistrial. The Court concluded that this standard was not satisfied when the prosecution asked a witness, who had never done business with plaintiff before, suggesting that it was "because he is a crook" was not intended to provoke a mistrial and therefore the double jeopardy clause did not bar a retrial.

F. Termination of the Case by Conviction

The general rule is that when a defendant appeals or collaterally attacks a conviction successfully, double jeopardy does not preclude a re-prosecution. When a defendant chooses to appeal from a conviction, he seeks to nullify the conviction. If successful, the courts treat the conviction as a nullity, meaning no trial ever occurred. Thus, the slate is wiped clean, the defendant never ran the gauntlet, and he can be tried "again." The following case provides some insight into this general rule.

Lockhart v. Nelson

488 U.S. 33 (1988).

CHIEF JUSTICE REHNQUIST delivered the opinion of the Court.

In this case a reviewing court set aside a defendant's conviction of enhanced sentence because certain evidence was erroneously admitted against him, and further held that the Double Jeopardy Clause forbade the State to retry him as a habitual offender because the remaining evidence adduced at trial was legally insufficient to support a conviction. Nothing suggests any misconduct in the prosecutor's submission of the evidence. We conclude that in cases such as this, where the evidence offered by the State and admitted by the trial court—whether erroneously or not—would have been sufficient to sustain a guilty verdict, the Double Jeopardy Clause does not preclude retrial.

Respondent Johnny Lee Nelson pleaded guilty in Arkansas state court to burglary, a class B felony, and misdemeanor theft. He was sentenced under Arkansas' habitual criminal statute, which provides that a defendant who is convicted of a class B felony and "who has previously been convicted of or found guilty of four [4] or more felonies," may be sentenced to an enhanced term of imprisonment of between 20 and 40 years. To have a convicted defendant's sentence enhanced under the statute, the State must prove beyond a reasonable doubt, at a separate sentencing hearing, that the defendant has the requisite number of prior felony convictions.

At respondent's sentencing hearing, the State introduced, without objection from the defense, certified copies of four prior felony convictions. The case was submitted to the jury, which found that the State had met its burden of proving four prior convictions and imposed an enhanced sentence. The State courts upheld the enhanced sentence on both direct and collateral review, despite respondent's protestations that one of the convictions relied upon by the State had been pardoned.

After finding that one conviction had been pardoned upon a writ of *habeas corpus*, the State desired to resentence the defendant as a habitual offender based on a different conviction. The District Court decided that the Double Jeopardy Clause prevented the State from attempting to resentence respondent as a habitual offender on the burglary charge. The Court of Appeals for the Eighth Circuit affirmed. The Court of Appeals reasoned that the pardoned conviction was not admissible under state law, and that "without it, the state has failed to provide sufficient evidence" to sustain the enhanced sentence. We granted certiorari to review this interpretation of the Double Jeopardy Clause.

It has long been settled that the Double Jeopardy Clause's general prohibition against successive prosecutions does not prevent the government from retrying a defendant who succeeds in getting his first conviction set aside, through direct appeal or collateral attack, because of some error in the proceedings leading to conviction. *United States v. Ball*, 163 U.S. 662 (1896). This rule is necessary in order to ensure the "sound administration of justice": "Corresponding to the right of an accused to be given a fair trial is the societal interest in punishing one whose guilt is clear after he has obtained such a trial. It would be a high price indeed for society to pay were every accused granted immunity from punishment because of any defect sufficient to constitute reversible error in the proceedings leading to conviction."

Permitting retrial after a conviction has been set aside also serves the interests of defendants, for "it is at least doubtful that appellate courts would be as zealous as they now are in protecting against the effects of improprieties at the trial or pretrial stage if they knew that reversal of a conviction would put the accused irrevocably beyond the reach of further prosecution." *Ibid.* In *Burks v. United States*, 437 U.S. 1 (1978), we recognized an exception to the general rule—when a defendant's conviction is reversed by an appellate court on the sole ground that the evidence was insufficient to sustain the jury's verdict, the Double Jeopardy Clause bars a retrial on the same charge. *Burks* was based on the view that an appellate court's reversal for insufficiency of the evidence is a determination that the government's case against the defen-

What's That?

What is a felony? While the term lies comfortably within the popular culture, its legal definition does not. A felony generally refers to a serious crime for which the potential incarceration is more than one year. The key is not what the accused actually receives as a sentence, but what the accused could receive. Thus, a charge of aggravated battery, with a sentence of two years, would be a felony even if the accused were released on probation after a conviction. Note that lesser offenses, for which incarceration could occur up to one year, are called misdemeanors.

dant was so lacking that the trial court should have entered a judgment of acquittal, rather than submitting the case to the jury. *Burks* was careful to point out that a reversal based solely on evidentiary insufficiency has fundamentally different implications, for double jeopardy purposes, than a reversal based on such ordinary "trial errors" as the "incorrect receipt or rejection of evidence." While the former is in effect a finding "that the government has failed to prove its case" against the defendant, the latter "implies nothing with respect to the guilt or innocence of the defendant," but is simply "a determination that he has been convicted through a judicial *process* which is defective in some fundamental respect."

It appears that this case is a situation described in *Burks* as reversal for "trial error"—the trial court erred in admitting a particular piece of evidence, and without it there was insufficient evidence to support a judgment of conviction. But with that evidence, there was enough to support the sentence: the court and jury had certified copies of four prior felony convictions, and that is sufficient to support a verdict of enhancement under the statute. The fact that one of the convictions had been later pardoned by the Governor vitiated its legal effect, but it did not deprive the certified copy of that conviction of its probative value under the statute. It is clear from our opinion in *Burks* that a reviewing court must consider all of the evidence admitted by the trial court in deciding whether retrial is permissible under the Double Jeopardy Clause—indeed, that was the *ratio decidendi* of *Burks*, and the overwhelming majority of appellate courts have agreed.

Permitting retrial in this instance is not the sort of governmental oppression at which the Double Jeopardy Clause is aimed; rather, it serves the interest of the defendant by affording him an opportunity to "obtain a fair readjudication of his guilt free from error." Had defendant offered evidence at the sentencing hearing to prove that the conviction had become a nullity by reason of the pardon, the trial judge would presumably have allowed the prosecutor an opportunity to offer evidence of another prior conviction to support the habitual offender charge. Our holding today merely recreates the situation that would have been obtained if the trial court had excluded the evidence of the conviction because of the showing of a pardon.

The judgment of the Court of Appeals is accordingly *reversed*.

JUSTICE MARSHALL, with whom JUSTICE BRENNAN and JUSTICE BLACKMUN join, dissenting.

The Court's analysis of this issue should begin with the recognition that, in deciding when the double jeopardy bar should apply, we are balancing two weighty interests: the defendant's interest in repose and society's interest in the orderly administration of justice. *See, e.g., United States v. Tateo.* It would seem that the defendant's interest is every bit as great in this situation as in *Burks.* Society's interest, however, would appear to turn on a number of variables. The chief one is the likelihood that retrying the defendant will lead to conviction. In appraising this likelihood, one might inquire into whether prosecutors tend in close cases to hold back probative evidence of a defendant's guilt; if they do not, there would be scant societal interest in permitting retrial given that the State's remaining evidence is, by definition, insufficient. Alternatively, one might inquire as to why the evidence was deemed inadmissible. Where

Practice Pointer

Should the defense attorney appeal issues of trial error as well as issues relating to evidentiary insufficiency? In practice, a convicted defendant will seek reversal for any reason regardless of the Double Jeopardy consequences. After *Burks* and *Nelson*, the risk in offering judges multiple grounds for reversal may lead judges to reverse for trial error because of the possibility of a new trial. Of course, there may not be another trial. Instead, a prosecutor may be willing to plea bargain because the witnesses' memories are faded, public sentiment about the type of offense has changed, or simply for judicial economy purposes.

evidence was stricken for reasons having to do with its unreliability, it would seem curious to include it in the sufficiency calculus. Inadmissible hearsay evidence, for example, or evidence deemed defective or nonprobative as a matter of law thus might not be included. By contrast, evidence stricken in compliance with evidentiary rules grounded in other public policies—the policy of encouraging subsequent remedial measures embodied in Federal Rule of Evidence 407, for example, or the policy of deterring unconstitutional searches and seizures embodied in the exclusionary rule—might more justifiably be included in a double jeopardy sufficiency analysis.

FYI

Suppose that a state has two degrees of murder and the jury is instructed on both degrees. The jury convicts on the less serious murder charge, which is reversed on appeal for trial error. At a retrial, what can be the maximum charge against the defendant? In *Morris v. Mathews*, 475 U.S. 237 (1986), the Court held that if the trial court erred and retried and convict the defendant on the more serious charge at a second trial, the appellate court can reduce the charge from a jeopardy-barred offense of the more serious charge to the permissible, less serious charge. By contrast, if the second trial for the jeopardy-barred offense, *e.g.*, murder, results in a conviction for the less serious charge which was not jeopardy-barred, *e.g.*, voluntary manslaughter, a retrial must occur because of the possible prejudicial effect on the jury of prosecuting the accused on a higher charge. *Price v. Georgia*, 398 U.S. 323 (1970).

Point for Discussion

The Thirteenth-Juror Reversal

Unlike *Burks*, *Tibbs v. Florida*, 457 U.S. 31 (1982), held that when an appellate court reverses a conviction because the verdict is against the weight of the evidence, there can be a retrial because such a reversal assumes that there was sufficient evidence at the first trial. The appellate judge simply disagreed with the way in which the jury decided the case.

G. Retrials & Increased Penalties

If there is a retrial and the prosecution seeks and the judge provides increased penalties, does this violate double jeopardy principles? This issue, overlapping with vindictive prosecution, was resolutely answered in *North Carolina v. Pearce*, 395 U.S. 711, 722 (1969), where Justice Stewart, for the Court, held:

Neither the double jeopardy provision nor the Equal Protection Clause imposes an absolute bar to a more severe sentence upon reconviction. A trial judge is not constitutionally precluded from imposing a new sentence, whether greater or less than the original sentence, in the light of events subsequent to the first trial that may have thrown new light upon the defendant's "life, health, habits, conduct, and mental and moral propensities." *Williams v. New York*, 337 U.S. 241. Such information may come to the judge's attention from evidence adduced at the second trial itself, from a new presentence investigation, from the defendant's prison record, or possibly from other sources. The freedom of a sentencing judge to consider the defendant's conduct subsequent to the first conviction in imposing a new sentence is no more than consonant with the principle, fully approved in *Williams*, that a State may adopt the "prevalent modern philosophy of penology that the punishment should fit the offender and not merely the crime."

The Court recognized that this principle has limits, particularly in the form of the Due Process Clause of the Fourteenth Amendment. Justice Stewart observed: "It can hardly be doubted that it would be a flagrant violation of the Fourteenth Amendment for a state trial court to follow an announced practice of imposing a heavier sentence upon every reconvicted defendant for the explicit purpose of punishing the defendant for his having succeeded in getting his original conviction set aside. Where the original conviction has been set aside because of a constitutional error, the imposition of such a punishment, "penalizing those who choose to exercise" constitutional rights, "would be patently unconstitutional." *United States v. Jackson*, 390 U.S. 570, 581. The very threat inherent in the existence of such a punitive policy would, with respect to those still in prison, serve to "chill the exercise of basic constitutional rights." But even if the first conviction has been set aside for non-constitutional error, the imposition of a penalty upon the defendant for having successfully pursued a statutory right of appeal or collateral remedy would be no less a violation of due process of law. A court is "without right to put a price on an appeal. A defendant's exercise of a right of appeal must be free and unfettered. It is unfair to use the great power given to the court to determine sentence to place a defendant in the dilemma of making an unfree choice."

Due process of law requires that vindictiveness against a defendant for having successfully attacked his first conviction must play no part in the sentence he receives after a new trial. Since the fear of such vindictiveness may unconstitutionally deter a defendant's exercise of the right to appeal or collaterally attack his first conviction, due process also requires that a defendant be freed of apprehension of such a retaliatory motivation on the part of the sentencing judge. In order to assure the absence of such a motivation, whenever a judge imposes a more severe sentence upon a defendant after a new trial, the reasons for doing so must affirmatively appear. Those reasons must be based upon objective information concerning identifiable conduct on the part of the defendant occurring after the time of the original sentencing proceeding. And the factual data upon which the increased sentence is based must be made part of the record, so that the constitutional legitimacy of the increased sentence may be fully reviewed on appeal.

Points for Discussion

a. Sentencing Considerations

A court sentencing a defendant after retrial can consider any event committed before the original sentencing, such as a conviction. *Texas v. McCullough*, 475 U.S. 134 (1986); *Wasman v. United States*, 468 U.S. 559 (1984). When a jury imposes the second sentence, the jury's independence minimizes the possibility that prosecutorial vindictiveness will influence the sentence. *Chaffin v. Stynchcombe*, 412 U.S. 17 (1973). When the court imposes sentence, the Double Jeopardy Clause applies, because the judge could retaliate against the defendant for taking an appeal by imposing a higher sentence on retrial. However, the presumption of vindictiveness does not apply when the initial sentence was based on a guilty plea and the higher sentence follows from a trial on the merits. *Alabama v. Smith*, 490 U.S. 794 (1989). The availability of an appeal by the defendant does not prohibit a higher punishment on a trial *de novo* on the same charge. *Colten v. Kentucky*, 407 U.S. 104 (1972). However, a higher offense cannot be charged in the *de novo* appeal. *Thigpen v. Roberts*, 468 U.S. 27 (1984); *Blackledge v. Perry*, 417 U.S. 21 (1974). The prosecution may also appeal a sentence imposed by the judge without violation of double jeopardy. *Pennsylvania v. Goldhammer*, 474 U.S. 28 (1985); *United States v. DiFrancesco*, 449 U.S. 117 (1980).

b. Double Jeopardy & Sentencing Considerations

The double jeopardy prohibition of multiple prosecutions for the same offense limits a court's ability to impose or alter sentences. *See Ex parte Lange*, 85 U.S. (18 Wall.) 163, 21 L.Ed. 872 (1873) (defendant cannot be subjected to another sentence after suffering fully one punishment for the offense). A sentence imposed at a proceeding sufficiently similar to a trial may be sufficiently final to invoke the protection of the Double Jeopardy Clause. For example, if a life sentence is imposed in a

Food for Thought

Can a court increase the sentence when an appellate court rules that the first sentence was invalid, unlawful or erroneous? *See, e.g., Jones v. Thomas*, 491 U.S. 376 (1989). Can a trial judge increase a valid sentence after the defendant begins to serve the sentence? *Compare United States v. Arrellano-Rios*, 799 F.2d 520 (9th Cir.1986) *with United States v. Lopez*, 706 F.2d 108 (2d Cir.1983).

bifurcated sentencing proceeding for a capital offense that resembles a trial on guilt or innocence, the Double Jeopardy Clause prohibits the imposition of the death penalty following a successful appeal and retrial. *Bullington v. Missouri*, 451 U.S. 430 (1981). When a jury's verdict in a capital sentencing proceeding is merely advisory, a court may impose the death penalty despite the jury's verdict of life imprisonment. *Spaziano v. Florida*, 468 U.S. 447 (1984).

FYI

Does *Bullington* extend to enhancement/recidivist proceedings on the theory that because such proceedings resemble trials, a decision not to enhance acts as an acquittal on the factual findings necessary to enhance? No, said the Court in *Monge v. California*, 524 U.S. 721 (1998). *Bullington* is limited to capital cases due to its unique character, such that it produces a "heightened interest in accuracy."

In *Schiro v. Farley*, 510 U.S. 222 (1994), the trial court found defendant guilty of murder while committing rape but made no finding on a count of intentional murder. It then imposed the death penalty after finding a statutory aggravating circumstance of intentionally killing while committing rape. The Court rejected the defendant's claim that the jury's failure to convict him on the intentional murder count operated as an acquittal of intentional murder and that double jeopardy prohibited the use of the intentional murder aggravating circumstance for sentencing purposes. The Court distinguished *Bullington* by noting that the case referred only to second capital sentencing proceedings.

Executive Summary

Double Jeopardy Clause. The Double Jeopardy Clause protects criminal defendants from having to "run the gauntlet" of criminal proceedings or charges multiple times. Its purpose is to shield defendants against the potential oppression of successive prosecutions and to promote the finality of judgments.

Application of the Double Jeopardy Clause. This protection extends not only to successive prosecutions but also to convictions of multiple offenses considered to be the same offense.

Attachment of Double Jeopardy. Double jeopardy analysis usually commences with the question of whether jeopardy attaches. In the trial setting, jeopardy attaches when a jury is empanelled and sworn.

When Is Retrial Permitted? If jeopardy attaches, the next question is whether a retrial of a defendant is permitted. This question is not a mere formality but is nuanced and complex. Retrials of prosecutions are authorized by statute today but are limited by double jeopardy principles.

Retrials in Various Contexts. The issue of the permissibility of a retrial arises in different contexts, such as whether there has been an acquittal, mistrial, dismissal, or conviction. If there has been an acquittal, no retrial is generally permitted. If there has been a conviction that has been set aside, the initial conviction is generally considered a nullity, and a retrial is permitted.

Mistrials & Double Jeopardy. Mistrials usually can be retried if there was manifest necessity for the mistrial. If there has been a dismissal prior to a final judgment, a retrial is often permitted, unless the basis for the dismissal was insufficiency of the evidence. If the dismissal was grounds other than insufficiency of the evidence, such as prejudice or a judicial error, a fair conclusion of the proceedings through a retrial is generally considered to be appropriate.

Major Themes

a.   Attachment—What does it mean for jeopardy to "attach?" The line between jeopardy attaching and not is an important one, generally limiting the prosecution to a "use it or lose it" situation.

b.   Posture of Case—The applicability of Double Jeopardy depends on the posture of the case—for example, was the initial case a dismissal, mistrial, completed trial with acquittal or conviction, or a charging of multiple offenses arising out of the same conduct?

c.   Retrials—Even if jeopardy applies, retrials are sometimes permitted. The question of whether a retrial is permitted, and whether a higher sentence can be imposed on remand than in the first sentence, depends on the circumstances and the applicable rules.

For More Information

- RUSSELL L. WEAVER, JOHN M. BURKOFF, CATHERINE HANCOCK & STEVEN I. FRIEDLAND, PRINCIPLES OF CRIMINAL PROCEDURE Ch. 21 (8th ed. 2024).

Test Your Knowledge

To assess your understanding of the material in this chapter, click here to take a quiz.

CHAPTER 22

Post-Trial Motions &
Direct Appeals

There are significant differences between the trial and appellate stages of a criminal proceeding. The purpose of the trial stage from the State's point of view is to convert a criminal defendant from a person presumed innocent to one found guilty beyond a reasonable doubt. By contrast, it is ordinarily the defendant, rather than the State, who initiates the appellate process, seeking not to fend off the efforts of the State's prosecutor but rather to overturn a finding of guilt made by a judge or a jury below.

—*Ross v. Moffitt*, 417 U.S. 600, 610 (1974)

Take Note

Following conviction, the defendant has several avenues of relief available and has access to a number of forums where he can obtain review of his conviction. Motions to set aside the verdict and motions for a new trial are addressed to the trial court. Direct appeal lies to the state appellate courts, while *habeas corpus* petitions can be filed in both state and federal court. This chapter addresses the forms of judicial review in the order in which they normally arise, and highlights substantive differences between the forms of judicial review, as well as distinct procedural requirements relating to time and form. Post-conviction remedies are addressed in the next Chapter.

A. Review by the Trial Court

1. Trial *De Novo*

In most appeals, a higher court is asked to scrutinize the trial record for errors that would require reversal of the conviction. In some states, however, misdemeanor charges are tried in lower courts, such as police courts or magistrate courts, from which no record or transcript of the proceedings is available for review by a higher court. These lower courts are sometimes referred to as courts-not-of-record and usually operate without a jury and without all of the procedural safeguards provided in the trial of felony cases. A defendant convicted in such a lower court is often granted an absolute right to a trial *de novo* in a superior court, sometimes called a court-of-record. Although occasionally referred to as an appeal, the granting of a trial *de novo* is normally automatic upon the defendant's request. Thus, no error need be alleged as to the first trial, and a defendant who exercises his right to a trial *de novo* is not entitled to judicial review of the sufficiency of the evidence presented to the lower court. *Justices of Boston Municipal Court v. Lydon*, 466 U.S. 294 (1984).

Food for Thought

Why might some jurisdictions choose to have such a system? What are the benefits? What are the costs? Do the benefits outweigh the costs?

FYI

The right to a trial *de novo* generally exists even when the defendant pled guilty in the lower court. Neither the defendant's plea nor the lower court's judgment is admissible evidence at the trial *de novo*, but the defendant's prior testimony is admissible at the trial in the higher court. Due Process prohibits prosecutorial vindictiveness in increasing the charges at the trial *de novo*. *Blackledge v. Perry*, 417 U.S. 21 (1974); *Thigpen v. Roberts*, 468 U.S. 27 (1984). However, the punishment imposed at the trial *de novo* may be harsher than that imposed by the lower court. *Colten v. Kentucky*, 407 U.S. 104 (1972).

2. Motions for New Trial & to Set Aside the Verdict

Prior to appeal to an appellate court, the defense may ask the trial court to set aside the guilty verdict and/or for a new trial. The procedures for such motions are very specific to individual jurisdictions and are governed by statute. A motion to set aside the verdict can be made after a guilty verdict is returned, and the motion can be based on: 1) the insufficiency or weight of the evidence; 2) error committed during trial; or 3) newly discovered evidence. Motions to set aside the verdict because of insufficiency of the evidence or error occurring at trial require the trial judge to review the case, the evidence submitted, and any errors in dealing with the introduction of evidence.

FYI

In some jurisdictions, a motion to set aside the verdict is referred to as a "judgment NOV" or "judgment notwithstanding the verdict." It also may simply be a "motion for a new trial," depending upon the grounds.

Defendants making motions to set aside the verdict and for a new trial because of newly discovered evidence have a high burden. The courts generally require that defense counsel prove: 1) the evidence was discovered after the trial concluded; 2) the evidence could not, by the exercise of diligence, have been discovered before the trial terminated; 3) the evidence is material and likely to produce a different verdict at the new trial; and 4) the evidence is not merely cumulative, corroborative, or collateral.

Hypo 1: *New Evidence of Self-Defense*

A defendant charged with murder testified that the deceased said, "I will kill you," and reached into his right pocket. Defendant maintained that he acted in self-defense because he knew the deceased often carried a razor and a pistol, and defendant thought the deceased was reaching for a weapon. While the jury was deliberating, a spectator approached defense counsel and related that he had seen a knife in the deceased's hand. Following conviction, defense moves for a new trial based on this newly discovered evidence. What result? *See Connell v. Commonwealth*, 144 Va. 553, 131 S.E. 196 (1926).

Hypo 2: *Sister's Withheld Testimony*

The government charged defendant with knowingly purchasing a fully automatic M-16 rifle at a gun show and later selling it to a pawn shop. Defendant claimed that Rogers, his sister's boyfriend, was the one who purchased the M-16, and that the next time that he saw the rifle was when his sister asked him to pawn it on Rogers's behalf. Defendant did not dispute that he possessed and eventually transferred the firearm described in the indictment. But he argued that he was unaware at the time that the internal mechanism of the M-16 had been altered to convert it to a fully automatic weapon. At trial, the central issue was whether defendant knew that the M-16 was a fully automatic weapon when he sold it to the pawn shop. The jury found the government's evidence convincing and convicted defendant. Three weeks later, defendant's sister informed defense counsel that the M-16 belonged to Rogers, and that she had asked defendant to pawn it on Rogers's behalf. She further stated that neither she nor defendant knew that the M-16 had been converted into a machine gun. At the time of her brother's trial, she told defendant that she would not testify truthfully on his behalf because she was involved in an intimate relationship with Rogers and did not want to place her boyfriend in jeopardy. She decided to tell the truth after she broke up with Rogers. As defense counsel, how would you argue a motion for a new trial based on the information supplied by defendant's sister? As the prosecutor, on what grounds would you oppose the motion?

B. Direct Appeal in the State Courts

1. The Right to Appeal

The Court has noted, at least in dicta, that "a review by an appellate court of the final judgment in a criminal case, however grave the offense of which the accused is convicted, was not at common law and is not now a necessary element of due process."

> **FYI**
>
> There was no right to appeal in criminal cases at common law, and England did not permit appeals from a criminal conviction until 1907. Appeals as of right in federal courts were nonexistent for the first century of our nation, and appellate review of any sort was rarely allowed. The States did not generally recognize an appeal as of right until 1889.

McKane v. Durston, 153 U.S. 684 (1894). Justice Scalia cited *McKane* for the proposition that "there is no constitutional right to appeal," and "a State could, as far as the federal Constitution is concerned, subject its trial-court determinations to no review whatever." *Martinez v. Court of Appeal*, 528 U.S. 152 (2000). However, by statute or State constitution, a right of appeal is now universal for all significant convictions.

The distinction between a right of appeal and discretionary review by an appellate court is important because the U.S. Supreme Court has held that in felony cases, counsel must be provided to indigent persons exercising their state-given right to appeal. *Douglas v. California*, 372 U.S. 353 (1963). However, counsel need not be provided to indigent defendants seeking discretionary review. *Ross v. Moffitt*, 417 U.S. 600 (1974). The right to counsel on appeal stems from the due process and equal protection clauses of the Fourteenth Amendment, not from the Sixth Amendment. Thus, although the Sixth Amendment guarantees the defendant's right to self-representation at trial, there is no such right at the appellate stage. *Martinez v. Court of Appeal*, 528 U.S. 152 (2000).

> **Food for Thought**
>
> Given that a right of appeal is not constitutionally mandated, why do the States and the federal government nonetheless provide for at least one appeal as of right? What are the values or goals involved? Does the benefit only inure to the criminal defendant or is there also some benefit to the State or the criminal justice system generally?

The appellate process begins with defendant's filing of a notice or petition of appeal. Such notice informs the parties, the trial judge and the appellate court that the case is being appealed. All jurisdictions require that the notice of appeal be filed within a specified period of time. For example, in the federal system the notice of appeal must be filed within ten days of the date of judgment. At the time the notice of appeal is filed, or at a subsequent specified date, the parties must designate portions of the trial record that will be sent to the appellate court. The appellate court bases its review of the case on the trial record which commonly includes: 1) jury instructions given or refused by the trial judge; 2) exhibits offered in evidence; 3) any orders entered by the trial court; 4) any opinion or memorandum decision rendered by the trial judge; 5) any pretrial discovery material requested; and 6) the entire trial transcript or just portions in which the judge ruled upon objections to the introduction of evidence.

FYI

Most jurisdictions have created a two-tiered appellate structure in which the convicted defendant has a right of appeal to an intermediate appellate court; a further appeal to a higher court, usually the State Supreme Court, which may be discretionary.

Counsel also must alert the appellate court to the basis of appeal by filing a statement of issues that the appellate court is asked to resolve. These issues will be expanded upon in counsels' written briefs that summarize the factual background of the case and set forth relevant legal arguments. The appellate court, usually in its discretion, may hear oral arguments on the issues raised.

2. Standards of Review

The thorniest legal issue on appeal is what standard of review the appellate court must apply. As an initial matter, the standard of review will depend in part on whether defense counsel preserved the issue for appeal by making a contemporaneous objection. The contemporaneous objection requirement is designed to afford opposing counsel an opportunity to respond to the objection, to allow the trial court to rule in the first instance as to the propriety of the objection, and to preclude defense counsel from "sandbagging" the trial court by not calling possible errors to its attention.

Practice Pointer

Criminal defense attorneys need to be aware of the importance of preserving issues for appeal because an unpreserved issue will face a much higher standard of review on appeal. To preserve an issue, a defense attorney must make a contemporaneous objection to a ruling of the court and articulate the reasons for the objection. It is critical that a defense attorney's reasons include those that are federally-based (*i.e.,* constitutional claims) along with those that are state-based. Preserved federal issues are the only ones that may be reviewed on *habeas corpus*, discussed in the next Chapter.

Many appellate courts also require opposing counsel to state the basis for opposing the objection, and require the trial judge to "state on the record" the grounds on which his ruling is based. In *United States v. Williams*, 951 F.2d 1287 (D.C. Cir. 1991), the court explained the purpose of the federal version of the rule:

Rule 12(e) of the Federal Rules of Criminal Procedure commands the court to "state its essential findings on the record." The rule serves several functions. Findings on the record inform the parties and other interested persons of the grounds of the ruling, add discipline to the process of judicial decision-making and enable appellate courts properly to perform their reviewing function. If the district court not only fails to make "essential findings on the record," but also expresses nothing in the way of legal reasoning, if it simply announces a result, it may frustrate these objectives. We say "may" because there are cases in which the facts are so certain, and the legal consequences so apparent, that little guesswork is needed to determine the grounds for the ruling.

Williams was a case where guesswork was needed, however. The court had to balance a countervailing appellate rule that allowed a reviewing court to sustain the trial court's ruling "if there is any reasonable view of the evidence that will support it." Because the appellate court had nothing in the record to suggest a factual or legal basis for the ruling, however, the *Williams* court remanded the case for the factual findings required by Rule 12(e).

a. Harmless Error Review & Structural Error

Trial errors can be of constitutional dimension—a violation of a constitutional right of the defendant, such as the Sixth Amendment right to confront witnesses—or non-constitutional, such as an error excluding a piece of evidence contrary to state evidence rules. A trial error that is not of constitutional dimension is harmless when it plainly appears from the facts and circumstances of the case that the error did not affect the verdict. Reversal is required for a non-constitutional error only if it "had substantial and injurious effect or influence in determining the jury's verdict." *United States v. Lane*, 474 U.S. 438 (1986).

Application of the harmless error doctrine to constitutional error depends upon the nature of the error, *i.e.,* whether the error is a "structural error" or not. Structural errors "are so intrinsically harmful as to require automatic reversal (*i.e.,* "affect substantial rights") without regard to their effect on the outcome." *Neder v. United States*, 527 U.S. 1 (1999). They are the type of errors whose effect is impossible to measure. The Court has recognized a limited number of structural errors requiring automatic reversal. They include: 1) unlawful exclusion of members of the defendant's race from a grand jury, *Vasquez v. Hillery*, 474 U.S. 254 (1986), 2) exclusion of a juror reluctant to impose the death penalty (but not opposed under all circumstances), *Gray v. Mississippi*, 481 U.S. 648 (1987), 3) absolute denial of the right to a public trial, *Waller v. Georgia*, 467 U.S. 39 (1984), 4) denial of the right of self-representation, *McKaskle v. Wiggins*, 465 U.S. 168 (1984), 5) a trial presided over by a biased judge, *Tumey v. Ohio*, 273 U.S. 510 (1927), 6) absolute denial of the right to counsel, *Gideon v.*

Wainwright, 372 U.S. 335 (1963), and 7) a constitutionally inadequate jury instruction on reasonable doubt, *Sullivan v. Louisiana*, 508 U.S. 275 (1993).

Constitutional errors that are not structural are treated differently depending on whether they are raised on direct appeal or collateral review. On collateral review (*e.g., habeas corpus* petitions), trial errors require reversal of the conviction only if the defendant proves "actual prejudice," *i.e.*, the error had a "substantial and injurious effect or influence in determining the jury's verdict." *Brecht v. Abrahamson*, 507 U.S. 619 (1993). On direct review, however, *Chapman v. California* held that trial errors require reversal of the conviction unless the reviewing court finds such errors to be harmless "beyond a reasonable doubt."

Food for Thought

Can you see why the errors listed as "structural" cannot be subject to harmless error analysis? Do the structural errors requiring automatic reversal reflect more serious errors than the constitutional errors that are subject to harmless error analysis (*i.e.*, right of confrontation, right to effective assistance of counsel, right to be present at all critical stages of the trial).

Chapman v. California

386 U.S. 18 (1967).

JUSTICE BLACK delivered the opinion of the Court.

Petitioners, Ruth Elizabeth Chapman and Thomas LeRoy Teale, were convicted in a California state court upon a charge that they robbed, kidnaped, and murdered a bartender. She was sentenced to life imprisonment and he to death. At the time of the trial, Art I, § 13, of the State's Constitution provided that 'in any criminal case, whether the defendant testifies or not, his failure to explain or to deny by his testimony any evidence or facts in the case against him may be commented upon by the court and by counsel, and may be considered by the court or the jury.' Both petitioners in this case chose not to testify at their trial, and the State's attorney prosecuting them took full advantage of his right under the State Constitution to comment upon their failure to testify, filling his argument to the jury from beginning to end with numerous references to their silence and inferences of their guilt resulting therefrom. The trial court also charged the jury that it could draw adverse inferences from petitioners' failure to testify. Shortly after the trial, but before petitioners' cases had been considered on appeal, this Court decided *Griffin v. State of*

Hear It

You can listen to the oral argument in *Chapman* at: http://www.oyez.org/cases/1960-1969/1966/1966_95.

California, 380 U.S. 609, which held California's constitutional provision and practice invalid on the ground that they put a penalty on the exercise of a person's right not to be compelled to be a witness against himself, guaranteed by the Fifth Amendment to the United States Constitution and made applicable to California and the other States by the Fourteenth Amendment. On appeal, the State Supreme Court, admitting that petitioners had been denied a federal constitutional right by the comments on their silence, nevertheless affirmed, applying the State Constitution's harmless-error provision, which forbids reversal unless 'the court shall be of the opinion that the error complained of has resulted in a miscarriage of justice.'

We are urged to hold that all federal constitutional errors, regardless of the facts and circumstances, must always be deemed harmful. Such a holding would require an automatic reversal of their convictions. We decline to adopt any such rule. All 50 States have harmless-error statutes or rules, and the United States long ago through its Congress established for its courts the rule that judgments shall not be reversed for 'errors or defects which do not affect the substantial rights of the parties.' None of these rules on its face distinguishes between federal constitutional errors and errors of state law or federal statutes and rules. All of these rules, state or federal, serve a very useful purpose insofar as they block setting aside convictions for small errors or defects that have little, if any, likelihood of having changed the result of the trial. We conclude that there may be some constitutional errors which in the setting of a particular case are so unimportant and insignificant that they may, consistent with the Federal Constitution, be deemed harmless, not requiring the automatic reversal of the conviction.

In fashioning a harmless-constitutional-error rule, we must recognize that harmless-error rules can work very unfair and mischievous results when, for example, highly important and persuasive evidence, or argument, though legally forbidden, finds its way into a trial in which the question of guilt or innocence is a close one. What harmless-error rules all aim at is a rule that will save the good in harmless-error practices while avoiding the bad, so far as possible.

The federal rule emphasizes 'substantial rights' as do most others. The California constitutional rule emphasizes 'a miscarriage of justice,' but the California courts have neutralized this to some extent by emphasis, and perhaps overemphasis, upon the court's view of 'overwhelming evidence.' We prefer the approach of this Court in deciding what was harmless error in our recent case of *Fahy v. State of Connecticut*, 375 U.S. 85. There we said: 'The question is whether there is a reasonable possibility that the evidence complained of might have contributed to the conviction.' Although our prior cases have indicated that there are some constitutional rights so basic to a fair trial that their infraction can never be treated as harmless error, this statement in *Fahy* itself belies any belief that all trial errors which violate the Constitution automatically call for reversal. At the same time, like the federal harmless-error statute, it emphasizes an intention not to treat as harmless those constitutional errors that 'affect substantial rights' of a party. An error in admitting plainly relevant evidence which possibly influenced the jury adversely to a litigant cannot, under *Fahy*, be conceived of as harmless. Certainly error, constitutional error, in illegally admitting highly prejudicial evidence or comments, casts on someone other than the person prejudiced by it a burden to show that it was harmless. It is for that reason that the original common-law harmless-error rule put the burden on the beneficiary of the error either to prove that there was no injury or to suffer a reversal of his erroneously obtained judgment. There is little, if any, difference between our statement in *Fahy v. State of Connecticut* about 'whether there is a reasonable possibility that the evidence complained of might have contributed to the conviction' and requiring the beneficiary of a constitutional error to prove beyond a reasonable doubt that the error complained of did not contribute to the verdict obtained. We do no more than adhere to the meaning of our *Fahy* case when we hold, as we now do, that before a federal constitutional error can be held harmless, the court must be able to declare a belief that it was harmless beyond a reasonable doubt. While appellate courts do not ordinarily have the original task of applying such a test, it is a familiar standard to all courts, and its adoption will provide a more workable standard, although achieving the same result as that aimed at in our *Fahy* case.

Applying the foregoing standard, we have no doubt that the error in these cases was not harmless to petitioners. To reach this conclusion one need only glance at the prosecutorial comments compiled from the record by petitioners' counsel and (with minor omissions) set forth in the Appendix. The California Supreme Court fairly summarized the extent of these comments as follows:

> Such comments went to the motives for the procurement and handling of guns purchased by Mrs. Chapman, funds or the lack thereof in Mr. Teale's possession immediately prior to the killing, the amount of intoxicating liquors consumed by defendants at the Spot Club and other taverns, the circumstances of the shooting in the automobile and the removal of the victim's body therefrom, who fired the fatal shots, why defendants used a false registration at a motel shortly after the killing, the meaning of a letter written by Mrs. Chapman several days after the killing, why Teale had a loaded weapon in his possession when apprehended, the meaning of statements made by Teale after his apprehension, why certain clothing and articles of personal property were shipped by defendants to Missouri, what clothing Mrs. Chapman wore at the time of the killing, conflicting statements as to Mrs. Chapman's whereabouts immediately preceding the killing and, generally, the overall commission of the crime.

Thus, the state prosecutor's argument and the trial judge's instruction to the jury continuously and repeatedly impressed the jury that from the failure of petitioners to testify, to all intents and purposes, the inferences from the facts in evidence had to be drawn in favor of the State—in short, that by their silence petitioners had served as irrefutable witnesses against themselves. Though the case in which this occurred presented a reasonably strong 'circumstantial web of evidence' against petitioners, it was also a case in which, absent the constitutionally forbidden comments, honest, fair-minded jurors might very well have brought in not-guilty verdicts. Under these circumstances, it is impossible for us to say that the State has demonstrated, beyond a reasonable doubt, that the prosecutor's comments and the trial judge's instruction did not contribute to petitioners' convictions. Such a machine-gun repetition of a denial of constitutional rights, designed and calculated to make petitioners' version of the evidence worthless, can no more be considered harmless than the introduction against a defendant of a coerced confession. Petitioners are entitled to a trial free from the pressure of unconstitutional inferences.

Reversed and remanded.

Points for Discussion

a.   Applying Harmless Error Anticipatorily at Trial?

In *Hackney v. Commonwealth*, 28 Va.App. 288, 504 S.E.2d 385 (1998), defendant was charged with grand larceny and possession of a firearm by a convicted felon. In light of well-settled precedent that justice requires separate trials "where evidence of one crime is not admissible in the trial of the others," the defendant filed a motion to sever the charge of possession of a firearm by a convicted felon from the larceny charge. The trial judge and defense counsel had the following discussion:

Food for Thought

Once an appellate court finds there is constitutional error, *Chapman* states that the prosecution must bear the burden of proving the error was harmless. Why is that so? Since the defendant was convicted and no longer presumed innocent, should the defendant bear the burden on all issues on appeal, including showing prejudice? What are the values *Chapman* is espousing by placing the burden on the prosecution?

THE COURT: The Commonwealth is going to ask the question, "Have you ever been convicted of a felony or a misdemeanor involving lying, cheating and stealing?" They're going to ask that question at some point during the trial as well.

DEFENSE COUNSEL: If he takes the stand.

THE COURT: If he takes the stand.

DEFENSE COUNSEL: If he takes the stand.

THE COURT: And the Court certainly can't rule that out. Previous cases recognized that if the defendant testifies, prior convictions are admissible for impeachment purposes, thus rendering harmless any error in denying a motion to sever the charges. I think the Court would have to overrule Counsel's motion here.

During its case-in-chief, the prosecution introduced prior convictions for three grand larceny and burglary offenses committed by defendant in order to prove a required element of the firearm charge, namely, that defendant was a convicted felon. Defendant testified in his defense to the larceny and firearm charges. On cross-examination, the prosecution elicited for impeachment purposes, testimony from the defendant that he had been previously convicted of three felonies. The jury found defendant guilty of grand larceny and possession of a firearm by a convicted felon. A panel of the appellate court held that in light of the defendant's decision to testify, the trial court's refusal to sever the charges was harmless error. Upon a rehearing en banc, the full court reversed the panel's decision:

> We hold that, as a matter of policy, we will not condone a trial court's clear error in refusing to sever the possession of a firearm by a felony charge predicated on the assumption that an accused will testify and render the error harmless. The harmless error doctrine is applicable only upon appellate review or in the trial court upon consideration of a motion to set aside a verdict. When applicable, the harmless error doctrine enables an appellate court or a trial court when considering a motion to set aside a verdict to ignore the effect of an erroneous ruling when an error clearly has had no impact upon the verdict or sentence in a case. The harmless error doctrine should not be used prospectively by a trial court as a basis to disregard an established rule of law.

The Court held that the trial court's refusal to sever was not harmless beyond a reasonable doubt.

b. Correct Burden Allocation

In *Gamache v. California*, 562 U.S. 1083 (2010), the Court denied certiorari, but four Justices expressed concern about the denial because, contrary to *Chapman*, the California Supreme Court stated that *defendant* was required "to demonstrate prejudice under the usual standard for ordinary trial error." Justice Sotomayor objected, stating: "It is not clear what the court intended in allocating the burden to the defendant to demonstrate prejudice, but if it meant to convey that the defendant bore the burden of persuasion, that would contravene *Chapman*. The allocation of the burden of proving harmlessness can be outcome determinative in some cases. With all that is at stake in capital cases, in future cases the California courts should take care to ensure that their burden allocation conforms to the commands of *Chapman*."

> ### Hypo: *Harmless Error & Jury Instructions*
>
> Defendant, who was charged with robbery, was positively identified by two victims (a cashier at a storage facility and a cashier at a convenience store). In addition, a security camera recorded his face and voice during one of the encounters. During his jury instructions, the judge failed to inform the jury of the elements or facts that must be shown in order to prove the crime of robbery (taking another's property, from his possession, in his presence, against his will, through force or fear). The judge did inform the jurors of the required mental state and the need to find that defendant used a weapon in the crime. Can this error be regarded as harmless? *See People v. Merritt*, 2 Cal.5th 819, 392 P.3d 421 (Cal. 2017).

b.   Plain Error Review

When a defendant fails to object to an error at trial, whether one of constitutional or non-constitutional dimension, but later calls the error to the attention of the appellate court, the standard of review is for plain error, which is a much higher standard of review than harmless error. An appellate court may review the record for plain error and may reverse the conviction to attain the ends of justice.

United States v. Olano

507 U.S. 725 (1993).

JUSTICE O'CONNOR delivered the opinion of the Court.

The question is whether the presence of alternate jurors during jury deliberations was a "plain error" that the Court of Appeals was authorized to correct under Federal Rule of Criminal Procedure 52(b).

Each of the respondents, Guy W. Olano, Jr., and Raymond M. Gray, served on the board of directors of a savings and loan association. In 1986, the two were indicted in the Western District of Washington on multiple federal charges for their participation in an elaborate loan "kickback" scheme. Their joint jury trial with five other codefendants commenced in March 1987. All of the parties agreed that 14 jurors would be selected to hear the case, and that the 2 alternates would be identified before deliberations began.

Hear It

You can listen to the oral argument in *Olano* at: http://www.oyez.org/cases/1990-1999/1992/1992_91_1306.

The matter arose again the next day, in an ambiguous exchange between Gray's counsel and the District Court:

> THE COURT: Have you given any more thought as to whether you want the alternates to go in and not participate, or do you want them out?

> MR. ROBISON counsel for Gray: We would ask they not.

One day later, on May 28, the last day of trial, the District Court for a third time asked the defendants whether they wanted the alternate jurors to retire into the jury room. Counsel for defendant Davy Hilling gave an unequivocal, affirmative answer.

> THE COURT: Well, Counsel, I received your alternates. Do I understand that the defendants now—it's hard to keep up with you, Counsel. It's sort of a day by day—but that's all right. You do all agree that all fourteen deliberate?

> Okay. Do you want me to instruct the two alternates not to participate in deliberation?

> MR. KELLOGG counsel for Hilling: That's what I was on my feet to say. It's my understanding that the conversation was the two alternates go back there instructed that they are not to take part in any fashion in the deliberations.

The District Court concluded that Hilling's counsel was speaking for the other defendants as well as his own client. None of the other counsel intervened during the colloquy between the District Court and Hilling's counsel on May 28, nor did anyone object later the same day when the court instructed the jurors that the two alternates would be permitted to attend but not participate in deliberations.

Both respondents were convicted on a number of charges. They appealed to the United States Court of Appeals for the Ninth Circuit. The Court of Appeals reversed certain counts for insufficient evidence and then considered whether the presence of alternate jurors during jury deliberations violated Federal Rule of Criminal Procedure 24(c): An alternate juror who does not replace a regular juror shall be discharged after the jury retires to consider its verdict.

Because respondents had not objected to the alternates' presence, the court applied a "plain error" standard under Rule 52(b). The court found that Rule 24(c) was violated in the instant case, because "the district court did not obtain individual waivers from each defendant personally, either orally or in writing." It then held that the presence of alternates in violation of Rule 24(c) was "inherently prejudicial" and reversible per se:

We cannot fairly ascertain whether in a given case the alternate jurors followed the district court's prohibition on participation. However, even if they heeded the letter of the court's instructions and remained orally mute throughout, it is entirely possible that their attitudes, conveyed by facial expressions, gestures or the like, may have had some effect upon the decision of one or more jurors.

Finally, in a footnote, the court decided that "because the violation is inherently prejudicial and because it infringes upon a substantial right of the defendants, it falls within the plain error doctrine." We granted certiorari to clarify the standard for "plain error" review by the courts of appeals under Rule 52(b).

"No procedural principle is more familiar to this Court than that a constitutional right," or a right of any other sort, "may be forfeited in criminal as well as civil cases by the failure to make timely assertion of the right before a tribunal having jurisdiction to determine it." *Yakus v. United States*, 321 U.S. 414, 444 (1944). Federal Rule of Criminal Procedure 52(b) provides a court of appeals a limited power to correct errors that were forfeited because not timely raised in district court.

Although "a rigid and undeviating judicially declared practice under which courts of review would invariably and under all circumstances decline to consider all questions which had not previously been specifically urged would be out of harmony with the rules of fundamental justice," there must be an "error" that is "plain" and that "affects substantial rights." Moreover, Rule 52(b) leaves the decision to correct the forfeited error within the sound discretion of the court of appeals, and the court should not exercise that discretion unless the error "seriously affects the fairness, integrity or public reputation of judicial proceedings." *United States v. Young*, 470 U.S. 1, 15 (1985).

Rule 52(b) defines a single category of forfeited-but-reversible error. Although it is possible to read the Rule in the disjunctive, as creating two separate categories—"plain errors" and "defects affecting substantial rights"—that reading is surely wrong. As we explained in *Young*, the phrase "error or defect" is more simply read as "error." The forfeited error "may be noticed" only if it is "plain" and "affects substantial rights." More precisely, a court of appeals may correct the error (either vacating for a new trial, or reversing outright) only if it meets these criteria.

The first limitation on appellate authority under Rule 52(b) is that there indeed be an "error." Deviation from a legal rule is "error" unless the rule has been waived. For example, a defendant who knowingly and voluntarily pleads guilty in conformity with the requirements of Rule 11 cannot have his conviction vacated by court of appeals on the grounds that he ought to have had a trial. Because the right to trial is waivable, and because the defendant who enters a valid guilty plea waives that right, his conviction without a trial is not "error."

Waiver is different from forfeiture. Whereas forfeiture is the failure to make the timely assertion of a right, waiver is the "intentional relinquishment or abandonment of a known right." Whether a particular right is waivable; whether the defendant must participate personally in the waiver; whether certain procedures are required for waiver; and whether the defendant's choice must be particularly informed or voluntary, all depend on the right at stake. Mere forfeiture, as opposed to waiver, does not extinguish an "error" under Rule 52(b). If a legal rule was violated during the district court proceedings, and if the defendant did not waive the rule, then there has been an "error" within the meaning of Rule 52(b) despite the absence of a timely objection.

The second limitation on appellate authority under Rule 52(b) is that the error be "plain." "Plain" is synonymous with "clear" or, equivalently, "obvious." We need not consider the special case where the error was unclear at the time of trial but becomes clear on appeal because the applicable law has been clarified. At a minimum, court of appeals cannot correct an error pursuant to Rule 52(b) unless the error is clear under current law.

The third and final limitation on appellate authority under Rule 52(b) is that the plain error "affect substantial rights." This is the same language employed in Rule 52(a), and in most cases it means that the error must have been prejudicial: It must have affected the outcome of the district court proceedings. When the defendant has made a timely objection to an error and Rule 52(a) applies, a court of appeals nor-

> **FYI**
>
> In *Henderson v. United States*, 568 U.S. 266 (2013), the Court held that an error is "plain" for "plain error" review, as long as the law was settled at the time of appellate review. The Court reasoned that adopting the "time of review" standard as opposed to the "time of error" standard puts appellants on equal footing and allows the appellate court to apply present law.

mally engages in a specific analysis of the district court record—a so-called "harmless error" inquiry—to determine whether the error was prejudicial. Rule 52(b) normally requires the same kind of inquiry, with one important difference: It is the defendant rather than the Government who bears the burden of persuasion with respect to prejudice. In most cases, a court of appeals cannot correct the forfeited error unless the defendant shows that the error was prejudicial. This burden shifting is dictated by a subtle but important difference in language between the two parts of Rule 52: While Rule 52(a) precludes error correction only if the error "does not affect substantial rights," Rule 52(b) authorizes no remedy unless the error does "affect substantial rights."

Rule 52(b) is permissive, not mandatory. If the forfeited error is "plain" and "affects substantial rights," the court of appeals has authority to order correction, but is not required to do so. The language of the Rule ("may be noticed"), the nature of forfeiture, and the established appellate practice that Congress intended to continue all point to this conclusion. "In criminal cases, where the life, or as in this case the liberty, of the defendant is at stake, the courts of the United States, in the exercise of a sound discretion, may notice forfeited error."

The Court of Appeals should correct a plain forfeited error affecting substantial rights if the error "seriously affects the fairness, integrity or public reputation of judicial proceedings." As we explained, the "standard laid down in *United States v. Atkinson* was codified in Federal Rule of Criminal Procedure 52(b)," and we repeatedly have quoted the *Atkinson* language in describing plain-error review. An error may "seriously affect the fairness, integrity or public reputation of judicial proceedings" independent of the defendant's innocence. Conversely, a plain error affecting substantial rights does not, without more, satisfy the *Atkinson* standard, for otherwise the discretion afforded by Rule 52(b) would be illusory.

With these basic principles in mind, we turn to the instant case. The Government essentially concedes that the "error" was "plain." We therefore focus our attention on whether the error "affected substantial rights" within the meaning of Rule 52(b), and conclude that it did not. The presence of alternate jurors during jury deliberations is not the kind of error that "affects substantial rights" independent of its prejudicial impact. Nor have respondents made a specific showing of prejudice. Respondents have made no specific showing that the alternate jurors in this case either participated in the jury's deliberations or "chilled" deliberation by the regular jurors. Nor will we presume prejudice for purposes of the Rule 52(b) analysis here. The Court of Appeals was incorrect in finding the error "inherently prejudicial." Until the close of trial, the 2 alternate jurors were indistinguishable from the 12 regular jurors. Along with the regular jurors, they commenced their office with an oath, received the normal initial admonishment, heard the same evidence and arguments, and were not identified as alternates until after the District Court gave a final set of instructions. In those instructions, the District Court specifically enjoined the jurors that "according to the law, the alternates must not participate in the deliberations," and reiterated, "we are going to ask that you not participate." The Court of Appeals should not have supposed that this injunction was contravened. "It is the almost invariable assumption of the law that jurors follow their instructions." "We presume that jurors, conscious of the gravity of their task, attend closely the particular language of the trial court's instructions in a criminal case and strive to understand, make sense of, and follow the instructions given them." Nor do we think that the mere presence of alternate jurors entailed a sufficient risk of "chill" to justify a presumption of prejudice on that score. In sum, respondents have not met their burden of showing

Take Note

As reiterated by the Court in *United States v. Marcus*, 560 U.S. 258 (2010), plain error analysis requires a "reasonable probability that the error affected the outcome of the trial," not just "any possibility no matter how likely."

prejudice under Rule 52(b). Because the conceded error in this case did not "affect substantial rights," the Court of Appeals had no authority to correct it. The judgment of the Court of Appeals is reversed, and the case is remanded for further proceedings consistent with this opinion.

c. Review for Sufficiency of the Evidence

The one claim that a defendant can make without concern about preserving the issue at trial is that the jury or judge convicted him based upon insufficient evidence. In *In re Winship*, 397 U.S. 358 (1970), the Court held that the requirement that the prosecution prove every element of the charged offense beyond a reasonable doubt is essential to Fourteenth Amendment due process. In *Jackson v. Virginia*, 443 U.S. 307 (1979), the Court discussed how that requirement should be viewed on appeal:

> After *Winship* the critical inquiry on review of the sufficiency of the evidence to support a criminal conviction must be not simply to determine whether the jury was properly instructed, but to determine whether the record evidence could reasonably support a finding of guilt beyond a reasonable doubt. But this inquiry does not require a court to "ask itself whether it believes that the evidence at the trial established guilt beyond a reasonable doubt." Instead, the relevant question is whether, after viewing the evidence in the light most favorable to the prosecution, *any* rational trier of fact could have found the essential elements of the crime beyond a reasonable doubt. This familiar standard gives full play to the responsibility of the trier of fact fairly to resolve conflicts in the testimony, to weigh the evidence, and to draw reasonable inferences from the basic facts to ultimate facts.

> **Take Note**
>
> The "*any* rational trier of fact" standard makes appeals on the basis of insufficiency of the evidence very difficult to sustain: in essence, the prosecution must have neglected to produce *any* credible evidence in support of an element of the offense. If this were the case, a defense attorney should win a motion for a directed verdict or a motion to set aside the verdict, as described above in Part A.2.

> Once a defendant has been found guilty of the crime charged, the fact finder's role as weigher of the evidence is preserved through a legal conclusion that upon judicial review *all of the evidence* is to be considered in the light most favorable to the prosecution. The criterion thus impinges upon "jury" discretion only to the extent necessary to guarantee the fundamental protection of due process of law.

3. Waiver of the Right to Appeal

As with all rights, a defendant can waive his right to appeal. For example, defendants can waive their right to appeal as part of a plea bargain. In *United States v. Wenger*, 58 F.3d 280 (7th Cir. 1995), the defendant waived his right to appeal his sentence in return for a plea and then in fact appealed, claiming that the trial judge did not make a specific inquiry as to whether he knowingly and voluntarily waived that right. The Seventh Circuit stated:

> Defendant has appealed, despite his promise not to do so. Waivers of appeal are enforceable. Defendant asks us to establish a procedural citadel around the right of appeal, so that waiver will be accepted only following elaborate warnings after the fashion of those used for the most vital constitutional rights. *See Johnson v. Zerbst*, 304 U.S. 458 (1938) (sixth amendment right to counsel); Fed.R.Crim.P. 11(c). But other rights may be surrendered without warnings of any kind and with considerably less formality. E.g., *Schneckloth v. Bustamonte*, 412 U.S. 218 (1973) (fourth amendment right to privacy); *United States v. Mezzanatto*, 513 U.S. 196 (1995) (right to exclude from evidence proffer made as part of plea negotiations). The right to appeal is in the latter category—not simply because it depends on a statute rather than the Constitution but because it has long been seen as the kind of right that depends on assertion. A litigant who does not take a timely appeal has forfeited any entitlement to appellate review. Our legal system makes no appeal the default position. A defendant who finds this agreeable need do nothing. All the waiver in a plea agreement does is to make that outcome a part of the parties' bargain, so that a defendant inclined against appeal or willing to forgo it—perhaps to put an unpleasant episode behind him more quickly—may obtain a concession from the prosecutor. In this case the prosecutor agreed to support a downward departure for acceptance of responsibility, a boon that usually would be unavailable to a defendant arrested (as defendant was) for an intervening offense.

> Empty promises are worthless promises; if defendants could retract their waivers (the practical effect, if the procedural hurdles to an effective waiver were set too high) then they could not obtain concessions by promising not to appeal. Although any defendant would like to obtain the concession and exercise the right as well, prosecutors cannot be fooled in the long run. Right holders are better off if they can choose between exercising the right and exchanging that right for something they value more highly. Defendant exchanged the right to appeal for prosecutorial concessions; he cannot have his cake and eat it too.

In *United States v. Han*, 181 F. Supp. 2d 1039 (N.D. Cal. 2002), the court held that a waiver of the right to appeal a sentence that is made as part of a plea agreement is a waiver of an unknown error, that is, one which has yet to occur. In light of the requirement that a waiver must be knowing and voluntary, a sentence limited only by the statutory maximum and constitutional constraints does not allow the defendant a fair opportunity to contemplate the *actual*, not theoretical, range of sentence that may be imposed. Accordingly, "a plea agreement containing a waiver of judicial review, should, at the very least, set forth a maximum sentence which the defendant would accept based upon certain assumptions as they relate to sentencing factors, including criminal history." The court offered the following as "standard language of a waiver of appeal" that could be used in plea agreements:

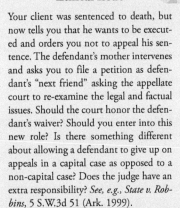

> In exchange for the government's concessions in this plea agreement, defendant waives, to the full extent of the law, any right to appeal or collaterally attack the conviction and sentence, including any restitution order, unless the Court imposes a sentence in excess of ___ months. If the custodial sentence exceeds ___ months, the defendant may appeal, but the government will be free to support on appeal the sentence actually imposed.

Ethical Issue

Your client was sentenced to death, but now tells you that he wants to be executed and orders you not to appeal his sentence. The defendant's mother intervenes and asks you to file a petition as defendant's "next friend" asking the appellate court to re-examine the legal and factual issues. Should the court honor the defendant's waiver? Should you enter into this new role? Is there something different about allowing a defendant to give up on appeals in a capital case as opposed to a non-capital case? Does the judge have an extra responsibility? *See, e.g., State v. Robbins,* 5 S.W.3d 51 (Ark. 1999).

A defendant may also forfeit his appeal as a sanction for escaping from the penal institution holding him. *Molinaro v. New Jersey*, 396 U.S. 365 (1970). However, the Court held that a fugitive defendant does not forfeit his right to appeal if he absconds while his case is pending in trial court but is recaptured before sentencing and appeal. *Ortega-Rodriguez v. United States*, 507 U.S. 234 (1993).

4. Ethics & the Frivolous Appeal

In *Smith v. Robbins*, 528 U.S. 259 (2000), Justice Souter observed that "No one has a right to a wholly frivolous appeal, against which the judicial system's first line of defense is its lawyers. Being officers of the court, members of the bar are bound 'not to clog the courts with frivolous motions or appeals.' " 528 U.S. at 294 (Souter, J., dissenting).

In *Anders v. California*, 386 U.S. 738 (1967), the Court suggested that when an attorney appointed to represent an indigent defendant on direct appeal finds the case wholly frivolous, he should: 1) advise the court and request permission to withdraw; 2) submit a brief referring to anything in the record that might arguably support the appeal; 3) furnish a copy of the brief to the defendant in time to allow him to raise any points that he chooses; and 4) request the court to conduct a full examination and decide whether the case is wholly frivolous.

California replaced an *Anders* brief with a *Wende* brief that provides that "counsel, upon concluding that an appeal would be frivolous, files a brief with the appellate court that summarizes the procedural and factual history of the case, with citation of the record. He also attests that he has reviewed the record, explained his evaluation of the case to his client, provided the client with a copy of the brief, and informed the client of his right to file a *pro se* supplemental brief. He further requests that the court independently examine the record for arguable issues."

The majority in *Smith v. Robbins, supra* approved the California approach: "The procedure we sketched in *Anders v. California*, is a prophylactic one; the States are free to adopt different procedures, so long as those procedures adequately safeguard a defendant's right to appellate counsel" and the State provides a review process that "reasonably ensures that an indigent's appeal will be resolved in a way that is related to the merit of that appeal." In dissent Justice Souter maintained:

> The rub is that although counsel may properly refuse to brief a frivolous issue and a court may just as properly deny leave to take a frivolous appeal, there needs to be some reasonable assurance that the lawyer has not relaxed his partisan instinct prior to refusing, in which case the court's review could never compensate for the lawyer's failure of advocacy. A simple statement by counsel that an appeal has no merit, coupled with an appellate court's endorsement of counsel's conclusion, gives no affirmative indication that anyone has sought out the appellant's best arguments or championed his cause to the degree contemplated by the adversary system. It is owing to

the importance of assuring that an adversarial, not an inquisitorial system is at work that I disagree with the Court's statement today that our cases approve of any state procedure that "reasonably ensures that an indigent's appeal will be resolved in a way that is related to the merit of that appeal." A purely inquisitorial system could satisfy that criterion, and so could one that appoints counsel only if the appellate court deems it useful. But we have rejected the former and have explicitly held the latter unconstitutional.

Make the Connection

A defendant who fails to obtain a reversal on direct appeal may make collateral attacks on the conviction, such as a petition for a writ of *habeas corpus* discussed in the next chapter.

528 U.S. at 294, 296 (Souter, J., dissenting).

5. Appeals of Last Resort

As a supplement to judicial review, all jurisdictions grant a convicted defendant an opportunity to appeal to executive authority for a pardon or grant of clemency. For example, Article 2, Section 2, Clause 1 of the U.S. Constitution gives the President "Power to grant Reprieves and Pardons for Offences against the United States, except in Cases of Impeachment."

FYI

President Gerald Ford gave former President Richard Nixon a "full pardon" for his role in the Watergate scandal. The President also has the power to "forgive the convicted person in part or entirely, to reduce a penalty in terms of a specified number of years, or to alter it with conditions which are in themselves constitutionally unobjectionable." *Schick v. Reed*, 419 U.S. 256 (1974).

Executive Summary

Trials *De Novo*. Some misdemeanor courts allow a defendant to try a case in front of a magistrate and then, if he loses, have a trial *de novo* in a superior court.

Post-Trial Motions. Defendants making motions to set aside the verdict and for a new trial because of newly discovered evidence have a high burden.

One Appeal as of Right. Most jurisdictions provide for one appeal of a criminal conviction as a matter of right.

Discretionary Appeals. A subsequent appeal may be heard only when the court exercises its discretion to accept the case.

Standards of Review. The standard of review on appeal depends both upon the kind of error alleged—whether constitutional or not—and whether it was preserved at trial.

Waiver of Right to Appeal. A defendant can waive his right to appeal.

Major Themes

a. Structural or Reversible Error—Automatic reversal is required in the rare case of a "structural error," a handful of scenarios where the effect of a trial error of constitutional dimension is impossible to measure. If not structural, a trial error of constitutional dimension is reversible unless the prosecution can prove the error was harmless beyond a reasonable doubt.

b. Plain Error—If the defendant failed to preserve an error for appeal, the standard of review is for "plain error," and the defendant bears the burden of proving a reasonable probability that the error affected the outcome.

c. Insufficient Evidence—A reversal for insufficiency of the evidence must meet a high burden—viewing the facts in the light most favorable to the prosecution, the appellate court must find that no reasonable juror could have found the defendant guilty beyond a reasonable doubt.

For More Information

- RUSSELL L. WEAVER, JOHN M. BURKOFF, CATHERINE HANCOCK & STEVEN I. FRIEDLAND, PRINCIPLES OF CRIMINAL PROCEDURE Ch. 21 (8th ed. 2024).

- MAYER BROWN LLP, FEDERAL APPELLATE PRACTICE (2d ed. 2013).

- JAMES WILLIAM MOORE ET AL., MOORE'S FEDERAL PRACTICE (3d ed. 1977–date).

- CHARLES WRIGHT & ARTHUR MILLER, FEDERAL PRACTICE AND PROCEDURE (Rev. ed. 1971–date).

- WAYNE R. LAFAVE, JEROLD H. ISRAEL, NANCY J. KING & ORIN S. KERR, CRIMINAL PROCEDURE (6th ed. 2017).

Test Your Knowledge

To assess your understanding of the material in this chapter, click here to take a quiz.

CHAPTER 23

Collateral Remedies

A. Introduction

A defendant who fails on direct appeal may file a collateral attack on the conviction, the most common form being a *habeas corpus* petition. Petitioning for a writ of *habeas corpus* is a collateral attack: it is not a continuation of the criminal process but a civil suit brought to challenge the legality of the restraint under which a person is held. The petitioner in this civil suit, having lost the presumption of innocence upon conviction, has the burden to prove that his confinement is illegal. The respondent in a *habeas* action is the prisoner's custodian—the warden or other prison official. *Habeas corpus* has been called "the most celebrated writ in the English law," and the Court paid homage to this "Great Writ of Liberty" in *Fay v. Noia*, 372 U.S. 391 (1963):

> **It's Latin to Me**
>
> *Habeas corpus* is a Latin term meaning "you have the body."

> We do well to bear in mind the extraordinary prestige of the Great Writ in Anglo-American jurisprudence. Received into our own law in the colonial period, given explicit recognition in the Federal Constitution, Art. I, section 9, cl. 2, incorporated in the first grant of federal court jurisdiction, *habeas corpus* was early confirmed by Chief Justice Marshall to be a "great constitutional privilege." Although in form the Great Writ is simply a mode of procedure, its history is inextricably intertwined with the growth of fundamental rights of personal liberty. For its function has been to provide a prompt and efficacious remedy for whatever society deems to be intolerable restraints. Its root principle is that in a civilized society, government must always be accountable to the judiciary for a man's imprisonment: if the imprisonment cannot be shown to conform with fundamental requirements of law, the

> **FYI**
>
> Most states have *habeas corpus*-like proceedings that closely follow federal *habeas corpus* discussed in the remainder of this chapter. Failure to prevail in state *habeas* proceedings will not bar a subsequent federal *habeas* action.

individual is entitled to his immediate release. Thus, there is nothing novel in the fact that today *habeas corpus* in the federal courts provides a mode for the redress of denials of due process of law. Vindication of due process is precisely its historic office.

However grand the rhetoric in *Fay v. Noia*, the reality is that merely filing a *habeas corpus* petition does not ensure that a federal court will review the merits of the petitioner's claim. As you will see, the Court—beginning in the 1970s—and Congress in 1996 greatly narrowed the ability to achieve post-conviction relief for unlawful confinement.

1. Factual Basis for Claim

In the following case, the Court discusses one of the procedural hurdles to getting a hearing on a federal *habeas* petition: the requirement that petitioner must have developed the factual basis of his claim in state proceedings.

Williams v. Taylor

529 U.S. 420 (2000).

JUSTICE KENNEDY delivered the opinion of the Court.

Petitioner Michael Wayne Williams received a capital sentence for the murders of Morris Keller, Jr., and Keller's wife, Mary Elizabeth. Petitioner later sought a writ of *habeas corpus* in federal court. Accompanying his petition was a request for an evidentiary hearing on constitutional claims which, he alleged, he had been unable to develop in state-court proceedings. The question is whether 28 U.S.C. § 2254(e)(2) bars the evidentiary hearing petitioner seeks. If petitioner "has failed to develop the factual basis of his claims in State court proceedings," his case is subject to § 2254(e)(2), and he may not receive a hearing because he concedes his inability to satisfy the statute's further stringent conditions for excusing the deficiency.

Hear It

You can listen to the oral argument in *Williams v. Taylor* at: http://www.oyez.org/cases/1990-1999/1999/1999_99_6615.

Petitioner filed a *habeas* petition in the United States District Court for the Eastern District of Virginia on November 20, 1996. The petition raised three claims. First, petitioner claimed the prosecution had violated *Brady v. Maryland*, 373 U.S. 83 (1963), in failing to disclose a report of a confidential pre-trial psychiatric examination of prosecution witness Cruse. Second, petitioner alleged his trial was rendered unfair by the seating of a juror who at *voir dire* had not revealed possible sources of bias. Finally, petitioner alleged one of the prosecutors committed misconduct in failing to reveal his knowledge of the juror's possible bias. [The district court dismissed the petition, deciding that petitioner could not satisfy § 2254(e)(2)'s requirements.] The Court of Appeals concluded petitioner could not satisfy the statute's conditions for excusing his failure to develop the facts and held him barred from receiving an evidentiary hearing.

On October 18, 1999, petitioner filed an application for stay of execution and a petition for a writ of certiorari. On October 28, we stayed petitioner's execution and granted certiorari to decide whether § 2254(e)(2) precludes him from receiving an evidentiary hearing on his claims. We now affirm in part and reverse in part. Section 2254(e)(2), the provision which controls whether petitioner may receive an evidentiary hearing in federal district court on the claims that were not developed in the Virginia courts, becomes the central point of our analysis. It provides as follows:

"If the applicant has failed to develop the factual basis of a claim in State court proceedings, the court shall not hold an evidentiary hearing on the claim unless the applicant shows that—

"(A) the claim relies on—

"(i) a new rule of constitutional law, made retroactive to cases on collateral review by the Supreme Court, that was previously unavailable; or

"(ii) a factual predicate that could not have been previously discovered through the exercise of due diligence; and

"(B) the facts underlying the claim would be sufficient to establish by clear and convincing evidence that but for constitutional error, no reasonable fact finder would have found the applicant guilty of the underlying offense."

By the terms of its opening clause the statute applies only to prisoners who have "failed to develop the factual basis of a claim in State court proceedings." If the prisoner has failed to develop the facts, an evidentiary hearing cannot be granted unless the prisoner's case meets the other conditions of § 2254(e)(2). Here, petitioner concedes his case does not comply with § 2254(e)(2)(B), so he may receive an evidentiary hearing only if his claims fall outside the opening clause.

We start with the language of the statute. Section 2254(e)(2) begins with a conditional clause, "if the applicant has failed to develop the factual basis of a claim in State court proceedings," which directs attention to the prisoner's efforts in state court. We ask first whether the factual basis was indeed developed in state court, a question susceptible, in the normal course, of a simple yes or no answer. Here the answer is no.

The Commonwealth would have the analysis begin and end there. Under its no-fault reading of the statute, if there is no factual development in the state court, the federal *habeas* court may not inquire into the reasons for the default when determining whether the opening clause of § 2254(e)(2) applies. We do not agree with the Commonwealth's interpretation of the word "failed." We do not deny "fail" is sometimes used in a neutral way, not importing fault or want of diligence. So the phrase "We fail to understand his argument" can mean simply "We cannot understand his argument." This is not the sense in which the word "failed" is used here, however.

We give the words of a statute their "ordinary, contemporary, common meaning," absent an indication Congress intended them to bear some different import. In its customary and preferred sense, "fail" connotes some omission, fault, or negligence on the part of the person who has failed to do something. To say a person has failed in a duty implies he did not take the necessary steps to fulfill it. He is, as a consequence, at fault and bears responsibility for the failure. In this sense, a person is not at fault when his diligent efforts to perform an act are thwarted, for example, by the conduct of another or by happenstance. Fault lies, in those circumstances, either with the person who interfered with the accomplishment of the act or with no one at all. We conclude Congress used the word "failed" in the sense just described. Had Congress intended a no-fault standard, it would have had no difficulty in making its intent plain. It would have had to do no more than use, in lieu of the phrase "has failed to," the phrase "did not."

Under the opening clause of § 2254(e)(2), a failure to develop the factual basis of a claim is not established unless there is lack of diligence, or some greater fault, attributable to the prisoner or the prisoner's counsel. If there has been no lack of diligence at the relevant stages in the state proceedings, the prisoner has not "failed to develop" the facts under § 2254(e)(2)'s opening clause, and he will be excused from showing compliance with the balance of the subsection's requirements. We find lack of diligence as to one of the three claims but not as to the other two. Petitioner did not exercise the diligence required to preserve the claim that nondisclosure of Cruse's psychiatric report was in contravention of *Brady v. Maryland*. The report concluded Cruse "had little recollection of the murders of the Kellers, other than vague memories, as he was intoxicated with alcohol and marijuana at the time." The report had been prepared in September 1993, before petitioner was tried; yet it was not mentioned by petitioner until he filed his federal *habeas* petition and attached a copy of the report. Petitioner explained that an investigator for his federal *habeas* counsel discovered the report in Cruse's court file but state *habeas* counsel had not seen it when he had reviewed the

Food for Thought

Is it right that a defendant's claim should stand or fall based on the diligence of his or her counsel? What if the attorney was known for laziness or inept work, or was a public defender with a burdensome caseload?

same file. State *habeas* counsel averred as follows: "Prior to filing petitioner's *habeas corpus* petition with the Virginia Supreme Court, I reviewed the Cumberland County court files of petitioner and of his co-defendant, Jeffrey Cruse. I have reviewed the attached psychiatric evaluation of Jeffrey Cruse. I have no recollection of seeing this report in Mr. Cruse's court file when I examined the file. Given the contents of the report, I am confident that I would remember it."

The trial court was not satisfied with this explanation for the late discovery. Nor are we. We conclude petitioner has met the burden of showing he was diligent in efforts to develop the facts supporting his juror bias and prosecutorial misconduct claims in collateral proceedings before the Virginia Supreme Court. Petitioner's claims are based on two of the questions posed to the jurors by the trial judge at *voir dire*. First, the judge asked prospective jurors, "Are any of you related to the following people who may be called as witnesses?" Then he read the jurors a list of names, one of which was "Deputy Sheriff Claude Meinhard." Bonnie Stinnett, who would later become the jury foreperson, had divorced Meinhard in 1979, after a 17-year marriage with four children. Stinnett remained silent, indicating the answer was "no." Meinhard, as the officer who investigated the crime scene and interrogated Cruse, would later become the prosecution's lead-off witness at trial.

After reading the names of the attorneys involved in the case, including one of the prosecutors, Robert Woodson, Jr., the judge asked, "Have you or any member of your immediate family ever been represented by any of the aforementioned attorneys?" Stinnett again said nothing, despite the fact Woodson had represented her during her divorce from Meinhard. In an affidavit she provided in the federal *habeas* proceedings, Stinnett claimed "she did not respond to the judge's first question because she did not consider herself 'related' to Claude Meinhard in 1994 at *voir dire*. Once our marriage ended in 1979, I was no longer related to him." As for Woodson's earlier representation of her, Stinnett explained as follows: "When Claude and I divorced in 1979, the divorce was uncontested and Mr. Woodson drew up the papers so that the divorce could be completed. Since neither Claude nor I was contesting anything, I didn't think Mr. Woodson 'represented' either one of us." Woodson provided an affidavit in which he admitted "he was aware that Juror Bonnie Stinnett was the ex-wife of then Deputy Sheriff Claude Meinhard and he was aware that they had been divorced for some time." Woodson stated, however, "to his mind, people who are related only by marriage are no longer 'related' once the marriage ends in divorce." Woodson also "had no recollection of having been involved as a private attorney in the divorce proceedings between Claude Meinhard and Bonnie Stinnett." He explained that "whatever his involvement was in the 1979 divorce, by the time of trial in 1994 he had completely forgotten about it."

Ethical Issue

Even if the prosecutor had a semantic point, should he have raised the marriage and divorce himself? Why or why not?

In ordering an evidentiary hearing on the juror bias and prosecutorial misconduct claims, the District Court concluded the factual basis of the claims was not reasonably available to petitioner's counsel during state *habeas* proceedings. The Court of Appeals held state *habeas* counsel was not diligent because petitioner's investigator on federal *habeas* discovered the relationships upon interviewing two jurors who referred in passing to Stinnett as "Bonnie Meinhard." The investigator later confirmed Stinnett's prior marriage to Meinhard by checking Cumberland County's public records. ("The documents supporting petitioner's Sixth Amendment claims have been a matter of public record since Stinnett's divorce became final in 1979. Indeed, because petitioner's federal *habeas* counsel located those documents, there is little reason to think that his state *habeas* counsel could not have done so as well"). We should be surprised, to say the least, if a district court familiar with the standards of trial practice were to hold that in all cases diligent counsel must check public records containing personal information pertaining to each and every juror. Because of Stinnett and Woodson's silence, there was no basis for an investigation into Stinnett's marriage history. Section 2254(e)(2) does not apply to petitioner's related claims of juror bias and prosecutorial misconduct.

The decision of the Court of Appeals is affirmed in part and reversed in part. The case is remanded for further proceedings consistent with this opinion.

Points for Discussion

a. Hearing, Bail, & Appeal

If a federal district court grants a hearing on a *habeas* petition, both the petitioner and the government must be given the opportunity to present evidence. Upon denial of the petition, the petitioner will be remanded to custody. If the court grants the petition, the petitioner shall be discharged from custody, but the court may suspend execution of its order to allow the government to appeal or to institute a new trial within a specified period of time. The court also has authority to admit the petitioner to bail, pending the government's appeal or initiation of a new trial. When deciding whether to grant release pending appeal to a state prisoner who has won *habeas* relief a federal court may consider: 1) the risk that the prisoner may flee; 2) the danger the prisoner may pose to the public; 3) the state's interest in continuing custody and rehabilitation; and 4) the prisoner's interest in release pending appeal. *Hilton v. Braunskill*, 481 U.S. 770 (1987).

b. Access to *Habeas*

The writ of *habeas corpus* may be suspended under the circumstances described in Art. I, § 2, cl. 2 of the Constitution: "The Privilege of the Writ of *Habeas Corpus* shall not be suspended unless when in Cases of Rebellion or Invasion the public Safety may require it."

c. No Statutory Right to Competency in *Habeas* Proceeding

In *Ryan v. Gonzales*, 568 U.S. 57 (2013), the Court held that the federal *habeas* statute did not create a right of competency simply because it gave the defendant a right to counsel. Whereas the two rights are connected at the trial level, in that an incompetent defendant cannot effectively aid in the defense of his case by counsel at trial, at the *habeas* level, a competent defendant is not necessary to aid counsel because the review is a backward-looking, records-based process.

> **FYI**
>
> In *Boumediene v. Bush*, 553 U.S. 723 (2008), the Court held that, in the case of enemy combatants held at Guantanamo Bay, Cuba, Congress had violated the Suspension Clause by improperly denying access to *habeas corpus* relief.

2. AEDPA Time Limits

At common law any person illegally detained could use the writ of *habeas corpus* to make repeated efforts to gain his freedom: "*Res judicata* did not attach to a court's denial of *habeas* relief. Instead, a renewed application could be made to every other judge or court in the realm, and each court or judge was bound to consider the question of the prisoner's right to a discharge independently, and not to be influenced by the previous decisions refusing discharge." *McCleskey v. Zant*, 499 U.S. 467 (1991). The common law courts tolerated multiple petitions and petitions filed years after the initial trial because the writ of *habeas corpus* originally applied only to prisoners confined under federal authority and not under state authority, and review was limited primarily to testing the jurisdiction of the sentencing court. The scope of the writ later expanded beyond its original narrow purview to encompass review of constitutional error that had occurred in both state and federal proceedings leading to conviction. *See* Section C of this Chapter. The expanded coverage of the writ led the Court to formulate the doctrines of exhaustion and procedural default as means of limiting abusive and repetitive *habeas* petitions. In 1996, Congress passed The Antiterrorism and Effective Death Penalty Act (AEDPA) which incorporated and expanded upon these doctrines. The current statutory provisions of the writ are found in 28 U.S.C.A. §§ 2241–2266.

Prior to enactment of the AEDPA there was no time limit on the filing of a writ of *habeas corpus*. Some courts applied the doctrine of laches on a case-by-case basis, *see e.g., Walker v. Mitchell*, 224 Va. 568, 299 S.E.2d 698 (1983) (six-and-a-half-year delay in filing a *habeas corpus* petition), but it did not operate as an effective statute of limitations due to the requirement that the government prove actual prejudice

What's That?

The "doctrine of laches" is based on the maxim that "equity aids the vigilant and not those who slumber on their rights." *Black's Law Dictionary*. When applied, a party's legal claim will not be enforced or allowed if delay in asserting the right or claim prejudiced the adverse party.

from the delay, *see id.* ("prejudice cannot be presumed solely from the passage of time").

In order to promote speedy punishment and the finality of criminal justice proceedings, AEDPA created a rigid one-year limitation for filing a petition for *habeas corpus* relief. The limitation period begins to run on the latest date of the following: 1) when the judgment of conviction becomes final; 2) when a state action impeding making a motion was removed; 3) when a right asserted was initially recognized by the Supreme Court and made retroactive; or 4) when the facts supporting the claim presented could have been discovered through due diligence. *See* 28 U.S.C. § 2244(d)(1).

Because the AEDPA limited the time for seeking *habeas* relief, case law has focused on the limitations period. For example, in *Johnson v. United States*, 544 U.S. 295 (2005), the Court held that the limitations period began to run when the petitioner received notice of the order vacating the state conviction that was used to enhance the federal sentence, provided that petitioner showed due diligence in seeking to vacate the state conviction. An application for state collateral review tolls the one-year limitations period during the interval between a lower state court's decision on collateral review and the filing of a notice of appeal to a higher state court. *Carey v. Saffold*, 536 U.S. 214 (2002). Judicial review of a state court judgment that is not part of a direct review, such as when a state prisoner requests that the trial court use its discretion to reduce his sentence, tolls the federal *habeas* statute of limitations. *Wall v. Kholi*, 562 U.S. 545 (2011). As for the third exception to the time limit for filing, the Court has held that any claim is time-barred if more than twelve months pass before the rule is held to be retroactive. *Dodd v. United States*, 545 U.S. 353 (2005).

If the *habeas* petition is filed in due time, a state prisoner seeking *habeas* review in a federal court must meet four requirements: 1) custody; 2) a violation of federal law; 3) exhaustion of other remedies; and 4) the absence of procedural default.

Hypo: *Tolling the AEDPA Time Limit?*

Suppose that the prosecution wrongfully withholds potentially exculpatory evidence contradicting a key witness' testimony that he had never provided false information to the government. By the time that defendant found out about the withheld evidence, he had already sought and been denied *habeas* relief within the one-year time limit. If defendant can argue that his trial was fundamentally unfair because of the withheld evidence, should he have the right to file a second or successive *habeas* petition? *See Scott v. United States*, 890 F.3d 1239 (11th Cir. 2018).

B. Custody

A person is in custody when he is presently serving a sentence for the conviction challenged by the writ, or when he has been released from confinement subject to the control of the parole board, probation officer, or a court that imposed a suspended sentence. In the latter case, a writ of *habeas corpus* is available if the conditions of release "significantly restrain" the petitioner's liberty. *Jones v. Cunningham*, 371 U.S. 236 (1963); *Hensley v. Municipal Court*, 411 U.S. 345 (1973). A prisoner serving consecutive sentences is "in custody" for purposes of challenging any of the sentences. *Peyton v. Rowe*, 391 U.S. 54 (1968). The writ may not be used to attack a conviction that imposed a fine or collateral civil disability and did not result in incarceration. Nor may the petitioner attack a sentence that has been fully served unless the prisoner is serving another sentence that was enhanced by the challenged sentence.

Garlotte v. Fordice

515 U.S. 39 (1995).

JUSTICE GINSBURG delivered the opinion of the Court.

To petition a federal court for *habeas corpus* relief from a state court conviction, the applicant must be "in custody in violation of the Constitution or laws or treaties of the United States." In *Peyton v. Rowe*, 391 U.S. 54 (1968), we held that the governing federal pre-

Hear It

You can listen to the oral argument in *Garlotte* at: http://www.oyez.org/cases/ 1990-1999/1994/1994_94_6790.

scription permits prisoners incarcerated under consecutive state court sentences to apply for federal *habeas* relief from sentences they had not yet begun to serve. We said in *Peyton* that, for purposes of *habeas* relief, consecutive sentences should be treated as a continuous series; a prisoner is "in custody in violation of the Constitution," we explained, "if any consecutive sentence the prisoner is scheduled to serve was imposed as the result of a deprivation of constitutional rights."

The case before us is appropriately described as *Peyton*'s complement, or *Peyton* in reverse. Like the *habeas* petitioners in *Peyton*, petitioner Harvey Garlotte is incarcerated under consecutive sentences. Unlike the *Peyton* petitioners, Garlotte does not challenge a conviction underlying a sentence yet to be served. Instead, Garlotte seeks to attack a conviction underlying the sentence that ran first in a consecutive series, a sentence already served, but one that nonetheless persists to postpone Garlotte's eligibility for parole. Following *Peyton*, we do not desegregate Garlotte's sentences, but comprehend them as composing a continuous stream. We therefore hold that Garlotte remains "in custody" under all of his sentences until all are served, and now may attack the conviction underlying the sentence scheduled to run first in the series.

On September 16, 1985, at a plea hearing held in a Mississippi trial court, Harvey Garlotte entered simultaneous guilty pleas to one count of possession with intent to distribute marijuana and two counts of murder. Pursuant to a plea agreement, the State recommended that Garlotte be sentenced to a prison term of three years on the marijuana count, to run consecutively with two concurrent life sentences on the murder counts. The court imposed the sentences in this order: the three-year sentence first, then, consecutively, the concurrent life sentences. Garlotte wrote to the trial court seven months after the September 16, 1985 hearing, asking for permission to withdraw his guilty plea on the marijuana count. The court's reply notified Garlotte of the Mississippi statute under which he could pursue post-conviction collateral relief. Garlotte unsuccessfully moved for relief. Nearly two years after the denial of Garlotte's motion, the Mississippi Supreme Court rejected his appeal. On January 18, 1989, the Mississippi Supreme Court denied further post-conviction motions filed by Garlotte. By this time, Garlotte had completed the period of incarceration set for the marijuana offense, and had commenced serving the life sentences.

On October 6, 1989, Garlotte filed a *habeas corpus* petition in the United States District Court for the Southern District of Mississippi, naming as respondent Kirk Fordice, the Governor of Mississippi. Adopting the recommendation of a federal magistrate judge, the District Court denied Garlotte's petition on the merits. Before the United States Court of Appeals for the Fifth Circuit, the State argued for the first time that the District Court lacked jurisdiction over Garlotte's petition. The State asserted that Garlotte, prior to the District Court filing, had already served the prison time imposed for the marijuana conviction; therefore, the State maintained, Garlotte was no longer "in custody" under that conviction within the meaning of the federal *habeas* statute. Garlotte countered that he remained "in custody" until all sentences were served, emphasizing that the marijuana conviction continued to postpone the date on which he would be eligible for parole. Adopting the State's position, the Fifth Circuit dismissed Garlotte's *habeas* petition for want of jurisdiction.

The Courts of Appeals have divided over the question whether a person incarcerated under consecutive sentences remains "in custody" under a sentence that (1) has been completed in terms of prison time served, but (2) continues to postpone the prisoner's date of potential release. We granted certiorari to resolve this conflict, and now reverse.

Had the Mississippi trial court ordered that Garlotte's life sentences run before his marijuana sentence—an option about which the prosecutor expressed indifference—*Peyton* unquestionably would have instructed the District Court to entertain Garlotte's present *habeas* petition. Because the marijuana term came first, and Garlotte filed his *habeas* petition after prison time had run on the marijuana sentence, Mississippi urges that *Maleng v. Cook*, 490 U.S. 488 (1989) (per curiam), rather than *Peyton*, controls. The question presented in *Maleng* was "whether a *habeas* petitioner remains 'in custody' under a conviction after the sentence imposed for it has fully expired, merely because of the possibility that the prior conviction will be used to enhance the sentences imposed for any subsequent crimes of which he is convicted." We held that the potential use of a conviction to enhance a sentence for subsequent offenses did not suffice to render a person "in custody" within the meaning of the *habeas* statute.

Maleng recognized that we had "very liberally construed the 'in custody' requirement for purposes of federal *habeas*," but stressed that the Court had "never extended it to the situation where a *habeas* petitioner suffers no present restraint from a conviction." "Almost all States have habitual offender statutes, and many States provide for specific enhancement of subsequent sentences on the basis of prior convictions,"; hence, the construction of "in custody" urged by the *habeas* petitioner in *Maleng* would have left nearly all convictions perpetually open to collateral attack. The *Maleng* petitioner's interpretation, we therefore commented, "would read the 'in custody' requirement out of the statute."

Take Note

As a remedy of last resort, a convicted person no longer subject to confinement may seek a common law writ of *coram nobis* to challenge his prior conviction. *See United States v. Morgan*, 346 U.S. 502 (1954). For example, in *Korematsu v. United States*, 323 U.S. 214 (1944), the Court upheld the conviction of an American citizen of Japanese ancestry for being in a location designated as off limits to all persons of Japanese ancestry. Forty years later, in *Korematsu v. United States*, 584 F. Supp. 1406 (N.D.Cal.1984), a federal district court granted a writ of *coram nobis* and vacated the conviction on grounds that the government had mislead the courts as to the military necessity of wartime relocation and internment of civilians in 1944.

Unlike the *habeas* petitioner in *Maleng*, Garlotte is serving consecutive sentences. In *Peyton*, we held that "a prisoner serving consecutive sentences is 'in custody' under any one of them" for purposes of the *habeas* statute. Having construed the statutory term "in custody" to require that consecutive sentences be viewed in the aggregate, we will not now adopt a different construction simply because the sentence imposed under the challenged conviction lies in the past rather than in the future.

Mississippi urges, as a prime reason for its construction of the 'in custody' requirement, that allowing a *habeas* attack on a sentence nominally completed would "encourage and reward delay in the assertion of *habeas* challenges." Mississippi argues that Garlotte's reading of the words "in custody" would undermine the expeditious adjudication rationale of *Peyton*.

It's Latin to Me

Coram nobis is Latin for "in our presence; before us." A writ of *coram nobis* is directed at the trial court alleged to have made an error of fact or law.

Our holding today is unlikely to encourage delay. A prisoner naturally prefers release sooner to later. Further, because the *habeas* petitioner generally bears the burden of proof, delay is apt to disadvantage the petitioner more than the State. Nothing in this record suggests that Garlotte has been dilatory in challenging his marijuana conviction. Finally, under *Habeas Corpus* Rule 9(a), a district court may dismiss a *habeas* petition if the State "has been prejudiced in its ability to respond to the petition by inexcusable delay in its filing."

Under *Peyton*, we view consecutive sentences in the aggregate, not as discrete segments. Invalidation of Garlotte's marijuana conviction would advance the date of his eligibility for release from present incarceration. Garlotte's challenge, which will shorten his term of incarceration if he proves unconstitutionality, implicates the core purpose of *habeas* review. We therefore hold that Garlotte was "in custody" under his marijuana conviction when he filed his federal *habeas* petition. Accordingly, the judgment of the Court of Appeals for the Fifth Circuit is reversed, and the case is remanded for proceedings consistent with this opinion.

JUSTICE THOMAS, with whom THE CHIEF JUSTICE joins, dissenting.

In my view, *Peyton* ought to be construed as limited to situations in which a *habeas* petitioner challenges a yet unexpired sentence. This would satisfy *Peyton*'s policy concerns by permitting challenges to unserved sentences at an earlier time. More importantly, this interpretation would also make sense of *Maleng v. Cook*'s proper insistence that the *habeas* statute does not permit prisoners to challenge expired convictions. The majority, however, relies upon broad language in one opinion to ignore language in another. Given the statute's text and the oddity of asserting that Garlotte is still serving time under the expired marijuana conviction, I would read *Peyton* narrowly. I dissent.

C. Violations of Federal Law

Only federal issues are cognizable in federal *habeas* proceedings; state constitutional or statutory violations are not. *See Rivera v. Illinois*, 556 U.S. 148 (2009) ("A mere error of state law is not a denial of due process. The Due Process Clause, our decisions instruct, safeguards not the meticulous observance of state procedural prescriptions, but 'fundamental elements of fairness in a criminal trial.' "). The most common *habeas corpus* claims are federal constitutional claims involving ineffective assistance of counsel, illegal confessions obtained by the police, improper judicial or prosecutorial conduct, and insufficient evidence. In most cases errors concerning the admissibility of evidence or instructions to the jury do not amount to constitutional violations. The writ of *habeas corpus* focuses on the legality of the prisoner's detention under the Due Process Clause of the Fourteenth Amendment, rather than his ultimate guilt or innocence.

Although 28 U.S.C. § 2254 speaks of a "violation of the Constitution or laws or treaties of the United States," almost all federal *habeas* petitions allege a violation of the Constitution. A conviction obtained in violation of a federal statute does not warrant *habeas* review unless the statutory violation qualifies as a "fundamental defect which inherently results in a complete miscarriage of justice, or an omission inconsistent with the rudimentary demands of fair procedure." *Reed v. Farley*, 512 U.S. 339 (1994). Most statutory violations simply do not rise to that high standard to invoke *habeas* jurisdiction.

The breadth of coverage of federal *habeas* review of state court convictions increased dramatically throughout history and through the Warren Court of the 1960s: "The writ of *habeas corpus* known to the Framers was quite different from that which exists today. The first Congress made the writ of *habeas corpus* available only to prisoners confined under the authority of the United States, not under state authority. It was not until 1867 that Congress made the writ generally available in 'all cases where any person may be restrained of his or her liberty in violation of the constitution, or of any treaty or law of the United States.' And it was not until well into this century that this Court interpreted that provision to allow a final judgment of conviction in a state court to be collaterally attacked on *habeas*." *Felker v. Turpin*, 518 U.S. 651 (1996).

In the following case, the Court limited the judicial availability of federal *habeas* relief in Fourth Amendment cases, its first step to rein in federal judges reared on the Warren Court's "judicial activism" and distrust of state courts.

The Warren Court's willingness to increase the scope of federal *habeas* review of state court convictions was partially premised on a belief that the state courts could not be trusted to protect the constitutional rights of criminal defendants. In the landmark case of *Gideon v. Wainwright*, 372 U.S. 335, 351 (1963), Justice Harlan expressed dissatisfaction with how many state courts' discharge of their "front-line responsibility for the enforcement of constitutional rights." The Burger and Rehnquist Courts, however, embraced the concept of a "new federalism" and resurrected faith in the state courts as protectors of individual freedom. "The battle over *habeas* is driven, in the main, not by relatively sterile concerns for federalism and congested federal dockets, but by an ideological resistance to the Warren Court's innovative interpretations of substantive federal rights." Larry Yackle, *The Habeas Hagioscope*, 66 S. CAL. L. REV. 2331 (1993).

Stone v. Powell

428 U.S. 465 (1976).

JUSTICE POWELL delivered the opinion of the Court.

[Respondent Powell was arrested for violating a vagrancy ordinance, but was later charged with murder and convicted on the basis of evidence seized during a search pursuant to the vagrancy arrest. Powell asserted that the vagrancy ordinance was unconstitutional and the subsequent arrest and search were illegal.]

Respondent alleges violations of Fourth Amendment rights guaranteed them through the Fourteenth Amendment. The question is whether state prisoners who have been afforded the opportunity for full and fair consideration of their reliance upon the exclusionary rule with respect to seized evidence by the state courts at trial and on direct review may invoke their claim again on federal *habeas corpus* review. The answer is to be found by weighing the utility of the exclusionary rule against the costs of extending it to collateral review of Fourth Amendment claims.

> **Hear It**
>
> You can listen to the oral argument in *Stone v. Powell* at: http://www.oyez.org/cases/1970-1979/1975/1975_74_1055.

The costs of applying the exclusionary rule even at trial and on direct review are well known: the focus of the trial, and the attention of the participants therein, are diverted from the ultimate question of guilt or innocence that should be the central concern in a criminal proceeding. Moreover, the physical evidence sought to be excluded is typically reliable and often the most probative information bearing on the guilt or innocence of the defendant. Application of the rule thus deflects the truth finding process and often frees the guilty. The disparity in particular cases between the error committed by the police officer and the windfall afforded a guilty defendant by application of the rule is contrary to the idea of proportionality that is essential to the concept of justice. Thus, although the rule is thought to deter unlawful police activity in part through the nurturing of respect for Fourth Amendment values, if applied indiscriminately it may well have the opposite effect of generating disrespect for the law and administration of justice. These long-recognized costs of the rule persist when a criminal conviction is sought to be overturned on collateral review on the ground that a search-and-seizure claim was erroneously rejected by two or more tiers of state courts.

Make the Connection

This weighing of costs and benefits should sound familiar to students of the Fourth Amendment. The Court has used the same cost/benefit analysis to restrict application of the exclusionary rule to violations of the Fourth Amendment, including exclusion of evidence at trial.

Evidence obtained by police officers in violation of the Fourth Amendment is excluded at trial in the hope that the frequency of future violations will decrease. Despite the absence of supportive empirical evidence, we have assumed that the immediate effect of exclusion will be to discourage law enforcement officials from violating the Fourth Amendment by removing the incentive to disregard it. More importantly, over the long term, this demonstration that our society attaches serious consequences to violation of constitutional rights is thought to encourage those who formulate law enforcement policies, and the officers who implement them, to incorporate Fourth Amendment ideals into their value system.

We adhere to the view that these considerations support the implementation of the exclusionary rule at trial and its enforcement on direct appeal of state-court convictions. But the additional contribution, if any, of the consideration of search-and-seizure claims of state prisoners on collateral review is small in relation to the costs. To be sure, each case in which such claim is considered may add marginally to an awareness of the values protected by the Fourth Amendment. There is no reason to believe, however, that the overall educative effect of the exclusionary rule would be appreciably diminished if search-and-seizure claims could not be raised in federal *habeas corpus* review of state convictions. Nor is there reason to assume that any specific disincentive already created by the risk of exclusion of evidence at trial or the reversal of convictions on direct review would be enhanced if there were the further risk that a conviction obtained in state court and affirmed on direct review might be overturned in collateral proceedings often occurring years after the incarceration of the defendant. The view that the deterrence of Fourth Amendment

Food for Thought

Even if review of a Fourth Amendment violation on collateral review would not have significant deterrent effects, is there any other value favoring a review of a claimed Fourth Amendment violation?

violations would be furthered rests on the dubious assumption that law enforcement authorities would fear that federal *habeas* review might reveal flaws in a search or seizure that went undetected at trial and on appeal. Even if one rationally could assume that some additional incremental deterrent effect would be presented in isolated cases, the resulting advance of the legitimate goal of furthering Fourth Amendment rights would be outweighed by the acknowledged costs to other values vital to a rational system of criminal justice.

In sum, we conclude that where the State has provided an opportunity for full and fair litigation of a Fourth Amendment claim, a state prisoner may not be granted federal *habeas corpus* relief on the ground that evidence obtained in an unconstitutional search or seizure was introduced at his trial. In this context the contribution of the exclusionary rule, if any, to the effectuation of the Fourth Amendment is minimal, and the substantial societal costs of application of the rule persist with special force.

MR. JUSTICE BRENNAN, with whom MR. JUSTICE MARSHALL concurs, dissenting.

It is simply inconceivable that a constitutional deprivation suddenly vanishes after the appellate process has been exhausted. Federal *habeas corpus* review of Fourth Amendment claims of state prisoners was merely one manifestation of the principle that "conventional notions of finality in criminal litigation cannot be permitted to defeat the manifest federal policy that federal constitutional rights of personal liberty shall not be denied without the fullest opportunity for plenary federal judicial review." *Fay v. Noia*, 372 U.S. 391, 424 (1963). This Court's precedents have been "premised in large part on a recognition that the availability of collateral remedies is necessary to insure the integrity of proceedings at and before trial where constitutional rights are at stake. Our decisions leave no doubt that the federal *habeas* remedy extends to state prisoners alleging that unconstitutionally obtained evidence was admitted against them at trial."

Food for Thought

Should every convicted defendant have at least one opportunity to litigate federal constitutional claims in federal court? In theory, a defendant convicted in state court could petition the Supreme Court for certiorari to review the conviction—without having to show that the state denied him a full and fair hearing on the constitutional claim. In practice, the Court is unlikely to grant certiorari. Should federal *habeas* be used to allow the lower federal courts to conduct the type of review that the Court is unable to provide because of its heavy caseload? On the other hand, if it is a perversion of federalist principles to have federal district courts essentially serve as appellate courts for the states who have "fully and fairly litigated" the federal issue, why shouldn't *Stone* apply to all claims of violation of federal law? What role does factual innocence play in defining *habeas* jurisdiction?

The only result of today's holding will be that denials by the state courts of claims by state prisoners of violations of their Fourth Amendment rights will go unreviewed by a federal tribunal. I fear that the same treatment ultimately will be accorded state prisoners' claims of violations of other constitutional rights; thus the potential ramifications of this case for federal *habeas* jurisdiction generally are ominous. The Court, no longer content just to restrict forthrightly the constitutional rights of the citizenry, has embarked on a campaign to water down even such constitutional rights as it purports to acknowledge by the device of foreclosing resort to the federal *habeas* remedy for their redress.

Points for Discussion

a. *Miranda* Claims

In *Withrow v. Williams*, 507 U.S. 680 (1993), the Court declined an opportunity to apply *Stone v. Powell* to *Miranda v. Arizona*, 384 U.S. 436 (1966), despite the fact that *Miranda*'s exclusionary rule, like that of the Fourth Amendment rule, is designed to deter police violations and is arguably unrelated to accurate fact-finding. Nevertheless, the *Withrow* Court found that a federal court can hear a petition concerning a *Miranda* violation. In rejecting an extension of *Stone,* the Court stated that "prophylactic though it may be," *Miranda* safeguards the constitutional right against self-incrimination, a fundamental right that is not "necessarily divorced from the correct ascertainment of guilt." Justice Souter also noted that eliminating *Miranda habeas* claims would result in the substitution of due process voluntariness claims in their place. *See Miller v. Fenton*, 474 U.S. 104 (1985) ("the voluntariness of a confession is a legal question requiring independent federal determination upon a federal writ of *habeas corpus*").

b. Grand Jury Discrimination

In *Rose v. Mitchell*, 443 U.S. 545 (1979), the Court held that a claim of racial discrimination in the selection of a state grand jury is cognizable on federal *habeas corpus*, even though the claimed error did not affect the determination of guilt and had been heard by the state court. The Court distinguished *Stone* on three grounds. First, the Court was unwilling to assume that state judges could fairly consider claims of grand jury discrimination, since those claims required the state courts to review their own procedures rather than those of the police. Second, the right to an indictment by a grand jury free from discrimination in its selection process is a personal constitutional right rather than a judicially created remedy. Third, state courts could be expected to respond to a determination that their grand jury selection procedures failed to meet constitutional requirements, *i.e.*, deterrence is effective.

Take Note

Although the opinion in *Stone v. Powell* led to speculation that defendants might be denied *habeas corpus* review of other constitutional claims, this did not happen. The Court did not extend its limiting principle to constitutional violations impacting the guilt determination. For example, in *Jackson v. Virginia*, 443 U.S. 307 (1979), the Court held that a claim that a prisoner was convicted on insufficient evidence is cognizable on federal *habeas corpus* review as a violation of due process. Unlike the Fourth Amendment, which operates to exclude evidence that would have aided in the truth-finding function, whether the prosecution's evidence met the reasonable doubt standard of proof related to the accuracy of fact-finding. *Jackson's* holding, however, limited *habeas* relief to a showing that no rational trier of fact, viewing the evidence in the light most favorable to the prosecution, "could have found the essential elements of the crime beyond a reasonable doubt."

Hypo: *Using* Kimmelman

Your client was convicted in State court based largely on evidence obtained from a warrantless search of his residence. Following direct appeal, your client fired his trial counsel and retained you. Your review of the trial transcript convinces you that the State court incorrectly applied Fourth Amendment precedent and that the federal courts would not uphold the warrantless search. Is there any way that you can obtain federal review of the search without running afoul of *Stone*? Consider whether *Stone's* rationale can be reconciled with *Kimmelman v. Morrison*, 477 U.S. 365 (1986): "The constitutional rights of criminal defendants are granted to the innocent and the guilty alike. Consequently, we decline to hold either that the guarantee of effective assistance of counsel belongs solely to the innocent or that it attaches only to matters affecting the determination of actual guilt." In *Kimmelman*, the Court ruled that *Stone* did not preclude Sixth Amendment ineffective assistance of counsel claims based on defense counsel's failure to move to suppress illegally seized evidence. The Court emphasized that, unlike the Fourth Amendment exclusionary rule, Sixth Amendment rights are fundamental trial rights, going to the fairness of the judicial process. Although the Fourth Amendment claim was one element of proof of the Sixth Amendment claim, "the two claims have separate identities and reflect different constitutional values." Moreover, "in general, no comparable, meaningful opportunity exists for the full and fair litigation of a *habeas* petitioner's ineffective assistance claims at trial and on direct review." Is it possible for you to use *Kimmelman* to create "backdoor" access to federal review of Fourth Amendment issues by combining the Fourth Amendment claim with a Sixth Amendment claim that trial counsel was ineffective in raising the Fourth Amendment claim?

c. *Stone v. Powell* & AEDPA

To what extent has *Stone* been extended by AEDPA's provision that *habeas* relief will not be granted with respect to any claim that was adjudicated on the merits in state court unless the state adjudication "resulted in a decision that was contrary to, or involved an unreasonable application of, clearly established Federal law, as determined by the Supreme Court of the United States"? Is there a distinction between the "contrary to" category and the "unreasonable application" category? Consider the following case.

Williams v. Taylor

529 U.S. 362 (2000).

JUSTICE STEVENS announced the judgment of the Court and delivered the opinion of the Court with respect to Parts, I, III, and IV, and an opinion with respect to Parts II and V. JUSTICE SOUTER, JUSTICE GINSBURG, and JUSTICE BREYER join this opinion in its entirety. JUSTICE O'CONNOR and JUSTICE KENNEDY join Parts I, III, and IV of this opinion.

The questions presented are whether Terry Williams' constitutional right to the effective assistance of counsel as defined in *Strickland v. Washington*, 466 U.S. 668 (1984), was violated, and whether the judgment of the Virginia Supreme Court refusing to set aside his

Hear It

You can listen to the oral argument in *(Terry) Williams* at: http://www.oyez.org/cases/1990-1999/1999/1999_98_8384.

death sentence "was contrary to, or involved an unreasonable application of, clearly established Federal law, as determined by the Supreme Court of the United States," within the meaning of 28 U.S.C. § 2254(d)(1) (1994 ed., Supp. III). We answer both questions affirmatively.

I

In September 1986, Williams was convicted of robbery and capital murder. The jury found a probability of future dangerousness and unanimously fixed Williams' punishment at death. The trial judge concluded that such punishment was "proper" and "just" and imposed the death sentence. The Virginia Supreme Court affirmed the conviction and sentence. In 1988 Williams filed for state collateral relief in the Danville Circuit Court. Judge Ingram (the same judge who presided over Williams' trial and sentencing) held an evidentiary hearing on Williams' claim that trial counsel had been ineffective. Based on the evidence, Judge Ingram found that Williams' conviction was valid, but that his trial attorneys had been ineffective during sentencing. Among the evidence that had not been presented at trial were documents prepared in connection with Williams' commitment when he was 11 years old that dramatically described mistreatment, abuse, and neglect during his early childhood, as well as testimony that he was "borderline mentally retarded," had suffered repeated head injuries, and might have mental impairments organic in origin. The *habeas* hearing also revealed that the same experts who had testified on the State's behalf at trial believed that Williams, if kept in a "structured environment," would not pose a future danger to society. Judge Ingram found that counsel's failure to discover and present this and other significant mitigating evidence was "below the range expected of reasonable, professional competent assistance of counsel." Counsel's performance thus "did not measure up to the standard required under the holding of *Strickland v. Washington*, 466 U.S. 668 (1984), and if it had, there is a reasonable probability that the result of the sentencing phase would have been different." Judge Ingram therefore recommended that Williams be granted a rehearing on the sentencing phase of his trial.

The Virginia Supreme Court did not accept that recommendation. Although it assumed, without deciding, that trial counsel had been ineffective, it disagreed with the trial judge's conclusion that Williams had suffered sufficient prejudice to warrant relief. Treating the prejudice inquiry as a mixed question of law and fact, the Virginia Supreme Court accepted the factual determination that available evidence in mitigation had not been presented at the trial, but held that the trial judge had misapplied the law in two respects. First, relying on *Lockhart v. Fretwell*, 506 U.S. 364 (1993), the court held that it was wrong for the trial judge to rely "on mere outcome determination" when assessing prejudice. Second, it construed the trial judge's opinion as having "adopted a *per se* approach" that would establish prejudice whenever any mitigating evidence was omitted. The court then reviewed the prosecution evidence supporting the "future dangerousness" aggravating circumstance, reciting Williams' criminal history, including the several most recent offenses to which he had confessed. In comparison, it found that the excluded mitigating evidence—which it characterized as merely indicating "that numerous people, mostly relatives, thought that defendant was nonviolent and could cope very well in a structured environment,"—"barely would have altered the profile of this defendant that was presented to the jury." The court concluded that there was no reasonable possibility that the omitted evidence would have affected the jury's sentencing recommendation, and that Williams had failed to demonstrate that his sentencing proceeding was fundamentally unfair.

Having exhausted his state remedies, Williams sought a federal writ of *habeas corpus* pursuant to 28 U.S.C. § 2254. After reviewing the state *habeas* hearing transcript and the state courts' findings of fact and conclusions of law, the federal trial judge agreed with the Virginia trial judge: The death sentence was constitutionally infirm. After noting that the Virginia Supreme Court had not addressed the question whether trial counsel's performance at the sentencing hearing fell below the range of competence demanded of lawyers in criminal cases, the District judge began by addressing that issue in detail. He identified five categories of mitigating evidence that counsel had failed to introduce, and he rejected the argument that counsel's failure to conduct an adequate investigation had been a strategic decision to rely almost entirely on the fact that Williams had voluntarily confessed.

According to Williams' trial counsel's testimony before the state *habeas* court, counsel did not fail to seek Williams' juvenile and social services records because he thought they would be counterproductive, but because counsel erroneously believed that "state law didn't permit it." Counsel also acknowledged in the course of the hearings that information about Williams' childhood would have been important in mitigation. And counsel's failure to contact a potentially persuasive character witness was likewise not a conscious strategic choice, but simply a failure to return that witness' phone call offering his service. Finally, even if counsel neglected to conduct such an investigation at the time as part of a tactical decision, the District Judge found, tactics as a matter of reasonable performance could not justify the omissions.

Turning to the prejudice issue, the judge determined that there was "a reasonable probability that, but for counsel's unprofessional errors, the result of the proceeding would have been different." He found that the Virginia Supreme Court had erroneously assumed that *Lockhart* had modified the *Strickland* standard for determining prejudice, and that it had made an important error of fact in discussing its finding of no prejudice. Having introduced his analysis of Williams' claim with the standard of review applicable on *habeas* appeals provided by 28 U.S.C. § 2254(d), the judge concluded that those errors established that the Virginia Supreme Court's decision "was contrary to, or involved an unreasonable application of, clearly established Federal law" within the meaning of § 2254(d)(1).

The Federal Court of Appeals reversed. It construed § 2254(d)(1) as prohibiting the grant of *habeas corpus* relief unless the state court "decided the question by interpreting or applying the relevant precedent in a manner that reasonable jurists would all agree is unreasonable." Applying that standard, it could not say that the Virginia Supreme Court's decision on the prejudice issue was an unreasonable application of the tests developed in either *Strickland* or *Lockhart*. It explained that the evidence that Williams presented a future danger to society was "simply overwhelming," it endorsed the Virginia Supreme Court's interpretation of *Lockhart*, and it characterized the state court's understanding of the facts in this case as "reasonable." We granted certiorari.

II

Over the years, the federal *habeas corpus* statute has been repeatedly amended, but the scope of that jurisdictional grant remains the same. It is well settled that the fact that constitutional error occurred in the proceedings that led to a state-court conviction may not alone be sufficient reason for concluding that a prisoner is entitled to the remedy of *habeas. See, e.g., Stone v. Powell.* On the other hand, errors that undermine confidence in the fundamental fairness of the state adjudication certainly justify the issuance of the federal writ. The deprivation of the right to the effective assistance of counsel recognized in *Strickland* is such an error.

The warden here contends that federal *habeas corpus* relief is prohibited by the amendment to 28 U.S.C. § 2254, enacted as a part of the Antiterrorism and Effective Death Penalty Act of 1996 (AEDPA). The relevant portion of that amendment provides:

> "(d) An application for a writ of *habeas corpus* on behalf of a person in custody pursuant to the judgment of a State court shall not be granted with respect to any claim that was adjudicated on the merits in State court proceedings unless the adjudication of the claim—

> "(1) resulted in a decision that was contrary to, or involved an unreasonable application of, clearly established Federal law, as determined by the Supreme Court of the United States."

The message that Congress intended to convey by using the phrases, "contrary to" and "unreasonable application of" is not entirely clear. The prevailing view in the Circuits is that the former phrase requires *de novo* review of 'pure' questions of law and the latter requires some sort of "reasonability" review of so-called mixed questions of law and fact.

We are not persuaded that the phrases define two mutually exclusive categories of questions. Most constitutional questions that arise in *habeas corpus* proceedings—and therefore most "decisions" to be made—require the federal judge to apply a rule of law to a set of facts, some of which may be disputed and some undisputed. For example, an erroneous conclusion that particular circumstances established the voluntariness of a confession, or that there exists a conflict of interest when one attorney represents multiple defendants, may well be described either as "contrary to" or as an "unreasonable application of" the governing rule of law. AEDPA plainly sought to ensure a level of "deference to the determinations of state courts," provided those determinations did not conflict with federal law or apply federal law in an unreasonable way. Congress wished to curb delays, to prevent "retrials" on federal *habeas*, and to give effect to state convictions to the extent possible under law. When federal courts are able to fulfill these goals within the bounds of the law, AEDPA instructs them to do so.

In sum, the statute directs federal courts to attend to every state-court judgment with utmost care, but it does not require them to defer to the opinion of every reasonable state-court judge on the content of federal law. If, after carefully weighing all the reasons for accepting a state court's judgment, a federal court is convinced that a prisoner's custody—or, as in this case, his sentence of death—violates the Constitution, that independent judgment should prevail. Otherwise the federal "law as determined by the Supreme Court of the United States" might be applied by the federal courts one way in Virginia and another way in California. In light of the well-recognized interest in ensuring that federal courts interpret federal law in a uniform way, we are convinced that Congress did not intend the statute to produce such a result.

III

In this case, Williams contends that he was denied his constitutionally guaranteed right to the effective assistance of counsel when his trial lawyers failed to investigate and to present substantial mitigating evidence to the sentencing jury. The threshold question under AEDPA is whether Williams seeks to apply a rule of law that was clearly established at the time his state-court conviction became final. That question is easily answered because the merits of his claim are squarely governed by our holding in *Strickland v. Washington.*

The rule set forth in *Strickland* qualifies as "clearly established Federal law, as determined by the Supreme Court of the United States." That the *Strickland* test "of necessity requires a case-by-case examination of the evidence," obviates neither the clarity of the rule nor the extent to which the rule must be seen as "established" by this Court. This Court's precedent "dictated" that the Virginia Supreme Court apply the *Strickland* test at the time that court entertained Williams' ineffective-assistance claim. And it can hardly be said that recognizing the right to effective counsel "breaks new ground or imposes a new obligation on the States." Williams is therefore entitled to relief if the Virginia Supreme Court's decision rejecting his ineffective-assistance claim was either "contrary to, or involved an unreasonable application of," that established law. It was both.

IV

The Virginia Supreme Court erred in holding that our decision in *Lockhart v. Fretwell*, modified or in some way supplanted the rule set down in *Strickland*. The trial judge analyzed the ineffective assistance claim under the correct standard; the Virginia Supreme Court did not. We are also persuaded, unlike the Virginia Supreme Court, that counsel's unprofessional service prejudiced Williams within the meaning of *Strickland*.

In our judgment, the state trial judge was correct both in his recognition

Food for Thought

Are you persuaded? Having covered ineffective assistance of counsel in Chapter 3, *supra*, has the Court made it at clear what sort of deficient performance and prejudice will result in a Sixth Amendment violation? Is it really "clearly established law"? And was the lower court's decision really "contrary to" *Strickland*? How much do you think the outcome in this case has to do with the fact that the deficient performance was in the penalty phase of a capital proceeding, as opposed to a less serious case?

of the established legal standard for determining counsel's effectiveness, and in his conclusion that the entire post-conviction record, viewed as a whole and cumulative of mitigation evidence presented originally, raised "a reasonable probability that the result of the sentencing proceeding would have been different" if competent counsel had presented and explained the significance of all the available evidence. It follows that the Virginia Supreme Court rendered a "decision that was contrary to, or involved an unreasonable application of, clearly established Federal law."

Accordingly, the judgment of the Court of Appeals is reversed, and the case is remanded for further proceedings consistent with this opinion.

JUSTICE O'CONNOR delivered the opinion of the Court with respect to Part II, concurred in part, and concurred in the judgment. JUSTICE KENNEDY joins this opinion in its entirety. THE CHIEF JUSTICE and JUSTICE THOMAS join this opinion with respect to Part II. JUSTICE SCALIA joins this opinion with respect to Part II.

Before 1996, this Court held that a federal court entertaining a state prisoner's application for *habeas* relief must exercise its independent judgment when deciding both questions of constitutional law and mixed constitutional questions (*i.e.*, application of constitutional law to fact). In other words, a federal *habeas* court owed no deference to a state court's resolution of such questions of law or mixed questions. If today's case were governed by the federal *habeas* statute prior to Congress' enactment of AEDPA in 1996, I would agree with Justice Stevens that Williams' petition for *habeas* relief must be granted if we, in our independent judgment, were to conclude that his Sixth Amendment right to effective assistance of counsel was violated.

II

Section 2254(d)(1) defines two categories of cases in which a state prisoner may obtain federal *habeas* relief with respect to a claim adjudicated on the merits in state court. Under the statute, a federal court may grant a writ of *habeas corpus* if the relevant state-court decision was either (1) "contrary to clearly established Federal law, as determined by the Supreme Court of the United States," or (2) "involved an unreasonable application of clearly established Federal law, as determined by the Supreme Court of the United States." The Court of Appeals for the Fourth Circuit properly accorded both the "contrary to" and "unreasonable application" clauses independent meaning. With respect to the first of the two statutory clauses, the Fourth Circuit held in *Green* that a state-court decision can be "contrary to" this Court's clearly established precedent in two ways. First, a state-court decision is contrary to this Court's precedent if the state court arrives at a conclusion opposite to that reached by this Court on a question of law. Second, a state-court decision is also contrary to this Court's precedent if the state court confronts facts that are materially indistinguishable from a relevant Supreme Court precedent and arrives at a result opposite to ours.

The word "contrary" is commonly understood to mean "diametrically different," "opposite in character or nature," or "mutually opposed." The text of § 2254(d)(1) suggests that the state court's decision must be substantially different from the relevant precedent of this Court. The Fourth Circuit's interpretation of the "contrary to" clause accurately reflects this textual meaning. A state-court decision will certainly be contrary to our clearly established precedent if the state court applies a rule that contradicts the governing law set forth in our cases. Take, for example, our decision in *Strickland v. Washington*. If a state court were to reject a prisoner's claim of ineffective assistance of counsel on the grounds that the prisoner had not established by a preponderance of the evidence that the result of his criminal proceeding would have been different, that decision would be "diametrically different," "opposite in character or nature," and "mutually opposed" to our clearly established precedent because we held in *Strickland* that the prisoner need only demonstrate a "reasonable probability that the result of the proceeding would have been different." A state-court decision will also be contrary to this Court's clearly established precedent if the state court confronts a set of facts that are materially indistinguishable from a decision of this Court and nevertheless arrives at a result different from our precedent. In either of these two scenarios, a federal court will be unconstrained by § 2254(d)(1) because the state-court decision falls within that provision's "contrary to" clause.

On the other hand, a run-of-the-mill state-court decision applying the correct legal rule from our cases to the facts of a prisoner's case would not fit comfortably within § 2254(d)(1)'s "contrary to" clause. Assume, for example, that a state-court decision on a prisoner's ineffective-assistance claim correctly identifies *Strickland* as the controlling legal authority and, applying that framework, rejects the prisoner's claim. Quite clearly, the state-court decision would be in accord with our decision in *Strickland* as to the legal prerequisites for establishing an ineffective-assistance claim, even assuming the federal court considering the prisoner's *habeas* application might reach a different result applying the *Strickland* framework itself. It is difficult to describe such a run-of-the-mill state-court decision as "diametrically different" from, "opposite in character or nature" from, or "mutually opposed" to *Strickland*, our clearly established precedent. Although the state-court decision may be contrary to the federal court's conception of how *Strickland* ought to be applied in that particular case, the decision is not "mutually opposed" to *Strickland* itself.

The Fourth Circuit's interpretation of the "unreasonable application" clause of § 2254(d)(1) is generally correct. A state-court decision can involve an "unreasonable application" of this Court's clearly established precedent in two ways. First, a state-court decision involves an unreasonable application of this Court's precedent if the state court identifies this Court's cases but unreasonably applies it to the facts of the particular state prisoner's case. Second, a state-court decision also involves an unreasonable application of this Court's precedent if the state court either unreasonably extends a legal principle from our precedent to a new context where it should not apply or unreasonably refuses to extend that principle to a new context where it should apply.

There remains the task of defining what exactly qualifies as an "unreasonable application" of law under § 2254(d)(1). Stated simply, a federal *habeas* court making the "unreasonable application" inquiry should ask whether the state court's application of clearly established federal law was objectively unreasonable. The federal *habeas* court should not transform the inquiry into a subjective one by resting its determination on the simple fact that at least one of the Nation's jurists has applied the relevant federal law in the same manner the state court did in the *habeas* petitioner's case. Under § 2254(d)(1)'s "unreasonable application" clause, then, a federal *habeas* court may not issue the writ simply because that court concludes in its independent judgment that the relevant state-court decision applied clearly established federal law erroneously or incorrectly. Rather, that application must also be unreasonable.

In sum, § 2254(d)(1) places a new constraint on the power of a federal *habeas* court to grant a state prisoner's application for a writ of *habeas corpus* with respect to claims adjudicated on the merits in state court. Under § 2254(d)(1), the writ may issue only if one of the following two conditions is satisfied—the state-court adjudication resulted in a decision that (1) "was contrary to clearly established Federal law, as determined by the Supreme Court of the United States," or (2) "involved an unreasonable application of clearly established Federal law, as determined by the Supreme Court of the United States." Under the "contrary to" clause, a federal *habeas* court may grant the writ if the state court arrives at a conclusion opposite to that reached by this Court on a question of law or if the state court decides a case differently than this Court has on a set of materially indistinguishable facts. Under the "unreasonable application" clause, a federal *habeas* court may grant the writ if the state court identifies the correct governing legal principle from this Court's decisions but unreasonably applies that principle to the facts of the prisoner's case.

> **FYI**
>
> Justice Kennedy was the only Justice in the majority of all the 2007 *habeas corpus* cases decided by a vote of 5–4 under AEDPA.

III

Although I disagree with Justice Stevens concerning the standard we must apply under § 2254(d)(1) in evaluating Williams' claims on *habeas*, the Virginia Supreme Court's adjudication of Williams' claim of ineffective assistance of counsel resulted in a decision that was

> **Food for Thought**
>
> As a matter of statutory interpretation of the phrases "contrary to" and "unreasonable application of," which group of justices has it right? Did you count the votes? Part II that you just read is the controlling interpretation.

both contrary to and involved an unreasonable application of this Court's clearly established precedent. I believe that the Court's discussion in Parts III and IV is correct and that it demonstrates the reasons that the Virginia Supreme Court's decision in Williams' case, even under the interpretation of § 2254(d)(1) I have set forth above, was both contrary to and involved an unreasonable application of our precedent. Accordingly, although I disagree with the interpretation of § 2254(d)(1) set forth in Part II of Justice Stevens' opinion, I join Parts I, III, and IV of the Court's opinion and concur in the judgment of reversal.

> **FYI**
>
> In *Carey v. Musladin*, 549 U.S. 70 (2006), the victim's family members sat in the audience during the trial wearing buttons displaying the victim's image. The defendant argued it denied him a fair trial. The Court held that there was no "clearly established" federal law on the effect on a defendant's fair-trial rights of such spectator conduct. While the Court had held that there was inherent prejudice in certain government-sponsored conduct (*e.g.*, requiring the defendant to wear prison clothing, *see Estelle v. Williams*, 425 U.S. 501 (1976)), the Court had never addressed a claim that private-actor courtroom conduct was so inherently prejudicial that it deprived a defendant of a fair trial.

Points for Discussion

a. No Mitigating Evidence

In *Schriro v. Landrigan*, 550 U.S. 465 (2007), the Court upheld the denial of an evidentiary hearing in a case where the defendant refused to permit his counsel to present mitigating evidence at the penalty phase of a capital case. Under § 2254's deferential standards, the federal district court did not abuse its discretion in denying the petition for *habeas* relief because, regardless of what information defense counsel might have produced, the defendant would not have permitted him to present it.

> **Ethical Issue**
>
> A capital defense attorney's decision not to present mitigating evidence at the penalty phase of a capital case will likely help to secure a death verdict for her client. Should the decision be left up to the client? Why or why not?

b. Death Penalty *Voir Dire*

In *Uttecht v. Brown*, 551 U.S. 1 (2007), the Court emphasized the AEDPA's "independent, high standard" before a *habeas corpus* writ can issue to set aside a state court ruling. At trial, defense counsel did not object to the removal for cause of a juror whose *voir dire* responses raised a question about his ability to consider the death penalty but which were not necessarily conclusive grounds for cause. The Court held that a reviewing court should consider the entire *voir dire* as well as the questioning of the particular juror. Where "there is lengthy questioning of a prospective juror, and the trial court has supervised a diligent and thoughtful *voir dire*, the trial court has broad discretion." Here, the trial court's decision "was not contrary to, or an unreasonable application of, clearly established federal law" under 28 U.S.C. § 2254(d).

Take Note

The Court held in *Abdul-Kabir v. Quarterman*, <u>550 U.S. 233 (2007)</u>, and *Brewer v. Quarterman*, <u>550 U.S. 286 (2007)</u>, that the state courts' decisions in those cases were "contrary to" and "involved an unreasonable application of, clearly established Federal law, as determined by the Supreme Court of the United States." In both cases, the trial court's jury instructions prevented the jury from giving meaningful consideration and effect to relevant mitigating evidence during the capital trial's penalty phase, contrary to clear precedent in *Penry v. Lynaugh*, <u>492 U.S. 302 (1989)</u>.

c. Court Precedents

"Clearly established federal law, as determined by the Court" means law established in the Court's precedents and not in federal circuit precedents. *See Parker v. Matthews*, <u>567 U.S. 37 (2012)</u> (per curiam) (reversing Sixth Circuit's use of a multi-step analysis for prosecutorial misconduct rather than the Court's more general standard). In addition, a Court case that was decided after the state court's findings does not qualify as "clearly established" for purposes of deference to the state court's findings. *See Greene v. Fisher*, 565 U.S. 34 (2011).

d. State Court Record Controls

When a federal court concludes that a state court's judgment is contrary to established federal law, or involves an unreasonable application of federal law, under 28 U.S.C. § 2254(d), it must be based on the record that was before the state court that decided the claim. *See Cullen v. Pinholster*, <u>563 U.S. 170 (2011)</u>.

FYI

When a state court denies post-conviction relief, but does not state its reasons, the denial nevertheless qualifies as an "adjudication on the merits" under § 2254(d), and therefore deserves deference. *See Harrington v. Richter*, <u>562 U.S. 86 (2011)</u>. The Court has taken to using *per curiam* opinions in unargued cases to reverse and chastise lower courts for their failure to sufficiently defer to state courts under AEDPA. For example, in *Parker v. Matthews*, 567 U.S.37 (2012) (per curiam), the Court reversed a lower court's findings of insufficiency of the evidence and prosecutorial misconduct, and opined as follows: "In this *habeas* case, the [federal circuit court] set aside two 29-year-old murder convictions based on the flimsiest of rationales. The court's decision is a textbook example of what the Antiterrorism and Effective Death Penalty Act of 1996 (AEDPA) proscribes: 'using federal *habeas corpus* review as a vehicle to second-guess the reasonable decisions of state courts.' " *See also Coleman v. Johnson*, <u>566 U.S. 650 (2012)</u> (per curiam reversal of lower court's finding of insufficiency of the evidence).

D. Exhaustion of Remedies

Before a federal court will review a constitutional claim in a *habeas corpus* proceeding that seeks review of a state conviction, the claim first must be fairly presented to the state court system by properly pursuing a claim throughout the entire state appellate process. 28 U.S.C. § 2254(b)(1)(A). Exhaustion of remedies includes the presentation of claims to the state supreme court even though its review is discretionary, *O'Sullivan v. Boerckel*, 526 U.S. 838 (1999), and even though that court does not address her claim in a written opinion, *e.g.*, the court denies discretionary review, *Dye v. Hofbauer*, 546 U.S. 1 (2005). In order to have fairly presented the claim, a petitioner must have presented a substantially equivalent claim to the state courts as it presented to the federal courts. The state court need not actually address the claim in a written opinion to satisfy this requirement.

The exhaustion requirement does not preclude *habeas* review; it merely delays such review. In *Rose v. Lundy*, 455 U.S. 509 (1982), the Court held that, when faced with a petition that combines unexhausted and exhausted claims, a federal district court must either dismiss the petition without prejudice to allow the petitioner to return to the state court to exhaust the remaining claims and then return to present all of the claims together in a single petition, or must allow the petitioner to drop the unexhausted claims. Because of the strict one-year time limitation for filing, a federal district court has discretion to stay a "mixed" petition while unexhausted claims are presented to a state court, and to return to federal court for review of the perfected petition without being time barred. *Rhines v. Weber*, 544 U.S. 269 (2005).

Take Note

This strict exhaustion requirement exists because of federalism concerns which suggest that federal courts should not allow a state prisoner to bypass the state courts and initiate the first review of his conviction in the federal courts.

If petitioner fails to exhaust state remedies, the federal court may dismiss the petition until such time as the petitioner has exhausted available state remedies. The only exceptions to the exhaustion of remedies doctrine are when there is an absence of available state remedies or special circumstances render such remedies ineffective to protect the rights of the petitioner. Because the exhaustion of state remedies doctrine is based on comity and is not a jurisdictional requirement, the government may waive the requirement. 28 U.S.C. § 2254(b)(1), (3).

Points for Discussion

a. Denial on the Merits

In light of the stringent requirements for exhaustion of remedies, why would any federal district court apply AEDPA's provision that the "application for a writ of *habeas corpus* may be denied on the merits, notwithstanding the failure of the applicant to exhaust the remedies available in the courts of the State"? The Court advised that the district court "should determine whether the interests of comity and federalism will be better served by addressing the merits forthwith or by requiring a series of additional state and district court proceedings before reviewing the merits of the petitioner's claim." *Granberry v. Greer*, 481 U.S. 129 (1987).

b. Equitable Principles

In addition to interests of comity and federalism, federal *habeas corpus* has traditionally been governed by equitable principles. Consider the situation in *Whittlesey v. Circuit Court*, 897 F.2d 143 (4th Cir. 1990). Whittlesey was convicted and sentenced by a Maryland State court in 1978. In 1980 he escaped from prison, committed other crimes in Florida and began serving a 136-year sentence in the Florida State Prison. In 1986, he filed a petition for post-conviction relief in Maryland state court. The state court dismissed Whittlesey's petition without prejudice because his presence could not be secured for a post-conviction hearing. (Whittlesey sought unsuccessfully to invoke the Interstate Agreement on Detainers as a means of transfer to Maryland for a hearing). In 1987, Whittlesey filed a federal petition for *habeas corpus*, raising the same issues he had raised in his state petitions. The federal district court dismissed the petition without prejudice on the ground that Whittlesey had not exhausted his state post-conviction remedies. On appeal to the circuit court, Whittlesey argued:

> (1) that he had complied with § 2254(b)'s exhaustion requirement. By its own terms § 2254(b) requires only that an applicant for *habeas* relief have exhausted the state court remedies available to him, and that since Whittlesey is unable to return for the hearing there are no remedies available.

> (2) that his petition falls within the futility exception of § 2254(b), which provides that a *habeas* writ may be granted despite a failure to exhaust state court remedies if "there is either an absence of available State corrective process or the existence of circumstances rendering such process ineffective to protect the rights of the prisoner." Whittlesey emphasized that since he is serving a 136-year sentence in Florida, it would be futile for him to wait until he has been released from prison in Florida to pursue his Maryland post-conviction remedy.

A majority of the Fourth Circuit panel held that Whittlesey had not exhausted his remedies because, "the doors of the Maryland state courts stand open for him to present his complaints; that he is unable to enter through those doors until completion of his Florida sentence is the price he must pay for having escaped from the Maryland prison and committed offenses in Florida. It is his own criminal misconduct which has denied Maryland courts the opportunity to hold a hearing, develop a record, and thereby address his claims on the merits. We will not command the district court to review his *habeas* petition when his own unlawful acts have prevented the state courts from reviewing his claims."

The dissent maintained that "this is one of those hard cases that invites the making of bad law—specifically bad exhaustion law. A prisoner who escapes from incarceration in state A only to be incarcerated for conviction of another crime in state B while still a fugitive from state A makes an instinctively unattractive petitioner for federal *habeas* relief from the original incarceration." The fact of the escape, however, has no more legal relevance to the availability of a federal *habeas* forum than do any other of the usual run of unsavory events and prior conduct that exist in the backgrounds of many federal *habeas* petitioners. " 'What else could the petitioner do?' And the answer, 'Nothing,' as obviously satisfies the ultimate concerns of comity underlying the exhaustion requirement. Whittlesey could spend the rest of his life in a Florida prison without the opportunity to litigate his constitutional claims. That is not right. Whittlesey has exhausted the state remedies that are available to him at the present time. He has the right to a federal *habeas* forum to present his constitutional claims."

E. Abuse of the Writ & Procedural Default

1. Successive Petitions as an Abuse of the Writ

The AEDPA establishes procedures for the disposition of second or successive petitions which must pass through a "gatekeeping" system requiring petitioner to seek an authorization order from a three-judge panel in the appropriate court of appeals before a district court may hear the petition. 28 U.S.C. § 2244(b)(3). In order to obtain an authorization order, a petitioner must make a *prima facie* showing that 1) the claim was not presented in a previous federal *habeas* petition, 2) this new claim relies on a new rule of constitutional law that was previously unavailable, or its factual basis "could not have been discovered previously through the exercise of due diligence," and 3) the facts underlying the claim, if proven and viewed in light of the whole evidence, show by clear and convincing evidence that, but for the constitutional error, no reasonable juror would have found the petitioner guilty of the offense. The panel's certification decision is not appealable and is not subject to rehearing.

Slack v. McDaniel

529 U.S. 473 (2000).

JUSTICE KENNEDY delivered the opinion of the Court.

Petitioner Antonio Slack was convicted of second-degree murder in Nevada state court in 1990. His direct appeal was unsuccessful. On November 27, 1991, Slack filed a petition for writ of *habeas corpus* in federal court under 28 U.S.C. § 2254. Early in the federal proceeding, Slack decided to litigate claims he had not yet presented to the Nevada courts. He could not raise the claims in federal court because, under the exhaustion of remedies rule, a federal court was required to dismiss a petition presenting claims not yet litigated in state court. Accordingly, Slack filed a motion seeking to hold his federal petition in abeyance while he returned to state court to exhaust the new claims. Without objection by the State, the District Court ordered the *habeas* petition dismissed "without prejudice." The order, dated February 19, 1992, further stated, "Petitioner is granted leave to file an application to renew upon exhaustion of all State remedies." After an unsuccessful round of state postconviction proceedings, Slack filed a new federal *habeas* petition on May 30, 1995. The District Court later appointed counsel, directing him to file an amended petition or a notice of intention to proceed with the current petition. On December 24, 1997, counsel filed an amended petition presenting 14 claims for relief. The State moved to dismiss the petition because it was a mixed petition, that is to say a petition raising some claims which had been presented to the state courts and some which had not. As its second ground, the State cited *Farmer v. McDaniel*, 98 F. 3d 1548 (C.A.9 1996), and contended that claims Slack had not raised in his 1991 federal *habeas* petition must be dismissed as an abuse of the writ.

Hear It

You can listen to the oral argument in *Slack* at: http://www.oyez.org/cases/1990-1999/1999/1999_98_6322.

The District Court granted the State's motion. First, the court relied on *Farmer* to hold that Slack's 1995 petition was "a second or successive petition," even though his 1991 petition had been dismissed without prejudice for a failure to exhaust state remedies. The court then invoked the abuse of the writ doctrine to dismiss with prejudice the claims Slack had not raised in the 1991 petition. This left Slack with four claims, each having been raised in the 1991 petition; but one of these had not yet been presented to the state courts. The court therefore dismissed Slack's remaining claims because they were in a mixed petition. Here, Slack seeks to challenge the dismissal of claims as abusive; he does not contend that all claims presented in the amended petition were exhausted. The District Court dismissed claims Slack failed to raise in his 1991 petition based on its conclusion that Slack's 1995 petition was a second or successive *habeas* petition. This conclusion was wrong. A *habeas* petition filed in the district court after an initial *habeas* petition was unadjudicated on its merits and dismissed for failure to exhaust state remedies is not a second or successive petition.

The phrase "second or successive petition" is a term of art given substance in our prior *habeas corpus* cases. The decision in *Rose v. Lundy*, 455 U.S., at 510, instructs us in reaching our understanding of the term. *Rose* held that a federal district court must dismiss *habeas corpus* petitions containing both exhausted and unexhausted claims. The opinion, however, contemplated that the prisoner could return to federal court after the requisite exhaustion. It was only if a prisoner declined to return to state court and decided to proceed with his exhausted claims in federal court that the possibility arose that a subsequent petition would be considered second or successive and subject to dismissal as an abuse of the writ. A petition filed after a mixed petition has been dismissed under *Rose* before the district court adjudicated any claims is to be treated as "any other first petition" and is not a second or successive petition.

The State complains that this rule is unfair. The filing of a mixed petition in federal court requires it to appear and to plead failure to exhaust. The petition is then dismissed without prejudice, allowing the prisoner to make a return through the state courts to exhaust new claims. The State expresses concern that, upon exhaustion, the prisoner would return to federal court but again file a mixed petition, causing the process to repeat itself. In this manner, the State contends, a vexatious litigant could inject undue delay into the collateral review process. To the extent the tactic would become a problem, it can be countered without upsetting the established meaning of a second or successive petition. First, the State remains free to impose proper procedural bars to restrict repeated returns to state court for postconviction proceedings. Second, provisions of AEDPA may bear upon the question in cases to which the Act applies. AEDPA itself demonstrates that Congress may address matters relating to exhaustion and mixed petitions through means other than rules governing "second or successive" petitions. E.g., 28 U.S.C. § 2254(b)(2). Third, the Rules of Civil Procedure, applicable as a general matter to *habeas* cases, vest the federal courts with due flexibility to prevent vexatious litigation. We reject the State's argument that refusing to give a new meaning to the established term "second or successive" opens the door to the abuses described.

It is so ordered.

Points for Discussion

a. Goal of Relitigation

In *Felker v. Turpin*, 518 U.S. 651 (1996), the Court upheld the limits on second or successive petitions as "a modified *res judicata* rule, a restraint on what is called in *habeas corpus* practice 'abuse of the writ.' " However, in *Calderon v. United States District Court*, 163 F. 3d 530 (9th Cir., en banc, 1998), the Ninth Circuit stated:

> We reject the panel majority's use of *res judicata* because it contravenes the longstanding rule that *res judicata* has no application in *habeas corpus*. The entire point of a *habeas* petition that challenges a state conviction is to relitigate issues that were raised in the state case and resolved against the petitioner. Obviously, then, *res judicata*, in the traditional sense of that doctrine cannot apply in *habeas corpus*; otherwise, nearly every *habeas* petition would be barred by the original trial. Federal courts have created a doctrine known as "abuse of the writ" that serves as a substitute for *res judicata* by limiting the availability of successive *habeas* petitions when a prior one has been denied. The reason why successive petitions are often deemed abusive is that the first petition provided an adequate opportunity for the petitioner to raise all of his claims, and the petitioner simply chose not to take advantage of that opportunity. Abuse of the writ evolved as a judicially created equitable doctrine, but it is now codified by the AEDPA.
>
> We also reject the State's argument that the traditional rule against applying *res judicata* in *habeas* cases has somehow been abrogated by the AEDPA. Even after the AEDPA, federal *habeas* relief exists in order to relitigate claims that were previously decided in state court, so it is quite fanciful to suggest that the AEDPA *sub silento* introduced *res judicata* into *habeas* law. Further, the AEDPA includes specific provisions to govern successive *habeas* petitions, and *res judicata* would render those provisions largely superfluous. We conclude that even after the AEDPA, the rule is as it has always been: *Res judicata* does not apply to *habeas* cases.

It's Latin to Me

In Latin, *res judicata* means "a thing adjudged." The doctrine of *res judicata* generally bars relitigation of claims between parties that were already decided on final judgment.

FYI

The doctrines of exhaustion and abuse of the writ are defenses invoked by the State to bar defendants who file multiple *habeas* petitions. May a prosecutor take a pro-active stance to bar possible *habeas* petitions? For example, if State law does not provide for a life-without-parole sentence, may the prosecutor plea bargain for the defendant's waiver of the right to file a *habeas* petition challenging a life sentence? Is such a waiver accomplished by the following plea agreement: "Defendant agrees that he will never apply, orally or in writing for parole, commutation of sentence, reprieve, or any other form of relief from life imprisonment. He understands this means he will be sentenced to serve the remainder of his natural life in the penitentiary. In consideration of the State waiving the death penalty, defendant also hereby gives up his right to ask for the Superior Court Sentence Review panel to review any sentence imposed upon him. He hereby states that the sentence of life imprisonment for his participation in the criminal acts is not excessive." In *Allen v. Thomas*, 161 F. 3d 667 (11th Cir. 1998), the Eleventh Circuit noted the absence of any published decisions addressing plea-bargained waivers of the right to seek federal *habeas* review. The court held that if such a waiver is constitutionally permissible, it did not occur in this case because the defendant did not make a knowing and intelligent waiver of the right to seek federal *habeas* review. The catch-all phrase—"or any other form of relief from life imprisonment"—is far too general to constitute a valid waiver of a specific right. *Id.* See also *United States v. Goodman*, 165 F. 3d 169 (2d Cir.1999).

b. "Second or Successive" Application

Any claim presented in a second or successive application must be dismissed if that issue was previously presented. Claims presented in the second or successive application that were not previously presented also must be dismissed, subject to statutory exceptions under § 2244(b)(2)(A)–(B). The filing of such permitted claims in a second or successive application must be authorized by the Court of Appeals under § 2244(b)(3)(A). In addition to *Slack v. McDaniel*, several other Court decisions have attempted to define the scope of the phrase "second or successive" application. For example, *Panetti v. Quarterman*, 551 U.S. 930 (2007) created an exception for a second application raising a claim that would have been unripe had the petitioner presented it in his first application. In *Magwood v. Patterson*, 561 U.S. 320 (2010), the Court addressed the issue of "whether an application is 'second or successive' if it challenges a new judgment." In *Burton v. Stewart*, 549 U.S. 147 (2007), the Court held that because both of the petitioner's *habeas* petitions had challenged the same judgment, the second petition was statutorily precluded. However, *Burton* acknowledged that the result might have been different if a new judgment had intervened between the *habeas* petitions. In *Magwood*, there was such an intervening judgment. Thus, Magwood's second petition was his first application to challenge the intervening judgment when the trial court had conducted a full resentencing.

2. Procedural Default

In *Justus v. Murray*, 897 F.2d 709 (4th Cir.1990), the court distinguished between procedural default and exhaustion as follows: "The doctrine of exhaustion and the procedural default rule are two different things. Exhaustion generally requires that before a federal court will review a constitutional claim in *habeas*, the claim must first be fairly presented to the state court system. The procedural default rule requires that if a state court rejects a *habeas* petitioner's federal constitutional challenge on the adequate and independent state ground that the claim is defaulted under a state procedural rule, a federal *habeas* court is ordinarily precluded from reviewing that claim unless the petitioner can show cause for the default and prejudice resulting from it." The consequence of procedural default is that the petitioner may be barred from judicial review of the forfeited claims in both state and federal courts. The most common form of procedural default is the defendant's failure to present a federal constitutional claim to the trial court and thus preserve the issue for appellate review. Unlike *Stone v. Powell* which bars federal *habeas* relief only when Fourth Amendment issues are given a full and fair hearing in the state courts, if there is a procedural bar, there is no hearing on the constitutional challenge in *any* state or federal court.

Wainwright v. Sykes

433 U.S. 72 (1977).

MR. JUSTICE REHNQUIST delivered the opinion of the Court.

Respondent Sykes was convicted of third-degree murder after a jury trial in the Circuit Court of DeSoto County. He testified at trial that on the evening of January 8, 1972, he told his wife to summon the police because he had just shot Willie Gilbert. When the police arrived at respondent's trailer home, they found Gilbert dead of a shotgun wound, lying a few feet from the front porch. Shortly after their arrival, respondent came from across the road and volunteered that he had shot Gilbert, and a few minutes later respondent's wife approached the police and told them the same thing. Sykes was immediately arrested and taken to the police station. Once there, he was read his *Miranda* rights, declined to seek the aid of counsel and indicated a desire to talk. He then made a statement, which was admitted into evidence at trial through the testimony of the two officers who heard it, to the effect that he had shot Gilbert from the front porch of his trailer home. There were several references during the trial to respondent's consumption of alcohol during the preceding day and to his apparent state of intoxication, facts which were acknowledged by the officers who arrived at the scene. At no time during the trial, however, was the admissibility of any of respondent's statements challenged by his counsel on the ground that respondent had not understood the *Miranda* warnings. Nor did the trial judge question their admissibility on his own motion or hold a fact-finding hearing bearing on that issue. Respondent appealed his conviction, but apparently did not challenge the admissibility of the inculpatory statements. He later filed in the trial court a motion to vacate the conviction and, in the State District Court of Appeals and Supreme Court, petitions for *habeas corpus*. These filings, apparently for the first time, challenged the statements made to police on grounds of involuntariness. In all of these efforts respondent was unsuccessful. Having failed in the Florida courts, respondent initiated the present action under 28 U.S.C. § 2254, asserting the inad-

Hear It

You can listen to the oral argument in *Sykes* at: http://www.oyez.org/cases/1970-1979/1976/1976_75_1578.

missibility of his statements by reason of his lack of understanding of the *Miranda* warnings.

The simple legal question before the Court calls for a construction of the language of 28 U.S.C. § 2254(a), which provides that the federal courts shall entertain an application for a writ of *habeas corpus* "in behalf of a person in custody pursuant to the judgment of a state court only on the ground that he is in custody in violation of the Constitution or laws or treaties of the United States."

The area of controversy which has developed has concerned the reviewability of federal claims which the state court has declined to pass on because not presented in the manner prescribed by its procedural rules. The adequacy of such an independent state procedural ground to prevent federal *habeas* review of the underlying federal issue has been treated very differently than where the state-law ground is substantive. The pertinent decisions marking the Court's somewhat tortuous efforts to deal with this problem are: *Ex parte Spencer*, 228 U.S. 652 (1913); *Brown v. Allen*, 344 U.S. 443 (1953); *Fay v. Noia*; *Davis v. United States*, 411 U.S. 233 (1973); and *Francis v. Henderson*, 425 U.S. 536 (1976).

In *Fay v. Noia*, respondent Noia sought federal *habeas* to review a claim that his state-court conviction had resulted from the introduction of a coerced confession in violation of the Fifth Amendment to the United States Constitution. While the convictions of his two codefendants were reversed on that ground in collateral proceedings following their appeals, Noia did not appeal and the New York courts ruled that his subsequent *coram nobis* action was barred on account of that failure. This Court held that petitioner was nonetheless entitled to raise the claim in federal *habeas*, and thereby overruled its decision 10 years earlier in *Brown v. Allen*: "The doctrine under which state procedural defaults are held to constitute an adequate and independent state law ground barring direct Supreme Court review is not to be extended to omit the power granted the federal courts under the federal *habeas* statute." As a matter of comity but not of federal power, the Court acknowledged "a limited discretion in the federal judge to deny relief to an applicant who had deliberately by-passed the orderly procedure of the state courts and in so doing has forfeited his state court remedies." The Court made clear that the waiver must be knowing and "an intentional relinquishment or abandonment of a known right or privilege." Noting petitioner's "grisly choice" between acceptance of his life sentence and pursuit of an appeal which might culminate in a sentence of death, the Court concluded that there had been no deliberate bypass of the right to have the federal issues reviewed through a state appeal.

Florida procedure did, consistently with the United States Constitution, require that respondents' confession be challenged at trial or not at all, and thus his failure to timely object to its admission amounted to an independent and adequate state procedural ground which would have prevented direct review here. We thus come to the crux of this case. Shall the rule of *Francis v. Henderson*, barring federal *habeas* review absent a showing of "cause" and "prejudice" attendant to a state procedural waiver, be applied to a waived objection to the admission of a confession at trial? We answer that question in the affirmative. Since *Brown v. Allen*, it has been the rule that the federal *habeas* petitioner who claims he is detained pursuant to a final judgment of a state court in violation of the United States Constitution is entitled to have the federal *habeas* court make its own independent determination of his federal claim, without being bound by the determination on the merits of that claim reached in the state proceedings. This rule of *Brown v. Allen* is in no way changed by our holding today. Rather, we deal only with contentions of federal law which were not resolved on the merits in the state proceeding due to respondent's failure to raise them there as required by state procedure. We leave open for resolution in future decisions the precise definition of the "cause" and "prejudice" standard, and note here only that it is narrower than the standard set forth in dicta in *Fay v. Noia*, which would make federal *habeas* review generally available to state convicts absent a knowing and deliberate waiver of the federal constitutional contention. It is the sweeping language of *Fay v. Noia*, going far beyond the facts of the case eliciting it, which we today reject.

The reasons for our rejection are several. The contemporaneous-objection rule itself is by no means peculiar to Florida, and deserves greater respect than *Fay* gives it, both for the fact that it is employed by a coordinate jurisdiction within the federal system and for the many interests which it serves in its own right. A contemporaneous objection enables the record to be made with respect to the constitutional claim when the recollections of witnesses are freshest, not years later in a federal *habeas* proceeding. It enables the judge who observed the demeanor of those witnesses to make the factual determinations necessary for properly deciding the federal constitutional question.

A contemporaneous-objection rule may lead to the exclusion of the evidence objected to, thereby making a major contribution to finality in criminal litigation. Without the evidence claimed to be vulnerable on federal constitutional grounds, the jury may acquit the defendant, and that will be the end of the case; or it may nonetheless convict the defendant, and he will have one less federal constitutional claim to assert in his federal *habeas* petition. If the state trial judge admits the evidence in question after a full hearing, the federal *habeas* court will gain significant guidance from the state ruling in this regard. Subtler considerations as well militate in favor of honoring a state contemporaneous-objection rule. An objection on the spot may force the prosecution to take a hard look at its whole card, and even if the prosecutor thinks that the state trial judge will admit the evidence he must contemplate the possibility of reversal by the state appellate courts or the ultimate issuance of a federal writ of *habeas corpus* based on the impropriety of the state court's rejection of the federal constitutional claim.

We think that the rule of *Fay v. Noia*, broadly stated, may encourage "sandbagging" on the part of defense lawyers, who may take their chances on a verdict of not guilty in a state trial court with the intent to raise their constitutional claims in a federal *habeas* court if their initial gamble does not pay off. The refusal of federal *habeas* courts to honor contemporaneous-objection rules may also make state courts themselves less stringent in their enforcement. Under the rule of *Fay v. Noia*, state appellate courts know that a federal constitutional issue raised for the first time in the proceeding before them may well be decided in any event by a federal *habeas* tribunal. Thus, their choice is between addressing the issue notwithstanding the petitioner's failure to timely object, or else face the prospect that the federal *habeas* court will decide the question without the benefit of their views. The failure of the federal *habeas* courts generally to require compliance with a contemporaneous-objection rule tends to detract from the perception of the trial of a criminal case in state court as a decisive and portentous event.

We believe the adoption of the *Francis* rule in this situation will have the salutary effect of making the state trial on the merits the "main event," so to speak, rather than a "tryout" for what will later be the determinative federal *habeas* hearing. There is nothing in the Constitution or in the language of § 2254 which requires that the state trial on the issue of guilt or innocence be devoted largely to the testimony of fact witnesses directed to the elements of the state crime, while only later will there occur in a federal *habeas* hearing a full airing of the federal constitutional claims which were not raised in the state proceedings. If a criminal defendant thinks that an action of the state trial court is about to deprive him of a federal constitutional right there is every reason for following state procedure in making known his objection.

Food for Thought

Are you persuaded? If Sykes' defaulted issue had been failure to object to a coerced confession, as in *Fay v. Noia*, with some strong evidence that the confession was involuntary, as opposed to a failure to understand *Miranda* warnings, do you think the Court would have reached out to change the rule? Is a state evidentiary rule like the "contemporaneous objection rule" sufficient to waive review of serious constitutional deficiencies? Is the failure to make a contemporaneous objection ineffective assistance of counsel?

The "cause" and "prejudice" exception of the *Francis* rule will afford an adequate guarantee that the rule will not prevent a federal *habeas* court from adjudicating for the first time the federal constitutional claim of a defendant who in the absence of such an adjudication will be the victim of a miscarriage of justice. Whatever precise content may be given those terms by later cases, we feel confident in holding without further elaboration that they do not exist here. Respondent advanced no explanation whatever for his failure to object at trial, and, as the proceeding unfolded, the trial judge is certainly not to be faulted for failing to question the admission of the confession himself. The other evidence of guilt presented at trial was substantial to a degree that would negate any possibility of actual prejudice resulting to the respondent from the admission of his inculpatory statement.

MR. JUSTICE BRENNAN, with whom MR. JUSTICE MARSHALL joins, dissenting.

I believe that *Fay's* commitment to enforcing intentional but not inadvertent procedural defaults offers a realistic measure of protection for the *habeas corpus* petitioner seeking federal review of federal claims that were not litigated before the State. When one pierces the surface justifications for a harsher rule posited by the Court, no standard stricter than *Fay's* deliberate-bypass test is realistically defensible. Punishing a lawyer's unintentional errors by closing the federal courthouse door to his client is both a senseless and misdirected method of deterring the slighting of state rules. It is senseless because unplanned and unintentional action of any kind generally is not subject to deterrence; and, to the extent that it is hoped that a threatened sanction addressed to the defense will induce greater care and caution on the part of trial lawyers, thereby forestalling negligent conduct or error, the potential loss of all valuable state remedies would be sufficient to this end. It is a misdirected sanction because even if the penalization of incompetence or carelessness will encourage more thorough legal training and trial preparation, the *habeas* applicant, as opposed to his lawyer, hardly is the proper recipient of such a penalty. Especially with fundamental constitutional rights at stake, no fictional relationship of principal-agent or the like can justify holding the criminal defendant accountable for the naked errors of his attorney. This is especially true, when so many indigent defendants are without any realistic choice in selecting who ultimately represents them at trial.

Points for Discussion

a. Procedural Default & Prejudice

In *Murray v. Carrier*, 477 U.S. 478 (1986), Justice O'Connor explained the cause and prejudice requirement:

> We think that the question of cause for a procedural default does not turn on whether counsel erred or on the kind of error counsel may have made. So long as a defendant is represented by counsel whose performance is not constitutionally ineffective under the standard established in *Strickland v. Washington*, we discern no inequity in requiring him to bear the risk of attorney error that results in a procedural default. Instead, the existence of cause for a procedural default must ordinarily turn on whether the prisoner can show that some objective factor external to the defense impeded counsel's efforts to comply with the State's procedural rule. Without attempting an exhaustive catalog of such objective impediments to compliance with a procedural rule, a showing that the factual or legal basis for

a claim was not reasonably available to, counsel, or that "some interference by officials," made compliance impracticable, would constitute cause under this standard. Similarly, if the procedural default is the result of ineffective assistance of counsel, the Sixth Amendment itself requires that responsibility for the default be imputed to the State, which may not "conduct trials at which persons who face incarceration must defend themselves without adequate legal assistance." Ineffective assistance of counsel, then, is cause for a procedural default.

Make the Connection

In Chapter 3, you learned that a successful ineffective assistance of counsel claim is difficult: it requires not only proof of deficient performance but also proof of a reasonable likelihood that the outcome of the trial would have been different. Failing to make a contemporaneous objection, while dooming a petitioner's ability to make the claim on *habeas*, will not necessarily be ineffective assistance of counsel.

Respondent does not dispute that the cause and prejudice test applies to procedural defaults on appeal, as we plainly indicated in *Reed v. Ross*. *Reed*, which involved a claim that was defaulted on appeal, held that a *habeas* petitioner could establish cause for a procedural default if his claim is "so novel that its legal basis is not reasonably available to counsel." That holding would have been entirely unnecessary to the disposition of the prisoner's claim if the cause and prejudice test were inapplicable to procedural defaults on appeal.

We see little reason why counsel's failure to detect a colorable constitutional claim should be treated differently from a deliberate but equally prejudicial failure by counsel to raise such a claim. The fact that the latter error can be characterized as a misjudgment, while the former is easily described as an oversight, is much too tenuous a distinction to justify a regime of evidentiary hearings into counsel's state of mind in failing to raise a claim on appeal.

The real thrust of respondent's arguments appears to be that on appeal it is inappropriate to hold defendants to the errors of their attorneys. Were we to accept that proposition, defaults on appeal would presumably be governed by a rule equivalent to *Fay v. Noia*'s "deliberate bypass" standard, under which only personal waiver by the defendant would require enforcement of a procedural default. We express no opinion as to whether counsel's decision not to take an appeal at all might require treatment under such a standard, but, for the reasons already given, we hold that counsel's failure to raise a particular claim on appeal is to be scrutinized under the cause and prejudice standard when that failure is treated as a procedural default by the state courts. Attorney error short of ineffective assistance of counsel does not constitute cause for a procedural default even when that default occurs on appeal rather than at trial. To the contrary, cause for a procedural default on appeal ordinarily requires a showing of some external impediment preventing counsel from constructing or raising the claim.

The *habeas* petitioner must show "not merely that the errors at trial created a possibility of prejudice, but that they worked to his actual and substantial disadvantage, infecting his entire trial with error of constitutional dimensions." Such a showing of pervasive actual prejudice can hardly be thought to constitute anything other than a showing that the prisoner was denied "fundamental fairness" at trial. "In appropriate cases" the principles of comity and finality that inform the concepts of cause and prejudice "must yield to the imperative of correcting a fundamentally unjust incarceration." We remain confident that, for the most part, "victims of a fundamental miscarriage of justice will meet the cause-and-prejudice standard." But we do not pretend that this will always be true. In an extraordinary case, where a constitutional violation has probably resulted in the conviction of one who is actually innocent, a federal *habeas* court may grant the writ even in the absence of a showing of cause for the procedural default.

Make the Connection

Justice O'Connor leaves an opening for a miscarriage of justice if a claim is not allowed to proceed for a person who is probably actually innocent or a victim of "a fundamentally unjust conviction." As discussed in Part F below, while the Court pays lip service to the potential issue of executing or incarcerating the innocent, the standards for such a showing are insurmountably high and not well-defined.

b. State Court Review of Ineffective Assistance of Counsel Claims

In *Edwards v. Carpenter*, 529 U.S. 446 (2000), the Court held that a claim of ineffective assistance of counsel must be presented first to the State courts before the claim can serve as cause to excuse the procedural default of another *habeas* claim. In turn, a procedurally defaulted ineffective-assistance-of-counsel claim can be excused if the petitioner can satisfy the cause and prejudice standard with respect to the ineffective assistance claim itself.

While in *Coleman v. Thompson*, 501 U.S. 722 (1991), the Court held that counsel's failure to file timely notice of appeal in state court does not qualify as cause for procedural default on a claim, since the prisoner bears the risk of the negligence of his agent, the Court made an exception to that general rule in *Martinez v. Ryan*, 566 U.S. 1 (2012). In *Martinez*, the Court held that where, under state law, the initial-review collateral proceeding is the first proceeding when a prisoner may raise ineffective assistance claims, it is the equivalent of a direct appeal for those claims. Therefore, there is "cause" for a default on those claims if there is no counsel or deficient counsel at that initial-review collateral proceeding. As the dissent noted, this is the functional equivalent to requiring that the state provide counsel for collateral proceedings that provide the first occasion to raise a claim of ineffective assistance of counsel.

In *Trevino v. Thaler*, 569 U.S. 413 (2013), the Court extended the *Martinez* exception regarding procedural default to a situation when a State's procedural framework, by reason of its design and operation, makes it highly unlikely that a defendant will have a meaningful opportunity to raise an ineffective-assistance-of-trial-counsel claim on direct appeal. In that event, the Court held the defendant may raise an ineffective assistance claim in a federal *habeas* court.

c.   **Cause & Prejudice**

How does the "cause-and-prejudice" standard differ from the "fundamental miscarriage of justice" standard for excusing a procedural default? "Prejudice" is a stricter standard than the "plain error" doctrine applicable to direct review because direct appeal is designed to afford a means for the *prompt* redress of miscarriages of justice. This standard "is out of place when a prisoner launches a collateral attack against a criminal conviction after society's legitimate interest in the finality of the judgment has been perfected by the expiration of the time allowed for direct review or by the affirmance of the conviction on appeal." Thus in *United States v. Frady*, 456 U.S. 152 (1982), prejudice did not follow simply from the fact that a jury instruction was erroneous (The instruction equated intent with malice and stated that the law presumes malice from the use of a weapon). The Court held that petitioner failed to show that the error "worked to his actual and substantial disadvantage, infecting his entire trial with error of constitutional dimensions," *i.e.,* prejudice must be evaluated by the effect of the error in the context of the whole trial, and the petitioner failed to contradict strong evidence that he had acted with malice.

Cause. In *Reed v. Ross*, 468 U.S. 1 (1984), the Court stated that cause existed for the defendant's failure to raise a due process challenge to shifting the burden of proof to the defendant on an issue of malice, because "burden shifting" was not held unconstitutional until several years after the procedural default. "Where a constitutional claim is so novel that its legal basis is not reasonably available to counsel, a defendant has cause for his failure to raise the claim in accordance with applicable state procedures." In contrast, in *Murray v. Carrier*, 477 U.S. 478 (1986), the Court found that the type of discovery claim in question "had been percolating in lower courts for years" at the time of the defendant's default. When the claim was actually raised in the defendant's case, it was not so novel as to excuse a procedural default.

Food for Thought

If petitioner can show "cause" under *Reed* because the "new rule" of law could not have been reasonably anticipated, does the petitioner then run afoul of *Teague v. Lane*, 489 U.S. 288 (1989), which held that "new rules of law" generally should not be applied retroactively to cases on "collateral review" such as *habeas corpus*? Professor Arkin characterized the interaction between *Reed* and *Teague* as "The Prisoner's Dilemma:" "If a petitioner is able to show that his claim is based on a 'new' rule of law, the *habeas* court will excuse his state procedural default, assuming petitioner can show actual prejudice. But, having shown that the rule under which he seeks relief was not available to him at the time he should have raised it in the state courts, the petitioner may well have won the battle under *Wainwright* only to lose the war to *Teague*. Under most circumstances, the petitioner will have shown that the very rule under which he seeks relief is not retroactive unless he can fit it into one of the two [extremely limited] *Teague* exceptions." Arkin, *The Prisoner's Dilemma: Life in the Lower Federal Courts After Teague v. Lane*, 69 N. CAR. L. REV. 371, 408 (1991). The two exceptions recognized in *Teague* are: 1) where the new rule places certain kinds of private conduct beyond the power of legislatures to proscribe, and 2) where the new rule requires procedures that are "implicit in the concept of ordered liberty" such as the right to counsel.

d. Apparent Futility

Suppose defense counsel says that she did not raise an issue in the state court proceedings because the state court would have been unsympathetic to the claim. Does the apparent futility of making an objection constitute cause? No, said the Court in *Engle v. Isaac*, 456 U.S. 107 (1982). The Court also rejected adoption of a rule requiring trial counsel to exercise "extraordinary vision" or to object to every aspect of the proceedings in the hope that some aspect might make a latent constitutional claim: "We have long recognized that the Constitution guarantees criminal defendants only a fair trial and a competent attorney. It does not insure that defense counsel will recognize and raise every conceivable constitutional claim. Where the basis of a constitutional claim is available, and other defense counsel have perceived and litigated that claim, the demands of comity and finality counsel against labeling alleged unawareness of the objection as a cause for a procedural default."

e. State Interference as Cause

In *Strickler v. Greene*, 527 U.S. 263 (1999), the Court explained the definition of "cause" when the failure to pursue a *Brady* claim will excuse the petitioner's default. A petitioner must prove that: 1) the prosecutor confirmed disclosure of all *Brady* material; 2) petitioner's reliance on the prosecutor's representations was reasonable; and 3) the prosecutor withheld evidence favorable to the defense. In *Amadeo v. Zant*, 486 U.S. 214 (1988), the Court held that governmental concealment of evidence that women and African Americans were intentionally under represented on jury lists constituted cause for the defendant's failure to raise a timely challenge to the jury panel.

Hypo: *Lawyers Gone AWOL*

Cory Maples was found guilty of murder and sentenced to death. Maples sought post-conviction relief in Alabama state court alleging, among other things, ineffective assistance of counsel. His petition was written by two *pro bono* attorneys, both associated with the New York offices of the Sullivan & Cromwell law firm. As required by state law, the two attorneys engaged a lawyer in Alabama to move their admission *pro hac vice*. The Alabama lawyer did, but made clear that he would have no substantive involvement in the case. While Maples' state post-conviction petition was pending, his two lawyers left Sullivan & Cromwell. Their new employment disabled them from representing Maples. They did not inform Maples of their departure, and no other Sullivan & Cromwell attorney entered an appearance or otherwise notified the court. The trial court denied Maples' petition and notices of the order were posted to the two lawyers at Sullivan & Cromwell's address. When those postings were returned, unopened, the trial court clerk attempted no further mailing. The Alabama attorney also received a copy of the order, but did not act on it. With no attorney of record acting on Maples' behalf, the 42-day period Maples had to file a notice of appeal expired. About a month later, an Alabama Assistant Attorney General sent a letter directly to Maples. The letter informed Maples of the missed deadline and notified him that he had four weeks remaining to file a federal *habeas* petition. Thereafter, Maples sought federal *habeas* relief. Does cause exist for Maples' procedural default? *Maples v. Thomas*, 565 U.S. 266 (2012); *see also Luna v. Kernan*, 784 F.3d 640 (9th Cir. 2015) (addressing similar issue of "egregious" attorney misconduct, but short of abandonment, leading to failure to meet one-year deadline).

F. Claims of Actual Innocence as "Gateways" to Federal *Habeas Corpus* Review

A common misperception, at least among the lay public, is that federal courts and ultimately the U.S. Supreme Court, sit as courts of last resort to correct any and all injustice done to American citizens. As Justice Scalia, a frequent critic of expansive federal *habeas* review, explained in *Bousley v. United States*, 523 U.S. 614 (1998), it "would be marvelously inspiring to be able to boast that we have a criminal-justice system in which a claim of 'actual innocence' will always be heard, no matter how late it is brought forward, and no matter how much the failure to bring it forward at the proper time is defendant's own fault. But of course we do not have such a system, and no society unwilling to devote unlimited resources to repetitive criminal litigation ever could."

In *Herrera v. Collins*, <u>506 U.S. 390 (1993)</u>, the Court refused to recognize a claim of factual innocence as a free-standing constitutional claim subject to review on federal *habeas corpus*. Herrera was convicted of capital murder and sentenced to death. Ten years later, he filed a petition for federal *habeas corpus* relief, claiming that newly discovered evidence (that his dead brother had committed the murders) showed that he was actually innocent of the crimes. The Court stated that, after a final judgment, the presumption of innocence is no longer applicable. Moreover, a new claim of innocence is factually based, and *habeas corpus* relief is not a proper remedy for correcting factual errors. Instead, a request for executive clemency is a proper remedy for innocence claims based upon new evidence that is discovered after the time for filing a new trial motion. The *Herrera* Court then assumed:

> for the sake of argument in deciding this case, that in a capital case a truly persuasive demonstration of 'actual innocence' made after trial would render the execution of a defendant unconstitutional, and justify federal *habeas* relief if there were no state avenues open to process such a claim. But because of the very disruptive effect that entertaining claims of actual innocence would have on the need for finality in capital cases, and the enormous burden that having to retry cases based on often stale evidence would place on the States, the threshold showing for such an assumed right would necessarily be extraordinarily high.

The Court stated that Herrera failed to meet the Court's standard, because his affidavits were based mostly on hearsay, were obtained without the benefit of cross-examination, contained inconsistencies, and failed to overcome the strong trial proof of guilt.

Food for Thought

Why did the Court only assume "for the sake of argument" that it would be a violation of the Eighth Amendment's prohibition on "cruel and unusual punishment" to execute a person who is factually innocent? Would it be? Why the reticence?

Claims of innocence, however, are a vital component to petitioners' attempts to gain *habeas* review otherwise barred by the procedural default rule. In *Schlup v. Delo*, <u>513 U.S. 298 (1995)</u>, the Court described the nature of the role of innocence as a gateway requirement:

> As a preliminary matter, it is important to explain the difference between Schlup's claim of actual innocence and the claim of actual innocence asserted in *Herrera*. In *Herrera*, the petitioner advanced his claim of innocence to support a novel substantive constitutional claim, namely that the

execution of an innocent person would violate the Eighth Amendment. Under petitioner's theory in *Herrera*, even if the proceedings that had resulted in his conviction and sentence were entirely fair and error-free, his innocence would render his execution a "constitutionally intolerable event." Schlup's claim of innocence, on the other hand, is procedural, rather than substantive. His constitutional claims are based not on his innocence, but rather on his contention that the ineffectiveness of his counsel and the withholding of evidence by the prosecution denied him the full panoply of protections afforded to criminal defendants by the Constitution. Schlup, however, faces procedural obstacles that he must overcome before a federal court may address the merits of those constitutional claims. Because Schlup has been unable to establish "cause and prejudice" sufficient to excuse his failure to present his evidence in support of his first federal petition, Schlup may obtain review of his constitutional claims only if he falls within the "narrow class of cases implicating a fundamental miscarriage of justice." Schlup's claim of innocence is offered only to bring him within this "narrow class of cases."

Schlup's claim thus differs in at least two important ways from that presented in *Herrera*. First, Schlup's claim of innocence does not by itself provide a basis for relief. Instead, his claim for relief depends critically on the validity of his *Strickland* and *Brady* claims. Schlup's claim of innocence is thus "not itself a constitutional claim, but instead a gateway through which a *habeas* petitioner must pass to have his otherwise barred constitutional claim considered on the merits." Schlup's conviction may not be entitled to the same degree of respect as one, such as Herrera's, that is the product of an error-free trial. Without any new evidence of innocence, even the existence of a concededly meritorious constitutional violation is not in itself sufficient to establish a miscarriage of justice that would allow a *habeas* court to reach the merits of a barred claim. However, if a petitioner such as Schlup presents evidence of innocence so strong that a court cannot have confidence in the outcome of the trial unless the court is also satisfied that the trial was free of nonharmless constitutional error, the petitioner should be allowed to pass through the gateway and argue the merits of his underlying claims.

Points for Discussion

a. Actual Innocence Showing

In *Bousley v. United States*, 523 U.S. 614 (1998), Bousley pleaded guilty to drug and firearm charges, but reserved the right to challenge the quantity of drugs used in calculating his sentence. He unsuccessfully appealed his sentence, but did not challenge the plea's validity. He sought *habeas* relief, claiming that his guilty plea lacked a factual basis because the evidence did not show a connection between the firearms in the bedroom of the house and the garage where the drug trafficking occurred. The district court dismissed the petition. While Bousley's appeal was pending, the Court held that a conviction for using a firearm requires the prosecution to show "active employment of the firearm." In affirming dismissal of the *habeas* petition, the Eighth Circuit rejected Bousley's argument that the new Supreme Court case should be applied retroactively. Despite the fact that Bousley had procedurally defaulted on his claims, the Court held that Bousley should be permitted to make an actual innocence showing. The Court stated that actual innocence means factual innocence, not mere legal insufficiency. The prosecution is not limited to the existing record but may present any admissible evidence of petitioner's guilt. The actual innocence showing also must extend to charges that the prosecution had dropped or abandoned in the course of plea bargaining.

Food for Thought

What must be shown in support of an argument for actual innocence, thereby warranting relief from the procedural default rule? In *House v. Bell*, 547 U.S. 518 (2006), the Court held that petitioner had satisfied the difficult showing required by *Schlup*, and that his federal *habeas* proceeding therefore could go forward. DNA testing established that semen on the murder victim's clothing came from her husband rather than from House, the defendant; that evidence was the only forensic evidence linking House to the murder. In addition, House in his post-trial proceedings had presented evidence that the murder victim's husband had confessed to the murder. The Court found this to be the "rare" case when, if the jury had heard all the conflicting evidence, it likely would have viewed the record as creating reasonable doubt. Nonetheless, while House gained an opportunity for his petition to be heard, his strong showing was "not a case of conclusive exoneration" that *Herrera* contemplated would be necessary for relief as a free-standing claim. Do you agree?

b. Innocence Overcomes AEDPA's Statute of Limitations

In *McQuiggin v. Perkins*, 569 U.S. 383 (2013), the Court held that proof of actual innocence can overcome AEDPA's one-year statute of limitations for filing petitions, but the untimeliness will bear on the credibility of the evidence proffered to show actual innocence.

Executive Summary

AEDPA's Limitations on the Writ of *Habeas Corpus*. The Antiterrorism and Effective Death Penalty Act of 1996 (AEDPA) severely limited the availability of federal *habeas corpus* relief.

A Civil Action. A collateral attack on a criminal conviction requires filing a separate lawsuit, which is civil in nature.

Time Limit on Filing. AEDPA has a one-year limitation for filing a petition for relief, and generally it prohibits the filing of successive petitions.

Exhaustion of State Remedies. Before filing a federal *habeas* petition, as a matter of comity a person must exhaust state remedies by presenting the claim to the state's highest court.

Requirement of Custody. A person may obtain federal *habeas* relief only if he is in custody, which includes significant restraints on personal liberty as well as physical incarceration.

Claims on *Habeas* Must Be "Federal." Federal *habeas* relief is available only for *federal* (not state) constitutional or statutory violations.

No Collateral Attack for Fourth Amendment Violations. If a person's Fourth Amendment claim was heard in state court, it cannot be considered by a federal court in a *habeas* proceeding.

Requirement to Preserve Issue or Show Cause and Prejudice. Failure to preserve an issue for appellate review precludes consideration in a *habeas corpus* proceeding unless there was cause for and actual prejudice from the failure to preserve the issue, or unless the petitioner can prove actual innocence.

Major Themes

a. Constitutional Errors—*Habeas corpus* is a collateral attack on a conviction that is a civil action brought by the convicted person against the party responsible for his or her custody, alleging federal constitutional errors in the trial or sentencing process.

b. Procedural Barriers—While known as "the Great Writ," the Court began to create more substantive and procedural barriers to federal *habeas* review of state convictions beginning in the 1970s, and those barriers were enhanced by Congress in 1996 through passage of AEDPA.

c. Attorney Errors—Many prisoners never receive a federal *habeas* hearing on their federal constitutional claims, even if the errors may be serious and the prisoner may be innocent, due to their or their counsel's failure to meet all of the procedural requirements, whether through neglect or oversight.

For More Information

- RUSSELL L. WEAVER, JOHN M. BURKOFF, CATHERINE HANCOCK & STEVEN I. FRIEDLAND, PRINCIPLES OF CRIMINAL PROCEDURE Ch. 22 (8th ed. 2024).

- RANDY HERTZ & JAMES S. LIEBMAN, FEDERAL *HABEAS CORPUS* PRACTICE & PROCEDURE (6th ed. 2011).

- WAYNE R. LAFAVE, JEROLD H. ISRAEL, NANCY J. KING & ORIN S. KERR, CRIMINAL PROCEDURE (6th ed. 2017).

Test Your Knowledge

To assess your understanding of the material in this chapter, click here to take a quiz.

Index

References are to pages.

Page numbers 1–38 and 163–840, set out below,
are found in Weaver, Burkoff, and Hancock's
Criminal Procedure, A Contemporary Approach (4th ed. 2024).